the Integration of Technology in the

MW00679780

Online Tutoring from SmarThinking In partnership with SmarThinking, we offer personalized, online tutoring during typical homework hours. Every new text comes with a one-semester passkey that will allow access to three types of services:

- **Live help** provides access to 20 hours a week of real-time, one-on-one instruction. With Internet access, students may interact live online with an experienced SmarThinking "e-structor" (online tutor) between 9 AM and 1 AM EST, every Sunday through Thursday.
- **Questions anytime** enables students to submit questions 24 hours a day, 7 days a week, for response by an e-structor within 24 hours. Students can even submit spreadsheets for personalized feedback within 24 hours.
- **Independent Study Resources** are available around the clock and provide access to additional educational services, ranging from interactive web sites to Frequently Asked Questions posed to SmarThinking e-structors.

NEW! Introduction to Financial Accounting An interactive multi-media product that provides practical, intuitive instruction on fundamental accounting concepts. This CD-ROM combines video, audio, and text in an interactive simulation. The user learns accounting by recording a series of business transactions for a real-world company. Each transaction is described and recorded in everyday business language and reconciled to financial statements prepared in accordance with Generally Accepted Accounting Principles ("GAAP"). An accounting coach tutors students as they proceed through the program. They are not able to move ahead without correctly completing each transaction, and they receive a performance evaluation at the end of the program. This program is designed to help students:

- Understand fundamental accounting terminology
- Become intelligent readers of financial statements
- Value, record, and classify business transactions
- Assess how business decisions affect profits and liquidity

The Needles Accounting Resource Center at http://accounting.college.hmco.com

For Students

- **NEW! ACE,** an online self-quizzing program, with over 1,000 new questions, that allows students to check their mastery of the topics covered in each chapter
- **Research Activities** based on the material covered in each chapter
- **Toys "R" Us Annual Report Activities** that make use of the latest Toys "R" Us financial statements
- **Links** to the web sites of over 200 real companies and annual reports referenced in the book
- **A List of Business Readings** from leading periodicals
- **Check Figures** for end-of-chapter problems

For Instructors

- **NEW!** A brand new set of **PowerPoint Slides** that will enhance classroom presentation of text material; the new slides are concise, contain lots of examples of transactions, and explain the accounting process in clear, easy-to-follow steps
- **Text previews,** which highlight new features and provide demonstrations of supplements
- **Sample syllabi** from other first-year accounting faculty
- ***Accounting Instructors' Report*** newsletter, which explores a wide range of contemporary teaching issues
- **Electronic Solutions,** fully functioning Excel spreadsheets for all text exercises, problems, and cases from the printed Instructor's Solutions Manual

Teaching Accounting Online This online training course from Faculty Development Programs provides suggestions for integrating new technologies into accounting education. Available within Blackboard.com, the course includes the following modules: Designing Course Basics; Be the Student; Common Online Tools; Designing Teaching Strategies; Designing Learning Activities; Designing Outcomes Assessment; and Delivering a Course. For more information, contact your Houghton Mifflin sales representative or our Faculty Services Center at (800) 733-1717.

2005e

NINTH EDITION

PRINCIPLES OF ACCOUNTING

VOLUME I: CHAPTERS 1-13

Belverd E. Needles, Jr., Ph.D., C.P.A., C.M.A.
DePaul University

Marian Powers, Ph.D.
Northwestern University

Susan V. Crosson, M.S. Accounting, C.P.A.
Santa Fe Community College, Florida

Houghton Mifflin Company
Boston New York

ɔ Jennifer, Jeffrey, Annabelle, and Abigail
ò Bruce, Brent, and Courtney Crosson and in loving memory of Helen and Bryce Van Valkenburgh

ɜenior Sponsoring Editor: Bonnie Binkert
Senior Development Editor: Margaret M. Kearney
Project Editor: Claudine Bellanton
Editorial Assistants: Lisa Goodman and Rachel Zanders
Senior Production/Design Coordinator: Sarah L. Ambrose
Senior Manufacturing Coordinator: Priscilla J. Bailey
Marketing Manager: Todd Berman

Custom Publishing Editor: Kyle Henderson
Custom Publishing Production Manager: Kathleen McCourt
Project Coordinator: Kim Gavrilles

Photo Credits: page 3, ©Edward Holub/CORBIS; page 5, Courtesy of Intel Corporation; page 45, ©DigitalVision/PictureQuest; page 89, ©Getty Images; page 129, ©Ed Kashi/CORBIS; page 167, ©Getty Images; page 169, Courtesy of Claire's Stores, Inc.; page 213, © Mark Richards/PhotoEdit; page 323, ©Lester Lefkowitz/Getty Images; page 365, ©Bruce Ayres/Getty Images; page 403, © Jose Luis Pelaez, Inc./CORBIS; page 441, ©BananaStock/Picturequest; page 443, Courtesy of J.C. Penney Company, Inc.; page 479, ©Ed Young/CORBIS; page 481, Courtesy of Fermi National Accelerator Laboratory; page 525, ©Getty Images; page 557, ©Arthur Tilley/Getty Images; page 593, ©AP/Wide World Photos; page 629, ©Todd Gipstein/CORBIS; page 669, ©Getty Images, page 709, ©DigitalVision/PictureQuest; page 711, Courtesy of Goodyear Tire & Rubber Company; page 751, ©AP/Wide World Photos; page 793, © AFP/Getty Images; page 795, Courtesy of United Parcel Service; page 835, © Scott Olson/ Getty Images; page 883, ©Don Smetzer/Getty Images; page 925, Courtesy of England , Inc.; page 965, ©Steve Kagan/Getty Images; page 1003, ©Stephen Marks/Getty Images; page 1005, Courtesy of Enterprise Rent-A-Car, page 1049, © Sergio Piumatti; page 1091, ©Ken Redding/CORBIS; page 1093, Courtesy of Harley Davidson, Inc., page 1129, ©David Young-Wolff/Getty Images.

The Toys "R" Us Annual Report (excerpts and complete) for the year ended February 1, 2003, which appears at the end of Chapter 6, pages 267-302, is reprinted by permission.

The 2002 Annual Report from Walgreens, which appears at the end of Chapter 6, pages 303-321, is reprinted with permission of Walgreen Co.

Printed in the United States of America.

ISBN-13: 978-0-618-49644-0
ISBN-10: 0-618-49644-0
N-03356

6 7 8 9 – CCI – 06

Houghton Mifflin
Custom Publishing

222 Berkeley Street • Boston, MA 02116

Address all correspondence and order information to the above address.

BRIEF CONTENTS

1 Uses of Accounting Information and the Financial Statements 2

2 Measuring Business Transactions 44

3 Measuring Business Income 88

4 Completing the Accounting Cycle 128

5 Merchandising Operations 166

6 Financial Reporting and Analysis 212

Supplement to Chapter 6 How to Read an Annual Report 257

7 Accounting Information Systems 322

8 Internal Control 364

9 Short-Term Financial Assets 402

10 Inventories 440

11 Long-Term Assets 478

12 Current Liabilities 524

13 Partnerships 556

Appendix A International Accounting 1173

Appendix B Long-Term Investments 1180

Appendix C The Time Value of Money 1187

Appendix D Future Value and Present Value Tables 1200

CONTENTS

Preface xxi
To the Student xxxiii
About the Authors xxxviii
Check Figures xxxix

1 Uses of Accounting Information and the Financial Statements 2

■ DECISION POINT Walgreen Co. 2

ACCOUNTING AS AN INFORMATION SYSTEM 4

Business Goals, Activities, and Performance Measures 4

■ VIDEO CASE Intel Corporation 5

■ FOCUS ON BUSINESS PRACTICE
How Do Performance Measures Relate to Executive Bonuses? 7

Financial and Management Accounting 7

Processing Accounting Information 7

■ FOCUS ON BUSINESS PRACTICE
What Does Walgreens Have to Say about Itself? 7

■ FOCUS ON BUSINESS PRACTICE
How Did Accounting Develop? 8

DECISION MAKERS: THE USERS OF ACCOUNTING INFORMATION 8

Management 9

Users with a Direct Financial Interest 9

■ FOCUS ON BUSINESS PRACTICE
What Does the CFO Do? 10

Users with an Indirect Financial Interest 10

Governmental and Not-for-Profit Organizations 10

ACCOUNTING MEASUREMENT 11

What Is Measured? 11

Business Transactions as the Object of Measurement 11

Money Measure 11

The Concept of Separate Entity 12

FORMS OF BUSINESS ORGANIZATION 12

Sole Proprietorships 13

Partnerships 13

Corporations 13

■ FOCUS ON BUSINESS PRACTICE
Are Most Corporations Big or Small Businesses? 13

FINANCIAL POSITION AND THE ACCOUNTING EQUATION 14

Assets 15

Liabilities 15

Owners' Equity 15

Some Illustrative Transactions 16

COMMUNICATION THROUGH FINANCIAL STATEMENTS 19

The Income Statement 22

The Statement of Owner's Equity 22

The Balance Sheet 22

The Statement of Cash Flows 22

GENERALLY ACCEPTED ACCOUNTING PRINCIPLES 23

Financial Statements, GAAP, and the Independent CPA's Report 23

Organizations That Influence Current Practice 24

PROFESSIONAL ETHICS AND THE ACCOUNTING PROFESSION 25

■ FOCUS ON BUSINESS ETHICS
Good Ethics = Good Business! 25

Chapter Review 26 Review of Learning Objectives 26
Review of Concepts and Terminology 27 Review Problem 29
Answer to Review Problem 30

Chapter Assignments 30 Questions 30 Short Exercises 31
Exercises 33 Problems 36 Alternate Problems 38

Skills Development Cases 39

Financial Reporting and Analysis Cases 41

2 Measuring Business Transactions 44

■ DECISION POINT Continental Airlines, Inc. & The Boeing Co. 44

MEASUREMENT ISSUES 46

The Recognition Issue 46

■ FOCUS ON BUSINESS PRACTICE
Accounting Policies: Where Do You Find Them? 46

The Valuation Issue 47

■ FOCUS ON INTERNATIONAL BUSINESS
No Dollar Amount: How Can That Be? 47

■ FOCUS ON BUSINESS PRACTICE
Is It Always Cost? 48

The Classification Issue 48

ACCOUNTS AND THE CHART OF ACCOUNTS 48
Owner's Equity Accounts 50
Account Titles 50

THE DOUBLE-ENTRY SYSTEM: THE BASIC METHOD OF ACCOUNTING 51
The T Account 51
The T Account Illustrated 52
Analyzing and Processing Transactions 52

TRANSACTION ANALYSIS ILLUSTRATED 54
- FOCUS ON BUSINESS ETHICS
  Are Financial Statements Always Truthful? 56

THE TRIAL BALANCE 61
- FOCUS ON BUSINESS TECHNOLOGY
  Are All Trial Balances Created Equal? 62

RECORDING AND POSTING TRANSACTIONS 63
The General Journal 63
The General Ledger 64
Some Notes on Presentation 66
Chapter Review 66 Review of Learning Objectives 66 Review of Concepts and Terminology 67 Review Problem 68 Answer to Review Problem 69
Chapter Assignments 72 Questions 72 Short Exercises 73 Exercises 75 Problems 78 Alternate Problems 81
Skills Development Cases 83
Financial Reporting and Analysis Cases 85

3 Measuring Business Income 88

- DECISION POINT Kelly Services 88

PROFITABILITY MEASUREMENT: THE ROLE OF BUSINESS INCOME 90
Net Income 90
Revenues 90
Expenses 90

INCOME MEASUREMENT ISSUES 91
The Accounting Period Issue 91
- FOCUS ON BUSINESS PRACTICE
  Fiscal Year-Ends Vary 91

The Continuity Issue 91
The Matching Issue 92

ACCRUAL ACCOUNTING 92
- FOCUS ON BUSINESS ETHICS
  Aggressive Accounting or Deception? You Judge. 93

Recognizing Revenues When Earned 93
Recognizing Expenses When Incurred 93
Adjusting the Accounts 93
Accrual Accounting and Performance Measures 94

THE ADJUSTMENT PROCESS 95
Type 1: Allocating Recorded Costs Between Two or More Accounting Periods (Deferred Expenses) 96
- FOCUS ON INTERNATIONAL BUSINESS
  Who Needs Accounting Knowledge? 99

Type 2: Recognizing Unrecorded Expenses (Accrued Expense) 100
Type 3: Allocating Recorded Unearned Revenues Between Two or More Accounting Periods (Deferred Revenues) 101
Type 4: Recognizing Unrecorded Revenues (Accrued Revenues) 103
- FOCUS ON BUSINESS TECHNOLOGY
  Ecommerce: What's Its Impact? 104

A Note About Journal Entries 104

USING THE ADJUSTED TRIAL BALANCE TO PREPARE FINANCIAL STATEMENTS 104
- FOCUS ON BUSINESS TECHNOLOGY
  Entering Adjustments With the Touch of a Button 104

CASH FLOWS FROM ACCRUAL-BASED INFORMATION 107
Chapter Review 108 Review of Learning Objectives 108 Review of Concepts and Terminology 109 Review Problem 110 Answer to Review Problem 111
Chapter Assignments 114 Questions 114 Short Exercises 114 Exercises 115 Problems 118 Alternate Problems 122
Skills Development Cases 124
Financial Reporting and Analysis Cases 125

4 Completing the Accounting Cycle 128

- DECISION POINT Dell Computer Corporation 128

OVERVIEW OF THE ACCOUNTING CYCLE 130

CLOSING ENTRIES 130
Required Closing Entries 132
The Accounts After Closing 136
- FOCUS ON INTERNATIONAL BUSINESS
  Closing Doesn't Have to Be Such a Headache. 139

THE POST-CLOSING TRIAL BALANCE 139

REVERSING ENTRIES: THE OPTIONAL FIRST STEP IN THE NEXT ACCOUNTING PERIOD 140

THE WORK SHEET: AN ACCOUNTANT'S TOOL 141
Preparing the Work Sheet 142

Using the Work Sheet 144

■ FOCUS ON BUSINESS TECHNOLOGY
Using Electronic Work Sheets 146

Chapter Review 147 Review of Learning Objectives 147 Review of Concepts and Terminology 147 Review Problem 148 Answer to Review Problem 149

Chapter Assignments 149 Questions 149 Short Exercises 150 Exercises 152 Problems 155 Alternate Problems 159

Skills Development Cases 161

Financial Reporting and Analysis Cases 163
Comprehensive Problem: Joan Miller Advertising Agency 164

5 Merchandising Operations 166

■ DECISION POINT Target Stores 166

MANAGEMENT ISSUES IN MERCHANDISING BUSINESSES 168

Cash Flow Management 168

■ VIDEO CASE Claire's Stores, Inc. 169

■ FOCUS ON BUSINESS TECHNOLOGY
Credit Cards or Debit Cards? 170

Profitability Management 170

Choice of Inventory System 171

■ FOCUS ON BUSINESS TECHNOLOGY
Bar Codes—How Have They Influenced Choice of Inventory Systems? 172

Control of Merchandising Operations 172

INCOME STATEMENT FOR A MERCHANDISING CONCERN 173

Net Sales 174

Cost of Goods Sold 174

Gross Margin 175

Operating Expenses 176

Net Income 176

TERMS OF SALE 176

■ FOCUS ON BUSINESS TECHNOLOGY
How Are Web Sales DOING? 177

APPLYING THE PERPETUAL INVENTORY SYSTEM 178

Transactions Related to Purchases of Merchandise 178

Transactions Related to Sales of Merchandise 179

■ FOCUS ON BUSINESS PRACTICE
Are Sales Returns Worth Accounting For? 180

APPLYING THE PERIODIC INVENTORY SYSTEM 181

Cost of Goods Sold 181

Transactions Related to Purchases of Merchandise 182

Transactions Related to Sales of Merchandise 184

THE MERCHANDISING WORK SHEET AND CLOSING ENTRIES: THE PERPETUAL INVENTORY SYSTEM 185

Adjustments Columns 185

Omission of Adjusted Trial Balance Columns 185

Income Statement and Balance Sheet Columns 186

Adjusting Entries 187

Closing Entries 187

THE MERCHANDISING WORK SHEET AND CLOSING ENTRIES: THE PERIODIC INVENTORY SYSTEM 188

Income Statement and Balance Sheet Columns 188

Closing Entries 190

ACCOUNTING FOR DISCOUNTS 191

Sales Discounts 191

Purchases Discounts 191

Chapter Review 192 Review of Learning Objectives 192 Review of Concepts and Terminology 193 Review Problem 195 Answer to Review Problem 195

Chapter Assignments 197 Questions 197 Short Exercises 198 Exercises 199 Problems 202 Alternate Problems 206

Skills Development Cases 208

Financial Reporting and Analysis Cases 210

6 Financial Reporting and Analysis 212

■ DECISION POINT General Mills, Inc. 212

OBJECTIVES OF FINANCIAL INFORMATION 214

QUALITATIVE CHARACTERISTICS OF ACCOUNTING INFORMATION 214

CONVENTIONS THAT HELP IN THE INTERPRETATION OF FINANCIAL INFORMATION 216

Comparability and Consistency 216

■ FOCUS ON BUSINESS PRACTICE
How Much Is Material? It's Not Only a Matter of Numbers. 217

Materiality 217

Conservatism 217

■ FOCUS ON BUSINESS PRACTICE
When is "Full Disclosure" Too Much? It's a Matter of Cost and Benefits. 218

Full Disclosure 218

Cost-Benefit 218

MANAGEMENT'S RESPONSIBILITY FOR ETHICAL REPORTING 219

■ FOCUS ON BUSINESS ETHICS
...onable Accounting Practices Are Under Scrutiny. 220

CLASSIFIED BALANCE SHEET 220

Assets 220

Liabilities 223

Owner's Equity 223

Reading and Graphing Real Company Balance Sheets 224

FORMS OF THE INCOME STATEMENT 226

Reading and Graphing Real Company Income Statements 228

USING CLASSIFIED FINANCIAL STATEMENTS 230

Evaluation of Liquidity 230

Evaluation of Profitability 231

■ FOCUS ON BUSINESS PRACTICE
Who is Right: The Credit-Worthiness Analyst or the Profitability Analyst? 232

■ FOCUS ON BUSINESS PRACTICE
To What Level of Profitability Should a Company Aspire? 235

Chapter Review 237 Review of Learning Objectives 237 Review of Concepts and Terminology 238 Review Problem 240 Answer to Review Problem 240

Chapter Assignments 241 Questions 241 Short Exercises 242 Exercises 243 Problems 246 Alternate Problems 249

Skills Development Cases 250

Financial Reporting and Analysis Cases 252

Supplement to Chapter 6 How to Read an Annual Report 257

THE COMPONENTS OF AN ANNUAL REPORT 257

Letter to the Stockholders 257

Financial Highlights 258

Description of the Company 258

Management's Discussion and Analysis 258

Financial Statements 258

Notes to the Financial Statements 260

Report of Management's Responsibilities 261

Report of Certified Public Accountants 261

Supplementary Information Notes 263

THE ANNUAL REPORT PROJECT 264

7 Accounting Information Systems 322

■ DECISION POINT RR Donnelley 322

ACCOUNTING INFORMATION SYSTEMS: PRINCIPLES OF DESIGN 324

Cost-Benefit Principle 324

Control Principle 324

■ FOCUS ON BUSINESS PRACTICE
How Much Is a Used Computerized Accounting System Worth? 325

Compatibility Principle 325

Flexibility Principle 325

COMPUTERIZED ACCOUNTING SYSTEMS 325

Spreadsheet Software 325

■ FOCUS ON BUSINESS TECHNOLOGY
Networking: How to Get It Done 326

GENERAL LEDGER SYSTEMS 326

Structure of General Ledger Systems 326

ACCOUNTANTS, BUSINESSES, AND THE INTERNET 328

■ FOCUS ON BUSINESS TECHNOLOGY
Top Ten Technological Challenges Businesses FACE 329

■ FOCUS ON BUSINESS PRACTICE
B to B and EDI: How Much Can They SAVE? 329

■ FOCUS ON BUSINESS TECHNOLOGY
E2K: How Much Time Can It Save? 330

ROLE OF SPECIAL-PURPOSE JOURNALS IN AN ACCOUNTING INFORMATION SYSTEM 330

■ FOCUS ON BUSINESS TECHNOLOGY
Why Are Customer Numbers Necessary? 330

■ FOCUS ON BUSINESS TECHNOLOGY
How Can Accounting Information Systems Help Satisfy Customers? 331

TYPES OF SPECIAL-PURPOSE JOURNALS 333

Sales Journal 333

Purchases Journal 335

Cash Receipts Journal 338

Cash Payments Journal 340

■ FOCUS ON BUSINESS ETHICS
Why Is Confidentiality Important to Accountants? 342

Transactions That Are Not Recorded in a Special-Purpose Journal 343

The Flexibility of Special-Purpose Journals 343

Chapter Review 344 Review of Learning Objectives 344 Review of Concepts and Terminology 344 Review Problem 346 Answer to Review Problem 346

Chapter Assignments 348 Questions 348 Short Exercises 349 Exercises 350 Problems 354 Alternate Problems 357

Skills Development Cases 360

Financial Reporting and Analysis Cases 362

8 Internal Control 364

■ DECISION POINT Oxford Health Plans, Inc. 364

INTERNAL CONTROL: BASIC COMPONENTS AND CONTROL ACTIVITIES 366

Management's Responsibility for Internal Control 366

Components of Internal Control 366

Control Activities 367

■ FOCUS ON BUSINESS ETHICS
Which Frauds Are Most Common? 367

Limitations of Internal Control 368

INTERNAL CONTROL OVER MERCHANDISING TRANSACTIONS 368

Internal Control and Management Goals 369

Control of Cash Sales Receipts 370

■ FOCUS ON BUSINESS TECHNOLOGY
How Do Computers Influence Internal Controls? 370

Control of Purchases and Cash Disbursements 371

■ FOCUS ON BUSINESS ETHICS
Throw It or Shred It? 374

PREPARING A BANK RECONCILIATION 375

Illustration of a Bank Reconciliation 376

Recording Transactions After Reconciliation 377

PETTY CASH PROCEDURES 378

Establishing the Petty Cash Fund 378

Making Disbursements from the Petty Cash Fund 378

Reimbursing the Petty Cash Fund 379

VOUCHER SYSTEMS 380

Components of a Voucher System 380

■ FOCUS ON BUSINESS PRACTICE
Which Is More Important: B to C or B to B? 380

Operation of a Voucher System 383

Chapter Review 386 Review of Learning Objectives 386 Review of Concepts and Terminology 386 Review Problem 388 Answer to Review Problem 389

Chapter Assignments 389 Questions 389 Short Exercises 391 Exercises 392 Problems 394 Alternate Problems 398

Skills Development Cases 399

Financial Reporting and Analysis Cases 401

9 Short-Term Financial Assets 402

■ DECISION POINT Pioneer Corporation 402

MANAGEMENT ISSUES RELATED TO SHORT-TERM FINANCIAL ASSETS 404

Managing Cash Needs During Seasonal Cycles 404

■ FOCUS ON BUSINESS PRACTICE
What a Difference a Year Makes! 405

Setting Credit Policies 405

■ FOCUS ON BUSINESS PRACTICE
Why Powerful Buyers Can Cause Headaches for Small Businesses 405

Financing Receivables 407

CASH AND CASH EQUIVALENTS 408

■ FOCUS ON BUSINESS ETHICS
What About the Unlawful Use of EFT? 409

SHORT-TERM INVESTMENTS 409

Held-to-Maturity Securities 410

Trading Securities 410

Available-for-Sale Securities 412

Dividend and Interest Income 412

ACCOUNTS RECEIVABLE 413

Uncollectible Accounts and the Direct Charge-Off Method 413

Uncollectible Accounts and the Allowance Method 414

■ FOCUS ON BUSINESS PRACTICE
Selling Goods and Services is Only Half the Problem. 415

Estimating Uncollectible Accounts Expense 415

■ FOCUS ON INTERNATIONAL BUSINESS
Why Companies in Emerging Economies Must Adapt Accounting Practices 416

Writing Off an Uncollectible Account 419

Recovery of Accounts Receivable Written Off 419

NOTES RECEIVABLE 420

Computations for Promissory Notes 420

■ FOCUS ON BUSINESS PRACTICE
How Long Is a Year? It Depends. 421

Accounting Entries for Promissory Notes 422

Chapter Review 424 Review of Learning Objectives 424 Review of Concepts and Terminology 425 Review Problem 426 Answer to Review Problem 427

Chapter Assignments 427 Questions 427 Short Exercises 428 Exercises 429 Problems 432 Alternate Problems 434

Skills Development Cases 436

Financial Reporting and Analysis Cases 438

10 Inventories 440

- DECISION POINT J.C. Penney Company, Inc. 440

MANAGEMENT ISSUES ASSOCIATED WITH ACCOUNTING FOR INVENTORIES 442

Applying the Matching Rule to Inventories 442

- VIDEO CASE J.C. Penney Company, Inc. 443

Assessing the Impact of Inventory Decisions 443

Evaluating the Level of Inventory 444

- FOCUS ON BUSINESS TECHNOLOGY Dell's Inventory Turnover Can Make Your Head Spin. 444
- FOCUS ON BUSINESS TECHNOLOGY What a Headache! 446

INVENTORY COST AND GOODS FLOW 446

Merchandise in Transit 446

Merchandise on Hand Not Included in Inventory 447

Goods Flow Versus Cost Flow 447

METHODS OF PRICING INVENTORY AT COST UNDER THE PERIODIC INVENTORY SYSTEM 447

Specific Identification Method 448

Average-Cost Method 448

First-In, First-Out (FIFO) Method 449

Last-In, First-Out (LIFO) Method 449

- FOCUS ON BUSINESS PRACTICE What's a "Category Killer?" 450

PRICING INVENTORY UNDER THE PERPETUAL INVENTORY SYSTEM 451

- FOCUS ON BUSINESS TECHNOLOGY More Companies Enjoy LIFO! 452

COMPARISON AND IMPACT OF INVENTORY DECISIONS AND MISSTATEMENTS 453

Effects on the Financial Statements 454

Effects on Income Taxes 454

- FOCUS ON BUSINESS PRACTICE Does a Company's Accounting Method Affect Management's Operating Decisions? 455

Effects of Misstatements in Inventory Measurement 455

- FOCUS ON BUSINESS ETHICS The Temptation to Overstate Inventories 456

Inventory Measurement and Cash Flows 457

VALUING INVENTORY AT THE LOWER OF COST OR MARKET (LCM) 457

- FOCUS ON BUSINESS PRACTICE How Bad Can It Get? 458

Item-by-Item Method 458

Major Category Method 458

VALUING INVENTORY BY ESTIMATION 459

Retail Method of Inventory Estimation 459

Gross Profit Method of Inventory Estimation 460

Chapter Review 461 Review of Learning Objectives 461 Review of Concepts and Terminology 462 Review Problem 463 Answer to Review Problem 463

Chapter Assignments 466 Questions 466 Short Exercises 467 Exercises 468 Problems 471 Alternate Problems 472

Skills Development Cases 473

Financial Reporting and Analysis Cases 475

11 Long-Term Assets 478

- DECISION POINT H. J. Heinz Company 478

MANAGEMENT ISSUES RELATED TO ACCOUNTING FOR LONG-TERM ASSETS 480

- VIDEO CASE Fermi National Accelerator Laboratory 481

Deciding to Acquire Long-Term Assets 481

Financing Long-Term Assets 483

Applying the Matching Rule to Long-Term Assets 484

ACQUISITION COST OF PROPERTY, PLANT, AND EQUIPMENT 485

The Importance of Classifying Expenditures Correctly 485

General Approach to Acquisition Costs 485

- FOCUS ON BUSINESS ETHICS Is It an Asset or Expense? The Answer Matters. 487

ACCOUNTING FOR DEPRECIATION 487

Factors That Affect the Computation of Depreciation 488

- FOCUS ON BUSINESS PRACTICE The Useful Life of an Aircraft Is How Long? 488

Methods of Computing Depreciation 489

- FOCUS ON BUSINESS PRACTICE Accelerated Methods Save Money! 492

DISPOSAL OF DEPRECIABLE ASSETS 492

Discard or Sale of Plant Assets 492

Exchanges of Plant Assets 494

ACCOUNTING FOR NATURAL RESOURCES 496

Depletion 496

Depreciation of Closely Related Plant Assets 497

Development and Exploration Costs in the Oil and Gas Industry 497

ACCOUNTING FOR INTANGIBLE ASSETS 498

- FOCUS ON BUSINESS PRACTICE Take a Closer Look at Subscriber Lists! 500

Research and Development Costs 500

- FOCUS ON INTERNATIONAL BUSINESS Lack of Comparability is a Real Problem! 500

Computer Software Costs 501
Leasehold Improvements 501
Goodwill 501
■ FOCUS ON BUSINESS PRACTICE
Wake up, Goodwill Is Growing! 502
SPECIAL PROBLEMS OF DEPRECIATING PLANT ASSETS 502
Depreciation for Partial Years 502
Revision of Depreciation Rates 503
Group Depreciation 504
Special Types of Capital Expenditures 504
Cost Recovery for Federal Income Tax Purposes 505
Chapter Review 505 Review of Learning Objectives 505 Review of Concepts and Terminology 506 Review Problem 508 Answer to Review Problem 509
Chapter Assignments 510 Questions 510 Short Exercises 511 Exercises 512 Problems 514 Alternate Problems 516
Skills Development Cases 518
Financial Reporting and Analysis Cases 520

12 Current Liabilities 524

■ DECISION POINT US Airways, Inc. 524
MANAGEMENT ISSUES RELATED TO ACCOUNTING FOR CURRENT LIABILITIES 526
Managing Liquidity and Cash Flows 526
■ FOCUS ON BUSINESS PRACTICE
Debt Problems Can Plague Even Well-Known Companies. 528
Recognition of Liabilities 528
Valuation of Liabilities 528
Classification of Liabilities 528
Disclosure of Liabilities 529
COMMON CATEGORIES OF CURRENT LIABILITIES 529
Definitely Determinable Liabilities 529
■ FOCUS ON BUSINESS PRACTICE
Small Businesses Offer Benefits, Too. 532
Estimated Liabilities 535
■ FOCUS ON BUSINESS PRACTICE
Those Little Coupons Can Add Up. 536
■ FOCUS ON BUSINESS PRACTICE
Are Frequent-Flier Miles a Liability or a Revenue? 537
CONTINGENT LIABILITIES AND COMMITMENTS 538
PAYROLL ACCOUNTING ILLUSTRATED 538
Computation of an Employee's Take-Home Pay 538
Payroll Register 540
Recording the Payroll 541
Employee Earnings Record 541
■ FOCUS ON BUSINESS ETHICS Why Is Payroll Fraud Common? 542
Recording Payroll Taxes 542
Payment of Payroll and Payroll Taxes 542
Chapter Review 543 Review of Learning Objectives 543 Review of Concepts and Terminology 543 Review Problem 544 Answer to Review Problem 544
Chapter Assignments 545 Questions 545 Short Exercises 546 Exercises 547 Problems 549 Alternate Problems 551
Skills Development Cases 552
Financial Reporting and Analysis Cases 555

13 Partnerships 556

■ DECISION POINT KPMG LLP 556
PARTNERSHIP CHARACTERISTICS 558
Voluntary Association 558
■ FOCUS ON INTERNATIONAL BUSINESS
How Do Partnerships Facilitate International Investment? 559
■ FOCUS ON BUSINESS PRACTICE
Corporations That Look Like Partnerships 559
■ FOCUS ON BUSINESS PRACTICE
How Do Limited Partnerships Help Finance Big Projects? 560
Other Forms of Association 560
■ FOCUS ON BUSINESS TECHNOLOGY
Joint Ventures and the Internet 560
ACCOUNTING FOR PARTNERS' EQUITY 561
DISTRIBUTION OF PARTNERSHIP INCOME AND LOSSES 562
Stated Ratios 562
Capital Balance Ratios 563
Salaries, Interest, and Stated Ratios 564
■ FOCUS ON BUSINESS PRACTICE
What Are the Risks of Being a Partner in an Accounting Firm? 566
DISSOLUTION OF A PARTNERSHIP 567
Admission of a New Partner 567
Withdrawal of a Partner 570
■ FOCUS ON BUSINESS PRACTICE
Can Withdrawal of Partners Harm a Partnership? 570
Death of a Partner 572
LIQUIDATION OF A PARTNERSHIP 572
Gain on Sale of Assets 573
Loss on Sale of Assets 575

Chapter Review 577 Review of Learning Objectives 577 Review of Concepts and Terminology 579 Review Problem 579 Answer to Review Problem 580

Chapter Assignments 581 Questions 581 Short Exercises 582 Exercises 583 Problems 584

Alternate Problems 586

Skills Development Cases 588

Financial Reporting and Analysis Cases 589

Appendix A International Accounting 1173

Appendix B Long-Term Investments 1180

Appendix C The Time Value of Money 1187

Appendix D Future Value and Present Value Tables 1200

Endnotes 1207

Company Name Index 1212

Subject Index 1215

PREFACE

Recent business and accounting events underscore the fact that accounting matters. Now, more than ever before, accounting students need to learn how to create, analyze, and use financial statements if they are going to be successful managers in the future. They also need to understand how a company's accounting information system works. *Principles of Accounting,* 2005e (9th edition) does just that. It continues a long tradition of teaching students that a company's financial statements and the accounting information system that provides the supporting data are key to guiding a company's prosperity.

We believe that in order to read and interpret financial statements, students have to learn how to think critically. That is why in *Principles of Accounting* we continue to seek ways to help students think critically about what they are reading, how they might make a financial or managerial decision, and what roles they might play as future users of financial accounting information systems. Students also have to learn how to analyze and interpret data—where did the numbers come from? What is the significance of the numbers? What do the numbers reveal about the financial health of the company? Again, we stress the importance of critical analysis in *Principles of Accounting,* 2005e.

Principles of Accounting continues to be the leading text for students—both business and accounting majors—with no previous training in accounting or business. It is part of a well-integrated text and technology program that includes an array of print and electronic support materials for students and professors. The text consists of 27 chapters; the first 18 cover financial accounting, and the remaining 9 chapters focus on managerial accounting.

Principles of Accounting was revised with these major objectives in mind:

- **To support new instructional technologies in today's business environment**
- **To provide a framework for making successful and ethical business decisions**
- **To present real-world events and relevant business practices**
- **To develop skills and abilities critical to life-long learning**

NEW INSTRUCTIONAL TECHNOLOGIES IN TODAY'S BUSINESS ENVIRONMENT

New technologies are a driving force behind business growth and accounting education today. We have therefore developed an integrated text and technology program dedicated to helping instructors take advantage of the opportunities created by new instructional technologies. Our goal with the new 2005 edition is to expand and seamlessly integrate the technology package so users can gain experience with technology tools basic to business. Whether an instructor wants to present a user or procedural orientation, incorporate new instructional strategies, develop students' core skills and competencies, or integrate technology into the classroom, the new 2005e text provides a total solution, making it the leading choice among instructors of first-year financial and managerial accounting courses.

Technology Supplements on the Web

NEW! ***Eduspace®*** Eduspace powered by Blackboard™ is Houghton Mifflin's online homework system. The system enables students to complete homework assignments online. After students complete the assignment, they submit it electronically and immediately receive feedback on their answers. Eduspace offers a wealth of other student and instructor resources, including HMTesting (our computerized test bank), brand new PowerPoint slide presentations, and a complete course manual.

SmarThinking Houghton Mifflin and SmarThinking have partnered to provide state-of-the-art, live, online tutoring. Tutors can assist students with all examples, exercises, problems, and cases found in the text and related student supplements. An interactive interface allows tutors and students to share, annotate, and manipulate resources in real time to help illustrate concepts. A SmarThinking password is available for free and can be packaged with every new copy of the textbook.

The Needles Accounting Resource Center Web Site The Needles Accounting Resource Center Web Site (http://accounting.college.hmco.com) provides a wealth of free resources for instructors and students. For example, students can access ACE, the very popular online self-testing program that allows them to take sample quizzes and check their mastery of the chapter material. Over 1,200 new questions have been added to the ACE quizzes. An ACE icon at the end of each learning objective section reminds students to check out the ACE online review quizzes. Other resources include

- links to the web sites of over 200 real companies
- a list of relevant readings from leading business and accounting periodicals (such as *BusinessWeek, Forbes, The Wall Street Journal,* and *The Journal of Accountancy*), which examine current business issues, the accounting profession, and career options in a broad context.
- research activities, which present extended investigations of topics covered in the text.
- Toys "R" Us annual report activities, which make use of the latest Toys "R" Us financial statements.

For instructors, the Needles Accounting Resource Center Web Site offers:

- a completely revised set of PowerPoint slides, which contain classroom presentation materials, discussion questions, and figures from the text.
- electronic solutions, available both on the web site and on a CD-ROM, which are fully functioning Excel spreadsheets for exercises, problems, and selected cases in the text.
- sample syllabi, demonstrating how other instructors organize and teach the introductory course.
- the *Accounting Instructors' Report* newsletter, which explores a wide range of contemporary teaching issues.
- Faculty Development Programs' online training, which provides suggestions for integrating new technologies into the classroom or teaching online.

NEW! **Wall Street Journal *Subscription*** Students whose instructors have adopted the WSJ version of *Principles of Accounting* will receive, packaged with their book, a registration card for a 10-week print and online subscription to the *Wall Street Journal.* Students fill out and return the registration card to initiate subscription privileges. The text package also includes a copy of the *Wall Street Journal Student Subscriber Handbook,* which explains how to use both print and online versions of the newspaper.

Technology Supplements on CD-ROMs

NEW! ***HMAccounting Tutor*** This new student tutorial CD-ROM, specifically developed for use with *Principles of Accounting,* 2005e, reinforces understanding of accounting concepts covered in the text. Organized by chapter and learning objective, this software program enables students to study more efficiently and learn interactively. The program includes

- demonstration problems with voice-over narration that illustrate important concepts.
- interactive tutorials that allow students to cover text concepts at their own pace.
- Internet case taken directly from the 2005 text, which contain a link to a portal page for information the student needs to complete the cases.
- an interactive quizzing function to reinforce learning.
- a built-in glossary with on-screen pop-up definitions.

NEW! ***Mastering the Accounting Cycle: A Bridge Tutorial*** This new, stand-alone tutorial CD-ROM emphasizes accounting transactions, presents a review of the debit and credit mechanism, and provides a foundation for the preparation and use of financial statements. The CD contains four demonstration problems that show the connection between the balance sheet, income statement, and cash flow statement. It also has an interactive quizzing function and a built-in glossary.

HMClassPrep with HMTesting CD-ROM This instructor CD contains the computerized version of the test bank as well as other useful instructor aids.

The *computerized test bank* allows instructors to select, edit, and add questions, or generate randomly selected questions to produce a test master for easy duplication. Test questions are organized by learning objective and can be compiled using key words from the text. Online Testing and Gradebook functions allow instructors to administer tests via their school's network or over the Web, set up classes, record grades from tests or assignments, analyze grades, and compile class and individual statistics. This program can be used on both PCs and Macintosh computers. (A printed version of the test bank is also available upon request.)

Other Instructor Aids on HMClassPrep include

- the complete ***Course Manual*** (course planning matrix, time/difficulty chart, chapter-by-chapter instructional materials, and review quizzes).
- the ***Solutions Manual*** (a complete set of solutions to all exercises, problems, and selected cases in the text; also available in print).
- ***PowerPoint Slides*** (brand new PowerPoint slide presentations for every chapter)
- five-minute ***video cases*** tied to the in-text cases, highlighting real companies.
- ***check figures*** for end-of-chapter problems.
- ***web links*** to the Needles Accounting Resource Center Web Site at (http://accounting.college.hmco.com).

NEW! ***Windows General Ledger Software on the Student CD-ROM*** Completely updated for *Principles of Accounting,* 2005e, Houghton Mifflin's Windows General Ledger software offers coverage of accounting concepts and procedures in an extremely simple and user-friendly computerized environment. Most of the text problems in Chapters 1-18 can be solved using this program. The new GLS has an updated interface and expanded features—such as the ability to export files to Peachtree. The GLS software is included on the Student CD, which comes free with new texts purchased from Houghton Mifflin.

Also on the Student CD are check figures for the text problems, the video cases that accompany *Principles of Accounting,* and a full glossary.

Fingraph Financial Analyst CD-ROM This CD contains the educational version of a patented software program used by financial analysts and certified public accountants to analyze and summarize the financial performance of companies. The financial data reported by over 20 well-known companies have been summarized and loaded into Microsoft Excel spreadsheets that can be accessed through the Needles Accounting Resource Center Web Site at http://accounting.college.hmco.com. Students can also enter data obtained from the annual report of any company. The Fingraph software enables students to prepare financial analyses of real companies in a very short time. The software accommodates a variety of learning styles; analyses are presented in tabular, graphic, and written formats. Most of the financial chapters of *Principles of Accounting,* 2005e contain a case designed to be worked in conjunction with the CD-ROM database, in which students analyze balance sheets, income statements, and statements of cash flows of real companies.

Introduction to Financial Accounting: The Language of Business CD-ROM Bel Needles and Marian Powers developed this competency-based, interactive CD in partnership with Learning Insights. The software is designed to teach accounting to people who have little or no financial background, especially business majors and nonfinancial managers who need to learn the financial impact of operating decisions.

Electronic Working Papers CD-ROM This CD is an electronic version of the printed Working Papers for exercises, problems, and selected cases in the text. By working on these Excel-based templates, students not only learn accounting but also the basic skills required for spreadsheet applications.

A Framework for Successful and Ethical Decision Making

We know that most instructors want to place more emphasis on critical analysis and on how managers use accounting information to make decisions. We also know that ethical decision making is an important topic in light of the new focus on corporate governance. We are proud to continue our long tradition of emphasizing ethical decision making. At the end of each chapter we present at least one short case, based on real public companies, in which students must address an authentic, work-related, ethical dilemma directly related to the chapter content. The cases reveal how managers must account for their business decisions. Also, we have added within the text several new Focus on Business Ethics boxes that feature examples of how real companies have faced ethical issues.

Comparative Financial Analysis

We have expanded the use of financial information in performance evaluation and measurement by introducing a new comparison case at the end of most of the financial chapters. Students compare Walgreens and Toys "R" Us, using both companies' financial statements, which are bound into the text at the end of Chapter 6. The comparison cases require students to compute ratios, make assumptions, report on the effect of seasonal sales, and describe each company's inventory management system, to name a few tasks. Again, *Principles of Accounting* continues to stress the important role of financial statements in revealing useful information about companies.

Cash Flow

We emphasize the effect of business activities on cash flow throughout the financial chapters. Beginning in Chapter 1, we introduce the statement of cash flows, and we point out the difference between income measurement and cash flow in various chapters, reinforcing it through assignments. An icon in the margin calls attention to cash flow discussions.

Key Ratios

Starting in Chapter 6, we examine financial analysis ratios and integrate them in subsequent financial chapters at appropriate points. We bring all the ratios together in a comprehensive financial analysis of Sun Microsystems, Inc., in Chapter 18. An icon %in the margin calls attention to key ratio presentations.

Management Accounting Coverage

Co-author Susan Crosson has heavily revised most of the managerial chapters (Chapters 19-27). Her efforts were directed at helping students gain confidence in their ability to understand and apply accounting concepts once they leave the classroom and enter the workplace. For example, rather than focusing on the technical details of cost accounting, the managerial chapters emphasize the management cycle critical to operating a successful business. The managerial chapters also emphasize the approaches learned from the most progressive companies, such as how to manage supply chains, analyze value chains, operate in a just-in-time environment, utilize activity-based management, apply the theory of constraints, and focus on quality.

Today, management's use of information goes far beyond computing the cost of products and services. This book explores the full range of innovative managerial systems in a value-centered economy in which managers must make critical decisions concerning product quality, customer service, and long-term relationships. The text discusses the latest in management models and technology, plus it emphasizes that performance measurement, evaluation, and compensation are essential to a manager's success in today's competitive environment. Service businesses, where many students will ultimately work, receive expanded emphasis within the text discussion and the chapter assignments.

Real-World Events and Business Practices

Working toward our goal of reflecting current business practice in a context that is relevant and exciting to students, we have incorporated the following real-world elements of the text.

Actual Financial Statements

To enhance students' appreciation for the usefulness and relevance of accounting information, we include excerpts from annual reports of real companies and articles about them in business journals. In total, we cite more than 200 publicly held companies in the text so that students can apply the concepts to real companies. These companies are identified by a URL in the margin of the text or by a URL within the end-of-chapter case text.

The complete annual report of Toys "R" Us and the financial statements and notes of Walgreen Company appear at the end of Chapter 6. Chapter 6 also presents the financial statements of Dell Computer Corporation in graphical form using the Fingraph Financial Analysis CD-ROM software. Chapter 18 features the financial statements of Sun Microsystems, Inc. to illustrate comprehensive financial analysis. Several of the Financial Reporting and Analysis Cases ask students to select real companies and access their financial statements on the Internet or through the Needles Accounting Resource Center Web Site at http://accounting.college.hmco.com to research the information needed to answer the questions.

Updated Decision Points

Every chapter begins with a Decision Point based on excerpts from a real company's annual report or from articles in the business press. In addition to introducing the concepts to be covered in the chapter, the Decision Point presents a situation that requires a decision by management and then demonstrates how the decision can be made using accounting information. The 2005 edition features several new Decision Points, among them Walgreens, Kelly Services, Cisco, Kraft, Coach, Palm, and Amazon.com. All of the other Decision Points have been revised and updated with the most recent financial information available.

New Focus on Business Boxes

Always a popular feature in the Needles accounting series, the Focus on Business boxes have been redesigned and over a third of them have been replaced with newsworthy feature stories. These boxes contain short summaries of items that show the relevance of accounting in four areas:

- Focus on Business Practice
- Focus on International Business
- Focus on Business Technology
- Focus on Business Ethics

Real-World Graphic Illustrations

We present graphs and tables illustrating how actual business practices relate to chapter topics. Many of these illustrations are based on data from studies of 600 annual reports published in *Accounting Trends and Techniques.* Beginning with Chapter 6, most chapters display a graphic that shows selected ratios for selected industries based on Dun & Bradstreet data. Service industry examples include advertising agencies and interstate trucking companies. Merchandising industry examples include auto and home supply companies and grocery stores. Manufacturing industry examples include machinery and computer companies. All graphs and tables have been updated with the most recent data available.

International Accounting

Recognizing the global economy in which all businesses operate today, we incorporate international accounting examples throughout the text. Each chapter includes a Financial Reporting and Analysis Case or a Managerial Reporting and Analysis Case that features an international company. Some examples include Harrods (British), Heineken (Dutch), Pioneer Corporation (Japan), and Roche (Swiss).

Video Cases

Two new 5-minute video vignettes (Claire's Boutiques and J. C. Penney) have been added to the series of video cases. Each video highlights a real company and is accompanied by an in-text case, which serves as an introduction to the chapter in which it is found. The videos work equally well as individual or group assignments, and all include a critical-thinking component and a writing assignment. The following video cases are included in the 2005 edition.

Intel Corporation (Chapter 1) examines the business goals of liquidity and profitability and the business activities of financing, investing, and operating.

Claire's Stores, Inc. (Chapter 5) describes a merchandising operation that has to regulate its inventories and generate a satisfactory gross margin in order to achieve profitability.

J.C. Penney Company, Inc. (Chapter 10) focuses on the management issues associated with accounting for inventories.

Fermi National Accelerator Laboratory (Chapter 11) demonstrates the importance of long-term assets to a unique scientific laboratory.

Goodyear Tire & Rubber Company (Chapter 17) describes the vision and objectives of the world's largest tire and rubber company and how Goodyear will need strong cash flows to carry out its objectives.

Enterprise Rent-A-Car (Chapter 24) presents the budgeting process in the management cycle and describes the master budget process for a service company.

Harley-Davidson, Inc. (Chapter 26) demonstrates how a company uses the concepts of responsibility accounting and the balanced scorecard in its performance management and evaluation system.

Competency-Based Skill Development for Life-Long Learning

Our goal in *Principles of Accounting,* 2005e is to provide the most comprehensive and flexible set of assignments to promote the development of critical knowledge and abilities while still providing the necessary technical skills required of future managers and accountants. Whether you favor more traditional assignments or cases that enhance a broader set of student skills, or a combination of both, we provide ample competency-based assignments—clearly identified—to meet your goals.

We also continue to integrate conceptual learning with procedural learning, especially in our end-of-chapter problems. We have added an analysis component to most of our problem requirements so students learn why a transaction was recorded or how the information in a particular financial statement is used to evaluate liquidity or profitability. In the managerial chapters, students not only make decisions but also must support them with reasoned explanations. We continue to stress the meaning behind the numbers in the financial and managerial reports—the message they contain.

Building Your Knowledge Foundation

This section consists of a variety of questions, exercises, and problems designed to develop basic knowledge, comprehension, and application of the concepts and techniques in the chapter.

- *Questions (Q):* Fifteen to 25 review questions cover the essential topics of the chapter.
- *Short Exercises (SE):* These ten very brief exercises are suitable for classroom use.
- *Exercises (E):* An average of 15 single topic exercises stress application.
- *Problems (P):* These five extensive applications of chapter topics often cover more than one Learning Objective. Most problems in the 2005 edition contain analysis components in which students are asked to explain how the numbers relate to the concepts covered in the chapter. Most problems in the financial chapters can be solved using our General Ledger Software for Windows. These problems are marked with the following icon:
- *Alternate Problems (P):* An alternative set of the most popular problems has been developed based on feedback from our study of users' syllabi.

Skills Development (SD) Cases, Financial Reporting and Analysis (FRA) Cases, and Managerial Reporting and Analysis (MRA) Cases

The Accounting Education Change Commission, the American Accounting Association, The American Institute of CPAs, and the Institute of Management Accountants have all called for the development of a broader set of skills among business and accounting graduates. The ten or more cases in this section answer this need by requiring students to work on their critical-thinking and communication skills, analytical skills, and writing skills. Most of the cases are based on real companies. All require critical-thinking and communication skills in the form of writing. At least one assignment in each chapter requires students to practice good business communication skills by writing a memorandum that reports results and offers recommendations. In addition, all cases are suitable for development of interpersonal skills through group activities. Certain cases are especially appropriate for group activities; they have specific instructions for applying a group methodology. We use icons to identify these cases, as well as to provide guidance in the best use of other assignments. The following is a list of those icons:

Cash Flow icons indicate assignments dealing with cash flow; they also indicate text discussions of cash flow.

Communication icons identify assignments designed to help students develop their ability to understand and communicate accounting information successfully.

Critical Thinking icons indicate assignments intended to strengthen student's critical-thinking skills.

Ethics icons identify assignments that address ethical issues.

Group Activity icons identify assignments especially appropriate for groups or teamwork.

International icons indicate cases involving international companies.

Key Ratio icons indicate the presence of financial analysis ratios in both the text and assignments.

Memorandum icons identify cases that require students to write short business memorandums.

Each case has a specific purpose, as described in the following paragraphs:

Conceptual Analysis Designed so that a written solution is appropriate, these short cases are based on real companies and address conceptual accounting issues.

Ethical Dilemma The inclusion of ethics training in the business and accounting curriculum has become very important in light of the accounting scandals that have rocked corporate America. Every chapter in *Principles of Accounting,* 2005e contains a short case, often based on a real company, in which students must address an ethical dilemma directly related to the chapter content.

Research Activity Each chapter has a case that asks students to do research using business periodicals, annual reports, newspaper articles, the library, and the Internet. Some cases are designed to improve students' interviewing and observation skills through field activities at actual businesses.

Decision-Making Practice Students practice decision making after extracting relevant data from a case and making computations as necessary. Students' role as decision maker may be from the perspective of a manager, investor, analyst, or creditor.

Interpreting Financial (Management) Reports These short cases are abstracted from business articles and annual reports of well-known companies such as Kmart, Sears, IBM, Toys "R" Us, Chrysler, and many others. All require students to extract relevant data, make computations, and interpret the results.

International Company Each chapter has an international case that focuses on a foreign company that has had an accounting experience compatible with chapter content.

Toy "R" Us Annual Report Students read and analyze the actual annual report of Toys "R" Us, which is printed at the end of Chapter 6.

Comparison Case: Toys "R" Us and Walgreen Co. This is a new case, which appears in most of the financial chapters. Students are asked to compare Toys "R" Us and Walgreens in a number of different ways. Using the Toy "R" Us Annual Report and the financial statements of Walgreens, both of which appear at the end of Chapter 6, students learn how to find information, perform various financial analyses, and then compare the results.

Fingraph Financial Analyst Most of the financial chapters have a case that requires students to use the Fingraph Financial Analyst CD-ROM. Students can use the Fingraph software to do tabular, graphic, or written analyses. Students can obtain financial data from more than 20 companies by accessing the Needles Accounting Resource Center Web Site at http://accounting.college.hmco.com/students, or they can obtain data from any company of their choice.

Internet Case Each chapter features an Internet case, which asks students to research a topic on the Internet, answer critical- and analytical-thinking questions, and then prepare a written or oral report on their findings.

Excel Spreadsheet Analysis These assignments in the managerial accounting chapters provide opportunities for written communication, interpretation, and analysis.

The Annual Report Project Because the use of real companies' annual reports is the most rapidly growing type of term project in the financial accounting course, we provide an annual report project that we have used in our own classes for several years. Depending on how comprehensive you want the project to be, we have developed four assignment options, including the use of the Fingraph Financial Analyst CD-ROM software.

ORGANIZATION OF *PRINCIPLES OF ACCOUNTING,* 2005E

The chapter organization of *Principles of Accounting,* 2005e reflects an early introduction of financial statements and the relationship of financial accounting to the major activities of a business. *Chapters 1-6* introduce performance measurements, cash flow effects, and ratio analysis, making the integration of these key management techniques throughout the text possible. *Chapters 7-8* cover accounting information systems and internal control, key topics in today's business environment. *Chapters 9-12* are about measuring and reporting assets and current liabilities. *Chapters 13-16* focus on accounting for partnerships and corporations. *Chapters 17-18* conclude the financial chapters by covering the statement of cash flows and emphasizing financial performance evaluation.

Chapters 19-20 introduce the fundamentals of management accounting and cost concepts. *Chapters 21-22* explore cost-based and activity-based systems for management accounting. *Chapters 23-24* focus on information analysis for planning, including cost behavior analysis and the budgeting process. *Chapters 25-26* cover performance measurement using standard costing and performance management and evaluation. *Chapter 27* concludes the managerial chapters with an analysis of decision making.

All 27 chapters of *Principles of Accounting,* 2005e have been thoroughly reviewed and edited. A new and fresh design will engage students as they proceed through the text.

Pedagogical Color

A consistent color scheme throughout the text presents inputs to the accounting system (source documents) in orange, the processing of accounting data (working papers and accounting forms) in green, and outputs of the system (financial statements) in blue.

Stop and Think Questions

We have introduced new "Stop and Think" questions, tied to each learning objective, to motivate students to read actively and think critically. These questions—accompanied by a short answer—are designed to help students think about what they are reading. They can also serve as a valuable review device or as the basis for class discussions.

Pedagogical Annotations

These annotations appear in Chapter 1 only. They introduce each pedagogical element of the text—Learning Objectives, Decision Points, Content Annotations, and Chapter Reviews, to name a few. They describe the purpose of the pedagogy and provide usage suggestions so that students can derive maximum benefit when reading and studying the text.

Content Annotations

These marginal annotations appear throughout the text, offering material that enriches the text discussion as well as strategies and tips for mastering text content. Content annotations fall into the following categories:

- *Key Points* briefly summarize main concepts or ideas.
- *Enrichment Notes* offer interesting insights—such as historical perspectives—to heighten students' appreciation of the material.
- *Terminology Notes* provide succinct definition of key terms and concepts used in the text discussion.
- *Business-World Examples* are short anecdotes drawn from real businesses to help students see the day-to-day relevance of accounting in real companies.
- *Ethical Considerations* highlight practices or behaviors that might engender ethical concern.
- *Study Notes* provide useful strategies and tips to help students avoid common pitfalls.

Related Text Assignments

In the 2005 edition, we have added a list of related text assignments to each learning objective. Students can now see which questions (Q), Short Exercises (SE), exercises (E), Problems (P), Skills Development (SD) Cases, and Financial (Managerial) Reporting and Analysis (FRA/MRA) Cases reinforce a particular learning objective.

ACKNOWLEDGMENTS

The success we have enjoyed over the years with *Principles of Accounting* is due in no small way to the countless comments and suggestions we have received from colleagues, attendees of our annual Conference on Accounting Education, and students who have used our book. While there are too many of you to name individually, we do wish to recognize those who have made special contributions to the 2005 edition of *Principles of Accounting.* We therefore thank Edward H. Julius (California Lutheran University) for his meticulous work on the Study Guide and Test Bank; Gayle Richardson (Bakersfield College) for her contribution to the Test Bank; Gail Mestas for creating the PowerPoint slides; Cathy Larson for her accuracy review of the text and solutions; Jacquie Commanday for her assistance with the Course Manual; and Sarah Evans for her developmental editing of the text and Course Manual and page layout.

We also recognize the constant support we have received over the years and particularly for this edition from senior sponsoring editor, Bonnie Binkert; senior development editor, Margaret Kearney; project editor, Claudine Bellanton; and editorial associate, Jim Dimock.

Others who have been supportive and have had an impact on this book through their reviews, suggestions, and class testing are:

Daneen Adams *Santa Fe Community College*
Gregory D. Barnes *Clarion University*
Mohamed E. Bayou *The University of Michigan—Dearborn*
Charles M. Betts *Delaware Technical and Community College*
Michael C. Blue *Bloomsburg University*
Gary R. Bower *Community College of Rhode Island*
Lee Cannell *El Paso Community College*
John D. Cunha *University of California—Berkeley*
Mark W. Dawson *Duquesne University*
Patricia A. Doherty *Boston University*
Lizabeth England *American Language Academy*
David Fetyko *Kent State University*
Sue Garr *Wayne State University*
Roxanne Gooch *Cameron University*
Christine Uber Grosse *The American Graduate School of International Management*
Dennis A. Gutting *Orange County Community College*
John Hancock *University of California—Davis Graduate School of Management*
Yvonne Hatami *Borough of Manhattan Community College*
Harry Hooper *Santa Fe Community College*
Marianne James *California State University, Los Angeles*
Edward H. Julius *California Lutheran University*
Howard A. Kanter *DePaul University*
Debbie Luna *El Paso Community College*
Kevin McClure *ESL Language Center*
Geroge McGowan
Gail A. Mestas
Jenine Moscove
Beth Brooks Patel *University of California—Berkeley*
LaVonda Ramey *Schoolcraft College*
Roberta Rettner *American Ways*
Gayle Richardson *Bakersfield College*
James B. Rosa *Queensborough Community College*
Donald Shannon *DePaul Univeristy*
S. Murray Simons *Northeastern University*

Marion Taube *University of Pittsburgh*
Kathleen Villani *Queensborough Community College*
Vicki Vorell *Cuyahoga Community College*
John Weber *DeVry Institute*
Kay Westerfield *University of Oregon*
Andy Williams *Edmunds Community College*

Finally, we want to identify and thank the facilitators for the last five years of COAE (Conference on Accounting Education) and congratulate our recent Technology Award winners:

2003 COAE Facilitators
Charlene Abendroth, California State University
Daneen Adams, Santa Fe Community College
Richard Fern, Eastern Kentucky University
Terry Grant, Mississippi College
Yvonne Hatami, Borough of Manhattan Community College
Rodger Holland, Columbus State University

2002 COAE Facilitators
Sharon Bell, University of North Carolina—Pembroke
Mark Henry, the Victoria College
Harry Hooper, Santa Fe Community College
Richard Irvine, Pensacola Junior College
Nancy Kelly, Middlesex Community College
Paul Mihalek, University of Hartford
Paul Weitzel, Eastern Shore Community College

2001 COAE Facilitators
Salvador Aceves, University of San Francisco
Betty Habershon, Prince George's Community College
Jim Mazza, Heald College
Roselyn Morris, Southwest Texas State University
Ginger Parker, Creighton University
David Rogers, Mesa State College
Jeanne Yamamura, University of Nevada—Reno

2000 COAE Facilitators
Mary Falkey, Prince Georges Community College
Kathy Otero, University of Texas—El Paso
Hubert Gill, University of North Florida
Rick Turpin, University of Tennessee
Lyle Hicks, Danville Area Community College
John Weber, DeVry University

1999 COAE Facilitators
Sidney Askew, Borough of Manhattan Community College
Dahli Gray, Morgan State University
Clarence Coleman, Jr., Francis Marion College
Karen Novey, Robert Morris College
James Dougher, DeVry Institute
Miriam Keller-Perkins, Berkeley College
Suzanne Wright, Penn State University

COAE Technology Award Winners
2003 - Elizabeth Murphy, DePaul University
2002 - Vicki Vorell, Cuyahoga Community College
2001 - Roselyn E. Morris, Southwest Texas State University

—B.N., M.P., and S.C.

To the Student

How to Study Accounting Successfully

The introductory accounting course is fundamental to the business curriculum and to success in the business world beyond college. Whether you are majoring in accounting or in another business discipline, it is one of the most important classes you will take. The course has multiple purposes because its students have diverse interests, backgrounds, and reasons for taking it. What are your goals in studying accounting? Being clear about your goals can contribute to your success in this course.

Success in this class also depends on your desire to learn and your willingness to work hard. It depends on your understanding of how the text complements the way your instructor teaches and the way you learn. A familiarity with how this text is structured will help you to study more efficiently, make better use of classroom time, and improve your performance on examinations and other assignments.

To be successful in the business world after you graduate, you will need a broad set of skills, which may be summarized as follows:

Technical/Analytical Skills A major objective of your accounting course is to give you a firm grasp of the essential business and accounting terminology and techniques that you will need to succeed in a business environment. With this foundation, you then can begin to develop the higher-level perception skills that will help you acquire further knowledge on your own.

An even more crucial objective of this course is to help you develop analytical skills that will allow you to evaluate data. An important aspect of analytical skills is the ability to use technology effectively in making analyses. Well-developed analytical and decision-making skills are among the professional skills most highly valued by employers and will serve you well throughout your academic and professional careers.

Communication Skills Another skill highly prized by employers is the ability to express oneself in a manner that others correctly understand. This can include writing skills, speaking skills, and presentation skills. Communication skills are developed through particular tasks and assignments and are improved through constructive criticism. Reading skills and listening skills support the direct communication skills.

Interpersonal Skills Effective interaction between two people requires a solid foundation of interpersonal skills. The success of such interaction depends on empathy, or the ability to identify with and understand the problems, concerns, and motives of others. Leadership, supervision, and interviewing skills also facilitate a professional's interaction with others.

Personal/Self Skills Personal/self skills form the foundation for growth in the use of all other skills. To succeed, a professional must take initiative, possess self-confidence, show independence, and be ethical in all areas of life. Personal/self skills can be enhanced significantly by the formal learning process and by peers and mentors who provide models upon which one can build. Accounting is just one course in your entire curriculum, but it can play an important role in your skill development. Your instructor is interested in helping you gain both a knowledge of accounting and the more general skills you will need to succeed in the business world. The following sections describe how you can get the most out of this course.

The Teaching/Learning Cycle™

Both teaching and learning have natural, parallel, and mutually compatible cycles. This teaching/learning cycle, as shown in Figure 1, interacts with the basic structure of learning objectives in this text.

The Teaching Cycle The inner (tan) circle in Figure 1 shows the steps an instructor takes in teaching a chapter. Your teacher *assigns* material, *presents* the subject in lecture, *explains* by going over assignments and answering questions, *reviews* the subject prior to an exam, and *assesses* your knowledge and understanding using examinations and other means of evaluation.

The Learning Cycle Moving outward, the next circle (green) in Figure 1 shows the steps you should take in studying a chapter. You should *preview* the material, *read* the chapter, *apply* your understanding by working the assignments, *review* the chapter, and *recall* and *demonstrate* your knowledge and understanding of the material in examinations and other assessments.

Integrated Learning Objectives Your textbook supports the teaching/learning cycle through the use of integrated learning objectives. Learning objectives are simply statements of what you should be able to do after you have completed a chapter. In Figure 1, the outside (blue) circle shows how learning objectives are integrated into your text and other study aids and how they interact with the teaching/learning cycle.

1. Learning objectives listed at the beginning of each chapter aid your teacher in making assignments and help you preview the chapter.
2. Each learning objective is referenced in the margin of the text at the point where that subject is covered. A list of related text assignments below each learning objective identifies the end-of-chapter exercises, problems, and cases that relate to that objective.
3. Every exercise, problem, and case in the end-of-chapter assignments shows the applicable learning objective(s) so you can refer to the text if you need help.
4. A summary of the key points for each learning objective, a list of new concepts and terms referenced by learning objectives, and a review problem covering key learning objectives assist you in reviewing each chapter. The Study Guide, also organized by learning objectives, provides additional review.

Why Students Succeed Students succeed in their accounting course when they coordinate their personal learning cycle with their instructor's cycle. Students who do a good job of previewing their assignments, reading the chapters before the instructor is ready to present them, preparing homework assignments before they are discussed in class, and reviewing carefully will ultimately achieve their potential on exams. To ensure that your learning cycle is synchronized with your instructor's teaching cycle, check your study habits against the following suggestions.

Previewing the Chapter

1. Read the learning objectives at the beginning of the chapter. These learning objectives specifically describe what you should be able to do after completing the chapter.
2. Study your syllabus. Know where you are in the course and where you are going. Know the rules of the course.
3. Realize that in an accounting course, each assignment builds on previous ones. If you do poorly in Chapter 1, you may have difficulty in Chapter 2 and be lost in Chapter 3.

FIGURE 1
The Teaching/Learning Cycle™ with integrated Learning Objectives

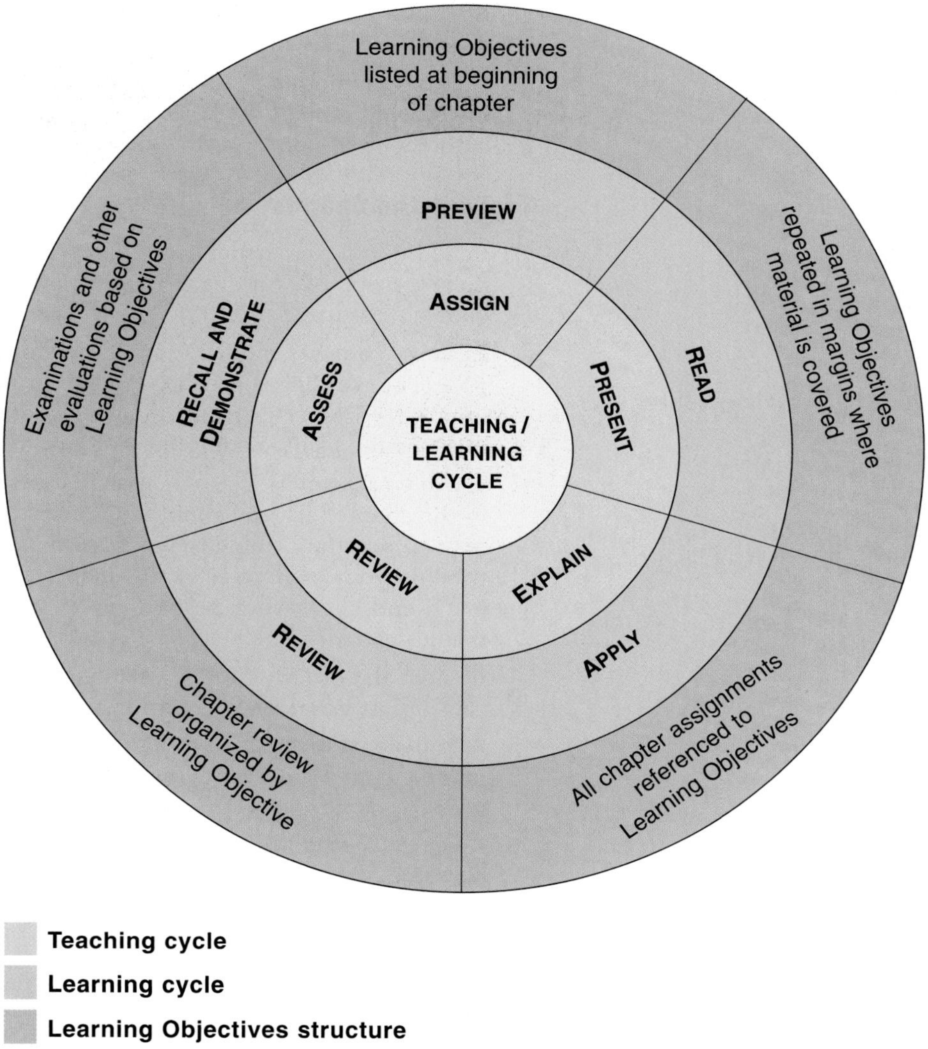

Reading the Chapter

1. As you read each chapter, be aware of the learning objectives in the margins. They will tell you why the material is relevant.
2. Allow yourself plenty of time to read the text. Accounting is a technical subject. Accounting books are so full of information that almost every sentence is important.
3. Strive to understand not only how each procedure is done, but also why it is done. Accounting is logical and requires reasoning. If you understand why something is done in accounting, there is little need to memorize.
4. Relate each new topic to its learning objective and be able to explain it in your own words.
5. Be aware of colors as you read. They are designed to help you understand the text. (For handy reference, the use of color is also explained on the back cover of the book.)
   Orange: All source documents and inputs are in orange.
   Green: All accounting forms, working papers, and accounting processes are shown in green.

Blue: All financial statements, the output or final product of the accounting process, are shown in blue.

6. If there is something you do not understand, prepare specific questions for your instructor. Pinpoint the topic or concept that confuses you. Some students keep a notebook of points with which they have difficulty.

Applying the Chapter

1. In addition to understanding why each procedure is done, you must be able to do it yourself by working exercises, problems, and cases. Accounting is a "do-it-yourself" course.
2. Read assignments and instructions carefully. Each assignment has a specific purpose. The wording is precise, and a clear understanding of it will save time and improve your performance. Acquaint yourself with the end-of-chapter assignment materials by reading the description of them in the Preface.
3. Try to work exercises, problems, and cases without referring to their discussions in the chapter. If you cannot work an assignment without looking in the chapter, you will not be able to work a similar problem on an exam. After you have tried on your own, refer to the chapter (based on the learning objective reference) and check your answer. Try to understand any mistakes you may have made.
4. Be neat and orderly. Sloppy calculations, messy papers, and general carelessness cause most errors on accounting assignments.
5. Allow plenty of time to work the chapter assignments. You will find that assignments seem harder and that you make more errors when you are feeling pressed for time.
6. Keep up with your class. Check your work against the solutions presented in class. Find your mistakes. Be sure you understand the correct solutions.
7. Note the part of each exercise, problem, or case that causes you difficulty so you can ask for help.
8. Attend class. Most instructors design classes to help you and to answer your questions. Absence from even one class can hurt your performance.

Reviewing the Chapter

1. Read the summary of learning objectives in the chapter review. Be sure you know the definitions of all the words in the review of concepts and terminology.
2. Review all assigned exercises, problems, and cases. Know them cold. Be sure you can work the assignments without the aid of the book.
3. Determine the learning objectives for which most of the problems were assigned. They refer to topics that your instructor is most likely to emphasize on an exam. Scan the text for such learning objectives and pay particular attention to the examples and illustrations.
4. Look for and scan other similar assignments that cover the same learning objectives. They may be helpful on an exam.
5. Review quizzes. Similar material will often appear on longer exams.
6. Attend any labs or visit any tutors your school provides, or see your instructor during office hours to get assistance. Be sure to have specific questions ready.

Taking Examinations

1. Arrive at class early so you can get the feel of the room and make a last-minute review of your notes.

2. Have plenty of sharp pencils and your calculator (if allowed) ready.
3. Review the exam quickly when it is handed out to get an overview of your task. Start with a part you know. It will give you confidence and save time.
4. Allocate your time to the various parts of the exam, and stick to your schedule. Every exam has time constraints. You need to move ahead and make sure you attempt all parts of the exam.
5. Read the questions carefully. Some may not be exactly like your homework assignments. They may approach the material from a slightly different angle to test your understanding and ability to reason, rather than your ability to memorize.
6. To avoid unnecessary errors, be neat, use good form, and show calculations.
7. Relax. If you have followed the above guidelines, your effort will be rewarded.

Preparing Other Assignments

1. Understand the assignment. Written assignments, term papers, computer projects, oral presentations, case studies, group activities, individual field trips, video critiques, and other activities are designed to enhance skills beyond your technical knowledge. It is essential to know exactly what your instructor expects. Know the purpose, audience, scope, and expected end product.
2. Allow plenty of time. "Murphy's Law" applies to such assignments: If anything can go wrong, it will.
3. Prepare an outline of each report, paper, or presentation. A project that is done well always has a logical structure.
4. Write a rough draft of each paper and report, and practice each presentation. Professionals always try out their ideas in advance and thoroughly rehearse their presentations. Good results are not accomplished by accident.
5. Make sure that each paper, report, or presentation is of professional quality. Instructors appreciate attention to detail and polish. A good rule of thumb is to ask yourself: Would I give this work to my boss?

About the Authors

Central to the success of any accounting text is the expertise of its author team. This team brings a wealth of classroom teaching experience, relevant business insight, and pedagogical expertise, as well as first-hand knowledge of today's students.

Belverd E. Needles, Jr., PhD, CPA, CMA
DePaul University

During his more than 30 years of teaching beginning accounting students, Belverd Needles has been an acknowledged innovator in accounting education. He has won teaching and education awards from DePaul University, the American Accounting Association, the Illinois CPA Society, the American Institute of CPAs, and the national honorary society, Beta Alpha Psi. The Conference on Accounting Education, started by Dr. Needles and sponsored by Houghton Mifflin, is in its 20th year; it has helped more than 2,000 beginning accounting instructors improve their teaching. Dr. Needles is editor of the *Accounting Instructors' Report*, in its 19th year, a newsletter that thousands of accounting teacher's rely on for new ideas in accounting education.

Marian Powers, PhD
Northwestern University

With more than 25 years of teaching experience, Marian Powers has taught beginning accounting at every level, from large lecture halls of 250 students to small classes of graduate students. She is a dynamic teacher who incorporates a variety of instructional strategies designed to broaden students' skills and experiences in critical thinking, group interaction, and communication. Consistently, Dr. Powers receives the highest ratings from students. She also brings practical experience to her students, including examples of how managers in all levels of business use and evaluate financial information. In recent years, Dr. Powers has concentrated on executive education. She has taught thousands of executives from leading companies around the world how to read and analyze the financial statements of their own companies and those of their competitors.

Susan Crosson, MS, CPA
Santa Fe Community College (Florida)

Susan Crosson, with more than 25 years of teaching at the college and university level, is recognized for her pedagogical expertise in teaching managerial accounting. Currently at Santa Fe Community College in Florida, Professor Crosson has a reputation for being able to engage university students in very large course sections and for encouraging community college students to master accounting. She believes in integrating technology into accounting education and actively uses the Internet to teach online, blended, and on-campus courses. Professor Crosson continues to promote the improvement of accounting education by serving the American Accounting Association and the Florida Institute of CPAs on a variety of committees, task forces, and sections. She is a past recipient of an IMA Faculty Development Grant to blend technology into the classroom, the Florida Association of Community Colleges Professor of the Year Award for Instructional Excellence, and the University of Oklahoma's Halliburton Education Award for Excellence.

Check Figures

Chapter 1 Problems
P 1. Total assets: $21,640
P 2. Total assets: $141,200
P 3. Total assets: $8,060
P 4. Total assets: $143,800
P 5. Total assets: $10,240
P 6. Total assets: $27,450
P 7. Total assets: $115,000
P 8. Total assets: $48,750

Chapter 2 Problems
P 1. No check figure
P 2. Trial balance totals: $21,100
P 3. Trial balance totals: $7,400
P 4. Trial balance totals: $23,100
P 5. Trial balance totals: $47,030
P 6. No check figure
P 7. Trial balance totals: $21,080
P 8. Trial balance totals: $61,420

Chapter 3 Problems
P 1. No check figure
P 2. No check figure
P 3. Adjusted Trial Balance: $212,334
P 4. Adjusted Trial Balance: $26,040
P 5. Adjusted Trial Balance: $29,778
P 6. No check figure
P 7. No check figure
P 8. Adjusted Trial Balance: $121,792

Chapter 4 Problems
P 1. Total assets: $627,800
P 2. Total assets: $56,808
P 3. Oct. Adjusted Trial Balance: $10,288; Total assets: $9,024; Post-Closing Trial Balance: $9,094; Nov. Adjusted Trial Balance: $10,858; Total assets: $9,204; Post-Closing Trial Balance: $9,344
P 4. Total assets: $17,808
P 5. Total assets: $123,574
P 6. Total assets: $193,858
P 7. Total assets: $6,943
P 8. Total assets: $350,868
Comprehensive Problem: Adjusted Trial Balance Totals: $41,260; Total assets: $34,250; Net income: $2,130

Chapter 5 Problems
P 1. Net income: $5,261
P 2. No check figure
P 3. Net income: $71,823
P 4. No check figure
P 5. Net Income: $67,480; Total assets: $244,530
P 6. Net income: $23,812; Total assets: $66,336
P 7. No check figure
P 8. Net income: $30,870
P.9. No check figure
P10. Net income: $3,435
P11. No check figure

Chapter 6 Problems
P 1. No check figure
P 2. Net income (loss): ($1,720)
P 3. Total assets: $595,600
P 4. Current Ratio: 20x4, 2.3; 20x3, 3.5; Return on Assets: 20x4, 12.5%; 20x3 11.0%
P 5. Net income: $72,260; Total assets: $1,083,800
P 6. No check figure
P 7. Net income: $63,626
P 8. Current Ratio: 20x5, 2.0; 20x4, 2.6; Return on Assets: 20x5, 14.8%; 20x4, 13.2%

Chapter 7 Problems
P 1. Maher Company's Total Accounts Receivable: $870; Maher Company's Total Accounts Payable: $2,100
P 2. Cash total in cash receipts journal: $23,340; Cash total in cash payments journal: $17,012
P 3. Accounts Payable total: $22,418
P 4. Trial Balance: $91,616
P 5 Trial Balance: $61,116
P 6. Simons Company's Total Accounts Receivable: $3,020; Simons Company's Total Accounts Payable: $2,600
P 7. Cash total in cash receipts journal: $66,968; Cash total in cash payments journal: $28,644
P 8. Trial Balance: $84,584

Chapter 8 Problems
P 1. Adjusted book balance: $3,930
P 2. Adjusted book balance: $149,473.28
P 3. No check figure
P 4. No check figure
P 5. Total Unpaid Vouchers: $6,216
P 6. No check figure
P 7. Adjusted book balance: $27,242.80
P 8. No check figure

Chapter 9 Problems
P 1. Short-term investments (at market): $354,000
P 2. No check figure
P 3. Amount of adjustment: $73,413
P 4. No check figure
P 5. Short-term investments (at market): $903,875
P 6. No check figure
P 7. Amount of adjustment: $9,533
P 8. No check figure

Chapter 10 Problems
P 1. 1. Cost of goods available for sale: $157,980
P 2. 1. Cost of goods sold for March: $4,578; for April: $15,457
P 3. 1. Cost of goods sold for March: $4,560; for April: $15,424
P 4. Estimated inventory shortage at cost: $6,052; at retail: $8,900
P 5. Estimated loss of inventory in fire: $653,027
P 6. Cost of goods available for sale: $10,560,000

P 7. 1. Cost of goods sold for April: $9,660; for May: $22,119
P 8. 1. Cost of goods sold for April: $9,580; for May: $21,991

Chapter 11 Problems
P 1. Total cost: Land: $361,950; Land Improvements: $71,000; Building: $691,800; Furniture and Equipment: $105,400
P 2. 1. Depreciation, Year 3: a. $165,000; b. $132,000; c. $90,000
P 3. Total Depreciation Expense: 20x5: $13,280; 20x6: $18,760; 20x7: $15,728
P 4. a. Gain on Sale of Road Grader: $1,800; b. Loss on Sale of Road Grader: $2,200; c. Gain on Exchange of Road Grader: $1,800; d. Loss on Exchange of Road Grader: $2,200; e. No gain recognized
P 5. Part A. c. Amortization Expense: $492,000; d. Loss on Exclusive License: $1,476,000; Part B. d. Leasehold Amortization Expense: $1,575; e. Leasehold Improvements Amortization Expense: $2,500
P 6. Totals: Land: $852,424; Land Improvements: $333,120; Buildings: $1,667,880; Machinery: $2,525,280; Expense: $36,240
P 7. 1. Depreciation, Year 3: a. $54,250; b. $81,375; c. $53,407
P 8. Total Depreciation Expense: 20x4: $71,820; 20x5: $103,092; 20x6: $84,072

Chapter 12 Problems
P 1. No check figure
P 2. No check figure
P 3. 1.b. Estimated Product Warranty Liability: $20,160
P 4. 3. Payroll Taxes Expense: $44,221.38
P 5. Net Pay, total: $8,176.32
P 6. No check figure
P 7. 1.b. Estimated Product Warranty Liability: $10,800
P 8. 3. Payroll Taxes Expense: $31,938.70

Chapter 13 Problems
P 1. 2.f. Rivera's income, 20x1: $42,600
P 2. 3. Naomi's share of income: $32,160
P 3. 1.d. Connie, Capital: $48,000
P 4. Cash distribution to Caruso: $336,000
P 5. Cash distribution to Menzer: $254,800
P 6. 1. Jacob's share of income: $225,000
P 7. d. Bob, Capital: $94,000
P 8. 1. Cash distribution to Susi: $104,400

Chapter 14 Problems
P 1. 2. Total stockholders' equity: $175,700
P 2. 1. 20x5 Total dividends: Preferred, $60,000; Common, $34,000
P 3. No check figure
P 4. 2. Total stockholders' equity: $950,080
P 5. 2. Total stockholders' equity: $330,375
P 6. 2. Total stockholders' equity: $1,488,000
P 7. 1. 20x3 Total dividends: Preferred, $420,000; Common, $380,000
P 8. 2. Total stockholders' equity: $475,040

Chapter 15 Problems
P 1. 2. Difference in net income: $48,800
P 2. 1. Income before extraordinary items and cumulative effect of accounting change: $108,000
P 3. 1. Income from continuing operations, December 31, 20x3: $551,250
P 4. 2. Total stockholders' equity, December 31, 20x3: $1,157,000
P 5. 2. Retained earnings: $231,500; Total stockholders' equity: $1,321,500
P 6. 1. Income before extraordinary items and cumulative effect of accounting change: $205,000
P 7. 2. Total stockholders' equity, December 31, 20x5: $2,964,000
P 8. 2. Retained earnings: $207,500; Total stockholders' equity: $1,257,500

Chapter 16 Problems
P 1. 2. Bond Interest Expense: Nov. 30, $1,597,500; Dec. 31, $266,250
P 2. 1. Bond Interest Expense: Sept. 1, $754,400; Nov. 30, $377,071
P 3. Bond Interest Expense: June 30, 20x4, $144,666; Sept. 1, 20x4, $93,290
P 4. 2. Loss on early retirement: $2,261,293
P 5. Bond Interest Expense: Jan. 31, 20x4, $2,400,000; June 30, 20x4, $2,000,000
P 6. 2. Bond Interest Expense: Sept. 1, $192,800; Nov. 30, $96,400
P 7. 1. Bond Interest Expense: Nov. 30, $520,150; Dec. 31, $86,651
P 8. Bond Interest Expense: June 30, 20x3, $46,598; Sept. 30, 20x3, $96,900

Chapter 17 Problems
P 1. No check figure
P 2. 1. Net cash flows from: operating activities, $126,600; investing activities, ($25,800); financing activities, $14,000
P 3. 1. Net cash flows from: operating activities, ($32,600); investing activities, ($7,200); financing activities, $51,000
P 4. 1. Net cash flows from: operating activities, ($106,000); investing activities, $34,000; financing activities, $24,000
P 5. No check figure
P 6. 1. Net Cash flows from: operating activities, $274,000; investing activities, $3,000; financing activities, ($130,000)
P 7. 1. Net cash flows from: operating activities, $46,800; investing activities: ($14,400); financing activities, $87,000

Chapter 18 Problems
P 1. No check figure
P 2. Increase: d, h, i
P 3. 1.c. Receivable turnover, 20x5: 13.9 times; 20x4: 15.6 times; 1.e. Inventory turnover, 20x5: 3.9 times; 20x4: 3.8 times

P 4. 1.b. Quick ratio, Reynard: 0.4 times; Bouche: 1.0 times; 2.d. Return on equity, Reynard: 11.8%; Bouche: 8.8%
P 5. Increase: a, b, e, f, l, m
P 6. 1.a. Current ratio, 20x6: 1.9 times; 20x5: 1.0 times; 2.c. Return on assets, 20x6: 8.4%; 20x5: 6.6%

Chapter 19 Problems
P 1. No check figure
P 2. Projected Cost per Unit: $22.25
P 3. No check figure
P 4. No check figure
P 5. Total traffic flow goal, 24,184
P 6. No check figure
P 7. 2. Decrease in number of rejects: 202
P 8. Average output, week eight: 92,899

Chapter 20 Problems
P 1. 2. Total unit cost: $13.72
P 2. Cost of goods manufactured: $10,163,200
P 3. 2a. Gross Margin: $191,800; 2d. Cost of Goods Manufactured: $312,100
P 4. 2. Overhead applied to Job 2214: $29,717
P 5. 2. Total costs assigned to the Grater order, activity-based costing method: $69,280.40
P 6. 1. Predetermined overhead rate for 20x6: $5.014 per machine hour
P 7. 2. Total costs assigned to the Kent order, activity-based costing method: $41,805.60
P 8. 1c. Rigger II: $11,665; BioScout: $14,940

Chapter 21 Problems
P 1. b. $66,500; i. $57,800
P 2. 1. Manufacturing overhead applied, January 15: $108,000
P 3. 3. Costs of units sold: $14,834
P 4. 1. Cost per equivalent unit: $6.05; Ending inventory: $7,225
P 5. 1. Cost per equivalent unit: $2.00; Ending inventory: $5,372
P 6. 2. Cost of units sold: $89,647
P 7. 1. Contract revenue, Job Order No. P-12: $28,990
P 8. 1. Cost per equivalent unit: $7.00; Ending inventory: $37,200

Chapter 22 Problems
P 1. No check figure
P 2. 1. Product unit cost: $270.00; 4. Product unit cost: $280.47
P 3. 1a. Total materials handling cost rate: 30% per dollar of direct materials
P 4. 3. Total direct cost, toy car work cell: $17,000
P 5. 3. Cost of goods sold: $564,400
P 6. 1. Product unit cost: $878.25
P 7. 3. Product unit cost: $10.43
P 8. 3. Cost of goods sold: $391,520

Chapter 23 Problems
P 1. 4. Cost per Job: $81.56
P 2. 1. 7,500 Billable Hours
P 3. 1.a. 3,500 Units
P 4. 2. 190,000 Units
P 5. 3. $806.60 per Job
P 6. 1. 740 Systems
P 7. 1.a. 7,900 Units
P 8. 2. 418 Loans

Chapter 24 Problems
P 1. 1. Total manufacturing costs budgeted, November: $1,157,000
P 2. 8. Income from operations: $3,086
P 3. 1. Ending cash balance, August: $1,800
P 4. 1. Projected net income: $101,812
P 5. Ending cash balance, February, $19,555
P 6. 1. Net income: $1,860,830
P 7. 1. Ending cash balance, February: ($2,900)
P 8. 1. Net income: $52,404

Chapter 25 Problems
P 1. Total standard unit cost of front entrance: $8,510
P 2. 2. Flexible budget formula: Total Budgeted Costs = ($.35 x Units Produced) + $10,500
P 3. 1. Direct materials price variance—Metal: $832 (F); 2. Direct labor rate variance—Molding: $510 (F)
P 4. 1.b. Direct materials quantity variance: $3,720 (U); 1.h. Fixed overhead volume variance: $320 (F)
P 5. c. Actual variable overhead: $42,500
P 6. 1. Total standard direct materials cost per unit: $167.52
P 7. 1. Direct materials price variance—Liquid Plastic: $386 (F); 2. Direct labor rate variance—Trimming/Packing: $56 (U)
P 8. 1.a. Direct materials price variance—Chemicals: $12,200 (F); 1.e. Variable overhead spending variance: $100 (U)

Chapter 26 Problems
P 1. 1. Flexible Budget, Total Cost: $7,248,000
P 2. 2. Operating Income: $194,782
P 3. 1. Flexible Budget, Contribution margin: $88,200
P 4. 3. Economic value added for 20x8: $21,850
P 5. 1. Residual income: ($2,500)
P 6. 2. Operating Income: $418,555
P 7. 3a. Actual Return on Investment: 6.3%
P 8. 3. Economic value added: $126,000

Chapter 27 Problems
P 1. 3. Operating income from further processing, bagel sandwiches: $.50
P 2. 1. Segment margin for Book X: $223,560
P 3. 2. $68.20
P 4. 1. Net present value: $99,672
P 5. 1. HTZ Machine: 13.4 %; 2. XJS Machine: 5.5 years
P 6. 1. Total cost to buy: $1,293,750
P 7. 1. Contribution margin per hour for phone calls: $130
P 8. 1.a. Net present value: ($26,895)

Principles of Accounting

1

Chapter 1 explores the nature and environment of accounting, with special emphasis on the users and uses of accounting information.

Uses of Accounting Information and the Financial Statements

Learning Objectives

LO1 Define *accounting,* identify business goals and activities, and describe the role of accounting in making informed decisions.

LO2 Identify the many users of accounting information in society.

LO3 Explain the importance of business transactions, money measure, and separate entity to accounting measurement.

LO4 Identify the three basic forms of business organization.

LO5 Define *financial position,* state the accounting equation, and show how they are affected by simple transactions.

LO6 Identify the four financial statements.

LO7 State the relationship of generally accepted accounting principles (GAAP) to financial statements and the independent CPA's report, and identify the organizations that influence GAAP.

LO8 Define *ethics* and describe the ethical responsibilities of accountants.

Look to the learning objectives (LOs) as a guide to help you master the material. You will see many references to LOs throughout each chapter.

Look in the margin for reminders of key concepts or ideas.

KEY POINT: Management must have a good understanding of accounting to set financial goals and to make financial decisions. Management not only must understand how accounting information is compiled and processed but also must realize that accounting information is imperfect and should be interpreted with caution.

DECISION POINT

A USER'S FOCUS

Walgreen Co. <www.walgreens.com>, a nationwide chain of more than 3,800 drugstores and pharmacies, has been a retailing success story, with 28 years of record sales and earnings. During the past five years, Walgreens has opened or remodeled 2,094 stores and by 2010 plans to operate more than 7,000 stores. In fiscal 2002, sales in stores open more than a year rose 10.5 percent.

Why is Walgreens considered successful? Customers appreciate the quality of the products that the company sells and the large selection and good service that its stores offer. Investment companies and others with a financial stake in Walgreens evaluate the success of the company and its management in financial terms, such as those contained in the Financial Highlights from the company's annual report, shown on the opposite page.[1]

Net sales, net earnings, total assets, and stockholders' equity are common financial measures of all companies, large or small. These measures are used to evaluate a company's management and to compare the company to other companies. It is easy to see the large increases at Walgreens over the years in these measures, but what do the terms mean? What financial knowledge do Walgreens' managers need to measure progress toward their financial goals? What financial knowledge does anyone who is evaluating Walgreens in relation to other companies need to understand these measures?

Walgreens' managers must have a thorough knowledge of accounting to understand how the operations for which they are responsible contribute

What kind of information do the people with a financial stake in Walgreens need to have?

to the firm's overall financial health. People with a financial stake in the company, such as owners, investors, creditors, employees, attorneys, and governmental regulators, must also know accounting to evaluate the financial performance of a business. Anyone who aspires to any of these roles in a business requires mastery of accounting terminology and concepts, the process of producing financial information, and how that information is interpreted and analyzed. The purpose of this course and this textbook is to assist you in acquiring that mastery.

A Decision Point at the start of each chapter shows how leading businesses use the accounting information presented in their annual reports to make business decisions.

Walgreens' Financial Highlights
(In millions)

	2002	2001	2000	1999	1998
Net sales	**$28,681**	$24,623	$21,207	$17,839	$15,307
Net earnings	**1,019**	886	777	624	511
Total assets	**9,879**	8,834	7,104	5,907	4,902
Stockholders' equity	**6,230**	5,207	4,234	3,484	2,849

Accounting as an Information System

LO1 Define *accounting,* identify business goals and activities, and describe the role of accounting in making informed decisions.

RELATED TEXT ASSIGNMENTS
Q: 1, 2, 3, 4
E: 1
P: 4, 7
SD: 1, 5
FRA: 2, 4, 6, 7, 8

Each LO is stated in the margin to introduce the related text material. The list of Related Text Assignments will guide you to the appropriate questions, exercises, problems, and cases for that LO.

Today's accountant focuses on the ultimate needs of decision makers who use accounting information, whether those decision makers are inside or outside the business. **Accounting** "is not an end in itself,"[2] but *an information system that measures, processes, and communicates financial information about an identifiable economic entity.* An economic entity is a unit that exists independently—for example, a business, a hospital, or a governmental body. The central focus of this book is on business entities and business activities, although other economic units, such as hospitals and governmental units, are mentioned at appropriate points in the text and assignment material.

Accounting provides a vital service by supplying the information that decision makers need to make "reasoned choices among alternative uses of scarce resources in the conduct of business and economic activities."[3] As shown in Figure 1, accounting is a link between business activities and decision makers. First, accounting measures business activities by recording data about them for future use. Second, the data are stored until needed and then processed to become useful information. Third, the information is communicated, through reports, to decision makers. We might say that data about business activities are the input to the accounting system and that useful information for decision makers is the output.

Business Goals, Activities, and Performance Measures

Key terms are highlighted in blue and are followed by their definition.

A **business** is an economic unit that aims to sell goods and services to customers at prices that will provide an adequate return to its owners. The list on the opposite page contains the names of some very well-known businesses and the principal goods or services that they sell.

Figure 1
Accounting as an Information System

Figures illustrate relationships between concepts and/or processes.

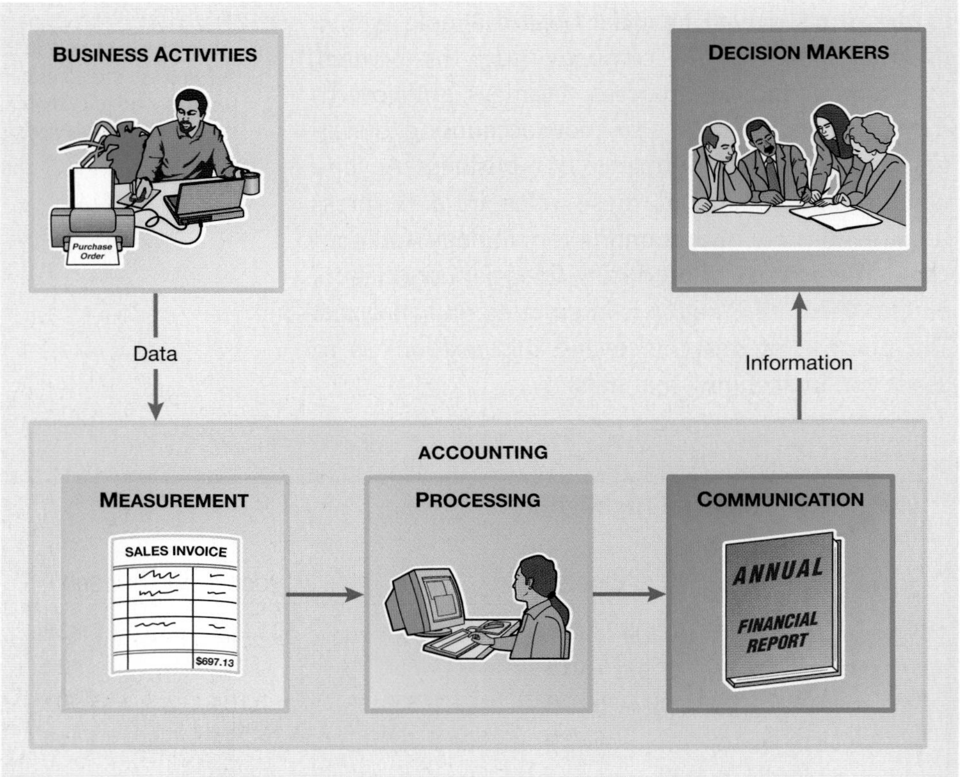

Stop and Think!
What makes accounting a valuable discipline?

The primary purpose of accounting is to provide decision makers with the financial information they need to make intelligent decisions. It is a valuable discipline because of the usefulness of the information it generates. ■

STOP AND THINK! questions enhance your critical thinking skills by challenging you to pause and reflect on the implications of the concepts and techniques presented in the text. The answers appear below each question.

Intel Corporation <www.intel.com>

OBJECTIVES

- To examine the principal activities of a business enterprise: financing, investing, and operating.
- To explore the principal performance goals of a business enterprise: liquidity and profitability.
- To relate these activities and goals to the financial statements.

BACKGROUND FOR THE CASE

Intel Corporation is one of the most successful companies in the world. In 1971, Intel introduced the world's first microprocessor, which made the personal computer (PC) possible. Today, Intel supplies the computing industry with chips, boards, systems, and software. Its principal products include:

- **Microprocessors.** Also called central processing units (CPUs), these are frequently described as the "brains" of a computer because they act as the central control for the processing of data in PCs. This category includes the famous Pentium® processor.
- **Networking and Communications Products.** These products enhance the capabilities and ease of use of PC systems by allowing users to talk to each other and to share information.
- **Semiconductor Products.** Semiconductors facilitate flash memory, making possible easily reprogrammable memory for computers, mobile phones, and many other products. Included in this category are embedded control chips that are programmed to regulate specific functions in such products as automobile engines, laser printers, disk drives, and home appliances.

In addition to PC users, Intel's customers include manufacturers of computers and computer systems, automobiles, and a wide range of industrial and telecommunications equipment.

For more information about Intel Corporation, visit the company's web site directly or access it through the Needles Accounting Resource Center Web Site at **http://accounting.college.hmco.com/students.**

REQUIRED

View the video on Intel Corporation that accompanies this book. As you are watching the video, take notes related to the following:

1. All businesses engage in three basic activities—financing, investing, and operating—but how they engage in them differs from company to company. Describe in your own words the nature of each of these activities and give as many examples as you can of how Intel engages in each activity.
2. To be successful, all businesses must achieve two performance objectives—liquidity and profitability. Describe in your own words the nature of each of these goals and describe how each applies to Intel.
3. Four financial statements apply to business enterprises. Which statements are most closely associated with the goal of liquidity? Which statement is most closely associated with the goal of profitability? Which statement shows the financial position of the company?

Video cases introduce key concepts and techniques presented in the chapter in the context of a real company.

www.generalmills.com	General Mills, Inc.	Food products
www.reebok.com	Reebok International Ltd.	Athletic footwear and clothing
www.sony.com	Sony Corp.	Consumer electronics
www.wendys.com	Wendy's International Inc.	Food service
www.hilton.com	Hilton Hotels Corp.	Hotels and resorts service
www.southwest.com	Southwest Airlines Co.	Passenger airline service

Icons are visual guides to key features of text and supporting study aids.

www.toyota.com

Despite their differences, all these businesses have similar goals and engage in similar activities, as shown in Figure 2. Each must take in enough money from customers to pay all the costs of doing business, with enough left over as profit for the owners to want to stay in the business. This need to earn enough income to attract and hold investment capital is the goal of **profitability**. In addition, businesses must meet the goal of liquidity. **Liquidity** means having enough cash available to pay debts when they are due. For example, Toyota may meet the goal of profitability by selling many cars at a price that earns a profit, but if its customers do not pay for their cars quickly enough to enable Toyota to pay its suppliers and employees, the

FIGURE 2
Business Goals and Activities

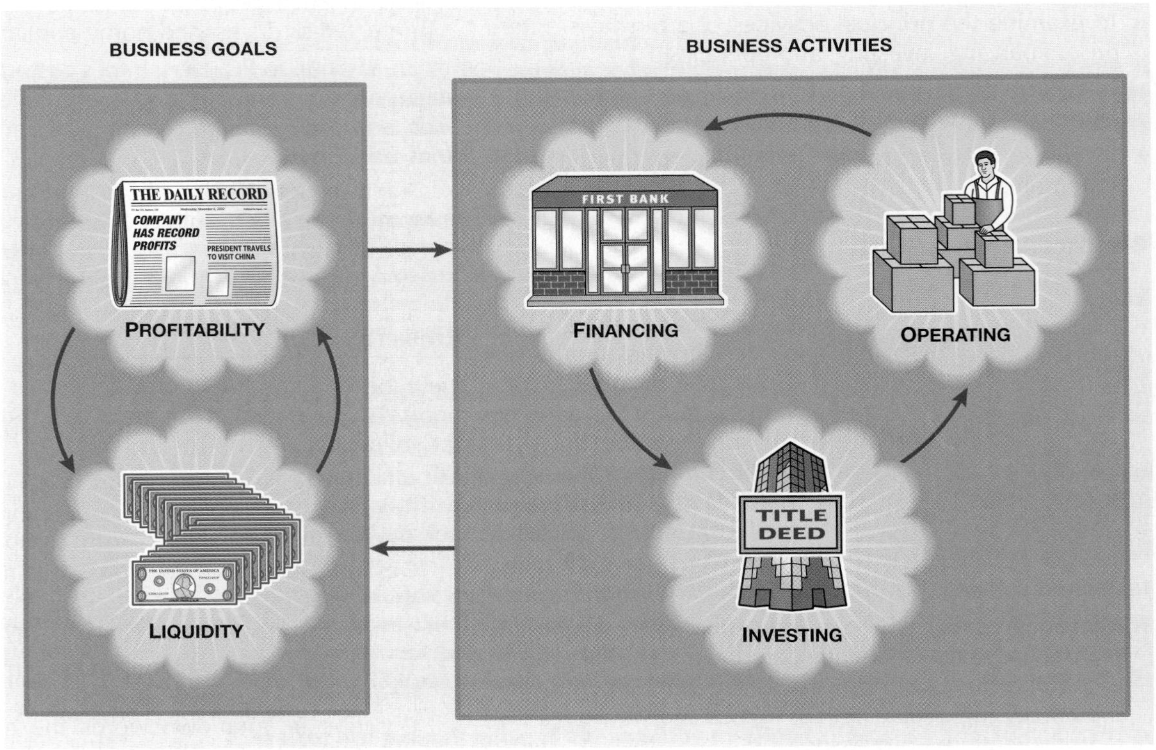

KEY POINT: Multiple financial goals signal that more than one measure of performance is of interest to users of accounting information. For example, lenders are concerned primarily with cash flow, and owners are concerned with earnings and dividends.

company may fail to meet the goal of liquidity. Both goals must be met if a company is to survive and be successful.

All businesses pursue their goals by engaging in similar activities. First, each business must engage in **financing activities** to obtain adequate funds, or capital, to begin and to continue operating. Financing activities include obtaining capital from owners and from creditors, such as banks and suppliers. They also include repaying creditors and paying a return to the owners. Second, each business must engage in **investing activities** to spend the capital it receives in ways that are productive and will help the business achieve its objectives. Investing activities include buying land, buildings, equipment, and other resources that are needed in the operation of the business, and selling these resources when they are no longer needed. Third, each business must engage in **operating activities**. In addition to the selling of goods and services to customers, operating activities include such actions as employing managers and workers, buying and producing goods and services, and paying taxes to the government.

An important function of accounting is to provide **performance measures**, which indicate whether managers are achieving their business goals and whether the business activities are well managed. It is important that these performance measures align with the goals of the business. For example, earned income is a measure of profitability, and cash flow is a measure of liquidity. Ratios of accounting measures are also used as performance measures. For instance, one performance measure for operating activities might be the ratio of expenses to the revenue of the business. A performance measure for financing activities might be the ratio of money owed by the business to total resources controlled by the company. Because managers are usually evaluated on whether targeted levels of specific performance measures are achieved, they must have a knowledge of accounting to understand how they are evaluated and how they can improve their performance. Furthermore,

The cash flow icon highlights discussion of cash as a measure of liquidity.

The key ratio icon highlights discussion of a measure used to evaluate a company's performance.

Focus on Business Practice

How Do Performance Measures Relate to Executive Bonuses?

A study of chief executive officers' bonus contracts shows that almost all companies use financial performance measures for determining annual bonuses. The most frequent measures are earnings per share, net income, operating income, return on equity, and cash flow. About one-third of the companies studied also use nonfinancial performance measures to determine bonuses. Examples of nonfinancial measures are customer satisfaction, product or service quality, nonfinancial strategic objectives, efficiency or productivity, and employee safety.[4]

because managers will act to achieve them, the targeted performance measures must be crafted in such a way as to motivate managers to take actions that are in the best interests of the owners of the business.

Financial and Management Accounting

Accounting's role of assisting decision makers by measuring, processing, and communicating information is usually divided into the categories of management accounting and financial accounting. Although there is considerable overlap in the functions of management accounting and financial accounting, the two can be distinguished by who the principal users of their information will be. **Management accounting** provides internal decision makers who are charged with achieving the goals of profitability and liquidity with information about financing, investing, and operating activities. Managers and employees who conduct the activities of the business need information that tells them how they have done in the past and what they can expect in the future. For example, The Gap, a retail clothing business, needs an operating report on each mall outlet that tells how much was sold at that outlet and what costs were incurred, and it needs a budget for each outlet that projects the sales and costs for the next year. **Financial accounting** generates reports and communicates them to external decision makers so that they can evaluate how well the business has achieved its goals. These reports to external users are called **financial statements**. Walgreens, whose stock is traded on the New York Stock Exchange, sends its financial statements to its owners (called *stockholders*), its banks and other creditors, and government regulators. Financial statements report directly on the goals of profitability and liquidity and are used extensively both inside and outside a business to evaluate the business's success. It is important for every person involved with a business to understand financial statements. They are a central feature of accounting and are the primary focus of this book.

www.gap.com

www.walgreens.com

Notations like these indicate that a direct link to the company's web site is available on the Needles Accounting Resource Center Web Site at **http://accounting.college.hmco.com/students**.

Processing Accounting Information

To avoid misunderstandings, it is important to distinguish accounting itself from the ways in which accounting information is processed by bookkeeping, computers, and management information systems.

Focus on Business boxes highlight the relevance of accounting in four different areas: business practice, business technology, business ethics, and international business.

Focus on Business Practice

What Does Walgreens Have to Say about Itself?

Walgreens <www.walgreens.com> reports its performance in meeting the major business objectives in its annual report.[5]

Liquidity: "A chunk of our positive cash position is due to a big improvement in inventory levels. . . . Short-term borrowings of $441 million were completely repaid during the year. For my money, the beauty of our 2002 balance sheet rivals Monet, showing a positive cash swing from borrowing to investing of nearly $900 million."

Profitablility: "We completed our 28th consecutive record year—and first billion-dollar earnings year—while opening 471 stores. . . ."

Walgreens' main business activities are shown at the right.

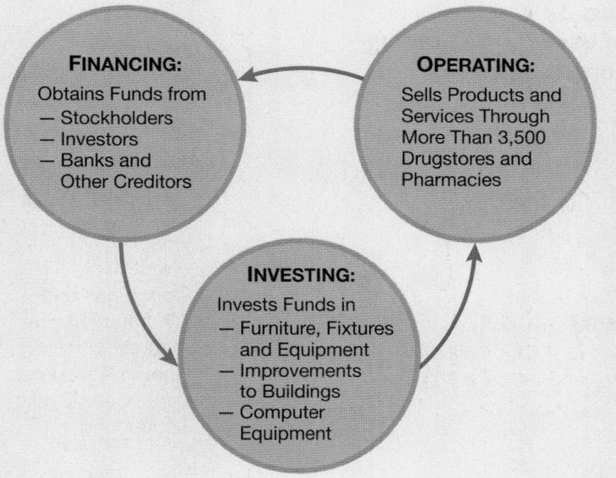

Focus on Business Practice

How Did Accounting Develop?

Accounting is a very old discipline. Forms of it have been essential to commerce for more than five thousand years. Accounting, in a version close to what we know today, gained widespread use in the 1400s, especially in Italy, where it was instrumental in the development of shipping, trade, construction, and other forms of commerce. This system of double-entry bookkeeping was documented by the famous Italian mathematician, scholar, and philosopher Fra Luca Pacioli. In 1494, Pacioli published his most important work, *Summa de Arithmetica, Geometrica, Proportioni et Proportionalita,* which contained a detailed description of accounting as practiced in that age. This book became the most widely read book on mathematics in Italy and firmly established Pacioli as the "Father of Accounting."

People often fail to understand the difference between accounting and bookkeeping. **Bookkeeping** is the process of recording financial transactions and keeping financial records. Mechanical and repetitive, bookkeeping is only a small—but important—part of accounting. Accounting, on the other hand, includes the design of an information system that meets the user's needs. The major goals of accounting are the analysis, interpretation, and use of information.

The **computer** is an electronic tool used to collect, organize, and communicate vast amounts of information with great speed. Accountants were among the earliest and most enthusiastic users of computers, and today they use microcomputers in all aspects of their work. It may appear that the computer is doing the accountant's job; in fact, it is only a tool that is instructed to do routine bookkeeping and to perform complex calculations.

KEY POINT: Computerized accounting information is only as reliable and useful as the data that go into the system. The accountant must have a thorough understanding of the concepts that underlie accounting to ensure the data's reliability and usefulness.

With the widespread use of the computer today, a business's many information needs are organized into what is called a **management information system (MIS)**. A management information system consists of the interconnected subsystems that provide the information needed to run a business. The accounting information system is the most important subsystem because it plays the key role of managing the flow of economic data to all parts of a business and to interested parties outside the business.

Check out ACE for a Review Quiz at http://accounting.college.hmco.com/students.

Decision Makers: The Users of Accounting Information

LO2 Identify the many users of accounting information in society.

RELATED TEXT ASSIGNMENTS
Q: 5, 6, 7, 8, 9
E: 1, 2
SD: 1, 2, 5

As shown in Figure 3, the people who use accounting information to make decisions fall into three categories: (1) those who manage a business; (2) those outside a business enterprise who have a direct financial interest in the business; and (3) those people, organizations, and agencies that have an indirect financial interest in the business. These categories apply to governmental and not-for-profit organizations as well as to profit-oriented ventures.

Figure 3
The Users of Accounting Information

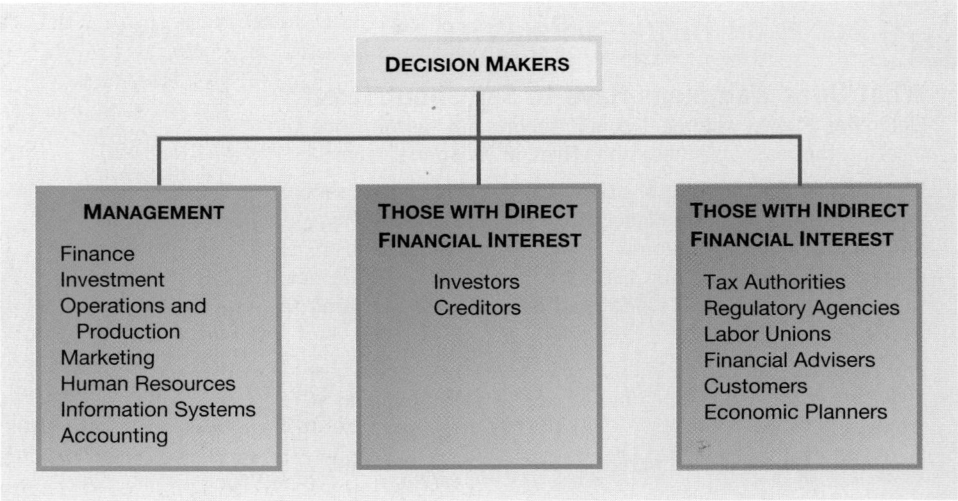

Management

Management refers to the people who have overall responsibility for operating a business and for meeting its profitability and liquidity goals. In a small business, management may consist solely of the owners. In a large business, management more often consists of people who have been hired to do the job. Managers must decide what to do, how to do it, and whether the results match their original plans. Successful managers consistently make the right decisions based on timely and valid information. To make good decisions, managers need answers to such questions as: What was the company's net income during the past quarter? Is the rate of return to the owners adequate? Does the company have enough cash? Which products are most profitable? What is the cost of manufacturing each product? Because so many key decisions are based on accounting data, management is one of the most important users of accounting information.

KEY POINT: Managers are internal users of accounting information.

In carrying out its decision-making process, management performs a set of functions that are essential to the operation of the business. Although large businesses have more elaborate operations than small ones, the same basic functions must be accomplished in all cases, and each requires accounting information for decision making. The basic management functions are:

Financing the business. Financial management obtains financial resources so that the company can begin and continue operating.

Investing the resources of the business. Asset management invests the financial resources of the business in productive assets that support the company's goals.

Producing goods and services. Operations and production management develops and produces goods and services.

Marketing goods and services. Marketing management sells, advertises, and distributes goods and services.

Managing employees. Human resource management encompasses the hiring, evaluation, and compensation of employees.

Providing information to decision makers. Information systems management captures data about all aspects of the company's operations, organizes the data into usable information, and provides reports to internal managers and appropriate outside parties. Accounting plays a key role in this function.

Users with a Direct Financial Interest

Another group of decision makers who need accounting information are those with a direct financial interest in a business. They depend on accounting to measure and report information about how a business has performed. Most businesses periodically publish a set of general-purpose financial statements that report their success in meeting the goals of profitability and liquidity. These statements show what has happened in the past, and they are important indicators of what will happen in the future. Many people outside the company carefully study these financial reports. The two most important outside groups are investors and creditors.

KEY POINT: The primary external users of accounting information are investors and creditors.

■ **Investors** Those who invest or may invest in a business and acquire a part ownership are interested in its past success and its potential earnings. A thorough study of a company's financial statements helps potential investors judge the prospects for a profitable investment. After investing, they must continually review their commitment, again by examining the company's financial statements.

■ **Creditors** Most companies borrow money for both long- and short-term operating needs. Creditors, those who lend money or deliver goods and services before being paid, are interested mainly in whether a company will have the cash to pay interest charges and to repay debt at the appropriate time. They study a

Focus on Business Practice

What Does the CFO Do?

John Connors, chief financial officer (CFO) of Microsoft <www.microsoft.com>, emphasizes that providing information to decision makers is an important accounting function:

> *The way I look at it, the [chief financial officer's] principal job is providing information that the business needs to make good decisions. . . . The real purpose is getting the information that managers need to do their jobs better, whether it is in sales and marketing, research and development, in the support groups, or operations.*[6]

company's liquidity and cash flow as well as its profitability. Banks, finance companies, mortgage companies, securities firms, insurance firms, suppliers, and other lenders must analyze a company's financial position before they make a loan.

Users with an Indirect Financial Interest

In recent years, society as a whole, through governmental and public groups, has become one of the largest and most important users of accounting information. Users who need accounting information to make decisions on public issues include tax authorities, regulatory agencies, and various other groups.

■ **Tax Authorities** Government at every level is financed through the collection of taxes. Under federal, state, and local laws, companies and individuals pay many kinds of taxes, including federal, state, and city income taxes; social security and other payroll taxes; excise taxes; and sales taxes. Each tax requires special tax returns and often a complex set of records as well. Proper reporting is generally a matter of law and can be very complicated. The Internal Revenue Code, for instance, contains thousands of rules governing the preparation of the accounting information used in computing federal income taxes.

■ **Regulatory Agencies** Most companies must report periodically to one or more regulatory agencies at the federal, state, and local levels. For example, all public corporations must report periodically to the **Securities and Exchange Commission (SEC)**. This body, set up by Congress to protect the public, regulates the issuing, buying, and selling of stocks in the United States. Companies listed on a stock exchange also must meet the special reporting requirements of their exchange.

www.sec.gov

■ **Other Groups** Labor unions study the financial statements of corporations as part of preparing for contract negotiations; a company's income and costs often play an important role in these negotiations. Those who advise investors and creditors—financial analysts, brokers, underwriters, lawyers, economists, and the financial press—also have an indirect interest in the financial performance and prospects of a business. Consumer groups, customers, and the general public have become more concerned about the financing and earnings of corporations as well as the effects that corporations have on inflation, the environment, social problems, and the quality of life. And economic planners, among them the President's Council of Economic Advisers and the Federal Reserve Board, use aggregated accounting information to set and evaluate economic policies and programs.

Stop and Think!

Why do managers in governmental and not-for-profit organizations need to understand financial information as much as managers in profit-seeking businesses?

Like managers of profit-seeking businesses, managers of governmental and not-for-profit organizations must report to those who fund them, and they must operate their organizations in a financially prudent way. ■

Governmental and Not-for-Profit Organizations

More than 30 percent of the U.S. economy is generated by governmental and not-for-profit organizations (hospitals, universities, professional organizations, and charities). The managers of these diverse entities need to understand and to use accounting information to perform the same functions as managers in businesses. They need to raise funds from investors, creditors, taxpayers, and donors, and to deploy scarce resources. They need to plan to pay for operations and to repay creditors on a timely basis. Moreover, they have an obligation to report their financial performance to legislators, boards, and donors, as well as to deal with tax authorities, regulators, and labor unions. Although most of the examples throughout this text focus on business enterprises, the same basic principles apply to governmental and not-for-profit organizations.

Check out ACE for a Review Quiz at http://accounting.college.hmco.com/students.

Accounting Measurement

LO3 Explain the importance of business transactions, money measure, and separate entity to accounting measurement.

RELATED TEXT ASSIGNMENTS
Q: 10
SE: 1
E: 3, 4, 5
SD: 3

TERMINOLOGY NOTE: *Measurement* means the analysis of transactions in terms of recognition, valuation, and classification. That is, it answers the question: How is this transaction best represented in the accounting records?

Terminology notes define terms used in the text.

Accounting is an information system that measures, processes, and communicates financial information. In this section, you begin the study of the measurement aspects of accounting. Here you learn what accounting actually measures and how certain transactions affect a company's financial position.

To make an accounting measurement, the accountant must answer four basic questions:

1. What is measured?
2. When should the measurement be made?
3. What value should be placed on what is measured?
4. How should what is measured be classified?

All these questions deal with basic assumptions and accepted accounting practice, and their answers establish what accounting is and what it is not. Accountants in industry, professional associations, public accounting, government, and academic circles debate the answers to these questions constantly, and the answers change as new knowledge and practice require. But the basis of today's accounting practice rests on a number of widely accepted concepts and conventions, which are described in this book. We begin by focusing on the first question: What is measured?

What Is Measured?

The world contains an unlimited number of things to measure and ways to measure them. Consider a machine that makes bottle caps. How many measurements of this machine could you make? You might start with size and then go on to location, weight, cost, and many other units of measurement. Some of these measurements are relevant to accounting; some are not. Every system must define what it measures, and accounting is no exception. Basically, financial accounting uses money measures to gauge the impact of business transactions on separate business entities. The concepts of business transactions, money measure, and separate entity are discussed in the next sections.

STOP AND THINK!
Are all economic events business transactions?
No, because not all economic events involve exchanges of value between a business and someone else. For example, when a customer places an order, it is an economic event, but until the order is fulfilled, no exchange of value has taken place. ■

Business Transactions as the Object of Measurement

Business transactions are economic events that affect the financial position of a business entity. Business entities can have hundreds or even thousands of transactions every day. These transactions are the raw material of accounting reports.

A transaction can be an exchange of value (a purchase, sale, payment, collection, or loan) between two or more independent parties. A transaction also can be an economic event that has the same effect as an exchange transaction but does not involve an exchange. Some examples of "nonexchange" transactions are losses from fire, flood, explosion, and theft; physical wear and tear on machinery and equipment; and the day-by-day accumulation of interest.

www.acehardware.com

To be recorded, a transaction must relate directly to a business entity. Suppose a customer buys a shovel from Ace Hardware but has to buy a hoe from a competing store because Ace is out of hoes. The transaction in which the shovel was sold is entered in Ace's records. However, the purchase of the hoe from the competitor is not entered in Ace's records because even though it indirectly affects Ace economically, it does not involve a direct exchange of value between Ace and the customer.

Money Measure

All business transactions are recorded in terms of money. This concept is termed **money measure**. Of course, information of a nonfinancial nature may be recorded, but it is through the recording of monetary amounts that the diverse transactions

TABLE 1. Examples of Foreign Exchange Rates

Tables give factual information referred to in the text.

Country	Price in $ U.S.	Country	Price in $ U.S.
Australia (dollar)	0.631	Hong Kong (dollar)	0.128
Brazil (real)	0.34	Japan (yen)	0.008
Britain (pound)	1.61	Mexico (peso)	0.10
Canada (dollar)	0.704	Russia (ruble)	0.032
Europe (euro)	1.12	Singapore (dollar)	0.565

Source: The Wall Street Journal, May 5, 2003.

and activities of a business are measured. Money is the only factor common to all business transactions, and thus it is the only practical unit of measure that can produce financial data that are alike and can be compared.

KEY POINT: The common unit of measurement in the United States for financial reporting purposes is the dollar.

The monetary unit a business uses depends on the country in which the business resides. For example, in the United States, the basic unit of money is the dollar. In Japan, it is the yen; in Europe, the euro; and in the United Kingdom, the pound. In international transactions, exchange rates must be used to translate from one currency to another. An **exchange rate** is the value of one currency in terms of another. For example, a British person purchasing goods from a U.S. company and paying in U.S. dollars must exchange British pounds for U.S. dollars before making payment. In effect, the currencies are goods that can be bought and sold. Table 1 illustrates the exchange rates for several currencies in dollars. It shows the exchange rate for British pounds as $1.61 per pound on a particular date. Like the prices of most goods, these prices change daily according to supply and demand for the currencies. For example, a few years earlier the exchange rate for British pounds was $1.43. Although our discussion in this book focuses on dollars, selected examples and certain assignments will be in foreign currencies.

Study notes provide useful tips on ways to avoid common pitfalls.

STUDY NOTE: For accounting purposes, a business is *always* separate and distinct from its owners, creditors, and customers. Note, however, that there is a difference between separate economic entity and separate legal entity.

THE CONCEPT OF SEPARATE ENTITY

For accounting purposes, a business is a **separate entity**, distinct not only from its creditors and customers but also from its owner or owners. It should have a completely separate set of records, and its financial records and reports should refer only to its own financial affairs. For example, the Jones Florist Company should have a bank account separate from the account of Kay Jones, the owner. Kay Jones may own a home, a car, and other property, and she may have personal debts, but these are not the Jones Florist Company's resources or debts. Kay Jones also may own another business, say a stationery shop. If she does, she should have a completely separate set of records for each business.

Check out ACE for a Review Quiz at http://accounting.college.hmco.com/students.

FORMS OF BUSINESS ORGANIZATION

LO4 Identify the three basic forms of business organization.

RELATED TEXT ASSIGNMENTS
Q: 11
SE: 2
E: 2

There are three basic forms of business organization: sole proprietorships, partnerships, and corporations. Accountants recognize each form as an economic unit separate from its owners, although legally only the corporation is considered separate from its owners. Other legal differences among the three forms are summarized in Table 2 and discussed briefly in the following sections. In this book, we begin with accounting for the sole proprietorship because it is the simplest form of accounting. At critical points, however, we call attention to its essential differences from accounting for partnerships and corporations.

TABLE 2. Comparative Features of the Forms of Business Organization

	Sole Proprietorship	Partnership	Corporation
1. Legal status	Not a separate legal entity	Not a separate legal entity	Separate legal entity
2. Risk of ownership	Owner's personal resources at stake	Partners' personal resources at stake	Limited to investment in corporation
3. Duration or life	Limited by choice or death of owner	Limited by choice or death of any partner	Indefinite, possibly unlimited
4. Transferability of ownership	Sale by owner establishes new company	Changes in any partner's percentage of interest requires new partnership	Transferable by sale of stock
5. Accounting treatment	Separate economic unit	Separate economic unit	Separate economic unit

SOLE PROPRIETORSHIPS

KEY POINT: In a sole proprietorship or partnership, the owners generally manage the business. In a corporation, however, there is a separation between ownership and management. The owners (stockholders) elect a board of directors to run the corporation for their benefit.

A **sole proprietorship** is a business owned by one person and is not incorporated. This form of organization gives the individual a means of controlling the business apart from his or her personal interests. Legally, however, the proprietorship is the same economic unit as the individual. The individual receives all profits or losses and is liable for all obligations of the business. Proprietorships represent the largest number of businesses in the United States, but they transact far less business in dollar terms than do corporations. In addition, they are typically the smallest in size. The life of a sole proprietorship ends when the owner wants it to or when the owner dies or becomes incapacitated.

PARTNERSHIPS

KEY POINT: A key disadvantage of a partnership is the unlimited liability of its owners. Unlimited liability can be avoided by organizing the business as a corporation.

A **partnership** is like a proprietorship in most ways except that it has more than one owner. A partnership is not a legal entity separate from the owner; it is an unincorporated association that brings together the talents and resources of two or more people. The partners share the profits and losses of the partnership according to an agreed-upon formula. Generally, any partner can obligate the partnership to another party, and the personal resources of each partner can be called on to pay the obligations of the partnership. In some cases, one or more partners limit their liability, but at least one partner must have unlimited liability. A partnership must be dissolved when ownership changes—for example, when a partner leaves or dies. For the business to continue as a partnership, a new partnership must be formed.

FOCUS ON BUSINESS PRACTICE

Are Most Corporations Big or Small Businesses?

Most people think of corporations as large national or global companies whose shares of stock are held by thousands of people and institutions. However, of the approximately 4 million corporations in the United States, only about 15,000 have stock that is publicly bought and sold. The vast majority of corporations are small businesses privately held by a few stockholders. Illinois alone has more than 250,000 corporations. Thus, the study of corporations is just as relevant to small businesses as it is to large ones.

CORPORATIONS

A **corporation** is a business unit chartered by the state and legally separate from its owners (the stockholders). The stockholders, whose ownership is represented by shares of stock, do not directly control the corporation's operations. Instead, they elect a board of directors to run the corporation for their benefit. In exchange for their limited involvement in the corporation's actual operations, stockholders enjoy limited liability; that is, their risk of loss is limited to the amount they paid for their shares. Thus, stockholders are often willing to invest in risky, but potentially

FIGURE 4
Number and Receipts of U.S. Proprietorships, Partnerships, and Corporations, 1999

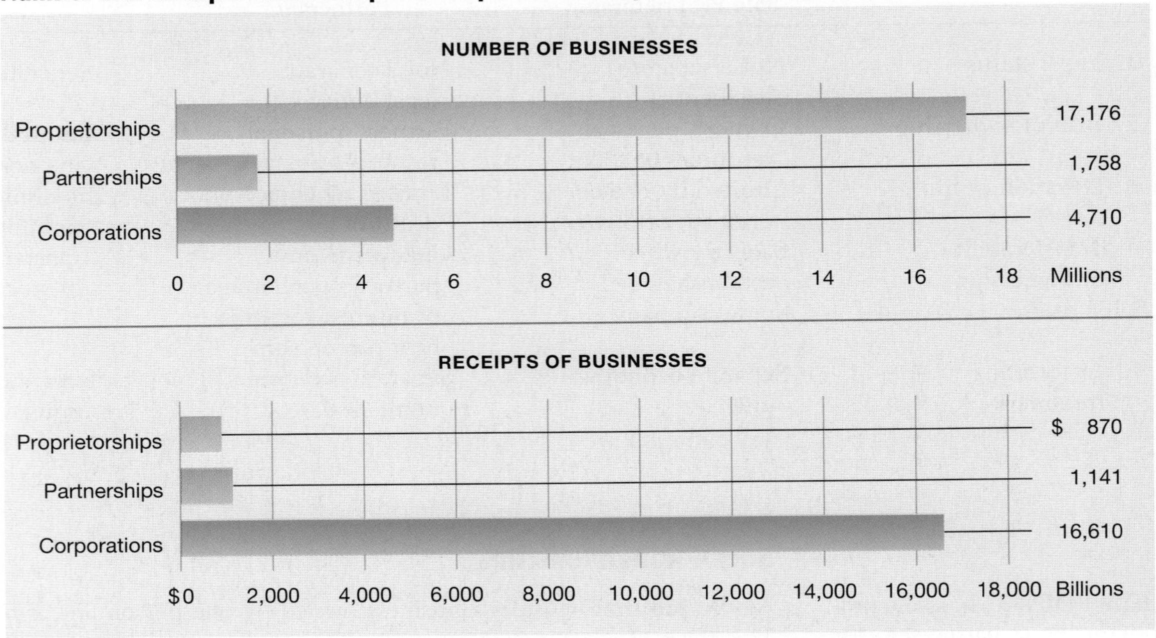

Source: U.S. Treasury Department, Internal Revenue Service, *Statistics of Income Bulletin,* Spring 2000.

STOP AND THINK!
Sole proprietorships, partnerships, and corporations differ legally; how and why does accounting treat them alike?
Accounting treats these business forms as entities separate from their owners because the financial performance of each must be measured and reported. ■

www.exxonmobil.com

profitable, activities. Also, because stockholders can sell their shares without dissolving the corporation, the life of a corporation is unlimited and not subject to the whims or health of a proprietor or a partner.

The characteristics of corporations make them very efficient in amassing capital, which enables them to grow extremely large. Even though corporations are fewer in number than sole proprietorships and partnerships, they contribute much more to the economy of the United States in monetary terms (see Figure 4). For example, in 1999, ExxonMobil generated more revenues than all but 30 of the world's countries.

Check out ACE for a Review Quiz at http://accounting.college.hmco.com/students.

FINANCIAL POSITION AND THE ACCOUNTING EQUATION

LO5 Define *financial position,* state the accounting equation, and show how they are affected by simple transactions.

RELATED TEXT ASSIGNMENTS
Q: 12, 13, 14, 15
SE: 3, 4, 5, 6, 7, 8, 9
E: 6, 7, 8, 9, 10, 11
P: 1, 2, 3, 5, 6, 8
SD: 6
FRA: 6, 8

Financial position refers to the economic resources that belong to a company and the claims against those resources at a point in time. Another term for claims is *equities.* Therefore, a company can be viewed as economic resources and equities:

Economic Resources = Equities

Every company has two types of equities, creditors' equities and owner's equity:

Economic Resources = Creditors' Equities + Owner's Equity

In accounting terminology, economic resources are called *assets* and creditors' equities are called *liabilities.* So the equation can be written like this:

Assets = Liabilities + Owner's Equity

This equation is known as the **accounting equation**. The two sides of the accounting equation must always be equal—that is, they must always be in balance. To evaluate the financial effects of business activities, it is important to understand their effects on this equation.

Assets

KEY POINT: Assets are the resources of a business, the essence of which is expected future benefits.

Assets are economic resources owned by a business that are expected to benefit future operations. Certain kinds of assets—for example, cash and money owed to the company by customers (called *accounts receivable*)—are monetary items. Other assets—inventories (goods held for sale), land, buildings, and equipment—are nonmonetary, physical items. Still other assets—the rights granted by patents, trademarks, or copyrights—are nonphysical.

Liabilities

KEY POINT: A liability is a debt or obligation that is satisfied with the payment of cash or the performance of a service.

Liabilities are present obligations of a business to pay cash, transfer assets, or provide services to other entities in the future. Among these obligations are debts of the business, amounts owed to suppliers for goods or services bought on credit (called *accounts payable*), borrowed money (for example, money owed on loans payable to banks), salaries and wages owed to employees, taxes owed to the government, and services to be performed.

As debts, liabilities are claims recognized by law. That is, the law gives creditors the right to force the sale of a company's assets if the company fails to pay its debts. Creditors have rights over owners and must be paid in full before the owners receive anything, even if payment of a debt uses up all the assets of a business.

Owner's Equity

Owner's equity represents the claims by the owner of a business to the assets of the business. It equals the residual interest, or *residual equity*, in the assets of an entity that remains after deducting the entity's liabilities. Theoretically, it is what would be left over if all the liabilities were paid, and it is sometimes said to equal **net assets**. By rearranging the accounting equation, we can define owner's equity this way:

$$\text{Owner's Equity} = \text{Assets} - \text{Liabilities}$$

The four types of transactions that affect owner's equity are shown in Figure 5. Two of these transactions, **owner's investments** and **owner's withdrawals**, are assets that the owner either puts into the business or takes out of the business. For instance, if the owner of Shannon Realty, John Shannon, takes cash out of his personal bank account and deposits it in the business bank account, he has made an owner's investment. The assets (cash) of the business increase, and John Shannon's equity in those assets also increases. Conversely, if John Shannon takes cash out of the business bank account and deposits it in his personal bank account, he has made a withdrawal from the business. The assets of the business decrease, and John Shannon's equity in the business also decreases.

STUDY NOTE: A mnemonic for remembering which types of accounts affect owner's equity is *WIRE:* Withdrawals, Investments, Revenues, and Expenses.

FIGURE 5
Four Types of Transactions That Affect Owner's Equity

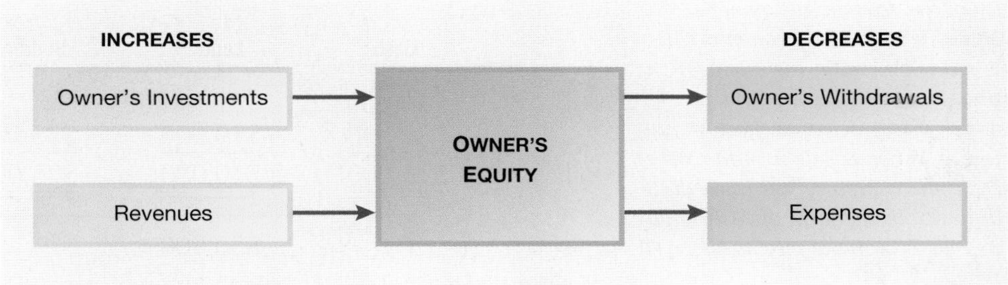

The other two types of transactions that affect owner's equity are revenues and expenses. Simply stated, **revenues** and **expenses** are the increases and decreases in owner's equity that result from operating a business. For example, the amount a customer pays (or agrees to pay in the future) to Shannon Realty in return for a service provided by the company is a revenue. The assets (cash or accounts receivable) of Shannon Realty increase, and the owner's equity in those assets also increases. On the other hand, the amount Shannon Realty pays out (or agrees to pay in the future) in the process of providing a service is an expense. Now the assets (cash) decrease or the liabilities (accounts payable) increase, and the owner's equity in the assets decreases.

Generally speaking, a company is successful if its revenues exceed its expenses. When the revenues exceed the expenses, the difference is called **net income**; when the expenses exceed the revenues, the difference is called **net loss**.

Some Illustrative Transactions

Let us now examine the effects of some of the most common business transactions on the accounting equation. Suppose that John Shannon opens Shannon Realty, a real estate agency, on December 1. During December, his business engages in the transactions described in the following paragraphs.

Owner's Investment John starts his business by depositing $50,000 in a bank account in the name of Shannon Realty. The transfer of cash from his personal account to the business account is an owner's investment. The first balance sheet of the new company would show the asset Cash and the owner's equity (John Shannon, Capital):

KEY POINT: The account name is "John Shannon, Capital," not "Owner's Equity" because capital accounts show the equity attributed to the specific owner.

Assets	=	Owner's Equity (OE)	
Cash		John Shannon, Capital	Type of OE Transaction
1. $50,000		$50,000	Owner's Investment

At this point, the company has no liabilities, and assets equal owner's equity. The labels Cash and John Shannon, Capital are called **accounts**. These are used by accountants to accumulate amounts that result from similar transactions. Transactions that affect owner's equity are identified by type so that similar types may later be grouped together on accounting reports.

KEY POINT: The purchase of an asset does not affect owner's equity.

Stop and Think!
From the standpoint of operating a business, why is the difference between making a sale for cash and making a sale on credit significant in terms of profitability and liquidity?
Both transactions affect profitability in the same way (owner's equity is increased); when a sale is made on credit, the business must wait to receive payment, which has a negative effect on liquidity. When a sale is made for cash, the company has immediate liquidity in the form of cash to pay its bills and make purchases. ■

Purchase of Assets with Cash John finds a good location and pays cash to purchase a lot for $10,000 and a small building on the lot for $25,000. This transaction does not change Shannon Realty's total assets, liabilities, or owner's equity, but it does change the composition of the assets—it decreases Cash and increases Land and Building:

	Assets			=	Owner's Equity	
	Cash	Land	Building		John Shannon, Capital	Type of OE Transaction
bal.	$50,000				$50,000	
2.	−35,000	+$10,000	+$25,000			
bal.	$15,000	$10,000	$25,000		$50,000	
		$50,000				

KEY POINT: Assets purchased on credit are recorded for the full amount at the time of the purchase.

PURCHASE OF ASSETS BY INCURRING A LIABILITY Assets do not always have to be purchased with cash. They may also be purchased on credit, that is, on the basis of an agreement to pay for them later. Suppose the company buys some office supplies for $500 on credit. This transaction increases the assets (Supplies) and increases the liabilities of Shannon Realty. This liability is designated by an account called Accounts Payable:

	Assets				=	Liabilities	+	Owner's Equity	
	Cash	Supplies	Land	Building		Accounts Payable		John Shannon, Capital	Type of OE Transaction
bal.	$15,000		$10,000	$25,000				$50,000	
3.		+$500				+$500			
bal.	$15,000	$500	$10,000	$25,000		$500		$50,000	
	$50,500					$50,500			

Notice that this transaction increases both sides of the accounting equation to $50,500.

KEY POINT: Payment of a liability does not affect owner's equity or the asset purchased on credit.

PAYMENT OF A LIABILITY If Shannon Realty later pays $200 of the $500 owed for the supplies, both assets (Cash) and liabilities (Accounts Payable) decrease, but Supplies is unaffected:

	Assets				=	Liabilities	+	Owner's Equity	
	Cash	Supplies	Land	Building		Accounts Payable		John Shannon, Capital	Type of OE Transaction
bal.	$15,000	$500	$10,000	$25,000		$500		$50,000	
4.	−200					−200			
bal.	$14,800	$500	$10,000	$25,000		$300		$50,000	
	$50,300					$50,300			

Notice that both sides of the accounting equation are still equal, although now at a total of $50,300.

KEY POINT: Revenues equal the price charged for the sale of goods or services.

REVENUES Shannon Realty earns revenues in the form of commissions by selling houses for clients. Sometimes these commissions are paid to Shannon Realty immediately in the form of cash, and sometimes the client agrees to pay the commission later. In either case, the commission is recorded when it is earned and Shannon Realty has a right to a current or future receipt of cash. First, assume that Shannon Realty sells a house and receives a commission of $1,500 in cash. This transaction increases both assets (Cash) and owner's equity (John Shannon, Capital):

	Assets				=	Liabilities	+	Owner's Equity	
	Cash	Supplies	Land	Building		Accounts Payable		John Shannon, Capital	Type of OE Transaction
bal.	$14,800	$500	$10,000	$25,000		$300		$50,000	
5.	+1,500							+1,500	Commissions Earned
bal.	$16,300	$500	$10,000	$25,000		$300		$51,500	
	$51,800					$51,800			

KEY POINT: Revenues are recorded when they are earned, not necessarily when payments are received.

Now assume that Shannon Realty sells a house, in the process earning a commission of $2,000, and agrees to wait for payment of the commission. Because the commission has been earned now, a bill or invoice is sent to the client, and the transaction is recorded now. This revenue transaction increases both assets and owner's equity as before, but a new asset account, Accounts Receivable, shows that Shannon Realty is awaiting receipt of the commission:

	Assets					= Liabilities +	Owner's Equity	
	Cash	Accounts Receivable	Supplies	Land	Building	Accounts Payable	John Shannon, Capital	Type of OE Transaction
bal.	$16,300		$500	$10,000	$25,000	$300	$51,500	
6.		+$2,000					+2,000	Commissions Earned
bal.	$16,300	$2,000	$500	$10,000	$25,000	$300	$53,500	

$53,800 = $53,800

As you progress in your study of accounting, you will be shown the use of separate accounts for revenues, like Commissions Earned.

COLLECTION OF ACCOUNTS RECEIVABLE Let us assume that a few days later Shannon Realty receives $1,000 from the client in transaction **6.** At that time, the asset Cash increases and the asset Accounts Receivable decreases:

	Assets					= Liabilities +	Owner's Equity	
	Cash	Accounts Receivable	Supplies	Land	Building	Accounts Payable	John Shannon, Capital	Type of OE Transaction
bal.	$16,300	$2,000	$500	$10,000	$25,000	$300	$53,500	
7.	+1,000	−1,000						
bal.	$17,300	$1,000	$500	$10,000	$25,000	$300	$53,500	

$53,800 = $53,800

Notice that this transaction does not affect owner's equity because the commission revenue was already recorded in transaction **6.** Also, notice that the balance of Accounts Receivable is $1,000, indicating that $1,000 is still to be collected.

EXPENSES Just as revenues are recorded when they are earned, expenses are recorded when they are incurred. Expenses can be paid in cash when they occur, or they can be paid later. If payment is going to be made later, a liability—for example, Accounts Payable or Wages Payable—increases. In both cases, owner's equity decreases. Assume that Shannon Realty pays $1,000 to rent some equipment for the office and $400 in wages to a part-time helper. These transactions reduce assets (Cash) and owner's equity (John Shannon, Capital):

	Assets					= Liabilities +	Owner's Equity	
	Cash	Accounts Receivable	Supplies	Land	Building	Accounts Payable	John Shannon, Capital	Type of OE Transaction
bal.	$17,300	$1,000	$500	$10,000	$25,000	$300	$53,500	
8.	−1,000						−1,000	Equipment Rental Expense
9.	−400						−400	Wages Expense
bal.	$15,900	$1,000	$500	$10,000	$25,000	$300	$52,100	

$52,400 = $52,400

Now assume that Shannon Realty has not paid a $300 bill for utilities expense incurred for December. In this case, the effect on owner's equity is the same as when the expense is paid in cash, but instead of a reduction in assets, there is an increase in liabilities (Accounts Payable):

	Assets					= Liabilities	+ Owner's Equity	
	Cash	Accounts Receivable	Supplies	Land	Building	Accounts Payable	John Shannon, Capital	Type of OE Transaction
bal.	$15,900	$1,000	$500	$10,000	$25,000	$300	$52,100	
10.						+300	−300	Utilities Expense
bal.	$15,900	$1,000	$500	$10,000	$25,000	$600	$51,800	
	$52,400					$52,400		

As you progress in your study of accounting, you will be shown the use of separate accounts for expenses, like Equipment Rental Expense, Wages Expense, and Utilities Expense.

STUDY NOTE: Owner's withdrawals do not qualify as expenses because they do not generate revenue.

OWNER'S WITHDRAWALS John now withdraws $600 in cash from Shannon Realty and deposits it in his personal account. This transaction reduces assets (Cash) and owner's equity (John Shannon, Capital). Although, as can be seen below, withdrawals have the same effect on the accounting equation as expenses (see transactions 8 and 9), it is important not to confuse them. Withdrawals are not expenses. Withdrawals are personal distributions of assets to the owner; expenses are incurred by the business in its operations.

	Assets					= Liabilities	+ Owner's Equity	
	Cash	Accounts Receivable	Supplies	Land	Building	Accounts Payable	John Shannon, Capital	Type of OE Transaction
bal.	$15,900	$1,000	$500	$10,000	$25,000	$600	$51,800	
11.	−600						−600	Owner's Withdrawal
bal.	$15,300	$1,000	$500	$10,000	$25,000	$600	$51,200	
	$51,800					$51,800		

SUMMARY Exhibit 1 (page 20) summarizes these 11 illustrative transactions.

Check out ACE for a Review Quiz at http://accounting.college.hmco.com/students.

COMMUNICATION THROUGH FINANCIAL STATEMENTS

LO6 Identify the four financial statements.

RELATED TEXT ASSIGNMENTS
Q: 16, 17, 18, 19, 20
SE: 10
E: 11, 12, 13, 14, 15
P: 4, 5, 7, 8
SD: 6
FRA: 3, 5, 7, 8

Financial statements are the primary means of communicating important accounting information about a business to those who have an interest in the business. It is helpful to think of these statements as models of the business enterprise because they show the business in financial terms. As is true of all models, however, financial statements are not perfect pictures of the real thing. Rather, they are the accountant's best effort to represent what is real. Four major financial statements are used to communicate accounting information about a business: the income statement, the statement of owner's equity, the balance sheet, and the statement of cash flows.

Exhibit 2 (page 21) illustrates the relationship among the four financial statements by showing how they would appear for Shannon Realty after the eleven sample transactions shown in Exhibit 1. The time period covered is the month of

Exhibits illustrate financial information.

EXHIBIT 1
Summary of Effects of Illustrative Transactions on Financial Position

	Assets					= Liabilities +	Owner's Equity	
	Cash	Accounts Receivable	Supplies	Land	Building	Accounts Payable	John Shannon, Capital	Type of Owner's Equity Transaction
1.	$50,000						$50,000	Owner's Investment
2.	−35,000			+$10,000	+$25,000			
bal.	$15,000			$10,000	$25,000		$50,000	
3.			+$500			+$500		
bal.	$15,000		$500	$10,000	$25,000	$500	$50,000	
4.	−200					−200		
bal.	$14,800		$500	$10,000	$25,000	$300	$50,000	
5.	+1,500						+$1,500	Commissions Earned
bal.	$16,300		$500	$10,000	$25,000	$300	$51,500	
6.		+$2,000					+2,000	Commissions Earned
bal.	$16,300	$2,000	$500	$10,000	$25,000	$300	$53,500	
7.	+1,000	−1,000						
bal.	$17,300	$1,000	$500	$10,000	$25,000	$300	$53,500	
8.	−1,000						−1,000	Equipment Rental Expense
9.	−400						−400	Wages Expense
bal.	$15,900	$1,000	$500	$10,000	$25,000	$300	$52,100	
10.						+300	−300	Utilities Expense
bal.	$15,900	$1,000	$500	$10,000	$25,000	$600	$51,800	
11.	−600						−600	Owner's Withdrawal
bal.	$15,300	$1,000	$500	$10,000	$25,000	$600	$51,200	
	$51,800					$51,800		

EXHIBIT 2
Income Statement, Statement of Owner's Equity, Balance Sheet, and Statement of Cash Flows for Shannon Realty

Shannon Realty
Income Statement
For the Month Ended December 31, 20xx

Revenues		
Commissions earned		$3,500
Expenses		
Equipment rental expense	$1,000	
Wages expense	400	
Utilities expense	300	
Total expenses		1,700
Net income		$1,800

Shannon Realty
Statement of Owner's Equity
For the Month Ended December 31, 20xx

John Shannon, Capital, December 1, 20xx		$ 0
Add: Investments by John Shannon	$50,000	
Net income for the month	1,800	51,800
Subtotal		$51,800
Less withdrawals by John Shannon		600
John Shannon, Capital, December 31, 20xx		$51,200

Shannon Realty
Statement of Cash Flows
For the Month Ended December 31, 20xx

Cash flows from operating activities		
Net income		$ 1,800
Adjustments to reconcile net income to net cash flows from operating activities		
Increase in accounts receivable	($ 1,000)*	
Increase in supplies	(500)	
Increase in accounts payable	600	(900)
Net cash flows from operating activities		$ 900
Cash flows from investing activities		
Purchase of land	($10,000)	
Purchase of building	(25,000)	
Net cash flows from investing activities		(35,000)
Cash flows from financing activities		
Investments by John Shannon	$50,000	
Withdrawals by John Shannon	(600)	
Net cash flows from financing activities		49,400
Net increase (decrease) in cash		$15,300
Cash at beginning of month		0
Cash at end of month		$15,300

Shannon Realty
Balance Sheet
December 31, 20xx

Assets		**Liabilities**	
Cash	$15,300	Accounts payable	$ 600
Accounts receivable	1,000		
Supplies	500	**Owner's Equity**	
Land	10,000	John Shannon, Capital	51,200
Building	25,000		
Total assets	$51,800	Total liabilities and owner's equity	$51,800

KEY POINT: Notice the sequence in which these financial statements must be prepared. The statement of owner's equity is a link between the income statement and the balance sheet, and the statement of cash flows is prepared last.

*Parentheses indicate a negative amount.

STOP AND THINK!
Which financial statement is most closely related to the goal of profitability, and which is most closely related to the goal of liquidity?
The income statement is most closely related to profitability; the statement of cash flows is most closely related to liquidity. ■

December 20xx. Notice that each statement is headed in a similar way. Each heading identifies the company and the kind of statement. The income statement, the statement of owner's equity, and the statement of cash flows give the time period to which they apply; the balance sheet gives the specific date to which it applies. Much of this book deals with developing, using, and interpreting more complete versions of these basic statements.

THE INCOME STATEMENT

TERMINOLOGY NOTE: The income statement is also called the *statement of earnings,* the *statement of operations,* or the *profit and loss statement.* Its purpose is to measure a company's performance over an accounting period.

The **income statement** summarizes the revenues earned and expenses incurred by a business over a period of time. Many people consider it the most important financial report because it shows whether or not a business achieved its profitability goal of earning an acceptable income. In Exhibit 2, Shannon Realty had revenues in the form of commissions earned of $3,500 ($2,000 of revenue earned on credit and $1,500 of cash). From this amount, total expenses of $1,700 were deducted (equipment rental expense of $1,000, wages expense of $400, and utilities expense of $300), to arrive at a net income of $1,800. To show that it applies to a period of time, the statement is dated "For the Month Ended December 31, 20xx."

THE STATEMENT OF OWNER'S EQUITY

TERMINOLOGY NOTE: The statement of owner's equity is also called the *capital statement.* It indicates changes in owner's capital over an accounting period.

The **statement of owner's equity** shows the change in the owner's capital over a period of time. In Exhibit 2, the beginning capital is zero because the company was started in this accounting period. During the month, John Shannon made an investment in the business of $50,000, and the company earned income (as shown on the income statement) of $1,800, for a total increase of $51,800. Deducted from this amount are the withdrawals for the month of $600, leaving an ending balance of $51,200 in the capital account.

THE BALANCE SHEET

TERMINOLOGY NOTE: The balance sheet is also called the *statement of financial position.* It represents two different views of a business: The left side shows the resources of the business; the right side shows who provided those resources (the creditors and the owners).

The purpose of a **balance sheet** is to show the financial position of a business on a certain date, usually the end of the month or year. For this reason, it often is called the *statement of financial position* and is dated as of a certain date. The balance sheet presents a view of the business as the holder of resources, or assets, that are equal to the claims against those assets. The claims consist of the company's liabilities and the owner's equity in the company. In Exhibit 2, Shannon Realty has several categories of assets, which total $51,800. These assets equal the total liabilities of $600 (Accounts Payable) plus the ending balance of owner's capital of $51,200. Notice that the owner's capital account amount on the balance sheet comes from the ending balance on the statement of owner's equity.

THE STATEMENT OF CASH FLOWS

KEY POINT: The purpose of the statement of cash flows is to explain the change in cash in terms of operating, investing, and financing activities over an accounting period. It provides valuable information that cannot be determined in an examination of the other three financial statements.

Whereas the income statement focuses on a company's profitability goal, the **statement of cash flows** is directed toward the company's liquidity goal. **Cash flows** are the inflows and outflows of cash into and out of a business. Net cash flows are the difference between the inflows and outflows. The statement of cash flows shows the cash produced by operating a business as well as important investing and financing transactions that take place during an accounting period. Notice in Exhibit 2 that the statement of cash flows for Shannon Realty explains how the Cash account changed during the period. Cash increased by $15,300. Operating activities produced net cash flows of $900, and financing activities produced net cash flows of $49,400. Investing activities used cash flows of $35,000.

This statement is related directly to the other three statements. Notice that net income comes from the income statement and that investments and withdrawals by

PARENTHETICAL NOTE: An entire chapter of this text is devoted to the statement of cash flows.

owners come from the statement of owner's equity. The other items in the statement represent changes in the balance sheet accounts: Accounts Receivable, Supplies, Accounts Payable, Land, and Building.

Check out ACE for a Review Quiz at http://accounting.college.hmco.com/students.

GENERALLY ACCEPTED ACCOUNTING PRINCIPLES

LO7 State the relationship of generally accepted accounting principles (GAAP) to financial statements and the independent CPA's report, and identify the organizations that influence GAAP.

RELATED TEXT ASSIGNMENTS
Q: 21, 22, 23
E: 1, 16
SD: 2
FRA: 1, 6

STOP AND THINK!
How do generally accepted accounting principles (GAAP) differ from the laws of science?
GAAP differ from the laws of science in that they are not unchanging but rather are constantly evolving. They may change as business conditions change or as improved methods are introduced. ■

To ensure that financial statements will be understandable to their users, a set of practices, called **generally accepted accounting principles (GAAP)**, has been developed to provide guidelines for financial accounting. Although the term has several meanings in the literature of accounting, perhaps this is the best definition: "Generally accepted accounting principles encompass the conventions, rules, and procedures necessary to define accepted accounting practice at a particular time."[7] In other words, GAAP arise from wide agreement on the theory and practice of accounting at a particular time. These "principles" are not like the unchangeable laws of nature found in chemistry or physics. They are developed by accountants and businesses to serve the needs of decision makers, and they can alter as better methods evolve or as circumstances change.

In this book, we present accounting practice, or GAAP, as it is today. We also try to explain the reasons or theory on which the practice is based. Both theory and practice are important to the study of accounting. However, you should realize that accounting is a discipline that is always growing, changing, and improving. Just as years of research are necessary before a new surgical method or lifesaving drug can be introduced, it may take years for new accounting discoveries to be implemented. As a result, you may encounter practices that seem contradictory. In some cases, we point out new directions in accounting. Your instructor also may mention certain weaknesses in current theory or practice.

FINANCIAL STATEMENTS, GAAP, AND THE INDEPENDENT CPA'S REPORT

Because financial statements are prepared by the management of a company and could be falsified for personal gain, all companies that sell ownership to the public and many companies that apply for sizable loans have their financial statements audited by an independent certified public accountant. **Certified public accountants (CPAs)** are licensed by all states for the same reason that lawyers and doctors are—to protect the public by ensuring the quality of professional service. One important attribute of certified public accountants is independence: They have no financial or other compromising ties with the companies they audit. This gives the public confidence in their work. The firms listed in Table 3 employ about 25 percent of all CPAs.

TABLE 3. Large International Certified Public Accounting Firms

Firm	Home Office	Some Major Clients
Deloitte & Touche	New York	General Motors, Procter & Gamble, Sears
Ernst & Young	New York	Coca-Cola, McDonald's
KPMG	New York	General Electric, Xerox
PricewaterhouseCoopers	New York	Du Pont, ExxonMobil, IBM, Ford

KEY POINT: The purpose of an audit is to lend credibility to a set of financial statements. The auditor does *not* attest to the absolute accuracy of the published information or to the value of the company as an investment. All he or she renders is an opinion, based on appropriate testing, about the fairness of the presentation of the financial information.

An independent CPA performs an **audit**, which is an examination of a company's financial statements and the accounting systems, controls, and records that produced them. The purpose of the audit is to ascertain that the financial statements have been prepared in accordance with generally accepted accounting principles. If the independent accountant is satisifed that this standard has been met, his or her report contains the following language:

> In our opinion, the financial statements . . . present fairly, in all material respects [the company's financial position] and are in conformity with generally accepted accounting principles.

This wording emphasizes the fact that accounting and auditing are not exact sciences. Because the framework of GAAP provides room for interpretation and the application of GAAP necessitates the making of estimates, the auditor can render an opinion or judgment only that the financial statements *present fairly* or conform *in all material respects* to generally accepted accounting principles. The accountant's report does not preclude minor or immaterial errors in the financial statements. However, it does imply that on the whole, investors and creditors can rely on those statements. Historically, auditors have enjoyed a strong reputation for competence and independence. As a result, banks, investors, and creditors are willing to rely on an auditor's opinion when deciding to invest in a company or to make loans to a company. The independent audit is an important factor in the worldwide growth of financial markets.

Organizations That Influence Current Practice

KEY POINT: The FASB is the primary source of GAAP.

KEY POINT: The AICPA is considered the primary organization of certified public accountants.

ENRICHMENT NOTE: The SEC imposes its own strict set of regulations on the companies it regulates, based in part on the standards set by the FASB.

Many organizations directly or indirectly influence GAAP, and they therefore influence much of what is contained in this book. The **Financial Accounting Standards Board (FASB)** is the most important body for developing and issuing rules on accounting practice. This independent body issues *Statements of Financial Accounting Standards*. The **American Institute of Certified Public Accountants (AICPA)** is the professional association of certified public accountants and influences accounting practice through the activities of its senior technical committees. The Securities and Exchange Commission (SEC) is an agency of the federal government that has the legal power to set and enforce accounting practices for companies whose securities are offered for sale to the general public. As such, it has enormous influence on accounting practice. The **Governmental Accounting Standards Board (GASB)**, which was established in 1984 under the same governing body as the Financial Accounting Standards Board, is responsible for issuing accounting standards for state and local governments.

With the growth of financial markets throughout the world, worldwide cooperation in the development of accounting principles has become a priority. The **International Accounting Standards Board (IASB)** has approved more than 30 international standards.

ENRICHMENT NOTE: The primary purpose of the tax law is to generate revenue for the operation of the government, not to measure business income.

U.S. tax laws that govern the assessment and collection of revenue for operating the federal government also influence accounting practice. Because a major source of the government's revenue is the income tax, the tax laws specify the rules for determining taxable income. These rules are interpreted and enforced by the **Internal Revenue Service (IRS)**. In some cases, the rules conflict with good accounting practice, but they still are an important influence on that practice. Businesses use certain accounting practices simply because they are required by the tax laws. Sometimes companies follow an accounting practice specified in the tax laws to take advantage of rules that can help them financially. Cases in which the tax laws affect accounting practice are noted throughout this book.

Check out ACE for a Review Quiz at http://accounting.college.hmco.com/students.

Professional Ethics and the Accounting Profession

LO8 Define *ethics* and describe the ethical responsibilities of accountants.

RELATED TEXT ASSIGNMENTS
Q: 24
SD: 4

Ethics is a code of conduct that applies to everyday life. It addresses the question of whether actions are right or wrong. Ethical actions are the product of individual decisions. You are faced with many situations involving ethical issues every day. Some may be potentially illegal—the temptation to take office supplies from your employer to use when you do homework, for example. Others are not illegal but are equally unethical—for example, deciding not to tell a fellow student who missed class that a test has been announced for the next class meeting. When an organization is said to act ethically or unethically, it means that individuals within the organization have made a decision to act ethically or unethically. When a company uses false advertising, cheats customers, pollutes the environment, treats employees poorly, or misleads investors by presenting false financial statements, members of management and other employees have made a conscious decision to act unethically. In the same way, ethical behavior within a company is a direct result of the actions and decisions of the company's employees.

Professional ethics is a code of conduct that applies to the practice of a profession. Like the ethical conduct of a company, the ethical actions of a profession are a collection of individual actions. As members of a profession, accountants have a responsibility, not only to their employers and clients but to society as a whole, to uphold the highest ethical standards. Historically, accountants have been held in high regard. For example, a survey of over one thousand prominent people in business, education, and government ranked the accounting profession second only to the clergy as having the highest ethical standards.[8] It is the responsibility of every person who becomes an accountant to uphold the high standards of the profession.

To ensure that its members understand the responsibilities of being professional accountants, the AICPA and each state have adopted codes of professional conduct that certified public accountants must follow. Fundamental to these codes is responsibility to the public, including clients, creditors, investors, and anyone else who relies on the work of the certified public accountant. In resolving conflicts among these groups, the accountant must act with integrity. **Integrity** means that the accountant is honest and candid and subordinates personal gain to service and the public trust. The accountant must also be objective. **Objectivity** means that he or she is impartial and intellectually honest. Furthermore, the accountant must be independent. **Independence** means avoiding all relationships that impair or even appear to impair the accountant's objectivity.

One way in which the auditor of a company maintains independence is by having no direct financial interest in the company and by not being an employee of the company. The accountant must exercise **due care** in all activities, carrying out professional responsibilities with competence and diligence. For example, an accountant must not accept a job for which he or she is not qualified, even at the risk of losing a client to another firm, and careless work is not acceptable. These broad principles are supported by more specific rules that public accountants must follow. (For instance, with certain exceptions, client information must be kept strictly confidential.) Accountants who violate the rules can be disciplined or even suspended from practice.

A professional association, the **Institute of Management Accountants (IMA)**, has formally adopted the Code of Professional Conduct for Management

Ethical issues are discussed in each chapter; they relate to real business situations that require ethical judgments.

Stop and Think!
What are some unethical ways in which a business may do its accounting or prepare its financial statements?
Unethical ways of accounting include recording business transactions that did not occur or being dishonest in recording those that did occur. Financial statements are unethically prepared when they misrepresent a company's financial situation or contain false information. ■

ENRICHMENT NOTE: The AICPA Code of Professional Ethics is a set of guidelines for appropriate professional behavior. The current guidelines were adopted in 1988 and are based on earlier standards.

Focus on Business Ethics

Good Ethics = Good Business!

Ethics is good business. Many companies, especially those that engage in international trade, adopt codes of ethics. Management sees such self-regulation as a way of avoiding fraud and litigation. A recent survey of 124 companies in 22 countries found that 78 percent of boards of directors had established ethics standards, a fourfold increase over a ten-year period. The study also found that codes of ethics help promote tolerance of diverse practices abroad. In addition, research has shown that over time, companies with codes of ethics tend to do much better in the stock market than those that have not adopted such codes.[9] The recent Enron bankruptcy is an example of the tragic results that can occur when a company's ethical system breaks down.

Accountants. This ethical code emphasizes that management accountants have a responsibility to be competent in their jobs, to keep information confidential except when authorized or legally required to disclose it, to maintain integrity and avoid conflicts of interest, and to communicate information objectively and without bias.[10]

Check out ACE for Review Quiz at http://accounting.college.hmco.com/students.

Chapter Review

The Chapter Review restates each learning objective and its main ideas.

REVIEW OF LEARNING OBJECTIVES

LO1 Define *accounting,* identify business goals and activities, and describe the role of accounting in making informed decisions.

Accounting is an information system that measures, processes, and communicates financial information about an identifiable entity for the purpose of making economic decisions. An important type of entity is the business which engages in operating, investing, and financing activities for the purpose of achieving the goals of profitability and liquidity. Management accounting focuses on the preparation of information primarily for internal use by management. Financial accounting is concerned with the development and use of accounting reports that are communicated to those outside the business as well as to management. Accounting is a tool that provides the information necessary to make reasoned choices among alternative uses of scarce resources in the conduct of business and economic activities.

LO2 Identify the many users of accounting information in society.

Accounting plays a significant role in society by providing information to managers of all institutions and to individuals with a direct financial interest in those institutions, including present or potential investors or creditors. Accounting information is also important to those with an indirect financial interest in the business—for example, tax authorities, regulatory agencies, and economic planners.

LO3 Explain the importance of business transactions, money measure, and separate entity to accounting measurement.

To make an accounting measurement, the accountant must determine what is measured, when the measurement should be made, what value should be placed on what is measured, and how what is measured should be classified. The objects of accounting measurement are business transactions that are measured in terms of money and are for separate entities. Relating these concepts, financial accounting uses money measure to gauge the impact of business transactions on a separate business entity.

LO4 Identify the three basic forms of business organization.

The three basic forms of business organization are sole proprietorships, partnerships, and corporations. Legally, sole proprietorships, which are formed by one individual, and partnerships, which are formed by more than one individual, are not separate from their owners. In accounting, however, they are treated as separate. Corporations, whose ownership is represented by shares of stock, are separate entities for both legal and accounting purposes.

LO5 Define *financial position,* state the accounting equation, and show how they are affected by simple transactions.

Financial position refers to the economic resources that belong to a company and the claims against those resources at a point in time. The accounting equation shows financial position as Assets = Liabilities + Owner's Equity. Business transactions affect financial position by decreasing or increasing assets, liabilities, or owner's equity in such a way that the accounting equation is always in balance.

LO6 Identify the four financial statements.

The four financial statements are the income statement, the statement of owner's equity, the balance sheet, and the statement of cash flows. They are the means by which accountants communicate the financial condition and activities of a business to those who have an interest in the business.

LO7 State the relationship of generally accepted accounting principles (GAAP) to financial statements and the independent CPA's report, and identify the organizations that influence GAAP.

Acceptable accounting practice consists of the conventions, rules, and procedures that make up generally accepted accounting principles at a particular time. GAAP are essential to the preparation and interpretation of financial statements and the independent CPA's report. Among the organizations that influence the formulation of GAAP are the Financial Accounting Standards Board, the American Institute of Certified Public Accountants, the Securities and Exchange Commission, and the Internal Revenue Service.

LO8 Define *ethics* and describe the ethical responsibilities of accountants.

All accountants are required to follow a code of professional ethics, the foundation of which is responsibility to the public. Accountants must act with integrity, objectivity, and independence, and they must exercise due care in all their activities.

Want more review? The student *Study Guide* provides a thorough review of each learning objective, a detailed outline, true/false and multiple-choice questions, and exercises. Answers are included. Ask for it at your bookstore.

Review of Concepts and Terminology

Each chapter has a glossary of the key concepts and terms defined in the chapter. The LO next to each term indicates the section in which it is discussed.

The following concepts and terms were introduced in this chapter:

LO1 **Accounting:** An information system that measures, processes, and communicates financial information about an identifiable economic entity.

LO5 **Accounting equation:** Assets = Liabilities + Owner's Equity.

LO5 **Accounts:** The labels used by accountants to accumulate the amounts produced from similar transactions.

LO7 **American Institute of Certified Public Accountants (AICPA):** The professional association of certified public accountants.

LO5 **Assets:** Economic resources owned by a business that are expected to benefit future operations.

LO7 **Audit:** An examination of a company's financial statements in order to render an independent professional opinion that they have been presented fairly, in all material respects, in conformity with generally accepted accounting principles.

LO6 **Balance sheet:** The financial statement that shows the assets, liabilities, and owner's equity of a business at a point in time. Also called a *statement of financial position*.

LO1 **Bookkeeping:** The process of recording financial transactions and keeping financial records.

LO1 **Business:** An economic unit that aims to sell goods and services to customers at prices that will provide an adequate return to its owners.

LO3 **Business transactions:** Economic events that affect the financial position of a business entity.

LO6 **Cash flows:** The inflows and outflows of cash into and out of a business.

LO7 **Certified public accountants (CPAs):** Public accountants who have met the stringent state licensing requirements.

LO1 **Computer:** An electronic tool for the rapid collection, organization, and communication of large amounts of information.

LO4 **Corporation:** A business unit granted a state charter recognizing it as a separate legal entity having its own rights, privileges, and liabilities distinct from those of its owners.

LO8 **Due care:** Competence and diligence in carrying out professional responsibilities.

LO8 **Ethics:** A code of conduct that addresses whether everyday actions are right or wrong.

LO3 **Exchange rate:** The value of one currency in terms of another.

LO5 **Expenses:** Decreases in owner's equity that result from operating a business.

LO1 **Financial accounting:** The process of generating and communicating accounting information in the form of financial statements to those outside the organization.

LO7 **Financial Accounting Standards Board (FASB):** The most important body for developing and issuing rules on accounting practice, called *Statements of Financial Accounting Standards.*

LO5 **Financial position:** The economic resources that belong to a company and the claims (equities) against those resources at a point in time.

LO1 **Financial statements:** The primary means of communicating important accounting information to users. They include the income statement, statement of owner's equity, balance sheet, and statement of cash flows.

LO1 **Financing activities:** Activities undertaken by management to obtain adequate funds to begin and to continue operating a business.

LO7 **Generally accepted accounting principles (GAAP):** The conventions, rules, and procedures that define accepted accounting practice at a particular time.

LO7 **Governmental Accounting Standards Board (GASB):** The board responsible for issuing accounting standards for state and local governments.

LO6 **Income statement:** The financial statement that summarizes the revenues earned and expenses incurred by a business over a period of time.

LO8 **Independence:** The avoidance of all relationships that impair or appear to impair an accountant's objectivity.

LO8 **Institute of Management Accountants (IMA):** A professional organization made up primarily of management accountants.

LO8 **Integrity:** Honesty, candidness, and the subordination of personal gain to service and the public trust.

LO7 **Internal Revenue Service (IRS):** The federal agency that interprets and enforces the tax laws governing the assessment and collection of revenue for operating the national government.

LO7 **International Accounting Standards Board (IASB):** The organization that encourages worldwide cooperation in the development of accounting principles; it has approved more than 30 international standards of accounting.

LO1 **Investing activities:** Activities undertaken by management to spend capital in ways that are productive and will help a business achieve its objectives.

LO5 **Liabilities:** Present obligations of a business to pay cash, transfer assets, or provide services to other entities in the future.

LO1 **Liquidity:** Having enough cash available to pay debts when they are due.

LO2 **Management:** The people who have overall responsibility for operating a business and meeting its goals.

LO1 **Management accounting:** The process of producing accounting information for the internal use of a company's management.

LO1 **Management information system (MIS):** The interconnected subsystems that provide the information needed to run a business.

LO3 **Money measure:** The recording of all business transactions in terms of money.

LO5 **Net assets:** Assets minus liabilities; owner's equity.

LO5 **Net income:** The difference between revenues and expenses when revenues exceed expenses.

LO5 **Net loss:** The difference between expenses and revenues when expenses exceed revenues.

LO8 **Objectivity:** Impartiality and intellectual honesty.

LO1 **Operating activities:** Activities undertaken by management in the course of running the business.

LO5 **Owner's equity:** The residual interest in the assets of a business entity that remains after deducting the entity's liabilities. Also called *residual equity*.

LO5 **Owner's investments:** The assets that the owner puts into the business.

LO5 **Owner's withdrawals:** The assets that the owner takes out of the business.

LO4 **Partnership:** A business that is owned by two or more people and that is not incorporated.

LO1 **Performance measures:** Indicators of whether managers are achieving business goals and whether the business activities are well managed.

LO8 **Professional ethics:** A code of conduct that applies to the practice of a profession.

LO1 **Profitability:** The ability to earn enough income to attract and hold investment capital.

LO5 **Revenues:** Increases in owner's equity that result from operating a business.

LO2 **Securities and Exchange Commission (SEC):** An agency of the U.S. government set up by Congress to protect the public by regulating the issuing, buying, and selling of stocks. It has the legal power to set and enforce accounting practices for firms whose securities are sold to the general public.

LO3 **Separate entity:** A business that is treated as distinct from its creditors, customers, and owners.

LO4 **Sole proprietorship:** A business that is owned by only one person and that is not incorporated.

LO6 **Statement of cash flows:** The financial statement that shows the inflows and outflows of cash from operating activities, investing activities, and financing activities over a period of time.

LO6 **Statement of owner's equity:** A financial statement that shows the change in owner's captial over a period of time.

Not sure you understand the techniques and calculations, or want to check if you are ready for a chapter test? The Review Problem models main computations or analyses presented in the chapter and other problem assignments. The answer is provided for immediate feedback.

REVIEW PROBLEM

The Effect of Transactions on the Accounting Equation

LO5 Charlene Rudek finished law school in June and immediately set up her own law practice. During the first month that the practice was operating, Rudek completed the following transactions:

a. Began the law practice by placing $2,000 in a bank account established for the business.
b. Purchased a law library for $900 cash.
c. Purchased office supplies for $400 on credit.
d. Accepted $500 in cash for completing a contract.
e. Billed clients $1,950 for services rendered during the month.
f. Paid $200 of the amount owed for office supplies.
g. Received $1,250 in cash from one client who had been billed previously for services rendered.
h. Paid rent expense for the month in the amount of $1,200.
i. Withdrew $400 from the practice for personal use.

REQUIRED

1. Show the effect of each of these transactions on the accounting equation by completing a table similar to Exhibit 1. Identify each owner's equity transaction.
2. Contrast the effects on cash flows of transactions **c** and **f** with transaction **b** and of transactions **e** and **g** with transaction **d**.

Answer to Review Problem

1. Table of effects of transactions on the accounting equation

	Assets				= Liabilities +	Owner's Equity	
	Cash	Accounts Receivable	Office Supplies	Law Library	Accounts Payable	C. Rudek, Capital	Type of OE Transaction
a.	$2,000					$2,000	Owner's Investment
b.	−900			+$900			
bal.	$1,100			$900		$2,000	
c.			+$400		+$400		
bal.	$1,100		$400	$900	$400	$2,000	
d.	+500					+ 500	Legal Fees Earned
bal.	$1,600		$400	$900	$400	$2,500	
e.		+$1,950				+1,950	Legal Fees Earned
bal.	$1,600	$1,950	$400	$900	$400	$4,450	
f.	−200				−200		
bal.	$1,400	$1,950	$400	$900	$200	$4,450	
g.	+1,250	−1,250					
bal.	$2,650	$ 700	$400	$900	$200	$4,450	
h.	−1,200					−1,200	Rent Expense
bal.	$1,450	$ 700	$400	$900	$200	$3,250	
i.	−400					−400	Owner's Withdrawal
bal.	$1,050	$ 700	$400	$900	$200	$2,850	
	$3,050				$3,050		

2. Transaction **c**, a purchase on credit, enables the company to use the asset immediately and to defer payment of cash. Cash is expended to partially pay for the asset in transaction **f**. The remainder is to be paid subsequently. This series of transactions contrasts with transaction **b**, in which cash is expended immediately for the asset. In each case, an asset is purchased, but the effects on cash flows differ.

   Transaction **e**, a sale on credit, allows the customer to pay later for services provided. This payment is partially received in transaction **g**, and the remainder is to be received later. These transactions contrast with transaction **d**, in which payment is received immediately for the services performed. In each case, the revenue is earned initially, but the effect on cash flows is different.

Chapter Assignments

Building Your Knowledge Foundation

Questions review key concepts, terminology, and topics of the chapter.

Questions

1. Why is accounting considered an information system?
2. What is the role of accounting in the decision-making process, and what broad business goals and activities does it help management achieve and manage?
3. Distinguish between management accounting and financial accounting.

4. Distinguish among these terms: *accounting, bookkeeping,* and *management information systems.*
5. Which decision makers use accounting information?
6. A business is an economic unit whose goal is to sell goods and services to customers at prices that will provide an adequate return to the business's owners. What functions must management perform to achieve that goal?
7. Why are investors and creditors interested in reviewing the financial statements of a company?
8. Among those who use accounting information are people and organizations that have an indirect interest in the business entity. Briefly describe these people and organizations.
9. Why has society as a whole become one of the largest users of accounting information?
10. Use the terms *business transactions, money measure,* and *separate entity* in a single sentence that demonstrates their relevance to financial accounting.
11. How do sole proprietorships, partnerships, and corporations differ?
12. Define *assets, liabilities,* and *owner's equity.*
13. Arnold Smith's company has assets of $22,000 and liabilities of $10,000. What is the amount of the owner's equity?
14. What four elements affect owner's capital? How?
15. Give examples of the types of transactions that (a) increase assets and (b) increase liabilities.
16. What is the function of the statement of owner's equity?
17. Why is the balance sheet sometimes called the statement of financial position?
18. Contrast the purpose of the balance sheet with that of the income statement.
19. A statement for an accounting period that ends in June can be headed "June 30, 20xx" or "For the Year Ended June 30, 20xx." Which heading is appropriate for (a) a balance sheet and (b) an income statement?
20. How does the income statement differ from the statement of cash flows?
21. What are GAAP? Why are they important to the readers of financial statements?
22. What do auditors mean by the phrase *in all material respects* when they state that financial statements "present fairly, in all material respects . . . in conformity with generally accepted accounting principles"?
23. What organization has the most influence on GAAP?
24. Discuss the importance of professional ethics in the accounting profession.

Short exercises are simple applications of chapter material for a single learning objective. If you need help locating the related text discussions, refer to the LO numbers in the margin. →

SHORT EXERCISES

SE 1. LO3 **Accounting Concepts**

Tell whether each of the following words or phrases relates most closely to (a) a business transaction, (b) a separate entity, or (c) a money measure:

1. Partnership
2. U.S. dollar
3. Payment of an expense
4. Corporation
5. Sale of an asset

SE 2. LO4 **Forms of Business Enterprises**

Match the descriptions on the left with the forms of business enterprise on the right:

_____ 1. Most numerous	a. Sole proprietorship
_____ 2. Commands most revenues	b. Partnership
_____ 3. Two or more co-owners	c. Corporation
_____ 4. Has stockholders	
_____ 5. Owned by one person	
_____ 6. Has a board of directors	

SE 3. **LO5 The Accounting Equation**

Determine the amount missing from each accounting equation below.

	Assets	=	Liabilities	+	Owner's Equity
1.	?		$25,000		$35,000
2.	$ 78,000		$42,000		?
3.	$146,000		?		$96,000

SE 4. **LO5 The Accounting Equation**

Use the accounting equation to answer each question below.

1. The assets of Sully Company are $480,000, and the liabilities are $360,000. What is the amount of the owner's equity?
2. The liabilities of Eva Company equal one-fifth of the total assets. The owner's equity is $80,000. What is the amount of the liabilities?

SE 5. **LO5 The Accounting Equation**

Use the accounting equation to answer each question below.

1. At the beginning of the year, Lanier Company's assets were $180,000, and its owner's equity was $100,000. During the year, the company's assets increased by $60,000, and its liabilities increased by $10,000. What was the owner's equity at the end of the year?
2. At the beginning of the year, Fanto Company had liabilities of $50,000 and owner's equity of $48,000. If assets increased by $20,000 and liabilities decreased by $15,000, what was the owner's equity at the end of the year?

SE 6. **LO5 The Accounting Equation and Net Income**

Use the following information and the accounting equation to determine the net income for the year for each alternative below.

	Assets	Liabilities
Beginning of the year	$ 70,000	$30,000
End of the year	100,000	50,000

1. No investments were made in the business, and no withdrawals were made during the year.
2. Investments of $10,000 were made in the business, but no withdrawals were made during the year.
3. No investments were made in the business, but withdrawals of $2,000 were made during the year.

SE 7. **LO5 The Accounting Equation and Net Income**

Meader Company had assets of $140,000 and liabilities of $60,000 at the beginning of the year, and assets of $200,000 and liabilities of $70,000 at the end of the year. During the year, there was an investment of $20,000 in the business, and withdrawals of $24,000 were made. What amount of net income did Meader Company earn during the year?

SE 8. **LO5 Effect of Transactions on the Accounting Equation**

On a sheet of paper, list the numbers **1** through **6,** with columns labeled Assets, Liabilities, and Owner's Equity. In the columns, indicate whether each transaction that follows caused an increase (+), a decrease (−), or no change (NC) in assets, liabilities, and owner's equity.

1. Purchased equipment on credit.
2. Purchased equipment for cash.
3. Billed customers for services performed.
4. Received and immediately paid a utility bill.
5. Received payment from a previously billed customer.
6. The owner made an additional investment.

SE 9. **LO5 Effect of Transactions on the Accounting Equation**

On a sheet of paper, list the numbers **1** through **6,** with columns labeled Assets, Liabilities, and Owner's Equity. In the columns, indicate whether each transaction below caused an increase (+), a decrease (−), or no change (NC) in assets, liabilities, and owner's equity.

1. Purchased supplies on credit.
2. Paid for previously purchased supplies.
3. Paid employee's weekly wages.
4. Cash withdrawal by owner.
5. Purchased a truck with cash.
6. Received a telephone bill to be paid next month.

SE 10. LO6 **Preparation and Completion of a Balance Sheet**

Use the following accounts and balances to prepare a balance sheet for Anatole Company at June 30, 20x1, using Exhibit 2 as a model:

Accounts Receivable	$ 800
Wages Payable	250
Owner's Capital	13,750
Building	10,000
Cash	?

Exercises are richer applications of all chapter material referenced by LOs. →

EXERCISES

E 1. LO1 LO2 LO7 **The Nature of Accounting**

Match the terms on the left with the descriptions on the right:

_____ 1. Bookkeeping
_____ 2. Creditors
_____ 3. Measurement
_____ 4. Financial Accounting Standards Board (FASB)
_____ 5. Tax authorities
_____ 6. Computer
_____ 7. Communication
_____ 8. Securities and Exchange Commission (SEC)
_____ 9. Investors
_____ 10. Processing
_____ 11. Management
_____ 12. Management information system

a. Function of accounting
b. Often confused with accounting
c. User(s) of accounting information
d. Organization that influences current practice
e. Tool that facilitates the practice of accounting

E 2. LO2 LO4 **Users of Accounting Information and Forms of Business Enterprise**

Vylex Pharmaceuticals has recently been formed to develop a new type of drug treatment for cancer. Previously a partnership, Vylex has now become a corporation. Identify the various groups that will have an interest in the financial statements of Vylex. What is the difference between a partnership and a corporation, and what advantages does the corporate form have over the partnership?

E 3. LO3 **Business Transactions**

Edgar owns and operates a minimart. State which of the actions below are business transactions. Explain why any other actions are not regarded as transactions.

1. Edgar reduces the price of a gallon of milk in order to match the price offered by a competitor.
2. Edgar pays a high school student cash for cleaning up the driveway behind the market.
3. Edgar fills his son's car with gasoline in payment for restocking the vending machines and the snack food shelves.
4. Edgar pays interest to himself on a loan he made to the business three years ago.

E 4. LO3 **Accounting Concepts**

Financial accounting uses money measures to gauge the impact of business transactions on a separate business entity. Tell whether each of the following words or phrases relates most closely to (a) a business transaction, (b) a separate entity, or (c) a money measure:

1. Corporation
2. Euro
3. Sales of products
4. Receipt of cash
5. Sole proprietorship
6. U.S. dollar
7. Partnership
8. Owner's investments
9. Japanese yen
10. Purchase of supplies

E 5. LO3 **Money Measure**

You have been asked to compare the sales and assets of four companies that make computer chips and to determine which company is the largest in each category. You have gathered the data shown at the top of the next page, but they cannot be used for direct comparison because each company's sales and assets are in its own currency.

Company (Currency)	Sales	Assets
Inchip (U.S. dollar)	20,000,000	13,000,000
Wong (Hong Kong dollar)	80,000,000	24,000,000
Mitzu (Japanese yen)	3,500,000,000	2,500,000,000
Works (Euro)	35,000,000	49,000,000

Assuming that the exchange rates in Table 1 are current and appropriate, convert all the figures to U.S. dollars and determine which company is the largest in sales and which is the largest in assets.

LO5 The Accounting Equation

E 6. Use the accounting equation to answer each question that follows. Show any calculations you make.

1. The assets of Caton Company are $800,000, and the owner's equity is $310,000. What is the amount of the liabilities?
2. The liabilities and owner's equity of Sung Company are $72,000 and $53,000, respectively. What is the amount of the assets?
3. The liabilities of Plumb Company equal one-third of the total assets, and owner's equity is $240,000. What is the amount of the liabilities?
4. At the beginning of the year, Wilde Company's assets were $220,000 and its owner's equity was $120,000. During the year, assets increased $60,000, and liabilities decreased $18,000. What is the owner's equity at the end of the year?

LO5 Owner's Equity Transactions

E 7. Identify the following transactions by marking each as an owner's investment (I), owner's withdrawal (W), revenue (R), expense (E), or not an owner's equity transaction (NOE):

a. Received cash for providing a service.
b. Took assets out of the business for personal expenses.
c. Received cash from a customer previously billed for a service.
d. Transferred assets to the business from a personal account.
e. Paid a service station for gasoline for a business vehicle.
f. Performed a service and received a promise of payment.
g. Paid cash to purchase equipment.
h. Paid cash to an employee for services performed.

LO5 Effect of Transactions on the Accounting Equation

E 8. During the month of April, Cosmos Corporation had the following transactions:

a. Paid salaries for April, $1,800.
b. Purchased equipment on credit, $3,000.
c. Purchased supplies with cash, $100.
d. Additional investment by owner, $4,000.
e. Received payment for services performed, $600.
f. Made partial payment on equipment purchased in transaction **b**, $1,000.
g. Billed customers for services performed, $1,600.
h. Cash withdrawal by owner, $1,500.
i. Received payment from customers billed in transaction **g**, $300.
j. Received utility bill, $70.

On a sheet of paper, list the letters **a** through **j**, with columns labeled Assets, Liabilities, and Owner's Equity. In the columns, indicate whether each transaction caused an increase (+), a decrease (−), or no change (NC) in assets, liabilities, and owner's equity.

LO5 Examples of Transactions

E 9. For each of the categories below, describe a transaction that would have the required effect on the elements of the accounting equation.

1. Increase one asset and decrease another asset.
2. Decrease an asset and decrease a liability.
3. Increase an asset and increase a liability.
4. Increase an asset and increase owner's equity.
5. Decrease an asset and decrease owner's equity.

LO5 Effect of Transactions on the Accounting Equation

E 10. The total assets and liabilities at the beginning and end of the year for Flag Company are listed below.

	Assets	Liabilities
Beginning of the year	$140,000	$ 55,000
End of the year	220,000	130,000

Determine Flag Company's net income or loss for the year under each of the following alternatives. The owner made

1. no investments in or withdrawals from the business during the year.
2. no investments in the business but withdrew $22,000 during the year.
3. an investment of $13,000 in the business but no withdrawals during the year.
4. an investment of $10,000 in the business and withdrew $22,000 during the year.

E 11. LO5 LO6 **Identification of Accounts**

1. Indicate whether each of the following accounts is an asset (A), a liability (L), or a part of owner's equity (OE):

   a. Cash
   b. Salaries Payable
   c. Accounts Receivable
   d. F. Wong, Capital
   e. Land
   f. Accounts Payable
   g. Supplies

2. Indicate whether each account below would be shown on the income statement (IS), the statement of owner's equity (OE), or the balance sheet (BS).

   a. Repair Revenue
   b. Automobile
   c. Fuel Expense
   d. Cash
   e. Rent Expense
   f. Accounts Payable
   g. F. Wong, Withdrawals

E 12. LO6 **Preparation of a Balance Sheet**

Listed in random order below are the balance sheet figures for the Solos Company as of December 31, 20xx.

Accounts Payable	$ 40,000	Accounts Receivable	$50,000
Building	90,000	Cash	20,000
N. Solos, Capital	170,000	Equipment	40,000
Supplies	10,000		

Sort the balances and prepare a balance sheet similar to the one in Exhibit 2.

E 13. LO6 **Completion of Financial Statements**

Complete the following independent sets of financial statements by determining the amounts that correspond to the letters. (Assume no new investments by the owner.)

Income Statement	Set A	Set B	Set C
Revenues	$1,100	$ g	$340
Expenses	a	5,200	m
Net income	$ b	$ h	$180
Statement of Owner's Equity			
Beginning balance	$2,900	$15,400	$200
Net income	c	1,600	n
Less withdrawals	200	i	o
Ending balance	$3,000	$ j	$ p
Balance Sheet			
Total assets	$ d	$21,000	$ q
Liabilities	$1,600	$ 5,000	$ r
Owner's equity	e	k	380
Total liabilities and owner's equity	$ f	$ l	$580

E 14. LO6 **Preparation of Financial Statements**

Ridge Company engaged in the following activities during the year: Service revenue, $52,800; Rent expense, $4,800; Wages expense, $33,080; Advertising expense, $5,400; Utilities expense, $3,600; and Sy Ridge, Withdrawals, $2,800. In addition, the year-end balances of selected accounts were as follows: Cash, $6,200; Accounts Receivable, $3,000; Supplies, $400; Land, $4,000; Accounts Payable, $1,800; and Sy Ridge, Capital, $8,680.

Using good form, prepare the income statement, statement of owner's equity, and balance sheet for Ridge Company (assume the year ends on June 30, 20x5). (**Hint:** The amount given for Sy Ridge, Capital is the beginning balance.)

E 15. LO6 **Statement of Cash Flows**

Waters Company began the year 20x4 with cash of $86,000. In addition to earning a net income of $50,000 and making an owner's withdrawal of $30,000 for his personal use,

Waters borrowed $120,000 from the bank and purchased equipment for $180,000 with cash. Also, Accounts Receivable increased by $12,000, and Accounts Payable increased by $18,000.

Determine the amount of cash on hand at the end of the year (December 31) by preparing a statement of cash flows similar to the one in Exhibit 2.

E 16. **LO7 Accounting Abbreviations**

Identify the accounting meaning of each of the following abbreviations: AICPA, SEC, GAAP, FASB, IRS, GASB, IASB, IMA, and CPA.

Problems are comprehensive applications of chapter material, often covering multiple learning objectives.

PROBLEMS

P 1. **LO5 Effect of Transactions on the Accounting Equation**

After receiving his degree in computer science, John Unger started his own business, Regency Business Services Company. The company completed the following transactions:

a. John deposited $18,000 in the bank to start the business and purchased a systems library with an additional investment of $1,840.
b. Paid current month's rent on an office, $720.
c. Purchased computers and other systems equipment for cash, $10,000.
d. Purchased computer supplies on credit, $1,200.
e. Received revenue from a client, $1,600.
f. Billed a client on completion of a short project, $1,420.
g. Paid wages, $800.
h. Received a partial payment from the client billed in transaction **f**, $160.
i. Withdrew cash for personal expenses, $500.
j. Made a partial payment on the computer supplies purchased in transaction **d**, $400.

REQUIRED ▶

1. Arrange the asset, liability, and owner's equity accounts in an equation similar to that in Exhibit 1, using the following account titles: Cash, Accounts Receivable, Computer Supplies, Equipment, Systems Library, Accounts Payable, and John Unger, Capital.
2. Show by addition and subtraction, as in Exhibit 1, the effects of the transactions on the accounting equation. Show new balances after each transaction, and identify each owner's equity transaction by type.
3. Contrast the effects on cash flows of transactions **d** and **j** with transaction **c** and of transactions **f** and **h** with transaction **e**.

Curious if you got the right answer? Look at the Check Figures section that precedes Chapter 1.

P 2. **LO5 Effect of Transactions on the Accounting Equation**

On October 1, Oscar Melendez started a new business, the Melendez Transport Company. During the month of October, the firm completed the following transactions:

a. Deposited $132,000 in a new bank account to establish Melendez Transport Company.
b. Purchased two trucks for cash, $86,000.
c. Purchased equipment on credit, $18,000.
d. Billed a customer for hauling goods, $2,400.
e. Received cash for hauling goods, $4,600.
f. Received cash payment from the customer billed in transaction **d**, $1,200.
g. Made a payment on the equipment purchased in transaction **c**, $10,000.
h. Paid wages in cash, $3,400.
i. Withdrew cash from the business for personal use, $2,400.

REQUIRED ▶

1. Arrange the asset, liability, and owner's equity accounts in an equation similar to that in Exhibit 1, using the following account titles: Cash, Accounts Receivable, Trucks, Equipment, Accounts Payable, and Oscar Melendez, Capital.
2. Show by addition and subtraction, as in Exhibit 1, the effects of the transactions on the accounting equation. Show new balances after each transaction, and identify each owner's equity transaction by type.

P 3. **LO5 Effect of Transactions on the Accounting Equation**

After completing his M.B.A., Sol Lindberg set up a consulting practice. At the end of his first month of operation, Lindberg had the following account balances: Cash, $2,930; Accounts Receivable, $1,400; Office Supplies, $270; Office Equipment, $4,200; Accounts Payable, $1,900; and Sol Lindberg, Capital, $6,900. Soon thereafter, the following transactions were completed:

a. Paid current month's rent, $800.
b. Made payment toward accounts payable, $450.

c. Billed clients for services performed, $800.
d. Received payment from clients billed last month, $1,000.
e. Purchased office supplies for cash, $80.
f. Paid part-time secretary's salary, $850.
g. Paid utilities expense, $90.
h. Paid telephone expense, $50.
i. Purchased additional office equipment for cash, $400.
j. Received cash from clients for services performed, $1,200.
k. Withdrew cash for personal expenses, $500.

REQUIRED ▶

1. Arrange the following asset, liability, and owner's equity accounts in an equation similar to that in Exhibit 1: Cash, Accounts Receivable, Office Supplies, Office Equipment, Accounts Payable, and Sol Lindberg, Capital.
2. Enter the beginning balances of the assets, liabilities, and owner's equity.
3. Show by addition and subtraction, as in Exhibit 1, the effects of the transactions on the accounting equation. Show new balances after each transaction, and identify each owner's equity transaction by type.

P 4.

LO1 Preparation of Financial
LO6 Statements

General ledger icons indicate that the problem can be solved using Houghton Mifflin General Ledger Software for Windows, with upgraded interface and available on the Student CD.

At the end of August 20xx, the Sheri Alexander, Capital account had a balance of $74,600. After operating during September, her Moon Valley Riding Club had the following account balances:

Cash	$17,400	Building	$60,000
Accounts Receivable	2,400	Horses	20,000
Supplies	2,000	Accounts Payable	35,600
Land	42,000		

In addition, the following transactions affected owner's equity:

Withdrawal by Sheri Alexander	$ 6,400	Salaries expense	$4,600
Investment by Sheri Alexander	32,000	Feed expense	2,000
Riding lesson revenue	12,400	Utilities expense	1,200
Locker rental revenue	3,400		

REQUIRED ▶

1. Using Exhibit 2 as a model, prepare an income statement, a statement of owner's equity, and a balance sheet for Moon Valley Riding Club. (**Hint:** The final balance of Sheri Alexander, Capital is $108,200).
2. Identify the links among the financial statements in part **1**.
3. Which of these statements are most closely associated with the goals of profitability and liquidity? Explain your answer. What other financial statement is helpful in evaluating liquidity?

P 5.

LO5 Effect of Transactions
LO6 on the Accounting Equation and Preparation of Financial Statements

Arrow Copying Service began operations and engaged in the following transactions during August 20xx:

a. Investment by owner, Myra Lomax, $10,000.
b. Paid current month's rent, $900.
c. Purchased copier for cash, $5,000.
d. Paid cash for paper and other copier supplies, $380.
e. Copying job payments received in cash, $1,780.
f. Copying job billed to major customer, $1,360.
g. Paid wages to part-time employees, $560.
h. Purchased additional copier supplies on credit, $280.
i. Received partial payment from customer in transaction **f**, $600.
j. Paid current month's utility bill, $180.
k. Made partial payment on supplies purchased in transaction **h**, $140.
l. Withdrew cash for personal use, $1,400.

REQUIRED ▶

1. Arrange the asset, liability, and owner's equity accounts in an equation similar to that in Exhibit 1, using these account titles: Cash, Accounts Receivable, Supplies, Copier, Accounts Payable, and M. Lomax, Capital.
2. Show by addition and subtraction, as in Exhibit 1, the effects of the transactions on the accounting equation. Show new balances after each transaction, and identify each owner's equity transaction by type.
3. Using Exhibit 2 as a guide, prepare an income statement, a statement of owner's equity, and a balance sheet for Arrow Copying Service. (Optional: Also prepare a statement of cash flows.)

ALTERNATE PROBLEMS

Looking for more practice? Alternate problems have the same format and learning objectives as the earlier problems.

P 6.

LO5 Effect of Transactions on the Accounting Equation

Rosa Partridge started The Creative Frames Shop in a small shopping center. In the first weeks of operation, the company completed the following transactions:

a. Deposited $21,000 in an account in the name of the company to start the business.
b. Paid the current month's rent, $1,500.
c. Purchased store equipment on credit, $10,800.
d. Purchased framing supplies for cash, $5,100.
e. Received framing revenue, $2,400.
f. Billed customers for services, $2,100.
g. Paid utilities expense, $750.
h. Received payment from customers in transaction **f**, $600.
i. Made payment on store equipment purchased in transaction **c**, $5,400.
j. Withdrew cash for personal expenses, $1,200.

REQUIRED

1. Arrange the following asset, liability, and owner's equity accounts in an equation similar to that in Exhibit 1: Cash, Accounts Receivable, Framing Supplies, Store Equipment, Accounts Payable, and Rosa Partridge, Capital.
2. Show by addition and subtraction, as in Exhibit 1, the effects of the transactions on the accounting equation. Show new balances after each transaction, and identify each owner's equity transaction by type.
3. Contrast the effects on cash flows of transactions **c** and **i** with transaction **d** and of transactions **f** and **h** with transaction **e**.

P 7.

LO1 Preparation of Financial
LO6 Statements

At the end of its first month of operation, March 20xx, Ellis Plumbing Company had the following account balances:

Cash	$58,600	Tools	$7,600
Accounts Receivable	10,800	Accounts Payable	8,600
Delivery Truck	38,000		

In addition, during the month of March, the following transactions affected owner's equity:

Original investment by J. Ellis	$40,000	Repair revenue	$ 5,600
Withdrawal by J. Ellis	4,000	Salaries expense	16,600
Further investment by J. Ellis	60,000	Rent expense	1,400
Contract revenue	23,200	Fuel expense	400

REQUIRED

1. Using Exhibit 2 as a model, prepare an income statement, a statement of owner's equity, and a balance sheet for Ellis Plumbing Company. (**Hint:** The final balance of J. Ellis, Capital is $106,400.)
2. Identify the links among the financial statements in part **1**.
3. Which financial statement is most closely associated with the goal of liquidity? Which with the goal of profitability? Explain your answers. What other statement is helpful in evaluating liquidity?

P 8.

LO5 Effect of Transactions
LO6 on the Accounting Equation and Preparation of Financial Statements

On April 1, 20xx, AAFast Taxi Service began operation. The company engaged in the following transactions during April:

a. Investment by owner, Madeline Curry, $42,000.
b. Purchased taxi for cash, $19,000.
c. Purchased uniforms on credit, $400.
d. Received taxi fares in cash, $3,200.
e. Paid wages to part-time drivers, $500.
f. Purchased gasoline during month for cash, $800.
g. Purchased car washes during month on credit, $120.
h. Further investment by owner, $5,000.
i. Paid part of the amount owed for the uniforms purchased in transaction **c**, $200.
j. Billed major client for fares, $900.
k. Paid for automobile repairs, $250.
l. Withdrew cash from business for personal use, $1,000.

REQUIRED

1. Arrange the asset, liability, and owner's equity accounts in an equation similar to that in Exhibit 1, using these account titles: Cash, Accounts Receivable, Uniforms, Taxi, Accounts Payable, and Madeline Curry, Capital.

2. Show by addition and subtraction, as in Exhibit 1, the effects of the transactions on the accounting equation. Show new balances after each transaction, and identify each owner's equity transaction by type.
3. Using Exhibit 2 as a guide, prepare an income statement, a statement of owner's equity, and a balance sheet for AAFast Taxi Service. (Optional: Also prepare a statement of cash flows.)

SKILLS DEVELOPMENT CASES

Conceptual Analysis

These cases focus on conceptual accounting issues encountered in the real business world.

LO1 Business Activities and
LO2 Management Functions

Communication icons identify cases that focus on understanding and communication accounting information successfully.

SD 1. J.C. Penney Company, Inc., <www.jcpenney.com> is America's largest department store company. According to its letter to stockholders, financial results didn't meet company expectations.

> J.C. Penney is implementing a number of strategic initiatives to ensure our competitiveness, to meet our growth objectives, and to provide a strong return on our stockholders' investment. These initiatives include: accelerated growth in our top 10 markets; expand our women's apparel and accessories business; speed merchandise to market; reduce our cost structure and enhance customer service.[11]

To achieve its strategy, J.C. Penney must organize its management into functions that relate to the principal activities of a business. Discuss the three basic activities J.C. Penney will engage in to achieve its goals, and suggest some examples of each. What is the role of J.C. Penney's management, and what functions must its management perform to accomplish these activities?

LO2 Users of Accounting
LO7 Information

Critical Thinking icons identify cases that reinforce critical thinking skills.

SD 2. Public companies report quarterly and annually on their success or failure in making a net income. The following item appeared in *The Wall Street Journal:* "Coca-Cola Co.'s <www.coca-cola.com> fourth-quarter net income plunged 27%, a dismal end to a disappointing year, as economic weakness in several overseas markets hurt sales of soft drinks."[12]

Discuss why each of the following individuals or groups might be interested in seeing the accounting reports that support this statement:

1. The management of Coca-Cola
2. The stockholders of Coca-Cola
3. The creditors of Coca-Cola
4. Potential stockholders of Coca-Cola
5. The Internal Revenue Service
6. The Securities and Exchange Commission
7. The Teamsters' union
8. A consumers' group called Public Cause
9. An economic adviser to the president of the United States

The financial statements of Coca-Cola are audited by a CPA firm. Why is the report of these independent auditors important to the users of Coca-Cola's financial statements?

Group Activity: Assign each of these users to a different group. Ask each group to discuss and present why its user needs accounting information.

LO5 Concept of an Asset

SD 3. Southwest Airlines Co. <www.southwest.com> is one of the most successful airlines in the United States. Its annual report contains this statement: "We are a company of People, not Planes. That is what distinguishes us from other airlines and other companies. At Southwest Airlines, People are our most important asset."[13] Are employees considered assets in the financial statements? Discuss in what sense Southwest considers its employees to be assets.

Ethical Dilemma

Ethical dilemmas provide practice in dealing with the tough choices people often face.

LO8 Professional Ethics

Ethics icons identify cases that address ethical issues.

SD 4. Discuss the ethical choices in the situations below. In each instance, describe the ethical dilemma, determine the alternative courses of action, and tell what you would do.

1. You are the payroll accountant for a small business. A friend asks you how much another employee is paid per hour.

2. As an accountant for the branch office of a wholesale supplier, you discover that several of the receipts the branch manager has submitted for reimbursement as selling expense actually stem from nights out with his spouse.
3. You are an accountant in the purchasing department of a construction company. When you arrive home from work on December 22, you find a large ham in a box marked "Happy Holidays—It's a pleasure to work with you." The gift is from a supplier who has bid on a contract your employer plans to award next week.
4. As an auditor with one year's experience at a local CPA firm, you are expected to complete a certain part of an audit in 20 hours. Because of your lack of experience, you know you cannot finish the job within that time. Rather than admit this, you are thinking about working late to finish the job and not telling anyone.
5. You are a tax accountant at a local CPA firm. You help your neighbor fill out her tax return, and she pays you $200 in cash. Because there is no record of this transaction, you are considering not reporting it on your tax return.
6. The accounting firm for which you work as a CPA has just won a new client, a firm in which you own 200 shares of stock that you received as an inheritance from your grandmother. Because it is only a small number of shares and you think the company will be very successful, you are considering not disclosing the investment.

Group Activity. Assign each case to a different group to resolve and report.

You are asked to gather information from the Internet or business publications and apply it to the accounting concepts in the chapter.

Research Activity

LO1 Need for Knowledge
LO2 of Accounting

SD 5. Locate an article about a company from one of the following sources: the business section of your local paper or a nearby metropolitan daily, *The Wall Street Journal, Business Week, Forbes,* or the Needles Accounting Resource Center Web Site at http://accounting.college.hmco.com/students. List all the financial and accounting terms used in the article. Bring the article to class and be prepared to discuss how a knowledge of accounting would help a reader understand the content of the article.

What are the relevant numbers, and what do they mean? Practice making business decisions based on accounting information.

Decision-Making Practice

LO5 Effect of Transactions
LO6 on the Balance Sheet

Memo icons identify cases that require short business memorandums.

SD 6. Instead of hunting for a summer job after finishing her junior year in college, Lucy Henderson organized a lawn service company in her neighborhood. To start her business on June 1, she deposited $1,350 in a new bank account in the name of her company. The $1,350 consisted of a $500 loan from her father and $850 of her own money. Using the money in this checking account, Henderson rented lawn equipment, purchased supplies, and hired neighborhood high school students to mow and trim the lawns of neighbors who had agreed to pay her for the service. At the end of each month, she mailed bills to her customers.

On August 31, Henderson was ready to dissolve her business and go back to school for the fall quarter. Because she had been so busy, she had not kept any records other than her checkbook and a list of amounts owed to her by customers.

Her checkbook had a balance of $1,760, and the amount owed to her by customers totaled $435. She expected these customers to pay her during October. She planned to return unused supplies to Suburban Landscaping Company for a full credit of $25. When she brought back the rented lawn equipment, Suburban Landscaping also would return a deposit of $100 she had made in June. She owed Suburban Landscaping $260 for equipment rentals and supplies. In addition, she owed the students who had worked for her $50, and she still owed her father $350. Although Henderson feels she did quite well, she is not sure just how successful she was. You have agreed to help her find out.

1. Prepare one balance sheet dated June 1 and another dated August 31 for Henderson Lawn Care Company.
2. Using information that can be inferred from comparing the balance sheets, write a memorandum to Lucy Henderson commenting on her company's performance in achieving profitability and liquidity. (Assume that she used none of the company's assets for personal purposes.) Also, mention the other two financial statements that would be helpful to her in evaluating these business goals.

FINANCIAL REPORTING AND ANALYSIS CASES

Interpreting Financial Reports

FRA 1. **LO7 Generally Accepted Accounting Principles**

J. P. Morgan Investment Management Inc. <www.jpmorgan.com> is the investment advisory service of the well-known investment bank J.P. Morgan Chase & Company. It makes investments worth billions of dollars in companies listed on the New York Stock Exchange and other stock markets. Generally accepted accounting principles (GAAP) are very important for J.P. Morgan's investment analysts. What are generally accepted accounting principles? Why are financial statements that have been prepared in accordance with GAAP and audited by an independent CPA useful for J.P. Morgan's investment analysts? What organizations influence GAAP? Explain how they do so.

FRA 2. **LO1 Operating Goals**

In May 2001, unable to get credit from enough of its lenders, housewares retailer Lechters, Inc., filed for Chapter 11 bankruptcy. It then secured new bank financing in the amount of $86 million. Suppliers, however, remained concerned about Lechters' ability to meet future obligations. Many retracted their term of sale, or the number of days the company had to pay for its merchandise, and asked for cash in advance or on delivery. Smaller home-furnishing retailers like Lechters struggle against big rivals, such as Bed Bath & Beyond, which are more valuable to suppliers and thus can demand better terms and pricing. In spite of these problems and an annual net loss of $101.8 million on sales of $405 million, management believed the company could eventually succeed with its strategy under the bankruptcy.[14] Which is more critical to the short-term survival of a company faced with Lechters' problems: liquidity or profitability? Which is more important in the long term? Explain your answers.

Using excerpts from business articles or annual reports of known companies, these cases ask you to extract relevant data, make computations, and interpret your results.

FRA 3. **LO6 Nature of Cash, Assets, and Net Income**

Charles Schwab Corporation <www.schwab.com> is a well-known financial services firm. Information for 2001 and 2000 from Schwab's annual report appears below.[15]

Charles Schwab Corporation
Condensed Balance Sheets
December 31, 2001 and 2000
(In millions)

	2001	2000
Assets		
Cash	$ 4,407	$ 4,876
Other assets	36,057	33,278
Total assets	$40,464	$38,154
Liabilities		
Total liabilities	$36,301	$33,924
Owner's Equity		
Owner's capital	$ 4,163	$ 4,230
Total liabilities and owner's equity	$40,464	$38,154

Three students who were looking at Charles Schwab's annual report were overheard to make the following comments:

Student A: What a great year Charles Schwab had in 2001! The company earned net income of $2,310,000,000 because its total assets increased from $38,154,000,000 to $40,464,000,000.

Student B: But the change in total assets isn't the same as net income! The company had a net loss of $469,000,000 because cash decreased from $4,876,000,000 to $4,407,000,000.

Student C: I see from the annual report that Charles Schwab had withdrawals (cash distributions to owners) of $209,000,000 in 2001. Don't you have to take that into consideration when analyzing the company's performance?

1. Comment on the interpretations of Students A and B, and then answer Student C's question.
2. Estimate Charles Schwab's net income for 2001. (**Hint:** Reconstruct the statement of owner's equity.)

Group Activity: After groups discuss **1,** have them compete to see which one can come up with the answer to **2** first.

Explore accounting issues facing international companies.

International Company

FRA 4.

LO1 The Goal of Profitability

International icons identify international cases.

In 1998, the celebrated Danish toy company Lego Group <www.lego.com> reported its first loss since the 1930s. In subsequent years, Lego's performance continued to be erratic with profits in 1999, but with a loss in 2000. While its bright plastic bricks were still famous around the globe, Lego was rapidly losing market share to computer and video games. The company's president said, "The Lego Group is not in critical condition, but action is needed. . . . We have to acknowledge that growth and innovation are not enough. We also have to be a profitable business."[16] Discuss the meaning of *profitability.* What other goal must a business achieve? Why is the goal of profitability important to Lego's president? What is the accounting measure of profitability, and on which statement is it determined?

Every chapter has a case on Toys "R" Us; the complete Toys "R" Us annual report for a recent year follows Chapter 6.

Toys "R" Us Annual Report

FRA 5.

LO6 The Four Basic Financial Statements

Refer to the Toys "R" Us <www.tru.com> annual report in the Supplement to Chapter 6 to answer the questions below. Keep in mind that every company, while following basic principles, adapts financial statements and terminology to its own special needs. Therefore, the complexity of the financial statements and the terminology in the Toys "R" Us statements will sometimes differ from those in the text. (Note that 2002 refers to the year ended February 1, 2003, and 2001 refers to the year ended February 2, 2002.)

1. What names does Toys "R" Us give its four basic financial statements? (Note that the word *consolidated* in the names of the financial statements means that these statements combine those of several companies owned by Toys "R" Us.)
2. Prove that the accounting equation works for Toys "R" Us on February 1, 2003, by finding the amounts for the following equation: Assets = Liabilities + Stockholders' Equity.
3. What were the total revenues of Toys "R" Us for the year ended February 1, 2003?
4. Was Toys "R" Us profitable in the year ended February 1, 2003? How much was net income (loss) in that year, and did it increase or decrease from the year ended February 2, 2002?
5. Did the company's cash and cash equivalents increase from February 2, 2002, to February 1, 2003? By how much? In what two places in the statements can this number be found or computed?
6. Did cash flows from operating activities, cash flows from investing activities, and cash flows from financing activities increase or decrease from 2001 to 2002?

Group Activity: Assign the above questions to in-class groups of three or four students. Set a time limit. The first group to answer all questions correctly wins.

Comparison cases ask you to read the financial statements of Toys "R" Us and Walgreens in the supplement to Chapter 6 and to compare these companies on key financial performance measures and financial disclosures.

Comparison Case: Toys "R" Us and Walgreen Co.

FRA 6.

LO1 Performance Measures
LO5 and Financial Statements
LO7

Refer to the Toys "R" Us <www.tru.com> annual report and the financial statements of Walgreen Co. <www.walgreens.com> in the Supplement to Chapter 6 to answer the following questions:

1. Which company is larger in terms of assets and in terms of revenues? What do you think is the best way to measure the size of a company?
2. Which company is more profitable in terms of net income? What is the trend of profitability over the past three years for both companies?
3. Which company has more cash? Which increased cash most in the last year? Which has more liquidity as measured by cash flows from operating activities?
4. Who is the auditor for each company? Why is the auditor's report that accompanies the financial statements important?

Use the professional software Fingraph® to analyze financial data.

Fingraph® Financial Analyst™

FRA 7.

LO1 Financial Statements,
LO6 Business Activities, and Goals

Choose a company from the list of Fingraph companies on the Needles Accounting Resource Center Web Site at http://accounting.college.hmco.com/students. Click on the company you selected to access the Microsoft Excel spreadsheet for that company. You will find the company's URL (Internet address) in the heading of the spreadsheet. Click on the URL for a link to the company's web site and annual report.

1. In the company's annual report, find a description of the business. What business is the company in? How would you describe its operating activities?
2. Find and identify the company's four basic financial statements. Which statement shows the resources of the business and the various claims to those resources? From the balance sheet, prove the accounting equation by showing that the company's assets equal its liabilities plus stockholders' equity. What is the company's largest category of assets? Which statement shows changes in all or part of the company's stockholders' equity during the year? Did the company pay any dividends in the last year?
3. Which statement is most closely associated with the company's profitability goal? How much net income did the company earn in the last year? Which statement is most closely associated with the company's liquidity goal? Did cash (and cash equivalents) increase in the last year? Which provided the most positive cash flows in the last year: operating, investing, or financing activities?
4. Prepare a one-page "executive summary" that highlights what you have learned from steps **1**, **2**, and **3**. An executive summary is a short, easy-to-read report that emphasizes important data and conclusions by putting them in numbered paragraphs or bulleted lists.

Use the Internet to research concepts and applications presented in the chapter.

Internet Case

FRA 8.

LO1 Financial Performance
LO5 Comparison of Two High-Tech Companies

Microsoft <www.microsoft.com> and Intel <www.intel.com> are two very successful high-tech corporations. Access their web sites using the URLs listed here or go to the Needles Accounting Resource Center Web Site at http://accounting.college.hmco.com/students for a link to their web sites. Access each company's annual report and locate the consolidated balance sheet and consolidated statement of income. Find the amount of total assets, revenues, and net income for the most recent year shown. Then compute net income to revenues (divide net income by revenues) and net income to total assets (divide net income by total assets) for both companies. Which company is larger? Which is more profitable?

2 Chapter 2 continues the exploration of accounting measurement by focusing on the problems of recognition, valuation, and classification and how they are solved in the measuring and recording of business transactions.

Measuring Business Transactions

Learning Objectives

LO1 Explain, in simple terms, the generally accepted ways of solving the measurement issues of recognition, valuation, and classification.

LO2 Describe the chart of accounts and recognize commonly used accounts.

LO3 Define *double-entry system* and state the rules for double entry.

LO4 Apply the steps for transaction analysis and processing to simple transactions.

LO5 Prepare a trial balance and describe its value and limitations.

LO6 Record transactions in the general journal and post transactions from the general journal to the ledger.

DECISION POINT

A USER'S FOCUS

Continental Airlines, Inc. <www.continental.com> & The Boeing Co. <www.boeing.com> In October 2000, Continental Airlines, Inc., announced that it had ordered 15 Boeing 757-300 jetliners.[1] The $1.2 billion order was part of an exclusive agreement Boeing negotiated with Continental. This exclusive 20-year agreement to purchase only Boeing aircraft was Boeing's fourth such agreement with a major airline and positioned the company favorably against Airbus, its European competitor. How should this important order have been recorded, if at all, in the records of Continental and Boeing? When should the purchase and sale that result from this order be recorded in the companies' records?

The order obviously was an important event, one with long-term consequences for both companies. But, as you will see in this chapter, it was not recorded in the accounting records of either company. At the time the order was placed, the aircraft were yet to be manufactured, and the first of them would not be delivered for several years. Even for "firm" orders, Boeing has cautioned that "an economic downturn could result in airline equipment requirements less than currently anticipated resulting in requests to negotiate the rescheduling or possible cancellation of firm orders."[2] The aircraft were not assets of Continental, and the company had not incurred a liability. No aircraft had been delivered or even built, so Continental was not obligated to pay at that point. And Boeing could not record any revenue until it manufactured and delivered the aircraft to Continental, and title to them shifted from Boeing to Continental.

When does Continental record the purchase of a new aircraft it orders from Boeing? When does Boeing record the revenue from the sale?

In fact, Boeing later experienced cancellation or extension of large, previously firm orders because of the economic slowdown in Asia,[3] and also because of the 9-11 attacks and the war in Iraq.

To understand and effectively use financial statements, it is important to know how to analyze events in order to determine the extent of their impact on those statements.

Measurement Issues

LO1 Explain, in simple terms, the generally accepted ways of solving the measurement issues of recognition, valuation, and classification.

RELATED TEXT ASSIGNMENTS
Q: 1, 2, 3, 4, 5
SE: 1, 2
E: 1, 2
P: 3, 4, 7
SD: 1, 2, 3
FRA: 4, 5

Business transactions are economic events that affect the financial position of a business entity. To measure a business transaction, the accountant must decide when the transaction occurred (the recognition issue), what value to place on the transaction (the valuation issue), and how the components of the transaction should be categorized (the classification issue).

These three issues—recognition, valuation, and classification—underlie almost every major decision in financial accounting today. They lie at the heart of accounting for pension plans, for mergers of giant companies, and for international transactions. In discussing the three basic issues, we follow generally accepted accounting principles and use an approach that promotes an understanding of the basic ideas of accounting. Keep in mind, however, that controversy does exist, and that solutions to some problems are not as cut-and-dried as they appear.

The Recognition Issue

TERMINOLOGY NOTE: In accounting, *recognize* means to record a transaction or event.

The **recognition** issue refers to the difficulty of deciding when a business transaction should be recorded. Often the facts of a situation are known, but there is disagreement about *when* the event should be recorded. Suppose, for instance, that a company orders, receives, and pays for an office desk. Which of the following actions constitutes a recordable event?

KEY POINT: A purchase should not be recognized (recorded) before title is transferred because until that point, the vendor has not fulfilled its contractual obligation and the buyer has no liability.

1. An employee sends a purchase requisition to the purchasing department.
2. The purchasing department sends a purchase order to the supplier.
3. The supplier ships the desk.
4. The company receives the desk.
5. The company receives the bill from the supplier.
6. The company pays the bill.

The answer to this question is important because the date on which a purchase is recorded affects amounts in the financial statements. According to accounting tradition, the transaction is recorded when title to the desk passes from the supplier to the purchaser, creating an obligation to pay. Thus, depending on the details of the shipping agreement, the transaction is recognized (recorded) at the time of either action **3** or action **4.** This is the guideline that we generally use in this book. However, in many small businesses that have simple accounting systems, the transaction is not recorded until the bill is received (action **5**) or paid (action **6**) because these are the implied points of title transfer. The predetermined time at which a transaction should be recorded is the **recognition point**.

The recognition issue is not always easy to resolve. Consider an advertising agency that prepares a major advertising campaign for a client. Employees may work on the campaign several hours a day for a number of weeks. They add value to the plan as they develop it. Should this added value be recognized as the campaign is being produced or at the time it is completed? Normally, the increase in value is recorded at the time the plan is finished and the client is billed for it. However, if a plan is going to take a long period to develop, the agency and the client may agree

FOCUS ON BUSINESS PRACTICE

Accounting Policies: Where Do You Find Them?

As noted in the Decision Point at the beginning of this chapter, Continental Airlines' <www.continental.com> order of jetliners from Boeing <www.boeing.com> was not an event that either company should have recorded as a transaction. But when do companies record such events as sales or purchase transactions? The answer to this question and others about a company's accounting policies may be found in the Summary of Significant Accounting Policies in the company's annual report. For example, under the heading "Sales and Other Operating Expenses," Boeing's Summary of Significant Accounting Policies states that "commercial aircraft sales are recorded as deliveries are made."[4]

that the client will be billed at key points during its development. A transaction is recorded at each billing.

Here are some more examples of the distinction between business events and transactions:

Business Events That Are *Not* Transactions	Business Events That *Are* Transactions
A customer inquires about the availability of a service.	A customer buys a service.
A company orders a product from a supplier.	A company receives a product previously ordered.
A company hires a new employee.	A company pays an employee for work performed.

THE VALUATION ISSUE

ENRICHMENT NOTE: The value of a transaction usually is based on a business document—a canceled check or an invoice. In general, appraisals or other subjective amounts are not recorded.

Valuation is perhaps the most controversial issue in accounting. The **valuation** issue focuses on assigning a monetary value to a business transaction. Generally accepted accounting principles state that the original cost (often called *historical cost*) is the appropriate value to assign to all business transactions—and therefore to all assets, liabilities, and components of owner's equity, including revenues and expenses, recorded by a business.

Cost is defined here as the exchange price associated with a business transaction at the point of recognition. According to this guideline, the purpose of accounting is not to account for value in terms of worth, which can change after a transaction occurs, but to account for value in terms of cost at the time of the transaction. For example, the cost of an asset is recorded when the asset is acquired, and the value is held at that level until the asset is sold, expires, or is consumed. In this context, *value* means the cost at the time of the transaction. The practice of recording transactions at cost is referred to as the **cost principle**.

Suppose that a person offers a building for sale at $120,000. It may be valued for real estate taxes at $75,000, and it may be insured for $90,000. One prospective buyer may offer $100,000 for the building, and another may offer $105,000. At this point, several different, unverifiable opinions of value have been expressed. Finally, suppose the seller and a buyer settle on a price and complete the sale for $110,000. All these figures are values of one kind or another, but only the last is sufficiently reliable to be used in the records. The market value of the building may vary over the years, but the building will remain on the new buyer's records at $110,000 until it is sold again. At that point, the accountant will record the new transaction at the new exchange price, and a profit or loss will be recognized.

STOP AND THINK!
Which is the most important issue in recording a transaction: recognition, valuation, or classification?

No issue is more important than another. Each must be resolved satisfactorily for a transaction to be recorded correctly.■

FOCUS ON INTERNATIONAL BUSINESS

No Dollar Amount: How Can That Be?

Determining the valuation of a sale or purchase transaction is often not difficult because it equals the amount of cash, or dollar amount, that changes hands. However, in some areas of the world, valuation is not so easy to determine. In a country where the currency is declining in value and inflation is high, companies often are forced to resort to barter transactions, in which one good or service is traded for another. In Russia, for example, perhaps as many as two-thirds of all transactions are barters. It is not uncommon for Russian companies to end up with piles of goods stacked around their offices and warehouses. In one case, an electric utility company provided a textile-machinery plant with electricity in exchange for wool blankets, which the plant had received in exchange for equipment sold to another company. Determining the value can be difficult in such cases because it becomes a matter of determining the fair value of the goods being traded.[5]

Focus on Business Practice

Is It Always Cost?

There are sometimes exceptions to the general rules of accounting. For instance, the cost principle is not followed in all parts of the financial statements. Investments, for example, are often accounted for at fair or market value because these investments are available for sale. The fair or market value is the best measure of the potential benefit to the company. Intel Corp. <www.intel.com>, the large microprocessor company, states in its annual report:

> *Investments designated as available-for-sale on the balance sheet date are reported at fair value.*[6]

The cost principle is used because the cost is verifiable. It results from the actions of independent buyers and sellers who come to an agreement on price. An exchange price is an objective price that can be verified by evidence created at the time of the transaction. It is this final price, verified by agreement of the two parties, at which the transaction is recorded.

The Classification Issue

The **classification** issue has to do with assigning all the transactions in which a business engages to appropriate categories, or accounts. Classification of debts can affect a company's ability to borrow money. And classification of purchases can affect its income; for example, purchases of tools may be considered repair expenses (a component of owner's equity) or equipment (assets).

KEY POINT: Assets, liabilities, and the components of owner's equity are not accounts, but account *classifications.* Cash is a type of asset account, and Notes Payable is a type of liability account.

Proper classification depends not only on correctly analyzing the effect of each transaction on the business, but also on maintaining a system of accounts that reflects that effect. The rest of this chapter explains the classification of accounts and the analysis and recording of transactions.

Check out ACE for a Review Quiz at http://accounting.college.hmco.com/students.

Accounts and the Chart of Accounts

LO2 Describe the chart of accounts and recognize commonly used accounts.

RELATED TEXT ASSIGNMENTS
Q: 6, 7, 8, 23
SE: 3
E: 3
FRA: 1, 6

Measuring business transactions often involves gathering large amounts of data. These data require a method of storage that allows businesspeople to retrieve transaction data quickly and in usable form—in other words, a filing system that classifies all transactions according to accounts. Recall that accounts are the basic storage units for accounting data and are used to accumulate amounts from similar transactions. An accounting system has a separate account for each asset, each liability, and each component of owner's equity, including revenues and expenses. Whether a company keeps records by hand or by computer, management must be able to refer to accounts so that it can study the company's financial history and plan for the future. A very small company may need only a few dozen accounts; a multinational corporation may need thousands.

In a manual accounting system, each account is kept on a separate page or card. These pages or cards are placed together in a book or file called the **general ledger**. In the computerized systems that most companies have today, accounts are maintained on magnetic tapes or disks. However, as a matter of convenience, accountants still refer to the group of company accounts as the *general ledger,* or simply the *ledger.*

KEY POINT: A chart of accounts is a table of contents for the ledger. Typically, it lists accounts in the order they appear in the ledger, which is usually the order in which they appear on the financial statements, and the numbering scheme allows for some flexibility.

To help identify accounts in the ledger and to make them easy to find, the accountant often numbers them. A list of these numbers with the corresponding account names is called a **chart of accounts**. A very simple chart of accounts appears in Exhibit 1. Notice that the first digit refers to the major financial statement classification. An account number that begins with the digit 1 represents an asset, an account number that begins with a 2 represents a liability, and so forth. The second and third digits refer to individual accounts. Also notice the gaps in the sequence of numbers. These gaps allow the accountant to expand the number of accounts.

In this chapter and in the next two, we refer to the accounts listed in Exhibit 1 as we discuss the sample case of the Joan Miller Advertising Agency.

EXHIBIT 1
Chart of Accounts for a Small Business

Account Number	Account Name	Description
		Assets
111	Cash	Money and any medium of exchange, including coins, currency, checks, postal and express money orders, and money on deposit in a bank
112	Notes Receivable	Amounts due from others in the form of promissory notes (written promises to pay definite sums of money at fixed future dates)
113	Accounts Receivable	Amounts due from others for revenues or sales on credit (sales on account)
115	Art Supplies	Prepaid expense; art supplies purchased and not used
116	Office Supplies	Prepaid expense; office supplies purchased and not used
117	Prepaid Rent	Prepaid expense; rent paid in advance and not used
118	Prepaid Insurance	Prepaid expense; insurance purchased and not expired; unexpired insurance
141	Land	Property owned for use in the business
142	Buildings	Structures owned for use in the business
143	Accumulated Depreciation, Buildings	Sum of the periodic allocation of the cost of buildings to expense
144	Art Equipment	Art equipment owned for use in the business
145	Accumulated Depreciation, Art Equipment	Sum of the periodic allocation of the cost of art equipment to expense
146	Office Equipment	Office equipment owned for use in the business
147	Accumulated Depreciation, Office Equipment	Sum of the periodic allocation of the cost of office equipment to expense
		Liabilities
211	Notes Payable	Amounts due to others in the form of promissory notes
212	Accounts Payable	Amounts due to others for purchases on credit (purchases on account)
213	Unearned Art Fees	Unearned revenue; advance deposits for artwork to be provided in the future
214	Wages Payable	Amounts due to employees for wages earned and not paid
221	Mortgage Payable	Amounts due on loans that are backed by the company's property and buildings
		Owner's Equity
311	Capital	Owner's investment in the company
312	Withdrawals	Assets withdrawn from the business by the owner for personal use
313	Income Summary	Temporary account used at the end of the accounting period to summarize the revenues and expenses for the period
		Revenues
411	Advertising Fees Earned	Revenues derived from performing advertising services
412	Art Fees Earned	Revenues derived from performing art services

(continued)

EXHIBIT 1
Chart of Accounts for a Small Business *(continued)*

Account Number	Account Name	Description
		Expenses
511	Wages Expense	Amounts earned by employees
512	Utilities Expense	Amounts for utilities, such as water, electricity, and gas, used
513	Telephone Expense	Amounts for telephone services used
514	Rent Expense	Amounts for rent on property and buildings used
515	Insurance Expense	Amounts for insurance expired
516	Art Supplies Expense	Amounts for art supplies used
517	Office Supplies Expense	Amounts for office supplies used
518	Depreciation Expense, Buildings	Amount of buildings' cost allocated to expense
519	Depreciation Expense, Art Equipment	Amount of art equipment cost allocated to expense
520	Depreciation Expense, Office Equipment	Amount of office equipment cost allocated to expense
521	Interest Expense	Amount of interest on debts

STOP AND THINK!
How would the asset accounts in the chart of accounts for Joan Miller Advertising Agency differ if it were a retail company that sold advertising products instead of a service company?

If it were a retail company, it would have an account for inventory.■

OWNER'S EQUITY ACCOUNTS

In the chart of accounts shown in Exhibit 1, the revenue and expense accounts are separated from the other owner's equity accounts. Figure 1 illustrates the relationships of these accounts to each other and to the financial statements. The distinctions among them are important for legal and financial reporting purposes.

First, for income tax reporting, financial reporting, and other purposes, the law requires that Capital and Withdrawals accounts be separated from revenues and expenses. The Capital account represents the owner's interest in the assets of the company. The Withdrawals account is used to record assets taken out of the business by the owner for personal use. These withdrawals are not described as salary or wages, although the owner may think of them as such, because there is no change in the ownership of the money withdrawn. In practice, the Withdrawals account often goes by other names, among them *Personal* and *Drawing*. Corporations do not use a Withdrawals account.

Second, management needs a detailed breakdown of revenues and expenses for budgeting and operating purposes. From these accounts, which are included on the income statement, management can identify the sources of all revenues and the nature of all expenses. In this way, accounting gives management information about whether it has achieved its primary goal of earning a net income.

ACCOUNT TITLES

The names of accounts often confuse beginning accounting students because some words are new or have technical meanings. Also, the same asset, liability, or owner's equity account can have different names in different companies. (Actually, this is not so strange. People, too, often are called different names by their friends, families, and associates.) For example, Fixed Assets, Plant and Equipment, Capital Assets, and Long-Lived Assets are all names for long-term asset accounts. Even the most acceptable names change over time, but out of habit, some companies continue to use names that are out of date.

FIGURE 1
Relationships of Owner's Equity Accounts

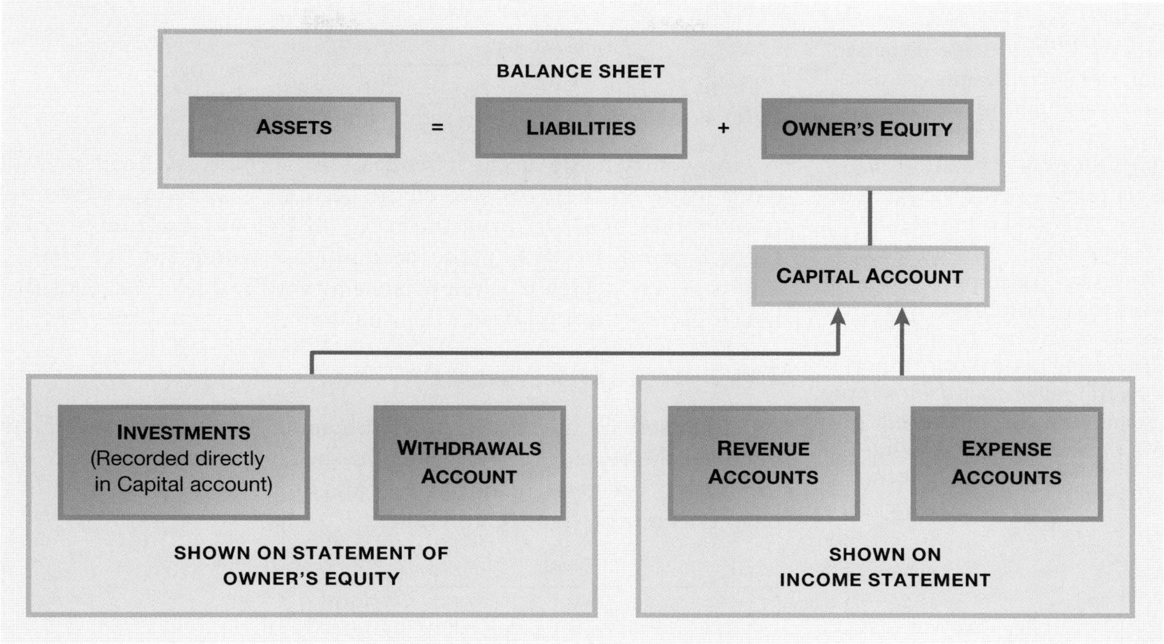

KEY POINT: Account names must be both concise and descriptive. Although some account names, such as Cash and Land, generally are fixed, others are not.

In general, an account title should describe what is recorded in the account. When you come across an account title that you do not recognize, examine the context of the name—whether it is classified as an asset, liability, or owner's equity component, including revenue or expense, on the financial statements—and look for the kind of transaction that gave rise to the account.

Check out ACE for a Review Quiz at http://accounting.college.hmco.com/students.

THE DOUBLE-ENTRY SYSTEM: THE BASIC METHOD OF ACCOUNTING

LO3 Define *double-entry system* and state the rules for double entry.

RELATED TEXT ASSIGNMENTS
Q: 9, 10, 11, 12, 13
SE: 2
FRA: 5

KEY POINT: Each transaction must include at least one debit and one credit, and the debit totals must equal the credit totals.

The double-entry system, the backbone of accounting, evolved during the Renaissance. The first systematic description of double-entry bookkeeping appeared in 1494, two years after Columbus discovered America, in a mathematics book by Fra Luca Pacioli. Goethe, the famous German poet and dramatist, referred to double-entry bookkeeping as "one of the finest discoveries of the human intellect." Werner Sombart, an eminent economist-sociologist, believed that "double-entry bookkeeping is born of the same spirit as the system of Galileo and Newton."

What is the significance of the double-entry system? The system is based on the *principle of duality*, which means that every economic event has two aspects—effort and reward, sacrifice and benefit, source and use—that offset or balance each other. In the **double-entry system**, each transaction must be recorded with at least one debit and one credit, so that the total dollar amount of debits and the total dollar amount of credits equal each other. Because of the way it is designed, the whole system is always in balance. All accounting systems, no matter how sophisticated, are based on the principle of duality.

THE T ACCOUNT

The T account is a good place to begin the study of the double-entry system. In its simplest form, an account has three parts: (1) a title, which describes the asset, the

KEY POINT: A T account is simply an abbreviated version of a ledger account. T accounts are used by accountants, instructors, students, and textbooks to quickly analyze a set of transactions; ledger accounts are used in the accounting records.

KEY POINT: Many students have preconceived ideas about what *debit* and *credit* mean. They think that *debit* means "decrease" (or implies something bad) and that *credit* means "increase" (or implies something good). It is important to realize that *debit* simply means "left side" and *credit* simply means "right side."

KEY POINT: Notice that the debits and credits do not act independently. That is, one is netted out against the other to produce the account balance.

liability, or the owner's equity account; (2) a left side, which is called the **debit** side; and (3) a right side, which is called the **credit** side. This form of an account, called a **T account** because it resembles the letter *T*, is used to analyze transactions. It looks like this:

Title of Account	
Debit (left) side	Credit (right) side

Any entry made on the left side of the account is a debit, or debit entry, and any entry made on the right side of the account is a credit, or credit entry. The terms *debit* (abbreviated Dr., from the Latin *debere*) and *credit* (abbreviated Cr., from the Latin *credere*) are simply the accountant's words for "left" and "right" (not for "increase" or "decrease"). We present a more formal version of the T account, the ledger account form, later in this chapter.

The T Account Illustrated

As discussed in the last chapter, Shannon Realty had several transactions that involved the receipt or payment of cash. These transactions can be summarized in the Cash account by recording receipts on the left (debit) side of the account and payments on the right (credit) side:

Cash			
(1)	50,000	(2)	35,000
(5)	1,500	(4)	200
(7)	1,000	(8)	1,000
		(9)	400
		(11)	600
	52,500		37,200
Bal.	15,300		

The cash receipts on the left total $52,500. (The total is written in small figures so that it cannot be confused with an actual debit entry.) The cash payments on the right side total $37,200. These totals are simply working totals, or **footings**. Footings, which are calculated at the end of each month, are an easy way to determine cash on hand. The difference in dollars between the total debit footing and the total credit footing is called the **balance**, or *account balance.* If the balance is a debit, it is written on the left side. If it is a credit, it is written on the right. Shannon Realty's Cash account has a debit balance of $15,300 ($52,500 − $37,200). This is the amount of cash the business has on hand at the end of the month.

Analyzing and Processing Transactions

The two rules of double-entry bookkeeping are that every transaction affects at least two accounts and that total debits must equal total credits. In other words, for every transaction, one or more accounts must be debited and one or more accounts must be credited, and the total dollar amount of the debits must equal the total dollar amount of the credits.

Look again at the accounting equation:

Assets = Liabilities + Owner's Equity

You can see that if a debit increases assets, then a credit must be used to decrease assets on the same side of the equal sign or increase liabilities or owner's equity on opposite sides of the equal sign. Likewise, if a credit decreases assets, then a debit must be used to increase assets or decrease liabilities or owner's equity. These rules can be shown as follows:

Assets		=	Liabilities		+	Owner's Equity	
Debit for increases (+)	Credit for decreases (−)		Debit for decreases (−)	Credit for increases (+)		Debit for decreases (−)	Credit for increases (+)

STOP AND THINK!
How are assets and expenses related, and why are the debit and credit effects for assets and expenses the same?

Assets and expenses are closely related because many assets are expenses that have not yet been used. Examples are prepaid assets and plant and equipment. As a result, debits increase *assets and expenses, and credits* decrease *assets and expenses. They appear on opposite sides of the accounting equation.* ■

1. Increases in assets are debited to asset accounts. Decreases in assets are credited to asset accounts.
2. Increases in liabilities and owner's equity are credited to liability and owner's equity accounts. Decreases in liabilities and owner's equity are debited to liability and owner's equity accounts.

One of the more difficult points to understand is the application of double-entry rules to the owner's equity components. The key is to remember that withdrawals and expenses are deductions from owner's equity. Thus, transactions that *increase* withdrawals or expenses *decrease* owner's equity. Consider this expanded version of the accounting equation:

$$\text{Assets} = \text{Liabilities} + \overbrace{\text{Capital} - \text{Withdrawals} + \text{Revenues} - \text{Expenses}}^{\text{Owner's Equity}}$$

This equation may be rearranged by shifting withdrawals and expenses to the left side, as follows:

Assets		+	Withdrawals		+	Expenses		=	Liabilities		+	Capital		+	Revenues	
+ (debits)	− (credits)		+ (debits)	− (credits)		+ (debits)	− (credits)		− (debits)	+ (credits)		− (debits)	+ (credits)		− (debits)	+ (credits)

Note that the rules for double entry for all the accounts on the left of the equal sign are just the opposite of the rules for all the accounts on the right of the equal sign. Assets, withdrawals, and expenses are increased by debits and decreased by credits. Liabilities, capital, and revenues are increased by credits and decreased by debits.

With this basic information about double entry, it is possible to analyze and process transactions by following the five steps illustrated in Figure 2. To show how the steps are applied, assume that on June 1, Koenig Art Supplies borrows $100,000 from its bank on a promissory note. The list that follows describes how this transaction is analyzed and processed.

FIGURE 2
Analyzing and Processing Transactions

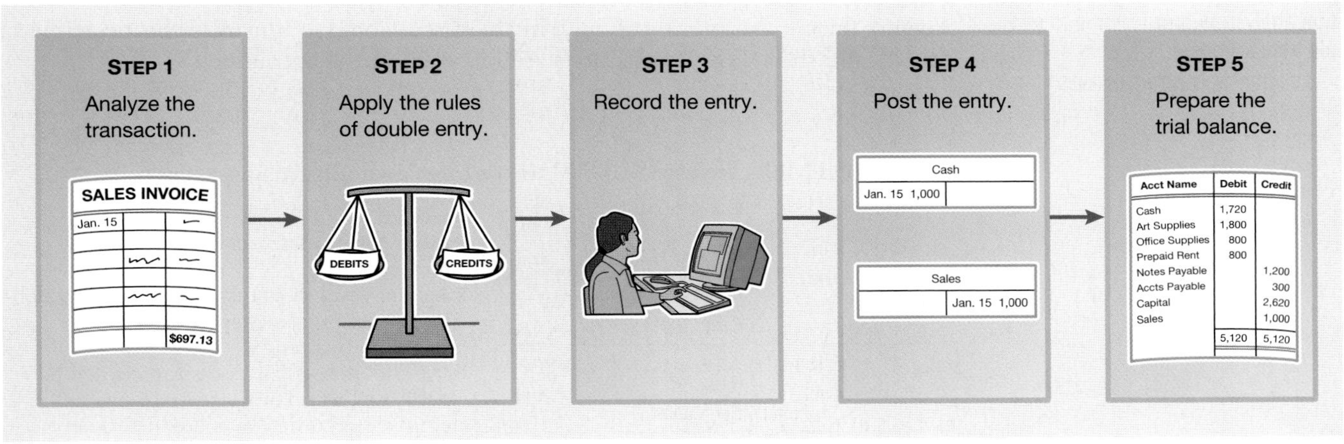

KEY POINT: Identifying the accounts involved in a transaction takes practice. Often, account names are not used in the description of a transaction.

1. *Analyze the transaction to determine its effect on assets, liabilities, and owner's equity.* In this case, both an asset (Cash) and a liability (Notes Payable) increase. A transaction is usually supported by some kind of **source document**—an invoice, receipt, check, or contract; here, it would be a copy of the signed note.
2. *Apply the rules of double entry.* Increases in assets are recorded by debits. Increases in liabilities are recorded by credits.
3. *Record the entry.* Transactions are recorded in chronological order in a journal. In one form of journal, which is explained in more detail later in this chapter, the date, debit account, and debit amount are recorded on one line and the credit account and credit amount, indented, on the next line, as follows:

A = L + OE
\+ \+

		Dr.	Cr.
June 1	Cash	100,000	
	Notes Payable		100,000
	Issued note payable for cash		

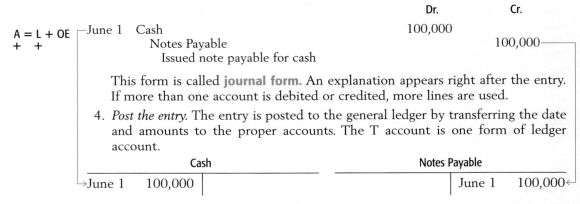

This form is called **journal form.** An explanation appears right after the entry. If more than one account is debited or credited, more lines are used.

4. *Post the entry.* The entry is posted to the general ledger by transferring the date and amounts to the proper accounts. The T account is one form of ledger account.

Cash

June 1 100,000	

Notes Payable

	June 1 100,000

In formal records, step **3** is never omitted. However, for purposes of analysis, accountants often bypass step **3** and record entries directly in T accounts because doing so clearly and quickly shows the effects of transactions on the accounts. Some of the assignments in this chapter use the same approach to emphasize the analytical aspects of double entry.

5. *Prepare the trial balance to confirm the balance of the accounts.* Periodically, accountants prepare a trial balance to confirm that the accounts are still in balance after the recording and posting of transactions. Preparation of the trial balance is explained later in this chapter.

Check out ACE for a Review Quiz at http://accounting.college.hmco.com/students.

TRANSACTION ANALYSIS ILLUSTRATED

LO4 Apply the steps for transaction analysis and processing to simple transactions.

RELATED TEXT ASSIGNMENTS
Q: 14, 15, 16, 20, 24
SE: 5, 6
E: 4, 5, 7, 12
P: 1, 2, 3, 4, 5, 6, 7, 8
SD: 2, 4, 5
FRA: 1, 2, 3, 5, 6

In the next few pages, we examine the transactions for Joan Miller Advertising Agency during the month of July. In the discussion, we illustrate the principle of duality and show how transactions are recorded in the accounts.

July 1: Joan Miller invests $20,000 to start her own advertising agency.

A = L + OE
\+ \+

		Dr.	Cr.
July 1	Cash	20,000	
	Joan Miller, Capital		20,000

Cash

July 1 20,000	

Joan Miller, Capital

	July 1 20,000

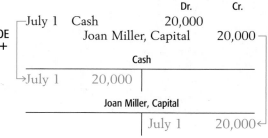

Transaction: Owner's investment.
Analysis: Assets increase. Owner's equity increases.
Rules: Increases in assets are recorded by debits. Increases in owner's equity are recorded by credits.
Entry: The increase in assets is recorded by a debit to Cash. The increase in owner's equity is recorded by a credit to Joan Miller, Capital.

Analysis: If Joan Miller had invested assets other than cash in the business, the appropriate asset accounts would be debited.

KEY POINT: Notice the exchange of one asset for another asset.

July 2: Rents an office, paying two months' rent, $1,600, in advance.

A = L + OE
\+
−

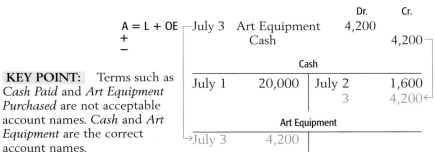

		Dr.	Cr.
July 2	Prepaid Rent	1,600	
	Cash		1,600

Cash

July 1	20,000	July 2	1,600

Prepaid Rent

July 2	1,600		

Transaction: Rent paid in advance.
Analysis: Assets increase. Assets decrease.
Rules: Increases in assets are recorded by debits. Decreases in assets are recorded by credits.
Entry: The increase in assets is recorded by a debit to Prepaid Rent. The decrease in assets is recorded by a credit to Cash.

July 3: Purchases art equipment, $4,200, with cash.

A = L + OE
\+
−

		Dr.	Cr.
July 3	Art Equipment	4,200	
	Cash		4,200

Cash

July 1	20,000	July 2	1,600
		3	4,200

Art Equipment

July 3	4,200		

Transaction: Purchase of equipment.
Analysis: Assets increase. Assets decrease.
Rules: Increases in assets are recorded by debits. Decreases in assets are recorded by credits.
Entry: The increase in assets is recorded by a debit to Art Equipment. The decrease in assets is recorded by a credit to Cash.

KEY POINT: Terms such as *Cash Paid* and *Art Equipment Purchased* are not acceptable account names. *Cash* and *Art Equipment* are the correct account names.

July 4: Orders art supplies, $1,800, and office supplies, $800.

Analysis: No entry is made because no transaction has occurred. According to the recognition issue, there is no liability until the supplies are shipped or received and there is an obligation to pay for them.

Compound Entry

July 5: Purchases office equipment, $3,000, from Morgan Equipment; pays $1,500 in cash and agrees to pay the rest next month.

A = L + OE
\+   +
−

		Dr.	Cr.
July 5	Office Equipment	3,000	
	Cash		1,500
	Accounts Payable		1,500

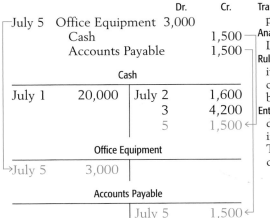

Cash

July 1	20,000	July 2	1,600
		3	4,200
		5	1,500

Office Equipment

July 5	3,000		

Accounts Payable

		July 5	1,500

Transaction: Purchase of equipment and partial payment.
Analysis: Assets increase. Assets decrease. Liabilities increase.
Rules: Increases in assets are recorded by debits. Decreases in assets are recorded by credits. Increases in liabilities are recorded by credits.
Entry: The increase in assets is recorded by a debit to Office Equipment. The decrease in assets is recorded by a credit to Cash. The increase in liabilities is recorded by a credit to Accounts Payable.

KEY POINT: Office equipment is recorded at the full $3,000, even though only half of it has been paid for.

Focus on Business Ethics

Are Financial Statements Always Truthful?

The accounting concepts related to recognition (when a transaction occurred), valuation (what value to place on the transaction), and classification (how the components of the transaction should be categorized) are not only important for good financial reporting; they are also designed to help a company's management fulfill its responsibilities to the owners and the public.

A prime example of this responsibility was recently demonstrated at Lucent Technologies <www.lucent.com>, a major telecommunications equipment manufacturer. After years of excellent results, Lucent surprised its investors by admitting that because of returns of equipment that distributors had been unable to sell, it was going to have to erase $452 million in equipment sales from the $679 million it had reported for the year.

The problem related to how and when Lucent recognizes proceeds from sales. The company's chief executive officer explained that to meet short-term growth targets, "We mortgaged future sales and revenue in a way we are paying for now."[7] In the aftermath, the company's stock dropped from $80 per share to less than $5 per share, and more than 10,000 employees were laid off.

July 6: Purchases art supplies, $1,800, and office supplies, $800, from Taylor Supply Company, on credit.

A = L + OE
\+ \+
\+

		Dr.	Cr.
July 6	Art Supplies	1,800	
	Office Supplies	800	
	Accounts Payable		2,600

Art Supplies

July 6	1,800		

Office Supplies

July 6	800		

Accounts Payable

		July 5	1,500
		6	2,600

Transaction: Purchase of supplies on credit.
Analysis: Assets increase. Liabilities increase.
Rules: Increases in assets are recorded by debits. Increases in liabilities are recorded by credits.
Entry: The increase in assets is recorded by debits to Art Supplies and Office Supplies. The increase in liabilities is recorded by a credit to Accounts Payable.

KEY POINT: Accounts Payable is used when there is a delay between purchase and payment.

July 8: Pays for a one-year life insurance policy, $960, with coverage effective July 1.

A = L + OE
\+
−

		Dr.	Cr.
July 8	Prepaid Insurance	960	
	Cash		960

Cash

July 1	20,000	July 2	1,600
		3	4,200
		5	1,500
		8	960

Prepaid Insurance

July 8	960		

Transaction: Insurance purchased in advance.
Analysis: Assets increase. Assets decrease.
Rules: Increases in assets are recorded by debits. Decreases in assets are recorded by credits.
Entry: The increase in assets is recorded by a debit to Prepaid Insurance. The decrease in assets is recorded by a credit to Cash.

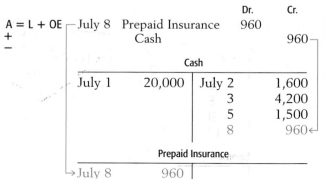

July 9: Pays Taylor Supply Company $1,000 of the amount owed.

A = L + OE
− −

		Dr.	Cr.
July 9	Accounts Payable	1,000	
	Cash		1,000

Cash

July 1	20,000	July 2	1,600
		3	4,200
		5	1,500
		8	960
		9	1,000

Accounts Payable

July 9	1,000	July 5	1,500
		6	2,600

KEY POINT: Accounts Payable, not Art Supplies or Office Supplies, is debited. Also, a liability usually is credited before it can be debited.

Transaction: Partial payment on a liability.
Analysis: Assets decrease. Liabilities decrease.
Rules: Decreases in liabilities are recorded by debits. Decreases in assets are recorded by credits.
Entry: The decrease in liabilities is recorded by a debit to Accounts Payable. The decrease in assets is recorded by a credit to Cash.

July 10: Performs a service for an automobile dealer by placing advertisements in a newspaper and collects a fee, $1,400.

A = L + OE
\+ \+

		Dr.	Cr.
July 10	Cash	1,400	
	Advertising Fees Earned		1,400

Cash

July 1	20,000	July 2	1,600
10	1,400	3	4,200
		5	1,500
		8	960
		9	1,000

Advertising Fees Earned

		July 10	1,400

Transaction: Revenue earned and cash collected.
Analysis: Assets increase. Owner's equity increases.
Rules: Increases in assets are recorded by debits. Increases in owner's equity are recorded by credits.
Entry: The increase in assets is recorded by a debit to Cash. The increase in owner's equity is recorded by a credit to Advertising Fees Earned.

July 12: Pays the secretary two weeks' wages, $1,200.

A = L + OE
− −

		Dr.	Cr.
July 12	Wages Expense	1,200	
	Cash		1,200

Cash

July 1	20,000	July 2	1,600
10	1,400	3	4,200
		5	1,500
		8	960
		9	1,000
		12	1,200

Wages Expense

July 12	1,200		

Transaction: Payment of wages expense.
Analysis: Assets decrease. Owner's equity decreases.
Rules: Decreases in owner's equity are recorded by debits. Decreases in assets are recorded by credits.
Entry: The decrease in owner's equity is recorded by a debit to Wages Expense. The decrease in assets is recorded by a credit to Cash.

STOP AND THINK!
In what way are unearned revenues the opposite of prepaid expenses?
With unearned revenues (a liability), cash is received in advance for a service to be performed later. With prepaid expenses (an asset), cash is paid in advance of receiving a service. ■

July 15: Accepts an advance fee, $1,000, for artwork to be done for another agency.

A = L + OE
\+ \+

		Dr.	Cr.
July 15	Cash	1,000	
	Unearned Art Fees		1,000

Cash

July 1	20,000	July 2	1,600
10	1,400	3	4,200
15	1,000	5	1,500
		8	960
		9	1,000
		12	1,200

Unearned Art Fees

		July 15	1,000

Transaction: Payment received for future services.
Analysis: Assets increase. Liabilities increase.
Rules: Increases in assets are recorded by debits. Increases in liabilities are recorded by credits.
Entry: The increase in assets is recorded by a debit to Cash. The increase in liabilities is recorded by a credit to Unearned Art Fees.

July 19: Performs a service by placing several major advertisements for Ward Department Stores. The fee, $4,800, is billed now but will be collected next month.

A = L + OE
\+ \+

		Dr.	Cr.
July 19	Accounts Receivable	4,800	
	Advertising Fees Earned		4,800

Accounts Receivable

July 19	4,800		

Advertising Fees Earned

		July 10	1,400
		19	4,800

Transaction: Revenue earned, to be received later.
Analysis: Assets increase. Owner's equity increases.
Rules: Increases in assets are recorded by debits. Increases in owner's equity are recorded by credits.
Entry: The increase in assets is recorded by a debit to Accounts Receivable. The increase in owner's equity is recorded by a credit to Advertising Fees Earned.

KEY POINT: Revenue is recognized even though payment has not been received yet. Accounts Receivable is used when there is a delay between the sale of services or merchandise and payment.

July 26: Pays the secretary two more weeks' wages, $1,200.

A = L + OE
− −

		Dr.	Cr.
July 26	Wages Expense	1,200	
	Cash		1,200

Cash

July 1	20,000	July 2	1,600
10	1,400	3	4,200
15	1,000	5	1,500
		8	960
		9	1,000
		12	1,200
		26	1,200

Wages Expense

July 12	1,200		
26	1,200		

Transaction: Payment of wages expense.
Analysis: Assets decrease. Owner's equity decreases.
Rules: Decreases in owner's equity are recorded by debits. Decreases in assets are recorded by credits.
Entry: The decrease in owner's equity is recorded by a debit to Wages Expense. The decrease in assets is recorded by a credit to Cash.

July 29: Receives and pays the utility bill, $200.

A = L + OE
− −

		Dr.	Cr.
July 29	Utilities Expense	200	
	Cash		200

Cash

July 1	20,000	July 2	1,600
10	1,400	3	4,200
15	1,000	5	1,500
		8	960
		9	1,000
		12	1,200
		26	1,200
		29	200

Utilities Expense

July 29	200		

Transaction: Payment of utilities expense.
Analysis: Assets decrease. Owner's equity decreases.
Rules: Decreases in owner's equity are recorded by debits. Decreases in assets are recorded by credits.
Entry: The decrease in owner's equity is recorded by a debit to Utilities Expense. The decrease in assets is recorded by a credit to Cash.

July 30: Receives (but does not pay) the telephone bill, $140.

A = L + OE
\+ −

		Dr.	Cr.
July 30	Telephone Expense	140	
	Accounts Payable		140

Accounts Payable

July 9	1,000	July 5	1,500
		6	2,600
		30	140

Telephone Expense

July 30	140		

KEY POINT: The expense and liability are recognized at this point, even though payment has not yet been made, because an expense has been incurred. Telephone services have been used, and the obligation to pay exists.

Transaction: Expense incurred, to be paid later.
Analysis: Liabilities increase. Owner's equity decreases.
Rules: Decreases in owner's equity are recorded by debits. Increases in liabilities are recorded by credits.
Entry: The decrease in owner's equity is recorded by a debit to Telephone Expense. The increase in liabilities is recorded by a credit to Accounts Payable.

July 31: Joan Miller withdraws $1,400 from the business for personal living expenses.

A = L + OE
− −

		Dr.	Cr.
July 31	Joan Miller, Withdrawals	1,400	
	Cash		1,400

Cash

July 1	20,000	July 2	1,600
10	1,400	3	4,200
15	1,000	5	1,500
		8	960
		9	1,000
		12	1,200
		26	1,200
		29	200
		31	1,400

Joan Miller, Withdrawals

July 31	1,400		

KEY POINT: Withdrawals are not considered an expense. Expenses are costs of operating a business, but withdrawals are assets that the owner takes out of the business.

Transaction: Owner's withdrawal for personal use.
Analysis: Assets decrease. Owner's equity decreases.
Rules: Decreases in owner's equity are recorded by debits. Decreases in assets are recorded by credits.
Entry: The decrease in owner's equity is recorded by a debit to Joan Miller, Withdrawals. The decrease in assets is recorded by a credit to Cash.

EXHIBIT 2
Summary of Transactions for Joan Miller Advertising Agency

Assets = Liabilities + Owner's Equity

Assets

Cash

July 1	20,000	July 2	1,600
10	1,400	3	4,200
15	1,000	5	1,500
		8	960
		9	1,000
		12	1,200
		26	1,200
		29	200
		31	1,400
	22,400		13,260
Bal.	9,140		

This account links to the statement of cash flows.

Accounts Receivable

July 19	4,800		

Art Supplies

July 6	1,800		

Office Supplies

July 6	800		

Prepaid Rent

July 2	1,600		

Prepaid Insurance

July 8	960		

Art Equipment

July 3	4,200		

Office Equipment

July 5	3,000		

Liabilities

Accounts Payable

July 9	1,000	July 5	1,500
		6	2,600
		30	140
	1,000		4,240
		Bal.	3,240

Unearned Art Fees

		July 15	1,000

Owner's Equity

Joan Miller, Capital

		July 1	20,000

Joan Miller, Withdrawals

July 31	1,400		

Advertising Fees Earned

		July 10	1,400
		19	4,800
		Bal.	6,200

Wages Expense

July 12	1,200		
26	1,200		
Bal.	2,400		

Utilities Expense

July 29	200		

Telephone Expense

July 30	140		

These accounts link to the income statement.

Exhibit 2 shows the transactions for July in their accounts and in relation to the accounting equation. Note that all transactions have been recorded on the date they are recognized. Most of these transactions involve either the receipt or payment of cash, as reflected in the Cash account. There are important exceptions, however. For instance, on July 19 Advertising Fees were earned, but receipt of cash for these fees will come later. Also, on July 5, 6, and 30 there were transactions recognized that totaled $4,240 in Accounts Payable. This means the company can wait to pay. At the end of the month, only the $1,000 recorded on July 9 had been paid. These lags between recognition of transactions and the subsequent cash inflows or outflows have an impact on achieving the goal of liquidity.

Check out ACE for a Review Quiz at http://accounting.college.hmco.com/students.

THE TRIAL BALANCE

LO5 Prepare a trial balance and describe its value and limitations.

RELATED TEXT ASSIGNMENTS
Q: 17, 18, 19, 24
SE: 4, 7, 8
E: 3, 6, 8, 9, 10, 11
P: 2, 3, 4, 5, 7, 8
SD: 5

KEY POINT: The trial balance is prepared at the end of the accounting period. It is an initial check that the ledger is in balance.

For every amount debited, an equal amount must be credited. This means that the total of debits and credits in the T accounts must be equal. To test this, the accountant periodically prepares a **trial balance**. Exhibit 3 shows a trial balance for Joan Miller Advertising Agency. It was prepared from the accounts in Exhibit 2.

A trial balance may be prepared at any time but is usually prepared on the last day of the month. Here are the steps in preparing a trial balance:

1. List each T account that has a balance, with debit balances in the left column and credit balances in the right column. Accounts are listed in the order in which they appear in the ledger.
2. Add each column.
3. Compare the totals of the columns.

In accounts in which increases are recorded by debits, the **normal balance** (the usual balance) is a debit balance; in accounts in which increases are recorded by credits, the normal balance is a credit balance. Table 1 summarizes the normal account balances of the major account categories. According to the table, the T account Accounts Payable (a liability) typically has a credit balance and is copied into the trial balance as a credit balance.

EXHIBIT 3
Trial Balance

KEY POINT: The accounts are listed in the same order as in the ledger. At this point, the Capital account does not reflect any revenues, expenses, or withdrawals for the period.

Joan Miller Advertising Agency
Trial Balance
July 31, 20xx

Cash	$ 9,140	
Accounts Receivable	4,800	
Art Supplies	1,800	
Office Supplies	800	
Prepaid Rent	1,600	
Prepaid Insurance	960	
Art Equipment	4,200	
Office Equipment	3,000	
Accounts Payable		$ 3,240
Unearned Art Fees		1,000
Joan Miller, Capital		20,000
Joan Miller, Withdrawals	1,400	
Advertising Fees Earned		6,200
Wages Expense	2,400	
Utilities Expense	200	
Telephone Expense	140	
	$30,440	$30,440

STOP AND THINK!
Under what conditions would net worth (assets minus liabilities) be negative?

Net worth would be negative if the net amount of all owner's equity accounts is a debit—in other words, if the total of withdrawals and expenses exceeds the total of capital and revenues. In this case, the company's liabilities exceed its assets and it is technically bankrupt. ■

TABLE 1. Normal Account Balances of Major Account Categories

	Increases Recorded by		Normal Balance	
Account Category	Debit	Credit	Debit	Credit
Assets	x		x	
Liabilities		x		x
Owner's Equity:				
Capital		x		x
Withdrawals	x		x	
Revenues		x		x
Expenses	x		x	

STUDY NOTE: A mnemonic for accounts with normal debit balances is AWE—Assets, Withdrawals, and Expenses.

Once in a while, a transaction leaves an account with a balance that is not "normal." For example, when a company overdraws its account at the bank, its Cash account (an asset) will show a credit balance instead of a debit balance. The "abnormal" balance should be copied into the trial balance columns as it stands, as a debit or a credit.

The trial balance proves whether or not the ledger is in balance. *In balance* means that the total of all debits recorded equals the total of all credits recorded. But the trial balance does not prove that the transactions were analyzed correctly or recorded in the proper accounts. For example, there is no way of determining from the trial balance that a debit should have been made in the Art Equipment account rather than the Office Equipment account. And the trial balance does not detect whether transactions have been omitted, because equal debits and credits will have been omitted. Also, if an error of the same amount is made in both a debit and a credit, it will not be discovered by the trial balance. The trial balance proves only that the debits and credits in the accounts are in balance.

If the debit and credit columns of the trial balance are not equal, look for one or more of the following errors: (1) a debit was entered in an account as a credit, or vice versa; (2) the balance of an account was computed incorrectly; (3) an error was made in carrying the account balance to the trial balance; or (4) the trial balance was summed incorrectly.

Other than simply adding the columns incorrectly, the two most common mistakes in preparing a trial balance are (1) recording an account with a debit balance as a credit, or vice versa, and (2) transposing two digits when transferring an amount to the trial balance (for example, entering $23,459 as $23,549). The first of these mistakes causes the trial balance to be out of balance by an amount evenly divisible by 2. The second causes the trial balance to be out of balance by a number divisible by 9. Thus, if a trial balance is out of balance and the addition has been verified, determine the amount by which the trial balance is out of balance and divide it first by 2 and then by 9. If the amount is divisible by 2, look in the trial balance for an amount that is equal to the quotient. If you find such an amount, it is probably in the wrong column. If the amount is divisible by 9, trace each amount to the ledger account balance, checking carefully for a transposition error. If neither of these techniques identifies the error, first recompute the balance of each account in the ledger.

FOCUS ON BUSINESS TECHNOLOGY

Are All Trial Balances Created Equal?

In computerized accounting systems, posting is done automatically, and the trial balance can be easily prepared as often as needed. Any accounts with abnormal balances are highlighted for investigation. Some general ledger software packages for small businesses list the trial balance amounts in a single column, with credit balances shown as minuses. In such cases, the trial balance is in balance if the total is zero.

Then, if you still have not found the error, retrace each posting from the journal to the ledger.

Check out ACE for a Review Quiz at http://accounting.college.hmco.com/students.

Recording and Posting Transactions

LO6 Record transactions in the general journal and post transactions from the general journal to the ledger.

RELATED TEXT ASSIGNMENTS
Q: 20, 21, 22, 23, 24
SE: 9, 10
E: 12, 13
P: 3, 5, 8

KEY POINT: The journal is a chronological record of events. Only the general journal is discussed in this chapter.

Let us now take a look at the formal process of recording transactions in the general journal and posting them to the ledger.

The General Journal

As you have seen, transactions can be entered directly into the accounts. But this method makes identifying individual transactions or finding errors very difficult because the debit is recorded in one account and the credit in another. The solution is to record all transactions chronologically in a **journal**. The journal is sometimes called the *book of original entry* because it is where transactions first enter the accounting records. Later, the debit and credit portions of each transaction can be transferred to the appropriate accounts in the ledger. A separate **journal entry** is used to record each transaction, and the process of recording transactions is called **journalizing**.

Most businesses have more than one kind of journal. The simplest and most flexible type is the **general journal**, the one we focus on in this chapter. Entries in the general journal include the following information about each transaction:

1. The date
2. The names of the accounts debited and the dollar amounts on the same lines in the debit column
3. The names of the accounts credited and the dollar amounts on the same lines in the credit column
4. An explanation of the transaction
5. The account identification numbers, if appropriate

Exhibit 4 displays two of the transactions for Joan Miller Advertising Agency that we discussed earlier. The procedure for recording transactions in the general journal is as follows:

1. Record the date by writing the year in small figures on the first line at the top of the first column, the month on the next line of the first column, and the day in the second column opposite the month. For subsequent entries on the same page for the same month and year, the month and year can be omitted.
2. Write the exact names of the accounts debited and credited in the Description column. Starting on the same line as the date, write the name(s) of the account(s) that are debited next to the left margin and indent the name(s) of the account(s) credited. The explanation is placed on the next line and is further indented. The explanation should be brief but sufficient to explain and identify the transaction. A transaction can have more than one debit or credit entry; this is called a **compound entry**. In a compound entry, all debit accounts are listed before any credit accounts. (The July 6 transaction of Joan Miller Advertising Agency in Exhibit 4 is an example of a compound entry.)
3. Write the debit amounts in the Debit column opposite the accounts to be debited, and write the credit amounts in the Credit column opposite the accounts to be credited.

STUDY NOTE: Check your journal for proper form. Frequent errors are forgetting to skip a space between entries, not indenting the credits, using the Post. Ref. column before posting is done, journalizing amounts that do not balance, entering a credit before a debit, and forgetting to enter the explanation.

EXHIBIT 4
The General Journal

A = L + OE
\+ +
\+

A = L + OE
\+
−

General Journal — Page 1

Date		Description	Post. Ref.	Debit	Credit
20xx					
July	6	Art Supplies		1,800	
		Office Supplies		800	
		Accounts Payable			2,600
		Purchase of art and office supplies on credit			
	8	Prepaid Insurance		960	
		Cash			960
		Paid one-year life insurance premium			

4. At the time the transactions are recorded, nothing is placed in the Post. Ref. (posting reference) column. (This column is sometimes called *LP* or *Folio.*) Later, if the company uses account numbers to identify accounts in the ledger, fill in the account numbers to provide a convenient cross-reference from the general journal to the ledger and to indicate that the entry has been posted to the ledger. If the accounts are not numbered, use a checkmark (✔).
5. It is customary to skip a line after each journal entry.

THE GENERAL LEDGER

The general journal is used to record the details of each transaction. The general ledger is used to update each account.

THE LEDGER ACCOUNT FORM The T account is a simple, direct means of recording transactions. In practice, a somewhat more complicated form of the account is needed in order to record more information. The **ledger account form**, which contains four columns for dollar amounts, is illustrated in Exhibit 5.

The account title and number appear at the top of the account form. As in the journal, the transaction date appears in the first two columns. The Item column is

EXHIBIT 5
Accounts Payable in the General Ledger

General Ledger

Accounts Payable — Account No. 212

Date		Item	Post. Ref.	Debit	Credit	Balance Debit	Balance Credit
20xx							
July	5		J1		1,500		1,500
	6		J1		2,600		4,100
	9		J1	1,000			3,100
	30		J2		140		3,240

EXHIBIT 6
Posting from the General Journal to the Ledger

General Journal — (2) Page 2

Date		Description	Post. Ref.	Debit	Credit
20xx	(2)	(1)	(5)	(3)	
July	30	Telephone Expense	513	140	
		Accounts Payable	212		140
		Received bill for telephone expense			

General Ledger

Accounts Payable — Account No. 212

Date		Item	Post. Ref.	Debit	Credit	Balance Debit	Balance Credit
20xx							
July	5		J1		1,500		1,500
	6		J1		2,600		4,100
	9		J1	1,000			3,100
	30		J2		140		3,240

General Ledger

Telephone Expense — Account No. 513

Date		Item	Post. Ref.	Debit	Credit	Balance Debit	Balance Credit
20xx						(4)	
July	30		J2	140		140	

A = L + OE
    +   −

STUDY NOTE: When posting, don't forget to use the Post. Ref. columns. They are critical for cross-referencing the components of entries.

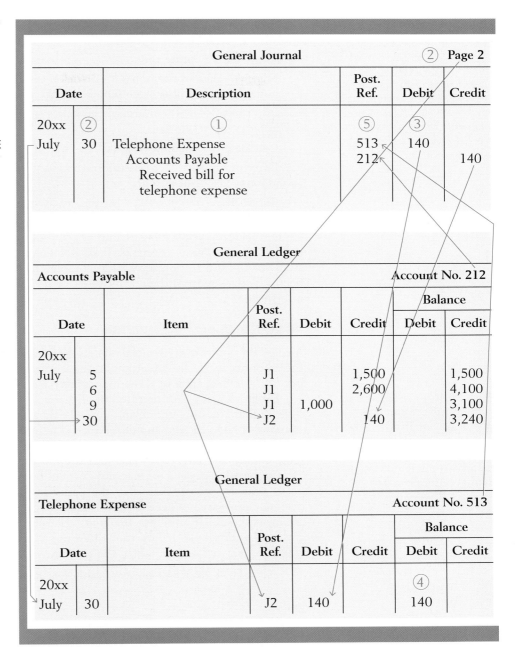

rarely used to identify transactions, because explanations already appear in the journal. The Post. Ref. column is used to note the journal page where the original entry for the transaction can be found. The dollar amount is entered in the appropriate Debit or Credit column, and a new account balance is computed in the final two columns after each entry. The advantage of this account form over the T account is that the current balance of the account is readily available.

STUDY NOTE: Posting is much like sorting mail. It is a tedious, but necessary, procedure, conveniently accomplished by a computer.

■ **POSTING TO THE LEDGER** After transactions have been entered in the journal, they must be transferred to the ledger. The process of transferring journal entry information from the journal to the ledger is called **posting**. Posting is usually done after several entries have been made—for example, at the end of each day or less frequently, depending on the number of transactions. As shown in Exhibit 6, through posting, each amount in the Debit column of the journal is transferred into the Debit column of the appropriate account in the ledger, and each amount in the

STOP AND THINK!
Why have both a journal and a ledger? Why not just record all entries in the ledger?

Transactions often need to be verified because mistakes occur. It is much easier to find a transaction and verify that it is correct when it is listed in chronological order in the journal. ■

Credit column of the journal is transferred into the Credit column of the appropriate account in the ledger. The steps in the posting process are as follows:

1. In the ledger, locate the debit account named in the journal entry.
2. Enter the date of the transaction and, in the Post. Ref. column of the ledger, the journal page number from which the entry comes.
3. Enter in the Debit column of the ledger account the amount of the debit as it appears in the journal.
4. Calculate the account balance and enter it in the appropriate Balance column.
5. Enter in the Post. Ref. column of the journal the account number to which the amount has been posted.
6. Repeat the same five steps for the credit side of the journal entry.

Notice that step **5** is the last step in the posting process for each debit and credit. In addition to serving as an easy reference between the journal entry and the ledger account, this entry in the Post. Ref. column of the journal indicates that all steps for the transaction have been completed. This allows accountants who have been called away from their work to easily find where they were before they were interrupted.

SOME NOTES ON PRESENTATION

A ruled line appears in financial reports before each subtotal or total to indicate that the amounts above are added or subtracted. It is common practice to use a double line under a final total to show that it has been checked, or verified.

KEY POINT: Placing a dash in the cents column is preferable to leaving it blank. (It's possible to infer from a blank cents column that the bookkeeper simply forgot to enter the figure for cents.)

Dollar signs ($) are required in all financial statements, including the balance sheet and income statement, and in the trial balance and other schedules. On these statements, a dollar sign should be placed before the first amount in each column and before the first amount in a column following a ruled line. Dollar signs in the same column are aligned. Dollar signs are not used in journals and ledgers.

On unruled paper, commas and decimal points are used in dollar amounts. On paper with ruled columns—like the paper in journals and ledgers—commas and decimal points are not needed. In this book, because most problems and illustrations are in whole dollar amounts, the cents column usually is omitted. When accountants deal with whole dollars, they often use a dash in the cents column to indicate whole dollars rather than taking the time to write zeros.

Check out ACE for a Review Quiz at http://accounting.college.hmco.com/students.

Chapter Review

REVIEW OF LEARNING OBJECTIVES

LO1 Explain, in simple terms, the generally accepted ways of solving the measurement issues of recognition, valuation, and classification.

To measure a business transaction, the accountant determines when the transaction occurred (the recognition issue), what value should be placed on the transaction (the valuation issue), and how the components of the transaction should be categorized (the classification issue). In general, recognition occurs when title passes, and a transaction is valued at the exchange price, the cost at the time the transaction is recognized. Classification refers to the categorizing of transactions according to a system of accounts.

LO2 Describe the chart of accounts and recognize commonly used accounts.

An account is a device for storing data from transactions. There is one account for each asset, liability, and component of owner's equity, including revenues and expenses. The ledger is a book or file containing all of a company's accounts, arranged according to a chart of accounts. Commonly used asset accounts are Cash, Notes Receivable, Accounts

Receivable, Prepaid Expenses, Land, Buildings, and Equipment. Common liability accounts are Notes Payable, Accounts Payable, Wages Payable, and Mortgage Payable. Common owner's equity accounts are Capital, Withdrawals, and revenue and expense accounts.

LO3 Define *double-entry system* and state the rules for double entry.

In the double-entry system, each transaction must be recorded with at least one debit and one credit, so that the total dollar amount of the debits equals the total dollar amount of the credits. The rules for double entry are (1) increases in assets are debited to asset accounts; decreases in assets are credited to asset accounts; and (2) increases in liabilities and owner's equity are credited to those accounts; decreases in liabilities and owner's equity are debited to those accounts.

LO4 Apply the steps for transaction analysis and processing to simple transactions.

The procedure for analyzing transactions is (1) analyze the effect of the transaction on assets, liabilities, and owner's equity; (2) apply the appropriate double-entry rule; (3) record the entry; (4) post the entry; and (5) prepare a trial balance.

LO5 Prepare a trial balance and describe its value and limitations.

A trial balance is used to check that the debit and credit balances are equal. It is prepared by listing each account with its balance in the Debit or Credit column. Then the two columns are added and the totals compared to test the balances. The major limitation of the trial balance is that even if debit and credit balances are equal, this does not guarantee that the transactions were analyzed correctly or recorded in the proper accounts.

LO6 Record transactions in the general journal and post transactions from the general journal to the ledger.

The general journal is a chronological record of all transactions. That record contains the date of each transaction, the names of the accounts and the dollar amounts debited and credited, an explanation of each entry, and the account numbers to which postings have been made. After transactions have been entered in the general journal, they are posted to the ledger. Posting is done by transferring each amount in the Debit column of the general journal to the Debit column of the appropriate account in the ledger, and transferring each amount in the Credit column of the general journal to the Credit column of the appropriate account in the ledger. After each entry is posted, a new balance is entered in the appropriate Balance column.

Review of Concepts and Terminology

The following concepts and terms were introduced in this chapter:

LO3 **Balance:** The difference in dollars between the total debit footing and the total credit footing of an account. Also called *account balance.*

LO2 **Chart of accounts:** A scheme that assigns a unique number to each account to facilitate finding the account in the ledger; also, the list of account numbers and titles.

LO1 **Classification:** The process of assigning transactions to the appropriate accounts.

LO6 **Compound entry:** An entry that has more than one debit or credit entry.

LO1 **Cost:** The exchange price associated with a business transaction at the point of recognition.

LO1 **Cost principle:** The practice of recording transactions at cost.

LO3 **Credit:** The right side of an account.

LO3 **Debit:** The left side of an account.

LO3 **Double-entry system:** The accounting system in which each transaction is recorded with at least one debit and one credit, so that the total dollar amount of debits and the total dollar amount of credits equal each other.

LO3 **Footings:** Working totals of columns of numbers. *To foot* means to total a column of numbers.

LO6 **General journal:** The simplest and most flexible type of journal.

LO2 **General ledger:** The book or file that contains all of the company's accounts, arranged in the order of the chart of accounts. Also called *ledger.*

LO6 **Journal:** A chronological record of all transactions; the place where transactions first enter the accounting records. Also called *book of original entry.*

LO6 **Journal entry:** Journal notations that record a single transaction.

LO3 **Journal form:** A form of journal in which the date, the debit account, and the debit amount of a transaction are recorded on one line and the credit account and credit amount on the next line.

LO6 **Journalizing:** The process of recording transactions in a journal.

LO6 **Ledger account form:** The form of account that has four dollar amount columns: one column for debit entries, one column for credit entries, and two columns (debit and credit) for showing the balance of the account.

LO5 **Normal balance:** The usual balance of an account; also the side (debit or credit) that increases the account.

LO6 **Posting:** The process of transferring journal entry information from the journal to the ledger.

LO1 **Recognition:** The determination of when a business transaction should be recorded.

LO1 **Recognition point:** The predetermined time at which a transaction should be recorded; usually, the point at which title passes to the buyer.

LO3 **Source document:** An invoice, check, receipt, or other document that supports a transaction.

LO3 **T account:** The simplest form of an account, used to analyze transactions.

LO5 **Trial balance:** A comparison of the total of debit and credit balances in the accounts to check that they are equal.

LO1 **Valuation:** The process of assigning a monetary value to a business transaction.

Review Problem

Transaction Analysis, General Journal, Ledger Accounts, and Trial Balance

LO4
LO5
LO6

After graduation from veterinary school, Laura Stors entered private practice. The transactions of the business through May 27 are as follows:

20xx

May	1	Laura Stors invested $2,000 in her business bank account.
	3	Paid $300 for two months' rent in advance for an office.
	9	Purchased medical supplies for $200 in cash.
	12	Purchased $400 of equipment on credit, making a 25 percent down payment.
	15	Delivered a calf for a fee of $35 (on credit).
	18	Made a partial payment of $50 on the equipment purchased May 12.
	27	Paid a utility bill of $40.

REQUIRED ▶

1. Record these transactions in the general journal.
2. Post the transactions to the following accounts in the ledger: Cash (111); Accounts Receivable (112); Medical Supplies (115); Prepaid Rent (117); Equipment (144); Accounts Payable (212); Laura Stors, Capital (311); Veterinary Fees Earned (411); and Utilities Expense (512).
3. Prepare a trial balance as of May 31.
4. How does the transaction of May 15 relate to recognition and cash flows? Also compare the transactions of May 9 and May 27 with regard to classification.

Answer to Review Problem

1. Journal entries recorded

General Journal — **Page 1**

Date		Description	Post. Ref.	Debit	Credit
20xx					
May	1	Cash	111	2,000	
		Laura Stors, Capital	311		2,000
		Deposited $2,000 in the business bank account			
	3	Prepaid Rent	117	300	
		Cash	111		300
		Paid two months' rent in advance for an office			
	9	Medical Supplies	115	200	
		Cash	111		200
		Purchased medical supplies for cash			
	12	Equipment	144	400	
		Accounts Payable	212		300
		Cash	111		100
		Purchased equipment on credit, paying 25 percent down			
	15	Accounts Receivable	112	35	
		Veterinary Fees Earned	411		35
		Fee on credit for delivery of a calf			
	18	Accounts Payable	212	50	
		Cash	111		50
		Partial payment for equipment purchased May 12			
	27	Utilities Expense	512	40	
		Cash	111		40
		Paid utility bill			

2. Transactions posted to the ledger accounts

General Ledger

Cash — Account No. 111

Date		Item	Post. Ref.	Debit	Credit	Balance Debit	Balance Credit
20xx							
May	1		J1	2,000		2,000	
	3		J1		300	1,700	
	9		J1		200	1,500	
	12		J1		100	1,400	
	18		J1		50	1,350	
	27		J1		40	1,310	

Accounts Receivable — Account No. 112

Date		Item	Post. Ref.	Debit	Credit	Balance Debit	Balance Credit
20xx							
May	15		J1	35		35	

Medical Supplies — Account No. 115

Date		Item	Post. Ref.	Debit	Credit	Balance Debit	Balance Credit
20xx							
May	9		J1	200		200	

Prepaid Rent — Account No. 117

Date		Item	Post. Ref.	Debit	Credit	Balance Debit	Balance Credit
20xx							
May	3		J1	300		300	

Equipment — Account No. 144

Date		Item	Post. Ref.	Debit	Credit	Balance Debit	Balance Credit
20xx							
May	12		J1	400		400	

Accounts Payable — Account No. 212

Date		Item	Post. Ref.	Debit	Credit	Balance Debit	Balance Credit
20xx May	12		J1		300		300
	18		J1	50			250

Laura Stors, Capital — Account No. 311

Date		Item	Post. Ref.	Debit	Credit	Balance Debit	Balance Credit
20xx May	1		J1		2,000		2,000

Veterinary Fees Earned — Account No. 411

Date		Item	Post. Ref.	Debit	Credit	Balance Debit	Balance Credit
20xx May	15		J1		35		35

Utilities Expense — Account No. 512

Date		Item	Post. Ref.	Debit	Credit	Balance Debit	Balance Credit
20xx May	27		J1	40		40	

3. Trial balance prepared

Laura Stors, Veterinarian Trial Balance May 31, 20xx		
Cash	$1,310	
Accounts Receivable	35	
Medical Supplies	200	
Prepaid Rent	300	
Equipment	400	
Accounts Payable		$ 250
Laura Stors, Capital		2,000
Veterinary Fees Earned		35
Utilities Expense	40	
	$2,285	$2,285

4. The transaction is recorded, or recognized, on May 15, even though no cash is received. The revenue is earned because the service was provided to and accepted by the buyer. The customer now has an obligation to pay the provider of the service. It is recorded as an accounts receivable because the customer has been allowed to pay later. The transaction on May 9 is classified as an asset, Medical Supplies, because these supplies will benefit the company in the future. The transaction on May 27 is classified as an expense, Utilities Expense, because the utilities have already been used and will not benefit the company in the future.

Chapter Assignments

Building Your Knowledge Foundation

Questions

1. What three issues underlie most accounting measurement decisions?
2. Why is recognition an issue for accountants?
3. A customer asks the owner of a store to save an item for him and says that he will pick it up and pay for it next week. The owner agrees to hold it. Should this transaction be recorded as a sale? Explain your answer.
4. Why is it practical for accountants to rely on original cost for valuation purposes?
5. Under the cost principle, changes in value after a transaction is recorded are not usually recognized in the accounts. Comment on this possible limitation of using original cost in accounting measurements.
6. What is an account, and how is it related to the ledger?
7. Tell whether each of the following accounts is an asset account, a liability account, or an owner's equity account:

   a. Notes Receivable
   b. Land
   c. Withdrawals
   d. Mortgage Payable
   e. Prepaid Rent
   f. Insurance Expense
   g. Service Revenue

8. In the owner's equity accounts, why do accountants maintain separate accounts for revenues and expenses rather than using the Capital account?
9. Why is the system of recording entries called the double-entry system? What is significant about this system?
10. "Double-entry accounting refers to entering a transaction in both the journal and the ledger." Comment on this statement.
11. "Debits are bad; credits are good." Comment on this statement.
12. What are the rules of double entry for (a) assets, (b) liabilities, and (c) owner's equity?
13. Why are the rules of double entry the same for liabilities and owner's equity?
14. What is the meaning of the statement, "The Cash account has a debit balance of $500"?
15. Explain why debits, which decrease owner's equity, also increase expenses, which are a component of owner's equity.
16. What are the five steps in analyzing and processing a transaction?
17. What does a trial balance prove?
18. What is the normal balance of Accounts Payable? Under what conditions could Accounts Payable have a debit balance?
19. Is it possible for errors to be present even though a trial balance balances? Explain your answer.
20. Is it a good idea to forgo the journal and enter a transaction directly into the ledger? Explain your answer.
21. In recording entries in a journal, which is written first, the debit or the credit? How is indentation used in the journal?
22. What is the relationship between the journal and the ledger?
23. Describe each of the following:
    a. Account
    b. Journal
    c. Ledger
    d. Book of original entry
    e. Post. Ref. column
    f. Journalizing
    g. Posting
    h. Footings
    i. Compound entry
24. List the following six items in sequence to illustrate the flow of events through the accounting system:
    a. Analysis of the transaction
    b. Debits and credits posted from the journal to the ledger
    c. Occurrence of the business transaction
    d. Preparation of the financial statements
    e. Entry made in the journal
    f. Preparation of the trial balance

Short Exercises

LO1 Recognition

SE 1. Which of the following events would be recognized and entered in the accounting records of Heller Company? Why?

Jan. 10 Heller Company places an order for office supplies.
Feb. 15 Heller Company receives the office supplies and a bill for them.
Mar. 1 Heller Company pays for the office supplies.

LO1 LO3 Recognition, Valuation, and Classification

SE 2. Tell how the concepts of recognition, valuation, and classification apply to this transaction:

Cash				Supplies			
		June 1	250	June 1	250		

LO2 Classification of Accounts

SE 3. Tell whether each of the accounts that follows is an asset, a liability, a revenue, an expense, or none of these.

a. Accounts Payable
b. Supplies
c. Withdrawals
d. Fees Earned
e. Supplies Expense
f. Accounts Receivable
g. Unearned Revenue
h. Equipment

LO5 Normal Balances

SE 4. Tell whether the normal balance of each account in **SE 3** is a debit or a credit.

LO4 Transaction Analysis

SE 5. For each transaction below, tell which account is debited and which account is credited.

May 2 Deric Norman started a computer programming business, Norman's Programming Service, by investing $5,000.
5 Purchased a computer for $2,500 in cash.
7 Purchased supplies on credit for $300.
19 Received cash for programming services performed, $500.
22 Received cash for programming services to be performed, $600.
25 Paid the rent for May, $650.
31 Billed a customer for programming services performed, $250.

LO4 Recording Transactions in T Accounts

SE 6. Set up T accounts and record each transaction in **SE 5.** Determine the balance of each account.

LO5 Preparing a Trial Balance

SE 7. From the T accounts created in **SE 6,** prepare a trial balance dated May 31, 20x5.

LO5 Correcting Errors in a Trial Balance

SE 8. The trial balance that follows is out of balance. Assuming all balances are normal, place the accounts in proper order and correct the trial balance so that debits equal credits.

Duncan Boating Service
Trial Balance
January 31, 20x5

Cash	$2,000	
Accounts Payable	400	
Fuel Expense	800	
Unearned Service Revenue	250	
Accounts Receivable		$1,300
Prepaid Rent		150
Ann Duncan, Capital		1,500
Service Revenue	1,750	
Wages Expense		300
Ann Duncan, Withdrawals	650	
	$5,850	$3,250

LO6 Recording Transactions in the General Journal

SE 9. Prepare a general journal form like the one in Exhibit 4 and label it Page 4. Record the following transactions in the journal:

Sept. 6 Billed a customer for services performed, $1,900.
16 Received partial payment from the customer billed on Sept. 6, $900.

LO6 Posting to the Ledger Accounts

SE 10. Prepare ledger account forms like the ones in Exhibit 5 for the following accounts: Cash (111), Accounts Receivable (113), and Service Revenue (411). Post the transactions that are recorded in **SE 9** to the ledger accounts, at the same time making the proper posting references.

EXERCISES

LO1 Recognition

E 1. Which of the following events would be recognized and recorded in the accounting records of Raymond Company on the date indicated?

Feb.	17	Raymond Company offers to purchase a tract of land for $280,000. There is a high likelihood that the offer will be accepted.
Mar.	7	Raymond Company receives notice that its rent will be increased from $1,000 per month to $1,200 per month effective April 1.
Apr.	28	Raymond Company receives its utility bill for the month of April. The bill is not due until May 10.
May	19	Raymond Company places a firm order for new office equipment costing $42,000.
June	27	The office equipment ordered on May 19 arrives. Payment is not due until September 1.

LO1 Application of Recognition Point

E 2. Azarian's Body Shop uses a large amount of supplies in its business. The following table summarizes selected transaction data for orders of supplies purchased:

Order	Date Shipped	Date Received	Amount
a	April 28	May 7	$300
b	May 8	13	750
c	10	16	400
d	15	21	600
e	25	June 1	750
f	June 3	9	500

Determine the total purchases of supplies for May alone if:

1. Azarian's Body Shop recognizes purchases when orders are shipped.
2. Azarian's Body Shop recognizes purchases when orders are received.

LO2 LO5 Classification of Accounts

E 3. Listed below are the ledger accounts of Geehan Service Company:

a. Cash
b. Accounts Receivable
c. Deb Geehan, Capital
d. Deb Geehan, Withdrawals
e. Service Revenue
f. Prepaid Rent
g. Accounts Payable
h. Investments in Securities
i. Wages Payable
j. Land
k. Supplies Expense
l. Prepaid Insurance
m. Utilities Expense
n. Fees Earned
o. Unearned Revenue
p. Office Equipment
q. Rent Payable
r. Notes Receivable
s. Interest Expense
t. Notes Payable
u. Supplies
v. Interest Receivable

Complete the following table, indicating with two Xs for each account its classification and its normal balance (whether a debit or credit increases the account):

	Type of Account						Normal Balance (increases balance)	
			Owner's Equity					
Item	Asset	Liability	Owner's Capital	Owner's Withdrawals	Revenue	Expense	Debit	Credit
a.	x						x	

LO4 Transaction Analysis

E 4. Analyze transactions **a–g**, following the example on the next page.

a. Liz Cruse established Cruse's Crop Shop by placing $2,400 in a bank account.
b. Paid two months' rent in advance, $840.
c. Purchased supplies on credit, $120.
d. Received cash for scrapbooking services, $100.
e. Paid for supplies purchased in **c**.
f. Paid utility bill, $72.
g. Took cash out of the business for personal expenses, $100.

Example:

a. The asset Cash was increased. Increases in assets are recorded by debits. Debit Cash, $2,400. A component of owner's equity, Liz Cruse, Capital, was increased. Increases in owner's equity are recorded by credits. Credit Liz Cruse, Capital, $2,400.

LO4 Recording Transactions in T Accounts

E 5. Open the following T accounts: Cash; Repair Supplies; Repair Equipment; Accounts Payable; Jessie Sturchio, Capital; Jessie Sturchio, Withdrawals; Repair Fees Earned; Salaries Expense; and Rent Expense. Record the following transactions for the month of June directly in the T accounts; use the letters to identify the transactions in your T accounts. Determine the balance in each account.

a. Jessie Sturchio opened Porcelain Cup Repair Service by investing $4,300 in cash and $1,600 in repair equipment.
b. Paid $400 for the current month's rent.
c. Purchased repair supplies on credit, $500.
d. Purchased additional repair equipment for cash, $300.
e. Paid salary to a helper, $450.
f. Paid $200 of amount purchased on credit in **c.**
g. Accepted cash for repairs completed, $1,860.
h. Withdrew $600 from business for living expenses.

LO5 Trial Balance

E 6. After recording the transactions in **E 5,** prepare a trial balance in proper sequence for Porcelain Cup Repair Service as of June 30, 20xx.

LO4 Analysis of Transactions

E 7. Explain each transaction **(a–h)** entered in the following T accounts:

Cash

a.	60,000	b.	15,000
g.	1,500	e.	3,000
h.	900	f.	4,500

Accounts Receivable

c.	6,000	g.	1,500

Equipment

b.	15,000	h.	900
d.	9,000		

Accounts Payable

f.	4,500	d.	9,000

K. LeMaster, Capital

		a.	60,000

Service Revenue

		c.	6,000

Wages Expense

e.	3,000		

LO5 Preparing a Trial Balance

E 8. The accounts of Rounds Service Company as of October 31, 20xx, are listed below in alphabetical order. The amount of Accounts Payable is omitted.

Accounts Payable	$?	Land	$10,400
Accounts Receivable	6,000	Notes Payable	40,000
Building	68,000	Pete Rounds, Capital	62,900
Cash	18,000	Prepaid Insurance	2,200
Equipment	24,000		

Prepare a trial balance with the proper heading (see Exhibit 3) and with the accounts listed in the chart of accounts sequence (see Exhibit 1). Compute the balance of Accounts Payable.

LO5 Effects of Errors on a Trial Balance

E 9. Which of the following errors would cause a trial balance to have unequal totals? Explain your answers.

a. A payment to a creditor was recorded as a debit to Accounts Payable for $172 and as a credit to Cash for $127.
b. A payment of $200 to a creditor for an account payable was debited to Accounts Receivable and credited to Cash.
c. A purchase of office supplies of $560 was recorded as a debit to Office Supplies for $56 and as a credit to Cash for $56.
d. A purchase of equipment for $600 was recorded as a debit to Supplies for $600 and as a credit to Cash for $600.

LO5 Correcting Errors in a Trial Balance

E 10. The trial balance for Fradin Services at the end of September follows. It does not balance because of a number of errors. Fradin's accountant compared the amounts in the

Fradin Services
Trial Balance
September 30, 20xx

Cash	$ 3,840	
Accounts Receivable	5,660	
Supplies	120	
Prepaid Insurance	180	
Equipment	8,400	
Accounts Payable		$ 4,540
F. Fradin, Capital		11,560
F. Fradin, Withdrawals		700
Revenues		5,920
Salaries Expense	2,600	
Rent Expense	600	
Advertising Expense	340	
Utilities Expense	26	
	$21,766	$22,720

trial balance with the ledger, recomputed the account balances, and compared the postings. He found the following errors:

a. The balance of Cash was understated by $400.
b. A cash payment of $420 was credited to Cash for $240.
c. A debit of $120 to Accounts Receivable was not posted.
d. Supplies purchased for $60 were posted as a credit to Supplies.
e. A debit of $180 to Prepaid Insurance was not posted.
f. The Accounts Payable account had debits of $5,320 and credits of $9,180.
g. The Notes Payable account, with a credit balance of $2,400, was not included in the trial balance.
h. The debit balance of F. Fradin, Withdrawals was listed in the trial balance as a credit.
i. A $200 debit to F. Fradin, Withdrawals was posted as a credit.
j. The actual balance of Utilities Expense, $260, was listed as $26 in the trial balance.

Prepare a correct trial balance.

LO5 Preparing a Trial Balance

E 11. The Breadloaf Construction Company builds foundations for buildings and parking lots. The following alphabetical list shows the company's account balances as of November 30, 20xx.

Accounts Payable	$ 11,700	Notes Payable	$60,000
Accounts Receivable	30,360	Office Trailer	6,600
Cash	?	Prepaid Insurance	13,800
Construction Supplies	5,700	Revenue Earned	52,200
Equipment	73,500	Supplies Expense	21,600
G. Breadloaf, Capital	120,000	Utilities Expense	1,260
G. Breadloaf, Withdrawals	23,400	Wages Expense	26,400

Prepare a trial balance for the company with the proper heading and with the accounts in balance sheet sequence. Determine the correct balance for the Cash account on November 30, 20xx.

LO4 Analysis of Unfamiliar
LO6 Transactions

E 12. Managers and accountants often encounter transactions with which they are unfamiliar. Use your analytical skills to analyze and record in journal form the transactions below, which have not yet been discussed in the text.

a. Purchased merchandise inventory on account, $1,600.
b. Purchased marketable securities for cash, $4,800.

c. Returned part of merchandise inventory purchased in **a** for full credit, $500.
d. Sold merchandise inventory on account, $1,600 (record sale only).
e. Purchased land and a building for $600,000. Payment is $120,000 cash, and there is a thirty-year mortgage for the remainder. The purchase price is allocated as follows: $200,000 to the land and $400,000 to the building.
f. Received an order for $24,000 in services to be provided. With the order was a deposit of $8,000.

LO6 Recording Transactions in the General Journal and Posting to the Ledger Accounts

E 13. Open a general journal form like the one in Exhibit 4, and label it Page 10. After opening the form, record the following transactions in the journal:

Dec. 14 Purchased an item of equipment for $6,000, paying $2,000 as a cash down payment.
28 Paid $3,000 of the amount owed on the equipment.

Prepare three ledger account forms like the one shown in Exhibit 5. Use the following account numbers: Cash, 111; Equipment, 144; and Accounts Payable, 212. Then post the two transactions from the general journal to the ledger accounts, being sure to make proper posting references.

Assume that the Cash account has a debit balance of $8,000 on the day prior to the first transaction.

PROBLEMS

LO4 Transaction Analysis

P 1. The following accounts are applicable to Connie's Scrapbooking Barn:

1. Cash
2. Accounts Receivable
3. Supplies
4. Prepaid Insurance
5. Equipment
6. Notes Payable
7. Accounts Payable
8. Capital
9. Withdrawals
10. Service Revenue
11. Rent Expense
12. Repair Expense

Connie's Scrapbooking Barn completed the following transactions:

	Debit	Credit
a. Paid for supplies purchased on credit last month.	7	1
b. Billed customers for services performed.		
c. Paid the current month's rent.		
d. Purchased supplies on credit.		
e. Received cash from customers for services performed but not yet billed.		
f. Purchased equipment on account.		
g. Received a bill for repairs.		
h. Returned part of the equipment purchased in **f** for a credit.		
i. Received payments from customers previously billed.		
j. Paid the bill received in **g**.		
k. Received an order for services to be performed.		
l. Paid for repairs with cash.		
m. Made a payment to reduce the principal of the note payable.		
n. Withdrew cash for personal expenses.		

REQUIRED ▶ Analyze each transaction and show the accounts affected by entering the corresponding numbers in the appropriate debit or credit column as shown in transaction **a.** Indicate no entry, if appropriate.

LO4 Transaction Analysis,
LO5 T Accounts, and Trial Balance

P 2. Kyle Piu established a small business, Computer Skills Training Center, to teach spreadsheet analysis, word processing, and other techniques on microcomputers.

a. Piu began by transferring the following assets to the business:

Cash	$9,200
Furniture	3,100
Microcomputers	7,300

b. Paid the first month's rent on a small storefront, $580.
c. Purchased computer software on credit, $750.
d. Paid for an advertisement in the school newspaper, $100.
e. Received enrollment applications from five students for a five-day course that is to start next week. Each student will pay $200 if he or she actually begins the course.
f. Paid wages to a part-time helper, $150.
g. Received cash payment from three of the students enrolled in **e,** $600.
h. Billed the two other students in **e,** who attended but did not pay in cash, $400.
i. Paid the utility bill for the current month, $110.
j. Made a payment on the software purchased in **c,** $250.
k. Received payment from one student billed in **h,** $200.
l. Purchased a second microcomputer for cash, $4,700.
m. Transferred cash to personal checking account, $300.

REQUIRED ▶

1. Set up the following T accounts: Cash; Accounts Receivable; Software; Furniture; Microcomputers; Accounts Payable; Kyle Piu, Capital; Kyle Piu, Withdrawals; Tuition Revenue; Wages Expense; Utilities Expense; Rent Expense; and Advertising Expense.
2. Record the transactions by entering debits and credits directly in the T accounts, using the transaction letter to identify each debit and credit.
3. Prepare a trial balance using the current date.
4. Contrast the effects on cash flows of transactions **c** and **j** with **d** and of transactions **h** and **k** with transaction **g.**

LO1 Transaction Analysis,
LO4 General Journal, Ledger
LO5 Accounts, and Trial Balance
LO6

P 3. Dee Strong began an office-cleaning business on October 1 and engaged in the following transactions during the month:

Oct.	1	Began business by transferring $6,000 from her personal bank account to the business bank account.
	2	Ordered cleaning supplies, $500.
	3	Purchased cleaning equipment for cash, $1,400.
	4	Leased a van by making two months' lease payment in advance, $600.
	7	Received the cleaning supplies ordered on October 2 and agreed to pay half the amount in ten days and the rest in thirty days.
	9	Paid for repairs on the van with cash, $40.
	12	Received cash for cleaning offices, $480.
	17	Paid half the amount owed on supplies purchased on October 7, $250.
	21	Billed customers for cleaning offices, $670.
	24	Paid cash for additional repairs on the van, $40.
	27	Received $300 from the customers billed on October 21.
	31	Withdrew $350 from the business for personal use.

REQUIRED ▶

1. Prepare journal entries to record the above transactions in the general journal (Pages 1 and 2). Use the accounts listed below.
2. Set up the following ledger accounts and post the journal entries to the accounts: Cash (111); Accounts Receivable (113); Cleaning Supplies (115); Prepaid Lease (116); Cleaning Equipment (141); Accounts Payable (211); Dee Strong, Capital (311); Dee Strong, Withdrawals (312); Cleaning Revenues (411); and Repair Expense (511).
3. Prepare a trial balance for Strong's Office-Cleaning Service as of October 31, 20xx.
4. Compare and contrast how the issues of recognition, valuation, and classification are settled in the transactions of October 7 and 9.

LO1 LO4 LO5 Transaction Analysis, Journal Form, T Accounts, and Trial Balance

P 4. Ben Aronson is a house painter. During the month of June, he completed the following transactions:

June	3	Began his business with equipment valued at $2,460 and placed $14,200 in a business checking account.
	5	Purchased a used truck costing $3,800. Paid $1,000 in cash and signed a note for the balance.
	7	Purchased supplies on account for $640.
	8	Completed a painting job and billed the customer $960.
	10	Received $300 in cash for painting two rooms.
	11	Hired an assistant to work with him at $12 per hour.
	12	Purchased supplies for $320 in cash.
	13	Received a $960 check from the customer billed on June 8.
	14	Paid $800 for an insurance policy for eighteen months' coverage.
	16	Billed a customer $1,240 for a painting job.
	18	Paid the assistant $300 for twenty-five hours' work.
	19	Paid $80 for a tune-up for the truck.
	20	Paid for the supplies purchased on June 7.
	21	Purchased a new ladder (equipment) for $120 and supplies for $580, on account.
	23	Received a telephone bill for $120, due next month.
	24	Received $660 in cash from the customer billed on June 16.
	25	Transferred $600 to a personal checking account.
	26	Received $720 in cash for painting a five-room apartment.
	28	Paid $400 on the note signed for the truck.
	29	Paid the assistant $360 for thirty hours' work.

REQUIRED

1. Prepare entries to record these transactions in journal form.
2. Set up the following T accounts and post all the journal entries: Cash; Accounts Receivable; Supplies; Prepaid Insurance; Equipment; Truck; Notes Payable; Accounts Payable; Ben Aronson, Capital; Ben Aronson, Withdrawals; Painting Fees Earned; Wages Expense; Telephone Expense; and Repair Expense.
3. Prepare a trial balance for Aronson Painting Service as of June 30, 20xx.
4. Compare how recognition applies to the transactions of June 8 and 10 and their effects on cash flow and how classification applies to the transactions of June 14 and 18.

LO4 LO5 LO6 Transaction Analysis, General Journal, Ledger Accounts, and Trial Balance

P 5. The Jump-Start Child Development Company provides babysitting and child-care programs. On August 31, 20xx, the company had the following trial balance:

Jump-Start Child Development Company
Trial Balance
August 31, 20xx

Cash (111)	$ 3,740	
Accounts Receivable (113)	3,400	
Equipment (141)	2,080	
Buses (143)	34,800	
Notes Payable (211)		$30,000
Accounts Payable (212)		3,280
Lisa Corvelli, Capital (311)		10,740
	$44,020	$44,020

During the month of September, the company completed the following transactions:

Sept.	3	Paid this month's rent, $540.
	5	Received cash fees for this month's services, $1,300.
	7	Purchased supplies on account, $170.
	8	Reimbursed the bus driver for gas expenses, $80.
	9	Ordered playground equipment, $2,000.
	10	Paid part-time assistants for two weeks' services, $460.
	12	Made a payment on account, $340.
	13	Received payments from customers on account, $2,400.
	15	Billed customers who had not yet paid for this month's services, $1,400.
	16	Paid for the supplies purchased on September 7.
	18	Purchased playground equipment for cash, $2,000.
	19	Withdrew cash for personal expenses, $220.
	20	Contributed equipment to the business, $580.
	21	Paid this month's utility bill, $290.
	24	Paid part-time assistants for two weeks' services, $460.
	25	Received payment for one month's services from customers previously billed, $1,000.
	26	Purchased gas for the bus on account, $70.
	29	Paid for a one-year insurance policy, $580.

REQUIRED

1. Enter these transactions in the general journal (Pages 17 and 18).
2. Open accounts in the ledger for the accounts in the trial balance and the following accounts: Supplies (115); Prepaid Insurance (116); Lisa Corvelli, Withdrawals (312); Service Revenue (411); Rent Expense (511); Gasoline Expense (512); Wages Expense (513); and Utilities Expense (514).
3. Enter the August 31, 20xx, account balances from the trial balance.
4. Post the entries to the ledger accounts. Be sure to make the appropriate posting references in the journal and ledger as you post.
5. Prepare a trial balance as of September 30, 20xx.
6. What does the trial balance prove? If it is in balance, does this mean there are no errors?

Alternate Problems

LO4 Transaction Analysis

P 6. The following accounts are applicable to Smiley's Landscaping Service, a company that maintains condominium grounds:

1. Cash
2. Accounts Receivable
3. Supplies
4. Prepaid Insurance
5. Equipment
6. Accounts Payable
7. Capital
8. Withdrawals
9. Landscaping Services Revenue
10. Wages Expense
11. Rent Expense
12. Utilities Expense

Smiley's Landscaping Service completed the following transactions:

	Debit	Credit
a. Received cash from customers billed last month.	1	2
b. Made a payment on accounts payable.		
c. Purchased a new one-year insurance policy in advance.		
d. Purchased supplies on credit.		

	Debit	Credit
e. Billed a client for landscaping services.	______	______
f. Made a rent payment for the current month.	______	______
g. Received cash from customers for landscaping services.	______	______
h. Paid wages for the staff.	______	______
i. Ordered equipment.	______	______
j. Paid the current month's utility bill.	______	______
k. Received and paid for the equipment ordered in **i.**	______	______
l. Returned for full credit some of the supplies purchased in **d** because they were defective.	______	______
m. Paid for supplies purchased in **d,** less the return in **l.**	______	______
n. Withdrew cash for personal expenses.	______	______

REQUIRED ▶ Analyze each transaction and show the accounts affected by entering the corresponding numbers in the appropriate debit or credit columns as shown in transaction **a.** Indicate no entry, if appropriate.

LO1 Transaction Analysis, LO4 Journal Form, T Accounts, LO5 and Trial Balance

P 7. Marcus Stahl won a concession to rent bicycles in the local park during the summer. In the month of May, Stahl completed the following transactions for his bicycle rental business:

May	3	Began business by placing $14,400 in a business checking account.
	6	Purchased supplies on account for $300.
	7	Purchased ten bicycles for $5,000, paying $2,400 down and agreeing to pay the rest in thirty days.
	9	Received $940 in cash for rentals during the first week of operation.
	10	Purchased a small shed to hold the bicycles and to use for other operations for $5,800 in cash.
	11	Paid $800 in cash for shipping and installation costs (considered an addition to the cost of the shed) to place the shed at the park entrance.
	14	Received $1,000 in cash for rentals during the second week of operation.
	15	Hired a part-time assistant to help out on weekends at $8 per hour.
	16	Paid a maintenance person $150 to clean the grounds.
	18	Paid the assistant $160 for a weekend's work.
	19	Paid $300 for the supplies purchased on May 6.
	20	Paid a $110 repair bill on bicycles.
	21	Received $1,100 in cash for rentals during the third week of operation.
	23	Paid the assistant $160 for a weekend's work.
	24	Billed a company $220 for bicycle rentals for an employees' outing.
	26	Paid the $200 fee for May to the Park District for the right to the bicycle concession.
	28	Received $820 in cash for rentals during the week.
	30	Paid the assistant $160 for a weekend's work.
	31	Transferred $1,000 to a personal checking account.

REQUIRED ▶
1. Prepare entries in journal form to record these transactions.
2. Set up the following T accounts and post all the journal entries: Cash; Accounts Receivable; Supplies; Shed; Bicycles; Accounts Payable; Marcus Stahl, Capital; Marcus Stahl, Withdrawals; Rental Revenue; Wages Expense; Maintenance Expense; Repair Expense; and Concession Fee Expense.
3. Prepare a trial balance for Stahl Rentals as of May 31, 20xx.
4. Compare how recognition applies to the transactions of May 24 and 28 and their effects on cash flows and how classification applies to the transactions of May 11 and 16.

LO4 Transaction Analysis, LO5 General Journal, Ledger LO6 Accounts, and Trial Balance

P 8. Samantha Young Company is a marketing firm. The company's trial balance as of April 30, 20xx, appears on the opposite page.

During the month of May, the company completed the following transactions:

May	3	Paid rent for May, $1,300.
	5	Received cash from customers on account, $4,600.
	6	Ordered supplies, $760.
	8	Billed customers for services provided, $5,600.

Samantha Young Company
Trial Balance
April 30, 20xx

Cash (111)	$20,400	
Accounts Receivable (113)	11,000	
Supplies (115)	1,220	
Office Equipment (141)	8,400	
Accounts Payable (211)		$ 5,200
Samantha Young, Capital (311)		35,820
	$41,020	$41,020

May 10 Made a payment on accounts payable, $2,200.
13 Received the supplies ordered on May 6 and agreed to pay for them in 30 days, $760.
15 Paid salaries for the first half of May, $3,800.
16 Discovered some of the supplies were not as ordered and returned them for a full credit, $160.
18 Received cash from a customer for services provided, $9,600.
22 Paid the utility bill for May, $320.
23 Paid the telephone bill for May, $240.
27 Received a bill, to be paid in June, for advertisements placed in the local newspaper during the month of May to promote Samantha Young Company, $1,400.
28 Billed a customer for services provided, $5,400.
30 Paid salaries for the last half of May, $3,800.
31 Withdrew cash for personal use, $2,400.

REQUIRED

1. Enter these transactions in the general journal (Pages 22 and 23).
2. Open accounts in the ledger for the accounts in the trial balance and the following accounts: Samantha Young, Withdrawals (312); Marketing Fees (411); Salaries Expense (511); Rent Expense (512); Utilities Expense (513); Telephone Expense (514); and Advertising Expense (515).
3. Enter the April 30 account balances from the trial balance in the appropriate ledger account.
4. Post the journal entries to the ledger accounts. Be sure to make the appropriate posting references in the journal and ledger as you post.
5. Prepare a trial balance as of May 31, 20xx.
6. What does the trial balance prove? If it is in balance, does this mean there are no errors?

SKILLS DEVELOPMENT CASES

Conceptual Analysis

LO1 Valuation Issue

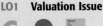

SD 1. Nike, Inc., <www.nike.com> manufactures athletic shoes and other sports-related products. In one of its annual reports, Nike made the following statement: "Property, plant, and equipment are recorded at cost."[8] Given that the property, plant, and equipment undoubtedly were purchased over several years and that the current value of those assets was likely to be very different from their original cost, explain what authoritative basis there is for Nike's carrying the assets at cost. Does accounting generally recognize

changes in value after the purchase of property, plant, and equipment? Assume you are a Nike accountant. Write a memo to management explaining the rationale underlying Nike's approach.

SD 2.
LO1 LO4 **Valuation and Classification Issues for Dot-Coms**

The dot-com business has raised many issues about accounting practices, some of which are of great concern to both the SEC and the FASB. Important ones relate to the valuation and classification of revenue transactions. Many dot-com companies seek to report as much revenue as possible because revenue growth is seen as a key performance measure for these companies. Amazon.com is a good example. Consider the following situations:

a. An Amazon.com <www.amazon.com> customer orders and pays $28 for a Gameboy® electronic game on the Internet. Amazon sends an email to the company that makes the product, which sends the Gameboy to the customer. Amazon collects $28 from the customer and pays $24 to the other company. Amazon never owns the Gameboy.
b. Amazon agrees to place a banner advertisement on its web site for another dot-com company. Instead of paying cash for the advertisement, the other company agrees to let Amazon advertise on its web site.
c. Assume the same facts as in situation **b** except that Amazon agrees to accept the other company's stock in this barter transaction. Over the next six months, the price of the stock received goes down.

Discuss the valuation and classification issues that arise in each of these situations, including how Amazon should account for each transaction.

Group Activity: Divide the class into groups. Assign each group one of the above cases so that one-third of the groups have each case. Debrief and discuss.

Ethical Dilemma

SD 3.
LO1 **Recognition Point and Ethical Considerations**

Jerry Hasbrow, a sales representative for Penn Office Supplies, is compensated on a commission basis and receives a substantial bonus for meeting his annual sales goal. The company's recognition point for sales is the day of shipment. On December 31, Hasbrow realizes he needs sales of $2,000 to reach his sales goal and receive the bonus. He calls a purchaser for a local insurance company, whom he knows well, and asks him to buy $2,000 worth of copier paper today. The purchaser says, "But Jerry, that's more than a year's supply for us." Hasbrow says, "Buy it today. If you decide it's too much, you can return however much you want for full credit next month." The purchaser says, "Okay, ship it."

The paper is shipped on December 31 and recorded as a sale. On January 15, the purchaser returns $1,750 worth of paper for full credit (approved by Hasbrow) against the bill. Should the shipment on December 31 be recorded as a sale? Discuss the ethics of Jerry Hasbrow's action.

Group Activity: Divide the class into informal groups to discuss and report on the ethical issues of this case.

Research Activity

SD 4.
LO4 **Transactions in a Business Article**

Locate an article on a company you recognize or on a company in a business that interests you in one of the following sources: a recent issue of a business publication (such as *Barron's, Fortune, The Wall Street Journal, BusinessWeek,* or *Forbes*) or the Needles Accounting Resource Center Web Site at http://accounting.college.hmco.com/students. Read the article carefully, noting any references to transactions in which the company engages. These may be normal transactions (such as sales or purchases) or unusual transactions (such as a merger or the purchase of another company). Bring a copy of the article to class and be prepared to describe how you would analyze and record the transactions you have noted.

Decision-Making Practice

LO4 **Transaction Analysis**
LO5 **and Evaluation of a Trial Balance**

SD 5. Ben Obi hired an attorney to help him start Obi Repairs Company. On June 1, Obi invested $23,000 in cash in the business. When he paid the attorney's bill of $1,400, the attorney advised him to hire an accountant to keep his records. However, Obi was so busy that it was June 30 before he asked you to straighten out his records. Your first task is to develop a trial balance based on the June transactions, which are described in the next two paragraphs.

After making the investment and paying the attorney, Obi borrowed $10,000 from the bank. He later paid $520, which included interest of $120, on this loan. He also purchased a pickup truck in the company's name, paying $5,000 down and financing $14,800. The first payment on the truck is due July 15. Obi then rented an office and paid three months' rent, $1,800, in advance. Credit purchases of office equipment for $1,400 and repair tools for $1,000 must be paid for by July 13.

In June, Obi Repairs completed repairs of $2,600, of which $800 were cash transactions. Of the credit transactions, $600 were collected during June, and $1,200 remained to be collected at the end of June. Wages of $800 were paid to employees. On June 30, the company received a $150 bill for June utilities and a $100 check from a customer for work to be completed in July.

1. Record the June transactions in journal form.
2. Set up T accounts, post the journal entries to the T accounts, and determine the balance of each account.
3. Prepare a June 30 trial balance for Obi Repairs Company.
4. Ben Obi is unsure how to evaluate the trial balance. His Cash account balance is $24,980, which exceeds his original investment of $23,000 by $1,980. Did he make a profit of $1,980? Explain why the Cash account is not an indicator of business earnings. Cite specific examples to show why it is difficult to determine net income by looking solely at figures in the trial balance.

FINANCIAL REPORTING AND ANALYSIS CASES

Interpreting Financial Reports

LO2 **Interpreting a Bank's**
LO4 **Financial Statements**

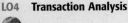

FRA 1. Mellon Bank <www.mellon.com> is a large bank holding company. Selected accounts from a recent annual report are as follows (in millions):[9]

Cash and Due from Banks	$ 3,506
Loans to Customers	26,369
Securities Available for Sale	7,910
Deposits by Customers	36,890

1. Indicate whether each of the accounts just listed is an asset, a liability, or a component of owner's equity on Mellon Bank's balance sheet.
2. Assume that you are in a position to do business with this large company. Prepare the entry on Mellon Bank's books in journal form to record each of the following transactions:
   a. You sell securities in the amount of $2,000 to the bank.
   b. You deposit the $2,000 received in step **a** in the bank.
   c. You borrow $5,000 from the bank.

International Company

LO4 **Transaction Analysis**

FRA 2. Ajinomoto Company <www.ajinomoto.com>, a Japanese company with operations in 22 countries, is primarily engaged in the manufacture and sale of food products. The following selected aggregate cash transactions were reported in the statement of cash flows in Ajinomoto's annual report (amounts in millions of yen):[10]

Purchase of property, plant, and equipment	¥46,381
Proceeds from issuance of long-term debt	10,357
Repayment of long-term debt	11,485

Prepare entries in journal form to record the above transactions.

Toys "R" Us Annual Report

FRA 3.

LO4 **Transaction Analysis**

Refer to the balance sheet in the Toys "R" Us <www.tru.com> annual report in the Supplement to Chapter 6. Prepare T accounts for the accounts Cash and Cash Equivalents, Accounts and Other Receivables, Prepaid Expenses and Other Current Assets, Accounts Payable, and Income Taxes Payable. Properly place the balance of the account at February 1, 2003, in the T accounts. Below are some typical transactions in which Toys "R" Us would engage. Analyze each transaction, enter it in the T accounts, and determine the balance of each account. Assume all entries are in thousands.

a. Paid cash in advance for certain expenses, $20,000.
b. Received cash from customers billed previously, $35,000.
c. Paid cash for income taxes previously owed, $70,000.
d. Paid cash to suppliers for amounts owed, $120,000.

Comparison Case: Toys "R" Us and Walgreen Co.

FRA 4.

LO1 **Recognition, Valuation, and Classification**

Refer to the Summary of Significant Accounting Policies in the notes to the financial statements in the Toys "R" Us <www.tru.com> annual report and to the financial statements of Walgreens <www.walgreens.com> to answer these questions:

1. How does the concept of recognition apply to advertising costs for both Toys "R" Us and Walgreens?
2. How does the concept of valuation apply to property and equipment for both companies?
3. How does the concept of classification apply to cash and cash equivalents for both companies?

Discuss any differences that you may observe.

Fingraph® Financial Analyst™

FRA 5.

LO1 **Transaction Identification**
LO3
LO4

Choose a company from the list of Fingraph companies on the Needles Accounting Resource Center Web Site at http://accounting.college.hmco.com/students. Click on the company you selected to access the Microsoft Excel spreadsheet for that company. You will find the company's URL (Internet address) in the heading of the spreadsheet. Click on the URL for a link to the company's web site and annual report.

1. From the company's annual report, determine the industry(ies) in which the company operates.
2. Find the summary of significant accounting policies that follows the financial statements. In these policies, find examples of the application of recognition, valuation, and classification.
3. Identify six types of transactions the company would commonly engage in. Are any of these transactions more common in the industry in which the company operates than in other industries? For each transaction, tell what account would typically be debited and what account would be credited.
4. Prepare a one-page executive summary that highlights what you have learned from steps 1, 2, and 3.

Internet Case

FRA 6.

LO2 **Comparison of**
LO4 **Contrasting Companies**

Sun Microsystems <www.sun.com> and Oracle Corporation <www.oracle.com> are leading computer and software companies. Go to their web sites directly using the URLs shown here, or go to the Needles Accounting Resource Center Web Site at http://accounting.college.hmco.com/students for a link to their web sites. Access each company's annual report and find its balance sheet.

1. What differences and similarities do you find in the account titles used by Sun Microsystems and those used by Oracle? What differences and similarities do you find in the account titles used by the two companies and the account titles used in this text?
2. Although the companies are in the same general industry, their businesses differ. How are these differences reflected on the balance sheets? What types of transactions resulted in the differences?

3 Chapter 3 defines the accounting concept of business income, discusses the role of adjusting entries in the measurement of income, and demonstrates the preparation of financial statements.

Measuring Business Income

Learning Objectives

LO1 Define *net income* and its two major components, *revenues* and *expenses.*

LO2 Explain how the income measurement issues of accounting period, continuity, and matching are resolved.

LO3 Define *accrual accounting* and explain three broad ways of accomplishing it.

LO4 State four principal situations that require adjusting entries and prepare typical adjusting entries.

LO5 Prepare financial statements from an adjusted trial balance.

Supplemental Objective

SO6 Analyze cash flows from accrual-based information.

DECISION POINT

A USER'S FOCUS

Kelly Services <www.kellyservices.com> Kelly Services is one of the most successful temporary employment agencies. During any given year, Kelly incurs various operating expenses that are recorded as expenses when they are paid. However, at the end of the year, some expenses—including, for example, the wages of employees during the last days before the end of the year—will have been incurred but will not be paid until the next year. If these expenses are not accounted for correctly, they will appear in the wrong year—the year in which they are paid instead of the year in which Kelly benefited from them. The result is a misstatement of the company's income, a key profitability performance measure. How is this problem avoided?

According to the concepts of accrual accounting and the matching rule, which you will learn in this chapter, the amount of expenses that have been incurred but not paid must be determined and then recorded as expenses of the current year with corresponding liabilities to be paid the next year. The accompanying figure shows the liabilities, called *accrued liabilities,* that resulted from this process at Kelly Services.[1] Total accrued liabilities for payroll and related expenses, accrued insurance, and income and other taxes were $227,033,000 in 2001 and $257,215,000 in 2002. If these items had not been recorded in their respective years, income would have been misstated by a significant amount.

How does Kelly Services record wages that have been incurred in December but won't be paid until January?

Financial Highlights: Notes to the Financial Statements

3. ACCRUED LIABILITIES

(In thousands)

	2002	2001
Payroll and related expenses	**$181,686**	$154,813
Accrued insurance	**27,912**	24,071
Income and other taxes	**47,617**	48,149
Total accrued liabilities	**$257,215**	$227,033

PROFITABILITY MEASUREMENT: THE ROLE OF BUSINESS INCOME

LO1 Define *net income* and its two major components, *revenues* and *expenses.*

RELATED TEXT ASSIGNMENTS
Q: 1
SD: 5
FRA: 5

KEY POINT: Accounting measures and reports a business's profitability. The extent of the reported profit or loss communicates the company's success or failure in meeting this business goal.

Profitability is one of the two major goals of a business (the other being liquidity). For a business to succeed, or even to survive, it must earn a profit. The word **profit**, though, has many meanings. One is the increase in owner's equity that results from business operations. However, even this definition can be interpreted differently by economists, lawyers, businesspeople, and the public. Because the word *profit* has more than one meaning, accountants prefer to use the term *net income,* which can be precisely defined from an accounting point of view. Net income is reported on the income statement and is a performance measure used by management, owners, and others to monitor a business's progress in meeting the goal of profitability. Readers of income statements need to understand how the accountant defines net income and to be aware of its strengths and weaknesses as a measure of company performance.

NET INCOME

STOP AND THINK!
When a company has net income, what happens to assets and/or liabilities?
Owner's equity increases, but there is also an increase in assets and/or a decrease in liabilities. ■

Net income is the net increase in owner's equity that results from the operations of a company and is accumulated in the Owner's Capital account. Net income, in its simplest form, is measured by the difference between revenues and expenses when revenues exceed expenses:

$$\text{Net Income} = \text{Revenues} - \text{Expenses}$$

When expenses exceed revenues, a **net loss** occurs.

REVENUES

Revenues are increases in owner's equity resulting from selling goods, rendering services, or performing other business activities. Revenues are inflows usually of cash or receivables, received in exchange for products or services. In the simplest case, revenues equal the price of goods sold or services rendered over a specific period of time. When a business delivers a product or provides a service to a customer, it usually receives either cash or a promise to pay cash in the near future. The promise to pay is recorded in either Accounts Receivable or Notes Receivable. The revenue for a given period equals the total of cash and receivables from goods and services provided to customers during that period.

KEY POINT: The essence of revenue is that something has been *earned* through the sale of goods or services. That is why cash received through a loan does not constitute revenue.

Liabilities generally are not affected by revenues, and some transactions that increase cash and other assets are not revenues. For example, a bank loan increases liabilities and cash but does not produce revenue. The collection of accounts receivable, which increases cash and decreases accounts receivable, does not produce revenue either. Remember that when a sale on credit takes place, the asset account Accounts Receivable increases; at the same time, an owner's equity revenue account increases. So counting the collection of the receivable as revenue later would be counting the same sale twice.

Not all increases in owner's equity arise from revenues. Owner's investments increase owner's equity but are not revenue.

EXPENSES

KEY POINT: The primary purpose of an expense is to generate revenue.

Expenses are decreases in owner's equity resulting from the costs of selling goods, rendering services, or performing other business activities. In other words, expenses are the costs of the goods and services used up in the course of earning revenues. Often called the *cost of doing business,* expenses include the costs of goods sold, of activities needed to carry on a business, and of attracting and serving customers.

Examples include salaries, rent, advertising, telephone service, expired or used assets, and depreciation (allocation of cost) of a building or office equipment.

Just as not all cash receipts are revenues, not all cash payments are expenses. A cash payment to reduce a liability does not result in an expense. The liability, however, may have come from incurring a previous expense, such as advertising, that is to be paid later. There may also be two steps before an expenditure of cash becomes an expense. For example, prepaid expenses and plant assets (such as machinery and equipment) are recorded as assets when they are acquired. Later, as their usefulness expires in the operation of the business, their cost is allocated to expenses. In fact, expenses sometimes are called *expired costs.*

Not all decreases in owner's equity arise from expenses. Owner withdrawals decrease owner's equity, but they are not expenses.

BUSINESS-WORLD EXAMPLE: Income measurement is difficult in many industries because of the uncertainties associated with their revenues and expenses. For example, cereal companies must recognize the expense associated with the anticipated redemption of box-tops and coupons during the period of the sale. And construction companies must estimate their revenues based on a project's percentage of completion.

Check out ACE for a Review Quiz at http://accounting.college.hmco.com/students.

Income Measurement Issues

LO2 Explain how the income measurement issues of accounting period, continuity, and matching are resolved.

RELATED TEXT ASSIGNMENTS
Q: 2, 3, 4
SE: 1
E: 1
SD: 1, 3
FRA: 1, 3, 5, 6

Several issues must be addressed in the measurement of income. These include the accounting period issue, the continuity issue, and the matching issue.

The Accounting Period Issue

The **accounting period issue** addresses the difficulty of assigning revenues and expenses to a short period of time, such as a month or a year. Not all transactions can be easily assigned to specific time periods. Purchases of buildings and equipment, for example, have effects that extend over many years. Accountants solve this problem by estimating the number of years the buildings or equipment will be in use and the cost that should be assigned to each year. In the process, they make an assumption about **periodicity**: that the net income for any period of time less than the life of the business, although tentative, is still a useful estimate of the entity's profitability for the period.

Generally, to make comparisons easier, the time periods are of equal length. Financial statements may be prepared for any time period. Accounting periods of less than one year—for example, a month or a quarter—are called *interim periods.* The 12-month accounting period used by an organization is called its **fiscal year**. Many organizations use the calendar year, January 1 to December 31, for their fiscal year. Others find it convenient to choose a fiscal year that ends during a slack season rather than a peak season. In this case, the fiscal year corresponds to the yearly cycle of business activity. The time period should always be noted in the financial statements.

Focus on Business Practice

Fiscal Year-Ends Vary.

The table below shows the diverse fiscal years used by some well-known companies. Many governmental and educational units use fiscal years that end June 30 or September 30.

Company	Last Month of Fiscal Year
Caesars World Inc. <www.caesarsworld.com>	July
The Walt Disney Company <www.disney.go.com>	September
Fleetwood Enterprises, Inc. <www.fleetwood.com>	April
H.J. Heinz, Inc. <www.heinz.com>	March
Kelly Services <www.kellyservices.com>	December
MGM-UA Communications Co. <www.mgm.com>	August
Toys "R" Us <www.tru.com>	January

The Continuity Issue

The process of measuring business income requires that certain expense and revenue transactions be allocated over several accounting periods. The number of accounting periods raises the **continuity issue**. How long will the business entity last? Many businesses survive less than five years, and in any given year, thousands of businesses go bankrupt. To prepare financial

BUSINESS-WORLD EXAMPLE: The continuity assumption is set aside when an organization is formed for a limited venture, such as a World's Fair or the Olympics.

statements for an accounting period, the accountant must make an assumption about the ability of the business to survive. Specifically, unless there is evidence to the contrary, the accountant assumes that the business will continue to operate indefinitely—that it is a **going concern**. Justification for all the techniques of income measurement rests on the assumption of continuity. For example, this assumption allows the cost of certain assets to be held on the balance sheet until a future year, when it will become an expense on the income statement.

Another example has to do with the value of assets on the balance sheet. The accountant records assets at cost and does not record subsequent changes in their value. But the value of assets to a going concern is much higher than the value of assets to a firm facing bankruptcy. In the latter case, the accountant may be asked to set aside the assumption of continuity and to prepare financial statements based on the assumption that the firm will go out of business and sell all of its assets at liquidation value—that is, for what they will bring in cash.

The Matching Issue

KEY POINT: Although the cash basis often is used for tax purposes, it seldom produces an accurate measurement of a business's performance for financial reporting purposes.

Revenues and expenses can be accounted for on a cash received and cash paid basis. This practice is known as the **cash basis of accounting**. Individuals and some businesses may use it for income tax purposes. Under this method, revenues are reported in the period in which cash is received, and expenses are reported in the period in which cash is paid. Taxable income, therefore, is calculated as the difference between cash receipts from revenues and cash payments for expenses.

Although the cash basis of accounting works well for some small businesses and many individuals, it does not meet the needs of most businesses. As explained above, revenues can be earned in a period other than the one in which cash is received, and expenses can be incurred in a period other than the one in which cash is paid. To measure net income adequately, revenues and expenses must be assigned to the appropriate accounting period. The accountant solves this problem by applying the **matching rule**:

> Revenues must be assigned to the accounting period in which the goods are sold or the services performed, and expenses must be assigned to the accounting period in which they are used to produce revenue.

Stop and Think!
Why must a company that gives a guaranty or warranty with its product or service show an expense in the year of sale rather than in a later year when a repair or replacement is made?

To measure a company's performance (net income) accurately, each expense (in this case, guaranty or warranty expense) must be matched with the related revenue in the year in which the product or service was sold. Otherwise, net income will be overstated, and the related liability will be understated. ■

Direct cause-and-effect relationships seldom can be demonstrated for certain, but many costs appear to be related to particular revenues. The accountant recognizes these expenses and the related revenues in the same accounting period. Examples are the costs of goods sold and sales commissions. When there is no direct means of connecting expenses and revenues, the accountant tries to allocate costs in a systematic way among the accounting periods that benefit from the costs. For example, a building is converted from an asset to an expense by allocating its cost over the years that the company benefits from its use.

Check out ACE for a Review Quiz at http://accounting.college.hmco.com/students.

Accrual Accounting

LO3 Define *accrual accounting* and explain three broad ways of accomplishing it.

RELATED TEXT ASSIGNMENTS
Q: 5, 6, 7, 8
SE: 1
E: 1, 2
P: 2, 7
SD: 1, 2, 3
FRA: 3

To apply the matching rule, accountants have developed accrual accounting. **Accrual accounting** "attempts to record the financial effects on an enterprise of transactions and other events and circumstances . . . in the periods in which those transactions, events, and circumstances occur rather than only in the periods in which cash is received or paid by the enterprise."[2] That is, accrual accounting consists of all the techniques developed by accountants to apply the matching rule. It is done in the following general ways: (1) by recording revenues when earned, (2) by recording expenses when incurred, and (3) by adjusting the accounts.

Focus on Business Ethics

Aggressive Accounting or Deception? You Judge.

Accounting principles, such as revenue recognition and the matching rule, should not be applied in a way that will distort or obscure financial information. Accounting practices are meant to inform readers of financial statements, not to deceive them. In recent years, the Securities and Exchange Commission <www.sec.gov> has been waging a public campaign against corporate accounting practices that manage or manipulate earnings to meet the expectations of Wall Street analysts.[3] Corporations engage in such practices in the hope of avoiding shortfalls that might cause serious declines in their stock price. The following describes a few of the corporate accounting practices that the SEC has challenged:

- Lucent Technologies <www.lucent.com> sold telecommunications equipment to companies from which there was no reasonable expectation of payment because of the companies' poor financial condition.
- America Online (AOL) <www.aol.com> recorded advertising as an asset rather than as an expense.
- Eclipsys <www.eclipsys.com> recorded software contracts as revenue even though it had not yet rendered the services.
- KnowledgeWare <knowledgeware.itil.com> recorded revenue from sales of software even though it told customers they did not have to pay until they had the software.

KEY POINT: Accrual accounting is a set of *procedures* (such as journal entries) devised to follow the *guideline* known as the matching rule.

Recognizing Revenues When Earned

The process of determining when revenue is earned, and consequently when it should be recorded, is called **revenue recognition**. The Securities and Exchange Commission has said that all the following conditions must exist before revenue is recognized:

- Persuasive evidence of an arrangement exists.
- Delivery has occurred or services have been rendered.
- The seller's price to the buyer is fixed or determinable.
- Collectibility is reasonably assured.[4]

For example, when Joan Miller Advertising Agency bills a customer for placing an advertisement, it is recorded as revenue because the transaction meets these four criteria. It is agreed that the customer owes for the service, the service has been rendered, the parties understand the price, and there is a reasonable expectation that the customer will pay the bill. Revenue is recorded by debiting Accounts Receivable and crediting Advertising Fees Earned. Note that it is not necessary for cash to be collected for revenue to be recorded. There only needs to be a reasonable expectation that it will be paid.

Recognizing Expenses When Incurred

Expenses are recorded when there is an agreement to purchase goods or services, the goods have been delivered or the services rendered, a price is established or can be determined, and the goods or services have been used to produce revenue. For example, when Joan Miller Advertising Agency receives its telephone bill, the expense is recognized both as having been incurred and as helping to produce revenue. The transaction is recorded by debiting Telephone Expense and crediting Accounts Payable. Until the bill is paid, Accounts Payable serves as a holding account. Notice that recognition of the expense does not depend on the payment of cash.

Adjusting the Accounts

A third application of accrual accounting is adjusting the accounts. Adjustments are necessary because the accounting period, by definition, ends on a particular day. The balance sheet must list all assets and liabilities as of the end of that day, and the income statement must contain all revenues and expenses applicable to the period ending on that day. Although operating a business is a continuous process, there

EXHIBIT 1
Trial Balance for Joan Miller Advertising Agency

Joan Miller Advertising Agency
Trial Balance
July 31, 20xx

Cash	$ 9,140	
Accounts Receivable	4,800	
Art Supplies	1,800	
Office Supplies	800	
Prepaid Rent	1,600	
Prepaid Insurance	960	
Art Equipment	4,200	
Office Equipment	3,000	
Accounts Payable		$ 3,240
Unearned Art Fees		1,000
Joan Miller, Capital		20,000
Joan Miller, Withdrawals	1,400	
Advertising Fees Earned		6,200
Wages Expense	2,400	
Utilities Expense	200	
Telephone Expense	140	
	$30,440	$30,440

ENRICHMENT NOTE: The accountant waits until the end of an accounting period to update certain revenues and expenses even though the revenues and expenses theoretically have changed during the period. There usually is no need to adjust them until the end of the period, when the financial statements are prepared. In fact, it would be impractical, even impossible, to adjust the accounts each time they are affected.

must be a cutoff point for the periodic reports. Some transactions invariably span the cutoff point; thus, some accounts need adjustment.

For example, some of the accounts in the end-of-the-period trial balance for Joan Miller Advertising Agency (Exhibit 1) do not show the correct balances for preparing the financial statements. The July 31 trial balance lists prepaid rent of $1,600. At $800 per month, this represents rent for the months of July and August. So on July 31, one-half of the $1,600, or $800, represents rent expense for July; the remaining $800 represents an asset that will be used in August. An adjustment is needed to reflect the $800 balance in the Prepaid Rent account on the balance sheet and the $800 rent expense on the income statement. As you will see on the following pages, several other accounts in the Joan Miller Advertising Agency trial balance do not reflect their correct balances. Like the Prepaid Rent account, they need to be adjusted.

ACCRUAL ACCOUNTING AND PERFORMANCE MEASURES

Accrual accounting can be difficult to understand. The related adjustments take time to calculate and enter in the records. Also, adjusting entries do not affect cash flows in the current period because they never involve the Cash account. You might ask, "Why go to all the trouble of making them? Why worry about them?" The Securities and Exchange Commission, in fact, has identified issues related to accrual accounting and adjustments as an area of utmost importance because of the potential for abuse and misrepresentation.[5]

STOP AND THINK!
Is accrual accounting more closely related to a company's goal of profitability or liquidity?
It is more closely related to profitability because the purpose of accrual accounting is to measure net income. Cash accounting is more closely related to the goal of liquidity. ■

All adjustments are important because they are necessary to measure key profitability performance measures. Adjusting entries affect net income on the income statement, and they affect profitability comparisons from one accounting period to the next. They also affect assets and liabilities on the balance sheet and thus provide information about a company's *future* cash inflows and outflows. This information is needed to assess management's short-term goal of achieving sufficient liquidity to meet its need for cash to pay ongoing obligations. The potential for abuse arises because considerable judgment underlies the application of adjusting entries. Misuse of this judgment can result in misleading measures of performance.

Check out ACE for a Review Quiz at http://accounting.college.hmco.com/students.

THE ADJUSTMENT PROCESS

LO4 State four principal situations that require adjusting entries and prepare typical adjusting entries.

RELATED TEXT ASSIGNMENTS
Q: 9, 10, 11, 12, 13, 14, 15, 16, 17, 18, 19, 20
SE: 2, 3, 4, 5, 6
E: 1, 3, 4, 5, 6, 7, 8, 9
P: 1, 2, 3, 4, 5, 6, 7, 8
SD: 1, 2, 3, 4, 5
FRA: 1, 2, 4, 5, 6, 7

KEY POINT: Each adjusting entry must include at least one balance sheet account and one income statement account. By definition, it cannot include a debit or a credit to Cash.

KEY POINT: Adjusting entries never involve the Cash account and thus never affect cash flows.

Accountants use **adjusting entries** to apply accrual accounting to transactions that span more than one accounting period. There are four situations in which adjusting entries are required, as illustrated in Figure 1. As shown, each situation affects one balance sheet account and one income statement account. Adjusting entries never involve the Cash account. The four types of adjusting entries may be stated as follows:

1. Costs have been recorded that must be allocated between two or more accounting periods. Examples are prepaid rent, prepaid insurance, supplies, and costs of a building. The adjusting entry in this case involves an asset account and an expense account.
2. Expenses have been incurred but are not yet recorded. Examples are the wages earned by employees in the current accounting period but after the last pay period. The adjusting entry involves an expense account and a liability account.
3. Revenues have been recorded that must be allocated between two or more accounting periods. An example is payments collected for services yet to be rendered. The adjusting entry involves a liability account and a revenue account.
4. Revenues have been earned but are not yet recorded. An example is fees earned but not yet collected or billed to customers. The adjusting entry involves an asset account and a revenue account.

Accountants often refer to adjusting entries as deferrals or accruals. A **deferral** is the postponement of the recognition of an expense already paid (Type 1 adjustment) or of a revenue received in advance (Type 3 adjustment). Recording of the receipt or payment of cash precedes the adjusting entry. An **accrual** is the recognition of a revenue (Type 4 adjustment) or expense (Type 2 adjustment) that has arisen but has not yet been recorded. No cash was received or paid prior to the adjusting entry; this will occur in a future accounting period. Once again, we use Joan Miller Advertising Agency to illustrate the kinds of adjusting entries that most businesses make.

FIGURE 1
The Four Types of Adjustments

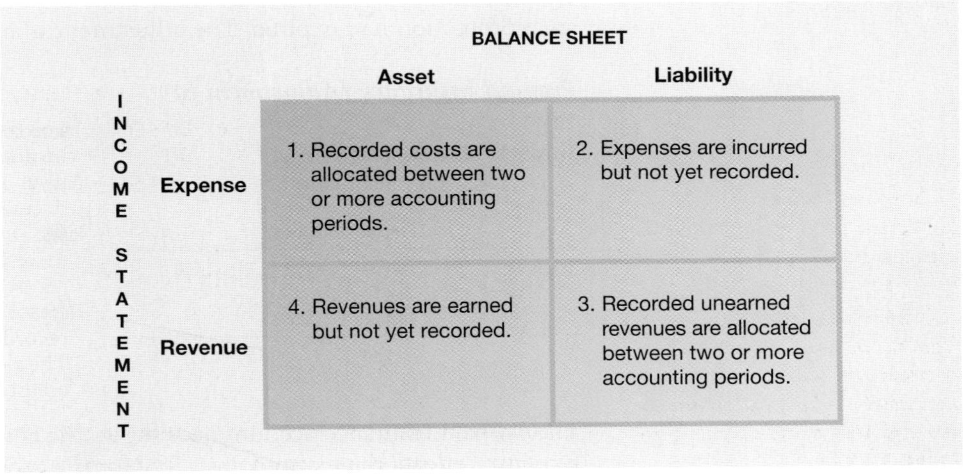

BALANCE SHEET
Asset
Liability
INCOME STATEMENT
Expense
Revenue
1. Recorded costs are allocated between two or more accounting periods.
2. Expenses are incurred but not yet recorded.
4. Revenues are earned but not yet recorded.
3. Recorded unearned revenues are allocated between two or more accounting periods.

TYPE 1: ALLOCATING RECORDED COSTS BETWEEN TWO OR MORE ACCOUNTING PERIODS (DEFERRED EXPENSES)

Companies often make expenditures that benefit more than one period. These expenditures are usually debited to an asset account. At the end of the accounting period, the amount that has been used is transferred from the asset account to an expense account. Two of the more important kinds of adjustments are those for prepaid expenses and the depreciation of plant and equipment.

KEY POINT: The expired portion of a prepayment is converted to an expense; the unexpired portion remains an asset.

■ **PREPAID EXPENSES** Expenses paid in advance are called **prepaid expenses**. They include rent, insurance, and supplies. At the end of an accounting period, some or all of these goods or services will have been used up or expired. An adjusting entry to reduce the asset and increase the expense is always required. As Figure 2 shows, the amount of the adjustment equals the cost of the goods or services used up or expired. If adjusting entries for prepaid expenses are not made at the end of a period, both the balance sheet and income statement will be incorrect; assets will be overstated, and expenses will be understated. Owner's equity on the balance sheet and net income on the income statement will be overstated.

At the beginning of the month, Joan Miller Advertising Agency paid two months' rent in advance, which resulted in an asset: the right to occupy the office for two months. As each day in the month passed, part of the asset's cost expired and became an expense. By July 31, one-half of the asset's cost had expired and should be treated as an expense. Here is the analysis of this economic event:

Prepaid Rent (Adjustment a)

A = L + OE
− −

		Dr.	Cr.
July 31	Rent Expense	800	
	Prepaid Rent		800

Prepaid Rent

July 2	1,600	July 31	800

Rent Expense

July 31	800		

Transaction: Expiration of one month's rent.
Analysis: Assets decrease. Owner's equity decreases.
Rules: Decreases in owner's equity are recorded by debits. Decreases in assets are recorded by credits.
Entries: The decrease in owner's equity is recorded by a debit to Rent Expense. The decrease in assets is recorded by a credit to Prepaid Rent.

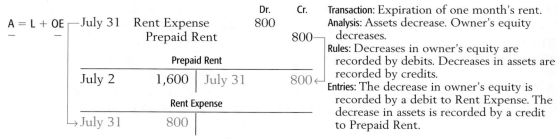

The Prepaid Rent account now has a balance of $800, which represents one month's rent paid in advance. The Rent Expense account reflects the $800 expense for the month of July. Besides rent, Joan Miller Advertising Agency prepaid expenses for insurance, art supplies, and office supplies, all of which call for adjusting entries.

On July 8, the agency purchased a one-year life insurance policy, paying for it in advance. Like prepaid rent, prepaid insurance offers benefits (in this case, protection) that expire day by day. By the end of the month, one-twelfth of the insurance protection had expired. The adjustment is analyzed and recorded like this:

Prepaid Insurance (Adjustment b)

A = L + OE
− −

		Dr.	Cr.
July 31	Insurance Expense	80	
	Prepaid Insurance		80

Prepaid Insurance

July 8	960	July 31	80

Insurance Expense

July 31	80		

Transaction: Expiration of one month's life insurance.
Analysis: Assets decrease. Owner's equity decreases.
Rules: Decreases in owner's equity are recorded by debits. Decreases in assets are recorded by credits.
Entries: The decrease in owner's equity is recorded by a debit to Insurance Expense. The decrease in assets is recorded by a credit to Prepaid Insurance.

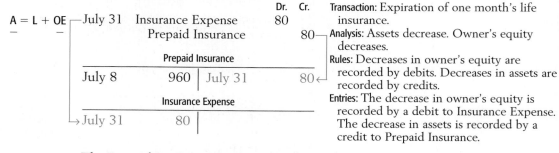

The Prepaid Insurance account now shows the correct balance, $880, and Insurance Expense reflects the expired cost, $80 for the month of July.

FIGURE 2
Adjustment for Prepaid (Deferred) Expenses

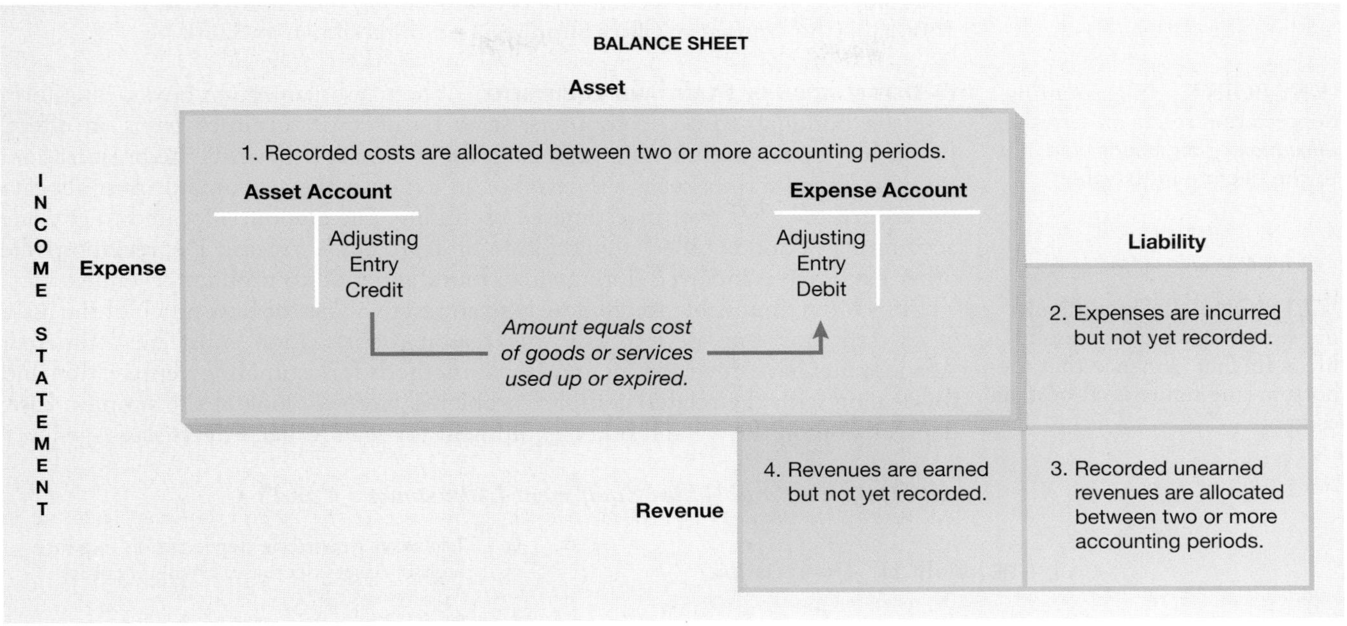

KEY POINT: Notice that the cost of supplies consumed is inferred, not observed.

Early in July, the agency purchased art supplies and office supplies, some of which it consumed during the month. These supplies are not accounted for each day because the financial statements are not prepared until the end of the month and the recordkeeping would involve too much work. Instead, Joan Miller makes a careful inventory of the supplies at the end of the month, recording the number and cost of those not yet consumed and that are thus still assets of the agency.

Suppose the inventory shows that art supplies costing $1,300 and office supplies costing $600 are still on hand. This means that of the $1,800 of art supplies originally purchased, $500 worth were used up (became an expense) in July. Of the original $800 of office supplies, $200 worth were consumed. These transactions are analyzed and recorded as follows:

Art Supplies and Office Supplies (Adjustments c and d)

			Dr.	Cr.
A = L + OE (− −)	July 31	Art Supplies Expense	500	
		Art Supplies		500
A = L + OE (− −)	July 31	Office Supplies Expense	200	
		Office Supplies		200

Art Supplies

July 6	1,800	July 31	500

Art Supplies Expense

July 31	500		

Office Supplies

July 6	800	July 31	200

Office Supplies Expense

July 31	200		

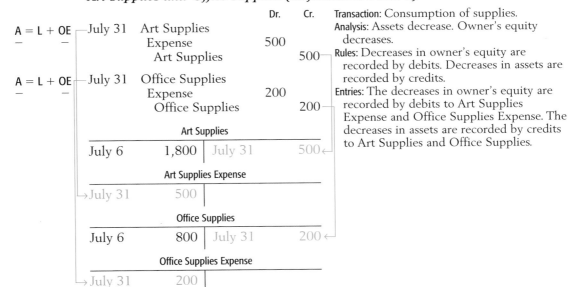

Transaction: Consumption of supplies.
Analysis: Assets decrease. Owner's equity decreases.
Rules: Decreases in owner's equity are recorded by debits. Decreases in assets are recorded by credits.
Entries: The decreases in owner's equity are recorded by debits to Art Supplies Expense and Office Supplies Expense. The decreases in assets are recorded by credits to Art Supplies and Office Supplies.

The asset accounts Art Supplies and Office Supplies now reflect the correct balances, $1,300 and $600, respectively, of supplies that are yet to be consumed. In addition, the amount of art supplies used up during the month of July is shown as $500, and the amount of office supplies used up is shown as $200.

KEY POINT: In accounting, depreciation refers only to the *allocation* of an asset's cost, not to the decline in its value.

KEY POINT: The difficulty in estimating an asset's useful life is further evidence that the bottom-line figure is, at best, an estimate.

DEPRECIATION OF PLANT AND EQUIPMENT When an organization buys a long-term asset—a building, trucks, computers, store fixtures, or furniture—it is, in effect, prepaying for the usefulness of that asset for as long as it benefits the organization. Because a long-term asset is a deferral of an expense, the accountant must allocate the cost of the asset over its estimated useful life. The amount allocated to any one accounting period is called **depreciation** or *depreciation expense.* Depreciation, like other expenses, is incurred during an accounting period to produce revenue.

It is often impossible to tell how long an asset will last or how much of the asset is used in any one period. For this reason, depreciation must be estimated. Accountants have developed a number of methods for estimating depreciation and for dealing with the related complex problems. Here we look at the simplest case, depreciation on the art and office equipment for Joan Miller Advertising Agency.

Art Equipment and Office Equipment (Adjustments e and f)

			Dr.	Cr.
A = L + OE − −	July 31	Depreciation Expense, Art Equipment	70	
		Accumulated Depreciation, Art Equipment		70
A = L + OE − −	July 31	Depreciation Expense, Office Equipment	50	
		Accumulated Depreciation, Office Equipment		50

Transaction: Recording depreciation expense.
Analysis: Assets decrease. Owner's equity decreases.
Rules: Decreases in owner's equity are recorded by debits. Decreases in assets are recorded by credits.
Entries: The owner's equity is decreased by debits to Depreciation Expense, Art Equipment and Depreciation Expense, Office Equipment. The assets are decreased by credits to Accumulated Depreciation, Art Equipment and Accumulated Depreciation, Office Equipment.

Art Equipment

July 3	4,200		

Accumulated Depreciation, Art Equipment

		July 31	70

Office Equipment

July 5	3,000		

Accumulated Depreciation, Office Equipment

		July 31	50

Depreciation Expense, Art Equipment

July 31	70		

Depreciation Expense, Office Equipment

July 31	50		

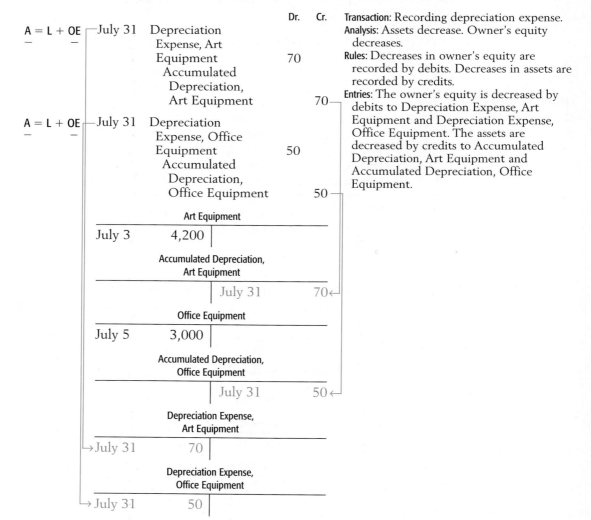

Suppose, for example, that Joan Miller estimates that the art equipment and office equipment for which she paid $4,200 and $3,000, respectively, will last five years (60 months) and will have zero value at the end of that time. The monthly

FIGURE 3
Adjustment for Depreciation

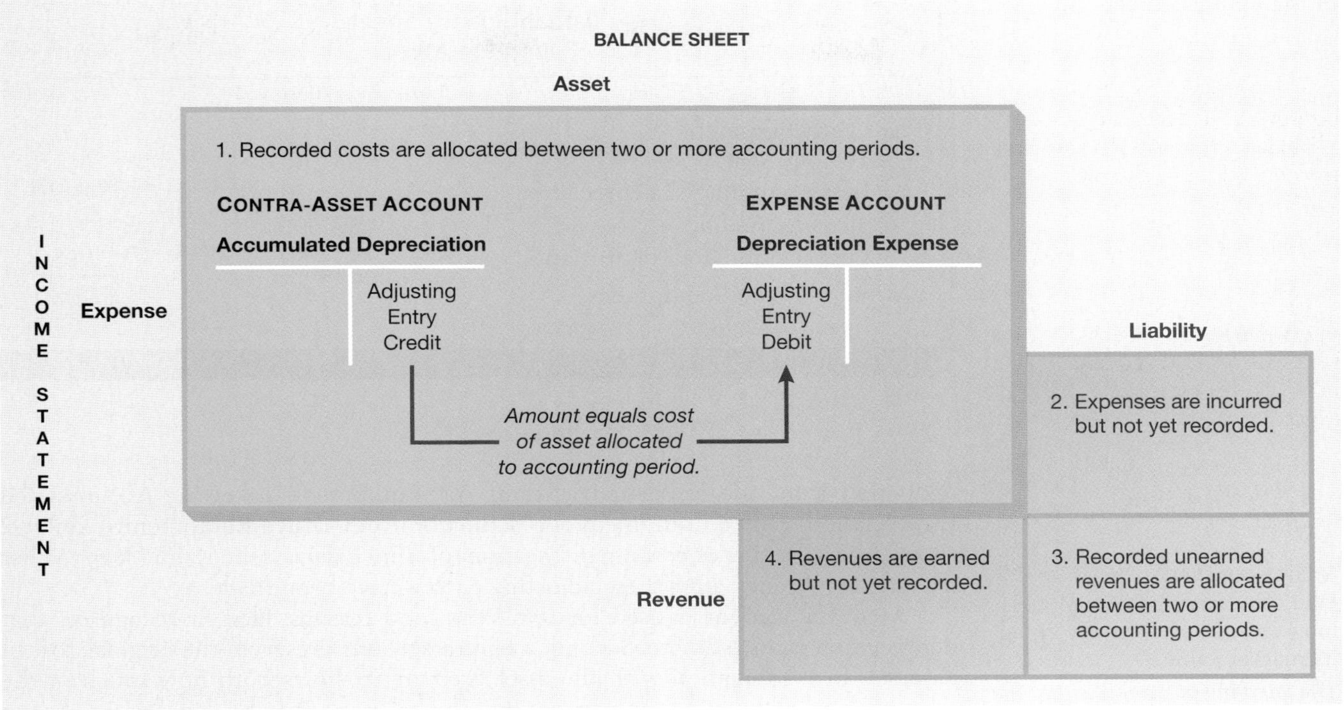

depreciation of art equipment and office equipment is $70 ($4,200 ÷ 60 months) and $50 ($3,000 ÷ 60 months), respectively. These amounts represent the costs allocated to July, and they are the amounts by which the asset accounts must be reduced and the expense accounts increased (reducing owner's equity).

■ **ACCUMULATED DEPRECIATION—A CONTRA ACCOUNT** Notice that in the previous analysis, the asset accounts are not credited directly. Instead, as shown in Figure 3, new accounts—Accumulated Depreciation, Art Equipment; and Accumulated Depreciation, Office Equipment—are credited. These **accumulated depreciation accounts** are contra-asset accounts used to total the past depreciation expense on specific long-term assets. A **contra account** is a separate account that is paired with a related account—in this case an asset account. The balance of the contra account is shown on the financial statement as a deduction from the related account.

There are several types of contra accounts. In this case, the balance of Accumulated Depreciation, Art Equipment is shown on the balance sheet as a

FOCUS ON INTERNATIONAL BUSINESS

Who Needs Accounting Knowledge?

The privatization of businesses in Eastern Europe and the republics of the former Soviet Union has created a great need for Western accounting knowledge. Many managers from these countries are anxious to study accounting. Under the old governmental systems, the concept of net income as Westerners know it did not exist because the state owned everything and there was no such thing as income.

The new businesses, because they are private, require accounting systems that recognize the importance of net income. In these new systems, it is necessary to make adjusting entries to record such things as depreciation and accrued expenses. Many Eastern European businesses have been suffering losses for years without knowing it and, as a result, are now in poor financial condition.

EXHIBIT 2
Plant and Equipment Section of the Balance Sheet

Joan Miller Advertising Agency
Partial Balance Sheet
July 31, 20xx

Plant and equipment		
Art equipment	$4,200	
Less accumulated depreciation	70	$4,130
Office equipment	$3,000	
Less accumulated depreciation	50	2,950
Total plant and equipment		$7,080

deduction from the associated account Art Equipment. Likewise, Accumulated Depreciation, Office Equipment is a deduction from Office Equipment. Exhibit 2 shows the plant and equipment section of the balance sheet for Joan Miller Advertising Agency after these adjusting entries have been made.

STOP AND THINK!
Will the carrying value of a long-term asset normally equal its market value?
The carrying value will equal the market value of the asset only by coincidence because the goal of recording depreciation is to allocate the cost of the asset over its life, not to determine its market value. ■

A contra account is used for two very good reasons. First, it recognizes that depreciation is an estimate. Second, a contra account preserves the original cost of an asset. In combination with the asset account, it shows both how much of the asset has been allocated as an expense and the balance left to be depreciated. As the months pass, the amount of the accumulated depreciation grows, and the net amount shown as an asset declines. In six months, Accumulated Depreciation, Art Equipment will show a balance of $420; when this amount is subtracted from the balance of Art Equipment, a net amount of $3,780 will remain. The net amount is called the **carrying value**, or *book value*, of the asset.

TYPE 2: RECOGNIZING UNRECORDED EXPENSES (ACCRUED EXPENSES)

At the end of an accounting period, there usually are expenses that have been incurred but not recorded in the accounts. These expenses require adjusting entries. One such case is interest on borrowed money. Each day, interest accumulates on the debt. As shown in Figure 4, at the end of the accounting period, an adjusting entry is made to record this accumulated interest, which is an expense of the period, and the corresponding liability to pay the interest. Other common unrecorded expenses are taxes, wages, and utilities. As the expense and the corresponding liability accumulate, they are said to *accrue*—hence the term **accrued expenses**.

■ **ACCRUED WAGES** Suppose the calendar for the month of July looks like the calendar that follows.

July

Su	M	T	W	Th	F	Sa
	1	2	3	4	5	6
7	8	9	10	11	12	13
14	15	16	17	18	19	20
21	22	23	24	25	26	27
28	29	30	31			

FIGURE 4
Adjustment for Unrecorded (Accrued) Expenses

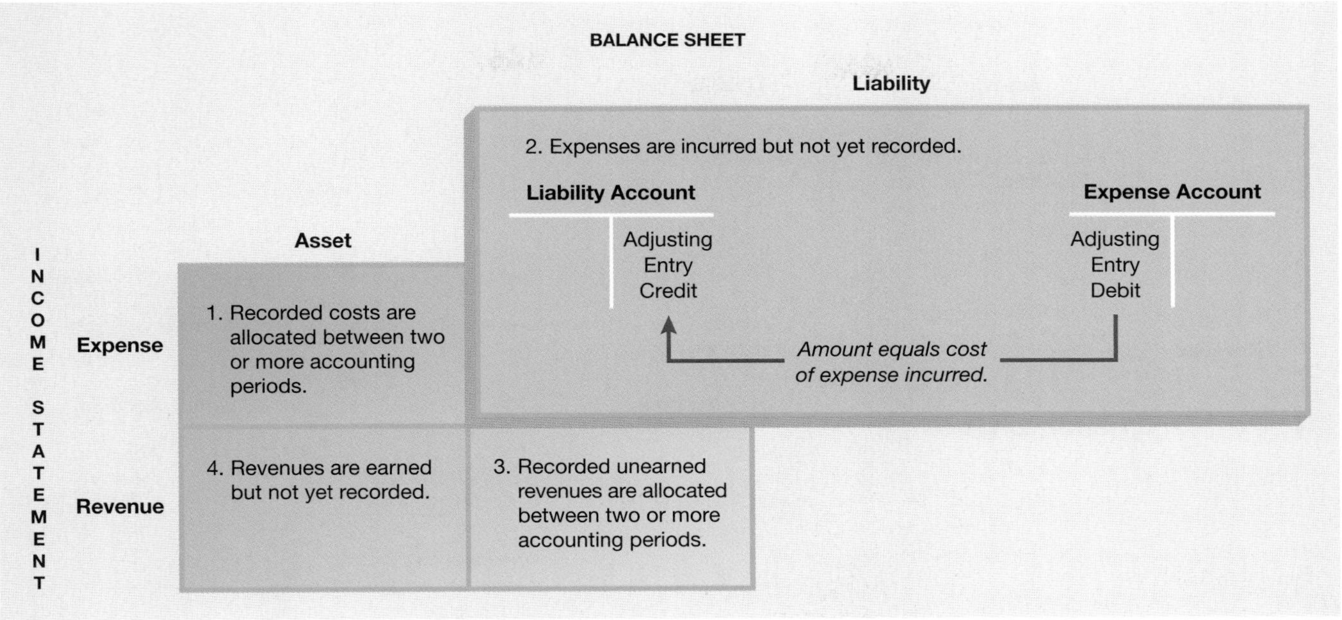
BALANCE SHEET
Liability
2. Expenses are incurred but not yet recorded.
Liability Account
Adjusting Entry Credit
Expense Account
Adjusting Entry Debit
Amount equals cost of expense incurred.
Asset
INCOME STATEMENT
Expense
1. Recorded costs are allocated between two or more accounting periods.
Revenue
4. Revenues are earned but not yet recorded.
3. Recorded unearned revenues are allocated between two or more accounting periods.

By the end of business on July 31, the secretary at Joan Miller Advertising Agency will have worked three days (Monday, Tuesday, and Wednesday) beyond the last biweekly pay period, which ended on July 26. The employee has earned the wages for these days, but she will not be paid until the regular payday in August. The wages for these three days are rightfully an expense for July, and the liabilities should reflect that the company owes the secretary for those days. Because the secretary's wage rate is $1,200 every two weeks, or $120 per day ($1,200 ÷ 10 working days), the expense is $360 ($120 × 3 days).

Accrued Wages (Adjustment g)

A = L + OE
    +   −

		Dr.	Cr.
July 31	Wages Expense	360	
	Wages Payable		360

Wages Payable

		July 31	360

Wages Expense

July 12	1,200		
26	1,200		
31	360		

Transaction: Accrual of unrecorded expense.
Analysis: Liabilities increase. Owner's equity decreases.
Rules: Decreases in owner's equity are recorded by debits. Increases in liabilities are recorded by credits.
Entries: The decrease in owner's equity is recorded by a debit to Wages Expense. The increase in liabilities is recorded by a credit to Wages Payable.

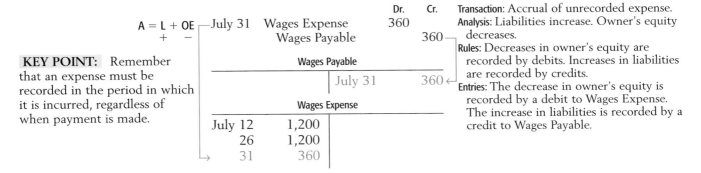

KEY POINT: Remember that an expense must be recorded in the period in which it is incurred, regardless of when payment is made.

The liability of $360 is now reflected correctly in the Wages Payable account. The actual expense incurred for wages during July, $2,760, is also correct.

TYPE 3: ALLOCATING RECORDED UNEARNED REVENUES BETWEEN TWO OR MORE ACCOUNTING PERIODS (DEFERRED REVENUES)

Just as expenses can be paid before they are used, revenues can be received before they are earned. When a company receives revenues in advance, it has an obligation

FIGURE 5
Adjustment for Unearned (Deferred) Revenues

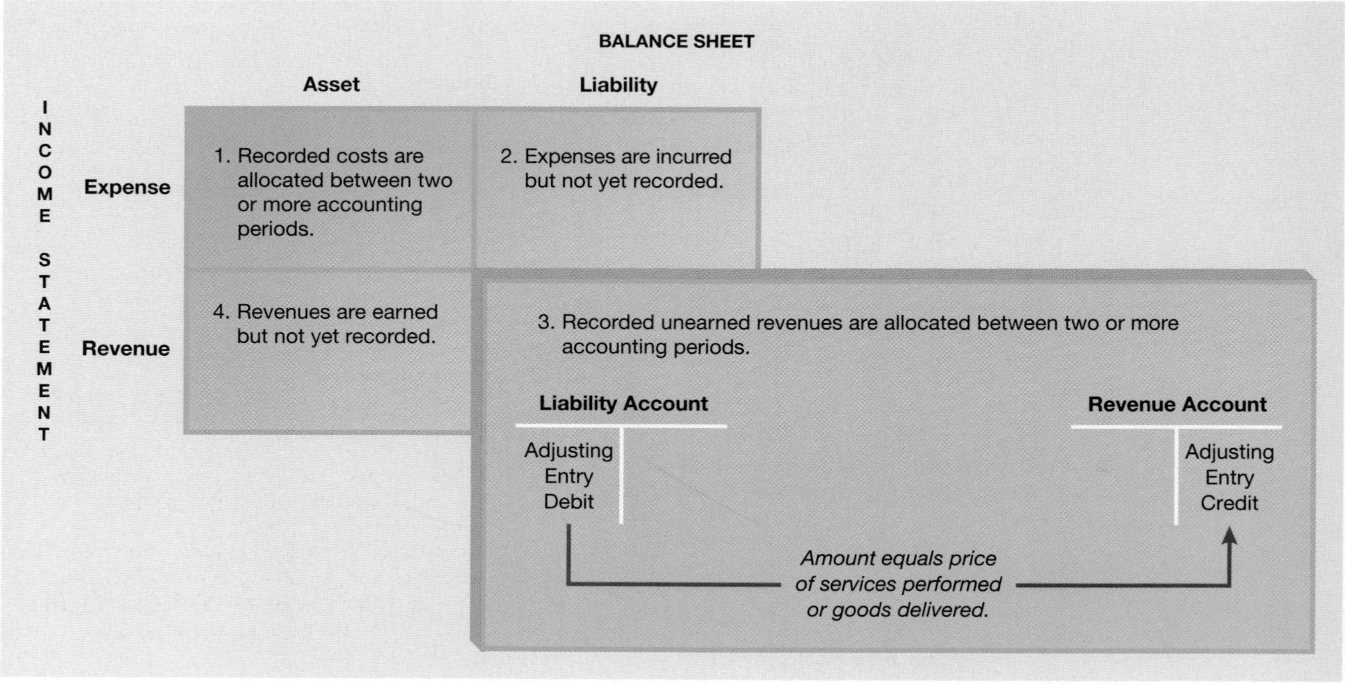

KEY POINT: Unearned Revenue is a liability because there is an obligation to deliver goods or perform a service, or to return the payment. Once the goods have been delivered or the service performed, the liability is converted into revenue.

to deliver goods or perform services. Therefore, **unearned revenues** are shown in a liability account. For example, publishing companies usually receive payment in advance for magazine subscriptions, and these receipts are recorded in a liability account. If the company fails to deliver the magazines, subscribers are entitled to their money back. As the company delivers each issue of the magazine, it earns a part of the advance payments. This earned portion must be transferred from the Unearned Subscriptions (liability) account to the Subscription Revenue account, as shown in Figure 5.

During the month of July, Joan Miller Advertising Agency received $1,000 as an advance payment for advertising designs to be prepared for another agency. Assume that by the end of the month, $400 of the design was completed and accepted by the other agency. Here is the transaction analysis:

Unearned Art Fees (Adjustment h)

A = L + OE
    − +

		Dr.	Cr.
July 31	Unearned Art Fees	400	
	Art Fees Earned		400

Unearned Art Fees

July 31	400	July 15	1,000

Art Fees Earned

		July 31	400

Transaction: Performance of services paid for in advance.
Analysis: Liabilities decrease. Owner's equity increases.
Rules: Decreases in liabilities are recorded by debits. Increases in owner's equity are recorded by credits.
Entries: The decrease in liabilities is recorded by a debit to Unearned Art Fees. The increase in owner's equity is recorded by a credit to Art Fees Earned.

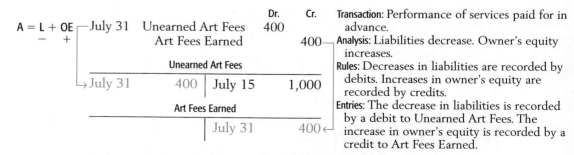

The liability account Unearned Art Fees now reflects the amount of work still to be performed, $600. The revenue account Art Fees Earned reflects the services performed and the revenue earned for them during July, $400.

TYPE 4: RECOGNIZING UNRECORDED REVENUES (ACCRUED REVENUES)

STUDY NOTE: When distinguishing between unearned revenues and accrued revenues, be aware that with accrued revenues, cash is not received in advance or by the end of the period.

Accrued revenues are revenues for which a service has been performed or goods delivered but for which no entry has been recorded. Any revenues earned but not recorded during the accounting period call for an adjusting entry that debits an asset account and credits a revenue account, as shown in Figure 6. For example, the interest on a note receivable is earned day by day but may not be received until another accounting period. Interest Receivable should be debited and Interest Income should be credited for the interest accrued at the end of the current period.

Suppose that Joan Miller Advertising Agency has agreed to place a series of advertisements for Marsh Tire Company and that the first ad appears on July 31, the last day of the month. The fee of $200 for this advertisement, which has been earned but not recorded, should be recorded this way:

Accrued Advertising Fees (Adjustment i)

A = L + OE
\+   +

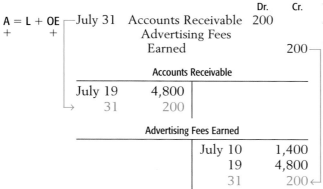

		Dr.	Cr.
July 31	Accounts Receivable	200	
	Advertising Fees Earned		200

Accounts Receivable

July 19	4,800		
31	200		

Advertising Fees Earned

		July 10	1,400
		19	4,800
		31	200

Transaction: Accrual of unrecorded revenue.
Analysis: Assets increase. Owner's equity increases.
Rules: Increases in assets are recorded by debits. Increases in owner's equity are recorded by credits.
Entries: The increase in assets is recorded by a debit to Accounts Receivable. The increase in owner's equity is recorded by a credit to Advertising Fees Earned.

FIGURE 6
Adjustment for Unrecorded (Accrued) Revenues

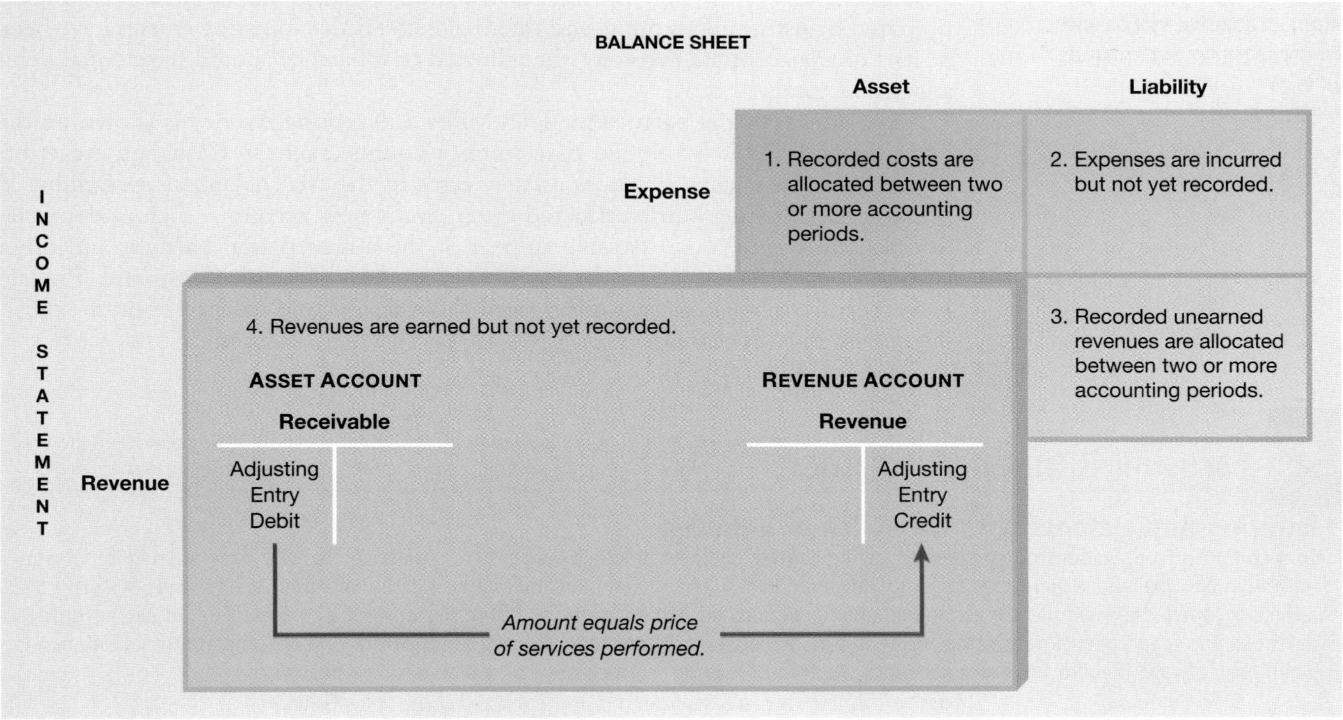
BALANCE SHEET
Asset
Liability
Expense
1. Recorded costs are allocated between two or more accounting periods.
2. Expenses are incurred but not yet recorded.
INCOME STATEMENT
Revenue
4. Revenues are earned but not yet recorded.
3. Recorded unearned revenues are allocated between two or more accounting periods.
ASSET ACCOUNT
Receivable
Adjusting Entry Debit
REVENUE ACCOUNT
Revenue
Adjusting Entry Credit
Amount equals price of services performed.

Focus on Business Technology

Ecommerce: What's Its Impact?

Electronic commerce has received much attention in recent years. Sales and purchases involving Internet-based companies like Amazon.com <www.amazon.com> and Travelocity.com <www.travelocity.com> have grown steadily. The total value of goods and services traded over the Internet was $433 billion in 2002, of which $94 billion were retail sales.[6] It is important to realize that when transactions are made electronically, they are analyzed and recorded just as if they had taken place in a physical store. Internet companies require insurance, employee payrolls, buildings, and other assets and liabilities, and they must make the adjusting entries in the same way as any other business.

Now both the asset and the revenue accounts show the correct balance: The $5,000 in Accounts Receivable is owed to the company, and the $6,400 in Advertising Fees Earned has been earned by the company during July. Marsh Tire Company will be billed for the series of advertisements when they are completed.

A Note About Journal Entries

Thus far, we have presented a full analysis of each journal entry. The analyses showed you the thought process behind each entry. By now, you should be fully aware of the effects of transactions on the accounting equation and the rules of debit and credit. For this reason, in the rest of the book, we present journal entries without full analysis.

Check out ACE for a Review Quiz at http://accounting.college.hmco.com/students.

Using the Adjusted Trial Balance to Prepare Financial Statements

LO5 Prepare financial statements from an adjusted trial balance.

RELATED TEXT ASSIGNMENTS
Q: 21
SE: 7, 8
E: 10
P: 4, 5

After adjusting entries have been recorded and posted, an **adjusted trial balance** is prepared by listing all accounts and their balances. If the adjusting entries have been posted to the accounts correctly, the adjusted trial balance should have equal debit and credit totals.

The adjusted trial balance for Joan Miller Advertising Agency is shown on the left side of Exhibit 3. Notice that some accounts, such as Cash and Accounts Payable, have the same balances as they have in the trial balance (see Exhibit 1) because no adjusting entries affected them. Some new accounts, such as depreciation accounts and Wages Payable, appear in the adjusted trial balance, and other accounts, such as Art Supplies, Office Supplies, Prepaid Rent, and Prepaid Insurance, have balances that differ from those in the trial balance because adjusting entries did affect them.

Focus on Business Technology

Entering Adjustments With the Touch of a Button

In a computerized accounting system, adjusting entries can be entered just like any other transactions. However, when the adjusting entries are similar for each accounting period, such as those for insurance expense and depreciation expense, or when they always involve the same accounts, such as those for accrued wages, the computer can be programmed to display them automatically. All the accountant has to do is verify the amounts or enter the correct amounts. The adjusting entries are then entered and posted, and the adjusted trial balance is prepared with the touch of a button.

EXHIBIT 3
Relationship of Adjusted Trial Balance to Income Statement

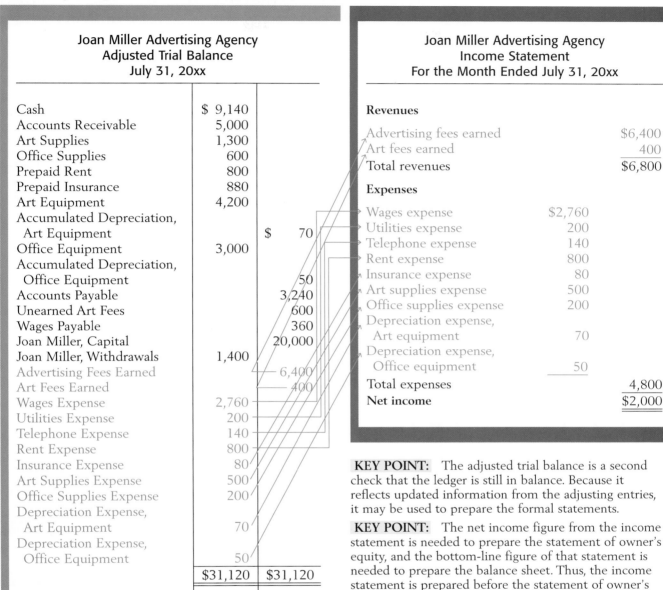

Joan Miller Advertising Agency
Adjusted Trial Balance
July 31, 20xx

Cash	$ 9,140	
Accounts Receivable	5,000	
Art Supplies	1,300	
Office Supplies	600	
Prepaid Rent	800	
Prepaid Insurance	880	
Art Equipment	4,200	
Accumulated Depreciation, Art Equipment		$ 70
Office Equipment	3,000	
Accumulated Depreciation, Office Equipment		50
Accounts Payable		3,240
Unearned Art Fees		600
Wages Payable		360
Joan Miller, Capital		20,000
Joan Miller, Withdrawals	1,400	
Advertising Fees Earned		6,400
Art Fees Earned		400
Wages Expense	2,760	
Utilities Expense	200	
Telephone Expense	140	
Rent Expense	800	
Insurance Expense	80	
Art Supplies Expense	500	
Office Supplies Expense	200	
Depreciation Expense, Art Equipment	70	
Depreciation Expense, Office Equipment	50	
	$31,120	$31,120

Joan Miller Advertising Agency
Income Statement
For the Month Ended July 31, 20xx

Revenues		
Advertising fees earned		$6,400
Art fees earned		400
Total revenues		$6,800
Expenses		
Wages expense	$2,760	
Utilities expense	200	
Telephone expense	140	
Rent expense	800	
Insurance expense	80	
Art supplies expense	500	
Office supplies expense	200	
Depreciation expense, Art equipment	70	
Depreciation expense, Office equipment	50	
Total expenses		4,800
Net income		$2,000

KEY POINT: The adjusted trial balance is a second check that the ledger is still in balance. Because it reflects updated information from the adjusting entries, it may be used to prepare the formal statements.

KEY POINT: The net income figure from the income statement is needed to prepare the statement of owner's equity, and the bottom-line figure of that statement is needed to prepare the balance sheet. Thus, the income statement is prepared before the statement of owner's equity, and that statement is prepared before the balance sheet.

KEY POINT: Notice that the adjusted trial balance figure for Joan Miller, Capital does not reflect net income or withdrawals during the period. The balance is updated when the closing entries are prepared (see Chapter 4).

Using the adjusted trial balance, the financial statements can be easily prepared. The income statement is prepared from the revenue and expense accounts, as shown in Exhibit 3. Then, as shown in Exhibit 4, the statement of owner's equity and the balance sheet are prepared. Notice that the net income from the income statement is combined with withdrawals on the statement of owner's equity to give the net change in the Joan Miller, Capital account. The resulting balance of Joan Miller, Capital on July 31 is used on the balance sheet, as are the asset and liability accounts.

Check out ACE for a Review Quiz at http://accounting.college.hmco.com/students.

EXHIBIT 4
Relationship of Adjusted Trial Balance to Balance Sheet and Statement of Owner's Equity

Joan Miller Advertising Agency
Adjusted Trial Balance
July 31, 20xx

Cash	$ 9,140	
Accounts Receivable	5,000	
Art Supplies	1,300	
Office Supplies	600	
Prepaid Rent	800	
Prepaid Insurance	880	
Art Equipment	4,200	
Accumulated Depreciation, Art Equipment		$ 70
Office Equipment	3,000	
Accumulated Depreciation, Office Equipment		50
Accounts Payable		3,240
Unearned Art Fees		600
Wages Payable		360
Joan Miller, Capital		20,000
Joan Miller, Withdrawals	1,400	
Advertising Fees Earned		6,400
Art Fees Earned		400
Wages Expense	2,760	
Utilities Expense	200	
Telephone Expense	140	
Rent Expense	800	
Insurance Expense	80	
Art Supplies Expense	500	
Office Supplies Expense	200	
Depreciation Expense, Art Equipment	70	
Depreciation Expense, Office Equipment	50	
	$31,120	$31,120

Joan Miller Advertising Agency
Balance Sheet
July 31, 20xx

Assets		
Cash		$ 9,140
Accounts receivable		5,000
Art supplies		1,300
Office supplies		600
Prepaid rent		800
Prepaid insurance		880
Art equipment	$ 4,200	
Less accumulated depreciation	70	4,130
Office equipment	$ 3,000	
Less accumulated depreciation	50	2,950
Total assets		$24,800
Liabilities		
Accounts payable	$ 3,240	
Wages payable	360	
Unearned art fees	600	
Total liabilities		$ 4,200
Owner's Equity		
Joan Miller, Capital		20,600
Total liabilities and owner's equity		$24,800

Joan Miller Advertising Agency
Statement of Owner's Equity
For the Month Ended July 31, 20xx

Joan Miller, Capital, July 1, 20xx		—
Add: Investment by Joan Miller	$20,000	
Net income	2,000	$22,000
Subtotal		$22,000
Less withdrawals		1,400
Joan Miller, Capital, July 31, 20xx		$20,600

From Income Statement in Exhibit 3

STOP AND THINK!
In Exhibit 4, why is the balance of Joan Miller, Capital in the adjusted trial balance different from the balance of the same account on the balance sheet?
The balance of Joan Miller, Capital in the adjusted trial balance does not reflect the amounts from Joan Miller, withdrawals and the revenue and expense accounts (net income), as reflected in the statement of owner's equity. ■

CASH FLOWS FROM ACCRUAL-BASED INFORMATION

SO6 Analyze cash flows from accrual-based information.

RELATED TEXT ASSIGNMENTS
Q: 22
SE: 9, 10
E: 11, 12, 13
FRA: 6

Management has the short-range goal of achieving sufficient liquidity to meet its needs for cash to pay its ongoing obligations. It is important for managers to be able to use accrual-based financial information to analyze cash flows in order to plan payments to creditors and assess the need for short-term borrowing.

Every revenue or expense account on the income statement has one or more related accounts on the balance sheet. For instance, Supplies Expense is related to Supplies, Wages Expense is related to Wages Payable, and Art Fees Earned is related to Unearned Art Fees. As we have shown, these accounts are related through adjusting entries whose purpose is to apply the matching rule in the measurement of net income. The cash flows generated or paid by company operations may also be determined by analyzing these relationships. For example, suppose that after receiving the financial statements in Exhibits 3 and 4, management wants to know how much cash was expended for art supplies. On the income statement, Art Supplies Expense is $500, and on the balance sheet, Art Supplies is $1,300. Because July was the company's first month of operation, there was no prior balance of art supplies, so the amount of cash expended for art supplies during the month was $1,800. The cash flow used to purchase art supplies ($1,800) was much greater than the amount expensed in determining income ($500). In planning for August, management can anticipate that the cash needed may be less than the amount expensed because, given the large inventory of art supplies, it will probably not be necessary to buy art supplies for more than a month. Understanding these cash flow effects enables management to better predict the business's need for cash in August.

The general rule for determining the cash flow received from any revenue or paid for any expense (except depreciation, which is a special case not covered here) is to determine the potential cash payments or cash receipts and deduct the amount not paid or received. The application of the general rule varies with the type of asset or liability account, which is shown as follows:

Type of Account	Potential Payment or Receipt	Not Paid or Received	Result
Prepaid Expense	Ending Balance + Expense for the Period	− Beginning Balance	= Cash Payments for Expenses
Unearned Revenue	Ending Balance + Revenue for the Period	− Beginning Balance	= Cash Receipts from Revenues
Accrued Payable	Beginning Balance + Expense for the Period	− Ending Balance	= Cash Payments for Expenses
Accrued Receivable	Beginning Balance + Revenue for the Period	− Ending Balance	= Cash Receipts from Revenues

STUDY NOTE: Balance sheet T accounts also work well for calculating cash receipts and cash payments. You have three pieces of information about the balance sheet account and must solve for one unknown. This approach reinforces the concept of normal balances. After the accrual number is entered, solve for the unknown cash effect.

For instance, assume that on May 31 a company had a balance of $480 in Prepaid Insurance and that on June 30 the balance was $670. If the insurance expense during June was $120, the amount of cash expended on insurance during June can be computed as follows:

Prepaid Insurance at June 30	$670
Insurance Expense during June	120
Potential cash payments for insurance	$790
Less Prepaid Insurance at May 31	480
Cash payments for insurance during June	$310

The beginning balance is deducted because it was paid in a prior accounting period. Note that the cash payments equal the expense plus the increase in the balance of the Prepaid Insurance account [$120 + ($670 − $480) = $310]. In this case, the cash paid was almost three times the amount of insurance expense. In future months, cash payments are likely to be less than the expense.

Check out ACE for a Review Quiz at http://accounting.college.hmco.com/students.

Chapter Review

Review of Learning Objectives

LO1 Define *net income* and its two major components, *revenues* and *expenses.*

Net income is the net increase in owner's equity that results from the operations of a company. Net income equals revenues minus expenses, unless expenses exceed revenues, in which case a net loss results. Revenues equal the price of goods sold and services rendered during a specific period. Expenses are the costs of goods and services used up in the process of producing revenues.

LO2 Explain how the income measurement issues of accounting period, continuity, and matching are resolved.

The accounting period issue recognizes that net income measurements for short periods of time are necessarily tentative. The continuity issue recognizes that even though businesses face an uncertain future, without evidence to the contrary, accountants must assume that a business will continue indefinitely. The matching issue has to do with the difficulty of assigning revenues and expenses to a period of time. It is addressed by applying the matching rule: Revenues must be assigned to the accounting period in which the goods are sold or the services performed, and expenses must be assigned to the accounting period in which they are used to produce revenue.

LO3 Define *accrual accounting* and explain three broad ways of accomplishing it.

Accrual accounting consists of all the techniques developed by accountants to apply the matching rule. Three broad ways of accomplishing it are by recognizing revenues when earned, recognizing expenses when incurred, and adjusting the accounts.

LO4 State four principal situations that require adjusting entries and prepare typical adjusting entries.

Adjusting entries are required when (1) recorded costs have to be allocated between two or more accounting periods, (2) unrecorded expenses exist, (3) recorded unearned revenues must be allocated between two or more accounting periods, and (4) unrecorded revenues exist. The preparation of adjusting entries is summarized as follows:

Type of Adjusting Entry	Type of Account: Debited	Type of Account: Credited	Balance Sheet Account Examples
1. Allocating recorded costs (previously paid, expired)	Expense	Asset (or contra-asset)	Prepaid Rent Prepaid Insurance Supplies Accumulated Depreciation, Buildings Accumulated Depreciation, Equipment
2. Accrued expenses (incurred, not paid)	Expense	Liability	Wages Payable Interest Payable
3. Allocating recorded unearned revenues (previously received, earned)	Liability	Revenue	Unearned Fees
4. Accrued revenues (earned, not received)	Asset	Revenue	Accounts Receivable Interest Receivable

LO5 Prepare financial statements from an adjusted trial balance.

An adjusted trial balance is prepared after adjusting entries have been posted to the accounts. Its purpose is to test whether the adjusting entries are posted correctly before the financial statements are prepared. The income statement is prepared from the revenue and expense accounts in the adjusted trial balance. The balance sheet is prepared from the asset and liability accounts in the adjusted trial balance and from the statement of owner's equity.

Supplemental Objective

SO6 Analyze cash flows from accrual-based information.

Cash flow information relates to management's liquidity goal. The general rule for determining the cash flow effect of any revenue or expense (except depreciation, which is a special case not covered here) is to determine the potential cash payments or cash receipts and deduct the amount not paid or received.

Review of Concepts and Terminology

The following concepts and terms were introduced in this chapter:

LO2 **Accounting period issue:** The difficulty of assigning revenues and expenses to a short period of time.

LO4 **Accrual:** The recognition of an expense or revenue that has arisen but has not yet been recorded.

LO3 **Accrual accounting:** The attempt to record the financial effects of transactions and other events in the periods in which those transactions or events occur, rather than only in the periods in which cash is received or paid by the business; all the techniques developed by accountants to apply the matching rule.

LO4 **Accrued expenses:** Expenses incurred but not recognized in the accounts; unrecorded expenses.

LO4 **Accrued revenues:** Revenues for which a service has been performed or goods delivered but for which no entry has been made; unrecorded revenues.

LO4 **Accumulated depreciation accounts:** Contra-asset accounts used to accumulate the depreciation expense of specific long-lived assets.

LO5 **Adjusted trial balance:** A trial balance prepared after all adjusting entries have been recorded and posted to the accounts.

LO4 **Adjusting entries:** Entries made to apply accrual accounting to transactions that span more than one accounting period.

LO4 **Carrying value:** The unexpired portion of the cost of an asset. Also called *book value.*

LO2 **Cash basis of accounting:** Accounting for revenues and expenses on a cash received and cash paid basis.

LO2 **Continuity issue:** The difficulty associated with not knowing how long a business entity will survive.

LO4 **Contra account:** An account whose balance is subtracted from an associated account in the financial statements.

LO4 **Deferral:** The postponement of the recognition of an expense that already has been paid or of a revenue that already has been received.

LO4 **Depreciation:** The portion of the cost of a tangible long-term asset allocated to any one accounting period. Also called *depreciation expense.*

LO1 **Expenses:** Decreases in owner's equity resulting from the costs of goods and services used up in the course of earning revenues. Also called *cost of doing business* or *expired costs.*

LO2 **Fiscal year:** Any 12-month accounting period used by an economic entity.

LO2 **Going concern:** The assumption, unless there is evidence to the contrary, that a business entity will continue to operate indefinitely.

LO2 **Matching rule:** Revenues must be assigned to the accounting period in which the goods are sold or the services performed, and expenses must be assigned to the accounting period in which they are used to produce revenue.

LO1 **Net income:** The net increase in owner's equity that results from business operations and is accumulated in the owner's Capital account; revenues less expenses when revenues exceed expenses.

LO1 **Net loss:** The net decrease in owner's equity that results from business operations when expenses exceed revenues. It is accumulated in the owner's Capital account.

LO2 **Periodicity:** The recognition that net income for any period less than the life of the business, although tentative, is still a useful measure.

LO4 **Prepaid expenses:** Expenses paid in advance that have not yet expired; an asset account.

LO1 **Profit:** The increase in owner's equity that results from business operations.

LO3 **Revenue recognition:** In accrual accounting, the process of determining when revenue is earned.

LO1 **Revenues:** Increases in owner's equity resulting from selling goods, rendering services, or performing other business activities.

LO4 **Unearned revenues:** Revenues received in advance for which the goods have not yet been delivered or the services performed; a liability account.

REVIEW PROBLEM

Determining Adjusting Entries, Posting to T Accounts, Preparing Adjusted Trial Balance, and Preparing Financial Statements

LO4
LO5 The following is the unadjusted trial balance for Certified Answering Service on December 31, 20x5:

Certified Answering Service
Trial Balance
December 31, 20x5

Cash	$2,160	
Accounts Receivable	1,250	
Office Supplies	180	
Prepaid Insurance	240	
Office Equipment	3,400	
Accumulated Depreciation, Office Equipment		$ 600
Accounts Payable		700
Unearned Revenue		460
James Neal, Capital		4,870
James Neal, Withdrawals	400	
Answering Service Revenue		2,900
Wages Expense	1,500	
Rent Expense	400	
	$9,530	$9,530

The following information is also available:

a. Insurance that expired during December amounted to $40.
b. Office supplies on hand at the end of December totaled $75.

c. Depreciation for the month of December totaled $100.
d. Accrued wages at the end of December totaled $120.
e. Revenues earned for services performed in December but not yet billed on December 31 totaled $300.
f. Revenues earned in December for services performed that were paid in advance totaled $160.

REQUIRED ▶
1. Prepare T accounts for the accounts in the trial balance and enter the balances.
2. Determine the required adjusting entries and record them directly to the T accounts. Open new T accounts as needed.
3. Prepare an adjusted trial balance.
4. Prepare an income statement, a statement of owner's equity, and a balance sheet for the month ended December 31, 20x5.

Answer to Review Problem

1. T accounts set up and amounts from trial balance entered
2. Adjusting entries recorded

Cash

Bal.	2,160		

Accounts Receivable

Bal.	1,250		
(e)	300		
Bal.	1,550		

Office Supplies

Bal.	180	(b)	105
Bal.	75		

Prepaid Insurance

Bal.	240	(a)	40
Bal.	200		

Office Equipment

Bal.	3,400		

Accumulated Depreciation, Office Equipment

		Bal.	600
		(c)	100
		Bal.	700

Accounts Payable

		Bal.	700

Unearned Revenue

(f)	160	Bal.	460
		Bal.	300

Wages Payable

		(d)	120

James Neal, Capital

		Bal.	4,870

James Neal, Withdrawals

Bal.	400		

Answering Service Revenue

		Bal.	2,900
		(e)	300
		(f)	160
		Bal.	3,360

Wages Expense

Bal.	1,500		
(d)	120		
Bal.	1,620		

Rent Expense

Bal.	400		

Insurance Expense

(a)	40		

Office Supplies Expense

(b)	105		

Depreciation Expense, Office Equipment

(c)	100		

3. Adjusted trial balance prepared

Certified Answering Service
Adjusted Trial Balance
December 31, 20x5

Cash	$ 2,160	
Accounts Receivable	1,550	
Office Supplies	75	
Prepaid Insurance	200	
Office Equipment	3,400	
Accumulated Depreciation, Office Equipment		$ 700
Accounts Payable		700
Unearned Revenue		300
Wages Payable		120
James Neal, Capital		4,870
James Neal, Withdrawals	400	
Answering Service Revenue		3,360
Wages Expense	1,620	
Rent Expense	400	
Insurance Expense	40	
Office Supplies Expense	105	
Depreciation Expense, Office Equipment	100	
	$10,050	$10,050

4. Financial statements prepared

Certified Answering Service
Income Statement
For the Month Ended December 31, 20x5

Revenues		
Answering service revenue		$3,360
Expenses		
Wages expense	$1,620	
Rent expense	400	
Insurance expense	40	
Office supplies expense	105	
Depreciation expense, office equipment	100	
Total expenses		2,265
Net income		$1,095

Financial statements prepared (*continued*)

Certified Answering Service
Statement of Owner's Equity
For the Month Ended December 31, 20x5

James Neal, Capital, November 30, 20x5	$4,870
Net income	1,095
Subtotal	$5,965
Less withdrawals	400
James Neal, Capital, December 31, 20x5	$5,565

Financial statements prepared (*continued*)

Certified Answering Service
Balance Sheet
December 31, 20x5

Assets		
Cash		$2,160
Accounts receivable		1,550
Office supplies		75
Prepaid insurance		200
Office equipment	$3,400	
Less accumulated depreciation	700	2,700
Total assets		$6,685
Liabilities		
Accounts payable		$ 700
Unearned revenue		300
Wages payable		120
Total liabilities		$1,120
Owner's Equity		
James Neal, Capital		5,565
Total liabilities and owner's equity		$6,685

Chapter Assignments

BUILDING YOUR KNOWLEDGE FOUNDATION

QUESTIONS

1. Why does the accountant use the term *net income* instead of *profit?*
2. Why does the need for an accounting period cause problems?
3. What is the significance of the continuity assumption?
4. "The matching rule is the most significant concept in accounting." Do you agree with this statement? Explain your answer.
5. What are the conditions for recognizing revenue?
6. What is the difference between the cash basis and the accrual basis of accounting?
7. In what three ways is accrual accounting accomplished?
8. Why are adjusting entries necessary?
9. What are the four situations that require adjusting entries? Give an example of each.
10. "Some assets are expenses that have not expired." Explain this statement.
11. What do plant and equipment, office supplies, and prepaid insurance have in common?
12. What is the difference between accumulated depreciation and depreciation expense?
13. What is a contra account? Give an example.
14. Why are contra accounts used to record depreciation?
15. How does unearned revenue arise? Give an example.
16. Where does unearned revenue appear in the financial statements?
17. What accounting problem does a magazine publisher who sells three-year subscriptions have?
18. Under what circumstances does a company have accrued revenues? Give an example. What asset arises when the adjustment is made?
19. What is an accrued expense? Give two examples.
20. "Why worry about adjustments? Doesn't it all come out in the wash?" Discuss these questions.
21. Why is the income statement usually the first statement prepared from the adjusted trial balance?
22. To what management goals do the measurements of net income and cash flow relate?

SHORT EXERCISES

SE 1. LO2 LO3 **Accrual Accounting Concepts**

Match the concepts of accrual accounting on the right with the assumptions or actions on the left:

1. Assumes expenses can be assigned to the accounting period in which they are used to produce revenues
2. Assumes a business will last indefinitely
3. Assumes revenues are earned at a point in time
4. Assumes net income measured for a short period of time, such as one quarter, is a useful measure

a. Periodicity
b. Going concern
c. Matching rule
d. Revenue recognition

SE 2. LO4 **Adjustment for Prepaid Insurance**

The Prepaid Insurance account began the year with a balance of $230. During the year, insurance in the amount of $570 was purchased. At the end of the year (December 31), the amount of insurance still unexpired was $350. Make the year-end entry in journal form to record the adjustment for insurance expense for the year.

SE 3. LO4 **Adjustment for Supplies**

The Supplies account began the year with a balance of $190. During the year, supplies in the amount of $490 were purchased. At the end of the year (December 31), the inventory of supplies on hand was $220. Make the year-end entry in journal form to record the adjustment for supplies expense for the year.

SE 4. LO4 **Adjustment for Depreciation**

The depreciation expense on office equipment for the month of March is $50. This is the third month that the office equipment, which cost $950, has been owned. Prepare the adjusting entry in journal form to record depreciation for March and show the balance sheet presentation for office equipment and related accounts after the adjustment.

SE 5. LO4 **Adjustment for Accrued Wages**

Wages are paid each Saturday for a six-day work week. Wages are currently running $690 per week. Make the adjusting entry required on June 30, assuming July 1 falls on a Tuesday.

SE 6. LO4 **Adjustment for Unearned Revenue**

During the month of August, deposits in the amount of $550 were received for services to be performed. By the end of the month, services in the amount of $380 had been performed. Prepare the necessary adjustment for Service Revenue at the end of the month.

SE 7. LO5 **Preparation of an Income Statement from an Adjusted Trial Balance**

The adjusted trial balance for Hailston Company on December 31, 20x3, contains the following accounts and balances: Owner's Capital, $4,300; Withdrawals, $350; Service Revenue, $2,600; Rent Expense, $400; Wages Expense, $900; Utilities Expense, $200; Telephone Expense, $50; and Insurance Expense, $350. Prepare an income statement in proper form for the month of December.

SE 8. LO5 **Preparation of a Statement of Owner's Equity**

Using the data in **SE 7,** prepare a statement of owner's equity for Hailston Company.

SE 9. SO6 **Determination of Cash Flows**

Wages Payable was $590 at the end of May and $920 at the end of June. Wages Expense for June was $2,300. How much cash was paid for wages during June?

SE 10. SO6 **Determination of Cash Flows**

Unearned Revenue was $1,300 at the end of November and $900 at the end of December. Service Revenue was $5,100 for the month of December. How much cash was received for services provided during December?

EXERCISES

E 1. LO2 LO3 LO4 **Applications of Accounting Concepts Related to Accrual Accounting**

The accountant for Sparks Company makes the assumptions or performs the activities listed below. Tell which of the following concepts of accrual accounting most directly relates to each assumption or action: (a) periodicity, (b) going concern, (c) matching rule, (d) revenue recognition, (e) deferral, and (f) accrual.

1. In estimating the life of a building, assumes that the business will last indefinitely
2. Records a sale when the customer is billed
3. Postpones the recognition of a one-year insurance policy as an expense by initially recording the expenditure as an asset
4. Recognizes the usefulness of financial statements prepared on a monthly basis even though they are based on estimates
5. Recognizes, by making an adjusting entry, wages expense that has been incurred but not yet recorded
6. Prepares an income statement that shows the revenues earned and the expenses incurred during the accounting period

E 2. LO3 **Application of Conditions for Revenue Recognition**

Four conditions must be met before revenue should be recognized. In each of the following cases, tell which condition has *not* been met:

a. Company A accepts a contract to perform services in the future for $1,000.
b. Company B ships products to another company worth $1,500 without an order from the other company but tells the company that it can return the products if it does not sell them.
c. Company C performs services totaling $5,000 for a company that is in financial difficulty.
d. Company D agrees to work out a price later for services that it performs for another company.

E 3. LO4 **Adjusting Entry for Unearned Revenue**

Green Mountain Company of Montpelier, Vermont, publishes a monthly magazine featuring local restaurant reviews and upcoming social, cultural, and sporting events. Subscribers pay for subscriptions either one year or two years in advance. Cash received from subscribers is credited to an account called Magazine Subscriptions Received in

Advance. On December 31, 20x3, the end of the company's fiscal year, the balance of this account was $1,000,000. Expiration of subscriptions revenue is as follows:

During 20x3	$200,000
During 20x4	500,000
During 20x5	300,000

Prepare the adjusting entry in journal form for December 31, 20x3.

E 4. LO4 **Adjusting Entries for Prepaid Insurance**

An examination of the Prepaid Insurance account shows a balance of $4,112 at the end of an accounting period, before adjustment. Prepare entries in journal form to record the insurance expense for the period under the following independent assumptions:

1. An examination of the insurance policies shows unexpired insurance that cost $1,974 at the end of the period.
2. An examination of the insurance policies shows that insurance that cost $694 has expired during the period.

E 5. LO4 **Supplies Account: Missing Data**

Each of the following columns represents a Supplies account:

	a	b	c	d
Supplies on hand, October 1	$396	$ 651	$294	$?
Supplies purchased during the month	78	?	261	2,892
Supplies consumed during the month	291	1,458	?	2,448
Supplies on hand, October 31	?	654	84	1,782

1. Determine the amounts indicated by the question marks.
2. Make the adjusting entry for column **a,** assuming supplies purchased are debited to an asset account.

E 6. LO4 **Adjusting Entry for Accrued Salaries**

Hasterson has a five-day work week and pays salaries of $70,000 each Friday.

1. Make the adjusting entry required on July 31, assuming that August 1 falls on a Wednesday.
2. Make the entry to pay the salaries on August 3.

E 7. LO4 **Revenue and Expense Recognition**

Swan Company produces computer software that is sold by Celestial Systems Company. Swan receives a royalty of 15 percent of sales. Royalties are paid by Celestial Systems and received by Swan semiannually on May 1 for sales made July through December of the previous year and on November 1 for sales made January through June of the current year. Royalty expense for Celestial Systems and royalty income for Swan in the amount of $12,000 were accrued on December 31, 20x2. Cash in the amounts of $12,000 and $20,000 was paid and received on May 1 and November 1, 20x3, respectively. Software sales during the July to December 20x3 period totaled $300,000.

1. Calculate the amount of royalty expense for Celestial Systems and royalty income for Swan during 20x3.
2. Record the appropriate adjusting entry made by each company on December 31, 20x3.

E 8. LO4 **Adjusting Entries**

Prepare year-end adjusting entries for each of the following:

1. Office Supplies had a balance of $168 on January 1. Purchases debited to Office Supplies during the year amount to $830. A year-end inventory reveals supplies of $570 on hand.
2. Depreciation of office equipment is estimated to be $4,260 for the year.
3. Property taxes for six months, estimated at $1,750, have accrued but have not been recorded.
4. Unrecorded interest receivable on U.S. government bonds is $1,700.
5. Unearned Revenue has a balance of $1,800. Services for $600 received in advance have now been performed.
6. Services totaling $400 have been performed; the customer has not yet been billed.

E 9. LO4 **Accounting for Revenue Received in Advance**

Hiski Jurgen, a lawyer, was paid $72,000 on April 1 to represent a client in certain real estate negotiations over the next 12 months.

1. Record the entries required in Jurgen's records on April 1 and at the end of the year, December 31.
2. How would this transaction be reflected on the income statement and balance sheet on December 31?

E 10. **LO5 Preparation of Financial Statements**

Prepare the monthly income statement, statement of owner's equity, and balance sheet for Sparkle Bright Services from the data provided in this adjusted trial balance.

Sparkle Bright Services
Adjusted Trial Balance
August 31, 20xx

Cash	$ 4,590	
Accounts Receivable	2,592	
Prepaid Insurance	380	
Prepaid Rent	200	
Cleaning Supplies	152	
Cleaning Equipment	3,200	
Accumulated Depreciation, Cleaning Equipment		$ 320
Truck	7,200	
Accumulated Depreciation, Truck		720
Accounts Payable		420
Wages Payable		80
Unearned Janitorial Revenue		920
Jim Harrington, Capital		15,034
Jim Harrington, Withdrawals	2,000	
Janitorial Revenue		14,620
Wages Expense	5,680	
Rent Expense	1,200	
Gas, Oil, and Other Truck Expenses	580	
Insurance Expense	380	
Supplies Expense	2,920	
Depreciation Expense, Cleaning Equipment	320	
Depreciation Expense, Truck	720	
	$32,114	$32,114

E 11. **SO6 Determination of Cash Flows**

After adjusting entries had been made, the 20x4 and 20x5 balance sheets of Akbar Company showed the following asset and liability amounts at the end of each year:

	20x4	20x5
Prepaid insurance	$1,450	$1,200
Wages payable	1,100	600
Unearned fees	950	2,100

From the accounting records, the following amounts of cash disbursements and cash receipts for 20x5 were determined:

Cash disbursed to pay insurance premiums	$1,900
Cash disbursed to pay wages	9,750
Cash received for fees	4,450

Calculate the amount of insurance expense, wages expense, and fees earned that should be reported on the 20x5 income statement.

E 12. **SO6 Determination of Cash Flows**

Sun Newspaper Agency delivers morning, evening, and Sunday city newspapers to subscribers who live in the suburbs. Customers can pay a yearly subscription fee in advance (at a savings) or pay monthly after delivery of their newspapers. The following data are available for the Subscriptions Receivable and Unearned Subscriptions accounts at the beginning and end of October 20xx

	October 1	October 31
Subscriptions Receivable	$ 7,600	$ 9,200
Unearned Subscriptions	22,800	19,600

The income statement shows subscriptions revenue for October of $44,800. Determine the amount of cash received from customers for subscriptions during October. Why is this calculation important to management?

E 13. **SO6 Relationship of Expenses to Cash Paid**

The income statement for Gemini Company included the following expenses for 20xx:

Rent expense	$ 5,200
Interest expense	7,800
Salaries expense	83,000

Listed below are the related balance sheet account balances at year end for last year and this year:

	Last Year	This Year
Prepaid rent	—	$ 900
Interest payable	$1,200	—
Salaries payable	5,000	9,600

1. Compute the cash paid for rent during the year.
2. Compute the cash paid for interest during the year.
3. Compute the cash paid for salaries during the year.

PROBLEMS

P 1. **LO4 Determining Adjustments**

At the end of its fiscal year, the trial balance for Desabrais Cleaners appears as follows:

Desabrais Cleaners
Trial Balance
September 30, 20x4

Cash	$ 11,788	
Accounts Receivable	26,494	
Prepaid Insurance	3,400	
Cleaning Supplies	7,374	
Land	18,000	
Building	185,000	
Accumulated Depreciation, Building		$ 45,600
Accounts Payable		20,400
Unearned Dry Cleaning Revenue		1,600
Mortgage Payable		110,000
Lucille Desabrais, Capital		56,560
Lucille Desabrais, Withdrawals	10,000	
Dry Cleaning Revenue		120,334
Laundry Revenue		37,300
Wages Expense	101,330	
Cleaning Equipment Rental Expense	6,000	
Telephone Expense	4,374	
Interest Expense	11,000	
Other Expenses	7,034	
	$391,794	$391,794

The following information is also available:

a. A study of the company's insurance policies shows that $680 is unexpired at the end of the year.
b. An inventory of cleaning supplies shows $1,244 on hand.

c. Estimated depreciation on the building for the year is $12,800.
d. Accrued interest on the mortgage payable amounts to $1,000.
e. On September 1, the company signed a contract, effective immediately, with Kings County Hospital to dry clean, for a fixed monthly charge of $400, the uniforms used by doctors in surgery. The hospital paid for four months' service in advance.
f. Sales and delivery wages are paid on Saturday. The weekly payroll is $2,520. September 30 falls on a Thursday and the company has a six-day pay week.

REQUIRED ▶ All adjustments affect one balance sheet account and one income statement account. For each of the above situations, show the accounts affected, the amount of the adjustment (using a + or − to indicate an increase or decrease), and the balance of the account after the adjustment in the following format:

Balance Sheet Account	Amount of Adjustment (+ or −)	Balance after Adjustment	Income Statement Account	Amount of Adjustment (+ or −)	Balance after Adjustment

P 2. LO3 LO4 **Preparing Adjusting Entries**

On June 30, the end of the current fiscal year, the following information was available to aid the Worcester Company's accountants in making adjusting entries:

a. Among the liabilities of the company is a mortgage payable in the amount of $240,000. On June 30, the accrued interest on this mortgage amounted to $12,000.
b. On Friday, July 2, the company, which is on a five-day workweek and pays employees weekly, will pay its regular salaried employees $19,200.
c. On June 29, the company completed negotiations and signed a contract to provide services to a new client at an annual rate of $3,600.
d. The Supplies account showed a beginning balance of $1,615 and purchases during the year of $3,766. The end-of-year inventory revealed supplies on hand of $1,186.
e. The Prepaid Insurance account showed the following entries on June 30:

Beginning Balance	$1,530
January 1	2,900
May 1	3,366

The beginning balance represents the unexpired portion of a one-year policy purchased the previous year. The January 1 entry represents a new one-year policy, and the May 1 entry represents the additional coverage of a three-year policy.

f. The following table contains the cost and annual depreciation for buildings and equipment, all of which were purchased before the current year:

Account	Cost	Annual Depreciation
Buildings	$185,000	$ 7,300
Equipment	218,000	21,800

g. On June 1, the company completed negotiations with another client and accepted a payment of $21,000, representing one year's services paid in advance. The $21,000 was credited to Services Collected in Advance.
h. The company calculated that as of June 30 it had earned $3,500 on a $7,500 contract that will be completed and billed in August.

REQUIRED ▶
1. Prepare adjusting entries for each item listed above.
2. Explain how the conditions for revenue recognition are applied to transactions **c** and **h**.

P 3. LO4 **Determining Adjusting Entries, Posting to T Accounts, and Preparing an Adjusted Trial Balance**

The trial balance for the Omega Advisory Company on March 31, 20x4, appears at the top of the next page.

The following information is also available:

a. Ending inventory of office supplies, $172.
b. Prepaid rent expired, $1,400.
c. Depreciation of office equipment for the period, $1,200.
d. Interest accrued on the note payable, $1,200.
e. Salaries accrued at the end of the period, $400.
f. Fees still unearned at the end of the period, $2,820.
g. Fees earned but not billed, $1,200.

REQUIRED ▶
1. Open T accounts for the accounts in the trial balance plus the following: Interest Payable; Salaries Payable; Office Supplies Expense; Depreciation Expense, Office Equipment; and Interest Expense. Enter the balances shown on the trial balance.

Omega Advisory Company Trial Balance March 31, 20x4		
Cash	$25,572	
Accounts Receivable	49,680	
Office Supplies	1,982	
Prepaid Rent	2,800	
Office Equipment	13,400	
Accumulated Depreciation, Office Equipment		$ 3,200
Accounts Payable		3,640
Notes Payable		20,000
Unearned Service Revenue		5,720
James Georgios, Capital		58,774
James Georgios, Withdrawals	30,000	
Service Revenue		117,000
Salaries Expense	66,000	
Utilities Expense	3,500	
Rent Expense	15,400	
	$208,334	$208,334

2. Determine the adjusting entries and post them directly to the T accounts.
3. Prepare an adjusted trial balance.

LO4 LO5 Determining Adjusting Entries and Tracing Their Effects to Financial Statements

P 4. Here is the trial balance for Broadway Dance Studio at the end of its current fiscal year.

Broadway Dance Studio Trial Balance October 31, 20x4		
Cash (111)	$ 1,028	
Accounts Receivable (112)	517	
Supplies (115)	170	
Prepaid Rent (116)	400	
Prepaid Insurance (117)	360	
Equipment (141)	4,100	
Accumulated Depreciation, Equipment (142)		$ 400
Accounts Payable (211)		380
Unearned Dance Fees (213)		900
Margrit Berger, Capital (311)		2,500
Margrit Berger, Withdrawals (312)	12,000	
Dance Fees (411)		20,995
Wages Expense (511)	3,200	
Rent Expense (512)	2,200	
Utilities Expense (515)	1,200	
	$25,175	$25,175

Margrit Berger made no investments in the business during the year. The following information is available to assist in the preparation of adjusting entries:

a. An inventory of supplies reveals $92 still on hand.

b. The prepaid rent reflects the rent for October plus the rent for the last month of the lease.
c. Prepaid insurance consists of a two-year policy purchased on May 1, 20x4.
d. Depreciation on equipment is estimated at $800.
e. Accrued wages are $65 on October 31.
f. Two-thirds of the unearned dance fees have been earned by October 31.

REQUIRED ▶

1. Record the adjusting entries in the general journal (Page 53).
2. Open ledger accounts for the accounts in the trial balance plus the following: Wages Payable (212); Supplies Expense (513); Insurance Expense (514); and Depreciation Expense, Equipment (516). Record the balances shown on the trial balance.
3. Post the adjusting entries from the general journal to the ledger accounts, showing the correct references.
4. Prepare an adjusted trial balance, an income statement, a statement of owner's equity, and a balance sheet.

P 5.
LO4 Determining Adjusting Entries
LO5 and Tracing Their Effects to Financial Statements

Having graduated from college with a degree in accounting, Bonnie Vitali opened a small tax-preparation service. At the end of its second year of operation, Vitali Tax Service had the trial balance shown below.

Vitali Tax Service
Trial Balance
December 31, 20x4

Cash	$ 2,268	
Accounts Receivable	1,031	
Prepaid Insurance	240	
Office Supplies	782	
Office Equipment	4,100	
Accumulated Depreciation, Office Equipment		$ 410
Copier	3,000	
Accumulated Depreciation, Copier		360
Accounts Payable		635
Unearned Service Revenue		219
Bonnie Vitali, Capital		5,439
Bonnie Vitali, Withdrawals	6,000	
Service Revenue		21,926
Office Salaries Expense	8,300	
Advertising Expense	650	
Rent Expense	2,400	
Telephone Expense	218	
	$28,989	$28,989

The following information was also available:

a. Office supplies on hand, December 31, 20x4, were $227.
b. Insurance still unexpired amounted to $120.
c. Estimated depreciation of office equipment was $410.
d. Estimated depreciation of the copier was $360.
e. The telephone expense for December was $19. Bill was received but not recorded.
f. The services for all unearned tax fees had been performed by the end of the year.

REQUIRED ▶

1. Open T accounts for the accounts in the trial balance plus the following: Insurance Expense; Office Supplies Expense; Depreciation Expense, Office Equipment; and Depreciation Expense, Copier. Record the balances shown in the trial balance.
2. Determine the adjusting entries and post them directly to the T accounts.
3. Prepare an adjusted trial balance, an income statement, a statement of owner's equity, and a balance sheet.

Alternate Problems

P 6. LO4 **Determining Adjustments**

At the end of the first three months of operation, the trial balance of Beacon County Answering Service appears as shown below. Ven Lien, the owner of Beacon County, has hired an accountant to prepare financial statements to determine how well the company is doing after three months. Upon examining the accounting records, the accountant finds the following items of interest:

a. An inventory of office supplies reveals supplies on hand of $133.
b. The Prepaid Rent account includes the rent for the first three months plus a deposit for April's rent.
c. Depreciation on the equipment for the first three months is $208.
d. The balance of the Unearned Answering Service Revenue account represents a 12-month service contract paid in advance on February 1.
e. On March 31, accrued wages total $80.

The balance of the Capital acccount represents investments by Ven Lien.

Beacon County Answering Service
Trial Balance
March 31, 20xx

Cash	$ 3,482	
Accounts Receivable	4,236	
Office Supplies	903	
Prepaid Rent	800	
Equipment	4,700	
Accounts Payable		$ 2,673
Unearned Answering Service Revenue		888
Ven Lien, Capital		5,933
Ven Lien, Withdrawals	2,130	
Answering Service Revenue		9,002
Wages Expense	1,900	
Office Cleaning Expense	345	
	$18,496	$18,496

REQUIRED ▶ All adjustments affect one balance sheet account and one income statement account. For each of the above situations, show the accounts affected, the amount of the adjustment (using a + or − to indicate an increase or decrease), and the balance of the account after the adjustment in the following format.

Balance Sheet Account	Amount of Adjustment (+ or −)	Balance after Adjustment	Income Statement Account	Amount of Adjustment (+ or −)	Balance after Adjustment

P 7. LO3 LO4 **Preparing Adjusting Entries**

On May 31, the end of the current fiscal year, the following information was available to help Lightfoot Company's accountants make adjusting entries:

a. The Supplies account showed a beginning balance of $4,348. Purchases of supplies during the year totaled $9,052. The end-of-year inventory revealed supplies on hand that cost $2,794.
b. The Prepaid Insurance account showed the following on May 31:

Beginning Balance	$ 7,160
February 1	8,400
April 1	14,544

The beginning balance represents the portion of a one-year policy that remained unexpired at the beginning of the current fiscal year. The February 1 entry represents a new one-year policy, and the April 1 entry represents additional coverage in the form of a three-year policy.

c. The following table contains the cost and annual depreciation for buildings and equipment, all of which were purchased before the current year:

Account	Cost	Annual Depreciation
Buildings	$572,000	$29,000
Equipment	748,000	79,800

d. On March 1, the company completed negotiations with a client and accepted payment of $33,600, which represented one year's services paid in advance. The $33,600 was credited to Unearned Service Revenue.
e. The company calculated that as of May 31, it had earned $8,000 on a $22,000 contract that will be completed and billed in September.
f. Among the liabilities of the company is a note payable in the amount of $600,000. On May 31, the accrued interest on this note amounted to $30,000.
g. On Saturday, June 2, the company, which is on a six-day workweek, will pay its regular salaried employees $24,600.
h. On May 29, the company completed negotiations and signed a contract to provide services to a new client at an annual rate of $35,000.

REQUIRED

1. Prepare adjusting entries for each item listed above.
2. Explain how the conditions for revenue recognition are applied to transactions **e** and **h**.

P 8. This is the trial balance for Wu's Transcription Services on December 31, 20x4:

LO4 Determining Adjusting Entries, Posting to T Accounts, and Preparing an Adjusted Trial Balance

Wu's Transcription Services
Trial Balance
December 31, 20x4

Cash	$ 16,500	
Accounts Receivable	8,250	
Office Supplies	2,662	
Prepaid Rent	1,320	
Office Equipment	9,240	
Accumulated Depreciation, Office Equipment		$ 1,540
Accounts Payable		5,940
Notes Payable		11,000
Unearned Service Revenue		2,970
Stephanie Wu, Capital		24,002
Stephanie Wu, Withdrawals	22,000	
Service Revenue		72,600
Salaries Expense	49,400	
Rent Expense	4,400	
Utilities Expense	4,280	
	$118,052	$118,052

The following information is also available:

a. Ending inventory of office supplies, $264.
b. Prepaid rent expired, $440.
c. Depreciation of office equipment for the period, $660.
d. Accrued interest expense at the end of the period, $550.
e. Accrued salaries at the end of the month, $330.
f. Fees still unearned at the end of the period, $1,166.
g. Fees earned but unrecorded, $2,200.

REQUIRED

1. Open T accounts for the accounts in the trial balance plus the following: Interest Payable; Salaries Payable; Office Supplies Expense; Depreciation Expense, Office Equipment; and Interest Expense. Enter the account balances.
2. Determine the adjusting entries and post them directly to the T accounts.
3. Prepare an adjusted trial balance.

Skills Development Cases

Conceptual Analysis

SD 1.

LO2 LO3 LO4 **Importance of Adjustments**

Never Flake Company, which operated in the northeastern part of the United States, provided a rust-prevention coating for the underside of new automobiles. The company advertised widely and offered its services through new car dealers. When a dealer sold a new car, the dealer's salesperson attempted to sell the rust-prevention coating as an option. The protective coating was supposed to make cars last longer in the severe northeastern winters. An important selling point was Never Flake's warranty, which stated that the company would repair any damage due to rust at no charge for as long as the buyer owned the car.

During the 1990s, Never Flake was very successful in generating enough cash to continue operations. But in 2001 the company suddenly declared bankruptcy. Company officials said that the firm had only $5.5 million in assets against liabilities of $32.9 million. Most of the liabilities represented potential claims under the company's lifetime warranty. It seemed that owners were keeping their cars longer now than previously. Therefore, more damage was being attributed to rust. Discuss what accounting decisions could have helped Never Flake to survive under these circumstances.

Group Activity: Divide the class into groups to discuss this case. Then debrief as a class by asking a person from each group to comment.

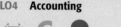

SD 2.

LO3 LO4 **Application of Accrual Accounting**

The Lyric Opera of Chicago <www.lyricopera.com> is one of the largest and best-managed opera companies in the United States. Managing opera productions requires advance planning, including the development of scenery, costumes, and stage properties and the sale of tickets. To measure how well the company is operating in any given year, accrual accounting must be applied to these and other transactions. At year end, April 30, 2001, Lyric Opera's balance sheet showed Deferred Production Costs of $1,639,949 and Deferred Ticket Revenue of $19,100,781.[7] Be prepared to discuss what accounting policies and adjusting entries are applicable to these accounts. Why are they important to Lyric Opera's management?

Ethical Dilemma

SD 3.

LO2 LO3 LO4 **Importance of Adjustments**

Central Appliance Service Company has achieved fast growth in the St. Louis area by selling service contracts on large appliances, such as washers, dryers, and refrigerators. For a fee, Central Appliance agrees to provide all parts and labor on an appliance after the regular warranty runs out. For example, by paying a fee of $200, a person who buys a dishwasher can add two years (years 2 and 3) to the regular one-year (year 1) warranty on the appliance. In 2004, the company sold service contracts in the amount of $1.8 million, all of which applied to future years. Management wanted all the sales recorded as revenues in 2004, contending that the amount of the contracts could be determined and the cash had been received.

Discuss whether you agree with the logic of Central Appliance's management. How would you record the cash receipts? What assumptions do you think should be made? Would you consider it unethical to follow management's recommendation? Who might be hurt or helped by this action?

Research Activity

SD 4.

LO4 **Real-World Observation of Business Activities**

Choose a company with which you are familiar. Visit the company and observe its operations. For example, it can be where you work, where you eat, or where you buy things. Identify at least two sources of revenue for the company and six types of expenses. For each type of revenue and each type of expense, determine whether it is probable that an adjusting entry is required at the end of the accounting period and specify whether the adjusting entry is a deferred revenue, deferred expense, accrued revenue, or accrued expense.

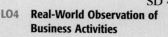

Decision-Making Practice

SD 5.
LO1 Adjusting Entries and
LO4 Performance Evaluation

Ginny Baxter, the owner of a newsletter for managers of hotels and restaurants, has prepared the following condensed amounts from her company's financial statements for 20x3:

Revenues	$346,000
Expenses	282,000
Net income	$ 64,000
Total assets	$172,000
Liabilities	$ 48,000
Owner's equity	124,000
Total liabilities and owner's equity	$172,000

Given these figures, Baxter is planning to withdraw $50,000 for personal expenses. However, Baxter's accountant has found that the following items were overlooked:

a. Although the balance of the Printing Supplies account is $32,000, only $14,000 in supplies is on hand at the end of the year.
b. Depreciation of $20,000 on equipment has not been recorded.
c. Wages of $9,400 have been earned by Baxter's employees but not recognized in the accounts.
d. A liability account called Unearned Subscriptions has a balance of $16,200, although it has been determined that one-third of these subscriptions have been mailed to subscribers.

1. Prepare the necessary adjusting entries.
2. Recast the condensed financial statement figures after you have made the necessary adjustments.
3. Discuss the performance of Baxter's business after the adjustments have been made. (**Hint:** Compare net income to revenues (divide net income by revenues) and total assets (divide net income by total assets) before and after the adjustments.) Do you think that making the withdrawal is advisable?

FINANCIAL REPORTING AND ANALYSIS CASES

Interpreting Financial Reports

FRA 1.
LO2 Analysis of an Asset Account
LO4

The Walt Disney Company <www.disney.go.com> is engaged in the financing, production, and distribution of motion pictures and television programming. In Disney's annual report, the balance sheet contains an asset called Film and Television Costs. Film and Television Costs, which consist of the cost associated with producing films and television programs less the amount expensed, were $3,606,000,000. The statement of cash flows reveals that the amount of film and television costs expensed (amortized) during the year was $2,469,000,000. The amount spent for new film productions was $2,679,000,000.[8]

1. What are Film and Television Costs, and why would they be classified as an asset?
2. Prepare an entry in T account form to record the amount the company spent on new film and television production during the year (assume all expenditures are paid for in cash).
3. Prepare an adjusting entry in T account form to record the expense for film and television productions.
4. Suggest a method by which The Walt Disney Company might have determined the amount of the expense in **3** in accordance with the matching rule.

FRA 2.
LO4 Identification of Accruals

H.J. Heinz Company, <www.heinz.com>, a major food company, had a net income in 2001 of $478,012,000 and the following current liabilities at the end of 2001:[9]

Current Liabilities (in thousands):	2001
Short-term debt	$1,555,869
Portion of long-term debt due within one year	314,965
Accounts payable	962,497
Salaries and wages	54,036
Accrued marketing	146,138
Accrued restructuring costs	134,550
Other accrued liabilities	388,582
Income taxes	98,460
Total current liabilities	$3,655,097

1. Which of the current liabilities definitely arose as the result of an adjusting entry at the end of the year? Which ones may partially have arisen from an adjusting entry? Which ones probably did not arise from an adjusting entry?
2. What effect do adjustments that create new liabilities have on net income or loss? Based on your answer in **1**, what percentage of current liabilities was definitely the result of an adjusting entry? Assuming the adjusting entries for these items had not been performed, what would Heinz's net income or loss have been?

International Company

FRA 3.
LO2 LO3 **Account Identification and Accrual Accounting**

Takashimaya Company, Ltd. <www.takashimaya.co.jp> is Japan's largest department store chain. An account on Takashimaya's balance sheet called Gift Certificates contains ¥41,657 million ($404 million).[10] Is this account an asset or a liability? What transaction gives rise to the account? How is this account an example of the application of accrual accounting? Explain the conceptual issues that must be resolved for an adjusting entry to be valid.

Toys "R" Us Annual Report

FRA 4.
LO4 **Analysis of Balance Sheet and Adjusting Entries**

Refer to the balance sheet in the Toys "R" Us <www.tru.com> annual report in the Supplement to Chapter 6. Examine the accounts listed in the current assets, property and equipment, and current liabilities sections. Which accounts are most likely to have had year-end adjusting entries? Describe the nature of the adjusting entries. For more information about the property and equipment section, refer to the notes to the consolidated financial statements.

Comparison Case: Toys "R" Us and Walgreen Co.

FRA 5.
LO1 LO2 LO4 **Depreciation Expense and Estimates**

Depreciation expense is recorded by an adjusting entry and is one of the most important expenses for many companies. In the Supplement to Chapter 6, refer to the Summary of Significant Accounting Policies in the notes to the financial statements in the Toys "R" Us <www.tru.com> annual report and to Walgreens' <www.walgreens.com> financial statements to answer these questions:

1. Where is depreciation (and amortization) expense disclosed on the financial statements for each company? Note that depreciation expense is not listed on Walgreens' income statement. Does this mean it is not a factor in computing net income for the company? (Also, note that amortization expense is similar to depreciation expense and is often included with it.)
2. Determine the importance of depreciation and amortization expense to each company by dividing depreciation and amortization expense by net sales. Why do you think the percentages are small?
3. Each company has a statement on the "Use of Estimates" in its Summary of Significant Accounting Policies. Read these statements and tell how important estimates are to the determination of depreciation expense. What assumptions do accountants make that allow these estimates to be made?

Fingraph® Financial Analyst™

FRA 6. **LO2 LO4 SO6 Income Measurement and Adjustments**

Choose a company from the list of Fingraph companies on the Needles Accounting Resource Center Web Site at http://accounting.college.hmco.com/students. Click on the company you selected to access the Microsoft Excel spreadsheet for that company. You will find the company's URL (Internet address) in the heading of the spreadsheet. Click on the URL for a link to the company's web site and annual report.

1. Identify the type of fiscal year that the company uses. Do you think the year end corresponds to the company's natural business year?
2. Find the company's balance sheet. From the asset accounts and liability accounts, find four examples of accounts that might have been related to an adjusting entry at the end of the year. For each example, tell whether it is a deferral or an accrual and suggest an income statement account that might be associated with it.
3. Find the summary of significant accounting policies that appears following the financial statements. In these policies, find examples of the application of going concern and accrual accounting. Explain your choices of examples.
4. Prepare a one-page executive summary that highlights what you have learned from parts **1**, **2**, and **3**.

Internet Case

FRA 7. **LO4 Comparison of Accrued Expenses**

How important are accrued expenses? Randomly choose four different companies from the Needles Accounting Resource Center Web Site at http://accounting.college.hmco.com/students. Use the links to get to each company's web site and annual report. For each company, find the section of the balance sheet labeled "Current Liabilities" and identify the current liabilities that are accrued expenses (sometimes called *accrued liabilities*). More than one account may be involved. On a pad, write the information you find in four columns: name of company, total current liabilities, total accrued liabilities, and total accrued liabilities as a percentage of total current liabilities. Write a memorandum to your instructor listing the companies you chose, telling how you obtained their reports, reporting the data you have gathered in the form of a table, and stating a conclusion, with reasons, as to the importance of accrued expenses to the companies you studied. (**Hint:** Compute the average percentage of total accrued expenses for the four companies.)

4 Chapter 4 focuses on the preparation of closing entries and the completion of the accounting cycle.

Completing the Accounting Cycle

LEARNING OBJECTIVES

LO1 State all the steps in the accounting cycle.
LO2 Explain and prepare closing entries.
LO3 Prepare the post-closing trial balance.
LO4 Prepare reversing entries as appropriate.
LO5 Prepare and use a work sheet.

DECISION POINT

A USER'S FOCUS

Dell Computer Corporation <www.dell.com> Dell Computer Corporation is the world's largest computer company. As a company whose shares are publicly traded, Dell must prepare both annual and quarterly financial statements for its stockholders and file them with the Securities and Exchange Commission. Note the interim income statement from Dell's quarterly report that appears here.[1] It shows that Dell's net revenue (sales) for the three months ended November 1, 2002, was greater than that for the same period of the preceding year by almost $1.7 billion, and net income increased approximately 31 percent from $429,000,000 to $561,000,000 for the same period.

Whether required by law or not, the preparation of *interim financial statements* every quarter, or even every month, is a good idea for all businesses because such reports give management an ongoing view of a company's financial performance. What are the costs and time involved in preparing interim financial statements?

The preparation of interim financial statements throughout the year requires more effort than the preparation of a single set of financial statements for the entire year. Each time the financial statements are prepared, adjusting entries must be determined, prepared, and recorded. Also, the ledger accounts must be prepared to begin the next accounting period. These procedures are time-consuming and costly. However, the advantages of preparing interim financial statements, even when they are not required, usually outweigh the costs, because such statements give management timely information for making decisions that will improve operations. This

Why is it important for a large company like Dell Computer Corporation to prepare interim financial statements?

chapter explains the accounting information systems used to process data and prepare financial statements at the end of an accounting period, whether that period is a month, a quarter, or a year.

Financial Highlights: Interim Income Statement
(Unaudited—in millions)

	Three Months Ended	
	November 1, 2002	November 2, 2001
Net revenue	$9,144	$7,468
Cost of revenue	7,482	6,155
Gross margin	1,662	1,313
Operating expenses:		
Selling, general and administrative	787	662
Research, development and engineering	117	107
Total operating expenses	904	769
Operating income	758	544
Investment and other income (loss), net	44	51
Income before income taxes	802	595
Income tax provision	241	166
Net income	$ 561	$ 429

OVERVIEW OF THE ACCOUNTING CYCLE

LO1 State all the steps in the accounting cycle.

RELATED TEXT ASSIGNMENTS
Q: 1
SE: 1
P: 3
SD: 1, 3, 4, 5
FRA: 2, 3, 5

The **accounting cycle** is a series of steps in the accounting system whose purpose is to measure business activities in the form of transactions and to transform these transactions into financial statements that will communicate useful information to decision makers. The steps in the accounting cycle, illustrated in Figure 1, are as follows:

1. *Analyze* business transactions from source documents.
2. *Record* the entries in the journal.
3. *Post* the entries to the ledger and prepare a trial balance.
4. *Adjust* the accounts and prepare an adjusted trial balance.
5. *Close* the accounts and prepare a post-closing trial balance.
6. *Prepare* financial statements.

You are already familiar with steps 1 through 4 and 6. Step 5 is covered in this chapter.

The order of these six steps can vary to some extent depending on the system in place. For instance, the financial statements (step 6) may be completed before the closing entries are prepared (step 5). In fact, in a computerized system, step 6 usually must be performed before step 5. The important point is that all these steps must be accomplished to complete the accounting cycle. At key points in the accounting cycle, trial balances are prepared to ensure that the ledger remains in balance.

STOP AND THINK!
Why is the accounting cycle called a "cycle"?
It is so called because its steps are repeated each accounting period. Step 1 of one period follows step 6 of the prior period. ■

KEY POINT: Steps 1 through 3 are carried out throughout the period, whereas steps 4 through 6 are carried out at the end of the period only.

Check out ACE for a Review Quiz at http://accounting.college.hmco.com/students.

CLOSING ENTRIES

LO2 Explain and prepare closing entries.

RELATED TEXT ASSIGNMENTS
Q: 2, 3, 4, 5
SE: 2, 3, 4, 5, 6, 9
E: 1, 8
P: 1, 2, 3, 4, 5, 6, 7, 8
SD: 4, 5
FRA: 1, 2, 4

Balance sheet accounts are considered **permanent accounts**, or *real accounts,* because they carry their end-of-period balances into the next accounting period. On the other hand, revenue and expense accounts are considered **temporary accounts**, or *nominal accounts,* because they begin each accounting period with a zero balance, accumulate a balance during the period, and are then cleared by means of closing entries.

Closing entries are journal entries made at the end of an accounting period. They have two purposes. First, closing entries set the stage for the next accounting period by clearing revenue, expense, and withdrawal accounts of their balances. Remember that the income statement reports net income (or loss) for a single accounting period and shows revenues and expenses for that period only. For the income statement to present the activity of a single accounting period, the revenue and expense accounts must begin each new period with zero balances. The zero balances are obtained by using closing entries to clear the balances in the revenue and expense accounts at the end of each accounting period. The Withdrawals account is closed in a similar manner.

Second, closing entries summarize a period's revenues and expenses. This is done by transferring the balances of revenue and expense accounts to the **Income Summary** account. This temporary account, which appears in the chart of accounts between the Withdrawals account and the first revenue account, provides a place to summarize all revenues and expenses. It is used only in the closing process and never appears in the financial statements.

STOP AND THINK!
Could closing entries be done without using the Income Summary account?
Since the Income Summary account is used to accumulate a balance (steps 1 and 2) that is subsequently transferred to Capital (step 3), it would be possible to eliminate the use of the Income Summary account by closing the accounts in steps 1 and 2 directly to the Capital account and eliminating step 3. ■

FIGURE 1
Overview of the Accounting Cycle

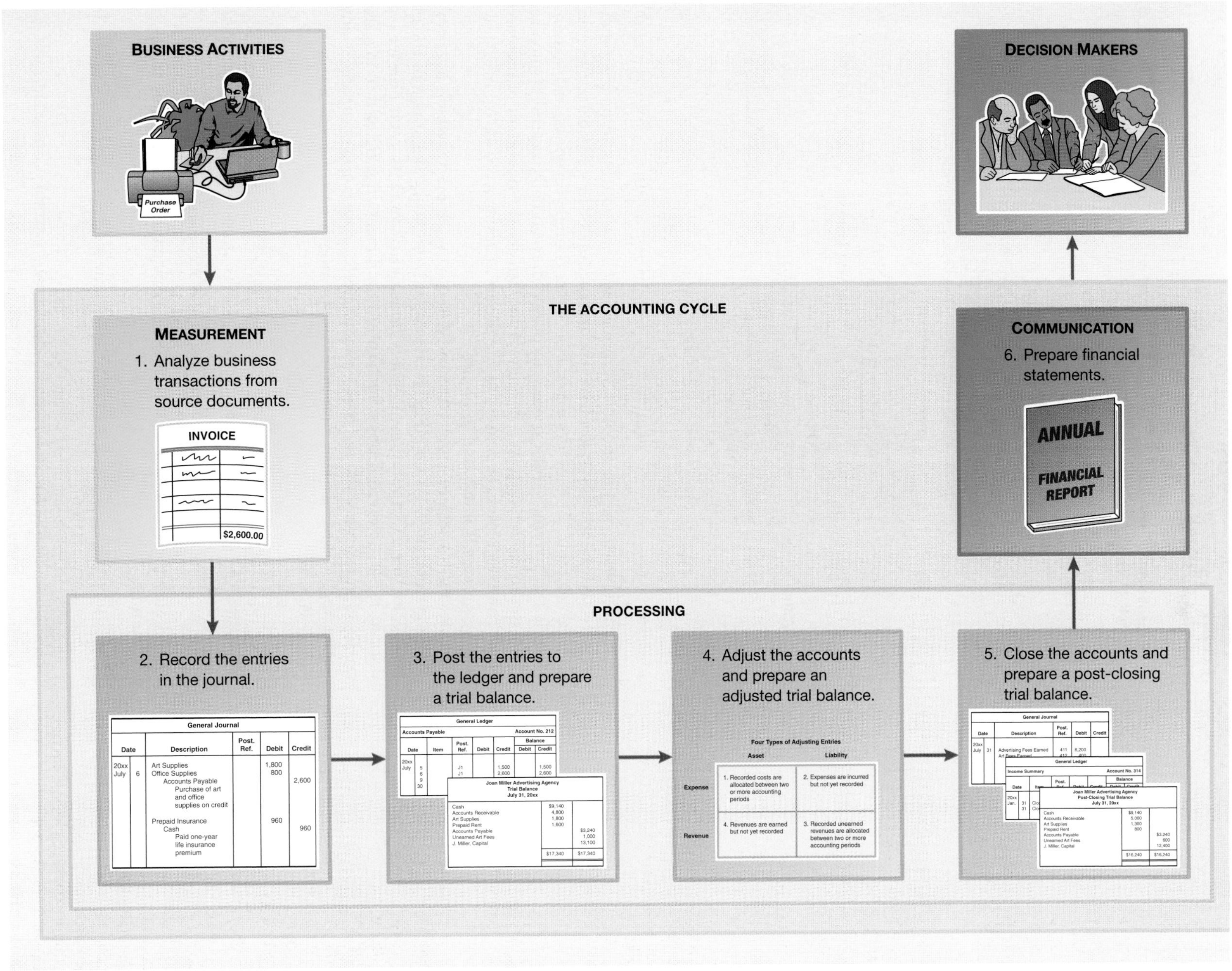

FIGURE 2
Overview of the Closing Process

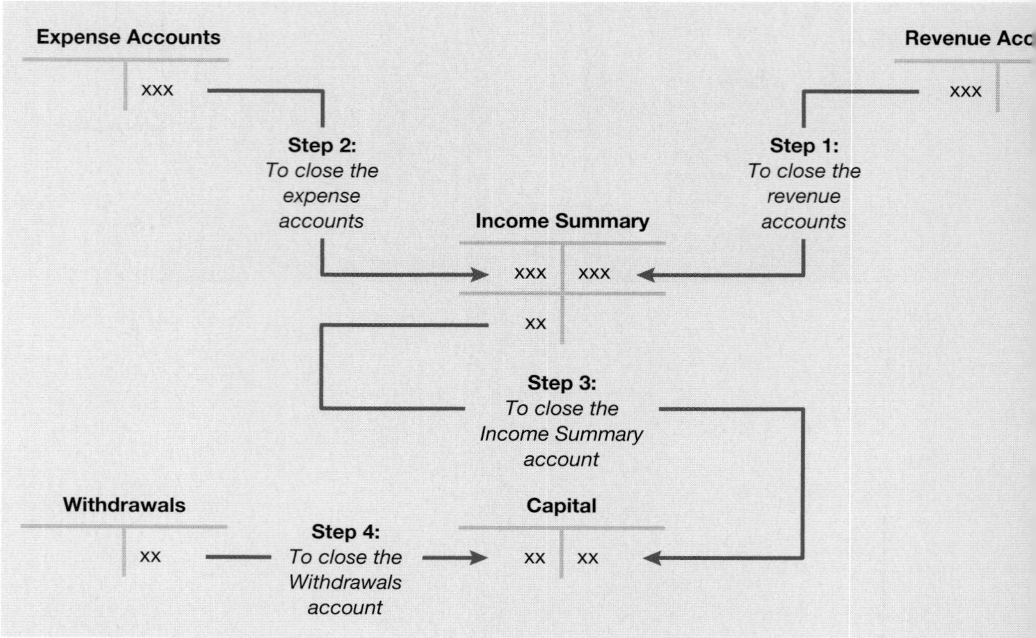

The balance of the Income Summary account equals the net income or loss reported on the income statement. The net income or loss is then transferred to the Capital account. This is done because even though revenues and expenses are recorded in revenue and expense accounts, they actually represent increases and decreases in owner's equity. Closing entries transfer the net effect of increases (revenues) and decreases (expenses) to the owner's capital account. An overview of the closing process is illustrated in Figure 2.

Closing entries are required at the end of any period for which financial statements are prepared. As noted in the Decision Point at the beginning of the chapter, Dell Computer Corporation prepares financial statements each quarter; when it does so, it must close its books. Such interim information is helpful to investors and creditors in assessing the ongoing financial performance of a company. Many companies, including Dell, also close their books monthly to give management a more timely view of ongoing operations.

www.dell.com

REQUIRED CLOSING ENTRIES

There are four important steps in closing the accounts:

1. Closing the credit balances from the income statement accounts to the Income Summary account
2. Closing the debit balances from the income statement accounts to the Income Summary account
3. Closing the Income Summary account balance to the Capital account
4. Closing the Withdrawals account balance to the Capital account

Each step is accomplished by a closing entry. All the data needed to record the closing entries are found in the adjusted trial balance.

ENRICHMENT NOTE: It is not absolutely necessary to use the Income Summary account when preparing closing entries. However, it does simplify the procedure. The Income Summary account is opened and closed with the preparation of closing entries.

EXHIBIT 1
Preparing Closing Entries from the Adjusted Trial Balance

Joan Miller Advertising Agency
Adjusted Trial Balance
July 31, 20xx

Cash	$ 9,140	
Accounts Receivable	5,000	
Art Supplies	1,300	
Office Supplies	600	
Prepaid Rent	800	
Prepaid Insurance	880	
Art Equipment	4,200	
Accumulated Depreciation, Art Equipment		$ 70
Office Equipment	3,000	
Accumulated Depreciation, Office Equipment		50
Accounts Payable		3,240
Unearned Art Fees		600
Wages Payable		360
Joan Miller, Capital		20,000
Joan Miller, Withdrawals	1,400	
Advertising Fees Earned		6,400
Art Fees Earned		400
Wages Expense	2,760	
Utilities Expense	200	
Telephone Expense	140	
Rent Expense	800	
Insurance Expense	80	
Art Supplies Expense	500	
Office Supplies Expense	200	
Depreciation Expense, Art Equipment	70	
Depreciation Expense, Office Equipment	50	
	$31,120	$31,120

Entry 1:

July 31	Advertising Fees Earned	411	6,400	
	Art Fees Earned	412	400	
	Income Summary	313		6,800
	Closed the revenue accounts			

Entry 2:

July 31	Income Summary	313	4,800	
	Wages Expense	511		2,760
	Utilities Expense	512		200
	Telephone Expense	513		140
	Rent Expense	514		800
	Insurance Expense	515		80
	Art Supplies Expense	516		500
	Office Supplies Expense	517		200
	Depreciation Expense, Art Equipment	519		70
	Depreciation Expense, Office Equipment	520		50
	Closed the expense accounts			

Income Summary

July 31	4,800	July 31	6,800
July 31	2,000	Bal.	0

Entry 3:

July 31	Income Summary	313	2,000	
	Joan Miller, Capital	311		2,000
	Closed the Income Summary account			

Entry 4:

July 31	Joan Miller, Capital	311	1,400	
	Joan Miller, Withdrawals	312		1,400
	Closed the Withdrawals account			

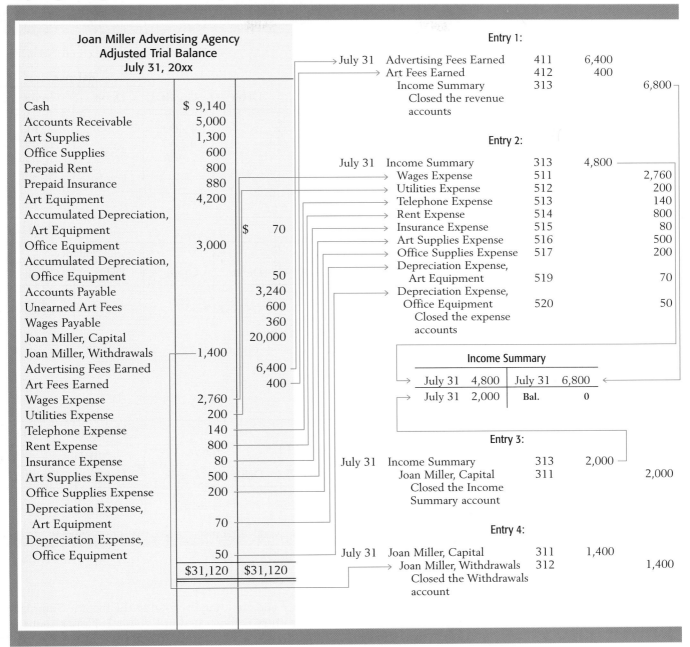

The relationships of the four kinds of entries to the adjusted trial balance are shown in Exhibit 1.

■ **STEP 1: CLOSING THE CREDIT BALANCES FROM INCOME STATEMENT ACCOUNTS TO THE INCOME SUMMARY ACCOUNT** On the credit side of the adjusted trial balance in Exhibit 1, two revenue accounts show balances: Advertising Fees Earned and Art Fees Earned. To close these two accounts, an entry must be made debiting each

EXHIBIT 2
Posting the Closing Entry of the Credit Balances from the Income Statement Accounts to the Income Summary Account

Advertising Fees Earned — Account No. 411

Date	Item	Post. Ref.	Debit	Credit	Balance Debit	Balance Credit
July 10		J2		1,400		1,400
19		J2		4,800		6,200
31	Adj. (j)	J3		200		6,400
31	Closing	J4	6,400			—

Art Fees Earned — Account No. 412

Date	Item	Post. Ref.	Debit	Credit	Balance Debit	Balance Credit
July 31	Adj. (i)	J3		400		400
31	Closing	J4	400			—

6,400
400
6,800

Income Summary — Account No. 313

Date	Item	Post. Ref.	Debit	Credit	Balance Debit	Balance Credit
July 31	Closing	J4		6,800		6,800

KEY POINT: The Income Summary account now reflects the account balances that the revenue accounts contained before they were closed.

account in the amount of its balance and crediting the total to the Income Summary account. The effect of posting the entry is illustrated in Exhibit 2. Notice that the entry (1) sets the balances of the revenue accounts to zero and (2) transfers the total revenues to the credit side of the Income Summary account.

■ STEP 2: CLOSING THE DEBIT BALANCES FROM INCOME STATEMENT ACCOUNTS TO THE INCOME SUMMARY ACCOUNT Several expense accounts show balances on the debit side of the adjusted trial balance in Exhibit 1. A compound entry is needed to credit each of these expense accounts for its balance and to debit the Income Summary account for the total. The effect of posting the closing entry is shown in Exhibit 3. Notice how the entry (1) reduces the expense account balances to zero and (2) transfers the total of the account balances to the debit side of the Income Summary account.

EXHIBIT 3

Posting the Closing Entry of the Debit Balances from the Income Statement Accounts to the Income Summary Account

Wages Expense — Account No. 511

Date	Item	Post. Ref.	Debit	Credit	Balance	
					Debit	Credit
July 12		J2	1,200		1,200	
26		J2	1,200		2,400	
31	Adj. (g)	J3	360		2,760	
31	Closing	J4		2,760	—	

Utilities Expense — Account No. 512

Date	Item	Post. Ref.	Debit	Credit	Balance	
					Debit	Credit
July 29		J2	200		200	
31	Closing	J4		200	—	

Telephone Expense — Account No. 513

Date	Item	Post. Ref.	Debit	Credit	Balance	
					Debit	Credit
July 30		J2	140		140	
31	Closing	J4		140	—	

Rent Expense — Account No. 514

Date	Item	Post. Ref.	Debit	Credit	Balance	
					Debit	Credit
July 31	Adj. (a)	J3	800		800	
31	Closing	J4		800	—	

Insurance Expense — Account No. 515

Date	Item	Post. Ref.	Debit	Credit	Balance	
					Debit	Credit
July 31	Adj. (b)	J3	80		80	
31	Closing	J4		80	—	

Art Supplies Expense — Account No. 516

Date	Item	Post. Ref.	Debit	Credit	Balance	
					Debit	Credit
July 31	Adj. (c)	J3	500		500	
31	Closing	J4		500	—	

Office Supplies Expense — Account No. 517

Date	Item	Post. Ref.	Debit	Credit	Balance	
					Debit	Credit
July 31	Adj. (d)	J3	200		200	
31	Closing	J4		200	—	

Income Summary — Account No. 313

Date	Item	Post. Ref.	Debit	Credit	Balance	
					Debit	Credit
July 31	Closing	J4		6,800		6,800
31	Closing	J4	4,800			2,000

2,760
200
140
800
80
500
200
50
70
4,800

Depreciation Expense, Art Equipment — Account No. 519

Date	Item	Post. Ref.	Debit	Credit	Balance	
					Debit	Credit
July 31	Adj. (e)	J3	70		70	
31	Closing	J4		70	—	

Depreciation Expense, Office Equipment — Account No. 520

Date	Item	Post. Ref.	Debit	Credit	Balance	
					Debit	Credit
July 31	Adj. (f)	J3	50		50	
31	Closing	J4		50	—	

KEY POINT: The credit balance of the Income Summary account at this point ($2,000) represents the key performance measure of net income.

STEP 3: CLOSING THE INCOME SUMMARY ACCOUNT BALANCE TO THE CAPITAL ACCOUNT

After the entries closing the revenue and expense accounts have been posted, the balance of the Income Summary account equals the net income or loss for the period. Since revenues are represented by the credit to Income Summary and expenses are represented by the debit to Income Summary, a net income is indicated by a credit balance (where revenues exceed expenses) and a net loss by a

EXHIBIT 4
Posting the Closing Entry of the Income Summary Account Balance to the Capital Account

Income Summary — Account No. 313

Date	Item	Post. Ref.	Debit	Credit	Balance Debit	Balance Credit
July 31	Closing	J4		6,800		6,800
31	Closing	J4	4,800			2,000
31	Closing	J4	2,000			—

Joan Miller, Capital — Account No. 311

Date	Item	Post. Ref.	Debit	Credit	Balance Debit	Balance Credit
July 1		J1		20,000		20,000
31	Closing	J4		2,000		22,000

KEY POINT: In a net loss situation, debit the Capital account (to reduce it) and credit Income Summary (to close it).

CLARIFICATION NOTE: If a net loss has been incurred, the Income Summary account would contain a debit balance when the income statement accounts are closed to it.

debit balance (where expenses exceed revenues). At this point, the Income Summary account balance, whatever its nature, must be closed to the Capital account, as shown in Exhibit 1. The effect of posting the closing entry when the company has a net income is shown in Exhibit 4. Notice the dual effect of (1) closing the Income Summary account and (2) transferring the balance, net income in this case, to Joan Miller's Capital account.

■ STEP 4: CLOSING THE WITHDRAWALS ACCOUNT BALANCE TO THE CAPITAL ACCOUNT

The Withdrawals account shows the amount by which capital is reduced during the accounting period by withdrawals of cash or other assets from the business for the owner's personal use. The debit balance of the Withdrawals account is closed to the Capital account, as illustrated in Exhibit 1. The effect of this closing entry, as shown in Exhibit 5, is to (1) close the Withdrawals account and (2) transfer the balance to the Capital account.

THE ACCOUNTS AFTER CLOSING

STUDY NOTE: A good way to review is to examine each ledger account and determine where it fits (if at all) into the adjusting and closing procedures. The Cash account, for example, is never part of adjusting or closing entries.

After all the steps in the closing process have been completed and all closing entries have been posted to the accounts, everything is ready for the next accounting period. The ledger accounts of Joan Miller Advertising Agency, as they appear at this point, are shown in Exhibit 6. The revenue, expense, and Withdrawals accounts (temporary accounts) have zero balances. The Capital account has been increased to reflect the agency's net income and decreased for the owner's withdrawals. The balance sheet accounts (permanent accounts) show the correct balances, which are carried forward to the next period.

EXHIBIT 5
Posting the Closing Entry of the Withdrawals Account Balance to the Capital Account

Joan Miller, Withdrawals — Account No. 312

Date	Item	Post. Ref.	Debit	Credit	Balance Debit	Balance Credit
July 31		J2	1,400		1,400	
31	Closing	J4		1,400	—	

Joan Miller, Capital — Account No. 311

Date	Item	Post. Ref.	Debit	Credit	Balance Debit	Balance Credit
July 1		J1		20,000		20,000
31	Closing	J4		2,000		22,000
31	Closing	J4	1,400			20,600

EXHIBIT 6
The Accounts After Closing Entries Are Posted

Cash					Account No. 111	
		Post.			Balance	
Date	Item	Ref.	Debit	Credit	Debit	Credit
July 1		J1	20,000		20,000	
2		J1		1,600	18,400	
4		J1		4,200	14,200	
5		J1		1,500	12,700	
8		J1		960	11,740	
9		J1		1,000	10,740	
10		J2	1,400		12,140	
12		J2		1,200	10,940	
15		J2	1,000		11,940	
26		J2		1,200	10,740	
29		J2		200	10,540	
31		J2		1,400	9,140	

Accounts Receivable					Account No. 113	
		Post.			Balance	
Date	Item	Ref.	Debit	Credit	Debit	Credit
July 19		J2	4,800		4,800	
31	Adj. (i)	J3	200		5,000	

Art Supplies					Account No. 115	
		Post.			Balance	
Date	Item	Ref.	Debit	Credit	Debit	Credit
July 6		J1	1,800		1,800	
31	Adj. (c)	J3		500	1,300	

Office Supplies					Account No. 116	
		Post.			Balance	
Date	Item	Ref.	Debit	Credit	Debit	Credit
July 6		J1	800		800	
31	Adj. (d)	J3		200	600	

Prepaid Rent					Account No. 117	
		Post.			Balance	
Date	Item	Ref.	Debit	Credit	Debit	Credit
July 2		J1	1,600		1,600	
31	Adj. (a)	J3		800	800	

Prepaid Insurance					Account No. 118	
		Post.			Balance	
Date	Item	Ref.	Debit	Credit	Debit	Credit
July 8		J1	960		960	
31	Adj. (b)	J3		80	880	

Art Equipment					Account No. 144	
		Post.			Balance	
Date	Item	Ref.	Debit	Credit	Debit	Credit
July 4		J1	4,200		4,200	

Accumulated Depreciation, Art Equipment					Account No. 145	
		Post.			Balance	
Date	Item	Ref.	Debit	Credit	Debit	Credit
July 31	Adj. (e)	J3		70		70

Office Equipment					Account No. 146	
		Post.			Balance	
Date	Item	Ref.	Debit	Credit	Debit	Credit
July 5		J1	3,000		3,000	

Accumulated Depreciation, Office Equipment					Account No. 147	
		Post.			Balance	
Date	Item	Ref.	Debit	Credit	Debit	Credit
July 31	Adj. (f)	J3		50		50

Accounts Payable					Account No. 212	
		Post.			Balance	
Date	Item	Ref.	Debit	Credit	Debit	Credit
July 5		J1		1,500		1,500
6		J1		2,600		4,100
9		J1	1,000			3,100
30		J2		140		3,240

Unearned Art Fees					Account No. 213	
		Post.			Balance	
Date	Item	Ref.	Debit	Credit	Debit	Credit
July 15		J2		1,000		1,000
31	Adj. (h)	J3	400			600

Wages Payable					Account No. 214	
		Post.			Balance	
Date	Item	Ref.	Debit	Credit	Debit	Credit
July 31	Adj. (g)	J3		360		360

(continued)

EXHIBIT 6
The Accounts After Closing Entries Are Posted *(continued)*

Joan Miller, Capital					Account No. 311	
		Post.			Balance	
Date	Item	Ref.	Debit	Credit	Debit	Credit
July 1		J1		20,000		20,000
31	Closing	J4		2,000		22,000
31	Closing	J4	1,400			20,600

Joan Miller, Withdrawals					Account No. 312	
		Post.			Balance	
Date	Item	Ref.	Debit	Credit	Debit	Credit
July 31		J2	1,400		1,400	
31	Closing	J4		1,400	—	

Income Summary					Account No. 313	
		Post.			Balance	
Date	Item	Ref.	Debit	Credit	Debit	Credit
July 31	Closing	J4		6,800		6,800
31	Closing	J4	4,800			2,000
31	Closing	J4	2,000			—

Advertising Fees Earned					Account No. 411	
		Post.			Balance	
Date	Item	Ref.	Debit	Credit	Debit	Credit
July 10		J2		1,400		1,400
19		J2		4,800		6,200
31	Adj. (i)	J3		200		6,400
31	Closing	J4	6,400			—

Art Fees Earned					Account No. 412	
		Post.			Balance	
Date	Item	Ref.	Debit	Credit	Debit	Credit
July 31	Adj. (h)	J3		400		400
31	Closing	J4	400			—

Wages Expense					Account No. 511	
		Post.			Balance	
Date	Item	Ref.	Debit	Credit	Debit	Credit
July 12		J2	1,200		1,200	
26		J2	1,200		2,400	
31	Adj. (g)	J3	360		2,760	
31	Closing	J4		2,760	—	

Utilities Expense					Account No. 512	
		Post.			Balance	
Date	Item	Ref.	Debit	Credit	Debit	Credit
July 29		J2	200		200	
31	Closing	J4		200	—	

Telephone Expense					Account No. 513	
		Post.			Balance	
Date	Item	Ref.	Debit	Credit	Debit	Credit
July 30		J2	140		140	
31	Closing	J4		140	—	

Rent Expense					Account No. 514	
		Post.			Balance	
Date	Item	Ref.	Debit	Credit	Debit	Credit
July 31	Adj. (a)	J3	800		800	
31	Closing	J4		800	—	

Insurance Expense					Account No. 515	
		Post.			Balance	
Date	Item	Ref.	Debit	Credit	Debit	Credit
July 31	Adj. (b)	J3	80		80	
31	Closing	J4		80	—	

Art Supplies Expense					Account No. 516	
		Post.			Balance	
Date	Item	Ref.	Debit	Credit	Debit	Credit
July 31	Adj. (c)	J3	500		500	
31	Closing	J4		500	—	

Office Supplies Expense					Account No. 517	
		Post.			Balance	
Date	Item	Ref.	Debit	Credit	Debit	Credit
July 31	Adj. (d)	J3	200		200	
31	Closing	J4		200	—	

Depreciation Expense, Art Equipment					Account No. 519	
		Post.			Balance	
Date	Item	Ref.	Debit	Credit	Debit	Credit
July 31	Adj. (e)	J3	70		70	
31	Closing	J4		70	—	

Depreciation Expense, Office Equipment					Account No. 520	
		Post.			Balance	
Date	Item	Ref.	Debit	Credit	Debit	Credit
July 31	Adj. (f)	J3	50		50	
31	Closing	J4		50	—	

FOCUS ON INTERNATIONAL BUSINESS

Closing Doesn't Have to Be Such a Headache.

For companies with extensive international operations, like Caterpillar Inc. <www.caterpillar.com>, Dow Chemical <www.dow.com>, Phillips Petroleum <www.phillips66.com>, Gillette <www.gillette.com>, and Bristol-Myers Squibb <www.bms.com>, closing the records and preparing financial statements on a timely basis used to be a problem. It was common practice for foreign divisions of companies like these to end their fiscal year one month before the end of the fiscal year of their counterparts in the United States. This gave them the extra time they needed to perform closing procedures and mail the results back to U.S. headquarters to be used in preparation of the company's overall financial statements. Such an arrangement is usually unnecessary today because high-speed computers and electronic communications make it possible for companies to close records and prepare financial statements for both foreign and domestic operations in less than a week.

Check out ACE for a Review Quiz at http://accounting.college.hmco.com/students.

THE POST-CLOSING TRIAL BALANCE

LO3 Prepare the post-closing trial balance.

RELATED TEXT ASSIGNMENTS
Q: 6, 7
P: 3
SD: 4

Because it is possible to make errors in posting the closing entries to the ledger accounts, it is necessary to determine that all temporary accounts have zero balances and to double-check that total debits equal total credits by preparing a new trial balance. This final trial balance, called the **post-closing trial balance**, is shown in Exhibit 7 for Joan Miller Advertising Agency. Notice that only the balance sheet accounts show balances because the income statement accounts and the Withdrawals account have all been closed.

EXHIBIT 7
Post-Closing Trial Balance

Joan Miller Advertising Agency
Post-Closing Trial Balance
July 31, 20xx

Cash	$ 9,140	
Accounts Receivable	5,000	
Art Supplies	1,300	
Office Supplies	600	
Prepaid Rent	800	
Prepaid Insurance	880	
Art Equipment	4,200	
Accumulated Depreciation, Art Equipment		$ 70
Office Equipment	3,000	
Accumulated Depreciation, Office Equipment		50
Accounts Payable		3,240
Unearned Art Fees		600
Wages Payable		360
Joan Miller, Capital		20,600
	$24,920	$24,920

STOP AND THINK!
Why does the post-closing trial balance contain only balance sheet accounts?
All the income statement, or temporary, accounts and the Withdrawals account have been closed, thus leaving only the balance sheet, or permanent, accounts to carry over to the next accounting period. ■

KEY POINT: Notice that Joan Miller, Capital now reflects the correct month-end balance, $20,600.

Check out ACE for a Review Quiz at http://accounting.college.hmco.com/students.

Reversing Entries: The Optional First Step in the Next Accounting Period

LO4 Prepare reversing entries as appropriate.

RELATED TEXT ASSIGNMENTS
Q: 8, 9
SE: 7, 8
E: 2, 7
P: 4, 5, 8
SD: 2, 4

At the end of each accounting period, adjusting entries are made to bring revenues and expenses into conformity with the matching rule. A **reversing entry** is a general journal entry made on the first day of a new accounting period; it is the exact reverse of an adjusting entry made at the end of the previous accounting period. Reversing entries are optional. They simplify the bookkeeping process for transactions involving certain types of adjustments. Not all adjusting entries can be reversed. Under the recording system used in this book, only adjustments for accruals (accrued revenues and accrued expenses) are reversed. Deferrals should not be reversed because such reversals would not simplify the bookkeeping process in future accounting periods.

KEY POINT: Reversing entries are the opposite of adjusting entries and are dated the first day of the new period. They apply only to certain adjusting entries and are never required.

To see how reversing entries can be helpful, consider the adjusting entry made in the records of Joan Miller Advertising Agency to accrue wages expense:

A = L + OE
  + −

July 31	Wages Expense	360	
	Wages Payable		360
	Accrued unrecorded wages		

When the secretary is paid on the next regular payday, the accountant would make this entry:

A = L + OE
− − −

Aug. 9	Wages Payable	360	
	Wages Expense	840	
	Cash		1,200
	Paid two weeks' wages to secretary, $360 of which accrued in the previous period		

Stop and Think!
Why are reversing entries helpful?
Reversing entries enable the bookkeeper to continue preparing routine entries early in the new period. (More complex entries are needed when reversing entries are not used.) ■

Notice that when the payment is made, if there is no reversing entry, the accountant must look in the records to find out how much of the $1,200 applies to the current accounting period and how much is applicable to the previous period. This may seem easy in our example, but think how difficult and time-consuming it would be if a company had hundreds of employees working on different schedules. A reversing entry helps solve the problem of applying revenues and expenses to the correct accounting period. It is exactly what its name implies: a reversal made by debiting the credits and crediting the debits of a previously made adjusting entry.

For example, notice the following sequence of entries and their effects on the ledger account Wages Expense:

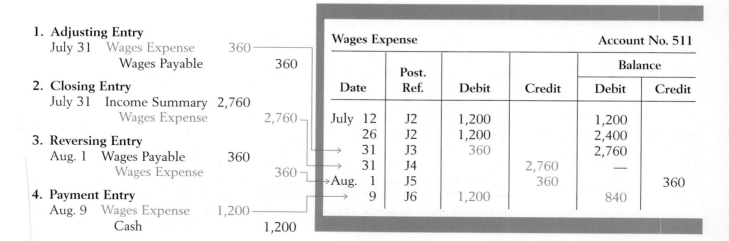

1. **Adjusting Entry**

July 31	Wages Expense	360	
	Wages Payable		360

2. **Closing Entry**

July 31	Income Summary	2,760	
	Wages Expense		2,760

3. **Reversing Entry**

Aug. 1	Wages Payable	360	
	Wages Expense		360

4. **Payment Entry**

Aug. 9	Wages Expense	1,200	
	Cash		1,200

Wages Expense — **Account No. 511**

Date		Post. Ref.	Debit	Credit	Balance Debit	Balance Credit
July	12	J2	1,200		1,200	
	26	J2	1,200		2,400	
	31	J3	360		2,760	
	31	J4		2,760	—	
Aug.	1	J5		360		360
	9	J6	1,200		840	

Entry **1** adjusted Wages Expense to accrue $360 in the July accounting period.

Entry **2** closed the $2,760 in Wages Expense for July to Income Summary, leaving a zero balance.

KEY POINT: Notice the abnormal credit balance as of August 1. This situation is "corrected" with the August 9 entry, an entry the bookkeeper can easily make.

Entry **3,** the reversing entry, set up a credit balance of $360 on August 1 in Wages Expense, which is the expense recognized through the adjusting entry in July (and also reduced the liability account Wages Payable to a zero balance). The reversing entry always sets up an abnormal balance in the income statement account and produces a zero balance in the balance sheet account.

Entry **4** recorded the $1,200 payment of two weeks' wages as a debit to Wages Expense, automatically leaving a balance of $840, which represents the correct wages expense to date in August. The reversing entry simplified the process of making the payment entry on August 9.

Reversing entries apply to any accrued expenses or revenues. In the case of Joan Miller Advertising Agency, wages expense was the only accrued expense. The adjusting entry for accrued revenue (advertising fees earned) would require the following reversing entry:

A = L + OE				
− −	Aug. 1	Advertising Fees Earned	200	
		Accounts Receivable		200
		Reversed the adjusting entry for accrued fees earned		

When the series of advertisements is finished, the company can credit all the proceeds to Advertising Fees Earned without regard to the amount accrued in the previous period. The credit will automatically be reduced to the amount earned during August by the $200 debit in the account.

As noted earlier, under our system of recording, reversing entries apply only to accruals. They do not apply to deferrals, such as the entries that involve supplies, prepaid rent, prepaid insurance, depreciation, and unearned art fees.

Check out ACE for a Review Quiz at http://accounting.college.hmco.com/students.

THE WORK SHEET: AN ACCOUNTANT'S TOOL

LO5 Prepare and use a work sheet.

RELATED TEXT ASSIGNMENTS
Q: 10, 11, 12, 13, 14, 15, 16, 17, 18, 19
SE: 9
E: 3, 4, 5, 6, 7, 8
P: 4, 5, 8
SD: 4

Accountants must collect relevant data to determine what should be included in financial reports. For example, they must examine insurance policies to see how much prepaid insurance has expired, examine plant and equipment records to determine depreciation, take an inventory of supplies on hand, and calculate the amount of accrued wages. These calculations, along with other computations, analyses, and preliminary drafts of statements, make up the accountants' **working papers**.

Working papers are important for two reasons. First, they help accountants organize their work and thus avoid omitting important data or steps that affect the financial statements. The second reason is that they provide evidence of past work so that accountants or auditors can retrace their steps and support the information in the financial statements.

KEY POINT: The work sheet is extremely useful when an accountant must prepare numerous adjustments. It is not a financial statement, it is not required, and it is not made public.

The **work sheet** is a special kind of working paper. It is often used as a preliminary step in recording adjusting and closing entries and the preparation of financial statements. Using a work sheet lessens the possibility of leaving out an adjustment, helps the accountant check the arithmetical accuracy of the accounts, and facilitates the preparation of financial statements. The work sheet is never published and is rarely seen by management. It is a tool for the accountant. Because preparing a work sheet is a very mechanical process, many accountants use a microcomputer for this purpose. In some cases, accountants use a spreadsheet program to prepare the work sheet. In other cases, they use a general ledger system to prepare financial statements from the adjusted trial balance.

Preparing the Work Sheet

KEY POINT: For complicated end-of-period situations, the work sheet is ideal because incorrect information can be erased along the way. As a result, the correctly completed work sheet can be used to facilitate the preparation of formal adjusting and closing entries. which can be corrected only with additional formal entries.

So far, adjusting entries for Joan Miller Advertising Agency have been entered directly in the journal and posted to the ledger, and the financial statements have been prepared from the adjusted trial balance. The process has been relatively simple because of the small size of Joan Miller's company. For larger companies, which may require many adjusting entries, a work sheet is essential. To illustrate the preparation of the work sheet, we continue with our example of the Joan Miller Advertising Agency.

A common form of work sheet has one column for account names and/or numbers and ten more columns with the headings shown in Exhibit 8. Notice that the work sheet is identified by a heading that consists of the name of the company, the title "Work Sheet," and the period of time covered (as on the income statement).

Preparation of a work sheet involves the following five steps:

KEY POINT: The work sheet Trial Balance columns take the place of the "traditional" trial balance.

1. **Enter and total the account balances in the Trial Balance columns.** The titles and balances of the accounts as of July 31 are copied directly from the ledger into the Trial Balance columns, as shown in Exhibit 8. When accountants use a work sheet, they do not have to prepare a separate trial balance.

2. **Enter and total the adjustments in the Adjustments columns.** The required adjustments are entered in the Adjustments columns of the work sheet, as shown in Exhibit 9. As each adjustment is entered, a letter is used to identify its debit and credit parts. The first adjustment, identified by the letter **a,** is to recognize rent expense, which results in a debit to Rent Expense and a credit to Prepaid Rent. In practice, this letter may be used to reference supporting computations or documentation underlying the adjusting entry and may simplify the recording of adjusting entries in the general journal.

   If an adjustment calls for an account that has not been used in the trial balance, the new account is added below the accounts listed in the trial balance. The trial balance includes only those accounts that have balances. For example, Rent Expense has been added in Exhibit 9. The only exception to this rule is the Accumulated Depreciation accounts, which have a zero balance only in the initial period of operation. Accumulated Depreciation accounts are listed immediately after their associated asset accounts.

   When all the adjustments have been made, the two Adjustments columns must be totaled. This procedure proves that the debits and credits of the adjustments are equal, and it generally reduces errors in the preparation of the work sheet.

3. **Enter and total the adjusted account balances in the Adjusted Trial Balance columns.** Exhibit 10 shows the adjusted trial balance. It is prepared by combining the amount of each account in the original Trial Balance columns with the corresponding amount in the Adjustments columns and entering each result in the Adjusted Trial Balance columns.

   STUDY NOTE: Crossfooting is far more difficult than adding and subtracting vertically, especially when you must pay particular attention to debits versus credits. It is normal to be uncomfortable with crossfooting at first, but you will quickly become accustomed to it.

   Exhibit 10 contains examples of **crossfooting**, or adding and subtracting a group of numbers horizontally. The first line shows Cash with a debit balance of $9,140. Because there are no adjustments to the Cash account, $9,140 is entered in the debit column of the Adjusted Trial Balance columns. On the second line, Accounts Receivable shows a debit of $4,800 in the Trial Balance columns. Since there is a debit of $200 from Adjustment **i** in the Adjustments column, it is added to the $4,800 and carried over to the debit column of the Adjusted Trial Balance columns at $5,000. On the next line, Art Supplies shows a debit of

$1,800 in the Trial Balance columns and a credit of $500 from adjustment **c** in the Adjustments columns. Subtracting $500 from $1,800 results in a $1,300 debit balance in the Adjusted Trial Balance columns. This process is followed for all the accounts, including those added below the trial balance totals. The Adjusted Trial Balance columns are then footed (totaled) to check the accuracy of the crossfooting.

STOP AND THINK!
Under what circumstances would the Income Statement and Balance Sheet columns balance when initially totaled?
When net income equals exactly $0.■

4. **Extend the account balances from the Adjusted Trial Balance columns to the Income Statement columns or the Balance Sheet columns.** Every account in the adjusted trial balance is either a balance sheet account or an income statement account. Each account is extended to its proper place as a debit or credit in either the Income Statement columns or the Balance Sheet columns. The result of extending the accounts is shown in Exhibit 11. Revenue and expense accounts are copied to the Income Statement columns. Assets, liabilities, and the Capital and Withdrawal accounts are extended to the Balance Sheet columns. To avoid overlooking an account, the accounts are extended line by line, beginning with the first line (which is Cash) and not omitting any subsequent lines. For instance, the Cash debit balance of $9,140 is extended to the debit column of the Balance Sheet columns; the Accounts Receivable debit balance of $5,000 is extended to the same debit column, and so forth. Each amount is carried across to only one column.

5. **Total the Income Statement columns and the Balance Sheet columns. Enter the net income or net loss in both pairs of columns as a balancing figure, and recompute the column totals.** This last step, shown in Exhibit 12, is necessary in order to compute net income or net loss and to prove the arithmetical accuracy of the work sheet.

Net income (or net loss) is equal to the difference between the total debits and credits of the Income Statement columns. It also equals the difference between the total debits and credits of the Balance Sheet columns:

Revenues (Income Statement credit column total)	$6,800
Expenses (Income Statement debit column total)	(4,800)
Net Income	$2,000

In this case, revenues (credit column) exceed expenses (debit column). Thus, the company has a net income of $2,000. The same difference is shown between the total debits and credits of the Balance Sheet columns.

The $2,000 is entered in the debit side of the Income Statement columns to balance the columns, and it is entered in the credit side of the Balance Sheet columns to balance the columns. Remember that the excess of revenues over expenses (net income) increases owner's equity and that increases in owner's equity are recorded by credits.

When a net loss occurs, the opposite rule applies. The excess of expenses over revenues—net loss—is placed in the credit side of the Income Statement columns as a balancing figure. It is then placed in the debit side of the Balance Sheet columns because a net loss decreases owner's equity, and decreases in owner's equity are recorded by debits.

As a final check, the four columns are totaled again. If the Income Statement columns and the Balance Sheet columns do not balance, an account may have been extended or sorted to the wrong column, or an error may have been made in adding the columns. Of course, equal totals in the two pairs of columns are not absolute proof of accuracy. If an asset has been carried to the Income Statement debit column (or an expense has been carried to the Balance Sheet debit column) or a similar error with revenues or liabilities has been made, the work sheet will still balance, but the net income figure will be wrong.

USING THE WORK SHEET

STUDY NOTE: Theoretically, adjusting entries can be recorded before the financial statements are prepared or even before the work sheet is completed. However, they always precede the preparation of formal closing entries. It is in the preparation of formal adjusting entries that the value of identification letters becomes apparent.

The completed work sheet assists the accountant in (1) recording the adjusting entries, (2) recording the closing entries in the general journal to prepare the records for the next period, and (3) preparing the financial statements.

■ **RECORDING THE ADJUSTING ENTRIES** For Joan Miller Advertising Agency, the adjustments were determined while completing the work sheet because they are essential to the preparation of the financial statements. The adjusting entries could have been recorded in the general journal at that point.

Recording the adjusting entries with appropriate explanations in the general journal, shown in Exhibit 13, is an easy step. The information can be copied from the work sheet. Adjusting entries are then posted to the general ledger.

EXHIBIT 13
Adjustments from Work Sheet Entered in the General Journal

General Journal — Page 3

Date		Description	Post. Ref.	Debit	Credit
20xx					
July	31	Rent Expense	514	800	
		Prepaid Rent	117		800
		Recognized expiration of one month's rent			
	31	Insurance Expense	515	80	
		Prepaid Insurance	118		80
		Recognized expiration of one month's insurance			
	31	Art Supplies Expense	516	500	
		Art Supplies	115		500
		Recognized art supplies used during the month			
	31	Office Supplies Expense	517	200	
		Office Supplies	116		200
		Recognized office supplies used during the month			
	31	Depreciation Expense, Art Equipment	519	70	
		Accumulated Depreciation, Art Equipment	145		70
		Recorded depreciation of art equipment for a month			
	31	Depreciation Expense, Office Equipment	520	50	
		Accumulated Depreciation, Office Equipment	147		50
		Recorded depreciation of office equipment for a month			
	31	Wages Expense	511	360	
		Wages Payable	214		360
		Accrued unrecorded wages			
	31	Unearned Art Fees	213	400	
		Art Fees Earned	412		400
		Recognized performance of services paid for in advance			
	31	Accounts Receivable	113	200	
		Advertising Fees Earned	411		200
		Accrued advertising fees earned but unrecorded			

EXHIBIT 14
Income Statement for Joan Miller Advertising Agency

Joan Miller Advertising Agency
Income Statement
For the Month Ended July 31, 20xx

Revenues		
Advertising fees earned		$6,400
Art fees earned		400
Total revenues		$6,800
Expenses		
Wages expense	$2,760	
Utilities expense	200	
Telephone expense	140	
Rent expense	800	
Insurance expense	80	
Art supplies expense	500	
Office supplies expense	200	
Depreciation expense, art equipment	70	
Depreciation expense, office equipment	50	
Total expenses		4,800
Net income		$2,000

KEY POINT: Notice the ease with which the income statement can be prepared now that the work sheet has been completed.

RECORDING THE CLOSING ENTRIES The four closing entries for Joan Miller Advertising Agency are entered in the journal and posted to the ledger, as illustrated in Exhibits 1 through 5. All accounts that need to be closed, except for Withdrawals, may be found in the Income Statement columns of the work sheet.

PREPARING THE FINANCIAL STATEMENTS Once the work sheet has been completed, preparing the financial statements is simple because the account balances have been sorted into Income Statement and Balance Sheet columns. The income statement in Exhibit 14 was prepared from the account balances in the Income Statement columns of Exhibit 12. The account balances for the statement of owner's equity in Exhibit 15 and the balance sheet in Exhibit 16 were drawn from the Balance Sheet columns of

EXHIBIT 15
Statement of Owner's Equity for Joan Miller Advertising Agency

Joan Miller Advertising Agency
Statement of Owner's Equity
For the Month Ended July 31, 20xx

Joan Miller, Capital, July 1, 20xx		—
Add: Investment by Joan Miller	$20,000	
Net income	2,000	$22,000
Subtotal		$22,000
Less withdrawals		1,400
Joan Miller, Capital, July 31, 20xx		$20,600

EXHIBIT 16
Balance Sheet for Joan Miller Advertising Agency

Joan Miller Advertising Agency
Balance Sheet
July 31, 20xx

Assets		
Cash		$ 9,140
Accounts receivable		5,000
Art supplies		1,300
Office supplies		600
Prepaid rent		800
Prepaid insurance		880
Art equipment	$ 4,200	
Less accumulated depreciation	70	4,130
Office equipment	$ 3,000	
Less accumulated depreciation	50	2,950
Total assets		$24,800
Liabilities		
Accounts payable	$ 3,240	
Unearned art fees	600	
Wages payable	360	
Total liabilities		$ 4,200
Owner's Equity		
Joan Miller, Capital, July 31, 20xx		20,600
Total liabilities and owner's equity		$24,800

the work sheet in Exhibit 12. Notice that the total assets and the total liabilities and owner's equity in the balance sheet are not the same as the totals of the Balance Sheet columns in the work sheet. The reason is that the Accumulated Depreciation and Withdrawals accounts have normal balances that appear in different columns from their associated accounts on the balance sheet. In addition, the owner's Capital account on the balance sheet is the amount determined on the statement of owner's equity. At this point, the financial statements have been prepared from the work sheet, not from the ledger accounts. For the ledger accounts to show the correct balances, the adjusting entries must be journalized and posted to the ledger.

FOCUS ON BUSINESS TECHNOLOGY

Using Electronic Work Sheets

The work sheet is a good application for electronic spreadsheet software programs like Lotus and Microsoft Excel. Constructing a work sheet using spreadsheet software takes time, but once it is done, the work sheet can be used over and over. The principal advantage of electronic preparation over manual preparation is that each time a number is entered or revised, the entire electronic work sheet is updated automatically, without the possibility of addition or extension mistakes. For example, if an error in an adjusting entry is corrected, the proper extensions to the other columns are made, all columns are re-added, and net income is recomputed. Of course, the software is purely mechanical. People are still responsible for inputting the correct numbers and equations initially.

Check out ACE for a Review Quiz at http://accounting.college.hmco.com/students.

Chapter Review

Review of Learning Objectives

LO1 State all the steps in the accounting cycle.

The steps in the accounting cycle are (1) analyze business transactions from source documents, (2) record the entries in the journal, (3) post the entries to the ledger and prepare a trial balance, (4) adjust the accounts and prepare an adjusted trial balance, (5) close the accounts and prepare a post-closing trial balance, and (6) prepare the financial statements.

LO2 Explain and prepare closing entries.

Closing entries have two purposes. First, they clear the balances of all temporary accounts (revenue, expense, and owner's Withdrawals accounts) so that they have zero balances at the beginning of the next accounting period. Second, they summarize a period's revenues and expenses in the Income Summary account so that the net income or loss for the period can be transferred as a total to owner's Capital. In preparing closing entries, first the revenue and expense account balances are transferred to the Income Summary account. Then the balance of the Income Summary account is transferred to the owner's Capital account. And, finally, the balance of the owner's Withdrawals account is transferred to the owner's Capital account.

LO3 Prepare the post-closing trial balance.

As a final check on the balance of the ledger and to ensure that all temporary (nominal) accounts have been closed, a post-closing trial balance is prepared after the closing entries are posted to the ledger accounts.

LO4 Prepare reversing entries as appropriate.

Reversing entries are optional entries made on the first day of a new accounting period in order to simplify routine bookkeeping procedures. They reverse certain adjusting entries made in the previous period. As used in this text, they apply only to accruals.

LO5 Prepare and use a work sheet.

There are five steps in the preparation of a work sheet: (1) Enter and total the account balances in the Trial Balance columns; (2) enter and total the adjustments in the Adjustments columns; (3) enter and total the adjusted account balances in the Adjusted Trial Balance columns; (4) extend the account balances from the Adjusted Trial Balance columns to the Income Statement or Balance Sheet columns; and (5) total the Income Statement and Balance Sheet columns, enter the net income or net loss in both pairs of columns as a balancing figure, and recompute the column totals. A work sheet is useful in (1) recording the adjusting entries, (2) recording the closing entries, and (3) preparing the financial statements. The balance sheet and income statement can be prepared directly from the Balance Sheet and Income Statement columns of the completed work sheet. The statement of owner's equity is prepared using owner's Withdrawals, net income, additional investments, and the beginning balance of of the owner's Capital account.

Review of Concepts and Terminology

The following concepts and terms were introduced in this chapter:

LO1 **Accounting cycle:** The sequence of steps followed in the accounting system to measure business transactions and transform them into financial statements; it includes analyzing and recording transactions, posting entries, adjusting and closing the accounts, and preparing financial statements.

LO2 **Closing entries:** Entries made at the end of an accounting period that set the stage for the next accounting period by clearing the temporary accounts of their balances and transferring them to owner's Capital; they summarize a period's revenues and expenses.

LO5 **Crossfooting:** Adding and subtracting numbers across a row.

LO2 **Income Summary:** A temporary account used during the closing process that holds a summary of all revenues and expenses before the net income or loss is transferred to the owner's Capital account.

LO2 **Permanent accounts:** Balance sheet accounts; accounts whose balances can extend past the end of an accounting period. Also called *real accounts*.

LO3 **Post-closing trial balance:** A trial balance prepared at the end of the accounting period after all adjusting and closing entries have been posted; a final check on the balance of the ledger to ensure that all temporary accounts have zero balances and that total debits equal total credits.

LO4 **Reversing entry:** An entry made on the first day of an accounting period that is the exact reverse of an adjusting entry made on the last day of the previous period.

LO2 **Temporary accounts:** Accounts that show the accumulation of revenues and expenses over one accounting period; at the end of the accounting period, these account balances are transferred to owner's equity. Also called *nominal accounts.*

LO5 **Working papers:** Documents used by accountants to organize their work and to support the information in the financial statements.

LO5 **Work sheet:** A type of working paper used as a preliminary step in recording adjusting and closing entries and in the preparation of financial statements.

REVIEW PROBLEM

Preparation of Closing Entries

LO2 At the end of the current fiscal year, the adjusted trial balance for Westwood Movers Company is as follows:

Westwood Movers Company
Adjusted Trial Balance
June 30, 20xx

Cash	$ 14,200	
Accounts Receivable	18,600	
Packing Supplies	10,400	
Prepaid Insurance	7,900	
Land	4,000	
Building	80,000	
Accumulated Depreciation, Building		$ 7,500
Trucks	106,000	
Accumulated Depreciation, Trucks		27,500
Accounts Payable		7,650
Unearned Storage Fees		5,400
Mortgage Payable		70,000
Art Burton, Capital		104,740
Art Burton, Withdrawals	18,000	
Moving Services Earned		159,000
Storage Fees Earned		26,400
Driver Wages Expense	94,000	
Fuel Expense	19,000	
Office Wages Expense	14,400	
Office Equipment Rental Expense	3,000	
Utilities Expense	4,450	
Insurance Expense	4,200	
Depreciation Expense, Building	4,000	
Depreciation Expense, Trucks	6,040	
	$408,190	$408,190

REQUIRED ▶ Prepare the necessary closing entries.

ANSWER TO REVIEW PROBLEM

Closing entries prepared

June 30	Moving Services Earned	159,000	
	Storage Fees Earned	26,400	
	Income Summary		185,400
	Closed the revenue accounts		
30	Income Summary	149,090	
	Driver Wages Expense		94,000
	Fuel Expense		19,000
	Office Wages Expense		14,400
	Office Equipment Rental Expense		3,000
	Utilities Expense		4,450
	Insurance Expense		4,200
	Depreciation Expense, Building		4,000
	Depreciation Expense, Trucks		6,040
	Closed the expense accounts		
30	Income Summary	36,310	
	Art Burton, Capital		36,310
	Closed the Income Summary account and transferred balance to the Capital account		
30	Art Burton, Capital	18,000	
	Art Burton, Withdrawals		18,000
	Closed the Withdrawals account		

Chapter Assignments

BUILDING YOUR KNOWLEDGE FOUNDATION

QUESTIONS

1. Resequence the following activities **a** through **f** to indicate the correct order of the accounting cycle:
   a. The transactions are entered in the journal.
   b. The financial statements are prepared.
   c. The transactions are analyzed from the source documents.
   d. The adjusting entries are prepared.
   e. The closing entries are prepared.
   f. The transactions are posted to the ledger.
2. What are the two purposes of closing entries?
3. What is the difference between adjusting entries and closing entries?
4. What is the purpose of the Income Summary account?
5. Which of the following accounts do not show a balance after the closing entries are prepared and posted?
   a. Insurance Expense
   b. Accounts Receivable
   c. Commission Revenue
   d. Prepaid Insurance
   e. Owner's Withdrawals
   f. Supplies
   g. Supplies Expense
   h. Owner's Capital
6. What is the significance of the post-closing trial balance?

7. Which of the following accounts would you expect to find in the post-closing trial balance?
   a. Insurance Expense
   b. Accounts Receivable
   c. Commission Revenue
   d. Prepaid Insurance
   e. Owner's Withdrawals
   f. Supplies
   g. Supplies Expense
   h. Owner's Capital
8. How do reversing entries simplify the bookkeeping process?
9. To what types of adjustments do reversing entries apply? To what types do they not apply?
10. Why are working papers important to accountants?
11. Why are work sheets never published and rarely seen by management?
12. Can the work sheet be used as a substitute for the financial statements? Explain your answer.
13. What is the normal balance (debit or credit) of the following accounts?
    a. Cash
    b. Accounts Payable
    c. Prepaid Rent
    d. Sam Jones, Capital
    e. Commission Revenue
    f. Sam Jones, Withdrawals
    g. Rent Expense
    h. Accumulated Depreciation, Office Equipment
    i. Office Equipment
14. Why should the Adjusted Trial Balance columns of the work sheet be totaled before the adjusted amounts are carried to the Income Statement and Balance Sheet columns?
15. What sequence should be followed in extending the amounts in the Adjusted Trial Balance columns to the Income Statement and Balance Sheet columns? Discuss your answer.
16. Do the Income Statement columns and the Balance Sheet columns of the work sheet balance after the amounts from the Adjusted Trial Balance columns are extended?
17. Do the totals of the Balance Sheet columns of the work sheet agree with the totals on the balance sheet? Explain your answer.
18. Should adjusting entries be posted to the ledger accounts before or after the closing entries? Explain your answer.
19. At the end of the accounting period, does the posting of adjusting entries to the ledger precede or follow the preparation of the work sheet?

SHORT EXERCISES

LO1 Accounting Cycle

SE 1. Resequence the following activities to indicate the usual order of the accounting cycle:

a. Close the accounts.
b. Analyze the transactions.
c. Post the entries to the ledger.
d. Prepare the financial statements.
e. Adjust the accounts.
f. Record the transactions in the journal.
g. Prepare the post-closing trial balance.
h. Prepare the initial trial balance.
i. Prepare the adjusted trial balance.

LO2 Closing Revenue Accounts

SE 2. Assume that at the end of the accounting period there are credit balances of $3,400 in Patient Services Revenues and $1,800 in Laboratory Fees Revenues. Prepare the required closing entry in journal form. The accounting period ends December 31.

SE 3. LO2 **Closing Expense Accounts**

Assume that dedit balances at the end of the accounting period are $1,400 in Rent Expense, $1,100 in Wages Expense, and $500 in Other Expenses. Prepare the required closing entry in journal form. The accounting period ends December 31.

SE 4. LO2 **Closing the Income Summary Account**

Assuming that total revenues were $5,200 and total expenses were $3,000, prepare the entry in journal form to close the Income Summary account to the H. Blake, Capital account. The accounting period ends December 31.

SE 5. LO2 **Closing the Withdrawals Account**

Assuming that withdrawals during the accounting period were $800, prepare the entry in journal form to close the H. Blake, Withdrawals account to the H. Blake, Capital account. The accounting period ends December 31.

SE 6. LO2 **Posting Closing Entries**

Show the effects of the transactions in **SE 2, SE 3, SE 4,** and **SE 5** by entering beginning balances in appropriate T accounts and recording the transactions. Assume that the H. Blake, Capital account has a beginning balance of $1,300.

SE 7. LO4 **Preparation of Reversing Entries**

Below, indicated by letters, are the adjusting entries at the end of March.

Account Name	Debit	Credit
Prepaid Insurance		(a) 180
Accumulated Depreciation, Office Equipment		(b) 1,050
Salaries Expense	(c) 360	
Insurance Expense	(a) 180	
Depreciation Expense, Office Equipment	(b) 1,050	
Salaries Payable		(c) 360
	1,590	1, 590

Prepare the required reversing entry in journal form.

SE 8. LO4 **Effects of Reversing Entries**

Assume that prior to the adjustments in **SE 7**, Salaries Expense had a debit balance of $1,800 and Salaries Payable had a zero balance. Prepare a T account for each of these accounts. Enter the beginning balance; post the adjustment for accrued salaries, the appropriate closing entry, and the reversing entry; and enter the transaction in the T accounts for a payment of $480 for salaries on April 3.

SE 9. LO2 LO5 **Preparing Closing Entries from a Work Sheet**

Prepare the required closing entries in journal form for the year ended December 31, using the following items from the Income Statement columns of a work sheet and assuming that withdrawals by the owner, M. Dye, were $6,000:

	Income Statement	
Account Name	Debit	Credit
Repair Revenue		32,860
Wages Expense	12,260	
Rent Expense	1,800	
Supplies Expense	6,390	
Insurance Expense	1,370	
Depreciation Expense, Repair Equipment	2,020	
	23,840	32,860
Net Income	9,020	
	32,860	32,860

Exercises

E 1. **LO2 Preparation of Closing Entries**

The adjusted trial balance for the Featherstone Real Estate Company at the end of its fiscal year is shown below. Prepare the required closing entries in journal form.

Featherstone Real Estate Company
Adjusted Trial Balance
December 31, 20xx

Cash	$ 7,275	
Accounts Receivable	2,325	
Prepaid Insurance	585	
Office Supplies	440	
Office Equipment	6,300	
Accumulated Depreciation, Office Equipment		$ 765
Automobile	6,750	
Accumulated Depreciation, Automobile		750
Accounts Payable		1,700
Unearned Management Fees		1,500
V. Featherstone, Capital		14,535
V. Featherstone, Withdrawals	7,000	
Sales Commissions Earned		31,700
Office Salaries Expense	13,500	
Advertising Expense	2,525	
Rent Expense	2,650	
Telephone Expense	1,600	
	$50,950	$50,950

E 2. **LO4 Reversing Entries**

Selected September T accounts for Weins Company are presented below.

Supplies

9/1 Bal.	860	9/30 Adjust.	1,280
Sept. purchases	940		
Bal.	520		

Supplies Expense

9/30 Adjust.	1,280	9/30 Closing	1,280
Bal.	—		

Wages Payable

		9/30 Adjust.	640
		Bal.	640

Wages Expense

Sept. wages	3,940	9/30 Closing	4,580
9/30 Adjust.	640		
Bal.	—		

1. In which of the accounts would a reversing entry be helpful? Why?
2. Prepare the appropriate reversing entry.
3. Prepare the entry to record a payment on October 3 for wages totaling $3,140. How much of this amount represents wages expense for October?

E 3. **LO5 Preparation of a Trial Balance**

The following alphabetical list presents the accounts and balances for Jessica's Dresses on June 30, 20x4. All the accounts have normal balances.

Accounts Payable	$15,420
Accounts Receivable	7,650
Accumulated Depreciation, Office Equipment	1,350
Advertising Expense	1,800

Cash	7,635
J. Alaria, Capital	30,630
J. Alaria, Withdrawals	27,000
Office Equipment	15,510
Prepaid Insurance	1,680
Rent Expense	7,200
Revenue from Commissions	57,900
Supplies	825
Wages Expense	36,000

Prepare the trial balance by listing the accounts in the correct order, with the balances in the appropriate debit or credit column.

LO5 Completion of a Work Sheet

E 4. The following is a highly simplified alphabetical list of trial balance accounts and their normal balances for the month ended March 31, 20xx:

Trial Balance Accounts and Balances

Accounts Payable	$4	Prepaid Insurance	$ 2
Accounts Receivable	7	Service Revenue	23
Accumulated Depreciation, Office Equipment	1	Supplies	4
Cash	4	Terri Julius, Capital	12
Office Equipment	8	Terri Julius, Withdrawals	6
		Unearned Revenues	3
		Utilities Expense	2
		Wages Expense	10

1. Prepare a work sheet, entering the trial balance accounts in the order in which they would normally appear and entering the balances in the correct debit or credit column.
2. Complete the work sheet using the following information:
   a. Expired insurance, $1.
   b. Of the unearned revenues balance, $2 has been earned by the end of the month.
   c. Estimated depreciation on office equipment, $1.
   d. Accrued wages, $1.
   e. Unused supplies on hand, $1.

LO5 Preparation of a Statement of Owner's Equity

E 5. The Capital, Withdrawals, and Income Summary accounts for Sariah's Clip Shop are shown in T account form below. The closing entries have been recorded for the year ended December 31, 20x4.

Sariah Abdul, Capital

12/31/x4	4,500	12/31/x3	13,000
		12/31/x4	9,500
		Bal.	18,000

Income Summary

12/31/x4	21,500	12/31/x4	31,000
12/31/x4	9,500		
Bal.	—		

Sariah Abdul, Withdrawals

4/1/x4	1,500	12/31/x4	4,500
7/1/x4	1,500		
10/1/x4	1,500		
Bal.	—		

Prepare a statement of owner's equity for Sariah's Clip Shop.

LO5 Adjusting Entries and Preparation of a Balance Sheet

E 6. In the partial work sheet that follows, the Trial Balance and Income Statement columns have been completed. All amounts shown are in dollars.

Account Name	Trial Balance Debit	Trial Balance Credit	Income Statement Debit	Income Statement Credit
Cash	14			
Accounts Receivable	24			
Supplies	22			
Prepaid Insurance	16			
Building	50			
Accumulated Depreciation, Building		16		
Accounts Payable		8		
Unearned Revenues		4		
T. L., Capital		64		
Revenues		88		92
Wages Expense	54		60	
	180	180		
Insurance Expense			8	
Supplies Expense			16	
Depreciation Expense, Building			4	
Wages Payable				
			88	92
Net Income			4	
			92	92

1. Show the adjustments that have been made in journal form without explanation.
2. Prepare a balance sheet.

E 7. LO4 LO5 **Preparation of Adjusting and Reversing Entries from Work Sheet Columns**

The items that appear below are from the Adjustments columns of a work sheet dated June 30, 20xx.

Account Name	Adjustments Debit	Adjustments Credit
Prepaid Insurance		(a) 240
Office Supplies		(b) 630
Accumulated Depreciation, Office Equipment		(c) 1,400
Accumulated Depreciation, Store Equipment		(d) 2,200
Office Salaries Expense	(e) 240	
Store Salaries Expense	(e) 480	
Insurance Expense	(a) 240	
Office Supplies Expense	(b) 630	
Depreciation Expense, Office Equipment	(c) 1,400	
Depreciation Expense, Store Equipment	(d) 2,200	
Salaries Payable		(e) 720
	5,190	5,190

1. Prepare the adjusting entries in journal form.
2. Where required, prepare appropriate reversing entries in journal form.

E 8. LO2 LO5 **Preparation of Closing Entries from the Work Sheet**

The items that follow are from the Income Statement columns of the work sheet for O'Malley Repair Shop for the year ended December 31, 20xx.

Account Name	Income Statement	
	Debit	Credit
Repair Revenue		25,620
Wages Expense	8,110	
Rent Expense	1,200	
Supplies Expense	4,260	
Insurance Expense	915	
Depreciation Expense, Repair Equipment	1,345	
	15,830	25,620
Net Income	9,790	
	25,620	25,620

Prepare entries in journal form to close the revenue, expense, Income Summary, and Withdrawals accounts. O'Malley withdrew $5,000 during the year.

PROBLEMS

LO2 Closing Entries Using T Accounts and Preparation of Financial Statements

P 1. The adjusted trial balance for Applewilde Tennis Club at the end of the company's fiscal year appears below.

Applewilde Tennis Club
Adjusted Trial Balance
June 30, 20x5

Cash	$ 26,200	
Prepaid Advertising	9,600	
Supplies	1,200	
Land	100,000	
Building	645,200	
Accumulated Depreciation, Building		$ 260,000
Equipment	156,000	
Accumulated Depreciation, Equipment		50,400
Accounts Payable		73,000
Wages Payable		29,000
Property Taxes Payable		22,500
Unearned Revenues, Locker Fees		3,000
Susan Wilde, Capital		471,150
Susan Wilde, Withdrawals	54,000	
Revenues from Court Fees		678,100
Revenues from Locker Fees		9,600
Wages Expense	351,000	
Maintenance Expense	51,600	
Advertising Expense	39,750	
Utilities Expense	64,800	
Supplies Expense	26,000	
Depreciation Expense, Building	30,000	
Depreciation Expense, Equipment	12,000	
Property Taxes Expense	22,500	
Miscellaneous Expense	6,900	
	$1,596,750	$1,596,750

REQUIRED

1. Prepare T accounts and enter the balances for Susan Wilde, Capital; Susan Wilde, Withdrawals; Income Summary; and all revenue and expense accounts.
2. Enter the four required closing entries in the T accounts, labeling the components *a*, *b*, *c*, and *d*, as appropriate.
3. Prepare an income statement, a statement of owner's equity, and a balance sheet. Assume no additional investments by the owner.
4. Explain why closing entries are necessary at the end of the accounting period.

P 2.

LO2 **Closing Entries Using Journal Form and Preparation of Financial Statements**

Lakeside Campgrounds, owned by Anthony Fabrizzi, rents out campsites in a wooded park. The adjusted trial balance for Lakeside Campgrounds on May 31, 20x5, the end of the current fiscal year, is as follows:

Lakeside Campgrounds
Adjusted Trial Balance
May 31, 20x5

Cash	$ 2,040	
Accounts Receivable	3,660	
Supplies	114	
Prepaid Insurance	594	
Land	15,000	
Building	45,900	
Accumulated Depreciation, Building		$ 10,500
Accounts Payable		1,725
Wages Payable		825
Anthony Fabrizzi, Capital		46,535
Anthony Fabrizzi, Withdrawals	18,000	
Campsite Rentals		44,100
Wages Expense	11,925	
Insurance Expense	1,892	
Utilities Expense	900	
Supplies Expense	660	
Depreciation Expense, Building	3,000	
	$103,685	$103,685

REQUIRED

1. Record the closing entries in journal form.
2. From the information given, prepare an income statement, a statement of owner's equity, and a balance sheet. Assume no additional investments by the owner.
3. Assuming that Wages Payable represents wages accrued at the end of the accounting period, record the optional reversing entry on June 1.

P 3.

LO1 LO2 LO3 **The Complete Accounting Cycle Without a Work Sheet: Two Months (second month optional)**

On October 1, 20xx, Jason Dauphinais opened Dauphinais Appliance Service. During the month, he completed the following transactions for the company:

Oct.	1	Began business by depositing $5,000 in a bank account.
	1	Paid the rent for a store for one month, $425.
	1	Paid the premium on a one-year insurance policy, $480.
	2	Purchased repair equipment from Fitzgerald Company, $4,200. Terms were $600 down and $300 per month for one year. First payment is due November 1.
	5	Purchased repair supplies from Deane Company on credit, $468.
	8	Paid cash for an advertisement in a local newspaper, $60.
	15	Received cash repair revenue for the first half of the month, $400.
	21	Paid Deane Company on account, $225.
	31	Received cash repair revenue for the second half of October, $975.
	31	Withdrew cash for personal expenses, $300.

REQUIRED FOR OCTOBER ▶

1. Prepare entries in journal form to record the October transactions.
2. Open the following accounts: Cash (111); Prepaid Insurance (117); Repair Supplies (119); Repair Equipment (144); Accumulated Depreciation, Repair Equipment (145); Accounts Payable (212); J. Dauphinais, Capital (311); J. Dáuphinais, Withdrawals (312); Income Summary (313); Repair Revenue (411); Store Rent Expense (511); Advertising Expense (512); Insurance Expense (513); Repair Supplies Expense (514); and Depreciation Expense, Repair Equipment (515). Post the October entries to the ledger accounts.
3. Using the following information, record adjusting entries in journal form and post to the ledger accounts:
   a. One month's insurance has expired.
   b. The remaining inventory of unused repair supplies is $169.
   c. The estimated depreciation on repair equipment is $70.
4. From the accounts in the ledger, prepare an adjusted trial balance. (*Note:* Normally a trial balance is prepared before adjustments but is omitted here to save time.)
5. From the adjusted trial balance, prepare an income statement, a statement of owner's equity, and a balance sheet for October.
6. Prepare and post closing entries.
7. Prepare a post-closing trial balance.

(Optional) During November, Jason Dauphinais completed these transactions for Dauphinais Appliance Service:

Nov.	1	Paid the monthly rent, $425.
	1	Made the monthly payment to Fitzgerald Company, $300.
	6	Purchased additional repair supplies on credit from Deane Company, $863.
	15	Received cash repair revenue for the first half of the month, $914.
	20	Paid cash for an advertisement in the local newspaper, $60.
	23	Paid Deane Company on account, $600.
	30	Received cash repair revenue for the last half of the month, $817.
	30	Withdrew cash for personal expenses, $300.

REQUIRED FOR NOVEMBER ▶

8. Prepare and post entries in journal form to record the November transactions.
9. Using the following information, record adjusting entries in journal form and post to the ledger accounts:
   a. One month's insurance has expired.
   b. The inventory of unused repair supplies is $413.
   c. The estimated depreciation on repair equipment is $70.
10. From the accounts in the ledger, prepare an adjusted trial balance.
11. From the adjusted trial balance, prepare the November income statement, statement of owner's equity, and balance sheet.
12. Prepare and post closing entries.
13. Prepare a post-closing trial balance.

P 4. LO2 LO4 LO5 **Preparation of a Work Sheet, Financial Statements, and Adjusting, Closing, and Reversing Entries**

Jacqueline Woo opened her executive search service on July 1, 20x4. Some customers paid for her services after they were rendered, and others paid in advance for one year of service. After six months of operation, Woo wanted to know how her business stood. The trial balance on December 31 appears at the top of the next page.

REQUIRED ▶

1. Enter the trial balance amounts in the Trial Balance columns of a work sheet. Remember that accumulated depreciation is listed with its asset account. Complete the work sheet using the following information:
   a. One year's rent had been paid in advance when Woo began business.
   b. Inventory of unused office supplies, $75.
   c. One-half year's depreciation on office equipment, $900.
   d. Service rendered that had been paid for in advance, $863.
   e. Executive search services rendered during the month but not yet billed, $270.
   f. Wages earned by employees but not yet paid, $188.
2. Prepare an income statement, a statement of owner's equity, and a balance sheet.

Jacqueline Woo Executive Search Service
Trial Balance
December 31, 20x4

Cash	$ 713	
Accounts Receivable	1,000	
Prepaid Rent	1,800	
Office Supplies	413	
Office Equipment	15,750	
Accounts Payable		$ 3,173
Unearned Revenues		1,823
Jacqueline Woo, Capital		10,000
Jacqueline Woo, Withdrawals	5,200	
Search Revenue		20,140
Utilities Expense	1,260	
Wages Expense	9,000	
	$35,136	$35,136

3. Prepare adjusting, closing, and, if required, reversing entries.
4. What is your evaluation of Jacqueline Woo's first six months in business?

LO2 Preparation of a Work Sheet,
LO4 Financial Statements, and
LO5 Adjusting, Closing, and Reversing Entries

P 5. The following trial balance was taken from the ledger of McIntire Express Delivery Company on August 31, 20x4, the end of the company's fiscal year:

McIntire Express Delivery Company
Trial Balance
August 31, 20x4

Cash	$ 5,036	
Accounts Receivable	14,657	
Prepaid Insurance	2,670	
Delivery Supplies	7,350	
Office Supplies	1,230	
Land	7,500	
Building	98,000	
Accumulated Depreciation, Building		$ 26,700
Trucks	51,900	
Accumulated Depreciation, Trucks		15,450
Office Equipment	7,950	
Accumulated Depreciation, Office Equipment		5,400
Accounts Payable		4,698
Unearned Lockbox Fees		4,170
Mortgage Payable		36,000
Matt McIntire, Capital		64,365
Matt McIntire, Withdrawals	15,000	
Delivery Services Revenue		141,735
Lockbox Fees Earned		14,400
Truck Drivers' Wages Expense	63,900	
Office Salaries Expense	22,200	
Gas, Oil, and Truck Repairs Expense	15,525	
	$312,918	$312,918

REQUIRED ▶

1. Enter the trial balance amounts in the Trial Balance columns of a work sheet and complete the work sheet using the following information:
   a. Expired insurance, $1,530.
   b. Inventory of unused delivery supplies, $715.
   c. Inventory of unused office supplies, $93.
   d. Estimated depreciation, building, $7,200.
   e. Estimated depreciation, trucks, $7,725.
   f. Estimated depreciation, office equipment, $1,350.
   g. The company credits the lockbox fees of customers who pay in advance to the Unearned Lockbox Fees account. Of the amount credited to this account during the year, $2,815 had been earned by August 31.
   h. Lockbox fees earned but unrecorded and uncollected at the end of the accounting period, $408.
   i. Accrued but unpaid truck drivers' wages at the end of the year, $960.
2. Prepare an income statement, a statement of owner's equity, and a balance sheet. Assume no additional investments by Matt McIntire.
3. Prepare adjusting, closing, and, if required, reversing entries.

ALTERNATE PROBLEMS

LO2 Closing Entries Using T Accounts and Preparation of Financial Statements

P 6. The adjusted trial balance for Hartford Go-Cart Lanes at the end of the company's fiscal year is as follows:

Hartford Go-Cart Lanes
Adjusted Trial Balance
December 31, 20x4

Cash	$ 16,214	
Accounts Receivable	7,388	
Supplies	156	
Prepaid Insurance	300	
Land	5,000	
Building	100,000	
Accumulated Depreciation, Building		$ 27,200
Equipment	125,000	
Accumulated Depreciation, Equipment		33,000
Accounts Payable		30,044
Notes Payable		70,000
Unearned Revenues		300
Wages Payable		3,962
Property Taxes Payable		10,000
Tom Wells, Capital		60,813
Tom Wells, Withdrawals	24,000	
Revenues		618,263
Wages Expense	381,076	
Advertising Expense	30,200	
Maintenance Expense	84,100	
Supplies Expense	1,148	
Insurance Expense	1,500	
Depreciation Expense, Building	4,800	
Depreciation Expense, Equipment	11,000	
Utilities Expense	42,200	
Miscellaneous Expense	9,500	
Property Taxes Expense	10,000	
	$853,582	$853,582

REQUIRED ▶

1. Prepare T accounts and enter the balances for Tom Wells, Capital; Tom Wells, Withdrawals; Income Summary; and all revenue and expense accounts.
2. Enter in the T accounts the four required closing entries, labeling the components *a*, *b*, *c*, and *d* as appropriate.
3. Prepare an income statement, a statement of owner's equity, and a balance sheet.
4. Explain why closing entries are necessary at the end of the accounting period.

P 7. LO2 **Closing Entries Using Journal Form and Preparation of Financial Statements**

Do-It-Yourself Trailer Rental rents small trailers by the day for local moving jobs. This is its adjusted trial balance at the end of the current fiscal year:

Do-It-Yourself Trailer Rental
Adjusted Trial Balance
June 30, 20x5

Cash	$ 692	
Accounts Receivable	972	
Supplies	119	
Prepaid Insurance	360	
Trailers	12,000	
Accumulated Depreciation, Trailers		$ 7,200
Accounts Payable		271
Wages Payable		200
Selena Perez, Capital		5,694
Selena Perez, Withdrawals	7,200	
Trailer Rentals Revenue		45,546
Wages Expense	23,400	
Insurance Expense	720	
Supplies Expense	266	
Depreciation Expense, Trailers	2,400	
Other Expenses	10,782	
	$58,911	$58,911

REQUIRED ▶

1. From the information given, record closing entries in journal form.
2. Prepare an income statement, a statement of owner's equity, and a balance sheet. Assume no additional investments by Selena Perez.

P 8. LO2 LO4 LO5 **Preparation of a Work Sheet, Financial Statements, and Adjusting, Closing, and Reversing Entries**

At the end of the current fiscal year, the trial balance of Flynn Theater appeared as shown at the top of the opposite page.

REQUIRED ▶

1. Enter the trial balance amounts in the Trial Balance columns of a work sheet and complete the work sheet using the following information.
   a. Expired insurance, $8,700.
   b. Inventory of unused office supplies, $122.
   c. Inventory of unused cleaning supplies, $234.
   d. Estimated depreciation, building, $7,000.
   e. Estimated depreciation, theater furnishings, $18,000.
   f. Estimated depreciation, office equipment, $1,580.
   g. The company credits all gift books sold during the year to the Gift Books Liability account. A gift book is a booklet of ticket coupons purchased in advance as a gift. The recipient redeems the coupons at some point in the future. On December 31, it was estimated that $18,900 worth of the gift books had been redeemed.
   h. Accrued but unpaid usher wages at the end of the accounting period, $430.
2. Prepare an income statement, a statement of owner's equity, and a balance sheet. Assume no additional investments by Danielle Flynn.
3. Prepare adjusting, closing, and, when possible, reversing entries from the work sheet.

Flynn Theater
Trial Balance
December 31, 20x5

Cash	$ 15,900	
Accounts Receivable	9,272	
Prepaid Insurance	9,800	
Office Supplies	390	
Cleaning Supplies	1,795	
Land	10,000	
Building	200,000	
Accumulated Depreciation, Building		$ 19,700
Theater Furnishings	185,000	
Accumulated Depreciation, Theater Furnishings		32,500
Office Equipment	15,800	
Accumulated Depreciation, Office Equipment		7,780
Accounts Payable		22,753
Gift Books Liability		20,950
Mortgage Payable		150,000
Danielle Flynn, Capital		156,324
Danielle Flynn, Withdrawals	30,000	
Ticket Sales Revenue		205,700
Theater Rental Revenue		22,600
Usher Wages Expense	92,000	
Office Wages Expense	12,000	
Utilities Expense	56,350	
	$638,307	$638,307

SKILLS DEVELOPMENT CASES

Conceptual Analysis

SD 1.
LO1 Interim Financial Statements

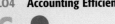

Ocean Oil Services Company provides services for drilling operations off the coast of Louisiana. The company has a significant amount of debt to River National Bank in Baton Rouge. The bank requires the company to provide it with quarterly financial statements. Explain what is involved in preparing financial statements every quarter.

SD 2.
LO4 Accounting Efficiency

Way Heaters Company manufactures industrial heaters used in making candy. It sells its heaters to some customers on credit with generous terms specifying payment six months after purchase and an interest rate based on current bank rates. Because the interest on the loans accrues a little every day but is not paid until the note's due date, an adjusting entry must be made at the end of each accounting period to debit Interest Receivable and credit Interest Income for the amount of the interest accrued but not paid to date. The company prepares financial statements every month. Keeping track of what has been accrued in the past is time-consuming because the notes carry different dates and interest rates. Discuss what the accountant can do to simplify the process of making the adjusting entry for accrued interest each month.

Ethical Dilemma

SD 3.
LO1 Ethics and Time Pressure

Jay Wheeler, an accountant for WB Company, has made adjusting entries and is preparing the adjusted trial balance for the first six months of the year. Financial statements must be delivered to the bank by 5 P.M. to support a critical loan agreement. By noon, Wheeler has been unable to balance the adjusted trial balance. The figures are off by $1,320, so he increases the balance of the owner's Capital account by $1,320. He closes the accounts, prepares the statements, and sends them to the bank on time. Wheeler hopes that no one will notice the problem and believes that he can find the error and correct it by the end of next month. Are Wheeler's actions ethical? Why or why not? Did he have other alternatives?

Research Activity

SD 4. **Interview of a Local Businessperson** (LO1, LO2, LO3, LO4, LO5)

Arrange to spend about an hour interviewing the owner, manager, or accountant of a local service or retail business. Your goal is to learn as much as you can about the accounting cycle of the person's business. Ask the interviewee to show you his or her accounting records and to tell you how such transactions as sales, purchases, payments, and payroll are handled. Examine the documents used to support the transactions. Look at any journals, ledgers, or work sheets. Does the business use a computer? Does it use its own accounting system, or does it use an outside or centralized service? Does it use the cash or the accrual basis of accounting? When does it prepare adjusting entries? When does it prepare closing entries? How often does it prepare financial statements? Does it prepare reversing entries? How do its procedures differ from those described in the text? When the interview is finished, organize and write up your findings and be prepared to present them in class.

Group Activity: Divide the class into groups and have each group investigate a different type of business, such as a shoe store, grocery store, hardware store, and fast-food restaurant. Have the groups give presentations in class.

Decision-Making Practice

SD 5. **Conversion from Accrual to Cash Statement** (LO1, LO2)

Adele, owner of Adele's Secretarial Service, is puzzled by the income statement that appears below. She knows she withdrew $15,600 in cash from the company for personal expenses; yet the cash balance in the company's bank account increased from $460 to $3,100 from last June 30 to this June 30. She wants to know how her net income could be less than the cash she took out of the business if there is an increase in the cash balance. Her accountant has completed the closing entries and shows her the balance sheets for June 30, 20x4, and June 30, 20x3. He explains that besides the change in the cash balance, Accounts Receivable decreased by $1,480 and Accounts Payable increased by $380 (supplies are the only items Adele buys on credit). The only other asset or liability account that changed during the year was Accumulated Depreciation, Office Equipment, which increased by $2,200.

Adele's Secretarial Service
Income Statement
For the Year Ended June 30, 20x4

Revenues		
Word processing services		$20,980
Expenses		
Rent expense	$2,400	
Depreciation expense, office equipment	2,200	
Supplies expense	960	
Other expenses	1,240	
Total expenses		6,800
Net income		$14,180

1. Verify the cash balance increase by preparing a statement that lists the receipts of cash and the expenditures of cash during the year.
2. Write a memorandum to Adele explaining why the accountant is answering her question by pointing out year-to-year changes in the balance sheet. Include an explanation of your treatment of depreciation expense.

FINANCIAL REPORTING AND ANALYSIS CASES

Interpreting Financial Reports

LO2 Closing Entries

FRA 1. H&R Block, Inc., <www.hrblock.com> is the world's largest tax preparation service firm. Adapted information from the statement of earnings (in thousands, without earnings per share information) in its annual report for the year ended April 30, 2002, follows.[2] The firm reported distributing cash in the amount of $115,725 to the owners in 2002.

Revenues	
Service revenues	$2,333,064
Other revenues	986,084
Total revenues	$3,319,148
Expenses	
Employee compensation and benefits	$1,308,705
Occupancy and equipment expense	305,387
Depreciation expense	155,386
Marketing and advertising expense	155,729
Supplies, freight, and postage expense	75,710
Bad debt	76,804
Interest expense	116,141
Other operating expenses	408,446
Total expenses	$2,602,308
Earnings before income taxes	$ 716,840
Income taxes	282,435
Net earnings	$ 434,405

1. Prepare in journal form the closing entries H&R Block would have made on April 30, 2002. Treat income taxes as an expense and cash distributions as withdrawals.
2. Based on the way you handled expenses and cash distributions in step **1** and their ultimate effect on the owner's capital, what theoretical reason can you give for not including expenses and cash distributions in the same closing entry?

International Company

LO1 Accounting Cycle and Closing
LO2 Entries

FRA 2. Nestlé S.A. <www.nestle.com>, maker of such well-known products as Nescafé, Lean Cuisine, and Perrier, is one of the largest and most internationally diverse companies in the world. Only 2 percent of its $81.4 billion in revenues comes from its home country of Switzerland; the rest comes from sales in almost every other country. Nestlé has over 224,000 employees in 70 countries, and many of its divisions operate as separate companies.[3] How would the accounting cycle, including the closing process, be the same for Nestlé as for Joan Miller Advertising Agency? How would it differ?

Toys "R" Us Annual Report

LO1 Fiscal Year, Closing Process, and Interim Reports

FRA 3. Refer to the notes to the financial statements in the Toys "R" Us <www.tru.com> annual report. When does Toys "R" Us end its fiscal year? For what reasons might it have chosen this date? From the standpoint of completing the accounting cycle, what advantages does this date have? Does Toys "R" Us prepare interim financial statements? What are the implications of interim financial statements for the accounting cycle?

Comparison Case: Toys "R" Us and Walgreen Co.

FRA 4.
LO2 **Interim Financial Reporting and Seasonality**

Both Walgreens <www.walgreens.com> and Toys "R" Us <www.tru.com> provide quarterly financial information in their financial statements. Quarterly financial reports provide important information about the "seasonality" of a company's operations. *Seasonality* refers to how dependent a company is on sales during one season of the year, such as the Christmas season, and it affects a company's need to plan for cash flows and inventory. From the quarterly financial information for Walgreens and for Toys "R" Us in the Supplement to Chapter 6, determine which company has more seasonal sales and income by calculating for the most recent year the percentage of quarterly net sales and net earnings to annual net sales and net earnings. Discuss the results.

Fingraph® Financial Analyst™

This activity is not applicable to this chapter.

Internet Case

FRA 5.
LO1 **Interim Financial Statements**

Go to Dell Computer Corporation's web site <www.dell.com> and find the latest quarterly financial report. Compare the results of the latest quarter available to you with the results in the Decision Point at the beginning of this chapter. Are Dell's net revenue (sales) and net income greater or less in the more recent quarter? What other information do you find in the quarterly report?

Comprehensive Problem: Joan Miller Advertising Agency

This comprehensive problem involving the Joan Miller Advertising Agency covers all the learning objectives in this chapter and in the chapters on measuring business transactions and measuring business income. To complete the problem, you may sometimes have to refer to this material.

The July 31, 20xx, post-closing trial balance for the Joan Miller Advertising Agency appears on the facing page. During August, the agency engaged in these transactions:

Aug. 1 Received an additional investment of cash from Joan Miller, $6,300.
2 Purchased additional office equipment with cash, $1,200.
5 Received art equipment transferred to the business from Joan Miller, $1,400.
6 Purchased additional office supplies with cash, $90.
7 Purchased additional art supplies on credit from Taylor Supply Company, $450.
8 Completed the series of advertisements for Marsh Tire Company that began on July 31 (see page 103) and billed Marsh Tire Company for the total services performed, including the accrued revenues (fees receivable) that had been recognized in an adjusting entry in July, $800.
9 Paid the secretary for two weeks' wages, $1,200.
12 Paid the amount due to Morgan Equipment for the office equipment purchased last month, $1,500.
13 Accepted an advance in cash for artwork to be done for another agency, $1,600.
14 Purchased a copier (office equipment) from Morgan Equipment for $2,100, paying $350 in cash and agreeing to pay the rest in equal payments over the next five months.
15 Performed advertising services and received a cash fee, $1,450.
16 Received payment on account from Ward Department Stores for services performed last month, $2,800.

Joan Miller Advertising Agency
Post-Closing Trial Balance
July 31, 20xx

Cash	$ 9,140	
Accounts Receivable	5,000	
Art Supplies	1,300	
Office Supplies	600	
Prepaid Rent	800	
Prepaid Insurance	880	
Art Equipment	4,200	
Accumulated Depreciation, Art Equipment		$ 70
Office Equipment	3,000	
Accumulated Depreciation, Office Equipment		50
Accounts Payable		3,240
Unearned Art Fees		600
Wages Payable		360
Joan Miller, Capital		20,600
	$24,920	$24,920

Aug. 19 Paid amount due for the telephone bill that was received and recorded at the end of July, $140.
20 Performed advertising services for Ward Department Stores and agreed to accept payment next month, $3,200.
21 Performed art services for cash, $580.
22 Received and paid the utility bill for August, $220.
23 Paid the secretary for two weeks' wages, $1,200.
26 Paid the rent for September in advance, $800.
27 Received the telephone bill for August, which is to be paid next month, $160.
30 Paid cash to Joan Miller as a withdrawal for personal expenses, $1,400.

REQUIRED

1. Record entries in journal form and post to the ledger accounts the optional reversing entries on August 1 for Wages Payable and Accounts Receivable (see Adjustment **g** on page 101 and Adjustment **i** on page 103). (Begin the general journal on Page 5.)
2. Record the transactions for August in journal form.
3. Post the August transactions to the ledger accounts.
4. Prepare a trial balance in the Trial Balance columns of a work sheet.
5. Prepare adjusting entries and complete the work sheet using the information below.
   a. One month's prepaid rent has expired, $800.
   b. One month's prepaid insurance has expired, $80.
   c. An inventory of art supplies reveals $600 still on hand on August 31.
   d. An inventory of office supplies reveals $410 still on hand on August 31.
   e. Depreciation on art equipment for August is calculated to be $100.
   f. Depreciation on office equipment for August is calculated to be $100.
   g. Art services performed for which payment had been received in advance totaled $1,300.
   h. Advertising services performed that will not be billed until September total $290.
   i. Three days' wages had accrued by the end of August (assume a five-day week).
6. From the work sheet prepare an income statement, a statement of owner's equity, and a balance sheet.
7. Record the adjusting entries in journal form, and post them to the ledger accounts.
8. Record the closing entries in journal form, and post them to the ledger accounts.
9. Prepare a post-closing trial balance.

5 Chapter 5 introduces merchandising accounting, including the operating cycle and the perpetual and periodic inventory systems for merchandising businesses.

Merchandising Operations

Learning Objectives

LO1 Identify the management issues related to merchandising businesses.

LO2 Compare the income statements for service and merchandising concerns, and define the components of the merchandising income statement.

LO3 Define and distinguish the terms of sale for merchandising transactions.

LO4 Prepare an income statement and record merchandising transactions under the perpetual inventory system.

LO5 Prepare an income statement and record merchandising transactions under the periodic inventory system.

Supplemental Objectives

SO6 Prepare a work sheet and closing entries for a merchandising concern using the perpetual inventory system.

SO7 Prepare a work sheet and closing entries for a merchandising concern using the periodic inventory system.

SO8 Apply sales and purchases discounts to merchandising transactions.

DECISION POINT

A USER'S FOCUS

Target Stores <www.target.com> Merchandising businesses have two key decisions to make: the price at which they sell merchandise and the level of service they provide. A department store may set the price of its merchandise at a relatively high level and provide a great deal of service. A discount store, on the other hand, may price its merchandise at a relatively low level and provide limited service. Target Stores, a division of Target Corp., is a successful discount retailer, as the figures in the Financial Highlights show.[1] What decisions did Target Stores' management make about pricing and service to achieve this success?

Target distinguishes itself from other discounters by providing its customers with high-quality, name-brand merchandise, superior service, a convenient shopping experience, and competitive prices. Target's merchandise might be sold at full price in specialty stores; Target sells it at prices that are competitive with those of other discount stores that sell less well-known merchandise. Target's chief executive officer says, "We continue to open stores across the country. . . . Even in our most populated states, our market presence has expanded by 40 percent [since 1997] indicating ample opportunity for profitable growth well into the future."[2]

What decisions did Target's management make about pricing and service that resulted in Target's becoming a leading discount retailer?

Financial Highlights

(In millions, except stores and square feet)

	2002	2001
Revenues	**$43,917**	$39,826
Net earnings	**1,654**	1,386
Stores	**1,475**	1,381
Retail square feet*	**176,525**	161,624

*In thousands, reflects total square feet, less office, warehouse, and vacant space.

Management Issues in Merchandising Businesses

LO1 Identify the management issues related to merchandising businesses.

RELATED TEXT ASSIGNMENTS
Q: 1, 2, 3, 4, 5, 6, 7
SE: 1
E: 1, 2
P: 1, 3, 8, 10
SD: 1, 2, 4
FRA: 3, 4, 5, 6

Up to this point you have studied business and accounting issues related to the simplest type of business—the service business. **Service businesses**, such as advertising agencies and law firms, perform services for fees or commissions. **Merchandising businesses**, on the other hand, earn income by buying and selling goods. These companies, whether wholesale or retail, use the same basic accounting methods as service companies, but the buying and selling of goods adds to the complexity of the process. As a foundation for discussing the accounting issues of merchandising businesses, we must first identify the management issues involved in running such a business.

Cash Flow Management

Cash flow management involves planning a company's receipts and payments of cash. If a company is not able to pay its bills when they are due, it may be forced out of business. This is particularly true for merchandising businesses, which differ from service businesses in that they must have goods on hand so that they are available for sale to customers. These goods are called **merchandise inventory**.

KEY POINT: The operating cycle is average day's inventory on hand plus the average number of days to collect credit sales.

Merchandising businesses engage in a series of transactions called the **operating cycle**, which is illustrated in Figure 1. The transactions in the operating cycle consist of (1) purchases of merchandise inventory for cash or on credit, (2) payment for purchases made on credit, (3) sales of merchandise inventory for cash or on credit, and (4) collection of cash from credit sales. Purchases of merchandise are usually made on credit, so the merchandiser has a period of time before payment is due, but this period is generally less than the time it takes to sell the merchandise. To finance the inventory until it is sold and the resulting cash is collected, management must plan for cash flows from within the company or from borrowing.

The need for cash flow management is demonstrated in Figure 2, which shows the financing period. Sometimes referred to as the *cash gap*, the **financing period** is the amount of time from the purchase of inventory until it is sold and payment is collected, less the amount of time creditors give the company to pay for the inventory. Thus, if it takes 60 days to sell inventory, 60 days to collect for the sale, and creditors' payment terms are 30 days, the financing period is 90 days. During the

Figure 1
The Operating Cycle of Merchandising Businesses

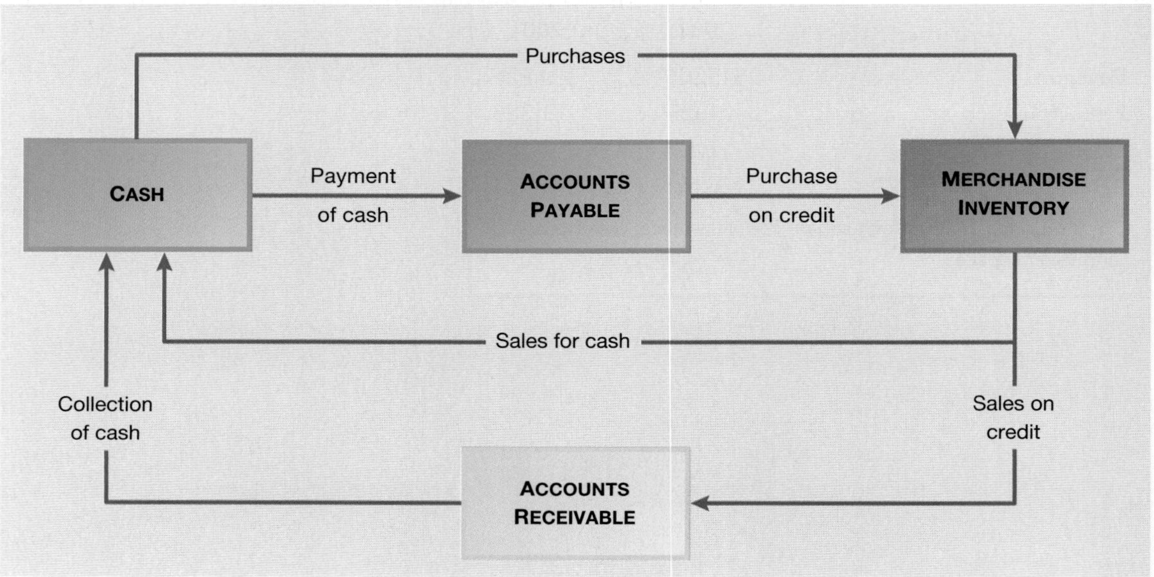

Claire's Stores, Inc. <www.clairestores.com>

OBJECTIVES

- To become familiar with the nature of merchandising operations.
- To identify the management issues associated with a merchandising business.
- To show how gross margin and operating expenses affect the business goal of profitability.

BACKGROUND FOR THE CASE

Claire's Stores, Inc. is a leading international retailer offering value-priced costume jewelry, accessories, and cosmetics to fashion-aware teens and young adults. Claire's Accessories is the company's core business. In the 1980s, the company sold its capital-intensive manufacturing businesses to concentrate on the specialty retailing of women's fashion accessories. The company has grown steadily and now has about 2,200 stores throughout North America, Europe, and Japan. Claire's Accessories stores are approximately 1,000 square feet in size in North America and 600 square feet in Europe and Japan. Claire's expansion into Europe has been particularly successful, with high store traffic and sales per square foot at 250 percent of that in North America. Keys to the company's success are the merchandising and marketing practices that reinforce its position as the place for customers to find new accessories. Constant product testing, test placement of successful items in all departments, and an efficient distribution system all enable Claire's to make quick responses to "what's new." The company's North American distribution center receives and ships merchandise on the same day, and the retail outlets receive shipments three to five times per week.

For more information about Claire's Stores, Inc., visit the company's web site through the Needles Accounting Resource Center Web Site at **http://accounting.college.hmco.com/students**.

REQUIRED

View the video on Claire's Stores, Inc., that accompanies this book. As you are watching the video, take notes related to the following questions:

1. All merchandising companies have inventories. What is inventory, and why is it important to implement controls over it? Identify the types of products that Claire's Accessories stores typically have in inventory and some ways in which the company might control its inventory.
2. All merchandising companies have an operating cycle. Describe the operating cycle and explain how Claire's successfully manages its operating cycle.
3. All merchandising companies try to achieve the goal of profitability by producing a satisfactory gross margin and maintaining acceptable levels of operating expenses. Describe how Claire's operations affect gross margin and operating expenses in a way that enables the company to achieve superior profitability.

financing period, the company will be without cash from this series of transactions and will need either to have funds available internally or to borrow from a bank.

www.dillards.com

The financing period for a merchandising company can be less than 120 days. For example, Dillard Dept. Stores, Inc., a successful chain of U.S. department stores, has a financing period of 101 days. It consists of inventory on hand for an average

FIGURE 2
The Financing Period

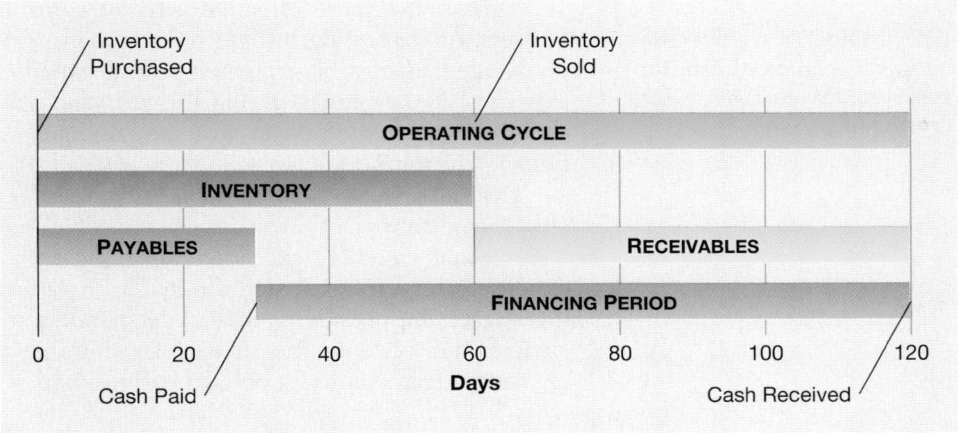

Focus on Business Technology

Credit Cards or Debit Cards?

An increasing percentage of merchandising transactions are conducted electronically. Credit cards have long been in use, but debit, purchase, and Smart cards are becoming integral parts of the so-called cashless society. The debit card allows consumers to access their bank accounts for ATM transactions or with any seller that accepts major credit cards. The price of the sale is withdrawn immediately from the customer's account when purchases are made at grocery stores, drugstores, gas stations, dry cleaners, or hardware stores. The purchase card, the business equivalent of a debit card, allows employees to purchase merchandise for their business. Smart cards have an embedded integrated circuit that stores information, such as prepaid amounts from which purchases are deducted at the point of purchase.

www.target.com

of 102 days, plus an average of 42 days to collect its receivables, minus an average of 43 days to pay for its merchandise. Target, on the other hand, has a much shorter financing period, only 29 days. Its period consists of inventory on hand for an average of 61 days, plus an average of 20 days to collect its receivables, minus an average of 52 days to pay for its merchandise. Target derives its advantage from selling most of its merchandise for cash, which results in very low receivables.

Stop and Think!
Can a company have a "negative" financing period?
Yes, if its merchandise is held for a very short time, if its sales are made mostly for cash, or if it has long terms to pay its suppliers. For example, Dell makes its computers to order (resulting in small inventories), sells on credit cards (which reduces accounts receivable), and takes 30 days or more to pay its suppliers. ■

As Target demonstrates, a company can help its cash flow by reducing its financing period. Many retailers, including Target, do this by selling as much as possible for cash. Cash sales include sales on bank credit cards, such as Visa or MasterCard, and on debit cards, which draw directly on the purchaser's bank account. They are considered cash sales because funds from them are available to the merchandiser immediately. In the case of credit sales, the company must wait a period of time before receiving the cash. Small retail stores may have mostly cash sales and very few credit sales, whereas large wholesale concerns may have almost all credit sales. Most merchandising businesses, however, have a combination of cash and credit sales.

Profitability Management

In addition to managing cash flow, management must achieve a satisfactory level of profitability. It must sell merchandise at a price that exceeds its cost by a sufficient margin to pay operating expenses and have enough left to provide sufficient income, or profitability. **Profitability management** is a complex activity that includes, first, achieving a satisfactory gross margin and, second, maintaining acceptable levels of operating expenses. Achieving a satisfactory gross margin depends on setting appropriate prices for merchandise and purchasing merchandise at favorable prices and terms. Maintaining acceptable levels of operating expenses depends on controlling expenses and operating efficiently.

KEY POINT: An operating budget is a financial plan for achieving the goal of profitability.

One of the more effective ways of controlling expenses is to use operating budgets. An **operating budget** reflects management's operating plans and consists of detailed listings of projected selling expenses and general and administrative expenses. At key times during the year and at the end of the year, management should compare the budget with actual expenses and make adjustments to operations as appropriate.

Exhibit 1 shows an operating budget for Fenwick Fashions Company, a merchandising company that we use as an example throughout this chapter. Fenwick's total selling expenses exceeded the budget by only $80, but four of its selling expense categories exceeded the budget by a total of $2,080. Management should investigate the possibility that underspending in advertising of $2,000 hid inefficiencies and waste in other areas. Also, sales may have been penalized by not spending the budgeted amount on advertising. Total general and administrative expenses

EXHIBIT 1
An Example of an Operating Budget

Fenwick Fashions Company
Operating Budget
For the Year Ended December 31, 20x3

Operating Expenses	Budget	Actual	Difference Under (Over) Budget
Selling expenses			
Sales salaries expense	$22,000	$22,500	($ 500)
Freight out expense	5,500	5,740	(240)
Advertising expense	12,000	10,000	2,000
Insurance expense, selling	800	1,600	(800)
Store supplies expense	1,000	1,540	(540)
Total selling expenses	$41,300	$41,380	($ 80)
General and administrative expenses			
Office salaries expense	$23,000	$26,900	($3,900)
Insurance expense, general	2,100	4,200	(2,100)
Office supplies expense	500	1,204	(704)
Depreciation expense, building	2,600	2,600	—
Depreciation expense, office equipment	2,000	2,200	(200)
Total general and administrative expenses	$30,200	$37,104	($6,904)
Total operating expenses	$71,500	$78,484	($6,984)

exceeded the budget by $6,904. Management should determine why large differences occurred for office salaries expense, insurance expense, and office supplies expense. The amount of insurance expense is usually set by the insurance company; thus, an error in the initial budgeting of insurance expense may have caused the unfavorable result. The operating budget helps management focus on specific areas that need attention.

CHOICE OF INVENTORY SYSTEM

Another issue the management of a merchandising business must address is the choice of inventory system. Management must choose the system or combination of systems that is best for achieving the company's goals. There are two basic systems of accounting for the many items in the merchandise inventory: the perpetual inventory system and the periodic inventory system.

KEY POINT: Under the perpetual inventory system, the Merchandise Inventory account and the Cost of Goods Sold account are updated with every sale.

Under the **perpetual inventory system**, continuous records are kept of the quantity and, usually, the cost of individual items as they are bought and sold. The detailed data available from the perpetual inventory system enable management to respond to customers' inquiries about product availability, to order inventory more effectively and thus avoid running out of stock, and to control the financial costs associated with investments in inventory. Under this system, the cost of each item

Focus on Business Technology

Bar Codes—How Have They Influenced Choice of Inventory Systems?

Many grocery stores, which traditionally used the periodic inventory system, now employ bar coding to update the physical inventory as items are sold. At the checkout counter, the cashier scans the electronic marking on each product, called a *bar code* or *universal product code* (UPC), into the cash register, which is linked to a computer that records the sale. Bar coding has become common in all types of retail companies, and in manufacturing firms and hospitals as well. It has also become a major factor in the increased use of the perpetual inventory system. Interestingly, some retail businesses now use the perpetual inventory system for keeping track of the physical flow of inventory and the periodic inventory system for preparing their financial statements.

is recorded in the Merchandise Inventory account when it is purchased. As merchandise is sold, its cost is transferred from the Merchandise Inventory account to the Cost of Goods Sold account. Thus, at all times the balance of the Merchandise Inventory account equals the cost of goods on hand, and the balance in Cost of Goods Sold equals the cost of merchandise sold to customers.

KEY POINT: The valuation of ending inventory on the balance sheet is determined by multiplying the quantity of each inventory item by its unit cost.

Under the **periodic inventory system**, the inventory not yet sold, or on hand, is counted periodically, usually at the end of the accounting period. No detailed records of the inventory on hand are maintained during the accounting period. The figure for inventory on hand is accurate only on the balance sheet date. As soon as any purchases or sales are made, the inventory figure becomes a historical amount, and it remains so until the new ending inventory amount is entered at the end of the next accounting period.

Some retail and wholesale businesses use the periodic inventory system because it reduces the amount of clerical work. If a business is fairly small, management can maintain control over its inventory simply through observation or by using an offline system of cards or computer records. But for larger businesses, the lack of detailed records may lead to lost sales or high operating costs.

KEY POINT: Although computerization has made the perpetual inventory system more popular in recent years, a physical count still should be made periodically to ensure that the actual number of goods on hand matches the quantity indicated by the computer records.

Because of the difficulty and expense of accounting for the purchase and sale of each item, companies that sell items of low value in high volume have traditionally used the periodic inventory system. Examples of such companies are drugstores, automobile parts stores, department stores, and discount stores. In contrast, companies that sell items of high unit value, such as appliances or automobiles, have tended to use the perpetual inventory system. The distinction between high and low unit value for inventory systems has blurred considerably in recent years because of the widespread use of computers. Although the periodic inventory system is still widely used, use of the perpetual inventory system has increased greatly.

Control of Merchandising Operations

Buying and selling, the principal transactions of merchandising businesses, involve assets—cash, accounts receivable, and merchandise inventory—that are vulnerable to theft and embezzlement. One reason for this vulnerability is that cash and inventory may be fairly easy to steal. Another is the difficulty of monitoring the large number of transactions (including cash receipts, receipts on account, payments for purchases, and receipts and shipments of inventory) in which these assets are usually involved. If a merchandising company does not take steps to protect its assets, it may suffer high losses of cash and inventory. Management's responsibility is to establish an environment, accounting systems, and control procedures that will protect the company's assets. These systems and procedures are called **internal controls**.

Maintaining control over merchandise inventory is facilitated by taking a **physical inventory**. This process involves an actual count of all merchandise on hand. It can be a difficult task because it is easy to accidentally omit items or to count them twice. A physical inventory must be taken under both the periodic and the perpetual inventory systems. Under the perpetual inventory system, the records need to be compared with the physical inventory to determine whether any inventory shortages exist.

Merchandise inventory includes all goods intended for sale that are owned by a business, regardless of where they are located—on shelves, in storerooms, in warehouses, or in trucks between warehouses and stores. It also includes goods in transit from suppliers if title to the goods has passed to the merchant. Ending inventory does not include merchandise that has been sold but not yet delivered to customers or goods that cannot be sold because they are damaged or obsolete. If the damaged or obsolete goods can be sold at a reduced price, however, they should be included in ending inventory at their reduced value.

The actual count is usually taken after the close of business on the last day of the fiscal year. To facilitate taking the physical inventory, many companies end their fiscal year in a slow season, when inventories are at relatively low levels. Retail department stores often end their fiscal year in January or February, for example. After hours, at night, or on the weekend, employees count all items and record the results on numbered inventory tickets or sheets, following procedures to ensure no items will be missed. Sometimes a store closes for all or part of a day for inventory taking. The use of bar coding to take inventory electronically has greatly facilitated the process in many companies.

ENRICHMENT NOTE: Inventory shortages can result from honest mistakes, such as accidentally tagging inventory with the wrong number.

Most companies experience losses of merchandise inventory from spoilage, shoplifting, and theft by employees. When such losses occur, the periodic inventory system provides no means of identifying them because the costs are automatically included in the cost of goods sold. For example, assume that a company has lost $1,250 in stolen merchandise during an accounting period. When the physical inventory is taken, the missing items are not in stock, so they cannot be counted. Because the ending inventory does not contain these items, the amount subtracted from goods available for sale is less than it would be if the goods were in stock. The cost of goods sold, then, is overstated by $1,250. In a sense, the cost of goods sold is inflated by the amount of merchandise that has been lost.

KEY POINT: An adjustment to the Merchandise Inventory account will be needed if the physical inventory reveals a difference between the actual inventory and the amount in the records.

The perpetual inventory system makes it easier to identify such losses. Because the Merchandise Inventory account is continuously updated for sales, purchases, and returns, the loss will show up as the difference between the inventory records and the physical inventory taken at the end of the accounting period. Once the amount of the loss has been identified, the ending inventory is updated by crediting the Merchandise Inventory account. The offsetting debit is usually an increase in Cost of Goods Sold because the loss is considered a cost that reduces the company's gross margin.

Check out ACE for a Review Quiz at http://accounting.college.hmco.com/students.

Income Statement for a Merchandising Concern

LO2 Compare the income statements for service and merchandising concerns, and define the components of the merchandising income statement.

RELATED TEXT ASSIGNMENTS
Q: 8, 9, 10
SE: 2
E: 3
SD: 4, 5
FRA: 1, 5

Many service companies require only a simple income statement. For those companies, as shown in Figure 3, net income represents the difference between revenues and expenses. But merchandising companies, because they buy and sell merchandise inventory, require a more complex income statement. As shown in Figure 3, the income statement for a merchandiser consists of three major parts: (1) net sales, (2) cost of goods sold, and (3) operating expenses. There is also a subtotal for gross margin.

The main difference between a merchandiser's income statement and the income statement of a service business is that the merchandiser must compute gross

FIGURE 3
The Components of Income Statements for Service and Merchandising Companies

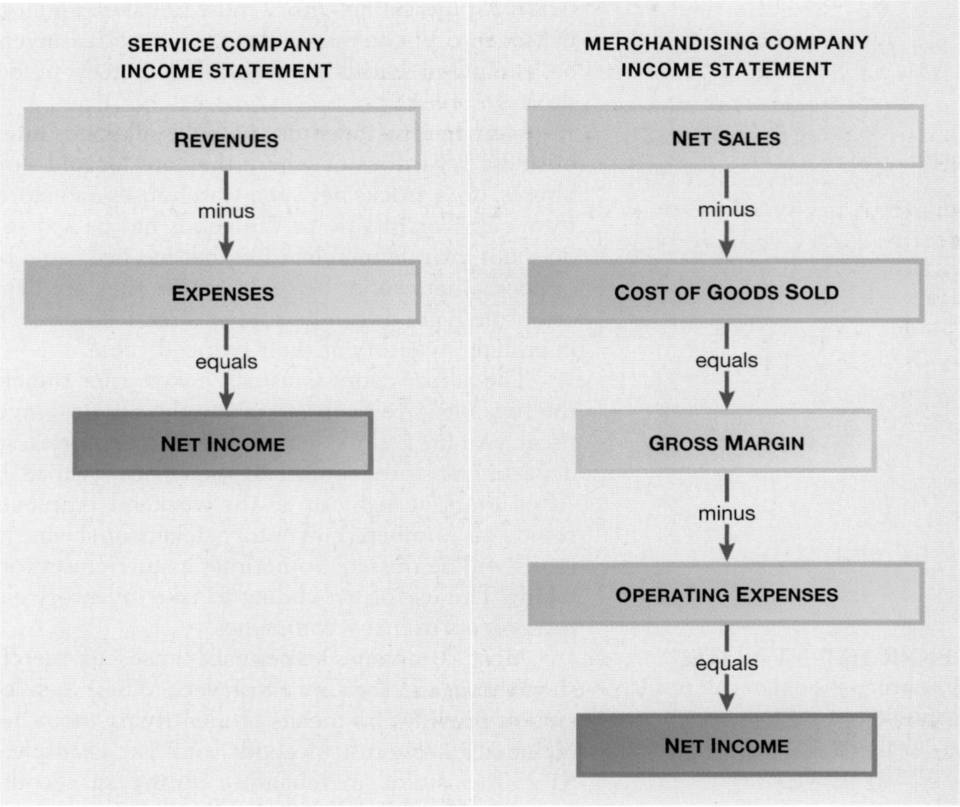

STOP AND THINK!
Why do merchandising companies have a more complex income statement than service companies?

Because merchandising companies buy and sell merchandising inventory, they require a Cost of Goods Sold account, which makes the income statement more complex. ■

margin before operating expenses are deducted. In the following discussion, the income statement for Fenwick Fashions Company, presented in Exhibit 2, will serve as an example of a merchandising income statement.

NET SALES

KEY POINT: A sale takes place when title to the goods transfers to the buyer.

The first major part of the merchandising income statement is **net sales**, often simply called *sales*. Net sales consist of the gross proceeds from sales of merchandise, or gross sales, less sales returns and allowances. **Gross sales** consist of total cash sales and total credit sales during an accounting period. Even though the cash may not be collected until the following accounting period under the revenue recognition rule, revenue is recorded as earned when title for merchandise passes from seller to buyer at the time of sale. **Sales Returns and Allowances** is a contra-revenue account used to accumulate cash refunds, credits on account, and allowances off selling prices made to customers who have received defective or otherwise unsatisfactory products. If other discounts or allowances are given to customers (see supplemental objective 8, for instance), they also should be deducted from gross sales.

Management, investors, and others often use the amount of sales and trends suggested by sales as indicators of a firm's progress. Increasing sales suggest growth; decreasing sales indicate the possibility of decreased future earnings and other financial problems. To detect trends, comparisons are frequently made between the net sales of different accounting periods.

COST OF GOODS SOLD

The second part of the income statement for a merchandiser or manufacturer is **cost of goods sold**, or simply *cost of sales*. Cost of goods sold is the amount a

EXHIBIT 2
Income Statement Under the Perpetual Inventory System

Fenwick Fashions Company
Income Statement
For the Year Ended December 31, 20x3

Net sales			
Gross sales			$246,350
Less sales returns and allowances			7,025
Net sales			$239,325
Cost of goods sold*			131,360
Gross margin			$107,965
Operating expenses			
Selling expenses			
Sales salaries expense	$22,500		
Freight out expense	5,740		
Advertising expense	10,000		
Insurance expense, selling	1,600		
Store supplies expense	1,540		
Total selling expenses		$41,380	
General and administrative expenses			
Office salaries expense	$26,900		
Insurance expense, general	4,200		
Office supplies expense	1,204		
Depreciation expense, building	2,600		
Depreciation expense, office equipment	2,200		
Total general and administrative expenses		37,104	
Total operating expenses			78,484
Net income			$ 29,481

*Freight in has been included in cost of goods sold.

KEY POINT: The matching rule precludes the cost of inventory from being expensed until the inventory has been sold.

merchandiser paid for the merchandise sold during an accounting period or the cost to a manufacturer of making the products sold during an accounting period.

GROSS MARGIN

KEY POINT: Gross margin is an important measure of profitability.

ENRICHMENT NOTE: When gross margin is insufficient to cover operating expenses, the company has suffered a net loss.

The difference between net sales and cost of goods sold on the merchandising income statement is **gross margin**, or *gross profit*. To be successful, merchants must sell goods for an amount greater than cost—that is, gross margin must be great enough to pay operating expenses and provide an adequate income. Management is interested in both the amount and the percentage of gross margin. The percentage of gross margin is computed by dividing the amount of gross margin by net sales. In the case of Fenwick Fashions, the amount of gross margin is $107,965 and the percentage of gross margin is 45.1 percent ($107,965 ÷ $239,325). This information is helpful in planning business operations. For instance, management may try to increase total sales dollars by reducing the selling price. This strategy reduces the percentage of gross margin, but it will work if the total items sold increase enough to raise the absolute amount of gross margin. This is the strategy of discount

www.samsclub.com
www.costco.com

www.neimanmarcus.com
www.tiffany.com

warehouse stores like Sam's Clubs and Costco Wholesale Corporation. On the other hand, management may keep a high gross margin and attempt to increase sales and the amount of gross margin by increasing operating expenses, such as advertising. This is the strategy followed by upscale specialty stores like Neiman Marcus and Tiffany & Co. Other strategies to increase gross margin include reducing cost of goods sold by better purchasing methods.

Operating Expenses

KEY POINT: The most common types of operating expenses are selling expenses and general and administrative expenses. They are deducted from gross margin on the income statement.

BUSINESS-WORLD EXAMPLE: Companies that are restructuring their operations often focus on reducing operating expenses.

The third major area of the merchandising income statement consists of **operating expenses**, which are the expenses other than cost of goods sold that are incurred in running a business. It is customary to group operating expenses into categories, such as selling expenses and general and administrative expenses. Selling expenses include the costs of storing goods and preparing them for sale, displaying, advertising, and otherwise promoting sales; making sales; and delivering goods to the buyer, if the seller bears the cost of delivery. The latter cost is often accumulated in an account called **Freight Out Expense** or *Delivery Expense*. Among the general and administrative expenses are general office expenses, which include expenses for accounting, personnel, credit and collections, and any other expenses that apply to overall operation. General occupancy expenses, such as rent expense, insurance expense, and utilities expense, are often classified as general and administrative expenses. However, they may also be allocated between the selling and the general and administrative categories. Careful planning and control of operating expenses can improve a company's profitability.

Net Income

Net income, the final figure or "bottom line" of the income statement, is what remains after operating expenses are deducted from gross margin. It is an important performance measure because it represents the amount of business earnings that accrue to the owners. It is the amount that is transferred to owner's equity from all the income-generating activities during the period. Both management and owners often use net income to measure whether a business has operated successfully during the past accounting period.

Check out ACE for a Review Quiz at http://accounting.college.hmco.com/students.

Terms of Sale

LO3 Define and distinguish the terms of sale for merchandising transactions.

RELATED TEXT ASSIGNMENTS
Q: 11, 12
SE: 3, 4
E: 4
FRA: 2, 6

KEY POINT: A trade discount applies to the list or catalogue price. A sales discount applies to the sales price.

When goods are sold on credit, both parties should understand the amount and timing of payment as well as other terms of the purchase, such as who pays delivery charges and what warranties or rights of return apply. Sellers quote prices in different ways. Many merchants quote the price at which they expect to sell their goods. Others, particularly manufacturers and wholesalers, quote prices as a percentage (usually 30 percent or more) off their list or catalogue prices. Such a reduction is called a **trade discount**. For example, if an article is listed at $1,000 with a trade discount of 40 percent, or $400, the seller records the sale at $600 and the buyer records the purchase at $600. The seller may raise or lower the trade discount depending on the quantity purchased. The list or catalogue price and related trade discount are used only to arrive at the agreed-upon price; they do not appear in the accounting records.

The terms of sale are usually printed on the sales invoice and thus constitute part of the sales agreement. Customary terms differ from industry to industry. In

Focus on Business Technology

How Are Web Sales Doing?

In spite of the well-publicized dot-com meltdown and the demise of "pure-play" Internet retailers like eToys.com and Pets.com, merchandise sales over the Internet are thriving. Internet sales amounted to $44.5 billion in 2001 and were expected to double in the next few years. As it has turned out, the most successful Internet retailing companies are established retailers that use the Internet to enhance their current operations. For example, mail-order catalogue companies like Lands' End <www.landsend.com> and L.L. Bean <www.llbean.com> have profitable Internet operations. Circuit City <www.circuitcity.com> allows customers to purchase online and pick up the products at stores near their homes. Office Depot <www.officedepot.com>, which focuses primarily on business-to-business Internet sales, has set up customized web pages for 37,000 corporate clients. These web sites allow customers to make online purchases or to check store inventories.[3] Although Internet transactions are recorded in the same way as on-site transactions, the technology adds a level of complexity to the transaction.

ENRICHMENT NOTE: Early collection also has the advantage of reducing the probability of a customer's defaulting.

some industries, payment is expected in a short period of time, such as 10 or 30 days. In these cases, the invoice is marked "n/10" ("net 10") or "n/30" ("net 30"), meaning that the amount of the invoice is due either 10 days or 30 days after the invoice date. If the invoice is due 10 days after the end of the month, it is marked "n/10 eom."

In some industries, it is customary to give a discount for early payment. This discount, called a **sales discount**, is intended to increase the seller's liquidity by reducing the amount of money tied up in accounts receivable. An invoice that offers a sales discount might be labeled "2/10, n/30," which means that the buyer either can pay the invoice within 10 days of the invoice date and take a 2 percent discount or can wait 30 days and pay the full amount of the invoice. It is almost always advantageous for a buyer to take the discount because the saving of 2 percent over a period of 20 days (from the eleventh day to the thirtieth day) represents an effective annual rate of 36.5 percent (365 days ÷ 20 days × 2% = 36.5%). Most companies would be better off borrowing money to take the discount. The practice of giving sales discounts has been declining because it is costly to the seller and because, from the buyer's viewpoint, the amount of the discount is usually very small in relation to the price of the purchase. Accounting for sales discounts is covered in Supplemental Objective 8.

In some industries, the seller usually pays transportation costs and charges a price that includes those costs. In other industries, it is customary for the purchaser to pay transportation charges. Special terms designate whether the seller or the purchaser pays the freight charges. **FOB shipping point** means that the seller places the merchandise "free on board" at the point of origin and the buyer bears the shipping costs. The title to the merchandise passes to the buyer at that point. For example, when the sales agreement for the purchase of a car says "FOB factory," the buyer must pay the freight from where the car was made to wherever he or she is located, and the buyer owns the car from the time it leaves the factory.

STOP AND THINK!
Assume a large shipment of uninsured merchandise to your company was destroyed when the delivery truck had an accident and burned. Would you want the terms to be FOB shipping point or FOB destination?

You would want the terms to be FOB destination because the loss of merchandise would be the responsibility of the shipper. If the terms were FOB shipping point, the merchandise would belong to you when it left the shipper and would be your loss. ■

On the other hand, **FOB destination** means that the seller bears the transportation costs to the place where the merchandise is delivered. The seller retains title until the merchandise reaches its destination and usually prepays the shipping costs, in which case the buyer makes no accounting entry for freight. The effects of these special shipping terms are summarized as follows:

Shipping Term	Where Title Passes	Who Pays the Cost of Transportation
FOB shipping point	At origin	Buyer
FOB destination	At destination	Seller

Many retailers allow customers to charge their purchases to a third-party company that the customer will pay later. These transactions are normally handled with credit cards. Five of the most widely used credit cards are American Express, Discover Card, Diners Club, MasterCard, and Visa. The customer establishes credit with the lender (the credit card issuer) and receives a plastic card to use in making charge purchases. If the seller accepts the card, an invoice is prepared and signed by the customer at the time of the sale. The seller then deposits the invoice in the bank and receives cash. Thus, the seller does not have to establish the customer's credit, collect from the customer, or tie up money in accounts receivable. As payment, the lender, rather than paying the total amount of the credit card sales, takes a discount of 2 to 6 percent. The discount is a selling expense for the merchandiser. For example, assume that a restaurant made sales of $1,000 on Visa credit cards and that Visa takes a 4 percent discount on the sales. Assume also that the sales invoices are deposited in a special Visa bank account in the name of the company, in much the same way that checks from cash sales are deposited. The sales are recorded as follows:

A = L + OE			
+ −	Cash	960	
+	Credit Card Discount Expense	40	
	Sales		1,000
	Made sales on Visa cards		

Check out ACE for a Review Quiz at http://accounting.college.hmco.com/students.

Applying the Perpetual Inventory System

LO4 Prepare an income statement and record merchandising transactions under the perpetual inventory system.

RELATED TEXT ASSIGNMENTS
Q: 13, 14, 16, 17
SE: 5, 6
E: 5, 6, 7
P: 1, 2, 8, 9
SD: 2
FRA: 2, 6

Exhibit 2 previously showed the income statement for Fenwick Fashions Company as it would appear if the company used the perpetual inventory system. The focal point of this income statement is cost of goods sold, which is deducted from net sales to arrive at gross margin. Under the perpetual inventory system, this account is continually updated during the accounting period as purchases, sales, and other inventory transactions take place. The Merchandise Inventory account on the balance sheet is updated at the same time.

Transactions Related to Purchases of Merchandise

The following sections illustrate the recording of typical transactions related to purchases of merchandise under the perpetual inventory system. Transactions related to sales made by Fenwick Fashions Company follow.

KEY POINT: The Merchandise Inventory account is increased when a purchase is made.

Purchases of Merchandise on Credit

Oct. 3 Received merchandise purchased on credit from Neebok Company, invoice dated October 1, terms n/10, FOB shipping point, $4,890.

A = L + OE				
+ +	Oct. 3	Merchandise Inventory	4,890	
		Accounts Payable		4,890
		Purchased merchandise from Neebok Company, terms n/10, FOB shipping point, invoice dated Oct. 1		

STOP AND THINK!
Under the perpetual inventory system, the Merchandise Inventory account is constantly updated. What would cause it to have the wrong balance?
The balance would be wrong if an error were made in updating the account or if merchandise had been lost or stolen. ■

Under the perpetual inventory system, the cost of merchandise purchased is placed in the Merchandise Inventory account at the time of purchase.

Transportation Costs on Purchases

Oct. 4 Received bill from Transfer Freight Company for transportation costs on October 3 shipment, invoice dated October 1, terms n/10, $160.

A = L + OE
  +   −

Oct. 4	Freight In	160	
	Accounts Payable		160
	Received transportation charges on Oct. 3 purchase, Transfer Freight Company, terms n/10, invoice dated Oct. 1		

KEY POINT: Freight in appears within the cost of goods sold section of the income statement, and Freight Out Expense appears as an operating expense.

Freight in, also called *transportation in*, is the transportation cost of receiving merchandise. Transportation costs are accumulated in a Freight In account because most shipments contain multiple items. It is usually not practical to identify the specific cost of shipping each item of inventory. In Exhibit 2, freight in is included in cost of goods sold. Theoretically, freight in should be allocated between ending inventory and cost of goods sold, but most companies choose to include the cost of freight in with the cost of goods sold on the income statement because it is a relatively small amount.

In some cases, the seller pays the freight charges and bills them to the buyer as a separate item on the invoice. When this occurs, the entries are the same as in the October 3 example, except that an additional debit is made to Freight In for the amount of the freight charges and Accounts Payable is increased by a like amount.

Purchases Returns and Allowances

Oct. 6 Returned merchandise received from Neebok Company on October 3 for credit, $480.

A = L + OE
−   −

Oct. 6	Accounts Payable	480	
	Merchandise Inventory		480
	Returned merchandise from purchase of Oct. 3 to Neebok Company for full credit		

If a seller sends the wrong product or one that is otherwise unsatisfactory, the buyer may be allowed to return the item for a cash refund or credit on account, or the buyer may be given an allowance off the sales price. Under the perpetual inventory system, the returned merchandise is removed from the Merchandise Inventory account.

Payments on Account

Oct. 10 Paid in full the amount due to Neebok Company for the purchase of October 3, part of which was returned on October 6.

A = L + OE
−   −

Oct. 10	Accounts Payable	4,410	
	Cash		4,410
	Made payment on account to Neebok Company $4,890 − $480 = $4,410		

Transactions Related to Sales of Merchandise

KEY POINT: The Cost of Goods Sold account is increased and the Merchandise Inventory account is decreased when a sale is made.

Under the perpetual inventory system, at the time of a sale, the cost of the merchandise is transferred from the Merchandise Inventory account to the Cost of Goods Sold account. In the case of a return of sold merchandise, the cost of the merchandise is transferred from Cost of Goods Sold back to Merchandise Inventory. Transactions related to sales made by Fenwick Fashions Company follow.

Sales of Merchandise on Credit

Oct. 7 Sold merchandise on credit to Gonzales Distributors, terms n/30, FOB destination, $1,200; the cost of the merchandise was $720.

A = L + OE
+   +
	Oct. 7	Accounts Receivable
		   Sales
		      Sold merchandise to Gonzales Distributors, terms n/30, FOB destination
			1,200	
				1,200

A = L + OE
−   −
		Cost of Goods Sold
		   Merchandise Inventory
		      Transferred cost of merchandise inventory sold to Cost of Goods Sold account
			720	
				720

KEY POINT: More entries are associated with a perpetual inventory system than with a periodic inventory system.

Under the perpetual inventory system, two entries are necessary. First, the sale is recorded. Second, Cost of Goods Sold is updated by a transfer from Merchandise Inventory. In the case of cash sales, Cash rather than Accounts Receivable is debited for the amount of the sale.

Payment of Delivery Costs

Oct. 8 Paid transportation costs for the sale on October 7, $78.

A = L + OE
−   −
	Oct. 8	Freight Out Expense
		   Cash
		      Paid delivery costs on Oct. 7 sale
			78	
				78

A seller will often absorb delivery or freight out costs in the belief that doing so will facilitate the sale of its products. These costs are accumulated in an account called Freight Out Expense, or *Delivery Expense*, which is shown as a selling expense on the income statement.

Returns of Merchandise Sold

Oct. 9 Return of merchandise sold on October 7 accepted from Gonzales Distributors for full credit and returned to merchandise inventory, $300; the cost of the merchandise was $180.

A = L + OE
−   −
	Oct. 9	Sales Returns and Allowances
		   Accounts Receivable
		      Accepted return of merchandise from Gonzales Distributors
			300	
				300

A = L + OE
+   +
	Oct. 9	Merchandise Inventory
		   Cost of Goods Sold
		      Transferred cost of merchandise returned to the Merchandise Inventory account
			180	
				180

Returns and allowances to customers for wrong or unsatisfactory merchandise are often an indicator of customer dissatisfaction. Such amounts are accumulated in a Sales Returns and Allowances account, which gives management a readily available

FOCUS ON BUSINESS PRACTICE

Are Sales Returns Worth Accounting For?

Some industries routinely have a high percentage of sales returns. More than 6 percent of all nonfood items sold in stores are eventually returned to vendors. This amounts to more than $100 billion a year, or more than the gross national product of two-thirds of the world's nations.[4] Book publishers like Simon & Schuster <www.simonsays.com> often have returns as high as 30 to 50 percent of books shipped because to gain the attention of potential buyers, large numbers of copies must be distributed to various outlets. Magazine publishers like AOL Time Warner <www.aoltw.com> expect to sell no more than 35 to 38 percent of the magazines they send to newsstands and other outlets.[5] In all these businesses, it pays for management to scrutinize the Sales Returns and Allowances account for ways to reduce returns and increase profitability.

KEY POINT: Because the Sales account is established with a credit, its contra account, Sales Returns and Allowances, is established with a debit.

measure of unsatisfactory products and dissatisfied customers. This contra-revenue account has a normal debit balance and is deducted from sales on the income statement. Under the perpetual inventory system, the cost of the merchandise must also be transferred from the Cost of Goods Sold account back into the Merchandise Inventory account. If an allowance is made instead of accepting a return, or if the merchandise cannot be returned to inventory and resold, this transfer is not made.

Receipts on Account

Nov. 5 Received payment in full from Gonzales Distributors for sale of merchandise on October 7, less the return on October 9.

A = L + OE				
+ −	Nov. 5	Cash	900	
		Accounts Receivable		900
		Received on account from Gonzales Distributors $1,200 − $300 = $900		

Check out ACE for a Review Quiz at http://accounting.college.hmco.com/students.

Applying the Periodic Inventory System

LO5 Prepare an income statement and record merchandising transactions under the periodic inventory system.

RELATED TEXT ASSIGNMENTS
Q: 13, 14, 15, 16, 17, 18
SE: 7, 8, 9
E: 8, 9, 10, 11
P: 3, 4, 7, 10, 11
SD: 2, 5
FRA: 2

Exhibit 3 shows the income statement for Fenwick Fashions Company as it would appear if the company used the periodic inventory system. A major feature of this income statement is the computation of cost of goods sold. Cost of goods sold must be computed because it is not updated for purchases, sales, and other transactions during the accounting period, as it is under the perpetual inventory system. Figure 4 illustrates the components of cost of goods sold.

Cost of Goods Sold

The method of computing cost of goods sold when using the periodic inventory method is sometimes confusing because it must take into account both merchandise inventory on hand at the beginning of the accounting period, called the **beginning inventory**, and merchandise inventory on hand at the end of the accounting period, called the **ending inventory**. The ending inventory appears on the balance sheet at the end of the accounting period and becomes the beginning inventory for the next accounting period.

To calculate cost of goods sold, the **goods available for sale** must first be determined. The goods available for sale during the year is the sum of two factors, beginning inventory and the net cost of purchases during the year. In this case, the goods available for sale is $179,660 ($52,800 + $126,860).

If a company sold all the goods available for sale during an accounting period, the cost of goods sold would equal the goods available for sale. In most businesses, however, some merchandise remains unsold and on hand at the end of the period. This merchandise, or ending inventory, must be deducted from the goods available for sale to determine the cost of goods sold. In the case of Fenwick Fashions Company, the ending inventory on December 31, 20x3, is $48,300. Thus, the cost of goods sold is $131,360 ($179,660 − $48,300).

An important component of the cost of goods sold section is **net cost of purchases**, which consists of net purchases plus any freight charges on the purchases. **Net purchases** equal total purchases less any deductions, such as purchases returns and allowances and any discounts allowed by suppliers for early payment (see supplemental objective 8). Because transportation charges, or freight in, are a necessary cost of receiving merchandise for sale, they are added to net purchases to arrive at the net cost of purchases, as shown in Exhibit 3.

EXHIBIT 3
Income Statement Under the Periodic Inventory System

ENRICHMENT NOTE:
Most published financial statements are condensed, eliminating much of the detail shown here.

Fenwick Fashions Company
Income Statement
For the Year Ended December 31, 20x3

Net sales			
Gross sales			$246,350
Less sales returns and allowances			7,025
Net sales			$239,325
Cost of goods sold			
Merchandise inventory, December 31, 20x2		$ 52,800	
Purchases	$126,400		
Less purchases returns and allowances	7,776		
Net purchases	$118,624		
Freight in	8,236		
Net cost of purchases		126,860	
Goods available for sale		$179,660	
Less merchandise inventory, December 31, 20x3		48,300	
Cost of goods sold			131,360
Gross margin			$107,965
Operating expenses			
Selling expenses			
Sales salaries expense	$ 22,500		
Freight out expense	5,740		
Advertising expense	10,000		
Insurance expense, selling	1,600		
Store supplies expense	1,540		
Total selling expenses		$ 41,380	
General and administrative expenses			
Office salaries expense	$ 26,900		
Insurance expense, general	4,200		
Office supplies expense	1,204		
Depreciation expense, building	2,600		
Depreciation expense, office equipment	2,200		
Total general and administrative expenses		37,104	
Total operating expenses			78,484
Net income			$ 29,481

TRANSACTIONS RELATED TO PURCHASES OF MERCHANDISE

The primary difference between the perpetual and periodic inventory systems is that in the perpetual inventory system, the Merchandise Inventory account is adjusted each time a purchase, sale, or other inventory transaction occurs, whereas in the periodic inventory system, the Merchandise Inventory account stays at its

FIGURE 4
The Components of Cost of Goods Sold

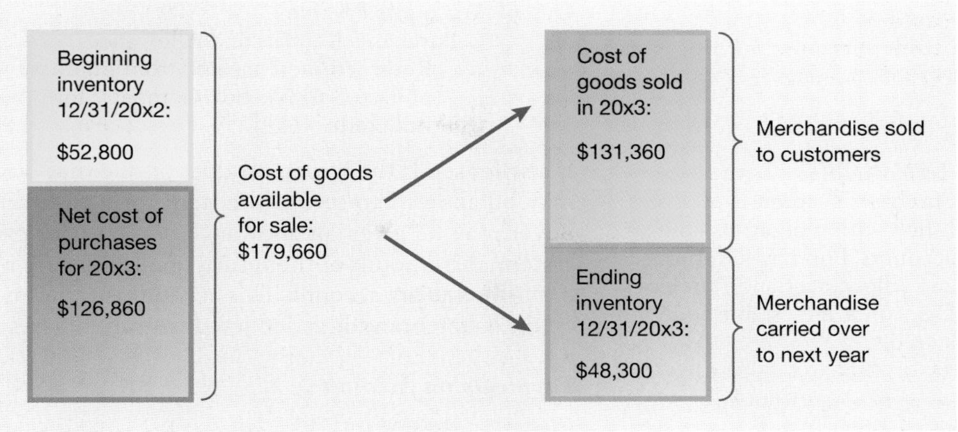

beginning balance until the physical inventory is recorded at the end of the period. In the periodic system, a Purchases account is used to accumulate the purchases of merchandise during the accounting period, and a Purchases Returns and Allowances account is used to accumulate returns of and allowances on purchases.

The following sections illustrate how purchase transactions made by Fenwick Fashions Company would be recorded under the periodic inventory system.

KEY POINT: The Purchases account is increased when a purchase is made under the periodic inventory system.

Purchases of Merchandise on Credit

Oct. 3 Received merchandise purchased on cedit from Neebok Company, invoice dated October 1, terms n/10, FOB shipping point, $4,890.

A = L + OE
    + −

Oct. 3	Purchases	4,890	
	Accounts Payable		4,890
	Purchased merchandise from Neebok Company, terms n/10, FOB shipping point, invoice dated Oct. 1		

Purchases is a temporary account used under the periodic inventory system. Its sole purpose is to accumulate the total cost of merchandise purchased for resale during an accounting period. (Purchases of other assets, such as equipment, are recorded in the appropriate asset account, not in the Purchases account.) The Purchases account does not indicate whether merchandise has been sold or is still on hand.

Transportation Costs on Purchases

Oct. 4 Received bill from Transfer Freight Company for transportation costs on October 3 shipment, invoice dated October 1, terms n/10, $160.

A = L + OE
    + −

Oct. 4	Freight In	160	
	Accounts Payable		160
	Received transportation charges on Oct. 3 purchase, Transfer Freight Company, terms n/10, invoice dated Oct. 1		

Transportation costs on purchases are usually accumulated in a Freight In account. In some cases, the seller pays the freight charges and bills them to the buyer as a separate item on the invoice. When this occurs, the entries are the same as in the October 3 example, except that a debit is made to Freight In for the amount of the freight charges and Accounts Payable is increased by a like amount.

ENRICHMENT NOTE: Accounts like Purchases and Purchases Returns and Allowances are used only in conjunction with a periodic inventory system.

Purchases Returns and Allowances

Oct. 6 Returned merchandise received from Neebok Company on October 3 for credit, $480.

A = L + OE
− +

Oct. 6	Accounts Payable	480	
	Purchases Returns and Allowances		480
	Returned merchandise from purchase of Oct. 3 to Neebok Company for full credit		

KEY POINT: Because the Purchases account is established with a debit, its contra accounts, Purchases Returns and Allowances and Purchases Discounts, are established with a credit.

If a seller sends the wrong product or one that is otherwise unsatisfactory, the buyer may be allowed to return the item for a cash refund or credit on account, or the buyer may be given an allowance off the sales price. Under the periodic inventory system, the amount of the return or allowance is recorded in the **Purchases Returns and Allowances** account. This account is a contra-purchases account with a normal credit balance, and it is deducted from purchases on the income statement.

Payments on Account

Oct. 10 Paid in full the amount due to Neebok Company for the purchase of October 3, part of which was returned on October 6.

A = L + OE
− −

Oct. 10	Accounts Payable	4,410	
	Cash		4,410
	Made payment on account to Neebok Company $4,890 − $480 = $4,410		

Transactions Related to Sales of Merchandise

The Cost of Goods Sold account, which is updated for sales and returns under the perpetual inventory system, is not used under the periodic inventory system because the Merchandise Inventory account is not updated until the end of the accounting period. Transactions related to Fenwick Fashions' sales follow.

Sales of Merchandise on Credit

Oct. 7 Sold merchandise on credit to Gonzales Distributors, terms n/30, FOB destination, $1,200; the cost of the merchandise was $720.

A = L + OE
\+ +

Oct. 7	Accounts Receivable	1,200	
	Sales		1,200
	Sold merchandise to Gonzales Distributors, terms n/30, FOB destination		

In the case of cash sales, Cash rather than Accounts Receivable is debited for the amount of the sale.

Payment of Delivery Costs

Oct. 8 Paid transportation costs for the sale on October 7, $78.

A = L + OE
− −

Oct. 8	Freight Out Expense	78	
	Cash		78
	Paid delivery costs on Oct. 7 sale		

Delivery costs are accumulated in the Freight Out Expense account. This account is shown as a selling expense on the income statement.

Returns of Merchandise Sold

Oct. 9 Return of merchandise sold on October 7 accepted from Gonzales Distributors for full credit and returned to merchandise inventory, $300.

A = L + OE
− −

Oct. 9	Sales Returns and Allowances	300	
	Accounts Receivable		300
	Accepted return of merchandise from Gonzales Distributors		

Returns and allowances to customers for wrong or unsatisfactory merchandise are accumulated in the Sales Returns and Allowances account. This account is a contra-revenue account with a normal debit balance and is deducted from sales on the income statement.

Receipts on Account

Nov. 5 Received payment in full from Gonzales Distributors for sale of merchandise on October 7, less the return on October 9.

A = L + OE	Nov. 5	Cash	900	
+		Accounts Receivable		900
−		Received on account from Gonzales Distributors $1,200 − $300 = $900		

Check out ACE for a Review Quiz at http://accounting.college.hmco.com/students.

The Merchandising Work Sheet and Closing Entries: The Perpetual Inventory System

SO6 Prepare a work sheet and closing entries for a merchandising concern using the perpetual inventory system.

RELATED TEXT ASSIGNMENTS
Q: 19, 20
SE: 10
E: 12
P: 5

The work sheet for a merchandising company is basically the same as for a service business, except that it includes the additional accounts needed to handle merchandising transactions. The treatment of these additional accounts differs depending on whether a company uses the perpetual or the periodic inventory system.

The accounts for a merchandising company using the perpetual inventory system generally include Sales, Sales Returns and Allowances, Cost of Goods Sold, and Freight In. The Merchandise Inventory account is up to date at the end of the accounting period and therefore is not involved in the closing process. The reason for this is that, under the perpetual inventory system, purchases of merchandise are recorded directly in the Merchandise Inventory account and costs are transferred from the Merchandise Inventory account to the Cost of Goods Sold account as merchandise is sold. The work sheet for Fenwick Fashions Company, assuming the company uses the perpetual inventory system, is shown in Exhibit 4. You are already familiar with the first step in preparing a work sheet, which is to enter the balances from the ledger accounts into the Trial Balance columns. Each of the other pairs of columns in the work sheet and the closing entries are discussed in the following paragraphs. Note that the ending merchandise inventory is $48,300 in both the Trial Balance and the Balance Sheet columns.

Adjustments Columns

The adjusting entries are entered in the Adjustments columns just as they are for service companies. Fenwick's adjusting entries involve insurance expired during the period (adjustment **a**), store and office supplies used during the period (adjustments **b** and **c**), and the depreciation of building and office equipment (adjustments **d** and **e**). No adjusting entry is made for merchandise inventory. After the adjusting entries are entered on the work sheet, the columns are totaled to prove that total debits equal total credits.

Omission of Adjusted Trial Balance Columns

KEY POINT: No inventory-related entries are entered in the Adjustments columns of the work sheet.

These two columns, which appear in the work sheet for a service company, can be omitted. They are optional and are used when there are many adjusting entries to record. When only a few adjusting entries are required, as is the case for Fenwick Fashions Company, these columns are not necessary and may be omitted to save time.

EXHIBIT 4
Work Sheet for Fenwick Fashions Company: Perpetual Inventory System

Fenwick Fashions Company
Work Sheet
For the Year Ended December 31, 20x3

	Trial Balance		Adjustments		Income Statement		Balance Sheet	
Account Name	Debit	Credit	Debit	Credit	Debit	Credit	Debit	Credit
Cash	29,410						29,410	
Accounts Receivable	42,400						42,400	
Merchandise Inventory	48,300						48,300	
Prepaid Insurance	17,400			(a) 5,800			11,600	
Store Supplies	2,600			(b) 1,540			1,060	
Office Supplies	1,840			(c) 1,204			636	
Land	4,500						4,500	
Building	20,260						20,260	
Accumulated Depreciation, Building		5,650		(d) 2,600				8,250
Office Equipment	8,600						8,600	
Accumulated Depreciation, Office Equipment		2,800		(e) 2,200				5,000
Accounts Payable		25,683						25,683
Gloria Fenwick, Capital		118,352						118,352
Gloria Fenwick, Withdrawals	20,000						20,000	
Sales		246,350				246,350		
Sales Returns and Allowances	7,025				7,025			
Cost of Goods Sold	123,124				123,124			
Freight In	8,236				8,236			
Sales Salaries Expense	22,500				22,500			
Freight Out Expense	5,740				5,740			
Advertising Expense	10,000				10,000			
Office Salaries Expense	26,900				26,900			
	398,835	398,835						
Insurance Expense, Selling			(a) 1,600		1,600			
Insurance Expense, General			(a) 4,200		4,200			
Store Supplies Expense			(b) 1,540		1,540			
Office Supplies Expense			(c) 1,204		1,204			
Depreciation Expense, Building			(d) 2,600		2,600			
Depreciation Expense, Office Equipment			(e) 2,200		2,200			
			13,344	13,344	216,869	246,350	186,766	157,285
Net Income					29,481			29,481
					246,350	246,350	186,766	186,766

INCOME STATEMENT AND BALANCE SHEET COLUMNS

KEY POINT: The Income Summary account does not appear on this work sheet.

After the Trial Balance columns have been totaled, the adjustments entered, and the equality of the columns proved, the balances are extended to the Income Statement and Balance Sheet columns. Again, begin with the Cash account at the top of the

EXHIBIT 5
Closing Entries for Fenwick Fashions Company: Perpetual Inventory System

General Journal — Page 10

Date		Description	Post. Ref.	Debit	Credit
20x3		*Closing entries:*			
Dec.	31	Income Summary		216,869	
		Sales Returns and Allowances			7,025
		Cost of Goods Sold			123,124
		Freight In			8,236
		Sales Salaries Expense			22,500
		Freight Out Expense			5,740
		Advertising Expense			10,000
		Office Salaries Expense			26,900
		Insurance Expense, Selling			1,600
		Insurance Expense, General			4,200
		Store Supplies Expense			1,540
		Office Supplies Expense			1,204
		Depreciation Expense, Building			2,600
		Depreciation Expense, Office Equipment			2,200
		Closed the temporary expense and revenue accounts having debit balances			
	31	Sales		246,350	
		Income Summary			246,350
		Closed the temporary revenue account having a credit balance			
	31	Income Summary		29,481	
		Gloria Fenwick, Capital			29,481
		Closed the Income Summary account			
	31	Gloria Fenwick, Capital		20,000	
		Gloria Fenwick, Withdrawals			20,000
		Closed the Withdrawals account			

sheet and move sequentially down the sheet, one account at a time, entering each account balance in the correct Income Statement or Balance Sheet column.

ADJUSTING ENTRIES

The adjusting entries from the work sheet are now entered into the general journal and posted to the ledger, as they would be in a service company. There is no difference in this procedure between a service company and a merchandising company.

CLOSING ENTRIES

Exhibit 5 shows the closing entries for Fenwick Fashions Company. The Cost of Goods Sold account is closed to Income Summary along with the expense accounts because the Cost of Goods Sold account has a debit balance. No closing entries affect the Merchandise Inventory account.

✓ Check out ACE for a Review Quiz at http://accounting.college.hmco.com/students.

The Merchandising Work Sheet and Closing Entries: The Periodic Inventory System

SO7 Prepare a work sheet and closing entries for a merchandising concern using the periodic inventory system.

RELATED TEXT ASSIGNMENTS
Q: 18, 19, 20
SE: 10
E: 13
P: 6

The accounts for a merchandising company using the periodic system generally include Sales, Sales Returns and Allowances, Purchases, Purchases Returns and Allowances, Freight In, and Merchandise Inventory. Like a service company's revenue and expense accounts, these accounts (except for Merchandise Inventory) are extended to the work sheet's Income Statement columns. During closing, they are transferred to the Income Summary account.

STUDY NOTE: The mnemonic BEE reflects the treatment of inventory in the Income Statement and Balance Sheet columns: Beginning, Ending, and Ending amounts, starting with the debit side of the Income Statement columns.

The Merchandise Inventory account requires special treatment under the periodic inventory system because purchases of merchandise are accumulated in the Purchases account. No entries are made to Merchandise Inventory during the accounting period. Thus, its balance is the same at the end of the period as at the beginning. To calculate net income, the closing entries must (1) remove the beginning inventory from the Merchandise Inventory account, (2) enter the ending inventory in the Merchandise Inventory account, and (3) transfer both inventory amounts to the Income Summary account. The following T accounts illustrate the flow of the inventory amounts for Fenwick Fashions.

Merchandise Inventory

Dec. 31, 20x2	Beg. Bal.	52,800	Dec. 31, 20x3	52,800
Dec. 31, 20x3	End. Bal.	48,300		

Income Summary

Dec. 31, 20x3	52,800	Dec. 31, 20x3	48,300

STUDY NOTE: Asset accounts are increased with debits and decreased with credits. Ending inventory must be established with a debit, and beginning inventory eliminated with a credit.

Beginning inventory ($52,800) is removed from the Merchandise Inventory account by a credit, leaving a zero balance, and transferred to the Income Summary account by a debit. Ending inventory ($48,300) is entered in the Merchandise Inventory account by a debit and recorded in the Income Summary account by a credit. The results of the two closing entries mirror the calculation of cost of goods sold, in which beginning inventory is added to net cost of purchases and ending inventory is then subtracted. When beginning inventory is debited to the Income Summary account, it is, in effect, added to net purchases because the balance in the Purchases account is also debited to Income Summary by a closing entry. And when ending inventory is credited to Income Summary, it is, in effect, deducted from the sum of beginning inventory and net cost of purchases. Keep these effects in mind while studying Fenwick Fashions' work sheet in Exhibit 6.

Income Statement and Balance Sheet Columns

KEY POINT: The Income Summary account does not appear on this work sheet.

As explained earlier, the Merchandise Inventory row requires special treatment. The beginning inventory balance of $52,800 (which is already in the trial balance) is extended to the debit column of the Income Statement columns, as in Exhibit 6. This procedure has the effect of adding beginning inventory to net purchases because the Purchases account is also in the debit column of the Income Statement columns. The ending inventory balance of $48,300 (which is determined by the physical inventory and is not in the trial balance) is then inserted in the credit column of the Income Statement columns. This has the effect of subtracting the ending inventory from goods available for sale in order to calculate the cost of goods sold. Finally, the ending merchandise inventory ($48,300) is inserted in the debit side of the Balance Sheet columns because it will appear on the balance sheet.

After all the items have been extended into the correct columns, the four columns are totaled. The net income or net loss is the difference between the debit

Exhibit 6
Work Sheet for Fenwick Fashions Company: Periodic Inventory System

Fenwick Fashions Company
Work Sheet
For the Year Ended December 31, 20x3

	Trial Balance		Adjustments		Income Statement		Balance Sheet	
Account Name	Debit	Credit	Debit	Credit	Debit	Credit	Debit	Credit
Cash	29,410						29,410	
Accounts Receivable	42,400						42,400	
Merchandise Inventory	52,800				52,800	48,300	48,300	
Prepaid Insurance	17,400			(a) 5,800			11,600	
Store Supplies	2,600			(b) 1,540			1,060	
Office Supplies	1,840			(c) 1,204			636	
Land	4,500						4,500	
Building	20,260						20,260	
Accumulated Depreciation, Building		5,650		(d) 2,600				8,250
Office Equipment	8,600						8,600	
Accumulated Depreciation, Office Equipment		2,800		(e) 2,200				5,000
Accounts Payable		25,683						25,683
Gloria Fenwick, Capital		118,352						118,352
Gloria Fenwick, Withdrawals	20,000						20,000	
Sales		246,350				246,350		
Sales Returns and Allowances	7,025				7,025			
Purchases	126,400				126,400			
Purchases Returns and Allowances		7,776				7,776		
Freight In	8,236				8,236			
Sales Salaries Expense	22,500				22,500			
Freight Out Expense	5,740				5,740			
Advertising Expense	10,000				10,000			
Office Salaries Expense	26,900				26,900			
	406,611	406,611						
Insurance Expense, Selling			(a) 1,600		1,600			
Insurance Expense, General			(a) 4,200		4,200			
Store Supplies Expense			(b) 1,540		1,540			
Office Supplies Expense			(c) 1,204		1,204			
Depreciation Expense, Building			(d) 2,600		2,600			
Depreciation Expense, Office Equipment			(e) 2,200		2,200			
			13,344	13,344	272,945	302,426	186,766	157,285
Net Income					29,481			29,481
					302,426	302,426	186,766	186,766

and credit Income Statement columns. In this case, Fenwick Fashions Company has earned a net income of $29,481, which is extended to the credit side of the Balance Sheet columns. The four columns are then added to prove that total debits equal total credits.

Closing Entries

Exhibit 7 shows the closing entries for Fenwick Fashions. Notice that Merchandise Inventory is credited for the amount of the beginning inventory ($52,800) in the first entry and debited for the amount of the ending inventory ($48,300) in the second entry. Otherwise, these closing entries are very similar to those for a service company except that the merchandising accounts also must be closed to Income Summary. All income statement accounts with debit balances, including the merchandising accounts of Sales Returns and Allowances, Purchases, and Freight In, are

Exhibit 7
Closing Entries for Fenwick Fashions Company: Periodic Inventory System

General Journal — Page 10

Date		Description	Post. Ref.	Debit	Credit
20x3		*Closing entries:*			
Dec.	31	Income Summary		272,945	
		Merchandise Inventory			52,800
		Sales Returns and Allowances			7,025
		Purchases			126,400
		Freight In			8,236
		Sales Salaries Expense			22,500
		Freight Out Expense			5,740
		Advertising Expense			10,000
		Office Salaries Expense			26,900
		Insurance Expense, Selling			1,600
		Insurance Expense, General			4,200
		Store Supplies Expense			1,540
		Office Supplies Expense			1,204
		Depreciation Expense, Building			2,600
		Depreciation Expense, Office Equipment			2,200
		Closed the temporary expense and revenue accounts having debit balances and removed the beginning inventory			
	31	Merchandise Inventory		48,300	
		Sales		246,350	
		Purchases Returns and Allowances		7,776	
		Income Summary			302,426
		Closed the temporary expense and revenue accounts having credit balances and established the ending inventory			
	31	Income Summary		29,481	
		Gloria Fenwick, Capital			29,481
		Closed the Income Summary account			
	31	Gloria Fenwick, Capital		20,000	
		Gloria Fenwick, Withdrawals			20,000
		Closed the Withdrawals account			

credited in the first entry. The total of these accounts ($272,945) equals the total of the debit column in the Income Statement columns of the work sheet. All income statement accounts with credit balances—Sales and Purchases Returns and Allowances—are debited in the second entry. The total of these accounts ($302,426) equals the total of the Income Statement credit column in the work sheet. The third and fourth entries are used to close the Income Summary account and transfer net income to the Capital account, and to close the Withdrawals account to the Capital account.

Check out ACE for a Review Quiz at http://accounting.college.hmco.com/students.

Accounting for Discounts

SO8 Apply sales and purchases discounts to merchandising transactions.

RELATED TEXT ASSIGNMENTS
Q: 21
SE: 11
E: 13, 14, 15, 16
P: 7
SD: 3

Sales Discounts

As mentioned earlier, sales discounts for early payment are customary in some industries. Because it usually is not possible to know at the time of the sale whether the customer will pay in time to take advantage of sales discounts, the discounts are recorded only at the time the customer pays. For example, assume that Fenwick Fashions Company sells merchandise to a customer on September 20 for $300, on terms of 2/10, n/60. This is the entry at the time of the sale:

A = L + OE
\+ +

Sept. 20	Accounts Receivable	300	
	Sales		300
	Sold merchandise on credit, terms 2/10, n/60		

KEY POINT: Accounts Receivable must be credited for the full $300 even though only $294 has been received.

The customer can take advantage of the sales discount any time on or before September 30, ten days after the date of the invoice. If the customer pays on September 29, the entry in Fenwick's records would look like this:

A = L + OE
\+ −
−

Sept. 29	Cash	294	
	Sales Discounts	6	
	Accounts Receivable		300
	Received payment for Sept. 20 sale; discount taken		

If the customer does not take advantage of the sales discount but waits until November 19 to pay for the merchandise, the entry would be as follows:

A = L + OE
\+
−

Nov. 19	Cash	300	
	Accounts Receivable		300
	Received payment for Sept. 20 sale; no discount taken		

At the end of the accounting period, the Sales Discounts account has accumulated all the sales discounts taken during the period. Because sales discounts reduce revenues from sales, Sales Discounts is a contra-revenue account with a normal debit balance that is deducted from sales on the income statement. Sales Discounts is treated the same as Sales Returns and Allowances on the work sheet and in the closing entries.

Purchases Discounts

Merchandise purchases are usually made on credit and sometimes involve **purchases discounts** for early payment. Purchases discounts are discounts taken for early payment for merchandise purchased for resale. They are to the buyer what sales discounts are to the seller. The amount of discounts taken is recorded in a separate account. Assume that Fenwick Fashions Company made a credit purchase of merchandise on November 12 for $1,500 with terms of 2/10, n/30 and returned

$200 in merchandise on November 14. When payment is made within the discount period, Fenwick's entry looks like this:

A = L + OE
− − +

Nov. 22	Accounts Payable		1,300	
	Purchases Discounts			26
	Cash			1,274
	Paid the invoice of Nov. 12			
	Purchase Nov. 12	$1,500		
	Less return Nov. 14	200		
	Net purchase	$1,300		
	Discount: 2%	26		
	Cash paid	$1,274		

KEY POINT: Accounts Payable must be debited for the full $1,300 even though only $1,274 has been paid.

If Fenwick does not pay for the purchase within the discount period, the entry would be as follows:

A = L + OE
− −

Dec. 12	Accounts Payable	1,300	
	Cash		1,300
	Paid the invoice of Nov. 12, less the return, on due date; no discount taken		

Like Purchases Returns and Allowances, Purchases Discounts is a contra-purchases account with a normal credit balance that is deducted from purchases on the income statement. If a company makes only a partial payment on an invoice, most creditors allow the company to take the discount applicable to the partial payment. The discount usually does not apply to freight, postage, taxes, or other charges that might appear on the invoice.

Check out ACE for a Review Quiz at http://accounting.college.hmco.com/students.

Chapter Review

Review of Learning Objectives

LO1 Identify the management issues related to merchandising businesses.

Merchandising companies differ from service companies in that they earn income by buying and selling goods. The buying and selling of goods adds to the complexity of the business and raises four issues that management must address. First, the series of transactions in which merchandising companies engage (the operating cycle) requires careful cash flow management. Second, to achieve the goal of profitability, management must price goods and control operating costs by using budgets to ensure an adequate income after operating expenses have been paid. Third, management must choose whether to use the perpetual or the periodic inventory system. Fourth, management must establish an internal control structure that protects the company's assets—its cash, merchandise inventory, and accounts receivable.

LO2 Compare the income statements for service and merchandising concerns, and define the components of the merchandising income statement.

In the simplest case, the income statement for a service company consists only of revenues and expenses. The income statement for a merchandising company has three major parts: (1) net sales, (2) cost of goods sold, and (3) operating expenses. Gross margin is the difference between revenues from net sales and the cost of goods sold. Net income is the "bottom line" after operating expenses are deducted from the gross margin.

LO3 Define and distinguish the terms of sale for merchandising transactions.

A trade discount is a reduction from the list or catalogue price of a product. A sales discount is a discount given for early payment of a sale on credit. FOB shipping point means that the buyer bears the cost of transportation and that title to the goods passes to the buyer at the shipping origin. FOB destination means that the seller bears the cost of transportation and that title does not pass to the buyer until the goods reach their destination.

LO4 Prepare an income statement and record merchandising transactions under the perpetual inventory system.

The Merchandise Inventory account is continuously adjusted by entering purchases, sales, and other inventory transactions as the transactions occur. Purchases increase the Merchandise Inventory account, and purchases returns decrease it. As goods are sold, their cost is transferred from the Merchandise Inventory account to the Cost of Goods Sold account.

LO5 Prepare an income statement and record merchandising transactions under the periodic inventory system.

When the periodic inventory system is used, the cost of goods sold section of the income statement must include the following elements:

$$\text{Gross Purchases} - \text{Purchases Returns and Allowances} + \text{Freight In} = \text{Net Cost of Purchases}$$

$$\text{Beginning Merchandise Inventory} + \text{Net Cost of Purchases} = \text{Goods Available for Sale}$$

$$\text{Goods Available for Sale} - \text{Ending Merchandise Inventory} = \text{Cost of Goods Sold}$$

Under the periodic inventory system, the Merchandise Inventory account stays at the beginning level until the physical inventory is recorded at the end of the accounting period. A Purchases account is used to accumulate purchases of merchandise during the accounting period, and a Purchases Returns and Allowances account is used to accumulate returns of and allowances on purchases.

Supplemental Objectives

SO6 Prepare a work sheet and closing entries for a merchandising concern using the perpetual inventory system.

Preparing a work sheet for a merchandising concern is much like preparing one for a service concern, except that there are additional accounts relating to merchandising transactions, such as Sales, Sales Returns and Allowances, Cost of Goods Sold, and Freight In. These accounts must be extended to the appropriate Income Statement columns. Also, since the Merchandise Inventory account is kept up to date, its ending balance is extended directly to the debit column of the Balance Sheet columns. There is no need to place it in the Income Statement columns. The closing entries for a merchandising concern under the perpetual inventory system are the same as those for a service business. There is no need to include the Merchandise Inventory account.

SO7 Prepare a work sheet and closing entries for a merchandising concern using the periodic inventory system.

The work sheet under the periodic inventory system is the same as under the perpetual inventory system with the exception that the beginning merchandise inventory from the trial balance is extended to the debit column of the Income Statement columns, and the ending balance of Merchandise Inventory is inserted in both the credit column of the Income Statement columns and the debit column of the Balance Sheet columns. The closing entries for a merchandising concern under the periodic inventory system are similar to those for a service business, with one exception. The exception is that the closing entries include a credit to Merchandise Inventory for the amount of the beginning inventory and a debit to Merchandise Inventory for the amount of the ending inventory.

SO8 Apply sales and purchases discounts to merchandising transactions.

Sales discounts are discounts for early payment. Terms of 2/10, n/30 mean that the buyer can take a 2 percent discount if the invoice is paid within ten days of the invoice date. Otherwise, the buyer is obligated to pay the full amount in 30 days. Discounts on sales are recorded in the Sales Discounts account, and discounts on purchases are recorded in the Purchases Discounts account.

Review of Concepts and Terminology

The following concepts and terms were introduced in this chapter:

LO5 **Beginning inventory:** Merchandise on hand at the start of an accounting period.

LO1 **Cash flow management:** The planning of a company's receipts and payments of cash.

LO2 **Cost of goods sold:** The amount a merchant paid for the merchandise sold during an accounting period. Also called *cost of sales*.

LO5 **Ending inventory:** Merchandise on hand at the end of an accounting period.

LO1 **Financing period:** The amount of time from the purchase of inventory until it is sold and payment is collected, less the amount of time creditors allow for payment of the inventory. Also called the *cash gap*.

LO3 **FOB destination:** A shipping term that means that the seller bears transportation costs to the place of delivery.

LO3 **FOB shipping point:** A shipping term that means that the buyer bears transportation costs from the point of origin.

LO4 **Freight in:** The transportation cost of receiving merchandise. Also called *transportation in*.

LO2 **Freight Out Expense:** The account that accumulates transportation charges on merchandise sold, which are shown as a selling expense. Also called *Delivery Expense*.

LO5 **Goods available for sale:** The sum of beginning inventory and the net cost of purchases during the period; the total goods available for sale to customers during an accounting period.

LO2 **Gross margin:** The difference between net sales and cost of goods sold. Also called *gross profit*.

LO2 **Gross sales:** Total sales for cash and on credit occurring during an accounting period.

LO1 **Internal controls:** The environment, accounting systems, and control procedures established by management and designed to safeguard the assets of a business and provide reliable accounting records.

LO1 **Merchandise inventory:** The goods on hand at any one time that are available for sale to customers.

LO1 **Merchandising businesses:** Businesses that earn income by buying and selling goods.

LO5 **Net cost of purchases:** Net purchases plus any freight charges on the purchases.

LO2 **Net income:** For merchandising companies, what is left after deducting operating expenses from gross margin.

LO5 **Net purchases:** Total purchases less any deductions, such as purchases returns and allowances and purchases discounts.

LO2 **Net sales:** The gross proceeds from sales of merchandise less sales returns and allowances and any discounts. Also called *sales* on income statements.

LO1 **Operating budget:** Management's operating plans as reflected by detailed listings of projected selling expenses and general and administrative expenses.

LO1 **Operating cycle:** A series of transactions that includes purchases of merchandise inventory for cash or on credit, payment for purchases made on credit, sales of merchandise inventory for cash or on credit, and collection of cash from the sales.

LO2 **Operating expenses:** The expenses other than cost of goods sold that are incurred in running a business.

LO1 **Periodic inventory system:** A system for determining inventory on hand by taking a physical count at the end of an accounting period.

LO1 **Perpetual inventory system:** A system for determining inventory on hand by keeping continuous records of the quantity and, usually, the cost of individual items as they are bought and sold.

LO1 **Physical inventory:** An actual count of all merchandise on hand.

LO1 **Profitability management:** The process of achieving a satisfactory gross margin and maintaining acceptable levels of operating expenses.

LO5 **Purchases:** A temporary account that is used under the periodic inventory system to accumulate the total cost of merchandise purchased for resale during an accounting period.

SO8 **Purchases discounts:** Discounts taken for prompt payment for merchandise purchased for resale; the Purchases Discounts account is a contra-purchases account.

LO5 **Purchases Returns and Allowances:** A contra-purchases account used under the periodic inventory system to accumulate cash refunds, credits on account, and other allowances made by suppliers.

LO3 **Sales discount:** A discount given to a buyer for early payment of a sale made on credit; the Sales Discounts account is a contra-revenue account.

LO2 **Sales Returns and Allowances:** A contra-revenue account used to accumulate cash refunds, credits on account, and other allowances made to customers who have received defective or otherwise unsatisfactory products.

LO1 **Service business:** Businesses that earn income by performing a service for fees or commissions.

LO3 **Trade discount:** A deduction (usually 30 percent or more) off a list or catalogue price that is not recorded in the accounting records.

REVIEW PROBLEM

Merchandising Transactions: Perpetual and Periodic Inventory Systems

LO4 Dawkins Company engaged in the following transactions during October.

LO5

Oct.	1	Sold merchandise to Ernie Devlin on credit, terms n/30, FOB shipping point, $1,050 (cost, $630).
	2	Purchased merchandise on credit from Ruland Company, terms n/30, FOB shipping point, $1,900.
	2	Paid Custom Freight $145 for freight charges on merchandise received.
	6	Purchased store supplies on credit from Arizin Supply House, terms n/30, $318.
	9	Purchased merchandise on credit from LNP Company, terms n/30, FOB shipping point, $1,800, including $100 freight costs paid by LNP Company.
	11	Accepted from Ernie Devlin a return of merchandise, which was returned to inventory, $150 (cost, $90).
	14	Returned for credit $300 of merchandise received on October 2.
	15	Returned for credit $100 of store supplies purchased on October 6.
	16	Sold merchandise for cash, $500 (cost, $300).
	22	Paid Ruland Company for purchase of October 2 less return of October 14.
	23	Received full payment from Ernie Devlin for his October 1 purchase, less return on October 11.

REQUIRED ▶

1. Prepare entries in journal form to record the transactions, assuming the perpetual inventory system is used.
2. Prepare entries in journal form to record the transactions, assuming the periodic inventory system is used.

ANSWER TO REVIEW PROBLEM

Accounts that differ under the two systems are highlighted.

		1. Perpetual Inventory System			2. Periodic Inventory System		
Oct.	1	Accounts Receivable	1,050		Accounts Receivable	1,050	
		Sales		1,050	Sales		1,050
		Sold merchandise on account to Ernie Devlin, terms n/30, FOB shipping point			Sold merchandise on account to Ernie Devlin, terms n/30, FOB shipping point		
		Cost of Goods Sold	630				
		Merchandise Inventory		630			
		Transferred cost of merchandise sold to Cost of Goods Sold account					

Date	1. Perpetual Inventory System	Debit	Credit	2. Periodic Inventory System	Debit	Credit
Oct. 2	Merchandise Inventory	1,900		Purchases	1,900	
	Accounts Payable		1,900	Accounts Payable		1,900
	Purchased merchandise on account from Ruland Company, terms n/30, FOB shipping point			Purchased merchandise on account from Ruland Company, terms n/30, FOB shipping point		
	Freight In	145		Freight In	145	
	Cash		145	Cash		145
	Paid freight on previous purchase			Paid freight on previous purchase		
6	Store Supplies	318		Store Supplies	318	
	Accounts Payable		318	Accounts Payable		318
	Purchased store supplies on account from Arizin Supply House, terms n/30			Purchased store supplies on account from Arizin Supply House, terms n/30		
9	Merchandise Inventory	1,700		Purchases	1,700	
	Freight In	100		Freight In	100	
	Accounts Payable		1,800	Accounts Payable		1,800
	Purchased merchandise on account from LNP Company, terms n/30, FOB shipping point, freight paid by supplier			Purchased merchandise on account from LNP Company, terms n/30, FOB shipping point, freight paid by supplier		
11	Sales Returns and Allowances	150		Sales Returns and Allowances	150	
	Accounts Receivable		150	Accounts Receivable		150
	Accepted return of merchandise from Ernie Devlin			Accepted return of merchandise from Ernie Devlin		
	Merchandise Inventory	90				
	Cost of Goods Sold		90			
	Transferred cost of merchandise returned to Merchandise Inventory account					
14	Accounts Payable	300		Accounts Payable	300	
	Merchandise Inventory		300	Purchases Returns and Allowances		300
	Returned portion of merchandise purchased from Ruland Company			Returned portion of merchandise purchased from Ruland Company		
15	Accounts Payable	100		Accounts Payable	100	
	Store Supplies		100	Store Supplies		100
	Returned store supplies (not merchandise) purchased on October 6 for credit			Returned store supplies (not merchandise) purchased on October 6 for credit		
16	Cash	500		Cash	500	
	Sales		500	Sales		500
	Sold merchandise for cash			Sold merchandise for cash		
	Cost of Goods Sold	300				
	Merchandise Inventory		300			
	Transferred cost of merchandise sold to Cost of Goods Sold account					
22	Accounts Payable	1,600		Accounts Payable	1,600	
	Cash		1,600	Cash		1,600
	Made payment on account to Ruland Company $1,900 − $300 = $1,600			Made payment on account to Ruland Company $1,900 − $300 = $1,600		
23	Cash	900		Cash	900	
	Accounts Receivable		900	Accounts Receivable		900
	Received payment on account of Ernie Devlin $1,050 − $150 = $900			Received payment on account of Ernie Devlin $1,050 − $150 = $900		

Chapter Assignments

BUILDING YOUR KNOWLEDGE FOUNDATION

QUESTIONS

1. What four issues must managers of merchandising businesses address?
2. What is the operating cycle of a merchandising business, and why is it important?
3. What is the primary difference between the operations of a merchandising business and those of a service business?
4. What is the difference between the perpetual inventory system and the periodic inventory system?
5. Under the periodic inventory system, how must the amount of inventory at the end of the year be determined?
6. What are the principal differences in the handling of merchandise inventory in the accounting records under the perpetual inventory system and the periodic inventory system?
7. Discuss this statement: "The perpetual inventory system is the best system because management always needs to know how much inventory it has."
8. What is the primary difference in the income statement of a merchandising company from that of a service company? Define *gross margin*. Why is it important?
9. During its first year in operation, Molinari Nursery had a cost of goods sold of $64,000 and a gross margin equal to 40 percent of sales. What was the dollar amount of the company's sales?
10. Could Molinari Nursery (in Question 9) have a net loss for the year? Explain your answer.
11. What is the difference between a trade discount and a sales discount?
12. Two companies quoted the following prices and terms on 50 units of product. Which supplier is quoting the better deal? Explain your answer.

	Price	Terms
Supplier A	$20 per unit	FOB shipping point
Supplier B	$21 per unit	FOB destination

13. What is the principal difference in accounting for the purchase and sale of merchandise under the perpetual inventory system and the periodic inventory system?
14. Is *freight in* an operating expense? Explain your answer.
15. Lorres Hardware purchased the following items: (a) a delivery truck, (b) two dozen hammers, (c) supplies for its office workers, and (d) a broom for the janitor. Which items should be debited to the Purchases account under the periodic inventory system?
16. Under which inventory system is a Cost of Goods Sold account maintained? Why?
17. Why is it advisable to maintain a Sales Returns and Allowances account when the same result could be obtained by debiting each return or allowance to the Sales account?
18. Why is special treatment of the Merchandise Inventory account at the end of the accounting period of particular importance in the determination of net income under the periodic inventory system? What must be achieved in the account?
19. What are the principal differences between the work sheet for a merchandising company and that for a service company? Discuss in terms of the periodic and the perpetual inventory systems.
20. What are the principal differences between the closing entries for a merchandising company using the perpetual inventory system and those for a company using the periodic inventory system?
21. What is the normal balance of the Sales Discounts account? Is it an asset, a liability, an expense, or a contra-revenue account?

Short Exercises

SE 1.
LO1 **Identification of Management Issues**

Identify each of the following decisions as most directly related to (a) cash flow management, (b) profitability management, (c) choice of inventory system, or (d) control of merchandising operations:

1. Determination of how to protect cash from theft or embezzlement
2. Determination of the selling price of goods for sale
3. Determination of policies governing sales of merchandise on credit
4. Determination of whether to use the periodic or the perpetual inventory system

SE 2.
LO2 **Merchandising Income Statement**

Using the following data, prepare an income statement for Martin's Hardware for the month ended February 28:

Cost of goods sold	$30,000
General and administrative expenses	8,000
Net sales	50,000
Selling expenses	7,000

SE 3.
LO3 **Terms of Sale**

A dealer buys tooling machines from a manufacturer and resells them to its customers.

a. The manufacturer sets a list or catalogue price of $6,000 for a machine. The manufacturer offers its dealers a 40 percent trade discount.
b. Freight charges are FOB shipping point. The cost of shipping a machine is $350.
c. The manufacturer offers a sales discount of 2/10, n/30. The sales discount does not apply to shipping costs.

What is the net cost of the tooling machine to the dealer, assuming it is paid for within ten days of purchase?

SE 4.
LO3 **Credit Card Sales Transaction**

Record in journal form the following transaction for Jenny's Crafts Store:

Apr. 19 A tabulation at the end of the day showed $400 in Visa® invoices, which are deposited in a special bank account at full value less 5 percent discount.

SE 5.
LO4 **Purchases of Merchandise: Perpetual Inventory System**

Record in journal form each of the following transactions, assuming the perpetual inventory system is used:

Aug. 2 Purchased merchandise on credit from Bean Company, invoice dated August 1, terms n/10, FOB shipping point, $2,300.
3 Received bill from Ace Shipping Company for transportation costs on August 2 shipment, invoice dated August 1, terms n/30, $210.
7 Returned damaged merchandise received from Bean Company on August 2 for credit, $360.
10 Paid in full the amount due to Bean Company for the purchase of August 2, part of which was returned on August 7.

SE 6.
LO4 **Sales of Merchandise: Perpetual Inventory System**

Record in journal form the following transactions, assuming the perpetual inventory system is used:

Aug. 4 Sold merchandise on credit to Konner Company, terms n/30, FOB destination, $1,200. (Cost = $720.)
5 Paid transportation costs for sale of August 4, $110.
9 Part of the merchandise sold on August 4 was accepted back from Konner Company for full credit and returned to the merchandise inventory, $350. (Cost = $210.)
Sept. 3 Received payment in full from Konner Company for merchandise sold on August 4, less the return on August 9.

SE 7.
LO5 **Purchases of Merchandise: Periodic Inventory System**

Record in journal form the transactions in SE 5, assuming the periodic inventory system is used.

SE 8.
LO5 **Cost of Goods Sold: Periodic Inventory System**

Using the following data and assuming cost of goods sold is $230,000, prepare the cost of goods sold section of a merchandising income statement (periodic inventory system), including computation of the amount of purchases for the month of October:

Freight in	$12,000
Merchandise inventory, Sept. 30, 20xx	33,000
Merchandise inventory, Oct. 31, 20xx	44,000
Purchases	?
Purchases returns and allowances	9,000

SE 9. LO5 **Sales of Merchandise: Periodic Inventory System**

Record in journal form the transactions in **SE 6** using the periodic inventory system.

SE 10. SO6 SO7 **Merchandise Inventory on the Work Sheet and in Closing Entries**

Forrester Company had beginning merchandise inventory of $14,800 and ending merchandise inventory of $19,200. Where would these numbers appear on the work sheet and in the closing entries under (1) the perpetual inventory system and (2) the periodic inventory system?

SE 11. SO8 **Sales and Purchases Discounts**

On April 15, Farid Company sold merchandise to Smarte Company for $1,500 on terms of 2/10, n/30. Record the entries in both Farid's and Smarte's records for (1) the sale, (2) a return of merchandise on April 20 of $300, and (3) payment in full on April 25. Assume both companies use the periodic inventory system.

EXERCISES

E 1. LO1 **Management Issues and Decisions**

The decisions that follow were made by the management of Shanahan Shoe Company. Indicate whether each decision pertains primarily to (a) cash flow management, (b) profitability management, (c) choice of inventory system, or (d) control of merchandise operations.

1. Decided to mark each item of inventory with a magnetic tag that sets off an alarm if the tag is removed from the store before being deactivated
2. Decided to reduce the credit terms offered to customers from 30 days to 20 days to speed up collection of accounts
3. Decided that the benefits of keeping track of each item of inventory as it is bought and sold would exceed the costs of such a system
4. Decided to raise the price of each item of inventory to achieve a higher gross margin to offset an increase in rent expense
5. Decided to purchase a new type of cash register that can be operated only by a person who knows a predetermined code
6. Decided to switch to a new cleaning service that will provide the same service at a lower cost

E 2. LO1 **Operating Budget**

The operating budget and actual performance for the six months ended June 30, 20x3, for Pacific Hardware Company appear below.

	Budget	Actual
Selling expenses		
Sales salaries expense	$ 90,000	$102,030
Sales supplies expense	2,000	1,642
Rent expense, selling space	18,000	18,000
Utilities expense, selling space	12,000	11,256
Advertising expense	15,000	21,986
Depreciation expense, selling fixtures	6,500	6,778
Total selling expenses	$143,500	$161,692
General and administrative expenses		
Office salaries expense	$ 50,000	$ 47,912
Office supplies expense	1,000	782
Rent expense, office space	4,000	4,000
Depreciation expense, office equipment	3,000	3,251
Utilities expense, office space	3,000	3,114
Postage expense	500	626
Insurance expense	2,000	2,700
Miscellaneous expense	500	481
Total general and administrative expenses	$ 64,000	$ 62,866
Total operating expenses	$207,500	$224,558

1. Prepare an operating report that shows budget, actual, and difference.
2. Discuss the results, identifying which differences most likely should be investigated by management.

LO2 Parts of the Income Statement: Missing Data

E 3. Compute the dollar amount of each item indicated by a letter in the following table. Treat each horizontal row of numbers as a separate problem.

Sales	Cost of Goods Sold	Gross Margin	Operating Expenses	Net Income (Loss)
$250,000	$ a	$ 80,000	$ b	$24,000
c	216,000	120,000	80,000	40,000
460,000	d	100,000	e	(2,000)
780,000	f	g	240,000	80,000

LO3 Terms of Sale

E 4. A household appliance dealer buys refrigerators from a manufacturer and resells them to its customers.

a. The manufacturer sets a list or catalogue price of $1,000 for a refrigerator. The manufacturer offers its dealers a 30 percent trade discount.
b. The manufacturer sells the machine under terms of FOB destination. The cost of shipping is $100.
c. The manufacturer offers a sales discount of 2/10, n/30. Sales discounts do not apply to shipping costs.

What is the net cost of the refrigerator to the dealer, assuming it is paid for within ten days of purchase?

LO4 Preparation of the Income Statement: Perpetual Inventory System

E 5. Using the selected account balances at December 31, 20xx, for City Rental that follow, prepare an income statement for the year ended December 31, 20xx. Show the detail of net sales. The company uses the perpetual inventory system, and Freight In has not been included in Cost of Goods Sold.

Account Name	Debit	Credit
Sales		$237,500
Sales Returns and Allowances	$ 11,750	
Cost of Goods Sold	140,000	
Freight In	6,750	
Selling Expenses	21,500	
General and Administrative Expenses	43,500	

LO4 Recording Purchases: Perpetual Inventory System

E 6. Give the entries to record each of the following transactions under the perpetual inventory system:

a. Purchased merchandise on credit, terms n/30, FOB shipping point, $2,500.
b. Paid freight on the shipment in transaction **a**, $135.
c. Purchased merchandise on credit, terms n/30, FOB destination, $1,400.
d. Purchased merchandise on credit, terms n/30, FOB shipping point, $2,600, which includes freight paid by the supplier of $200.
e. Returned part of the merchandise purchased in transaction **c**, $500.
f. Paid the amount owed on the purchase in transaction **a**.
g. Paid the amount owed on the purchase in transaction **d**.
h. Paid the amount owed on the purchase in transaction **c** less the return in **e**.

LO4 Recording Sales: Perpetual Inventory System

E 7. On June 15, Tunnale Company sold merchandise for $1,300 on terms of n/30 to Whist Company. On June 20, Whist Company returned some of the merchandise for a credit of $300, and on June 25, Whist paid the balance owed. Give Tunnale's entries to record the sale, return, and receipt of payment under the perpetual inventory system. The cost of the merchandise sold on June 15 was $750, and the cost of the merchandise returned to inventory on June 20 was $175.

E 8. **LO5 Preparation of the Income Statement: Periodic Inventory System**

Using the selected year-end account balances at December 31, 20x4, for the Atlanta General Store shown below, prepare a 20x4 income statement. Show the detail of net sales. The company uses the periodic inventory system. Beginning merchandise inventory was $52,000; ending merchandise inventory is $44,000.

Account Name	Debit	Credit
Sales		$594,000
Sales Returns and Allowances	$ 30,400	
Purchases	229,600	
Purchases Returns and Allowances		8,000
Freight In	11,200	
Selling Expenses	97,000	
General and Administrative Expenses	74,400	

E 9. **LO5 Merchandising Income Statement: Missing Data, Multiple Years**

Determine the missing data for each letter in the following three income statements for Leominster Wholesale Paper Company (in thousands):

	20x4	20x3	20x2
Gross sales	$ o	$ h	$286
Sales returns and allowances	24	19	a
Net sales	p	317	b
Merchandise inventory, beginning	q	i	38
Purchases	192	169	c
Purchases returns and allowances	31	j	17
Freight in	r	29	22
Net cost of purchases	189	k	d
Goods available for sale	222	212	182
Merchandise inventory, ending	39	l	42
Cost of goods sold	s	179	e
Gross margin	142	m	126
Selling expenses	t	78	f
General and administrative expenses	39	n	33
Total operating expenses	130	128	g
Net income	u	10	27

E 10. **LO5 Recording Purchases: Periodic Inventory System**

Using the data in **E 6,** give the entries to record each of the transactions under the periodic inventory system.

E 11. **LO5 Recording Sales: Periodic Inventory System**

Using the relevant data in **E 7,** give the entries to record each of the transactions under the periodic inventory system.

E 12. **SO6 Preparation of Closing Entries: Perpetual Inventory System**

Below are selected account balances of Linley Company for the year ended December 31, 20xx.

Account Name	Debit	Credit
Sales		$297,000
Sales Returns and Allowances	$ 15,200	
Cost of Goods Sold	113,000	
Freight In	5,600	
Selling Expenses	48,500	
General and Administrative Expenses	37,200	

Prepare closing entries, assuming that the owner of Linley Company, Sandra Linley, withdrew $40,000 for personal expenses during the year.

E 13. Selected account balances of the Lakeside Grocery Store for the year ended December 31, 20xx, follow.

SO7 Preparation of Closing Entries:
SO8 Periodic Inventory System

Account Name	Debit	Credit
Sales		$297,000
Sales Returns and Allowances	$ 11,000	
Sales Discounts	4,200	
Purchases	114,800	
Purchases Returns and Allowances		1,800
Purchases Discounts		2,200
Freight In	5,600	
Selling Expenses	48,500	
General and Administrative Expenses	37,200	

Beginning merchandise inventory was $26,000, and ending merchandise inventory is $22,000. Prepare closing entries, assuming that the owner of Lakeside Grocery, John Grover, withdrew $34,000 for personal expenses during the year.

E 14. Give the entries to record the following transactions engaged in by Ramos Company, which uses the periodic inventory system:

SO8 Sales Involving Discounts

Mar. 1 Sold merchandise on credit to Smythe Company, terms 2/10, n/30, FOB shipping point, $500.
3 Accepted a return from Smythe Company for full credit, $200.
10 Received payment from Smythe Company for the sale, less the return and discount.
11 Sold merchandise on credit to Smythe Company, terms 2/10, n/30, FOB shipping point, $800.
31 Received payment for amount due from Smythe Company for the sale of March 11.

E 15. Give the entries to record the following transactions engaged in by Amal Company, which uses the periodic inventory system:

SO8 Purchases Involving Discounts

July 2 Purchased merchandise on credit from Olney Company, terms 2/10, n/30, FOB destination, invoice dated July 1, $800.
6 Returned some merchandise to Olney Company for full credit, $100.
11 Paid Olney Company for purchase of July 2 less return and discount.
14 Purchased merchandise on credit from Olney Company, terms 2/10, n/30, FOB destination, invoice dated July 12, $900.
31 Paid amount owed Olney Company for purchase of July 14.

E 16. The Melody Company purchased $9,200 of merchandise, terms 2/10, n/30, from Mirro Company and paid for the merchandise within the discount period. Give the entries (1) by the Melody Company to record the purchase and payment and (2) by Mirro Company to record the sale and receipt of payment. Both companies use the periodic inventory system.

SO8 Purchases and Sales Involving Discounts

PROBLEMS

P 1. Selected accounts from the adjusted trial balance for Bear Camera Store at the end of the fiscal year, June 30, 20x4, follow.

LO1 Merchandising Income
LO4 Statement: Perpetual Inventory System

Bear Camera Store Partial Adjusted Trial Balance June 30, 20x4		
Sales		$433,912
Sales Returns and Allowances	$ 11,250	
Cost of Goods Sold	221,185	
Freight In	10,078	
Store Salaries Expense	107,550	
Office Salaries Expense	26,500	
Advertising Expense	18,200	
Rent Expense	14,400	
Insurance Expense	2,800	
Utilities Expense	8,760	
Store Supplies Expense	2,464	
Office Supplies Expense	1,814	
Depreciation Expense, Store Equipment	1,800	
Depreciation Expense, Office Equipment	1,850	

REQUIRED ▶

1. Prepare an income statement for Bear Camera Store. Freight In should be combined with Cost of Goods Sold. Store Salaries Expense; Advertising Expense; Store Supplies Expense; and Depreciation Expense, Store Equipment are selling expenses. The other expenses are general and administrative expenses. The company uses the perpetual inventory system. Show details of net sales and operating expenses.
2. Based on your knowledge at this point in the course, how would you use the income statement for Bear Camera Store to evaluate the company's profitability? What other financial statement should be considered and why?

P 2. Sweet Company engaged in the following transactions in July 20xx:

LO4 Merchandising Transactions: Perpetual Inventory System

July 1 Sold merchandise to Rick Lee on credit, terms n/30, FOB shipping point, $4,200 (cost, $2,520).
3 Purchased merchandise on credit from Cobalt Company, terms n/30, FOB shipping point, $7,600.
5 Paid Rapid Freight for freight charges on merchandise received, $580.
6 Purchased store supplies on credit from DGE Supply Company, terms n/20, $1,272.
8 Purchased merchandise on credit from Holt Company, terms n/30, FOB shipping point, $7,200, which includes $400 freight costs paid by Holt Company.
12 Returned some of the merchandise purchased on July 3 for credit, $1,200.
15 Sold merchandise on credit to Bob Wagner, terms n/30, FOB shipping point, $2,400 (cost, $1,440).
16 Returned some of the store supplies purchased on July 6 for credit, $400.
17 Sold merchandise for cash, $2,000 (cost, $1,200).
18 Accepted for full credit a return from Rick Lee and returned merchandise to inventory, $400 (cost, $240).
24 Paid Cobalt Company for purchase of July 3 less return of July 12.
25 Received full payment from Rick Lee for his July 1 purchase less the return on July 18.

REQUIRED ▶

1. Prepare entries in journal form to record the transactions, assuming use of the perpetual inventory system.
2. Why is it important to keep purchases of merchandise in a separate account from purchases of store supplies?

P 3. The data at the top of the next page are from Pat's Sports Equipment's adjusted trial balance on September 30, 20x5, the fiscal year end. The company's beginning merchandise inventory was $243,666; ending merchandise inventory is $229,992 for the period.

LO1 LO5 Merchandising Income Statement: Periodic Inventory System

Pat's Sports Equipment Partial Adjusted Trial Balance September 30, 20x5		
Sales		$1,301,736
Sales Returns and Allowances	$ 33,750	
Purchases	663,555	
Purchases Returns and Allowances		90,714
Freight In	30,234	
Store Salaries Expense	322,650	
Office Salaries Expense	79,500	
Advertising Expense	54,600	
Rent Expense	43,200	
Insurance Expense	8,400	
Utilities Expense	56,280	
Store Supplies Expense	1,392	
Office Supplies Expense	2,442	
Depreciation Expense, Store Equipment	5,400	
Depreciation Expense, Office Equipment	5,550	

REQUIRED ▶

1. Prepare an income statement for Pat's Sports Equipment. Store Salaries Expense; Advertising Expense; Store Supplies Expense; and Depreciation Expense, Store Equipment are selling expenses. The other expenses are general and administrative expenses. The company uses the periodic inventory system. Show details of net sales and operating expenses.
2. How would you use the income statement you prepared in **1** to evaluate the company's profitability? What other financial statements should be considered and why?

P 4. Use the relevant data in **P 2** for this problem.

LO5 Merchandising Transactions: Periodic Inventory System

REQUIRED ▶ Prepare entries in journal form to record the transactions, assuming use of the periodic inventory system.

P 5. The year-end trial balance at the top of the opposite page was taken from the ledger of the Clay Party Costumes Company at the end of its annual accounting period on June 30, 20x4. The company uses the perpetual inventory system.

SO6 Merchandiser's Work Sheet, Financial Statements, and Closing Entries: Perpetual Inventory System

REQUIRED ▶

1. Enter the trial balance on a work sheet, and complete the work sheet using the following information: ending store supplies inventory, $550; expired insurance, $2,400; estimated depreciation on store equipment, $5,000; sales salaries payable, $650; and accrued utilities expense, $100.
2. Prepare an income statement, a statement of owner's equity, and a balance sheet. Sales Salaries Expense; Other Selling Expenses; Store Supplies Expense; and Depreciation Expense, Store Equipment are all selling expenses.
3. From the work sheet, prepare the closing entries.

P 6. The trial balance at the bottom of the opposite page was taken from the ledger of East End Bookstore at the end of its annual accounting period. The company uses the periodic inventory system.

SO7 Merchandiser's Work Sheet, Financial Statements, and Closing Entries: Periodic Inventory System

REQUIRED ▶

1. Enter the trial balance on a work sheet, and complete the work sheet using this information: ending merchandise inventory, $33,227; ending store supplies inventory, $304; unexpired prepaid insurance, $200; estimated depreciation on store equipment, $4,300; sales salaries payable, $80; and accrued utilities expense, $150.

Clay Party Costumes Company
Trial Balance
June 30, 20x4

Cash	$ 7,050	
Accounts Receivable	24,830	
Merchandise Inventory	88,900	
Store Supplies	3,800	
Prepaid Insurance	4,800	
Store Equipment	151,300	
Accumulated Depreciation, Store Equipment		$ 25,500
Accounts Payable		38,950
Jarrott Clay, Capital		161,350
Jarrott Clay, Withdrawals	24,000	
Sales		475,250
Sales Returns and Allowances	4,690	
Cost of Goods Sold	231,840	
Freight In	10,400	
Sales Salaries Expense	64,600	
Rent Expense	48,000	
Other Selling Expenses	32,910	
Utilities Expense	3,930	
	$701,050	$701,050

East End Bookstore
Trial Balance
June 30, 20x3

Cash	$ 6,025	
Accounts Receivable	9,280	
Merchandise Inventory	29,450	
Store Supplies	1,911	
Prepaid Insurance	1,600	
Store Equipment	37,200	
Accumulated Depreciation, Store Equipment		$ 15,600
Accounts Payable		12,300
Ellen Donnelly, Capital		41,994
Ellen Donnelly, Withdrawals	12,000	
Sales		102,250
Sales Returns and Allowances	987	
Purchases	63,200	
Purchases Returns and Allowances		21,011
Freight In	2,261	
Sales Salaries Expense	21,350	
Rent Expense	3,600	
Other Selling Expenses	2,614	
Utilities Expense	1,677	
	$193,155	$193,155

2. Prepare an income statement, a statement of owner's equity, and a balance sheet. Sales Salaries Expense; Other Selling Expenses; Store Supplies Expense; and Depreciation Expense, Store Equipment are all selling expenses.
3. From the work sheet, prepare the closing entries.

P 7. **LO5 SO8 Merchandising Transactions, Including Discounts: Periodic Inventory System**

Kimbassa Authentics Company engaged in these transactions in January 20xx:

Jan. 2 Purchased merchandise on credit from Chang Company, terms 2/10, n/30, FOB destination, $7,400.
3 Sold merchandise on credit to B. St. Pierre, terms 1/10, n/30, FOB shipping point, $1,000.
5 Sold merchandise for cash, $700.
6 Purchased and received merchandise on credit from Oakland Company, terms 2/10, n/30, FOB shipping point, $4,200.
7 Received freight bill from North Port Express for shipment received on January 6, $570.
9 Sold merchandise on credit to R. Hayden, terms 1/10, n/30, FOB destination, $3,800.
10 Purchased merchandise from Chang Company, terms 2/10, n/30, FOB shipping point, $2,650, including freight costs of $150.
11 Received freight bill from North Port Express for sale to R. Hayden on January 9, $291.
12 Paid Chang Company for purchase of January 2.
13 Received payment in full for B. St. Pierre's purchase of January 3.
14 Paid Oakland Company half the amount owed on the January 6 purchase. A discount is allowed on partial payment.
15 Returned faulty merchandise worth $300 to Chang Company for credit against purchase of January 10.
16 Purchased office supplies from GHI Co., terms n/10, $478.
17 Received payment from R. Hayden for half of the purchase of January 9. A discount is allowed on partial payment.
18 Paid Chang Company in full for amount owed on purchase of January 10, less return on January 15.
19 Sold merchandise on credit to M. Perez, terms 2/10, n/30, FOB shipping point, $780.
20 Returned for credit several items of office supplies purchased on January 16, $128.
22 Issued a credit to M. Perez for returned merchandise, $180.
25 Paid for January 16 purchase, less return on January 20.
26 Paid North Port Express for freight charges of January 7 and 11.
27 Received payment of amount owed by M. Perez for purchase of January 19, less credit of January 22.
28 Paid Oakland Company for balance of January 6 purchase.
31 Sold merchandise for cash, $973.

REQUIRED ▶ Prepare entries in journal form to record the transactions, assuming that the periodic inventory system is used.

Alternate Problems

P 8. **LO1 LO4 Merchandising Income Statement: Perpetual Inventory System**

At the end of the fiscal year, August 31, 20x4, selected accounts from the adjusted trial balance for Holiday Merchandise were as shown at the top of the next page. The company uses the perpetual inventory system.

REQUIRED ▶

1. Using the information given, prepare an income statement for Holiday Merchandise. Combine Freight In with Cost of Goods Sold. Store Salaries Expense; Advertising Expense; Store Supplies Expense; and Depreciation Expense, Store Equipment are selling expenses. The other expenses are general and administrative expenses. Show details of net sales and operating expenses.

Holiday Merchandise Partial Adjusted Trial Balance August 31, 20x4		
Sales		$324,000
Sales Returns and Allowances	$ 4,000	
Cost of Goods Sold	122,800	
Freight In	4,600	
Store Salaries Expense	65,250	
Office Salaries Expense	25,750	
Advertising Expense	48,600	
Rent Expense	4,800	
Insurance Expense	2,400	
Utilities Expense	3,120	
Store Supplies Expense	5,760	
Office Supplies Expense	2,350	
Depreciation Expense, Store Equipment	2,100	
Depreciation Expense, Office Equipment	1,600	

2. Based on your knowledge at this point in the course, how would you use the income statement for Holiday Merchandise to evaluate the company's profitability? What other financial statement should be considered and why?

P 9. Garden Company engaged in the following transactions in October 20x4:

LO4 Merchandising Transactions: Perpetual Inventory System

Oct. 7 Sold merchandise on credit to Sonia Mendes, terms n/30, FOB shipping point, $6,000 (cost, $3,600).
8 Purchased merchandise on credit from DaCosta Company, terms n/30, FOB shipping point, $12,000.
9 Paid Jay Company for shipping charges on merchandise purchased on October 8, $508.
10 Purchased merchandise on credit from Paige Company, terms n/30, FOB shipping point, $19,200, including $1,200 freight costs paid by Paige.
13 Purchased office supplies on credit from Hayami Company, terms n/30, $4,800.
14 Sold merchandise on credit to Eliza Samms, terms n/30, FOB shipping point, $4,800 (cost, $2,880).
14 Returned damaged merchandise received from DaCosta Company on October 8 for credit, $1,200.
17 Received check from Sonia Mendes for her purchase of October 7.
18 Returned a portion of the office supplies purchased on October 13 for credit because the wrong items were sent, $800.
19 Sold merchandise for cash, $3,600 (cost, $2,160).
20 Paid Paige Company for purchase of October 10.
21 Paid DaCosta Company the balance from the transactions of October 8 and October 14.
24 Accepted from Eliza Samms a return of merchandise, which was put back in inventory, $400 (cost, $240).

REQUIRED ▶

1. Prepare entries in journal form to record the transactions, assuming the perpetual inventory system is used.
2. Why is it important to keep purchases of merchandise in a separate account from purchases of office supplies?

P 10. Selected accounts from the adjusted trial balance for Gourmet Gadgets Shop at the end of the fiscal year, March 31, 20x4, appear at the top of the next page. Gourmet Gadgets' merchandise inventory was $38,200 at the beginning of the year and $29,400 at the end of the year. The company uses the periodic inventory system.

LO1 Merchandising Income
LO5 Statement: Periodic Inventory System

Gourmet Gadgets Shop
Partial Adjusted Trial Balance
March 31, 20x4

Sales		$165,000
Sales Returns and Allowances	$ 2,000	
Purchases	70,200	
Purchases Returns and Allowances		2,600
Freight In	2,300	
Store Salaries Expense	32,625	
Office Salaries Expense	12,875	
Advertising Expense	24,300	
Rent Expense	2,400	
Insurance Expense	1,200	
Utilities Expense	1,560	
Store Supplies Expense	2,880	
Office Supplies Expense	1,175	
Depreciation Expense, Store Equipment	1,050	
Depreciation Expense, Office Equipment	800	

REQUIRED ▶

1. Using the information given, prepare an income statement for Gourmet Gadgets Shop. Store Salaries Expense; Advertising Expense; Store Supplies Expense; and Depreciation Expense, Store Equipment are selling expenses. The other expenses are general and administrative expenses. Show details of net sales and operating expenses.
2. Based on your knowledge at this point in the course, how would you use the income statement for Gourmet Gadgets Shop to evaluate the company's profitability? What other financial statements should be considered and why?

P 11. Use the relevant data in **P 9** for this problem.

LO5 **Merchandising Transactions: Periodic Inventory System**

REQUIRED ▶ Prepare entries in journal form to record the transactions, assuming the periodic inventory system is used.

SKILLS DEVELOPMENT CASES

Conceptual Analysis

SD 1. LO1 **Cash Flow Management**

Matson Audio and Video Source has operated in a middle-size Midwest city for 30 years. The company has always prided itself on individual attention to its customers. It carries a large inventory so it can offer a good selection and deliver purchases quickly. It accepts credit cards and checks in payment but also provides 90 days credit to reliable customers who have purchased from the company in the past. The company maintains good relations with suppliers by paying invoices soon after they are received. In the past year, the company has been strapped for cash and has had to borrow from the bank to pay its bills. An analysis of its financial statements reveals that, on average, inventory is on hand for 70 days before being sold and receivables are held for 90 days before being paid. Accounts payable are paid, on average, in 20 days. What are the operating cycle and the financing period, and how long are Matson's? In what three ways can Matson improve its cash flow management? Make a suggestion for implementing each.

SD 2. LO1 LO4 LO5 **Periodic Versus Perpetual Inventory Systems**

Books Unlimited is a well-established chain of 20 bookstores in eastern Michigan. In recent years the company has grown rapidly, adding five new stores in regional malls. Management has relied on the manager of each store to place orders keyed to the market in his or her region; the managers select from a master list of available titles provided by the central office. Every six months, a physical inventory is taken, and financial statements are prepared using the periodic inventory system. At that time, books that have not sold well are placed on sale or, whenever possible, returned to the publisher. As a result of the company's fast growth, there are many new store managers, and management has found that they are not as able to judge the market as are managers of the older, established stores. Thus, management is considering implementing a perpetual inventory system and carefully monitoring sales from the central office. Do you think Books Unlimited should switch to the perpetual inventory system or stay with the periodic inventory system? Discuss the advantages and disadvantages of each system.

Group Activity: Divide the class into groups. Ask half the groups to develop reasons to keep a periodic inventory system and half to list reasons to change to a perpetual inventory system. Debrief by writing parallel lists on the board.

Ethical Dilemma

SD 3.

SO8 Ethics and Purchases Discounts

The purchasing power of some customers is such that they can exert pressure on suppliers to go beyond the suppliers' customary allowances. For example, Wal-Mart <www.walmart.com> represents more than 10 percent of annual sales for many suppliers, including Fruit of the Loom <www.fruit.com>, Sunbeam <www.sunbeam.com>, Rubbermaid <www.rubbermaid.com>, and Coleman <www.coleman.com>. *Forbes* magazine reports that while many of these suppliers allow a 2 percent discount if bills are paid within 15 days, "Wal-Mart routinely pays its bills closer to 30 days and takes the 2 percent discount anyway on the gross amount of the invoice, not the net amount, which deducts for [trade] discounts and things like freight costs."[6]

Identify two ways in which Wal-Mart's practice benefits Wal-Mart. Do you think this practice is unethical, or is it just good cash management on the part of Wal-Mart? Are the suppliers harmed by it?

Research Activity

SD 4.

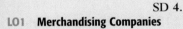

LO1 LO2 Merchandising Companies

Conduct an individual field trip by visiting any retail or wholesale business. It may be a business where you buy a product, a company where you work, or a family business. It is not necessary for you to talk to anyone at the business, but it may be helpful to do so. Determine why the business is a merchandising business. List the products or groups of products that the company sells. Does the company offer any services? How do services differ from merchandise? Make a list of the types of transactions the business engages in. Also identify and list all the operating expenses you can think of that would be relevant to this business. Organize your findings in the form of a memo to your instructor.

Decision-Making Practice

SD 5.

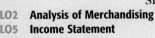

LO2 LO5 Analysis of Merchandising Income Statement

In 20x5, Les Solty opened a small retail store in a suburban mall. Called Solty Denim Company, the shop sold designer jeans. Solty worked 14 hours a day and controlled all aspects of the operation. All sales were for cash or bank credit card. The business was such a success that in 20x6, Solty decided to open a second store in another mall. Because the new shop needed his attention, he hired a manager to work in the original store with two sales clerks. During 20x6, the new store was successful, but the operations of the original store did not match the first year's performance.

Concerned about this turn of events, Solty compared the two years' results for the original store. The figures were as follows:

	20x6	20x5
Net sales	$325,000	$350,000
Cost of goods sold	225,000	225,000
Gross margin	$100,000	$125,000
Operating expenses	75,000	50,000
Net income	$ 25,000	$ 75,000

In addition, Solty's analysis revealed that the cost and selling price of jeans were about the same in both years and that the level of operating expenses was roughly the same in both years, except for the new manager's $25,000 salary. Sales returns and allowances were insignificant amounts in both years.

Studying the situation further, Solty discovered the following facts about the cost of goods sold:

	20x6	20x5
Purchases	$200,000	$271,000
Total purchases allowances	15,000	20,000
Freight in	19,000	27,000
Physical inventory, end of year	32,000	53,000

Still not satisfied, Solty went through all the individual sales and purchase records for the year. Both sales and purchases were verified. However, the 20x6 ending inventory should have been $57,000, given the unit purchases and sales during the year. After puzzling over all this information, Solty comes to you for accounting help.

1. Using Solty's new information, recompute the cost of goods sold for 20x5 and 20x6, and account for the difference in net income between 20x5 and 20x6.
2. Suggest at least two reasons for the discrepancy in the 20x6 ending inventory.

FINANCIAL REPORTING AND ANALYSIS CASES

Interpreting Financial Reports

FRA 1.

LO2 Comparison of Operating Performance

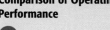

Wal-Mart <www.walmart.com> and Kmart <www.kmartcorp.com>, two of the largest retailers in the United States, have different approaches to retailing. Their success has been different also. At one time, Kmart was larger than Wal-Mart. Today, Wal-Mart is almost three times as large and Kmart has declared bankruptcy. You can see the difference by analyzing their respective income statements and merchandise inventories. Selected information from their annual reports for the year ended January 31, 2001, is presented below.[7] (All amounts are in millions.)

Wal-Mart: Net sales, $191,329; Cost of goods sold, $150,255; Operating expenses, $31,550; Ending inventory, $21,442

Kmart: Net sales, $37,028; Cost of goods sold, $29,658; Operating expenses, $7,415; Ending inventory, $6,412

1. Prepare a schedule computing the gross margin and income from operations for both companies as dollar amounts and as percentages of net sales. Also compute inventory as a percentage of the cost of goods sold.
2. From what you know about the different retailing approaches of these two companies, do the gross margins and incomes from operations you computed in **1** seem compatible with these approaches? What is it about the nature of Wal-Mart's operations that produces higher gross margin and lower operating expenses in percentages in comparison to Kmart? Which company's approach was more successful in the fiscal year ending January 31, 2001? Explain your answer.
3. Both companies have chosen a fiscal year that ends on January 31. Why do you suppose they made this choice? How realistic do you think the inventory figures are as indicators of inventory levels during the rest of the year? Which company appears to make the most efficient use of its inventory?

International Company

FRA 2.

LO3 LO4 LO5 British Terminology for Merchandising Transactions

Harrods <www.harrods.com> is a large British retailer with department stores throughout the United Kingdom and Europe. British and American merchandising terms differ. For instance, in the United Kingdom, the income statement is called the *profit and loss account*, sales is called *turnover,* merchandise inventory is called *stocks,* accounts receivable is called *debtors,* and accounts payable is called *creditors.* Of course, the amounts are stated in terms of the pound (£). In today's business world, it is important to understand terminology employed by professionals from other countries. Explain in your own words why the British may use the terms *profit and loss account, turnover, stocks, debtors,* and *creditors* rather than the American equivalents.

Toys "R" Us Annual Report

FRA 3.
LO1 Operating Cycle and Financing Period

Refer to the Toys "R" Us <www.tru.com> annual report in the Supplement to Chapter 6 and to Figures 1 and 2 in this chapter. Write a memorandum to your instructor briefly describing the Toys "R" Us operating cycle and financing period. This memorandum should identify the most common transactions in the operating cycle as it applies to Toys "R" Us. It should refer to the importance of accounts receivable, accounts payable, and merchandise inventory in the Toys "R" Us financial statements. Complete the memorandum by explaining why the operating cycle and financing period are favorable to the company.

Comparison Case: Toys "R" Us and Walgreen Co.

FRA 4.
LO1 Income Statement Analysis

Refer to the Toys "R" Us <www.tru.com> annual report and the financial statements of Walgreens <www.walgreens.com> in the Supplement to Chapter 6. Determine which company—Toys "R" Us or Walgreens—has more profitable merchandising operations by preparing a schedule that compares the companies based on net sales, cost of sales, gross margin, total operating expenses, and income from operations as a percentage of sales. (***Hint:*** You should put the income statements in comparable formats.) In addition, for each company, compute inventory as a percentage of the cost of sales. Which company has the highest prices in relation to costs of sales? Which company is more efficient in its operating expenses? Which company manages its inventory better? Overall, on the basis of the income statement, which company is more profitable? Explain your answers.

Fingraph® Financial Analyst™

FRA 5.
LO1 Income Statement Analysis
LO2

Choose any retail company from the list of Fingraph companies on the Needles Accounting Resource Center Web Site at http://accounting.college.hmco.com/students. Access the Microsoft Excel spreadsheets for the company you selected. Using the Fingraph CD-ROM software, display the Income Statements Analysis: Income from Operations in tabular and graphic form for the company.

Write an executive summary that analyzes the change in the company's income from operations from the first to the second year. In preparing the summary, focus on the reasons the change occurred by answering the following questions: Did the company's income from operations improve or decline from the first to the second year? What was the relationship of the change to the change in net sales? Was the change in income from operations primarily due to a change in gross margin or to a change in operating expenses? Suggest some possible reasons for the change in gross margin or operating expenses. Use percentages to support your answer.

Internet Case

FRA 6.
LO1 Comparison of Traditional
LO3 Merchandising with
LO4 Ecommerce

Ecommerce is a word coined to describe business conducted over the Internet. Ecommerce is similar in some ways to traditional retailing, but it presents new challenges. Choose a company with traditional retail outlets that is also selling over the Internet and go to its web site. Some examples are Wal-Mart <www.walmart.com>, Kmart <www.kmartcorp.com>, Toys "R" Us <www.tru.com>, Barnes & Noble <www.bn.com>, and Lands' End <www.landsend.com>. Investigate and list the steps a customer makes to purchase an item on the site. How do these steps differ from those in a traditional retail store? What are some of the accounting challenges in recording Internet transactions? Be prepared to discuss your results in class.

6

Chapter 6 introduces the objectives and qualitative aspects of financial information and demonstrates how much more useful classified financial statements are than simple financial statements in presenting information to statement users.

Financial Reporting and Analysis

Learning Objectives

LO1 State the objectives of financial reporting.

LO2 State the qualitative characteristics of accounting information and describe their interrelationships.

LO3 Define and describe the conventions of *comparability* and *consistency, materiality, conservatism, full disclosure,* and *cost-benefit.*

LO4 Explain management's responsibility for ethical financial reporting and define *fraudulent financial reporting.*

LO5 Identify and describe the basic components of a classified balance sheet.

LO6 Prepare multistep and single-step classified income statements.

LO7 Evaluate liquidity and profitability using classified financial statements.

DECISION POINT

A USER'S FOCUS

General Mills, Inc. <www.generalmills.com> The management of a corporation is judged by the company's financial performance. Financial performance is reported to stockholders and others outside the business in the company's annual report, which includes the financial statements and other relevant information. Performance measures are usually based on the relationships of key data in the financial statements. For large companies, this often means condensing a tremendous amount of information to a few numbers that management considers important. For example, what key measures does the management of General Mills, Inc., a successful food products company that recently acquired its long-time rival Pillsbury and offers such well-known brands as Cheerios, Wheaties, Hamburger Helper, and Progresso Soups, choose to focus on as its goals?

In its letter to shareholders, General Mills states its financial goals as follows:

> Our target is 7 percent compound annual sales growth between now and 2010. With this faster topline growth, . . . our Earnings Per Share (EPS) growth should accelerate, too. Our target is to deliver 11 to 15 percent annual earnings per share growth over the balance of this decade. We believe achieving these goals will represent superior performance when benchmarked against major consumer products companies.[1]

General Mills' management has thus set forth measurable performance goals by which it can be evaluated. The graph on the opposite page shows that the company reached its growth in sales target in only

What key performance measures does the management of General Mills choose to focus on as its goals?

one of the past three years. However, it reached its growth in EPS in all three years.

Of course, investors and creditors will want to do their own analysis of General Mills. This will require reading and interpreting the financial statements and calculating other ratios. However, the analysis will be meaningless unless the reader understands financial statements and generally accepted accounting principles, on which the statements are based. Also important to learning how to read and interpret financial statements is a comprehension of the categories and classifications used in balance sheets and income statements. Key financial ratios used in financial statement analysis are based on those categories. This chapter begins by describing the objectives, characteristics, and conventions that underlie the preparation of financial statements.

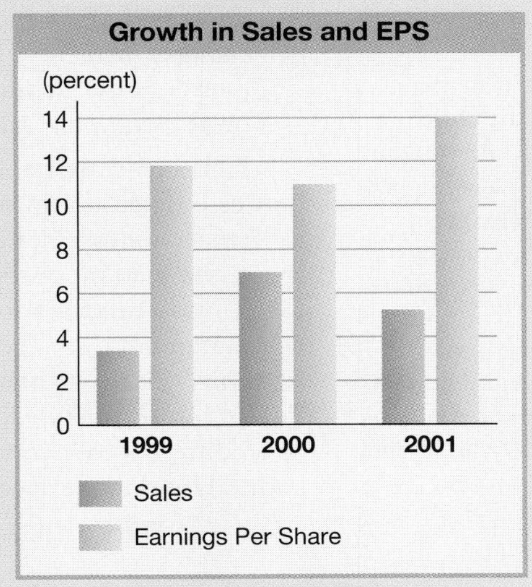

Objectives of Financial Information

LO1 State the objectives of financial reporting.

RELATED TEXT ASSIGNMENTS
Q: 1
SE: 1
E: 1

The United States has a highly developed exchange economy. In this kind of economy, most goods and services are exchanged for money or claims to money instead of being used or bartered by their producers. Most business is carried on through corporations, including many extremely large firms that buy, sell, and obtain financing in U.S. and world markets.

By issuing stocks and bonds that are traded in financial markets, businesses can raise capital for production and marketing activities. Investors are interested mainly in returns from dividends and increases in the market price of their investments. Creditors want to know if the business can repay a loan plus interest in accordance with required terms. Thus, both investors and creditors need to know if a company can generate adequate cash flows. Financial statements are important to both groups in making that judgment. They offer valuable information that helps investors and creditors judge a company's ability to pay dividends and repay debts with interest. In this way, the market puts scarce resources to work in the companies that can use them most efficiently.

The information needs of users and the general business environment are the basis for the three objectives of financial reporting established by the Financial Accounting Standards Board (FASB):[2]

KEY POINT: Although reading financial reports requires some understanding of business, it does not require the skills of a CPA.

1. *To furnish information that is useful in making investment and credit decisions.* Financial reporting should offer information that can help current and potential investors and creditors make rational investment and credit decisions. The reports should be in a form that makes sense to those who have some understanding of business and are willing to study the information carefully.
2. *To provide information useful in assessing cash flow prospects.* Financial reporting should supply information to help current and potential investors and creditors predict the amounts, timing, and risk of cash receipts from dividends or interest and proceeds from the sale, redemption, or maturity of stocks or loans.
3. *To provide information about business resources, claims to those resources, and changes in them.* Financial reporting should give information about the company's assets, liabilities, and stockholders' equity, and the effects of transactions on the company's assets, liabilities, and stockholders' equity.

STOP AND THINK!
How do the four basic financial statements meet the third objective of financial reporting?
The balance sheet provides information about a company's resources (assets) and claims to those resources (liabilities and owners' equity). The income statement, statement of cash flows, and statement of owner's equity provide information about changes in resources and claims to them. ■

Financial statements are the most important way of periodically presenting to parties outside the business the information that has been gathered and processed in the accounting system. For this reason, the financial statements—the balance sheet, the income statement, the statement of owner's equity, and the statement of cash flows—are the most important output of the accounting system. These financial statements are "general purpose" because of their wide audience. They are "external" because their users are outside the business. Because of a potential conflict of interest between managers, who must prepare the statements, and investors or creditors, who invest in or lend money to the business, these statements often are audited by outside accountants to increase confidence in their reliability.

Check out ACE for a Review Quiz at http://accounting.college.hmco.com/students.

Qualitative Characteristics of Accounting Information

LO2 State the qualitative characteristics of accounting information and describe their interrelationships.

RELATED TEXT ASSIGNMENTS
Q: 2
SE: 1
E: 1

It is easy for students in their first accounting course to get the idea that accounting is 100 percent accurate. This idea is reinforced by the fact that all the problems in this and other introductory books can be solved. The numbers all add up; what is supposed to equal something else does. Accounting seems very much like mathematics in its precision. In this book, the basics of accounting are presented in a simple form to help you understand them. In practice, however, accounting information

FIGURE 1
Qualitative Characteristics and the Conventions of Accounting Information

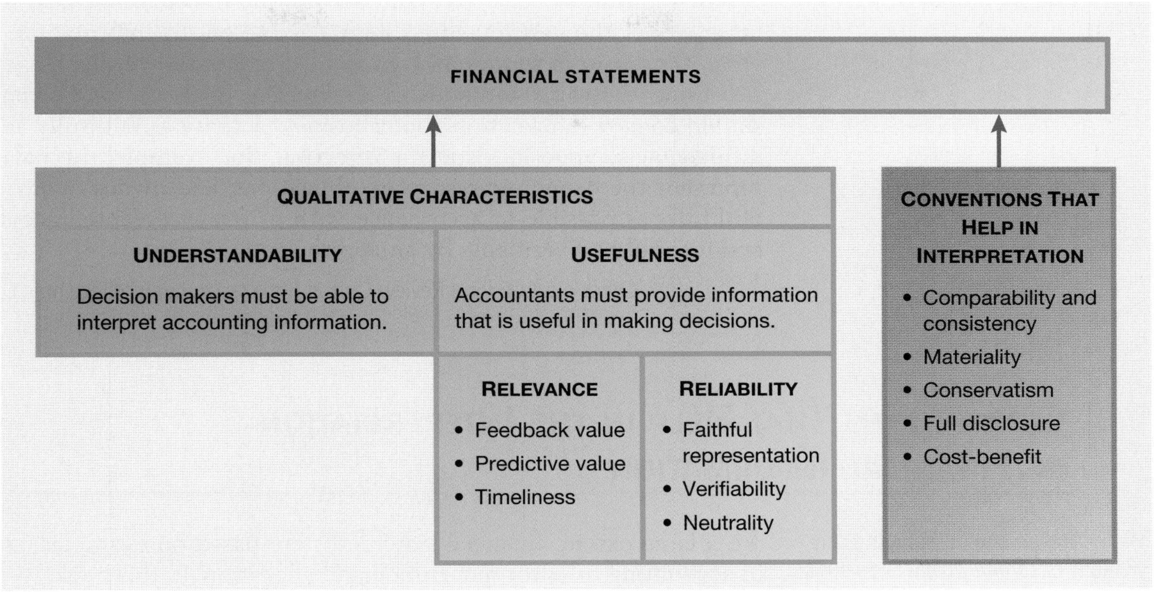

is neither simple nor precise, and it rarely satisfies all criteria. The FASB emphasizes this fact in the following statement:

> The information provided by financial reporting often results from approximate, rather than exact, measures. The measures commonly involve numerous estimates, classifications, summarizations, judgments and allocations. The outcome of economic activity in a dynamic economy is uncertain and results from combinations of many factors. Thus, despite the aura of precision that may seem to surround financial reporting in general and financial statements in particular, with few exceptions the measures are approximations, which may be based on rules and conventions, rather than exact amounts.[3]

STOP AND THINK!
What are some areas that require estimates to record transactions under the matching rule?
To record depreciation expense, it is necessary to estimate the useful life of the asset. To record the amount of unearned revenue that is now earned or the amount of accrued revenue on a project in process, it is necessary to estimate the amount of revenue earned. ■

KEY POINT: Financial statements should be free of material misstatements.

The goal of accounting information—to provide the basic data that different users need to make informed decisions—is an ideal. The gap between the ideal and the actual provides much of the interest and controversy in accounting. To facilitate interpretation, the FASB has described the **qualitative characteristics** of accounting information, which are standards for judging that information. In addition, there are generally accepted conventions for recording and reporting that simplify interpretation. The relationships among these concepts are shown in Figure 1.

The most important qualitative characteristics are understandability and usefulness. **Understandability** depends on both the accountant and the decision maker. The accountant prepares the financial statements in accordance with accepted practices, generating important information that is believed to be understandable. But the decision maker must interpret the information and use it in making decisions. The decision maker must judge what information to use, how to use it, and what it means.

For accounting information to meet the standard of **usefulness**, it must have two major qualitative characteristics: relevance and reliability. **Relevance** means that the information can affect the outcome of a decision. In other words, a different decision would be made if the relevant information were not available. To be relevant, information must provide feedback, help predict future conditions, and be timely. For example, the income statement provides information about how a company performed over the past year (feedback), and it helps in planning for the next year (prediction). To be useful, however, it also must be communicated soon enough after the end of the accounting period to enable the reader to make decisions (timeliness).

In addition to being relevant, accounting information must have **reliability**. In other words, the user must be able to depend on the information. It must represent what it is meant to represent. It must be credible and verifiable by independent parties using the same methods of measuring. It also must be neutral. Accounting should convey information about business activity as faithfully as possible without influencing anyone in a specific direction. For example, the balance sheet should represent the economic resources, obligations, and owner's equity of a business as faithfully as possible in accordance with generally accepted accounting principles, and it should be verifiable by an auditor.

Check out ACE for a Review Quiz at http://accounting.college.hmco.com/students.

Conventions That Help in the Interpretation of Financial Information

LO3 Define and describe the conventions of *comparability* and *consistency, materiality, conservatism, full disclosure,* and *cost-benefit.*

RELATED TEXT ASSIGNMENTS
Q: 3
SE: 2
E: 1, 2
P: 1, 6
SD: 1, 2

To a large extent, financial statements are based on estimates and the application of accounting rules for recognition and allocation. In this book, we point out a number of difficulties with financial statements. One is failing to recognize the changing value of the dollar caused by inflation. Another is treating intangibles, such as research and development costs, as assets if they are purchased outside the company and as expenses if they are developed within the company. Such problems do not mean that financial statements are useless; they are essential. However, users must know how to interpret them. To help in this interpretation, accountants depend on five **conventions**, or rules of thumb, in recording transactions and preparing financial statements: (1) comparability and consistency, (2) materiality, (3) conservatism, (4) full disclosure, and (5) cost-benefit.

Comparability and Consistency

Stop and Think!
How can financial information be consistent but not comparable?
Consistency in accounting applies only to the use of the accounting principles for presenting the financial information. It does not apply to the conditions that are represented in the financial statements. For example, changes in business operations or the economy may make financial information incomparable from year to year, even though the same accounting policies have been followed. ■

A characteristic that increases the usefulness of accounting information is comparability. Information about a company is more useful if it can be compared with similar facts about the same company over several time periods or about another company for the same time period. **Comparability** means that the information is presented in such a way that a decision maker can recognize similarities, differences, and trends over different time periods or between different companies.

Consistent use of accounting measures and procedures is important in achieving comparability. The **consistency** convention requires that once an accounting procedure is adopted by a company, it remain in use from one period to the next unless users of the financial statements are informed of the change. Thus, without a note to the contrary, the users can assume that there has been no change in the treatment of a particular transaction, account, or item that would affect the interpretation of the statements.

If management decides that a certain procedure is no longer appropriate and should be changed, or if reporting requirements change, generally accepted accounting principles require that the change and its dollar effect be described in the notes to the financial statements:

> The nature of and justification for a change in accounting principle and its effect on income should be disclosed in the financial statements of the period in which the change is made. The justification for the change should explain clearly why the newly adopted accounting principle is preferable.[4]

FOCUS ON BUSINESS PRACTICE

How Much Is Material? It's Not Only a Matter of Numbers.

The materiality issue has been a pet peeve of the SEC <www.sec.gov>, which contends that companies have increasingly abused the convention to protect their stocks from taking a pounding when earnings do not reach their targets. Over the years, companies have excluded from earnings any losses that they deem so small as to have virtually no effect on net income. Accountants and companies have typically used a rule of thumb of 5 percent of net income. The SEC has issued a new rule that puts stricter requirements on the use of materiality in that it calls for qualitative considerations in addition to quantitative guides. The percentage assessment is acceptable as an initial screening, but now companies cannot decline to book items in order to meet earnings estimates, preserve a growing earnings trend, convert a loss to a profit, increase management compensation, or hide an illegal transaction, such as a bribe.[5]

www.rmc.com

For example, Reynolds Metals Company changed its method of accounting for business start-up costs because the American Institute of Certified Public Accountants (AICPA) changed the requirements for accounting for this type of cost.[6]

MATERIALITY

BUSINESS-WORLD EXAMPLE: By definition, a $10 stapler is a long-term asset that, theoretically, should be capitalized and depreciated over its useful life. However, the convention of materiality allows the stapler to be expensed entirely in the year of purchase because its cost is small and writing it off in one year has no effect on anyone's decision making.

KEY POINT: Illegal acts involving even small dollar amounts should be investigated.

Materiality refers to the relative importance of an item or event. If an item or event is material, it is probably relevant to users of the financial statements. In other words, an item is material if users would have done something differently if they had not known about the item. The accountant is often faced with decisions about small items or events that make little difference to users no matter how they are handled. For example, a large company may decide that expenditures for durable items of less than $500 should be charged as expenses rather than recorded as long-term assets and depreciated.

In general, an item is material if there is a reasonable expectation that knowing about it would influence the decisions of users of financial statements. The materiality of an item normally is determined by relating its dollar value to an element of the financial statements, such as net income or total assets. Some accountants feel that when an item is 5 percent or more of net income, it is material. However, materiality also depends on the nature of the item, not just its value. For example, in a multimillion-dollar company, a mistake of $5,000 in recording an item may not be important, but the discovery of a $5,000 bribe or theft can be very important. Also, many small errors can combine into a material amount. Accountants judge the materiality of many things, and the users of financial statements depend on their judgments being fair and accurate. The SEC has recently questioned whether a desire to avoid showing certain items in the financial statements has influenced some companies' judgment about materiality.

CONSERVATISM

KEY POINT: The purpose of conservatism is not to produce the lowest net income and lowest asset value. It is a guideline for choosing among GAAP alternatives, and it should be used with care.

Accountants try to base their decisions on logic and evidence that lead to the fairest report of what happened. In judging and estimating, however, accountants often are faced with uncertainties. In these cases, they look to the convention of **conservatism**. This convention means that when accountants face major uncertainties about which accounting procedure to use, they generally choose the one that is least likely to overstate assets and income.

One of the most common applications of the conservatism convention is the use of the lower-of-cost-or-market method in accounting for inventories. Under this method, if an item's market value is greater than its cost, the more conservative cost figure is used. If the market value falls below the cost, the more conservative market value is used. The latter situation often occurs in the computer industry.

Conservatism can be a useful tool in doubtful cases, but its abuse leads to incorrect and misleading financial statements. Suppose that someone incorrectly applies

Focus on Business Practice

When Is "Full Disclosure" Too Much? It's a Matter of Cost and Benefits.

The large accounting firm of Ernst & Young <www.ey.com> reports that over a 20-year period, the total number of pages in the annual reports of 25 large, well-known companies has increased an average of 84 percent and the number of pages of notes has increased 325 percent—from 4 to 17 pages. Management's discussion and analysis increased 300 percent, from 3 pages to 12.[7] Because some people feel that "these documents are so daunting that people don't read them at all," the SEC allows companies to issue to the public "summary reports" in which the bulk of the notes can be reduced. Although more accessible and less costly, summary reports are controversial because many analysts feel that it is in the notes that one gets the detailed information necessary to understand complex business operations. One analyst remarked, "To banish the notes for fear they will turn off readers would be like eliminating fractions from math books on the theory that the average student prefers to work with whole numbers."[8] Where this controversy will end, nobody knows. Detailed reports still must be filed with the SEC, but more and more companies are providing summary reports to the public.

KEY POINT: Expensing a long-term asset in the period of purchase is not a GAAP alternative.

the conservatism convention by expensing a long-term asset of material cost in the period of purchase. In this case, there is no uncertainty. Income and assets for the current period would be understated, and income in future periods would be overstated. For this reason, accountants depend on the conservatism convention only when there is uncertainty about which accounting procedure to use.

Full Disclosure

ENRICHMENT NOTE: Significant events arising after the balance sheet date must be disclosed in the statements. Suppose a firm has purchased a piece of land for a future subdivision. Shortly after the end of its fiscal year, the firm is served papers to halt construction because the Environmental Protection Agency asserts that the land was once a toxic waste dump. This information, which obviously affects the users of the financial statements, must be disclosed in the statements for the just-ended fiscal year.

The convention of **full disclosure** requires that financial statements and their notes present all information that is relevant to the users' understanding of the statements. That is, the statements should offer any explanation needed to keep them from being misleading. Explanatory notes are considered an integral part of the financial statements. For instance, a change from one accounting procedure to another should be reported. In general, the form of the financial statements can affect their usefulness in making certain decisions—for example, the categories used to group accounts in the statements convey information about the accounts. Also, certain items, such as the amount of depreciation expense on the income statement and the accumulated depreciation on the balance sheet, are essential to the readers of financial statements.

Other examples of disclosures required by the FASB and other official bodies are the accounting procedures used in preparing the statements, important terms of the company's debt, commitments and contingencies, and important events taking place after the date of the statements. However, the statements can become so cluttered with notes that they impede rather than help understanding. Beyond required disclosures, the application of the full-disclosure convention is based on the judgment of management and of the accountants who prepare the financial statements.

In recent years, the principle of full disclosure also has been influenced by investors and creditors. To protect them, independent auditors, the stock exchanges, and the SEC have made more demands for disclosure by publicly owned companies. The SEC has been pushing especially hard for the enforcement of full disclosure. As a result, more and better information about corporations is available to the public today than ever before.

Cost-Benefit

The **cost-benefit** convention underlies all the qualitative characteristics and conventions. It holds that the benefits to be gained from providing accounting information should be greater than the costs of providing it. Of course, minimum levels of relevance and reliability must be reached if accounting information is to be useful. Beyond the minimum levels, however, it is up to the FASB and the SEC, which

BUSINESS-WORLD EXAMPLE: Firms use the convention of cost-benefit for both accounting and nonaccounting decisions. Department stores could almost completely stop shoplifting if they were to hire five times as many clerks to watch customers. The benefit would be reduced shoplifting. The cost would be reduced sales (customers do not like being watched closely) and increased wages expense. Although shoplifting is a serious problem for department stores, the benefit of reducing shoplifting in this way does not outweigh the cost.

require the information, and the accountant, who provides the information, to judge the costs and benefits in each case. Most of the costs of providing information fall at first on the preparers; the benefits are reaped by both preparers and users. Finally, both the costs and the benefits are passed on to society in the form of prices and social benefits from more efficient allocation of resources.

The costs and benefits of a particular requirement for accounting disclosure are both direct and indirect, immediate and deferred. For example, it is hard to judge the final costs and benefits of a far-reaching and costly regulation. The FASB, for instance, allows certain large companies to make a supplemental disclosure in their financial statements of the effects of changes in current costs. Most companies choose not to present this information because they believe the costs of producing and providing it exceed its benefits to the readers of their financial statements. Cost-benefit is a question faced by all regulators, including the FASB and the SEC. Even though there are no definitive ways of measuring costs and benefits, much of an accountant's work deals with these concepts.

Check out ACE for a Review Quiz at http://accounting.college.hmco.com/students.

Management's Responsibility for Ethical Reporting

LO4 Explain management's responsibility for ethical financial reporting and define *fraudulent financial reporting.*

RELATED TEXT ASSIGNMENTS
Q: 4
SD: 3, 4, 5

www.generalmills.com

The users of financial statements depend on the good faith of those who prepare these statements. This dependence places a duty on a company's management and its accountants to act ethically in the reporting process. That duty is often expressed in the report of management that accompanies financial statements. For example, the report of the management of General Mills, Inc., a company known for strong financial reporting and controls, states:

> The management . . . is responsible for the fairness and accuracy of the consolidated financial statements. The consolidated financial statements have been prepared in accordance with accounting principles that are generally accepted in the United States, using management's best estimates and judgments where appropriate.[9]

General Mills' management also tells how it meets this responsibility:

> Management has established a system of internal controls that provides reasonable assurance that assets are adequately safeguarded and transactions are recorded accurately in all material respects, in accordance with management's authorization. We maintain a strong audit program that independently evaluates the adequacy and effectiveness of internal controls.[10]

STOP AND THINK!
What is the difference between aggressive accounting and fraudulent financial reporting?
There is often a fine line between aggressive accounting, which is the use of legitimate accounting methods to achieve business purposes, and fraudulent financial reporting, which is the intentional misrepresentation of financial information. The former is acceptable, whereas the latter is unethical and sometimes illegal. ■

The intentional preparation of misleading financial statements is called **fraudulent financial reporting**.[11] It can result from the distortion of records (e.g., the manipulation of inventory records), falsified transactions (e.g., fictitious sales), or the misapplication of accounting principles (e.g., treating as an asset an item that should be expensed). There are a number of possible motives for fraudulent reporting—for instance, to obtain a higher price when a company is sold, meet the expectations of stockholders, or obtain a loan. Sometimes, the incentive is personal gain, such as additional compensation, promotion, or avoidance of penalties for poor performance. The personal costs of such actions can be high. Individuals who authorize or prepare fraudulent financial statements may face prison sentences and fines. A company's investors and lenders, employees, and customers suffer from fraudulent financial reporting as well.

www.worldcom.com
www.enron.com

Due to recent abuses in financial reporting that have come to light in companies like WorldCom and Enron, Congress passed the Sarbanes-Oxley Act in 2002. This legislation orders the SEC to draw up rules requiring chief executives and chief

Focus on Business Ethics

Questionable Accounting Practices Are Under Scrutiny.

There is a difference between management's choosing to follow accounting principles that are favorable to its actions and fraudulent financial reporting. Because of recent, highly visible accounting misstatements by such companies as WorldCom <www.worldcom.com>, Enron <www.enron.com>, Sunbeam Corporation <www.sunbeam.com>, and many others attempting to meet the earnings expectations of stock analysts, the SEC is cracking down on what it sees as the main abuses, which the chairman of the SEC has called "accounting hocus-pocus." These are cases in which real transactions are accounted for in such a way as to distort reality. Examples include one-time "big bath" restructuring charges that overstate current expenses to benefit future periods, creative acquisition accounting in mergers, writing off purchased research and development inappropriately, miscellaneous "cookie jar reserves" involving unrealistic assumptions about such items as sales returns and warranty costs, and the abuse of the materiality convention.[12] The SEC brings about 100 accounting actions each year. In recent times, executives at WorldCom and Sunbeam have been indicted. Executives at Enron are under investigation.[13]

financial officers of all 15,000 publicly traded companies to file statements each quarter swearing that, based on their knowledge, their company's quarterly and annual statements are accurate and complete. Violation can result in criminal penalties. To comply with this law and meet ethical reporting requirements, a company's accountants and auditors must apply financial accounting concepts in such a way as to present a fair view of the company's operations and financial position and to avoid misleading readers of the financial statements.

Check out ACE for a Review Quiz at http://accounting.college.hmco.com/students.

Classified Balance Sheet

LO5 Identify and describe the basic components of a classified balance sheet.

RELATED TEXT ASSIGNMENTS
Q: 5, 6, 7, 8, 9, 10, 11, 12, 13
SE: 3, 4
E: 3, 4
P: 3, 5
FRA: 4, 5

The balance sheets you have seen in the chapters thus far categorize accounts as assets, liabilities, and owner's equity. Because even a fairly small company can have hundreds of accounts, simply listing accounts in these broad categories is not particularly helpful to a statement user. Setting up subcategories within the major categories often makes financial statements much more useful. Investors and creditors study and evaluate the relationships among the subcategories. General-purpose external financial statements that are divided into subcategories are called **classified financial statements**.

The balance sheet presents the financial position of a company at a particular time. The subdivisions of the classified balance sheet shown in Exhibit 1 are typical of those used by most companies in the United States. The subdivisions under owner's equity depend, of course, on the form of business.

Assets

REAL-WORLD EXAMPLE: Examples of accounts that would be classified as "other assets" are long-term receivables and bond issue costs.

A company's assets are often divided into four categories: (1) current assets; (2) investments; (3) property, plant, and equipment; and (4) intangible assets. These categories are listed in the order of their presumed ease of conversion into cash. For example, current assets are usually more easily converted to cash than are property, plant, and equipment. For simplicity, some companies group investments, intangible assets, and other miscellaneous assets into a category called "**other assets**."

■ **Current Assets** **Current assets** are cash and other assets that are reasonably expected to be converted to cash, sold, or consumed within one year or within the normal operating cycle of the business, whichever is longer. The normal operating cycle of a company is the average time needed to go from cash to cash. For example,

EXHIBIT 1
Classified Balance Sheet for Shafer Auto Parts Company

Shafer Auto Parts Company
Balance Sheet
December 31, 20xx

Assets			
Current assets			
Cash		$10,360	
Short-term investments		2,000	
Notes receivable		8,000	
Accounts receivable		35,300	
Merchandise inventory		60,400	
Prepaid insurance		6,600	
Store supplies		1,060	
Office supplies		636	
Total current assets			$124,356
Investments			
Land held for future use			5,000
Property, plant, and equipment			
Land		$ 4,500	
Building	$20,650		
Less accumulated depreciation	8,640	12,010	
Delivery equipment	$18,400		
Less accumulated depreciation	9,450	8,950	
Office equipment	$ 8,600		
Less accumulated depreciation	5,000	3,600	
Total property, plant, and equipment			29,060
Intangible assets			
Trademark			500
Total assets			$158,916
Liabilities			
Current liabilities			
Notes payable		$15,000	
Accounts payable		23,883	
Salaries payable		2,000	
Current portion of mortgage payable		1,800	
Total current liabilities			$ 42,683
Long-term liabilities			
Mortgage payable			17,800
Total liabilities			$ 60,483
Owner's Equity			
Fred Shafer, Capital			98,433
Total liabilities and owner's equity			$158,916

cash is used to buy merchandise inventory, which is sold for cash or for a promise of cash if the sale is made on account. If a sale is made on account, the resulting receivable must be collected before the cycle is completed.

www.boeing.com

KEY POINT: Use one year as the current period unless the normal operating cycle happens to be longer.

The normal operating cycle for most companies is less than one year, but there are exceptions. Boeing Company, for example, can take more than one year to make commerical aircraft. The cost of those aircraft are considered current asssets while they are being made because they will be sold in the current operating cycle. The payments for a television set or a refrigerator can be extended over 24 or 36 months, but these receivables are still considered current assets.

Cash is obviously a current asset. Short-term investments, notes and accounts receivable, and inventory are also current assets because they are expected to be converted to cash within the next year or during the normal operating cycle. On the balance sheet, they are listed in the order of their ease of conversion into cash.

KEY POINT: A firm does not consume prepaid expenses, but it does enjoy the benefit of the space rented, the insurance protection provided, and so forth.

Prepaid expenses, such as rent and insurance paid in advance, and inventories of supplies bought for use rather than for sale also should be classified as current assets. Such assets are current in the sense that if they had not been bought earlier, a current outlay of cash would be needed to obtain them.[14]

KEY POINT: For an investment to be classified as current, management must intend to sell it within the next year or the current operating cycle, and it must be readily marketable.

In deciding whether an asset is current or noncurrent, the idea of "reasonable expectation" is important. For example, Short-Term Investments, also called "Marketable Securities," is an account used for temporary investments of "idle" cash—that is, cash not immediately required for operating purposes. Management can reasonably expect to sell these securities as cash needs arise over the next year or operating cycle. Investments in securities that management does not expect to sell within the next year and that do not involve the temporary use of idle cash should be shown in the investments category of a classified balance sheet.

STOP AND THINK!
Why is it that land held for future use and equipment not currently used in the business are classified as investments rather than as property, plant, and equipment?
They are classified as investments because doing so helps users of financial statements assess the performance of the company using such measures as return on assets. Also, the investment category gives users some idea of resources the company may be able to draw on without disturbing the current business operations. ■

■ **INVESTMENTS** The **investments** category includes assets, usually long term, that are not used in the normal operation of the business and that management does not plan to convert to cash within the next year. Items in this category are securities held for long-term investment, long-term notes receivable, land held for future use, plant or equipment not used in the business, and special funds established to pay off a debt or buy a building. Also included are large permanent investments in another company for the purpose of controlling that company.

■ **PROPERTY, PLANT, AND EQUIPMENT** **Property, plant, and equipment** are tangible long-term assets used in the continuing operation of the business. They represent a place to operate (land and buildings) and the equipment to produce, sell, deliver, and service the company's goods. They are therefore also called *operating assets* or, sometimes, *fixed assets, tangible assets, long-lived assets,* or *plant assets.* Through depreciation, the costs of these assets (except land) are spread over the periods they benefit. Past depreciation is recorded in the Accumulated Depreciation accounts. The order in which property, plant, and equipment are listed on the balance sheet is not the same everywhere. In practice, accounts are often combined to make the financial statements less cluttered. For example:

Property, Plant, and Equipment

Land		$ 4,500
Buildings and equipment	$47,650	
Less accumulated depreciation	23,090	24,560
Total property, plant, and equipment		$29,060

Many companies simply show a single line with a total for property, plant, and equipment and provide the details in a note to the financial statements.

The property, plant, and equipment category also includes natural resources owned by the company, such as forest lands, oil and gas properties, and coal mines, if they are used in the regular course of business. If they are not, they are listed in the investments category, as noted above.

Intangible Assets **Intangible assets** are long-term assets with no physical substance whose value stems from the rights or privileges they extend to their owners. Examples are patents, copyrights, goodwill, franchises, and trademarks. These assets are recorded at cost, which is spread over the expected life of the right or privilege.

Liabilities

Liabilities are divided into two categories, based on when the liabilities fall due: current liabilities and long-term liabilities.

BUSINESS-WORLD EXAMPLE: The portion of a mortgage paid monthly for 120 months that is due during the next year or the current operating cycle would be classified as a current liability. The portion due after the next year or the current operating cycle would be classified as a long-term liability.

Current Liabilities The category of **current liabilities** consists of obligations due to be paid or performed within one year or within the normal operating cycle of the business, whichever is longer. Current liabilities are typically paid from current assets or by incurring new short-term liabilities. They include notes payable, accounts payable, the current portion of long-term debt, salaries and wages payable, taxes payable, and customer advances (unearned revenues).

Long-Term Liabilities The debts of a business that fall due more than one year in the future or beyond the normal operating cycle, which will be paid out of noncurrent assets, are **long-term liabilities**. Mortgages payable, long-term notes, bonds payable, employee pension obligations, and long-term lease liabilities generally fall into the category of long-term liabilities.

Owner's Equity

The terms *owner's equity, proprietorship, capital,* and *net worth* are used interchangeably. They all stand for the owner's interest in the company. The first three terms are preferred to *net worth* because most assets are recorded at original cost rather than at current value. For this reason, the ownership section will not represent "worth." It is really a claim against the assets of the company.

Although the form of business organization does not usually affect the accounting treatment of assets and liabilities, the equity section of the balance sheet differs depending on whether the business is a sole proprietorship, a partnership, or a corporation.

Sole Proprietorship You are already familiar with the owner's equity section of a sole proprietorship, like the one shown in the balance sheet for Shafer Auto Parts Company in Exhibit 1:

Owner's Equity	
Fred Shafer, Capital	$98,433

KEY POINT: The only difference in equity between a sole proprietorship and a partnership is in the number of capital accounts.

Partnership The equity section of the balance sheet for a partnership is called *partners' equity* and is much like that for the sole proprietorship. It might appear as follows:

Partners' Equity		
A. J. Martin, Capital	$21,666	
R. C. Moore, Capital	35,724	
Total partners' equity		$57,390

■ **CORPORATION** Corporations are by law separate, legal entities that are owned by their stockholders. The equity section of a balance sheet for a corporation is called stockholders' equity and has two parts: contributed, or paid-in, capital and retained earnings. It might appear like this:

Stockholders' Equity

Contributed capital		
Common stock, $10 par value, 5,000 shares authorized, issued, and outstanding	$50,000	
Paid-in capital in excess of par value	10,000	
Total contributed capital		$60,000
Retained earnings		37,500
Total stockholders' equity		$97,500

Remember that owner's equity accounts show the sources of and claims on assets. Of course, the claims are not on any particular asset but on the assets as a whole. It follows, then, that a corporation's contributed and earned capital accounts measure its stockholders' claims on assets and also indicate the sources of the assets. The **contributed capital**, also called *paid-in capital*, accounts reflect the amounts of assets invested by stockholders. Generally, contributed capital is shown on corporate balance sheets by two amounts: (1) the face, or par, value of issued stock and (2) the amounts paid in, or contributed, in excess of the par value per share. In the illustration above, stockholders invested amounts equal to the par value of the outstanding stock (5,000 × $10) plus $10,000 more.

The **Retained Earnings** account is sometimes called *Earned Capital* because it represents the stockholders' claim to the assets that are earned from operations and reinvested in corporate operations. Distributions of assets to shareholders, which are called *dividends*, reduce the Retained Earnings account balance just as withdrawals of assets by the owner of a business lower the Capital account balance. Thus the Retained Earnings account balance, in its simplest form, represents the earnings of the corporation less dividends paid to stockholders over the life of the business.

READING AND GRAPHING REAL COMPANY BALANCE SHEETS

Although financial statements usually follow the same general form as illustrated for Shafer Auto Parts Company, no two companies have statements that are exactly alike. The balance sheet of Dell Computer Corporation, the world's leading direct seller of computer systems, is a good example of some of the variations. As shown in Exhibit 2, it provides data for two years so that the change from one year to the next can be evaluated. Note that its major classifications are similar but not identical to Shafer's. For instance, Shafer's assets include investments and intangible assets categories, whereas Dell has an asset category called "other non-current assets," which is a small amount of its total assets. Also note that Dell has a category called "other liabilities." Because this category appears after long-term debt, it represents longer-term liabilities, due more than one year from the balance sheet dates.

www.dell.com

Dell's stockholders' equity section also differs from the owner's equity section of Shafer Auto Parts Company because it is a corporation. However, it is possible to look at the total stockholders' equity and know that this amount relates to the stockholders' claims on the company and is similar to the capital account for Shafer.

When we look at columns of numbers, it is sometimes difficult to see the patterns. Graphic presentation of the numbers can be helpful in visualizing the changes taking place in a company's financial position. Figure 2, which was prepared with the Fingraph® Financial Analyst™ CD-ROM software that accompanies this text, is a graphic presentation of a portion of the balance sheet shown in Exhibit 2. Total

EXHIBIT 2
Balance Sheet for Dell Computer Corporation

Dell Computer Corporation
Consolidated Statement of Financial Position
(in millions)

	January 31, 2003	February 1, 2002
ASSETS		
Current assets:		
Cash and cash equivalents	$ 4,232	$ 3,641
Short-term investments	406	273
Accounts receivable, net	2,586	2,269
Inventories	306	278
Other	1,394	1,416
Total current assets	8,924	7,877
Property, plant and equipment, net	913	826
Investments	5,267	4,373
Other non-current assets	366	459
Total assets	$15,470	$13,535
LIABILITIES AND STOCKHOLDERS' EQUITY		
Current liabilities:		
Accounts payable	$ 5,989	$ 5,075
Accrued and other	2,944	2,444
Total current liabilities	8,933	7,519
Long-term debt	506	520
Other liabilities	1,158	802
Total liabilities	10,597	8,841
Stockholders' equity:		
Common stock and capital in excess of $.01 par value; shares authorized: 7,000; shares issued: 2,681 and 2,654, respectively	6,018	5,605
Treasury stock, at cost; 102 and 52 shares, respectively	(4,539)	(2,249)
Retained earnings	3,486	1,364
Other comprehensive income (loss)	(33)	38
Other	(59)	(64)
Total stockholders' equity	4,873	4,694
Total liabilities and stockholders' equity	$15,470	$13,535

Source: Dell Computer Corporation, *Annual Report,* 2002.

assets and its components are graphed on the left side, and total liabilities and its components, together with total stockholders' equity, are on the right. The composition of the assets and liabilities, their relation to stockholders' equity, and the changes in them from 2001 to 2002 are easily seen. These graphs show that overall Dell was relatively stable in both totals and components from 2001 to 2002, but overall the assets increased. Also note that the graphic presentation of the balance sheet reduces the detailed clutter of the statement. For instance, all current assets are combined and represented by a single component line.

FIGURE 2
Graphic Presentation of Dell Computer Corporation's Balance Sheet

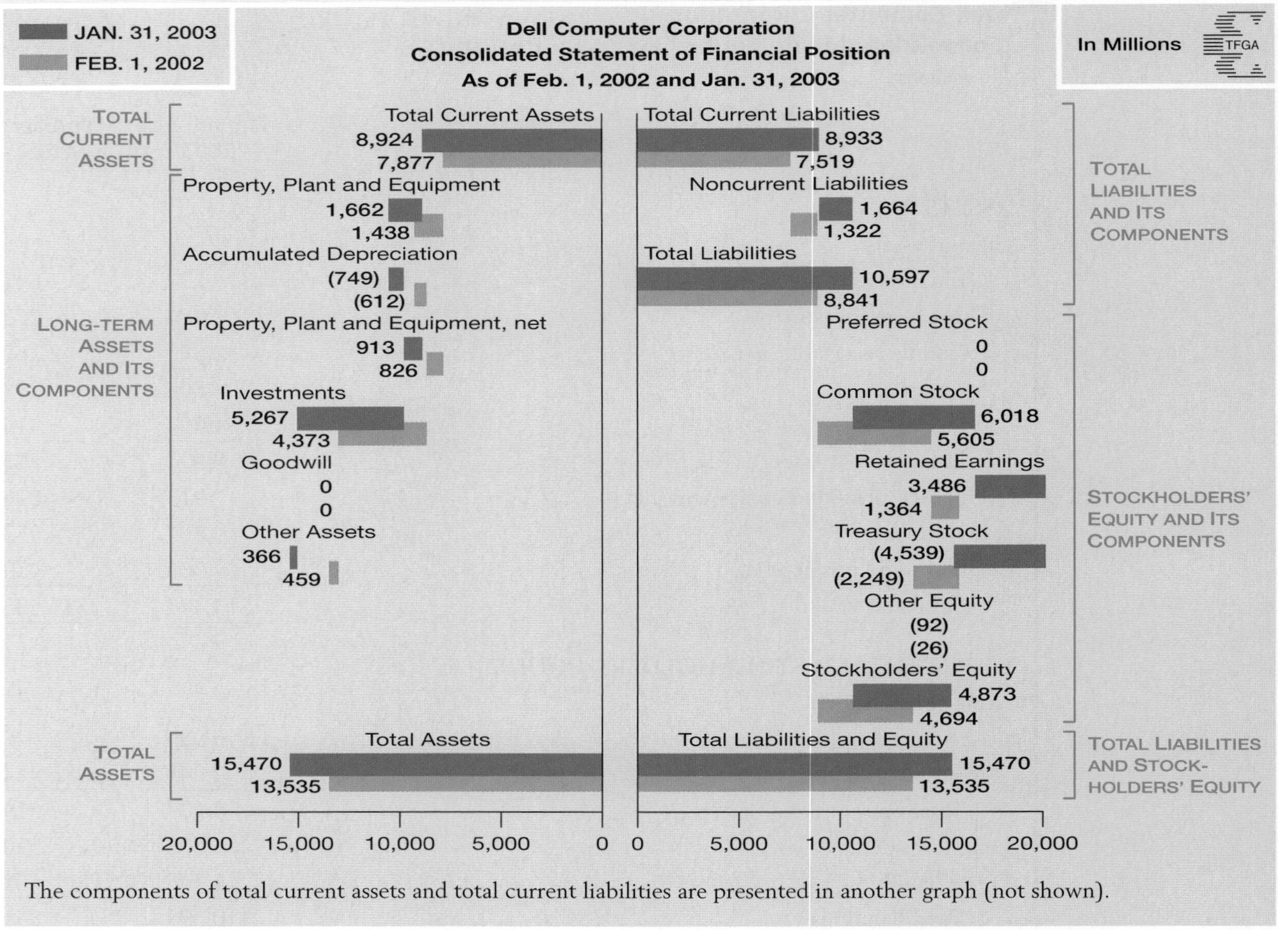

The components of total current assets and total current liabilities are presented in another graph (not shown).

Check out ACE for a Review Quiz at http://accounting.college.hmco.com/students.

FORMS OF THE INCOME STATEMENT

LO6 Prepare multistep and single-step classified income statements.

RELATED TEXT ASSIGNMENTS
Q: 14, 15
SE: 5, 6, 7
E: 5, 6, 7
P: 2, 5, 7
FRA: 5

For internal management, a detailed income statement is helpful in analyzing the company's performance. But for external reporting purposes, the income statement is usually presented in condensed form. **Condensed financial statements** present only the major categories of the detailed financial statements. The two common forms of the condensed income statement are the multistep and single-step forms. The **multistep form**, illustrated in Exhibit 3, derives net income in the same step-by-step fashion as a detailed income statement, but it gives only the totals of significant categories. Usually, it shows some breakdown for operating expenses, such as the totals for selling expenses and general and administrative expenses. In the Shafer Auto Parts Company statement, gross margin less operating expenses is called **income from operations** and a new section, **other revenues and expenses**, has been added to include nonoperating revenues and expenses. The latter section includes revenues from investments (such as dividends and interest from stocks, bonds, and savings accounts) and interest earned on credit or notes extended to customers. It

EXHIBIT 3
Condensed Multistep Income Statement for Shafer Auto Parts Company

BUSINESS-WORLD EXAMPLE: The multistep income statement is a valuable analytical tool that is often overlooked. Analysts frequently convert a single-step statement into a multistep one because the latter separates operating sources of income from nonoperating ones. Investors want income to result primarily from operations, not from one-time gains or losses.

KEY POINT: Financial analysts often focus on income from operations as a key profitability measure.

Shafer Auto Parts Company
Income Statement
For the Year Ended December 31, 20xx

Net sales		$289,656
Cost of goods sold		181,260
Gross margin		$108,396
Operating expenses		
Selling expenses	$54,780	
General and administrative expenses	34,504	
Total operating expenses		89,284
Income from operations		$ 19,112
Other revenues and expenses		
Interest income	$ 1,400	
Less interest expense	2,631	
Excess of other expenses over other revenues		1,231
Net income		$ 17,881

also includes interest expense and other expenses that result from borrowing money or from credit extended to the company. If the company has other revenues and expenses not related to normal business operations, they too are included in this part of the income statement. Thus, an analyst who wants to compare two companies independent of their financing methods—that is, before considering other revenues and expenses—would focus on income from operations.

The **single-step form** of income statement, illustrated in Exhibit 4, derives net income in a single step by putting the major categories of revenues in the first part

EXHIBIT 4
Condensed Single-Step Income Statement for Shafer Auto Parts Company

STOP AND THINK!
Which is the better measure of a company's performance: income from operations or net income?

Neither measure is better than the other. Both measure different aspects of profitability. Income from operations measures the income from a company's ongoing operations before considering issues of financing (interest expense), nonoperating revenues, and income taxes. Net income measures whether a business has been operating successfully. ■

Shafer Auto Parts Company
Income Statement
For the Year Ended December 31, 20xx

Revenues		
Net sales		$289,656
Interest income		1,400
Total revenues		$291,056
Costs and expenses		
Cost of goods sold	$181,260	
Selling expenses	54,780	
General and administrative expenses	34,504	
Interest expense	2,631	
Total costs and expenses		273,175
Net income		$ 17,881

of the statement and the major categories of costs and expenses in the second part. The multistep form and the single-step form both have advantages. The multistep form shows the components that are used in deriving net income; the single-step form has the advantage of simplicity. Approximately an equal number of large U.S. companies use each form in their public reports.

Net income from the income statement becomes an element of the statement of owner's equity.

READING AND GRAPHING REAL COMPANY INCOME STATEMENTS

Income statements, like balance sheets, vary among companies. You will rarely, if ever, find an income statement exactly like the one for Shafer Auto Parts Company. You will encounter terms and structure that differ, such as those on the multistep income statement for Dell Computer Corporation in Exhibit 5, in which management provides three years of data for comparison purposes. You may also encounter components that are not covered in this chapter. If this occurs, refer to the index at the end of the book to find the topic and read about it.

www.dell.com

Figure 3, which was prepared with the Fingraph® Financial Analyst™ CD-ROM software that is available with this text, is a graphic presentation of a portion of

EXHIBIT 5
Income Statement for Dell Computer Corporation

Dell Computer Corporation
Consolidated Statement of Income
(in millions, except per share amounts)

	Fiscal Year Ended		
	January 31, 2003	February 1, 2002	February 2, 2001
Net revenue	$35,404	$31,168	$31,888
Cost of revenue	29,055	25,661	25,445
Gross margin	6,349	5,507	6,443
Operating expenses:			
Selling, general and administrative	3,050	2,784	3,193
Research, development and engineering	455	452	482
Special charges	—	482	105
Total operating expenses	3,505	3,718	3,780
Operating income	2,844	1,789	2,663
Investment and other income (loss), net	183	(58)	531
Income before income taxes and cumulative effect of change in accounting principle	3,027	1,731	3,194
Provision for income taxes	905	485	958
Income before cumulative effect of change in accounting principle	2,122	1,246	2,236
Cumulative effect of change in accounting principle, net	—	—	(59)
Net income	$ 2,122	$ 1,246	$ 2,177

Source: Dell Computer Corporation, *Annual Report,* 2002.

FIGURE 3
Graphic Presentation of a Portion of Dell Computer Corporation's Income Statement

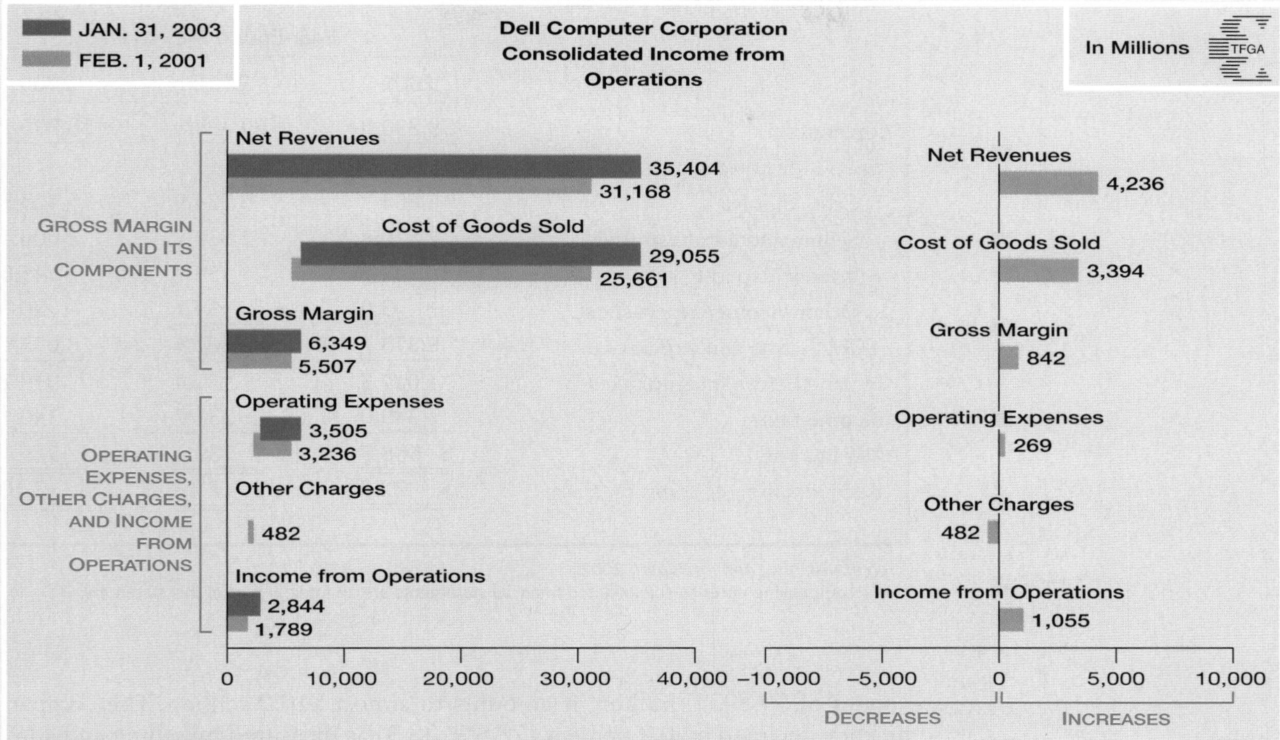

Other components and net income are presented in another graph (not shown).

Dell's income statement. It helps show the company's progress in meeting its profitability objectives. On the left side of the graph are the components of income from operations, beginning with net revenues at the top and ending with income from operations at the bottom. The right side graphs the percentage changes in the components. Increases are shown on the right of the vertical column, and decreases are shown on the left. Except for special charges, there was little change in the components from 2001 to 2002 but overall the company grew during the year.

www.nike.com

Exhibit 6 shows the single-step income statement used by Nike, Inc., the footwear company. When a company uses the single-step form, most analysts will still calculate gross margin, income from operations, and each component's percentage of revenues. Such calculations for Nike would be as follows (in millions):

	2002	Percent	2001	Percent
Revenues	$9,893.0	100.0	$9,488.8	100.0
Cost of sales	6,004.7	60.7	5,784.9	61.0
Gross margin	$3,888.3	39.3	$3,703.9	39.0
Selling and administrative expenses	2,820.4	28.5	2,689.7	28.3
Income from operations	$1,067.9	10.8	$1,014.2	10.7

This analysis shows that Nike's income from operations increased slightly, from 10.7 to 10.8 percent. The difference of 0.1 percent may not seem like a lot; however on

EXHIBIT 6
Single-Step Income Statement for Nike, Inc.

Nike, Inc.
Consolidated Statements of Income
(In millions, except per share data)

	Year Ended May 31,		
	2002	2001	2000
Revenues	**$9,893.0**	$9,488.8	$8,995.1
Costs and expenses:			
Costs of sales	**6,004.7**	5,784.9	5,403.8
Selling and administrative	**2,820.4**	2,689.7	2,606.4
Interest expense	**47.6**	58.7	45.0
Other income/expense, net	**3.0**	34.1	20.7
Total costs and expenses	**8,875.7**	8,567.4	8,075.9
Income before income taxes	**1,017.3**	921.4	919.2
Income taxes	**349.0**	331.7	340.1
Net income	**$ 668.3**	$ 589.7	$ 579.1
Basic income per common share	**$ 2.50**	$ 2.18	$ 2.10

Source: Nike, Inc., *Annual Report,* 2002.
The accompanying notes to consolidated financial statements are an integral part of this statement.

revenues of $9,893.0 million, it amounts to almost $10.0 million. The company's efficiency declined by 0.2 percent (28.5 − 28.3) as measured by selling and administrative expenses, but this was more than offeset by the increase in gross margin of 0.3 percent (39.3 minus 39.0).

Check out ACE for a Review Quiz at http://accounting.college.hmco.com/students.

USING CLASSIFIED FINANCIAL STATEMENTS

LO7 Evaluate liquidity and profitability using classified financial statements.

RELATED TEXT ASSIGNMENTS
Q: 16, 17, 18, 19, 20
SE: 8, 9
E: 8, 9, 10
P: 4, 5, 8
SD: 6
FRA: 1, 2, 3, 4, 5, 6, 7, 8

Earlier in this chapter, you learned that the objectives of financial reporting established by the Financial Accounting Standards Board are to provide information that is useful in making investment and credit decisions, in judging cash flow prospects, and in understanding business resources, claims to those resources, and changes in them. These objectives are related to two important goals of management: maintaining adequate liquidity and achieving satisfactory profitability. Investors and creditors base their decisions largely on their assessment of a company's potential liquidity and profitability. The following analysis shows how ratios make use of the components in classified financial statements to reflect a company's performance with respect to these important goals.

EVALUATION OF LIQUIDITY

KEY POINT: It is imperative that accounts be classified correctly before the ratios are computed. If accounts are not classified correctly, the ratios will not be correct.

Liquidity means having enough money on hand to pay bills when they are due and to take care of unexpected needs for cash. Two measures of liquidity are working capital and the current ratio.

■ **WORKING CAPITAL** The first measure, **working capital**, is the amount by which total current assets exceed total current liabilities. This is an important measure of liquidity because current liabilities are debts that must be paid or obligations that

FIGURE 4
Average Current Ratio for Selected Industries

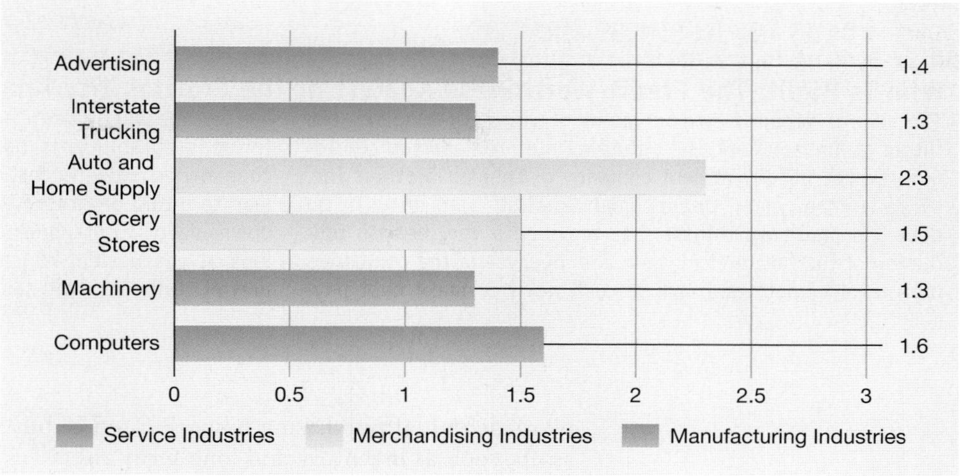

Source: Data from Dun & Bradstreet, *Industry Norms and Key Business Ratios,* 2001–2002.

must be performed within one year, and current assets are assets that will be realized in cash or used up within one year or one operating cycle, whichever is longer. By definition, current liabilities are paid out of current assets. So the excess of current assets over current liabilities is the net current assets, or working capital, on hand to continue business operations. Working capital can be used to buy inventory, obtain credit, and finance expanded sales. Lack of working capital can lead to a company's failure.

For Shafer Auto Parts Company, working capital is computed as follows:

Current assets	$124,356
Less current liabilities	42,683
Working capital	$ 81,673

BUSINESS-WORLD EXAMPLE: Some successful firms, such as McDonald's, manage to have very low current ratios by carefully planning their cash flows.

CURRENT RATIO The second measure of liquidity, the current ratio, is closely related to working capital and is believed by many bankers and other creditors to be a good indicator of a company's ability to pay its bills and to repay outstanding loans. The **current ratio** is the ratio of current assets to current liabilities. For Shafer Auto Parts Company, it would be computed like this:

$$\text{Current Ratio} = \frac{\text{Current Assets}}{\text{Current Liabilities}} = \frac{\$124{,}356}{\$42{,}683} = 2.9$$

ENRICHMENT NOTE: It is inadvisable to have too high a current ratio because the firm could probably use the excess funds more effectively to increase its overall profit.

Thus, Shafer has $2.90 of current assets for each $1.00 of current liabilities. Is that good or bad? The answer requires the comparison of this year's ratio with ratios for earlier years and with similar measures for successful companies in the same industry. The average current ratio varies widely from industry to industry, as shown in Figure 4. For the advertising industry, which has no merchandise inventory, the current ratio is 1.4. In contrast, auto and home supply, which carries large merchandise inventories, has an average current ratio of 2.3. The current ratio for Shafer Auto Parts Company, 2.9, exceeds the average for its industry. A very low current ratio, of course, can be unfavorable, but so can a very high one. The latter may indicate that the company is not using its assets effectively.

EVALUATION OF PROFITABILITY

Just as important as paying bills on time is **profitability**—the ability to earn a satisfactory income. As a goal, profitability competes with liquidity for managerial attention because liquid assets, although important, are not the best profit-producing resources. Cash, for example, means purchasing power, but a satisfactory profit can

Focus on Business Practice

Who Is Right: The Credit-Worthiness Analyst or the Profitability Analyst?

The answer depends on your point of view. For example, the future of Amazon.com, the online retailer, has sparked controversy in the big investment company of Lehman Brothers Inc. <www.lehman.com>. One Lehman analyst, who focuses on debt and credit worthiness, has provided a very bearish prediction of the future of Amazon.com because of the company's high level of debt and lack of cash flows to make debt payments. Another Lehman analyst, who focuses on growth and future profitability, is bullish on Amazon.com because the company is growing fast and reducing costs, which should lead to future profitability. Credit analysts tend to look at the downside of future prospects, whereas profitability analysts look at the upside. Which view of Amazon.com's future will prevail? Only time will tell.[15]

be made only if purchasing power is used to buy profit-producing (and less liquid) assets, such as inventory and long-term assets.

Among the common measures of a company's ability to earn income are (1) profit margin, (2) asset turnover, (3) return on assets, (4) debt to equity ratio, and (5) return on equity. To evaluate a company meaningfully, one must relate its current profit performance to its past performance and prospects for the future, as well as to the averages for other companies in the same industry.

Profit Margin The **profit margin** shows the percentage of each sales dollar that results in net income. It is figured by dividing net income by net sales. It should not be confused with gross margin, which is not a ratio but rather the amount by which revenues exceed the cost of goods sold.

Shafer Auto Parts Company has a profit margin of 6.2 percent:

$$\text{Profit Margin} = \frac{\text{Net Income}}{\text{Net Sales}} = \frac{\$17{,}881}{\$289{,}656} = .062\ (6.2\%)$$

On each dollar of net sales, Shafer made 6.2 cents. A difference of 1 or 2 percent in a company's profit margin can mean the difference between a fair year and a very profitable one.

KEY POINT: Average total assets equals assets at the beginning of the year plus assets at the end of the year, divided by 2.

Asset Turnover **Asset turnover** measures how efficiently assets are used to produce sales. Computed by dividing net sales by average total assets, it shows how many dollars of sales were generated by each dollar of assets. A company with a higher asset turnover uses its assets more productively than one with a lower asset turnover. Average total assets is computed by adding total assets at the beginning of the year to total assets at the end of the year and dividing by 2.

Assuming that total assets for Shafer Auto Parts Company were $148,620 at the beginning of the year, its asset turnover is computed as follows:

$$\text{Asset Turnover} = \frac{\text{Net Sales}}{\text{Average Total Assets}}$$

$$= \frac{\$289{,}656}{(\$158{,}916 + \$148{,}620) \div 2} = \frac{\$289{,}656}{\$153{,}768} = 1.9 \text{ times}$$

Shafer produces $1.90 in sales for each $1.00 invested in average total assets. This ratio shows a meaningful relationship between an income statement figure and a balance sheet figure.

Return on Assets Both the profit margin and the asset turnover ratios have some limitations. The profit margin ratio does not take into consideration the assets necessary to produce income, and the asset turnover ratio does not take into account the amount of income produced. The **return on assets** ratio overcomes these deficiencies by relating net income to average total assets. For Shafer Auto Parts, it is computed like this:

FIGURE 5
Average Profit Margin for Selected Industries

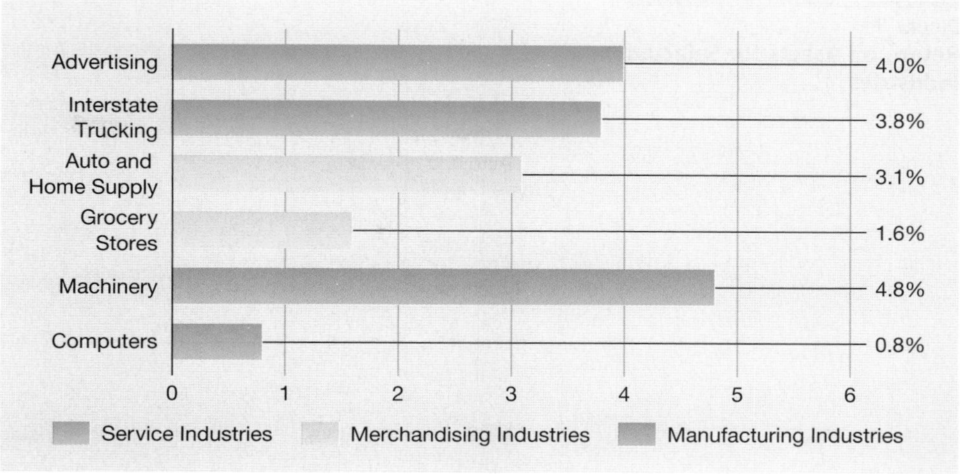

Source: Data from Dun & Bradstreet, *Industry Norms and Key Business Ratios,* 2001–2002.

$$\text{Return on Assets} = \frac{\text{Net Income}}{\text{Average Total Assets}}$$

$$= \frac{\$17{,}881}{(\$158{,}916 + \$148{,}620) \div 2} = \frac{\$17{,}881}{\$153{,}768} = .116\ (11.6\%)$$

KEY POINT: Return on assets is one of the most widely used measures of profitability because it reflects both the profit margin and asset turnover.

For each dollar invested, Shafer's assets generated 11.6 cents of net income. This ratio indicates the income-generating strength (profit margin) of the company's resources and how efficiently the company is using all its assets (asset turnover).

Return on assets, then, combines profit margin and asset turnover as follows:

$$\frac{\text{Net Income}}{\text{Net Sales}} \times \frac{\text{Net Sales}}{\text{Average Total Assets}} = \frac{\text{Net Income}}{\text{Average Total Assets}}$$

$$\text{Profit Margin} \times \text{Asset Turnover} = \text{Return on Assets}$$

$$6.2\% \times 1.9 \text{ times} = 11.8\%^*$$

*The slight difference between 11.6 and 11.8 is due to rounding.

Thus, a company's management can improve overall profitability by increasing the profit margin, the asset turnover, or both. Similarly, in evaluating a company's overall profitability, the financial statement user must consider the interaction of both ratios to produce return on assets.

Careful study of Figures 5, 6, and 7 shows the different ways in which the selected industries combine profit margin and asset turnover to produce return on

FIGURE 6
Asset Turnover for Selected Industries

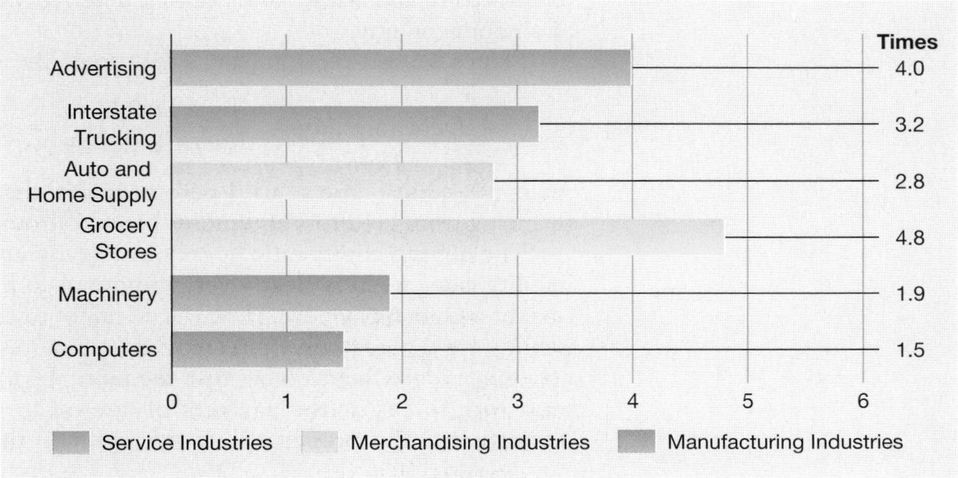

Source: Data from Dun & Bradstreet, *Industry Norms and Key Business Ratios,* 2001–2002.

FIGURE 7
Return on Assets for Selected Industries

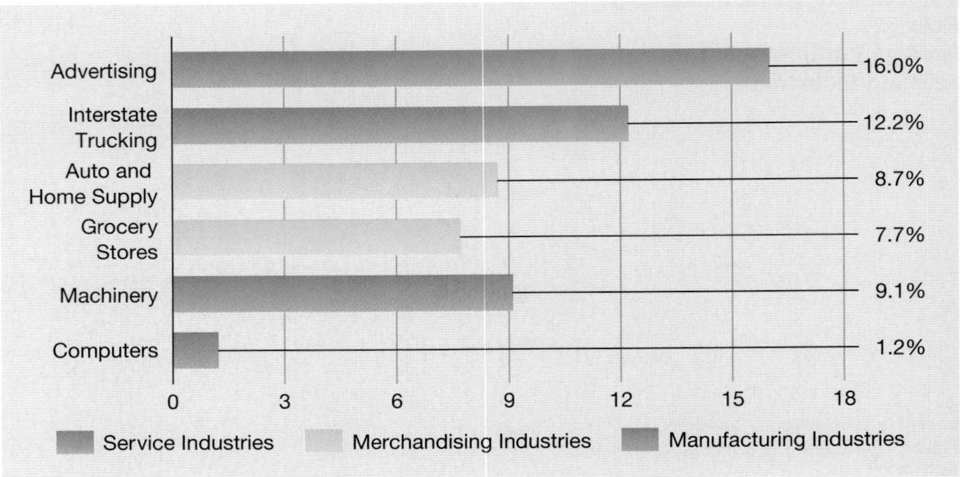

Source: Data from Dun & Bradstreet, *Industry Norms and Key Business Ratios,* 2001–2002.

STOP AND THINK!
Why is it important to compare a company's financial performance with industry averages?

When calculating ratios to measure performance, analysts need benchmarks to measure whether the performance was good or bad. Past performance of the company is one measure, but a better measure is the financial performance of similar companies. This is done by examining industry averages. ■

KEY POINT: A company with a low debt to equity ratio has a better chance of surviving in rough times. Debt requires additional expenses (interest) that must be paid.

assets. For instance, by comparing the return on assets for grocery stores and machinery manufacturers, you can see how they achieve it in very different ways. The grocery store industry has a profit margin of 1.6 percent, which when multiplied by an asset turnover of 4.8 times, gives a return on assets of 7.7 percent. The machinery industry, on the other hand, has a higher profit margin, 4.8 percent, and a lower asset turnover, 1.9 times, and produces a return on assets of 9.1 percent.

Shafer's profit margin of 6.2 percent is well above the auto and home supply industry average of 3.1 percent, but its asset turnover of 1.9 times lags behind the industry average of 2.8 times. Shafer is sacrificing asset turnover to achieve a higher profit margin. It is clear that this strategy is working, because Shafer's return on assets of 11.6 percent exceeds the industry average of 8.7 percent.

■ **DEBT TO EQUITY RATIO** Another useful measure of profitability is the **debt to equity ratio**, which shows the proportion of the company financed by creditors in comparison with that financed by owners. This ratio is computed by dividing total liabilities by owner's equity. Since the balance sheets of many companies do not show total liabilities, a short way of determining total liabilities is to deduct owner's equity from total assets. A debt to equity ratio of 1.0 means that total liabilities equal owner's equity—that half of the company's assets are financed by creditors. A ratio of 0.5 means that one-third of the assets are financed by creditors. A company with a high debt to equity ratio is at risk in poor economic times because it must continue to repay creditors. Owner's investments, on the other hand, do not have to be repaid, and withdrawals can be deferred when the company suffers because of a poor economy.

Shafer Auto Parts Company's debt to equity ratio is computed as follows:

$$\text{Debt to Equity} = \frac{\text{Total Liabilities}}{\text{Owner's Equity}} = \frac{\$60{,}483}{\$98{,}433} = .614\ (61.4\%)$$

A debt to equity ratio of 61.4 percent means that Shafer receives less than half its financing from creditors and more than half from its owner, Fred Shafer.

The debt to equity ratio does not fit neatly into either the liquidity or the profitability category. It is clearly very important to liquidity analysis because it relates to debt and its repayment. However, the debt to equity ratio is also relevant to profitability for two reasons. First, creditors are interested in the proportion of the business that is debt financed because the more debt a company has, the more profit it must earn to ensure the payment of interest to its creditors. Second, an owner is interested in the proportion of the business that is debt financed because the

FIGURE 8
Average Debt to Equity Ratio for Selected Industries

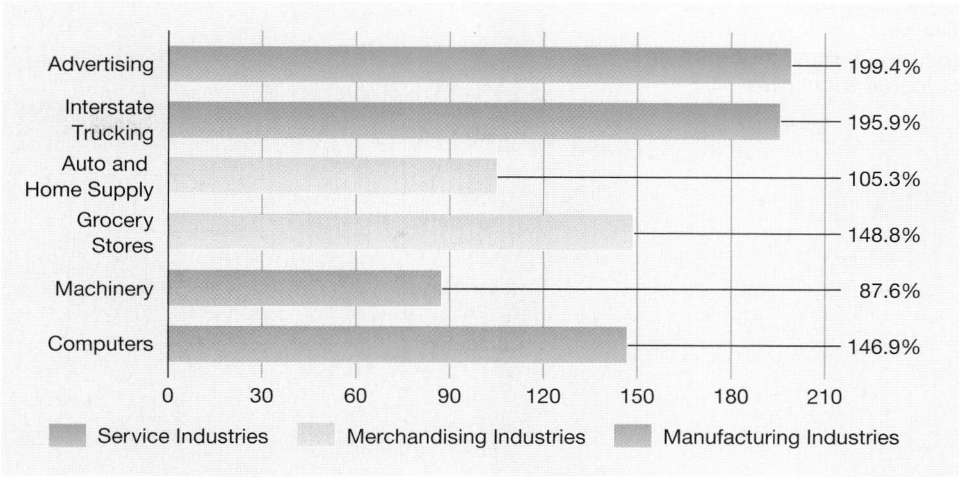

Source: Data from Dun & Bradstreet, *Industry Norms and Key Business Ratios,* 2001–2002.

amount of interest that must be paid on the debt affects the amount of profit that is left to provide a return on the owner's investments. The debt to equity ratio also shows how much expansion is possible by borrowing additional long-term funds. Figure 8 shows that the debt to equity ratio in our selected industries varies from a low of 87.6 percent in the machinery industry to a high of 199.4 percent in the advertising industry.

RETURN ON EQUITY Of course, Fred Shafer is interested in how much he has earned on his investment in the business. His **return on equity** is measured by the ratio of net income to average owner's equity. Taking the ending owner's equity from the balance sheet and assuming that beginning owner's equity is $100,553, Shafer's return on equity is computed as follows:

$$\text{Return on Equity} = \frac{\text{Net Income}}{\text{Average Owner's Equity}}$$

$$= \frac{\$17{,}881}{(\$98{,}433 + \$100{,}553) \div 2} = \frac{\$17{,}881}{\$99{,}493} = .180\ (18.0\%)$$

In 20xx, Shafer Auto Parts Company earned 18.0 cents for every dollar invested by the owner, Fred Shafer.

Whether this is an acceptable return depends on several factors, such as how much the company earned in previous years and how much other companies in the

FOCUS ON BUSINESS PRACTICE

To What Level of Profitability Should a Company Aspire?

At one time, a company earning a 20 percent return on equity ranked among the elite. Only Disney <www.disney.go.com>, Wal-Mart <www.walmart.com>, Coca-Cola <www.coca-cola.com>, and a few other companies were able to achieve this level of profitability. However, in the first quarter of 1995, for the first time, the average company of the Standard & Poor's 500 companies made a return on equity of 20.12 percent. *The Wall Street Journal* described this performance as "akin to the average ball player hitting .350."[16] This meant that stockholders' equity would double every four years.

Why did this happen? First, a good business environment and cost cutting led to more profitable operations. Second, special charges and other accounting transactions reduced stockholders' equity for many companies. In this way, the denominator of the ratio is reduced, thus increasing the ratio.

Until 2000, the number of companies with a return on equity of more than 20 percent continued to increase, but during the recession of 2001 and 2002, this number declined. When earnings are declining, companies tend to emphasize measures of performance other than profitability.

FIGURE 9
Average Return on Equity for Selected Industries

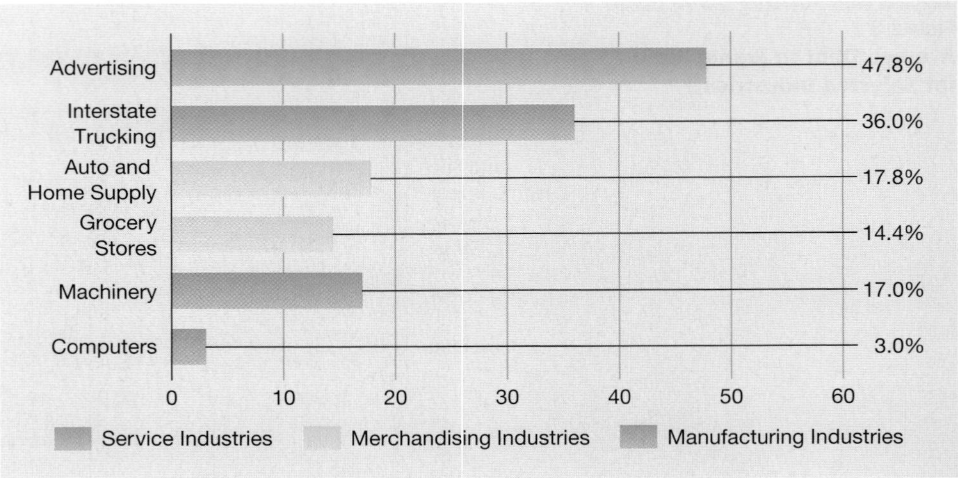

Source: Data from Dun & Bradstreet, *Industry Norms and Key Business Ratios,* 2001–2002 .

same industry earned. As measured by return on equity (Figure 9), the advertising industry is the most profitable of our sample industries, with a return on equity of 47.8 percent. Shafer Auto Parts Company's average return on equity of 18.0 percent is slightly more than the average of 17.8 percent for the auto and home supply industry.

FIGURE 10
Graphic Presentation of Dell Computer Corporation's Profitability Ratios

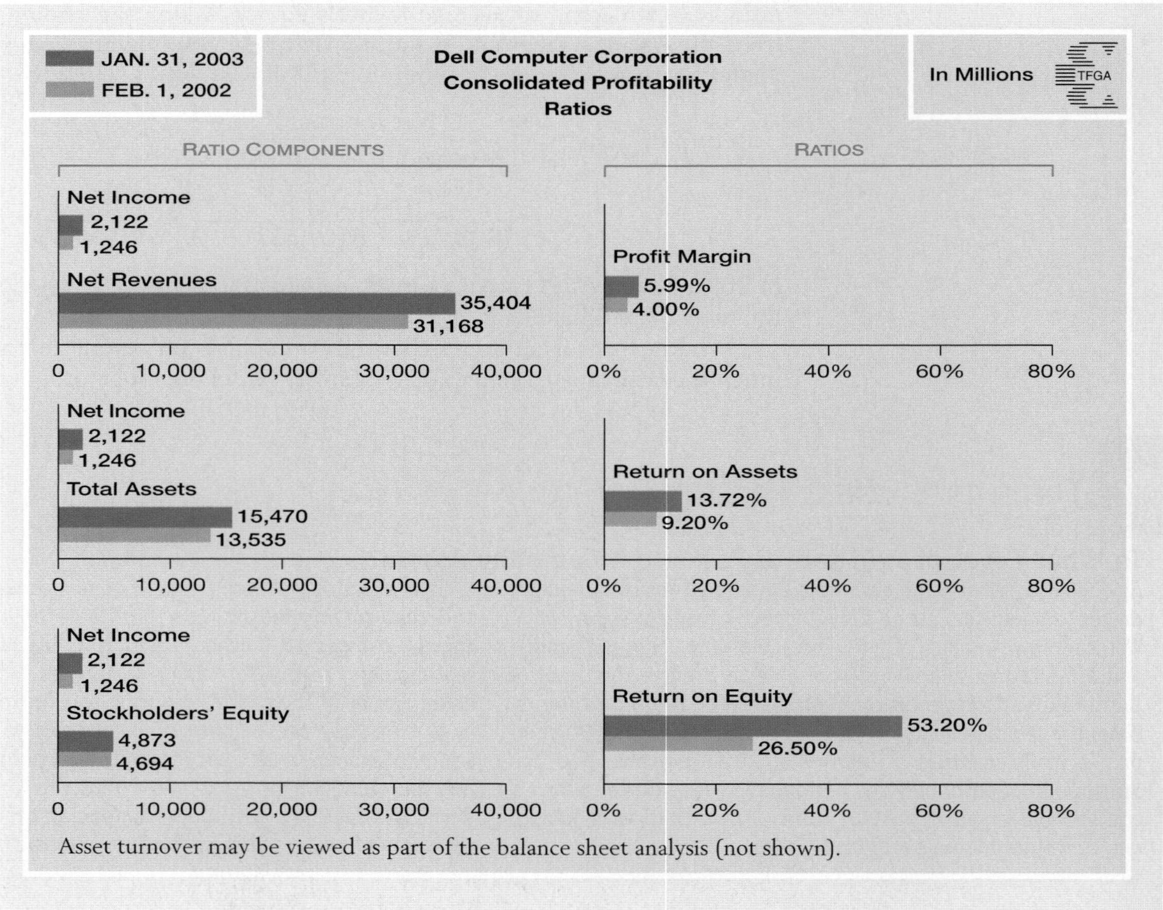

Asset turnover may be viewed as part of the balance sheet analysis (not shown).

www.dell.com

■ **GRAPHING RATIO ANALYSIS** Figure 10, prepared with the Fingraph® Financial Analyst™ software that is available with this text, graphically presents Dell Computer Corporation's profitability ratios involving net income. It helps us visualize the progress of the company in meeting its profitability objectives. On the left of the figure are the components of the ratios. On the right are the ratios for the past two years. Notice that the changes in return on equity and return on assets are linked to changes in profit margin or asset turnover. The Fingraph Financial Analyst CD-ROM software graphs all the ratios used in this book and provides narrative analysis. The asset turnover ratio is shown graphically with the Fingraph balance sheet analysis.

✓ Check out ACE for a Review Quiz at http://accounting.college.hmco.com/students.

Chapter Review

REVIEW OF LEARNING OBJECTIVES

LO1 State the objectives of financial reporting.

The objectives of financial reporting are (1) to furnish information that is useful in making investment and credit decisions, (2) to provide information that can be used to assess cash flow prospects, and (3) to provide information about business resources, claims to those resources, and changes in them.

LO2 State the qualitative characteristics of accounting information and describe their interrelationships.

Understandability depends on the knowledge of the user and the ability of the accountant to provide useful information. Usefulness is a function of two primary characteristics: relevance and reliability. Information is relevant when it affects the outcome of a decision. Information that is relevant has feedback value and predictive value, and is timely. To be reliable, information must represent what it is supposed to represent and be verifiable and neutral.

LO3 Define and describe the conventions of *comparability* and *consistency, materiality, conservatism, full disclosure,* and *cost-benefit.*

Because accountants' measurements are not exact, certain conventions are applied in current practice to help users interpret financial statements. The first of these conventions is comparability and consistency. Consistency requires the use of the same accounting procedures from period to period and enhances the comparability of financial statements. The second is materiality, which has to do with the relative importance of an item. The third is conservatism, which entails using the procedure that is least likely to overstate assets and income. The fourth is full disclosure, which means including all relevant information in the financial statements. The fifth is cost-benefit, which suggests that above a minimum level of information, additional information should be provided only if the benefits derived from the information exceed the costs of providing it.

LO4 Explain management's responsibility for ethical financial reporting and define *fraudulent financial reporting.*

Management is responsible for the preparation of financial statements in accordance with generally accepted accounting principles and for the internal controls that provide assurance that this objective is achieved. Fraudulent financial reporting is the intentional preparation of misleading financial statements.

LO5 Identify and describe the basic components of a classified balance sheet.

The classified balance sheet is subdivided as follows:

Assets	Liabilities
Current assets	Current liabilities
Investments	Long-term liabilities
Property, plant, and equipment	**Owner's Equity**
Intangible assets	(Content depends on the
(Other assets)	form of business)

A current asset is an asset that can reasonably be expected to be realized in cash or consumed during the next year or the normal operating cycle, whichever is longer. Investments are assets, usually long term, that are not used in the normal operation of a business. Property, plant, and equipment are tangible long-term assets used in day-to-day operations. Intangible assets are long-term assets with no physical substance whose value stems from the rights or privileges they extend to the owners. A current liability is an obligation that can reasonably be expected to be paid or performed during the next year or the normal operating cycle, whichever is longer. Long-term liabilities are debts that fall due more than one year in the future or beyond the normal operating cycle. The equity section of the balance sheet for a corporation differs from that for a proprietorship or partnership in that it has subdivisions of contributed capital (the value of assets invested by stockholders) and retained earnings (stockholders' claim to assets earned from operations and reinvested in operations).

LO6 Prepare multistep and single-step classified income statements.

Classified income statements for external reporting can be in multistep or single-step form. The multistep form arrives at net income through a series of steps; the single-step form arrives at net income in a single step. There is usually a separate section in the multistep form for other revenues and expenses.

LO7 Evaluate liquidity and profitability using classified financial statements.

One use of classified financial statements is to evaluate a company's liquidity and profitability. Two measures of liquidity are working capital and the current ratio. Five measures of profitability are profit margin, asset turnover, return on assets, debt to equity ratio, and return on equity. Referring to industry averages aids interpretation of these ratios.

Review of Concepts and Terminology

The following concepts and terms were introduced in this chapter:

LO7 **Asset turnover:** A measure of profitability that shows how efficiently assets are used to produce sales; net sales divided by average total assets.

LO5 **Classified financial statements:** General-purpose external financial statements that are divided into subcategories.

LO3 **Comparability:** The convention of presenting information in a way that enables decision makers to recognize similarities, differences, and trends over different time periods or between different companies.

LO6 **Condensed financial statements:** Financial statements for external reporting that present only the major categories of information.

LO3 **Conservatism:** The convention that when faced with two equally acceptable alternatives, the accountant must choose the one least likely to overstate assets and income.

LO3 **Consistency:** The convention requiring that once an accounting procedure is adopted, it not be changed from one period to the next unless users of the financial statements are informed of the change.

LO5 **Contributed capital:** The accounts that reflect the owner's investment in a corporation. Also called *paid-in capital.*

LO3 **Conventions:** Rules of thumb, or general principles, for recording transactions and preparing financial statements.

LO3 **Cost-benefit:** The convention that the benefits gained from providing accounting information should be greater than the costs of providing that information.

LO5 **Current assets:** Cash and other assets that are reasonably expected to be converted to cash, sold, or consumed within one year or within a normal operating cycle, whichever is longer.

LO5 **Current liabilities:** Obligations due to be paid or performed within one year or within the normal operating cycle, whichever is longer.

LO7 **Current ratio:** A measure of liquidity; current assets divided by current liabilities.

LO7 **Debt to equity ratio:** A measure of profitability that shows the relationship of assets financed by creditors to those financed by owners; total liabilities divided by owner's equity.

LO4 **Fraudulent financial reporting:** The intentional preparation of misleading financial statements.

LO3 **Full disclosure:** The convention requiring that financial statements and their notes present all information relevant to the users' understanding of the statements.

LO6 **Income from operations:** Gross margin less operating expenses. Also called *operating income.*

LO5 **Intangible assets:** Long-term assets with no physical substance whose value stems from the rights or privileges they extend to their owners.

LO5 **Investments:** Assets, usually long term, that are not used in the normal operation of a business and that management does not intend to convert to cash within the next year.

LO7 **Liquidity:** Having enough money on hand to pay bills when they are due and to take care of unexpected needs for cash.

LO5 **Long-term liabilities:** Debts that fall due more than one year in the future or beyond the normal operating cycle.

LO3 **Materiality:** The convention that refers to the relative importance of an item or event in a financial statement and its influence on the decisions of the users of financial statements.

LO6 **Multistep form:** A form of condensed income statement that arrives at net income in the same steps as a detailed income statement but presents only the totals of significant categories.

LO5 **Other assets:** A balance sheet category that some companies use to group all assets other than current assets and property, plant, and equipment.

LO6 **Other revenues and expenses:** The section of a multistep income statement that includes revenues and expenses not related to business operations. Also called *nonoperating revenues and expenses.*

LO7 **Profitability:** The ability of a business to earn a satisfactory income.

LO7 **Profit margin:** A measure of profitability that shows the percentage of each sales dollar that results in net income; net income divided by net sales.

LO5 **Property, plant, and equipment:** Tangible long-term assets used in the continuing operation of a business. Also called *operating assets, fixed assets, tangible assets, long-lived assets,* or *plant assets.*

LO2 **Qualitative characteristics:** Standards for judging the information that accountants give to decision makers.

LO2 **Relevance:** The qualitative characteristic of information that bears directly on the outcome of a decision.

LO2 **Reliability:** The qualitative characteristic of information that represents what it is supposed to represent and is verifiable and neutral.

LO5 **Retained Earnings:** The account that reflects the stockholders' claim to the assets earned from operations and reinvested in corporate operations. Also called *Earned Capital.*

LO7 **Return on assets:** A measure of profitability that shows how efficiently a company uses its assets to produce income; net income divided by average total assets.

LO7 **Return on equity:** A measure of profitability that relates the amount earned by a business to the owner's investment in the business; net income divided by average owner's equity.

LO6 **Single-step form:** A form of condensed income statement that arrives at net income in a single step.

LO2 **Understandability:** The qualitative characteristic of information that communicates an intended meaning.

LO2 **Usefulness:** The qualitative characteristic of information that is relevant and reliable.

LO7 **Working capital:** A measure of liquidity that shows the net current assets on hand to continue business operations; total current assets minus total current liabilities.

Review Problem

Analyzing Liquidity and Profitability Using Ratios

LO7 Flavin Shirt Company has faced increased competition from overseas shirtmakers in recent years. Presented below is summary information for the last two years:

	20x5	20x4
Current assets	$ 200,000	$ 170,000
Total assets	880,000	710,000
Current liabilities	90,000	50,000
Long-term liabilities	150,000	50,000
Owner's equity	640,000	610,000
Sales	1,200,000	1,050,000
Net income	60,000	80,000

Total assets and owner's equity at the beginning of 20x4 were $690,000 and $590,000, respectively.

REQUIRED ▶ Use (1) liquidity analysis and (2) profitability analysis to document the declining financial position of Flavin Shirt Company.

Answer to Review Problem

1. Liquidity analysis

	Current Assets	Current Liabilities	Working Capital	Current Ratio
20x4	$170,000	$50,000	$120,000	3.40
20x5	200,000	90,000	110,000	2.22
Decrease in working capital			$ 10,000	
Decrease in current ratio				1.18

Both working capital and the current ratio declined from 20x4 to 20x5 because the $40,000 increase in current liabilities ($90,000 − $50,000) was greater than the $30,000 increase in current assets.

2. Profitability analysis

	Net Income	Sales	Profit Margin	Average Total Assets	Asset Turnover	Return on Assets	Average Owner's Equity	Return on Equity
20x4	$80,000	$1,050,000	7.6%	$700,000[1]	1.50	11.4%	$600,000[3]	13.3%
20x5	60,000	1,200,000	5.0	795,000[2]	1.51	7.5	625,000[4]	9.6
Increase (decrease)	($20,000)	$ 150,000	(2.6)%	$ 95,000	0.01	(3.9)%	$ 25,000	(3.7)%

[1]($710,000 + $690,000) ÷ 2
[2]($880,000 + $710,000) ÷ 2
[3]($610,000 + $590,000) ÷ 2
[4]($640,000 + $610,000) ÷ 2

Net income decreased by $20,000 despite an increase in sales of $150,000 and an increase in average total assets of $95,000. The results were decreases in profit margin from 7.6 percent to 5.0 percent and in return on assets from 11.4 percent to 7.5 percent. Asset turnover showed almost no change and so did not contribute to the decline in profitability. The decrease in return on equity, from 13.3 percent to 9.6 percent, was not as great as the decrease in return on assets because the growth in total assets was financed by debt instead of by owner's equity, as shown by the capital structure analysis below.

	Total Liabilities	Owner's Equity	Debt to Equity Ratio
20x4	$100,000	$610,000	16.4%
20x5	240,000	640,000	37.5
Increase	$140,000	$ 30,000	21.1%

Total liabilities increased by $140,000, while owner's equity increased by $30,000. As a result, the amount of the business financed by debt in relation to the amount of the business financed by owner's equity increased from 20x4 to 20x5.

Chapter Assignments

Building Your Knowledge Foundation

Questions

1. What are the three objectives of financial reporting?
2. What are the qualitative characteristics of accounting information, and what is their significance?
3. What are the accounting conventions? How does each help in the interpretation of financial information?
4. Who is responsible for the preparation of reliable financial statements, and what is a principal way of achieving this objective?
5. What is the purpose of classified financial statements?
6. What are four common categories of assets?
7. What criteria must an asset meet to be classified as current? Under what condition is an asset considered current even though it will not be realized as cash within a year? What are two examples of assets that fall into this category?
8. In what order should current assets be listed?
9. What is the difference between a short-term investment in the current assets section of the balance sheet and a security in the investments section?
10. What is an intangible asset? Give at least three examples.
11. Name the two major categories of liabilities.
12. What are the primary differences between the equity section of the balance sheet for a sole proprietorship or partnership and the corresponding section for a corporation?
13. Explain the difference between contributed capital and retained earnings.
14. Explain how the multistep form of income statement differs from the single-step form. What are the relative merits of each?

15. Why are other revenues and expenses separated from operating revenues and expenses on the multistep income statement?
16. Define *liquidity,* and name two measures of liquidity.
17. How is the current ratio computed, and why is it important?
18. Which is the more important goal: liquidity or profitability? Explain your answer.
19. Name five measures of profitability.
20. "Return on assets is a better measure of profitability than profit margin." Evaluate this statement.

SHORT EXERCISES

SE 1.
LO1 LO2 **Objectives and Qualitative Characteristics**

Identify each of the following statements as either an objective (O) of financial information or a qualitative (Q) characteristic of accounting information:

1. Information about business resources, claims to those resources, and changes in them should be provided.
2. Decision makers must be able to interpret accounting information.
3. Information that is useful in making investment and credit decisions should be furnished.
4. Accounting information must be relevant and reliable.
5. Information useful in assessing cash flow prospects should be provided.

SE 2.
LO3 **Accounting Conventions**

State which of the accounting conventions—comparability and consistency, materiality, conservatism, full disclosure, or cost-benefit—is being followed in each of the cases listed below.

1. Management provides detailed information about the company's long-term debt in the notes to the financial statements.
2. A company does not account separately for discounts received for prompt payment of accounts payable because few of these transactions occur and the total amount of the discounts is small.
3. Management eliminates a weekly report on property, plant, and equipment acquisitions and disposals because no one finds it useful.
4. A company follows the policy of recognizing a loss on inventory when the market value of an item falls below its cost but does nothing if the market value rises.
5. When several accounting methods are acceptable, management chooses a single method and follows that method from year to year.

SE 3.
LO5 **Classification of Accounts: Balance Sheet**

Tell whether each of the following accounts is a current asset; an investment; property, plant, and equipment; an intangible asset; a current liability; a long-term liability; owner's equity; or not on the balance sheet:

1. Delivery Trucks
2. Accounts Payable
3. Note Payable (due in 90 days)
4. Delivery Expense
5. T. Woo, Capital
6. Prepaid Insurance
7. Trademark
8. Investment to Be Held Six Months
9. Interest Payable
10. Factory Not Used in Business

SE 4.
LO5 **Classified Balance Sheet**

Using the following accounts, prepare a classified balance sheet at year end, May 31, 20xx: Accounts Payable, $400; Accounts Receivable, $550; Accumulated Depreciation, Equipment, $350; Cash, $100; Equipment, $2,000; Franchise, $100; Investments (long-term), $250; Merchandise Inventory, $300; Notes Payable (long-term), $200; R. Strong, Capital, ?; Wages Payable, $50.

SE 5.
LO6 **Classification of Accounts: Income Statement**

Tell whether each of the following accounts is part of net sales, cost of goods sold, operating expenses, other revenues and expenses, or is not on the income statement:

1. Delivery Expense
2. Interest Expense
3. Unearned Revenue
4. Sales Returns and Allowances
5. Cost of Goods Sold
6. Depreciation Expense
7. Investment Income
8. Withdrawals

SE 6.
LO6 **Single-Step Income Statement**

Using the following accounts, prepare a single-step income statement at year end, May 31, 20xx: Cost of Goods Sold, $280; General Expenses, $150; Interest Expense, $70; Interest Income, $30; Net Sales, $800; Selling Expenses, $185.

SE 7. **LO6 Multistep Income Statement**

Using the accounts presented in **SE 6,** prepare a multistep income statement.

SE 8. **LO7 Liquidity Ratios**

Using the following accounts and balances taken from a year-end balance sheet, compute working capital and the current ratio:

Accounts Payable	$ 7,000
Accounts Receivable	10,000
Cash	4,000
J. Matson, Capital	20,000
Marketable Securities	2,000
Merchandise Inventory	12,000
Notes Payable in Three Years	13,000
Property, Plant, and Equipment	40,000

SE 9. **LO7 Profitability Ratios**

Using the following information from a balance sheet and an income statement, compute the (1) profit margin, (2) asset turnover, (3) return on assets, (4) debt to equity ratio, and (5) return on equity. (The previous year's total assets were $100,000 and owner's equity was $70,000.)

Total assets	$120,000
Total liabilities	30,000
Total owner's equity	90,000
Net sales	130,000
Cost of goods sold	70,000
Operating expenses	45,000

EXERCISES

E 1. **LO1 LO2 LO3 Financial Accounting Concepts**

The lettered items below represent a classification scheme for the concepts of financial accounting. Match each numbered term with the letter of the category in which it belongs.

a. Decision makers (users of accounting information)
b. Business activities or entities relevant to accounting measurement
c. Objectives of accounting information
d. Accounting measurement considerations
e. Accounting processing considerations
f. Qualitative characteristics
g. Accounting conventions
h. Financial statements

1. Conservatism
2. Verifiability
3. Statement of cash flows
4. Materiality
5. Reliability
6. Recognition
7. Cost-benefit
8. Understandability
9. Business transactions
10. Consistency
11. Full disclosure
12. Furnishing information that is useful to investors and creditors
13. Specific business entities
14. Classification
15. Management
16. Neutrality
17. Internal accounting control
18. Valuation
19. Investors
20. Timeliness
21. Relevance
22. Furnishing information that is useful in assessing cash flow prospects

E 2. **LO3 Accounting Concepts and Conventions**

Each of the statements below violates a convention in accounting. State which of the following accounting conventions is violated: comparability and consistency, materiality, conservatism, full disclosure, or cost-benefit.

1. A series of reports that are time-consuming and expensive to prepare is presented to the board of directors each month even though the reports are never used.
2. A company changes its method of accounting for depreciation.
3. The company in **2** does not indicate in the financial statements that the method of depreciation was changed, nor does it specify the effect of the change on net income.

4. A new office building next to the factory is debited to the Factory account because it represents a fairly small dollar amount in relation to the factory.
5. The asset account for a pickup truck still used in the business is written down to what the truck could be sold for even though the carrying value under conventional depreciation methods is higher.

E 3. **LO5 Classification of Accounts: Balance Sheet**

The lettered items below represent a classification scheme for a balance sheet, and the numbered items are account titles. Match each account with the letter of the category in which it belongs.

a. Current assets
b. Investments
c. Property, plant, and equipment
d. Intangible assets
e. Current liabilities
f. Long-term liabilities
g. Owner's equity
h. Not on balance sheet

1. Patent
2. Building Held for Sale
3. Prepaid Rent
4. Wages Payable
5. Note Payable in Five Years
6. Building Used in Operations
7. Fund Held to Pay Off Long-Term Debt
8. Inventory
9. Prepaid Insurance
10. Depreciation Expense
11. Accounts Receivable
12. Interest Expense
13. Unearned Revenue
14. Short-Term Investments
15. Accumulated Depreciation
16. M. Capelli, Capital

E 4. **LO5 Classified Balance Sheet Preparation**

The following data pertain to a corporation: Cash, $31,200; Investment in Six-Month Government Securities, $16,400; Accounts Receivable, $38,000; Inventory, $40,000; Prepaid Rent, $1,200; Investment in Corporate Securities (long-term), $20,000; Land, $8,000; Building, $70,000; Accumulated Depreciation, Building, $14,000; Equipment, $152,000; Accumulated Depreciation, Equipment, $17,000; Copyright, $6,200; Accounts Payable, $51,000; Revenue Received in Advance, $2,800; Bonds Payable, $60,000; Common Stock, $10 par, 10,000 shares authorized, issued, and outstanding, $100,000; Paid-in Capital in Excess of Par Value, $50,000; and Retained Earnings, $88,200.

Prepare a classified balance sheet; omit the heading.

E 5. **LO6 Classification of Accounts: Income Statement**

Using the classification scheme below for a multistep income statement, match each account with the letter of the category in which it belongs.

a. Net sales
b. Cost of goods sold
c. Selling expenses
d. General and administrative expenses
e. Other revenues and expenses
f. Not on income statement

1. Purchases
2. Sales Discounts
3. Merchandise Inventory (beginning)
4. Interest Income
5. Advertising Expense
6. Office Salaries Expense
7. Freight Out Expense
8. Prepaid Insurance
9. Utilities Expense
10. Sales Salaries Expense
11. Rent Expense
12. Purchases Returns and Allowances
13. Freight In
14. Depreciation Expense, Delivery Equipment
15. Wages Payable
16. Interest Expense

E 6. **LO6 Preparation of Income Statements**

The following data pertain to a sole proprietorship: Sales, $405,000; Cost of Goods Sold, $220,000; Selling Expenses, $90,000; General and Administrative Expenses, $60,000; Interest Expense, $4,000; and Interest Income, $3,000.

1. Prepare a condensed single-step income statement.
2. Prepare a condensed multistep income statement.

E 7. **LO6 Multistep Income Statement**

A condensed single-step income statement for Harrington Housewares Company appears at the top of the next page. Present the information in a condensed multistep

Harrington Housewares Company Income Statement For the Year Ended June 30, 20xx		
Revenues		
Net sales		$1,197,132
Interest income		5,720
Total revenues		$1,202,852
Costs and expenses		
Cost of goods sold	$777,080	
Selling expenses	203,740	
General and administrative expenses	100,688	
Interest expense	13,560	
Total costs and expenses		1,095,068
Net income		$ 107,784

income statement, and tell what insights can be obtained from the multistep form as opposed to the single-step form.

LO7 Liquidity Ratios

E 8. The following accounts and balances are from the general ledger of Swan Company.

Accounts Payable	$ 49,800
Accounts Receivable	30,600
Cash	4,500
Current Portion of Long-Term Debt	30,000
Long-Term Investments	31,200
Marketable Securities	37,800
Merchandise Inventory	76,200
Notes Payable, 90 days	45,000
Notes Payable, 2 years	60,000
Notes Receivable, 90 days	78,000
Notes Receivable, 2 years	30,000
Prepaid Insurance	1,200
Property, Plant, and Equipment	180,000
C. Swan, Capital	84,900
Salaries Payable	2,550
Supplies	1,050
Property Taxes Payable	3,750
Unearned Revenue	2,250

Compute the (1) working capital and (2) current ratio.

LO7 Profitability Ratios

E 9. The following end-of-year amounts are from the financial statements of Laliberte Company: Total assets, $852,000; Total liabilities, $344,000; Owner's equity, $508,000; Net sales, $1,564,000; Cost of goods sold, $972,000; Operating expenses, $404,000; and Withdrawals, $80,000. During the past year, total assets increased by $150,000. Total owner's equity was affected only by net income and withdrawals.

Compute (1) profit margin, (2) asset turnover, (3) return on assets, (4) debt to equity ratio, and (5) return on equity.

LO7 Computation of Ratios

E 10. A simplified balance sheet and income statement for a sole proprietorship appear at the top of the next page. Total assets and owner's equity at the beginning of 20xx were $360,000 and $280,000, respectively.

1. Compute the following liquidity measures: (a) working capital and (b) current ratio.
2. Compute the following profitability measures: (a) profit margin, (b) asset turnover, (c) return on assets, (d) debt to equity ratio, and (e) return on equity.

Balance Sheet
December 31, 20xx

Assets		Liabilities	
Current assets	$100,000	Current liabilities	$ 40,000
Investments	20,000	Long-term liabilities	60,000
Property, plant, and equipment	293,000	Total liabilities	$100,000
Intangible assets	27,000	**Owner's Equity**	
		P. Cavafy, Capital	340,000
Total assets	$440,000	Total liabilities and owner's equity	$440,000

Income Statement
For the Year Ended December 31, 20xx

Net sales	$820,000
Cost of goods sold	500,000
Gross margin	$320,000
Operating expenses	270,000
Net income	$ 50,000

PROBLEMS

LO3 Accounting Conventions

P 1. In each case below, accounting conventions *may* have been violated.

1. After careful study, Hawthorne Company, which has offices in 40 states, decided to change its method of depreciating office furniture. The new method is adopted for the current year, and the change is noted in the financial statements.
2. In the past, Ruggio Corporation has recorded operating expenses in general accounts for each classification (e.g., Salaries Expense, Depreciation Expense, and Utilities Expense). Management has determined that despite the additional recordkeeping costs, the company's income statement should break down each operating expense into its components of selling expense and administrative expense.
3. Connie Watts, Pine Corporation's auditor, discovered that a company officer had authorized the payment of a $3,000 bribe to a local government official. Pine's management argued that because the item was so small in relation to the size of the company ($3 million in sales), the illegal payment should not be disclosed.
4. Dearleap Bookstore built a small addition to its main building to house a new computer games section. Because no one could be sure that the section would succeed, the accountant took a conservative approach and recorded the addition as an expense.
5. Since its origin ten years ago, Hsu Company has used the same generally accepted inventory method. Because there has been no change in the inventory method, the company does not declare in its financial statements what inventory method it uses.

REQUIRED ▶ In each case, identify the convention that applies, state whether the treatment is in accord with the convention and generally accepted accounting principles, and briefly explain your answer.

LO6 Forms of the Income Statement

P 2. The July 31, 20x5, year-end income statement accounts that follow are for Inge Robotics Company. Beginning merchandise inventory was $172,800 and ending merchandise inventory is $145,000. Inge Robotics Company is a sole proprietorship.

Account Name	Debit	Credit
Sales		$922,200
Sales Returns and Allowances	$ 53,800	
Purchases	449,000	
Purchases Returns and Allowances		23,840
Freight In	34,800	
Sales Salaries Expense	124,320	
Sales Supplies Expense	3,280	
Rent Expense, Selling Space	14,400	
Utilities Expense, Selling Space	5,920	
Advertising Expense	33,600	
Depreciation Expense, Delivery Equipment	8,800	
Office Salaries Expense	58,480	
Office Supplies Expense	19,520	
Rent Expense, Office Space	4,800	
Utilities Expense, Office Space	2,000	
Postage Expense	4,640	
Insurance Expense	5,360	
Miscellaneous Expense	2,880	
General Management Salaries Expense	84,000	
Interest Expense	11,200	
Interest Income		840

REQUIRED ▶

1. Prepare (a) a detailed income statement, (b) a condensed income statement in multi-step form, and (c) a condensed income statement in single-step form.
2. Which form is most useful to management? Which is most useful to an investor?

LO5 Classified Balance Sheet

P 3. The following information is taken from the July 31, 20x4, post-closing trial balance of Theopoulos Machine Company.

Account Name	Debit	Credit
Cash	$ 31,000	
Short-Term Investments	33,000	
Notes Receivable	10,000	
Accounts Receivable	276,000	
Merchandise Inventory	145,000	
Prepaid Rent	1,600	
Prepaid Insurance	4,800	
Sales Supplies	1,280	
Office Supplies	440	
Deposit for Future Advertising	3,680	
Building, Not in Use	49,600	
Land	22,400	
Delivery Equipment	41,200	
Accumulated Depreciation, Delivery Equipment		$ 28,400
Franchise Fee	4,000	
Accounts Payable		114,600
Salaries Payable		5,200
Interest Payable		840
Long-Term Notes Payable		80,000
Pete Theopoulos, Capital		394,960

REQUIRED ▶ From the information provided, prepare a classified balance sheet for Theopoulos Machine Company.

P 4. **LO7 Ratio Analysis: Liquidity and Profitability**

O'Malley Products Company has been disappointed with its operating results for the past two years. As the accountant for the company, you have the following information available to you.

	20x4	20x3
Current assets	$ 45,000	$ 35,000
Total assets	145,000	110,000
Current liabilities	20,000	10,000
Long-term liabilities	20,000	—
Owner's equity	105,000	100,000
Net sales	262,000	200,000
Net income	16,000	11,000

Total assets and owner's equity at the beginning of 20x3 were $90,000 and $80,000, respectively.

REQUIRED ▶

1. Compute the following liquidity measures for 20x3 and 20x4: (a) working capital and (b) current ratio. Comment on the differences between the years.
2. Compute the following measures of profitability for 20x3 and 20x4: (a) profit margin, (b) asset turnover, (c) return on assets, (d) debt to equity ratio, and (e) return on equity. Comment on the change in performance from 20x3 to 20x4.

P 5. **LO5 LO6 LO7 Classified Financial Statement Preparation and Evaluation**

Folino Company is in the auto supply business. At the December 31, 20x6, year end, the following financial information was available from the income statement: administrative expenses, $175,600; cost of goods sold, $700,840; interest expense, $45,280; interest income, $5,600; net sales, $1,428,780; and selling expenses, $440,400.

The following information was available from the balance sheet (after closing entries were made): accounts payable, $65,200; accounts receivable, $209,600; accumulated depreciation, delivery equipment, $34,200; accumulated depreciation, store fixtures, $84,440; cash, $56,800; Cindy Folino, Capital, $718,600; delivery equipment, $177,000; inventory, $273,080; investment in Tsung Corporation (long-term), $112,000; investment in U.S. government securities (short-term), $79,200; long-term notes payable, $200,000; short-term notes payable, $100,000; prepaid expenses, $11,520; and store fixtures, $283,240.

Total assets on December 31, 20x5, were $1,048,800 and withdrawals for the year were $120,000.

REQUIRED ▶

1. From the information above, prepare (a) an income statement in single-step form, (b) a statement of owner's equity, and (c) a classified balance sheet.
2. From the statements you have prepared, compute the following measures: (a) working capital and current ratio (for liquidity); and (b) profit margin, asset turnover, return on assets, debt to equity ratio, and return on equity (for profitability).
3. Using the industry averages for the auto and home supply business in Figures 4–9 in this chapter, determine whether Folino Company needs to improve its liquidity or its profitability. Explain your answer, making recommendations as to specific areas on which Folino Company should concentrate.

P 6. **LO3 Accounting Conventions**

In each case below, accounting conventions *may* have been violated.

1. Mt. Shasta Manufacturing Company uses the cost method for computing the balance sheet amount of inventory unless the market value of the inventory is less than the cost, in which case the market value is used. At the end of the current year, the market value is $221,000, and the cost is $240,000. Mt. Shasta uses the $221,000 figure to compute current assets because management feels it is the more cautious approach.
2. Herlihan Company has annual sales of $15,000,000. It follows the practice of charging any items costing less than $300 to expenses in the year purchased. During the current year, it purchased several chairs for the executive conference rooms at $291 each, including freight. Although the chairs were expected to last for at least ten years, they were charged as an expense in accordance with company policy.
3. Svrcek Company closed its books on December 31, 20x4, before preparing its annual report. A day later, a fire destroyed one of its two factories. Although Svrcek

Company had fire insurance and would not suffer a loss on the building, it expected a significant decrease in sales in 20x5 because of the fire. The company did not report the fire damage in its 20x4 financial statements because the fire did not affect that year's operations.

4. Geehan Chemical Company spends a substantial portion of its profits on research and development. The company has been reporting its $7,500,000 expenditure for research and development as a lump sum, but management recently decided to begin classifying the expenditures by project even though the recordkeeping costs will increase.
5. During the current year, Kern Company changed from one generally accepted method of accounting for inventories to another method.

REQUIRED ▶ In each case, identify the convention that applies, state whether the treatment is in accord with the convention and generally accepted accounting principles, and briefly explain why.

ALTERNATE PROBLEMS

LO6 Forms of the Income Statement

P 7. The income statement accounts from the June 30, 20x5, year-end adjusted trial balance of Kansas City Appliance Company follow. Beginning merchandise inventory was $175,200 and ending merchandise inventory is $157,650. The company is a sole proprietorship.

Account Name	Debit	Credit
Sales		$541,230
Sales Returns and Allowances	$ 15,298	
Purchases	212,336	
Purchases Returns and Allowances		6,159
Freight In	11,221	
Sales Salaries Expense	102,030	
Sales Supplies Expense	1,642	
Rent Expense, Selling Space	18,000	
Utilities Expense, Selling Space	11,256	
Advertising Expense	21,986	
Depreciation Expense, Selling Fixtures	6,778	
Office Salaries Expense	47,912	
Office Supplies Expense	782	
Rent Expense, Office Space	4,000	
Depreciation Expense, Office Equipment	3,251	
Utilities Expense, Office Space	3,114	
Postage Expense	626	
Insurance Expense	2,700	
Miscellaneous Expense	481	
Interest Expense	3,600	
Interest Income		800

REQUIRED ▶

1. From the information provided, prepare the following:
   a. a detailed income statement,
   b. a condensed income statement in multistep form, and
   c. a condensed income statement in single-step form.
2. Which of these forms do you think is most useful to management and which is most useful to investment analysts?

P 8. LO7 **Ratio Analysis: Liquidity and Profitability**

Below is a summary of data from the income statements and balance sheets for Leominster Plastics Company for 20x4 and 20x5.

	20x5	20x4
Current assets	$ 366,000	$ 310,000
Total assets	2,320,000	1,740,000
Current liabilities	180,000	120,000
Long-term liabilities	800,000	580,000
Owner's equity	1,340,000	1,040,000
Net sales	4,600,000	3,480,000
Net income	300,000	204,000

Total assets and owner's equity at the beginning of 20x4 were $1,360,000 and $840,000, respectively.

REQUIRED

1. Compute the following liquidity measures for 20x4 and 20x5: (a) working capital and (b) current ratio. Comment on the differences between the years.
2. Compute the following measures of profitability for 20x4 and 20x5: (a) profit margin, (b) asset turnover, (c) return on assets, (d) debt to equity ratio, and (e) return on equity. Comment on the change in performance from 20x4 to 20x5.

SKILLS DEVELOPMENT CASES

Conceptual Analysis

SD 1. LO3 **Accounting Conventions**

Central Parking, which operates a seven-story parking building in downtown Chicago, has a calendar year end. It serves daily and hourly parkers, as well as monthly parkers, who pay a fixed monthly rate in advance. The company traditionally has recorded all cash receipts as revenues when received. Most monthly parkers pay in full during the month prior to that in which they have the right to park. The company's auditors have said that beginning in 20x5, the company should consider recording the cash receipts from monthly parking on an accrual basis, crediting Unearned Revenues. Total cash receipts for 20x5 were $2,500,000, and the cash receipts received in 20x5 and applicable to January 20x6 were $125,000. Discuss the relevance of the accounting conventions of consistency, materiality, and full disclosure to the decision to record the monthly parking revenues on an accrual basis.

SD 2. LO3 **Materiality**

Sophia Electronics, Inc., operates a chain of consumer electronics stores in the Atlanta area. This year the company achieved annual sales of $50 million, on which it earned a net income of $2 million. At the beginning of the year, management implemented a new inventory system that enabled it to track all purchases and sales. At the end of the year, a physical inventory revealed that the actual inventory was $80,000 below what the new system indicated it should be. The inventory loss, which probably resulted from shoplifting, is reflected in a higher cost of goods sold. The problem concerns management but seems to be less important to the company's auditors. What is materiality? Why might the inventory loss concern management more than it does the auditors? Do you think the amount is material?

Ethical Dilemma

SD 3. LO4 **Ethics and Financial Reporting**

Sensor Software, located outside Boston, develops computer software and licenses it to financial institutions. The firm uses an aggressive accounting method that records revenues from the software it has developed on a percentage of completion basis. Consequently, revenue for partially completed projects is recognized based on the proportion of the project that is completed. If a project is 50 percent completed, then 50 percent of the contracted revenue is recognized. In 20x4, preliminary estimates for a $5 million project are that the project is 75 percent complete. Because the estimate of completion is a matter of judgment, management asks for a new report showing the project to be 90 percent complete. The change will enable senior managers to meet their financial goals for the year and thus receive substantial year-end bonuses. Do you think management's action is ethical? If you were the company controller and were asked to prepare the new report, would you do it? What action would you take?

Group Activity: Use in-class groups to debate the ethics of the action.

SD 4.
LO4 **Ethics and Financial Reporting**

The SEC is conducting an investigation into possible fraudulent accounting practices at Lucent Technologies, Inc. <www.lucent.com>. The probe focuses on whether Lucent improperly booked $679 million in revenue. The SEC is looking at how Lucent recognized revenue on sales to its distribution partners, who may not have sold the products or even may not have been able to sell the products. This practice is known as "stuffing the channels." In an adjustment, the company took back $452 million in revenue it had sent to its distribution partners but never actually sold to end customers. Normal accounting practice does not allow recording as revenue shipments to distributors on consignment—that is, with the right of return if not sold. It is not clear what rights of return exist in this case, but analysts have been critical of Lucent's aggressive practice. Lucent maintains the practice is legal.[17] What is the difference between aggressive accounting and fraudulent financial reporting? Can Lucent's revenue recognition practice be legal but also fraudulent?

Research Activity

SD 5.
LO4 **Accounting and Fraud**

Most university and public libraries have access to indexes of leading newspapers, such as *The Wall Street Journal* and *The New York Times*, on CD-ROM. Go to a library and do a search for a recent year using the key words "accounting and fraud," "accounting and restatement," or "accounting and irregularities." Choose one of the articles you find and read it. What company is involved, and how is accounting connected with the fraud, restatement, or irregularity? Describe the situation. Does it involve an apparently legal or illegal activity? Does it involve fraudulent financial reporting? Explain your answer, and be prepared to discuss it in class.

Decision-Making Practice

SD 6.
LO7 **Financial Analysis for Loan Decision**

Steve Sulong was recently promoted to loan officer at First National Bank. He has authority to issue loans up to $50,000 without approval from a higher bank official. This week two small companies, Handy Harvey Company, and Sheila's Fashions Company, have each submitted a proposal for a six-month, $50,000 loan. To prepare financial analyses of the two companies, Sulong has obtained the information summarized below.

Handy Harvey Company, is a local lumber and home improvement company. Because sales have increased so much during the past two years, owner Harvey Cushing has had to raise additional working capital, especially as represented by receivables and inventory. The $50,000 loan is needed to ensure that the company has enough working capital for the next year. Handy Harvey began the year with total assets of $740,000 and owner's equity of $260,000. During the past year, the company had a net income of $40,000 on net sales of $760,000. Handy Harvey's unclassified balance sheet as of the current date appears as follows:

Assets		Liabilities and Owner's Equity	
Cash	$ 30,000	Accounts payable	$200,000
Accounts receivable (net)	150,000	Notes payable (short term)	100,000
Inventory	250,000	Notes payable (long term)	200,000
Land	50,000	H. Cushing, Capital	300,000
Buildings (net)	250,000		
Equipment (net)	70,000		
Total assets	$800,000	Total liabilities and owner's equity	$800,000

Sheila's Fashions has for three years been a successful clothing store for young professional women. The leased store is located in the downtown financial district. Owner Sheila Willard's loan proposal asks for $50,000 to pay for stocking a new line of women's suits during the coming season. At the beginning of the year, the company had total assets of $200,000 and total owner's equity of $114,000. Over the past year, the company earned a net income of $36,000 on net sales of $480,000. The firm's unclassified balance sheet at the current date is as follows:

Assets		Liabilities and Owner's Equity	
Cash	$ 10,000	Accounts payable	$ 80,000
Accounts receivable (net)	50,000	Accrued liabilities	10,000
Inventory	135,000	S. Willard, Capital	150,000
Prepaid expenses	5,000		
Equipment (net)	40,000		
Total assets	$240,000	Total liabilities and owner's equity	$240,000

1. Prepare a financial analysis of each company's liquidity before and after receiving the proposed loan. Also compute profitability ratios before and after, as appropriate. Write a brief summary of the effect of the proposed loan on each company's financial position.
2. Assume you are Sulong and can make a loan to only one of these companies. Write a memorandum to the bank's vice president outlining your decision and naming the company to which you would lend $50,000. Be sure to state what positive and negative factors could affect each company's ability to pay back the loan in the next year. Also indicate what other information of a financial or nonfinancial nature would be helpful in making a final decision.

FINANCIAL REPORTING AND ANALYSIS CASES

Interpreting Financial Reports

FRA 1.
LO7 Comparison of Profitability

Two of the largest chains of grocery stores in the United States are Albertson's Inc. <www.albertsons.com> and the Great Atlantic & Pacific Tea Company (A&P) <www.aptea.com>. In a recent fiscal year, Albertson's had a net income of $765 million, and A&P had a net income of $14 million. It is difficult to judge which company is more profitable from those figures alone because they do not take into account the relative sales, sizes, and investments of the companies. Data (in millions) to complete a financial analysis of the two companies follow:[18]

	Albertson's	A&P
Net sales	$36,762	$10,151
Beginning total assets	15,719	3,335
Ending total assets	16,078	3,309
Beginning total liabilities	10,017	2,489
Ending total liabilities	10,394	2,512
Beginning stockholders' equity	5,702	846
Ending stockholders' equity	5,684	797

1. Determine which company was more profitable by computing profit margin, asset turnover, return on assets, debt to equity ratio, and return on equity for the two companies. Comment on the relative profitability of the two companies.

2. What do the ratios tell you about the factors that go into achieving an adequate return on assets in the grocery industry? For industry data, refer to Figures 5 through 9 in this chapter.
3. How would you characterize the use of debt financing in the grocery industry and the use of debt by the two companies?

Group Activity: Assign each ratio or company to a group, and hold a class discussion.

FRA 2.
LO7 **Evaluation of Profitability**

Carla Cruz is the owner and president of Cruz Tapestries, which wholesales fine tapestries to retail stores. Because Cruz was not satisfied with the company earnings in 20x3, she raised prices in 20x4, increasing gross margin from sales from 30 percent in 20x3 to 35 percent in 20x4. Cruz is pleased that net income went up from 20x3 to 20x4, as shown in the following comparative income statements:

	20x4	20x3
Revenues		
Net sales	$611,300	$693,200
Costs and expenses		
Cost of goods sold	$397,345	$485,240
Selling and administrative expenses	169,199	166,504
Total costs and expenses	$566,544	$651,744
Net income	$ 44,756	$ 41,456

Total assets for Cruz Tapestries at year end for 20x2, 20x3, and 20x4 were $623,390, $693,405, and $768,455, respectively.

Has Cruz Tapestries' profitability really improved? (**Hint:** Compute profit margin and return on assets, and comment.) What factors has Cruz overlooked in evaluating the profitability of the company? (**Hint:** Compute asset turnover and comment on the role it plays in profitability.)

FRA 3.
LO7 **Financial Analysis with Industry Comparison**

Exhibits 2 and 5 in this chapter contain the comparative balance sheet and income statement for Dell Computer Corporation <www.dell.com>. Assume you are the chief financial officer.

1. Compute liquidity ratios (working capital and current ratio) and profitability ratios (profit margin, asset turnover, return on assets, debt to equity ratio, and return on equity) for 2001 and 2002 and show the industry ratios (except working capital) from Figures 4 to 9 in this chapter. Use income from continuing operations and end-of-year assets and stockholders' equity to compute the ratios.
2. Write a memorandum to the board of directors in executive summary form describing changes in Dell's liquidity and profitability performance from 2001 to 2002 compared with the industry averages.

International Company

FRA 4.
LO5 LO7 **Interpretation and Analysis of British Financial Statements**

Presented on the next page are the classified balance sheets for the British company GlaxoSmithKline PLC <www.gsk.com>, a pharmaceutical firm with marketing and manufacturing operations in 57 countries.[19]

In the United Kingdom, the format of classified financial statements usually differs from that used in the United States. To compare the financial statements of companies in different countries, it is important to know how to interpret a variety of formats.

GlaxoSmithKline PLC and Subsidiaries
Consolidated Balance Sheets

	2000 £m	1999 £m
Goodwill	170	160
Intangible assets	966	926
Tangible assets	6,642	6,402
Investments	2,544	1,804
Fixed assets	10,322	9,292
Equity investments	171	52
Stocks	2,277	2,243
Debtors	5,399	4,828
Liquid investments	2,138	1,780
Cash at bank	1,283	579
Current assets	11,268	9,482
Loans and overdrafts	(2,281)	(2,819)
Other creditors	(6,803)	(5,629)
Creditors: amounts due within one year	(9,084)	(8,448)
Net current assets	2,184	1,034
Total assets less current liabilities	12,506	10,326
Loans	(1,751)	(1,897)
Other creditors	(143)	(147)
Creditors: amounts due after one year	(1,894)	(2,044)
Provisions for liabilities and charges	(1,657)	(1,675)
Net assets	8,955	6,607
Called up share capital	1,556	1,549
Share premium account	30	—
Other reserves	6,125	3,915
Equity shareholders' funds	7,711	5,464
Non-equity minority interest	1,039	961
Equity minority interests	205	182
Capital employed	8,955	6,607

1. For each line on GlaxoSmithKline's balance sheet, indicate the corresponding term that would be found on a U.S. balance sheet. (For this exercise, consider Provisions for liabilities and Charges to be long-term liabilities.) What is the focus or rationale behind the format of the U.K. balance sheet?
2. Assuming that GlaxoSmithKline earned a net income of £4,147 million and £2,543 million in 2000 and 1999, respectively, compute the current ratio, debt to equity

ratio, return on assets, and return on equity for 2000 and 1999. (Use year-end amounts to compute ratios.)

Toys "R" Us Annual Report

FRA 5.

LO5 LO6 LO7 Reading and Analyzing an Annual Report

Refer to the Toys "R" Us <www.tru.com> annual report to answer the following questions. (Note that 2001 refers to the year ended February 2, 2002, and 2002 refers to the year ended February 1, 2003.)

1. Consolidated balance sheets: (a) Did the amount of working capital increase or decrease from 2001 to 2002? By how much? (b) Did the current ratio improve from 2001 to 2002? (c) Does the company have long-term investments or intangible assets? (d) Did the debt to equity ratio of Toys "R" Us change from 2001 to 2002? (e) What is the contributed capital for 2002? How does contributed capital compare with retained earnings?
2. Consolidated statements of earnings: (a) Does Toys "R" Us use a multistep or single-step income statement? (b) Is it a comparative statement? (c) What is the trend of net earnings? (d) How significant are income taxes for Toys "R" Us? (e) Did the profit margin increase from 2001 to 2002? (f) Did asset turnover improve from 2001 to 2002? (g) Did the return on assets increase from 2001 to 2002? (h) Did the return on equity increase from 2001 to 2002? Total assets and total stockholders' equity for 2000 may be obtained from the financial highlights.
3. Multistep income statement: In the 1987 Toys "R" Us annual report, management stated that the company's "[operating] expense levels were among the best controlled in retailing [at] 18.8 percent. . . .We were able to operate with lower merchandise margins and still increase our earnings and return on sales."[20] Prepare a multistep income statement for Toys "R" Us down to income from operations for 2001 and 2002, and compute the ratios of gross margin, operating expenses, and income from operations to net sales. Comment on whether the company continued, as of 2002, to maintain the level of performance indicated by management in 1987. In 1987, gross margin was 31.2 percent and income from operations was 12.4 percent of net sales.

Comparison Case: Toys "R" Us and Walgreen Co.

FRA 6.

LO7 Financial Analysis Comparison: Toys "R" Us vs. Walgreens

Compare the financial performance of Toys "R" Us <www.tru.com> and Walgreens <www.walgreens.com> on the basis of liquidity and profitability for 2002 and 2001. Use the following ratios: working capital, current ratio, debt to equity ratio, profit margin, asset turnover, return on assets, and return on equity. In 2000, Walgreens' total assets were $7,103,700,000, and total stockholders' equity was $4,234,000,000. Comment on the relative performance of the two companies. (If you have done **FRA 5,** use the computations you made in that solution for Toys "R" Us.) In general, how does Walgreens' performance compare with the performance of Toys "R" Us with respect to liquidity and profitability? What distinguishes Walgreens' profitability performance from that of Toys "R" Us?

Fingraph® Financial Analyst™

FRA 7.

LO7 Analysis of Dell Computer Corporation or Toys "R" Us

Choose one or both of the following analyses:

1. *Alternative to FRA 3:* Analyze the balance sheet and income statement of Dell Computer Corporation <www.dell.com> using Fingraph Financial Analyst CD-ROM software. To do this assignment, you will need to enter the data from Dell's financial statements shown in this chapter. Complete part 1 of **FRA 3.** Prepare the memorandum required in part 2 of **FRA 3** separately.
2. *Alternative to FRA 5:* Refer to the Toys "R" Us <www.tru.com> annual report in the Supplement to this chapter. Analyze the Toys "R" Us balance sheet and income statement using Fingraph Financial Analyst CD-ROM software. Your instructor will specify which year to analyze. Complete requirements 1, 2, and 3 of **FRA 5.**

Internet Case

FRA 8.
LO7 **Annual Reports and Financial Analysis**

Select a large, well-known company and access its annual report online. Or, choose a company on the Needles Accounting Resource Center Web Site at http://accounting.college.hmco.com/students and use the links provided there to access the company's web site and its annual report. In the annual report of the company you have chosen, identify the four basic financial statements and the notes to the financial statements. Perform a liquidity analysis, including the calculation of working capital and the current ratio. Perform a profitability analysis, calculating profit margin, asset turnover, return on assets, debt to equity ratio, and return on equity. Be prepared to present your findings in class.

Supplement to Chapter 6

How to Read an Annual Report

More than 4 million corporations are chartered in the United States. Most of these are small, family-owned businesses. They are called *private* or *closely held corporations* because their common stock is held by only a few people and is not available for sale to the public. Larger companies usually find it desirable to raise investment funds from many investors by issuing common stock to the public. These companies are called *public companies.* Although they are fewer in number than private companies, their total economic impact is much greater.

Public companies must register their common stock with the Securities and Exchange Commission (SEC), which regulates the issuance and subsequent trading of the stock of public companies. One important responsibility of the management of public companies under SEC rules is to report each year to the company's stockholders on the financial performance of the company. This report, called an *annual report*, contains the annual financial statements and other information about the company. Annual reports, which are a primary source of financial information about public companies, are distributed to all the company's stockholders and filed with the SEC. When filed with the SEC, the annual report is called the 10-K because a Form 10-K is used to file the report. The general public may obtain an annual report by calling or writing the company or accessing it online at the company's web site. If a company has filed its 10-K electronically with the SEC, it may be accessed at **http://www.sec.gov/edgar.shtml**. Many libraries also maintain files of annual reports or have them available on electronic media, such as *Compact Disclosure.*

This supplement describes the major sections of the typical annual report and contains the annual report of one of the most successful retailers of this generation, Toys "R" Us, Inc. In addition to operating stores that sell toys and other items for children, the company has a chain of stores that sell children's clothes, called Kids "R" Us and a chain of stores devoted exclusively to babies, called Babies "R" Us. The Toys "R" Us annual report should be referred to in completing the case assignments related to the company in each chapter. For purposes of comparison, the supplement also includes the financial statements and notes to the financial statements of Walgreens, one of the largest drugstore chains in the United States.

The Components of an Annual Report

In addition to listing the corporation's directors and officers, an annual report contains a letter to the stockholders, a multiyear summary of financial highlights, a description of the company, management's discussion of operating results and financial conditions, the financial statements, notes to the financial statements, a report of management's responsibilities, the auditors' report, and supplementary information notes.

Letter to the Stockholders

Traditionally, an annual report begins with a letter in which the top officers of the corporation tell stockholders about the performance and prospects of the company. In its 2002 annual report, the president and chief executive officer of Toys "R" Us wrote to the stockholders about the highlights of the past year, the key priorities for the new year, store format and redeployment plans, corporate citizenship, and other aspects of the business. He reported on results as follows:

> 2002 was a year of encouraging progress, but a time of disappointments as well. Three divisions in our portfolio of businesses—Babies "R" Us, Toys "R" Us International, and Toysrus.com—enjoyed the best performances in their history. Those results, coupled with improved expense discipline, resulted in a 19% gain in net earnings, before restructuring and other charges in 2001, for Toys "R" Us, Inc. However, weaker results in Toys "R" Us U.S. and Kids "R" Us were very disappointing, despite progress in strategic execution in both divisions. . . .
>
> Nonetheless, we were encouraged by the progress we made in the execution of our strategy, which we believe further strengthened our ability to improve our performance in 2003 and beyond.

Financial Highlights

The financial highlights section of an annual report presents key statistics for a ten-year period and is often accompanied by graphs. The Toys "R" Us annual report, for example, gives key figures for operations, financial position, and number of stores at year end. Note that the financial highlights section often includes nonfinancial data, such as the number of stores.

Description of the Company

An annual report contains a detailed description of the products and divisions of the company. Some analysts tend to scoff at this section of the annual report because it often contains glossy photographs and other image-building material, but it should not be overlooked because it may provide useful information about past results and future plans.

Management's Discussion and Analysis

Management also presents a discussion and analysis of financial condition and results of operations. In this section, management explains the difference from one year to the next. For example, the management of Toys "R" Us describes the company's net sales in the following way:

> ***Comparison of Fiscal Year 2002 to 2001***
> We reported consolidated net sales of $11.3 billion for the 52-week fiscal year ended February 1, 2003 versus $11.0 billion for the 52-week fiscal year ended February 2, 2002, or a 3% increase in consolidated net sales. Our consolidated net sales were $11.2 billion for 2002, after excluding the impact of foreign currency translation, representing a 1% increase over 2001 net sales.

Its management of cash flows is described as follows:

> The seasonal nature of our business typically causes cash balances to decline from the beginning of the year through October as inventory increases for the holiday selling season and funds are used for construction of new stores, remodeling and other initiatives that normally occur in this period. The fourth quarter, including the holiday season, accounts for more than 40% of our net sales and substantially all of our operating earnings.

Financial Statements

All companies present four basic financial statements in their annual reports. As you can see in the annual report included with this supplement, Toys "R" Us presents statements of earnings (income statements), balance sheets, statements of cash flows, and statements of stockholders' equity (retained earnings).

The headings of all Toys "R" Us financial statements are preceded by the word *consolidated*. A corporation issues *consolidated* financial statements when it consists of more than one company and has combined their data for reporting purposes. For example, Toys "R" Us has combined the financial data of Kids "R" Us and Babies "R" Us with those of the Toys "R" Us stores.

Toys "R" Us provides several years of data for each financial statement: two years for the balance sheet and three years for the others. Financial statements presented in this fashion are called *comparative financial statements*. Such statements are in accordance with generally accepted accounting principles and help readers assess the company's performance over several years.

You may notice that the fiscal year for Toys "R" Us ends on the Saturday nearest the end of January, rather than on the same date each year. The reason is that Toys "R" Us is a retail company. It is common for retailers to end their fiscal years at a slow period after the busiest time of year.

In a note at the bottom of each page of the financial statements, Toys "R" Us reminds the reader that the accompanying notes are an integral part of the statements and must be consulted in interpreting the data.

STATEMENTS OF EARNINGS Toys "R" Us uses a multistep form of the income statement that shows gross margin as the difference between net sales and cost of sales (goods sold). Total operating expenses are deducted from gross margin to arrive at operating earnings (income). Interest expense is shown separately, and income taxes are deducted in another step. *Net earnings* is an alternative name for *net income*. The company also discloses the earnings per share, which is the net earnings divided by the weighted average number of shares of common stock held by stockholders during the year.

BALANCE SHEETS Toys "R" Us has a typical balance sheet for a merchandising company. In the assets and liabilities sections, the company separates out the current assets and the current liabilities. Current assets will become available as cash or be used up in the next year; current liabilities will have to be paid or satisfied in the next year. These groupings help in understanding the company's liquidity.

Several items in the stockholders' equity section need additional explanation. Common stock represents the number of shares outstanding at par value. Additional paid-in capital represents amounts invested by stockholders in excess of the par value of the common stock. Treasury shares is a deduction from stockholders' equity that represents the cost of previously issued shares that have been bought back and held by the company.

STATEMENTS OF CASH FLOWS Whereas the income statement reflects a company's profitability, the statement of cash flows reflects its liquidity. This statement provides information about a company's cash receipts, cash payments, and investing and financing activities during an accounting period.

Refer to the consolidated statements of cash flows in the Toys "R" Us annual report. The first major section shows cash flows from operating activities. It begins with the net earnings (income) from the consolidated statements of earnings and adjusts that figure to a figure that represents the net cash from operating activities. Among the adjustments are increases for depreciation and amortization, which are expenses that do not require the use of cash, and increases and decreases for the changes in the working capital accounts. In the year ended February 1, 2003, Toys "R" Us had net earnings of $229,000,000, and its net cash from operating activities was $574,000,000. Added to net income are such expenses as depreciation and amortization. Two small negative items were more than offset by a positive amount associated with deferred income taxes. Accounts and other receivables showed little change. Increases in merchandise inventories, prepaid expenses, and other operating assets contributed to declines in cash, as did a decrease in income taxes payable. An increase of $112,000,000 in accounts payable, accrued expenses, and other liabilities was a significant source of cash.

The second major section of the consolidated statements of cash flows is cash flows from investing activities. The main item in this category is capital expenditures, net, of $388,000,000. This figure demonstrates that Toys "R" Us is a growing company.

The third major section of the consolidated statements of cash flows is cash flows from financing activities. You can see here that the sources of cash from financing are long-term borrowings of $548,000,000 and issuance of stock of $266,000,000, which were helpful in making debt repayments of $141,000,000. In total, the company generated $613,000,000 in cash from financing activities during the year.

At the bottom of the consolidated statements of cash flows, the net effect of the operating, investing, and financing activities on the cash balance may be seen. Toys "R" Us had an increase in cash and cash equivalents during the year of $740,000,000 and ended the year with $1,023,000,000 of cash and cash equivalents on hand.

The supplemental disclosures of cash flow information show income tax and interest payments for the last three years.

■ **STATEMENTS OF STOCKHOLDERS' EQUITY** Instead of a simple statement of retained earnings, Toys "R" Us presents a *statement of stockholders' equity*. This statement explains the changes in five components of stockholders' equity.

NOTES TO THE FINANCIAL STATEMENTS

To meet the requirements of full disclosure, a company must add *notes to the financial statements* to help users interpret some of the more complex items. The notes are considered an integral part of the financial statements. In recent years, the need for explanation and further details has become so great that the notes often take more space than the statements themselves. The notes to the financial statements include a summary of significant accounting policies and explanatory notes.

■ **SUMMARY OF SIGNIFICANT ACCOUNTING POLICIES** Generally accepted accounting principles require that the financial statements include a *Summary of Significant Accounting Policies.* In most cases, this summary is presented in the first note to the financial statements or as a separate section just before the notes. In this summary, the company tells which generally accepted accounting principles it has followed in preparing the statements. For example, in the Toys "R" Us report, the company states the principles followed for property and equipment:

> Property and equipment are recorded at cost. Leasehold improvements represent capital improvements made to leased locations. Depreciation and amortization are provided using the straight-line method over the estimated useful lives of the assets or, where applicable, the terms of the respective leases, whichever is shorter.

Other important accounting policies listed by Toys "R" Us deal with fiscal year; reclassification; principles of consolidation; use of estimates; revenue recognition; advertising costs; cash and cash equivalents; merchandise inventories; credits and allowances received from vendors; cost of sales and selling, general, and administrative expenses; costs of computer software; financial instruments; and stock options.

■ Explanatory Notes Other notes explain some of the items in the financial statements. For example, Toys "R" Us showed the details of its Property and Equipment account, which is reproduced below.

Property and Equipment

	Useful Life (in years)	February 1, 2003	February 2, 2002
Land		$ 825	$ 811
Buildings	45–50	2,009	1,980
Furniture and equipment	5–20	1,786	1,800
Leasehold improvements	12½–35	1,726	1,542
Costs of computer software	5	192	127
Construction in progress		33	41
Leased property and equipment under capital lease		53	53
		6,624	6,354
Less accumulated depreciation and amortization		1,861	1,810
		$4,763	$4,544

Other notes had to do with restricted cash, merchandise inventories, goodwill, investment in Toys–Japan, seasonal financing and long-term debt, derivative instruments and hedging activities, issuance of common stock and equity security units, stockholders' equity, earnings per share, stock purchase warrants, leases, taxes on income, stock options, replacement of certain stock option grants with restricted stock, profit-sharing plan, Toysrus.com, segments, restructuring and other charges, gain from initial public offering of Toys–Japan, subsequent events, and other matters.

Report of Management's Responsibilities

A statement of management's responsibility for the financial statements and the internal control structure may accompany the financial statements. The management report of Toys "R" Us acknowledges management's responsibility for the integrity and objectivity of the financial information and for the system of internal controls. It mentions the company's internal audit program and its distribution of company policies to employees. It also mentions the Audit Committee of the Board of Directors and states that the company's financial statements have been audited.

Report of Certified Public Accountants

The *independent auditors' report* deals with the credibility of the financial statements. This report by independent certified public accountants gives the accountants' opinion about how fairly these statements have been presented. Using financial statements prepared by managers without an independent audit would be like having a judge hear a case in which he or she was personally involved. Management, through its internal accounting system, is logically responsible for recordkeeping because it needs similar information for its own use in operating the business. The

Figure 11
Auditors' Report for Toys "R" Us, Inc.

REPORT OF INDEPENDENT AUDITORS

To the Board of Directors and Stockholders
Toys"R"Us, Inc.

① We have audited the accompanying consolidated balance sheets of Toys"R"Us, Inc. and subsidiaries as of February 1, 2003 and February 2, 2002, and the related consolidated statements of earnings, stockholders' equity and cash flows for each of the three years in the period ended February 1, 2003. These financial statements are the responsibility of the company's management. Our responsibility is to express an opinion on these financial statements based on our audits.

② We conducted our audits in accordance with auditing standards generally accepted in the United States. Those standards require that we plan and perform the audit to obtain reasonable assurance about whether the financial statements are free of material misstatement. An audit includes examining, on a test basis, evidence supporting the amounts and disclosures in the financial statements. An audit also includes assessing the accounting principles used and significant estimates made by management, as well as evaluating the overall financial statement presentation. We believe that our audits provide a reasonable basis for our opinion.

③ In our opinion, the financial statements referred to above present fairly, in all material respects, the consolidated financial position of Toys"R"Us, Inc. and subsidiaries at February 1, 2003 and February 2, 2002, and the consolidated results of their operations and their cash flows for each of the three years in the period ended February 1, 2003, in conformity with accounting principles generally accepted in the United States.

④ As discussed in the note entitled "Goodwill," the company adopted SFAS No. 142, Goodwill and Other Intangible Assets, effective February 3, 2002.

Ernst & Young LLP
New York, New York
March 5, 2003

Source: Reprinted by permission of Toys "R" Us. The notes to the financial statement, which are an integral part of the report, are not included.

certified public accountants, acting independently, add the necessary credibility to management's figures for interested third parties. They report to the board of directors and the stockholders rather than to management.

In form and language, most auditors' reports are like the one shown in Figure 11. Usually such a report is short, but its language is very important. The report is usually divided into three parts, but it can have a fourth part if there is a need for further explanation.

1. The first paragraph identifies the financial statements subject to the auditors' report. This paragraph also identifies responsibilities. Company management is responsible for the financial statements, and the auditor is responsible for expressing an opinion on the financial statements based on the audit.
2. The second paragraph, or *scope section,* states that the examination was made in accordance with generally accepted auditing standards. These standards call for an acceptable level of quality in ten areas established by the American Institute of Certified Public Accountants. This paragraph also contains a brief description of the objectives and nature of the audit.
3. The third paragraph, or *opinion section,* states the results of the auditors' examination. The use of the word *opinion* is very important because the auditor does not certify or guarantee that the statements are absolutely correct. To do so would go beyond the truth, since many items, such as depreciation, are based on estimates. Instead, the auditors simply give an opinion about whether, overall, the financial statements "present fairly," in all material respects, the financial position, results of operations, and cash flows. This means that the statements are

prepared in accordance with generally accepted accounting principles. If, in the auditors' opinion, the statements do not meet accepted standards, the auditors must explain why and to what extent.

4. The optional fourth paragraph mentions the adoption of a new accounting standard.

Supplementary Information Notes

In recent years, the FASB and the SEC have ruled that certain supplemental information must be presented with financial statements. Examples are the quarterly reports that most companies present to their stockholders and to the SEC. These quarterly reports, called *interim financial statements,* are in most cases reviewed but not audited by the company's independent CPA firm. In its annual report, Toys "R" Us presents unaudited quarterly financial data from its 2002 quarterly statements, which are shown in the following table (for the year ended February 1, 2003; dollars in millions, except per share amounts):

	First Quarter	Second Quarter	Third Quarter	Fourth Quarter
Year Ended February 1, 2003				
Net Sales	$2,095	$2,070	$2,271	$4,869
Gross Margin	682	670	722	1,432
Net (Loss)/Earnings	(4)	(17)	(28)	278
Basic (Loss)/ Earnings per Share	$ (0.02)	$ (0.08)	$ (0.13)	$ 1.31
Diluted (Loss)/ Earnings per Share	$ (0.02)	$ (0.08)	$ (0.13)	$ 1.30

Interim data are presented for the prior year as well. Toys "R" Us also provides supplemental information on the market price of its common stock during the years and data on its store locations.

The Annual Report Project

Many instructors assign a term project that requires reading and analyzing a real annual report. The Annual Report Project described here has proved successful in the authors' classes. It may be used with the annual report of any company, including the Toys "R" Us annual report and the financial statements from the Walgreen Co. annual report that are provided with this supplement.

The extent to which financial analysis is required depends on the point in the course at which the Annual Report Project is assigned. Several options are provided in Instruction 3E, below.

INSTRUCTIONS:

1. Select any company from the list of Fingraph companies on the Needles Accounting Resource Center Web Site at http://accounting.college. hmco.com/students. Click on the company to access the Microsoft Excel spreadsheet for that company. Then click on the URL in the heading of the spreadsheet for a link to the company's web site and annual report. You may also obtain the annual report of a company of your own choice and access the company's annual report online or obtain it through your library or another source.
2. Library and Internet Research

   Go to the library or the Needles Accounting Resource Center Web Site (http://accounting.college.hmco.com/students) to learn about the company you have chosen and the industry in which it operates. Find at least two articles or other references to the industry and the company and summarize your findings.

   Also, access the company's Internet home page directly or through the Needles Accounting Resource Center. Review the company's products and services and find its financial information. Summarize what you have learned.
3. Your term project should consist of five or six double-spaced pages organized according to the following outline:

   A. Introduction

   Identify your company by writing a summary that includes the following elements:
   - Name of the chief executive officer
   - Location of the home office
   - Ending date of latest fiscal year
   - Description of the principal products or services that the company provides
   - Main geographic area of activity
   - Name of the company's independent accountants (auditors). In your own words, explain what the accountants said about the company's financial statements.
   - The most recent price of the company's stock and its dividend per share. Be sure to provide the date for this information.

   B. Industry Situation and Company Plans

   Describe the industry and its outlook; then summarize the company's future plans based on your library research and on reading the annual report. Be sure to read the letter to the stockholders. Include relevant information about the company's plans from that discussion.

C. Financial Statements

Income Statement: Is the format more like a single-step or multistep format? Determine gross profit, income from operations, and net income for the last two years; comment on the increases or decreases in these amounts.

Balance Sheet: Show that Assets = Liabilities + Stockholders' Equity for the past two years.

Statement of Cash Flows: Are cash flows from operations more or less than net income for the past two years? Is the company expanding through investing activities? What is the company's most important source of financing? Overall, has cash increased or decreased over the past two years?

D. Accounting Policies

What are the significant accounting policies, if any, relating to revenue recognition, cash, short-term investments, merchandise inventories, and property and equipment?

What are the topics of the notes to the financial statements?

E. Financial Analysis

For the past two years, calculate and discuss the significance of the following ratios:

Option (a): Basic (After Completing Chapters 1–6)

Liquidity Ratios
- Working capital
- Current ratio

Profitability Ratios
- Profit margin
- Asset turnover
- Return on assets
- Debt to equity ratio
- Return on equity

Option (b): Basic with Enhanced Liquidity Analysis (After Completing Chapters 1–10)

Liquidity Ratios
- Working capital
- Current ratio
- Receivable turnover
- Average days' sales uncollected
- Inventory turnover
- Average days' inventory on hand
- Operating cycle

Profitability Ratios
- Profit margin
- Asset turnover
- Return on assets
- Debt to equity ratio
- Return on equity

Option (c): Comprehensive (After Completing Chapters 1–18)

Liquidity Ratios
- Working capital
- Current ratio
- Receivable turnover
- Average days' sales uncollected
- Inventory turnover

- Average days' inventory on hand
- Payables turnover
- Average days' payable
- Operating cycle
- Financing period

Profitability Ratios
- Profit margin
- Asset turnover
- Return on assets
- Return on equity

Long-Term Solvency Ratios
- Debt to equity ratio
- Interest coverage

Cash Flow Adequacy
- Cash flow yield
- Cash flows to sales
- Cash flows to assets
- Free cash flow

Market Strength Ratios
- Price/earnings per share
- Dividends yield

Option (d): Comprehensive Using Fingraph® Financial Analyst™ Software on the CD-ROM That Accompanies This Text

Annual Report 2002

Shaping *our future and* *our brands*

This annual report is for the year ended February 1, 2003. Pages 1–5 and 20–48 reprinted by permission of Toys "R" Us, Inc.

Company Profile

We are one of the world's leading retailers of toys, children's apparel and baby products based on our consolidated net sales in 2002. As of February 1, 2003, we operated 1,595 "R"Us retail stores worldwide. These consist of 1,051 United States locations comprised of 681 toy stores under the name "Toys"R"Us," 183 infant-toddler stores under the name "Babies"R"Us," 146 children's clothing stores under the name "Kids"R"Us," 37 educational specialty stores under the name "Imaginarium" and 4 "Geoffrey" stores that include products from Toys"R"Us, Kids"R"Us and Babies"R"Us as well as many interactive events. Internationally, as of February 1, 2003, we operated 544 stores, including licensed and franchised stores, under the "R"Us name. We also sell merchandise through Internet sites at www.toysrus.com, www.babiesrus.com, www.imaginarium.com and www.giftsrus.com. Toys"R"Us, Inc. is incorporated in the state of Delaware.

Our History

Toys"R"Us got its start in 1948 when founder Charles Lazarus opened a baby furniture store, Children's Bargain Town, in Washington D.C. Lazarus quickly realized the potential of fulfilling customer's requests for baby toys and toys for older children.

In 1957, Lazarus introduced a "supermarket environment." That same year, the Toys"R"Us name made its debut, complete with a backwards "R". By 1966, Lazarus had four stores with approximately $12 million in annual sales. Around this time, Lazarus sold his stores to retail conglomerate Interstate Stores. He maintained responsibility for running Toys"R"Us, which continued to grow profitably. Interstate, however, faced major difficulties and was forced to declare bankruptcy. During this critical period, Lazarus led and restructured the company. In 1978, when Interstate emerged from bankruptcy it was renamed Toys"R"Us, Inc.

The 1980s were a time of major expansion for Toys"R"Us, Inc. In 1983, the company had 169 toy stores in 26 states and had added four stores under its new Kids"R"Us brand. The company opened its first international stores in Singapore and Canada in 1984. Just 10 years later, the company completed its 1993 fiscal year with 581 U.S. toy stores, 217 Kids"R"Us stores and 234 stores in international locations. In 2001, Toys"R"Us opened its flagship store in Times Square.

In 1996, the company opened its first Babies"R"Us store. The acquisition of Baby Superstore in 1997 added 76 locations and helped Babies"R"Us become the undisputed leader in the juvenile market. Imaginarium was acquired in 1998 to bring the learning and educational toy categories to the "R"Us family of retail stores. Between 2000 and 2002, Imaginarium boutiques were added to U.S. toy stores as part of the division's Mission Possible renovation. In addition, Imaginarium also operates 37 freestanding locations.

Geoffrey the Giraffe was first introduced in 1960. However, he didn't receive his name until 1970 when a contest was held among company associates to name him. In 2000, Geoffrey was reintroduced, in his current animatronic form, as the company's lovable wisecracking "spokesanimal." Today he's one of the world's most recognized icons by kids and grown-ups alike, representative of a worldwide chain of stores that has forever changed the way the world shops for toys.

financial highlights

Toys"R"Us, Inc. and Subsidiaries

(Dollars in millions, except per share data)	Fiscal Year Ended									
	Feb. 1, 2003	Feb. 2, 2002	Feb. 3, 2001	Jan. 29, 2000	Jan. 30, 1999	Jan. 31, 1998	Feb. 1, 1997	Feb. 3, 1996	Jan. 28, 1995	Jan. 29, 1994
Operations										
Total Enterprise Sales*	**$13,067**	$12,630	$12,774	$12,118	$11,459	$11,315	$10,113	$9,498	$8,819	$8,018
Net Sales	**11,305**	11,019	11,332	11,862	11,170	11,038	9,932	9,427	8,746	7,946
Net Earnings/(Loss)	**229**	67	404	279	(132)	490	427	148	532	483
Basic Earnings/(Loss) Per Share	**1.10**	0.34	1.92	1.14	(0.50)	1.72	1.56	0.54	1.88	1.66
Diluted Earnings/(Loss) Per Share	**1.09**	0.33	1.88	1.14	(0.50)	1.70	1.54	0.53	1.85	1.63
Financial Position at Year End										
Working Capital	**$ 1,182**	$ 657	$ 575	$ 35	$ 106	$ 579	$ 619	$ 326	$ 484	$ 633
Real Estate - Net	**2,398**	2,313	2,348	2,342	2,354	2,435	2,411	2,336	2,271	2,036
Total Assets	**9,397**	8,076	8,003	8,353	7,899	7,963	8,023	6,738	6,571	6,150
Long-Term Debt	**2,139**	1,816	1,567	1,230	1,222	851	909	827	785	724
Stockholders' Equity	**4,030**	3,414	3,418	3,680	3,624	4,428	4,191	3,432	3,429	3,148
Common Shares Outstanding	**212.5**	196.7	197.5	239.3	250.6	282.4	287.8	273.1	279.8	289.5
Number of Stores at Year End										
Toys"R"Us – U.S.	**681**	701	710	710	704	700	682	653	618	581
Toys"R"Us – International**	**544**	507	491	462	452	441	396	337	293	234
Babies"R"Us – U.S.	**183**	165	145	131	113	98	82	–	–	–
Kids"R"Us – U.S.	**146**	184	198	205	212	215	212	213	204	217
Imaginarium – U.S.	**37**	42	37	40	–	–	–	–	–	–
Geoffrey – U.S.	**4**	–	–	–	–	–	–	–	–	–
Total Stores	**1,595**	1,599	1,581	1,548	1,481	1,454	1,372	1,203	1,115	1,032

**Total enterprise sales consist of all Toys"R"Us branded net sales, which include net sales from all the company's stores and from the company's internet businesses, in addition to net sales from licensed and franchised stores.*

***Includes licensed and franchised stores.*

contents

Financial Highlights . . . . *page 1*

Letter to Our Shareholders . . . . *page 3*

Divisional Highlights . . . . *page 7*

Corporate Philanthropy and Corporate Responsibility . . . . *page 19*

Management's Discussion and Analysis of Results of Operations and Financial Condition . . . . . . *page 22*

Financial Statements . . . . *page 31*

Report of Management and Report of Independent Auditors . . . . *page 45*

Directors and Officers . . . . *page 46*

Quarterly Financial Data and Market Information . . . . . . *page 48*

Store Locations, Corporate Data and Stockholder Information . . . . *page 49*

Building our portfolio of brands

TOYS R US® KIDS R US® BABIES R US

letter to our shareholders

Performance and Progress

A year in review

John Eyler
Chairman and Chief
Executive Officer

2002 was a year of encouraging progress, but a time of disappointments as well. Three divisions in our portfolio of businesses – Babies"R"Us, Toys"R"Us International and Toysrus.com – enjoyed the best performances in their history. Those results, coupled with improved expense discipline resulted in a 19% gain in net earnings, before restructuring and other charges in 2001, for Toys"R"Us, Inc. However, weaker results in Toys"R"Us U.S. and Kids"R"Us were very disappointing, despite progress in strategic execution in both divisions.

The performance of our U.S. toy stores did not meet our expectations. Our comparable store sales declined 1% for the year and, in a difficult retail environment, our operating earnings declined as well.

Nonetheless, we were encouraged by the progress we made in the execution of our strategy; which we believe further strengthened our ability to improve our performance in 2003 and beyond. For example, by working closely with our vendors last year, we gained market share in core toy, defined as the Boys and Girls, Learning (i.e. Imaginarium) and Preschool categories. Our core toy sales outpaced toy industry performance, as reported by the Toy Industry Association, by 4% for the year.

We continued to improve our in-stock position, content, presentation and service levels. In addition, we experienced significant improvements in customer satisfaction scores related to pricing and value perception. Both messages were effectively reinforced through our award-winning television commercials featuring our charismatic "spokesanimal," Geoffrey the Giraffe.

We enjoyed historically high levels of success in several of our divisions in 2002. Babies"R"Us and Toys"R"Us International both turned in record-setting operating earnings for the fourth quarter and full year of 2002. In addition, Toysrus.com achieved operating profitability in the fourth quarter – a full year ahead of schedule. Our Kids"R"Us division has been struggling in its stand-alone stores for some time now, but we have seen positive results from sourcing apparel through Kids"R"Us for our Babies"R"Us stores as well as our Toys"R"Us/Kids"R"Us combo stores. Currently, our total apparel business represents approximately $900 million in sales per year, at above company average profit margins, and we expect continued growth. Approximately 65% of these sales come from exclusive products that generate higher margins than nationally branded items. We'll talk about these divisions in greater detail in this report.

Geoffrey the Giraffe helped boost consumer awareness for Toys"R"Us in 2002.

maginarium® TOYSRUS.COM® Geoffrey™

We worked diligently in 2002 to improve our productivity, reduce expenses and enhance our financial strength.

We took steps to strengthen our balance sheet and improve our liquidity. As a result, we had substantial excess liquidity in early November during our seasonal borrowing peak, and ended the fiscal year with more than $1 billion in cash.

We reduced capital spending significantly in 2002. Net capital expenditures were $398 million in 2002 as compared to $705 million in 2001.

We made solid progress on our commitment to reduce selling, general and administrative (SG&A) expenses by 200 basis points by 2005. We were able to achieve a reduction of 70 basis points in 2002, so we're approximately a third of the way to achieving our four-year objectives in the first year.

We will also continue to find ways to strengthen and expand our portfolio, and, in fact, made progress in the development of new businesses for the future in 2002. Our test of Toys"R"Us ToyBox, our store concept within grocery stores which first opened in the summer of 2001, is generating positive results. By the end of the year, we expanded our initial test to more than 30 stores, and we are currently evaluating further expansion opportunities for 2003.

The customer response to our recently launched Geoffrey stores has been positive.

We also launched Geoffrey, which is a combination Toys"R"Us, Kids"R"Us and Babies"R"Us store, in four smaller markets in 2002. The customer response has been positive, and we've already derived some key learnings from Geoffrey that may be applicable to our other divisions. We plan to move forward carefully with this concept, but we are encouraged by the results we've seen.

Challenges for 2003

We are committed to doing all it takes to turn the U.S. toy stores around and to expand further on the successes that we've seen. This progress clearly indicates that we are on the right track with our strategies. Our challenge and our commitment is to build on what we've accomplished. We will accelerate execution of our merchandising, presentation, customer service, pricing and advertising efforts designed to drive traffic and increase profitable sales. Knowing that we also need the support of our vendor community to succeed, we continue to work in partnership with them to build excitement for their brands and to re-energize underperforming product categories.

We will accelerate execution of our strategies in 2003.

We will also continue to improve our cost effectiveness to reduce our SG&A even further in 2003. In March, we reduced our national headquarters staff by approximately 200 positions, or 10%. We also announced that we would combine our Kids"R"Us and Babies"R"Us management teams into one group. This will help Kids"R"Us reduce its operating costs. In addition, we will ensure that our balance sheet remains strong and that we have ample liquidity now and into the future.

Babies"R"Us registers more expectant parents than any other retailer in the U.S.

I think it truly says something about the strength of our portfolio that even in a year where we did not see the kind of success we expected in the largest division of our company, we were still able to announce a meaningful earnings increase. As we look to the future, I'm very proud of the steps that we've taken to manage the business in an undeniably difficult operating environment.

Conclusion

As I write this letter, our associates from all divisions and all disciplines are working with tremendous commitment to make ours a more profitable organization. They share my absolute conviction that in 2003 we will seize upon every opportunity to drive sales and profits across every division. Given the solid improvement in our earnings in 2002, despite very difficult and uncertain economic and world environments, we believe we have ample evidence that we're on the right track. We will build on that progress, and we will not stop until we can deliver a better value for your investment and repay your faith in our company.

John H. Eyler, Jr.
Chairman, President and Chief Executive Officer
March 29, 2003

Responding
to our
World

The Demand for Corporate **Responsibility**

Corporate Governance

Corporate governance is a joint responsibility requiring the involvement of and interaction between the Board of Directors and the senior management of the company.

Toys"R"Us, Inc. is fortunate to have a talented Board of Directors committed to the success of the company. For example, during fiscal year 2002, 11 Board meetings and 34 additional Board committee meetings were held. At several of the Board meetings, the Board met in executive session, outside the presence of senior management, to further discuss and examine issues of importance to the company.

After many months of careful research, investigation and thought, the Board adopted Corporate Governance Guidelines of the company in March 2002 to reflect the Board's commitment to monitor the effectiveness of policy and decision-making, both at the Board and management level, and to enhance stockholder value over the long term. Those Guidelines covered such issues as conflicts of interest, the compensation of the company's Chief Executive Officer and other Board members, the process and criteria for selecting Board members and the requirements that the Audit, Compensation and former Corporate Governance Committees be comprised solely of independent Board members and that independent Board members constitute a substantial majority of the Board.

In the past year, the Board has adopted Amended and Restated Corporate Governance Guidelines of the company that further address those issues and cover such issues as director orientation and continuing education and the Board's retention of independent advisors, as well as the requirement that the new Corporate Governance and Nominating Committee be comprised solely of independent Board members. The current Guidelines and committee charters are published in the company's proxy materials filed with the SEC in 2003.

The Toys"R"Us Board of Directors is fully engaged in and focused on the strategic issues facing our business. Each year, the Board devotes one meeting to develop, discuss and refine the company's long-range operating plan and overall corporate strategy. Following the Board's annual strategic meeting, the Board reviews the progress of one or more strategic initiatives at each scheduled meeting. Through the established procedures, the Board, consistent with good corporate governance, encourages the long-term success of the company by exercising sound and independent business judgment on the strategic issues that are important to the company's business.

Code of Conduct for Suppliers

There is growing concern in the global community about working conditions in many nations, including the United States, which may fall below the basic standards of fair and humane treatment. In an effort to source products in a manner that is both socially responsible and profitable, Toys"R"Us, Inc. developed its Code of Conduct for Suppliers program in 1997.

Implementation of the Code and the use of SA8000®, an independent monitoring and factory certification program, enable the company and its business partners to continually improve their performance in relation to workers' rights, labor standards and other human rights issues integral to the manufacturing process.

Developed by Social Accountability International (SAI) in 1998 and currently in use by businesses and governments around the world, SA8000® assessments are widely recognized by trade unions and non-governmental organizations as a powerful tool for creating environments where both workers and management benefit. Facilities in more than 20 nations and 15 industries have been SA8000® certified.

Participation in the Toys"R"Us Code of Conduct program and compliance with all of its provisions is mandatory for all suppliers who sell products, for the purpose of resale, to any Toys"R"Us, Inc. division. The company will terminate its business relationship with any supplier that elects not to participate in the Code of Conduct program or fails to abide by any of its stated provisions.

The Toys"R"Us Code of Conduct includes provisions covering the following issues: Child Labor, Forced Labor, Worker Environment, Working Conditions, Discrimination, Wages & Hours, and Freedom of Association.

Suppliers must post copies of the Toys"R"Us Code of Conduct for all workers to view. The company also encourages suppliers to implement their own Code of Conduct that meets or exceeds the provisions of the Toys"R"Us, Inc. program.

Inquiries about the Toys"R"Us Code of Conduct can be directed to: Vice President of Product Development, Safety Assurance & Imports, Toys"R"Us, Inc., 461 From Road, Paramus, NJ 07652.

Management's Discussion and Analysis

of Results of Operations and Financial Condition

RESULTS OF OPERATIONS

Comparison of Fiscal Year 2002 to 2001

We reported consolidated net sales of $11.3 billion for the 52-week fiscal year ended February 1, 2003 versus $11.0 billion for the 52-week fiscal year ended February 2, 2002, or a 3% increase in consolidated net sales. Our consolidated net sales were $11.2 billion for 2002, after excluding the impact of foreign currency translation, representing a 1% increase over 2001 net sales.

Total enterprise sales consist of all Toys"R"Us branded net sales from all of our stores and from our internet businesses, and the net sales from international licensed and franchised stores. We believe that enterprise sales are useful in analyzing the worldwide strength of our family of brands:

(In billions)	2002	2001	2000
Consolidated net sales	**$ 11.3**	$ 11.0	$ 11.3
Licensed and franchised net sales	**1.8**	1.6	1.5
Total enterprise sales	**$ 13.1**	$ 12.6	$ 12.8

Our consolidated comparable store sales, in local currencies, were flat for the fourth quarter and the fiscal year. Comparable store sales for our U.S. toy store division declined 1% for both the fourth quarter and the full year. Video game sales, which include sales of video hardware, software and accessories, were the primary factor contributing to these decreases. The video game category posted an 18% decline for the fourth quarter and a 13% decline for the year. The introduction of three video platforms (X-Box, Gamecube and Gameboy Advance) drove strong video sales in 2001. The performance of the video game category was also negatively impacted by significant reductions in the retail prices of video game platforms this year, such as the reduction in retail price from $299 to $199 for X-Box and PlayStation 2, and a reduction in retail price from $199 to $149 for Gamecube. Video game sales accounted for approximately 19% of our total U.S. toy store sales, excluding apparel sales, in the fourth quarter of 2002, down from 22% in 2001. Juvenile product sales in our U.S. toy stores declined 8% for the full year, mainly due to a shift of some sales to Babies"R"Us stores in the same markets. However, our core toy sales, which include boys and girls, learning and preschool toy categories, increased 3% in 2002.

Our International division reported comparable toy store sales increases, in local currencies, of 5% for the fourth quarter and 6% for the full year. These increases were primarily driven by the strong performance of our toy stores in the United Kingdom and Spain. We continued to expand the presence of in-store shops, such as Universe of Imagination (learning and educational products), Animal Alley (plush), Teentronics (electronic entertainment products) and Babies"R"Us (newborn and infant products). In addition, the penetration of exclusive products in the International division continues to grow, and, as a result, contributed to the improvement of our gross margin in this division.

Our Babies"R"Us division reported 12% net sales growth for the full year, primarily driven by the opening of 19 new Babies"R"Us stores in the United States this year. This division reported a 2% increase in comparable store sales for the fourth quarter and a 3% increase for the full year. A variety of initiatives helped to drive sales and guest traffic, including the rollout of extended apparel sizing to all stores and the addition of in-store photo studios in 21 Babies"R"Us stores.

Toysrus.com reported a net sales increase of 11% for the fourth quarter and 23% for the full year. Growth in the on-line toy business and the Babiesrus.com (baby products), Imaginarium.com (learning products) and the new Giftsrus.com (personalized gifts) on-line stores were factors in the sales performance of Toysrus.com.

We record the costs associated with operating our distribution network as a part of selling, general and administrative expenses (SG&A), including those costs that primarily relate to moving merchandise from distribution centers to stores. Therefore, our consolidated gross margin may not be comparable to some other retailers which include similar costs in their cost of sales. Our consolidated gross margin, as a percentage of sales, increased by 0.4% for the fourth quarter and was flat at 31.0% for the full year. Our consolidated gross margin for the fourth quarter of 2001 included $27 million of store closing markdowns, which were recorded as part of the restructuring and other charges announced in January 2002. Credits and allowances from vendors, which are netted against our cost of sales, have a positive impact on our consolidated gross margin. These credits and allowances increased our consolidated gross margin by 0.4% for the year, primarily in support of our increased promotional activities. Our U.S. toy store division reported a 0.7% decline in gross margin for the fourth quarter and a 0.8% decline for the full year. These declines were primarily attributed to the impact of increased promotional activity, such as our "Low Price Super Stars" pricing campaign, as well as the impact of higher markdowns recorded to keep our inventories fresh. Our International toy store division reported a 0.3% increase in gross margin to 32.2% for the year, primarily due to our continued emphasis on exclusive products which carry higher margins. Our Babies"R"Us division reported a 1.0% improvement in gross margin to 36.0%, primarily due to a shift in sales mix to higher margin import product. Gross margin for Toysrus.com improved 2.7% to 24.8%, reflecting an ongoing mix shift toward higher margin juvenile and learning products, as well as lower markdowns due to decreased inventory levels this year.

Our consolidated SG&A, as a percentage of net sales, increased 0.3% to 18.3% for the fourth quarter of 2002. This increase was primarily due to an increase in net advertising expense as a result of our decision to defer certain of our advertising activities to this year's fourth quarter. Our consolidated SG&A, as a percentage of sales, decreased 0.7% to 24.0% for the full year, primarily as a result of our continued focus on expense control. During 2002, we implemented shared services in a variety of functional groups, which, along with other efforts, helped us to achieve the overall reduction in SG&A as a percentage of sales. Advertising allowances, which are netted against

SG&A and have a positive impact on our SG&A, did not significantly vary year over year. SG&A for our U.S. toy store division decreased in absolute dollars, however it remained flat as a percentage of sales at 22.6% for the year. SG&A for the Babies"R"Us division decreased 0.2% to 23.6% for the year, primarily as a function of expense control coupled with higher sales productivity. SG&A for our International toy store business was reduced by 0.2% to 22.6% for the year. SG&A for Toysrus.com decreased for the year, due to lower fulfillment costs associated with product bundling, and a reduction in net advertising costs. The SG&A decrease, as well as an increase in Toysrus.com's net sales for the year, contributed to the overall reduction in consolidated SG&A, as a percentage of sales.

Depreciation and amortization increased by $9 million to $317 million for the year. Depreciation and amortization for 2001 included $13 million related to the amortization of goodwill. We ceased amortizing this goodwill on February 3, 2002 when we adopted the provisions of Statement of Financial Accounting Standard No. 142, "Goodwill and Other Intangible Assets,"(SFAS No. 142) (see the section "Recent Accounting Pronouncements"). Therefore, excluding the 2001 goodwill amortization, depreciation and amortization increased by $22 million for the year. This increase was primarily due to our Mission Possible store remodeling program, new store openings, and strategic investments to improve our management information systems. These increases were partially offset by the impact of closed stores. As part of the restructuring initiatives announced in January 2002, we closed 37 Kids"R"Us stores and 27 Toys"R"Us stores in the United States.

Interest expense, net of interest income, increased by $4 million to $23 million for the fourth quarter of 2002 and increased by $1 million to $110 million for the full year. These increases in net interest expense are mainly attributable to increased long-term borrowings, partly offset by increased cash investments, lower short-term borrowings and a decrease in interest rates.

Our effective tax rate was 36.5% versus 26.9% in the prior year. Our 2001 effective tax rate was impacted by the reversal of prior years' charges included in restructuring and other charges recorded in 2001.

Foreign currency translation had a 3% favorable impact on our consolidated net earnings for the fourth quarter of 2002 and a 4% favorable impact on our consolidated net earnings for the full year of 2002. Inflation did not have a significant impact on our full year consolidated net earnings for 2002.

Fourth Quarter Results

Our business is highly seasonal, with net sales and net earnings typically highest in the fourth quarter due to the inclusion of the holiday selling season. Fourth quarter 2002 net earnings were $278 million compared with $158 million in 2001. Diluted earnings per share were $1.30 for the fourth quarter of 2002 compared with $0.78 in 2001. Total consolidated comparable store sales, in local currencies, were flat in the fourth quarter of 2002 compared with an increase of 2% in 2001. Our results for 2001 included restructuring and other charges of $213 million ($126 million, net of taxes). Excluding the impact of these charges, net earnings were $284 million and diluted earnings per share were $1.39 for the fourth quarter of 2001.

Fourth Quarter Net Sales by Segment

(In millions)	**2002**	2001	2000
Toys"R"Us – U.S.	**$3,114**	$3,202	$3,270
Toys"R"Us – International	**1,069**	915	907
Babies"R"Us	**381**	342	335
Toysrus.com[1]	**193**	174	140
Other[2]	**112**	126	147
Total	**$4,869**	$4,759	$4,799

Fourth Quarter Operating Earnings by Segment

(In millions)	**2002**	2001	2000
Toys"R"Us – U.S.[3]	**$ 271**	$ 331	$ 335
Toys"R"Us – International	**157**	131	128
Babies"R"Us	**40**	29	29
Toysrus.com, net of minority interest[4]	**3**	(17)	(54)
Other[3], [5]	**(9)**	(35)	(13)
Restructuring and other charges	**–**	(186)	–
Total	**$ 462**	$ 253	$ 425

(1) Includes the sales of Toysrus.com – Japan.

(2) Includes the sales of the Kids"R"Us and Geoffrey divisions.

(3) Includes markdowns related to the store closings announced as part of the restructuring in 2001.

(4) Includes the operations of Toysrus.com – Japan, net of minority interest.

(5) Includes corporate expenses, the operating results of the Kids"R"Us and Geoffrey divisions and the equity in net earnings of Toys"R"Us – Japan, Ltd. (Toys – Japan).

Comparison of Fiscal Year 2001 to 2000

We reported consolidated net sales of $11.0 billion for the 52-week fiscal year ended February 2, 2002 versus $11.3 billion for the 53-week fiscal year ended February 3, 2001. Net sales of Toys – Japan, which has been accounted for on the "equity method" since its initial public offering, are included in our consolidated net sales in the first quarter of 2000 and excluded from our net sales thereafter. Our consolidated net sales were $11.0 billion for both years, after excluding sales of Toys – Japan. Currency translation did not have a significant impact on our consolidated net sales in 2001.

Total enterprise sales, which consist of all Toys"R"Us branded net sales from all of our stores and from our internet businesses, and the net sales from international licensed and franchised stores, were $12.6 billion in 2001 versus $12.8 billion in 2000.

Our consolidated comparable store sales, in local currencies, declined 1%. Comparable store sales for our U.S. toy store division increased 2% for the fourth quarter and declined 1% for the fiscal year. Video game sales were the primary drivers of the fourth quarter increase due to the introduction of X-Box, Gamecube and Gameboy Advance in the latter half of the year. Video game sales accounted for approximately 22% of our total U.S. toy store sales, excluding apparel sales, in the fourth quarter of 2001 as compared to 18% in the fourth quarter of the prior year. We had 433 stores in the Mission Possible format by the start of the 2001 holiday season, which also contributed to the comparable store sales increase in the fourth quarter. This gain partially offset the negative impact of 268 stores under construction during the first nine months of 2001 that were retrofitted to the Mission Possible format, as well as the negative impact resulting from the events of the September 11th terrorist attacks. Our International division reported comparable toy store sales increases of 5%, in local currencies, primarily driven by the performance of our toy stores in the United Kingdom, which reported double-digit comparable store sales growth. Our Babies"R"Us division reported 8% net sales growth, primarily driven by the opening of 20 new Babies"R"Us stores in the United States this year, as well as a 2% comparable store sales increase. Toysrus.com reported a net sales increase of 24% for the fourth quarter and 54% for the full year, which continued to reflect increases in its market share and the impact of the Toysrus.com alliance with Amazon.com that began in 2000.

Our consolidated gross margin, as a percentage of net sales, remained flat at 31.0%. Our consolidated margin for 2001 included $27 million of store closing markdowns, which were recorded as part of the restructuring and other charges announced in January 2002, and our consolidated margin for 2000 included $10 million of markdowns resulting from the alliance between Toysrus.com and Amazon.com. Excluding the impact of these items, our consolidated gross margin would have increased from 31.0% to 31.2%. Credits and allowances from our vendors, which are netted against our gross margin and have a positive impact on our cost of sales, did not vary significantly. Gross margin for the U.S. toy store division decreased 0.2% to 30.1% due to the impact of $15 million in store closing markdowns, that we recorded with the 2001 restructuring and other charges. The Babies"R"Us division reported a 1.2% improvement in gross margin to 35.0%, primarily due to a favorable sales shift to higher margin juvenile import and proprietary product. Our International toy store business reported a 0.2% increase in gross margin to 31.9%, primarily due to our continued emphasis on exclusive products.

Our consolidated SG&A, as a percentage of net sales, remained flat at 24.7% for the full year. Our consolidated SG&A for 2000 included $85 million of non-recurring charges related to the alliance between Toysrus.com and Amazon.com. Excluding these charges, our 2000 consolidated SG&A would have been 24.0% of sales. A reduction in advertising allowances, which are netted against SG&A and have a positive impact on SG&A, accounted for 0.3% of the increase in consolidated SG&A. SG&A for our U.S. toy store division increased 1.1% to 22.6%, reflecting the strategic investments we made in our business, including the renovation of our U.S. toy stores to the Mission Possible format and certain guest focused initiatives, both of which accounted for approximately 1.0% of this increase. Additional SG&A expenses resulting from the September 11th events accounted for approximately 0.1% of this increase. SG&A for our International toy store business increased 0.1% to 22.8%. SG&A for the Babies"R"Us division increased 0.4% to 23.8%, primarily attributable to increased payroll costs to support our emphasis on guest focused initiatives.

Depreciation and amortization increased by $18 million, primarily due to the Mission Possible store remodeling program, continued new store expansion and strategic investments to improve our management information systems.

Interest expense decreased by $10 million, primarily due to lower interest rates, partially offset by the impact of higher average total debt outstanding during the year. Interest and other income decreased by $15 million, primarily due to lower average investments outstanding, as well as lower interest rates.

Our effective tax rate declined to 26.9% from 36.5%. The reduction in our effective tax rate was due to the impact of the restructuring and other charges recorded in 2001.

Neither foreign currency exchange nor inflation had a significant impact on our consolidated net earnings in 2001.

Restructuring and Other Charges

In January 2002, we announced plans to reposition our business and, as part of this plan, we closed 27 non-Mission Possible format Toys"R"Us stores and 37 Kids"R"Us stores. In conjunction with the Kids"R"Us store closings in most all of these locations, we converted the nearest Toys"R"Us store into a Toys"R"Us/Kids"R"Us combo store.

As part of this plan, we eliminated approximately 1,700 staff positions in our stores and our headquarters. In addition, these plans included the costs of consolidating five of our store support center facilities into our new headquarters in Wayne, New Jersey, in 2003.

The costs associated with the facilities' consolidation, elimination of positions, and other actions designed to improve efficiency in support functions were $79 million, of which $15 million related to severance. The costs associated with store closings were $73 million for Kids"R"Us and $85 million for Toys"R"Us, of which $27 million was recorded in cost of sales. The fair value of the facilities to be consolidated and stores identified for closure were obtained from third party appraisals. We also reversed $24 million of previously accrued charges ($11 million from the 1998 charge and $13 million from the 1995 charge) that we determined to be no longer needed. Accordingly, based on these actions, we recorded $213 million of pre-tax ($126 million after-tax) restructuring and other charges in the fourth quarter of the fiscal year ending February 2, 2002. Details on the components of the charges are as follows:

Description (in millions)	Initial charge	Utilized in 2001	Reserve balance at 2/02/02	Utilized in 2002	Adjustments to charge in 2002	Reserve balance at 2/01/03
Store closing:						
Lease commitments	$ 52	$ –	$ 52	$ (11)	$ –	$ 41
Severance	4	–	4	(4)	–	–
Write-down of property and equipment	75	(75)	–	–	–	–
Markdowns	27	–	27	(27)	–	–
Store support center consolidation:						
Lease commitments	28	–	28	–	11*	39
Write-down of property and equipment	29	(29)	–	–	–	–
Severance	15	–	15	(9)	(1)	5
Other	7	(7)	–	–	–	–
Total restructuring and other charges	**$237**	**$(111)**	**$126**	**$ (51)**	**$ 10**	**$ 85**

**In the fourth quarter of 2002, we determined that the reserve for lease costs for the disposition of one of our store support center facilities needed to be increased and, accordingly, recorded an additional charge of $11 million.*

In 2000, Toysrus.com, our internet subsidiary, recorded $118 million in non-recurring charges as a result of the transition to its co-branded on-line store with Amazon.com, of which $10 million was included in cost of sales and $108 million was included in SG&A. These costs and charges related primarily to the closure of three distribution centers, as well as web-site asset write-offs and other costs. We had remaining lease commitment reserves of $3 million at February 1, 2003, that will be utilized in 2003 and thereafter.

We previously announced strategic initiatives to reposition our worldwide business and recorded related restructuring and other charges of $698 million in 1998 and $396 million in 1995 to complete these initiatives. As of February 1, 2003, we substantially completed all announced initiatives. We reversed reserves of $10 million in the fourth quarter of 2002 that were determined to no longer be needed. We also reversed reserves of $29 million in 2001, $24 million of which were reversed in the fourth quarter of 2001 and is discussed above, and $11 million in 2000 that were determined to no longer be needed. We had $42 million of reserves remaining at February 1, 2003, primarily for long-term lease commitments that will be utilized in 2003 and thereafter.

We believe that the remaining reserves at February 1, 2003 are reasonable estimates of what is required to complete all remaining initiatives.

Liquidity and Capital Resources

Our contractual obligations mainly consist of operating leases related to real estate used in the operation of our business and long-term debt. The table below shows the amounts we are obligated to pay for operating leases and principal amounts due under long-term debt issuances by fiscal period:

Contractual Obligations at February 1, 2003 (in millions)

	Amounts due in Fiscal 2003	Amounts due in Fiscal 2004 and Fiscal 2005	Amounts due in Fiscal 2006 and Fiscal 2007	Amounts due subsequent to 2007	Total
Operating leases*	$ 317	$ 615	$ 552	$ 1,786	$ 3,270
Sub-leases to third parties	17	26	20	40	103
Net operating lease obligations	300	589	532	1,746	3,167
Capital lease obligations	6	9	2	1	18
Long-term debt	367	541	697**	723	2,328
Minimum royalty obligations	14	7	–	–	21
Other obligations	2	4	–	–	6
Total contractual obligations	**$ 689**	**$ 1,150**	**$ 1,231**	**$ 2,470**	**$ 5,540**

**Includes synthetic lease obligation for our new headquarters facility in Wayne, New Jersey as described in the section "Critical Accounting Policies" and the note to our consolidated financial statements entitled "LEASES."*

***Includes $390 million of equity security units, due 2007, which we are obligated to remarket in 2005. See the section "Financing Activities" and the note to our consolidated financial statements entitled "ISSUANCE OF COMMON STOCK AND EQUITY UNITS."*

We are in compliance with all covenants associated with the above contractual obligations. The covenants include, among other things, requirements to provide financial information and public filings, and to comply with specified financial ratios. Non-compliance with associated covenants could give rise to accelerated payments, requirements to provide collateral, or changes in terms contained in the respective agreements.

At February 1, 2003, we had available over $1 billion of cash and cash equivalents. Our current portion of long-term debt of $379 million at February 1, 2003 includes a 475 million Swiss Franc note, due on January 28, 2004. In addition, our long-term debt at February 1, 2003 includes a 500 million Euro bond, due on February 13, 2004. See the section "Other Matters" and the note to our consolidated financial statements entitled "SUBSEQUENT EVENTS" for a discussion regarding the registration of $800 million of debt securities in March 2003 and the sale and issuance of $400 million of notes in April 2003.

We have $985 million in unsecured committed revolving credit facilities from a syndicate of financial institutions. These credit facilities are available for seasonal borrowings. There were no outstanding balances under these credit facilities at the end of fiscal 2002, 2001 or 2000. Additionally, we have lines of credit with various banks to meet certain of the short-term financing needs of our foreign subsidiaries. The following table shows our commercial commitments with their related expirations and availability:

Commercial Commitments at February 1, 2003 (in millions)

	Amount of commitment expiration per fiscal period					
	Total amounts committed	Fiscal 2003	Fiscal 2004 and Fiscal 2005	Fiscal 2006 and Fiscal 2007	Fiscal 2008 and subsequent	Amounts available at February 1, 2003
Unsecured revolving credit facilities:						
Facility expiring in September 2006	$ 685	$ –	$ –	$ 685	$ –	$ 685
364-day facility expiring August 25, 2003	300	300	–	–	–	300
Total unsecured revolving credit facilities	$ 985	$ 300	$ –	$ 685	$ –	$ 985

Cash requirements for operating and investing activities will be met primarily through use of our exisiting cash and cash equivalents, cash flows from operating activities, and utilization of our unsecured committed revolving credit facilities. At February 1, 2003, we had in place stand-by letters of credit of $360 million, primarily as a guarantee for a debt obligation and $75 million of outstanding letters of credit related to import merchandise.

Credit Ratings

	Moody's	Standard & Poor's
Long-term debt	Baa3	BBB-
Commercial paper	P-3	A-3
Outlook	Negative	Stable
Date of last rating update	March 19, 2003	March 5, 2003

Our debt instruments do not contain provisions requiring acceleration of payment upon a debt rating downgrade. We continue to be confident in our ability to refinance maturing debt. Other credit ratings for our debt are available; however we disclosed above only ratings of the two largest nationally recognized statistical rating organizations because we believe these are the most relevant to our business.

The seasonal nature of our business typically causes cash balances to decline from the beginning of the year through October as inventory increases for the holiday selling season and funds are used for construction of new stores, remodeling and other initiatives that normally occur in this period. The fourth quarter, including the holiday season, accounts for more than 40% of our net sales and substantially all of our operating earnings.

Operating Activities

Our net cash inflows from operating activities increased to $574 million in 2002 from net cash inflows of $504 million in 2001 and net cash outflows of $151 in 2000. Net earnings, as adjusted for non-cash items, of $600 million in 2002 and $425 million in 2001 were the primary drivers of the net cash inflows from operations in those years. The net cash outflows from operations in 2000 were primarily driven by an increase in merchandise inventories of $486 million, and a net decrease in accounts payable, accrued expenses and other liabilities of $178 million, and was partially offset by net earnings, as adjusted for non-cash items, of $444 million for that year.

Investing Activities

Capital expenditures, net of dispositions, were $398 million in 2002, $705 million in 2001 and $402 million in 2000. Capital expenditures during these periods include investments to: open 55 new Babies"R"Us stores in the United States; open 18 new Toys"R"Us stores internationally; reformat our existing Toys"R"Us store base in the United States to our Mission Possible format and remodel 41 existing Kids"R"Us stores to our R-Generation store format; convert 286 existing Toys"R"Us stores into Toys"R"Us/Kids"R"Us combo stores; improve and enhance our management information systems.

During 2003, we plan to reduce our capital expenditures for our business to less than $350 million. We plan to open approximately 20 new Babies"R"Us stores in the United States and approximately five new international Toys"R"Us stores, and we also plan to continue to improve and enhance our management information systems in 2003.

Financing Activities

Net cash inflows from financing activities were $613 million in 2002, primarily driven by net long-term borrowings of $407 million, as well as proceeds received from the issuance of our common stock and contracts to purchase common stock totaling $266 million. In May 2002, we issued 14,950,000 shares of our common stock at a price of $17.65 per share and received net proceeds of $253 million. On the same date, we issued 8,050,000 equity security units with a stated amount of $50 per unit and received net proceeds of $390 million. Each security unit consists of a contract to purchase, for $50, a specified number of shares of Toys"R"Us common stock in August 2005, and a senior note due in 2007 with a principal amount of $50. The fair value of the contract to purchase shares of Toys"R"Us common stock was estimated at $1.77 per equity security unit. The fair value of the senior note was estimated at $48.23 per equity security unit. Interest on the senior notes is payable quarterly at an initial rate of 6.25%. We are obligated to remarket the notes in May 2005 at the then prevailing interest rate for similar notes. If the remarketing were not to be successful, we would be entitled to take possession of the senior notes, and the holder's obligation under the contracts to purchase shares of our common stock would be deemed to have been satisfied. The net proceeds from these public offerings were used to refinance short-term borrowings and for other general corporate purposes.

Net cash inflows from financing activities were $191 million in 2001, primarily as a result of net borrowings of $216 million during the year. In July 2001, we issued and sold $750 million of notes, comprised of $500 million of notes bearing interest at 7.625% per annum, maturing in 2011, and $250 million of notes bearing interest at 6.875% per annum, maturing in 2006. The proceeds from these notes were used to reduce outstanding commercial paper obligations. Simultaneously with the sale of the notes, we entered into interest rate swap agreements. As a result of the interest rate swap agreements, interest on the $500 million notes accrues at an effective rate of LIBOR plus 1.5120% and interest on the $250 million notes accrues at an effective rate of LIBOR plus 1.1515%. In October 2002, we terminated a portion of the interest rate swap agreeements and received a payment of $27 million, which is being amortized over the remaining lives of the related notes. Concurrently, we entered into new interest rate swap agreements. Of the $500 million notes, $200 million accrues interest at an effective rate of LIBOR plus 3.06%, and $125 million of the $250 million notes accrues interest at an effective rate of LIBOR plus 3.54%. Interest is payable on both notes semi-annually on February 1 and August 1 of each year. In February 2001, we borrowed 500 million EURO through the public issuance of a EURO bond bearing interest at 6.375% per annum. The obligation was swapped into a $466 million fixed rate obligation with an effective rate of 7.43% per annum with interest payments due annually and principal due February 13, 2004.

Net cash outflows from financing activities were $2 million for 2000. Net borrowings for 2000 were $521 million and were used primarily to repurchase 42 million shares of our common stock, to fund increased inventory levels, and to fund our Toysrus.com internet subsidiary. In 2000, we received a total of $97 million from SOFTBANK Venture Capital and affiliates representing their 20% minority interest investment in Toysrus.com.

Other Matters

On March 24, 2003, we filed a "shelf" registration statement with the Securities and Exchange Commission giving us the capability to sell up to $800 million of debt securities that would be used to repay outstanding debt and for general corporate purposes. In April 2003, we sold and issued $400 million in notes bearing interest at a coupon rate of 7.875%, maturing on April 15, 2013. The notes were sold at a price of 98.305%, resulting in an effective yield of 8.125%. Simultaneously with the sale of the notes, we entered into interest rate swap agreements. As a result of these swap agreements, interest will accrue at the effective rate of LIBOR plus 3.622%. Interest is payable semi-annually commencing on October 15, 2003. We plan to use the proceeds from these notes for the repayment of indebtedness maturing in the 2004 calendar year, and pending such repayment, for working capital needs and other general corporate purposes.

In August 2000, eleven purported class action lawsuits were filed (six in the United States District Court for the District of New Jersey, three in the United States District Court for the Northern District of California, one in the United States District Court for the Western District of Texas and one in the Superior Court of the State of California, County of San Bernardino), against us and our affiliates Toysrus.com, Inc. and Toysrus.com, LLC. In September 2000, three additional purported class action lawsuits were filed (two in the United States District Court for the District of New Jersey and one in the United States District Court for the Western District of Texas). These actions generally purport to bring claims under federal privacy and computer fraud statutes, as well as under state statutory and common law, on behalf of all persons who have visited one or more of our websites and either made an online purchase or allegedly had information about them unlawfully "intercepted," "monitored," "transmitted," or "used." All the suits (except one filed in the United States District Court for the District of New Jersey) also named Coremetrics, Inc. (Coremetrics) as a defendant. Coremetrics is an internet marketing company with whom we have an agreement. These suits seek damages in unspecified amounts and other relief under state and federal law.

With Coremetrics, we filed a joint application with the Multidistrict litigation panel which resulted in all of the federal actions being consolidated and transferred to the United States District Court for the Northern District of California. Plaintiffs voluntarily dismissed the action in the Superior Court of the State of California, County of San Bernardino without prejudice. On October 16, 2001, plaintiffs filed an amended complaint in the United States District Court for the Northern District of California. We believe that we have substantial defenses to all of these claims. On November 13, 2002, we entered into a settlement agreement with plaintiffs in connection with all causes of action. This settlement agreement is subject to the court's review and approval and will not have a material impact on our consolidated financial statements.

We are party to certain other litigation, which, in our judgment, based in part on the opinion of legal counsel, will not have a material adverse effect on our consolidated financial statements.

In August 2000, Toysrus.com entered into a 10-year strategic alliance with Amazon.com to operate a co-branded toy and video game on-line store, which was launched in the third quarter of 2000. In addition, a co-branded baby products on-line store was launched in May 2001 and a co-branded creative and learning products on-line store was launched in July 2001. Under this alliance, Toysrus.com and Amazon.com are responsible for specific aspects of the on-line stores. Toysrus.com is responsible for merchandising, marketing and content for the co-branded store. Toysrus.com also identifies, buys, owns and manages the inventory. Amazon.com handles web-site development, order fulfillment, guest service, and the housing of Toysrus.com's inventory in Amazon.com's U.S. distribution centers. Also in August 2000, Amazon.com was granted a warrant entitling it to acquire up to 5% (subject to dilution under certain circumstances) of the capital of Toysrus.com at the then market value. This warrant has not been exercised.

We recorded a non-operating gain of $315 million ($200 million net of taxes) resulting from the initial public offering of shares of Toys – Japan, which was completed in April 2000. Of this gain, $91 million resulted from an adjustment to the basis of our investment in Toys – Japan, and $224 million was related to the sale of a portion of company-owned common stock of Toys – Japan, for which we received net cash proceeds of $267 million. In connection with this transaction, we recorded a provision for current income taxes of $82 million and a provision for deferred income taxes of $33 million. As a result of this transaction, our ownership percentage in the common stock of Toys – Japan was reduced from 80% to 48%. Toys – Japan is a licensee of our company.

Quantitative and Qualitative Disclosures About Market Risks

We are exposed to market risk from potential changes in interest rates and foreign exchange rates. The countries in which we own assets and operate stores are politically stable, and we regularly evaluate these risks and have taken the following measures to mitigate these risks: our foreign exchange risk management objectives are to stabilize cash flow from the effects of foreign currency fluctuations; we do not participate in speculative hedges; and we will, whenever practical, offset local investments in foreign currencies with liabilities denominated in the same currencies. We also enter into derivative financial instruments to hedge a variety of risk exposures, including interest rate and currency risks.

Our foreign currency exposure is primarily concentrated in the United Kingdom, Europe, Canada, Australia and Japan. We face currency exposures that arise from translating the results of our worldwide operations into U.S. dollars from exchange rates that have fluctuated from the beginning of the period. We also face transactional currency exposures relating to merchandise that we purchase in foreign currencies. We enter into forward exchange contracts to minimize and manage the currency risks associated with these transactions. The counter-parties to these contracts are highly rated financial institutions and we do not have significant exposure to any one counter-party. Gains or losses on these derivative instruments are largely offset by the gains or losses on the underlying hedged transactions. For foreign currency derivative instruments, market risk is determined by calculating the impact on fair value of an assumed one-time change in foreign rates relative to the U.S. dollar. Fair values were estimated based on market prices, where available, or dealer quotes. With respect to derivative instruments outstanding at February 1, 2003, a 10% appreciation of the U.S. dollar would have increased pre-tax earnings in 2002 by $39 million, while a 10% depreciation of the U.S. dollar would have decreased pre-tax earnings in 2002 by $42 million. Comparatively, considering our derivative instruments outstanding at February 2, 2002, a 10% appreciation of the U.S. dollar would have increased pre-tax earnings in 2001 by $13 million, while a 10% depreciation of the U.S. dollar would have decreased pre-tax earnings in 2001 by $13 million.

We are faced with interest rate risks resulting from interest rate fluctuations. We have a variety of fixed and variable rate debt instruments. In an effort to manage interest rate exposures, we strive to achieve an acceptable balance between fixed and variable rate debt and have entered into interest rate swaps to maintain that balance. For interest rate derivative instruments, market risk is determined by calculating the impact to fair value of an assumed one-time change in interest rates across all maturities. Fair values were estimated based on market prices, where available, or dealer quotes. A change in interest rates on variable rate debt is assumed to impact earnings and cash flow, but not the fair value of debt. A change in interest rates on fixed rate debt is assumed to impact the fair value of debt, but not earnings and cash flow. Based on our overall interest rate exposure at February 1, 2003 and February 2, 2002, a 1% increase in interest rates would have decreased pre-tax earnings by $15 million in 2002 and $11 million in 2001, respectively. A 1% decrease in interest rates would have increased pre-tax earnings by $15 million in 2002 and $11 million in 2001. A 1% increase in interest rates would decrease the fair value of our long-term debt at February 1, 2003 and February 2, 2002 by approximately $90 million and $79 million, respectively. A 1% decrease in interest rates would increase the fair value of our long-term debt at February 1, 2003 and February 2, 2002 by approximately $98 million and $87 million, respectively.

See notes to our consolidated financial statements for additional discussion of our outstanding derivative financial instruments at February 1, 2003.

Critical Accounting Policies

Our consolidated financial statements have been prepared in accordance with accounting principles generally accepted in the United States. The preparation of these financial statements requires us to make certain estimates and assumptions that affect the reported amounts of assets, liabilities, revenues and expenses, and the related disclosure of contingent assets and liabilities as of the date of the financial statements and during the applicable periods. We base these estimates on historical experience and on other various assumptions that we believe to be reasonable under the circumstances. Actual results may differ materially from these estimates under different assumptions or conditions and could have a material impact on our consolidated financial statements.

We believe the following are some of the critical accounting policies that include significant judgments and estimates used in the preparation of our consolidated financial statements.

Inventories and Vendor Allowances:
Merchandise inventories for the U.S. toy store division, which represent approximately 60% of total merchandise inventories, are stated at the lower of LIFO (last-in, first-out) cost or market value, as determined by the retail inventory method. All other merchandise inventories are stated at the lower of FIFO (first-in, first-out) cost or market value, as determined by the retail inventory method.

We receive various types of merchandise and other types of allowances from our vendors, which are based on negotiated terms. We use estimates at interim periods to record our provisions for inventory shortage and to record vendor funded merchandise allowances. These estimates are based on available data and other factors and are adjusted to actual amounts at the completion of our physical inventories and finalization of all vendor allowances.

Deferred Tax Assets:
As part of the process of preparing our consolidated financial statements, we are required to estimate our income taxes in each of the jurisdictions in which we operate. This process involves estimating our actual current tax exposure, together with assessing temporary differences resulting from differing treatment of items for tax and accounting purposes. These differences result in deferred tax assets and liabilities, which are included within our consolidated balance sheet. The measurement of deferred tax assets is adjusted by a valuation allowance to recognize the extent to which, more likely than not, the future tax benefits will be recognized.

At February 1, 2003, we recorded deferred tax assets, net of valuation allowances, of $317 million. We believe it is more likely than not that we will be able to realize these assets through the reduction of future taxable income. We base this belief upon the levels of taxable income historically generated by our businesses, as well as projections of future taxable income. If future levels of taxable income are not consistent with our expectations, we may be required to record an additional valuation allowance, which could reduce our net earnings by a material amount.

Derivatives and Hedging Activities:
We enter into derivative financial arrangements to hedge a variety of risk exposures, including interest rate and currency risks associated with our long-term debt, as well as foreign currency risk relating to import merchandise purchases. We account for these hedges in accordance with SFAS No. 133, "Accounting for Derivative Instruments and Hedging Activities," and we record the fair value of these instruments within our consolidated balance sheet. Gains and losses from derivative financial instruments are largely offset by gains and losses on the underlying transactions. At February 1, 2003, we increased the carrying amount of our long-term debt by $172 million, representing the fair value of debt in excess of the carrying amount on that date. Also at February 1, 2003, we recorded derivative assets of $158 million and derivative liabilities of $10 million. While we intend to continue to meet the conditions for hedge accounting, if hedges were not to be highly effective in offsetting cash flows attributable to the hedged risk, the changes in the fair value of the derivatives used as hedges could have a material effect on our consolidated financial statements.

Insurance Risks:
We insure a substantial portion of our general liability and workers' compensation risks through a wholly-owned insurance subsidiary, in addition to third party insurance coverage. Provisions for losses related to self-insured risks are based upon independent actuarially determined estimates. While we believe these provisions for losses to be adequate, the ultimate liabilities may be in excess of, or less than, the amounts recorded.

Stock Options:
We account for stock options under Accounting Principles Board Opinion No. 25, "Accounting for Stock Issued to Employees", which does not require compensation costs related to stock options to be recorded in net income, as all options granted under the various stock option plans had an exercise price equal to the market value of the underlying common stock at grant date. SFAS No. 148 "Accounting for Stock-Based Compensation – Transition and Disclosure – an amendment of SFAS No. 123," provides guidance on acceptable approaches to the implementation of SFAS No. 123, and requires more prominent disclosures of pro forma net earnings and earnings per share determined as if the fair value method of accounting for stock options had been applied in measuring compensation cost. Stock options are further detailed in the note to our consolidated financial statements entitled "STOCK OPTIONS."

Synthetic Lease:
Our new corporate headquarters facility, located in Wayne, New Jersey, is financed under a lease arrangement commonly referred to as a "synthetic lease." Under this lease, unrelated third parties, arranged by Wachovia Development Corporation, a multi-purpose real estate investment company, will fund up to $125 million for the acquisition and construction of the facility. Upon completion of the construction, which is expected to be in 2003, we will begin to pay rent on the facility until the lease expires in 2011. The rent will be based on a mix of fixed and variable interest rates, which will be applied against the final amount funded. Upon expiration of the lease, we would expect to either: renew the lease arrangement; purchase the facility from the lessor; or remarket the property on behalf of the owner. The lease agreement provides the lessor with a residual value guarantee equal to the funding for the acquisition and construction of the facility. Under accounting principles generally accepted in the United States, this arrangement is required to be treated as an operating lease for accounting purposes and as a financing for tax purposes.

Recent Accounting Pronouncements

In 2002, the FASB Emerging Issues Task Force issued EITF issue No. 02-16, "Accounting by a Reseller for Cash Consideration Received from a Vendor" (EITF 02-16). EITF 02-16 considers vendor allowances as a reduction in the price of a vendor's product that should be recognized as a reduction of cost of sales. Advertising allowances that are received for specific, identifiable and incremental costs are considered a reduction of advertising expenses and should be recognized as a reduction of SG&A. The provisions of EITF 02-16 are effective for all new arrangements, or modifications to existing arrangements, beginning after December 31, 2002. We are currently evaluating the potential impact of the provisions of EITF 02-16 on our consolidated financial statements for 2003.

In January 2003, the Financial Accounting Standards Board (FASB) issued Interpretation No. 46, "Consolidation of Variable Interest Entities" (FIN 46), which will require the consolidation of entities that are controlled by a company through interests other than voting interests. Under the requirements of this interpretation, an entity that maintains a majority of the risks or rewards associated with Variable Interest Entities (VIEs), commonly known as special purpose entities, is effectively in the same position as the parent in a parent-subsidiary relationship. Disclosure requirements of VIEs are effective in all financial statements issued after January 31, 2003. The consolidation requirements apply to all VIEs created after January 31, 2003. FIN 46 requires public companies to apply the consolidation requirements to VIEs that existed prior to February 1, 2003 and remained in existence as of the beginning of annual or interim periods beginning after June 15, 2003. Our new corporate headquarters facility, located in Wayne, New Jersey, is leased from unrelated third parties, arranged by a multi-purpose real estate investment company that we do not control. In addition, we do not have the majority of the associated risks or rewards. Accordingly, we believe that FIN 46 will have no impact on the accounting for this synthetic lease. The synthetic lease is discussed above and in the note to our consolidated financial statements entitled "LEASES." We believe that FIN 46 will not have a material impact on our consolidated financial statements.

In November 2002, the FASB issued Interpretation No. 45, "Guarantor's Accounting and Disclosure Requirements for Guarantees, Including Indirect Guarantees of Indebtedness of Others" (FIN 45), which imposes new disclosure and liability-recognition requirements for financial guarantees, performance guarantees, indemnifications and indirect guarantees of the indebtedness of others. FIN 45 requires certain guarantees to be recorded at fair value. This is different from previous practice, where a liability would typically be recorded only when a loss is probable and reasonably estimable. The initial recognition and initial measurement provisions are applicable on a prospective basis to guarantees issued or modified after December 31, 2002. FIN 45 also requires new disclosures, even when the likelihood of making any payments under the guarantee is remote. The disclosure requirements are effective for interim and annual periods ending after December 15, 2002. We have procedures to identify guarantees contained in the various legal documents and agreements that have been executed, and those to be executed in the future, that fall within the scope of FIN 45. We expect that FIN 45 will not have a material impact on our consolidated financial statements.

In July 2002, the FASB issued SFAS No. 146, "Accounting for Costs Associated with Exit or Disposal Activities" (SFAS No. 146), which addresses the recognition, measurement, and reporting of costs associated with exit or disposal activities and supercedes Emerging Issues Task Force issue No. 94-3, "Liability Recognition for Certain Employee Termination Benefits and Other Costs to Exit an Activity (including Certain Costs Incurred in a Restructuring)," (EITF No. 94-3). The fundamental difference between SFAS No. 146 and EITF No. 94-3 is the requirement that a liability for a cost associated with an exit or disposal activity be recognized when the liability is incurred rather than at the date an entity commits to an exit plan. A fundamental conclusion of SFAS No. 146 is that an entity's commitment to a plan, by itself, does not create an obligation that meets the definition of a liability. SFAS No. 146 also establishes that the initial measurement of a liability recognized be recorded at fair value. The provisions of this statement are effective for exit or disposal activities that are initiated after December 31, 2002, with early application encouraged. We believe that the adoption of this pronouncement will not have a significant effect on our consolidated financial statements.

In August 2001, the FASB issued SFAS No. 144, "Accounting for the Impairment or Disposal of Long-Lived Assets" (SFAS No. 144), which addresses financial accounting and reporting for the impairment or disposal of long-lived assets and supersedes SFAS No. 121, "Accounting for the Impairment of Long-Lived Assets and for Long-Lived Assets to be Disposed Of." We adopted SFAS No. 144 as of February 3, 2002 and the adoption did not have a significant effect on our consolidated financial statements.

In July 2001, the FASB issued SFAS No. 142, "Goodwill and Other Intangible Assets" (SFAS No. 142), which is effective for fiscal years beginning after December 15, 2001. SFAS No. 142 changes the accounting for goodwill from an amortization method to an impairment only approach. We adopted this pronouncement on February 3, 2002. As a result of this adoption, amortization of $348 million of goodwill, which was to be amortized ratably through 2037, ceased. Based on the historical and projected operating results of the reporting units to which the goodwill relates, we determined that no impairment of this goodwill exists. Application of the non-amortization provisions of SFAS No. 142 resulted in an increase in net earnings of $2 million for the fourth quarter of 2002 and $8 million for the 2002 fiscal year.

Forward Looking Statements

This annual report contains "forward looking" statements within the meaning of Section 27A of the Securities Act of 1933, as amended, and Section 21E of the Securities Exchange Act of 1934, which are intended to be covered by the safe harbors created thereby. All statements that are not historical facts, including statements about our beliefs or expectations, are forward-looking statements. We generally identify these statements by words or phrases such as "anticipate," "estimate," "plan," "expect," "believe," "intend," "foresee," "will," "may," and similar words or phrases. These statements discuss, among other things, our strategy, store openings and renovations, future performance and anticipated cost savings, results of our restructuring, anticipated international development and other goals and targets. Such statements involve risks and uncertainties that exist in our operations and business environment that could render actual outcomes and results materially different than predicted. Our forward-looking statements are based on assumptions about many factors, including, but not limited to, ongoing competitive pressures in the retail industry, changes in consumer spending and consumer preferences, general economic conditions in the United States and other jurisdictions in which we conduct our business (such as interest rates, currency exchange rates and consumer confidence) and normal business uncertainty. While we believe that our assumptions are reasonable at the time forward-looking statements were made, we caution that it is impossible to predict the actual outcome of numerous factors and, therefore, readers should not place undue reliance on such statements. Forward-looking statements speak only as of the date they are made, and we undertake no obligation to update such statements in light of new information or future events that involve inherent risks and uncertainties. Actual results may differ materially from those contained in any forward-looking statement.

Consolidated Statements of Earnings

Toys"R"Us, Inc. and Subsidiaries

(in millions, except per share data)	**February 1, 2003**	February 2, 2002	Year Ended February 3, 2001
Net sales	**$ 11,305**	$ 11,019	$ 11,332
Cost of sales	**7,799**	7,604	7,815
Gross margin	**3,506**	3,415	3,517
Selling, general and administrative expenses	**2,718**	2,721	2,801
Depreciation and amortization	**317**	308	290
Restructuring and other charges	**–**	186	–
Total operating expenses	**3,035**	3,215	3,091
Operating earnings	**471**	200	426
Other (expense) income:			
Interest expense	**(119)**	(117)	(127)
Interest and other income	**9**	8	23
Gain from IPO of Toys – Japan	**–**	–	315
Earnings before income taxes	**361**	91	637
Income taxes	**132**	24	233
Net earnings	**$ 229**	$ 67	$ 404
Basic earnings per share	**$ 1.10**	$ 0.34	$ 1.92
Diluted earnings per share	**$ 1.09**	$ 0.33	$ 1.88

See notes to consolidated financial statements.

Consolidated Balance Sheets

Toys"R"Us, Inc. and Subsidiaries

(In millions)	February 1, 2003	February 2, 2002
Assets		
Current Assets:		
Cash and cash equivalents	$ 1,023	$ 283
Restricted cash	60	–
Accounts and other receivables	202	210
Merchandise inventories	2,190	2,041
Prepaid expenses and other current assets	85	97
Total current assets	3,560	2,631
Property and Equipment:		
Real estate, net	2,398	2,313
Other, net	2,365	2,231
Total property and equipment	4,763	4,544
Goodwill, net	348	348
Derivative assets	158	42
Other assets	568	511
	$ 9,397	$ 8,076
Liabilities and Stockholders' Equity		
Current Liabilities:		
Short-term borrowings	$ –	$ –
Accounts payable	896	878
Accrued expenses and other current liabilities	824	738
Income taxes payable	279	319
Current portion of long-term debt	379	39
Total current liabilities	2,378	1,974
Long-term debt	2,139	1,816
Deferred income taxes	545	447
Derivative liabilities	10	122
Other liabilities	282	276
Minority interest in Toysrus.com	13	27
Stockholders' Equity:		
Common stock	30	30
Additional paid-in capital	414	444
Retained earnings	5,457	5,228
Accumulated other comprehensive loss	(149)	(267)
Treasury shares, at cost	(1,722)	(2,021)
Total stockholders' equity	4,030	3,414
	$ 9,397	$ 8,076

See notes to consolidated financial statements.

Consolidated Statements of Cash Flows

Toys"R"Us, Inc. and Subsidiaries

(In millions)	February 1, 2003	February 2, 2002	Year Ended February 3, 2001
Cash Flows from Operating Activities			
Net earnings	**$ 229**	$ 67	$ 404
Adjustments to reconcile net earnings to net cash from operating activities:			
Depreciation and amortization	**317**	308	290
Deferred income taxes	**99**	(6)	67
Minority interest in Toysrus.com	**(14)**	(24)	(52)
Other non-cash items	**(31)**	(29)	50
Restructuring and other charges	**–**	109	–
Gain from initial public offering of Toys – Japan	**–**	–	(315)
Changes in operating assets and liabilities:			
Accounts and other receivables	**8**	15	(69)
Merchandise inventories	**(100)**	217	(486)
Prepaid expenses and other operating assets	**(18)**	36	(54)
Accounts payable, accrued expenses and other liabilities	**112**	(241)	(178)
Income taxes payable	**(28)**	52	192
Net cash from operating activities	**574**	504	(151)
Cash Flows from Investing Activities			
Capital expenditures, net	**(398)**	(705)	(402)
Net proceeds from sale of Toys – Japan common stock	**–**	–	267
Reduction in cash due to deconsolidation of Toys – Japan	**–**	–	(15)
Net cash from investing activities	**(398)**	(705)	(150)
Cash Flows from Financing Activities			
Short-term borrowings, net	**–**	(588)	419
Long-term borrowings	**548**	1,214	147
Long-term debt repayment	**(141)**	(410)	(45)
Proceeds from issuance of stock and contracts to purchase stock	**266**	–	–
Increase in restricted cash	**(60)**	–	–
Exercise of stock options	**–**	19	2
Proceeds received from investors in Toysrus.com	**–**	–	97
Share repurchase program	**–**	(44)	(632)
Issuance of stock warrants	**–**	–	10
Net cash from financing activities	**613**	191	(2)
Effect of exchange rate changes on cash and cash equivalents	**(49)**	18	(6)
Cash and Cash Equivalents			
Increase/(decrease) during year	**740**	8	(309)
Beginning of year	**283**	275	584
End of year	**$ 1,023**	$ 283	$ 275
Supplemental Disclosures of Cash Flow Information			
Income tax payments (refunds), net	**$ 32**	$ (22)	$ (2)
Interest payments	**$ 93**	$ 85	$ 128

See notes to consolidated financial statements.

Consolidated Statements of Stockholders' Equity

Toys"R"Us, Inc. and Subsidiaries

	Common Stock							
	Issued		In Treasury		Additional paid-in capital	Accumulated other comprehensive loss	Retained earnings	Total stockholders' equity
(In millions)	Shares	Amount	Shares	Amount				
Balance, January 29, 2000	300.4	$ 30	(61.1)	$ (1,423)	$ 453	$ (137)	$ 4,757	$ 3,680
Net earnings for the year	–	–	–	–	–	–	404	404
Foreign currency translation adjustments	–	–	–	–	–	(74)	–	(74)
Comprehensive income								330
Share repurchase program	–	–	(42.1)	(632)	–	–	–	(632)
Issuance of restricted stock, net	–	–	–	50	(21)	–	–	29
Exercise of stock options, net	–	–	0.3	4	(3)	–	–	1
Issuance of stock warrants	–	–	–	–	10	–	–	10
Balance, February 3, 2001	300.4	$ 30	(102.9)	$ (2,001)	$ 439	$ (211)	$ 5,161	$ 3,418
Net earnings for the year	–	–	–	–	–	–	67	67
Foreign currency translation adjustments	–	–	–	–	–	(55)	–	(55)
Unrealized loss on hedged transactions	–	–	–	–	–	(1)	–	(1)
Comprehensive income								11
Share repurchase program	–	–	(2.1)	(44)	–	–	–	(44)
Issuance of restricted stock, net	–	–	0.5	5	4	–	–	9
Exercise of stock options, net	–	–	0.8	19	1	–	–	20
Balance, February 2, 2002	300.4	$ 30	(103.7)	$ (2,021)	$ 444	$ (267)	$ 5,228	$ 3,414
Net earnings for the year	–	–	–	–	–	–	229	229
Foreign currency translation adjustments	–	–	–	–	–	127	–	127
Unrealized loss on hedged transactions	–	–	–	–	–	(9)	–	(9)
Comprehensive income								347
Common stock equity offering	–	–	14.9	301	(35)	–	–	266
Issuance of restricted stock, net	–	–	0.9	(2)	5	–	–	3
Balance, February 1, 2003	**300.4**	**$ 30**	**(87.9)**	**$ (1,722)**	**$ 414**	**$ (149)**	**$ 5,457**	**$ 4,030**

See notes to consolidated financial statements.

Notes to Consolidated Financial Statements

Toys"R"Us, Inc. and Subsidiaries

(Amounts in millions, except per share data)

SUMMARY OF SIGNIFICANT ACCOUNTING POLICIES

Fiscal Year

The company's fiscal year ends on the Saturday nearest to January 31. References to 2002, 2001, and 2000 are for the 52 weeks ended February 1, 2003 and February 2, 2002 and the 53 weeks ended February 3, 2001.

Reclassification

Certain reclassifications have been made to prior periods to conform to current presentations.

Principles of Consolidation

The consolidated financial statements include the accounts for the company and its subsidiaries. All material intercompany balances and transactions have been eliminated. Assets and liabilities of foreign operations are translated at current rates of exchange at the balance sheet date while results of operations are translated at average rates in effect for the period. Unrealized translation gains or losses are shown as a component of accumulated other comprehensive loss within stockholders' equity.

Use of Estimates

The preparation of financial statements in conformity with accounting principles generally accepted in the United States requires management to make estimates and assumptions that affect the amounts reported in the consolidated financial statements and accompanying notes. Actual results could differ from those estimates.

Revenue Recognition

The company recognizes sales revenue at the time the guest takes possession of merchandise or at the point of sale in our stores, or at the time of delivery for products purchased from our web-sites. Layaway transactions are recognized as revenue when the guest satisfies all payment obligations and takes possession of the merchandise. Revenues from the sale of gift cards and issuance of store credits are recognized as they are redeemed.

Advertising Costs

Net advertising costs are included in selling, general and administrative expenses and are expensed at the point of first broadcast or distribution. Net advertising costs were $147, $160, and $135 for 2002, 2001 and 2000, respectively.

Cash and Cash Equivalents

The company considers its highly liquid investments with original maturities of less than three months to be cash equivalents.

Merchandise Inventories

Merchandise inventories for the U.S. toy store division, which represent approximately 60% of total inventories, are stated at the lower of LIFO (last-in, first-out) cost or market, as determined by the retail inventory method. All other merchandise inventories are stated at the lower of FIFO (first-in, first-out) cost or market, as determined by the retail inventory method.

Credits and Allowances Received from Vendors

Credits and allowances are received from vendors and are related to formal agreements negotiated with such vendors. These credits and allowances are predominantly for cooperative advertising, promotions, and volume related purchases. These credits and allowances, excluding advertising allowances, are netted against cost of sales. The company's policy is to recognize credits, that are related directly to inventory purchases, as the related inventory is sold. Cooperative advertising allowances offset the cost of cooperative advertising that is agreed to by the company and its vendors, and are netted against advertising expenses included in selling, general and administrative expenses. The company's policy is to recognize cooperative advertising allowances in the period that the related advertising media is run.

Cost of Sales and Selling, General and Administrative Expenses

The significant components of the line item "Cost of sales" include the cost to acquire merchandise from vendors; freight in; markdowns; provision for inventory shortages; and discounts and allowances related to merchandise inventories.

The significant components of the line item "Selling, general and administrative expenses" include store payroll and related payroll benefits; rent and other store operating expenses; net advertising expenses; costs associated with operating the company's distribution network that primarily relate to moving merchandise from distribution centers to stores; and other corporate-related expenses.

Property and Equipment

Property and equipment are recorded at cost. Leasehold improvements represent capital improvements made to leased locations. Depreciation and amortization are provided using the straight-line method over the estimated useful lives of the assets or, where applicable, the terms of the respective leases, whichever is shorter. Accelerated depreciation methods are used for income tax reporting purposes with recognition of deferred income taxes for the resulting temporary differences. The company periodically evaluates the need to recognize impairment losses relating to long-lived assets. If indications of impairment exist and if the value of the assets are impaired, an impairment loss would be recognized.

Costs of Computer Software

The company capitalizes certain costs associated with computer software developed or obtained for internal use in accordance with the provisions of Statement Of Position No. 98-1, "Accounting for the Costs of Computer Software Developed or Obtained for Internal Use," issued by the American Institute of Certified Public Accountants. The company's policy provides for the capitalization of costs from the acquisition of external materials and services associated with developing or obtaining internal use computer software. Certain payroll costs for employees that are directly associated with internal use computer software projects are capitalized once specific criteria are met. The amount of payroll costs capitalized is limited to the time directly spent on computer software projects. Costs associated with preliminary stage activities, training, maintenance and all other post-implementation stage activities are expensed as incurred. All costs capitalized in connection with internal use computer software projects are amortized on a straight-line basis over a useful life of five years.

Financial Instruments

The company adopted the provisions of Statement of Financial Accounting Standards No. 133, "Accounting for Derivative Instruments and Hedging Activities" (SFAS No. 133), as amended, effective February 4, 2001, as discussed in the footnote entitled "DERIVATIVE INSTRUMENTS AND HEDGING ACTIVITIES." This statement requires that all derivatives be recorded on the balance sheet at fair value and that changes in fair value be recognized currently in earnings unless specific hedge accounting criteria is met.

The company enters into forward foreign exchange contracts to minimize the risk associated with currency movement relating to its short-term intercompany loan program with foreign subsidiaries. Gains and losses, which offset the movement in the underlying transactions, are recognized as part of such transactions. Gross deferred unrealized losses on the forward contracts were not material at either February 1, 2003 or at February 2, 2002. The related receivable, payable and deferred gain or loss are included on a net basis in the balance sheet. The company had $205 and $108 of short-term outstanding forward contracts at February 1, 2003 and February 2, 2002, maturing in 2003 and 2002, respectively. These contracts are entered into with counter-parties that have high credit ratings and with which the company has the contractual right to net forward currency settlements.

Stock Options

The company accounts for stock options in accordance with the provisions of Accounting Principles Board Opinion No. 25, "Accounting for Stock Options Issued to Employees" (APB 25). The company has adopted the disclosure only provisions of SFAS No. 123 "Accounting for Stock Based Compensation" (FAS 123), issued in 1995.

In accordance with the provisions of SFAS No. 123, the company applies APB Opinion No. 25 and related interpretations in accounting for its stock option plans and, accordingly, does not recognize compensation cost. If the company had elected to recognize compensation cost based on the fair value of the options granted at grant date as prescribed by SFAS No. 123, net earnings and earnings per share would have been reduced to the pro forma amounts indicated in the following table:

	2002	2001	2000
Net earnings – as reported	**$ 229**	$ 67	$ 404
Net earnings – pro forma	**190**	28	385
Basic earnings per share – as reported	**1.10**	0.34	1.92
Basic earnings per share – pro forma	**0.92**	0.14	1.83
Diluted earnings per share – as reported	**1.09**	0.33	1.88
Diluted earnings per share – pro forma	**0.91**	0.14	1.79

The weighted-average fair value at the date of grant for options granted in 2002, 2001, 2000 was $6.42, $9.16 and $5.88, respectively. The fair value of each option grant is estimated on the date of grant using the Black-Scholes option pricing model. As there were a number of options granted during the years of 2000 through 2002, a range of assumptions are provided below:

	2002	2001	2000
Expected stock price volatility	**.407 –.507**	.407 –.567	.434 –.585
Risk-free interest rate	**2.6% – 5.0%**	3.6% – 5.1%	5.0% – 6.8%
Weighted average expected life of options	**5 years**	5 years	5 years

The effects of applying SFAS No. 123 and the results obtained through the use of the Black-Scholes option pricing model are not necessarily indicative of future values.

RESTRICTED CASH

The company had restricted cash of $60 at February 1, 2003. Included in this amount is $45 being used as support for a letter of credit in exchange for reduced letter of credit fees. This letter of credit partially supports the company's 475 Swiss Franc note, due January 28, 2004. The remaining $15 relates to a pending real estate transaction that is expected to close in 2003.

MERCHANDISE INVENTORIES

Merchandise inventories for the U.S. toy store division are stated at the lower of LIFO (last-in, first-out) cost or market. If inventories had been valued at the lower of FIFO (first-in, first-out) cost or market, inventories would show no change at February 1, 2003 or February 2, 2002.

	February 1, 2003	February 2, 2002
Toys"R"Us – U.S.	**$ 1,387**	$ 1,328
Toys"R"Us – International	**362**	278
Babies"R"Us	**287**	282
Toysrus.com	**34**	52
Other	**120**	101
	$ 2,190	$ 2,041

PROPERTY AND EQUIPMENT

	Useful life (in years)	February 1, 2003	February 2, 2002
Land		$ 825	$ 811
Buildings	45-50	2,009	1,980
Furniture and equipment	5-20	1,786	1,800
Leasehold improvements	12½-35	1,726	1,542
Costs of computer software	5	192	127
Construction in progress		33	41
Leased property and equipment under capital lease		53	53
		6,624	6,354
Less accumulated depreciation and amortization		1,861	1,810
		$ 4,763	$ 4,544

GOODWILL

In July 2001, the Financial Accounting Standards Board ("FASB") issued SFAS No. 142, "Goodwill and Other Intangible Assets" (SFAS No. 142), which is effective for fiscal years beginning after December 15, 2001. SFAS No. 142 changes the accounting for goodwill from an amortization method to an impairment only approach. The company adopted this pronouncement on February 3, 2002. As a result of this adoption, amortization of $348 of goodwill, which was to be amortized ratably through 2037, ceased. The carrying amount of goodwill at February 1, 2003 relates to the acquisition of Baby Super Stores, Inc. in 1997 ($319), which is now part of the Babies"R"Us division, and the acquisition of Imaginarium Toy Centers, Inc. in 1999 ($29), which is part of the Toys"R"Us – U.S. division. Based on the estimated fair market values (calculated using historical operating results of the reporting units to which the goodwill relates and relative industry multiples) of these divisions compared with the related book values, the company has determined that no impairment of this goodwill exists. Application of the non-amortization provisions of SFAS No. 142 resulted in an increase in net earnings of $8 for 2002. Had the non-amortization provisions of SFAS No. 142 been applied for 2001 and 2000, the company would have reported net earnings of $75 and $412, respectively, and diluted earnings per share of $0.36 and $1.92, respectively.

INVESTMENT IN TOYS – JAPAN

The company is accounting for its 48% ownership investment in the common stock of Toys – Japan on the "equity method" of accounting since the initial public offering in April 2000. Toys – Japan operates as a licensee of the company. As part of the initial public offering, Toys – Japan issued 1.3 shares of common stock to the public at a price of 12,000 yen or $113.95 per share. In November 2001, the common stock of Toys - Japan split 3 for 1. The company's accounting policy for the sales of subsidiaries' stock is to recognize gains or losses for value received in excess of or less than its basis in such subsidiary. No similar issuances of subsidiaries' stock are contemplated at this time. The carrying value of the investment is reflected on the consolidated balance sheets as part of "Other Assets" and was $140 and $123 at February 1, 2003 and February 2, 2002, respectively. At February 1, 2003, the quoted market value of the company's investment was $188, which exceeds the carrying value of the investment. The valuation represents a mathematical calculation based on the closing quotation published by the Tokyo over-the-counter market and is not necessarily indicative of the amount that could be realized upon sale. The company is a guarantor of 80% of a 10 billion yen ($84) loan from third parties in Japan with an annual rate of 6.47%, due in 2012, for which Toys – Japan is the borrower.

SEASONAL FINANCING AND LONG-TERM DEBT

	February 1, 2003	February 2, 2002
7.625% notes, due fiscal 2011	$ 554	$ 505
6.875% notes, due fiscal 2006	267	254
500 Euro bond, due February 13, 2004	538	431
475 Swiss Franc note, due January 28, 2004[(a)]	348	277
Equity Security Units	408	–
8¾% debentures, due fiscal 2021, net of expenses[(b)]	198	198
Note at an effective cost of 2.32% due in semi-annual installments through fiscal 2005[(c)]	158	126
Industrial revenue bonds, net of expenses	21	34
Obligation under capital leases	18	21
Mortgage notes at annual interest rates from 10.16% to 11.00%	8	9
	2,518	1,855
Less current portion	379	39
	$ 2,139	$ 1,816

Long-term debt balances as of February 1, 2003 and February 2, 2002 have been impacted by certain interest rate and currency swaps that have been designated as fair value and cash flow hedges, as discussed in the note entitled, "DERIVATIVE INSTRUMENTS AND HEDGING ACTIVITIES."

(a) Supported by a 475 Swiss Franc bank letter of credit. This note has been converted by an interest rate and currency swap to a floating rate, U.S. dollar obligation at 3 month LIBOR.

(b) Fair value was $192 and $204 at February 1, 2003 and February 2, 2002, respectively. The fair value was estimated using quoted market rates for publicly traded debt and estimated interest rates for non-public debt.

(c) Amortizing note secured by the expected future yen cash flows from license fees due from Toys – Japan.

On May 28, 2002, the company completed public offerings of Toys"R"Us common stock and equity security units, as described in the note entitled "ISSUANCE OF COMMON STOCK AND EQUITY SECURITY UNITS."

In February 2001, the company issued and sold 500 EURO through the public issuance of a EURO bond bearing interest at 6.375% per annum. Through the use of derivative instruments, this obligation was swapped into a $466 fixed rate obligation at an effective rate of 7.43% per annum with interest payments due annually and principal due on February 13, 2004.

In July 2001, the company issued and sold $750 of notes comprised of $500 of notes bearing interest at 7.625% per annum, maturing in August 2011, and $250 of notes bearing interest at 6.875% per annum, maturing in August 2006. Simultaneously with the issuance of these notes, the company entered into interest rate swap agreements. As a result of the interest rate swap agreements, interest on the $500 notes will accrue at the rate of LIBOR plus 1.5120% per annum and interest on the $250 notes accrues at the rate of LIBOR plus 1.1515% per annum. Interest is payable on both notes semi-annually on February 1 and August 1, commencing on February 1, 2002. In October 2002, the company terminated a portion of the interest rate swap agreements and received a payment of $27, which is being amortized over the lives of the related notes. Concurrently, the company entered into new interest rate swap agreements. Of the $500 notes, $200 accrues interest at the rate of LIBOR plus 3.06%, and $125 of the $250 notes accrues interest at the rate of LIBOR plus 3.54%.

As of February 1, 2003, the company had $985 in unsecured committed revolving credit facilities from a syndicate of financial institutions. These credit facilities consist of a $685 facility expiring September 2006 and a $300 facility expiring on August 25, 2003. The facilities are used for seasonal borrowings and to support the company's domestic commercial paper borrowings. As of February 1, 2003, all of the $685 facility expiring September 2006 and all of the $300 facility expiring on August 25, 2003 were available.

The annual maturities of long-term debt at February 1, 2003 are as follows:

	Annual maturities	Fair value hedging adjustment	Annual maturities, including fair value hedging adjustment
2003	$ 373	$ 6	$ 379
2004	499	75	574
2005	51	–	51
2006	279	17	296
2007	420*	19	439
2008 and subsequent	724	55	779
	$ 2,346	$ 172	$ 2,518

Long-term debt balances as of February 1, 2003 have been impacted by certain interest rate and currency swaps that have been designated as fair value and cash flow hedges, as discussed in the note entitled, "DERIVATIVE INSTRUMENTS AND HEDGING ACTIVITIES."

**Includes $390 of equity security units, due 2007, which the company is obligated to remarket in 2005. See the note entitled "ISSUANCE OF COMMON STOCK AND EQUITY SECURITY UNITS."*

DERIVATIVE INSTRUMENTS AND HEDGING ACTIVITIES

The company is exposed to market risk from potential changes in interest rates and foreign exchange rates. The company continues to regularly evaluate these risks and continues to take measures to mitigate these risks, including, among other measures, entering into derivative financial instruments to hedge a variety of risk exposures including interest rate and currency risks. The company enters into forward exchange contracts to minimize and manage the currency risks related to its import merchandise purchase program. The company enters into interest rate swaps to manage interest rate risk and strives to achieve what it believes is an acceptable balance between fixed and variable rate debt.

The company purchases forward exchange contracts to minimize and manage the foreign currency risks related to its import merchandise purchase program. The counter-parties to these contracts are highly rated financial institutions and the company does not have significant exposure to any one counter-party. These forward exchange contracts are designated as cash flow hedges, as defined by SFAS No. 133, and are effective as hedges. Accordingly, changes in the effective portion of the fair value of these forward exchange contracts are included in other comprehensive income. Once the hedged transactions are completed, or when merchandise is sold, the unrealized gains and losses on the forward contracts are reclassified from accumulated other comprehensive income and recognized in earnings. The unrealized losses related to the import merchandise purchase program contracts, that were recorded in other comprehensive income, were not material at February 1, 2003 or February 2, 2002.

The company is faced with interest rate risks resulting from interest rate fluctuations. The company has a variety of fixed and variable rate debt instruments. In an effort to manage interest rate exposures, the company strives to achieve an acceptable balance between fixed and variable rate debt and has entered into interest rate swaps to maintain that balance.

On May 28, 2002, the company entered into an interest rate swap agreement on its Equity-Linked Securities. Under the agreement, the company will pay interest at a variable rate in exchange for fixed rate payments, effectively transforming these debentures to floating rate obligations. This swap is designated as a highly effective fair value hedge, as defined by SFAS No. 133. Changes in the fair value of the interest rate swap offset changes in the fair value of the fixed rate debt due to changes in market interest rates with some ineffectiveness present. The amount of ineffectiveness did not have a material effect on earnings.

On March 19, 2002, the company refinanced a note payable originally due in 2005 and increased the amount outstanding to $160 from $100. This borrowing is repayable in semi-annual installments of principal and interest, with the final installment due on February 20, 2008. The effective cost of this borrowing is 2.23% and is secured by expected future cash flows from license fees due from Toys – Japan. The company also entered into a contract to swap yen to U.S. dollars, within exact terms of the loan. This cross currency swap has been designated as a foreign currency cash flow hedge, as defined by SFAS No. 133, and is effective as a hedge.

In July 2001, the company entered into interest rate swap agreements on its 7.625% $500 notes, due August 1, 2011, and its 6.875% $250 notes, due August 1, 2006. Under these agreements, the company will pay interest at a variable rate in exchange for fixed rate payments, effectively transforming the debentures to floating rate obligations. These swaps are designated as highly effective fair value hedges, as defined by SFAS No. 133. Changes in the fair value of the interest rate swaps perfectly offset changes in the fair value of the fixed rate debt due to changes in market interest rates. As such, there were no ineffective hedge portions recognized in earnings during 2001.

In February 2001, the company issued and sold 500 EURO through the public issuance of a EURO bond bearing interest at 6.375% per annum. The obligation was swapped into a $466 fixed rate obligation with an effective rate of 7.43% per annum with interest payments due annually and principal due February 13, 2004. This cross currency swap is designated as a cash flow hedge, as defined by SFAS No. 133, and is effective as a hedge. The portion of the fair value of the swap attributable to changes in the spot rate is matched in earnings against changes in the fair value of debt.

The company entered into a Swiss Franc floating rate loan with a financial institution in January 1999, due January, 28 2004. The company also entered into a contract to swap U.S. dollars to Swiss Francs, within exact terms of the loan. This cross currency swap has been designated as a foreign currency fair value hedge, as defined by SFAS No. 133, and is effective as a hedge.

The company increased the carrying amount of its long-term debt by $172 at February 1, 2003, representing the fair value of debt in excess of the carrying amount on that date. Also at February 1, 2003, the company recorded derivative assets of $158 and derivative liabilities of $10, representing the fair value of these derivatives at that date.

ISSUANCE OF COMMON STOCK AND EQUITY SECURITY UNITS

On May 28, 2002, the company completed public offerings of Toys"R"Us common stock and equity security units. On that date, the company issued 15.0 shares of its common stock at a price of $17.65 per share and received net proceeds of $253. Also on that date, the company issued 8.0 equity security units with a stated amount of $50 per unit and received net proceeds of $390. Each security unit consists of a contract to purchase, for $50, a specified number of shares of Toys"R"Us common stock in August 2005, and a senior note due in 2007 with a principal amount of $50. The fair value of the contract to purchase shares of Toys"R"Us common stock was estimated at $1.77 per equity security unit. The fair value of the senior note was estimated at $48.23 per equity security unit. Interest on the senior notes is payable quarterly at an initial rate of 6.25%, which commenced in August 2002. The company is obligated to remarket the notes in May 2005 at the then prevailing market interest rate for similar notes. If the remarketing were not to be successful, the company would be entitled to take possession of the senior notes, and the holder's obligation under the contracts to purchase shares of Toys"R"Us common stock would be deemed to have been satisfied. The proceeds allocated to the purchase contracts were recorded in stockholders' equity on the consolidated balance sheet. The fair value of the senior notes is reflected as long-term debt on the consolidated balance sheet. The net proceeds from the public offerings were used to refinance short-term borrowings and for other general corporate purposes. As a result of the interest rate swap agreements, interest on the senior notes will accrue at the rate of LIBOR plus 3.43% per annum. Interest is payable quarterly each year, beginning in August 2002.

STOCKHOLDERS' EQUITY

The common shares of the company, par value $0.10 per share, were as follows:

	February 1, 2003	February 2, 2002
Authorized shares	**650.0**	650.0
Issued shares	**300.4**	300.4
Treasury shares	**87.9**	103.7
Issued and outstanding shares	**212.5**	196.7

EARNINGS PER SHARE

The following table sets forth the computation of basic and diluted earnings per share:

	2002	2001	2000
Numerator:			
Net earnings available to common stockholders	**$ 229**	$ 67	$ 404
Denominator for basic earnings per share – weighted average shares	**207.6**	197.6	210.9
Impact of dilutive securities	**2.0**	8.4	4.1
Denominator for diluted earnings per share – weighted average shares	**209.6**	206.0	215.0
Basic earnings per share	**$ 1.10**	$ 0.34	$ 1.92
Diluted earnings per share	**$ 1.09**	$ 0.33	$ 1.88

Options to purchase approximately 32.5, 10.3 and 3.0 shares of common stock were outstanding during 2002, 2001 and 2000, respectively, but were not included in the computation of diluted earnings per share because the option exercise prices were greater than the average market price of the common shares.

STOCK PURCHASE WARRANTS

The company issued 1.2 stock purchase warrants to SOFTBANK Venture Capital and affiliates ("SOFTBANK") for $8.33 per warrant. Each warrant gives the holder thereof the right to purchase one share of Toys"R"Us common stock at an exercise price of $13 per share, until the expiration date of February 24, 2010. In addition, the company granted a warrant on August 9, 2000 entitling Amazon.com to acquire up to 5% (subject to dilution under certain circumstances) of the capital of Toysrus.com at the then market value. As of February 1, 2003, none of these warrants have been exercised.

LEASES

The company leases a portion of the real estate used in its operations. Most leases require the company to pay real estate taxes and other expenses; some require additional amounts based on percentages of sales.

Minimum rental commitments under noncancelable operating leases having a term of more than one year as of February 1, 2003 are as follows:

	Gross minimum rentals	Sublease income	Net minimum rentals
2003	$ 317	$ 17	$ 300
2004	314	14	300
2005	301	12	289
2006	285	11	274
2007	267	9	258
2008 and subsequent	1,786	40	1,746
	$ 3,270	$ 103	$ 3,167

Total rent expense, net of sublease income, was $267, $261 and $291 in 2002, 2001 and 2000, respectively. The company remains contingently liable for lease payments related to the sub-lease of locations to third parties. To the extent that sub-lessees fail to perform, the company's total net rent expense would be increased.

The company's new corporate headquarters facility, located in Wayne, New Jersey, is financed under a lease arrangement commonly referred to as a "synthetic lease." Under this lease, unrelated third parties, arranged by Wachovia Development Corporation, a multi-purpose real estate investment company, will fund up to $125 for the acquisition and construction of the facility. Upon completion of the construction, which is expected to be in 2003, the company will begin to pay rent on the facility until the lease expires in 2011. The rent will be based on a mix of fixed and variable interest rates that will be applied against the final amount funded. Upon expiration of the lease, the company would expect to either: renew the lease arrangement; purchase the facility from the lessor; or remarket the property on behalf of the owner. The lease agreement provides the lessor with a residual value guarantee equal to the funding for the acquisition and construction of the facility. Under accounting principles generally accepted in the United States, this arrangement is required to be treated as an operating lease for accounting purposes and as a financing for tax purposes.

TAXES ON INCOME

The provisions for income taxes consist of the following:

	2002	2001	2000
Current:			
Federal	$ 4	$ 63	$ 120
Foreign	31	10	36
State	(2)	9	10
	$ 33	$ 82	$ 166
Deferred:			
Federal	62	(61)	50
Foreign	23	16	13
State	14	(13)	4
	99	(58)	67
Total tax provision	$ 132	$ 24	$ 233

At February 1, 2003 and February 2, 2002, the company had gross deferred tax assets, before valuation allowances, of $612 and $576, respectively, and gross deferred tax liabilities of $600 and $484, respectively. Deferred tax assets of $32 and $45 were included in "Prepaid Expenses and Other Current Assets" at February 1, 2003 and February 2, 2002, respectively. Deferred tax assets, net of valuation allowances, of $285 and $245 were included in "Other Assets" at February 1, 2003 and February 2, 2002, respectively. Deferred tax liabilities of $55 and $36 were included in "Accrued Expenses and Other Current Liabilities" at February 1, 2003 and February 2, 2002, respectively. The tax effects of temporary differences and carryforwards that give rise to significant portions of deferred tax assets and liabilities consist of the following:

	February 1, 2003	February 2, 2002
Deferred tax assets:		
Foreign loss carryforwards	$ 305	$ 296
Restructuring	116	131
Other	143	115
Depreciation and amortization	30	22
Derivative instruments and hedging activities	11	–
LIFO reserves	7	12
Valuation allowances, related to foreign loss carryforwards	(295)	(287)
	$ 317	$ 289
Deferred tax liabilities:		
Depreciation and amortization	$ (404)	$ (344)
Other	(169)	(131)
LIFO reserves	(27)	(9)
	$ (600)	$ (484)
Net deferred liabilities	$ (283)	$ (195)

On February 1, 2003, the company had foreign loss carryforwards available to reduce future taxable income of certain foreign subsidiaries. The foreign loss carryforwards, as well as the related tax benefits associated with the foreign loss carryforwards, will expire as follows:

Expiration	Net operating loss carryforwards	Tax benefit
1 – 5 years	$ 208	$ 71
6 – 7 years	9	4
Indefinitely	572	230
	$ 789	$ 305

At February 1, 2003, the company had valuation allowances of $295 against the tax benefit of foreign loss carryforwards of $305.

A reconciliation of the federal statutory tax rate with the effective tax rate follows:

	2002	2001	2000
Statutory tax rate	35.0%	35.0%	35.0%
State income taxes, net of federal income tax benefit	1.4	1.8	1.4
Foreign taxes, net of valuation allowance	(2.4)	(9.4)	1.1
Reversal of deferred tax asset	–	(6.5)	–
Subpart F income	1.5	5.4	0.6
Amortization of goodwill	–	3.5	0.5
Other, net	1.0	(2.9)	(2.1)
Effective tax rate	36.5%	26.9%	36.5%

Deferred income taxes are not provided on un-remitted earnings of foreign subsidiaries that are intended to be indefinitely invested. Exclusive of amounts that, if remitted, would result in little or no tax under current U.S. tax laws, unremitted earnings were approximately $607 at February 1, 2003. Net income taxes of approximately $120 would be due if these earnings were remitted.

STOCK OPTIONS

The company has stock option plans (the "Plans") that provide for the granting of options to purchase the company's common stock. The Plans cover employees and directors of the company and provide for the issuance of non-qualified options, incentive stock options, performance share options, performance units, stock appreciation rights, restricted shares, restricted units and unrestricted shares. The Plans provide for a variety of vesting dates with the majority of the options vesting approximately three years from the date of grant, 50% over the first two years and the remaining 50% over three years. Options granted to directors are exercisable one-third on a cumulative basis commencing on the third, fourth and fifth anniversaries from the date of the grant.

The exercise price per share of all options granted has been the average of the high and low market price of the company's common stock on the date of grant. All options must be exercised within ten years from the date of grant.

At February 1, 2003, an aggregate of 47.7 shares of authorized common stock were reserved for all of the Plans noted above, including 1.6 shares reserved for the future issuance of restricted shares, restricted units, performance units, unrestricted shares and 2 shares reserved for the restricted shares of units granted but not yet vested. Of these amounts, 11.5 were available for future grants. All outstanding options expire at dates ranging from February 17, 2003 to December 30, 2012.

Stock option transactions are summarized as follows:

	Shares	Exercise price per share	Weighted-average exercise price
Outstanding at January 29, 2000	39.8	$ 11.69 – $ 40.94	$ 24.59
Granted	7.5	10.25 – 26.25	15.29
Exercised	(0.4)	14.78 – 22.06	18.96
Canceled	(22.2)	14.63 – 40.94	28.60
Outstanding at February 3, 2001	24.7	$ 10.25 – $ 40.94	$ 18.36
Granted	8.6	15.53 – 38.36	28.03
Exercised	(1.1)	14.63 – 25.44	16.21
Canceled	(1.6)	11.50 – 39.88	24.26
Outstanding at February 2, 2002	30.6	$ 10.25 – $ 40.94	$ 20.39
Granted	6.0	9.83 – 20.41	20.08
Exercised	0.0	0.00 – 0.00	0.00
Canceled	(4.0)	10.25 – 38.19	19.62
Outstanding at February 1, 2003	**32.6**	**$ 9.83 – $40.94**	**$20.43**

The following table summarizes information about stock options outstanding at February 1, 2003:

	Outstanding			Exercisable (Vested)	
Range of exercise prices	Number of options	Weighted average remaining years of contractual life	Weighted average exercise price	Number of options	Weighted average exercise price
$ 9.83 – $14.99	2.0	6	$12.83	1.9	$12.84
$15.00 – $19.99	15.2	6	$17.60	12.6	$17.81
$20.00 – $24.99	7.3	8	$21.00	3.4	$21.47
$25.00 – $29.99	7.1	7	$25.85	3.7	$26.08
$30.00 – $40.94	1.0	4	$35.57	1.0	$35.57
Outstanding at February 1, 2003	32.6	7	$20.43	22.6	$20.07

Options exercisable and the weighted-average exercise prices were 11.3 and $19.60 at February 3, 2001; 16.1 and $20.74 at February 2, 2002; and 22.6 and $20.07 at February 1, 2003, respectively.

At February 1, 2003 and February 2, 2002, Toysrus.com, the company's internet subsidiary, had approximately 11.3 stock options outstanding to both employees and non-employees of the company. This represents approximately 11% of the authorized common stock of Toysrus.com at February 1, 2003 and February 2, 2002. These outstanding options, with exercise prices ranging between $0.30 and $2.25 per share, entitle each option holder the right to purchase one share of the common stock of Toysrus.com.

The company utilizes a restoration feature to encourage the early exercise of certain options and retention of shares, thereby promoting increased employee ownership. This feature provides for the grant of new options when previously owned shares of company stock are used to exercise existing options. Restoration option grants are non-dilutive, as they do not increase the combined number of shares of company stock and options held by an employee prior to exercise. The new options are granted at a price equal to the fair market value on the date of the new grant and generally expire on the same date as the original options that were exercised.

REPLACEMENT OF CERTAIN STOCK OPTION GRANTS WITH RESTRICTED STOCK

In 2000, the company authorized the exchange of certain stock options having an exercise price above $22 per share for an economically equivalent grant of restricted stock. The exchange, which was voluntary, replaced approximately 14.4 options with approximately 1.7 restricted shares. Shares of restricted stock resulting from the exchange vest over a period of three years. One-half of the grant vested on April 1, 2002 and the remainder vests on April 1, 2003. Accordingly, the company recognizes compensation expense throughout the vesting period of the restricted stock. The company recorded $3 in compensation expense related to this restricted stock in 2002 and $8 in both 2001 and 2000.

PROFIT SHARING PLAN

The company has a profit sharing plan with a 401(k) salary deferral feature for eligible domestic employees. The terms of the plan call for annual contributions by the company as determined by the Board of Directors, subject to certain limitations. The profit sharing plan may be terminated at the company's discretion. Provisions of $34, $46 and $50 have been charged to earnings in 2002, 2001 and 2000, respectively.

TOYSRUS.COM

Toysrus.com operates a co-branded toy and video game on-line store (Toysrus.com), a co-branded baby products on-line store (Babiesrus.com), and a co-branded learning products and information on-line store (Imaginarium.com) under a strategic alliance with Amazon.com.

The Toysrus.com strategic alliance with Amazon.com was launched in the third quarter of 2000 and expires in 2010. Under this alliance, each company is responsible for specific aspects of the on-line stores. Toysrus.com is responsible for merchandising, marketing and content for the co-branded stores. Toysrus.com also identifies, buys, owns and manages the inventory. Amazon.com handles web-site development, order fulfillment, customer service, and the housing of Toysrus.com's inventory in Amazon.com's U.S. distribution centers. The company recognizes revenue for Toysrus.com at the point in time when merchandise is shipped to customers, in accordance with the shipping terms (FOB shipping point) that exist under the agreement with Amazon.com.

Toysrus.com also opened a personalized gifts for all ages on-line store (Giftsrus.com) in November 2002. Visitors can choose from hundreds of products, ranging from exclusive stuffed animals, toys, clothing, home décor, and keepsakes, have them personalized with messages, monogrammed, hand-painted or engraved, gift wrapped, and then delivered. Giftsrus.com does not operate as part of the strategic alliance with Amazon.com.

In February 2000, the company entered into an agreement with SOFTBANK that included an investment of $60 by SOFTBANK in Toysrus.com. Accordingly, the company records a 20% minority interest in the net losses of Toysrus.com in selling, general and administrative expenses. Toysrus.com received additional capital contributions of $37 from SOFTBANK, representing its proportionate share of funding required for the operations of Toysrus.com.

SEGMENTS

The company's reportable segments are Toys"R"Us – U.S., which operates toy stores in 49 states and Puerto Rico; Toys"R"Us – International, which operates, licenses or franchises toy stores in 29 countries outside the United States; Babies"R"Us, which operates stores in 35 states; and Toysrus.com, the company's internet subsidiary.

Information on segments and reconciliation to earnings before income taxes, are as follows:

	February 1, 2003	February 2, 2002	February 3, 2001
Net sales			
Toys"R"Us – U.S.	**$ 6,743**	$ 6,877	$ 7,073
Toys"R"Us – International	**2,161**	1,889	1,872
Babies"R"Us	**1,595**	1,421	1,310
Toysrus.com(1)	**340**	277	180
Other(2)	**466**	555	897
Total	**$11,305**	$11,019	$11,332
Operating earnings			
Toys"R"Us – U.S.(3)	**$ 280**	$ 308	$ 431
Toys"R"Us – International	**160**	131	124
Babies"R"Us	**174**	138	120
Toysrus.com, net of minority interest(4)	**(37)**	(76)	(212)
Other(3), (5)	**(106)**	(115)	(37)
Restructuring and other charges	**–**	(186)	–
Operating earnings	**$ 471**	$ 200	$ 426
Interest expense, net	**(110)**	(109)	(104)
Gain from IPO of Toys – Japan	**–**	–	315
Earning before income taxes	**$ 361**	$ 91	$ 637
Identifiable assets			
Toys"R"Us – U.S.	**$ 5,513**	$ 5,412	$ 5,384
Toys"R"Us – International	**1,430**	1,146	1,235
Babies"R"Us	**758**	574	486
Toysrus.com	**58**	84	141
Other(6)	**1,638**	860	757
Total	**$ 9,397**	$ 8,076	$ 8,003
Depreciation and amortization			
Toys"R"Us – U.S.	**$ 176**	$ 166	$ 143
Toys"R"Us – International	**49**	41	42
Babies"R"Us	**24**	29	26
Toysrus.com	**4**	6	6
Other(6)	**64**	66	73
Total	**$ 317**	$ 308	$ 290

(1) Includes the net sales of Toysrus.com – Japan.

(2) Includes the net sales of the Kids"R"Us and Geoffrey divisions, and the net sales of the Toys – Japan division prior to its initial public offering on April 24, 2000.

(3) Includes markdowns related to the store closings announced as part of the restructuring in 2001.

(4) Includes the operations of Toysrus.com – Japan, net of minority interest.

(5) Includes corporate expenses, the operating results of the Kids"R"Us and Geoffrey divisions, and the equity in net earnings of Toys – Japan.

(6) Includes the Kids"R"Us and Geoffrey divisions, as well as corporate assets and related depreciation.

RESTRUCTURING AND OTHER CHARGES

In January 2002, the company announced plans to reposition its business, and as part of this plan, the company closed 27 non-Mission Possible format Toys"R"Us stores and closed 37 Kids"R"Us stores. In conjuction with the Kids"R"Us store closings in most of these locations, the company converted the nearest Toys"R"Us store into a Toys"R"Us/Kids"R"Us combo store.

As part of this plan, the company eliminated approximately 1,700 staff positions in its stores and its headquarters. In addition, these plans include the cost of consolidating five of the company's store support center facilities into its new headquarters in Wayne, New Jersey in 2003.

The costs associated with the facilities consolidation, elimination of positions, and other actions designed to improve efficiency in support functions were $79, of which $15 related to severance. The costs associated with store closings were $73 for Kids"R"Us and $85 for Toys"R"Us, of which $27 was recorded in cost of sales. The fair value of the facilities to be consolidated and store closings were obtained from third party appraisals. The company also reversed $24 of previously accrued charges ($11 from the 1998 charge and $13 from the 1995 charge) that the company determined to be no longer needed. Accordingly, based on these actions, the company recorded $213 million of pre-tax ($126 after-tax) restructuring and other charges in the fourth quarter of its fiscal year ending February 2, 2002. Details on the components of the charges are as follows:

Description	Initial charge	Utilized in 2001	Reserve balance at 2/02/02	Utilized in 2002	Adjustments to charge in 2002	Reserve balance at 2/01/03
Store closing:						
Lease commitments	$ 52	$ –	$ 52	$ (11)	$ –	$ 41
Severance	4	–	4	(4)	–	–
Write-down of property and equipment	75	(75)	–	–	–	–
Markdowns	27	–	27	(27)	–	–
Store support center consolidation:						
Lease commitments	28	–	28	–	11*	39
Write-down of property and equipment	29	(29)	–	–	–	–
Severance	15	–	15	(9)	(1)	5
Other	7	(7)	–	–	–	–
Total restructuring and other charges	**$237**	**$(111)**	**$ 126**	**$ (51)**	**$ 10**	**$ 85**

**In the fourth quarter of 2002, we determined that a reserve for lease costs for the disposition of one of our store support center facilities was no longer adequate and, accordingly, recorded an additional charge of $11 million.*

In 2000, Toysrus.com the company's internet subsidiary, recorded $118 in non-recurring charges as a result of the transition to its co-branded on-line store with Amazon.com, of which, $10 were included in cost of sales and $108 were included in selling, general and administrative expenses. These costs and charges related primarily to the closure of three distribution centers, as well as web-site asset write-offs and other costs. The company had remaining lease commitment reserves of $3 at February 1, 2003, that will be utilized in 2003 and thereafter.

The company previously announced strategic initiatives to reposition its worldwide business and recorded related restructuring and other charges of $698 in 1998 and $396 in 1995 to complete these initiatives. As of February 1, 2003, the company had substantially completed all announced initiatives. The company reversed unused reserves of $10 in the fourth quarter of 2002, and also reversed unused reserves of $29 in 2001, $24 of which were reversed in the fourth quarter of 2001 and are discussed above, and $11 in 2000, as these reserves were concluded to be no longer necessary. The company had $42 of reserves remaining at February 1, 2003, primarily for long-term lease commitments that will be utilized in 2003 and thereafter. The company believes that remaining reserves at February 1, 2003 are reasonable estimates of what is required to complete all remaining initiatives.

GAIN FROM INITIAL PUBLIC OFFERING OF TOYS – JAPAN

The company recorded a pre-tax non-operating gain of $315 ($200 net of taxes) in the first quarter of fiscal 2000 resulting from the initial public offering of shares of Toys – Japan. Of this gain, $91 resulted from an adjustment to the basis of the company's investment in Toys – Japan and $224 was related to the sale of a portion of the company-owned common stock of Toys – Japan, for which the company received net cash proceeds of $267. In connection with this transaction, the company recorded a provision for current income taxes of $82 and a provision for deferred income taxes of $33, respectively. As a result of this transaction, the company's ownership percentage in the common stock of Toys – Japan was reduced from 80% to 48%. Toys – Japan is a licensee of the company.

SUBSEQUENT EVENTS

On March 24, 2003, the company filed a "shelf" registration statement with the Securities and Exchange Commission, giving the company the capability to sell up to $800 of debt securities that would be used to repay outstanding debt and for general corporate purposes. In April 2003, the company sold and issued $400 million in notes bearing interest at a coupon rate of 7.875%, maturing on April 15, 2013. The notes were sold at a price of 98.305%, resulting in an effective yield of 8.125%. Simultaneously with the sale of the notes, we entered into interest rate swap agreements. As a result of these swap agreements, interest will accrue at the rate of LIBOR plus 3.622%. Interest is payable semi-annually commencing on October 15, 2003. The company plans to use the proceeds from these notes for the repayment of indebtedness maturing in the 2004 calendar year, and pending such repayment, for working capital needs and other general corporate purposes.

On March 5, 2003 the company announced that it would be eliminating approximately 200 positions in its store support facilities in 2003, representing approximately 10% of total headquarters staff.

OTHER MATTERS

In August 2000, eleven purported class action lawsuits were filed (six in the United States District Court for the District of New Jersey, three in the United States District Court for the Northern District of California, one in the United States District Court for the Western District of Texas and one in the Superior Court of the State of California, County of San Bernardino), against the company and our affiliates Toysrus.com, Inc. and Toysrus.com, LLC. In September 2000, three additional purported class action lawsuits were filed (two in the United

States District Court for the District of New Jersey and one in the United States District Court for the Western District of Texas). These actions generally purport to bring claims under federal privacy and computer fraud statutes, as well as under state statutory and common law, on behalf of all persons who have visited one or more of the company's web sites and either made an online purchase or allegedly had information about them unlawfully "intercepted," "monitored," "transmitted," or "used." All the suits (except one filed in the United States District Court for the District of New Jersey) also named Coremetrics, Inc. ("Coremetrics"), as a defendant. Coremetrics is an internet marketing company with whom the company has an agreement. These suits seek damages in unspecified amounts and other relief under state and federal law.

With Coremetrics the company filed a joint application with the Multidistrict litigation panel which resulted in all of the federal actions being consolidated and transferred to the United States District Court for the Northern District of California. Plaintiffs voluntarily dismissed the action in the Superior Court of the State of California, County of San Bernardino without prejudice. On October 16, 2001, plaintiffs filed an amended complaint in the United States District Court for the Northern District of California. The company believes that it has substantial defenses to all of these claims. On November 13, 2002, the company entered into a settlement agreement with plaintiffs in connection with all causes of action. This settlement agreement is subject to the court's review and approval and will not have a material impact on the company's consolidated financial statements.

RECENT ACCOUNTING PRONOUNCEMENTS

In 2002, the FASB Emerging Issues Task Force issued EITF issue No. 02-16, "Accounting by a Reseller for Cash Consideration Received from a Vendor" (EITF 02-16). EITF 02-16 considers vendor allowances as a reduction in the price of a vendor's product that should be recognized as a reduction of cost of sales. Advertising allowances that are received for specific, identifiable and incremental costs are considered a reduction of advertising expenses and should be recognized as a reduction of SG&A. The provisions of EITF 02-16 are effective for all new arrangements, or modifications to existing arrangements, beginning after December 31, 2002. The company is currently evaluating the potential impact of the provisions of EITF 02-16 on its consolidated financial statements for 2003.

In January 2003, the FASB issued Interpretation No. 46, "Consolidation of Variable Interest Entities" (FIN 46), which will require the consolidation of entities that are controlled by a company through interests other than voting interests. Under the requirements of this interpretation, an entity that maintains a majority of the risks or rewards associated with Variable Interest Entities ("VIEs"), commonly known as special purpose entities, is effectively in the same position as the parent in a parent-subsidiary relationship. Disclosure requirements of VIEs are effective in all financial statements issued after January 31, 2003. The consolidation requirements apply to all VIEs created after January 31, 2003. FIN 46 requires public companies to apply the consolidation requirements to VIEs that existed prior to February 1, 2003 and remained in existence as of the beginning of annual or interim periods beginning after June 15, 2003. The company's new corporate headquarters facility, located in Wayne, New Jersey, is leased from unrelated third parties, arranged by a multi-purpose real estate investment company that the company does not control. In addition the company does not have the majority of the associated risks or rewards. Accordingly, the company believes that FIN 46 will have no impact on the accounting for the synthetic lease for such facility. The synthetic lease is discussed in the note entitled "LEASES." The company believes that FIN 46 will not have a material impact on its consolidated financial statements.

In November 2002, the FASB issued Interpretation No. 45, "Guarantor's Accounting and Disclosure Requirements for Guarantees, Including Indirect Guarantees of Indebtedness of Others" (FIN 45), which imposes new disclosure and liability-recognition requirements for financial guarantees, performance guarantees, indemnifications and indirect guarantees of the indebtedness of others. FIN 45 requires certain guarantees to be recorded at fair value. This is different from previous practice, where a liability would typically be recorded only when a loss was probable and reasonably estimable. The initial recognition and initial measurements provisions are applicable on a prospective basis to guarantees issued or modified after December 31, 2002. FIN 45 also requires additional disclosures, even when the likelihood of making any payments under the guarantee is remote. The disclosure requirements are effective for interim and annual periods ending after December 15, 2002. The company instituted procedures to identify guarantees contained in the various legal documents and agreements, already executed and those to be executed in the future that fall within the scope of FIN 45. The company expects that FIN 45 will not have a material impact on its consolidated financial statements.

In July 2002, the FASB issued SFAS No. 146 "Accounting for Costs Associated with Exit or Disposal Activities" (SFAS No. 146), which addresses the recognition, measurement, and reporting of costs associated with exit or disposal activities and supercedes Emerging Issues Task Force Issue No. 94-3, "Liability Recognition for Certain Employee Termination Benefits and Other Costs to Exit an Activity (including Certain Costs Incurred in a Restructuring)" (EITF No. 94.3). The fundamental difference between SFAS No. 146 and EITF No. 94-3 is the requirement that a liability for a cost associated with an exit or disposal activity be recognized when the liability is incurred rather than at the date an entity commits to an exit plan. A fundamental conclusion of SFAS No. 146 is that an entity's commitment to a plan, by itself, does not create an obligation that meets the definition of a liability. SFAS No. 146 also establishes that the initial measurement of a liability recognized be recorded at fair value. The provisions of this statement are effective for exit or disposal activities that are initiated after December 31, 2002, with early application encouraged. The company believes that adoption of this pronouncement will not have a significant effect on the company's consolidated financial statements.

In August 2001, the FASB issued SFAS No. 144, "Accounting for the Impairment or Disposal of Long-Lived Assets" (SFAS No. 144), which addresses financial accounting and reporting for the impairment or disposal of long-lived assets and supersedes SFAS No. 121, "Accounting for the Impairment of Long-Lived Assets and for Long-Lived Assets to be Disposed Of." The company adopted SFAS No. 144 as of February 3, 2002. The adoption did not have a significant effect on the company's consolidated financial statements.

Report of Management

Responsibility for the integrity and objectivity of the financial information presented in this Annual Report resides with the management of Toys"R"Us. The accompanying financial statements have been prepared from accounting records which management believes fairly and accurately reflect the operations and financial position of the company.

Management has established a system of internal controls to provide reasonable assurance that assets are maintained and accounted for in accordance with its policies and that transactions are recorded accurately on the company's books and records. The company's disclosure controls provide reasonable assurance that appropriate information is accumulated and communicated to senior management to allow decisions regarding accurate, complete and timely financial disclosures.

The company's comprehensive internal audit program provides for constant evaluation of the adequacy of the adherence to management's established policies and procedures. The company has distributed to key employees its policies for conducting business affairs in a lawful and ethical manner.

The Audit Committee of the Board of Directors, which is comprised solely of outside directors, provides oversight of the financial reporting process through periodic meetings with our independent auditors, internal auditors, and management.

The financial statements of the company have been audited by Ernst & Young LLP, the company's independent auditors, in accordance with auditing standards generally accepted in the United States, including a review of financial reporting matters and internal controls to the extent necessary to express an opinion on the consolidated financial statements.

John H. Eyler, Jr.
Chairman, President and
Chief Executive Officer
March 5, 2003

Louis Lipschitz
Executive Vice President
and Chief Financial Officer

Report of Independent Auditors

The Board of Directors and Stockholders
Toys"R"Us, Inc.

We have audited the accompanying consolidated balance sheets of Toys"R"Us, Inc. and subsidiaries as of February 1, 2003 and February 2, 2002, and the related consolidated statements of earnings, stockholders' equity and cash flows for each of the three years in the period ended February 1, 2003. These financial statements are the responsibility of the company's management. Our responsibility is to express an opinion on these financial statements based on our audits.

We conducted our audits in accordance with auditing standards generally accepted in the United States. Those standards require that we plan and perform the audit to obtain reasonable assurance about whether the financial statements are free of material misstatement. An audit includes examining, on a test basis, evidence supporting the amounts and disclosures in the financial statements. An audit also includes assessing the accounting principles used and significant estimates made by management, as well as evaluating the overall financial statement presentation. We believe that our audits provide a reasonable basis for our opinion.

In our opinion, the financial statements referred to above present fairly, in all material respects, the consolidated financial position of Toys"R"Us, Inc. and subsidiaries at February 1, 2003 and February 2, 2002, and the consolidated results of their operations and their cash flows for each of the three years in the period ended February 1, 2003, in conformity with accounting principles generally accepted in the United States.

As discussed in the note entitled "Goodwill", the company adopted SFAS No. 142, Goodwill and Other Intangible Assets, effective February 3, 2002.

Ernst & Young LLP

Ernst & Young LLP
New York, New York
March 5, 2003

The Board of Directors

Charles Lazarus
Chairman Emeritus and founder
Toys"R"Us, Inc.
Board member since 1969

Charles Lazarus, founder of Toys"R"Us, Inc., is a pioneer of off-price specialty retailing. He opened his first retail establishment totally dedicated to children's needs in 1948 in Washington D.C. Mr. Lazarus continued to lead Toys"R"Us, Inc. as Chairman of the Board and Chief Executive Officer until 1994. Under his leadership, the company expanded internationally and launched its Kids"R"Us and Babies"R"Us brands. Mr. Lazarus remained Chairman of the Board from 1994 until 1998 when he became Chairman Emeritus.

Mr. Lazarus is a Director of Loral Space Systems and has served on the boards of Wal-Mart and Automatic Data Processing. He also served on the Advisory Board for Trade Policy under both President George Bush and President Bill Clinton. He is a member of the Toy Industry Hall of Fame.

John H. Eyler, Jr. [1]
Chairman, President and
Chief Executive Officer
Toys"R"Us, Inc.
Board member since 2000

John H. Eyler Jr. joined Toys"R"Us, Inc. as President and Chief Executive Officer in January 2000. He was named Chairman of the Board in 2001. Prior to joining the company, Mr. Eyler was Chairman and Chief Executive Officer of FAO Schwarz in New York, where he had been employed since 1992.

Mr. Eyler's previous positions include Chief Executive Officer of Chicago's Hartmarx retail subsidiary, and Chairman and Chief Executive Officer of MainStreet, a division of Federated Department Stores, Inc.

He serves on the Board of Directors for the National Retail Federation and The Andre Agassi Charitable Foundation. Mr. Eyler is also on the Board of NYC 2012, an effort to bring the 2012 Olympic Games to New York City. He holds a degree in Finance from the University of Washington and an M.B.A. from Harvard Business School.

RoAnn Costin [2]
President
Reservoir Capital Management, Inc.
Board member since 1996

RoAnn Costin is the President of Reservoir Capital Management, Inc., an investment advisory firm. She has worked in investment management since 1981, holding the position of Senior Vice President, Investment Manager for The Putnam Companies and Portfolio Manager for State Street Research and Management, Inc.

Ms. Costin holds an M.B.A. from the Stanford University Graduate School of Business and a B.A. in Government from Harvard University. In addition to Toys"R"Us, Inc., she serves on the Board of Directors for the Paul Taylor Dance Company in New York and on the Board of Trustees for The Boston Conservatory.

Roger N. Farah [1,4]
President and Chief Operating Officer
Polo Ralph Lauren
Board member since 2001

Roger N. Farah, has been President and Chief Operating Officer of Polo Ralph Lauren and a member of its Board of Directors since 2000.

From 1994 to 2000, Mr. Farah was Chairman of the Board and Chief Executive Officer of Venator Group, Inc. Prior to that, he held positions as President and Chief Operating Officer of Macy's Inc., Chairman and Chief Executive Officer of Federated Merchandising Services, and Chairman and Chief Executive Officer of Rich's Department Stores. From 1998 until 2000, he served on the Board of Directors at Liz Claiborne, Inc.

Mr. Farah received his B.S. in Economics from the University of Pennsylvania, Wharton School. He currently serves on the Wharton School's Board of Directors.

Peter A. Georgescu [2,4]
Chairman Emeritus
Young & Rubicam, Inc.
Board member since 2001

Peter A. Georgescu is Chairman Emeritus of Young & Rubicam, Inc. where he served as the company's Chairman and CEO from 1994 until 2000. He also served as President of Young and Rubicam Advertising and President of the company's former International division. Under Mr. Georgescu's tenure, Young & Rubicam transformed from a private to a publicly-held company and built an extensive database for global branding.

Mr. Georgescu also serves on the Board of Directors for EMI Group PLC, International Flavors & Fragrances Inc. and Levi Strauss & Co. He is Vice Chairman/Director of New York Presbyterian Hospital and a Director of A Better Chance. He received his B.A. from Princeton and an M.B.A. from the Stanford Business School. He was elected to the Advertising Hall of Fame in 2001.

Michael Goldstein [1]
Chairman, The Toys"R"Us
Children's Fund, Inc.
Board member since 1989

Michael Goldstein is Chairman of The Toys"R"Us Children's Fund, Inc. and Toys"R"Us.com, Inc. He has spent 19 years with Toys"R"Us, Inc. serving as both Chairman of the Board and Chief Executive Officer. Prior to 1983, Mr. Goldstein held positions as Sr. Executive Vice President-Operations & Finance with Lerner Stores Corporation and as a Partner with Ernst & Young.

Mr. Goldstein is a Director of Finlay Enterprises, Inc., United Retail Group, 4 Kids Entertainment, Inc. and Columbia House. He is President-elect of the 92nd Street Y, a Director of The Special Contributions Fund of the NAACP, and serves on the Advisory Boards of the For All Kids Foundation, USA Tennis Foundation and the New York Restoration Project. Mr. Goldstein is President and Director of the Northside Center for Child Development. He serves on the Board and Executive Committee of Reading is Fundamental and on the Board and Executive Committee of the Queens College Foundation. He is an inductee into the Toy Industry Hall of Fame and was appointed by President George W. Bush to serve on the Advisory Committee for Trade Policy and Negotiation. He is a graduate of Queens College with a B.S. in Economics.

Calvin Hill [3]
Consultant
Board member since 1997

Calvin Hill is a consultant to The Dallas Cowboys Football Club, Mental Health Management, Inc., Fleet Financial Services and Alexander & Associates, Inc. Mr. Hill was Vice President with the Baltimore Orioles from 1987 to 1994, also serving on its Board of Directors. From 1993 to 2000, he served on President Bill Clinton's Council on Physical Fitness.

Mr. Hill currently serves on the Boards of the Rand Corporation Drug Policy and Research Center, the NCAA Foundation, Duke Divinity School, and International Special Olympics. He launched his professional athletic career with the Dallas Cowboys in 1969 and has played professional football in both the World Football League and the NFL. He is a graduate of Yale University.

Nancy Karch [2,4]
Senior Partner (retired)
McKinsey & Company
Board member since 2000

Nancy Karch is a retired Director of the international consulting firm McKinsey & Company and a member of the McKinsey Advisory Council, comprised of former partners who provide advice to the firm. During 26 years with McKinsey, she held several leadership positions, including Managing Partner of the Retail and Consumer Industries Sector, and Managing Partner of McKinsey Southeast United States.

Ms. Karch is a recognized expert in the field of general merchandise retailing and an active speaker in the retailing and consumer goods fields. She also serves on the Board of Directors of Liz Claiborne, Inc., Gillette, and the Corporate Executive Board, a business research firm. Ms. Karch holds a B.A. in mathematics from Cornell University, an M.S. in mathematics from Northeastern University, and an M.B.A. from Harvard Business School.

company officers

Norman S. Matthews [1,3,4]
Consultant
Board member since 1996

Norman S. Matthews has worked in consulting and venture capital since 1989. Prior to that he held various executive positions with Federated Department stores, including President, Vice Chairman and Executive Vice President. He was also Chairman of Federated's Gold Circle Stores Division.

In addition to Toys"R"Us, Inc., Mr. Matthews serves on the Board of Directors for The Progressive Corporation, Sunoco, Eye Care Centers of America, Finlay Enterprises, Inc., Galyan's Trading Company, and Henry Schein, Inc. He holds a B.A. degree from Princeton University and an M.B.A. from Harvard Business School.

Arthur B. Newman [1,2,3]
Senior Managing Director,
The Blackstone Group, L.P.
Board member since 1997

Arthur B. Newman has been a Senior Managing Director and head of The Restructuring Group of The Blackstone Group, L.P., a private investment bank, since 1991. Previously, Mr. Newman was a Managing Director and head of the Restructuring and Reorganization Group of Chemical Bank and a senior partner at Ernst & Young. Mr. Newman has been an advisor in many of this country's largest reorganizations, including AMF Bowling, Arch Wireless, The Charter Company, Chiquita Banana, Dow Corning Corporation, Eastern Airlines, Exide Technologies, Global Crossing, Iridium, LTV Corporation, Levitz Furniture, Macy's, Manville Corporation, Mobile Media Corporation, Montgomery Ward, Texaco, Inc., White Motor Corporation and the Wickes Corporation.

Mr. Newman is a member of the America College of Bankruptcy and was the recipient of the 1990 award by the Bankruptcy & Reorganization Group, Lawyers Division of UJA-Federation. Mr. Newman holds a B.S. degree in economics and an M.B.A. from Rutgers University. He is a certified public accountant in New York.

1 Executive Committee
2 Audit Committee
3 Compensation & Organizational Development Committee
4 Corporate Governance and Nominating Committee

Corporate and Administrative Officers

John H. Eyler, Jr.
Chairman, President and Chief Executive Officer

Francesca L. Brockett
Executive Vice President – Strategic Planning & Business Development

Michael D'Ambrose
Executive Vice President – Human Resources

Karen Duvall
Executive Vice President – Supply Chain

John Holohan
Executive Vice President – Chief Information Officer

Christopher K. Kay
Executive Vice President – Operations & General Counsel, Corporate Secretary

Warren F. Kornblum
Executive Vice President – Chief Marketing Officer

Louis Lipschitz
Executive Vice President – Chief Financial Officer

Jon W. Kimmins
Sr. Vice President – Treasurer

Dorvin D. Lively
Sr. Vice President – Corporate Controller

Peter W. Weiss
Sr. Vice President – Taxes

Rebecca A. Caruso
Vice President – Corporate Communications

Ursula H. Moran
Vice President – Investor Relations

Divisional Officers

Richard L. Markee
Executive Vice President and President – Specialty Businesses and International Operations

Raymond L. Arthur
President – Toysrus.com

John Barbour
Executive Vice President and President – Toys"R"Us International

James E. Feldt
Executive Vice President and President – Merchandising and Marketing, Toys"R"Us U.S.

Elliott Wahle
President – Babies"R"Us & Kids"R"Us

Joan W. Donovan
Sr. Vice President – General Merchandise Manager, Toys"R"Us International

Jonathan M. Friedman
Sr. Vice President – Chief Financial Officer, Toys"R"Us U.S.

Andrew R. Gatto
Sr. Vice President – Product Development, Toys"R"Us U.S.

Steven J. Krajewski
Sr. Vice President – Operations, Toys"R"Us U.S.

James G. Parros
Sr. Vice President – Stores & Distributions Center Operations, Kids"R"Us

David Schoenbeck
Sr. Vice President – Operations, Babies"R"Us

Pamela B. Wallack
Sr. Vice President – General Merchandise Manager, Babies"R"Us & Kids"R"Us

International Country Presidents and Managing Directors

David Rurka
Managing Director – Toys"R"Us U.K.

Jacques LeFoll
President – Toys"R"Us France

Monika Merz
President – Toys"R"Us Canada

John Schryver
Managing Director – Toys"R"Us Australia

Michael C. Taylor
Managing Director – Toys"R"Us Central Europe

Antonio Urcelay
Managing Director – Toys"R"Us Iberia

A Heartfelt Tribute

After decades of much appreciated leadership and service, Charles Lazarus and Michael Goldstein will be leaving the Board at the end of this year's (2002-2003) term. Charles and Mike have both served many years as Chief Executive Officer and as Chairman of the Board of Directors of Toys"R"Us, Inc., where they both played significant roles in the growth of the company. Thereafter, they served the company with distinction as members of the Board of Directors. We are extremely grateful for their leadership, their inspiration, their compassion and their commitment to the Toys"R"Us family of stockholders, colleagues and guests.

Quarterly Financial Data and Market Information

Toys"R"Us, Inc. and Subsidiaries

Quarterly Financial Data

(In millions except per share data)

The following table sets forth certain unaudited quarterly financial information:

	First Quarter	Second Quarter	Third Quarter	Fourth Quarter
Year Ended February 1, 2003				
Net Sales	$ 2,095	$ 2,070	$ 2,271	$ 4,869
Gross Margin	682	670	722	1,432
Net (Loss)/Earnings	(4)	(17)	(28)	278
Basic (Loss)/ Earnings per Share	$ (0.02)	$ (0.08)	$ (0.13)	$ 1.31
Diluted (Loss)/ Earnings per Share	$ (0.02)	$ (0.08)	$ (0.13)	$ 1.30

	First Quarter	Second Quarter	Third Quarter	Fourth Quarter[a]
Year Ended February 2, 2002				
Net Sales	$ 2,061	$ 2,021	$ 2,178	$ 4,759
Gross Margin	665	661	710	1,379
Net (Loss)/Earnings	(18)	(29)	(44)	158
Basic (Loss)/ Earnings per Share	$ (0.09)	$ (0.15)	$ (0.22)	$ 0.80
Diluted (Loss)/ Earnings per Share	$ (0.09)	$ (0.15)	$ (0.22)	$ 0.78

(a) Includes restructuring and other charges of $213 ($126 net of tax, or $0.61 per share).

Market Information

The company's common stock is listed on the New York Stock Exchange. The following table reflects the high and low prices (rounded to the nearest hundredth) based on New York Stock Exchange trading since February 3, 2001.

The company has not paid any cash dividends, however, the Board of Directors of the company periodically reviews this policy.

The company had approximately 30,736 Stockholders of Record on March 12, 2003.

		High	Low
2001	1st Quarter	$ 26.52	$ 23.00
	2nd Quarter	31.00	22.30
	3rd Quarter	25.10	16.81
	4th Quarter	24.00	18.25
2002	1st Quarter	$ 20.31	$ 16.18
	2nd Quarter	18.28	12.58
	3rd Quarter	14.09	8.70
	4th Quarter	13.81	9.04

Why Walgreens?

2002 ANNUAL REPORT

This annual report is for the year ended August 31, 2002. Pages 1–5 and 18–31 reprinted by permission of Walgreen Co.

Financial Highlights

For the Years Ended August 31, 2002 and 2001

(In Millions, except per share data)	**2002**	2001	Increase
Net Sales	**$28,681.1**	$24,623.0	16.5%
Net Earnings	**$ 1,019.2**	$ 885.6	15.1%
Net Earnings per Common Share (diluted)	**$ .99**	$ .86	15.1%
Shareholders' Equity	**$ 6,230.2**	$ 5,207.2	19.6%
Return on Average Shareholders' Equity	**17.8%**	18.8%	
Closing Stock Price per Common Share	**$ 34.75**	$ 34.35	
Total Market Value of Common Stock	**$ 35,616**	$ 35,017	1.7%
Dividends Declared per Common Share	**$ .145**	$ .140	3.6%
Average Shares Outstanding (diluted)	**1,032.3**	1,028.9	0.3%

Questions and Answers for Our Shareholders

November 18, 2002

Chairman L. Daniel Jorndt (left) with president and chief executive officer David W. Bernauer.

"Beautifully boring" – that was the description of Walgreens and other companies who made *Bloomberg Personal Finance's* "Profit Champ" list this fall. Each of the 51 firms recognized has achieved increased earnings per share for at least 10 consecutive years. In Walgreens case, the streak is approaching three decades.

During this past rocky year, when the bears ruled the stock market and economic news turned morning coffee bitter, we completed our 28th consecutive record year – and first billion-dollar earnings year – while opening 471 stores and investing nearly $1 billion in new stores, distribution centers and technology improvements. And in a world where cash is now king, we ended 2002 with over $400 million in the bank, nearly $3 billion in owned real estate, virtually no debt and the wherewithal to self-finance accelerating growth and customer service innovations. As one analyst commented recently: "Profits are opinion, but cash is a fact."

It was a record year, but fourth quarter earnings came in a penny light of expectations. Why?

Dave Bernauer: Pure and simple, this was a sales problem. Prescriptions were excellent – up 20 percent for the quarter and more than 21 percent for the year. But fourth quarter front-end – non-pharmacy – sales were anemic, particularly for promotional and summer seasonal merchandise. Those weak sales held our profit below Wall Street's expectations. A company with our stock market valuation isn't allowed a toe-stub, and our stock took a hit.

Why the weak sales?

Dan Jorndt: The easiest culprit is the economy, but we're not taking that bait. One of the beauties of our admittedly "boring" business is its staying power – we sell everyday, consumable items that people *need* more than *want.* Some times are tougher than others, but since the mid-1970s – through recessions and boom times – we've never had a down year. So when sales are tight, we look in the mirror…and adjust. We've made lots of corrections, especially in our advertising, to ensure that fall and holiday sales are more "Walgreen-like," that is, good, strong front-end sales.

Quite frankly, we got out of balance this summer. We were less promotion-oriented, which helped increase our gross profits, but hurt the top sales line. Advertising is always a delicate balance and we're moving the pendulum a little more in favor of traffic building. But we're seeking middle ground. Walgreens is not a retailer that sacrifices all to drive sales. We will get the top line moving...sensibly.

Walgreens keeps adding stores despite the economic slowdown. Is this smart?
Bernauer: There's never been a better time for us to expand. We have the sites, the cash, the people...and America has the need. The only retail segment where sales are outpacing store growth is drugstores. In 2001, the number of retail prescriptions climbed 5 percent, while drugstore outlets grew only 1 percent. Although we're the largest prescription provider in the nation, we still fill only 12 percent of the total, which gives us outstanding growth opportunity.

What about Wal*Mart?
Bernauer: What about *any* competitor? Any store that sells what we sell is on our radar screen. Our strategy has always been to define our segment – convenient healthcare and basic need retailing – and do it better than anyone else. We've seriously – and successfully – competed head-on with Wal*Mart for a quarter century now. They're not new competition. They *are* excellent, respected competition...and they're also one of the few retailers expanding at the same pace we are. Top competitors like Wal*Mart make us better. We watch them... they watch us.

Inventory was high going into fiscal 2002. How did you end up?
Bernauer: A chunk of our positive cash position is due to a big improvement in inventory levels. We had a bad case of indigestion last year, but ended 2002 with inventories up just 5 percent, despite a 16.5 percent sales increase and opening a record 363 net new stores plus new distribution centers in Jupiter, Florida, and Waxahachie, Texas. More importantly, we didn't just blow out product with severe price cuts. We used our systems to attack overages on an orderly basis without hurting gross profit margins and in-stock conditions.

Short-term borrowings of $441 million were completely repaid during the year. For my money, the beauty of our 2002 balance sheet rivals Monet, showing a positive cash swing from borrowing to investing of nearly $900 million.

Walgreens Net Store Growth
Number of stores by year

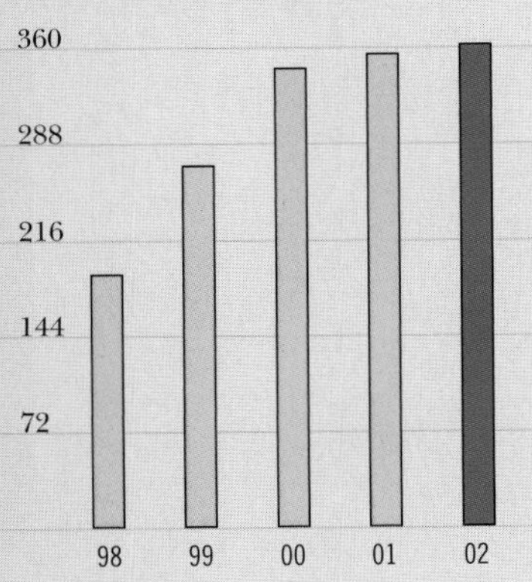

Walgreens versus Competition
Net store growth, 2000-2002

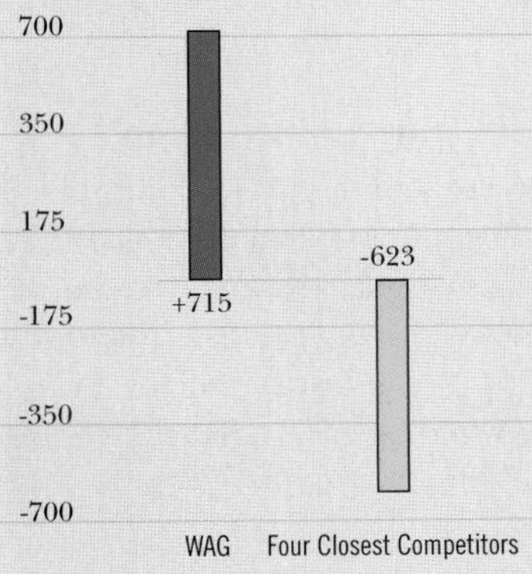

Source: Published company reports

3,883 AND GROWING
Walgreens is the most "national" – and fastest growing – drugstore chain in America. In 2002, we filled 361 million prescriptions – 12 percent of the U.S. retail market and more per store than all major competitors. Our stores average $7.1 million or $654 per square foot in annual sales. Looking ahead, in 2003 we plan to open 450 new stores (approximately 360 net), add 12,000 new jobs and open our third new distribution center in just two years.

Dan Jorndt retires in January after 40 years with Walgreens. Since 1990 he's served as president, CEO and then chairman, leading this company through its period of greatest expansion and innovation. Dan Jorndt's two favorite words are "thank you." On behalf of all shareholders, we thank him for his leadership, honesty, retail savvy, tough decisions, long days and nights, sense of humor and the example he's set. Quite simply, he's made all of those whose lives he's touched a little richer. We wish him and his wife, Pat, the best — and most active — of retirements.

What was the impact of generic drug introductions last year?
Jorndt: Very positive. Generics save money for patients and their providers, both private insurance companies and state Medicaid plans. For Walgreens, while the higher mix of generics to brands slowed our top-line sales growth trend slightly last year, it had a healthy impact on the bottom line. The most important metric in pharmacy is the number of prescriptions. We filled 361 million in 2002, up almost 12 percent from the previous year, and more than double the national increase.

Is there still a pharmacist shortage?
Bernauer: There is a shortage...a big one. But aside from a few markets, we're in good shape. At the end of fiscal 2002, we had 1,600 more pharmacists working for us than a year ago. We're meeting ongoing needs and staffing over 360 net new drugstores a year. We also have the pharmacists to cover 900 24-hour stores. That's more than half of *all* 24-hour pharmacies in America.

If you could stress just one thing to shareholders this year, what would it be?
Jorndt: The quality of our earnings. Warren Buffet has a good quote: "It's only when the tide goes out that you learn who's been swimming naked." A lot of skinny-dippers have surfaced in the past year, bringing down high-flying companies and millions of shareholders. Believe me, we at Walgreens have our swimsuits on, and they're those scratchy knee-to-neck getups beach lovers wore in the 1920s. More boring than bikinis and thongs? You'd better believe it. But accounting works best when it's boring.

Our earnings are all about quality. Our financial statements are straightforward...what you see is what you get. We pay as we go and, other than store leases, everything is on our balance sheet. With no one-time charges and virtually no debt, WAG made the "Top 10" on a recent Merrill Lynch list of firms with quality earnings.

What worries you?
Bernauer: Mostly, stuff that's difficult to control. That includes the current economy as well as government actions. As our population ages, healthcare costs are going up, up, up. This will require government at all levels to make some very tough decisions about resource allocation. We believe it's our job to invest, create jobs, serve customer needs and get a return for these efforts, a return on which we pay significant taxes. It's the government's job to provide social

WHAT ARE WE WORTH?

As of August 31, 2002, Walgreens market capitalization was $35.6 billion. That ranks us third among U.S. retailers and third in the world. In terms of sales volume, we rank No. 78 in the *Fortune 100*. Walgreens has paid dividends in every quarter since 1933 and has raised them for 27 consecutive years. Since 1980, we've had seven two-for-one stock splits.

Sales
Billions of dollars

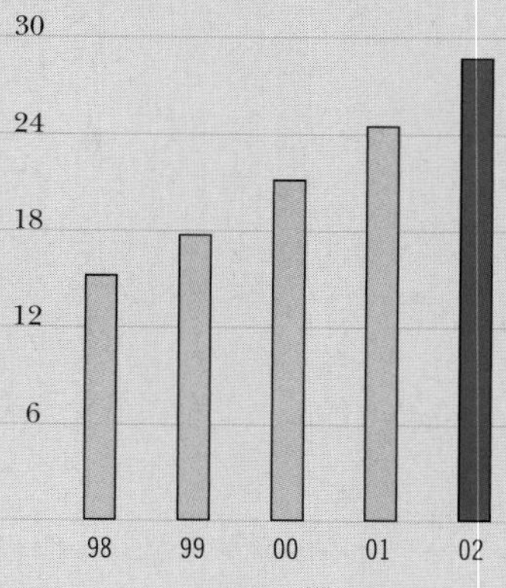

Earnings
Millions of dollars

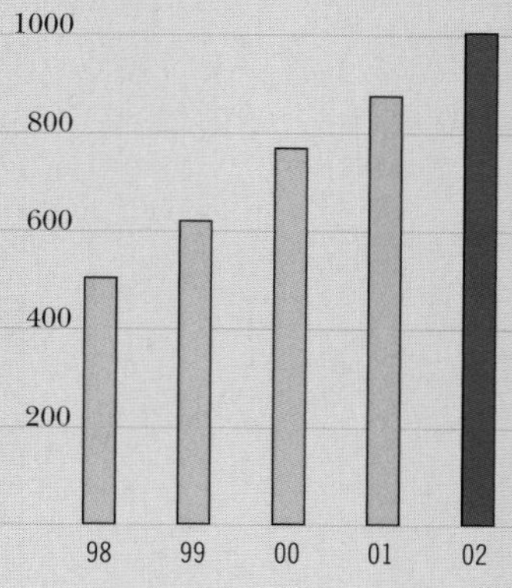

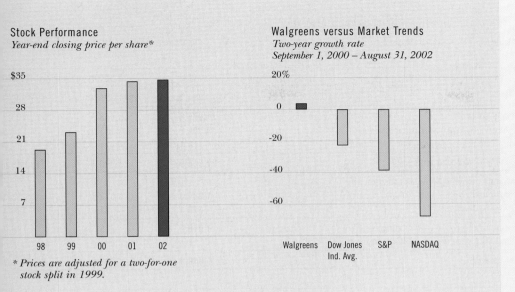

Stock Performance
*Year-end closing price per share**

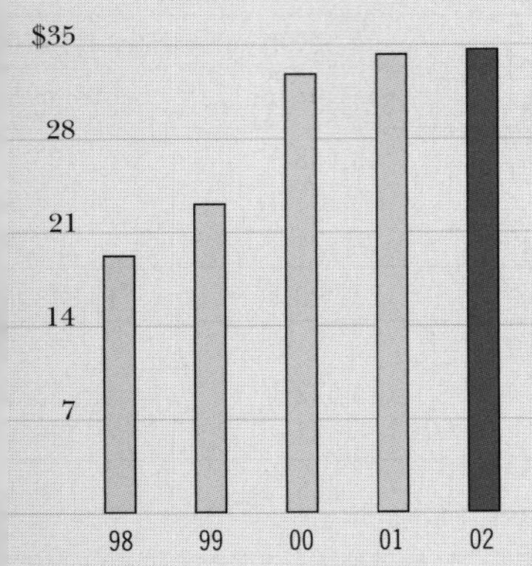

* *Prices are adjusted for a two-for-one stock split in 1999.*

Walgreens versus Market Trends
Two-year growth rate
September 1, 2000 – August 31, 2002

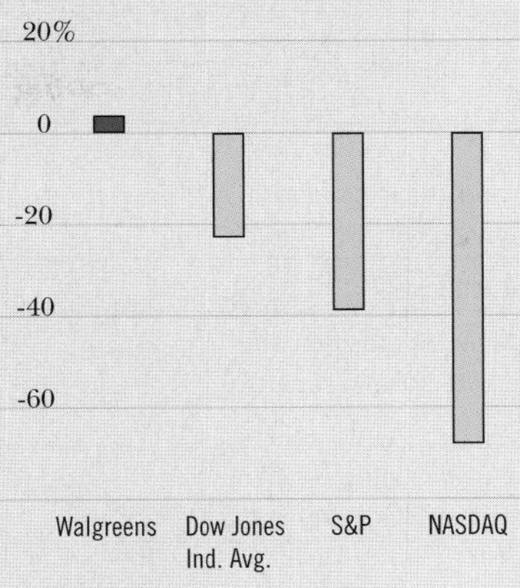

WALGREENS STOCK PERFORMANCE

10 YEARS
On August 31, 1992, 100 shares of Walgreen stock sold for $3,838. Ten years later, on August 31, 2002, those 100 shares, having split three times, were 800 shares worth $27,800, for a gain of 624 percent.

20 YEARS
On August 31, 1982, 100 shares of Walgreen stock sold for $3,600. Twenty years later, those 100 shares, having split six times, were 6,400 shares worth $222,400, for a gain of 6,078 percent.

services. Although pharmacy consumes only 10 percent of the nation's healthcare bill and is the most cost-effective form of treatment, there have been moves recently to slash state Medicaid reimbursement to levels below the filling cost. We and other community pharmacies cannot accept plans – public or private – on which we lose money.

Jeffrey A. Rein will become president and chief operating officer in January 2003.

January marks a new era, as Dan Jorndt retires and Dave Bernauer adds "chairman" to his CEO position. What will change?
Jorndt: I've had a great 40-year run with this company, but it's time for new blood. Same core strategy, same execution...someone else calling the shots. These moves are part of our long-term succession plan. We're blessed in not having to go outside for CEOs. Dave Bernauer and our new president, Jeff Rein, are both pharmacists who started in the stores and have spent long careers here. They, and what I call the "new generation" of Walgreen leaders behind them, are among the top retailers in the country. These men and women know drugstores inside out and bring amazing energy and relentless character to their work. It will be a pleasure to watch their progress.

IN A TOUGH BUSINESS ENVIRONMENT, where confidence in corporate America has plummeted, we feel compelled to say, "No, Chicken Little, the sky isn't falling." We read volumes about the failures...while the thousands of successful companies receive little press. We can't solve the world's ills, but we can promise you, our shareholders and employees, that we'll do our level best to restore faith in what's good about American business. At Walgreens, we know who we are and what we're about. We have a competitive format and clearly defined strategy...a growing demand for our products and services...healthy cash and inventory positions...superior real estate and technology...and motivated, seasoned people at every level. Thanks for your faith in our long-term future...it's a solid one.

L. Daniel Jorndt
Chairman

David W. Bernauer
President and Chief Executive Officer

Eleven-Year Summary of Selected Consolidated Financial Data

Walgreen Co. and Subsidiaries (Dollars in Millions, except per share data)

Fiscal Year		2002	2001	2000
Net Sales		**$28,681.1**	$24,623.0	$21,206.9
Costs and Deductions	Cost of sales	**21,076.1**	18,048.9	15,465.9
	Selling, occupancy and administration	**5,980.8**	5,175.8	4,516.9
	Other (income) expense *(1)*	**(13.1)**	(24.4)	(39.2
	Total Costs and Deductions	**27,043.8**	23,200.3	19,943.6
Earnings	Earnings before income tax provision and cumulative effect of accounting changes	**1,637.3**	1,422.7	1,263.3
	Income tax provision	**618.1**	537.1	486.4
	Earnings before cumulative effect of accounting changes	**1,019.2**	885.6	776.9
	Cumulative effect of accounting changes *(2)*	**—**	—	—
	Net Earnings	**$ 1,019.2**	$ 885.6	$ 776.9
Per Common Share *(3)*	Net earnings *(2)*			
	Basic	**$ 1.00**	$ .87	$ .77
	Diluted	**.99**	.86	.76
	Dividends declared	**.15**	.14	.14
	Book value	**6.08**	5.11	4.19
Non-Current Liabilities	Long-term debt	**$ 11.2**	$ 20.8	$ 18.2
	Deferred income taxes	**176.5**	137.0	101.6
	Other non-current liabilities	**505.7**	457.2	446.2
Assets and Equity	Total assets	**$ 9,878.8**	$ 8,833.8	$ 7,103.7
	Shareholders' equity	**6,230.2**	5,207.2	4,234.0
	Return on average shareholders' equity	**17.8%**	18.8%	20.1%
Drugstore Units	Year-end: Units *(4)*	**3,883**	3,520	3,165

(1) Fiscal 2002, 2001 and 2000 include pre-tax income of $6.2 million ($.004 per share), $22.1 million ($.01 per share) and $33.5 million ($.02 per share), respectively, from the partial payments of the brand name prescription drugs litigation settlement. Fiscal 1998 includes a pre-tax gain of $37.4 million ($.02 per share) from the sale of the company's long-term care pharmacy business.

(2) Fiscal 1998 includes the after-tax $26.4 million ($.03 per share) charge from the cumulative effect of accounting chang for system development costs. Fiscal 1993 includes the after-tax $23.6 million ($.02 per share) costs from the cumulativ effect of accounting changes for postretirement benefits and income taxes.

(3) Per share data have been adjusted for two-for-one stock splits in 1999, 1997 and 1995.

(4) Units include mail service facilities.

1999	1998	1997	1996	1995	1994	1993	1992
$17,838.8	$15,306.6	$13,363.0	$11,778.4	$10,395.1	$9,235.0	$8,294.8	$7,475.0
12,978.6	11,139.4	9,681.8	8,514.9	7,482.3	6,614.4	5,959.0	5,377.7
3,844.8	3,332.0	2,972.5	2,659.5	2,392.7	2,164.9	1,929.6	1,738.8
(11.9)	(41.9)	(3.9)	(2.9)	(3.6)	(2.7)	6.5	5.5
16,811.5	14,429.5	12,650.4	11,171.5	9,871.4	8,776.6	7,895.1	7,122.0
1,027.3	877.1	712.6	606.9	523.7	458.4	399.7	353.0
403.2	339.9	276.1	235.2	202.9	176.5	154.4	132.4
624.1	537.2	436.5	371.7	320.8	281.9	245.3	220.6
—	(26.4)	—	—	—	—	(23.6)	—
$ 624.1	$ 510.8	$ 436.5	$ 371.7	$ 320.8	$ 281.9	$ 221.7	$ 220.6
$ .62	$ .51	$ .44	$ .38	$ .33	$ .29	$ .23	$ .22
.62	.51	.44	.37	.32	.29	.23	.22
.13	.13	.12	.11	.11	.09	.08	.07
3.47	2.86	2.40	2.08	1.82	1.60	1.40	1.25
$ 18.0	$ 13.6	$ 3.3	$ 3.4	$ 2.4	$ 1.8	$ 6.2	$ 18.7
74.8	89.1	112.8	145.2	142.3	137.7	144.2	171.8
405.8	369.9	279.2	259.9	237.6	213.8	176.2	103.8
$ 5,906.7	$ 4,901.6	$ 4,207.1	$ 3,633.6	$ 3,252.6	$2,872.8	$2,506.0	$2,346.9
3,484.3	2,848.9	2,373.3	2,043.1	1,792.6	1,573.6	1,378.8	1,233.3
19.7%	19.6%	19.8%	19.4%	19.1%	19.1%	18.8%	19.1%
2,821	2,549	2,358	2,193	2,085	1,968	1,836	1,736

Management's Discussion and Analysis of Results of Operations and Financial Condition

Results of Operations

Fiscal 2002 was the 28th consecutive year of record sales and earnings. Net earnings were $1.019 billion or $.99 per share (diluted), an increase of 15.1% from last year's earnings of $885.6 million or $.86 per share. Included in this year's results was a $6.2 million pre-tax gain ($.004 per share) for a partial payment of the company's share of the brand name prescription drugs antitrust litigation settlement. Last year's results included a $22.1 million ($.01 per share) comparable payment. Excluding these gains, fiscal year earnings rose 16.5%.

Total net sales increased by 16.5% to $28.7 billion in fiscal 2002 compared to increases of 16.1% in 2001 and 18.9% in 2000. Drugstore sales increases resulted from sales gains in existing stores and added sales from new stores, each of which include an indeterminate amount of market-driven price changes. Comparable drugstore (those open at least one year) sales were up 10.5% in 2002, 10.5% in 2001 and 11.7% in 2000. New store openings accounted for 9.6% of the sales gains in 2002, 11.3% in 2001 and 10.6% in 2000. The company operated 3,883 drugstores as of August 31, 2002, compared to 3,520 a year earlier.

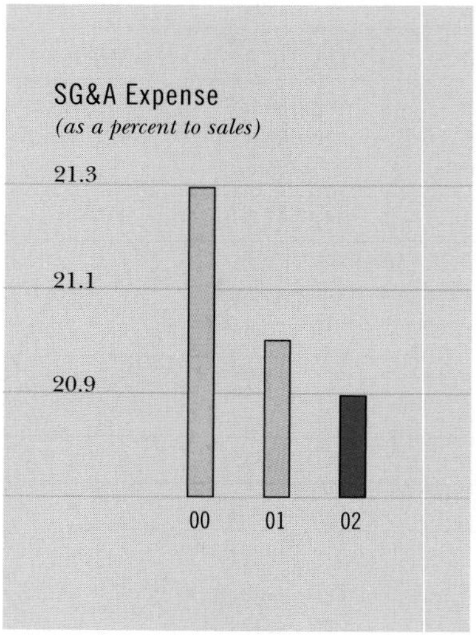

Prescription sales increased 21.2% in 2002, 20.9% in 2001 and 25.3% in 2000. Comparable drugstore prescription sales were up 16.3% in 2002, 17.6% in 2001 and 19.0% in 2000. Prescription sales were 59.8% of total sales for fiscal 2002 compared to 57.5% in 2001 and 55.2% in 2000. Third party sales, where reimbursement is received from managed care organizations and government and private insurance, were 89.8% of pharmacy sales in 2002, 88.4% in 2001 and 86.1% in 2000. Pharmacy sales trends are expected to continue primarily because of increased penetration in existing markets, availability of new drugs and demographic changes such as the aging population.

Gross margins as a percent of total sales were 26.5% in 2002, 26.7% in 2001 and 27.1% in 2000. The decrease in gross margin was caused by a number of factors. Non-pharmacy margins declined as a result of more aggressive advertising and in-store promotions. Although prescription margins increased, due in part to the shift to more generic medications, the trend in sales mix continued toward pharmacy, which carries lower margins than the rest of the store. Within the pharmacy, third party sales, which typically have lower profit margins than cash prescriptions, continue to become a larger portion of prescription sales.

The company uses the last-in, first-out (LIFO) method of inventory valuation. The effective LIFO inflation rates were 1.42% in 2002, 1.93% in 2001 and 1.36% in 2000, which resulted in charges to cost of sales of $55.9 million in 2002, $62.8 million in 2001 and $38.8 million in 2000. Inflation on prescription inventory was 4.3% in 2002, 4.9% in 2001 and 3.5% in 2000.

Selling, occupancy and administration expenses were 20.9% of sales in fiscal 2002, 21.0% of sales in fiscal 2001 and 21.3% of sales in fiscal 2000. The decrease in fiscal 2002, as a percent to sales, was caused by lower store direct expenses, which were partially offset by higher occupancy costs. The decline in fiscal 2001 resulted from lower advertising and headquarters expense. Fixed costs continue to be spread over a larger base of stores.

Interest income net of interest expense increased in 2002 principally due to higher investment levels. Average net investment levels were approximately $162 million in 2002, $31 million in 2001 and $64 million in 2000.

The fiscal 2002 and 2001 effective income tax rates were 37.75% compared to 38.50% in 2000. The decrease in rates compared to 2000 was principally the result of lower state income taxes and the settlement of various IRS matters.

Critical Accounting Policies

The consolidated financial statements are prepared in accordance with accounting principles generally accepted in the United States of America and include amounts based on management's prudent judgments and estimates. Actual results may differ from these estimates. Management believes that any reasonable deviation from those judgments and estimates would not have a material impact on the company's consolidated financial position or results of operations. However, to the extent that the estimates used differ from actual results, adjustments to the statement of earnings and corresponding balance sheet accounts would be necessary. Some of the more significant estimates include liability for closed locations, liability for insurance reserves, vendor allowances, allowance for doubtful accounts, and cost of sales. The company uses the following techniques to determine estimates:

Liability for closed locations – The present value of future rent obligations and other related costs to the first lease option date or estimated sublease date.

Liability for insurance reserves – Incurred losses by policy year extended by historical growth factors to derive ultimate losses.

Vendor allowances – Vendor allowances are principally received as a result of meeting defined purchase levels or promoting vendors' products. Those received as a result of purchase levels are accrued as a reduction of merchandise purchase prices over the incentive period based on estimates. Those received for promoting vendors' products are offset against advertising expense and result in a reduction of selling, occupancy and administration expense.

Allowance for doubtful accounts – Based on both specific receivables and historic write-off percents.

Cost of sales – Based primarily on point-of-sale scanning information with an estimate for shrinkage and adjusted based on periodic inventories.

Financial Condition

Cash and cash equivalents were $449.9 million at August 31, 2002, compared to $16.9 million at August 31, 2001. Short-term investment objectives are to minimize risk, maintain liquidity and maximize after-tax yields. To attain these objectives, investment limits are placed on the amount, type and issuer of securities. Investments are principally in top-tier money market funds, tax exempt bonds and commercial paper.

Net cash provided by operating activities for fiscal 2002 was $1.5 billion compared to $719.2 million a year ago. The change between periods was principally due to tighter control over inventory levels. The company's profitability is the principal source for providing funds for expansion and remodeling programs, dividends to shareholders and funding for various technological improvements.

Capital Expenditures
Fiscal Year 2003
We plan to spend $1.021 billion.

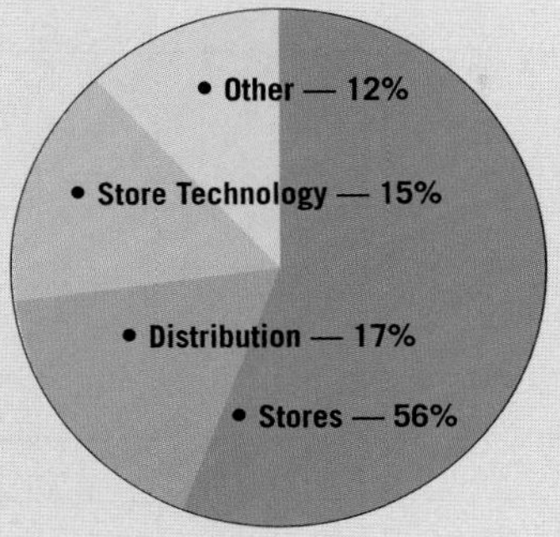

Net cash used for investing activities was $551.9 million in fiscal 2002 and $1.1 billion in 2001. Additions to property and equipment were $934.4 million compared to $1.2 billion last year. During the year, 471 new or relocated drugstores were opened. This compares to 474 new or relocated drugstores opened in the same period last year. New stores are owned or leased. There were 150 owned locations opened during the year or under construction at August 31, 2002, versus 245 for the same period last year. During the year, two new distribution centers opened, one in West Palm Beach (Jupiter), Florida, and the other in the Dallas metropolitan area.

During fiscal 2002, the company entered into two sale-leaseback transactions. These transactions involved 86 drugstore locations and resulted in proceeds of $302 million.

Capital expenditures for fiscal 2003 are expected to exceed $1 billion. The company expects to open more than 450 new stores in fiscal 2003 and have a total of 7,000 drugstores by the year 2010. The company is continuing to relocate stores to more convenient and profitable freestanding locations. In addition to new stores, a significant portion of the expenditures will be made for technology and distribution centers. A new distribution center is under construction in Ohio. Another is planned in Southern California.

Net cash used for financing activities was $488.9 million compared to $419.4 million provided a year ago. The change was principally due to payments of short-term borrowings this year versus proceeds from borrowings last year. There were no short-term borrowings at August 31, 2002, compared to $440.7 million at August 31, 2001. Borrowings were needed during each year to support working capital needs and store and distribution center growth, which included purchases of new store property, equipment and inventory. At August 31, 2002, the company had a syndicated bank line of credit facility of $600 million to support the company's short-term commercial paper program. On July 2, 2002, the company deregistered the remaining $100 million of unissued authorized debt securities, previously filed with the Securities and Exchange Commission.

Recent Accounting Pronouncements

During the first quarter of 2002, the company adopted Statement of Financial Accounting Standards (SFAS) No. 142, "Goodwill and Other Intangible Assets." Under this pronouncement, goodwill is no longer amortized but periodically tested for impairment. No significant impact to the consolidated financial position or results of operations occurred as a result of adopting this standard.

The adoption of SFAS No. 144, "Accounting for the Impairment or Disposal of Long-Lived Assets," resulted in additional disclosures which can be found under "Impaired Assets and Liabilities for Store Closings" in the Summary of Major Accounting Policies.

During the fourth quarter of 2002, the company early adopted SFAS No. 146, "Accounting for Costs Associated with Exit or Disposal Activity." As a result, beginning in June 2002, the remaining lease obligations for closed locations were no longer recognized at the time management made the decision to close the location but were recognized at the time of closing. The adoption of this pronouncement did not have a material impact in the fourth quarter and is not expected to have a material impact on the company's consolidated financial position or results of operations in the future.

Cautionary Note Regarding Forward-Looking Statements

Certain statements and projections of future results made in this report constitute forward-looking information that is based on current market, competitive and regulatory expectations that involve risks and uncertainties. Those risks and uncertainties include changes in economic conditions generally or in the markets served by the company; consumer preferences and spending patterns; changes in state or federal legislation or regulations; the availability and cost of real estate and construction; competition; and risks of new business areas. Please see Walgreen Co.'s Form 10-K for the period ended August 31, 2002, for a discussion of certain other important factors as they relate to forward-looking statements. Actual results could differ materially.

Consolidated Statements of Earnings and Shareholders' Equity

Walgreen Co. and Subsidiaries for the Years Ended August 31, 2002, 2001 and 2000 (Dollars in Millions, except per share data)

	Earnings	2002	2001	2000
Net Sales		**$28,681.1**	$24,623.0	$21,206.9
Costs and Deductions	Cost of sales	**21,076.1**	18,048.9	15,465.9
	Selling, occupancy and administration	**5,980.8**	5,175.8	4,516.9
		27,056.9	23,224.7	19,982.8
Other (Income) Expense	Interest income	**(6.9)**	(5.4)	(6.1)
	Interest expense	—	3.1	.4
	Other income	**(6.2)**	(22.1)	(33.5)
		(13.1)	(24.4)	(39.2)
Earnings	Earnings before income tax provision	**1,637.3**	1,422.7	1,263.3
	Income tax provision	**618.1**	537.1	486.4
	Net Earnings	**$ 1,019.2**	$ 885.6	$ 776.9
Net Earnings per Common Share	Basic	**$ 1.00**	$ .87	$ .77
	Diluted	**.99**	.86	.76
	Average shares outstanding	**1,022,554,460**	1,016,197,785	1,007,393,572
	Dilutive effect of stock options	**9,716,486**	12,748,828	12,495,236
	Average shares outstanding assuming dilution	**1,032,270,946**	1,028,946,613	1,019,888,808

	Common Stock		Paid-in	Retained
Shareholders' Equity	Shares	Amount	Capital	Earnings
Balance, August 31, 1999	1,004,022,258	$78.4	$258.9	$3,147.0
Net earnings	—	—	—	776.9
Cash dividends declared ($.135 per share)	—	—	—	(136.1)
Employee stock purchase and option plans	6,796,632	.6	108.3	—
Balance, August 31, 2000	1,010,818,890	79.0	367.2	3,787.8
Net earnings	—	—	—	885.6
Cash dividends declared ($.14 per share)	—	—	—	(142.5)
Employee stock purchase and option plans	8,606,162	.6	229.5	—
Balance, August 31, 2001	**1,019,425,052**	**79.6**	**596.7**	**4,530.9**
Net earnings	—	—	—	**1,019.2**
Cash dividends declared ($.145 per share)	—	—	—	**(148.4)**
Employee stock purchase and option plans	**5,483,224**	**.5**	**151.7**	—
Balance, August 31, 2002	**1,024,908,276**	**$80.1**	**$748.4**	**$5,401.7**

The accompanying Summary of Major Accounting Policies and the Notes to Consolidated Financial Statements are integral parts of these statements.

Consolidated Balance Sheets

Walgreen Co. and Subsidiaries at August 31, 2002 and 2001 (Dollars in Millions)

	Assets	2002	2001
Current Assets	Cash and cash equivalents	$ 449.9	$ 16.9
	Accounts receivable, net	954.8	798.3
	Inventories	3,645.2	3,482.4
	Other current assets	116.6	96.3
	Total Current Assets	5,166.5	4,393.9
Non-Current Assets	Property and equipment, at cost, less accumulated depreciation and amortization	4,591.4	4,345.3
	Other non-current assets	120.9	94.6
	Total Assets	$9,878.8	$8,833.8

	Liabilities and Shareholders' Equity	2002	2001
Current Liabilities	Short-term borrowings	$ —	$ 440.7
	Trade accounts payable	1,836.4	1,546.8
	Accrued expenses and other liabilities	1,017.9	937.5
	Income taxes	100.9	86.6
	Total Current Liabilities	2,955.2	3,011.6
Non-Current Liabilities	Deferred income taxes	176.5	137.0
	Other non-current liabilities	516.9	478.0
	Total Non-Current Liabilities	693.4	615.0
Shareholders' Equity	Preferred stock, $.0625 par value; authorized 32 million shares; none issued	—	—
	Common stock, $.078125 par value; authorized 3.2 billion shares; issued and outstanding 1,024,908,276 in 2002 and 1,019,425,052 in 2001	80.1	79.6
	Paid-in capital	748.4	596.7
	Retained earnings	5,401.7	4,530.9
	Total Shareholders' Equity	6,230.2	5,207.2
	Total Liabilities and Shareholders' Equity	$9,878.8	$8,833.8

The accompanying Summary of Major Accounting Policies and the Notes to Consolidated Financial Statements are integral parts of these statements.

Consolidated Statements of Cash Flows

Walgreen Co. and Subsidiaries for the Years Ended August 31, 2002, 2001 and 2000 (In Millions)

Fiscal Year		2002	2001	2000
Cash Flows from Operating Activities	Net earnings	**$1,019.2**	$ 885.6	$ 776.9
	Adjustments to reconcile net earnings to net cash provided by operating activities –			
	Depreciation and amortization	**307.3**	269.2	230.1
	Deferred income taxes	**22.9**	46.9	21.0
	Income tax savings from employee stock plans	**56.8**	67.3	38.5
	Other	**(8.6)**	2.1	13.6
	Changes in operating assets and liabilities –			
	Inventories	**(162.8)**	(651.6)	(368.2)
	Trade accounts payable	**289.6**	182.8	233.7
	Accounts receivable, net	**(170.6)**	(177.3)	(135.4)
	Accrued expenses and other liabilities	**75.0**	82.2	101.2
	Income taxes	**14.3**	(5.4)	28.6
	Other	**30.7**	17.4	31.7
	Net cash provided by operating activities	**1,473.8**	719.2	971.7
Cash Flows from Investing Activities	Additions to property and equipment	**(934.4)**	(1,237.0)	(1,119.1)
	Disposition of property and equipment	**368.1**	43.5	22.9
	Net proceeds from corporate-owned life insurance	**14.4**	59.0	58.8
	Net cash used for investing activities	**(551.9)**	(1,134.5)	(1,037.4)
Cash Flows from Financing Activities	(Payments of) proceeds from short-term borrowings	**(440.7)**	440.7	—
	Cash dividends paid	**(147.0)**	(140.9)	(134.6)
	Proceeds from employee stock plans	**111.1**	126.1	79.2
	Other	**(12.3)**	(6.5)	(7.9)
	Net cash (used for) provided by financing activities	**(488.9)**	419.4	(63.3)
Changes in Cash and Cash Equivalents	Net increase (decrease) in cash and cash equivalents	**433.0**	4.1	(129.0)
	Cash and cash equivalents at beginning of year	**16.9**	12.8	141.8
	Cash and cash equivalents at end of year	**$ 449.9**	$ 16.9	$ 12.8

The accompanying Summary of Major Accounting Policies and the Notes to Consolidated Financial Statements are integral parts of these statements.

Summary of Major Accounting Policies

Description of Business

The company is principally in the retail drugstore business and its operations are within one reportable segment. Stores are located in 43 states and Puerto Rico. At August 31, 2002, there were 3,880 retail drugstores and 3 mail service facilities. Prescription sales were 59.8% of total sales for fiscal 2002 compared to 57.5% in 2001 and 55.2% in 2000.

Basis of Presentation

The consolidated statements include the accounts of the company and its subsidiaries. All significant intercompany transactions have been eliminated. The consolidated financial statements are prepared in accordance with accounting principles generally accepted in the United States of America and include amounts based on management's prudent judgments and estimates. While actual results may differ from these estimates, management does not expect the differences, if any, to have a material effect on the consolidated financial statements.

Cash and Cash Equivalents

Cash and cash equivalents include cash on hand and all highly liquid investments with an original maturity of three months or less. The company's cash management policy provides for the bank disbursement accounts to be reimbursed on a daily basis. Checks issued but not presented to the banks for payment of $317 million and $233 million at August 31, 2002 and 2001, respectively, are included in cash and cash equivalents as reductions of other cash balances.

Financial Instruments

The company had approximately $37 million and $53 million of outstanding letters of credit at August 31, 2002 and 2001, respectively, which guaranteed foreign trade purchases. Additional outstanding letters of credit of $84 million and $71 million at August 31, 2002 and 2001, respectively, guaranteed payments of casualty claims. The casualty claim letters of credit are annually renewable and will remain in place until the casualty claims are paid in full. The company pays a nominal facility fee to the financing bank to keep this line of credit facility active. The company also had purchase commitments of approximately $70 million and $162 million at August 31, 2002 and 2001, respectively, related to the purchase of store locations. There were no investments in derivative financial instruments during fiscal 2002 and 2001.

Inventories

Inventories are valued on a lower of last-in, first-out (LIFO) cost or market basis. At August 31, 2002 and 2001, inventories would have been greater by $693.5 million and $637.6 million, respectively, if they had been valued on a lower of first-in, first-out (FIFO) cost or market basis. Included in inventory are product cost and in-bound freight. Cost of sales is primarily derived based upon point-of-sale scanning information with an estimate for shrinkage and adjusted based on periodic inventories. At August 31, 2001 and 2000, the company experienced lower inventory levels in certain LIFO pools compared with the previous year-end inventory levels which caused a liquidation of LIFO inventories which were carried at lower costs prevailing in prior years. The effect of this liquidation was a reduction in cost of sales of $4.2 million in fiscal 2001 and $3.1 million in fiscal 2000.

Vendor Allowances

The company receives vendor allowances principally as a result of meeting defined purchase levels or promoting vendors' products. Those received as a result of purchase levels are accrued as a reduction of merchandise purchase price over the incentive period and result in a reduction of cost of sales. Those received for promoting vendors' products are offset against advertising expense and result in a reduction of selling, occupancy and administration expense.

Property and Equipment

Depreciation is provided on a straight-line basis over the estimated useful lives of owned assets. Leasehold improvements and leased properties under capital leases are amortized over the estimated physical life of the property or over the term of the lease, whichever is shorter. Estimated useful lives range from 12½ to 39 years for land improvements, buildings and building improvements and 5 to 12½ years for equipment. Major repairs, which extend the useful life of an asset, are capitalized in the property and equipment accounts. Routine maintenance and repairs are charged against earnings. The composite method of depreciation is used for equipment; therefore, gains and losses on retirement or other disposition of such assets are included in earnings only when an operating location is closed, completely remodeled or impaired. Fully depreciated property and equipment are removed from the cost and related accumulated depreciation and amortization accounts.

Property and equipment consists of *(In Millions)*:

	2002	2001
Land and land improvements		
Owned stores	**$1,080.4**	$1,109.2
Distribution centers	**57.8**	38.7
Other locations	**9.3**	18.6
Buildings and building improvements		
Owned stores	**1,185.9**	1,156.6
Leased stores (leasehold improvements only)	**425.6**	411.1
Distribution centers	**364.9**	309.1
Other locations	**58.2**	70.6
Equipment		
Stores	**1,609.6**	1,440.3
Distribution centers	**499.4**	350.2
Other locations	**464.9**	462.7
Capitalized system development costs	**144.1**	117.4
Capital lease properties	**17.8**	18.8
	5,917.9	5,503.3
Less: accumulated depreciation and amortization	**1,326.5**	1,158.0
	$4,591.4	$4,345.3

The company capitalizes application stage development costs for significant internally developed software projects, including "SIMS Plus," an inventory management system, and "Basic Department Management," a marketing system. These costs are amortized over a five-year period. Amortization of these costs was $19.5 million in 2002, $17.3 million in 2001 and $13.1 million in 2000. Unamortized costs as of August 31, 2002 and 2001, were $73.2 million and $66.1 million, respectively.

Revenue Recognition

For all sales other than third party pharmacy sales, the company recognizes revenue at the time of the sale. For third party sales, revenue is recognized at the time the prescription is filled, adjusted by an estimate for those that will be unclaimed by customers. Customer returns are immaterial.

Impaired Assets and Liabilities for Store Closings

The company tests long-lived assets for impairment whenever events or circumstances indicate. Store locations that have been open at least five years are periodically reviewed for impairment indicators. Once identified, the amount of the impairment is computed by comparing the carrying value of the assets to the fair value, which is based on the discounted estimated future cash flows. Included in selling, occupancy and administration expense were impairment charges of $8.4 million in 2002, $9.7 million in 2001, and $15.1 million in 2000.

Summary of Major Accounting Policies

(continued)

During the fourth quarter of fiscal 2002, the company implemented SFAS No. 146, "Accounting for Costs Associated with Exit or Disposal Activities." Since implementation, the present value of expected future lease costs are charged against earnings when the location is closed. Prior to this, the liability was recognized at the time management made the decision to relocate or close the store.

Insurance

The company obtains insurance coverage for catastrophic exposures as well as those risks required to be insured by law. It is the company's policy to retain a significant portion of certain losses related to worker's compensation, property losses, business interruptions relating from such losses and comprehensive general, pharmacist and vehicle liability. Provisions for these losses are recorded based upon the company's estimates for claims incurred. The provisions are estimated in part by considering historical claims experience, demographic factors and other actuarial assumptions.

Pre-Opening Expenses

Non-capital expenditures incurred prior to the opening of a new or remodeled store are charged against earnings as incurred.

Advertising Costs

Advertising costs, which are reduced by the portion funded by vendors, are expensed as incurred. Net advertising expenses which are included in selling, occupancy and administration expense were $64.5 million in 2002, $54.1 million in 2001 and $76.7 million in 2000.

Stock-Based Compensation Plans

As permitted by SFAS No. 123, the company applies Accounting Principles Board (APB) Opinion No. 25 and related interpretations in accounting for its plans. Under APB 25, compensation expense is recognized for stock option grants if the exercise price is below the fair value of the underlying stock at the date of grant. The company complies with the disclosure provisions of SFAS No. 123, which requires presentation of pro forma information applying the fair-value based method of accounting.

Income Taxes

The company provides for federal and state income taxes on items included in the Consolidated Statements of Earnings regardless of the period when such taxes are payable. Deferred taxes are recognized for temporary differences between financial and income tax reporting based on enacted tax laws and rates.

Earnings Per Share

In fiscal year 2002 and 2001, the diluted earnings per share calculation excluded certain stock options, because the options' exercise price was greater than the average market price of the common shares for the year. If they were included, anti-dilution would have resulted. At August 31, 2002 and August 31, 2001, options to purchase 3,186,227 and 3,316,906 common shares granted at a price ranging from $35.90 to $45.625 and $36.875 to $45.625 per share were excluded from the fiscal year 2002 and 2001 calculations, respectively.

Notes to Consolidated Financial Statements

Interest Expense

The company capitalized $8.5 million, $15.6 million and $4.0 million of interest expense as part of significant construction projects during fiscal 2002, 2001 and 2000, respectively. Interest paid, net of amounts capitalized, was $.3 million in 2002, $3.4 million in 2001 and $.2 million in 2000.

Other Income

In fiscal 2002, 2001 and 2000, the company received partial payments of the brand name prescription drug antitrust litigation settlement for pre-tax income of $6.2 million ($.004 per share), $22.1 million ($.01 per share) and $33.5 million ($.02 per share), respectively. These payments, which are now concluded, were a result of a pharmacy class action against drug manufacturers, which resulted in a $700 million settlement for all recipients.

Leases

Although some locations are owned, the company generally operates in leased premises. Original non-cancelable lease terms typically are 20-25 years and may contain escalation clauses, along with options that permit renewals for additional periods. The total amount of the minimum rent is expensed on a straight-line basis over the term of the lease. In addition to minimum fixed rentals, most leases provide for contingent rentals based upon sales.

Minimum rental commitments at August 31, 2002, under all leases having an initial or remaining non-cancelable term of more than one year are shown below *(In Millions)*:

2003	$ 897.9
2004	943.3
2005	933.4
2006	914.0
2007	895.0
Later	10,659.2
Total minimum lease payments	**$15,242.8**

The above minimum lease payments include minimum rental commitments related to capital leases amounting to $10.7 million at August 31, 2002. Total minimum lease payments have not been reduced by minimum sublease rentals of approximately $49.1 million on leases due in the future under non-cancelable subleases.

During fiscal 2002, the company entered into two sale-leaseback transactions. The properties were sold at net book value and resulted in proceeds of $302 million. The related leases are accounted for as operating leases.

Rental expense was as follows *(In Millions)*:

	2002	2001	2000
Minimum rentals	**$873.0**	$730.1	$605.7
Contingent rentals	**23.6**	26.2	31.4
Less: Sublease rental income	**(11.1)**	(10.4)	(7.6)
	$885.5	$745.9	$629.5

Notes to Consolidated Financial Statements

(continued)

Income Taxes

The provision for income taxes consists of the following *(In Millions)*:

	2002	2001	2000
Current provision –			
Federal	**$510.2**	$417.1	$400.9
State	**85.0**	73.1	64.5
	595.2	490.2	465.4
Deferred provision –			
Federal	**24.0**	47.1	17.7
State	**(1.1)**	(.2)	3.3
	22.9	46.9	21.0
	$618.1	$537.1	$486.4

The deferred tax assets and liabilities included in the Consolidated Balance Sheets consist of the following *(In Millions)*:

	2002	2001
Deferred tax assets –		
Employee benefit plans	**$106.2**	$146.3
Accrued rent	**56.5**	52.7
Insurance	**82.7**	68.3
Inventory	**35.6**	28.1
Other	**95.3**	39.0
	376.3	334.4
Deferred tax liabilities –		
Accelerated depreciation	**401.9**	341.7
Inventory	**98.9**	92.9
Other	**14.7**	16.1
	515.5	450.7
Net deferred tax liabilities	**$139.2**	$116.3

Income taxes paid were $528.0 million, $432.1 million and $398.4 million during the fiscal years ended August 31, 2002, 2001 and 2000, respectively. The difference between the statutory income tax rate and the effective tax rate is principally due to state income tax provisions.

Short-Term Borrowings

The company obtained funds through the placement of commercial paper, as follows *(Dollars in Millions)*:

	2002	2001	2000
Average outstanding during the year	**$250.2**	$304.9	$14.0
Largest month-end balance	**689.0**	461.2	98.0
	(Nov)	(Nov)	(Nov)
Weighted-average interest rate	**2.3%**	5.2%	5.9%

At August 31, 2002, the company had a syndicated bank line of credit facility of $600 million to support the company's short-term commercial paper program. On July 2, 2002, the company deregistered the remaining $100 million of unissued authorized debt securities, previously filed with the Securities and Exchange Commission.

Contingencies

The company is involved in various legal proceedings incidental to the normal course of business. Company management is of the opinion, based upon the advice of General Counsel, that although the outcome of such litigation cannot be forecast with certainty, the final disposition should not have a material adverse effect on the company's consolidated financial position or results of operations.

Capital Stock

The company's common stock is subject to a Rights Agreement under which each share has attached to it a Right to purchase one one-hundredth of a share of a new series of Preferred Stock, at a price of $37.50 per Right. In the event an entity acquires or attempts to acquire 15% of the then outstanding shares, each Right, except those of an acquiring entity, would entitle the holder to purchase a number of shares of common stock pursuant to a formula contained in the Agreement. These non-voting Rights will expire on August 21, 2006, but may be redeemed at a price of $.0025 per Right at any time prior to a public announcement that the above event has occurred.

As of August 31, 2002, 102,738,392 shares of common stock were reserved for future stock issuances under the company's various employee benefit plans. Preferred stock of 10,249,083 shares has been reserved for issuance upon the exercise of Preferred Share Purchase Rights.

Stock Compensation Plans

The Walgreen Co. Executive Stock Option Plan provides to key employees the granting of options to purchase company common stock over a 10-year period, at a price not less than the fair market value on the date of the grant. Under this Plan, options may be granted until October 9, 2006, for an aggregate of 38,400,000 shares of common stock of the company. Compensation expense related to the plan was less than $1 million in fiscal 2002, $1.4 million in fiscal 2001 and less than $1 million in fiscal 2000. The options granted during fiscal 2002, 2001 and 2000 have a minimum three-year holding period.

The Walgreen Co. Stock Purchase/Option Plan (Share Walgreens) provides for the granting of options to purchase company common stock over a period of 10 years to eligible employees upon the purchase of company shares subject to certain restrictions. Under the terms of the Plan, the option price cannot be less than 85% of the fair market value at the date of grant. Compensation expense related to the Plan was $10.9 million in fiscal 2002, $9.6 million in fiscal 2001 and less than $1 million in fiscal 2000. Options may be granted under this Plan until September 30, 2012, for an aggregate of 42,000,000 shares of common stock of the company. The options granted during fiscal 2002, 2001 and 2000 have a two-year holding period.

The Walgreen Co. Restricted Performance Share Plan provides for the granting of up to 32,000,000 shares of common stock to certain key employees, subject to restrictions as to continuous employment except in the case of death, normal retirement or total and permanent disability. Restrictions generally lapse over a four-year period from the date of grant. Compensation expense is recognized in the year of grant. Compensation expense related to the Plan was $5.4 million in fiscal 2002, $3.6 million in fiscal 2001 and $5.1 million in fiscal 2000. The number of shares granted was 81,416 in 2002, 61,136 in 2001 and 84,746 in 2000.

Under the Walgreen Co. 1982 Employees Stock Purchase Plan, eligible employees may purchase company stock at 90% of the fair market value at the date of purchase. Employees may purchase shares through cash purchases, loans or payroll deductions up to certain limits. The aggregate number of shares for which all participants have the right to purchase under this Plan is 64,000,000.

On May 11, 2000, substantially all employees, in conjunction with opening the company's 3,000th store, were granted a stock option award to purchase from 75 to 500 shares, based on years of service. The stock option award, issued at fair market value on the date of the grant, represents a total of 14,859,275 shares of Walgreen Co. common stock. The options vest after three years and are exercisable up to 10 years after the grant date.

The Walgreen Co. Broad Based Employee Stock Option Plan provides for the granting of options to eligible employees to purchase common stock over a 10-year period, at a price not less than the fair market value on the date of the grant, in connection with the achievement of store opening milestones. Options may be granted for an aggregate of 15,000,000 shares of company common stock until all options have either been exercised or have expired. There is a holding period of three years for options granted under this plan.

Notes to Consolidated Financial Statements

(continued)

A summary of information relative to the company's stock option plans follows:

	Options Outstanding		Options Exercisable	
	Shares	Weighted-Average Exercise Price	Shares	Weighted-Average Exercise Price
August 31, 1999	28,479,238	$ 7.89		
Granted	17,040,383	28.43		
Exercised	(5,055,842)	5.59		
Canceled/Forfeited	(1,086,118)	27.39		
August 31, 2000	39,377,661	$16.55	19,267,211	$6.45
Granted	5,354,388	36.68		
Exercised	(5,532,895)	5.75		
Canceled/Forfeited	(2,943,030)	28.02		
August 31, 2001	**36,256,124**	**$20.24**	**14,824,227**	**$7.40**
Granted	**2,886,365**	**34.05**		
Exercised	**(3,525,955)**	**7.28**		
Canceled/Forfeited	**(1,315,499)**	**30.32**		
August 31, 2002	**34,301,035**	**$22.35**	**13,786,657**	**$9.71**

Net options granted as a percentage of outstanding shares at fiscal year-end were 0.2% in fiscal 2002, 0.2% in fiscal 2001 and 1.6% in fiscal 2000.

The following table summarizes information concerning currently outstanding and exercisable options:

	Options Outstanding			Options Exercisable	
Range of Exercise Prices	Number Outstanding at 8/31/02	Weighted-Average Remaining Contractual Life	Weighted-Average Exercise Price	Number Exercisable at 8/31/02	Weighted-Average Exercise Price
$ 4 to 14	11,511,707	3.13 yrs.	$ 7.64	11,511,707	$ 7.64
15 to 30	14,869,487	7.31	26.65	2,212,570	19.81
31 to 46	7,919,841	8.48	35.67	62,380	34.17
$ 4 to 46	34,301,035	6.18 yrs.	$22.35	13,786,657	$ 9.71

The company applies Accounting Principles Board (APB) Opinion No. 25 and related interpretations in accounting for its plans. Accordingly, no compensation expense has been recognized based on the fair value of its grants under these plans. Had compensation costs been determined consistent with the method of SFAS No. 123 for options granted in fiscal 2002, 2001 and 2000, pro forma net earnings and net earnings per common share would have been as follows *(In Millions, except per share data)*:

	2002	2001	2000
Net earnings			
As reported	**$1,019.2**	$885.6	$776.9
Pro forma	**958.7**	833.3	754.3
Net earnings per common share – Basic			
As reported	**1.00**	.87	.77
Pro forma	**.94**	.82	.75
Net earnings per common share – Diluted			
As reported	**.99**	.86	.76
Pro forma	**.93**	.81	.74

The weighted-average fair value and exercise price of options granted for fiscal 2002, 2001 and 2000 were as follows:

	2002	2001	2000
Granted at market price –			
Weighted-average fair value	**$13.60**	$14.28	$12.17
Weighted-average exercise price	**34.40**	32.88	28.44
Granted below market price –			
Weighted-average fair value	**11.86**	20.78	10.56
Weighted-average exercise price	**33.21**	38.78	24.12

The fair value of each option grant used in the pro forma net earnings and net earnings per share was determined using the Black-Scholes option pricing model with weighted-average assumptions used for grants in fiscal 2002, 2001 and 2000:

	2002	2001	2000
Risk-free interest rate	**4.56%**	6.16%	6.64%
Average life of option (years)	**7**	7	7
Volatility	**27.58%**	25.95%	25.86%
Dividend yield	**.22%**	.16%	.27%

Retirement Benefits

The principal retirement plan for employees is the Walgreen Profit-Sharing Retirement Trust to which both the company and the employees contribute. The company's contribution, which is determined annually at the discretion of the Board of Directors, has historically related to pre-tax income. The profit-sharing provision was $145.7 million in 2002, $126.6 million in 2001 and $112.4 million in 2000.

The company provides certain health and life insurance benefits for retired employees who meet eligibility requirements, including age and years of service. The costs of these benefits are accrued over the period earned. The company's postretirement health and life benefit plans currently are not funded.

Components of net periodic benefit costs *(In Millions)*:

	2002	2001	2000
Service cost	**$ 6.0**	$ 4.8	$ 4.7
Interest cost	**10.5**	8.7	7.7
Amortization of actuarial loss	**1.4**	.3	—
Amortization of prior service cost	**(0.4)**	—	—
Total postretirement benefit cost	**$17.5**	$13.8	$12.4

Change in benefit obligation *(In Millions)*:

	2002	2001
Benefit obligation at September 1	**$142.7**	$118.6
Service cost	**6.0**	4.8
Interest cost	**10.5**	8.7
Amendments	**—**	(7.1)
Actuarial loss	**72.6**	23.1
Benefit payments	**(6.6)**	(6.3)
Participants contributions	**1.2**	.9
Benefit obligation at August 31	**$226.4**	$142.7

Notes to Consolidated Financial Statements

(continued)

Change in plan assets *(In Millions)*:

	2002	2001
Plan assets at fair value at September 1	**$ —**	$ —
Plan participants contributions	**1.2**	.9
Employer contributions	**5.4**	5.4
Benefits paid	**(6.6)**	(6.3)
Plan assets at fair value at August 31	**$ —**	$ —

Funded status *(In Millions)*:

	2002	2001
Funded status	**$(226.4)**	$(142.7)
Unrecognized actuarial loss	**99.1**	27.9
Unrecognized prior service cost	**(6.7)**	(7.1)
Accrued benefit cost at August 31	**$(134.0)**	$(121.9)

The discount rate assumptions used to compute the postretirement benefit obligation at year-end were 7.0% for 2002 and 7.5% for 2001.

Future benefit costs were estimated assuming medical costs would increase at a 9% annual rate decreasing to 5.25% over the next seven years and then remaining at a 5.25% annual growth rate thereafter. A one percentage point change in the assumed medical cost trend rate would have the following effects *(In Millions)*:

	1% Increase	1% Decrease
Effect on service and interest cost	$ 4.0	$ (3.0)
Effect on postretirement obligation	49.0	(37.8)

Supplementary Financial Information

Included in the Consolidated Balance Sheets captions are the following assets and liabilities *(In Millions)*:

	2002	2001
Accounts receivable –		
Accounts receivable	**$ 974.9**	$819.2
Allowances for doubtful accounts	**(20.1)**	(20.9)
	$ 954.8	$798.3
Accrued expenses and other liabilities –		
Accrued salaries	**$ 323.8**	$272.7
Taxes other than income taxes	**179.9**	155.5
Profit sharing	**143.3**	122.1
Other	**370.9**	387.2
	$1,017.9	$937.5

Summary of Quarterly Results *(Unaudited)*

(Dollars in Millions, except per share data)

		Quarter Ended				
		November	February	May	August	Fiscal Year
Fiscal 2002	Net sales	**$6,559.4**	**$7,488.5**	**$7,397.9**	**$7,235.3**	**$28,681.1**
	Gross profit	**1,697.9**	**2,033.9**	**1,937.2**	**1,936.0**	**7,605.0**
	Net earnings	**185.9**	**326.6**	**259.0**	**247.7**	**1,019.2**
	Per Common Share – Basic	**$ .18**	**$ .32**	**$ .25**	**$ .25**	**$ 1.00**
	Diluted	**.18**	**.32**	**.25**	**.24**	**.99**
Fiscal 2001	Net sales	$5,614.2	$6,429.0	$6,296.2	$6,283.6	$24,623.0
	Gross profit	1,488.1	1,770.8	1,651.6	1,663.6	6,574.1
	Net earnings	158.4	296.9	213.4	216.9	885.6
	Per Common Share – Basic	$ .16	$ .29	$ .21	$ .21	$ .87
	Diluted	.15	.29	.21	.21	.86

Comments on Quarterly Results: In further explanation of and supplemental to the quarterly results, the 2002 fourth quarter LIFO adjustment was a credit of $9.9 million compared to a 2001 charge of $2.8 million. If the 2002 interim results were adjusted to reflect the actual inventory inflation rates and inventory levels as computed at August 31, 2002, earnings per share would have increased in the first quarter by $.01 and decreased in the fourth quarter by $.01. Similar adjustments in 2001 would have increased earnings per share in the second quarter by $.01 and decreased earnings per share in the fourth quarter by $.01.

The quarter ended November 30, 2001, includes the pre-tax income of $5.5 million (less than $.01 per share) from the partial payment of the brand name prescription drugs antitrust litigation settlement. The quarter ended August 31, 2002, includes the pre-tax income of $.7 million (less than $.01 per share). The quarter ended February 28, 2001, includes the pre-tax income of $22.1 million ($.01 per share) from the second partial payment.

Common Stock Prices

Below is the New York Stock Exchange high and low sales price for each quarter of fiscal 2002 and 2001.

		Quarter Ended				
		November	February	May	August	Fiscal Year
Fiscal 2002	High	**$36.00**	**$40.70**	**$40.29**	**$39.49**	**$40.70**
	Low	**28.70**	**30.72**	**36.10**	**30.20**	**28.70**
Fiscal 2001	High	$45.75	$45.00	$45.29	$42.40	$45.75
	Low	32.75	35.38	37.13	31.00	31.00

Reports of Independent Public Accountants

To the Board of Directors and Shareholders of Walgreen Co.:
We have audited the accompanying consolidated balance sheet of Walgreen Co. and subsidiaries (the "Company") as of August 31, 2002, and the related consolidated statements of earnings, shareholders' equity, and cash flows for the year then ended. These consolidated financial statements are the responsibility of the Company's management. Our responsibility is to express an opinion on these consolidated financial statements based on our audit. The consolidated financial statements of the Company for the years ended August 31, 2001 and 2000 were audited by other auditors who have ceased operations. Those auditors expressed in their report dated September 28, 2001 an unqualified opinion on those statements.

We conducted our audit in accordance with auditing standards generally accepted in the United States of America. Those standards require that we plan and perform the audit to obtain reasonable assurance about whether the consolidated financial statements are free of material misstatement. An audit includes examining, on a test basis, evidence supporting the amounts and disclosures in the financial statements. An audit also includes assessing the accounting principles used and significant estimates made by management, as well as evaluating the overall financial statement presentation. We believe that our audit provides a reasonable basis for our opinion.

In our opinion, such consolidated financial statements present fairly, in all material respects, the financial position of Walgreen Co. and subsidiaries as of August 31, 2002, and the results of their operations and their cash flows for the year then ended, in conformity with accounting principles generally accepted in the United States of America.

Deloitte & Touche LLP

Deloitte & Touche LLP
Chicago, Illinois
September 27, 2002

To the Board of Directors and Shareholders of Walgreen Co.:
We have audited the accompanying consolidated balance sheets of Walgreen Co. (an Illinois corporation) and Subsidiaries as of August 31, 2001 and 2000, and the related consolidated statements of earnings, shareholders' equity and cash flows for each of the three years in the period ended August 31, 2001. These financial statements are the responsibility of the company's management. Our responsibility is to express an opinion on these financial statements based on our audits.

We conducted our audits in accordance with auditing standards generally accepted in the United States. Those standards require that we plan and perform the audit to obtain reasonable assurance about whether the financial statements are free of material misstatement. An audit includes examining, on a test basis, evidence supporting the amounts and disclosures in the financial statements. An audit also includes assessing the accounting principles used and significant estimates made by management, as well as evaluating the overall financial statement presentation. We believe that our audits provide a reasonable basis for our opinion.

In our opinion, the financial statements referred to above present fairly, in all material respects, the financial position of Walgreen Co. and Subsidiaries as of August 31, 2001 and 2000 and the results of their operations and their cash flows for each of the three years in the period ended August 31, 2001 in conformity with accounting principles generally accepted in the United States.

Arthur Andersen LLP

Arthur Andersen LLP (1)
Chicago, Illinois
September 28, 2001

(1) This report is a copy of the previously issued report covering fiscal years 2001 and 2000. The predecessor auditor has not reissued their report.

Management's Report

The primary responsibility for the integrity and objectivity of the consolidated financial statements and related financial data rests with the management of Walgreen Co. The financial statements were prepared in conformity with accounting principles generally accepted in the United States of America appropriate in the circumstances and included amounts that were based on management's most prudent judgments and estimates relating to matters not concluded by fiscal year-end. Management believes that all material uncertainties have been either appropriately accounted for or disclosed. All other financial information included in this annual report is consistent with the financial statements.

The firm of Deloitte & Touche LLP, independent public accountants, was engaged to render a professional opinion on Walgreen Co.'s consolidated financial statements as of August 31, 2002. Their report contains an opinion based on their audit, which was made in accordance with auditing standards generally accepted in the United States of America and procedures, which they believed were sufficient to provide reasonable assurance that the consolidated financial statements, considered in their entirety, are not misleading and do not contain material errors. The financial statements for the years ended August 31, 2001 and 2000 were audited by other auditors whose report expressed an unqualified opinion on those statements.

Four outside members of the Board of Directors constitute the company's Audit Committee, which meets at least quarterly and is responsible for reviewing and monitoring the company's financial and accounting practices. Deloitte & Touche LLP and the company's General Auditor meet alone with the Audit Committee, which also meets with the company's management to discuss financial matters, auditing and internal accounting controls.

The company's systems are designed to provide an effective system of internal accounting controls to obtain reasonable assurance at reasonable cost that assets are safeguarded from material loss or unauthorized use and transactions are executed in accordance with management's authorization and properly recorded. To this end, management maintains an internal control environment which is shaped by established operating policies and procedures, an appropriate division of responsibility at all organizational levels, and a corporate ethics policy which is monitored annually. The company also has an Internal Control Evaluation Committee, composed primarily of senior management from the Accounting and Auditing Departments, which oversees the evaluation of internal controls on a company-wide basis. Management believes it has appropriately responded to the internal auditors' and independent public accountants' recommendations concerning the company's internal control system.

David W. Bernauer
President
and Chief Executive Officer

William M. Rudolphsen
Controller
and Chief Accounting Officer

Roger L. Polark
Senior Vice President
and Chief Financial Officer

Board of Directors

As of November 18, 2002

Directors

L. Daniel Jorndt*
Chairman
Elected 1990

David W. Bernauer*
President and
Chief Executive Officer
Elected 1999

William C. Foote
Chairman of the Board,
Chief Executive Officer
and President
USG Corporation
Elected 1997

James J. Howard
Chairman Emeritus
Xcel Energy, Inc.
Elected 1986

Alan G. McNally
Chairman
Harris Bankcorp Inc.
Elected 1999

Cordell Reed
Former Senior Vice President
Commonwealth Edison Co.
Elected 1994

David Y. Schwartz
Former Partner
Arthur Andersen LLP
Elected 2000

John B. Schwemm
Former Chairman and
Chief Executive Officer
R.R. Donnelley & Sons Co.
Elected 1985

Marilou M. von Ferstel
Former Executive Vice President
and General Manager
Ogilvy Adams & Rinehart
Elected 1987

Charles R. Walgreen III
Chairman Emeritus
Elected 1963

* *L. Daniel Jorndt will retire in January 2003. David W. Bernauer will become chairman and chief executive officer. Jeffrey A. Rein will become president and chief operating officer. George J. Riedl will become senior vice president–Marketing.*

Committees

Audit Committee
John B. Schwemm,
Chairman
William C. Foote
David Y. Schwartz
Marilou M. von Ferstel

Compensation Committee
Cordell Reed,
Chairman
James J. Howard
John B. Schwemm

Finance Committee
David Y. Schwartz,
Chairman
David W. Bernauer
L. Daniel Jorndt
Alan G. McNally
Cordell Reed
Charles R. Walgreen III

Nominating and Governance Committee
William C. Foote,
Chairman
James J. Howard
Alan G. McNally
John B. Schwemm
Marilou M. von Ferstel

Officers

As of November 18, 2002

Corporate

Chairman
L. Daniel Jorndt*

President
David W. Bernauer*
Chief Executive Officer

Executive Vice Presidents
Jerome B. Karlin
Store Operations
Jeffrey A. Rein*
Marketing

Senior Vice Presidents
R. Bruce Bryant
Western Store Operations
George C. Eilers
Eastern Store Operations
J. Randolph Lewis
Distribution & Logistics
Julian A. Oettinger
General Counsel and
Corporate Secretary
Roger L. Polark
Chief Financial Officer
William A. Shiel
Facilities Development
Trent E. Taylor
Chief Information Officer
Mark A. Wagner
Central Store Operations

Vice Presidents
John W. Gleeson
Corporate Strategy and Treasurer
Dana I. Green
Human Resources
Dennis R. O'Dell
Health Services
Gregory D. Wasson
President
Walgreens Health Initiatives

Operational and Divisional

Store Operations Vice Presidents
James F. Cnota
Kermit R. Crawford
George C. Eilers Jr.
Debra M. Ferguson
John J. Foley
David L. Gloudemans
John W. Grant
Frank C. Grilli
William M. Handal
Patrick E. Hanifen
Barry L. Markl
Richard Robinson
Michael D. Tovian
Kevin P. Walgreen
Christine D. Whelan
Bruce C. Zarkowsky
Barry W. Zins

Divisional Vice Presidents
Thomas L. Bergseth
Facilities Planning and Design
Donald A. Churchill
Construction and Facilities
Thomas J. Connolly
Real Estate
Robert M. Kral
Operations/Merchandising Development
Laurie L. Meyer
Corporate Communications
Allan M. Resnick
Law
George J. Riedl*
Purchasing
Robert E. Rogan
Distribution Centers
Jerry A. Rubin
Real Estate
William M. Rudolphsen
Controller
James M. Schultz
Performance Development
Craig M. Sinclair
Advertising
Patrick W. Tupa
Real Estate
Terry R. Watkins
Distribution Centers
Kenneth R. Weigand
Employee Relations
Denise K. Wong
Supply Chain Systems
Chester G. Young
General Auditor
Robert G. Zimmerman
Vice President – Administration
Walgreens Health Initiatives

7

Chapter 7 focuses on the principles of designing accounting information systems and on the preparation and the role and types of special-purpose journals.

Accounting Information Systems

Learning Objectives

LO1 Identify the principles of designing accounting information systems.

LO2 Describe the use and structure of spreadsheet software and general ledger systems in computerized accounting systems.

LO3 Explain how accountants and businesses use the Internet.

LO4 Describe the role of special-purpose journals and their relationship to controlling accounts and subsidiary ledgers.

LO5 Construct and use a sales journal, purchases journal, cash receipts journal, and cash payments journal.

DECISION POINT

A USER'S FOCUS

RR Donnelley <www.rrdonnelley.com> With sales of more then $6 billion per year, RR Donnelley is one of the largest printing firms in the world. Most of the catalogues and magazines you receive in the mail are printed in Donnelley's plants.

Donnelley recently decided it needed a new accounting information system. Like all companies, it wanted a system that would provide more than just financial statements—one that would enable it to be more competitive and more responsive to customers' needs. The system also had to be flexible enough to deal with Donnelley's expanding business, and its benefits had to outweigh its costs. In addition, it had to be compatible with Donnelley's operations so that it could be put in place without causing schedules to break down. Such problems are not uncommon; for example, when Hershey Foods <www.hersheys.com>, a major supplier of chocolate candy, implemented its new software system during the peak Halloween season, key retailers failed to receive shipments. If Donnelley did not print and ship magazines and catalogues on time, it would have highly dissatisfied customers. How did Donnelley implement an accounting information system that met all these needs?

Donnelley's managers went to a Dutch software firm that had experience in developing programs for the printing industry. They tested the Dutch firm's software and formed a dedicated team of 55 Donnelley personnel to work with the software company. The result was a Web-based system that manages printing presses and binding lines and that allows customers

Why did RR Donnelley choose a software vendor with expertise in the printing industry to design its Web-based accounting information system?

to enter their own orders, check the status of jobs remotely, and do away with paper-order processing. By selecting a software vendor with large-scale printing expertise, Donnelley's managers obtained a system that fulfilled the company's needs. Because the system did not need extensive customization, it not only saved Donnelley money, but also facilitated implementation.[1]

Accounting Information Systems: Principles of Design

LO1 Identify the principles of designing accounting information systems.

RELATED TEXT ASSIGNMENTS
Q: 1, 2
SE: 1
SD: 1
FRA: 1, 2, 3

Accounting information systems summarize financial data about a business and organize the data into useful forms. Accountants communicate the results to management. The means by which an accounting system accomplishes these objectives is called **data processing**. Management uses the resulting information to make a variety of business decisions.

As businesses have grown larger and more complex, the role of accounting information systems has grown. Today, many organizations use comprehensive, computerized information systems that integrate financial and nonfinancial information about customers, operations, and suppliers in a single database. Though integrated with a wide variety of other information, accounting information serves as the base for these integrated information systems, which are known as **enterprise resource planning (ERP) systems**. Three companies that specialize in ERP software are the German-based company SAP and the U.S.-based companies PeopleSoft and Oracle.

www.sap.com
www.peoplesoft.com
www.oracle.com

ERP systems are most often set up, monitored, and operated by accountants. The primary purpose of these systems is to integrate all functions of a company to provide timely information to decision makers throughout the organization. For this reason, accountants must understand all phases of their company's operations as well as the latest developments in systems design and technology. Additionally, while a computerized accounting system may automate many or all bookkeeping functions, it does not eliminate the need to understand the accounting process. In fact, it is impossible to use any accounting information system, manual or computerized, without a basic knowledge of accounting.

Stop and Think!
Certainly, it is important to make right decisions and avoid wrong decisions, but what is the cost of making no decisions?
The cost can be high. For example, assume a product suddenly becomes so popular that it will soon be sold out. If the retailer's accounting information system is not set up to provide this information to the sales manager quickly, the sales manager's failure to make the decision to reorder could cause the company to lose valuable sales. ■

The design of an accounting information system involves four general principles: (1) the cost-benefit principle, (2) the control principle, (3) the compatibility principle, and (4) the flexibility principle.

Cost-Benefit Principle

The most important systems principle, the **cost-benefit principle**, holds that the benefits derived from an accounting information system must be equal to or greater than the system's cost. In addition to performing certain routine tasks—preparing payroll and tax reports and financial statements, and maintaining internal control—the accounting system may be called upon to provide other information that management wants or needs. The benefits from that information must be weighed against both the tangible and the intangible costs of gathering it. In the Decision Point at the beginning of this chapter, we saw how Donnelley's new system significantly improved customer service while reducing costs.

Among the tangible costs are those for personnel, forms, and equipment. One of the intangible costs is the cost of wrong decisions stemming from the lack of good information. For instance, wrong decisions can lead to loss of sales, production stoppages, or inventory losses. Some companies have spent thousands of dollars on computerized systems that do not offer enough benefits. On the other hand, some have failed to realize the important benefits that could be gained from investing in more advanced systems. It is the job of the accountant and the systems designer or analyst to weigh the costs and benefits.

KEY POINT: The cost of making a wrong decision is an intangible cost that can easily be overlooked in designing an accounting system. It is the systems analyst's job to strike the optimal balance between expected benefits and costs.

Control Principle

The **control principle** requires that an accounting information system provide all the features of internal control needed to protect a firm's assets and to ensure that data are reliable. For example, before expenditures are made, a responsible member of management should approve them.

KEY POINT: An accounting information system should help protect the company's assets and provide reliable data.

Focus on Business Practice

How Much Is a Used Computerized Accounting System Worth?

Apparently, a second-hand computerized accounting system has value in the marketplace, if it's a good one. When it declared bankruptcy, the old-line retailer Montgomery Ward had many problems, but accounting, inventory, and sales software wasn't one of them. When the company auctioned off its custom-designed software system, bids started at $100 million.[2]

Compatibility Principle

The **compatibility principle** holds that the design of an accounting information system must be in harmony with the organizational and human factors of the business. Donnelley, as explained in the Decision Point, chose a software supplier with experience in the printing industry to ensure the compatibility of its new system.

The organizational factors of business have to do with the nature of a company's business and the formal roles its units play in meeting business objectives. For example, a company can organize its marketing efforts by region or by product. If a company is organized by region, its accounting information system should report revenues and expenses by region. If a company is organized by product, its system should report revenues and expenses first by product and then by region.

KEY POINT: A systems analyst must carefully consider a business's activities, objectives, and performance measures, as well as the behavioral characteristics of its employees.

The human factors of business have to do with the people within the organization and their abilities, behaviors, and personalities. The interest, support, and competence of a company's employees are very important to the success or failure of systems design. In changing systems or installing new ones, the accountant must deal with the people who are carrying out or supervising existing procedures. Such people must understand, accept, and, in many cases, be trained in the new procedures. The new system cannot succeed unless the system and the people in the organization are compatible.

Flexibility Principle

KEY POINT: To work effectively with a computerized accounting system, you must understand how a manual accounting system works. A computerized system functions exactly like a manual system, except that it processes information at lightning speed.

The **flexibility principle** holds that an accounting information system must be flexible enough to allow for growth in the volume of transactions and for organizational changes. Businesses do not stay the same. They grow, they offer new products, they add new branch offices, they sell existing divisions, or they make other changes that require adjustments in the accounting system. A carefully designed accounting system allows a business to grow and change without having to make major alterations in the system. For example, the chart of accounts should be designed to accommodate the addition of new asset, liability, owner's equity, revenue, and expense accounts.

Check out ACE for a Review Quiz at http://accounting.college.hmco.com/students.

Computerized Accounting Systems

LO2 Describe the use and structure of spreadsheet software and general ledger systems in computerized accounting systems.

RELATED TEXT ASSIGNMENTS
Q: 3, 4, 5, 6
SE: 2
SD: 1, 2, 3

Businesses use computerized systems for accounting and many other purposes. Large, multinational companies have vast computer resources and use very powerful computers that are linked together to provide communication and data transfer around the world. However, even in these large companies and in most small companies, the microcomputer, or PC, is a critical element in the processing of information. It has become even more critical as companies have expanded their use of the Internet to communicate and transact business directly with vendors, suppliers, and clients. Two kinds of microcomputer programs on which accountants rely heavily are spreadsheet software and general ledger systems.

Spreadsheet Software

Spreadsheet software is used to analyze data. A **spreadsheet** is a computerized grid of columns and rows into which the user places data or formulas related to

FOCUS ON BUSINESS TECHNOLOGY

Networking: How to Get It Done

Many businesses achieve the computing power of mainframes (large computers) by linking many microcomputers in a network. In a daisy chain network, the microcomputers are linked in a type of circle, or daisy chain. With this network, a person may have to go through several other microcomputers to reach a file or communicate with a person at another computer. In a home base, or star, network, all microcomputers are linked to a central switching point, or home base. A separate microcomputer called a *server* contains all the common data files, such as the accounting records. The server is also connected to the home base. All users can access accounting records and other data files by going through the home base. This type of network is faster and more efficient than the daisy chain network.

financial planning, cost estimating, and other accounting tasks. Windows® Excel and Lotus are popular commercial spreadsheet programs used for financial analysis and other purposes.

GENERAL LEDGER SYSTEMS

KEY POINT: Five kinds of transactions—credit sales, credit purchases, cash receipts, cash payments, and miscellaneous—are common in the typical business. In a manual system, a separate journal should be used for each type of transaction, and a general journal should be used for all other transactions. In a computerized system, a separate function is chosen for each type.

STOP AND THINK!
Why is knowledge of accounting necessary when a computerized general ledger system will do the steps in the accounting cycle automatically?
Knowledge of accounting is necessary for two reasons. First, transactions must be entered in the proper way and in the proper accounts. Second, an understanding of the financial statements that the system produces is a necessary component in making business decisions. ■

General ledger systems is the terminology commonly used to identify the group of integrated software programs that accountants use to perform major functions, such as accounting for sales and accounts receivable, purchases and accounts payable, cash receipts and disbursements, and payroll.

Today, most general ledger systems are written using the Windows® operating system, which has a **graphical user interface (GUI)**. A graphical user interface employs symbols, called **icons**, to represent operations. Examples of icons include a file folder, eraser, hourglass, and magnifying glass. The keyboard can be used in the traditional way, or a *mouse* or *trackball* may be used. When a program uses Windows as its graphical user interface, the program is termed *Windows-compatible.* The visual format and the ability to use a mouse or trackball make Windows-compatible software easy to use. Figure 1 shows how Peachtree Complete Accounting™ for Windows (PCW) uses a combination of text and icons. It is an example of what a graphical user interface looks like on your computer.

One of the benefits of Windows-compatible programs is that they use standardized terms and operations. Once you have mastered one Windows-compatible program, such as Peachtree Complete Accounting, you will be able to use other Windows-compatible applications.

Three software programs available for this book are (1) General Ledger Software, (2) Peachtree Complete Accounting for Windows, and (3) Quickbooks®. General Ledger Software is used to work end-of-chapter problems. It is designed for educational use and cannot be purchased commercially. Peachtree Complete and Quickbooks can be purchased through retail stores. They, too, can be used with selected end-of-chapter problems.

STRUCTURE OF GENERAL LEDGER SYSTEMS

Most general ledger systems are organized so that each module performs a major task of the accounting information system. Figure 2 shows a typical configuration of general ledger systems. Note that there is a software module for each major accounting function: sales/accounts receivable, purchases/accounts payable, cash receipts, cash disbursements, payroll, and general journal. When these features interact with one another, the software is called an *integrated program*.

Source documents, or written evidence, should support each transaction entered into the accounting system. Source documents verify that a transaction occurred and provide the details of the transaction. For example, a customer's invoice should support each sale on account, and a vendor's invoice should support each purchase. Even though the transactions are recorded in a computer file

FIGURE 1
Graphical User Interface

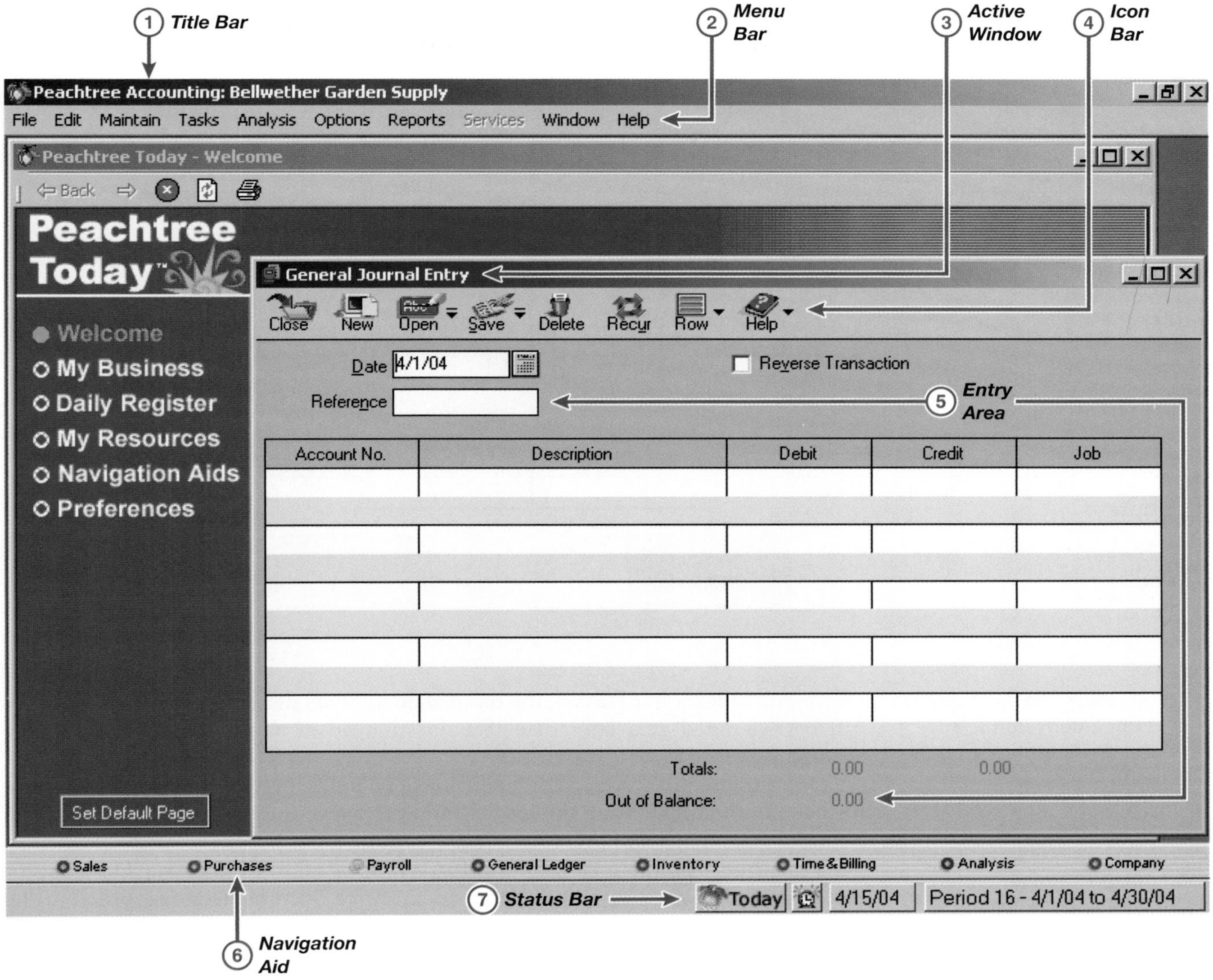

(1) ***Title Bar:*** The title bar at the top of the screen identifies the program and the company under consideration.

(2) ***Menu Bar:*** When you click on one of the menu bar headings, a submenu of options opens. You select an option with a mouse or by holding down the <Alt> key and pressing the letter underlined in the desired option.

(3) ***Active Window:*** This bar shows what window is open, or "active." Here, the "General Journal Entry" window is active.

(4) ***Icon Bar:*** The icon bar shows visual images that pertain to the window. Some icons are common to all windows, whereas others are specific to a particular window. You click on an icon to perform the associated function.

(5) ***Entry Area:*** This part of the screen is where you enter informatior for the journal entry.

(6) ***Navigation Aid:*** The navigation aid offers a graphical supplement to the menu bar. The major functions of the program are represented as icons or pictures that show you how tasks flow through the system.

(7) ***Status Bar:*** The gray bar (screen colors may vary) at the bottom of the window shows the current date and the current accounting period.

Source: "Graphical User Interface" from *Peachtree Complete Accounting™ for Windows®*. Reprinted by permission of Peachtree Software.

FIGURE 2
Computerized Accounting System Using a General Ledger System

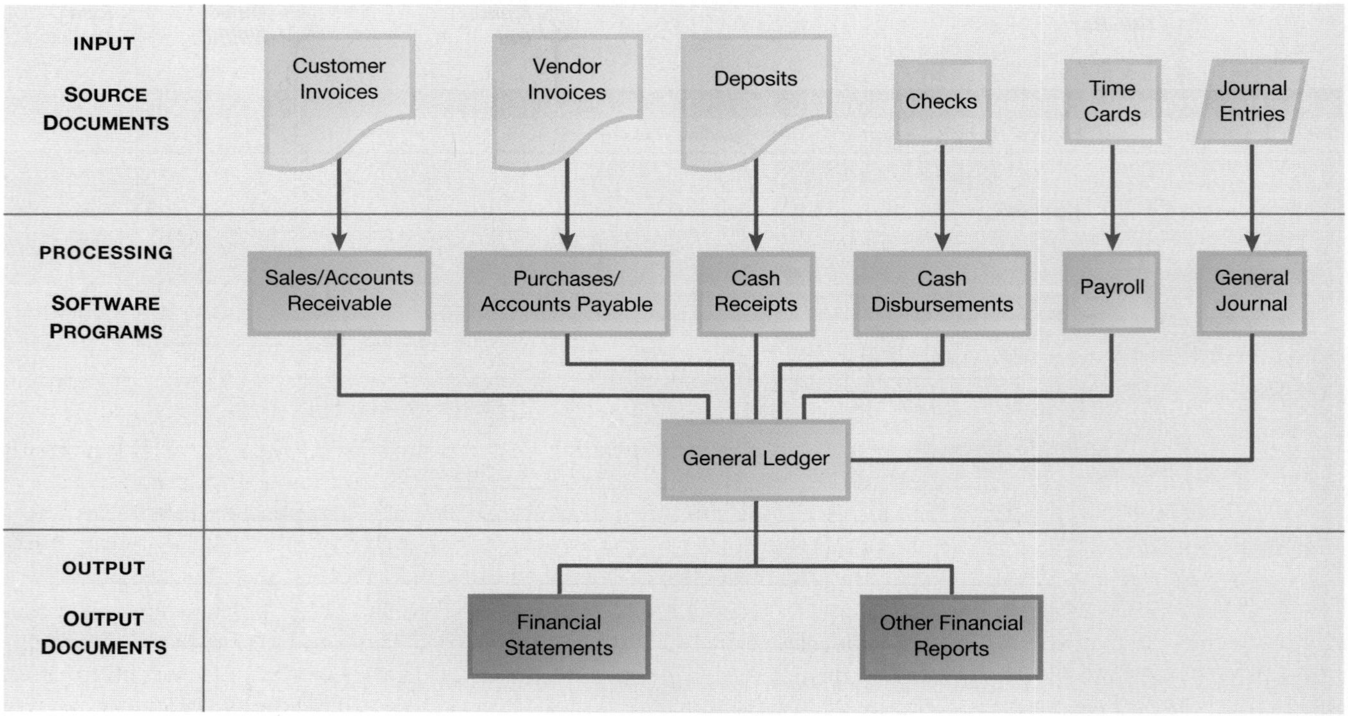

KEY POINT: At least one source document should support each business transaction entered in the records. The accounting system should provide easy reference to the source documents to facilitate subsequent examination (e.g., by an auditor). For instance, canceled checks should be filed by check number.

(on floppy disks or hard disks), the original documents should be stored so that they can be examined at a later date if a question arises about the accuracy of the accounting records.

After transactions are processed in a general ledger system, there is a procedure for posting them, updating the ledgers, and preparing the trial balance. Finally, the financial statements and other accounting reports are printed.

Peachtree Complete Accounting for Windows allows either *batch* posting or *real-time* posting. In a batch posting system, source documents are recorded in the appropriate journal and saved; posting is done at the end of the day, week, or month. In a real-time posting system, documents are posted as they are recorded in the journal. The basic goal of a general ledger system is to make accounting tasks less time-consuming and more accurate and dependable. However, it is important to understand just what the computer is accomplishing. Knowledge of the underlying accounting process helps ensure that the accounting records are accurate and that the assets of the business are protected.

Check out ACE for a Review Quiz at http://accounting.college.hmco.com/students.

ACCOUNTANTS, BUSINESSES, AND THE INTERNET

LO3 Explain how accountants and businesses use the Internet.

RELATED TEXT ASSIGNMENTS
Q: 7
SE: 3
SD: 5
FRA: 1

The **Internet** is the world's largest computer network. The Internet allows any computer on the network to communicate with any other computer on the network. Computer access to the Internet is generally gained via a modem connected to a phone line or cable.

Most people are well aware of the Internet's ability to provide access to the World Wide Web (WWW), electronic mail (email), and electronic bulletin boards. Recent research shows that even businesses with fewer than ten employees are users of the Internet. More than 50 percent of these small businesses have Internet

Focus on Business Technology

The Top Ten Technological Challenges Businesses Face

Every year, the American Institute of Certified Public Accountants publishes a list of the ten most important technological challenges facing businesses. In recent years, the list has emphasized the growing role of the Internet in business activities. In 2003, the list identified the following items as the top ten technological priorities:[3]

1. Information Security
2. Business Information Management
3. Application Integration
4. Web Services
5. Disaster Recovery Planning
6. Wireless Technologies
7. Intrusion Detection
8. Remote Connectivity
9. Customer Relationship Management
10. Privacy

access, and more than 20 percent have their own web sites.[4] Among the ways in which accountants and businesses of all sizes use the Internet are the following:

- **Financial reporting.** Companies today commonly make their financial statements available on the Internet. Large companies are required to file their financial information electronically with the SEC, and it is available on Edgar, the SEC's online warehouse of financial information. Additionally, most companies publish electronic versions of their annual reports on their web sites.

www.sec.gov/edgar.shtml

Stop and Think!
Why do you think small businesses may be reluctant to establish their own web sites?
There are several possible reasons. A web site is costly to set up and maintain; management may lack knowledge or expertise about web sites and may fail to see their benefits; or the business may be of a type that would not benefit from the principal features of a web site. ■

- **XBRL.** **Extensible Business Reporting Language (XBRL)** is a new computer language developed by accountants and others for the express purpose of identifying and communicating financial information. It allows businesses to post information on the Web in a uniform way so that users can access the information, summarize it, perform computations, and format the output in any manner they wish.
- **Ecommerce.** **Electronic commerce (ecommerce)** is the conduct of business transactions on computer networks, including the Internet. Most people are familiar with the buying and selling of products from business to consumers (B to C) on the Internet, but the Internet is used far more widely in business-to-business (B to B) and business to government (B to G) transactions. These transactions include buying and selling products and services, collecting receivables, and paying bills.
- **EDI.** Ecommerce is often facilitated through private links, referred to as **Electronic Data Interchange (EDI).** For example, companies in many industries, such as retail chemicals, oil, and automobile parts, have formed private networks to use EDI for buying and selling goods and services.
- **Supply-chain management.** **Supply-chain management** is a system that uses the Internet to track the supplies and materials a manufacturer will need on a day-to-day—sometimes hour-to-hour—basis. Such a system may also link the manufacturer to its customers.

Focus on Business Practice

B to B and EDI: How Much Can They Save?

An officer of Target Corporation <www.target.com>, the large discount retailer, is quoted as saying, B to B is "real, and it's big, and it's growing. In five years all of our purchasing activity will be done over the Internet." Most executives agree with this statement. Sales and purchases that in the past would have been made by telephone or fax are now transacted by electronic data interchange (EDI). For example, Target participates in a worldwide Retail Exchange, an electronic marketplace formed by over 50 large retailers, including J.C. Penney <www.jcpenney.com> and Safeway Inc. <www.safeway.com>. The purpose of the Retail Exchange is to provide a market for online sales and purchases. When Target wants to purchase something—for instance, fax paper, cleaning products, or jeans—it posts its needs, and other companies bid on the business. Retailers participating in the exchange have seen a 12 to 15 percent reduction in purchasing costs. Even greater reductions are likely because at present only about 50 percent of purchases are made this way.[5]

Focus on Business Technology

E2K: How Much Time Can It Save?

E2K, or event-to-knowledge, is the concept of the time it takes to turn the results of a transaction, such as a sale or a purchase, into useful information for managers. It involves the application of the just-in-time management philosophy to accounting. The goal of just-in-time accounting (JITA) is to reduce the time it takes to produce and distribute financial reports from days or weeks to a single business day so that managers receive them when they need them, or "just in time." Cisco Systems <www.cisco.com>, the large software company, believes it has achieved a breakthrough with a "virtual close" program that gives managers the financial results of one day by 2 P.M. the next day. A reduction in E2K time means that managers have more time to consider the information and can thus make better decisions.[6]

- E2K. **Event-to-knowledge (E2K) management** means that the Internet is used to get information to users within and outside a company in the quickest possible way after an event like a sale or a purchase has occurred.
- **Document-less transactions.** One of the limitations on the growth of electronic commerce is that although the transactions are conducted electronically, source documents, such as those used in general ledger systems, are still often needed to back up the transactions. For example, a purchase is made on the Internet, but a confirmation is emailed, faxed, or mailed to provide documentation of the transaction. Gradually, methods that eliminate the need for source documents are being developed.

Check out ACE for a Review Quiz at http://accounting.college.hmco.com/students.

Role of Special-Purpose Journals in an Accounting Information System

LO4 Describe the role of special-purpose journals and their relationship to controlling accounts and subsidiary ledgers.

RELATED TEXT ASSIGNMENTS
Q: 8, 9, 12
SE: 4, 6, 8, 9, 10
E: 1, 2, 5, 6, 7, 8
P: 1, 3, 4, 5, 6, 8
SD: 1, 4, 6

The method of accounting described in prior chapters, and presented in Figure 3, is a form of **manual data processing**. It has been a useful way to present basic accounting theory and practice in small businesses. Data are fed into the system manually by entering each transaction from a source document into the general journal. Then each debit and credit is posted to the correct ledger account. A work sheet is used as a tool to prepare the financial statements that are distributed to users. This system, although useful for explaining the basic concepts of accounting, is actually used in only the smallest of companies.

Companies involved in more transactions, perhaps hundreds or thousands every week or every day, must have a more efficient and economical way of recording transactions in the journal and posting entries to the ledger. The easiest approach is to group typical transactions into common categories and use an input device called a **special-purpose journal** for each category. Special-purpose journals promote efficiency, economy, and control. Although manual special-purpose journals are used by

Focus on Business Technology

Why Are Customer Numbers Necessary?

In manual accounting systems, subsidiary ledgers are often maintained in alphabetical order because that is a convenient way for people to organize information. With computers, however, numbers are much faster and easier to process than letters. For this reason, numbers are essential for all types of computer data processing. There are customer numbers, order numbers, social security numbers, product numbers, credit card numbers, and many more. When numbers are used, every account can be given a unique identification number. Then the potential confusion of having more than one Janet Smith or Juan Sanchez as customers can be avoided because each customer is assigned a different number.

FIGURE 3
Steps and Devices in a Manual Accounting System

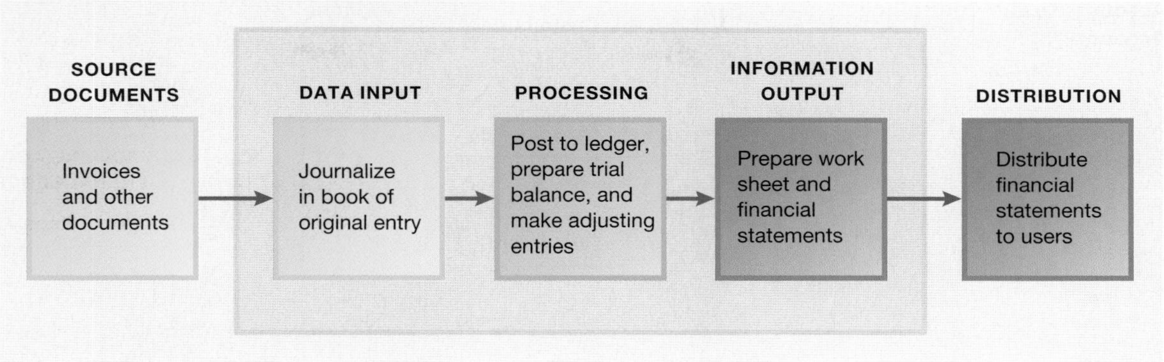

companies that have not yet computerized their systems, the concepts that underlie these journals also underlie the programs that drive computerized general ledger accounting systems.

Most business transactions—90 to 95 percent—fall into one of four categories. Each kind of transaction can be recorded in a special-purpose journal.

KEY POINT: Although a transaction could fall outside the four categories listed to the right, a transaction cannot fall into more than one category.

Transaction	Special-Purpose Journal	Posting Abbreviation
Sale of merchandise on credit	Sales journal	S
Purchase on credit	Purchases journal	P
Receipt of cash	Cash receipts journal	CR
Disbursement of cash	Cash payments journal	CP

Notice that these special-purpose journals correspond to the accounting functions shown in the computerized system in Figure 2, except for payroll.

The general journal is used to record transactions that do not fall into any of these special categories. For example, purchase returns, sales returns, and adjusting and closing entries are recorded in the general journal. (When transactions are posted from the general journal to the ledger accounts, the posting abbreviation used is *J*.)

Using special-purpose journals greatly reduces the work involved in entering and posting transactions in the general ledger. For example, in most cases, instead of posting every debit and credit for each transaction, only the total amounts of the transactions are posted. In addition, labor can be divided by assigning each journal to a different employee. This division of labor is important in establishing good internal control.

FOCUS ON BUSINESS TECHNOLOGY

How Can Accounting Information Systems Help Satisfy Customers?

Accounting information systems are obviously important for financial reporting, but they are increasingly becoming a means of providing good customer service as well. For instance, Walgreens, the world's largest prescription pharmacy company, has established direct communications with the insurance companies, employers, and government agencies that pay the bills of Walgreens' customers. From an accounting perspective, such links enhance Walgreens' profitability by eliminating rejected prescriptions, facilitating billing, and speeding collections. From the customers' point of view, instant communication with payers means faster service and immediate confirmation of payments—no forms, no paperwork, and no-hassle service.[7]

FIGURE 4
Relationship of Subsidiary Accounts to the Controlling Account

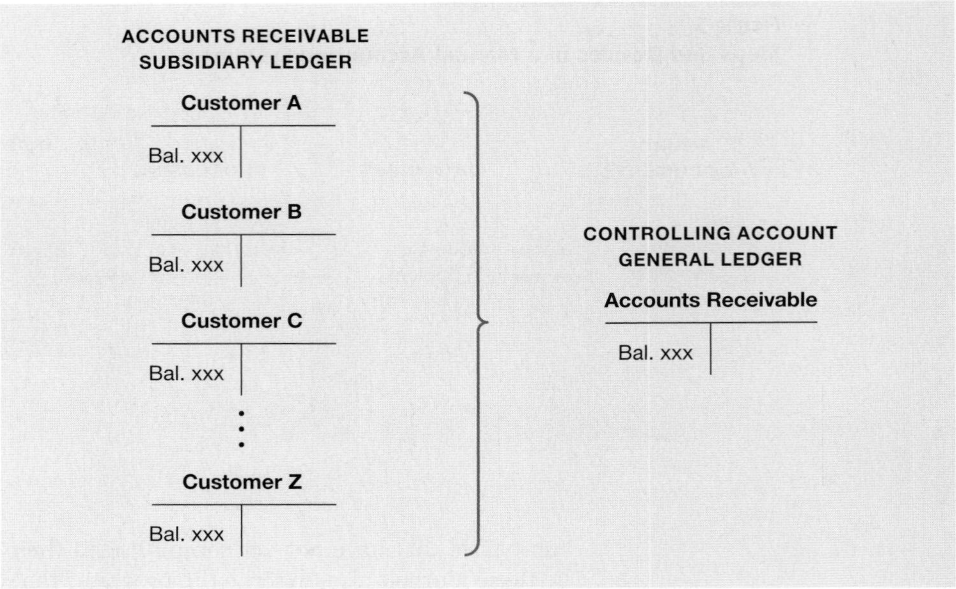

KEY POINT: Any general ledger account, such as Notes Payable or Buildings, that requires a detailed listing of individual balances would be a good candidate for a controlling account.

Controlling accounts and subsidiary ledgers contain important details about the figures in special-purpose journals and other books of original entry. A **controlling account**, also called a *control account*, is an account in the general ledger that maintains the total of the individual account balances in a subsidiary ledger. A **subsidiary ledger** is a ledger separate from the general ledger that contains a group of related accounts. The total of the balances in the subsidiary ledger accounts equals or ties in with the balance in the corresponding controlling account.

For example, up to this point we've used a single Accounts Receivable account. However, a single entry in Accounts Receivable does not tell us how much each customer has bought and how much each customer has paid or still owes. In practice, almost all companies that sell to customers on credit keep an individual accounts receivable record for each customer. If the company has 6,000 credit customers, there are 6,000 accounts receivable. To include all these accounts in the general ledger with the other asset, liability, and owner's equity accounts would make it very bulky. Consequently, most companies place individual customers' accounts in a separate, subsidiary ledger. In the accounts receivable subsidiary ledger, customers' accounts are filed either alphabetically or numerically (if account numbers are used).

STOP AND THINK!
When a customer calls customer service at a company to find out whether a recent payment was received and recorded, would the customer service representative refer to the general ledger or the subsidiary ledger?
The customer service representative would refer to the subsidiary ledger because that is where the customer's individual account would be located. ■

When a company puts individual customers' accounts in an accounts receivable subsidiary ledger, it still must maintain an Accounts Receivable account in the general ledger. This account controls in the sense that its balance must equal the total of the individual account balances in the subsidiary ledger, as shown in Figure 4. Transactions that involve accounts receivable, such as credit sales, must be posted to the individual customers' accounts daily. Postings to the controlling account in the general ledger are made at least once a month. When the amounts in the subsidiary ledger and the controlling account do not match, the accountant must find the error and correct it.

Most companies use an accounts payable subsidiary ledger as well. It is possible to use a subsidiary ledger for almost any account in the general ledger, such as Notes Receivable, Short-Term Investments, and Equipment, when management wants specific information on individual items.

Check out ACE for a Review Quiz at http://accounting.college.hmco.com/students.

TYPES OF SPECIAL-PURPOSE JOURNALS

LO5 Construct and use a sales journal, purchases journal, cash receipts journal, and cash payments journal.

RELATED TEXT ASSIGNMENTS
Q: 10, 11
SE: 5, 6, 7, 8, 9, 10
E: 2, 3, 4, 5, 6, 7, 8
P: 1, 2, 3, 4, 5, 6, 7, 8
SD: 6

As noted earlier, the four basic types of special-purpose journals are the sales journal, purchases journal, cash receipts journal, and cash payments journal.

SALES JOURNAL

The **sales journal** is designed to handle all credit sales. Cash sales are recorded in the cash receipts journal. Exhibit 1 illustrates a page from a typical sales journal and related ledger accounts. The page records six sales transactions involving five customers. Notice how the sales journal saves time:

1. Only one line is needed to record each transaction. Each entry consists of a debit to a customer in Accounts Receivable. The corresponding credit to Sales is understood.
2. The account names do not have to be written out because each entry automatically is debited to Accounts Receivable and credited to Sales.
3. No explanations are necessary because the function of the sales journal is to record credit sales only.
4. Only one amount—the total credit sales for the month—has to be posted. It is posted twice: once as a debit to Accounts Receivable and once as a credit to Sales. You can see the time this saves for the six transactions listed in Exhibit 1. Imagine the time saved when there are hundreds of sales transactions.

EXHIBIT 1
Sales Journal and Related Ledger Accounts

Sales Journal — Page 1

Date		Account Debited	Invoice Number	Post. Ref.	Amount (Debit Accounts Receivable/ Credit Sales)
July	1	Peter Clark	721	✓	750
	5	Georgetta Jones	722	✓	500
	8	Eugene Cumberland	723	✓	335
	12	Maxwell Gertz	724	✓	1,165
	18	Peter Clark	725	✓	1,225
	25	Michael Powers	726	✓	975
					4,950
					(114/411)

Post total at **end of month.**

Accounts Receivable — 114

Date		Post. Ref.	Debit	Credit	Balance Debit	Balance Credit
July	31	S1	4,950		4,950	

Sales — 411

Date		Post. Ref.	Debit	Credit	Balance Debit	Balance Credit
July	31	S1		4,950		4,950

KEY POINT: The checkmarks indicate daily postings to the subsidiary accounts, which normally are listed in alphabetical or numerical order. Also, the column totals are posted to the appropriate general ledger accounts at the end of the month.

STOP AND THINK!
If one wanted to know a company's total sales, would the sales journal be a good place to find this information?

Usually not. The sales journal shows only credit sales. Cash sales are recorded in the cash receipts journal. The best place to find total sales is in the Sales account in the general ledger after all postings have been made. ■

EXHIBIT 2
Relationship of Sales Journal, General Ledger, and Accounts Receivable Subsidiary Ledger and the Posting Procedure

KEY POINT: Accounts in the subsidiary ledger are maintained in alphabetical order. If account numbers are used to identify customers, the accounts would be listed in account number order.

KEY POINT: Subsidiary accounts are posted daily to prevent customers from exceeding their credit limits and to have up-to-date balances for customers wishing to pay their accounts.

Sales Journal — Page 1

Date		Account Debited	Invoice Number	Post. Ref.	Amount (Debit Accounts Receivable/ Credit Sales)
July	1	Peter Clark	721	✓	750
	5	Georgetta Jones	722	✓	500
	8	Eugene Cumberland	723	✓	335
	12	Maxwell Gertz	724	✓	1,165
	18	Peter Clark	725	✓	1,225
	25	Michael Powers	726	✓	975
					4,950
					(114/411)

Post total at **end of month** to general ledger accounts.

Post individual amounts **daily** to subsidiary ledger accounts.

General Ledger

Accounts Receivable — 114

Date		Post. Ref.	Debit	Credit	Balance Debit	Balance Credit
July	31	S1	4,950		4,950	

Sales — 411

Date		Post. Ref.	Debit	Credit	Balance Debit	Balance Credit
July	31	S1		4,950		4,950

Accounts Receivable Subsidiary Ledger

Peter Clark

Date		Post. Ref.	Debit	Credit	Balance
July	1	S1	750		750
	18	S1	1,225		1,975

Eugene Cumberland

Date		Post. Ref.	Debit	Credit	Balance
July	8	S1	335		335

Continue posting to Maxwell Gertz, Georgetta Jones, and Michael Powers.

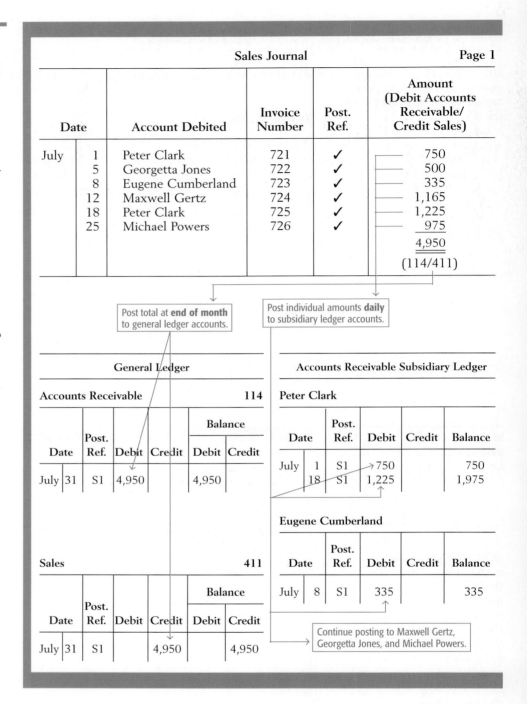

Exhibit 2 illustrates the procedure for using a sales journal:

1. Enter each sales invoice in the sales journal on a single line. Record the date, the customer's name, the invoice number, and the amount. No column is needed for the terms if the terms on all sales are the same.
2. At the end of each day, post each individual sale to the customer's account in the accounts receivable subsidiary ledger. As each sale is posted, place a checkmark (or customer account number, if used) in the Post. Ref. (posting reference) column of the sales journal to indicate that it has been posted. In the Post. Ref. column of each customer's account, place an *S* and the sales journal page number (*S1* means Sales Journal—Page 1) to indicate the source of the entry.

EXHIBIT 3
Schedule of Accounts Receivable

Mitchell's Used Car Sales
Schedule of Accounts Receivable
July 31, 20xx

Peter Clark	$1,975
Eugene Cumberland	335
Maxwell Gertz	1,165
Georgetta Jones	500
Michael Powers	975
Total Accounts Receivable	$4,950

KEY POINT: In theory, the sum of the account balances from the subsidiary accounts must equal the balance in the related general ledger controlling account. In practice, however, the equality is verified only at the end of the month, when the general ledger is posted.

KEY POINT: Columns can be added to a special-purpose journal for accounts that are commonly used.

3. At the end of the month, sum the Amount column in the sales journal to determine the total credit sales, and post the total to the general ledger accounts (debit Accounts Receivable and credit Sales). Place the numbers of the accounts debited and credited beneath the total in the sales journal to indicate that this step has been completed. In the general ledger, indicate the source of the entry in the Post. Ref. column of each account.
4. Verify the accuracy of the posting by adding the account balances of the accounts receivable subsidiary ledger and comparing the total with the balance of the Accounts Receivable controlling account in the general ledger. You can do this by listing the accounts in a schedule of accounts receivable, like the one in Exhibit 3, in the order in which the accounts are maintained. This step is performed after posting collections on account in the cash receipts journal.

Many cities and states require retailers to collect a sales tax from their customers and periodically remit the total collected to the city or state. In this case, an additional column is needed in the sales journal to record the credit to Sales Taxes Payable on credit sales. The form of the entry is shown in Exhibit 4. The procedure for posting to the ledger is exactly the same as described above, except that the total of the Sales Taxes Payable column must be posted as a credit to the Sales Taxes Payable account at the end of the month.

PURCHASES JOURNAL

The **purchases journal** is used to record purchases on credit. It can take the form of either a single-column journal or a multicolumn journal. In the single-column

EXHIBIT 4
Section of a Sales Journal with a Column for Sales Taxes

Sales Journal — Page 2

Date		Account Debited	Invoice Number	Post. Ref.	Debit: Accounts Receivable	Credits: Sales Taxes Payable	Credits: Sales
Aug.	1	Ralph P. Hake	727	✓	206	6	200

EXHIBIT 5
Relationship of Single-Column Purchases Journal to the General Ledger and the Accounts Payable Subsidiary Ledger

ENRICHMENT NOTE: The single-column purchases journal works exactly the same way as a sales journal, except that different ledger accounts are used.

Purchases Journal — Page 1

Date		Account Credited	Date of Invoice	Terms	Post. Ref.	Amount (Debit Purchases/ Credit Accounts Payable)
July	1	Jones Chevrolet	7/1	2/10, n/30	✓	2,500
	2	Marshall Ford	7/2	2/15, n/30	✓	300
	3	Dealer Sales	7/3	n/30	✓	700
	12	Thomas Auto	7/11	n/30	✓	1,400
	17	Dealer Sales	7/17	2/10, n/30	✓	3,200
	19	Thomas Auto	7/17	n/30	✓	1,100
						9,200
						(511/212)

Post individual amounts **daily.**

Post total at **end of month.**

General Ledger

Accounts Payable — 212

Date		Post. Ref.	Debit	Credit	Balance Debit	Balance Credit
July	31	P1		9,200		9,200

Purchases — 511

Date		Post. Ref.	Debit	Credit	Balance Debit	Balance Credit
July	31	P1	9,200		9,200	

Accounts Payable Subsidiary Ledger

Dealer Sales

Date		Post. Ref.	Debit	Credit	Balance
July	3	P1		700	700
	17	P1		3,200	3,900

Jones Chevrolet

Date		Post. Ref.	Debit	Credit	Balance
July	1	P1		2,500	2,500

Continue posting to Marshall Ford and Thomas Auto.

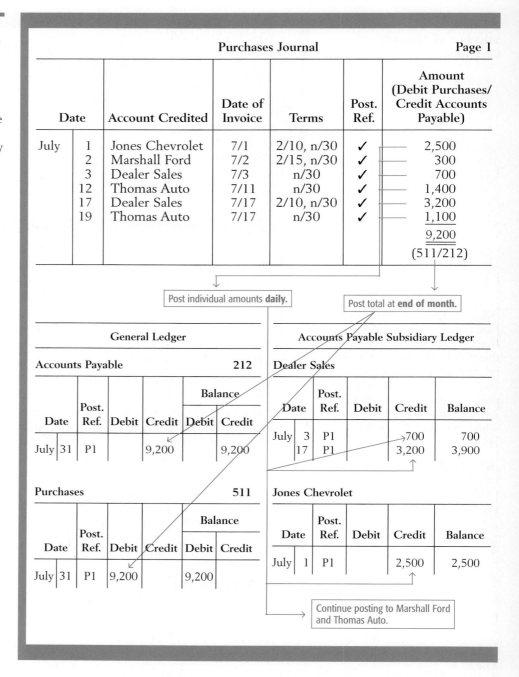

ENRICHMENT NOTE: It is easy to forget that a cash purchase is entered into the cash payments journal, not into the purchases journal.

journal shown in Exhibit 5, only credit purchases of merchandise for resale to customers are recorded. This kind of transaction is recorded with a debit to Purchases and a credit to Accounts Payable. When the single-column purchases journal is used, credit purchases of items other than merchandise are recorded in the general journal. Cash purchases are never recorded in the purchases journal; they are recorded in the cash payments journal, which we explain later.

Like the Accounts Receivable account, the Accounts Payable account in the general ledger is generally used as a controlling account. So that the company knows how much it owes each supplier, it keeps a separate account for each supplier in an accounts payable subsidiary ledger.

The procedure for using the purchases journal is much like that for using the sales journal:

1. Enter each purchase invoice in the purchases journal on a single line. Record the date, the supplier's name, the invoice date, the terms (if given), and the amount. It is not necessary to record the shipping terms in the terms column because they do not affect the payment date.
2. At the end of each day, post each individual purchase to the supplier's account in the accounts payable subsidiary ledger. As each purchase is posted, place a checkmark in the Post. Ref. column of the purchases journal to show that it has been posted. Also place a *P* and the page number of the purchases journal (*P1* stands for Purchases Journal—Page 1) in the Post. Ref. column of each supplier's account to show the source of the entry.
3. At the end of the month, sum the Amount column in the purchases journal, and post the total to the general ledger accounts (a debit to Purchases and a credit to Accounts Payable). Place the numbers of the accounts debited and credited beneath the totals in the purchases journal to show that this step has been carried out. In the general ledger, indicate the source of the entry in the Post. Ref. column of each account.
4. Check the accuracy of the posting by adding the account balances of the accounts payable subsidiary ledger and comparing the total with the balance of the Accounts Payable controlling account in the general ledger. This step can be done by preparing a schedule of accounts payable from the subsidiary ledger.

KEY POINT: The multicolumn purchases journal can accommodate the purchase of *anything* on credit. Each column total (except the total of Other Accounts) must be posted at the end of the month.

The single-column purchases journal can be expanded to record credit purchases of items other than merchandise by adding separate debit columns for other accounts that are used often. For example, the multicolumn purchases journal in Exhibit 6 has columns for Freight In, Store Supplies, Office Supplies, and Other Accounts. Here, the total credits to Accounts Payable ($9,637) equal the total debits to Purchases, Freight In, Store Supplies, Office Supplies, and Parts ($9,200 + $50 + $145 + $42 + $200). Again, the individual transactions in the Accounts

Exhibit 6
A Multicolumn Purchases Journal

Purchases Journal — Page 1

Date		Account Credited	Date of Invoice	Terms	Post. Ref.	Credit: Accounts Payable	Debits: Purchases	Freight In	Store Supplies	Office Supplies	Other Accounts: Account	Post. Ref.	Amount
July	1	Jones Chevrolet	7/1	2/10, n/30	✓	2,500	2,500						
	2	Marshall Ford	7/2	2/15, n/30	✓	300	300						
	2	Shelby Car Delivery	7/2	n/30	✓	50		50					
	3	Dealer Sales	7/3	n/30	✓	700	700						
	12	Thomas Auto	7/11	n/30	✓	1,400	1,400						
	17	Dealer Sales	7/17	2/10, n/30	✓	3,200	3,200						
	19	Thomas Auto	7/17	n/30	✓	1,100	1,100						
	25	Osborne Supply	7/21	n/10	✓	187			145	42			
	28	Auto Supply	7/28	n/10	✓	200					Parts	120	200
						9,637	9,200	50	145	42			200
						(212)	(511)	(514)	(132)	(133)			(✓)

Payable column are posted daily to the accounts payable subsidiary ledger, and the totals of each column in the purchases journal are posted monthly to the corresponding general ledger accounts. Entries in the Other Accounts column are posted individually to the named accounts, and the column total is not posted.

Cash Receipts Journal

KEY POINT: The cash receipts journal can accommodate *all* receipts of cash. Daily postings are made, not only to the subsidiary accounts, but also to the "other accounts." The Other Accounts column totals, therefore, are not posted at the end of the month. Only at the end of the month are the control account balances meaningful or correct.

All transactions involving receipts of cash are recorded in the **cash receipts journal**. Examples of these transactions are cash from cash sales and cash from credit customers in payment of their accounts. Although all cash receipts are alike in that they require a debit to Cash, they differ in that they require a variety of credit entries. Thus, the cash receipts journal must have several columns. The Other Accounts column is used to record credits to accounts not specifically represented by a column. The account numbers are entered in the Post. Ref. column, and the amounts are posted daily to the appropriate account in the general ledger.

The cash receipts journal shown in Exhibit 7 has three debit columns and three credit columns. The three debit columns are as follows:

1. *Cash* Each entry must have an amount in this column because each transaction involves a receipt of cash.
2. *Sales Discounts* This company allows a 2 percent discount for prompt payment. Therefore, it is useful to have a column for sales discounts. Notice that in the transactions of July 8 and 28, the debits to Cash and Sales Discounts equal the credits to Accounts Receivable.
3. *Other Accounts* The Other Accounts column (sometimes called *Sundry Accounts*) is used for transactions that involve both a debit to Cash and a debit to some account other than Sales Discounts.

These are the credit columns:

1. *Accounts Receivable* This column is used to record collections on account from customers. The name of the customer is written in the Account Debited/Credited column so that the payment can be entered in the corresponding account in the accounts receivable subsidiary ledger. Posting to the individual accounts receivable accounts is usually done daily so that each customer's balance is up to date.
2. *Sales* This column is used to record all cash sales during the month. Retail firms that use cash registers would make an entry at the end of each day for the total sales from each cash register for that day. The debit, of course, is in the Cash debit column.
3. *Other Accounts* This column is used for the credit portion of any entry that is neither a cash collection from accounts receivable nor a cash sale. The name of the account to be credited is indicated in the Account Debited/Credited column. For example, the transactions of July 1, 20, and 24 involve credits to accounts other than Accounts Receivable or Sales. These individual postings should be done daily (or weekly if there are just a few of them). If a company finds that it consistently is crediting a certain account in the Other Accounts column, it can add another credit column to the cash receipts journal for that particular account.

The procedure for posting the cash receipts journal, as shown in Exhibit 7, is as follows:

1. Post the transactions in the Accounts Receivable column daily to the individual accounts in the accounts receivable subsidiary ledger. The amount credited to the customer's account is the same as that credited to Accounts Receivable. A checkmark in the Post. Ref. column of the cash receipts journal indicates that the amount has been posted, and a *CR1* (Cash Receipts Journal—Page 1) in the

EXHIBIT 7
Relationship of the Cash Receipts Journal to the General Ledger and the Accounts Receivable Subsidiary Ledger

Cash Receipts Journal — Page 1

Date		Account Debited/Credited	Post. Ref.	Debits: Cash	Debits: Sales Discounts	Debits: Other Accounts	Credits: Accounts Receivable	Credits: Sales	Credits: Other Accounts
July	1	Henry Mitchell, Capital	311	20,000					20,000
	5	Sales		1,200				1,200	
	8	Georgetta Jones	✓	490	10		500		
	13	Sales		1,400				1,400	
	16	Peter Clark	✓	750			750		
	19	Sales		1,000				1,000	
	20	Store Supplies	132	500					500
	24	Notes Payable	213	5,000					5,000
	26	Sales		1,600				1,600	
	28	Peter Clark	✓	588	12		600		
				32,528	22		1,850	5,200	25,500
				(111)	(412)		(114)	(411)	(✓)

Post individual amounts in Accounts Receivable Susidiary Ledger column **daily.**

Post totals at **end of month.**

Total not posted.

Post individual amounts in Other Accounts column **daily.**

General Ledger

Cash — 111

Date		Post. Ref.	Debit	Credit	Balance: Debit	Balance: Credit
July	31	CR1	32,528		32,528	

Accounts Receivable — 114

Date		Post. Ref.	Debit	Credit	Balance: Debit	Balance: Credit
July	31	S1	4,950		4,950	
	31	CR1		1,850	3,100	

Store Supplies — 132

Date		Post. Ref.	Debit	Credit	Balance: Debit	Balance: Credit
Bal.					500	
July	20	CR1		500	—	

Accounts Receivable Subsidiary Ledger

Peter Clark

Date		Post. Ref.	Debit	Credit	Balance
July	1	S1	750		750
	16	CR1		750	—
	18	S1	1,225		1,225
	28	CR1		600	625

Georgetta Jones

Date		Post. Ref.	Debit	Credit	Balance
July	5	S1	500		500
	8	CR1		500	—

Continue posting to Notes Payable and Henry Mitchell, Capital.

Continue posting to Sales and Sales Discounts.

Post. Ref. column of each subsidiary ledger account indicates the source of the entry.

2. Post the debits/credits in the Other Accounts columns daily, or at convenient short intervals during the month, to the general ledger accounts. Write the account number in the Post. Ref. column of the cash receipts journal as the individual items are posted to indicate that the posting has been done, and write *CR1* in the Post. Ref. column of the general ledger account to indicate the source of the entry.
3. At the end of the month, total the columns in the cash receipts journal, as shown below. The sum of the Debits column totals must equal the sum of the Credits column totals:

Debits Column Totals		Credits Column Totals	
Cash	$32,528	Accounts Receivable	$ 1,850
Sales Discounts	22	Sales	5,200
Other Accounts	0	Other Accounts	25,500
Total Debits	$32,550	Total Credits	$32,550

This step is called *crossfooting.*

4. Post the Debits column totals as follows:
   a. *Cash* Posted as a debit to the Cash account.
   b. *Sales Discounts* Posted as a debit to the Sales Discounts account.
5. Post the Credits column totals as follows:
   a. *Accounts Receivable* Posted as a credit to the Accounts Receivable controlling account.
   b. *Sales* Posted as a credit to the Sales account.
6. Write the account numbers below each column in the cash receipts journal as they are posted to indicate that these steps have been completed. *CR1* is written in the Post. Ref. column of each account in the general ledger to indicate the source of the entry.
7. Notice that the total of the Other Accounts column is not posted because each entry was posted separately when the transaction occurred. The individual accounts were posted in step **2.** Place a checkmark at the bottom of the column to show that postings in that column have been made and that the total is not posted.

Cash Payments Journal

KEY POINT: The cash payments journal can accommodate *all* cash payments. It functions like the cash receipts journal, although it uses some different general ledger accounts.

All transactions involving payments of cash are recorded in the **cash payments journal** (also called the *cash disbursements journal*). Examples of these transactions are cash purchases and payments of obligations resulting from earlier purchases on credit. The form of the cash payments journal is much like that of the cash receipts journal.

The cash payments journal shown in Exhibit 8 has three credit columns and two debit columns.

The credit columns for the cash payments journal are as follows:

1. *Cash* Each entry must have an amount in this column because each transaction involves a payment of cash.
2. *Purchases Discounts* When purchases discounts are taken, they are recorded in this column.
3. *Other Accounts* This column is used to record credits to accounts other than Cash or Purchases Discounts. Notice that the July 31 transaction shows a purchase of Land for $15,000, with a check for $5,000 and a note payable for $10,000.

EXHIBIT 8
Relationship of the Cash Payments Journal to the General Ledger and the Accounts Payable Subsidiary Ledger

Cash Payments Journal — Page 1

Date		Ck. No.	Payee	Account Credited/Debited	Post. Ref.	Credits: Cash	Credits: Purchases Discounts	Credits: Other Accounts	Debits: Accounts Payable	Debits: Other Accounts
July	2	101	Sondra Tidmore	Purchases	511	400				400
	6	102	Daily Journal	Advertising Expense	612	200				200
	8	103	Siviglia Agency	Rent Expense	631	250				250
	11	104	Jones Chevrolet		✓	2,450	50		2,500	
	16	105	Charles Kuntz	Salaries Expense	611	600				600
	17	106	Marshall Ford		✓	294	6		300	
	24	107	Grabow & Co.	Prepaid Insurance	119	480				480
	27	108	Dealer Sales		✓	3,136	64		3,200	
	30	109	A&B Equipment Company	Office Equipment	144	900				400
				Service Equipment	146					500
	31	110	Burns Real Estate	Notes Payable	213	5,000		10,000		
				Land	141					15,000
						13,710	120	10,000	6,000	17,830
						(111)	(512)	(✓)	(212)	(✓)

Post individual amounts in Other Accounts column **daily**.

Post individual amounts in Accounts Payable Subsidiary Ledger column **daily**.

Post totals at **end of month.**

Totals not posted.

General Ledger

Cash — 111

Date		Post. Ref.	Debit	Credit	Balance: Debit	Balance: Credit
July	31	CR1	32,528		32,528	
	31	CP1		13,710	18,818	

Prepaid Insurance — 119

Date		Post. Ref.	Debit	Credit	Balance: Debit	Balance: Credit
July	24	CP1	480		480	

Continue posting to Land, Office Equipment, Service Equipment, Notes Payable, Purchases, Salaries Expense, Advertising Expense, and Rent Expense.

Continue posting to Purchases Discounts and Accounts Payable.

Accounts Payable Subsidiary Ledger

Dealer Sales

Date		Post. Ref.	Debit	Credit	Balance
July	3	P1		700	700
	17	P1		3,200	3,900
	27	CP1	3,200		700

Jones Chevrolet

Date		Post. Ref.	Debit	Credit	Balance
July	1	P1		2,500	2,500
	11	CP1	2,500		—

Marshall Ford

Date		Post. Ref.	Debit	Credit	Balance
July	2	P1		300	300
	17	CP1	300		—

The debit columns are as follows:

1. *Accounts Payable* This column is used to record payments to suppliers that have extended credit to the company. Each supplier's name is written in the Payee column so that the payment can be entered in the supplier's account in the accounts payable subsidiary ledger.
2. *Other Accounts* Cash can be expended for many reasons. Therefore, an Other Accounts or Sundry Accounts column is needed in the cash payments journal. The title of the account to be debited is written in the Account Credited/Debited column, and the amount is entered in the Other Accounts debit column. If a company finds that a particular account appears often in the Other Accounts column, it can add another debit column to the cash payments journal.

The procedure for posting the cash payments journal, shown in Exhibit 8, is as follows:

1. Post the transactions in the Accounts Payable column daily to the individual accounts in the accounts payable subsidiary ledger. Place a checkmark in the Post. Ref. column of the cash payments journal to indicate that the posting has been made.
2. Post the debits/credits in the Other Accounts debit/credit columns to the general ledger daily or at convenient short intervals during the month. Write the account number in the Post. Ref. column of the cash payments journal as the individual items are posted to indicate that the posting has been completed and *CP1* (Cash Payments Journal—Page 1) in the Post. Ref. column of each general ledger account.
3. At the end of the month, the columns are footed and crossfooted. That is, the sum of the Credits column totals must equal the sum of the Debits column totals, as follows:

Credits Column Totals		**Debits Column Totals**	
Cash	$13,710	Accounts Payable	$ 6,000
Purchases Discounts	120	Other Accounts	17,830
Other Accounts	10,000		
Total Credits	$23,830	Total Debits	$23,830

4. At the end of the month, post the column totals for Cash, Purchases Discounts, and Accounts Payable to their respective accounts in the general ledger. Write the account number below each column in the cash payments journal as it is

Focus on Business Ethics

Why Is Confidentiality Important to Accountants?

Confidentiality is an important issue in the design and use of accounting information systems. For example, computer operators and other employees who have access to accounting records may know customers' credit histories as well as what they have purchased, how much they owe the company, and how punctually they pay their bills. In many cases, customers may include friends, neighbors, and acquaintances. The payroll records also contain such sensitive information as salary levels. To avoid problems, it is good practice for businesses to restrict access to sensitive records to only those employees whose work depends on them and to make it clear that strict confidentiality must be maintained. The Institute of Management Accountants states that information should not be communicated to anyone inside or outside the company who is not authorized to receive it, except when disclosure is required by law.

EXHIBIT 9
Transactions Recorded in the General Journal

KEY POINT: The general journal is used only to record transactions that cannot be accommodated by the special-purpose journals. Whenever a controlling account is recorded, it must be "double posted" to the general ledger and the subsidiary accounts. All general journal entries are posted daily; column totals are neither obtained nor posted.

General Journal — Page 1

Date		Description	Post. Ref.	Debit	Credit
July	25	Accounts Payable, Thomas Auto	212/✓	700	
		Purchases Returns and Allowances	513		700
		Returned used car for credit; invoice date: 7/11			
	26	Sales Returns and Allowances	413	35	
		Accounts Receivable, Maxwell Gertz	114/✓		35
		Allowance for faulty tire			

posted to indicate that this step has been completed and *CP1* in the Post. Ref. column of each general ledger account. Place a checkmark under the total of each Other Accounts column in the cash payments journal to indicate that the postings in the column have been made and that the total is not posted.

Transactions That Are Not Recorded in a Special-Purpose Journal

Adjusting and closing entries are recorded in the general journal. Transactions that do not involve sales, purchases, cash receipts, or cash payments should also be recorded in the general journal. Usually, there are only a few of these transactions. Two examples of entries that do not fit in a special-purpose journal are a return of merchandise bought on account and an allowance from a supplier for credit.

These entries are shown in Exhibit 9. Notice that the entries include a debit or a credit to a controlling account (Accounts Payable or Accounts Receivable). The name of the customer or supplier also is given here. When this kind of debit or credit is made to a controlling account in the general ledger, the entry must be posted twice: once to the controlling account and once to the individual account in the subsidiary ledger. This procedure keeps the subsidiary ledger equal to the controlling account. Notice that the July 26 transaction is posted by a debit to Sales Returns and Allowances in the general ledger (shown by the account number 413), a credit to the Accounts Receivable controlling account in the general ledger (account number 114), and a credit to the Maxwell Gertz account in the accounts receivable subsidiary ledger (checkmark).

The Flexibility of Special-Purpose Journals

Special-purpose journals reduce and simplify the work of accounting and allow for the division of labor. Such journals should be designed to fit the business in which they are used. As noted earlier, if certain accounts show up often in the Other Accounts column of a journal, it is a good idea to add a column for them when a new page of a special-purpose journal is prepared. Also, if certain transactions appear repeatedly in the general journal, it is a good idea to set up a new special-purpose journal.

✓ Check out ACE for a Review Quiz at http://accounting.college.hmco.com/students.

Chapter Review

Review of Learning Objectives

LO1 Identify the principles of designing accounting information systems.

The developers of an accounting information system must keep in mind the four principles of systems design: the cost-benefit principle, the control principle, the compatibility principle, and the flexibility principle.

LO2 Describe the use and structure of spreadsheet software and general ledger systems in computerized accounting systems.

Most companies today have computerized accounting systems that use spreadsheet software and general ledger systems. Spreadsheet software, such as Windows® Excel and Lotus, is used widely by accountants for analysis of data. General ledger systems are a group of integrated software programs that perform major accounting functions, such as accounting for purchases and accounts payable, sales and accounts receivable, and payroll. Some software uses icons in a graphical user interface to guide the accountant through the tasks.

LO3 Explain how accountants and businesses use the Internet.

In addition to using the Internet for access to the Web, email, and electronic bulletin boards, accountants and businesses use it for financial reporting, Extensible Business Reporting Language (XBRL), electronic commerce (ecommerce), electronic data interchange (EDI), supply-chain management, event-to-knowledge management (E2K), and document-less transactions.

LO4 Describe the role of special-purpose journals and their relationship to controlling accounts and subsidiary ledgers.

The typical manual data processing system uses several special-purpose journals, each designed to record one kind of transaction. Recording only one kind of transaction in each journal reduces and simplifies the accounting task and allows for the division of labor. The division of labor is important for internal control. Subsidiary ledgers contain individual accounts of a specific kind, such as customers' accounts (accounts receivable) or suppliers' accounts (accounts payable). The individual account records are kept separately in a subsidiary ledger to avoid making the general ledger too bulky. The total of the balances of the subsidiary ledger accounts should equal the balance of the controlling account in the general ledger because the individual items are posted daily to the subsidiary ledger accounts and the column totals are posted to the general ledger account monthly from the special-purpose journal.

LO5 Construct and use a sales journal, purchases journal, cash receipts journal, and cash payments journal.

A special-purpose journal is constructed by devoting a single column to a particular account (for example, debits to Cash in the cash receipts journal and credits to Cash in the cash payments journal). Other columns in the journal depend on the kinds of transactions in which the company normally engages. Special-purpose journals also have columns for transaction dates, explanations or subsidiary account names, and posting references.

Review of Concepts and Terminology

The following concepts and terms were introduced in this chapter:

LO1 **Accounting information systems:** The processes that gather data, put them into useful form, and communicate the results to management.

LO5 **Cash payments journal:** A multicolumn special-purpose journal used to record payments of cash. Also called *cash disbursements journal.*

LO5 **Cash receipts journal:** A multicolumn special-purpose journal used to record transactions involving the receipt of cash.

LO1 **Compatibility principle:** The principle that holds that the design of an accounting information system must be in harmony with the organizational and human factors of the business.

LO4 **Controlling account:** An account in the general ledger that summarizes the total balance of a group of related accounts in a subsidiary ledger. Also called *control account*.

LO1 **Control principle:** The principle that holds that an accounting information system must provide all the features of internal control needed to protect the firm's assets and ensure that data are reliable.

LO1 **Cost-benefit principle:** The principle that holds that the benefits derived from an accounting information system must be equal to or greater than its cost.

LO1 **Data processing:** The means by which an accounting system gathers data, organizes them into useful forms for business decision making, and issues the resulting information to users.

LO3 **Electronic commerce (ecommerce):** The conduct of business transactions on computer networks, including the Internet.

LO3 **Electronic Data Interchange (EDI):** Private links that facilitate the conduct of electronic commerce.

LO1 **Enterprise resource planning (ERP) systems:** Comprehensive, computerized information systems that integrate financial and nonfinancial information about customers, operations, and suppliers in a single database.

LO3 **Event-to-knowledge (E2K) management:** A system that uses the Internet to get information to users within and outside a company in the quickest possible way after an event like a sale or a purchase has occurred.

LO3 **Extensible Business Reporting Language (XBRL):** A new computer language developed by accountants and others for the express purpose of identifying and communicating financial information.

LO1 **Flexibility principle:** The principle that holds that an accounting information system must be flexible enough to allow for growth in the volume of transactions and for organizational changes.

LO2 **General ledger systems:** A group of integrated software programs that accountants use to perform the major accounting functions.

LO2 **Graphical user interface (GUI):** The employment of symbols, called *icons*, to represent operations, which makes software easier to use.

LO2 **Icons:** Symbols representing operations that appear on a computer screen as part of a graphical user interface.

LO3 **Internet:** The world's largest computer network.

LO4 **Manual data processing:** A system of accounting in which each transaction is entered manually from a source document into the general journal (input device) and each debit and credit is posted manually to the correct ledger account (processor and memory device) for the eventual preparation of financial statements (output devices).

LO5 **Purchases journal:** A single-column or multicolumn special-purpose journal used to record all purchases on credit.

LO5 **Sales journal:** A type of special-purpose journal used to record credit sales.

LO2 **Source documents:** The written evidence that supports each accounting transaction for each major accounting function.

LO4 **Special-purpose journal:** An input device in an accounting system that is used to record a single type of transaction.

LO2 **Spreadsheet:** A computerized grid of columns and rows into which the user places data or formulas related to financial planning, cost estimating, and other accounting tasks.

LO4 **Subsidiary ledger:** A ledger separate from the general ledger that contains a group of related accounts; the total of the balances in the subsidiary ledger accounts must equal the balance of the related controlling account in the general ledger.

LO3 **Supply-chain management:** A system that uses the Internet to track the supplies and materials a manufacturer will need on a day-to-day basis.

Review Problem

Purchases Journal

LO1 LO4 LO5 Caraban Company is a retail seller of hiking and camping gear. The company is installing a manual accounting system, and the accountant is trying to decide whether to use a single-column or a multicolumn purchases journal. Here is a list of several transactions related to purchases in the month of January.

Jan. 5 Received a shipment of merchandise from Simons Corporation, terms 2/10, n/30, FOB shipping point, invoice dated January 4, $2,875.

10 Received a bill from Allied Freight for the freight charges on the January 5 shipment, terms n/30, invoice dated January 4, $416.

15 Returned some of the merchandise received from Simons Corporation because it was not what was ordered, $315.

20 Purchased store supplies of $56 and office supplies of $117 from Mason Company, terms n/30, invoice dated January 20.

25 Received a shipment from Thomas Manufacturing, $1,882, which included supplier-paid freight charges of $175, terms n/30, FOB shipping point, invoice dated January 23.

REQUIRED ▶

1. Record the transactions using a single-column purchases journal and a general journal, and show the posting reference for each journal entry. Use the following accounts: Store Supplies (116), Office Supplies (117), Accounts Payable (211), Purchases (611), Purchases Returns and Allowances (612), and Freight In (613).
2. Record the transactions using a multicolumn purchases journal and a general journal, total the purchases journal, and show the posting reference for each entry.
3. Using the principles of systems design, compare the single-column and multicolumn journals in terms of the number of entries and postings.

Answer to Review Problem

1. Record the transactions in a single-column purchases journal and the general journal. Show the posting references.

Purchases Journal — Page 1

Date		Account Credited	Date of Invoice	Terms	Post. Ref.	Amount
Jan.	5	Simons Corporation	1/4	2/10, n/30	✓	2,875

General Journal — Page 1

Date		Description	Post. Ref.	Debit	Credit
Jan.	10	Freight In	613	416	
		Accounts Payable, Allied Freight	211/✓		416
		Freight charges on Simons Corporation shipment, terms n/30, invoice dated January 4			
	15	Accounts Payable, Simons Corporation	211/✓	315	
		Purchases Returns and Allowances	612		315
		Returned merchandise not ordered			
	20	Store Supplies	116	56	
		Office Supplies	117	117	
		Accounts Payable, Mason Company	211/✓		173
		Purchased supplies, terms n/30, invoice dated January 20			
	25	Purchases	611	1,707	
		Freight In	613	175	
		Accounts Payable, Thomas Manufacturing	211/✓		1,882
		Purchased merchandise, terms n/30; supplier paid shipping, invoice dated January 23			

2. Record the transactions in a multicolumn purchases journal and the general journal. Total the purchases journal and show posting references.

Purchases Journal — Page 1

Date		Account Credited	Date of Invoice	Terms	Post. Ref.	Credit: Accounts Payable	Debits: Purchases	Debits: Freight In	Debits: Store Supplies	Debits: Office Supplies
Jan.	5	Simons Corporation	1/4	2/10, n/30	✓	2,875	2,875			
	10	Allied Freight	1/4	n/30	✓	416		416		
	20	Mason Company	1/20	n/30	✓	173			56	117
	25	Thomas Manufacturing	1/23	n/30	✓	1,882	1,707	175		
						5,346	4,582	591	56	117
						(211)	(611)	(613)	(116)	(117)

Each of these amounts is posted **daily** to the appropriate account in the subsidiary ledger.

Each of these totals is posted **monthly** to the applicable general ledger account.

General Journal **Page 1**

Date		Description	Post. Ref.	Debit	Credit
Jan.	15	Accounts Payable, Simons Corporation	211/✓	315	
		Purchases Returns and Allowances	612		315
		Returned merchandise not ordered			

This amount is posted both to the controlling account and to the subsidiary account.

This amount is posted to the general ledger account.

3. The single-column purchases journal requires four general journal entries plus one purchases journal entry, or 20 separate lines, including explanations. In addition, 15 postings to the general ledger and the accounts payable subsidiary ledger are necessary. (Also, the total of the purchases journal must be posted twice at the end of the month: once as a debit to Purchases and once as a credit to Accounts Payable.) The multicolumn purchases journal calls for just one general journal entry and four purchases journal entries. Only eight lines need to be written, and only seven postings must be made. (In addition, the column totals in the purchases journal must be posted at the end of the month.)

   In applying the cost-benefit principle, the benefits of the multicolumn purchases journal in terms of journalizing and posting time saved are clear from this analysis. In addition, there are fewer chances for error when using the multicolumn purchases journal. So the control principle is better achieved under the second system. It is not possible to decide which system better meets the compatibility principle because we do not know the relative proportion of transaction types. For instance, if the number of transactions like the one for January 5 exceeds all the others by ten to one, the first system may be more compatible with the needs of the company. On the other hand, if there are many transactions like those for January 10, 20, and 25, the second system may be more compatible. Finally, in terms of the flexibility principle, the multicolumn purchases journal is obviously more flexible because it can handle more kinds of transactions and can be expanded to include columns for other accounts if necessary.

Chapter Assignments

Building Your Knowledge Foundation

Questions

1. What is the relationship of accounting information systems to data processing?
2. Describe the four principles of accounting information systems design.
3. Why is a graphical user interface important to the successful use of general ledger systems?
4. Define and contrast *enterprise resource planning* (ERP) *systems*, *electronic commerce*, and *electronic data interchange* (EDI).
5. Data are the raw material of a computer system. Trace the flow of data through the different parts of a computerized accounting system.

6. How does a computerized accounting system using a general ledger system relate to the major accounting functions?
7. In what ways can the Internet assist businesses in their operations?
8. How do special-purpose journals save time in entering and posting transactions?
9. What is the purpose of the Accounts Receivable controlling account? What is its relationship to the accounts receivable subsidiary ledger?
10. Lake Transit had 1,700 sales on credit during the current month.
    a. If the firm uses a two-column general journal to record sales, how many times will the word *Sales* be written?
    b. How many postings to the Sales account will have to be made?
    c. If the firm uses a sales journal, how many times will the word *Sales* be written?
    d. How many postings to the Sales account will have to be made?
11. Why are the cash receipts journal and cash payments journal crossfooted? When is this step performed?
12. A company has the following accounts with balances: 18 asset accounts, including the Accounts Receivable account but not the individual customers' accounts; 200 customer accounts; 8 liability accounts, including the Accounts Payable account but not the individual creditors' accounts; 100 creditor accounts; and 35 owner's equity accounts, including income statement accounts—a total of 361 accounts. How many accounts in total would appear in the general ledger?

SHORT EXERCISES

SE 1. **LO1 Principles of Accounting Information System Design**

Indicate whether each of the following statements concerning a newly installed accounting information system is most closely related to the (a) cost-benefit principle, (b) control principle, (c) compatibility principle, or (d) flexibility principle:

1. Procedures are in place to ensure that the data entered into the system are reliable.
2. The system allows for growth in the number and types of transactions entered into by the company.
3. The system was installed after its costs were carefully weighed against the improved decision making that will result.
4. The system takes into account the various operations of the business and the capabilities of the people who will interact with the system.

SE 2. **LO2 Computerized Accounting System**

Assuming that a company uses a general ledger package for its computerized accounting system, indicate whether each of the following source documents would provide input to (a) sales/accounts receivable, (b) purchases/accounts payable, (c) cash receipts, (d) cash disbursements, (e) payroll, or (f) the general journal:

1. Deposit slips
2. Time cards
3. Vendor invoices
4. Checks issued
5. Customer invoices
6. Documents for other journal entries

SE 3. **LO3 Use of the Internet**

Define and contrast the following uses of the Internet:

1. Electronic commerce (ecommerce)
2. Electronic Data Interchange (EDI)
3. Supply-chain management

SE 4. **LO4 Transactions and Special-Purpose Journals**

Indicate whether each transaction listed below should be recorded in the (a) sales journal, (b) multicolumn purchases journal, (c) cash receipts journal, (d) cash payments journal, or (e) general journal:

1. Receipt on account
2. Purchase return on account
3. Sale on account
4. Purchase on account
5. Sale for cash
6. Payment on account

SE 5. **LO5 Sales Journal Transactions**

Using Exhibit 2 as a model, show how each of the following transactions should be entered in a sales journal. All terms are 2/10, n/30. If a transaction should not appear in the sales journal, tell where it should be recorded. Total and rule the journal.

Oct.	1	Sold merchandise to S. Rush on credit, invoice no. 301, $350.
	8	Sold merchandise to J. Sussman for cash, $150.
	15	Sold merchandise to F. Thomaso on credit, invoice no. 302, $200.

LO4 LO5 Sales Journal Postings and Subsidiary Ledger

SE 6. Assuming the transactions in **SE 5** are the only sales transactions for the month of October, describe all the postings that would be made from the sales journal to the general ledger and the accounts receivable subsidiary ledger.

LO5 Multicolumn Purchases Journal

SE 7. Using Exhibit 6 as a model, show how each of the following transactions should be entered in a multicolumn purchases journal. If a transaction should not appear in this journal, tell where it should be recorded. Total and rule the journal.

Oct. 2 Purchased merchandise on credit from Farmington Electronics, invoice dated October 1, terms 2/10, n/30, $500.
4 Purchased merchandise on credit from Ciarri Electrics, invoice dated October 2, terms 2/10, n/30, $650, including freight charges of $50.
6 Purchased supplies on credit from Avon Supplies, invoice dated October 5, terms n/30, $180, to be allocated one-third to store and two-thirds to office.
8 Purchased postage stamps at the post office for cash (check no. 101), $58.
9 Purchased equipment on credit from Simsbury Furniture Co., invoice dated October 9, terms n/EOM, $1,000.

LO4 LO5 Purchases Journal Postings and Subsidiary Ledger

SE 8. Assuming the transactions in **SE 7** are the only purchases transactions for the month of October, describe all the postings that would be made from the purchases journal to the general ledger and the accounts payable subsidiary ledger.

LO4 LO5 Cash Receipts Journal

SE 9. Using Exhibit 7 as a model, show how each of the following transactions should be entered in the cash receipts journal. If a transaction should not appear in this journal, tell where it should be recorded.

Oct. 8 Sold merchandise for cash to J. Sussman, $150.
9 Received payment on account from S. Rush, $350 less 2 percent discount.
17 F. Thomaso returned purchase of October 15 for full credit, $200.

Describe the postings that are required for each transaction.

LO4 LO5 Cash Payments Journal

SE 10. Using Exhibit 8 as a model, show how each of the following transactions should be entered in the cash payments journal. If a transaction should not appear in this journal, tell where it should be recorded.

Oct. 8 Issued check no. 101 to the U.S. Postal Service for postage, $58.
12 Issued check no. 102 to Farmington Electronics, $500 less 2 percent discount.

Describe the postings that are required for each transaction.

EXERCISES

LO4 Matching Transactions to Special-Purpose Journals

E 1. A company uses a single-column sales journal, a single-column purchases journal, a cash receipts journal, a cash payments journal, and a general journal. In which journal would each of the following transactions be recorded?

1. Sold merchandise on credit
2. Sold merchandise for cash
3. Gave a customer credit for merchandise purchased on credit and returned
4. Paid a creditor
5. Paid office salaries
6. Received a customer's payment for merchandise previously purchased on credit
7. Recorded adjusting and closing entries
8. Purchased merchandise on credit
9. Purchased sales department supplies on credit
10. Purchased office equipment for cash
11. Returned merchandise purchased on credit
12. Paid sales commissions

LO4 LO5 Characteristics of Special-Purpose Journals

E 2. Fallow Corporation uses a single-column sales journal, a single-column purchases journal, a cash receipts journal, a cash payments journal, and a general journal.

1. In which of the journals listed above would you expect to find the fewest transactions recorded?

2. At the end of the accounting period, to which account or accounts should the total of the sales journal be posted as a debit and/or credit?
3. At the end of the accounting period, to which account or accounts should the total of the purchases journal be posted as a debit and/or credit?
4. What two subsidiary ledgers would probably be associated with the journals listed above? From which journals would postings normally be made to each of the two subsidiary ledgers?
5. In which of the journals are adjusting and closing entries made?

LO5 Identifying the Content of a Special-Purpose Journal

E 3. Shown below is a page from a special-purpose journal.

				Debits		Credits		
Date		Account Debited/Credited	Post. Ref.	Cash	Sales Discount	Accounts Receivable	Sales	Other Accounts
		Balance Forward		79,598	1,574	20,408	8,564	52,200
May	25	Sally Juno	✓	980	20	1,000		
	26	Notes Receivable	115	2,240				2,000
		Interest Income	715					240
	27	Cash Sale		1,920			1,920	
	31	Kevin LaPorte	✓	400		400		
				85,138	1,594	21,808	10,484	54,440
				(111)	(412)	(114)	(411)	(√)

1. What kind of journal is this?
2. Explain each transaction.
3. Explain the following: (a) the numbers under the double rule, (b) the checkmarks entered in the Post. Ref. column, (c) the numbers 115 and 715 in the Post. Ref. column, and (d) the checkmark below the Other Accounts credit column.

LO5 Multicolumn Purchases Journal

E 4. Herlihy Company uses a multicolumn purchases journal similar to the one shown in Exhibit 6. During the month of July, Herlihy made the following purchases:

July 1 Purchased merchandise from Burlington Company on account for $5,400, invoice dated July 1, terms 2/10, n/30.

3 Received freight bill dated July 1 from SuLong Freight for merchandise purchased July 1, $350, terms n/30.

18 Purchased supplies from Leddin Company for $240; allocated half to the store and half to the office; invoice dated July 16, terms n/30.

23 Purchased merchandise from Valera Company on account for $1,974; total included freight in of $174; invoice dated July 20, terms n/30, FOB shipping point.

27 Purchased office supplies from Leddin Company for $96, invoice dated July 27, terms n/30.

31 Purchased a one-year insurance policy from Southbury Associates, $480, invoice dated July 31, terms n/30.

1. Set up a multicolumn purchases journal similar to the one in Exhibit 6 and label it page 1.
2. Enter the transactions listed above in the purchases journal. Then foot and crossfoot the columns.

LO4 LO5 Finding Errors in Special-Purpose Journals

E 5. A company records purchases in a single-column purchases journal and records purchases returns in its general journal. During the past month, an accounting clerk made each of the errors described below.

1. Correctly recorded a $191 purchase in the purchases journal but posted it to the creditor's account as a $119 purchase.
2. Made an error in totaling the Amount column of the purchases journal.
3. Posted a purchases return from the general journal to the Purchases Returns and Allowances account and the Accounts Payable account but did not post it to the creditor's account.
4. Made an error in determining the balance of a creditor's account.
5. Posted a purchases return to the Accounts Payable account but did not post it to the Purchases Returns and Allowances account.

Explain how each error might be discovered.

LO4 LO5 Posting from a Sales Journal

E 6. Figaro Company began business on June 1. The company maintains a sales journal. The sales journal at the end of the month is shown below.

Sales Journal — **Page 1**

Date		Account Debited	Invoice Number	Post. Ref.	Amount
June	3	Sue Longo	1001		516
	8	Ed Kohen	1002		951
	12	Ye Tang	1003		642
	18	Sue Longo	1004		291
	27	Gina Touloumos	1005		1,299
					3,699

1. Open general ledger accounts for Accounts Receivable (112) and Sales (411) and an accounts receivable subsidiary ledger with an account for each customer. Make the appropriate postings from the sales journal, inserting the posting references in the sales journal and in the ledger accounts as you work.
2. Prove the accounts receivable subsidiary ledger by preparing a schedule of accounts receivable.

LO4 LO5 Identification of Transactions

E 7. Conomacos Company uses a manual accounting system with a sales journal, purchases journal, cash receipts journal, cash payments journal, and general journal similar to those illustrated in the text. On October 31, the Sales account in the general ledger looked like this:

Sales — **Page 411**

Date		Item	Post Ref.	Debit	Credit	Balance	
						Debit	Credit
Oct.	31		S11		74,842		74,842
	31		CR7		42,414		117,256
	31		J17	117,256			—

On October 31, the M. Kern account in the accounts receivable subsidiary ledger looked like this:

M. Kern Account No. 10012

Date		Item	Post. Ref.	Debit	Credit	Balance
Oct.	8		S10	4,216		4,216
	12		J14		564	3,652
	18		CR6		1,000	2,652

1. Write an explanation of each entry in the Sales account; include the journal from which the entry was posted.
2. Write an explanation of each entry in the M. Kern account in the accounts receivable subsidiary ledger; include the journal from which the entry was posted.

LO4 LO5 **Identification of Transactions**

E 8. Randall Company uses a sales journal, single-column purchases journal, cash receipts journal, cash payments journal, and general journal similar to those shown in the text. On April 30, the D. Amir account in the accounts receivable subsidiary ledger appeared as shown below.

D. Amir

Date		Item	Post. Ref.	Debit	Credit	Balance
Mar.	31		S4	2,448		2,448
Apr.	7		J7		192	2,256
	12		CR5		600	1,656
	17		S6	684		2,340

On April 30, the Wong Company account in the accounts payable subsidiary ledger appeared as follows:

Wong Company

Date		Item	Post. Ref.	Debit	Credit	Balance
Apr.	18		P7		6,078	6,078
	20		J9	636		5,442
	25		CP8	5,442		—

1. Write an explanation of each entry that affected the D. Amir account receivable, including the journal from which the entry was posted.
2. Write an explanation of each entry that affected the Wong Company account payable, including the journal from which the entry was posted.

PROBLEMS

LO4 Special-Purpose Journals and
LO5 Subsidiary Ledgers

P 1. Maher Company is a small retail business that uses a manual accounting system similar to the one described in this chapter. At the end of April 20xx, the firm's accounts receivable and accounts payable subsidiary ledgers showed the following balances:

Accounts Receivable		Accounts Payable	
A. Barrel	$430	Bayle Company	$1,300
L. Lozocek	330	Centro Company	890
Total Accounts Receivable	$760	Total Accounts Payable	$2,190

During May, the company engaged in the following transactions:

May 2 Sold merchandise on credit to R. Woodman, a new customer, $570, terms 2/10, n/30, invoice no. 1001.
4 Received payment in full from L. Lozocek, no discount allowed.
5 Paid Bayle Company the full amount owed less a 2 percent discount, check no. 201.
8 Accepted a return of merchandise for credit from R. Woodman, $170.
9 Paid Centro Company the full amount owed, no discount allowed, check no. 202.
12 Received payment from R. Woodman for amount due less discount.
15 Received partial payment from A. Barrel, no discount allowed, $230.
22 Purchased merchandise from Bayle Company, $1,200, terms 2/10, n/30, FOB destination, invoice dated May 22.
23 Sold merchandise on credit to L. Lozocek, $670, terms 2/10, n/30, invoice no. 1002.
26 Purchased merchandise from Centro Company, $1,500, terms 2/10, n/30, FOB destination, invoice dated May 23.
31 Returned merchandise to Centro Company for full credit, $600.

REQUIRED

1. Prepare a single-column sales journal, a single-column purchases journal, a cash receipts journal, a cash payments journal, and a general journal similar to the ones illustrated in the chapter. Use Page 1 for all references.
2. Open the following general ledger accounts: Accounts Receivable (112) and Accounts Payable (211).
3. Open the following accounts receivable subsidiary ledger accounts: A. Barrel, L. Lozocek, and R. Woodman.
4. Open the following accounts payable subsidiary ledger accounts: Bayle Company and Centro Company.
5. Enter the transactions in the journals and post to the appropriate subsidiary ledger and general ledger accounts.
6. Foot and crossfoot the journals, and make the end-of-month postings applicable to Accounts Receivable and Accounts Payable.
7. Prove the control balances of Accounts Receivable and Accounts Payable by preparing schedules of accounts receivable and accounts payable.
8. When in the accounting cycle will (a) the total of all the customer accounts in the accounts receivable subsidiary ledger equal the balance of the accounts receivable controlling account and (b) the total of all the supplier accounts in the accounts payable subsidiary ledger equal the balance of the accounts payable controlling account?

LO5 Cash Receipts and Cash Payments Journals

P 2. Kimball Company is a small retail business that uses a manual data processing system similar to the one described in the chapter. Among its special-purpose journals are multicolumn cash receipts and cash payments journals. These were the cash transactions for Kimball Company during the month of November:

Nov. 1 Paid November rent to R. Carello, $1,000, with check no. 782.
3 Paid Stavos Wholesale on account, $2,300 less a 2 percent discount, check no. 783.
4 Received payment on account of $1,000, within the 2 percent discount period, from J. Walker.
5 Cash sales, $2,632.
8 Paid Moving Freight on account, $598, with check no. 784.

Nov. 9 The owner, Fred Kimball, invested an additional $10,000 in cash and a truck valued at $14,000 in the business.
11 Paid Escobedo Supply on account, $284, with check no. 785.
14 Cash sales, $2,834.
15 Paid Moving Freight $310 for the freight on a shipment of merchandise received today, with check no. 786.
16 Paid Ludman Company on account, $1,568 net a 2 percent discount, with check no. 787.
17 Received payment on account from P. Sivula, $120.
18 Cash sales, $1,974.
19 Received payment on a note receivable, $1,800 plus $36 interest.
20 Purchased office supplies from Escobedo Supply, $108, with check no. 788.
21 Paid a note payable in full to Kenington Bank, $4,100 including $100 interest, with check no. 789.
24 Cash sales, $2,964.
25 Paid $500 less a 2 percent discount to Stavos Wholesale, with check no. 790.
26 Paid sales clerk Tracy Dye $1,100 for her monthly salary, with check no. 791.
27 Purchased equipment from Standard Corporation for $16,000, paying $4,000 with check no. 792 and signing a note payable for the difference.
30 Fred Kimball withdrew $1,200 from the business, using check no. 793.

REQUIRED ▶
1. Enter these transactions in the cash receipts and cash payments journals.
2. Foot and crossfoot the journals.
3. If a manager wanted to know the total sales for the accounting period, where else would the manager need to refer to obtain the data needed?.

LO4 LO5 Purchases and General Journals

P 3. Meloon Lawn Supply Company uses a multicolumn purchases journal and a general journal similar to those illustrated in the text. The company also maintains an accounts payable subsidiary ledger. The items below represent the company's credit transactions for the month of July.

July 2 Purchased merchandise from Diego Fertilizer Company, $2,640.
3 Purchased office supplies of $166 and store supplies of $208 from Laronne Supply, Inc.
5 Purchased cleaning equipment from Whitman Company, $1,856.
7 Purchased display equipment from Laronne Supply, Inc., $4,700.
10 Purchased lawn mowers from Brandon Lawn Equipment Company, for resale, $8,400 (which included transportation charges of $350).
14 Purchased merchandise from Diego Fertilizer Company, $3,444.
18 Purchased a lawn mower from Brandon Lawn Equipment Company to be used in the business, $950 (which included transportation charges of $70).
23 Purchased store supplies from Laronne Supply, Inc., $54.
27 Returned a defective lawn mower purchased on July 10 for full credit, $750.

REQUIRED ▶
1. Enter the preceding transactions in the purchases journal and the general journal. Assume that all terms are n/30 and that invoice dates are the same as the transaction dates. Use Page 1 for all references.
2. Foot and crossfoot the purchases journal.
3. Open the following general ledger accounts: Store Supplies (116), Office Supplies (117), Lawn Equipment (142), Display Equipment (144), Cleaning Equipment (146), Accounts Payable (211), Purchases (611), Purchases Returns and Allowances (612), and Freight In (613). Open accounts payable subsidiary ledger accounts as needed. Post from the journals to the ledger accounts.

LO4 LO5 Comprehensive Use of Special-Purpose Journals

P 4. Ye Olde Book Store opened its doors for business on May 1. During May, the following transactions took place:

May 1 Linda Berrill began the business by depositing $42,000 in the new company's bank account.
3 Issued check no. C001 to Remax Rentals for one month's rent, $1,000.
4 Received a shipment of books from Chassman Books, Inc., invoice dated May 3, terms 5/10, n/60, FOB shipping point, $15,680.
5 Received a bill for freight from Menden Shippers for the previous day's shipment, terms n/30, $790.

May 6 Received a shipment from Lakeside Books, invoice dated May 6, terms 2/10, n/30, FOB shipping point, $11,300.
7 Issued check no. C002 to Pappanopoulos Freight for transportation charges on the previous day's shipment, $574.
8 Issued check no. C003 to Yun Chao Equipment Company for store equipment, $10,400.
9 Sold books to Midtown Center, terms 5/10, n/30, invoice no. 1001, $1,564.
10 Returned books to Chassman Books, Inc., for credit, $760.
11 Issued check no. C004 to WCAM for radio commercials, $470.
12 Issued check no. C005 to Chassman Books, Inc., for balance of amount owed less discount.
13 Cash sales for the first two weeks, $4,018. (For this problem, cash sales are recorded every two weeks, not daily as they are in actual practice.)
14 Issued check no. C006 to Lakeside Books, $6,000 less discount.
15 Signed a 90-day, 10 percent note for a bank loan and received $20,000 in cash.
15 Sold books to Steve Oahani, terms n/30, invoice no. 1002, $260.
16 Issued a credit memorandum to Midtown Center for returned books, $124.
17 Received full payment from Midtown Center of balance owed less discount.
18 Sold books to Missy Porter, terms n/30, invoice no. 1003, $194.
19 Received a shipment from Perspectives Publishing Company, invoice dated May 18, terms 5/10, n/60, $4,604.
20 Returned additional books purchased on May 4 to Chassman Books, Inc., for credit at gross price, $1,436.
21 Sold books to Midtown Center, terms 5/10, n/30, invoice no. 1004, $1,634.
23 Received a shipment from Chassman Books, Inc., invoice dated May 19, terms 5/10, n/60, FOB shipping point, $2,374.
24 Issued check no. C007 to Menden Shippers for balance owed on account plus shipping charges of $194 on previous day's shipment.
27 Cash sales for the second two weeks, $7,488.
29 Issued check no. C008 to Payroll for sales salaries for first four weeks of the month, $1,400.
31 Cash sales for the last four days of the month, $554.

REQUIRED ▶

1. Prepare a sales journal, a multicolumn purchases journal, a cash receipts journal, a cash payments journal, and a general journal. Use Page 1 for all journal references.
2. Open the following general ledger accounts: Cash (111); Accounts Receivable (112); Store Equipment (141); Accounts Payable (211); Notes Payable (212); Linda Berrill, Capital (311); Sales (411); Sales Discounts (412); Sales Returns and Allowances (413); Purchases (511); Purchases Discounts (512); Purchases Returns and Allowances (513); Freight In (514); Sales Salaries Expense (611); Advertising Expense (612); and Rent Expense (613).
3. Open accounts receivable subsidiary ledger accounts for Midtown Center, Steve Oahani, and Missy Porter.
4. Open accounts payable subsidiary ledger accounts for Chassman Books, Inc.; Lakeside Books; Menden Shippers; and Perspectives Publishing Company.
5. Enter the transactions in the journals and post as appropriate.
6. Foot and crossfoot the journals, and make the end-of-month postings.
7. Prepare a trial balance of the general ledger and prove the control balances of Accounts Receivable and Accounts Payable by preparing schedules of accounts receivable and accounts payable.

LO4 LO5 Comprehensive Use of Special-Purpose Journals

P 5. During October, Fahner Refrigeration Company completed the following transactions:

Oct. 1 Received merchandise from Tate Company, $5,000, invoice dated September 29, terms 2/10, n/30, FOB shipping point.
3 Issued check no. 230 to Wallace Realtors for October rent, $4,000.
4 Received merchandise from LaRocke Manufacturing, $10,800, invoice dated October 1, terms 2/10, n/30, FOB shipping point.
6 Issued check no. 231 to Babbitt Company for repairs, $1,120.
7 Received $800 credit memorandum pertaining to October 4 shipment from LaRocke Manufacturing for return of unsatisfactory merchandise.
8 Issued check no. 232 to Esmerelda Company for freight charges on October 1 and October 4 shipments, $368.

Oct. 9 Sold merchandise to J. Koppel, $2,000, terms 1/10, n/30, invoice no. 725.
10 Issued check no. 233 to Tate Company for full payment less discount.
11 Sold merchandise to K. Hanama for $2,500, terms 1/10, n/30, invoice no. 726.
12 Issued check no. 234 to LaRocke Manufacturing for balance of account less discount.
13 Purchased advertising on credit from WRRT, invoice dated October 13, $900, terms n/20.
15 Issued credit memorandum to K. Hanama for $100 for merchandise returned.
16 Cash sales for the first half of the month, $19,340. (For this problem, cash sales are recorded twice a month, not daily, as they are in actual practice.)
17 Sold merchandise to H. Blake, $1,400, terms 1/10, n/30, invoice no. 727.
18 Received check from J. Koppel for October 9 sale less discount.
19 Received check from K. Hanama for balance of account less discount.
20 Received merchandise from Tate Company, $5,600, invoice dated October 19, terms 2/10, n/30, FOB shipping point.
21 Received freight bill from Winters Company for merchandise received on October 20, invoice dated October 19, $1,140, terms n/5.
22 Issued check no. 235 for advertising purchase of October 13.
24 Received merchandise from LaRocke Manufacturing, $7,200, invoice dated October 23, terms 2/10, n/30, FOB shipping point.
25 Issued check no. 236 for freight charge of October 21.
26 Sold merchandise to J. Koppel, $1,600, terms 1/10, n/30, invoice no. 728.
28 Received credit memorandum from LaRocke Manufacturing for defective merchandise received October 24, $600.
29 Issued check no. 237 to Woo Company for purchase of office equipment, $700.
30 Issued check no. 238 to Tate Company for half of October 20 purchase less discount.
30 Received check in full from H. Blake, no discount allowed.
31 Cash sales for the last half of the month, $23,120.
31 Issued check no. 239 to Payroll for monthly sales salaries, $8,600.

REQUIRED ▶

1. Prepare a sales journal, a multicolumn purchases journal, a cash receipts journal, a cash payments journal, and a general journal for Fahner Refrigeration Company. Use Page 1 for all journal references.
2. Open the following general ledger accounts: Cash (111); Accounts Receivable (112); Office Equipment (141); Accounts Payable (211); Sales (411); Sales Discounts (412); Sales Returns and Allowances (413); Purchases (511); Purchases Discounts (512); Purchases Returns and Allowances (513); Freight In (514); Sales Salaries Expense (521); Advertising Expense (522); Rent Expense (531); and Repairs Expense (532).
3. Open accounts receivable subsidiary ledger accounts for H. Blake, K. Hanama, and J. Koppel.
4. Open accounts payable subsidiary ledger accounts for LaRocke Manufacturing, Tate Company, Winters Company, and WRRT.
5. Enter the transactions in the journals and post as appropriate.
6. Foot and crossfoot the journals, and make the end-of-month postings.
7. Prepare a trial balance of the general ledger and prove the control balances of Accounts Receivable and Accounts Payable by preparing schedules of accounts receivable and accounts payable.

Alternate Problems

P 6. **LO4 LO5 Special-Purpose Journals and Subsidiary Ledgers**

Simons Company, a small retail business, uses a manual accounting system similar to the one illustrated in this chapter. At the end of May 20xx, the accounts in the accounts receivable and accounts payable subsidiary ledgers showed the following balances:

Accounts Receivable		Accounts Payable	
T. Bacon	$ 870	Shalkor Inc.	$2,900
R. Banks	650	Ventman Company	460
Total Accounts Receivable	$1,520	Total Accounts Payable	$3,360

During June, the company engaged in the following transactions:

June 2 Sold merchandise on credit to R. Banks, $920, terms 2/10, n/30, invoice no. 4001.
4 Received payment in full from R. Banks for the amount due at the beginning of June less a 2 percent discount.
5 Paid Shalkor Inc. the full amount owed less a 2 percent discount, check no. 501.
8 Accepted a return of merchandise from R. Banks, $220.
9 Paid Ventman Company the full amount owed, no discount allowed, check no. 502.
12 Received payment from R. Banks for the amount due less the discount.
15 Received partial payment from T. Bacon, no discount allowed, $300.
22 Purchased merchandise from Ventman Company, $1,700, terms 2/10, n/30, FOB destination, invoice dated June 21.
23 Sold merchandise on credit to M. Abdul, $2,450, terms 2/10, n/30, invoice no. 4002.
26 Purchased merchandise from Shalkor Inc., $1,500, terms 2/10, n/30, FOB destination, invoice dated June 24.
30 Returned merchandise to Ventman Company for full credit, $600.

REQUIRED ▶

1. Prepare a sales journal, a single-column purchases journal, a cash receipts journal, a cash payments journal, and a general journal similar to the ones illustrated in the chapter. Use Page 1 for all references.
2. Open the following general ledger accounts: Accounts Receivable (112) and Accounts Payable (211).
3. Open accounts receivable subsidiary ledger accounts for M. Abdul, T. Bacon, and R. Banks.
4. Open accounts payable subsidiary ledger accounts for Shalkor Inc. and Ventman Company.
5. Enter the transactions in the journals and post to the appropriate subsidiary ledger and general ledger accounts.
6. Foot and crossfoot the journals, and make the end-of-month postings applicable to Accounts Receivable and Accounts Payable.
7. Prove the control balances of Accounts Receivable and Accounts Payable by preparing schedules of accounts receivable and accounts payable.
8. When in the accounting cycle will (a) the total of all the customer accounts in the accounts receivable subsidiary ledger equal the balance of the accounts receivable controlling account and (b) the total of all the supplier accounts in the accounts payable subsidiary ledger equal the balance of the accounts payable controlling account?

LO5 Cash Receipts and Cash Payments Journals

P 7. The items below detail all cash transactions by O'Malley Company for the month of October. The company uses multicolumn cash receipts and cash payments journals similar to those illustrated in the chapter.

Oct. 1 The owner, Michael O'Malley, invested $50,000 cash and $24,000 in equipment in the business.
2 Paid rent to Bellamy Agency, $600, with check no. 75.
3 Cash sales, $2,200.
6 Purchased store equipment for $5,000 from Quantum Company, with check no. 76.
7 Purchased merchandise for cash, $6,500, from Hoffman Company, with check no. 77.
8 Paid Boronski Company invoice, $1,800, less 2 percent discount, with check no. 78 (assume that a payable has already been recorded).
9 Paid advertising bill, $350, to WKBD, with check no. 79.
10 Cash sales, $3,910.
12 Received $800 on account from L. Saluna.
13 Purchased used truck for cash, $3,520, from Denecker Company, with check no. 80.
19 Received $4,180 from Precision Company, in settlement of a $4,000 note plus interest.

Oct. 20 Received $1,078 ($1,100 less $22 cash discount) from I. Fraden.
21 Paid O'Malley $2,000 from business for personal use by issuing check no. 81.
23 Paid Rinardi Company invoice, $2,500, less 2 percent discount, with check no. 82.
26 Paid Curran Company for freight on merchandise received, $60, with check no. 83.
27 Cash sales, $4,800.
28 Paid C. Shegley for monthly salary, $1,400, with check no. 84.
31 Purchased land from O. Dante for $20,000, paying $5,000 with check no. 85 and signing a note payable for $15,000.

REQUIRED ▶

1. Enter the preceding transactions in the cash receipts and cash payments journals.
2. Foot and crossfoot the journals.
3. If a manager wanted to know the total sales for the accounting period, where else would the manager need to refer to obtain the data needed?

LO4 Comprehensive Use of
LO5 Special-Purpose Journals

P 8. The following transactions were completed by Stackpole's Men's Wear during the month of May, its first month of operation:

May 1 Garrett Stackpole deposited $40,000 in the new company's bank account.
2 Issued check no. 101 to Bannister Realty for one month's rent, $2,400.
3 Received merchandise from Seagal Company, $14,000, invoice dated May 2, terms 2/10, n/60, FOB shipping point.
4 Received from Gallagher Company freight bill on merchandise purchased, $1,928, terms n/20.
5 Issued check no. 102 to Kenawahi Company for store equipment, $14,800.
6 Borrowed $16,000 from the bank on a 90-day, 9 percent note.
7 Cash sales for the first week, $3,964. (To shorten this problem, cash sales are recorded weekly instead of daily, as they would be in actual practice.)
8 Sold merchandise to Avon Old Farms School, $1,800, terms 2/10, n/30, invoice no. 1001.
9 Sold merchandise to Missy Cavanaugh, $600, terms n/20, invoice no. 1002.
10 Purchased advertising in the *Sentinel-Gazette*, $300, terms n/15.
11 Issued check no. 103 for purchase of May 3 less discount.
12 Issued a credit memorandum for merchandise returned by Missy Cavanaugh, $60.
15 Cash sales for the second week, $6,984.
16 Received merchandise from Seagal Company, $3,800, invoice dated May 15, terms 2/10, n/60, FOB shipping point.
17 Received from Gallagher Company freight bill on merchandise purchased, $524, terms n/20.
18 Received merchandise from Cronos Company, $2,800, invoice dated May 16, terms 1/10, n/60, FOB destination.
18 Received payment in full less discount from Avon Old Farms School.
20 Received a credit memorandum from Seagal Company for merchandise returned, $200.
21 Cash sales for the third week, $5,824.
23 Issued check no. 104 for the total amount owed Gallagher Company.
24 Sold merchandise to Avon Old Farms School, $1,368, terms 2/10, n/30, invoice no. 1003.
25 Issued check no. 105 in payment of the amount owed Seagal Company less discount.
26 Sold merchandise to Alicia Menotte, $744, terms n/20, invoice no. 1004.
27 Issued check no. 106 for the amount owed the *Sentinel-Gazette.*
28 Cash sales for the fourth week, $3,948.
31 Issued check no. 107 to Payroll for sales salaries for the month of May, $7,200.

REQUIRED ▶

1. Prepare a sales journal, a multicolumn purchases journal, a cash receipts journal, a cash payments journal, and a general journal. Use Page 1 for all journal references.
2. Open the following general ledger accounts: Cash (111); Accounts Receivable (112); Store Equipment (141); Accounts Payable (211); Notes Payable (212); Garrett Stackpole, Capital (311); Sales (411); Sales Discounts (412); Sales Returns and

Allowances (413); Purchases (511); Purchases Discounts (512); Purchases Returns and Allowances (513); Freight In (514); Sales Salaries Expense (611); Advertising Expense (612); and Rent Expense (613).

3. Open accounts receivable subsidiary ledger accounts for Avon Old Farms School, Missy Cavanaugh, and Alicia Menotte.
4. Open accounts payable subsidiary ledger accounts for Cronos Company, Gallagher Company, the *Sentinel-Gazette*, and Seagal Company.
5. Enter the transactions in the journals and post as appropriate.
6. Foot and crossfoot the journals, and make the end-of-month postings.
7. Prepare a trial balance of the general ledger and prove the control balances of Accounts Receivable and Accounts Payable by preparing schedules of accounts receivable and accounts payable.

SKILLS DEVELOPMENT CASES

Conceptual Analysis

LO1 Accounting System
LO2 Evaluation
LO4

SD 1. Asian Accent Interiors is an interior design company that was started three years ago by Agnes Hiramata. For the first two years of the company's life, Hiramata helped clients plan the decorating of their luxury apartments in Manhattan. Hiramata did not sell any furnishings herself but was paid an hourly fee plus a percentage of the total purchases made by her clients. Although the business was successful, it was very simple. And it required just a simple manual accounting system consisting of a general journal and a general ledger. During the past year, Hiramata expanded. She opened a second-floor studio and began displaying and selling selected furnishings. She hired her first employees and began buying and selling on credit. As the number of daily transactions multiplied, Hiramata began to find the manual accounting system very burdensome. It was taking far too much time to record and post all the transactions. The company does not have a computer at present, but Hiramata is thinking about buying one. She has come to you for help. Evaluate Hiramata's current accounting system in terms of the principles of systems design (excluding the control principle) and make a recommendation about the types of accounting systems Hiramata should consider installing. Write a memorandum to Hiramata providing your analysis and recommendation.

LO2 General Ledger Systems

SD 2. Fine Arts Gallery and Framing, located in the South Fork Mall, was established two years ago to provide framing services. At the time, Gary Hoben, the owner, set up an accounting system. His business is a sole proprietorship service business that uses a general journal and general ledger. Because all sales were for cash or by credit card and because Hoben made a practice of paying all bills by the end of the month, the gallery had few receivables or payables. Over the past year, however, Hoben has added an inventory of color prints and posters, which carry a high profit margin. In addition, the new suppliers offer generous terms for payment. As a result, Hoben has allowed customers who buy framed prints or posters to pay over a period of three months. With the increased number of transactions involving inventory, accounts receivable, and accounts payable, Hoben's general journal/general ledger accounting system is now outdated. What kind of accounting system could Hoben use to handle the increased number and complexity of the store's transactions?

LO2 Switching to a General Ledger Accounting System

SD 3. Krock's & Marici's operates a growing full-service bookstore in the Louisville area. The firm is known for excellent service and large inventories of books in a wide number of fields, such as art, history, business, technology, travel, fiction, and juvenile. To increase traffic and project a casual image, the company has a coffee shop in the bookstore. The owner's accountant has recommended that it install a general ledger software system. Describe a general ledger software system and identify the source documents, software function, and output documents that would constitute the system. What do you think the advantages of this system will be?

Ethical Dilemma

SD 4. LO4 **Confidentiality of Accounting Records**

Frank Santino is the accounting manager at the Ford and Toyota dealership in Petersburg, Texas, a town with a population of 50,000. At a barbecue, José Martinez, a close friend, mentions that he is planning to sell some land to Louis Johnson for $20,000 and will allow Johnson to pay him over a five-year period. Santino, who happened to have been reviewing the delinquent accounts at the dealership earlier in the day, knows that Johnson has a poor payment history and that his car may have to be repossessed. Martinez asks Santino what he thinks about the sale. What ethical issue is involved here? If you were Santino, would you warn Martinez about Johnson's credit record?

Research Activity

SD 5. LO3 **Using the Internet**

Assume you have been asked by your boss, the owner of a small dress shop, to investigate general ledger software for her business. Both Peachtree Software and Intuit Software, the publisher of Quickbooks®, have web pages. Access these web sites through the Needles Accounting Resource Center Web Site at http://accounting.college.hmco.com/students. Study the information you find, and write a summary of the information and its usefulness. Can you assess the differences in the software approaches of the two companies and their applicability to a small dress shop?

Decision-Making Practice

SD 6. LO4 LO5 **Design of Special-Purpose Journals**

RW Finer Foods Company, owned by Robert Washington, is a neighborhood grocery store that accepts cash or checks in payment for food. Known for its informality, the store has been very successful and has grown with the community. Along with that growth, however, has come an increase in the number of bad checks customers have written for purchases. Washington is concerned about the difficulty of accounting for these returned checks, so he has asked you to look into the problem.

In addition to a purchases journal and a cash payments journal, the company has a combination single-column sales and cash receipts journal. The combination journal has worked in the past because all sales are for cash (including checks), and almost all cash receipts represent sales transactions. Thus, the single column represents a debit to Cash and a credit to Sales.

The bad checks are recorded individually in the general journal by debiting Accounts Receivable and crediting Cash for the amount of the check. When a customer pays off a bad check, another entry is made in the general journal debiting Cash and crediting Accounts Receivable. Returned Check Revenue for the amount of $10, which represents reimbursement of the service charge by the bank, will be recorded in the Sales/Cash Receipts journal when the bad check is collected. Washington keeps the returned checks in an envelope. When a customer comes in to pay one off, Washington gives the check back. No other records of the returned checks are maintained.

In studying the problem, you discover that the company is averaging ten returned checks per day, totaling $1,000. As part of the solution, you recommend that Washington issue check-cashing cards to customers whose credit is approved in advance. The card must be presented when a customer offers a check in payment for groceries. You recommend further that a special-purpose journal be established for the returned checks and returned check revenue, that a subsidiary ledger be maintained, and that the combination sales/cash receipts journal be expanded.

1. Draw and label the columns for the new returned checks journal and the expanded sales/cash receipts journal.
2. Assume that there are 300 returned checks and 280 collections per month and that the records are closed each month. How many written lines can be saved each month by recording returned checks and subsequent collections in the special journals? How many postings can be saved each month? (Ignore the effect of the subsidiary ledger.)
3. Describe the nature and use of the subsidiary ledger. What advantages do you see in having a subsidiary ledger?
4. Assuming that it takes approximately two and a half minutes to make each entry and related postings under the old system of recording bad checks and one minute to

make each entry and related postings under the new system, what are the monthly savings if the cost is $20 an hour? What further, and possibly more significant, savings may be realized by using the new system?

Group Activity: After presenting parts **1** and **3** in class, divide the class into teams to work on parts **2** and **4**. Compare and discuss results.

Financial Reporting and Analysis Cases

Interpreting Financial Reports

FRA 1.
LO1 LO3 **Electronic Commerce on the Internet**

Amazon.com, <www.amazon.com> which describes itself as the "Earth's Biggest Bookstore," is the leading Internet book seller. It might be described as a "virtual" bookstore because it carries only a relatively few books in its Seattle warehouse, far fewer than the average superstore, like Borders or Barnes & Noble. Buyers choose from a selection of 2.5 million books on the Internet and give credit card information to place an order. Amazon.com verifies the information and electronically sends the order to a wholesaler that packages and sends the order, usually within one day. Ninety-five percent of the books Amazon.com sells are delivered by these wholesalers, which charge a wholesale markup for handling and shipping. The cost of having to rely on wholesalers for distribution is one reason that Amazon.com has not yet reached profitability in spite of its success. As a result, the company is planning to expand its own distribution capability, which it believes it can do at a lower cost.[8]

1. Define electronic commerce and describe generally how conducting business on the Internet differs from conducting business in a retail store.
2. Describe how you believe the four principles of systems design apply to Amazon.com's sale and distribution of books as compared to a more traditional bookstore.
3. What changes in the application of these principles will occur if Amazon.com begins to do more of its own distribution?

International Company

This category is not applicable to this chapter.

Toys "R" Us Annual Report

FRA 2.
LO1 **Principles of Accounting Systems Design**

In its Annual Report, the management of Toys "R" Us <www.tru.com> described the success of Toysrus.com, whose sales have increased by 23 percent in the past year, as follows:

> Toysrus.com recorded its first operating profit of $3 million during the fourth quarter of 2002 versus an operating loss of $(17) million for the prior year's fourth quarter. . . . A number of factors contributed to this significant improvement in operating performance including higher merchandise margins, . . . diligent expense control, reduced inventory levels, and increased integration between Babiesrus.com and Babies "R" Us stores

Explain how these efforts to improve operating results are facilitated by computer systems that comply with the principles of cost-benefit, control, compatibility, and flexibility. Give an example from this quote to support each principle.

Comparison Case

This category is not applicable to this chapter.

Fingraph® Financial Analyst™

This category is not applicable to this chapter.

Internet Case

FRA 3. LO1 **Accounting and Systems Careers**

Many accountants are involved in systems careers. Go to the Needles Accounting Resource Center Web Site at http://accounting.college.hmco.com/students. Under Companies Web Links, go to the annual reports on the web sites for PeopleSoft <www.peoplesoft.com>, Accenture (formerly Andersen Consulting) <www.accenture.com>, and PricewaterhouseCoopers <www.pwc.com>. Find information describing these firms' businesses and look for the sections on career opportunities that relate to accounting and systems. For each firm, summarize its business and the career opportunities and be prepared to discuss what you find in class.

8

Chapter 8 focuses on the basic components and control activities of an effective internal control system, with emphasis on internal control over merchandising transactions.

Internal Control

Learning Objectives

LO1 Define *internal control*, explain its basic components and limitations, and give examples of control activities.

LO2 Apply internal control activities to common merchandising transactions.

LO3 Demonstrate the control of cash by preparing a bank reconciliation.

Supplemental Objectives

SO4 Demonstrate the use of a simple imprest system.

SO5 Define *voucher system* and describe the components and operation of a voucher system.

DECISION POINT

A USER'S FOCUS

Oxford Health Plans, Inc. <www.oxhp.com> After a decade of rapid growth, Oxford Health Plans, Inc., surprised Wall Street analysts with losses of more than $200 million. How did disaster strike so quickly? Ironically, Oxford's dazzling growth was its undoing. Its systems were unable to handle the expanding business as it grew from 217,000 plan members to over 1.9 million. As Oxford was signing up hordes of new members, the company was unable to send out monthly bills to thousands of member accounts, and it couldn't track payments to hundreds of doctors and hospitals. As a result, uncollected receivables from customers tripled to more than $400 million. Also, amounts owed to caregivers soared to more than $650 million. As one analyst said, "If you drive a train at 150 miles an hour without good tracks, you derail".[1] What could Oxford's management have done to avoid these problems?

Problems with controls and systems are serious for all companies. At Oxford, they led to an inability to collect from members and to overpayments to caregivers, which contributed to the company's losses. Oxford's management was forced to institute new systems and internal controls over billing, accounts receivable, and cash receipts. Further, the company had to establish internal controls over accounts payable and cash disbursements so that it did not under- or overpay. Such controls are critical to managing cash, protecting revenues, and restraining costs. As you will see in the following section, these goals can be achieved through an internal control structure that

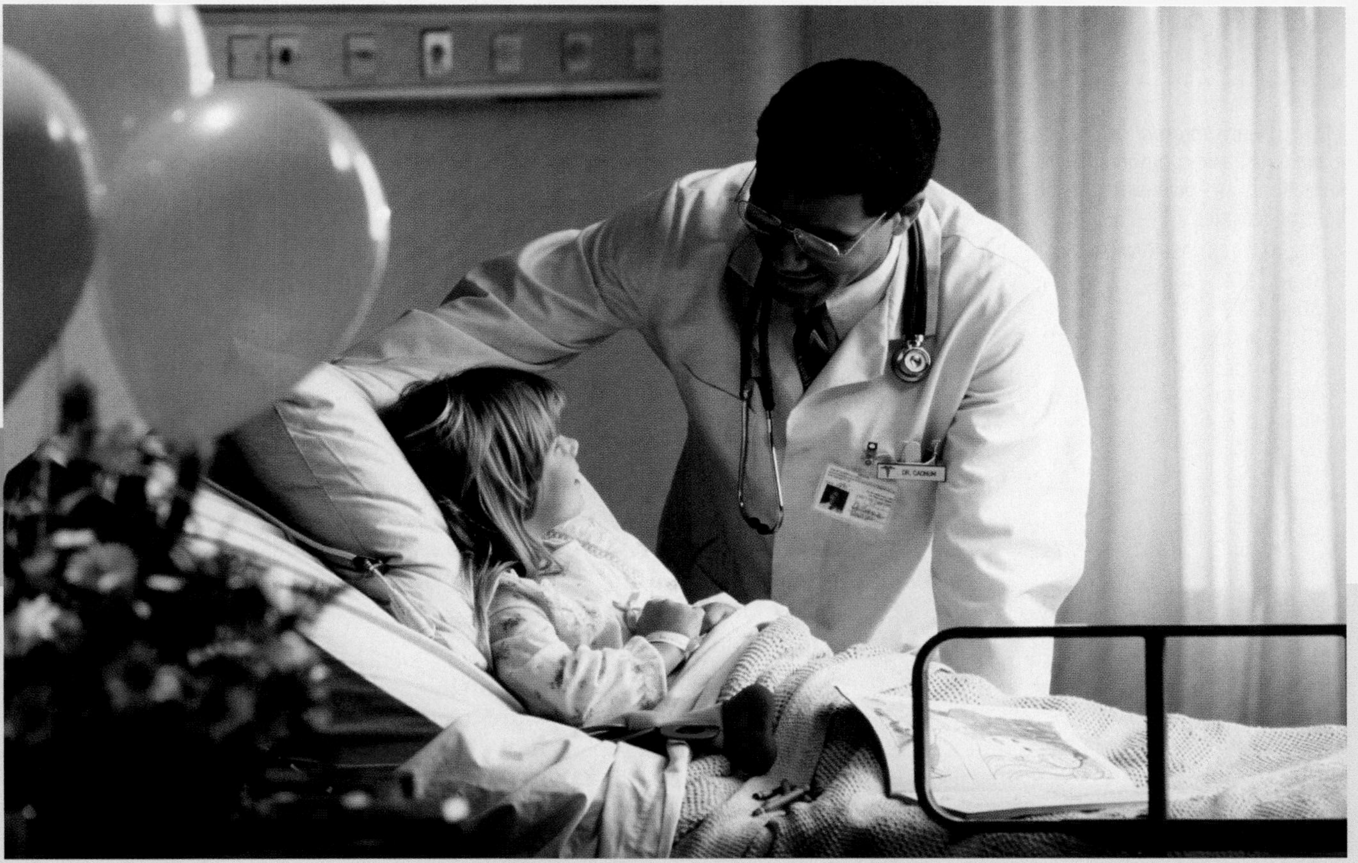

Why are good internal controls critical for a company like Oxford Health Plans, Inc.?

includes an accounting information system with procedures specifically designed to prevent losses. Fortunately, Oxford was able to resolve its systems and control weaknesses and is now a Fortune 500 company with annual revenues of almost $5 million.

INTERNAL CONTROL: BASIC COMPONENTS AND CONTROL ACTIVITIES

LO1 Define *internal control,* explain its basic components and limitations, and give examples of control activities.

RELATED TEXT ASSIGNMENTS
Q: 1, 2, 3, 4
SE: 1, 2, 3, 4
E: 1, 2, 3, 4, 5
P: 2, 4, 6, 7
SD: 1, 2, 4, 5
FRA: 1, 2, 3, 4

A merchandising company can have inaccurate accounting records as well as high losses of cash and inventory if it does not take steps to protect its assets. The best way to do this is to set up and maintain a good system of internal control.

MANAGEMENT'S RESPONSIBILITY FOR INTERNAL CONTROL

Management is responsible for establishing a satisfactory system of internal control. **Internal control** is defined as all the policies and procedures management uses to ensure the reliability of financial reporting, compliance with laws and regulations, and the effectiveness and efficiency of operations. In other words, management must safeguard the firm's assets and have reliable accounting records. It must ensure that employees comply with legal requirements and operate the company in the best way possible.

Management comments on its responsibility and effectiveness in achieving the goals of internal control in the "Report of Management" in the company's annual report to stockholders. A portion of this statement from the annual report of Circuit City Stores, Inc., follows:

www.circuitcity.com

KEY POINT: A good system of internal control safeguards a company's assets, produces reliable accounting records, promotes operational efficiency, and encourages adherence to management's policies.

> Management is responsible for maintaining an internal control structure designed to provide reasonable assurance that the books and records reflect the transactions of the Company and that the Company's established policies and procedures are carefully followed. Because of inherent limitations in any system, there can be no absolute assurance that errors or irregularities will not occur. Nevertheless, management believes that the internal control structure provides reasonable assurance that assets are safeguarded and that financial information is objective and reliable.[2]

COMPONENTS OF INTERNAL CONTROL

To accomplish the objectives of internal control, management must establish five interrelated components of internal control:[3]

1. *Control environment* The **control environment** is created by the overall attitude, awareness, and actions of management. It includes management's integrity and ethics, philosophy and operating style, organizational structure, method of assigning authority and responsibility, and personnel policies and practices. Personnel should be qualified to handle responsibilities, which means that employees must be trained and informed. For example, the manager of a retail store should train employees to follow prescribed procedures for handling cash sales, credit card sales, and returns and refunds.
2. *Risk assessment* **Risk assessment** is the identification of areas in which risks of loss of assets or inaccuracies in the accounting records are high so that adequate controls can be implemented. Among the greater risks in a retail store are that employees will take cash or that customers will shoplift merchandise.
3. *Information and communication* **Information and communication** relates to the accounting system established by management to identify, assemble, analyze, classify, record, and report a company's transactions, and to the need for clear communication of individual responsibilities in performing the accounting functions.
4. *Control activities* **Control activities** are the policies and procedures management puts in place to see that its directives are carried out. Control activities are discussed in more detail in the next section.

STOP AND THINK!
Which of the following accounts would be assigned a higher level of risk: Buildings or Merchandise Inventory?
Merchandise Inventory would because there is a greater risk of human error in recording the large number of transactions involved and because there is a greater risk of theft. ■

5. *Monitoring* **Monitoring** involves management's regular assessment of the quality of internal control, including periodic review of compliance with all policies and procedures. For example, large companies often have a staff of internal auditors who review the company's system of internal control to determine if it is working properly and if procedures are being followed. In smaller businesses, owners and managers conduct these reviews.

Control Activities

Control activities are a principal way in which companies implement internal control in an accounting information system. These activities safeguard a company's assets and ensure the reliability of accounting records. Control activities include the following:

1. *Authorization* All transactions and activities should be properly authorized by management. In a retail store, for example, some transactions, such as normal cash sales, are authorized routinely; others, such as issuing a refund, may require a manager's approval.
2. *Recording transactions* To facilitate preparation of financial statements and to establish accountability for assets, all transactions should be recorded. For example, in a retail store, the cash register records sales, refunds, and other transactions internally on a paper tape or computer disk so that the cashier can be held responsible for the cash received and the merchandise removed during his or her shift.
3. *Documents and records* Using well-designed documents helps ensure the proper recording of transactions. For example, to ensure that all transactions are recorded, invoices and other documents should be prenumbered, and all numbers should be accounted for.
4. *Physical controls* Physical controls permit access to assets only with management's authorization. For example, retail stores should use cash registers, and only the cashier responsible for the cash in a register should have access to it. Other employees should not be able to open the cash drawer if the cashier is not present. Likewise, warehouses and storerooms should be accessible only to authorized personnel. Access to accounting records, including those stored in company computers, should also be controlled.
5. *Periodic independent verification* The records should be periodically checked against the assets by someone other than the persons responsible for those records and assets. For example, at the end of each shift or day, the owner or store manager should count the cash in the cash drawer and compare the amount with the amount recorded on the tape or computer disk in the cash

Focus on Business Ethics

Which Frauds Are Most Common?

A survey of 5,000 large U.S. businesses disclosed that 21 percent suffered frauds in excess of $1 million. The most common were credit card frauds, check frauds, inventory theft, false invoices and phantom vendors, and expense account abuse. Major factors in allowing these frauds to take place were poor internal controls, management override of internal controls, and collusion. The most common methods of detection were notification by an employee, internal controls, internal auditor review, notification by a customer, and accidental discovery. Companies successful in preventing fraud have a good system of internal control and a formal code of ethics with a program to monitor compliance that includes a system for reporting incidents of fraud. These companies routinely communicate the existence of the program to their employees.[4]

register. Other examples of independent verification are the monthly bank reconciliation and periodic counts of physical inventory.

6. *Separation of duties* The organizational plan should separate functional responsibilities. Within a department, no one person should be in charge of authorizing transactions, operating the department, handling assets, and keeping records of assets. For example, in a stereo store, each employee should oversee only a single part of a transaction. A sales employee takes the order and creates an invoice. Another employee receives the customer's cash or credit card payment and issues a receipt. Once the customer has a paid receipt, and only then, a third employee obtains the item from the warehouse and gives it to the customer. A person in the accounting department subsequently records the sales from the tape or disk in the cash register, comparing them with the sales invoices and updating the inventory in the records. The separation of duties means that a mistake, careless or not, cannot be made without being seen by at least one other person.

KEY POINT: No control procedure can guarantee the prevention of theft. However, the more procedures there are in place, the less likely it is that a theft will occur.

7. *Sound personnel procedures* Sound practices should be followed in managing the people who carry out the functions of each department. Among those practices are supervision, rotation of key people among different jobs, insistence that employees take vacations, and bonding of personnel who handle cash or inventories. **Bonding** is the process of carefully checking an employee's background and insuring the company against theft by that person. Bonding does not guarantee against theft, but it does prevent or reduce economic loss if theft occurs. Prudent personnel procedures help ensure that employees know their jobs, are honest, and will find it difficult to carry out and conceal embezzlement over time.

Limitations of Internal Control

No system of internal control is without weaknesses. As long as control procedures are performed by people, the internal control system will be vulnerable to human error. Errors may arise from misunderstandings, mistakes in judgment, carelessness, distraction, or fatigue. Separation of duties can be defeated through collusion by employees who secretly agree to deceive the company. In addition, established procedures may be ineffective against employees' errors or dishonesty, and controls that were initially effective may become ineffective when conditions change.[5] In some cases, the costs of establishing and maintaining elaborate systems may exceed the benefits. In a small business, for example, active involvement by the owner can be a practical substitute for the separation of some duties.

Check out ACE for a Review Quiz at http://accounting.college.hmco.com/students.

Internal Control over Merchandising Transactions

LO2 Apply internal control activities to common merchandising transactions.

RELATED TEXT ASSIGNMENTS
Q: 5, 6, 7, 8, 16
SE: 4, 5
E: 5
P: 4, 6
SD: 1, 2, 4, 5
FRA: 1, 3

Sound internal control activities are needed in all aspects of a business, but particularly when assets are involved. Assets are especially vulnerable when they enter or leave a business. When sales are made, for example, cash or other assets enter the business, and goods or services leave the business. Activities must be set up to prevent theft during those transactions.

Likewise, purchases of assets and payments of liabilities must be controlled. The majority of those transactions can be safeguarded by adequate purchasing and payment systems. In addition, assets on hand, such as cash, investments, inventory, plant, and equipment, must be protected. Lack of adequate internal controls can lit-

www.oxhp.com

erally bring a company to its knees as we saw with Oxford Health Plans, Inc., in the Decision Point at the beginning of the chapter.

In this section, you will see how internal control activities are applied to such merchandising transactions as cash sales receipts, purchases, and cash payments. Similar activities are applicable to service and manufacturing businesses.

Internal Control and Management Goals

KEY POINT: Maintaining internal control is especially complex and difficult for a merchandiser. Management must not only establish controls for cash sales receipts, purchases, and cash payments, but also go to great lengths to manage and protect its inventory.

When a system of internal control is applied effectively to merchandising transactions, it can achieve important management goals. For example, two key goals for the success of a merchandising business are:

1. To prevent losses of cash or inventory owing to theft or fraud
2. To provide accurate records of merchandising transactions and account balances

Three broader goals for management are:

1. To keep enough inventory on hand to sell to customers without overstocking
2. To keep enough cash on hand to pay for purchases in time to receive discounts
3. To keep credit losses as low as possible by making credit sales only to customers who are likely to pay on time

One control used in meeting broad management goals is the cash budget, which projects future cash receipts and disbursements. By maintaining adequate cash balances, a company is able to take advantage of discounts on purchases, prepare to borrow money when necessary, and avoid the damaging effects of being unable to pay bills when they are due. By investing excess cash, the company can earn interest until the cash is needed.

KEY POINT: The separation of duties *can* be defeated through the collusion of two or more people.

A more specific accounting control is the separation of duties that involve the handling of cash. Such separation makes theft without detection extremely unlikely, unless two or more employees conspire. The separation of duties is easier in large businesses than in small ones, where one person may have to carry out several duties. The effectiveness of internal control over cash varies, based on the size and nature of the company. Most firms, however, should use the following procedures:

1. Separate the functions of authorization, recordkeeping, and custodianship of cash.
2. Limit the number of people who have access to cash.
3. Designate specific people who are responsible for handling cash.
4. Use banking facilities as much as possible, and keep the amount of cash on hand to a minimum.
5. Bond all employees who have access to cash.
6. Physically protect cash on hand by using cash registers, cashiers' cages, and safes.
7. Have a person who does not handle or record cash make periodic independent verifications of the cash on hand.
8. Record all cash receipts promptly.
9. Deposit all cash receipts promptly.
10. Make payments by check rather than by currency.
11. Have a person who does not authorize, handle, or record cash transactions reconcile the Cash account.

Notice that each of the foregoing procedures helps safeguard cash by making it more difficult for any one individual who has access to cash to steal or misuse it without being detected.

Control of Cash Sales Receipts

Cash receipts for sales of goods and services can be received by mail or over the counter in the form of checks, credit or debit cards, or currency. Whatever the source of the payments, cash should be recorded immediately upon receipt. This is usually done by making an entry in a cash receipts journal. Such a journal establishes a written record of cash receipts that should prevent errors and make theft more difficult.

Control of Cash Received Through the Mail Payment by mail is increasing because of the expansion of mail-order sales. Cash receipts that arrive by mail are vulnerable to theft by the employees who handle them. To control mailed receipts, companies should urge customers to pay by check or by credit card instead of with currency.

Cash received through the mail should be handled by two or more employees. The employee who opens the mail should make a list in triplicate of the money received. The list should contain each payer's name, the purpose for which the money was sent, and the amount. One copy goes with the cash to the cashier, who deposits the money. The second copy goes to the accounting department for recording. The third copy is kept by the person who opens the mail. Errors can be easily caught because the amount deposited by the cashier must agree with the amount received and the amount recorded in the cash receipts journal.

Stop and Think!
Why is it important to write down the amount of cash received through the mail or over the counter?
It is important because until there is a written record of the cash, there is no accountability. This is why some stores offer a reward to customers who report making a purchase without receiving a receipt. ■

Control of Cash Received over the Counter Two common tools for controlling cash sales receipts are cash registers and prenumbered sales tickets. The amount of a cash sale should be rung up on a cash register at the time of the sale. The cash register should be placed so that the customer can see the amount recorded. Each cash register should have a locked-in tape on which it prints the day's transactions. At the end of the day, the cashier counts the cash in the cash register and turns it in to the cashier's office. Another employee takes the tape out of the cash register and records the cash receipts for the day in the cash receipts journal. The amount of cash turned in and the amount recorded on the tape should agree; if not, any differences must be explained. Large retail chains commonly monitor cash receipts by having each cash register tied directly into a computer that records each transaction as it occurs. Whether the elements are performed manually or by computer, separating responsibility for cash receipts, cash deposits, and recordkeeping is necessary to ensure good internal control.

KEY POINT: The cashier should not be allowed to remove the cash register tape or to record the day's cash receipts.

In some stores, internal control is further strengthened by the use of prenumbered sales tickets and a central cash register or cashier's office, where all sales are rung up and collected by a person who does not participate in the sale. The sales-

Focus on Business Technology

How Do Computers Influence Internal Controls?

One of the more difficult challenges facing computer programmers is to build good internal controls into computerized accounting programs. Such computer programs must include controls that prevent unintentional errors as well as unauthorized access and tampering. The programs prevent errors through reasonableness checks (such as not allowing any transactions over a specified amount), mathematical checks that verify the arithmetic of transactions, and sequence checks that require documents and transactions to be in proper order. They typically use passwords and questions about randomly selected personal data to prevent unauthorized access to computer records. They may also use firewalls, which are strong electronic barriers to unauthorized access, as well as data encryption. Data encryption is a way of coding data so that if they are stolen, they are useless to the thief.

FIGURE 1
Internal Control for Purchasing and Paying for Goods and Services

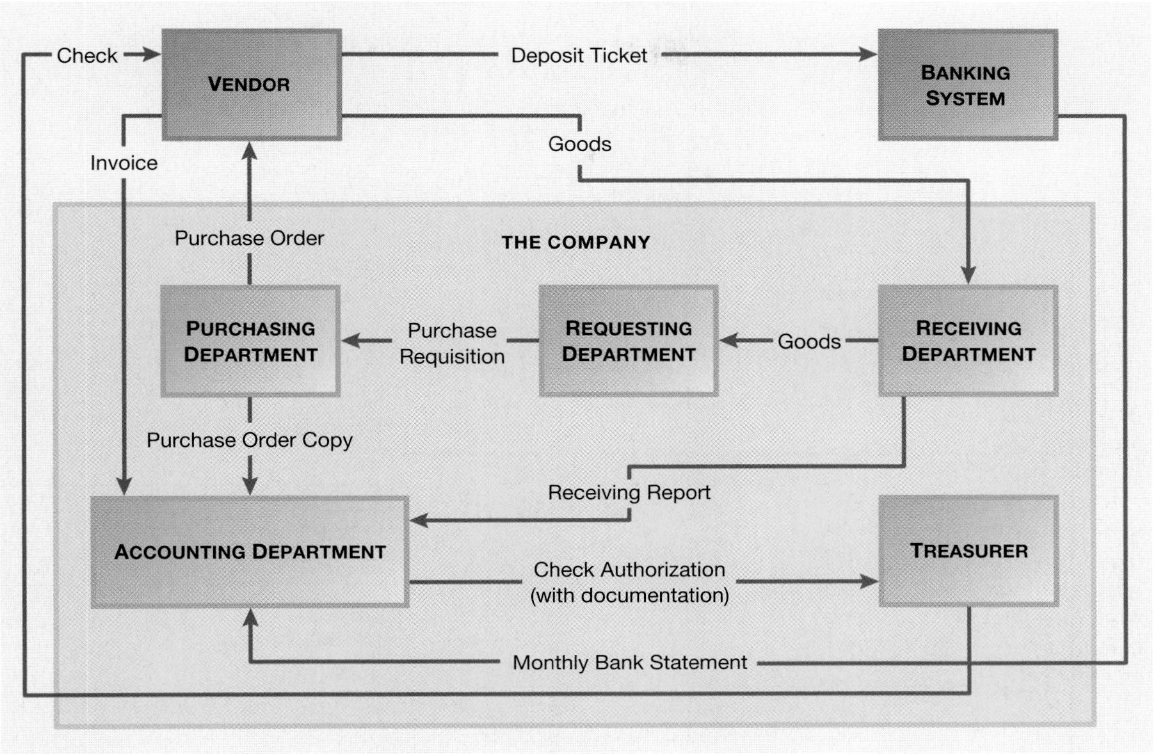

person completes a prenumbered sales ticket at the time of the sale, giving one copy to the customer and keeping a copy. At the end of the day, all sales tickets must be accounted for, and the sales total computed from the sales tickets should equal the total sales recorded on the cash register.

CONTROL OF PURCHASES AND CASH DISBURSEMENTS

Purchases and cash disbursements are particularly vulnerable to fraud and embezzlement. Lack of internal controls in these areas can cause other problems as well. For example, at Oxford Health Plans, Inc., discussed in this chapter's Decision Point, inadequate controls over cash disbursements resulted in overpayments that contributed to the company's huge losses, and failure to pay bills in a timely manner had a negative effect on the company's relations with caregivers.

www.oxhp.com

To avoid such situations, cash should be paid only after the receipt of specific authorization supported by documents that establish the validity and amount of the claim. In addition, maximum possible use should be made of the principle of separation of duties in the purchase of goods and services and the payment for them. The degree of separation of duties varies, depending on the size of the business. Figure 1 shows how separation of duties can be maximized in large companies. Five internal units (the requesting department, the purchasing department, the accounting department, the receiving department, and the treasurer) and two external contacts (the vendor and the banking system) all play a role in the internal control plan. Notice that business documents are also crucial components of the plan.

As shown in Figure 2, every action is documented and verified by at least one other person. Thus, the requesting department cannot work out a kickback scheme

Figure 2
Internal Control Plan for Purchases and Cash Disbursements

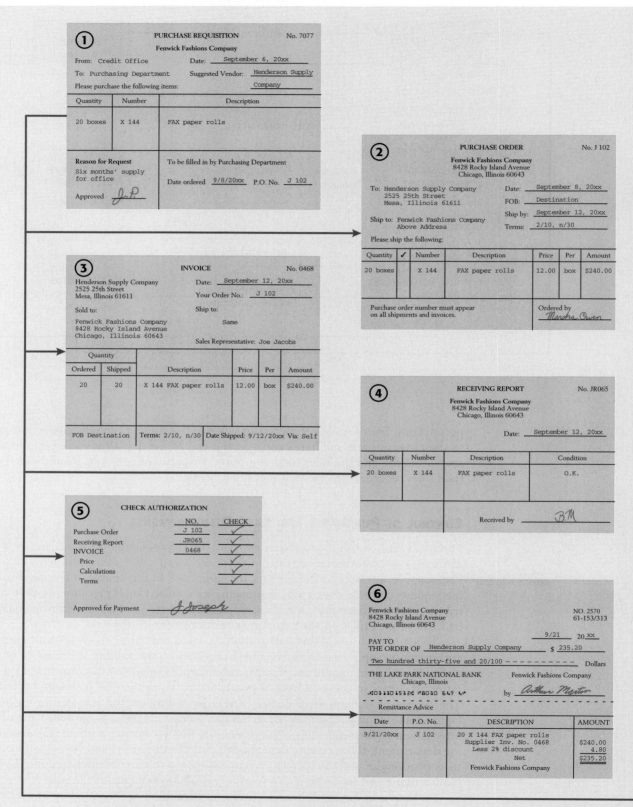

① PURCHASE REQUISITION No. 7077
Fenwick Fashions Company

From: Credit Office Date: September 6, 20xx
To: Purchasing Department Suggested Vendor: Henderson Supply Company
Please purchase the following items:

Quantity	Number	Description
20 boxes	X 144	FAX paper rolls

Reason for Request: Six months' supply for office
Approved: J.P.

To be filled in by Purchasing Department
Date ordered 9/8/20xx P.O. No. J 102

② PURCHASE ORDER No. J 102
Fenwick Fashions Company
8428 Rocky Island Avenue
Chicago, Illinois 60643

To: Henderson Supply Company
2525 25th Street
Mesa, Illinois 61611
Ship to: Fenwick Fashions Company
Above Address

Date: September 8, 20xx
FOB: Destination
Ship by: September 12, 20xx
Terms: 2/10, n/30

Please ship the following:

Quantity	✓	Number	Description	Price	Per	Amount
20 boxes		X 144	FAX paper rolls	12.00	box	$240.00

Purchase order number must appear on all shipments and invoices.
Ordered by Marsha Owen

③ INVOICE No. 0468
Henderson Supply Company
2525 25th Street
Mesa, Illinois 61611

Date: September 12, 20xx
Your Order No.: J 102

Sold to:
Fenwick Fashions Company
8428 Rocky Island Avenue
Chicago, Illinois 60643

Ship to: Same

Sales Representative: Joe Jacobs

Quantity		Description	Price	Per	Amount
Ordered	Shipped				
20	20	X 144 FAX paper rolls	12.00	box	$240.00

FOB Destination | Terms: 2/10, n/30 | Date Shipped: 9/12/20xx Via: Self

④ RECEIVING REPORT No. JR065
Fenwick Fashions Company
8428 Rocky Island Avenue
Chicago, Illinois 60643

Date: September 12, 20xx

Quantity	Number	Description	Condition
20 boxes	X 144	FAX paper rolls	O.K.

Received by B.M.

⑤ CHECK AUTHORIZATION

	NO.	CHECK
Purchase Order	J 102	✓
Receiving Report	JR065	✓
INVOICE	0468	✓
Price		✓
Calculations		✓
Terms		✓

Approved for Payment J. Joseph

⑥ Fenwick Fashions Company
8428 Rocky Island Avenue
Chicago, Illinois 60643
NO. 2570
61-153/313

9/21 20xx

PAY TO THE ORDER OF Henderson Supply Company $ 235.20
Two hundred thirty-five and 20/100 ---------- Dollars

THE LAKE PARK NATIONAL BANK
Chicago, Illinois
Fenwick Fashions Company
by Arthur Martin

⑆03130153⑆ ⑈8030 647 4⑈

Remittance Advice

Date	P.O. No.	DESCRIPTION	AMOUNT
9/21/20xx	J 102	20 X 144 FAX paper rolls Supplier Inv. No. 0468 Less 2% discount Net Fenwick Fashions Company	 $240.00 4.80 $235.20

Business Document	Prepared by	Sent to	Verification and Related Procedures
① Purchase requisition	Requesting department	Purchasing department	Purchasing verifies authorization.
② Purchase order	Purchasing department	Vendor	Vendor sends goods or services in accordance with purchase order.
③ Invoice	Vendor	Accounting department	Accounting receives invoice from vendor.
④ Receiving report	Receiving department	Accounting department	Accounting compares invoice, purchase order, and receiving report. Accounting verifies prices.
⑤ Check authorization	Accounting department	Treasurer	Accounting attaches check authorization to invoice, purchase order, and receiving report.
⑥ Check	Treasurer	Vendor	Treasurer verifies all documents before preparing check.
⑦ Bank statement	Buyer's bank	Accounting department	Accounting compares amount and payee's name on returned check with check authorization.

⑦

Statement of Account with
THE LAKE PARK NATIONAL BANK
Chicago, Illinois

Fenwick Fashions Company
8428 Rocky Island Avenue
Chicago, Illinois 60643

Checking Acct No
8030-647-4
Period covered
Sept.30-Oct.31,20xx

Previous Balance	Checks/Debits—No.	Deposits/Credits—No.	S.C.	Current Balance
$2,645.78	$4,319.33 --16	$5,157.12 --7	$12.50	$3,471.07

CHECKS/DEBITS			DEPOSITS/CREDITS		DAILY BALANCES	
Posting Date	Check No.	Amount	Posting Date	Amount	Date	Amount
					09/30	2,645.78
10/01	2564	100.00	10/01	586.00	10/01	2,881.78
10/01	2565	250.00	10/05	1,500.00	10/04	2,825.60
10/04	2567	56.18	10/06	300.00	10/05	3,900.46
10/05	2566	425.14	10/16	1,845.50	10/06	4,183.34
10/06	2568	17.12	10/21	600.00	10/12	2,242.34
10/12	2569	1,705.80	10/24	300.00CM	10/16	3,687.84
10/12	2570	235.20	10/31	25.62IN	10/17	3,589.09
10/16	2571	400.00			10/21	4,189.09
10/17	2572	29.75			10/24	3,745.59
10/17	2573	69.00			10/25	3,586.09
10/24	2574	738.50			10/28	3,457.95
10/24		5.00DM			10/31	3,471.07
10/25	2575	7.50				
10/25	2577	152.00				
10/28		118.14NSF				
10/28		10.00DM				
10/31		12.50SC				

Explanation of Symbols:

CM – Credit Memo
DM – Debit Memo
NSF – Non-Sufficient Funds
SC – Service Charge
EC – Error Correction
OD – Overdraft
IN – Interest on Average Balance

The last amount in this column is your balance.

Please examine; if no errors are reported within ten (10) days, the account will be considered to be correct.

FOCUS ON BUSINESS ETHICS

Throw It or Shred It?

What happens to all the paper—records and documents of all sorts—generated by a company's accounting system? Some of it, of course, must be saved for tax and legal purposes, but much of it is discarded after a time. Because accounting records and documents contain much information that companies want to keep confidential, management is reluctant to simply throw the paper in the trash. As a result, a nationwide industry of information-destruction firms has grown up and prospers. Companies such as DocuShred, Inc., <www.docushred.com> of Pennsylvania specialize in picking up paper and shredding it in a confidential way. Some shredding machines can make confetti of up to ten tons of paper per hour at seven to fifteen cents per pound. This method is cheaper, faster, and more secure than any method the companies themselves could employ. Data-destruction companies recycle about 95 percent of the shredded paper.[6] Of course, documents that may be the subject of an investigation should not be destroyed, as happened in the infamous case of Enron <www.enron.com> and its auditor, Arthur Andersen.

to make illegal payments to the supplier because the receiving department independently records receipts and the accounting department verifies prices. The receiving department cannot steal goods because the receiving report must equal the invoice. For the same reason, the supplier cannot bill for more goods than it ships. The accounting department's work is verified by the treasurer, and the treasurer ultimately is checked by the accounting department.

KEY POINT: A purchase requisition is not the same as a purchase order. A purchase requisition is sent to the purchasing department; a purchase order is sent to the vendor.

Figure 2 illustrates the typical sequence of documents used in an internal control plan for purchases and cash disbursements. To begin, the credit office (requesting department) of Fenwick Fashions Company fills out a formal request for a purchase, or **purchase requisition**, for 20 boxes of fax paper rolls (item 1). The department head approves it and forwards it to the purchasing department. The people in the purchasing department prepare a **purchase order**, as shown in item 2. The purchase order is addressed to the vendor (seller) and contains a description of the items ordered; the expected price, terms, and shipping date; and other shipping instructions. Fenwick Fashions Company does not pay any bill that is not accompanied by a purchase order number.

TERMINOLOGY NOTE: *Invoice* is the business term for "bill." Every business document must have a number for purposes of reference.

After receiving the purchase order, the vendor, Henderson Supply Company, ships the goods and sends an **invoice** or bill (item 3) to Fenwick Fashions Company. The invoice gives the quantity and description of the goods delivered, the price, and the terms of payment. If goods cannot all be shipped immediately, the estimated date for shipment of the remainder is indicated.

When the goods reach the receiving department of Fenwick Fashions Company, an employee writes the description, quantity, and condition of the goods on a form called a **receiving report** (item 4). The receiving department does not receive a copy of the purchase order or the invoice, so its employees do not know what should be received or its value. Thus, they are not tempted to steal any excess that may be delivered.

The receiving report is sent to the accounting department, where it is compared with the purchase order and the invoice. If everything is correct, the accounting department completes a **check authorization** and attaches it to the three supporting documents. The check authorization form shown in item 5 has a space for each item to be checked off as it is examined. Notice that the accounting department has all the documentary evidence for the transaction but does not have access to the assets purchased. Nor does it write the check for payment. This means that the people performing the accounting function cannot gain by falsifying documents in an effort to conceal fraud.

Finally, the treasurer examines all the documents and issues an order to the bank for payment, called a **check** (item 6), for the amount of the invoice less any appropriate discount. In some systems, the accounting department fills out the check so that all the treasurer has to do is inspect and sign it. The check is then sent to the supplier, with a remittance advice that shows what the check is for. A supplier who is not paid the proper amount will complain, of course, thus providing a form of outside control over the payment. Using a deposit ticket, the supplier deposits the check in the bank, which returns the canceled check with Fenwick Fashions Company's next bank statement (item 7). If the treasurer has made the check out for the wrong amount (or altered a pre-filled-in check), the problem will show up in the bank reconciliation.

There are many variations of the system just described. This example is offered as a simple system that provides adequate internal control.

Check out ACE for a Review Quiz at http://accounting.college.hmco.com/students.

PREPARING A BANK RECONCILIATION

LO3 Demonstrate the control of cash by preparing a bank reconciliation.

RELATED TEXT ASSIGNMENTS
Q: 9, 10
SE: 6, 7
E: 6, 7, 8
P: 1, 2, 7
SD: 3

ENRICHMENT NOTE:
Periodically, banks detect individuals who are *kiting*. Kiting is the illegal issuing of checks when there isn't enough money to cover them. Before one kited check clears the bank, a kited check from another account is deposited to cover it, making an endless circle.

STOP AND THINK!
How could a small business use information from bank statements and technology to reduce its cash management costs?

Using computer software to reconcile the cash balance with the bank statement will save time monthly. A detailed listing by category of all bank charges for previous periods may highlight areas where costs are controllable and could be reduced. Even small companies can save money by evaluating how they conduct business. ■

It is rare that the balance of a company's Cash account will exactly equal the cash balance shown on the bank statement. Certain transactions shown in the company's records may not have been recorded by the bank, and certain bank transactions may not appear in the company's records. Therefore, a necessary step in internal control is to prove both the balance shown on the bank statement and the balance of Cash in the accounting records.

A **bank reconciliation** is the process of accounting for the difference between the balance appearing on the bank statement and the balance of the Cash account in the company's records. This process involves making additions to and subtractions from both balances to arrive at the adjusted cash balance.

The most common transactions shown in the company's records but not entered in the bank's records are the following:

1. *Outstanding checks* These are checks that the company has issued and recorded but that do not yet appear on the bank statement.
2. *Deposits in transit* These are deposits mailed or taken to the bank but not received in time to be recorded on the bank statement.

Transactions that may appear on the bank statement but not in the company's records include the following:

1. *Service charges (SC)* Banks often charge a fee, or service charge, for the use of a checking account. Many banks base the service charge on a number of factors, such as the average balance of the account during the month or the number of checks drawn.
2. *NSF (nonsufficient funds) checks* An NSF check is a check that the company has deposited in its bank account but that is not paid when the bank presents it to the issuer's bank. The bank charges the company's account and returns the check so that the company can try to collect the amount due. If the bank has deducted the NSF check from the bank statement but the company has not deducted it from its book balance, an adjustment must be made in the bank reconciliation. The company usually reclassifies the NSF check from Cash to Accounts Receivable because it must now collect from the person or company that wrote the check.
3. *Miscellaneous debits and credits* Banks charge for other services as well, including stopping payment on checks and printing checks. The bank notifies the

depositor of each deduction by including a debit memorandum with the monthly statement. A bank will also sometimes serve as an agent in collecting on promissory notes for the depositor. In such a case, a credit memorandum will be included in the statement, along with a debit memorandum of the service charge.

4. *Interest income* Banks commonly pay interest on a company's average balance. Accounts that pay interest are sometimes called NOW or money market accounts. Such interest is reported on the bank statement.

An error by either the bank or the depositor will, of course, require immediate correction.

ILLUSTRATION OF A BANK RECONCILIATION

KEY POINT: The ending bank statement balance does not represent the amount that should appear on the balance sheet for cash. There are events and items, such as deposits in transit and outstanding checks, that the bank is unaware of at the cutoff date. This is why a bank reconciliation must be prepared.

Assume that the October bank statement for Fenwick Fashions Company indicates a balance on October 31 of $3,471.07, and that in its records, Fenwick Fashions Company has a cash balance on October 31 of $2,415.91. The purpose of a bank reconciliation is to identify the items that make up the difference between these amounts and to determine the correct cash balance. The bank reconciliation for Fenwick Fashions Company is shown in Exhibit 1. The numbered items in the exhibit refer to the following:

1. A deposit in the amount of $276.00 was mailed to the bank on October 31 and has not been recorded by the bank.
2. Five checks issued in October or prior months have not yet been paid by the bank, as follows:

Check No.	Date	Amount
551	Sept. 14	$150.00
576	Oct. 30	40.68
578	Oct. 31	500.00
579	Oct. 31	370.00
580	Oct. 31	130.50

3. The deposit for cash sales of October 6 was incorrectly recorded in Fenwick Fashions Company's records as $330.00. The bank correctly recorded the deposit as $300.00.

STUDY NOTE: A credit memorandum means that an amount was *added* to the bank balance; a debit memorandum means that an amount was *deducted*.

4. Among the returned checks was a credit memorandum showing that the bank had collected a promissory note from A. Jacobs in the amount of $280.00, plus $20.00 in interest on the note. A debit memorandum was also enclosed for the $5.00 collection fee. No entry had been made on Fenwick Fashions Company's records.
5. Also returned with the bank statement was an NSF check for $128.14. This check had been received from a customer named Arthur Clubb. The NSF check from Clubb was not reflected in the company's accounting records.
6. A debit memorandum was enclosed for the regular monthly service charge of $12.50. This service charge had not yet been recorded by Fenwick Fashions Company.
7. Interest earned by Fenwick Fashions Company on the average balance was reported as $15.62.

Note in Exhibit 1 that starting from their separate balances, both the bank and book amounts are adjusted to the amount of $2,555.89. This adjusted balance is the

EXHIBIT 1
Bank Reconciliation

Fenwick Fashions Company
Bank Reconciliation
October 31, 20xx

Balance per bank, October 31		$3,471.07
① Add deposit of October 31 in transit		276.00
		$3,747.07
② Less outstanding checks:		
No. 551	$150.00	
No. 576	40.68	
No. 578	500.00	
No. 579	370.00	
No. 580	130.50	1,191.18
Adjusted bank balance, October 31		**$2,555.89**
Balance per books, October 31		$2,415.91
Add:		
④ Note receivable collected by bank	$280.00	
④ Interest income on note	20.00	
⑦ Interest income	15.62	315.62
		$2,731.53
Less:		
③ Overstatement of deposit of October 6	$ 30.00	
④ Collection fee	5.00	
⑤ NSF check of Arthur Clubb	128.14	
⑥ Service charge	12.50	175.64
Adjusted book balance, October 31		**$2,555.89**

Note: The circled numbers refer to the items listed in the text.

KEY POINT: Even though the September 14 check was deducted on the September 30 reconciliation, it must be deducted again in each subsequent month in which it remains outstanding.

STUDY NOTE: It is possible to place an item in the wrong section of a bank reconciliation and still have it balance. The *correct* adjusted balance must be obtained.

amount of cash owned by the company on October 31 and thus is the amount that should appear on its October 31 balance sheet.

RECORDING TRANSACTIONS AFTER RECONCILIATION

KEY POINT: Notice that only those transactions the company has not recorded before receiving the bank statement are recorded.

The adjusted balance of cash differs from both the bank statement and Fenwick Fashions Company's records. The bank balance will automatically become correct when outstanding checks are presented for payment and the deposit in transit is received and recorded by the bank. Entries must be made, however, for the transactions necessary to update the book balance. All the items reported by the bank but not yet recorded by the company must be recorded in the general journal by means of the following entries:

A = L + OE
\+   +
−

Oct. 31	Cash	300.00	
	Notes Receivable		280.00
	Interest Income		20.00
	Note receivable of $280.00 and interest of $20.00 collected by bank from A. Jacobs		

KEY POINT: Every entry involves either a debit or a credit to Cash.

A = L + OE
+   +
	Oct. 31	Cash
		  Interest Income
		    Interest on average bank account balance
			15.62	15.62

A = L + OE
−   −
	31	Sales
		  Cash
		    Correction of error in recording a $300.00 deposit as $330.00
			30.00	30.00

A = L + OE
+
−
	31	Accounts Receivable
		  Cash
		    NSF check of Arthur Clubb returned by bank
			128.14	128.14

A = L + OE
−   −
	31	Bank Service Charges Expense
		  Cash
		    Bank service charge ($12.50) and collection fee ($5.00) for October
			17.50	17.50

It is acceptable to record these entries in one or two compound entries to save time and space.

Check out ACE for a Review Quiz at http://accounting.college.hmco.com/students.

Petty Cash Procedures

SO4 Demonstrate the use of a simple imprest system.

RELATED TEXT ASSIGNMENTS
Q: 11, 12, 13, 14, 15, 16
SE: 8
E: 9, 10
P: 3, 8

It is not always practical to make every disbursement by check. For example, it is sometimes necessary to make small payments of cash for such things as postage stamps, incoming postage, shipping charges due, or minor purchases of pens, paper, and the like.

For situations in which it is inconvenient to pay by check, most companies set up a **petty cash fund**. One of the best ways to control a petty cash fund is through the use of an **imprest system**. Under this system, a petty cash fund is established for a fixed amount. Each cash payment from the fund is documented by a voucher. The fund is periodically reimbursed, based on the vouchers, by the exact amount necessary to restore its original cash balance.

Establishing the Petty Cash Fund

Some companies have a regular cashier or other employee who administers the petty cash fund. To establish the fund, the company issues a check for an amount intended to cover two to four weeks of small expenditures. The check is cashed and the money placed in the petty cash box, drawer, or envelope.

The only entry required when the fund is established is to record the check.

A = L + OE
+
−
	Oct. 14	Petty Cash
		  Cash
		    To establish the petty cash fund
			100.00	100.00

Making Disbursements from the Petty Cash Fund

The custodian of the petty cash fund should prepare a **petty cash voucher**, or written authorization, for each expenditure, as shown in Figure 3. On each petty cash

FIGURE 3
Petty Cash Voucher

PETTY CASH VOUCHER

No. X 744

Date Oct. 23, 20xx

For Postage due

Charge to Postage Expense

Amount $2.86

W.S. — Approved by

Tom L. — Received by

KEY POINT: Even though withdrawals from petty cash are generally small, the cumulative total over time can represent a substantial amount. Accordingly, an effective system of internal control must be established for the management of the fund.

voucher, the custodian enters the date, amount, and purpose of the expenditure. The voucher is signed by the person who receives the payment.

The custodian should be informed that unannounced audits of the fund will be made occasionally. The cash in the fund plus the sum of the petty cash vouchers should at all times equal the amount shown in the Petty Cash account.

REIMBURSING THE PETTY CASH FUND

KEY POINT: When the petty cash fund is replenished, the Petty Cash account is neither debited nor credited. But if the size of the fund is changed, there should be an entry to Petty Cash.

At specified intervals, when the fund becomes low, and at the end of an accounting period, the petty cash fund is replenished by a check issued to the custodian for the exact amount of the expenditures. From time to time, there may be minor discrepancies in the amount of cash left in the fund at the time of reimbursement. In those cases, the amount of the discrepancy is recorded in a Cash Short or Over account—as a debit if short or as a credit if over.

Assume that after two weeks the petty cash fund established earlier has a cash balance of $14.27 and petty cash vouchers as follows: postage, $25.00; supplies, $30.55; and freight in, $30.00. The entry to replenish, or replace, the fund would be:

A = L + OE
\+ −
− −

Oct. 28	Postage Expense	25.00	
	Supplies	30.55	
	Freight In	30.00	
	Cash Short or Over	.18	
	Cash		85.73
	To replenish the petty cash fund		

Notice that the Petty Cash account was not affected by the entry to replenish the fund. The Petty Cash account is debited when the fund is established or the fund level is changed. Expense or asset accounts are debited each time the fund is replenished, including in this case $.18 to Cash Short or Over for a small cash shortage. In most cases, no further entries to the Petty Cash account are needed unless the firm wants to change the fixed amount of the fund.

The petty cash fund should be replenished at the end of an accounting period to bring it up to its fixed amount and ensure that changes in the other accounts involved are reflected in the current period's financial statements. If, through an oversight, the petty cash fund is not replenished at the end of the period, expenditures for the period still must appear on the income statement. They are shown through an adjusting entry debiting the expense accounts and crediting Petty Cash. The result is a reduction in the petty cash fund and the Petty Cash account by the amount of the adjusting entry. On the financial statements, the balance of the Petty Cash account is usually combined with other cash accounts.

Check out ACE for a Review Quiz at http://accounting.college.hmco.com/students.

VOUCHER SYSTEMS

SO5 Define *voucher system* and describe the components and operation of a voucher system.

RELATED TEXT ASSIGNMENTS
Q: 17, 18, 19, 20, 21
SE: 9, 10
P: 5

KEY POINT: The purpose of a voucher system is to control expenditures through mandatory documentation and written authorization.

A **voucher system** is any system that gives documentary proof of and written authorization for business transactions. In this section, we present a voucher system designed to keep the tightest possible control over a company's expenditures. It consists of records and procedures for systematically gathering, recording, and paying expenditures. The system provides strong internal control by separating duties and responsibilities in the following functions:

1. Authorization of expenditures
2. Receipt of goods and services
3. Validation of liability by examination of invoices from suppliers for correctness of prices, extensions (quantity times price), shipping costs, and credit terms
4. Payment of expenditure by check, taking discounts when possible

Under a voucher system, every liability must be recorded as soon as it is incurred. A written authorization, called a **voucher**, is prepared for each expenditure when it becomes an obligation to pay, and checks are written only for approved vouchers. No one person has the authority both to incur expenses and to issue checks. In large companies, the duties of authorizing expenditures, verifying receipt of goods and services, checking invoices, recording liabilities, and issuing checks are divided among different people. So, for both accounting and management control, every expenditure must be carefully and routinely reviewed and verified before payment. For each transaction, the written approval leaves a trail of documentary evidence, or what is called an **audit trail**.

COMPONENTS OF A VOUCHER SYSTEM

Although there is more than one way to set up a voucher system, most systems use (1) vouchers, (2) voucher checks, (3) a voucher register, and (4) a check register.

KEY POINT: A voucher serves the same purpose as a check authorization form.

■ **VOUCHERS** Any business can use vouchers to control expenditures. A voucher serves as the basis of an accounting entry. To facilitate tracking, all vouchers are sequentially numbered, and a separate voucher is attached to each bill as it comes in. In the cash disbursement system introduced earlier in this chapter, a voucher would replace the check authorization form. Figure 4 shows the front and back of a typical voucher. On the front is important information about the expenditure and the authorizing signatures required for payment. On the back of the voucher is

FOCUS ON BUSINESS PRACTICE

Which Is More Important: B to C or B to B?

E-tailing, the selling of business (goods) to consumers (B to C), gets the most publicity, but the most rapidly growing segment of business use of the Internet is business to business (B to B) transactions. It is projected that B to B transactions will exceed $14 trillion, compared with $7 trillion for B to C transactions. Industries leading in B to B transactions are automotive, chemicals, paper and office products, computers and electronics, and utilities. Manual voucher systems are obviously not sufficient for this heavy volume of activity. B to B voucher systems will require strong internal controls that ensure proper delivery, precise product specifications, high levels of customer service, and timely, accurate bill payment.[7]

FIGURE 4
Front and Back of a Typical Voucher Form

Thomas Appliance Company

Payee	Belmont Products	Voucher No.	704
Address	Gary, Indiana	Date Due	7/13
		Date Paid	7/13
Terms	2/10, n/30	Check No.	205

Date	Invoice No.	Description	Amount
7/3	XL1066	10 cases Model 70X14	1,200--

Approved M.N. — Controller   Approved A. Thomas — Treasurer

BACK OF VOUCHER

Account Debited	Acct. No.	Amount
Purchases	511	1,200.00
Freight In	512	
Rent Expense	631	
Salary Expense	611	
Utilities Expense	635	
Total		$1,200.00

Voucher No.	704
Payee	Belmont Products
Address	Gary, Indiana
Invoice Amount	1,200.00
Less Discount	24.00
Net	1,176.00
Date Due	7/13
Date Paid	7/13
Check No.	205

STUDY NOTE: A voucher not only provides for the necessary signatures but also includes information and document numbers that are important in creating an audit trail.

information about the accounts and amounts to be debited and credited. The voucher identifies the transaction by both voucher number and check number and is recorded in both the voucher register and the check register, as described in the following sections.

KEY POINT: Payment is made with a voucher check.

■ **VOUCHER CHECKS** Although regular checks can be used effectively with a voucher system, many businesses use a form of **voucher check**, which tells the payee the reason the check was issued. The information is written either on the check itself or on a detachable stub.

KEY POINT: All approved vouchers are recorded in the voucher register.

■ **VOUCHER REGISTER** The **voucher register** is the book of original entry in which vouchers are recorded after they have been approved. The voucher register takes the place of the purchases journal in companies that use special-purpose journals. There is one important difference between the two journals: All expenditures—expenses, payroll, plant, and equipment, as well as purchases of merchandise—are

EXHIBIT 2
Voucher Register

KEY POINT: The voucher register contains a Vouchers Payable column that functions exactly like the Accounts Payable column in a purchases journal.

Voucher Register

Date		Voucher No.	Payee	Payment Date	Payment Check No.	Credit Vouchers Payable	Debits Purchases	Debits Freight In	Debits Store Supplies
20xx									
July	1	701	Common Utility	7/6	203	75			
	2	702	Ade Realty	7/2	201	400			
	2	703	Buy Rite Supplies	7/6	202	25			
	3	704	Belmont Products	7/13	205	1,200	1,200		
	6	705	M&M Freight			60		60	
	7	706	J. Jay, Petty Cash	7/7	204	50			
	8	707	Belmont Products	7/18	208	600	600		
	11	708	M&M Freight			30		30	
	11	709	Mack Truck			5,600			
	12	710	Livingstone Wholesale	7/22	209	785	750	35	
	14	711	Payroll	7/14	206	2,200			
	17	712	First National Bank	7/17	207	4,250			
	20	713	Livingstone Wholesale			525	500	25	
	21	714	Belmont Products			400	400		
	24	715	M&M Freight			18		18	
	30	716	Payroll	7/30	210	2,200			
	31	717	J. Jay, Petty Cash	7/31	211	47		17	
	31	718	Maintenance Company			175			
	31	719	Store Supply Company			350			350
						18,990	3,450	185	350
						(211)	(511)	(512)	(116)

recorded in a voucher register; only purchases of merchandise on credit are recorded in a single-column purchases journal.

A voucher register appears in Exhibit 2. Notice that a column called Vouchers Payable replaces the Accounts Payable column. As you can see, the first entry in the voucher register records the receipt of a utility bill. It is recorded as a debit to Utilities Expense and a credit to Vouchers Payable (not Accounts Payable). On July 6, this utility bill was paid with check number 203.

KEY POINT: A check register serves the same purpose as a cash payments journal.

■ **CHECK REGISTER** In a voucher system, the **check register**, as shown in Exhibit 3, is the journal in which checks are listed as they are written. Consequently, it

ENRICHMENT NOTE: The Other Accounts column enables the voucher register to accommodate any type of expenditure. The total of the Other Accounts column is not posted because it represents several different accounts, each of which is posted the day the transaction is entered into the voucher register.

Page 1

Debits								
						Other Accounts		
Office Supplies	Sales Salaries Expense	Office Salaries Expense	Maintenance Expense, Selling	Maintenance Expense, Office	Utilities Expense	Name	No.	Amount
					75			
						Rent Expense	631	400
25								
						Petty Cash	121	50
						Trucks	148	5,600
	1,400	800						
						Notes Payable	212	4,000
						Interest Expense	645	250
	1,400	800						
20						Misc. Expense	649	10
			100	75				
45	2,800	1,600	100	75	75			10,310
(117)	(611)	(612)	(621)	(622)	(635)			(✓)

replaces the cash payments journal. Carefully study the connection between the voucher register and the check register. The incurrence of a liability is recorded in the voucher register; its payment is recorded in the check register.

Operation of a Voucher System

There are five steps in the operation of a voucher system:

1. *Preparing the voucher* A voucher is prepared for each expenditure. All documents—purchase orders, invoices, and receiving reports—should be attached to the voucher when it is submitted for approval.

EXHIBIT 3
Check Register

Check Register

Date		Check No.	Payee	Voucher No.	Debit: Vouchers Payable	Credits: Purchases Discounts	Credits: Cash
20xx							
July	2	201	Ade Realty	702	400		400
	6	202	Buy Rite Supplies	703	25		25
	6	203	Common Utility	701	75		75
	7	204	J. Jay, Petty Cash	706	50		50
	13	205	Belmont Products	704	1,200	24	1,176
	14	206	Payroll	711	2,200		2,200
	17	207	First National Bank	712	4,250		4,250
	18	208	Belmont Products	707	600	12	588
	22	209	Livingstone Wholesale	710	785	15	770
	30	210	Payroll	716	2,200		2,200
	31	211	J. Jay, Petty Cash	717	47		47
					11,832	51	11,781
					(211)	(513)	(111)

STUDY NOTE: The check register in Exhibit 3 assumes the use of the gross method to handle discounts.

Many companies pay their employees out of a separate payroll account. In such cases, a voucher is prepared to cover the total payroll. The check for the voucher is then deposited in the payroll account, and individual payroll checks are drawn on that account.

2. *Recording the voucher* All approved vouchers should be recorded in the voucher register, as shown in Exhibit 2. For example, the entry for Voucher 704 corresponds to the information that is presented in Figure 4. Vouchers that do not have appropriate approvals or supporting documents should be investigated immediately.

3. *Paying the voucher* After a voucher has been recorded, it is placed in an unpaid voucher file. Many companies file their vouchers by due date and by vendor within due date, so that checks can be written at the appropriate times. Such a practice ensures that all discounts for prompt payment can be taken. After payment, vouchers are filed by voucher number.

   A few days before a voucher is due, a check for the correct amount, accompanied by the voucher and supporting documents, is presented to the individual who is authorized to sign checks. The payment is entered in the check register, as shown in Exhibit 3. For example, Belmont Products is paid with check no. 205. Both the date of payment and the check number are then entered in the voucher register on the same line as the corresponding voucher. This information is helpful in the preparation of a schedule of unpaid vouchers, which is described in step **5**.

   Extra steps are required when there has been a purchase return or allowance that applies to a voucher. For example, suppose that part of a ship-

EXHIBIT 4
Schedule of Unpaid Vouchers

Thomas Appliance Company
Schedule of Unpaid Vouchers
July 31, 20xx

Payee	Voucher Number	Amount
M&M Freight	705	$ 60
M&M Freight	708	30
Mack Truck	709	5,600
Livingstone Wholesale	713	525
Belmont Products	714	400
M&M Freight	715	18
Maintenance Company	718	175
Store Supply Company	719	350
Total Unpaid Vouchers		$7,158

KEY POINT: The schedule total of $7,158 would appear as a liability on the July 31 balance sheet, usually labeled Accounts Payable.

ment of merchandise is defective and is returned to the supplier for credit. At the time the merchandise is returned or the allowance is given, an entry should be made in the general journal debiting Vouchers Payable and crediting Purchases Returns and Allowances, and a notation should be made on the voucher in the voucher file. At the time of payment, only the *net amount* of the voucher—the original amount less the return or allowance and any applicable discount—should be paid and recorded in the check register. Rather than noting the change on the voucher, some companies cancel the original voucher and prepare a new one for the amount to be paid.

4. *Posting the voucher and check registers* Posting the voucher and check registers is very similar to posting the purchases journal and cash payments journal. The only difference is that the Vouchers Payable account is substituted for the Accounts Payable account.

5. *Summarizing unpaid vouchers* Because the sum of the vouchers in the unpaid vouchers file should always equal the credit balance of the Vouchers Payable account, a subsidiary ledger is unnecessary. At the end of each accounting period, the unpaid voucher file should be totaled to prove the balance of the Vouchers Payable account. Exhibit 4 shows a schedule of unpaid vouchers, which is a list of all the unpaid vouchers according to the voucher register in Exhibit 2. The voucher register and the check register (Exhibit 3) are reconciled by simple subtraction:

Vouchers Payable credit from the voucher register	$18,990
Less Vouchers Payable debit from the check register	11,832
Vouchers Payable credit balance from the schedule of unpaid vouchers	$ 7,158

Sometimes the account title *Vouchers Payable* appears on a company's balance sheet. The preferred practice, however, is to use the more widely known and accepted term *Accounts Payable*, even when a voucher system is in place.

Check out ACE for a Review Quiz at http://accounting.college.hmco.com/students.

Chapter Review

Review of Learning Objectives

LO1 Define *internal control*, explain its basic components and limitations, and give examples of control activities.

Internal control consists of all the policies and procedures a company uses to ensure the reliability of financial reporting, compliance with laws and regulations, and the effectiveness and efficiency of operations. Internal control has five components: the control environment, risk assessment, information and communication, control activities, and monitoring. Examples of control activities are proper authorization of transactions; recording all transactions to facilitate preparation of financial statements and to establish accountability for assets; use of well-designed documents to ensure proper recording of transactions; physical controls; periodic checks of records and assets; separation of duties into the functions of authorization, operations, custody of assets, and recordkeeping; and use of sound personnel policies. A system of internal control relies on the people who implement it. Thus, the effectiveness of internal control is limited by the people involved. Human error, collusion, and failure to recognize changed conditions all can contribute to a system's failure.

LO2 Apply internal control activities to common merchandising transactions.

Certain procedures strengthen internal control over cash sales receipts, purchases, and cash disbursements. First, the functions of authorization, recordkeeping, and custody should be kept separate. Second, the accounting system should provide for physical protection of assets (especially cash and merchandise inventory), use of banking services, prompt recording and deposit of cash receipts, and payment by check. Third, the people who have access to cash and merchandise inventory should be specifically designated and their number limited. Fourth, employees who have access to cash or merchandise inventory should be bonded. Fifth, the Cash account should be reconciled each month, and unannounced audits of cash on hand should be made by an individual who does not authorize, handle, or record cash transactions.

LO3 Demonstrate the control of cash by preparing a bank reconciliation.

A bank reconciliation accounts for the difference between the balance that appears on the bank statement and the balance in the company's Cash account. It involves adjusting both balances to arrive at the adjusted cash balance. The bank balance is adjusted for outstanding checks and deposits in transit. The depositor's book balance is adjusted for service charges, NSF checks, interest earned, and miscellaneous debits and credits.

Supplemental Objectives

SO4 Demonstrate the use of a simple imprest system.

An imprest system is a method of controlling small cash expenditures by setting up a fund at a fixed amount and periodically reimbursing the fund by the amount necessary to restore the original balance. A petty cash fund, one example of an imprest system, is established by a debit to Petty Cash and a credit to Cash. It is replenished by debits to various expense or asset accounts and a credit to Cash. Each expenditure should be supported by a petty cash voucher.

SO5 Define *voucher system* and describe the components and operation of a voucher system.

A voucher system is any system that gives documentary proof of and written authorization for business transactions. It consists of authorizations (vouchers), voucher checks, a special journal to record the vouchers (voucher register), and a special journal to record the voucher checks (check register). The five steps in operating a voucher system are (1) preparing the voucher, (2) recording the voucher, (3) paying the voucher, (4) posting the voucher and check registers, and (5) summarizing unpaid vouchers.

Review of Concepts and Terminology

The following concepts and terms were introduced in this chapter:

SO5 **Audit trail:** The documentary evidence of written approval created by key people as they routinely review and verify an expenditure before payment is made.

LO3 **Bank reconciliation:** The process of accounting for the difference between the balance appearing on the bank statement and the balance of the Cash account in the company's records.

LO1 **Bonding:** The process of carefully checking an employee's background and insuring the company against theft by that person.

LO2 **Check:** A written order to a bank to pay the amount specified from funds on deposit.

LO2 **Check authorization:** A form prepared by the accounting department after it has compared the receiving report with the purchase order and the invoice. It permits the issuance of a check to pay the invoice.

SO5 **Check register:** In a voucher system, the journal in which voucher checks are listed as they are written.

LO1 **Control activities:** Policies and procedures established by management to ensure that the objectives of internal control are met.

LO1 **Control environment:** The overall attitude, awareness, and actions of management, as reflected in the company's philosophy and operating style, organizational structure, method of assigning authority and responsibility, and personnel policies and practices.

SO4 **Imprest system:** A system for controlling small cash disbursements by establishing a fund at a fixed amount and periodically reimbursing the fund by the amount necessary to restore the original cash balance.

LO1 **Information and communication:** The accounting system established by management and the communication of responsibilities with regard to the accounting system.

LO1 **Internal control:** All the policies and procedures a company uses to ensure the reliability of financial reporting, compliance with laws and regulations, and the effectiveness and efficiency of operations.

LO2 **Invoice:** A form sent to the purchaser by the vendor describing the goods delivered, the quantity, price, and terms of payment.

LO1 **Monitoring:** Management's regular assessment of the quality of internal control.

SO4 **Petty cash fund:** A fund for making small payments of cash when it is inconvenient to pay by check.

SO4 **Petty cash voucher:** A form signed by a person who receives a cash payment from a petty cash fund; lists the date, amount, and purpose of the expenditure.

LO2 **Purchase order:** A form prepared by a company's purchasing department and sent to a vendor describing the items ordered; the expected price, terms, and shipping date; and other shipping instructions.

LO2 **Purchase requisition:** A formal written request for a purchase, prepared by the requesting department in an organization and sent to the purchasing department.

LO2 **Receiving report:** A form prepared by the receiving department of a company describing the quantity and condition of goods received.

LO1 **Risk assessment:** The identification of areas in which risks of loss of assets or inaccuracies in the accounting records are high.

SO5 **Voucher:** A written authorization prepared for each business expenditure when it becomes a liability or obligation to pay.

SO5 **Voucher check:** A form of check, used in a voucher system, that describes the reason for issuing the check.

SO5 **Voucher register:** The book of original entry in which vouchers are recorded after they have been approved.

SO5 **Voucher system:** Any system that gives documentary proof of and written authorization for business transactions.

Review Problem

Bank Reconciliation

LO3 The information that follows comes from the records of the Maynard Company. The credit memorandum on April 15 is for the collection of a note and includes $100 in interest. Checks numbered 1714 for $210 and 1715 for $70 were outstanding on March 31.

From the Cash Receipts Journal — Page 14

Date		Debit Cash
Apr.	1	560
	10	1,440
	17	780
	30	2,900
		5,680

From the Cash Payments Journal — Page 18

Date		Check Number	Credit Cash
Apr.	4	1716	580
	6	1717	800
	17	1718	1,050
	25	1719	110
			2,540

From the General Ledger

Cash — Account No. 111

Date		Item	Post. Ref.	Debit	Credit	Balance Debit	Balance Credit
Mar.	31	Balance				4,200	
Apr.	30		CR14	5,680		9,880	
	30		CP18		2,540	7,340	

From the Company's Bank Statement

Checks and Other Debits: Date	Check Number	Amount	Deposits: Date	Amount	Balance: Date	Amount
					4/1	4,480
4/5	1714	210	4/2	560	4/2	5,040
4/5	1716	580	4/11	1,440	4/5	4,250
4/12	1717	800	4/15	1,500CM	4/11	5,690
4/28		20SC	4/17	780	4/12	4,890
			4/28	10IN	4/15	6,390
					4/17	7,170
					4/28	7,160

CM—Credit Memo SC—Service Charge IN—Interest

REQUIRED ▶ 1. Prepare a bank reconciliation as of April 30, 20xx.
2. Prepare the necessary entries in journal form.

Answer to Review Problem

1. Prepare a bank reconciliation.

Maynard Company
Bank Reconciliation
April 30, 20xx

Balance per bank, April 30, 20xx		$ 7,160
Add deposit of April 30, in transit		2,900
		$10,060
Less outstanding checks:		
No. 1715	$ 70	
No. 1718	1,050	
No. 1719	110	1,230
Adjusted bank balance, April 30, 20xx		$ 8,830
Balance per books, April 30, 20xx		$ 7,340
Add: Note collected by bank	$1,400	
Interest income on note	100	
Interest income	10	1,510
		$ 8,850
Less service charge		20
Adjusted book balance, April 30, 20xx		$ 8,830

2. Prepare the entries in journal form.

Apr. 30	Cash	1,500	
	Notes Receivable		1,400
	Interest Income		100
	Collection of note by bank		
30	Cash	10	
	Interest Income		10
	Interest on bank account		
30	Bank Service Charges Expense	20	
	Cash		20
	Bank service charge for April		

Chapter Assignments

Building Your Knowledge Foundation

Questions

1. Most people think of internal control as a means of making fraud harder to commit and easier to detect. What are some other important purposes of internal control?

2. What are the five components of internal control?
3. What are some examples of control activities?
4. Why is the separation of duties necessary to ensure sound internal control? What does this principle assume about the relationships of employees in a company and the possibility of two or more of them stealing from the company?
5. In a small business, it is sometimes impossible to separate duties completely. What are three other practices that a small business can follow to achieve the objectives of internal control over cash?
6. At Thrifty Variety Store, each sales clerk counts the cash in his or her cash drawer at the end of the day, then removes the cash register tape and prepares a daily cash form, noting any discrepancies. This information is checked by an employee in the cashier's office, who counts the cash, compares the total with the form, and then gives the cash to the cashier. What is the weakness in this system of internal control?
7. How does a movie theater control cash receipts?
8. For each of the following business documents, tell what department or person prepares it and what department or person receives it: purchase requisition, purchase order, invoice, receiving report, check authorization, check, deposit ticket, and bank statement.
9. Why is a bank reconciliation prepared?
10. Assume that each of the following items appeared on a bank reconciliation. Which item would be (1) an addition to the balance on the bank statement, (2) a deduction from the balance on the bank statement, (3) an addition to the balance on the books, or (4) a deduction from the balance on the books? Write the correct number next to each item.

    a. Outstanding checks
    b. Deposits in transit
    c. Bank service charge
    d. NSF check returned with statement
    e. Note collected by bank

    Which of the above items requires an entry?
11. What is the purpose of a petty cash fund? From the standpoint of internal control, what is the significance of the level at which the fund is established?
12. What account or accounts are debited when a petty cash fund is established? What account or accounts are debited when a petty cash fund is replenished?
13. What does a credit balance in the Cash Short or Over account indicate?
14. At the end of the day, the combined count of cash for all cash registers in a store reveals a cash shortage of $17.20. In what account would this cash shortage be recorded? Would the account be debited or credited?
15. Should a petty cash fund be replenished as of the last day of the accounting period? Explain your answer.
16. Explain how each of the following can contribute to internal control over cash: (a) a bank reconciliation; (b) a petty cash fund; (c) a cash register with printed receipts; (d) printed, prenumbered cash sales receipts; (e) regular vacations for the cashier; (f) two signatures on checks; and (g) prenumbered checks.
17. What is the greatest advantage of a voucher system?
18. Before a voucher for the purchase of merchandise is approved for payment, three documents should be compared to verify the amount of the liability. What are the three documents?
19. A company that presently uses a general journal, a sales journal, a purchases journal, a cash receipts journal, and a cash payments journal decides to adopt the voucher system. Which of the five journals would be changed or replaced? What would replace them?
20. What is the correct order for filing (a) unpaid vouchers and (b) paid vouchers?
21. When the voucher system is used, is there an Accounts Payable controlling account and an accounts payable subsidiary ledger? Be prepared to explain your answer.

Short Exercises

SE 1. LO1 **Purposes of Internal Control**

Ann Mogen owns a gourmet coffee shop. Identify four ways in which good internal controls can help her operate her business.

SE 2. LO1 **Components of Internal Control**

Schell Company is a men's clothing store. Indicate whether each of the following components of internal control is part of the (a) control environment, (b) risk assessment, (c) information and communication, (d) control activities, or (e) monitoring:

1. An organization plan calls for separation of duties in the handling of cash sales.
2. Charles Schell emphasizes to employees the importance of following specific procedures in the handling of cash.
3. All cash transactions are recorded automatically in the company's computer when the sales are rung up on the cash register.
4. Management identifies the ways clothes could be stolen.
5. Management observes that employees are following proper procedures.

SE 3. LO1 **Limitations of Internal Control**

Internal control is subject to several inherent limitations. Indicate whether each of the following situations is an example of (a) human error, (b) collusion, (c) changed conditions, or (d) cost-benefit considerations:

1. Effective separation of duties in a restaurant is impractical because the business is too small.
2. The cashier and the manager of a retail shoe store work together to circumvent the internal controls for the purpose of embezzling funds.
3. The cashier in a pizza shop does not understand the procedures for operating the cash register and thus fails to ring up all sales and to count the cash at the end of the day.
4. At a law firm, computer supplies were mistakenly delivered to the reception area instead of the receiving area because the supplier began using a different means of shipment. As a result, the receipt of supplies was not recorded.

SE 4. LO1 LO2 **Internal Control Activities**

Match the check-writing policy for a small business described below to these control activities:

a. Authorization
b. Recording transactions
c. Documents and records
d. Physical controls
e. Periodic independent verification
f. Separation of duties
g. Sound personnel policies

1. The person who writes the checks to pay bills is different from the persons who authorize the payments and who keep the records of the payments.
2. The checks are kept in a locked drawer. The only person who has the key is the person who writes the checks.
3. The person who writes the checks is bonded.
4. Once each month the owner compares and reconciles the amount of money shown in the accounting records with the amount in the bank account.
5. Each check is approved by the owner of the business before it is mailed.
6. A check stub recording pertinent information is completed for each check.
7. Every day, all checks are recorded in the accounting records, using the information on the check stubs.

SE 5. LO2 **Internal Control Documents for Purchases and Payments**

Indicate the letter of where each of the following documents would be prepared and the letter of where each document would be sent:

1. Purchase requisition	a. Requesting department
2. Receiving report	b. Purchasing department
3. Invoice	c. Receiving department
4. Check authorization	d. Accounting department
5. Check	e. Treasurer
	f. Supplier

SE 6. LO3 **Elements of a Bank Reconciliation**

When a bank reconciliation is performed, is each of the following items (a) an addition to the balance per bank, (b) a deduction from the balance per bank, (c) an addition to the balance per books, or (d) a deduction from the balance per books?

1. Service charges (by the bank)
2. Deposits in transit

3. Interest income (shown on bank statement)
4. Outstanding checks

SE 7. **LO3 Bank Reconciliation**

Prepare a bank reconciliation from the following information:

a. Balance per bank statement as of June 30, $2,586.58
b. Balance per books as of June 30, $1,308.87
c. Deposits in transit, $348.00
d. Outstanding checks, $1,611.11
e. Interest on average balance, $14.60

SE 8. **SO4 Petty Cash Fund**

A petty cash fund was established at $100. At the end of May, the fund has a cash balance of $36 and petty cash vouchers for postage, $29, and office supplies, $34. Prepare the entry on May 31 to replenish the fund.

SE 9. **SO5 Components of a Voucher System**

Identify which of the following statements describes the purpose of a (a) voucher, (b) voucher check, (c) voucher register, and (d) check register:

1. Provides a record of the payment of vouchers
2. Serves as a means of payment and notes the reason for the issuance of the payment
3. Provides a written authorization for each expenditure
4. Provides a record of all authorized expenditures

SE 10. **SO5 Operation of a Voucher System**

Arrange the following actions in the order in which they would take place in the operation of a voucher system:

1. A voucher check is written for each recorded voucher on the due date and is recorded in the check register.
2. A voucher is prepared authorizing each expenditure.
3. A list of unpaid vouchers is prepared to prove the balance of the Vouchers Payable account.
4. Each authorized voucher is recorded in the voucher register.
5. Column totals in the voucher register and the check register and individual items in the Other Accounts column of the voucher register are posted to the appropriate accounts.

EXERCISES

E 1. **LO1 Use of Accounting Records in Internal Control**

Careful scrutiny of accounting records and financial statements can lead to the discovery of fraud or embezzlement. Each of the following situations may indicate a possible breakdown in internal control. Indicate the nature of the possible fraud or embezzlement in each situation:

1. Wages expense for a branch office was 30 percent higher in 20x2 than in 20x1, even though the office was authorized to employ only the same four employees and raises were only 5 percent in 20x2.
2. Sales returns and allowances increased from 5 percent to 20 percent of sales in the first two months of 20x2, after record sales in 20x1 resulted in large bonuses for the sales staff.
3. Gross margin decreased from 40 percent of net sales in 20x1 to 30 percent in 20x2, even though there was no change in pricing. Ending inventory was 50 percent less at the end of 20x2 than it was at the beginning of the year. There is no immediate explanation for the decrease in inventory.
4. A review of daily records of cash register receipts shows that one cashier consistently accepts more discount coupons for purchases than do the other cashiers.

E 2. **LO1 Internal Control Activities**

Jessie's Video Store maintains the following policies with regard to purchases of new videotapes at each of its branch stores:

1. Employees are required to take vacations, and the duties of employees are rotated periodically.
2. Once each month a person from the home office visits each branch store to examine the receiving records and to compare the inventory of videos with the accounting records.
3. Purchases of new videos must be authorized by purchase order in the home office and paid for by the treasurer in the home office. Receiving reports are prepared in each branch and sent to the home office.

4. All new personnel receive one hour of training in how to receive and catalogue new videos.
5. The company maintains a perpetual inventory system that keeps track of all videos purchased, sold, and on hand.

Match the following control activities to each of the above policies. (Some may have several answers.)

a. Authorization
b. Recording transactions
c. Documents and records
d. Physical controls
e. Periodic independent verification
f. Separation of duties
g. Sound personnel policies

E 3. LO1 **Internal Control Evaluation**

Developing a convenient means of providing sales representatives with cash for their incidental expenses, such as entertaining a client at lunch, is a problem many companies face. Under one company's plan, the sales representatives receive advances in cash from the petty cash fund. Each advance is supported by an authorization from the sales manager. The representative returns the receipt for the expenditure and any unused cash, which is replaced in the petty cash fund. The cashier of the petty cash fund is responsible for seeing that the receipt and the cash returned equal the advance. When the petty cash fund is reimbursed, the amount of the representative's expenditure is debited to Direct Sales Expense.

What is the weak point in this system? What fundamental principle of internal control is being ignored? What improvement in the procedure can you suggest?

E 4. LO1 **Internal Control Evaluation**

An accountant is responsible for the following procedures: (1) receiving all cash; (2) maintaining the general ledger; (3) maintaining the accounts receivable subsidiary ledger that includes the individual records of each customer; (4) maintaining the journals for recording sales, purchases, and cash receipts; and (5) preparing monthly statements to be sent to customers. As a service to customers and employees, the company allows the accountant to cash checks of up to $50 with money from the cash receipts. When deposits are made, the checks are included in place of the cash receipts.

What weakness in internal control exists in this system?

E 5. LO1 LO2 **Internal Control Activities**

Ted Songe, who operates a small grocery store, has established the following policies with regard to the checkout cashiers:

1. Each cashier has his or her own cash drawer, to which no one else has access.
2. Each cashier may accept checks for purchases under $50 with proper identification. Checks over $50 must be approved by Songe before they are accepted.
3. Every sale must be rung up on the cash register and a receipt given to the customer. Each sale is recorded on a tape inside the cash register.
4. At the end of each day, Songe counts the cash in the drawer and compares it with the amount on the tape inside the cash register.

Match the following conditions for internal control to each of the policies listed above:

a. Transactions are executed in accordance with management's general or specific authorization.
b. Transactions are recorded as necessary to permit preparation of financial statements and maintain accountability for assets.
c. Access to assets is permitted only as allowed by management.
d. At reasonable intervals, the records of assets are compared with the existing assets.

E 6. LO3 **Bank Reconciliation**

Prepare a bank reconciliation from the following information:

a. Balance per bank statement as of August 31, $8,454.54
b. Balance per books as of August 31, $6,138.04
c. Deposits in transit, $1,134.42
d. Outstanding checks, $3,455.92
e. Bank service charge, $5.00

E 7. LO3 **Bank Reconciliation: Missing Data**

Compute the correct amounts to replace each letter in the following table:

Balance per bank statement	$ a	$26,700	$945	$5,970
Deposits in transit	1,800	b	150	375
Outstanding checks	4,500	3,000	c	225
Balance per books	10,350	28,200	675	d

LO3 Collection of a Note by a Bank

E 8. Haskell Corporation received a notice with its bank statement that the bank had collected a note for $4,000 plus $20 interest from L. Peters and credited Haskell Corporation's account for the total less a collection charge of $30.

Explain the effect that these items have on the bank reconciliation. Prepare an entry in journal form to record the information on the books of Haskell Corporation.

SO4 Petty Cash Entries

E 9. The petty cash fund of Sachs Company appeared as follows on July 31, 20xx (the end of the accounting period):

Cash on hand		$122.46
Petty cash vouchers		
Freight in	$45.72	
Postage	42.38	
Flowers for a sick employee	37.00	
Office supplies	52.44	177.54
Total		$300.00

Because there is cash on hand, is there a need to replenish the petty cash fund on July 31? Explain your answer. Prepare, in journal form, an entry to replenish the fund.

SO4 Petty Cash Transactions

E 10. A small company maintains a petty cash fund for minor expenditures. In June and July, the following transactions took place:

a. The fund was established in the amount of $100.00 on June 1 from the proceeds of check no. 2707.

b. On June 30, the petty cash fund had cash of $15.46 and the following receipts on hand: postage, $40.00; supplies, $24.94; delivery service, $12.40; and rubber stamp, $7.20. Check no. 2778 was drawn to replenish the fund.

c. On July 31, the petty cash fund had cash of $22.06 and these receipts on hand: postage, $34.20; supplies, $32.84; and delivery service, $6.40. The petty cash custodian could not account for the shortage. Check no. 2847 was drawn to replenish the fund.

Prepare entries in journal form necessary to record each transaction.

PROBLEMS

LO3 Bank Reconciliation

P 1. The information presented below and on the opposite page comes from the records of Costa Company:

From the Cash Receipts Journal — Page 9

Date	Debit Cash
Apr. 1	914
8	1,012
15	3,240
22	2,646
30	1,942
	9,754

From the Cash Payments Journal — Page 12

Date	Check Number	Credit Cash
Apr. 1	531	14
3	532	283
4	533	416
5	534	27
	535 (voided)	
6	536	5
11	537	5,746
12	538	709
21	539	1,246
22	540	76
		8,522

From the General Ledger

Cash						Account No. 111	
						Balance	
Date		Item	Post. Ref.	Debit	Credit	Debit	Credit
Mar.	31	Balance				2,465	
Apr.	30		CR9	9,754		12,219	
	30		CP12		8,522	3,697	

TURNBULL NATIONAL BANK — Statement of Costa Company, Jarvis and Oak Streets

Checks/Debits			Deposits/Credits		Daily Balances	
Posting Date	Check No.	Amount	Posting Date	Amount	Date	Amount
					4/01	3,785.00
4/03	500	100.00	4/03	914.00	4/03	4,099.00
4/03	505	500.00	4/09	1,012.00	4/05	3,625.00
4/05	530	460.00	4/16	3,240.00	4/07	3,209.00
4/05	531	14.00	4/23	2,646.00	4/09	4,194.00
4/07	533	416.00	4/27	408.00CM	4/13	4,174.00
4/09	534	27.00	4/30	42.00IN	4/15	3,267.00
4/13	536	5.00			4/16	6,507.00
4/13		15.00NSF			4/23	9,153.00
4/15	538	907.00			4/25	3,407.00
4/25	537	5,746.00			4/27	3,739.00
4/27	540	76.00			4/30	3,777.00
4/30		4.00SC				

Code: CM–Credit Memo IN–Interest NSF–Nonsufficient Funds
DM–Debit Memo SC–Service Charge

The NSF check was received from customer S. Tilvie for merchandise. The credit memorandum represents a $400 note, plus interest, collected by the bank. Check number 535 was prepared improperly and has been voided. Check number 538 for a purchase of merchandise was recorded incorrectly in the cash payments journal as $709 instead of $907. On April 1, the following checks were outstanding: no. 500 for $100, no. 505 for $500, no. 529 for $260, and no. 530 for $460.

REQUIRED ▶

1. Prepare a bank reconciliation as of April 30, 20xx.
2. Prepare the journal entries necessary to adjust the accounts.
3. What amount should appear on the balance sheet for Cash as of April 30?

LO1 LO3 Bank Reconciliation

P 2. The following information is available for Sultani Company as of November 30, 20xx:

a. Cash on the books as of November 30 amounted to $113,675.28. Cash on the bank statement for the same date was $141,717.08.
b. A deposit of $14,249.84, representing cash receipts of November 30, did not appear on the bank statement.
c. Outstanding checks totaled $7,293.64.

d. A check for $2,420.00 returned with the statement was recorded in the cash payments journal as $2,024.00. The check was for advertising.
e. The bank service charge for November amounted to $26.00.
f. The bank collected $36,400.00 for Sultani Company on a note. The face value of the note was $36,000.00.
g. An NSF check for $1,140.00 from a customer, Estelle Maxx, was returned with the statement.
h. The bank mistakenly deducted a check for $800.00 drawn by Mooney Corporation.
i. The bank reported a credit of $960.00 for interest on the average balance.

REQUIRED ▶

1. Prepare a bank reconciliation for Sultani Company as of November 30, 20xx.
2. Prepare the journal entries necessary from the reconciliation.
3. State the amount of cash that should appear on the balance sheet as of November 30.
4. What control activity in the internal control structure does the bank reconciliation accomplish? How does it accomplish this activity and how should the person to prepare the bank reconciliation be chosen?

P 3.
SO4 Petty Cash Transactions

A small company maintains a petty cash fund for minor expenditures. The following transactions occurred in June and July.

a. The fund was established in the amount of $300.00 on June 1 from the proceeds of check no. 1515.
b. On June 30, the petty cash fund had cash of $46.38 and the following receipts on hand: postage, $120.00; supplies, $74.82; delivery service, $37.20; and rubber stamp, $21.60. Check no. 1527 was drawn to replenish the fund.
c. On July 31, the petty cash fund had cash of $66.18 and the following receipts on hand: postage, $102.60; supplies, $98.52; and delivery service, $19.20. The petty cash custodian could not account for the shortage. Check no. 1621 was written to replenish the fund.

REQUIRED ▶ Prepare the journal entries necessary to record each transaction.

P 4.
LO1 LO2 Internal Control Procedures

Eyles Sports Shop is a small neighborhood sporting goods store. The shop's owner, Samantha Eyles, has set up a system of internal control over sales to prevent theft and to ensure the accuracy of the accounting records.

When a customer buys a product, the cashier writes up a sales invoice that describes the purchase, including the total price. All sales invoices are prenumbered sequentially.

If the sale is by credit card, the cashier runs the credit card through a scanner that verifies the customer's credit. The scanner prints out a receipt and a slip for the customer to sign. The signed slip is put in the cash register, and the customer is given the receipt and a copy of the sales invoice.

If the sale is by cash or check, the cashier rings it up on the cash register and gives change, if appropriate. Checks must be written for the exact amount of the purchase and must be accompanied by identification. The sale is recorded on a tape inside the cash register that cannot be accessed by the cashier. The cash register may be locked with a key. The cashier is the only person other than Eyles who has a key. The cash register must be locked when the cashier is not present. Refunds are made only with Eyles's approval, are recorded on prenumbered credit memorandum forms, and are rung up on the cash register.

At the end of each day, Eyles counts the cash and checks in the cash register and compares the total with the amount recorded on the tape inside the register. Eyles totals all the signed credit card slips and ensures that the total equals the amount recorded by the scanner. Eyles also makes sure that all sales invoices and credit memoranda are accounted for. Eyles prepares a bank deposit ticket for the cash, checks, and signed credit card slips, less $40 in change to be put in the cash register the next day, and removes the record of the day's credit card sales from the scanner. All the records are placed in an envelope that is sealed and sent to the company's accountant for verification and recording in the company records. On the way home, Eyles places the bank deposit in the night deposit box.

The company hires experienced cashiers who are bonded. The owner spends the first half-day with new cashiers, showing them the procedures and overlooking their work.

REQUIRED ▶ Give an example of how each of the following control procedures is applied to internal control over sales and cash at Eyles Sports Shop: authorization, recording transactions, documents and records, physical controls, periodic independent verification, separation of duties, and sound personnel procedures. Do not address controls over inventory.

P 5. During the month of July, Second Star Toy Shop had the following transactions.

SO5 Voucher System Transactions

July 1 Prepared voucher no. 205, payable to the petty cash cashier, to establish a petty cash fund, $500.

2 Issued check no. 330 for voucher no. 205.

3 Prepared voucher no. 206, payable to Fortunato Distributing, for a shipment of merchandise, $1,600, invoice dated July 3, terms 2/10, n/60, FOB shipping point. Fortunato prepaid freight of $120 and added it to the invoice, for a total of $1,720.

5 Prepared voucher no. 207, payable to Moynihan Realty, for July rent, $2,400.

5 Issued check no. 331 for voucher no. 207.

6 Prepared voucher no. 208, payable to Sheehan Distributors, for merchandise, $2,000, invoice dated July 6, terms 2/10, n/60, FOB shipping point.

7 Prepared voucher no. 209, payable to Gaines Express, for freight in on July 6 shipment, $128, terms n/10.

8 Prepared voucher no. 210, payable to Best Buy Hardware, for office equipment, $800, terms n/30.

10 Received credit memorandum from Sheehan Distributors for damaged merchandise returned, $200.

11 Prepared voucher no. 211, payable to Sheehan Distributors, for merchandise, $2,600, invoice dated July 10, terms 2/10, n/60, FOB shipping point.

12 Prepared voucher no. 212, payable to Gaines Express, for freight in on July 11, $188, terms n/10.

13 Issued check no. 332 for voucher no. 206.

14 Prepared voucher no. 213, payable to the company's owner, Patti Paul, for her personal expenses, $2,000.

16 Issued check no. 333 for voucher no. 213.

16 Issued check no. 334 for voucher no. 208. There was a return on July 10.

17 Issued check no. 335 for voucher no. 209.

18 Prepared vouchers no. 214, 215, 216, and 217, for $1,200 each, payable to Kusak Furniture, for office furniture having an invoice price of $4,800, terms one-fourth down and one-fourth each month for three months.

19 Issued check no. 336 for voucher no. 214.

19 Issued check no. 337 for voucher no. 211.

20 Issued check no. 338 for voucher no. 212.

21 Prepared voucher no. 218, payable to Mohansa Supply, $540 ($380 to be charged to Store Supplies and $160 to Office Supplies), terms n/10.

22 Prepared voucher no. 219, payable to Schmitt Videocassettes, for merchandise, $660, invoice dated July 20, terms 2/10, n/30, FOB shipping point. Freight paid by shipper and included in invoice total, $60.

23 Prepared voucher no. 220, payable to Southern National Bank, in payment of an $8,000 note plus $200 interest.

23 Issued check no. 339 for voucher no. 220.

25 Prepared voucher no. 221, payable to Hassad Insurance Company, for a one-year policy, $960.

26 Issued check no. 340 for voucher no. 221.

27 Prepared voucher no. 222, payable to Sheehan Distributors, for merchandise, $1,200, invoice dated July 26, terms 2/10, n/60, FOB shipping point.

28 Prepared voucher no. 223, payable to Gaines Express, for freight in on shipment of July 27, $76.

29 Prepared voucher no. 224, payable to the Payroll Account, for monthly salaries, $15,800 (to be divided as follows: Sales Salaries Expense, $8,800, and Office Salaries Expense, $7,000).

29 Issued check no. 341 for voucher no. 224.

30 Issued check no. 342 for voucher no. 219.

31 Prepared voucher no. 225 to reimburse the petty cash fund. A count of the fund revealed cash on hand of $100 and the following receipts: postage, $88; office supplies, $68; collect telegram, $12; flowers for sick employee, $60; and

delivery service, $108. The total of cash on hand and receipts was $64 less than the book balance of petty cash.

July31 Issued check no. 343 for voucher no. 225.

REQUIRED ▶

1. Record the transactions in a voucher register (Page 18), a check register (Page 12), and a general journal (Page 10). Record purchases at gross amounts. Total the voucher and check registers.
2. Prepare a Vouchers Payable account (211) and post those portions of the journal and register entries that affect this account. Assume the Vouchers Payable account had a zero balance on June 30.
3. Prove the balance of Vouchers Payable by preparing a schedule of unpaid vouchers.

Alternate Problems

P 6.

LO1 **Internal Control Procedures**
LO2

VueWay Printers makes printers for personal computers and maintains a factory outlet showroom through which it sells its products to the public. The company's management has set up a system of internal controls over the inventory of printers to prevent theft and to ensure the accuracy of the accounting records.

All printers in inventory at the factory outlet are kept in a secured warehouse behind the showroom, except for the sample printers on display. Only authorized personnel may enter the warehouse. When a customer buys a printer, a sales invoice is written in triplicate by the cashier and is marked "paid." The sales invoices are sequentially numbered, and all must be accounted for. The cashier sends the pink copy of the completed invoice to the warehouse, gives the blue copy to the customer, and keeps the green copy. The customer drives around to the warehouse entrance. The warehouse attendant takes the blue copy of the invoice from the customer and gives the customer the printer and the pink copy of the invoice.

The company maintains a perpetual inventory system for the printers at the outlet. The warehouse attendant at the outlet signs an inventory transfer sheet for each printer received. An accountant at the factory is assigned responsibility for maintaining the inventory records based on copies of the inventory transfer sheets and the sales invoices. The records are updated daily and may be accessed by computer but not modified by the sales personnel and the warehouse attendant. The accountant also sees that all prenumbered inventory transfer sheets are accounted for and compares copies of them with the ones signed by the warehouse attendant. Once every three months the company's internal auditor takes a physical count of the printer inventory and compares the results with the perpetual inventory records.

All new employees are required to read a sales and inventory manual and receive a two-hour training session about the internal controls. They must demonstrate that they can perform the functions required of them.

REQUIRED ▶

Give an example of how each of the following internal control procedures is applied to the printer inventory at VueWay Printers' outlet showroom: authorization, recording transactions, documents and records, physical controls, periodic independent verification, separation of duties, and sound personnel procedures. Do not address controls over cash.

P 7.

LO1 **Bank Reconciliation**
LO3

The following information is available for Manuel Suarez Company as of October 31, 20xx:

a. Cash on the books as of October 31 amounted to $21,327.08. Cash on the bank statement for the same date was $26,175.73.
b. A deposit of $2,610.47, representing cash receipts of October 31, did not appear on the bank statement.
c. Outstanding checks totaled $1,968.40.
d. A check for $960.00 returned with the statement was recorded incorrectly in the check register as $690.00. The check was made for a cash purchase of merchandise.
e. Bank service charges for October amounted to $12.50.
f. The bank collected for Manuel Suarez Company $6,120.00 on a note. The face value of the note was $6,000.00.
g. An NSF check for $91.78 from a client, Liz Fahll, came back with the statement.
h. The bank mistakenly charged to the company account a check for $425.00 drawn by another company.

i. The bank reported that it had credited the account for $170.00 in interest on the average balance for October.

REQUIRED ▶

1. Prepare a bank reconciliation for Manuel Suarez Company as of October 31, 20xx.
2. Prepare the journal entries necessary to adjust the accounts.
3. State the amount of cash that should appear on the balance sheet as of October 31.
4. What control activity in the internal control structure does the bank reconciliation accomplish? How does it accomplish this activity and how should the person to prepare the bank reconciliation be chosen?

P 8.

SO4 Petty Cash Transactions

The Appalachian Theater Company established a petty cash fund in its snack bar so that payment can be made for small deliveries on receipt. The following transactions occurred in July and August:

July 1 The fund was established in the amount of $400.00 from the proceeds of a check drawn for that purpose.

31 The petty cash fund has cash of $31.42 and the following receipts on hand: for merchandise received, $204.30; freight in, $65.74; laundry service, $84.00; and miscellaneous expense, $14.54. A check was drawn to replenish the fund.

Aug.31 The petty cash fund has cash of $55.00 and the following receipts on hand: merchandise, $196.84; freight in, $76.30; laundry service, $84.00; and miscellaneous expense, $7.86. The petty cash custodian cannot account for the excess cash in the fund. A check is drawn to replenish the fund.

REQUIRED ▶ In journal form, prepare the entries necessary to record each of these transactions.

SKILLS DEVELOPMENT CASES

Conceptual Analysis

SD 1.

LO1 LO2 Internal Control Lapse

Starbucks Corporation <www.starbucks.com> has accused an employee and her husband of embezzling $3.7 million by billing the company for services from a fictitious consulting firm. The employee and her husband created a phony company called RAD Services Inc. and charged Starbucks for work they never provided. The employee worked in the information technology department. RAD Services Inc. charged Starbucks for as much as $492,800 in consulting services in a single week.[8] For such a fraud to have taken place, certain control activities were likely not implemented. Identify and describe these activities.

SD 2.

LO1 LO2 System for Control of Supplies

Industrial Services Company provides maintenance services to factories in the West Bend, Wisconsin, area. The company, which buys large amounts of cleaning supplies, has consistently been over budget in its expenditures for those items. In the past, supplies were left open in the warehouse so that the on-site supervisors could take them as needed. Periodically, a clerk in the accounting department ordered additional supplies from a long-time supplier. The only records maintained were records of purchases. Once a year, an inventory of supplies was made for the preparation of the financial statements.

To solve the budgetary problem, management recently implemented a new system for controlling and purchasing supplies. Under the new system, the cleaning supplies were placed in a secured storeroom overseen by a supplies clerk. Supplies are requisitioned by the supervisors of specific jobs. Each job receives a predetermined amount of supplies based on a study of the needs of that job. In the storeroom, the supplies clerk notes the levels of supplies and completes a purchase requisition when supplies are needed. The purchase requisition goes to the purchasing clerk, a new position, who is solely responsible for authorizing purchases and who prepares the purchase orders for suppliers. The prices of several suppliers are constantly monitored to ensure that the lowest price is obtained. When supplies are received from a vendor, the supplies clerk checks them in and prepares a receiving report, which is sent to accounting, where each payment to a supplier is documented by the purchase requisition, the purchase order, and the receiving report. The accounting department also maintains a record of supplies inventory, supplies requisitioned by supervisors, and supplies received. Once each month, a physical inventory of cleaning supplies in the storeroom is made by the warehouse manager and compared against the supplies inventory records maintained by the accounting department.

Demonstrate how the new system applies or does not apply to each of the seven control activities described in this chapter. Is each new control activity an improvement over the old system?

Ethical Dilemma

SD 3. LO3 **Inflating the Cash Account and the Bank Reconciliation**

Jean McGuire is the accountant for Slate Company. Among her responsibilities are the payment of bills and the preparation of the monthly bank reconciliation. On December 31, year end, McGuire's boss, Lydia Grunwald, instructed her to write checks for all the outstanding bills so that their amounts could be deducted for income tax purposes. Since payment of all the outstanding bills would have overdrawn the company's checking account by $78,000, McGuire had to hold the checks until sufficient funds were received. On January 2, a check for $100,000 was received from a customer in payment of an account receivable. Grunwald did not want to report the negative balance of cash on the previous year's balance sheet. She thus instructed McGuire to record the receipt as of December 31 and to show the check as a deposit in transit on the bank reconciliation. The checks written by McGuire on December 31 were mailed on January 3 and listed as outstanding checks on the bank reconciliation. Which, if any, of McGuire's and Grunwald's actions are unethical? Who may be harmed by their actions? What alternative actions could McGuire have taken?

Research Activity

SD 4. LO1 LO2 **Internal Controls**

Go to a retail business, such as a bookstore, a clothing shop, a gift shop, a grocery, a hardware store, or a car dealership, in your local shopping area or a local shopping mall. Speak to someone who is knowledgeable about the store's internal controls. Find out the answers to the following questions, and be prepared to discuss your findings in class:

1. How does the company protect against inventory theft and loss?
2. What control activities, including authorization, recording transactions, documents and records, physical controls, periodic independent verification, separation of duties, and sound personnel policies, does the company use?
3. Can you see these control procedures in use?

Group Activity: Assign teams to carry out the above assignment.

Decision-Making Practice

SD 5. LO1 LO2 **Identifying Internal Control Weaknesses**

Fleet's is a retail store with several departments. Its internal control procedures for cash sales and purchases are described in the following paragraphs:

Cash sales. Every cash sale is rung up on the department cash register by the sales clerk assigned to that department. The cash register produces a sales slip that is given to the customer with the merchandise. A carbon copy of the sales ticket is made on a continuous tape locked inside the machine. At the end of each day, a "total" key is pressed, and the machine prints the total sales for the day on the continuous tape. Then, the sales clerk unlocks the machine, reads the total sales figure, and makes the entry in the accounting records for the day's cash sales. Next, she counts the cash in the drawer, places the basic $100 change fund back in the drawer, and gives the cash received to the cashier. Finally, she files the cash register tape and is ready for the next day's business.

Purchases. All goods are ordered by the purchasing agent upon the requests of the various department heads. When the goods are received, the receiving clerk prepares a receiving report in triplicate. One copy is sent to the purchasing agent, one copy is forwarded to the department head, and one copy is kept by the receiving clerk. Invoices are forwarded immediately to the accounting department to ensure payment before the discount period elapses. After payment, the invoice is forwarded to the purchasing agent for comparison with the purchase order and the receiving report and is then returned to the accounting office for filing.

Fleet's president has asked you to evaluate these control procedures for cash sales and purchases. Write a memorandum to the president identifying the significant internal control weakness for each of the above situations and in each case recommend changes that would improve the current system.

Financial Reporting and Analysis Cases

Interpreting Financial Reports

LO1 Effect of Ecommerce on
LO2 Internal Control

FRA 1. Many retailers, such as Crate & Barrel <www.crateandbarrel.com>, Eddie Bauer Inc. <www.eddiebauer.com>, and Sears, Roebuck and Co.<www.sears.com>, are selling to customers on the Internet. In what ways do Internet transactions differ from retail store transactions? How will each difference affect internal controls?

Group Activity: Divide the class into teams and ask each team to identify as many differences as they can. Debrief by asking each team to give one difference and describe its effect on internal controls. Write the results on the board. Continue until no team can add another difference.

International Company

LO1 Internal Control and Accounting Education in a Developing Country

FRA 2. Zambia, a country in southern Africa, has 8.5 million inhabitants. It has an elected government and is moving toward capital markets through privatization of government-owned business. For example, the government-owned beer company was recently sold to private interests for $13 million. One national priority calls for the training of competent professional accountants, and the Zambian Centre for Accountancy Studies has been established with the assistance of the World Bank. There are only about 250 native-born certified accountants in all of Zambia. A state with a comparable population in the United States would have more than 20,000 certified public accountants. One reason for placing a priority on the training of accountants is the importance of good internal controls to the development of a country like Zambia. What are the purposes of internal control, and what are some ways in which such controls would aid the development of a country like Zambia? What are some other reasons for making accounting education a high national priority?

Toys "R" Us Annual Report

LO1 Internal Control
LO2 Considerations

FRA 3. Refer to the annual report for Toys "R" Us <www.tru.com> in the Supplement to Chapter 6. How many stores did Toys "R" Us operate in the United States and abroad in the most recent year? The typical store contains a showroom where customers wheel carts down aisles to select items for purchase, a warehouse where larger items may be picked up after purchase, a bank of cash registers, and a service desk where returns and other unusual transactions can be authorized. Identify the main activities or transactions for which Toys "R" Us management would need to establish internal controls in each new store. Discuss the objectives of internal controls in each case.

Fingraph® Financial Analyst™

This activity is not appropriate for this chapter.

Comparison Case

The comparison case is not applicable to this chapter.

Internet Case

LO1 Comparison of Reports of Management on Internal Control

FRA 4. Through the Needles Accounting Resource Center Web site at http://accounting.hmco.com/students, go to the annual reports in the web sites for Tandy Corporation <www.tandy.com> and Circuit City Stores, Inc. <www.circuitcity.com>. Find the "Report of Management on Internal Accounting Controls" in the case of Tandy and "Management's Report" in the case of Circuit City in the companies' respective annual reports. A portion of the Circuit City's report is quoted in the text. Compare management statements. What similarities do you find in the content? What is a difference in the reports? Which company in your opinion, does a better job of explaining what management has done to fulfill its responsibility of internal control?

9

Chapter 9 focuses on management of, and accounting for, several types of short-term assets: cash and cash equivalents, short-term investments, accounts receivable, and notes receivable.

Short-Term Financial Assets

LEARNING OBJECTIVES

LO1 Identify and explain the management issues related to short-term financial assets.

LO2 Explain *cash, cash equivalents,* and the importance of electronic funds transfer.

LO3 Identify types of short-term investments and explain the financial reporting implications.

LO4 Define *accounts receivable* and apply the allowance method of accounting for uncollectible accounts.

LO5 Define *promissory note,* and compute and record promissory notes receivable.

DECISION POINT

A USER'S FOCUS

Pioneer Corporation <www.pioneer.co.jp> A company must use its assets to maximize income earned while maintaining liquidity. Pioneer Corporation, a leading Japanese manufacturer of electronics for home, commerce, and industry, manages about $2.4 billion in short-term financial assets. **Short-term financial assets** are assets that arise from cash transactions, the investment of cash, and the extension of credit. What is the composition of these assets? Why are they important to Pioneer's management?

Pioneer's short-term financial assets, as reported on the balance sheet in the company's annual report, are shown in the table on the opposite page.[1] These assets make up almost 41 percent of Pioneer's total assets, and they are very important to the company's strategy for meeting its goals. Effective asset management techniques ensure that these assets remain liquid and usable for the company's operations.

A commonly used ratio for measuring the adequacy of short-term financial assets is the quick ratio. The **quick ratio** is the ratio of short-term financial assets to current liabilities. Because Pioneer's current liabilities are (in millions) ¥177,825 ($1,434.1), its quick ratio is 1.39, which is computed as follows:

$$\text{Quick Ratio} = \frac{\text{Short-Term Financial Assets}}{\text{Current Liabilities}}$$

$$= \frac{\$1{,}995{,}200{,}000}{\$1{,}434{,}100{,}000} = 1.39$$

A quick ratio of about 1.0 has historically been the minimum common benchmark. However, it is more

How does Pioneer Electric, a leading manufacturer of electronics for the home, manage its short-term financial assets?

important to look at industry characteristics and at the trends for a particular company to see if the ratio is improving or not. A lower ratio may mean that a company is a very good manager of its short-term financial assets. Pioneer has maintained a quick ratio of over 1.0 for several years. Through good cash management, the company has not tied up excess funds in quick assets relative to current liabilities. This chapter emphasizes management of, and accounting for, short-term financial assets to achieve liquidity.

Financial Highlights
(In millions)

	Yen	Dollars
Cash and cash equivalents	¥121,127	$ 976.8
Short-term investments	1,598	12.9
Accounts receivable, net of allowances of ¥5,895 ($47.5)	116,594	940.3
Notes receivable	8,079	65.2
Total short-term financial assets	¥247,398	$1,995.2

Management Issues Related to Short-Term Financial Assets

LO1 Identify and explain the management issues related to short-term financial assets.

RELATED TEXT ASSIGNMENTS
Q: 1, 2
SE: 1, 2
E: 1, 2
P: 2, 6
SD: 1, 2, 3, 4, 5
FRA: 1, 3, 4, 5, 6

The management of short-term financial assets is critical to the goal of maintaining adequate liquidity. In dealing with short-term financial assets, management must address three key issues: managing cash needs during seasonal cycles, setting credit policies, and financing receivables.

Managing Cash Needs During Seasonal Cycles

Most companies experience seasonal cycles of business activity during the year. During some periods, sales are weak; during others, they are strong. There are also periods when expenditures are high and periods when expenditures are low. For toy companies, college textbook publishers, amusement parks, construction companies, and sports equipment companies, the cycles are dramatic, but all companies experience them to some degree.

www.homedepot.com

Seasonal cycles require careful planning of cash inflows, cash outflows, borrowing, and investing. Figure 1 shows the seasonal cycles typical of a home improvement company, such as The Home Depot, Inc. As you can see, cash receipts from sales are highest in the late spring, summer, and fall because that is when most people make home improvements. Sales are relatively low in the winter months. On the other hand, cash expenditures are highest in late winter and spring as the company builds up inventory for spring and summer selling. During the late summer, fall, and winter, the company has excess cash on hand that it needs to invest in a way that will earn a return but still permit access to cash as needed. During the late spring

Figure 1
Seasonal Cycles and Cash Requirements for a Home Improvement Company

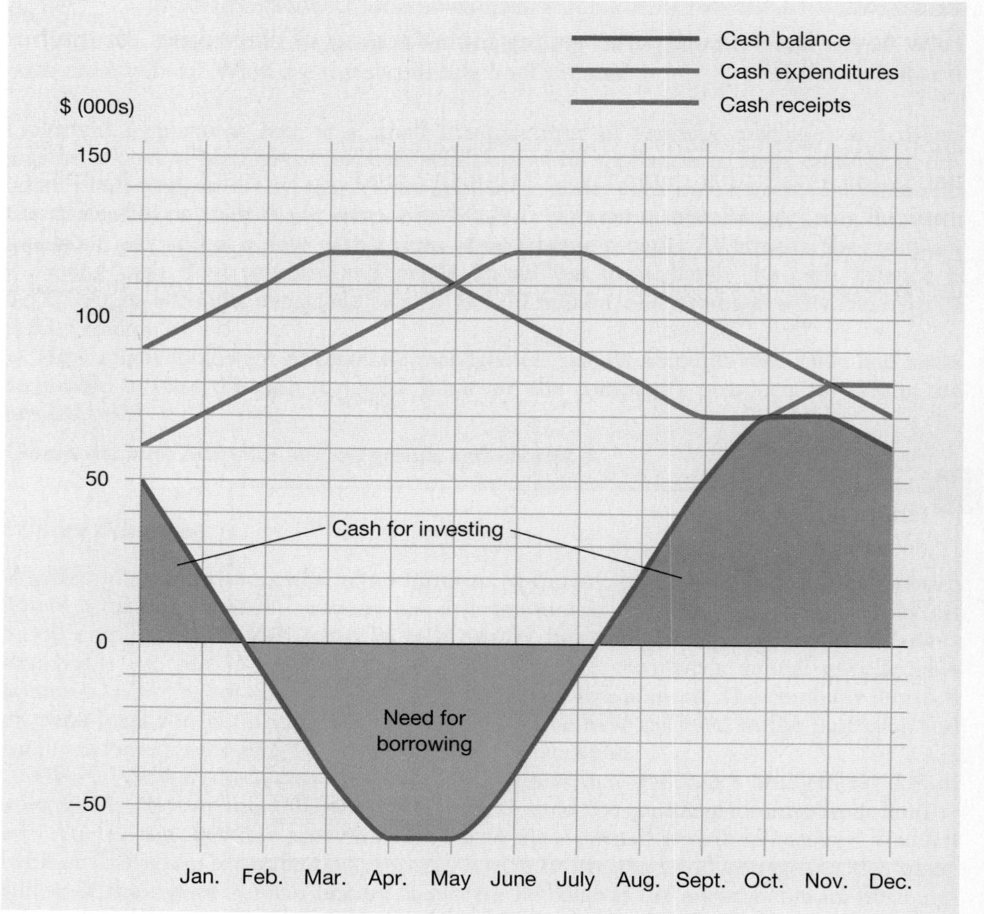

Focus on Business Practice

What a Difference a Year Makes!

It's hard to know how much cash reserve a company should have. Analysts are often critical of companies that build cash reserves because the cash is not earning as much as other assets might. But having a cash reserve may be a good thing, especially in a cyclical industry like the auto industry. For example, just about two years ago, the Big Three automakers—General Motors <www.gm.com>, Ford <www.ford.com>, and DaimlerChrysler <www.daimlerchrysler.com>—were awash in cash. However, in little over two years, the three companies went through $28 billion in cash through various purchases, losses, dividends, and share buybacks. Then, with increasing losses from rising costs, big rebates, and 0 percent financing, the companies were suddenly faced with a shortage of cash. As a result, Standard & Poor's lowered their credit ratings, which raises the interest cost of borrowing money. Perhaps the Big Three should have held on to some of that cash.[2]

ENRICHMENT NOTE: Here is a chance to apply the economic concept of profit maximization. Profit is maximized when marginal revenue equals marginal cost. Thus, credit policy should equate the additional gross profit from credit sales with the cost of credit sales (i.e., bad debts).

Stop and Think!
To increase sales, a company decides to increase its credit terms from 15 days to 30 days. What effect will this change in policy have on receivable turnover, average days' sales uncollected, and cash flows?

Receivable turnover will become smaller because average net accounts receivable will increase relative to sales. Consequently, the average days' sales uncollected will increase. This will have an adverse effect on cash flows because, on average, the company will have to wait longer to receive cash from sales. ■

and early summer, the company needs to plan for short-term borrowing to tide it over until cash receipts pick up later in the year. The discussion in this chapter of accounting for cash and cash equivalents and for short-term investments is directly related to managing the seasonal cycles of a business.

Setting Credit Policies

Companies that sell on credit do so to be competitive and to increase sales. In setting credit terms, management must keep in mind both the terms the company's competitors are offering and the needs of customers. Obviously, companies that sell on credit want to have customers who will pay the debts they incur. To increase the likelihood of selling only to customers who will pay on time, most companies develop control procedures and maintain a credit department. The credit department's responsibilities include the examination of each person or company that applies for credit and the approval or rejection of a credit sale to that customer. Typically, the credit department asks for information about the customer's financial resources and debts. It may also check personal references and credit bureaus for further information. Then, based on the information it has gathered, the credit department decides whether to extend credit to the customer.

Two common measures of the effect of a company's credit policies are **receivable turnover** and **average days' sales uncollected**. The receivable turnover reflects the relative size of a company's accounts receivable and the success of its credit and collection policies. It may also be affected by external factors, such as seasonal conditions and interest rates. It shows how many times, on average, the receivables were turned into cash during the accounting period. The average days' sales uncollected is a related measure that shows, on average, how long it takes to collect accounts receivable.

Focus on Business Practice

Why Powerful Buyers Can Cause Headaches for Small Businesses

Big buyers often have significant power over small suppliers, and their cash management decisions can cause severe cash flow problems for the little companies that depend on them. For instance, in an effort to control costs and optimize cash flow, Ameritech Corp. <www.ameritech.com> told 70,000 suppliers that it would begin paying its bills in 45 days instead of 30. Other large companies routinely take 90 days or more to pay. Some small suppliers are so anxious to get the big companies' business that they fail to realize the implications of the deals they make until it is too late. When Earthly Elements, Inc., accepted a $10,000 order for dried floral gifts from a national home shopping network, its management was ecstatic because the deal increased sales by 25 percent. But in four months, the resulting cash crunch forced the company to close down. When the shopping network finally paid for the big order six months later, it was too late to revive Earthly Elements.[3]

Turnover ratios usually consist of one balance sheet account and one income statement account. The receivable turnover is computed by dividing net sales by average net accounts receivable. Theoretically, the numerator should be net credit sales, but the amount of net credit sales is rarely made available in public reports, so total net sales is used. Pioneer Corporation, discussed in the Decision Point at the start of the chapter, had net sales in 2001 of $5,052,700,000. Its net trade accounts receivable in 2001 and 2000 were $940,300,000 and $805,564,000, respectively. Its receivable turnover is computed as follows:[4]

www.pioneer.co.jp

$$\text{Receivable Turnover} = \frac{\text{Net Sales}}{\text{Average Net Accounts Receivable}}$$

$$= \frac{\$5{,}052{,}700{,}000}{(\$940{,}300{,}000 + \$805{,}564{,}000) \div 2}$$

$$= \frac{\$5{,}052{,}700{,}000}{\$872{,}932{,}000} = 5.8 \text{ times}$$

To find the average days' sales uncollected, the number of days in a year is divided by the receivable turnover, as follows:

$$\text{Average Days' Sales Uncollected} = \frac{365 \text{ days}}{\text{Receivable Turnover}} = \frac{365 \text{ days}}{5.8} = 62.9 \text{ days}$$

Pioneer turns its receivables 5.8 times a year, for an average of every 62.9 days. While this turnover period is longer than that of many companies, it is not unusual for electronics companies because their credit terms allow retail outlets to receive and sell products before paying for them. This example demonstrates the need to interpret ratios in light of the specific industry's practice.

BUSINESS-WORLD EXAMPLE: For many businesses with seasonal sales activity, such as Nordstrom, Dillard, Marshall Field's, and Macy's, the fourth quarter produces more than 25 percent of annual sales. For such businesses, receivables are highest at the balance sheet date, resulting in an artificially low receivable turnover and high average days' sales uncollected.

As Figure 2 shows, the receivable turnover ratio varies substantially from industry to industry. Grocery stores, for example, have a high turnover because that type of business has few receivables; the turnover in interstate trucking is 11.4 times because the typical credit terms in that industry are 30 days. The turnover in the machinery and computer industries is lower because those industries tend to have longer credit terms.

Figure 3 shows the average days' sales uncollected for the industries listed in Figure 2. Grocery stores, which have the lowest ratio (3.8 days) require the least amount of receivables financing; the computer industry, with average days' sales uncollected of 52.9 days, requires the most.

FIGURE 2
Receivable Turnover for Selected Industries

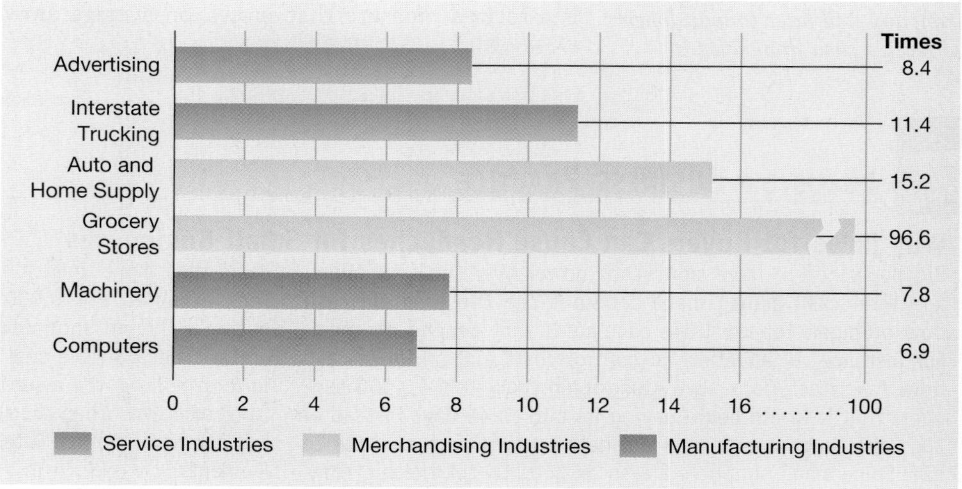

Source: Data from Dun and Bradstreet, *Industry Norms and Key Business Ratios,* 2001–2002.

FIGURE 3
Average Days' Sales Uncollected for Selected Industries

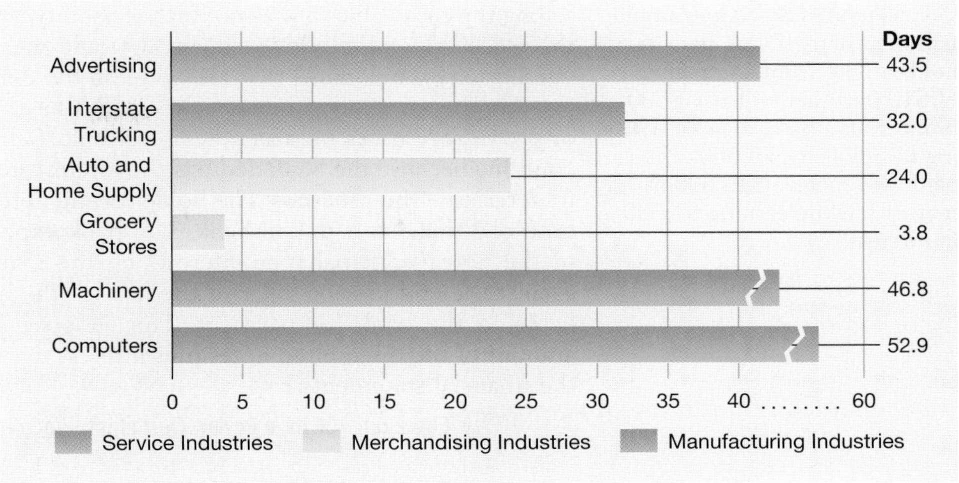

Source: Data from Dun and Bradstreet, *Industry Norms and Key Business Ratios,* 2001–2002.

FINANCING RECEIVABLES

Financial flexibility is important to most companies. Companies that have significant amounts of assets tied up in accounts receivable may be unwilling or unable to wait until cash from the receivables is collected. Many companies have set up finance companies to help their customers pay for the purchase of their products; for example, Ford has set up Ford Motor Credit Co. (FMCC), General Motors has set up General Motors Acceptance Corp. (GMAC), and Sears has set up Sears Roebuck Acceptance Corp. (SRAC). Some companies borrow funds by pledging their accounts receivable as collateral. If a company does not pay back its loan, the creditor can take the collateral (in this case, the accounts receivable) and convert it to cash to satisfy the loan.

www.ford.com
www.gm.com
www.sears.com

Companies can also raise funds by selling or transferring accounts receivable to another entity, called a **factor**. The sale or transfer of accounts receivable, called **factoring**, can be done with or without recourse. *With recourse* means that the seller of the receivables is liable to the purchaser if a receivable is not collected. *Without recourse* means that the factor that buys the accounts receivable bears any losses from uncollectible accounts. A company's acceptance of credit cards like Visa, MasterCard, or American Express is an example of factoring without recourse because the credit card issuers accept the risk of nonpayment.

KEY POINT: The receivable turnover and average days' sales uncollected will appear better for a company that factors receivables than for a company that does not factor.

The factor, of course, charges a fee for its service. The fee for sales with recourse is usually about 1 percent of the accounts receivable. The fee is higher for sales without recourse because the factor's risk is greater. In accounting terminology, the seller of the receivables with recourse is said to be contingently liable. A **contingent liability** is a potential liability that can develop into a real liability if a particular subsequent event occurs. In this case, the subsequent event would be nonpayment of the receivable by the customer. A contingent liability generally requires disclosure in the notes to the financial statements.

www.circuitcity.com

Circuit City Stores, Inc., is one of the nation's largest electronics and appliance retailers. To sell its products, the company offers generous terms through its installment programs, under which customers pay over a number of months. The company is growing rapidly and needs the cash from these installment receivables sooner than the customers have agreed to pay. To generate cash immediately from these receivables, the company sells them through a process called securitization. Under **securitization**, the company groups its receivables in batches and sells them at a discount to companies and investors. When the receivables are paid, the buyers of the receivables receive the full amount; their revenue is the amount of the discount. Circuit City sells all its receivables without recourse, which means that after

STUDY NOTE: An example will help here. If Company A holds a note from company B of $10,000 that will pay $600 in interest, a bank may be willing to buy it for $9,600. The bank will receive $10,600 at maturity while earning $1,000 in interest.

selling the receivables, it has no further liability, even if the customers do not pay. If the receivables were with recourse, it would mean that if a customer did not pay, Circuit City would have to make good on the debt.[5]

Another method of financing receivables is through the **discounting**, or selling, of promissory notes held as notes receivable. Selling notes receivable is called discounting because the bank deducts the interest from the maturity value of the note to determine the proceeds. The holder of the note (usually the payee) endorses the note and delivers it to the bank. The bank expects to collect the maturity value of the note (principal plus interest) on the maturity date but also has recourse against the endorser or seller of the note. If the maker fails to pay, the endorser is liable to the bank for payment. The endorser has a contingent liability in the amount of the discounted notes plus interest that must be disclosed in the notes to the financial statements.

Check out ACE for a Review Quiz at http://accounting.college.hmco.com/students.

CASH AND CASH EQUIVALENTS

LO2 Explain *cash, cash equivalents,* and the importance of electronic funds transfer.

RELATED TEXT ASSIGNMENTS
Q: 3, 4
SE: 3
E: 3
SD: 1
FRA: 4

ENRICHMENT NOTE: Most reporting practices are set by the FASB. This is an example of an SEC requirement for disclosure of information.

www.pioneer.co.jp

STOP AND THINK!
A cash register can be considered a type of impress system. If a cashier in a supermarket started the day with $100 in change, what should the amount of cash in the drawer equal at the end of the day?
The amount of cash in the drawer should equal the total cash sales less any refunds plus $100. ■

The annual report of Pioneer Corporation refers to *cash and cash equivalents.* Of the two terms, *cash* is the easier to understand. It is the most liquid of all assets and the most readily available to pay debts. On the balance sheet, **cash** normally consists of currency and coins on hand, checks and money orders from customers, and deposits in bank checking and savings accounts. Cash may also include a **compensating balance**, an amount that is not entirely free to be spent. A compensating balance is a minimum amount that a bank requires a company to keep in its bank account as part of a credit-granting arrangement. Such an arrangement restricts cash; in effect, increases the interest of the loan; and reduces a company's liquidity. Therefore, the SEC requires companies to disclose the amount of any compensating balances in a note to the financial statements.

The term *cash equivalents* is a little harder to understand. At times a company may find that it has more cash on hand than it needs to pay current obligations. Excess cash should not remain idle, especially during periods of high interest rates. Thus, management may periodically invest idle funds in time deposits or certificates of deposit at banks and other financial institutions, in government securities (such as U.S. Treasury notes), or in other securities. Such actions are rightfully called investments. However, if the investments have a term of 90 days or less when they are purchased, they are called **cash equivalents** because the funds revert to cash so quickly that they are regarded as cash on the balance sheet. Pioneer Corporation follows this practice. Its policy is stated as follows: "The Company considers all highly liquid investments with a maturity of 90 days or less when purchased to be cash equivalents. Cash equivalents are stated at cost, which approximates market value."[6] A survey of 600 large U.S. corporations found that 53 of them, or 9 percent, used the term *cash* as the balance sheet caption and 510, or 85 percent, used the phrase *cash and cash equivalents* or *cash and equivalents.* Twenty-seven companies, or 5 percent, combined cash with marketable securities.[7] The average amount of cash held can also vary by industry.

Most companies need to keep some currency and coins on hand. Currency and coins are needed for cash registers, for paying expenses that are impractical to pay by check, and for situations that require cash advances—for example, when sales representatives need cash for travel expenses. One way to control a cash fund or cash advances is through the use of an imprest system. A common form of imprest system is a petty cash fund, which is established at a fixed amount. Each cash payment from the fund is documented by a receipt. The fund is periodically reimbursed, based on the documented expenditures, by the exact amount necessary to restore its original cash balance. The person responsible for the petty cash fund must

FOCUS ON BUSINESS ETHICS

What About the Unlawful Use of EFT?

Electronic Funds Transfer (EFT) has made it easy to transfer funds around the world. It has facilitated the huge growth in international business, but what about the unlawful use of EFT? To combat the laundering of money by drug dealers, U.S. law requires banks to report cash transactions in excess of $10,000. However, terrorist groups have circumvented this law by electronically transferring amounts of less than $10,000. In response, the Treasury Department has set up rules that require banks to keep records about the sources and recipients of electronic transfers. But it is questionable how much effect this action will have. Since most of the millions of EFT transactions that occur every day look pretty much alike, looking for transactions that support illegal activities is like looking for a needle in a haystack.

always be able to account for its contents by having cash and receipts whose total equals the originally fixed amount.

All businesses rely on banks to control cash receipts and cash disbursements. Banks serve as safe depositories for cash, negotiable instruments, and other valuable business documents, such as stocks and bonds. The checking accounts that banks provide improve control by minimizing the amount of currency a company needs to keep on hand and by supplying permanent records of all cash payments. Banks also serve as agents in a variety of transactions, such as the collection and payment of certain kinds of debts and the exchange of foreign currencies.

www.walmart.com

Many companies commonly conduct transactions through a type of electronic communication called **electronic funds transfer (EFT)**. Instead of writing checks to pay for purchases or to repay loans, the company arranges to have cash transferred electronically from its bank to another company's bank. Wal-Mart Stores, Inc., for example, makes 75 percent of its payments to suppliers through EFT. The actual cash, of course, is not transferred. For the banks, an electronic transfer is simply a bookkeeping entry.

www.citigroup.com
www.bankone.com
www.bankofamerica.com

In serving customers, banks also offer automated teller machines (ATMs) for making deposits, withdrawing cash, transferring funds among accounts, and paying bills. Large consumer banks like Citibank, BankOne, and Bank of America process hundreds of thousands of ATM transactions each week. Many banks also give customers the option of paying bills over the telephone and with *debit cards.* When a customer makes a retail purchase using a debit card, the amount of the purchase is deducted directly from the buyer's bank account. The bank usually documents debit card transactions for the retailer, but the retailer must develop new internal controls to ensure that the transactions are recorded properly and that unauthorized transfers are not permitted. It is expected that within a few years, 25 percent of all retail activity will be handled electronically.

Check out ACE for a Review Quiz at http://accounting.college.hmco.com/students.

SHORT-TERM INVESTMENTS

LO3 Identify types of short-term investments and explain the financial reporting implications.

RELATED TEXT ASSIGNMENTS
Q: 5, 6
SE: 4, 5
E: 4, 5
P: 1, 5
SD: 1, 5, 6

When investments have a maturity of more than 90 days but are intended to be held only until cash is needed for current operations, they are called **short-term investments** or **marketable securities**. Investments intended to be held for more than one year are called *long-term investments.* Long-term investments are reported in an investments section of the balance sheet, not in the current assets section. Although long-term investments may be just as marketable as short-term assets, management intends to hold them for an indefinite period of time.

Securities that may be held as short-term or long-term investments fall into three categories, as specified by the Financial Accounting Standards Board: held-to-maturity securities, trading securities, and available-for-sale securities.[8] Trading securities are classified as short-term investments. Held-to-maturity securities and available-for-sale securities may be classified as either short-term or long-term investments, depending on their length to maturity or management's intent to hold them. The three categories of securities when held as short-term investments are discussed here.

Held-to-Maturity Securities

KEY POINT: Any broker costs or taxes paid to acquire securities are part of the cost of the securities.

Held-to-maturity securities are debt securities that management intends to hold to their maturity date and whose cash value is not needed until that date. Such securities are recorded at cost and valued on the balance sheet at cost adjusted for the effects of interest. For example, suppose that on December 1, 20x4, Webber Company pays $97,000 for U.S. Treasury bills, which are short-term debt of the federal government. The bills will mature in 120 days at $100,000. Webber would make the following entry:

A = L + OE
\+ −

20x4			
Dec. 1	Short-Term Investments	97,000	
	Cash		97,000
	Purchase of U.S. Treasury bills that mature in 120 days		

At Webber's year end on December 31, the entry to accrue the interest income earned to date would be as follows:

A = L + OE
\+ +

20x4			
Dec. 31	Short-Term Investments	750	
	Interest Income		750
	Accrual of interest on U.S. Treasury bills $3,000 × 30/120 = $750		

On December 31, the U.S. Treasury bills would be shown on the balance sheet as a short-term investment at their amortized cost of $97,750 ($97,000 + $750). When Webber receives the maturity value on March 31, 20x5, the entry is as follows:

A = L + OE
\+ +
−

20x5			
Mar. 31	Cash	100,000	
	Short-Term Investments		97,750
	Interest Income		2,250
	Receipt of cash at maturity of U.S. Treasury bills and recognition of related income		

Trading Securities

Trading securities are debt and equity securities bought and held principally for the purpose of being sold in the near term. Debt securities are to be redeemed at a specified time and pay a return in the form of interest. Equity securities are an ownership interest in an entity and are subject to market fluctuations. Return takes the form of dividends and increases in the price of the securities.

Trading securities are frequently bought and sold to generate profits on short-term changes in their prices. Trading securities are classified as current assets on the balance sheet and are valued at fair value, which is usually the same as market value—for example, when securities are traded on a stock exchange or in the over-the-counter market.

An increase or decrease in the fair value of the total trading portfolio (the group of securities held for trading purposes) is included in net income in the accounting period in which the increase or decrease occurs. For example, assume that Franklin Company purchases 10,000 shares of Exxon Mobil Corporation for $900,000 ($90 per share) and 5,000 shares of Texaco Inc. for $300,000 ($60 per share) on October 25, 20x4. The purchase is made for trading purposes; that is, management intends

www.exxonmobil.com
www.texaco.com

to realize a gain by holding the shares for only a short period. The entry to record the investment at cost follows:

A = L + OE + −	20x4 Oct. 25	Short-Term Investments Cash Investment in stocks for trading ($900,000 + $300,000 = $1,200,000)	1,200,000	 1,200,000

Assume that at year end Exxon Mobil's stock price has decreased to $80 per share and Texaco's has risen to $64 per share. The trading portfolio is now valued at $1,120,000:

Security	Market Value	Cost	Gain (Loss)
Exxon Mobil (10,000 shares)	$ 800,000	$ 900,000	
Texaco (5,000 shares)	320,000	300,000	
Totals	$1,120,000	$1,200,000	($80,000)

Because the current fair value of the portfolio is $80,000 less than the original cost of $1,200,000, an adjusting entry is needed, as follows:

A = L + OE − −	20x4 Dec. 31	Unrealized Loss on Investments Allowance to Adjust Short-Term Investments to Market Recognition of unrealized loss on trading portfolio	80,000	 80,000

KEY POINT: The Allowance to Adjust Short-Term Investments to Market account is never changed when securities are sold. It changes only with an adjusting entry at year end.

The unrealized loss will appear on the income statement as a reduction in income. The loss is unrealized because the securities have not been sold; unrealized gains are treated the same way if they occur. The Allowance to Adjust Short-Term Investments to Market account appears on the balance sheet as a contra-asset, as follows:

Short-term investments (at cost)	$1,200,000
Less allowance to adjust short-term investments to market	80,000
Short-term investments (at market)	$1,120,000
or, more simply,	
Short-term investments (at market value, cost is $1,200,000)	$1,120,000

If Franklin sells its 5,000 shares of Texaco for $70 per share on March 2, 20x5, a realized gain on trading securities is recorded as follows:

A = L + OE + + −	20x5 Mar. 2	Cash Short-Term Investments Realized Gain on Investments Sale of 5,000 shares of Texaco for $70 per share; cost was $60 per share	350,000	 300,000 50,000

The realized gain will appear on the income statement. Note that the realized gain is unaffected by the adjustment for the unrealized loss at the end of 20x4. The two transactions are treated independently. If the stock had been sold for less than cost, a realized loss on investments would have been recorded. Realized losses also appear on the income statement.

www.bp.com

Let's assume that during 20x5 Franklin buys 2,000 shares of BP Corporation at $64 per share and has no transactions involving Exxon Mobil. Also assume that by December 31, 20x5, the price of Exxon Mobil's stock has risen to $95 per share, or $5 per share more than the original cost, and that BP's stock price has fallen to $58, or $6 less than the original cost. The trading portfolio now can be analyzed as follows:

Security	Market Value	Cost	Gain (Loss)
Exxon Mobil (10,000 shares)	$ 950,000	$ 900,000	
BP (2,000 shares)	116,000	128,000	
Totals	$1,066,000	$1,028,000	$38,000

KEY POINT: The entry to the Allowance to Adjust Short-Term Investments to Market account is equal to the change in the market value. Compute the new allowance, and then compute the amount needed to change the account. The unrealized loss or gain is the other half of the entry.

The market value of the portfolio now exceeds the cost by $38,000 ($1,066,000 – $1,028,000). This amount represents the targeted ending balance for the Allowance to Adjust Short-Term Investments to Market account. Recall that at the end of 20x4, that account had a credit balance of $80,000, meaning that the market value of the trading portfolio was less than the cost. The account has no entries during 20x5 and thus retains its balance until adjusting entries are made at the end of the year. The adjustment for 20x5 must be $118,000—enough to result in a debit balance of $38,000 in the allowance account.

A = L + OE
\+ \+

20x5			
Dec. 31	Allowance to Adjust Short-Term Investments to Market	118,000	
	Unrealized Gain on Investments		118,000
	Recognition of unrealized gain on trading portfolio ($80,000 + $38,000 = $118,000)		

STOP AND THINK!
What would cause an Allowance to Adjust Short-Term Investments to Market account that has a negative (credit) balance at the beginning of the year to have a positive (debit) balance at the end of the year?
The total market value of the portfolio of trading securities would have increased enough during the year to exceed the negative (credit) balance at the beginning of the year. ■

The 20x5 ending balance of the allowance account may be determined as follows:

Allowance to Adjust Short-Term Investments to Market

Dec. 31, 20x5 adj.	118,000	Dec. 31, 20x4 bal.	80,000
Dec. 31, 20x5 bal.	38,000		

The balance sheet presentation of short-term investments is as follows:

Short-term investments (at cost)	$1,028,000
Plus allowance to adjust short-term investments to market	38,000
Short-term investments (at market)	$1,066,000

or, more simply,

Short-term investments (at market value, cost is $1,028,000)	$1,066,000

If the company also holds held-to-maturity securities, they are included in short-term investments at cost adjusted for the effects of interest if they will mature within one year.

AVAILABLE-FOR-SALE SECURITIES

www.pioneer.co.jp

Available-for-sale securities are debt and equity securities that do not meet the criteria for either held-to-maturity or trading securities. They are accounted for in exactly the same way as trading securities, except that the unrealized gain or loss is not reported on the income statement, but as a special item in the stockholders' equity section of the balance sheet. For example, Pioneer Corporation states in its annual report that "all debt securities and marketable equity securities held by the Company are classified as available-for-sale securities, and are carried at their fair values with unrealized gains and losses reported as a component of shareholders' equity."[9] This component is called accumulated other comprehensive income.

DIVIDEND AND INTEREST INCOME

Dividend and interest income for all three categories of investments appears in the other income and expenses section of the income statement.

Check out ACE for a Review Quiz at http://accounting.college.hmco.com/students.

Accounts Receivable

LO4 Define *accounts receivable* and apply the allowance method of accounting for uncollectible accounts.

RELATED TEXT ASSIGNMENTS
Q: 7, 8, 9, 10, 11, 12, 13, 14, 15, 16, 17
SE: 6, 7, 8
E: 6, 7, 8, 9, 10, 11
P: 2, 3, 6, 7
SD: 2, 4
FRA: 1, 2, 4, 7

The other major types of short-term financial assets are accounts receivable and notes receivable. Both result from credit sales to customers. Retailers like Sears, Roebuck and Co. have made credit available to nearly every responsible person in the United States. Every field of retail trade has expanded by allowing customers to make payments a month or more after the date of sale. What is not so apparent is that credit has expanded even more in the wholesale and manufacturing industries than at the retail level. The levels of accounts receivable in selected industries are shown in Figure 4.

Accounts receivable are short-term financial assets that arise from sales on credit to customers by wholesalers or retailers. This type of credit is often called **trade credit**. Terms on trade credit usually range from 5 to 60 days, depending on industry practice. For some companies that sell to consumers, **installment accounts receivable** constitute a significant portion of accounts receivable. Installment accounts receivable arise from the sale of goods on terms that allow the buyer to make a series of time payments. Department stores, appliance stores, furniture stores, used car companies, and other retail businesses often offer installment credit. Retailers like J.C. Penney Company, Inc., and Sears, Roebuck and Co. have millions of dollars in installment accounts receivable. Although the payment period may be 24 months or more, installment accounts receivable are classified as current assets if such credit policies are customary in the industry.

www.jcpenney.com
www.sears.com

On the balance sheet, the title "accounts receivable" is used for amounts arising from credit sales made to customers in the ordinary course of business. If loans or credit sales are made to employees, officers of the corporation, or owners, they should be shown separately, with an asset title like "receivables from employees," because of the increased risk of uncollectibility and conflict of interest.

Normally, individual customer accounts receivable have debit balances, but sometimes customers overpay their accounts either by mistake or in anticipation of future purchases. When these accounts show credit balances, the total of the credits should be shown on the balance sheet as a current liability because the amounts must be refunded if future sales are not made to those customers.

Uncollectible Accounts and the Direct Charge-Off Method

A company will always have some customers who cannot or will not pay their debts. The accounts owed by such customers are called **uncollectible accounts**, or *bad debts*, and are a loss or an expense of selling on credit. Why does a company sell

FIGURE 4
Accounts Receivable as a Percentage of Total Assets for Selected Industries

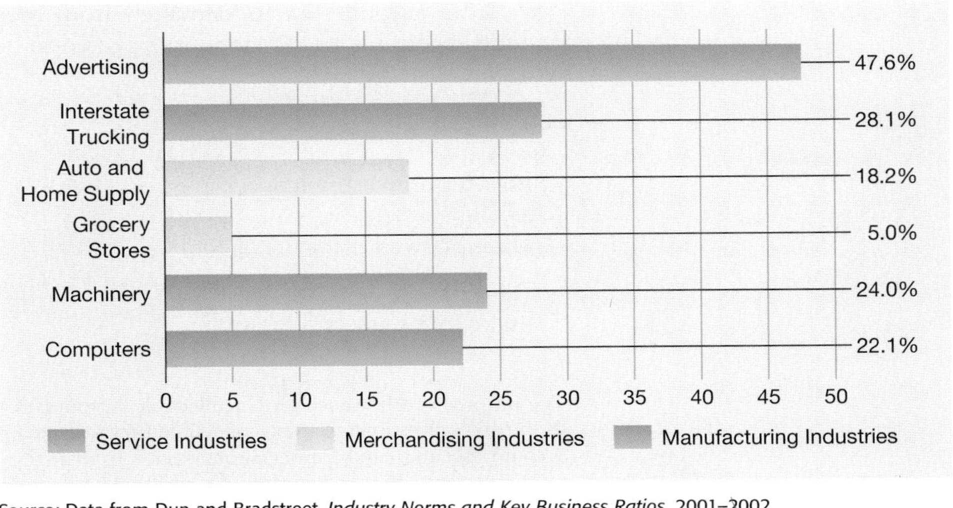

Source: Data from Dun and Bradstreet, *Industry Norms and Key Business Ratios,* 2001–2002.

on credit if it expects that some of its accounts will not be paid? The answer is that the company expects to sell much more than it would if it did not sell on credit, thereby increasing its earnings.

KEY POINT: The direct charge-off method does not conform to the matching rule.

Some companies recognize the loss from an uncollectible account receivable at the time it is determined to be uncollectible by reducing Accounts Receivable directly and increasing Uncollectible Accounts Expense. Many small companies use this method, called the **direct charge-off method**, because it is required in computing taxable income under federal tax regulations. However, companies that follow generally accepted accounting principles do not use it in their financial statements because it does not conform to the matching rule. The direct charge-off is often recorded in a different accounting period from the one in which the sale takes place. Companies that follow GAAP prefer the allowance method, which is explained in the next section.

Uncollectible Accounts and the Allowance Method

KEY POINT: The allowance method relies on an estimate of uncollectible accounts but is in accord with the matching rule.

Under the **allowance method** of accounting for uncollectible accounts, bad debt losses are matched against the sales they help to produce. As mentioned earlier, when management extends credit to increase sales, it knows that it will incur some losses from uncollectible accounts. Those losses are expenses that occur at the time sales on credit are made and should be matched to the revenues they help to generate. Of course, at the time the sales are made, management cannot identify which customers will not pay their debts, nor can it predict the exact amount of money that will be lost. Therefore, to observe the matching rule under generally accepted accounting principles, losses from uncollectible accounts must be estimated, and the estimate becomes an expense in the fiscal year in which the sales are made.

For example, let us assume that Cottage Sales Company made most of its sales on credit during its first year of operation, 20x4. At the end of the year, accounts receivable amounted to $100,000. On December 31, 20x4, management reviewed the collectible status of the accounts receivable. Approximately $6,000 of the $100,000 of accounts receivable were estimated to be uncollectible. Therefore, the uncollectible accounts expense for the first year of operation was estimated to be $6,000. The following adjusting entry would be made on December 31 of that year:

A = L + OE
− −

20x4			
Dec. 31	Uncollectible Accounts Expense	6,000	
	Allowance for Uncollectible Accounts		6,000
	To record the estimated uncollectible accounts expense for the year		

Uncollectible Accounts Expense appears on the income statement as an operating expense. **Allowance for Uncollectible Accounts** appears on the balance sheet as a contra account that is deducted from accounts receivable.* It reduces the accounts receivable to the amount expected to be realized, or collected, in cash, as follows:

Current assets		
Cash		$ 10,000
Short-term investments		15,000
Accounts receivable	$100,000	
Less allowance for uncollectible accounts	6,000	94,000
Inventory		56,000
Total current assets		$175,000

*The purpose of Allowance for Uncollectible Accounts is to reduce the gross accounts receivable to the amount estimated to be collectible (net realizable value). The purpose of another contra account, Accumulated Depreciation, is *not* to reduce the gross plant and equipment accounts to realizable value. Rather, its purpose is to show how much of the cost of the plant and equipment has been allocated as an expense to previous accounting periods.

FOCUS ON BUSINESS PRACTICE

Selling Goods and Services Is Only Half the Problem.

To be profitable, a company must not only sell goods and services; it must also generate cash flows by collecting on those sales. The latter has been a problem for the five leading North American manufacturers of telecommunications equipment. In the late 1990s, to make sales to start-up telecom companies, these manufacturers made loans of $17 billion to their customers. Nortel Networks <www.nortelnetworks.com> had $4.1 billion in customer financing; Cisco Systems <www.cisco.com>, $2.4 billion; Lucent Technologies <www.lucent.com>, $5.4 billion; Motorola <www.motorola.com>, $3.8 billion; and Qualcomm <www.qualcomm.com>, $1.18 billion. While not all of these loans were bad debts, many became so when the telecom industry experienced a major recession in 2001. All five companies had to increase their allowances for uncollectible accounts, actions that eliminated previously reported earnings and caused the companies' stock prices to fall.[10]

Accounts receivable may also be shown on the balance sheet as follows:

Accounts receivable (net of allowance for uncollectible accounts of $6,000)	$94,000

Or they may be shown at "net," with the amount of the allowance for uncollectible accounts identified in a note to the financial statements. The estimated uncollectible amount cannot be identified with any particular customer; therefore, it is credited to a separate contra-asset account—Allowance for Uncollectible Accounts.

KEY POINT: The accountant looks at the local economic conditions as well as national conditions in setting the estimated uncollectible accounts expense.

The allowance account often has other titles, such as *Allowance for Doubtful Accounts* and *Allowance for Bad Debts.* Once in a while, the older phrase *Reserve for Bad Debts* will be seen, but in modern practice it should not be used. *Bad Debts Expense* is a title often used for Uncollectible Accounts Expense.

STOP AND THINK!
How might the receivable turnover and the average days' sales uncollectible ratios reveal that management is consistently underestimating the amount of losses from uncollectible accounts?
A decrease in receivables turnover and an increase in average days' sales uncollectible from period to period, especially in the absence of changes in credit policies, might mean that management is underestimating the amount of losses from uncollectible accounts. ■

ESTIMATING UNCOLLECTIBLE ACCOUNTS EXPENSE

As noted, it is necessary to estimate the expense to cover the expected losses for the year. Of course, estimates can vary widely. If management takes an optimistic view and projects a small loss from uncollectible accounts, the resulting net accounts receivable will be larger than if management takes a pessimistic view. The net income will also be larger under the optimistic view because the estimated expense will be smaller. The company's accountant makes an estimate based on past experience and current economic conditions. For example, losses from uncollectible accounts are normally expected to be greater in a recession than during a period of economic growth. The final decision, made by management, on the amount of the expense will depend on objective information, such as the accountant's analyses, and on certain qualitative factors, such as how investors, bankers, creditors, and others may view the performance of the debtor company. Regardless of the qualitative considerations, the estimated losses from uncollectible accounts should be realistic.

Two common methods of estimating uncollectible accounts expense are the percentage of net sales method and the accounts receivable aging method.

KEY POINT: The percentage of net sales method can be described as the income statement method to emphasize that the percentage of the net sales calculated is the amount expensed. That is, any previous balance in the allowance account is irrelevant in preparing the adjustment.

■ **PERCENTAGE OF NET SALES METHOD** The **percentage of net sales method** asks the question, How much of this year's net sales will not be collected? The answer determines the amount of uncollectible accounts expense for the year. For example, the following balances represent the ending figures for Hassel Company for 20x9:

Sales			
		Dec. 31	645,000

Sales Returns and Allowances			
Dec. 31	40,000		

Sales Discounts			
Dec. 31	5,000		

Allowance for Uncollectible Accounts			
		Dec. 31	3,600

PARENTHETICAL NOTE: The percentage of net sales method, unlike the direct charge-off method, matches revenues with expenses.

Below are Hassel's actual losses from uncollectible accounts for the past three years:

Year	Net Sales	Losses from Uncollectible Accounts	Percentage
20x6	$ 520,000	$10,200	1.96
20x7	595,000	13,900	2.34
20x8	585,000	9,900	1.69
Total	$1,700,000	$34,000	2.00

In many businesses, net sales is understood to approximate net credit sales. If there are substantial cash sales, then net credit sales should be used because they generate accounts receivable. Hassel's management believes that uncollectible accounts will continue to average about 2 percent of net sales. The uncollectible accounts expense for the year 20x9 is therefore estimated to be

$$.02 \times (\$645{,}000 - \$40{,}000 - \$5{,}000) = .02 \times \$600{,}000 = \$12{,}000$$

The entry to record this estimate is as follows:

A = L + OE − −	20x9 Dec. 31	Uncollectible Accounts Expense	12,000	
		Allowance for Uncollectible Accounts		12,000
		To record uncollectible accounts expense at 2 percent of $600,000 net sales		

After the above entry is posted, Allowance for Uncollectible Accounts will have a balance of $15,600:

Allowance for Uncollectible Accounts

Debit	Credit	
	Dec. 31	3,600
	Dec. 31 adj.	12,000
	Dec. 31 bal.	15,600

The balance consists of the $12,000 estimated uncollectible accounts receivable from 20x9 sales and the $3,600 estimated uncollectible accounts receivable from previous years.

■ **ACCOUNTS RECEIVABLE AGING METHOD** The **accounts receivable aging method** asks the question, How much of the year-end balance of accounts receivable will not be collected? Under this method, the year-end balance of Allowance for Uncollectible Accounts is determined directly by an analysis of accounts receivable. The difference between the amount determined to be uncollectible and the actual balance of Allowance for Uncollectible Accounts is the expense for the year. In theory, this method should produce the same result as the percentage of net sales method, but in practice it rarely does.

The **aging of accounts receivable** is the process of listing each customer's receivable account according to the due date of the account. If the customer's account is past due, there is a possibility that the account will not be paid. And that possibility increases as the account extends further beyond the due date. The aging of accounts receivable helps management evaluate its credit and collection policies and alerts it to possible problems.

FOCUS ON INTERNATIONAL BUSINESS

Why Companies in Emerging Economies Must Adapt Accounting Practices

Companies in emerging economies do not always follow the accounting practices accepted in the United States. The Shanghai Stock Exchange is one of the fastest-growing stock markets in the world. Few Chinese companies acknowledge that uncollected receivables are not worth full value even when the receivables have been outstanding for a year or more. It is common practice in the United States to write off receivables more than six months old. Now that Chinese companies like Shanghai Steel Tube and Shanghai Industrial Sewing Machine are making their shares of stock available to outsiders, they must estimate uncollectible accounts in accordance with international accounting standards. Recognition of this expense could easily wipe out annual earnings.[11]

EXHIBIT 1
Analysis of Accounts Receivable by Age

Myer Company
Analysis of Accounts Receivable by Age
December 31, 20x5

Customer	Total	Not Yet Due	1–30 Days Past Due	31–60 Days Past Due	61–90 Days Past Due	Over 90 Days Past Due
A. Arnold	$ 150		$ 150			
M. Benoit	400			$ 400		
J. Connolly	1,000	$ 900	100			
R. Deering	250				$ 250	
Others	42,600	21,000	14,000	3,800	2,200	$1,600
Totals	$44,400	$21,900	$14,250	$4,200	$2,450	$1,600
Estimated percentage uncollectible		1.0	2.0	10.0	30.0	50.0
Allowance for Uncollectible Accounts	$ 2,459	$ 219	$ 285	$ 420	$ 735	$ 800

ENRICHMENT NOTE: The aging method is often superior to the percentage of net sales method during changing economic times. For example, during a recession, more bad debts occur. The aging method automatically reflects the economic change as accounts receivable age because customers are unable to pay. A company using the percentage of net sales method must anticipate the change and modify the percentage it uses.

KEY POINT: When the write-offs in an accounting period exceed the amount of the allowance, a debit balance in the Allowance for Uncollectible Accounts account results.

The aging of accounts receivable for Myer Company is illustrated in Exhibit 1. Each account receivable is classified as being not yet due or as being 1–30 days, 31–60 days, 61–90 days, or over 90 days past due. The estimated percentage uncollectible in each of these catagories is multiplied by the amount in each category in order to determine the estimated, or target, balance of Allowance for Uncollectible Accounts. In total, it is estimated that $2,459 of the $44,400 accounts receivable will not be collected.

Once the target balance for Allowance for Uncollectible Accounts has been found, it is necessary to determine how much the adjustment is. The amount of the adjustment depends on the current balance of the allowance account. Let us assume two cases for the December 31 balance of Myer Company's Allowance for Uncollectible Accounts: (1) a credit balance of $800 and (2) a debit balance of $800.

In the first case, an adjustment of $1,659 is needed to bring the balance of the allowance account to a $2,459 credit balance, calculated as follows:

Targeted balance for allowance for uncollectible accounts	$2,459
Less current credit balance of allowance for uncollectible accounts	800
Uncollectible accounts expense	$1,659

The uncollectible accounts expense is recorded as follows:

A = L + OE				
− −	20x5 Dec. 31	Uncollectible Accounts Expense	1,659	
		Allowance for Uncollectible Accounts		1,659
		To bring the allowance for uncollectible accounts to the level of estimated losses		

The resulting balance of Allowance for Uncollectible Accounts is $2,459, as follows:

Allowance for Uncollectible Accounts

		Dec. 31	800
		Dec. 31 adj.	1,659
		Dec. 31 bal.	2,459

In the second case, because Allowance for Uncollectible Accounts has a debit balance of $800, the estimated uncollectible accounts expense for the year will have to be $3,259 to reach the targeted balance of $2,459. This calculation is as follows:

Targeted balance for allowance for uncollectible accounts	$2,459
Plus current debit balance of allowance for uncollectible accounts	800
Uncollectible accounts expense	$3,259

The uncollectible accounts expense is recorded as follows:

A = L + OE
−   −

20x5			
Dec. 31	Uncollectible Accounts Expense	3,259	
	Allowance for Uncollectible Accounts		3,259
	To bring the allowance for uncollectible accounts to the level of estimated losses		

After this entry, Allowance for Uncollectible Accounts has a credit balance of $2,459:

Allowance for Uncollectible Accounts

Dec. 31	800	Dec. 31 adj.	3,259
		Dec. 31 bal.	2,459

■ **COMPARISON OF THE TWO METHODS** Both the percentage of net sales method and the accounts receivable aging method estimate the uncollectible accounts expense in accordance with the matching rule, but as shown in Figure 5, they do so in different ways. The percentage of net sales method is an income statement

FIGURE 5
Two Methods of Estimating Uncollectible Accounts

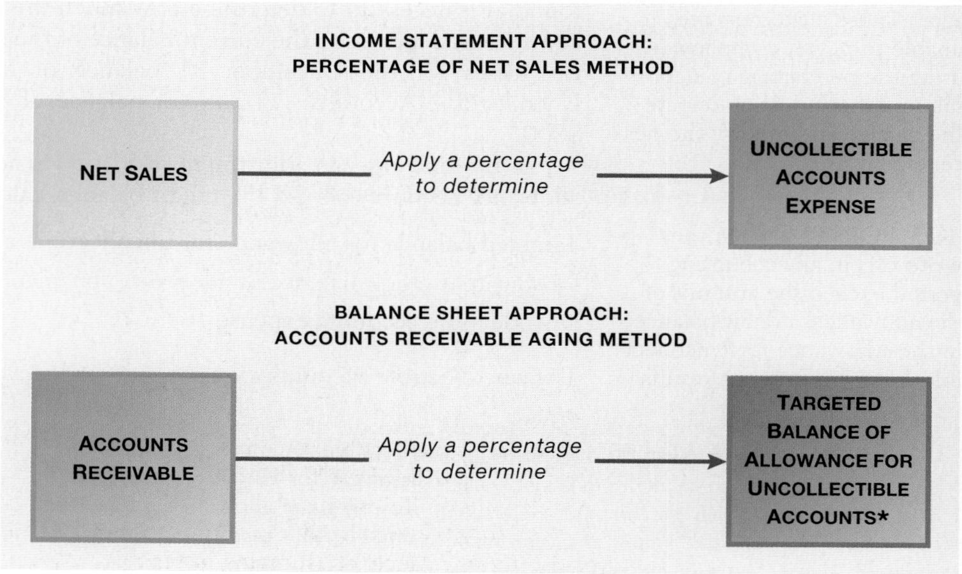

*Add current debit balance or subtract current credit balance to determine uncollectible accounts expense.

KEY POINT: Describing the aging method as the balance sheet method emphasizes that the computation is based on ending accounts receivable, rather than on net sales for the period.

approach. It assumes that a certain proportion of sales will not be collected, and this proportion is the *amount of Uncollectible Accounts Expense* for the accounting period. The accounts receivable aging method is a balance sheet approach. It assumes that a certain proportion of accounts receivable outstanding will not be collected. This proportion is the *targeted balance of the Allowance for Uncollectible Accounts account.* The expense for the accounting period is the difference between the targeted balance and the current balance of the allowance account.

■ WHY ACCOUNTS WRITTEN OFF WILL DIFFER FROM ESTIMATES Regardless of the method used to estimate uncollectible accounts, the total of accounts receivable written off in any given year will rarely equal the estimated uncollectible amount. The allowance account will show a credit balance when the total of accounts written off is less than the estimated uncollectible amount. The allowance account will show a debit balance when the total of accounts written off is greater than the estimated uncollectible amount.

WRITING OFF AN UNCOLLECTIBLE ACCOUNT

When it becomes clear that a specific account receivable will not be collected, the amount should be written off to Allowance for Uncollectible Accounts. Remember that the uncollectible amount was already accounted for as an expense when the allowance was established. For example, assume that on January 15, 20x6, R. Deering, who owes Myer Company $250, is declared bankrupt by a federal court. The entry to *write off* this account is as follows:

A = L + OE
+
−

20x6			
Jan. 15	Allowance for Uncollectible Accounts	250	
	Accounts Receivable		250
	To write off receivable from R. Deering as uncollectible; Deering declared bankrupt on January 15		

KEY POINT: When writing off an individual account, debit Allowance for Uncollectible Accounts, not Uncollectible Accounts Expense.

Although the write-off removes the uncollectible amount from Accounts Receivable, it does not affect the estimated net realizable value of accounts receivable. The write-off simply reduces R. Deering's account to zero and reduces Allowance for Uncollectible Accounts by a similar amount, as shown below:

	Balances Before Write-off	Balances After Write-off
Accounts receivable	$44,400	$44,150
Less allowance for uncollectible accounts	2,459	2,209
Estimated net realizable value of accounts receivable	$41,941	$41,941

RECOVERY OF ACCOUNTS RECEIVABLE WRITTEN OFF

Occasionally, a customer whose account has been written off as uncollectible will later be able to pay some or all of the amount owed. When this happens, two entries must be made: one to reverse the earlier write-off (which is now incorrect) and another to show the collection of the account. For example, assume that on September 1, 20x6, R. Deering, after his bankruptcy on January 15, notified Myer Company that he could pay $100 of his account and sent a check for $50. The entries to record this transaction are as follows:

	20x6			

A = L + OE
+
−
	Sept. 1	Accounts Receivable
		  Allowance for Uncollectible Accounts
		    To reinstate the portion of
		    the account of R. Deering
		    now considered collectible;
		    originally written off January 15
			100	100

A = L + OE
+
−
	Sept. 1	Cash
		  Accounts Receivable
		    Collection from R. Deering
			50	50

The collectible portion of R. Deering's account must be restored to his account and credited to Allowance for Uncollectible Accounts for two reasons. First, it turned out to be wrong to write off the full $250 on January 15 because only $150 was actually uncollectible. Second, the accounts receivable subsidiary account for R. Deering should reflect his ability to pay a portion of the money he owed despite his declaration of bankruptcy. Documentation of this action will give a clear picture of R. Deering's credit record for future credit action.

Check out ACE for a Review Quiz at http://accounting.college.hmco.com/students.

NOTES RECEIVABLE

LO5 Define *promissory note,* and compute and record promissory notes receivable.

RELATED TEXT ASSIGNMENTS
Q: 18, 19
SE: 9
E: 12, 13, 14, 15
P: 4, 8

A **promissory note** is an unconditional promise to pay a definite sum of money on demand or at a future date. The entity who signs the note and thereby promises to pay is called the *maker* of the note. The entity to whom payment is to be made is called the *payee.*

The promissory note illustrated in Figure 6 is dated May 20, 20x5, and is an unconditional promise by the maker, Samuel Mason, to pay a definite sum, or principal ($1,000), to the payee, Cook County Bank & Trust Company, on the future date of August 18, 20x5. The promissory note bears an interest rate of 8 percent. The payee regards all promissory notes it holds that are due in less than one year as **notes receivable** in the current assets section of the balance sheet. The maker regards them as **notes payable** in the current liabilities section of the balance sheet.

This portion of the chapter is concerned primarily with notes received from customers. The nature of a company's business generally determines how frequently it receives promissory notes from customers. Firms selling durable goods of high value, such as farm machinery and automobiles, will often accept promissory notes. Among the advantages of promissory notes are that they produce interest income and represent a stronger legal claim against a debtor than do accounts receivable. In addition, selling, or discounting, promissory notes to banks is a common financing method. Almost all companies occasionally receive a note, and many companies obtain notes receivable in settlement of past-due accounts.

COMPUTATIONS FOR PROMISSORY NOTES

In accounting for promissory notes, the following terms are important to remember: (1) *maturity date,* (2) *duration of note,* (3) *interest and interest rate,* and (4) *maturity value.*

MATURITY DATE The **maturity date** is the date on which a promissory note must be paid. This date must either be stated on the note or be determinable from the facts stated on the note. Among the most common statements of maturity date are the following:

1. A specific date, such as "November 14, 20xx"
2. A specific number of months after the date of the note, for example, "three months after date"

FIGURE 6
A Promissory Note

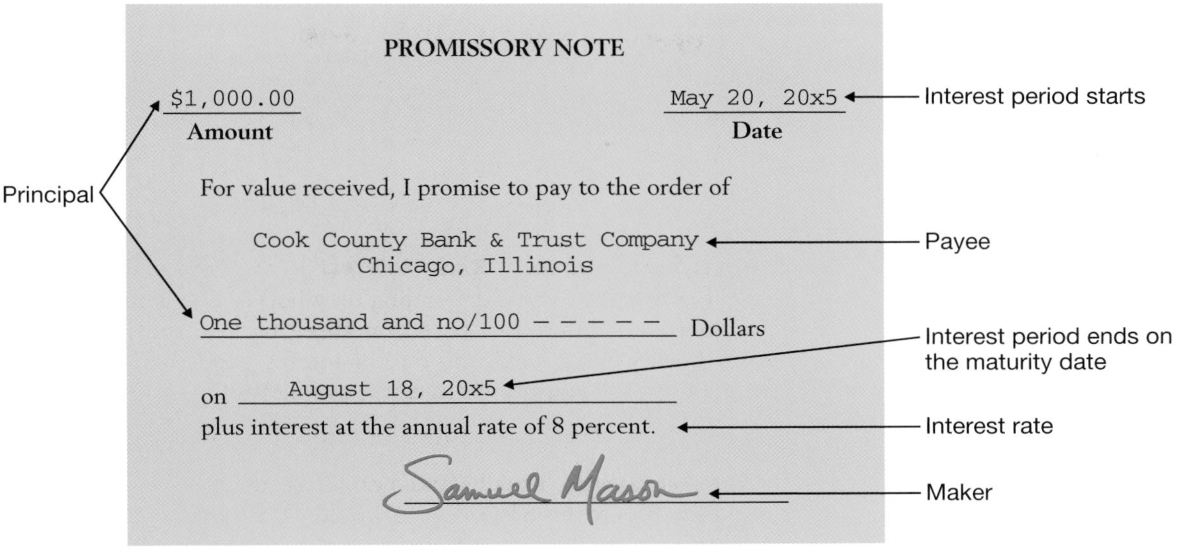

3. A specific number of days after the date of the note, for example, "60 days after date"

The maturity date is obvious when a specific date is stated. And when the maturity date is a number of months from the date of the note, one simply uses the same day in the appropriate future month. For example, a note that is dated January 20 and that is due in two months would be due on March 20.

When the maturity date is a specific number of days from the date of the note, however, the exact maturity date must be determined. In computing the maturity date, it is important to exclude the date of the note. For example, a note dated May 20 and due in 90 days would be due on August 18, computed as follows:

Days remaining in May (31 − 20)	11
Days in June	30
Days in July	31
Days in August	18
Total days	90

DURATION OF NOTE The **duration of note** is the length of time in days between a promissory note's issue date and its maturity date. Knowing the duration of the note is important because interest is calculated for the exact number of days. Identifying the duration is easy when the maturity date is stated as a specific number of days from the date of the note because the two numbers are the same.

FOCUS ON BUSINESS PRACTICE

How Long Is a Year? It Depends.

Most banks use a 365-day year to compute interest for all loans, but some use a 360-day year for commercial loans. For example, the brokerage firm of May SWS Securities <www.maysws.com> of Dallas, Texas, states in its customer loan agreement, "Interest is calculated on a 360-day basis." In Europe, use of a 360-day year is common. Financial institutions that use the 360-day basis earn slightly more interest than those that use the 365-day basis. In this book, we use a 360-day year to keep the computations simple.

STUDY NOTE: Another way to compute the duration of notes is to begin with the interest period, as follows:

90	Interest period
−11	days remaining in May (31 − 20)
79	
−30	days in June
49	
−31	days in July
18	due date in August

However, if the maturity date is stated as a specific date, the exact number of days must be determined. Assume that a note issued on May 10 matures on August 10. The duration of the note is 92 days, determined as follows:

Days remaining in May (31 − 10)	21
Days in June	30
Days in July	31
Days in August	10
Total days	92

INTEREST AND INTEREST RATE **Interest** is the cost of borrowing money or the return for lending money, depending on whether one is the borrower or the lender. The amount of interest is based on three factors: the principal (the amount of money borrowed or lent), the rate of interest, and the loan's length of time. The formula used in computing interest is as follows:

$$\text{Principal} \times \text{Rate of Interest} \times \text{Time} = \text{Interest}$$

Interest rates are usually stated on an annual basis. For example, the interest on a one-year, 8 percent, \$1,000 note would be \$80 (\$1,000 × 8/100 × 1 = \$80). If the term, or time period, of the note is three months instead of a year, the interest charge would be \$20 (\$1,000 × 8/100 × 3/12 = \$20).

When the term of a note is expressed in days, the exact number of days must be used in computing the interest. To keep the computation simple, let us compute interest on the basis of 360 days per year. Therefore, if the term of the above note were 45 days, the interest would be \$10, computed as follows: \$1,000 × 8/100 × 45/360 = \$10.

MATURITY VALUE The **maturity value** is the total proceeds of a promissory note—face value plus interest—at the maturity date. The maturity value of a 90-day, 8 percent, \$1,000 note is computed as follows:

$$\begin{aligned}\text{Maturity Value} &= \text{Principal} + \text{Interest}\\ &= \$1{,}000 + (\$1{,}000 \times 8/100 \times 90/360)\\ &= \$1{,}000 + \$20\\ &= \$1{,}020\end{aligned}$$

There are also so-called non-interest-bearing notes. The maturity value is the face value, or principal amount. In this case, the principal includes an implied interest cost.

ACCOUNTING ENTRIES FOR PROMISSORY NOTES

The accounting entries for promissory notes receivable fall into four groups: (1) recording receipt of a note, (2) recording collection on a note, (3) recording a dishonored note, and (4) recording adjusting entries.

KEY POINT: The entry to record receipt of a note does not include interest because no interest has yet been earned.

RECORDING RECEIPT OF A NOTE Assume that on June 1, a 30-day, 12 percent note is received from a customer, J. Halsted, in settlement of an existing account receivable of \$4,000. The entry for this transaction is as follows:

A = L + OE
\+
−

June 1	Notes Receivable	4,000	
	Accounts Receivable		4,000
	Received 30-day, 12 percent note in payment of account of J. Halsted		

RECORDING COLLECTION ON A NOTE When the note plus interest is collected 30 days later, the entry is as follows:

A = L + OE
\+ +
−

July 1	Cash	4,040	
	Notes Receivable		4,000
	Interest Income		40
	Collected 30-day, 12 percent note from J. Halsted		

STUDY NOTE: Dishonored notes are, in effect, not written off. The amounts are merely transferred to accounts receivable, which can be written off later.

■ **RECORDING A DISHONORED NOTE** When the maker of a note does not pay the note at maturity, the note is said to be dishonored. The holder, or payee, of a **dishonored note** should make an entry to transfer the total amount due from Notes Receivable to an account receivable from the debtor. If J. Halsted dishonors her note on July 1, the following entry would be made:

A = L + OE
\+ +
−

July 1	Accounts Receivable	4,040	
	Notes Receivable		4,000
	Interest Income		40
	30-day, 12 percent note dishonored by J. Halsted		

The interest earned is recorded because although J. Halsted did not pay the note, she is still obligated to pay both the principal and the interest.

Two things are accomplished by transferring a dishonored note receivable into an Accounts Receivable account. First, it leaves only notes that have not matured and are presumably negotiable and collectible in the Notes Receivable account. Second, it establishes a record in the borrower's accounts receivable account that he or she has dishonored a note receivable. Such information may be helpful in deciding whether to extend future credit to the customer.

ENRICHMENT NOTE: The interest rate on the account receivable is usually higher than the rate on the note.

STOP AND THINK!
Under what circumstances would an accrual of interest income on an interest-bearing note receivable not be required at the end of an accounting period?
It would not be required if the interest to date were paid on the last day of the accounting period. ■

■ **RECORDING ADJUSTING ENTRIES** A promissory note received in one period may not be due until a following accounting period. Because the interest on a note accrues by a small amount each day of the note's duration, it is necessary, according to the matching rule, to apportion the interest earned to the periods in which it belongs. For example, assume that on August 31 a 60-day, 8 percent, $2,000 note was received and that the company prepares financial statements monthly. The following adjusting entry is necessary on September 30 to show how the interest earned for September has accrued:

A = L + OE
\+ +

Sept. 30	Interest Receivable	13.33	
	Interest Income		13.33
	To accrue 30 days' interest earned on a note receivable $\$2,000 \times 8/100 \times 30/360 = \$13.33$		

The Interest Receivable account is a current asset on the balance sheet. When payment of the note plus interest is received on October 30, the following entry is made:*

A = L + OE
\+ +
−
−

Oct. 30	Cash	2,026.67	
	Notes Receivable		2,000.00
	Interest Receivable		13.33
	Interest Income		13.34
	Receipt of note receivable plus interest		

As can be seen from these transactions, both September and October receive the benefit of one-half the interest earned.

Check out ACE for a Review Quiz at http://accounting.college.hmco.com/students.

*Some firms may follow the practice of reversing the September 30 adjusting entry. Here we assume that a reversing entry is not made.

Chapter Review

Review of Learning Objectives

LO1 Identify and explain the management issues related to short-term financial assets.

In managing short-term financial assets, management must (1) consider the need for short-term investing and borrowing as the business's balance of cash fluctuates during seasonal cycles, (2) establish credit policies that balance the need for sales with the ability to collect, and (3) assess the need to increase cash flows through the financing of receivables.

LO2 Explain *cash, cash equivalents,* and the importance of electronic funds transfer.

Cash consists of coins and currency on hand, checks and money orders received from customers, and deposits in bank accounts. Cash equivalents are investments that have a term of 90 days or less. Conducting transactions through electronic funds transfer (EFT) is important because of its efficiency. It eliminates much of the paperwork associated with traditional recordkeeping.

LO3 Identify types of short-term investments and explain the financial reporting implications.

Short-term investments are classified as held-to-maturity securities, trading securities, or available-for-sale securities. Held-to-maturity securities are debt securities that management intends to hold to the maturity date; they are valued on the balance sheet at cost adjusted for the effects of interest. Trading securities are debt and equity securities bought and held principally for the purpose of being sold in the near term; they are valued at fair value or at market value. Unrealized gains or losses on trading securities appear on the income statement. Available-for-sale securities are debt and equity securities that do not meet the criteria for either held-to-maturity or trading securities. They are accounted for in the same way as trading securities, except that an unrealized gain or loss is reported as a special item in the stockholders' equity section of the balance sheet.

LO4 Define *accounts receivable* and apply the allowance method of accounting for uncollectible accounts.

Accounts receivable are amounts still to be collected from credit sales to customers. Because credit is offered to increase sales, uncollectible accounts associated with credit sales should be charged as expenses in the period in which the sales are made. However, because of the time lag between the sales and the time the accounts are judged uncollectible, the accountant must use the allowance method to match the amount of uncollectible accounts against revenues in any given period.

Uncollectible accounts expense is estimated by either the percentage of net sales method or the accounts receivable aging method. When the first method is used, bad debts are judged to be a certain percentage of net sales during the period. When the second method is used, certain percentages are applied to groups of accounts receivable that have been arranged by due dates.

Allowance for Uncollectible Accounts is a contra-asset account to Accounts Receivable. The estimate of uncollectible accounts is debited to Uncollectible Accounts Expense and credited to the allowance account. When an individual account is determined to be uncollectible, it is removed from Accounts Receivable by debiting the allowance account and crediting Accounts Receivable. If the written-off account should later be collected, the earlier entry should be reversed and the collection should be recorded in the normal way.

LO5 Define *promissory note,* and compute and record promissory notes receivable.

A promissory note is an unconditional promise to pay a definite sum of money on demand or at a future date. Companies selling durable goods of high value, such as farm machinery and automobiles, often accept promissory notes. Selling these notes to banks is a common financing method.

In accounting for promissory notes, it is important to know how to calculate the maturity date, duration of note, interest and interest rate, and maturity value. The accounting entries for promissory notes receivable fall into four groups: recording receipt of a note, recording collection on a note, recording a dishonored note, and recording adjusting entries.

REVIEW OF CONCEPTS AND TERMINOLOGY

The following concepts and terms were introduced in this chapter:

LO4 **Accounts receivable:** Short-term financial assets that arise from sales on credit at the wholesale or retail level.

LO4 **Accounts receivable aging method:** A method of estimating uncollectible accounts based on the assumption that a predictable proportion of each dollar of accounts receivable outstanding will not be collected.

LO4 **Aging of accounts receivable:** The process of listing each customer's receivable account according to the due date of the account.

LO4 **Allowance for Uncollectible Accounts:** A contra-asset account that reduces accounts receivable to the amount expected to be collected in cash. Also called *Allowance for Doubtful Accounts* and *Allowance for Bad Debts.*

LO4 **Allowance method:** A method of accounting for uncollectible accounts by expensing estimated uncollectible accounts in the period in which the related sales take place.

LO3 **Available-for-sale securities:** Debt and equity securities that do not meet the criteria for either held-to-maturity or trading securities.

LO1 **Average days' sales uncollected:** A ratio that shows on average how long it takes to collect accounts receivable; 365 days divided by receivable turnover.

LO2 **Cash:** Coins and currency on hand, checks and money orders from customers, and deposits in bank checking and savings accounts.

LO2 **Cash equivalents:** Short-term investments that will revert to cash in 90 days or less from the time they are purchased.

LO2 **Compensating balance:** A minimum amount that a bank requires a company to keep in its bank account as part of a credit-granting arrangement.

LO1 **Contingent liability:** A potential liability that can develop into a real liability if a particular subsequent event occurs.

LO4 **Direct charge-off method:** A method of accounting for uncollectible accounts by directly debiting an expense account when bad debts are discovered instead of using the allowance method; this method violates the matching rule but is required for federal income tax computations.

LO1 **Discounting:** A method of selling notes receivable in which the bank deducts the interest from the maturity value of the note to determine the proceeds.

LO5 **Dishonored note:** A promissory note that the maker cannot or will not pay at the maturity date.

LO5 **Duration of note:** The length of time in days between a promissory note's issue date and its maturity date.

LO2 **Electronic funds transfer (EFT):** The transfer of funds from one bank to another through electronic communication.

LO1 **Factor:** An entity that buys accounts receivable.

LO1 **Factoring:** The selling or transferring of accounts receivable.

LO3 **Held-to-maturity securities:** Debt securities that management intends to hold to their maturity or payment date and whose cash value is not needed until that date.

LO4 **Installment accounts receivable:** Accounts receivable that are payable in a series of time payments.

LO5 **Interest:** The cost of borrowing money or the return for lending money, depending on whether one is the borrower or the lender.

LO3 **Marketable securities:** Short-term investments intended to be held only until needed to pay current obligations. Also called *short-term investments.*

LO5 **Maturity date:** The date on which a promissory note must be paid.

LO5 **Maturity value:** The total proceeds of a promissory note—principal plus interest—at the maturity date.

LO5 **Notes payable:** Collective term for promissory notes owed by the entity (maker) who promises payment to other entities.

LO5 **Notes receivable:** Collective term for promissory notes held by the entity to whom payment is promised (payee).

LO4 **Percentage of net sales method:** A method of estimating uncollectible accounts based on the assumption that a predictable proportion of each dollar of sales will not be collected.

LO5 **Promissory note:** An unconditional promise to pay a definite sum of money on demand or at a future date.

LO1 **Quick ratio:** A ratio for measuring the adequacy of short-term financial assets; short-term financial assets divided by current liabilities.

LO1 **Receivable turnover:** A ratio for measuring the average number of times receivables were turned into cash during an accounting period; net sales divided by average net accounts receivable.

LO1 **Securitization:** The grouping of receivables into batches for sale at a discount to companies and investors.

LO1 **Short-term financial assets:** Assets that arise from cash transactions, the investment of cash, and the extension of credit.

LO3 **Short-term investments:** Temporary investments of excess cash that are intended to be held only until they are needed to pay current obligations. Also called *marketable securities.*

LO4 **Trade credit:** Credit granted to customers by wholesalers or retailers.

LO3 **Trading securities:** Debt and equity securities bought and held principally for the purpose of being sold in the near term.

LO4 **Uncollectible accounts:** Accounts receivable owed by customers who cannot or will not pay. Also called *bad debts.*

REVIEW PROBLEM

Estimating Uncollectible Accounts, Receivables Analysis, and Notes Receivable Transactions

LO1 LO4 LO5 The Farm Implement Company sells merchandise on credit and also accepts notes for payment. During the year ended June 30, the company had net sales of $1,200,000. At the end of the year, it had Accounts Receivable of $400,000 and a debit balance in Allowance for Uncollectible Accounts of $2,100. In the past, approximately 1.5 percent of net sales has proved uncollectible. Also, an aging analysis of accounts receivable reveals that $17,000 in accounts receivable appears to be uncollectible.

The Farm Implement Company sold a tractor to R. C. Sims. Payment was received in the form of a 90-day, 9 percent, $15,000 note dated March 16. On June 14, Sims dishonored the note. On June 29, the company received payment in full from Sims plus additional interest from the date of the dishonored note.

REQUIRED ▶

1. Compute Uncollectible Accounts Expense and determine the ending balance of Allowance for Uncollectible Accounts and Accounts Receivable, Net under (a) the percentage of net sales method and (b) the accounts receivable aging method.
2. Compute the receivable turnover and average days' sales uncollected using the data from the accounts receivable aging method in **1** and assuming that the prior year's net accounts receivable were $353,000.
3. Prepare entries in journal form relating to the note received from R. C. Sims.

Answer to Review Problem

1. Uncollectible Accounts Expense computed and balances determined
   a. Percentage of net sales method:

   Uncollectible Accounts Expense = 1.5 percent × $1,200,000 = $18,000

   Allowance for Uncollectible Accounts = $18,000 − $2,100 = $15,900

   Accounts Receivable, Net = $400,000 − $15,900 = $384,100

   b. Accounts receivable aging method:

   Uncollectible Accounts Expense = $2,100 + $17,000 = $19,100

   Allowance for Uncollectible Accounts = $17,000

   Accounts Receivable, Net = $400,000 − $17,000 = $383,000

2. Receivable turnover and average days' sales uncollected computed

$$\text{Receivable Turnover} = \frac{\$1,200,000}{(\$383,000 + \$353,000) \div 2} = 3.3 \text{ times}$$

$$\text{Average Days' Sales Uncollected} = \frac{365 \text{ days}}{3.3} = 110.6 \text{ days}$$

3. Entries related to the note prepared

A = L + OE
+   +
	Mar. 16	Notes Receivable
		  Sales
		  Tractor sold to R. C. Sims;
		  terms of note: 90 days, 9 percent
			15,000.00	
				15,000.00

A = L + OE
+   +
−
	June 14	Accounts Receivable
		  Notes Receivable
		  Interest Income
		    The note was dishonored by R. C. Sims
		    Maturity value:
		    $15,000 + ($15,000 × 9/100
		    × 90/360) = $15,337.50
			15,337.50	
				15,000.00
				337.50

A = L + OE
+   +
−
	June 29	Cash
		  Accounts Receivable
		  Interest Income
		    Received payment in full from R. C. Sims
		    $15,337.50 + ($15,337.50 × 9/100 ×
		    15/360)
		    $15,337.50 + $57.52 = $15,395.02
			15,395.02	
				15,337.50
				57.52

Chapter Assignments

Building Your Knowledge Foundation

Questions

1. Why does a business need short-term financial assets? What three issues does management face in dealing with short-term financial assets?
2. What is a factor, and what do the terms *factoring with recourse* and *factoring without recourse* mean?
3. What items are included in the Cash account? What is a compensating balance?

4. How do cash equivalents differ from cash? From short-term investments?
5. What are the three kinds of securities held as short-term investments, and how are they valued at the balance sheet date?
6. What are unrealized gains and losses on trading securities? On what statement are they reported?
7. Which of the following items should be in accounts receivable? If an item does not belong in accounts receivable, tell where on the balance sheet it does belong: (a) installment accounts receivable from regular customers, due monthly for three years; (b) debit balances in customers' accounts; and (c) receivables from employees; (d) credit balances in customers' accounts; and (e) receivables from officers of the company.
8. Why does a company sell on credit if it expects that some of the accounts will not be paid? What role does a credit department play in selling on credit?
9. What accounting rule is violated by the direct charge-off method of recognizing uncollectible accounts? Why?
10. According to generally accepted accounting principles, at what point in the cycle of selling and collecting does a loss on an uncollectible account occur?
11. Do the following terms differ in any way: *allowance for bad debts, allowance for doubtful accounts, allowance for uncollectible accounts?*
12. What is the effect on net income of management's taking an optimistic versus a pessimistic view of estimated uncollectible accounts?
13. In what ways is Allowance for Uncollectible Accounts similar to Accumulated Depreciation? In what ways is it different?
14. What is the reasoning behind the percentage of net sales method and the accounts receivable aging method of estimating uncollectible accounts?
15. What is the procedure for estimating uncollectible accounts that also gives management a view of the status of collections and the overall quality of accounts receivable?
16. After adjusting and closing the accounts at the end of the year, suppose that Accounts Receivable is $176,000 and Allowance for Uncollectible Accounts is $14,500. (a) What is the collectible value of Accounts Receivable? (b) If the $450 account of a bankrupt customer is written off in the first month of the new year, what will be the resulting collectible value of Accounts Receivable?
17. Why should an account that has been written off as uncollectible be reinstated if the amount owed is subsequently collected?
18. What is a promissory note? Who is the maker? Who is the payee?
19. What are the maturity dates of the following notes: (a) a three-month note that is dated August 16, (b) a 90-day note that is dated August 16, and (c) a 60-day note that is dated March 25?

SHORT EXERCISES

LO1 Management Issues

SE 1. Indicate whether each of the following actions is related to (a) managing cash needs during seasonal cycles, (b) setting credit policies, or (c) financing receivables:

1. Selling accounts receivable to a factor
2. Borrowing funds for short-term needs during slow periods
3. Conducting thorough checks of new customers' ability to pay
4. Investing cash that is not currently needed for operations

LO1 Short-Term Liquidity Ratios

SE 2. Ravena Company has cash of $20,000, short-term investments of $25,000, net accounts receivable of $45,000, inventory of $44,000, accounts payable of $60,000, and net sales of $360,000. Last year's net accounts receivable were $35,000. Ravena has no current liabilities other than accounts payable.

Compute the following ratios: quick ratio, receivable turnover, and average days' sales uncollected.

SE 3. **LO2 Cash and Cash Equivalents** Compute the amount of cash and cash equivalents on Dalester Company's balance sheet if on the balance sheet date, it has currency and coins on hand of $500, deposits in checking accounts of $3,000, U.S. Treasury bills due in 80 days of $30,000, and U.S. Treasury bonds due in 200 days of $50,000.

SE 4. **LO3 Held-to-Maturity Securities** On May 31, Levinson Company invested $49,000 in U.S. Treasury bills. The bills mature in 120 days at $50,000. Prepare entries to record the purchase on May 31; the adjustment to accrue interest on June 30, which is the end of the fiscal year; and the receipt of cash at the maturity date of September 28.

SE 5. **LO3 Trading Securities** Hi Light Corporation began investing in trading securities in 20x1. At the end of 20x1, it had the following trading portfolio:

Security	Cost	Market Value
C-Thru Rulers (10,000 shares)	$220,000	$330,000
Magenta (5,000 shares)	100,000	75,000
Totals	$320,000	$405,000

Prepare the necessary year-end adjusting entry on December 31 and the entry for the sale of all the Magenta shares on the following March 23 for $95,000.

SE 6. **LO4 Percentage of Net Sales Method** At the end of October, Yao Company's management estimates the uncollectible accounts expense to be 1 percent of net sales of $2,770,000. Give the entry to record the uncollectible accounts expense, assuming that the Allowance for Uncollectible Accounts has a debit balance of $14,000.

SE 7. **LO4 Accounts Receivable Aging Method** An aging analysis on June 30 of the accounts receivable of Multiview Corporation indicates that uncollectible accounts amount to $43,000. Give the entry to record uncollectible accounts expense under each of the following independent assumptions: (a) Allowance for Uncollectible Accounts has a credit balance of $9,000 before adjustment, and (b) Allowance for Uncollectible Accounts has a debit balance of $7,000 before adjustment.

SE 8. **LO4 Write-off of Accounts Receivable** Platt Company, which uses the allowance method, has an account receivable from Patty Greer of $4,400 that it deems to be uncollectible. Prepare the entries on May 31 to write off the account and on August 13 to record an unexpected receipt of $1,000 from Greer. The company does not expect to collect more from Greer.

SE 9. **LO5 Notes Receivable Entries** On August 25, Morgan Company received a 90-day, 9 percent note in settlement of an account receivable in the amount of $10,000. Record the receipt of the note, the accrual of interest at the end of the fiscal year on September 30, and the collection of the note on the due date.

EXERCISES

E 1. **LO1 Management Issues** Indicate whether each of the following actions is primarily related to (a) managing cash needs during seasonal cycles, (b) setting credit policies, or (c) financing receivables:

1. Buying a U.S. Treasury bill with cash that is not needed for a few months
2. Comparing receivable turnovers for two years
3. Setting a policy that allows customers to buy on credit
4. Selling notes receivable to a financing company
5. Borrowing funds for short-term needs during the period of the year when sales are low
6. Changing the terms for credit sales in an effort to reduce the average days' sales uncollected
7. Using a factor to provide operating funds
8. Establishing a department whose responsibility is to approve customers' credit

E 2. **LO1 Short-Term Liquidity Ratios** Using the following data from the financial statements of Renard Company, compute the quick ratio, the receivable turnover, and the average days' sales uncollected:

Current assets	
Cash	$ 70,000
Short-term investments	170,000
Notes receivable	240,000
Accounts receivable, net	200,000
Inventory	500,000
Prepaid assets	50,000
Total current assets	$1,230,000
Current liabilities	
Notes payable	$ 300,000
Accounts payable	150,000
Accrued liabilities	20,000
Total current liabilities	$ 470,000
Net sales	$1,600,000
Last period's accounts receivable, net	$ 180,000

E 3. **LO2 Cash and Cash Equivalents**

At year end, Tarski Company had currency and coins in cash registers of $2,800, money orders from customers of $5,000, deposits in checking accounts of $32,000, U.S. Treasury bills due in 80 days of $90,000, certificates of deposits at the bank that mature in six months of $100,000, and U.S. Treasury bonds due in one year of $50,000. Calculate the amount of cash and cash equivalents that will be shown on the company's year-end balance sheet.

E 4. **LO3 Held-to-Maturity Securities**

Valera Company experiences heavy sales in the summer and early fall, after which time it has excess cash to invest until the next spring. On November 1, 20x1, the company invested $194,000 in U.S. Treasury bills. The bills mature in 180 days at $200,000. Prepare entries to record the purchase on November 1; the adjustment to accrue interest on December 31, which is the end of the fiscal year; and the receipt of cash at the maturity date of April 30.

E 5. **LO3 Trading Securities**

Bolton Corporation, which has begun investing in trading securities, engaged in the following transactions:

Jan. 6	Purchased 7,000 shares of General Mills stock, $30 per share.
Feb. 15	Purchased 9,000 shares of Delta, $22 per share.

At year end on June 30, General Mills was trading at $40 per share, and Delta was trading at $18 per share.

Record the entries for the purchases. Then record the necessary year-end adjusting entry. (Include a schedule of the trading portfolio cost and market in the explanation.) Also record the entry for the sale of all the Delta shares on August 20 for $16 per share. Is the last entry affected by the June 30 adjustment?

E 6. **LO4 Percentage of Net Sales Method**

At the end of the year, Simonic Enterprises estimates the uncollectible accounts expense to be .7 percent of net sales of $30,300,000. The current credit balance of Allowance for Uncollectible Accounts is $51,600. Prepare the entry in journal form to record the uncollectible accounts expense. What is the balance of Allowance for Uncollectible Accounts after this adjustment?

E 7. **LO4 Accounts Receivable Aging Method**

Accounts Receivable of Soo Company shows a debit balance of $52,000 at the end of the year. An aging analysis of the individual accounts indicates estimated uncollectible accounts to be $3,350.

Prepare the entry in journal form to record the uncollectible accounts expense under each of the following independent assumptions: (a) Allowance for Uncollectible Accounts has a credit balance of $400 before adjustment, and (b) Allowance for Uncollectible Accounts has a debit balance of $400 before adjustment. What is the balance of Allowance for Uncollectible Accounts after each of these adjustments?

E 8. **LO4 Aging Method and Net Sales Method Contrasted**

At the beginning of 20xx, the balances for Accounts Receivable and Allowance for Uncollectible Accounts were $430,000 and $31,400, respectively. During the year, credit sales were $3,200,000, and collections on account were $2,950,000. In addition, $35,000 in uncollectible accounts were written off.

Using T accounts, determine the year-end balances of Accounts Receivable and Allowance for Uncollectible Accounts. Then make the year-end adjusting entry to record the uncollectible accounts expense and show the year-end balance sheet presentation of Accounts Receivable and Allowance for Uncollectible Accounts under each of the following conditions:

a. Management estimates the percentage of uncollectible credit sales to be 1.2 percent of total credit sales.
b. Based on an aging of accounts receivable, management estimates the end-of-year uncollectible accounts receivable to be $38,700.

Post the results of each of the entries to the T account for Allowance for Uncollectible Accounts.

E 9. LO4 **Aging Method and Net Sales Method Contrasted**

During 20x1, Alpine Supply Company had net sales of $2,850,000. Most of the sales were on credit. At the end of 20x1, the balance of Accounts Receivable was $350,000, and Allowance for Uncollectible Accounts had a debit balance of $12,000. Alpine Supply Company's management uses two methods of estimating uncollectible accounts expense: (a) The percentage of uncollectible sales is 1.5 percent of net sales, and (b) based on an aging of accounts receivable, the end-of-year uncollectible accounts total $35,000. Make the end-of-year adjusting entry to record the uncollectible accounts expense under each method, and tell what the balance of Allowance for Uncollectible Accounts will be after each adjustment. Why are the results different? Which method is likely to be more reliable?

E 10. LO4 **Aging Method and Net Sales Method Contrasted**

The Georgia Parts Company sells merchandise on credit. During the fiscal year ended July 31, the company had net sales of $4,600,000. At the end of the year, it had Accounts Receivable of $1,200,000 and a debit balance in Allowance for Uncollectible Accounts of $6,800. In the past, approximately 1.4 percent of net sales has proved uncollectible. Also, an aging analysis of accounts receivable reveals that $60,000 of the receivables appear to be uncollectible. Prepare entries in journal form to record uncollectible accounts expense using (a) the percentage of net sales method and (b) the accounts receivable aging method.

What is the resulting balance of Allowance for Uncollectible Accounts under each method? How would your answers under each method change if Allowance for Uncollectible Accounts had a credit balance of $6,800 instead of a debit balance? Why do the methods result in different balances?

E 11. LO4 **Accounts Receivable Transactions**

Assuming that the allowance method is used, prepare entries in journal form to record the following transactions:

July 12, 20x4	Sold merchandise to Erin Lane for $1,800, terms n/10.
Oct. 18, 20x4	Received $600 from Erin Lane on account.
May 8, 20x5	Wrote off as uncollectible the balance of the Erin Lane account when she declared bankruptcy.
June 22, 20x5	Unexpectedly received a check for $200 from Erin Lane.

E 12. LO5 **Interest Computations**

Determine the interest on the following notes:

a. $22,800 at 10 percent for 90 days
b. $16,000 at 12 percent for 60 days
c. $18,000 at 9 percent for 30 days
d. $30,000 at 15 percent for 120 days
e. $10,800 at 6 percent for 60 days

E 13. LO5 **Notes Receivable Transactions**

Prepare entries in journal form to record the following transactions:

Jan. 16	Sold merchandise to Rounds Corporation on account for $36,000, terms n/30.
Feb. 15	Accepted a 90-day, 10 percent, $36,000 note from Rounds Corporation in lieu of payment of account.
May 16	Rounds Corporation dishonored the note.
June 15	Received payment in full from Rounds Corporation, including interest at 10 percent from the date the note was dishonored.

E 14. LO5 **Adjusting Entries: Interest Income**

Prepare entries in journal form (assuming reversing entries were not made) to record the following:

Dec. 1	Received a 90-day, 12 percent note for $10,000 from a customer for a sale of merchandise.
31	Made end-of-year adjustment for interest income.
Mar. 1	Received payment in full for note and interest.

E 15.
LO5 Notes Receivable Transactions

Prepare entries in journal form to record these transactions:

Jan. 5 Accepted a 60-day, 10 percent, $4,800 note dated this day in granting a time extension on the past-due account of K. Napoli.
Mar. 6 K. Napoli paid the maturity value of her $4,800 note.
9 Accepted a 60-day, 12 percent, $3,000 note dated this day in granting a time extension on the past-due account of S. Plechette.
May 8 When asked for payment, S. Plechette dishonored his note.
June 7 S. Plechette paid in full the maturity value of the note plus interest at 12 percent for the period since May 8.

PROBLEMS

P 1.
LO3 Held-to-Maturity and Trading Securities

Lahore Distributions follows a policy of investing excess cash until it is needed. During 20x1 and 20x2, the company engaged in the following transactions:

20x1
Feb. 1 Invested $97,000 in 120-day U.S. Treasury bills that had a maturity value of $100,000.
Mar. 30 Purchased 20,000 shares of Baser Company common stock at $16 per share and 12,000 shares of Jim's Fruit, Inc., common stock at $10 per share as trading securities.
June 1 Received maturity value of U.S. Treasury bills in cash.
10 Received dividends of $.50 per share from Baser Company and $.25 per share from Jim's Fruit, Inc.
30 Made year-end adjusting entry for trading securities. Market price of Baser Company shares is $13 per share and of Jim's Fruit, Inc., shares is $12 per share.
Dec. 3 Sold all the shares of Baser Company for $12 per share.

20x2
Mar. 17 Purchased 15,000 shares of CPS, Inc., for $9 per share.
May 31 Invested $116,000 in 120-day U.S. Treasury bills that had a maturity value of $120,000.
June 10 Received dividend of $.30 per share from Jim's Fruit, Inc.
30 Made year-end adjusting entry for held-to-maturity securities.
30 Made year-end adjusting entry for trading securities. Market price of Jim's Fruit, Inc., shares is $6 per share, and market price of CPS, Inc., shares is $11 per share.

REQUIRED ▶

1. Prepare entries in journal form to record these transactions, assuming that Lahore Distributions' fiscal year ends on June 30.
2. Show the balance sheet presentation of Lahore Distributions' short-term investments on June 30, 20x2.

P 2.
LO1 Methods of Estimating
LO4 Uncollectible Accounts and Receivables Analysis

Cavanaugh Company had an Accounts Receivable balance of $320,000 and a credit balance in Allowance for Uncollectible Accounts of $16,700 at January 1, 20xx. During the year, the company recorded the following transactions:

a. Sales on account, $1,052,000
b. Sales returns and allowances by credit customers, $53,400
c. Collections from customers, $993,000
d. Worthless accounts written off, $19,800

The company's past history indicates that 2.5 percent of its net credit sales will not be collected.

REQUIRED ▶

1. Prepare T accounts for Accounts Receivable and Allowance for Uncollectible Accounts. Enter the beginning balances, and show the effects on these accounts of the items listed above, summarizing the year's activity. Determine the ending balance of each account.
2. Compute Uncollectible Accounts Expense and determine the ending balance of Allowance for Uncollectible Accounts under (a) the percentage of net sales method and (b) the accounts receivable aging method, assuming an aging of the accounts receivable shows that $24,000 may be uncollectible.

3. Compute the receivable turnover and average days' sales uncollected, using the data from the accounts receivable aging method in **2.**
4. How do you explain that the two methods used in **2** result in different amounts for Uncollectible Accounts Expense? What rationale underlies each method?

P 3. **LO4 Accounts Receivable Aging Method**

Avioni Fashions Store uses the accounts receivable aging method to estimate uncollectible accounts. On February 1, 20x1, the balance of the Accounts Receivable account was a debit of $446,341, and the balance of Allowance for Uncollectible Accounts was a credit of $43,000. During the year, the store had sales on account of $3,724,000, sales returns and allowances of $63,000, worthless accounts written off of $44,300, and collections from customers of $3,214,000. As part of the end-of-year (January 31, 20x2) procedures, an aging analysis of accounts receivable is prepared. The totals of the analysis, which is partially complete, follow:

Customer Account	Total	Not Yet Due	1–30 Days Past Due	31–60 Days Past Due	61–90 Days Past Due	Over 90 Days Past Due
Balance Forward	$793,791	$438,933	$149,614	$106,400	$57,442	$41,402

To finish the analysis, the following accounts need to be classified:

Account	Amount	Due Date
B. Sunni	$10,977	Jan. 15
S. Hoffman	9,314	Feb. 15 (next fiscal year)
D. Ywahoo	8,664	Dec. 20
P. Blaine	780	Oct. 1
K. Matson	14,810	Jan. 4
J. Laberge	6,316	Nov. 15
A. Ming	4,389	Mar. 1 (next fiscal year)
	$55,250	

From past experience, the company has found that the following rates are realistic for estimating uncollectible accounts:

Time	Percentage Considered Uncollectible
Not yet due	2
1–30 days past due	5
31–60 days past due	15
61–90 days past due	25
Over 90 days past due	50

REQUIRED ▶

1. Complete the aging analysis of accounts receivable.
2. Compute the end-of-year balances (before adjustments) of Accounts Receivable and Allowance for Uncollectible Accounts.
3. Prepare an analysis computing the estimated uncollectible accounts.
4. Prepare the entry in journal form to record Avioni Fashion Store's estimated uncollectible accounts expense for the year (round the adjustment to the nearest whole dollar).

P 4. **LO5 Notes Receivable Transactions**

Northern Importing Company engaged in the following transactions involving promissory notes:

Jan.	14	Sold merchandise to Maguire Company for $37,000, terms n/30.
Feb.	13	Received $8,400 in cash from Maguire Company and received a 90-day, 8 percent promissory note for the balance of the account.
May	14	Received payment in full from Maguire Company.
	15	Received a 60-day, 12 percent note from Rocky Mount Company in payment of a past-due account, $12,000.
July	14	When asked to pay, Rocky Mount Company dishonored the note.
	20	Received a check from Rocky Mount Company for payment of the maturity value of the note and interest at 12 percent for the six days beyond maturity.
	25	Sold merchandise to Trisha Geehan Company for $36,000, with payment of $6,000 cash down and the remainder on account.

July 31 Received a 45-day, 10 percent, $30,000 promissory note from Trisha Geehan Company for the outstanding account receivable.
Sept. 14 When asked to pay, Trisha Geehan Company dishonored the note.
25 Wrote off the Trisha Geehan Company account as uncollectible following news that the company had declared bankruptcy.

REQUIRED ▶ Prepare entries in journal form to record the above transactions.

ALTERNATE PROBLEMS

P 5. **LO3 Held-to-Maturity and Trading Securities**

During certain periods, Wong Suu Company invests its excess cash until it is needed. During 20x1 and 20x2, the company engaged in the following transactions:

20x1

Jan. 16 Invested $146,000 in 120-day U.S. Treasury bills that had a maturity value of $150,000.
Apr. 15 Purchased 10,000 shares of Morris Tools common stock at $40 per share and 5,000 shares of D'Alleinne Gas common stock at $30 per share as trading securities.
May 16 Received maturity value of U.S. Treasury bills in cash.
June 2 Received dividends of $2.00 per share from Morris Tools and $1.50 per share from D'Alleinne Gas.
30 Made year-end adjusting entry for trading securities. Market price of Morris Tools shares is $32 per share and of D'Alleinne Gas shares is $35 per share.
Nov. 14 Sold all the shares of Morris Tools for $42 per share.

20x2

Feb. 15 Purchased 9,000 shares of BSC Communications for $50 per share.
Apr. 1 Invested $195,500 in 120-day U.S. Treasury bills that had a maturity value of $200,000.
June 1 Received dividend of $2.20 per share from D'Alleinne Gas.
30 Made year-end adjusting entry for held-to-maturity securities.
30 Made year-end adjusting entry for trading securities. Market price of D'Alleinne Gas shares is $33 per share and of BSC Communications shares is $60 per share.

REQUIRED ▶

1. Prepare entries in journal form to record the preceding transactions, assuming that Wong Suu Company's fiscal year ends on June 30.
2. Show the balance sheet presentation of short-term investments on June 30, 20x2.

P 6. **LO1 LO4 Methods of Estimating Uncollectible Accounts and Receivables Analysis**

On December 31 of last year, the balance sheet of Vince Company had Accounts Receivable of $298,000 and a credit balance in Allowance for Uncollectible Accounts of $20,300. During the current year, Vince Company's records included the following selected activities: (a) sales on account, $1,195,000; (b) sales returns and allowances, $73,000; (c) collections from customers, $1,150,000; and (d) accounts written off as worthless, $16,000. In the past, 1.6 percent of Vince Company's net sales has been uncollectible.

REQUIRED ▶

1. Prepare T accounts for Accounts Receivable and Allowance for Uncollectible Accounts. Enter the beginning balances, and show the effects on these accounts of the items listed above, summarizing the year's activity. Determine the ending balance of each account.
2. Compute Uncollectible Accounts Expense and determine the ending balance of Allowance for Uncollectible Accounts under (a) the percentage of net sales method and (b) the accounts receivable aging method, assuming an aging of the accounts receivable shows that $20,000 may be uncollectible.
3. Compute the receivable turnover and average days' sales uncollected, using the data from the accounts receivable aging method in **2**.
4. How do you explain that the two methods used in **2** result in different amounts for Uncollectible Accounts Expense? What rationale underlies each method?

P 7. **LO4 Accounts Receivable Aging Method**

Pinero Company uses the accounts receivable aging method to estimate uncollectible accounts. The Accounts Receivable account had a debit balance of $88,430 and

Allowance for Uncollectible Accounts had a credit balance of $7,200 at the beginning of the year. During the year, the company had sales on account of $473,000, sales returns and allowances of $4,200, worthless accounts written off of $7,900, and collections from customers of $450,730. At the end of the year (December 31), a junior accountant for the company was preparing an aging analysis of accounts receivable. At the top of page 6 of the report, the following totals appeared:

Customer Account	Total	Not Yet Due	1–30 Days Past Due	31–60 Days Past Due	61–90 Days Past Due	Over 90 Days Past Due
Balance Forward	$89,640	$49,030	$24,110	$9,210	$3,990	$3,300

The following accounts remained to be classified to finish the analysis:

Account	Amount	Due Date
A. Miele	$ 930	Jan. 14 (next year)
L. Dzud	620	Dec. 24
P. Chao	1,955	Sept. 28
W. North	2,100	Aug. 16
B. Ojito	375	Dec. 14
J. Taub	2,685	Jan. 23 (next year)
D. Frost	295	Nov. 5
	$8,960	

From past experience, the company has found that the following rates are realistic to estimate uncollectible accounts:

Time	Percentage Considered Uncollectible
Not yet due	2
1–30 days past due	4
31–60 days past due	20
61–90 days past due	30
Over 90 days past due	50

REQUIRED ▶

1. Complete the aging analysis of accounts receivable.
2. Determine the end-of-year balances (before adjustments) of Accounts Receivable and Allowance for Uncollectible Accounts.
3. Prepare an analysis computing the estimated uncollectible accounts.
4. Prepare the entry in journal form to record the estimated uncollectible accounts expense for the year (round the adjustment to the nearest whole dollar).

P 8.
LO5 Notes Receivable Transactions

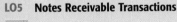

Carlotta Manufacturing Company sells engines. The company engaged in the following transactions involving promissory notes:

Jan.	10	Sold engines to Tilton Company for $60,000, terms n/10.
	20	Accepted a 90-day, 12 percent promissory note in settlement of the account from Tilton.
Apr.	20	Received payment from Tilton Company for the note and interest.
May	5	Sold engines to Marsden Company for $40,000, terms n/10.
	15	Received $8,000 cash and a 60-day, 13 percent note for $32,000 in settlement of the Marsden account.
July	14	When asked to pay, Marsden dishonored the note.
Aug.	2	Wrote off the Marsden account as uncollectible after receiving news that the company declared bankruptcy.
	5	Received a 90-day, 11 percent note for $30,000 from Carlson Company in settlement of an account receivable.
Nov.	3	When asked to pay, Carlson dishonored the note.
	9	Received payment in full from Carlson, including 15 percent interest for the six days since the note was dishonored.

REQUIRED ▶ Prepare entries in journal form to record the preceding transactions.

SKILLS DEVELOPMENT CASES

Conceptual Analysis

SD 1.

LO1 **Management of Cash**
LO2
LO3

Collegiate Publishing Company publishes college textbooks in the sciences and humanities. More than 50 percent of Collegiate Publishing's sales occur in July, August, and December. Its cash balances are largest in August, September, and January. During the rest of the year, its cash receipts are low. The company's treasurer keeps the cash in a bank checking account earning little or no interest and pays bills from this account as they come due. To survive periods when cash receipts are low, Collegiate Publishing Company sometimes borrows money, and it repays the loans in the months when cash receipts are largest.

A management consultant has suggested that Collegiate Publishing Company institute a new cash management plan under which cash would be invested in marketable securities as it is received and securities would be sold when the funds are needed. In this way, the company would earn income on the cash and might realize a gain through an increase in the value of the securities, thus reducing the need for borrowing. The president of the company has asked you to assess the plan. Write a memorandum to the president that lays out the accounting implications of the plan for cash and cash equivalents and for the three types of marketable securities. Include in your assessment any disadvantages the plan might have.

SD 2.

LO1 **Role of Credit Sales**
LO4

Mitsubishi Corp. <www.mitsubishi.com>, a broadly diversified Japanese corporation, instituted a credit plan called Three Diamonds for customers who buy its major electronic products, such as large-screen televisions and videotape recorders, from specified retail dealers.[12] Under the plan, approved customers who make purchases in July of one year do not have to make any payments until September of the next year and pay no interest during the intervening months. Mitsubishi pays the dealer the full amount less a small fee, sends the customer a Mitsubishi credit card, and collects from the customer at the specified time.

What was Mitsubishi's motivation for establishing such generous credit terms? What costs are involved? What are the accounting implications?

SD 3.

LO1 **Receivables Financing**

Goldstein Appliances, Inc., is a small manufacturer of washing machines and dryers located in central Michigan. Goldstein sells most of its appliances to large, established discount retail companies that market the appliances under their own names. Goldstein sells the appliances on trade credit terms of n/60. If a customer wants a longer term, however, Goldstein will accept a note with a term of up to nine months. At present, the company is having cash flow troubles and needs $5 million immediately. Its cash balance is $200,000, its accounts receivable balance is $2.3 million, and its notes receivable balance is $3.7 million.

How might Goldstein Appliance's management use its accounts receivable and notes receivable to raise the cash it needs? What are the company's prospects for raising the needed cash?

Group Activity: Assign to in-class groups and debrief.

Ethical Dilemma

SD 4.

LO1 **Ethics, Uncollectible Accounts,**
LO4 **and Short-Term Objectives**

Waddell Interiors, a successful retail furniture company, is located in an affluent suburb where a major insurance company has just announced a restructuring that will lay off 4,000 employees. Waddell Interiors sells quality furniture, usually on credit. Accounts Receivable are one of its major assets. Although the company's annual uncollectible accounts losses are not out of line, they represent a sizable amount. The company depends on bank loans for its financing. Sales and net income have declined in the past year, and some customers are falling behind in paying their accounts.

Henry Waddell, the owner of the business, knows that the bank's loan officer likes to see a steady performance. He has therefore instructed the company's controller to underestimate the uncollectible accounts this year to show a small growth in earnings. Waddell believes this action is justified because earnings in future years will average out the losses, and since the company has a history of success, he believes the adjustments are meaningless accounting measures anyway. Are Waddell's actions ethical? Would any parties be harmed by his actions? How important is it to try to be accurate in estimating losses from uncollectible accounts?

Group Activity: Assign in-class groups to debate the ethical issues of this case.

Research Activity

SD 5.
LO1 LO3 **Stock and Treasury Investments**

Locate the listing of New York Stock Exchange (NYSE) stocks in a recent issue of *The Wall Street Journal*. Find five companies whose names you recognize (such as IBM, McDonald's, or Ford). Write down the range of each company's stock price for the last year and the current closing price. Also note the dividend, if any, per share. How much did the market values of the common stocks you picked vary in the last year? Do these data demonstrate the need to value short-term investments of this type at market value? How does accounting for short-term investments in these common stocks differ from accounting for short-term investments in U.S. Treasury bills? How are dividends received on investments in these common stocks accounted for?

Be prepared to hand in your notes and to discuss the results of your investigation during class.

Decision-Making Practice

SD 6.
LO3 **Accounting for Short-Term Investments**

Jackson Christmas Tree Company's business—the growing and selling of Christmas trees—is seasonal. By January 1, after its heavy selling season, the company has cash on hand that will not be needed for several months. It has minimal expenses from January to October and heavy expenses during the harvest and shipping months of November and December. The company's management follows the practice of investing the idle cash in marketable securities, which can be sold as funds are needed for operations. The company's fiscal year ends on June 30.

On January 10 of the current year, Jackson has cash of $597,300 on hand. It keeps $20,000 on hand for operating expenses and invests the rest as follows:

$100,000 three-month Treasury bills	$ 97,800
1,000 shares of Ford Motor Co. ($50 per share)	50,000
2,500 shares of McDonald's ($50 per share)	125,000
2,100 shares of IBM ($145 per share)	304,500
Total short-term investments	$577,300

On February 10 and on May 10, Jackson receives quarterly cash dividends from each company in which it has invested: $.50 per share from Ford Motor Co., $.05 per share from McDonald's, and $.25 per share from IBM. The Treasury bills are redeemed at face value on April 10. On June 1, management sells 500 shares of McDonald's at $55 per share.

On June 30, the market values of the investments are as follows:

Ford Motor Co.	$ 61 per share
McDonald's	$ 46 per share
IBM	$140 per share

Jackson receives another quarterly dividend from each company on August 10. It sells all its remaining shares on November 1 at the following prices:

Ford Motor Co.	$ 55 per share
McDonald's	$ 44 per share
IBM	$160 per share

1. Record the investment transactions that occurred on January 10, February 10, April 10, May 10, and June 1. The Treasury bills are accounted for as held-to-maturity securities, and the stocks are trading securities. Prepare the required adjusting entry on June 30, and record the investment transactions on August 10 and November 1.
2. Explain how the short-term investments would be shown on the balance sheet on June 30.
3. After November 1, what is the balance of Allowance to Adjust Short-Term Investments to Market, and what will happen to this account next June?
4. What is your assessment of Jackson Christmas Tree Company's strategy with regard to idle cash?

Financial Reporting and Analysis Cases

Interpreting Financial Reports

FRA 1. LO1 LO4 **Role of Estimates in Accounting for Receivables**

CompuCredit <www.compucredit.com> is a credit card issuer in Atlanta. It prides itself on making credit cards available to almost anybody in a matter of seconds over the Internet. The cost to the consumer is an interest rate of 28 percent, about double that of companies that provide cards only to customers with good credit. CompuCredit has been successful. It has 1.9 million accounts and achieved an income of over $100 million in a recent year. To arrive at net income, the company estimates that 10 percent of its $1.3 billion in accounts receivable will not be paid; the industry average is 7 percent. Some analysts have been critical of CompuCredit for being too optimistic in its projections of losses.[13] Why are estimates necessary in accounting for receivables? If CompuCredit were to use the same estimate of losses as other companies in its industry, what would its net income have been for the year? How would one determine if CompuCredit's estimate of losses is reasonable?

FRA 2. LO4 **Accounting for Accounts Receivable**

Dodge Products Co. is a major consumer goods company that sells over 3,000 products in 135 countries. The company's annual report to the Securities and Exchange Commission presented the following data (in thousands) pertaining to net sales and accounts related to accounts receivable for 1999, 2000, and 2001.

	2001	2000	1999
Net sales	$4,910,000	$4,865,000	$4,888,000
Accounts receivable	523,000	524,000	504,000
Allowance for uncollectible accounts	18,600	21,200	24,500
Uncollectible accounts expense	15,000	16,700	15,800
Uncollectible accounts written off	19,300	20,100	17,700
Recoveries of accounts previously written off	1,700	100	1,000

1. Compute the ratio of Uncollectible Accounts Expense to Net Sales and to Accounts Receivable and the ratio of Allowance for Uncollectible Accounts to Accounts Receivable for 1999, 2000, and 2001.
2. Compute the receivable turnover and average days' sales uncollected for each year, assuming 1998 net accounts receivable were $465,000,000.
3. What is your interpretation of the ratios? Describe management's attitude toward the collectibility of accounts receivable over the three-year period.

International Company

FRA 3. LO1 **Comparison and Interpretation of Ratios**

Philips Electronics N.V. <www.philips.com> and Heineken N.V. <www.heinekencorp.nl> are two well-known Dutch companies. Philips is a large, diversified electronics, music, and media company, and Heineken makes a popular beer. Philips is about three and a half times bigger than Heineken. Its 2001 revenues were 32.3 billion euros, versus 9.1 billion euros for Heineken. Ratios can help in comparing and understanding companies. For example, the receivable turnovers for Philips and Heinken in 2000 and 2001 were as follows:[14]

	2001	2000
Philips	5.2 times	5.6 times
Heineken	7.7 times	7.9 times

What do the ratios tell you about the credit policies of the two companies? How long does it take each, on average, to collect a receivable? What do the ratios tell about the companies' relative needs for capital to finance receivables? Can you tell which company has a better credit policy? Explain your answers.

Toys "R" Us Annual Report

FRA 4. LO1 LO2 LO4 **Analysis of Short-Term Financial Assets**

Refer to the Toys "R" Us <www.tru.com> annual report in the Supplement to Chapter 6 to answer the following questions:

1. How much cash and cash equivalents did Toys "R" Us have on February 1,2003? Do you suppose most of that amount is cash in the bank or cash equivalents?

2. Toys "R" Us does not disclose an allowance for uncollectible accounts. How do you explain the lack of disclosure?
3. Compute the quick ratios for 2002 and 2001 and comment on them.
4. Compute receivable turnover and average days' sales uncollected for 2002 and 2001 and comment on Toys "R" Us credit policies. Accounts Receivable in 2000 were $225,000,000.

Comparison Case: Toys "R" Us and Walgreen Co.

FRA 5.
LO1 **Quick Ratio and Seasonality of Cash Flows**

Refer to the Toys "R" Us <www.tru.com> annual report and the financial statements of Walgreens <www.walgreens.com> in the Supplement to Chapter 6 to answer the following questions:

1. What is the quick ratio for both companies for the last two years? Comment on the results of your calculation. (If you were assigned **FRA 4**, use the calculation from that case for Toys "R" Us.)
2. Do you think the seasonal need for cash is different or the same for Toys "R" Us and Walgreens? Explain. Identify the place in the financial statements where the seasonality of sales is discussed.

Fingraph® Financial Analyst™

FRA 6.
LO1 **Comparison and Analysis of Short-Term Financial Assets**

Choose any two companies in the same industry from the list of Fingraph companies on the Needles Accounting Resource Center Web Site at http://accounting.college.hmco.com/students. The industry should be one in which accounts receivable is likely to be an important current asset—for example, manufacturing, consumer products, consumer food and beverage, or computers. Retail companies should be avoided because they usually have low accounts receivables. Access the Microsoft Excel spreadsheets for the companies you selected. Click on the URL at the top of each company's spreadsheet for a link to the company's web site and annual report.

1. In the summary of significant accounting policies or notes to the financial statements in the annual reports of the companies you have selected, find any reference to cash and cash equivalents, short-term (marketable) securities, and accounts receivable.
2. Using the Fingraph Financial Analyst CD-ROM software, display and print for the companies you have selected (a) the Current Assets and Current Liabilities Analysis page and (b) the Liquidity and Asset Utilization Analysis page in tabular and graphic form. Prepare a table that compares the quick ratio, receivable turnover, and average days' sales uncollected for both companies for two years.
3. Find and read the liquidity analysis section of management's discussion and analysis in each annual report.
4. Write a one-page executive summary that highlights the accounting policies for short-term financial assets and compares the short-term liquidity position of the two companies. Include your assessment of the companies' relative liquidity, and make reference to management's assessment. Include the Fingraph pages and your table with your report.

Internet Case

FRA 7.
LO4 **Comparison of J.C. Penney and Sears**

Access the annual reports of J.C. Penney, Inc. <www.jcpenney.com> and Sears, Roebuck and Co. <www.sears.com> directly, or go to the Needles Accounting Resource Center Web Site at http://accounting.college.hmco.com/students for a link to their web sites. Find the accounts receivable and marketable securities (if any) on each company's balance sheet and the notes related to these accounts in the notes to the financial statements. If either company has marketable securities, what is their cost and market value? Does the company currently have a gain or loss on the securities? Which company has the most accounts receivable as a percentage of total assets? What is the percentage of the allowance account to gross accounts receivable for each company? Which company experienced the highest loss rate on its receivables? Why do you think there is a difference? Do the companies finance their receivables? Be prepared to discuss your findings in class.

10

Chapter 10 presents the management issues associated with inventories, including the costing of inventories for financial reporting.

Inventories

Learning Objectives

LO1 Identify and explain the management issues associated with accounting for inventories.

LO2 Define *inventory cost* and relate it to goods flow and cost flow.

LO3 Calculate the pricing of inventory, using the cost basis under the periodic inventory system.

LO4 Apply the perpetual inventory system to the pricing of inventories at cost.

LO5 State the effects of inventory methods and misstatements of inventory on income determination, income taxes, and cash flows.

LO6 Apply the lower-of-cost-or-market (LCM) rule to inventory valuation.

Supplemental Objective

SO7 Estimate the cost of ending inventory using the retail method and gross profit method.

DECISION POINT

A USER'S FOCUS

J.C. Penney Company, Inc. <www.jcpenney.com> Managing inventory for profit is one of management's most complex and challenging tasks. In terms of dollars, the inventory of goods held for sale is one of the largest assets of a merchandising business. As may be seen in the financial highlights on the opposite page, J.C. Penney Company, Inc., a major retailer with department stores in all 50 states and Puerto Rico, devotes more than 27 percent, or \$4.9 billion, of its \$17.9 billion in assets to inventories. What challenges does J.C. Penney's management face in managing its inventory?

Not only must J.C. Penney's management purchase merchandise that customers will want to buy; it must also have the merchandise available in the right locations at the times when customers want to buy it. Management also must try to minimize the cost of inventory while maintaining quality. To these ends, J.C. Penney maintains purchasing offices in cities throughout the world, including Hong Kong, Taipei, Osaka, Seoul, Bangkok, Singapore, Bombay, and Florence. Further, because of the high cost of borrowing funds and storing inventory, management must control the amount of money tied up in inventory. Important accounting decisions include what assumptions to make about the flow of inventory costs, what prices to put on inventory, what inventory systems to use, and how to protect inventory against loss.

Proper management of inventory has helped J.C. Penney reduce its inventory (and total assets) and increase its level of retail sales. The company has

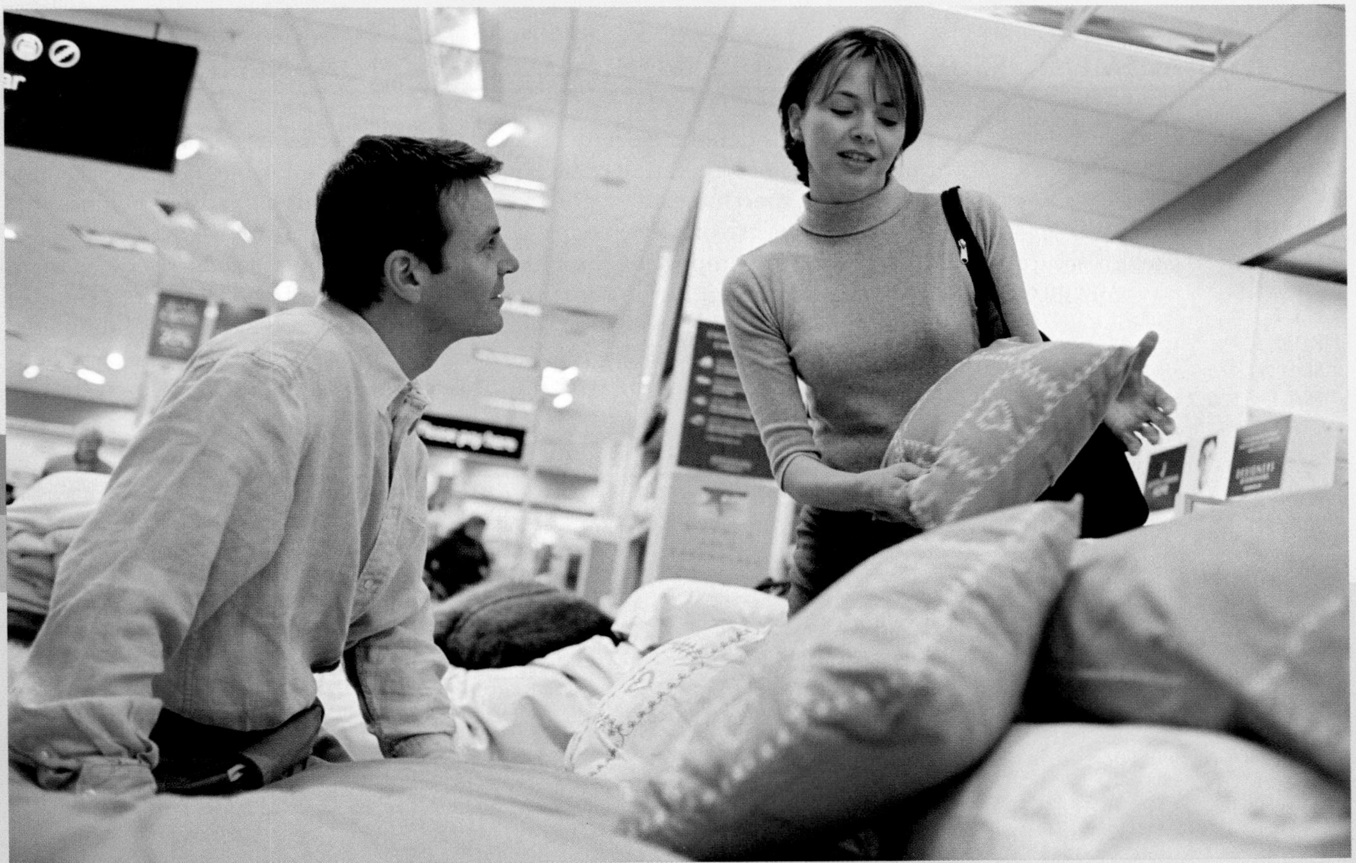

What challenges does J.C. Penney's management face in managing its inventory?

improved its income from operations from a negative $886 million in 2000 to a positive $584 million in 2002. The company plans to improve the profitability of its core department stores by further improving inventory management, controlling costs, and closing underperforming stores.[1]

Financial Highlights
(In millions)

	2002	2001	2000
Retail sales, net	$32,347	$32,004	$31,846
Cost of goods sold	22,573	22,789	23,031
(Loss)/income from operations	584	203	(886)
Merchandise inventories	4,945	4,930	5,269
Total assets	$17,867	$18,048	$19,742

Management Issues Associated with Accounting for Inventories

LO1 Identify and explain the management issues associated with accounting for inventories.

RELATED TEXT ASSIGNMENTS
Q: 1, 2, 3
SE: 1, 2
E: 1, 2
P: 1, 2, 6, 7
SD: 1, 4
FRA: 1, 4, 5, 6, 7

www.jcpenney.com
www.tru.com
www.itwinc.com

Inventory is considered a current asset because it is normally sold within a year or within a company's operating cycle. For a merchandising business like J.C. Penney or Toys "R" Us, **merchandise inventory** consists of all goods owned and held for sale in the regular course of business.

Inventories are important for manufacturing companies as well. Because manufacturers are engaged in the actual making of products, they have three kinds of inventory: raw materials to be used in the production of goods, partially completed products (often called *work in process*), and finished goods ready for sale. For example, in its annual report for the year 2002, Illinois Tool Works, Inc., disclosed the following inventories:[2]

Financial Highlights
(In thousands)

	2002	2001
Inventories		
Raw materials	$275,902	$287,067
Work in process	98,678	101,418
Finished goods	588,166	605,671
Total inventories	$962,746	$994,156

In manufacturing operations, the costs of the work in process and the finished goods inventories include not only the cost of the raw materials that go into the product, but also the cost of the labor used to convert the raw materials to finished goods and the overhead costs that support the production process. Included in this last category are such costs as indirect materials (e.g., paint, glue, and nails), indirect labor (such as the salaries of supervisors), factory rent, depreciation of plant assets, utilities costs, and insurance costs. The methods for maintaining and pricing inventory explained in this chapter are applicable to manufactured goods, but because the details of accounting for manufacturing companies are usually covered as a management accounting topic, this chapter focuses on accounting for merchandising firms.

Applying the Matching Rule to Inventories

The American Institute of Certified Public Accountants states, "A major objective of accounting for inventories is the proper determination of income through the process of matching appropriate costs against revenues."[3] Note that the objective is the proper determination of income through the matching of costs and revenues, not the determination of the most realistic inventory value. These two objectives are sometimes incompatible, in which case the objective of income determination takes precedence.

KEY POINT: Merchandise inventory affects both the income statement and the balance sheet.

The reason inventory accounting is so important to income measurement is linked to the way income is measured on the merchandising income statement. Recall that gross margin is computed as the difference between net sales and cost of goods sold and that cost of goods sold is dependent on the cost assigned to inventory or goods not sold. Because of those relationships, the higher the cost of ending inventory, the lower the cost of goods sold and the higher the resulting gross margin. Conversely, the lower the value assigned to ending inventory, the higher the cost of goods sold and the lower the gross margin. Because the amount of gross mar-

J.C. Penney Company, Inc.

<www.jcpenney.com>

OBJECTIVES

- To explain why merchandise inventories represent one of the most important assets of a retail company
- To understand the difference between goods flow and cost flow
- To identify and explain four methods of determining inventory cost
- To define and explain the lower-of-cost-or-market (LCM) rule

BACKGROUND FOR THE CASE

J.C. Penney Company, Inc., as profiled in the Decision Point in this chapter, is a major department store retailer. Merchandise inventories represent a substantial portion of the company's assets. J.C. Penney stores sell fashion at value prices. The company's target customers fall in the middle of the American population. They have a household income ranging from $30,000 to $80,000. The company's goal is "to be the customer's first choice for its products and services." The company faces intense competition not only from other department stores like Sears <www.sears.com> or Macy's <www.macys.com>, but also from discount stores like Target <www.target.com> and specialty stores like The Limited <www.limitedbrands.com>. To a great extent, J.C. Penney's future success depends on its ability to manage its inventory. Proper management of inventory has helped the company reduce its inventory (and total assets) and increase its level of retail sales, but the company still faces challenges. The company has announced plans to improve the profitability of its core department stores by further improving inventory management, controlling costs, and closing underperforming stores.

For more information about J.C. Penney Company, Inc., visit the company's web site through the Needles Accounting Resource Center Web Site at **http://accounting.college.hmco.com/students.**

REQUIRED

View the video on J.C. Penney Company, Inc., that accompanies this book. As you are watching the video, take notes related to the following questions:

1. Merchandise inventories make up more than 25 percent of J.C. Penney's assets. Explain how inventories affect the profitability of a retailer like J.C. Penney, and give both positive and negative reasons why the level of inventory is important to the company's operations.
2. Explain the difference between goods flow and cost flow as they relate to inventories, and tell which is more important in determining the cost of inventory.
3. Identify and explain the four methods of determining the cost of inventory available to J.C. Penney. Which method does J.C. Penney use?
4. What is the lower-of-cost-or-market (LCM) rule and why is it appropriate for J.C. Penney to use it? Why is LCM considered a conservative approach to inventory valuation?

gin has a direct effect on the amount of net income, the amount assigned to ending inventory directly affects the amount of net income. In effect, the value assigned to the ending inventory determines what portion of the cost of goods available for sale is assigned to cost of goods sold and what portion is assigned to the balance sheet as inventory to be carried over into the next accounting period.

ASSESSING THE IMPACT OF INVENTORY DECISIONS

Figure 1 summarizes the choices management has with regard to inventory systems and methods. The decisions usually result in different amounts of reported net income. Thus, the choices affect both the external evaluation of the company by investors and creditors and such internal evaluations as performance reviews, which determine bonuses and executive compensation. Because income is affected, the valuation of inventory may also have a considerable effect on the amount of income taxes paid. Federal income tax authorities have specific regulations about the acceptability of different methods. As a result, management is sometimes faced with balancing the goal of proper income determination with that of minimizing income taxes. Another consideration is that since the choice of inventory valuation method affects the amount of income taxes paid, it also affects a company's cash flows.

FIGURE 1
Management Choices in Accounting for Inventories

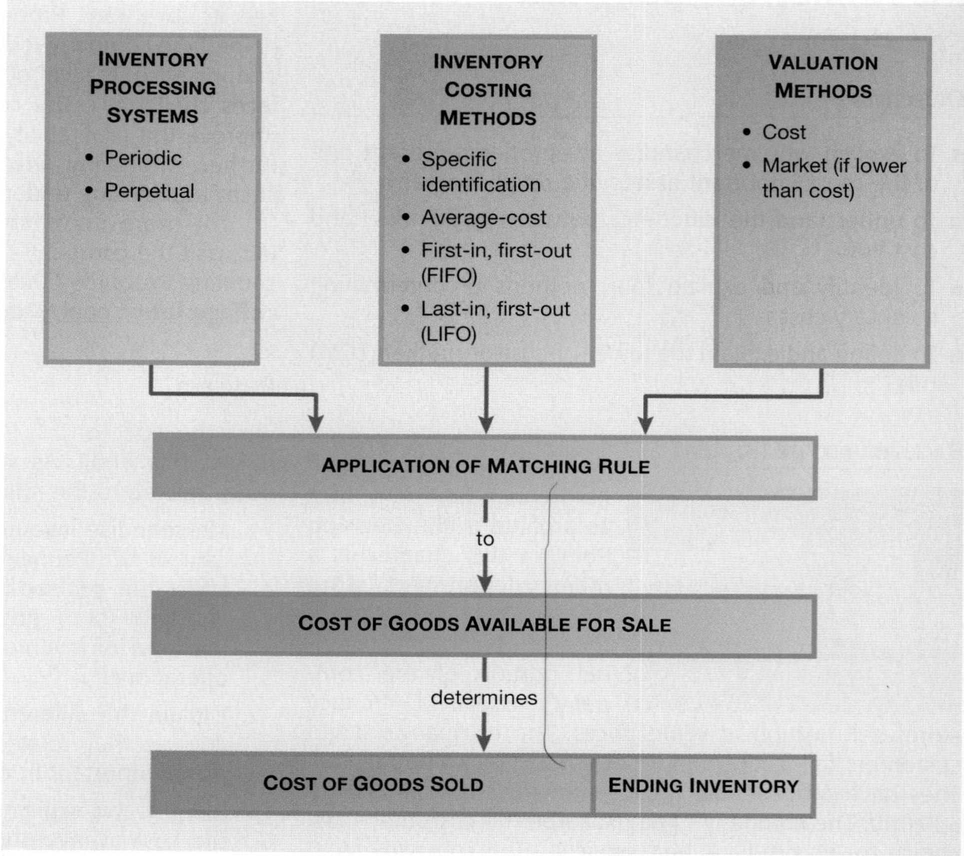

ENRICHMENT NOTE: Management considers the behavior of inventory prices over time when selecting inventory costing methods.

EVALUATING THE LEVEL OF INVENTORY

ENRICHMENT NOTE: Some of the costs associated with carrying inventory are insurance, property taxes, and storage costs. There is also the possibility of additional spoilage and employee theft.

The level of inventory has important economic consequences for a company. Ideally, a company should have a great variety and quantity on hand so that customers have a large choice and do not have to wait for an item to be restocked. Such an inventory policy is not costless, however. Handling and storage costs and the interest on the funds needed to maintain high inventory levels can be substantial. But low inventory levels may result in disgruntled customers and lost sales. Common measures for evaluating inventory levels are inventory turnover and its related measure, average days' inventory on hand. **Inventory turnover** is similar to receivable turnover. It indicates the number of times a company's average inventory is sold during an accounting period. It is computed by dividing cost of goods sold by average inventory. For example, J.C. Penny's cost of goods sold was

FOCUS ON BUSINESS TECHNOLOGY

Dell's Inventory Turnover Can Make Your Head Spin.

Dell Computer <www.dell.com> turns its inventory every six days. How can it do this when other companies have inventory on hand for 60, 100, or even more days? Technology and good inventory management are a big part of the answer.

Dell's speed from order to delivery sets the industry standard. Consider that a computer ordered by 9 A.M. can be delivered the next day by 9 P.M. How can Dell do this when it does not start ordering components and assembling computers until an order is placed? First, Dell's suppliers keep components warehoused just minutes from Dell's factories, making efficient, just-in-time operations possible. Another time and money saver is the handling of computer monitors. Monitors are no longer shipped first to Dell and then on to buyers. Dell sends an email message to a shipper, such as United Parcel Service <www.ups.com>, and the shipper picks up a monitor from a supplier and schedules it to arrive with the PC. In addition to contributing to a high inventory turnover, this practice saves Dell about $30 per monitor in freight costs. Dell is showing the world how to run a business in the cyber age by selling more than $1 million worth of computers a day on its web site.[4]

FIGURE 2
Inventory Turnover for Selected Industries

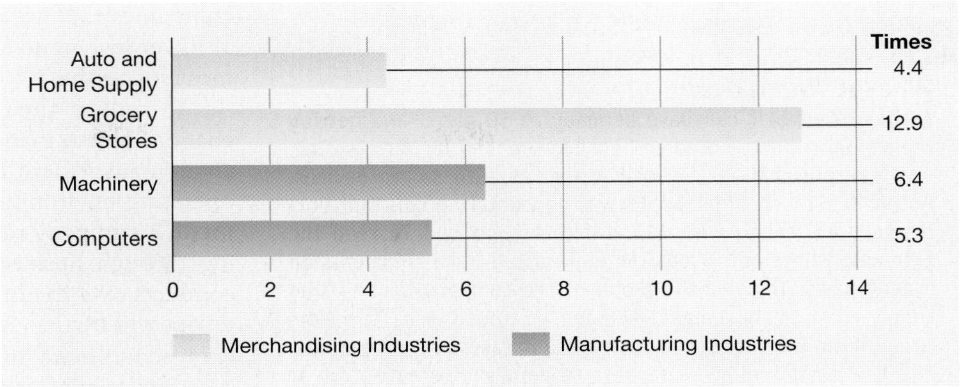

Source: Data from Dun & Bradstreet, *Industry Norms and Key Business Ratios,* 2001–2002.

ENRICHMENT NOTE:
Inventory turnover will be systematically higher if year-end inventory levels are low. For example, Toys "R" Us inventory levels on January 30 are at their lowest point of the year.

$22,573 million in 2002; its ending inventory was $4,945 million in 2002 and $4,930 million in 2001. Its inventory turnover is computed as follows:

$$\text{Inventory Turnover} = \frac{\text{Cost of Goods Sold}}{\text{Average Inventory}}$$

$$= \frac{\$22{,}573{,}000{,}000}{(\$4{,}945{,}000{,}000 + \$4{,}930{,}000{,}000) \div 2}$$

$$= \frac{\$22{,}573{,}000{,}000}{\$4{,}937{,}500{,}000} = 4.6 \text{ times}$$

The **average days' inventory on hand** indicates the average number of days required to sell the inventory on hand. It is found by dividing the number of days in a year by the inventory turnover, as follows:

$$\text{Average Days' Inventory on Hand} = \frac{\text{Number of Days in a Year}}{\text{Inventory Turnover}}$$

$$= \frac{365 \text{ days}}{4.6 \text{ times}} = 79.3 \text{ days}$$

STOP AND THINK!
Is it good or bad for a retail store to have a large inventory?
It depends. Obviously, a large inventory means customers have choices, and they are less likely to be disappointed because the items they want are out of stock. On the other hand, maintaining a large inventory is expensive, and if the items do not sell, they may have to be sold at a discount. The challenge to management is finding the right balance in the size of inventory. ■

J.C. Penney turned its inventory over 4.6 times in 2002, or, on average, every 79.3 days. These figures represent an improvement over the previous two years, and they are also reasonable because J.C. Penney is in a business in which fashions change every season, or about every 90 days. Management wants to sell all of each season's inventory within 80 to 90 days, even while purchasing inventory for the next season.

There are natural levels of inventory in every industry, as shown for selected merchandising and manufacturing industries in Figures 2 and 3. Nonetheless,

FIGURE 3
Average Days' Inventory on Hand for Selected Industries

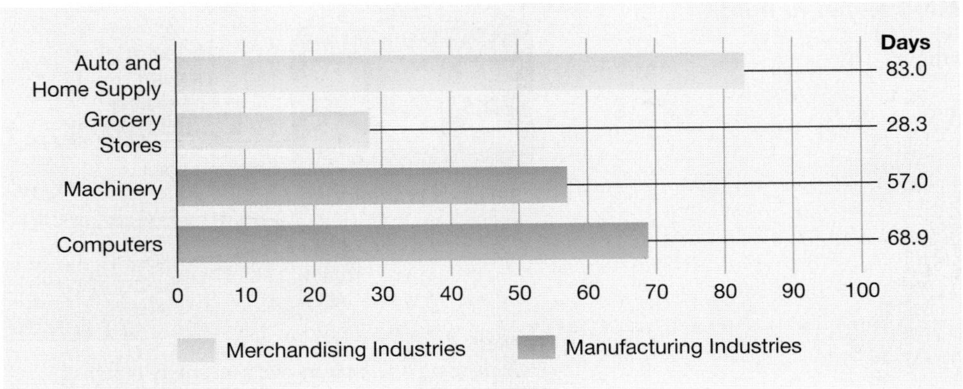

Source: Data from Dun & Bradstreet, *Industry Norms and Key Business Ratios,* 2001–2002.

Focus on Business Technology

What a Headache!

A single seat belt can have as many as 50 parts, and getting them from suppliers used to be a big problem for Autoliv, Inc. <www.autoliv.com>, a Swedish maker of auto safety devices. Autoliv's plant in Indianapolis was encountering constant bottlenecks in dealing with 125 different suppliers. To keep the production lines going required high-priced, rush shipments on a daily basis. To solve the problem, the company began using supply-chain management, keeping in touch with suppliers through the Internet rather than through faxes and phone calls. The new system allows suppliers to monitor the inventory at Autoliv and thus to anticipate problems. It also provides information on quantity and time of recent shipments, as well as continuously updated forecasts of parts that will be needed in the next 12 weeks. With the new system, Autoliv has reduced inventory by 75 percent and rush freight costs by 95 percent.[5]

companies that are able to maintain their inventories at lower levels and still satisfy customer needs are the most successful.

To reduce their levels of inventory, many merchandising and manufacturing companies use supply-chain management in conjunction with a just-in-time operating environment. With **supply-chain management**, a company manages its inventory and purchasing through business-to-business transactions that it conducts over the Internet. In a **just-in-time operating environment**, the company works closely with suppliers to coordinate and schedule shipments so that the shipments arrive just at the time they are needed. The benefits of using supply-chain management in a just-in-time operating environment are that the company has less money tied up in inventory, and the cost associated with carrying the inventory is reduced.

Check out ACE for a Review Quiz at http://accounting.college.hmco.com/students.

Inventory Cost and Goods Flow

LO2 Define *inventory cost* and relate it to goods flow and cost flow.

RELATED TEXT ASSIGNMENTS
Q: 4, 5, 6
SD: 5
FRA: 1

BUSINESS-WORLD EXAMPLE: When customers order merchandise from a catalogue company, they pay not only the price listed in the catalogue, but also such charges as shipping and insurance. Consequently, the cost is greater than the catalogue price.

According to the AICPA, "The primary basis of accounting for inventories is cost, which has been defined generally as the price paid or consideration given to acquire an asset."[6] This definition of **inventory cost** has generally been interpreted as including the following costs: invoice price less purchases discounts; freight in, including insurance in transit; and applicable taxes and tariffs. Other costs—for ordering, receiving, and storing—should in principle also be included in inventory cost, but in practice it is so difficult to allocate such costs to specific inventory items that they are instead usually considered expenses of the accounting period.

Merchandise in Transit

Because merchandise inventory includes all items owned by a company and held for sale, the status of any merchandise in transit, whether the company is selling it or buying it, must be examined to determine if the merchandise should be included in the inventory count. As Figure 4 illustrates, neither the seller nor the buyer has *phys-*

Figure 4
Merchandise in Transit

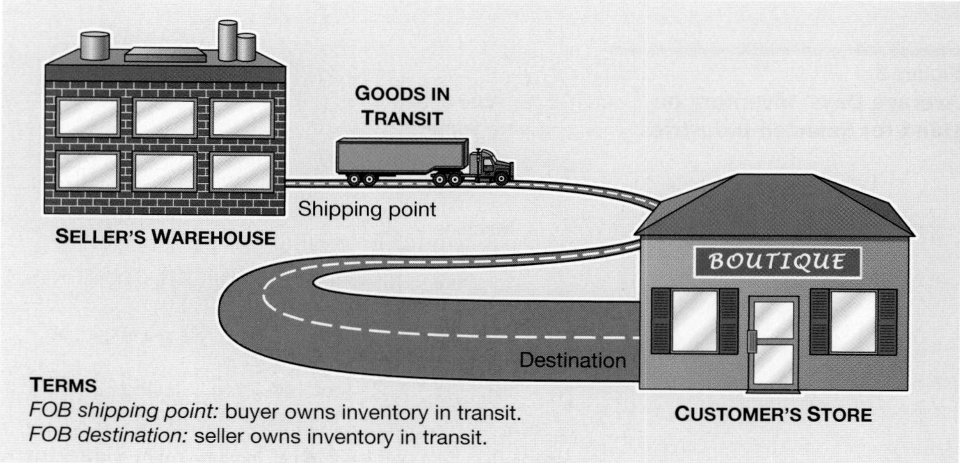

ical possession of merchandise in transit. Ownership of goods in transit is determined by the terms of the shipping agreement, which indicate when title passes. Outgoing goods shipped FOB (free on board) destination would be included in the seller's merchandise inventory, whereas those shipped FOB shipping point would not. Conversely, incoming goods shipped FOB shipping point would be included in the buyer's merchandise inventory, but those shipped FOB destination would not.

Merchandise on Hand Not Included in Inventory

KEY POINT: The consignor will count as inventory all merchandise placed (consigned) at other locations.

At the time a company takes a physical inventory, it may have merchandise on hand to which it does not hold title. One category of such goods is merchandise that has been sold and is awaiting delivery to the buyer. Since the sale has been completed, title to the goods has passed to the buyer, and the merchandise should be included in the inventory of the buyer, not of the seller. A second category is goods held on consignment. A **consignment** is merchandise that its owner (known as the *consignor*) places on the premises of another company (the *consignee*) with the understanding that payment is expected only when the merchandise is sold and that unsold items may be returned to the consignor. Title to consigned goods remains with the consignor until the consignee sells the goods. Consigned goods should not be included in the physical inventory of the consignee because they still belong to the consignor.

Goods Flow Versus Cost Flow

KEY POINT: The assumed flow of costs for inventory pricing does not have to correspond to the natural flow of goods.

The prices of most kinds of merchandise vary during the year. Identical lots of merchandise may have been purchased at different prices. Also, when identical items are bought and sold, it is often impossible to tell which have been sold and which are still in inventory. It is therefore necessary to make an assumption about the order in which items have been sold. Because the assumed order of sale may or may not be the same as the actual order of sale, the assumption is really about the *flow of costs* rather than the *flow of physical inventory.*

Stop and Think!
Which is more important from the standpoint of inventory costing: the flow of goods or the flow of costs?
Flow of costs is more important because inventory costing ignores the actual flow of goods and assumes a flow of costs. ■

The term **goods flow** refers to the actual physical movement of goods in the operations of a company, and the term **cost flow** refers to the association of costs with their *assumed* flow in the operations of a company. The assumed cost flow may or may not be the same as the actual goods flow. The possibility of a difference between cost flow and goods flow may seem strange at first, but it arises because several choices of assumed cost flow are available under generally accepted accounting principles. In fact, it is sometimes preferable to use an assumed cost flow that bears no relationship to goods flow because it gives a better estimate of income, which is the main goal of inventory valuation.

Check out ACE for a Review Quiz at http://accounting.college.hmco.com/students.

Methods of Pricing Inventory at Cost Under the Periodic Inventory System

LO3 Calculate the pricing of inventory, using the cost basis under the periodic inventory system.

RELATED TEXT ASSIGNMENTS
Q: 7, 8, 9
SE: 3, 4, 5, 6
E: 3, 4, 5, 7, 9
P: 1, 2, 6, 7
SD: 7

The value assigned to ending inventory is the result of two measurements: quantity and price. Quantity is determined by taking a physical inventory. The pricing of inventory is usually based on the assumed cost flow of the goods as they are bought and sold. Accountants usually price inventory by using one of the following generally accepted methods, each based on a different assumption of cost flow: (1) specific identification method; (2) average-cost method; (3) first-in, first-out (FIFO) method; and (4) last-in, first-out (LIFO) method. The choice of method depends on the nature of the business, the financial effects of the method, and the cost of implementing the method. To illustrate the four methods under the periodic inventory system, we use the following data for the month of June:

Inventory Data—June 30

June 1	Inventory	50 units @ $1.00	$ 50
6	Purchase	50 units @ $1.10	55
13	Purchase	150 units @ $1.20	180
20	Purchase	100 units @ $1.30	130
25	Purchase	150 units @ $1.40	210
Goods available for sale		500 units	$625
Sales		280 units	
On hand June 30		220 units	

Notice that a total of 500 units is available for sale at a total cost of $625. Stated simply, the problem of inventory pricing is to divide the $625 between the 280 units sold and the 220 units on hand. Recall that under the periodic inventory system, the inventory is not updated after each purchase and sale. Thus, it is not necessary to know when the individual sales take place.

SPECIFIC IDENTIFICATION METHOD

If the units in the ending inventory can be identified as coming from specific purchases, the **specific identification method** may be used. This method prices the inventory by identifying the cost of each item in ending inventory. For instance, if the June 30 inventory consisted of 50 units from the June 1 inventory, 100 units from the June 13 purchase, and 70 units from the June 25 purchase, the specific identification method would assign a cost of $268 to the inventory, as follows:

Periodic Inventory System—Specific Identification Method

50 units @ $1.00	$ 50	Cost of goods available for sale	$625
100 units @ $1.20	120		
70 units @ $1.40	98	→ Less June 30 inventory	268
220 units at a cost of	$268	Cost of goods sold	$357

BUSINESS-WORLD EXAMPLE: Even if it were possible to track each individual inventory item, a company would not do so because it would be excessively expensive to track which items were left in inventory. The cost would clearly exceed the benefit.

The specific identification method may appear logical, and it might be used in the purchase and sale of high-priced articles, such as automobiles and works of art, but it is not used by many companies because of two definite disadvantages. First, it is often difficult and impractical to keep track of the purchase and sale of individual items. Second, when a company deals in items that are identical but that it bought at different costs, deciding which items were sold becomes arbitrary; thus, the company can raise or lower income by choosing the lower- or higher-cost items.

AVERAGE-COST METHOD

BUSINESS-WORLD EXAMPLE: The physical flow of goods may sometimes seem to dictate a particular method, such as in a milk producer's operations in which the perishable nature of the product apparently requires a *physical flow* of FIFO. However, the milk producer's management can choose an inventory method based on an assumed *cost flow* that differs from FIFO, such as average-cost or LIFO.

Under the **average-cost method**, inventory is priced at the average cost of the goods available for sale during the period. Average cost is computed by dividing the total cost of goods available for sale by the total units available for sale. This gives an average unit cost that is applied to the units in ending inventory. In our illustration, the ending inventory would be $275, or $1.25 per unit, determined as follows:

Periodic Inventory System—Average-Cost Method

Cost of Goods Available for Sale ÷ Units Available for Sale = Average Unit Cost

$625 ÷ 500 units = $1.25

Ending inventory: 220 units @ $1.25 =	$275
Cost of goods available for sale	$625
Less June 30 inventory	275
Cost of goods sold	$350

The average-cost method tends to level out the effects of cost increases and decreases because the cost for the ending inventory calculated under this method is influenced by all the prices paid during the year and by the beginning inventory price. Some, however, criticize the average-cost method because they believe recent costs are more relevant for income measurement and decision making.

First-In, First-Out (FIFO) Method

The **first-in, first-out (FIFO) method** is based on the assumption that the costs of the first items acquired should be assigned to the first items sold. The costs of the goods on hand at the end of a period are assumed to be from the most recent purchases, and the costs assigned to goods that have been sold are assumed to be from beginning inventory and the earliest purchases. The FIFO method of determining inventory cost may be adopted by any business, regardless of the actual physical flow of goods, because the assumption is made regarding the flow of costs and not the flow of goods. In our illustration, the June 30 inventory would be $301 when the FIFO method is used. It is computed as follows:

Periodic Inventory System—First-In, First-Out Method

150 units @ $1.40 from purchase of June 25	$210
70 units @ $1.30 from purchase of June 20	91
220 units at a cost of	$301
Cost of goods available for sale	$625
Less June 30 inventory	301
Cost of goods sold	$324

ENRICHMENT NOTE: When you make a FIFO cost flow assumption, you use it even if you can prove that one of the first-purchased items is still in inventory. Let's say that for the first week of January, perfume was packaged in blue boxes, and then the company changed to red packaging. When you price inventory using the FIFO method, you assume the blue boxes (the older merchandise) were sold, even if you have some of them left in inventory.

The effect of the FIFO method is to value the ending inventory at the most recent costs and include earlier costs in cost of goods sold. During periods of consistently rising prices, the FIFO method yields the highest possible amount of net income because cost of goods sold will show the earliest costs incurred, which are lower during periods of inflation. Another reason for this result is that businesses tend to increase selling prices as costs rise, even when inventories were purchased before the price rise. The reverse effect occurs in periods of price decreases. Consequently, a major criticism of FIFO is that it magnifies the effects of the business cycle on income.

Last-In, First-Out (LIFO) Method

The **last-in, first-out (LIFO) method** of costing inventories is based on the assumption that the costs of the last items purchased should be assigned to the first items sold and that the cost of ending inventory reflects the cost of the goods purchased earliest. Under LIFO, the June 30 inventory would be $249,computed as follows:

Periodic Inventory System—Last-In, First-Out Method

50 units @ $1.00 from June 1 inventory	$ 50
50 units @ $1.10 from purchase of June 6	55
120 units @ $1.20 from purchase of June 13	144
220 units at a cost of	$249
Cost of goods available for sale	$625
Less June 30 inventory	249
Cost of goods sold	$376

BUSINESS-WORLD EXAMPLE: Physical flow under LIFO can be likened to the changes in a gravel pile. As gravel on top is sold, more is purchased and added on top. The gravel on the bottom may never be sold. Despite the physical flow of LIFO, any acceptable cost flow assumption may be made.

The effect of LIFO is to value inventory at the earliest prices and to include in cost of goods sold the cost of the most recently purchased goods. This assumption, of course, does not agree with the actual physical movement of goods in most businesses.

FIGURE 5
Impact of Cost Flow Assumptions on the Income Statement and Balance Sheet Using the Periodic Inventory System

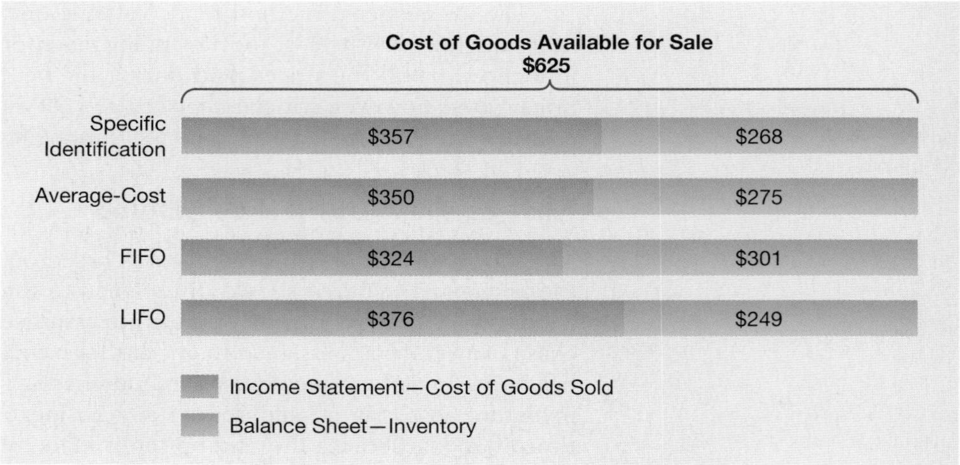

There is, however, a strong logical argument to support LIFO, based on the fact that a certain size of inventory is necessary in a going concern. When inventory is sold, it must be replaced with more goods. The supporters of LIFO reason that the fairest determination of income occurs if the current costs of merchandise are matched against current sales prices, regardless of which physical units of merchandise are sold. When prices are moving either upward or downward, the cost of goods sold will, under LIFO, show costs closer to the price level at the time the goods were sold. As a result, the LIFO method tends to show a smaller net income during inflationary times and a larger net income during deflationary times than other methods of inventory valuation. The peaks and valleys of the business cycle tend to be smoothed out. In inventory valuation, the flow of costs—and hence income determination—is more important than the physical movement of goods and balance sheet valuation.

An argument may also be made against LIFO. Because the inventory valuation on the balance sheet reflects earlier prices, it often gives an unrealistic picture of the current value of the inventory. Such balance sheet measures as working capital and current ratio may be distorted and must be interpreted carefully.

STOP AND THINK!
Under what condition would all four methods of inventory pricing produce exactly the same results?
They would produce the same results if there were no price changes after the purchase of beginning inventory. ■

Figure 5 summarizes the impact of the four inventory cost allocation methods on the cost of goods sold as reported on the income statement and on inventory as reported on the balance sheet when a company uses the periodic inventory system. In periods of rising prices, the FIFO method yields the highest inventory valuation, the lowest cost of goods sold, and hence a higher net income; the LIFO method yields the lowest inventory valuation, the highest cost of goods sold, and thus a lower net income.

Check out ACE for a Review Quiz at http://accounting.college.hmco.com/students.

FOCUS ON BUSINESS PRACTICE

What's a "Category Killer?"

A new type of retail company called the "category killer" seems to ignore the tenets of good inventory management. The category killers include Home Depot <www.homedepot.com>, Barnes & Noble <www.bn.com>, Wal-Mart <www.walmart.com>, Toys "R" Us <www.tru.com>, and Blockbuster Entertainment Corporation <www.blockbuster.com>. These retailers maintain huge inventories of the goods in which they specialize and sell them at such low prices that smaller competitors find it hard to compete. Although the category killers have large amounts of money tied up in inventories, they maintain very sophisticated just-in-time operating environments that require suppliers to meet demanding standards for delivery of products and reduction of inventory costs. Some suppliers are required to stock the shelves and keep track of inventory levels. By minimizing handling and overhead costs and buying at favorably low prices, the category killers achieve great success.

PRICING INVENTORY UNDER THE PERPETUAL INVENTORY SYSTEM

LO4 Apply the perpetual inventory system to the pricing of inventories at cost.

RELATED TEXT ASSIGNMENTS
Q: 10
SE: 7, 8, 9
E: 6, 7
P: 3, 8
SD: 5

The pricing of inventories under the perpetual inventory system differs from pricing under the periodic inventory system. The difference occurs because under the perpetual inventory system, a continuous record of quantities and costs of merchandise is maintained as purchases and sales are made. Under the periodic inventory system, only the ending inventory is counted and priced, and cost of goods sold is determined by deducting the cost of the ending inventory from the cost of goods available for sale. Under the perpetual inventory system, cost of goods sold is accumulated as sales are made and costs are transferred from the Inventory account to the Cost of Goods Sold account. The cost of the ending inventory is the balance of the Inventory account. To illustrate pricing methods under the perpetual inventory system, we use the same data as in the last section, but we add specific sales dates and amounts, as follows:

Inventory Data—June 30

June	1	Inventory	50 units @ $1.00
	6	Purchase	50 units @ $1.10
	10	Sale	70 units
	13	Purchase	150 units @ $1.20
	20	Purchase	100 units @ $1.30
	25	Purchase	150 units @ $1.40
	30	Sale	210 units
	30	Inventory	220 units

Pricing the inventory and cost of goods sold using the specific identification method is the same under the perpetual system as under the periodic system because cost of goods sold and ending inventory are based on the cost of the identified items sold and on hand. The perpetual system facilitates the use of the specific identification method because detailed records of purchases and sales are maintained.

Pricing the inventory and cost of goods sold using the average-cost method differs when the perpetual system is used. Under the periodic system, the average cost is computed for all goods available for sale during the month. Under the perpetual system, an average is computed after each purchase or series of purchases, as follows:

ENRICHMENT NOTE: An automated perpetual system has considerable costs. They include the costs of automating the system, maintaining the system, and taking a physical inventory to check against the perpetual records.

Perpetual Inventory System—Average-Cost Method

June	1	Inventory	50 units @ $1.00	$ 50.00
	6	Purchase	50 units @ $1.10	55.00
	6	Balance	100 units @ $1.05	$105.00
	10	Sale	70 units @ $1.05	(73.50)
	10	Balance	30 units @ $1.05	$ 31.50
	13	Purchase	150 units @ $1.20	180.00
	20	Purchase	100 units @ $1.30	130.00
	25	Purchase	150 units @ $1.40	210.00
	25	Balance	430 units @ $1.28*	$551.50
	30	Sale	210 units @ $1.28	(268.80)
	30	Inventory	220 units @ $1.29*	$282.70
Cost of goods sold			($73.50 + $268.80)	$342.30

*Rounded.

STOP AND THINK!
Under the perpetual inventory system, why is the cost of goods sold not determined by deducting the ending inventory from goods available for sale, as it is under the periodic method?

Under the perpetual inventory system, the cost of goods sold and the inventory balance are determined after every transaction. ■

The sum of the costs applied to sales becomes the cost of goods sold, $342.30. The ending inventory is the balance, or $282.70.

When pricing the inventory using the FIFO and LIFO methods, it is necessary to keep track of the components of inventory at each step of the way because as sales are made, the costs must be assigned in the proper order. To apply the FIFO method, the approach is as follows:

Perpetual Inventory System—FIFO Method

June 1	Inventory	50 units @ $1.00		$ 50.00
6	Purchase	50 units @ $1.10		55.00
10	Sale	50 units @ $1.00	($ 50.00)	
		20 units @ $1.10	(22.00)	(72.00)
10	Balance	30 units @ $1.10		$ 33.00
13	Purchase	150 units @ $1.20		180.00
20	Purchase	100 units @ $1.30		130.00
25	Purchase	150 units @ $1.40		210.00
30	Sale	30 units @ $1.10	($ 33.00)	
		150 units @ $1.20	(180.00)	
		30 units @ $1.30	(39.00)	(252.00)
30	Inventory	70 units @ $1.30	$ 91.00	
		150 units @ $1.40	210.00	$301.00
Cost of goods sold		($72.00 + $252.00)		$324.00

Note that the ending inventory of $301 and the cost of goods sold of $324 are the same as the figures computed earlier under the periodic inventory system. This will always occur because the ending inventory under both systems consists of the last items purchased—in this case, the entire purchase of June 25 and 70 units from the purchase of June 20.

To apply the LIFO method, the approach is as follows:

Perpetual Inventory System—LIFO Method

June 1	Inventory	50 units @ $1.00		$ 50.00
6	Purchase	50 units @ $1.10		55.00
10	Sale	50 units @ $1.10	($ 55.00)	
		20 units @ $1.00	(20.00)	(75.00)
10	Balance	30 units @ $1.00		$ 30.00
13	Purchase	150 units @ $1.20		180.00
20	Purchase	100 units @ $1.30		130.00
25	Purchase	150 units @ $1.40		210.00
30	Sale	150 units @ $1.40	($210.00)	
		60 units @ $1.30	(78.00)	(288.00)
30	Inventory	30 units @ $1.00	$ 30.00	
		150 units @ $1.20	180.00	
		40 units @ $1.30	52.00	$262.00
Cost of goods sold		($75.00 + $288.00)		$363.00

Note that the ending inventory of $262 includes 30 units from the beginning inventory, all units from the June 13 purchase, and 40 units from the June 20 purchase.

A comparison of the average-cost, FIFO, and LIFO methods using the perpetual inventory system is shown in Figure 6. The results are the same as under the periodic inventory system, but some amounts have changed. For example, LIFO has

Focus on Business Technology

More Companies Enjoy LIFO!

Using the LIFO method under the perpetual inventory system is a tedious process, especially if done manually. The development of faster and less expensive computer systems has made it easier for many companies to switch to LIFO and still use the perpetual inventory system. The availability of better technology may partially account for the increasing use of LIFO in the United States and may enable more companies to enjoy LIFO's economic benefits.

FIGURE 6
Impact of Cost Flow Assumptions on the Income Statement and Balance Sheet Using the Perpetual Inventory System

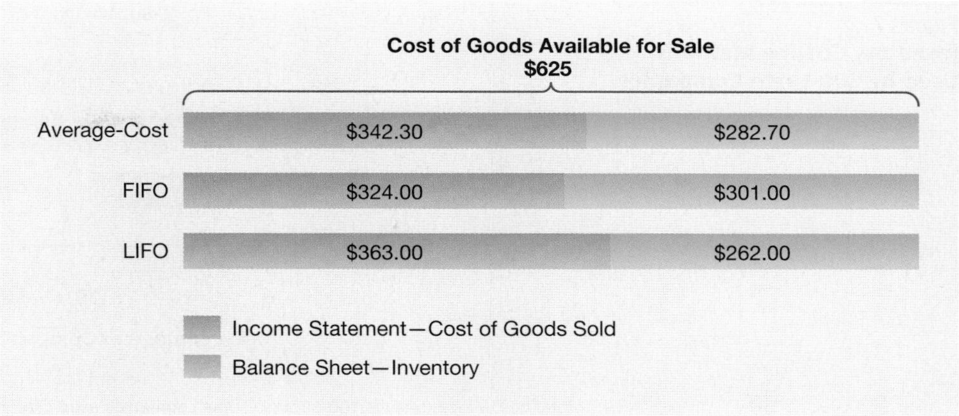

the lowest inventory valuation regardless of the inventory system used, but the amount is $262 using the perpetual system versus $249 using the periodic system.

Check out ACE for a Review Quiz at http://accounting.college.hmco.com/students.

COMPARISON AND IMPACT OF INVENTORY DECISIONS AND MISSTATEMENTS

LO5 State the effects of inventory methods and misstatements of inventory on income determination, income taxes, and cash flows.

RELATED TEXT ASSIGNMENTS
Q: 11, 12, 13, 14
SE: 10
E: 8, 9, 10
SD: 2, 4, 6, 7
FRA: 1, 2, 3, 4, 5, 8

Exhibit 1 shows how the specific identification, average-cost, FIFO, and LIFO methods of pricing inventory under both the periodic and the perpetual inventory systems affect gross margin. The exhibit uses the same data as before and assumes June sales of $500. Because the specific identification method is based on actual cost, it is the same under both systems.

Keeping in mind that June was a period of rising prices, we can see that LIFO, which charges the most recent, and, in this case, the highest, prices to cost of goods sold, resulted in the lowest gross margin under both systems. Conversely, FIFO, which charges the earliest, and, in this case, the lowest, prices to cost of goods sold,

EXHIBIT 1
Effects of Inventory Systems and Costing Methods on Gross Margin

		Periodic Inventory System			Perpetual Inventory System*		
	Specific Identification Method	Average-Cost Method	First-In, First-Out Method	Last-In, First-Out Method	Average-Cost Method	First-In, First-Out Method	Last-In, First-Out Method
Sales	$500	$500	$500	$500	$500	$500	$500
Cost of goods sold							
Beginning inventory	$ 50	$ 50	$ 50	$ 50			
Purchases	575	575	575	575			
Cost of goods available for sale	$625	$625	$625	$625			
Less ending inventory	268	275	301	249	$283†	$301	$262
Cost of goods sold	$357	$350	$324	$376	$342†	$324	$363
Gross margin	$143	$150	$176	$124	$158	$176	$137

*Ending inventory under the perpetual inventory system is provided for comparison only. It is not used in the computation of cost of goods sold.
†Rounded.

FIGURE 7
Inventory Costing Methods Used by 600 Large Companies

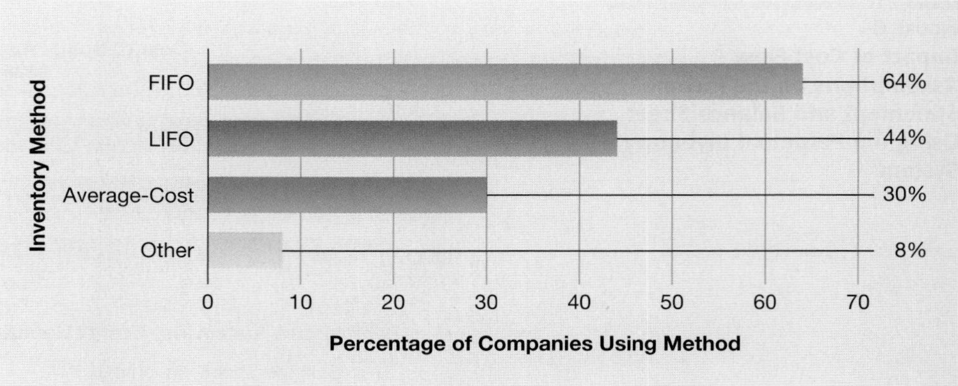

Total percentage exceeds 100 because some companies used different methods for different types of inventory.
Source: "Inventory Costing Methods Used by 600 Large Companies." Reprinted with permission from *Accounting Trends and Techniques.* Copyright © 2002 by the American Institute of Certified Public Accountants, Inc.

produced the highest gross margin. The gross margin under the average-cost method is in between the gross margins under LIFO and FIFO; thus, this method clearly has a less pronounced effect. Note that ending inventory and gross margin under FIFO are the same under both the periodic and the perpetual inventory systems.

During a period of declining prices, the reverse would occur. The LIFO method would produce a higher gross margin than the FIFO method. It is apparent that the method of inventory valuation has the greatest importance during prolonged periods of price changes in one direction, either up or down.

Because the specific identification method depends on the particular items sold, no generalization can be made about the effect of changing prices.

EFFECTS ON THE FINANCIAL STATEMENTS

KEY POINT: The assumption of inventory cost flows is necessary because of changes in merchandise prices.

Each of the four methods of inventory pricing is acceptable for use in published financial statements. The FIFO, LIFO, and average-cost methods are widely used, as can be seen in Figure 7, which shows the inventory costing methods used by 600 large companies. Each method has its advantages and disadvantages, and none can be considered best or perfect. The factors that should be considered in choosing an inventory method are the trend of prices and the effects of each method on financial statements, income taxes, and cash flows.

A basic problem in determining the best inventory measure for a particular company is that inventory affects both the balance sheet and the income statement. As we have seen, the LIFO method is best suited for the income statement because it matches revenues and cost of goods sold. But it is not the best measure of the current balance sheet value of inventory, particularly during a prolonged period of price increases or decreases. FIFO, on the other hand, is best suited to the balance sheet because the ending inventory is closest to current values and thus gives a more realistic view of the current financial assets of a business. Readers of financial statements must be alert to inventory methods and be able to assess their effects.

EFFECTS ON INCOME TAXES

The Internal Revenue Service has developed several rules for valuing inventories for federal income tax purposes. A company has a wide choice of methods, including specific identification, average-cost, FIFO, and LIFO, as well as lower-of-cost-or-market, discussed later in the chapter. But once a method has been chosen, it must be used consistently from one year to the next. The IRS must approve any change in the inventory valuation method for income tax purposes.* This requirement

*A single exception to this rule is that although taxpayers must notify the IRS of a change to LIFO from another method, they do not need to have advance IRS approval.

Focus on Business Practice

Does a Company's Accounting Method Affect Management's Operating Decisions?

It certainly does when taxes are involved! Research has shown that among firms that use the LIFO inventory method, those with high tax rates are more likely to buy extra inventory at year end than are those with low tax rates.[7] This behavior is predictable because LIFO deducts the most recent purchases, which are likely to have higher costs than earlier purchases, in determining taxable income. This action will result in lower income taxes.

KEY POINT: In periods of rising prices, LIFO results in lower net income and thus lower taxes.

agrees with the consistency convention, since changes in inventory method may cause income to fluctuate too much and would make income statements hard to interpret from year to year. A company may change its inventory method if there is a good reason for doing so. The nature and effect of the change must be shown on the company's financial statements.

Many accountants believe that using the FIFO and average-cost methods in periods of rising prices causes businesses to report more than their true profit, resulting in the payment of excess income taxes. The profit is overstated because cost of goods sold is understated relative to current prices. The company must buy replacement inventory at higher prices, but additional funds are also needed to pay income taxes. During the rapid inflation of 1979 to 1982, billions of dollars reported as profits and paid in income taxes were believed to be the result of poor matching of current costs and revenues under the FIFO and average-cost methods. Consequently, many companies, believing that prices would continue to rise, switched to the LIFO inventory method.

If a company uses the LIFO method in reporting income for tax purposes, the IRS requires that the same method be used in the accounting records. Also, the IRS will not allow the use of the lower-of-cost-or-market rule if LIFO is used to determine inventory cost. In such a case, only the LIFO cost can be used. This rule, however, does not preclude a company from using lower-of-LIFO-cost-or-market for financial reporting purposes (discussed later in this chapter).

Over a period of rising prices, a business that uses the LIFO method may find that for balance sheet purposes, its inventory is valued at a cost figure far below what it currently pays for the same items. Management must monitor this situation carefully, because if it should let the inventory quantity at year end fall below the beginning-of-the-year level, the company will find itself paying higher income taxes. Higher income before taxes results because the company expenses historical costs of inventory, which are below current costs. When this occurs, it is called a **LIFO liquidation** because sales have reduced inventories below the levels set in prior years; that is, units sold exceed units purchased for the period.

A LIFO liquidation may be prevented by making enough purchases prior to year end to restore the desired inventory level. Sometimes a LIFO liquidation cannot be avoided because products are discontinued or supplies are interrupted, as in the case of a strike. In a recent year, 27 out of 600 large companies reported a LIFO liquidation in which net income was increased because of the matching of older historical cost with present sales dollars.[8]

Effects of Misstatements in Inventory Measurement

The basic problem of separating goods available for sale into two components—goods sold and goods not sold—is that of assigning a cost to the goods not sold, the ending inventory. The portion of the goods available for sale not assigned to the ending inventory is used to determine the cost of goods sold.

Because the figures for ending inventory and cost of goods sold are related, a misstatement in the inventory figure at the end of the period will cause an equal misstatement in gross margin and income before income taxes on the income statement. The amount of assets and owner's equity on the balance sheet will also be misstated by the same amount. The consequences of overstatement and understatement of inventory are illustrated in the three simplified examples that follow. In each case, beginning inventory, net cost of purchases, and cost of goods available for sale have been stated correctly. In the first example, ending inventory has been stated correctly. In the second example, ending inventory is overstated by $6,000; in the third example, ending inventory is understated by $6,000.

Example 1. Ending Inventory Correctly Stated at $10,000

Cost of Goods Sold for the Year		Income Statement for the Year	
Beginning inventory	$12,000	Net sales	$100,000
Net cost of purchases	58,000	→ Cost of goods sold	60,000
Cost of goods available for sale	$70,000	Gross margin	$ 40,000
Ending inventory	10,000	Operating expenses	32,000
Cost of goods sold	$60,000 ←	Income before income taxes	$ 8,000

Example 2. Ending Inventory Overstated by $6,000

Cost of Goods Sold for the Year		Income Statement for the Year	
Beginning inventory	$12,000	Net sales	$100,000
Net cost of purchases	58,000	→ Cost of goods sold	54,000
Cost of goods available for sale	$70,000	Gross margin	$ 46,000
Ending inventory	16,000	Operating expenses	32,000
Cost of goods sold	$54,000 ←	Income before income taxes	$ 14,000

KEY POINT: A misstatement in inventory affects not only the current year, but also has the opposite effect on the next year.

Example 3. Ending Inventory Understated by $6,000

Cost of Goods Sold for the Year		Income Statement for the Year	
Beginning inventory	$12,000	Net sales	$100,000
Net cost of purchases	58,000	→ Cost of goods sold	66,000
Cost of goods available for sale	$70,000	Gross margin	$ 34,000
Ending inventory	4,000	Operating expenses	32,000
Cost of goods sold	$66,000 ←	Income before income taxes	$ 2,000

In all three examples, the total cost of goods available for sale was $70,000. The difference in income before income taxes resulted from how this $70,000 was divided between ending inventory and cost of goods sold.

KEY POINT: Inventory errors will correct (counterbalance) themselves over a two-year period.

Because the ending inventory in one period becomes the beginning inventory in the following period, it is important to recognize that a misstatement in inventory valuation affects not only the current period but also the following period. Over a two-year period, the errors in income before income taxes will offset, or counterbalance, each other. If we assume that Example 2 represents year 1, for instance, the overstatement of ending inventory in year 1 will cause a $6,000 overstatement of beginning inventory in year 2, resulting in an understatement of income by $6,000 in the second year.

Focus on Business Ethics

The Temptation to Overstate Inventories

Net income can be easily manipulated when accounting for inventory. For example, it is easy to overstate or understate inventory by including end-of-the-year purchase and sales transactions in the wrong fiscal year or by simply misstating inventory. In one spectacular case, Rite Aid Corp. <www.riteaid.com>, the large drugstore chain, falsified income by manipulating its computerized inventory system to cover losses from shrinkage, which includes shoplifting, employee theft, and spoilage. In another case, bookkeepers at RentWay, Inc. <www.rentway.com>, a company that rents furniture to apartment dwellers, boosted income artificially over several years by overstating inventory in small increments that were not noticed by top management.[9]

STOP AND THINK!
Why is misstatement of inventory one of the most common means of financial statement fraud?

For one thing, the value put on inventory has a direct dollar-for-dollar effect on net income. For another, it is relatively easy to falsify the value placed on the ending inventory and to cover up the falsification. ■

Because the total income before income taxes for the two years is the same, it may appear that one need not worry about inventory misstatements. However, the misstatements violate the matching rule. In addition, management, creditors, and investors make many decisions on an annual basis and depend on the accountant's determination of net income. The accountant has an obligation to make the net income figure for each year as useful as possible.

The effects of misstatements in inventory on income before income taxes are as follows:

Year 1	Year 2
Ending inventory overstated	**Beginning inventory overstated**
Cost of goods sold understated	Cost of goods sold overstated
Income before income taxes overstated	Income before income taxes understated
Ending inventory understated	**Beginning inventory understated**
Cost of goods sold overstated	Cost of goods sold understated
Income before income taxes understated	Income before income taxes overstated

A misstatement in inventory results in a misstatement in income before income taxes of the same amount. Thus, the measurement of inventory is important.

INVENTORY MEASUREMENT AND CASH FLOWS

www.internationalpaper.com

A company's inventory methods affect not only its reported profitability but also its reported liquidity and cash flows. In the case of a large company like International Paper Co., these effects can be complex and material. In a note on inventories, International Paper provides more detail about these effects:

> The last-in, first-out inventory method is used to value most of International Paper's U.S. inventories. Approximately 68% of total raw materials and finished products inventories were valued using this method. If the first-in, first-out method had been used, it would have increased total inventory balances by approximately $264 million and $250 million at December 31, 2000 and 1999, respectively.[10]

K/R

By using LIFO, the company usually reports a lower income before taxes. This will have a favorable effect on cash flows because of the lower amount of income taxes to be paid. The reader of the financial statements may determine what International Paper's inventory value would have been if it were valued at current prices under FIFO rather than older prices under LIFO. Thus, a more realistic comparison of the company's liquidity ratios can be made. For example, the more realistic FIFO figure would show a better short-term liquidity position as measured by the current ratio than the LIFO figures reported on the balance sheet would seem to indicate. However, the company's inventory turnover and average days' inventory on hand will be adversely affected if the more realistic FIFO figures are used.

Check out ACE for a Review Quiz at http://accounting.college.hmco.com/students.

VALUING INVENTORY AT THE LOWER OF COST OR MARKET (LCM)

LO6 Apply the lower-of-cost-or-market (LCM) rule to inventory valuation.

RELATED TEXT ASSIGNMENTS
Q: 15, 16
SE: 11
E: 11
SD: 3
FRA: 5

Although cost is usually the most appropriate basis for valuation of inventory, there are times when inventory may properly be shown in the financial statements at less than its cost. If the market value of inventory falls below its cost because of physical deterioration, obsolescence, or decline in price level, a loss has occurred. This loss may be recognized by writing the inventory down to **market**, or current replacement cost, of inventory. For a merchandising company, market is the amount that the company would pay at the present time for the same goods, purchased from the usual suppliers and in the usual quantities. The **lower-of-cost-or-market (LCM) rule**

FOCUS ON BUSINESS PRACTICE

How Bad Can It Get?

Pretty bad! When the lower-of-cost-or-market rule comes into play, it can be an indicator of how bad. For example, when the market for Internet and telecommunications equipment soured in 2001, Cisco Systems, Inc. <www.cisco.com>, found itself faced with probably the largest inventory loss in history. It had to write down to zero almost two-thirds of its $2.5 billion inventory, 80 percent of which consisted of raw materials that would never be made into final product. In another case, through poor management, a downturn in the economy, and underperforming stores, Kmart <www.kmartcorp.com> found itself with a huge amount of excess merchandise, including more than 5,000 truckloads of goods stored in parking lots, which it could not sell except at drastically reduced prices. The company had to mark down its inventory by $1 billion in order to sell it, resulting in a loss for the year.[12]

requires that when the replacement cost of inventory falls below historical cost, based on one of the conventional inventory costing methods, the inventory is written down to the lower value and a loss is recorded. This rule is an example of the application of the convention of conservatism because the loss is recognized before an actual transaction takes place. Under historical cost accounting, the inventory remains at cost until it is sold. It may help in applying the LCM rule to think of it as the "lower-of-cost-or-replacement-cost" rule.* Approximately 90 percent of 600 large companies report applying the LCM rule to their inventories.[11]

There are two basic methods of valuing inventories at the lower of cost or market accepted both by GAAP and the IRS for federal income tax purposes: (1) the item-by-item method and (2) the major category method. For example, a stereo shop could determine lower of cost or market for each kind of speaker, receiver, and turntable (item by item) or for all speakers, all receivers, and all turntables (major categories).

STOP AND THINK!
Given that the LCM rule is an application of the conservatism convention in the current accounting period, is the effect of this application also conservative in the next period?
It probably is not because a reduction in inventory in the current period resulting in lower net income will cause the beginning inventory in the next period to be smaller and will thus increase net income in that period. ■

STUDY NOTE: Cost must first be determined by the specific identification, FIFO, LIFO, or average-cost method before it can be compared with replacement cost.

ITEM-BY-ITEM METHOD

When the **item-by-item method** is used, cost and market values are compared for each item in inventory. Each individual item is then valued at its lower price, as shown in Table 1:

TABLE 1. Lower of Cost or Market with Item-by-Item Method

		Per Unit		
	Quantity	Cost	Market	Lower of Cost or Market
Category I				
Item a	200	$1.50	$1.70	$ 300
Item b	100	2.00	1.80	180
Item c	100	2.50	2.60	250
Category II				
Item d	300	5.00	4.50	1,350
Item e	200	4.00	4.10	800
Inventory at the lower of cost or market				$2,880

MAJOR CATEGORY METHOD

Under the **major category method**, the total cost and total market values for each category of items are compared. Each category is then valued at its lower amount, as shown in Table 2:

*In some cases, the *realizable value* of the inventory determines the *market value*—the amount for which the goods can be sold—rather than by the amount for which the goods can be replaced. The circumstances in which realizable value determines market value are encountered in practice only occasionally, and the valuation procedures are technical enough to be addressed in a more advanced accounting course.

TABLE 2. Lower of Cost or Market with Major Category Method

		Per Unit		Total		
	Quantity	Cost	Market	Cost	Market	Lower of Cost or Market
Category I						
Item a	200	$1.50	$1.70	$ 300	$ 340	
Item b	100	2.00	1.80	200	180	
Item c	100	2.50	2.60	250	260	
Totals				$ 750	$ 780	$ 750
Category II						
Item d	300	5.00	4.50	$1,500	$1,350	
Item e	200	4.00	4.10	800	820	
Totals				$2,300	$2,170	2,170
Inventory at the lower of cost or market						$2,920

Check out ACE for a Review Quiz at http://accounting.college.hmco.com/students.

VALUING INVENTORY BY ESTIMATION

SO7 Estimate the cost of ending inventory using the retail method and gross profit method.

RELATED TEXT ASSIGNMENTS
Q: 17, 18, 19
E: 12, 13
P: 4, 5
FRA: 5

It is sometimes necessary or desirable to estimate the value of ending inventory. The retail method and gross profit method are most commonly used for this purpose.

RETAIL METHOD OF INVENTORY ESTIMATION

The **retail method**, as its name implies, is used in retail merchandising businesses to estimate the cost of ending inventory by using the ratio of cost to retail price. There are two principal reasons for its use. First, since preparing financial statements each month requires a knowledge of the cost of inventory, the retail method can be used to estimate the cost without the time or expense of determining the cost of items in the inventory. Second, because items in a retail store normally have a price tag or a universal product code, it is common practice to take the physical inventory at retail from these price tags or codes and to reduce the total value to cost through use of the retail method. The term *at retail* means the amount of the inventory at the marked selling prices of the inventory items.

KEY POINT: When estimating inventory by the retail method, the inventory need not be counted.

When the retail method is used to estimate ending inventory, the records must show the beginning inventory at cost and at retail. The records must also show the amount of goods purchased during the period both at cost and at retail. The net sales at retail is, of course, the balance of the Sales account less returns and allowances. A simple example of the retail method is shown in Table 3.

Goods available for sale is determined both at cost and at retail by listing beginning inventory and net purchases for the period at cost and at their expected selling price, adding freight to the cost column, and totaling. The ratio of these two amounts (cost to retail price) provides an estimate of the cost of each dollar of retail sales value. The estimated ending inventory at retail is then determined by deducting sales for the period from the retail price of the goods that were available for sale during the period. The inventory at retail is then converted to cost on the basis of the ratio of cost to retail.

The cost of ending inventory may also be estimated by applying the ratio of cost to retail price to the total retail value of the physical count of the ending inventory.

TABLE 3. Retail Method of Inventory Estimation

	Cost	Retail
Beginning inventory	$ 40,000	$ 55,000
Net purchases for the period (excluding freight in)	107,000	145,000
Freight in	3,000	
Merchandise available for sale	$150,000	$200,000
Ratio of cost to retail price: $\frac{\$150,000}{\$200,000} = 75\%$		
Net sales during the period		160,000
Estimated ending inventory at retail		$ 40,000
Ratio of cost to retail	75%	
Estimated cost of ending inventory	$ 30,000	

STUDY NOTE: Freight in is not placed under the Retail column when using the retail method of inventory estimation because businesses automatically price their goods high enough to cover freight charges.

Applying the retail method in practice is often more difficult than this simple example because of such complications as changes in retail price during the year, different markups on different types of merchandise, and varying volumes of sales for different types of merchandise.

GROSS PROFIT METHOD OF INVENTORY ESTIMATION

The **gross profit method** (also known as the *gross margin method*) assumes that the ratio of gross margin for a business remains relatively stable from year to year. The gross profit method is used in place of the retail method when records of the retail prices of beginning inventory and purchases are not kept. It is considered acceptable for estimating the cost of inventory for interim reports, but it is not acceptable for valuing inventory in the annual financial statements. It is also useful in estimating the amount of inventory lost or destroyed by theft, fire, or other hazards. Insurance companies often use this method to verify loss claims.

As Table 4 shows, the gross profit method is simple to use. First, figure the cost of goods available for sale in the usual way (add purchases to beginning inventory). Second, estimate the cost of goods sold by deducting the estimated gross margin of 30 percent from sales. Finally, deduct the estimated cost of goods sold from the goods available for sale to arrive at the estimated cost of ending inventory.

BUSINESS-WORLD EXAMPLE: It is highly desirable to maintain financial records off site. If records were destroyed, it would be difficult, if not impossible, to reconstruct the data necessary for an insurance claim.

TABLE 4. Gross Profit Method of Inventory Estimation

1. Beginning inventory at cost		$ 50,000
Purchases at cost (including freight in)		290,000
Cost of goods available for sale		$340,000
2. Less estimated cost of goods sold		
Sales at selling price	$400,000	
Less estimated gross margin (30% × 400,000)	120,000	
Estimated cost of goods sold		280,000
3. Estimated cost of ending inventory		$ 60,000

Check out ACE for a Review Quiz at http://accounting.college.hmco.com/students.

Chapter Review

Review of Learning Objectives

LO1 Identify and explain the management issues associated with accounting for inventories.

Included in inventory are goods owned, whether produced or purchased, that are held for sale in the normal course of business. Manufacturing companies also include raw materials and work in process. Among the issues management must face in accounting for inventories are allocating the cost of inventories in accordance with the matching rule, assessing the impact of inventory decisions, and evaluating the level of inventory. The objective of accounting for inventories is the proper determination of income through the matching of costs and revenues, not the determination of the most realistic inventory value. Because the valuation of inventory has a direct effect on a company's net income, the choice of inventory systems and methods affects not only the amount of income taxes and cash flows, but also the external and internal evaluation of the company. The level of inventory as measured by the inventory turnover and its related measure, average days' inventory on hand, is important to managing the amount of investment a company needs.

LO2 Define *inventory cost* and relate it to goods flow and cost flow.

The cost of inventory includes (1) invoice price less purchases discounts; (2) freight in, including insurance in transit; and (3) applicable taxes and tariffs. Goods flow refers to the actual physical flow of merchandise, whereas cost flow refers to the assumed flow of costs in the operations of the business.

LO3 Calculate the pricing of inventory, using the cost basis under the periodic inventory system.

The value assigned to ending inventory is the result of two measurements: quantity and price. Quantity is determined by taking a physical inventory. The pricing of inventory is usually based on the assumed cost flow of the goods as they are bought and sold. One of four assumptions is usually made regarding cost flow. These assumptions are represented by four inventory methods. Inventory pricing can be determined by the specific identification method, which associates the actual cost with each item of inventory, but this method is rarely used. The average-cost method assumes that the cost of inventory is the average cost of goods available for sale during the period. The first-in, first-out (FIFO) method assumes that the costs of the first items acquired should be assigned to the first items sold. The last-in, first-out (LIFO) method assumes that the costs of the last items acquired should be assigned to the first items sold. The inventory method chosen may or may not be equivalent to the actual physical flow of goods.

LO4 Apply the perpetual inventory system to the pricing of inventories at cost.

The pricing of inventories under the perpetual and periodic inventory systems differs because under the perpetual system a continuous record of quantities and costs of merchandise is maintained as purchases and sales are made. Cost of goods sold is accumulated as sales are made and costs are transferred from the Inventory account to the Cost of Goods Sold account. The cost of the ending inventory is the balance of the Inventory account. The specific identification method and the FIFO method produce the same results under the perpetual and periodic inventory systems. The results differ for the average-cost method because an average is calculated after each purchase rather than at the end of the accounting period, and for the LIFO method because the cost components of inventory change constantly as goods are bought and sold.

LO5 State the effects of inventory methods and misstatements of inventory on income determination, income taxes, and cash flows.

During periods of rising prices, the LIFO method will show the lowest net income; FIFO, the highest; and average-cost, in between. The opposite effects occur in periods of falling prices. No generalization can be made regarding the specific identification method. The Internal Revenue Service requires that if LIFO is used for tax purposes, it must also be used for financial statements; it also does not allow the lower-of-cost-or-market rule to be applied to the LIFO method. If the value of ending inventory is understated or overstated, a corresponding error—dollar for dollar—will be made in income before income taxes. Furthermore, because the ending inventory of one period is the beginning inventory of the next, the misstatement affects two accounting periods, although the effects are opposite.

LO6 Apply the lower-of-cost-or-market (LCM) rule to inventory valuation.

The lower-of-cost-or-market rule can be applied to the above methods of determining inventory at cost. This rule states that if the replacement cost (market) of the inventory is lower than the inventory cost, the lower figure should be used. Valuation can be determined on an item-by-item or major category basis.

Supplemental Objective

SO7 Estimate the cost of ending inventory using the retail method and gross profit method.

Two methods of estimating the value of inventory are the retail method and the gross profit method. Under the retail method, inventory is determined at retail prices and is then reduced to estimated cost by applying a ratio of cost to retail price. Under the gross profit method, cost of goods sold is estimated by reducing sales by estimated gross margin. The estimated cost of goods sold is then deducted from the cost of goods available for sale to estimate the inventory.

Review of Concepts and Terminology

The following concepts and terms were introduced in this chapter:

LO3 **Average-cost method:** An inventory costing method in which inventory is priced at the average cost of the goods available for sale during the period.

LO1 **Average days' inventory on hand:** The average number of days required to sell the inventory on hand; number of days in a year divided by inventory turnover.

LO2 **Consignment:** Merchandise that its owner (the *consignor*) places on the premises of another company (the *consignee*) with the understanding that payment is expected only when the merchandise is sold and that unsold items may be returned to the consignor.

LO2 **Cost flow:** The association of costs with their assumed flow in the operations of a company.

LO3 **First-in, first-out (FIFO) method:** An inventory costing method based on the assumption that the costs of the first items acquired should be assigned to the first items sold.

LO2 **Goods flow:** The actual physical movement of goods in the operations of a company.

SO7 **Gross profit method:** A method of inventory estimation based on the assumption that the ratio of gross margin for a business remains relatively stable from year to year. Also called *gross margin method.*

LO2 **Inventory cost:** The price paid or consideration given to acquire an asset; includes invoice price less purchases discounts, plus freight in, plus applicable taxes and tariffs.

LO1 **Inventory turnover:** A ratio indicating the number of times a company's average inventory is sold during an accounting period; cost of goods sold divided by average inventory.

LO6 **Item-by-item method:** A lower-of-cost-or-market method of valuing inventory in which cost and market values are compared for each item in inventory and each item is then valued at its lower price.

LO1 **Just-in-time operating environment:** A system of reducing levels of inventory by working closely with suppliers to coordinate and schedule deliveries so that goods arrive just at the time they are needed.

LO3 **Last-in, first-out (LIFO) method:** An inventory costing method based on the assumption that the costs of the last items purchased should be assigned to the first items sold.

LO5 **LIFO liquidation:** The reduction of inventory below previous levels so that income is increased by the amount by which current prices exceed the historical cost of the inventory under LIFO.

LO6 **Lower-of-cost-or-market (LCM) rule:** A method of valuing inventory at an amount less than cost when the replacement cost falls below historical cost.

LO6 **Major category method:** A lower-of-cost-or-market method of valuing inventory in which the total cost and total market values for each category of items are compared and each category is then valued at its lower amount.

LO6 **Market:** Current replacement cost of inventory.

LO1 **Merchandise inventory:** All goods owned and held for sale in the regular course of business.

SO7 **Retail method:** A method of inventory estimation, used in retail merchandising businesses, in which inventory at retail value is reduced by the ratio of cost to retail price.

LO3 **Specific identification method:** An inventory costing method in which the price of inventory is computed by identifying the cost of each item in ending inventory as coming from a specific purchase.

LO1 **Supply-chain management:** A system of managing inventory and purchasing through business-to-business transactions conducted over the Internet.

Review Problem

Periodic and Perpetual Inventory Systems

LO1 LO3 LO4 The table below summarizes the beginning inventory, purchases, and sales of Psi Company's single product during January.

Date			Beginning Inventory and Purchases			
			Units	Cost	Total	Sales Units
Jan.	1	Inventory	1,400	$19	$26,600	
	4	Sale				300
	8	Purchase	600	20	12,000	
	10	Sale				1,300
	12	Purchase	900	21	18,900	
	15	Sale				150
	18	Purchase	500	22	11,000	
	24	Purchase	800	23	18,400	
	31	Sale				1,350
Totals			4,200		$86,900	3,100

REQUIRED ▶

1. Assuming that the company uses the periodic inventory system, compute the cost that should be assigned to ending inventory and to cost of goods sold using (a) the average-cost method, (b) the FIFO method, and (c) the LIFO method.
2. Assuming that the company uses the perpetual inventory system, compute the cost that should be assigned to ending inventory and to cost of goods sold using (a) the average-cost method, (b) the FIFO method, and (c) the LIFO method.
3. Compute inventory turnover and average days' inventory on hand under each of the inventory cost flow assumptions in **1.** What conclusion can be made from this comparison?

Answer to Review Problem

	Units	Amount
Beginning inventory	1,400	$26,600
Purchases	2,800	60,300
Available for sale	4,200	$86,900
Sales	3,100	
Ending inventory	1,100	

1. Periodic inventory system:

a. Average-cost method

Cost of goods available for sale	$86,900
Less ending inventory consisting of 1,100 units at $20.69*	22,759
Cost of goods sold	$64,141

*$86,900 ÷ 4,200 = $20.69 (rounded).

b. FIFO method

Cost of goods available for sale		$86,900
Less ending inventory consisting of		
Jan. 24 purchase (800 × $23)	$18,400	
Jan. 18 purchase (300 × $22)	6,600	25,000
Cost of goods sold		$61,900

c. LIFO method

Cost of goods available for sale	$86,900
Less ending inventory consisting of beginning inventory (1,100 × $19)	20,900
Cost of goods sold	$66,000

2. Perpetual inventory system:

a. Average-cost method

Date		Units	Cost*	Amount*
Jan. 1	Inventory	1,400	$19.00	$26,600
4	Sale	(300)	19.00	(5,700)
4	Balance	1,100	19.00	$20,900
8	Purchase	600	20.00	12,000
8	Balance	1,700	19.35	$32,900
10	Sale	(1,300)	19.35	(25,155)
10	Balance	400	19.36	$ 7,745
12	Purchase	900	21.00	18,900
12	Balance	1,300	20.50	$26,645
15	Sale	(150)	20.50	(3,075)
15	Balance	1,150	20.50	$23,570
18	Purchase	500	22.00	11,000
24	Purchase	800	23.00	18,400
24	Balance	2,450	21.62	$52,970
31	Sale	(1,350)	21.62	(29,187)
31	Inventory	1,100	21.62	$23,783
Cost of goods sold ($5,700 + $25,155 + $3,075 + $29,187)				$63,117

*Rounded.

b. FIFO method

Date		Units	Cost	Amount
Jan. 1	Inventory	1,400	$19	$26,600
4	Sale	(300)	19	(5,700)
4	Balance	1,100	19	$20,900
8	Purchase	600	20	12,000

Jan. 8	Balance	1,100	19	
		600	20	$32,900
10	Sale	(1,100)	19	
		(200)	20	(24,900)
10	Balance	400	20	$ 8,000
12	Purchase	900	21	18,900
12	Balance	400	20	
		900	21	$26,900
15	Sale	(150)	20	(3,000)
15	Balance	250	20	
		900	21	$23,900
18	Purchase	500	22	11,000
24	Purchase	800	23	18,400
24	Balance	250	20	
		900	21	
		500	22	
		800	23	$53,300
31	Sale	(250)	20	
		(900)	21	
		(200)	22	(28,300)
31	Inventory	300	22	
		800	23	$25,000
Cost of goods sold ($5,700 + $24,900 + $3,000 + $28,300)				$61,900

c. LIFO method

Date		Units	Cost	Amount
Jan. 1	Inventory	1,400	$19	$26,600
4	Sale	(300)	19	(5,700)
4	Balance	1,100	19	$20,900
8	Purchase	600	20	12,000
8	Balance	1,100	19	
		600	20	$32,900
10	Sale	(600)	20	
		(700)	19	(25,300)
10	Balance	400	19	$ 7,600
12	Purchase	900	21	18,900
12	Balance	400	19	
		900	21	$26,500
15	Sale	(150)	21	(3,150)
15	Balance	400	19	
		750	21	$23,350
18	Purchase	500	22	11,000
24	Purchase	800	23	18,400
24	Balance	400	19	
		750	21	
		500	22	
		800	23	$52,750
31	Sale	(800)	23	
		(500)	22	
		(50)	21	(30,450)
31	Inventory	400	19	
		700	21	$22,300
Cost of goods sold ($5,700 + $25,300 + $3,150 + $30,450)				$64,600

3. Ratios computed:

	Average-Cost	FIFO	LIFO
Cost of goods sold	$64,141	$61,900	$66,000
Average inventory	$24,680* ($22,759 + $26,600) ÷ 2	$25,800 ($25,000 + $26,600) ÷ 2	$23,750 ($20,900 + $26,600) ÷ 2
Inventory turnover	2.6 times ($64,141 ÷ $24,680)	2.4 times ($61,900 ÷ $25,800)	2.8 times ($66,000 ÷ $23,750)
Average days' inventory on hand	140.4 days (365 days ÷ 2.6 times)	152.1 days (365 days ÷ 2.4 times)	130.4 days (365 days ÷ 2.8 times)

*Rounded.

In periods of rising prices, the LIFO method will always result in a higher inventory turnover and lower average days' inventory on hand. When comparing inventory ratios for two or more companies, the inventory methods used by the companies should be considered.

Chapter Assignments

Building Your Knowledge Foundation

Questions

1. What is merchandise inventory, and what is the primary objective of inventory measurement?
2. How does inventory for a manufacturing company differ from that for a merchandising company?
3. Why is the level of inventory important, and what are two common measures of inventory level?
4. What items should be included in the cost of inventory?
5. Fargo Sales Company is very busy at the end of its fiscal year on June 30. It has an order for 130 units of product in its warehouse. Although the shipping department tries, it cannot ship the product by June 30, and title has not yet passed. Should the 130 units be included in the year-end count of inventory? Why or why not?
6. What is the difference between goods flow and cost flow?
7. Do the FIFO and LIFO inventory methods result in different quantities of ending inventory?
8. Under which method of cost flow are (a) the earliest costs assigned to inventory, (b) the latest costs assigned to inventory, and (c) the average costs assigned to inventory?
9. What are the relative advantages and disadvantages of FIFO and LIFO from management's point of view?
10. Why do you think it is more expensive to maintain a perpetual inventory system?
11. In periods of steadily rising prices, which inventory method—average-cost, FIFO, or LIFO—will give the (a) highest ending inventory cost, (b) lowest ending inventory cost, (c) highest net income, and (d) lowest net income?
12. May a company change its inventory cost method from year to year? Explain.
13. What is the relationship between income tax rules and the inventory valuation methods?
14. If the merchandise inventory is mistakenly overstated at the end of 20x0, what is the effect on the (a) 20x0 net income, (b) 20x0 year-end balance sheet value, (c) 20x1 net income, and (d) 20x1 year-end balance sheet value?
15. In the phrase *lower of cost or market*, what is meant by the word *market*?

16. What methods can be used to determine the lower of cost or market?
17. Does using the retail method mean that inventories are measured at retail value on the balance sheet? Explain.
18. For what reasons might management use the gross profit method of estimating inventory?
19. Which of the following inventory systems or methods do not require the taking of a physical inventory: (a) perpetual, (b) periodic, (c) retail, and (d) gross profit?

SHORT EXERCISES

LO1 Management Issues

SE 1. Indicate whether each of the following items is associated with (a) allocating the cost of inventories in accordance with the matching rule, (b) assessing the impact of inventory decisions, or (c) evaluating the level of inventory:

1. Calculating the average days' inventory on hand
2. Ordering a supply of inventory to satisfy customer needs
3. Calculating the income tax effect of an inventory method
4. Deciding the cost to place on ending inventory

LO1 Inventory Turnover and Average Days' Inventory on Hand

SE 2. During 20x1, Louisville Clothiers had beginning inventory of $240,000, ending inventory of $280,000, and cost of goods sold of $1,100,000. Compute the inventory turnover and average days' inventory on hand.

LO3 Specific Identification Method

SE 3. Assume the following data with regard to inventory for Ambrose Company:

Aug. 1	Inventory	80 units @ $10 per unit	$ 800
8	Purchase	100 units @ $11 per unit	1,100
22	Purchase	70 units @ $12 per unit	840
Goods available for sale		250 units	$2,740
Aug. 15	Sale	90 units	
28	Sale	50 units	
Inventory, Aug. 31		110 units	

Assuming that the inventory consists of 60 units from the August 8 purchase and 50 units from the purchase of August 22, calculate the cost of ending inventory and cost of goods sold.

LO3 Average-Cost Method–Periodic Inventory System

SE 4. Using the data in SE 3, calculate the cost of ending inventory and cost of goods sold according to the average-cost method under the periodic inventory system.

LO3 FIFO Method–Periodic Inventory System

SE 5. Using the data in SE 3, calculate the cost of ending inventory and cost of goods sold according to the FIFO method under the periodic inventory system.

LO3 LIFO Method–Periodic Inventory System

SE 6. Using the data in SE 3, calculate the cost of ending inventory and cost of goods sold according to the LIFO method under the periodic inventory system.

LO4 Average-Cost Method–Perpetual Inventory System

SE 7. Using the data in SE 3, calculate the cost of ending inventory and cost of goods sold according to the average-cost method under the perpetual inventory system.

LO4 FIFO Method–Perpetual Inventory System

SE 8. Using the data in SE 3, calculate the cost of ending inventory and cost of goods sold according to the FIFO method under the perpetual inventory system.

LO4 LIFO Method–Perpetual Inventory System

SE 9. Using the data in SE 3, calculate the cost of ending inventory and cost of goods sold according to the LIFO method under the perpetual inventory system.

LO5 Effects of Methods and Changing Prices

SE 10. Using Exhibit 1 as an example, prepare a table with seven columns that shows the ending inventory and cost of goods sold for each of the results from your calculations in SE 3 through SE 9. Comment on the results, including the effects of the different prices at which the merchandise was purchased. Which method(s) would result in the lowest income taxes?

SE 11. **LO6 Lower of Cost or Market** The following schedule is based on a physical inventory and replacement costs for one product line of men's shirts:

Item	Quantity	Cost per Unit	Market per Unit
Short sleeve	280	$24	$20
Long sleeve	190	28	29
Extra-long sleeve	80	34	35

Determine the value of this category of inventory at the lower of cost or market using (1) the item-by-item method and (2) the major category method.

EXERCISES

E 1. **LO1 Management Issues** Indicate whether each of the following items is associated with (a) allocating the cost of inventories in accordance with the matching rule, (b) assessing the impact of inventory decisions, or (c) evaluating the level of inventory:

1. Computing inventory turnover
2. Application of the just-in-time operating environment
3. Determining the effects of inventory decisions on cash flows
4. Apportioning the cost of goods available for sale to ending inventory and cost of goods sold
5. Determining the effects of inventory methods on income taxes
6. Determining the assumption about the flow of costs into and out of the company

E 2. **LO1 Inventory Ratios** SaveMore Discount Stores is assessing its levels of inventory for 20x2 and 20x3 and has gathered the following data:

	20x3	20x2	20x1
Ending inventory	$128,000	$108,000	$92,000
Cost of goods sold	640,000	600,000	

Compute the inventory turnover and average days' inventory on hand for 20x3 and 20x2 and comment on the results.

E 3. **LO3 Periodic Inventory System and Inventory Costing Methods** Paul's Farm Store recorded the following purchases and sales of fertilizer during the past year:

Jan. 1	Beginning inventory	250 cases @ $23	$ 5,750
Feb. 25	Purchased	100 cases @ $26	2,600
June 15	Purchased	400 cases @ $28	11,200
Aug. 15	Purchased	100 cases @ $26	2,600
Oct. 15	Purchased	300 cases @ $28	8,400
Dec. 15	Purchased	200 cases @ $30	6,000
Goods available for sale		1,350	$36,550
Total sales		1,000 cases	
Dec. 31	Ending inventory	350 cases	

Assume that Paul's Farm Store sold all of the June 15 purchase and 200 cases each from the January 1 beginning inventory, the October 15 purchase, and the December 15 purchase.

Determine the costs that should be assigned to ending inventory and cost of goods sold under each of the following assumptions: (1) costs are assigned by the specific identification method; (2) costs are assigned by the average-cost method; (3) costs are assigned by the FIFO method; (4) costs are assigned by the LIFO method. What conclusions can be drawn about the effect of each method on the income statement and the balance sheet of Paul's Farm Store? Round your answers to the nearest whole number and assume the periodic inventory system.

E 4. **LO3 Periodic Inventory System and Inventory Costing Methods** During its first year of operation, Bingham Company purchased 5,600 units of a product at $21 per unit. During the second year, it purchased 6,000 units of the same product at $24 per unit. During the third year, it purchased 5,000 units at $30 per unit.

Bingham Company managed to have an ending inventory each year of 1,000 units. The company uses the periodic inventory system.

Prepare cost of goods sold statements that compare the value of ending inventory and the cost of goods sold for each of the three years using (1) the FIFO inventory costing method and (2) the LIFO method. From the resulting data, what conclusions can you draw about the relationships between changes in unit price and changes in the value of ending inventory?

E 5. **LO3 Periodic Inventory System and Inventory Costing Methods**

In chronological order, the inventory, purchases, and sales of a single product for a recent month are as follows:

			Units	Amount per Unit
June	1	Beginning inventory	300	$30
	4	Purchase	800	33
	8	Sale	400	60
	12	Purchase	1,000	36
	16	Sale	700	60
	20	Sale	500	66
	24	Purchase	1,200	39
	28	Sale	600	66
	29	Sale	400	66

Using the periodic inventory system, compute the cost of ending inventory, cost of goods sold, and gross margin. Use the average-cost, FIFO, and LIFO inventory costing methods. Explain the differences in gross margin produced by the three methods. Round unit costs to cents and totals to dollars.

E 6. **LO4 Perpetual Inventory System and Inventory Costing Methods**

Using the data provided in **E 5** and assuming the perpetual inventory system, compute the cost of ending inventory, cost of goods sold, and gross margin. Use the average-cost, FIFO, and LIFO inventory costing methods. Explain the reasons for the differences in gross margin produced by the three methods. Round unit costs to cents and totals to dollars.

E 7. **LO3 LO4 Periodic and Perpetual Systems and Inventory Costing Methods**

During July 20x1, Downes, Inc., sold 250 units of its product Velt for $4,000. The following units were available:

	Units	Cost
Beginning inventory	100	$ 2
Purchase 1	40	4
Purchase 2	60	6
Purchase 3	70	8
Purchase 4	80	10
Purchase 5	90	12

A sale of 100 units was made after purchase 1, and a sale of 150 units was made after purchase 4. Of the units sold, 100 came from beginning inventory and 150 from purchases 3 and 4.

Determine goods available for sale and ending inventory in units. Then determine the costs that should be assigned to cost of goods sold and ending inventory under each of the following assumptions: (1) Costs are assigned under the periodic inventory system using (a) the specific identification method, (b) the average-cost method, (c) the FIFO method, and (d) the LIFO method. (2) Costs are assigned under the perpetual inventory system using (a) the average-cost method, (b) the FIFO method, and (c) the LIFO method. For each alternative, show the gross margin. Round unit costs to cents and totals to dollars.

E 8. **LO5 Effects of Inventory Methods on Cash Flows**

Lao Products, Inc., sold 120,000 cases of glue at $40 per case during 20x1. Its beginning inventory consisted of 20,000 cases at a cost of $24 per case. During 20x1, it purchased 60,000 cases at $28 per case and later 50,000 cases at $30 per case. Operating expenses were $1,100,000, and the applicable income tax rate was 30 percent.

Using the periodic inventory system, compute net income using the FIFO method and the LIFO method for costing inventory. Which alternative produces the larger cash flow? The company is considering a purchase of 10,000 cases at $30 per case just before the year end. What effect on net income and on cash flow will this proposed purchase have under each method? (**Hint:** What are the income tax consequences?)

LO3 Characteristics of Inventory
LO5 Costing Methods

E 9. Match each of the descriptions listed below to these inventory costing methods:

a. Specific identification
b. Average-cost
c. First-in, first-out (FIFO)
d. Last-in, first-out (LIFO)

1. Matches recent costs with recent revenues
2. Assumes that each item of inventory is identifiable
3. Results in the most realistic balance sheet valuation
4. Results in the lowest net income in periods of deflation
5. Results in the lowest net income in periods of inflation
6. Matches the oldest costs with recent revenues
7. Results in the highest net income in periods of inflation
8. Results in the highest net income in periods of deflation
9. Tends to level out the effects of inflation
10. Is unpredictable as to the effects of inflation

LO5 Effects of Inventory Errors

E 10. Condensed income statements for Earle Company for two years are shown below.

	20x5	20x4
Sales	$126,000	$105,000
Cost of goods sold	75,000	54,000
Gross margin	$ 51,000	$ 51,000
Operating expenses	30,000	30,000
Income before income taxes	$ 21,000	$ 21,000

After the end of 20x5, the company discovered that an error had resulted in a $9,000 understatement of the 20x4 ending inventory.

Compute the corrected income before income taxes for 20x4 and 20x5. What effect will the error have on income before income taxes and owner's equity for 20x6?

LO6 Lower-of-Cost-or-Market Rule

E 11. Rasmin Company values its inventory, shown below, at the lower of cost or market. Compute Rasmin's inventory value using (1) the item-by-item method and (2) the major category method.

		Per Unit	
	Quantity	Cost	Market
Category I			
Item aa	200	$ 2.00	$ 1.80
Item bb	240	4.00	4.40
Item cc	400	8.00	7.50
Category II			
Item dd	300	12.00	13.00
Item ee	400	18.00	18.20

SO7 Retail Method

E 12. Isabel's Dress Shop had net retail sales of $500,000 during the current year. The following additional information was obtained from the accounting records:

	At Cost	At Retail
Beginning inventory	$ 80,000	$120,000
Net purchases (excluding freight in)	280,000	440,000
Freight in	20,800	

1. Using the retail method, estimate the company's ending inventory at cost.
2. Assume that a physical inventory taken at year end revealed an inventory on hand of $36,000 at retail value. What is the estimated amount of inventory shrinkage (loss due to theft, damage, etc.) at cost using the retail method?

SO7 Gross Profit Method

E 13. Lance Borkowski was at home watching television when he received a call from the fire department telling him his store had burned. His business was a total loss. The insurance company asked him to prove his inventory loss. For the year, until the date of the fire, Borkowski's company had sales of $450,000 and purchases of $280,000. Freight in amounted to $13,700, and the beginning inventory was $45,000. It was Borkowski's custom to price goods to achieve a gross margin of 40 percent. Compute Borkowski's estimated inventory loss.

PROBLEMS

P 1. LO1 LO3 **Periodic Inventory System and Inventory Costing Methods**

The Champlain Cabinet Company sold 2,200 cabinets during 20x2 at $160 per cabinet. Its beginning inventory on January 1 was 130 cabinets at $56. Purchases made during the year were as follows:

February	225 cabinets @ $62
April	350 cabinets @ $65
June	700 cabinets @ $70
August	300 cabinets @ $66
October	400 cabinets @ $68
November	250 cabinets @ $72

The company's selling and administrative expenses for the year were $101,000, and the company uses the periodic inventory system.

REQUIRED

1. Prepare a schedule to compute the cost of goods available for sale.
2. Compute income before income taxes under each of the following inventory cost flow assumptions: (a) the average-cost method; (b) the FIFO method; and (c) the LIFO method.
3. Compute inventory turnover and average days' inventory on hand under each of the inventory cost flow assumptions in **2.** What conclusion can be made from this comparison?

P 2. LO1 LO3 **Periodic Inventory System and Inventory Costing Methods**

The inventory, purchases, and sales of Product ABO for March and April follow. The company closes its books at the end of each month and uses the periodic inventory system.

Mar.	1	Beginning inventory	60 units @ $49
	7	Sale	20 units
	10	Purchase	100 units @ $52
	19	Sale	70 units
	31	Ending inventory	70 units
Apr.	4	Purchase	120 units @ $53
	11	Sale	110 units
	15	Purchase	50 units @ $54
	23	Sale	80 units
	25	Purchase	100 units @ $55
	27	Sale	100 units
	30	Ending inventory	50 units

REQUIRED

1. Compute the cost of the ending inventory on March 31 and April 30 using the average-cost method. In addition, determine cost of goods sold for March and April. Round unit costs to cents and totals to dollars.
2. Compute the cost of the ending inventory on March 31 and April 30 using the FIFO method. In addition, determine cost of goods sold for March and April.
3. Compute the cost of the ending inventory on March 31 and April 30 using the LIFO method. In addition, determine cost of goods sold for March and April.
4. Do the cash flows from operations for March and April differ depending on the inventory costing method—average-cost, FIFO, or LIFO—used? Explain.

P 3. LO4 **Perpetual Inventory System and Inventory Costing Methods**

Use the data provided in **P 2,** but assume that the company uses the perpetual inventory system. (**Hint:** In preparing the solutions required below, it is helpful to determine the balance of inventory after each transaction, as shown in the Review Problem in this chapter.)

REQUIRED

1. Determine the cost of ending inventory and cost of goods sold for March and April using the average-cost method. Round unit costs to cents and totals to dollars.
2. Determine the cost of ending inventory and cost of goods sold for March and April using the FIFO method.
3. Determine the cost of ending inventory and cost of goods sold for March and April using the LIFO method.

P 4. SO7 **Retail Method**

Lopez Company operates a large discount store and uses the retail method to estimate the cost of ending inventory. Management suspects that in recent weeks there have been unusually heavy losses from shoplifting or employee pilferage. To estimate the amount of the loss, the company has taken a physical inventory and will compare the results with the estimated cost of inventory. Data from the accounting records of Lopez Company are as follows:

	At Cost	At Retail
October 1 beginning inventory	$51,488	$ 74,300
Purchases	71,733	108,500
Purchases returns and allowances	(2,043)	(3,200)
Freight in	950	
Sales		109,183
Sales returns and allowances		(933)
October 31 physical inventory at retail		62,450

REQUIRED ▶
1. Using the retail method, prepare a schedule to estimate the dollar amount of the store's month-end inventory at cost.
2. Use the store's cost to retail ratio to reduce the retail value of the physical inventory to cost.
3. Calculate the estimated amount of inventory shortage at cost and at retail.

P 5.
SO7 Gross Profit Method

Sabatino Sisters is a large retail furniture company that operates in two adjacent warehouses. One warehouse is a showroom, and the other is used to store merchandise. On the night of April 22, 20x2, a fire broke out in the storage warehouse and destroyed the merchandise stored there. Fortunately, the fire did not reach the showroom, so all the merchandise on display was saved.

Although the company maintained a perpetual inventory system, its records were rather haphazard, and the last reliable physical inventory had been taken on December 31. In addition, there was no control of the flow of the goods between the showroom and the warehouse. Thus, it was impossible to tell what goods should have been in either place. As a result, the insurance company required an independent estimate of the amount of loss. The insurance company examiners were satisfied when they were provided with the following information.

Merchandise inventory on December 31, 20x1	$ 727,400
Purchases, January 1 to April 22, 20x2	1,206,100
Purchases returns, January 1 to April 22, 20x2	(5,353)
Freight in, January 1 to April 22, 20x2	26,550
Sales, January 1 to April 22, 20x2	1,979,525
Sales returns, January 1 to April 22, 20x2	(14,900)
Merchandise inventory in showroom on April 22, 20x2	201,480
Average gross margin	44%

REQUIRED ▶ Prepare a schedule that estimates the amount of the inventory lost in the fire.

ALTERNATE PROBLEMS

P 6.
LO1 Periodic Inventory System and
LO3 Inventory Costing Methods

K/R

McDougal Company merchandises a single product called Gailen. The following data represent beginning inventory and purchases of Gailen during the past year: January 1 inventory, 68,000 units at $11.00; February purchases, 80,000 units at $12.00; March purchases, 160,000 units at $12.40; May purchases, 120,000 units at $12.60; July purchases, 200,000 units at $12.80; September purchases, 160,000 units at $12.60; and November purchases, 60,000 units at $13.00. Sales of Gailen totaled 786,000 units at $20.00 per unit. Selling and administrative expenses totaled $5,102,000 for the year, and McDougal Company uses the periodic inventory system.

REQUIRED ▶
1. Prepare a schedule to compute the cost of goods available for sale.
2. Compute income before income taxes under each of the following inventory cost flow assumptions: (a) the average-cost method; (b) the FIFO method; and (c) the LIFO method.
3. Compute inventory turnover and average days' inventory on hand under each of the inventory cost flow assumptions listed in **2.** What conclusion can be drawn from this comparison?

P 7.
LO1 Periodic Inventory System and
LO3 Inventory Costing Methods

The inventory of Product H and data on purchases and sales for a two-month period follow. The company closes its books at the end of each month. It uses a periodic inventory system.

Apr.	1	Beginning inventory	50 units @ $102
	5	Sale	30 units
	10	Purchase	100 units @ $110

Apr.	17	Sale	60 units
	30	Ending inventory	60 units
May	2	Purchase	100 units @ $108
	8	Sale	110 units
	14	Purchase	50 units @ $112
	18	Sale	40 units
	22	Purchase	60 units @ $117
	26	Sale	30 units
	30	Sale	20 units
	31	Ending inventory	70 units

REQUIRED

1. Compute the cost of ending inventory of Product H on April 30 and May 31 using the average-cost method. In addition, determine cost of goods sold for April and May. Round unit costs to cents and totals to dollars.
2. Compute the cost of the ending inventory on April 30 and May 31 using the FIFO method. In addition, determine cost of goods sold for April and May.
3. Compute the cost of the ending inventory on April 30 and May 31 using the LIFO method. In addition, determine cost of goods sold for April and May.
4. Do the cash flows from operations for April and May differ depending on the inventory costing method—average-cost, FIFO, or LIFO—used? Explain.

P 8. **LO4 Perpetual Inventory System and Inventory Costing Methods**

Use the data provided in **P 7,** but assume that the company uses the perpetual inventory system. (**Hint:** In preparing the solutions required below, it is helpful to determine the balance of inventory after each transaction, as shown in the Review Problem in this chapter.)

REQUIRED

1. Determine the cost of ending inventory and cost of goods sold for April and May using the average-cost method. Round unit costs to cents and totals to dollars.
2. Determine the cost of ending inventory and cost of goods sold for April and May using the FIFO method.
3. Determine the cost of ending inventory and cost of goods sold for April and May using the LIFO method.

Skills Development Cases

Conceptual Analysis

SD 1. **LO1 Evaluation of Inventory Levels**

J.C. Penney <www.jcpenney.com> has an inventory turnover of 4.6 times. Dell Computer Corporation <www.dell.com> has an inventory turnover of 75.7. Dell achieves its high turnover through supply-chain management in a just-in-time operating environment. Why is inventory turnover important to companies like J.C. Penney and Dell? Why are comparisons among companies important? Are J.C. Penney and Dell a good match for comparison? What are supply-chain management and a just-in-time operating environment? Why are they important to achieving a favorable inventory turnover?

SD 2. **LO5 LIFO Inventory Method**

Eighty-six percent of chemical companies use the LIFO inventory method for the costing of inventories, whereas only 9 percent of computer equipment companies use LIFO.[13] Describe the LIFO inventory method. What effects does it have on reported income, cash flows, and income taxes during periods of price changes? Why do you think so many chemical companies use LIFO while most companies in the computer industry do not?

SD 3. **LO6 LCM and Conservatism**

Exxon Mobil Corporation <www.exxonmobil.com> uses the LIFO inventory method for most of its inventories. The cost of inventories is heavily dependent on the cost of oil. In a recent year when the price of oil was down, Exxon Mobil, following the lower-of-cost-or-market (LCM) rule, wrote down its inventory by $325 million. In the next year, when the price of oil recovered, the company reported that market price exceeded the LIFO carrying values by $6.7 billion.[14] Explain why the LCM rule resulted in a writedown in the first year. What is the inconsistency between the first and second year treatment of the change in the price of oil? How does the accounting convention of conservatism explain the inconsistency? If the price of oil declines substantially in the third year, what will be the likely consequence?

Ethical Dilemma

SD 4.
LO1 LO5 Inventories, Income Determination, and Ethics

Flare, Inc., which has a December 31 year end, designs and sells fashions for young professional women. Sandra Mason, president of the company, feared that the forecasted 20x5 profitability goals would not be reached. She was pleased when Flare received a large order on December 30 from The Executive Woman, a retail chain of upscale stores for businesswomen. Mason immediately directed the controller to record the sale, which represented 13 percent of Flare's annual sales, but directed the inventory control department not to separate the goods for shipment until after January 1. Separated goods are not included in inventory because they have been sold. On December 31, the company's auditors arrived to observe the year-end taking of the physical inventory under the periodic inventory system. What will be the effect of Sandra Mason's action on Flare's 20x5 profitability? What will be the effect on Flare's 20x6 profitability? Was Mason's action ethical?

Research Activity

SD 5.
LO2 LO4 Retail Business Inventories

Make an appointment to visit a local retail business—a grocery, clothing, book, music, or appliance store—and interview the manager for 30 minutes about the company's inventory accounting system. The store may be a branch of a larger company. Ask the following questions, summarize your findings in a paper, and be prepared to discuss your results in class:

1. What is the physical flow of merchandise into the store, and what documents are used in connection with this flow?
2. What documents are prepared when merchandise is sold?
3. Does the store keep perpetual inventory records? If so, does it keep the records in units only, or does it keep track of cost as well? If not, what system does the store use?
4. How often does the company take a physical inventory?
5. How are financial statements generated for the store?
6. What method does the company use to cost its inventory for financial statements?

Group Activity: Assign teams to various types of businesses in your community.

Decision-Making Practice

SD 6.
LO5 Inventory Costing Methods, Income Taxes, and Cash Flows

The Osaka Trading Company began business in 20x4 for the purpose of importing and marketing an electronic component widely used in digital appliances. It is now December 20, 20x4, and Osaka Trading Company's management is considering its options. Among its considerations is whether to choose the FIFO or LIFO inventory method. Under the periodic inventory system, the effects on net income of using the two methods are as follows:

	FIFO Method	LIFO Method
Sales (500,000 units × $12)	$6,000,000	$6,000,000
Cost of goods sold		
Purchases		
200,000 × $4	$ 800,000	$ 800,000
400,000 × $6	2,400,000	2,400,000
Total purchases	$3,200,000	$3,200,000
Less ending inventory		
FIFO (100,000 × $6)	(600,000)	
LIFO (100,000 × $4)		(400,000)
Cost of goods sold	$2,600,000	$2,800,000
Gross margin	$3,400,000	$3,200,000
Operating expenses	2,400,000	2,400,000
Income before income taxes	$1,000,000	$ 800,000
Income taxes	300,000	240,000
Net income	$ 700,000	$ 560,000

Also, management has an option to purchase an additional 100,000 units of inventory before year end at a price of $8 per unit, the price that is expected to prevail during 20x5. The income tax rate applicable to the company in 20x4 is 30 percent.

Business conditions are expected to be favorable in 20x5, as they were in 20x4. Management has asked you for advice. Analyze the effects of making the additional purchase. Then prepare a memorandum to Osaka's management in which you compare cash outcomes under the four alternatives (Option 1: FIFO and LIFO and Option 2: FIFO and LIFO) and advise management which inventory method to choose and whether to order the additional inventory. Be prepared to discuss your recommendations in class.

LO3 LO5 FIFO versus LIFO Analysis

SD 7. Refrigerated Truck Sales Company (RTS Company) buys large refrigerated trucks from the manufacturer and sells them to companies and independent truckers who haul perishable goods over long distances. RTS has been successful in this specialized niche of the industry. Because of the high cost of the trucks and of financing inventory, RTS tries to maintain as small an inventory as possible. In fact, at the beginning of July the company had no inventory or liabilities, as shown on the balance sheet below.

On July 9, RTS took delivery of a truck at a price of $300,000. On July 19, an identical truck was delivered to the company at a price of $320,000. On July 28, the company sold one of the trucks for $390,000. During July, expenses totaled $30,000. All transactions were paid in cash.

RTS Company
Balance Sheet
July 1, 20x4

Assets		Stockholders' Equity	
Cash	$800,000	Common stock	$800,000
Total assets	$800,000	Total stockholders' equity	$800,000

1. Prepare income statements and balance sheets for RTS on July 31 using (a) the FIFO method of inventory valuation and (b) the LIFO method of inventory valuation. Assume an income tax rate of 40 percent. Explain the effects of each method on the financial statements.
2. Assume that the management of RTS Company follows the policy of declaring a cash dividend each period that is exactly equal to net income. What effects does this action have on each balance sheet prepared in **1**, and how do the resulting balance sheets compare with the balance sheet at the beginning of the month? Which inventory method, if either, do you feel is more realistic in representing RTS's income?
3. Assume that RTS receives notice of another price increase of $20,000 on refrigerated trucks, to take effect on August 1. How does this information relate to management's dividend policy, and how will it affect next month's operations?

FINANCIAL REPORTING AND ANALYSIS CASES

Interpreting Financial Reports

LO1 LO2 LO5 FIFO and LIFO

FRA 1. Hershey Foods Corp. <www.hersheys.com> is famous for its chocolate and confectionary products. In 2000, the company had net sales of $4,220 million, cost of goods sold of $2,471 million, and net income of $334 million. The company uses LIFO to determine cost of inventories. The following disclosure was made to show the relationship of LIFO cost to FIFO cost (dollars are in millions):[15]

	2000	1999
Raw materials	$264	$271
Goods in process	48	49
Finished goods	338	365
Inventories at FIFO	650	685
Adjustment to LIFO	(45)	(83)
Total inventories	$605	$602

1. Prepare a schedule comparing net income for 2000 using the LIFO and FIFO methods. Use a corporate income tax rate of 40 percent. Did prices of cocoa and sugar, the main ingredients of Hershey's products, go up or down in 2000? Explain.
2. Why do you suppose Hershey's management chooses to use the LIFO inventory method? On what economic conditions, if any, do those reasons depend? Given your calculations in **1**, do you believe the economic conditions relevant to Hershey were advantageous for using LIFO in 2000? Explain your answer.
3. Compute inventory turnover and average days' inventory on hand under the LIFO and FIFO methods. What conclusion can be drawn from this comparison?

LO5 Misstatement of Inventory

FRA 2. Crazy Eddie, Inc. <www.crazyeddie.com>, a discount consumer electronics chain, seemed to be missing $52 million in merchandise inventory. "It was a shock," the new management was quoted as saying. It was also one of the nation's largest swindles. Investors lost $145.6 million when the company declared bankruptcy. A count turned up only $75 million in inventory, compared with $126.7 million reported by former management. Net sales could account for only $6.7 million of the difference. At the time, it was not clear whether bookkeeping errors in prior years or an actual physical loss created the shortfall, although at least one store manager felt it was a bookkeeping error because security was strong. "It would be hard for someone to steal anything," he said. Former management was eventually fined $72.7 million.[16]

1. What is the effect of the misstatement of inventory on Crazy Eddie's reported earnings in prior accounting periods?
2. Is this a situation you would expect in a company that is experiencing financial difficulty? Explain.

LO5 LIFO Liquidation

FRA 3. Crane Company <www.crane.com> reported approximately $259 million and $236 million of inventories valued under the LIFO method in 2000 and 1999, respectively. As explained in the company's annual report:

> The reduction of inventory quantities has resulted in a liquidation of LIFO inventories acquired at lower costs prevailing in prior years. Liquidations have reduced cost of sales by $1.3 million in 2000, $2.7 million in 1999, and $.6 million in 1998. Replacement cost would have been higher by $21.4 million and $23.1 million at December 31, 2000 and 1999, respectively.[17]

Assume Crane's average income tax rates for 1999 and 2000 were 40 percent.

1. Explain why a reduction in the quantity of inventory resulted in an increase in net income. Would the same result have occurred if Crane had used the FIFO method to value inventory? Explain your answer.
2. What is the income tax effect of the LIFO liquidation? Is this a favorable outcome?

International Company

LO1 Comparison of Inventory
LO5 Levels and Methods

FRA 4. Yamaha Motor Co., Ltd. <www.yamaha-motor.co.jp> and Pioneer Corporation <www.pioneer.co.jp> are two large, diversified Japanese electronics companies. Both use the average-cost method and the lower-of-cost-or-market rule to account for inventories. The following data are for their 2001 fiscal years (in millions of yen):[18]

	Yamaha	Pioneer
Beginning inventory	¥139,625	¥ 91,517
Ending inventory	166,074	84,429
Cost of goods sold	668,992	447,389

Compare the inventory efficiency of Yamaha and Pioneer by computing the inventory turnover and average days' inventory on hand for both companies in 2001. Comment on the results. Most companies in the United States use the LIFO inventory method.

How would inventory method affect your evaluation if you were to compare Pioneer and Yamaha to a U.S. company? What could you do to make the results comparable?

Toys "R" Us Annual Report

FRA 5.

LO1 LO5 LO6 SO7 Retail Method and Inventory Ratios

Refer to the note related to inventories in the Toys "R" Us <www.tru.com> annual report in the Supplement to Chapter 6 to answer the following questions: What inventory method(s) does Toys "R" Us use? If LIFO inventories had been valued at FIFO, why would there be no difference? Do you think many of the company's inventories are valued at market? Few companies use the retail method; why do you think Toys "R" Us uses it? Compute and compare the inventory turnover and average days' inventory on hand for Toys "R" Us for 2001 and 2002. Beginning 2001 inventory was $1,902 million.

Comparison Case: Toys "R" Us and Walgreen Co.

FRA 6.

LO1 Inventory Efficiency

Refer to the financial statements for Toys "R" Us <www.tru.com> and Walgreens <www.walgreens.com> in the Supplement to Chapter 6. Beginning inventory for 2001 for Toys "R" Us was $2,307 million and for Walgreens, $2,830.8 million. Calculate inventory turnover and average days' inventory on hand for the past two years. If you did **FRA 5**, refer to your answer there for Toys "R" Us. Has either company improved its performance over the past two years? If so, what advantage does it have? Which company seems to make the most efficient use of inventory? Explain.

Fingraph® Financial Analyst™

FRA 7.

LO1 Comparative Analysis of Inventories and Operating Cycle

Select any two companies from the same industry from the list of Fingraph companies on the Needles Accounting Resource Center Web Site at http://accounting.college.hmco.com/students. Choose an industry, such as manufacturing, consumer products, consumer food and beverage, or computers, in which inventory is likely to be an important current asset. Access the Microsoft Excel spreadsheets for the companies you selected. Click on the URL at the top of each company's spreadsheet for a link to the company's web site and annual report.

1. In the annual reports of the companies you have selected, read any reference to inventories in the summary of significant accounting policies or notes to the financial statements. What inventory method does the company use? What are the changes in and the relative importance of raw materials, work in process, and finished goods inventories?
2. Using the Fingraph Financial Analyst CD-ROM software, display and print in tabular and graphic form the Liquidity and Asset Utilization Analysis page. Prepare a table that compares the inventory turnover and average days' inventory on hand for both companies for two years. Also include in your table the operating cycle by combining average days' inventory on hand with average days' sales uncollected.
3. Find and read references to inventories in the liquidity analysis section of management's discussion and analysis in each annual report.
4. Write a one-page executive summary that highlights the accounting policies for inventories, the relative importance and changes in raw materials, work in process, and finished goods, and compares the inventory utilization of the two companies, including reference to management's assessment. Comment specifically on the financing implications of the companies' relative operating cycles. Include the Fingraph page and your table with your report.

Internet Case

FRA 8.

LO5 Effect of LIFO on Income and Cash Flows

Maytag Corporation <www.maytag.com>, an appliance manufacturer, uses the LIFO inventory method. Go to its web site and select "About Maytag." Then select "Financial Center." After finding the income statement and inventory note, calculate what net income would have been had the company used FIFO. Calculate how much cash the company saved for the year and cumulatively by using LIFO. What is the difference between the LIFO and FIFO gross margin and profit margin results? Which reporting alternative is better for the company?

11

Chapter 11 explores the management issues associated with the acquisition, operation, and disposal of property, plant, and equipment, natural resources, and intangible assets, as well as the concepts and techniques of depreciation, depletion, and amortization.

Long-Term Assets

Learning Objectives

LO1 Identify the types of long-term assets and explain the management issues related to accounting for them.

LO2 Distinguish between capital and revenue expenditures, and account for the cost of property, plant, and equipment.

LO3 Define *depreciation* and compute depreciation under the straight-line, production, and declining-balance methods.

LO4 Account for the disposal of depreciable assets.

LO5 Identify the issues related to accounting for natural resources and compute depletion.

LO6 Identify the issues related to accounting for intangible assets, including research and development costs and goodwill.

Supplemental Objective

SO7 Apply depreciation methods to problems of partial years, revised rates, groups of similar items, special types of capital expenditures, and cost recovery.

DECISION POINT

A USER'S FOCUS

H. J. Heinz Company <www.heinz.com> The effects of management's decisions regarding long-term assets are most apparent in the areas of reported total assets, net income, and cash flows related to investing activities. How does one learn about the significance of those items to a company? An idea of the extent of a company's long-term assets and their importance can be gained from the financial statements. For example, the list of assets in the Financial Highlights is from the annual report of H. J. Heinz Company, one of the world's largest food companies. Of the company's $10 billion in total assets, property, plant, and equipment represent about 23 percent, and other noncurrent assets represent about 47 percent.

With 69 percent of Heinz's total assets classified as long-term, management's decisions regarding choice of expected useful life and residual value of the assets can have a material impact on the amount expensed on the income statement. The income statement shows that depreciation and amortization expenses associated with those assets are more than $207 million, or about 25 percent of net income. While depreciation and amortization expenses have no cash effect, the statement of cash flows indicates the amount paid for newly purchased property, plant, and equipment and to what extent a company is reinvesting in its operations. Heinz spent more than $213 million on new long-term assets. In addition to annual expense recognition, long-term assets are reviewed annually to determine if the assets have lost some of their service potential, resulting in asset impairment. Finally, disposals of long-term assets may result in

What do Heinz's financial statements reveal about the company's long-term assets?

gains or losses on the income statement. Each of these financial-statement issues falls within the scope of accounting for the acquisition, use, and disposal of long-term assets and the related management judgments.[1]

Financial Highlights (In thousands)

	2002	2001
Total Current Assets	$ 3,373,566	$3,116,814
Property, Plant, and Equipment:		
Land	$ 63,075	$ 54,774
Buildings and leasehold improvements	880,490	878,028
Equipment, furniture, and other	2,929,082	2,947,978
	3,872,647	3,880,780
Less accumulated depreciation	1,622,573	1,712,400
Total property, plant, and equipment, net	$ 2,250,074	$2,168,380
Other Noncurrent Assets:		
Goodwill (net of amortization: 2002—$393,972 and 2001—$334,907)	$ 2,528,942	$2,077,451
Trademarks (net of amortization: 2002—$144,884 and 2001—$118,254)	808,884	567,692
Other intangibles (net of amortization: 2002—$160,230 and 2001—$157,678)	152,249	120,749
Other noncurrent assets	1,164,639	984,064
Total other noncurrent assets	$ 4,654,714	$3,749,956
Total Assets	$10,278,354	$9,035,150

Management Issues Related to Accounting for Long-Term Assets

LO1 Identify the types of long-term assets and explain the management issues related to accounting for them.

RELATED TEXT ASSIGNMENTS
Q: 1, 2, 3, 4, 5, 6, 7
SE: 1
E: 1, 2
SD: 1, 6, 7
FRA: 3, 4, 5

Long-term assets are assets that (1) have a useful life of more than one year, (2) are acquired for use in the operation of a business, and (3) are not intended for resale to customers. For many years, it was common to refer to long-term assets as *fixed assets*, but use of this term is declining because the word *fixed* implies that they last forever. The relative importance of long-term assets to various industries is shown in Figure 1. Long-term assets range from 17.7 percent of total assets in the advertising industry to 51.2 percent in interstate trucking.

Although there is no strict rule for defining the useful life of a long-term asset, the most common criterion is that the asset be capable of repeated use for at least a year. Included in this category is equipment used only in peak or emergency periods, such as generators.

Assets not used in the normal course of business should not be included in this category. Thus, land held for speculative reasons or buildings no longer used in ordinary business operations should not be included in the property, plant, and equipment category. Instead, they should be classified as long-term investments.

Finally, if an item is held for resale to customers, it should be classified as inventory—not plant and equipment—no matter how durable it is. For example, a printing press held for sale by a printing press manufacturer would be considered inventory, whereas the same printing press would be considered plant and equipment if a printing company buys it for use in operations.

Long-term assets differ from current assets in that they support the operating cycle instead of being a part of it. They are also expected to benefit the business for a longer period than do current assets. Current assets are expected to be used up or converted to cash within one year or during the operating cycle, whichever is longer. Long-term assets are expected to last beyond that period. Long-term assets and their related expenses are summarized in Figure 2 on page 482.

Generally, long-lived assets are reported at carrying value, as presented in Figure 3 on page 482. **Carrying value** is the unexpired part of the cost of an asset, not its market value; it is also called *book value.* If a long-lived asset loses some or all of its revenue-generating potential before the end of its useful life, the asset may be deemed impaired, and its carrying value reduced. **Asset impairment** occurs when the sum of the expected cash flows from the asset is less than the carrying value of the asset.[2] Reducing carrying value to fair value, as measured by the present value

STUDY NOTE: For an asset to be classified as property, plant, and equipment, it must be "put in use." This means that it is available for its intended purpose. An emergency generator is "put in use" when it is available for emergencies, even if it is never used.

KEY POINT: A computer used in the office would be considered plant and equipment, whereas an identical computer held for sale to customers would be considered inventory.

Stop and Think!
Is carrying value ever the same as market value?
On the date of acquisition, the carrying value equals the current market value. After that, it would be a coincidence if it equaled the market value. ■

Figure 1
Long-Term Assets as a Percentage of Total Assets for Selected Industries

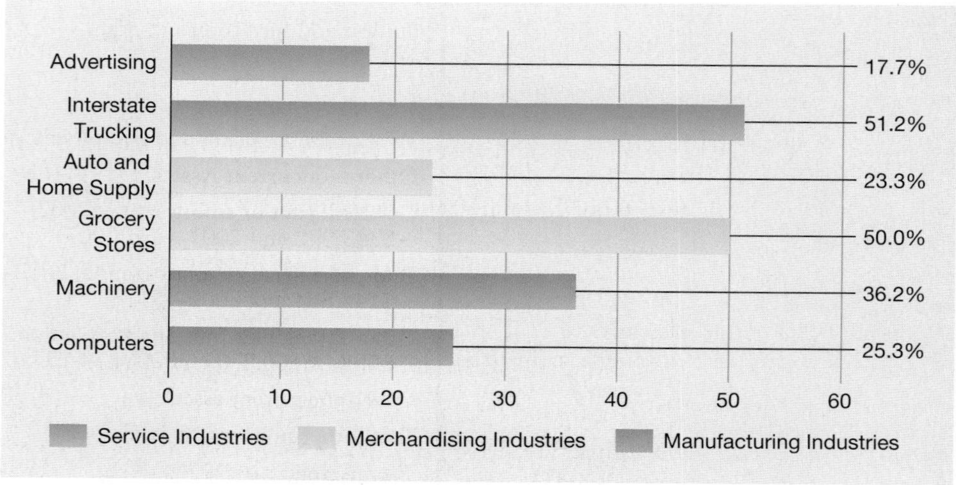

Source: Data from Dun & Bradstreet, *Industry Norms and Key Business Ratios,* 2001–02.

Fermi National Accelerator Laboratory <www.fnal.gov>

OBJECTIVES

- To describe the characteristics of long-term assets
- To identify the four issues that must be addressed in applying the matching rule to long-term assets
- To define depreciation and state the principal causes of depreciation
- To identify the issues related to intangible assets, including research and development

BACKGROUND FOR THE CASE

Fermi National Accelerator Laboratory (Fermilab), located 30 miles west of Chicago, is run by the U.S. Department of Energy. Its primary mission is to advance the understanding of the fundamental nature of matter and energy.

Fermilab operates the world's highest-energy particle accelerator, the Trevatron, or "atom-smasher." Circling through rings of magnets four miles in circumference, particle beams generate experimental conditions equivalent to those that existed in the first quadrillionth of a second after the birth of the universe. This capability to re-create such high energy levels places Fermilab at the frontier of global physics research. The facility provides leadership and resources for qualified experimenters to conduct basic research at the leading edge of high-energy physics and related disciplines. In the year 2000, with Collider Run II, scientists at Fermilab began probing the smallest dimensions that humans have ever examined. These scientists have the opportunity to make discoveries that could answer some important questions in particle physics.

Although a unit of the U.S. government, Fermilab is a financially independent nonprofit corporation with a governing body consisting of the presidents of 87 affiliated research universities. With annual revenues of about $300 million, consisting mostly of government contracts, and annual expenses of about $260 million, Fermilab faces the same management challenges as a for-profit corporation. It must make huge investments in long-term assets. Other than salaries, depreciation is the lab's largest expense. In addition, Fermilab creates intellectual capital through basic research that it shares with U.S. industry to encourage economic development.

For more information about Fermi National Accelerator Laboratory, visit its web site through the Needles Accounting Resource Center Web Site at **http://accounting.college.hmco.com/students** or directly through Fermilab's web site.

REQUIRED

View the video on Fermi National Accelerator Laboratory that accompanies this book. As you are watching the video, take notes related to the following questions:

1. What characteristics distinguish long-term assets? What are some examples of long-term assets at Fermilab?
2. What four issues must be addressed in applying the matching rule to long-term assets?
3. What is depreciation, and what are its two major causes?
4. What are research and development costs, and how does Fermilab account for them? How might this method understate the assets of Fermilab?

of future cash flows, is an application of conservatism. All long-term assets are subject to an asset impairment evaluation. A reduction in carrying value as a result of impairment is recorded as a loss.

www.amazon.com
www.cisco.com
www.lucent.com

Because of a slowdown in the growth of Internet, telecommunications, and technology companies, companies like Amazon.com, Cisco Systems, and Lucent Technologies took write-downs totaling billions of dollars. The carrying value of certain long-term tangible and intangible assets no longer exceeded the cash flows that they would help generate, due to declining revenues or slowing revenue growth. The write-downs caused the companies to report operating losses.[3]

DECIDING TO ACQUIRE LONG-TERM ASSETS

The decision to acquire a long-term asset involves a complex process. Methods of evaluating data to make rational decisions in this area are grouped under a topic called capital budgeting, which is usually covered as a managerial accounting topic. However, an awareness of the general nature of the problem can be helpful in

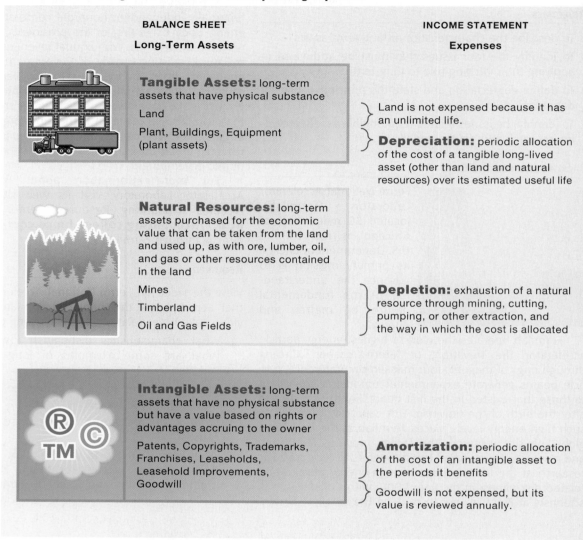

FIGURE 2
Classification of Long-Term Assets and Corresponding Expenses

BALANCE SHEET Long-Term Assets	INCOME STATEMENT Expenses
Tangible Assets: long-term assets that have physical substance Land Plant, Buildings, Equipment (plant assets)	Land is not expensed because it has an unlimited life. **Depreciation:** periodic allocation of the cost of a tangible long-lived asset (other than land and natural resources) over its estimated useful life
Natural Resources: long-term assets purchased for the economic value that can be taken from the land and used up, as with ore, lumber, oil, and gas or other resources contained in the land Mines Timberland Oil and Gas Fields	**Depletion:** exhaustion of a natural resource through mining, cutting, pumping, or other extraction, and the way in which the cost is allocated
Intangible Assets: long-term assets that have no physical substance but have a value based on rights or advantages accruing to the owner Patents, Copyrights, Trademarks, Franchises, Leaseholds, Leasehold Improvements, Goodwill	**Amortization:** periodic allocation of the cost of an intangible asset to the periods it benefits Goodwill is not expensed, but its value is reviewed annually.

KEY POINT: For an asset to be classified as intangible, it must lack physical substance, be long term, and (normally) represent a legal right or advantage.

understanding the accounting issues related to long-term assets. To illustrate the acquisition decision, let us assume that Irena Markova, M.D., is considering the purchase of a $5,000 computer system for her office. She estimates that if she purchases the computer, she can reduce the hours of a part-time employee sufficiently to save net cash flows of $2,000 per year for four years and that the computer will be worth $1,000 at the end of that period. These data are summarized as follows:

FIGURE 3
Carrying Value of Long-Term Assets on the Balance Sheet

Plant Assets	Natural Resources	Intangible Assets
Less Accumulated Depreciation	Less Accumulated Depletion	Less Accumulated Amortization
Carrying Value	Carrying Value	Carrying Value

	20x4	20x5	20x6	20x7
Acquisition cost	($5,000)			
Net annual savings in cash flows	2,000	$2,000	$2,000	$2,000
Disposal price				1,000
Net cash flows	($3,000)	$2,000	$2,000	$3,000

To place the cash flows on a comparable basis, it is helpful to use present value tables, such as Tables 3 and 4 in the appendix on future value and present value tables. Assuming that the appropriate interest rate is 10 percent compounded annually, the purchase may be evaluated as follows:

		Present Value
Acquisition cost	Present value factor = 1.000 1.000 × $5,000	($5,000)
Net annual savings in cash flows	Present value factor = 3.170 (Table 4: 4 periods, 10%) 3.170 × $2,000	6,340
Disposal price	Present value factor = .683 (Table 3: 4 periods, 10%) .683 × $1,000	683
Net present value		$2,023

As long as the net present value is positive, Dr. Markova will earn at least 10 percent on the investment. In this case, the return is greater than 10 percent because the net present value is a positive $2,023. Based on this analysis, Dr. Markova makes the decision to purchase. However, there are other important considerations that have to be taken into account, such as the costs of training and maintenance, and the possibility that because of unforeseen circumstances, the savings may not be as great as expected. In Dr. Markova's case, the decision to purchase is likely to be a good one because the net present value is both positive and large relative to the investment.

Information about a company's acquisitions of long-term assets may be found under investing activities in the statement of cash flows. For example, in referring to this section of its 2002 annual report, the management of H. J. Heinz Company makes the following statement:

www.heinz.com

> Capital expenditures totaled $213.4 million compared to $411.3 million last year. . . . In fiscal 2003, the company expects capital expenditures to be consistent with fiscal 2002.[4]

FINANCING LONG-TERM ASSETS

In addition to deciding whether to acquire a long-term asset, management must decide how to finance the asset if it is acquired. Some companies are profitable enough to pay for long-term assets out of cash flows from operations, but when financing is needed, some form of long-term arrangement related to the life of the asset is usually most appropriate. For example, an automobile loan generally spans 4 or 5 years, whereas a mortgage on a house may span as many as 30 years.

For a major long-term acquisition, a company may issue capital stock, long-term notes, or bonds. A good place to study a company's long-term financing is in the financing activities section of the statement of cash flows. For instance, in discussing this section, Ford Motor Company's management states, "At December 31, 2002, the Automotive sector had total debt of $14.2 billion, up $400 million from a year ago. The weighted average maturity of our long-term debt . . . is approximately 27 years."[5]

www.ford.com

FIGURE 4
Issues of Accounting for Long-Term Assets

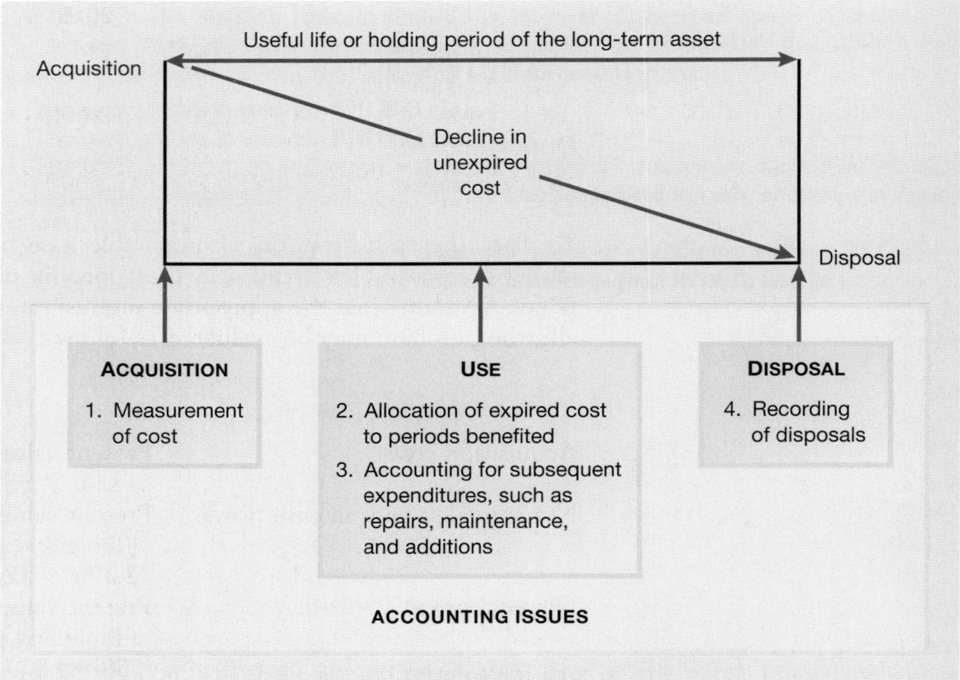

APPLYING THE MATCHING RULE TO LONG-TERM ASSETS

Accounting for long-term assets requires the proper application of the matching rule through the resolution of two important issues. The first is how much of the total cost to allocate to expense in the current accounting period. The second is how much to retain on the balance sheet as an asset to benefit future periods. To resolve these issues, four important questions about the acquisition, use, and disposal of each long-term asset must be answered (see Figure 4):

1. How is the cost of the long-term asset determined?
2. How should the expired portion of the cost of the long-term asset be allocated against revenues over time?
3. How should subsequent expenditures, such as repairs and additions, be treated?
4. How should disposal of the long-term asset be recorded?

STUDY NOTE: Useful life is measured by the service units a business expects to receive from an asset. It should not be confused with physical life, which is often much longer. If the management of a new business is having difficulty determining an asset's estimated useful life, it may obtain help from trade magazines. Nearly every industry has at least one.

Because of the long life of long-term assets and the complexity of the transactions relating to them, management has many choices and estimates to make. For example, acquisition cost may be complicated by group purchases, trade-ins, or construction costs. In addition, to allocate the cost of the asset to future periods effectively, management must estimate how long the asset will last and what it will be worth at the end of its use. In making such estimates, it is helpful to think of a long-term asset as a bundle of services to be used in the operation of the business over a period of years. A delivery truck may provide 100,000 miles of service over its life. A piece of equipment may have the potential to produce 500,000 parts. A building may provide shelter for 50 years. As each of those assets is purchased, the company is paying in advance for 100,000 miles, the capacity to produce 500,000 parts, or 50 years of service. In essence, each asset is a type of long-term prepaid expense. The accounting problem is to spread the cost of the services over the useful life of the asset. As the services benefit the company over the years, the cost becomes an expense rather than an asset.

Check out ACE for a Review Quiz at http://accounting.college.hmco.com/students.

ACQUISITION COST OF PROPERTY, PLANT, AND EQUIPMENT

LO2 Distinguish between capital and revenue expenditures, and account for the cost of property, plant, and equipment.

RELATED TEXT ASSIGNMENTS
Q: 8, 9, 10
SE: 2, 3
E: 3, 4, 5, 14
P: 1, 6
SD: 4, 5, 6
FRA: 3

Expenditure refers to a payment or an obligation to make future payment for an asset, such as a truck, or a service, such as a repair. Expenditures may be classified as capital expenditures or revenue expenditures. A **capital expenditure** is an expenditure for the purchase or expansion of a long-term asset. Capital expenditures are recorded in the asset accounts because they benefit several future accounting periods. A **revenue expenditure** is an expenditure related to the repair, maintenance, and operation of a long-term asset. These expenditures do not extend the asset's original useful life but are necessary to enable the asset to fulfill its original useful life. Revenue expenditures are recorded in the expense accounts because their benefits are realized in the current period.

STUDY NOTE: Although dyeing a carpet may make it look almost new, it is not considered a capital expenditure because even though the carpet looks better, its fibers are not stronger, and it probably will not last significantly longer than it would have before the color was changed.

STUDY NOTE: The cost of mailing lists may be recorded as an asset because the mailing lists will be used over and over and will benefit future accounting periods.

THE IMPORTANCE OF CLASSIFYING EXPENDITURES CORRECTLY

Careful distinction between capital and revenue expenditures is important to the proper application of the matching rule. For example, if the purchase of an automobile is mistakenly recorded as a revenue expenditure, the total cost of the automobile is recorded as an expense on the income statement. As a result, current net income is reported at a lower amount (understated) and assets are understated. In future periods net income will be overstated because depreciation expense is understated. Assets are also understated because the asset was completely expensed in the period that it was purchased. If, on the other hand, a revenue expenditure, such as the painting of a building, were charged to an asset account, the expense of the current period would be understated. Current net income and assets would be overstated by the same amount, and the net income of future periods would be understated because of the erroneous future depreciation expense that was recorded.

Determining when a payment is an expense and when it is an asset is a matter of judgment, in the exercise of which management takes a leading role. For example, inconsistencies have existed in accounting for the costs of computer programs that run the systems for businesses. Some companies immediately write off the expenditure as an expense, whereas others treat it as a long-term intangible asset and amortize it year after year. Companies spend billions of dollars a year on this type of software, and it is an important variable in the profitability of many companies. Although the AICPA has issued new rules to try to bring more standardization to these accounting issues, considerable latitude does still exist, such as in determining how long the economic life of the software will be.[6]

GENERAL APPROACH TO ACQUISITION COSTS

The acquisition cost of property, plant, and equipment includes all expenditures reasonable and necessary to get the asset in place and ready for use. For example, the cost of installing and testing a machine is a legitimate cost of the machine. However, if the machine is damaged during installation, the cost of repairs is an operating expense and not an acquisition cost.

KEY POINT: Expenditures necessary to prepare an asset for its intended use are a cost of the asset.

Cost is easiest to determine when a purchase is made for cash. In that case, the cost of the asset is equal to the cash paid for the asset plus expenditures for freight, insurance while in transit, installation, and other necessary related costs. If a debt is incurred in the purchase of the asset, the interest charges are not a cost of the asset, but a cost of borrowing the money to buy the asset. They are therefore an operating expense. An exception to this principle is that interest costs incurred during the construction of an asset are properly included as a cost of the asset.[7]

Expenditures like freight, insurance while in transit, and installation are included in the cost of the asset because they are necessary if the asset is to function. Following the matching rule, they are allocated to the useful life of the asset rather than charged as expenses in the current period.

For practical purposes, many companies establish policies defining when an expenditure should be recorded as an expense or an asset. For example, small expenditures for items that would normally be treated as assets may be treated as expenses because the amounts involved are not material in relation to net income. Thus, a wastebasket, which might last for years, would be recorded as a supplies expense rather than as a depreciable asset.

Some of the problems of determining the cost of long-lived plant assets are discussed in the next sections.

KEY POINT: Many costs may be incurred to prepare land for its intended use and condition. All such costs are a cost of land.

LAND There are often expenditures in addition to the purchase price of land that should be debited to the Land account. Some examples are commissions to real estate agents; lawyers' fees; accrued taxes paid by the purchaser; costs of preparing the land to build on, such as the costs of tearing down old buildings and draining, clearing, and grading the land; and assessments for local improvements, such as putting in streets and sewage systems. The cost of landscaping is usually debited to the Land account because such improvements are relatively permanent. Land is not subject to depreciation because it does not have a limited useful life.

ENRICHMENT NOTE: The costs of tearing down existing buildings can be major. For example, companies may spend millions of dollars imploding buildings so they can remove them and build new ones.

Let us assume that a company buys land for a new retail operation. It pays a net purchase price of $170,000, pays brokerage fees of $6,000 and legal fees of $2,000, pays $10,000 to have an old building on the site torn down, receives $4,000 salvage from the old building, and pays $1,000 to have the site graded. The cost of the land is $185,000:

Net purchase price		$170,000
Brokerage fees		6,000
Legal fees		2,000
Tearing down old building	$10,000	
Less salvage	4,000	6,000
Grading		1,000
Total cost		$185,000

LAND IMPROVEMENTS Some improvements to real estate, such as driveways, parking lots, and fences, have a limited life and are thus subject to depreciation. They should be recorded in an account called Land Improvements rather than in the Land account.

BUILDINGS When an existing building is purchased, its cost includes the purchase price plus all repairs and other expenditures required to put it in usable condition. Buildings are subject to depreciation because they have a limited useful life. When a business constructs its own building, the cost includes all reasonable and necessary expenditures, such as those for materials, labor, part of the overhead and other indirect costs, architects' fees, insurance during construction, interest on construction loans during the period of construction, lawyers' fees, and building permits. If outside contractors are used in the construction, the net contract price plus other expenditures necessary to put the building in usable condition are included in the cost.

ENRICHMENT NOTE: The electrical wiring and plumbing of a dental chair are included in the cost of the asset because they are a necessary cost of preparing the asset for use.

EQUIPMENT The cost of equipment includes all expenditures connected with purchasing the equipment and preparing it for use. Those expenditures include the invoice price less cash discounts; freight, including insurance; excise taxes and tariffs; buying expenses; installation costs; and test runs to ready the equipment for operation. Equipment is subject to depreciation.

Focus on Business Ethics

Is It an Asset or Expense? The Answer Matters.

Determining whether an expenditure is a long-term asset or an expense is not always as clear-cut as some might imagine. Management has considerable leeway in how to record transactions, but the financial statements must be prepared in accordance with generally accepted accounting principles and the result cannot be deceptive. If management's choices are questioned, the results can sometimes have drastic consequences.

For example, *The Wall Street Journal* reported that the chief financial officer of WorldCom <www.worldcom.com> used an unorthodox and unusually aggressive technique to account for one of the long-distance company's biggest expenses. The company recorded charges paid to local telephone networks to complete calls as long-term assets instead of operating expenses. This increased income in the year in question by deferring the costs to a future year, effectively turning a net loss for the year into a net income. In total, the company says that at least $3.8 billion was accounted for in this way. As a result of the report, the company's stock price dropped from a high of $64.50 to less than one dollar. The SEC filed civil fraud charges against WorldCom, saying the company "falsely portrayed itself as a profitable business."[8] Criminal charges may follow and the company will likely face bankruptcy.

This and other notable cases show that accounting is not a passive part of business that can be manipulated at will, but must be taken seriously. The financial statements must reveal the substance of the business's activities.

Stop and Think!
What incentive does a company have to allocate more of a group purchase price to the land rather than to the building?
A higher land valuation has the effect of increasing income because a smaller building valuation results in a lower amount to depreciate over its useful life. ■

■ **Group Purchases** Land and other assets are sometimes purchased for a lump sum. Because land is a nondepreciable asset that has an unlimited life, it must have a separate ledger account, and the lump-sum purchase price must be apportioned between the land and the other assets. For example, assume that a building and the land on which it is situated are purchased for a lump-sum payment of $85,000. The apportionment can be made by determining the price of each if purchased separately and applying the appropriate percentages to the lump-sum price. Assume that appraisals yield estimates of $10,000 for the land and $90,000 for the building if purchased separately. In that case, 10 percent of the lump-sum price, or $8,500, would be allocated to the land, and 90 percent, or $76,500, would be allocated to the building, as follows:

	Appraisal	Percentage	Apportionment
Land	$ 10,000	10% ($10,000 ÷ $100,000)	$ 8,500 ($85,000 × 10%)
Building	90,000	90% ($90,000 ÷ $100,000)	76,500 ($85,000 × 90%)
Totals	$100,000	100%	$85,000

Check out ACE for a Review Quiz at http://accounting.college.hmco.com/students.

Accounting for Depreciation

LO3 Define *depreciation* and compute depreciation under the straight-line, production, and declining-balance methods.

RELATED TEXT ASSIGNMENTS
Q: 11, 12, 13, 14, 15, 16
SE: 4, 5, 6
E: 5, 6, 7, 10
P: 2, 3, 7, 8
SD: 1, 2, 6
FRA: 1, 3, 5, 6

The AICPA describes depreciation accounting as follows:

> The cost of a productive facility is one of the costs of the services it renders during its useful economic life. Generally accepted accounting principles require that this cost be spread over the expected useful life of the facility in such a way as to allocate it as equitably as possible to the periods during which services are obtained from the use of the facility. This procedure is known as depreciation accounting, a system of accounting which aims to distribute the cost or other basic value of tangible capital assets, less salvage (if any), over the estimated useful life of the unit . . . in a systematic and rational manner. It is a process of allocation, not of valuation.[9]

This description contains several important points. First, all tangible assets except land have a limited useful life. Because of this, their costs must be distributed as expenses over the years they benefit. Physical deterioration and obsolescence are the major causes of the limited useful life of a depreciable asset. The

PARENTHETICAL NOTE: An older computer may be functioning as well as it did on the day of purchase, but it has become obsolete because much faster, more efficient computers are now available.

physical deterioration of tangible assets results from use and from exposure to the elements, such as wind and sun. Periodic repairs and a sound maintenance policy may keep buildings and equipment in good operating order and extract the maximum useful life from them, but every machine or building at some point must be discarded. Repairs do not eliminate the need for depreciation. **Obsolescence** is the process of becoming out of date. Because of fast-changing technology and fast-changing demands, machinery and even buildings often become obsolete before they wear out. Accountants do not distinguish between physical deterioration and obsolescence because they are interested in the length of an asset's useful life, not in what limits that useful life.

Second, the term *depreciation*, as used in accounting, does not refer to an asset's physical deterioration or decrease in market value over time. Depreciation means the allocation of the cost of a plant asset to the periods that benefit from the services of that asset. The term is used to describe the gradual conversion of the cost of the asset into an expense.

KEY POINT: Depreciation is the allocation of the acquisition cost of an asset, and any similarity between undepreciated cost and current market value is pure coincidence.

Third, depreciation is not a process of valuation. Accounting records are kept in accordance with the cost principle; they are not indicators of changing price levels. It is possible that because of an advantageous purchase and specific market conditions, the market value of a building may rise. Nevertheless, depreciation must continue to be recorded because it is the result of an allocation, not a valuation, process. Eventually, the building will wear out or become obsolete regardless of interim fluctuations in market value.

FACTORS THAT AFFECT THE COMPUTATION OF DEPRECIATION

Four factors affect the computation of depreciation: (1) cost, (2) residual value, (3) depreciable cost, and (4) estimated useful life.

■ **COST** As explained earlier in the chapter, cost is the net purchase price plus all reasonable and necessary expenditures to get the asset in place and ready for use.

KEY POINT: Residual value is the portion of an asset's acquisition cost expected to be recovered at the asset's disposal date.

■ **RESIDUAL VALUE** The **residual value** of an asset is its estimated net scrap, salvage, or trade-in value as of the estimated date of disposal. Other terms often used to describe residual value are *salvage value* and *disposal value.*

KEY POINT: It is depreciable cost, not acquisition cost, that is allocated over the useful life of a plant asset.

■ **DEPRECIABLE COST** The **depreciable cost** of an asset is its cost less its residual value. For example, a truck that costs $12,000 and has a residual value of $3,000 would have a depreciable cost of $9,000. Depreciable cost must be allocated over the useful life of the asset.

■ **ESTIMATED USEFUL LIFE** **Estimated useful life** is the total number of service units expected from a long-term asset. Service units may be measured in terms of years

FOCUS ON BUSINESS PRACTICE

The Useful Life of an Aircraft Is How Long?

Most airlines depreciate airplanes over an estimated useful life of 10 to 20 years. But how long will a properly maintained airplane really last? Western Airlines <www.westernairlines.com> paid $3.3 million for a new Boeing 737 in July 1968. More than 78,000 flights and 30 years later, this aircraft was still flying for Vanguard Airlines <www.flyvanguard.com>, a no-frills airline. Among the other airlines that have owned this aircraft during the course of its life are Piedmont, Delta <www.delta.com>, and US Airways <www.usairways.com>. Virtually every part of the plane has been replaced over the years. Boeing believes the plane could theoretically make double the number of flights before it is retired.

The useful lives of many types of assets can be extended indefinitely if the assets are correctly maintained, but proper accounting in accordance with the matching rule requires depreciation over a "reasonable" useful life. Each airline that owned the plane would have accounted for the plane in this way.

the asset is expected to be used, units expected to be produced, miles expected to be driven, or similar measures. In computing the estimated useful life of an asset, an accountant should consider all relevant information, including (1) past experience with similar assets, (2) the asset's present condition, (3) the company's repair and maintenance policy, (4) current technological and industry trends, and (5) local conditions, such as weather.

Depreciation is recorded at the end of the accounting period by an adjusting entry that takes the following form:

A = L + OE
−   −

Depreciation Expense, Asset Name	XXX	
Accumulated Depreciation, Asset Name		XXX
To record depreciation for the period		

Methods of Computing Depreciation

Many methods are used to allocate the cost of plant assets to accounting periods through depreciation. Each is proper for certain circumstances. The most common methods are (1) the straight-line method, (2) the production method, and (3) an accelerated method known as the declining-balance method.

CLARIFICATION NOTE: The straight-line depreciation method should be used when approximately equal asset benefit is obtained each year.

KEY POINT: Residual value and useful life are, at best, educated guesses.

Straight-Line Method When the **straight-line method** is used to calculate depreciation, the depreciable cost of the asset is spread evenly over the estimated useful life of the asset. The straight-line method is based on the assumption that depreciation depends only on the passage of time. The depreciation expense for each period is computed by dividing the depreciable cost (cost of the depreciating asset less its estimated residual value) by the number of accounting periods in the asset's estimated useful life. The rate of depreciation is the same in each year. Suppose, for example, that a delivery truck costs $10,000 and has an estimated residual value of $1,000 at the end of its estimated useful life of five years. The annual depreciation would be $1,800 under the straight-line method, calculated as follows:

$$\frac{\text{Cost} - \text{Residual Value}}{\text{Estimated Useful Life}} = \frac{\$10{,}000 - \$1{,}000}{5 \text{ years}} = \$1{,}800 \text{ per year}$$

The depreciation for the five years would be as follows:

Depreciation Schedule, Straight-Line Method

	Cost	Yearly Depreciation	Accumulated Depreciation	Carrying Value
Date of purchase	$10,000	—	—	$10,000
End of first year	10,000	$1,800	$1,800	8,200
End of second year	10,000	1,800	3,600	6,400
End of third year	10,000	1,800	5,400	4,600
End of fourth year	10,000	1,800	7,200	2,800
End of fifth year	10,000	1,800	9,000	1,000

There are three important points to note from the depreciation schedule for the straight-line depreciation method. First, the depreciation is the same each year. Second, the accumulated depreciation increases uniformly. Third, the carrying value decreases uniformly until it reaches the estimated residual value.

Production Method The **production method** of depreciation is based on the assumption that depreciation is solely the result of use and that the passage of time plays no role in the depreciation process. If we assume that the delivery truck in the previous example has an estimated useful life of 90,000 miles, the depreciation cost per mile would be determined as follows:

$$\frac{\text{Cost} - \text{Residual Value}}{\text{Estimated Units of Useful Life}} = \frac{\$10{,}000 - \$1{,}000}{90{,}000 \text{ miles}} = \$.10 \text{ per mile}$$

PARENTHETICAL NOTE: The production method is appropriate when a company has widely fluctuating rates of production. For example, carpet mills often close during the first two weeks in July. Charging a full month's depreciation would not achieve the goal of matching cost with revenue. Conversely, the same mills may run double shifts in September. At that time, twice the usual amount of depreciation should be charged.

If we assume that the use of the truck was 20,000 miles for the first year, 30,000 miles for the second, 10,000 miles for the third, 20,000 miles for the fourth, and 10,000 miles for the fifth, the depreciation schedule for the delivery truck would be as follows:

Depreciation Schedule, Production Method

	Cost	Miles	Yearly Depreciation	Accumulated Depreciation	Carrying Value
Date of purchase	$10,000	—	—	—	$10,000
End of first year	10,000	20,000	$2,000	$2,000	8,000
End of second year	10,000	30,000	3,000	5,000	5,000
End of third year	10,000	10,000	1,000	6,000	4,000
End of fourth year	10,000	20,000	2,000	8,000	2,000
End of fifth year	10,000	10,000	1,000	9,000	1,000

There is a direct relation between the amount of depreciation each year and the units of output or use. Also, the accumulated depreciation increases each year in direct relation to units of output or use. Finally, the carrying value decreases each year in direct relation to units of output or use until it reaches the estimated residual value.

Under the production method, the unit of output or use employed to measure the estimated useful life of each asset should be appropriate for that asset. For example, the number of items produced may be an appropriate measure for one machine, but the number of hours of use may be a better measure for another. The production method should be used only when the output of an asset over its useful life can be estimated with reasonable accuracy.

PARENTHETICAL NOTE: Accelerated depreciation is appropriate for assets that provide the greatest benefits in their early years. Under such a method, depreciation charges will be high in years when revenue generation from the asset is high.

■ DECLINING-BALANCE METHOD An **accelerated method** of depreciation results in relatively large amounts of depreciation in the early years of an asset's life and smaller amounts in later years. Such a method, which is based on the passage of time, assumes that many kinds of plant assets are most efficient when new, and so provide more and better service in the early years of their useful life. It is consistent with the matching rule to allocate more depreciation to earlier years than to later years if the benefits or services received in the earlier years are greater than those received later.

An accelerated method also recognizes that fast-changing technologies cause some equipment to become obsolescent and lose service value rapidly. Thus, it is realistic to allocate more to depreciation in earlier years than in later ones. Another argument in favor of an accelerated method is that repair expense is likely to be greater in later years than in earlier years. Thus, the total of repair and depreciation expense remains fairly constant over a period of years. This result naturally assumes that the services received from the asset are roughly equal from year to year.

The **declining-balance method** is the most common accelerated method of depreciation. Under this method, depreciation is computed by applying a fixed rate to the carrying value (the declining balance) of a tangible long-lived asset, resulting in higher depreciation charges during the early years of the asset's life. Though any fixed rate can be used, the most common rate is a percentage equal to twice the straight-line depreciation percentage. When twice the straight-line rate is used, the method is usually called the **double-declining-balance method**.

KEY POINT: The double-declining-balance method is the only method presented in which the residual value is not deducted before beginning the depreciation calculation.

In our earlier example, the delivery truck had an estimated useful life of five years. Consequently, under the straight-line method, the depreciation rate for each year was 20 percent (100 percent ÷ 5 years).

Under the double-declining-balance method, the fixed rate is 40 percent (2 × 20 percent). This fixed rate is applied to the *remaining carrying value* at the end of each year. Estimated residual value is not taken into account in figuring depreciation except in a year when calculated depreciation exceeds the amount necessary to

KEY POINT: Under the double-declining-balance method, depreciation in the last year rarely equals the exact amount needed to reduce carrying value to residual value. Depreciation in the last year is limited to the amount necessary to reduce carrying value to residual value.

PARENTHETICAL NOTE: An asset remains on the books as long as it is in use. Even if the asset is fully depreciated, the company should not remove it from the books until it is taken out of service.

bring the carrying value down to the estimated residual value. The depreciation schedule for this method is as follows:

Depreciation Schedule, Double-Declining-Balance Method

	Cost	Yearly Depreciation		Accumulated Depreciation	Carrying Value
Date of purchase	$10,000		—	—	$10,000
End of first year	10,000	(40% × $10,000)	$4,000	$4,000	6,000
End of second year	10,000	(40% × $6,000)	2,400	6,400	3,600
End of third year	10,000	(40% × $3,600)	1,440	7,840	2,160
End of fourth year	10,000	(40% × $2,160)	864	8,704	1,296
End of fifth year	10,000		296*	9,000	1,000

*Depreciation limited to amount necessary to reduce carrying value to residual value: $296 = $1,296 (previous carrying value) − $1,000 (residual value).

Note that the fixed rate is always applied to the carrying value at the end of the previous year. The depreciation is greatest in the first year and declines each year after that. Finally, the depreciation in the fifth year is limited to the amount necessary to reduce carrying value to residual value.

COMPARISON OF THE THREE METHODS A visual comparison may provide a better understanding of the three depreciation methods described above. Figure 5 compares yearly depreciation and carrying value under the three methods. In the left-hand graph, which shows yearly depreciation, straight-line depreciation is uniform at $1,800 per year over the five-year period. However, the double-declining-balance method begins at an amount greater than straight-line ($4,000) and decreases each year to amounts that are less than straight-line (ultimately, $296). The production method does not generate a regular pattern because of the random fluctuation of the depreciation from year to year. The three yearly depreciation patterns are reflected in the graph of carrying value. In that graph, each method starts in the same place (cost of $10,000) and ends at the same place (residual value of $1,000). It is the patterns during the useful life of the asset that differ for each method. For instance, the carrying value under the straight-line method is always greater than that under the double-declining-balance method, except at the beginning and end of useful life.

STOP AND THINK!
Which depreciation method would best reflect the risk of obsolescence from rapid technological changes?

An accelerated depreciation method is best. Companies facing rapid technological change use it to minimize the risk of obsolescence. ■

FIGURE 5
Graphic Comparison of Three Methods of Determining Depreciation

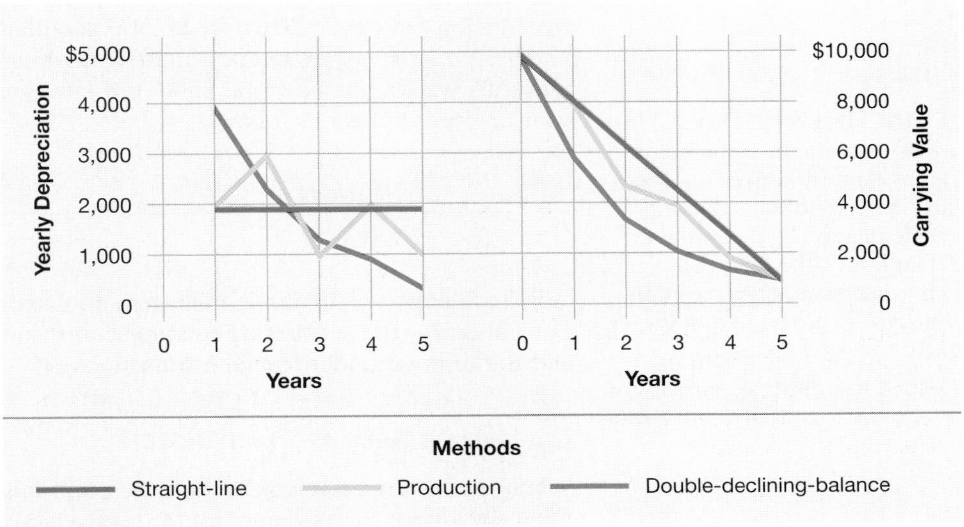

Focus on Business Practice

Accelerated Methods Save Money!

An AICPA study of 600 large companies found that the overwhelming majority used the straight-line method of depreciation for financial reporting purposes, as shown in Figure 6. Only about 13 percent used some type of accelerated method, and 5 percent used the production method. These figures tend to be misleading about the importance of accelerated depreciation methods, however, especially when it comes to income taxes. Federal income tax laws allow either the straight-line method or an accelerated method, and for tax purposes, about 75 percent of the 600 companies studied preferred using an accelerated method. Companies use different methods of depreciation for good reason. The straight-line method can be advantageous for financial reporting because it can produce the highest net income, and an accelerated method can be beneficial for tax purposes because it can result in lower income taxes.

Figure 6
Depreciation Methods Used by 600 Large Companies for Financial Reporting

CLARIFICATION NOTE: For financial reporting purposes, the objective is to measure performance accurately. For tax purposes, the objective is to minimize tax liability.

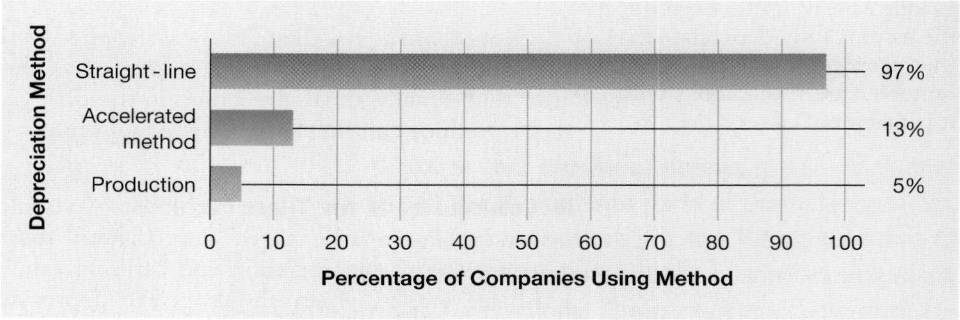

Total percentage exceeds 100 because some companies used different methods for different types of depreciable assets.

Check out ACE for a Review Quiz at http://accounting.college.hmco.com/students.

Disposal of Depreciable Assets

LO4 Account for the disposal of depreciable assets.

RELATED TEXT ASSIGNMENTS
Q: 17, 18
SE: 7, 8
E: 8, 9
P: 4
FRA: 6

ENRICHMENT NOTE: Plant assets may also be disposed of by involuntary conversion (e.g., fire, theft, mud slide, flood) or condemnation by a governmental authority. For financial reporting purposes, involuntary conversions are treated in the same way as if the assets were discarded or sold.

When plant assets are no longer useful because they are worn out or obsolete, they may be discarded, sold, or traded in on the purchase of new plant and equipment. For accounting purposes, a plant asset may be disposed of in one of three ways: It may be (1) discarded, (2) sold for cash, or (3) exchanged for another asset. To illustrate how each of these cases is recorded, assume that MGC Company purchased a machine on January 2, 20x0, for $6,500 and planned to depreciate it on a straight-line basis over an estimated useful life of ten years. The residual value at the end of ten years was estimated to be $500. On January 2, 20x7, the balances of the relevant accounts appear as follows:

Machinery			Accumulated Depreciation, Machinery	
6,500				4,200

On September 30, 20x7, management disposes of the asset. The next few sections illustrate the accounting treatment to record depreciation for the partial year and the disposal under several assumptions.

Discard or Sale of Plant Assets

When a plant asset is discarded or disposed of in some other way, it is first necessary to record depreciation expense for the partial year up to the date of disposal. This step is required because the asset was used until that date and, under the matching rule, the accounting period should receive the proper allocation of depreciation expense.

In this illustration, MGC Company disposes of the machinery on September 30. The entry to record the depreciation for the first nine months of 20x7 (nine-twelfths of a year) is as follows:

A = L + OE
− −

Sept. 30	Depreciation Expense, Machinery	450	
	Accumulated Depreciation, Machinery		450
	To record depreciation up to date of disposal		
	$\frac{\$6{,}500 - \$500}{10} \times \frac{9}{12} = \$450$		

KEY POINT: When it disposes of an asset, a company must do two things. First, it must bring the depreciation up to date. Second, it must remove all evidence of ownership of the asset, including the contra account Accumulated Depreciation.

The relevant accounts appear as follows after the entry is posted:

Machinery		Accumulated Depreciation, Machinery	
6,500			4,650

After updating the depreciation, it is then necessary to remove the carrying value of the asset as shown in the following sections.

■ DISCARDED PLANT ASSETS A plant asset rarely lasts exactly as long as its estimated life. If it lasts longer than its estimated life, it is not depreciated past the point at which its carrying value equals its residual value. The purpose of depreciation is to spread the depreciable cost of an asset over the estimated life of the asset. Thus, the total accumulated depreciation should never exceed the total depreciable cost. If an asset remains in use beyond the end of its estimated life, its cost and accumulated depreciation remain in the ledger accounts. Proper records will thus be available for maintaining control over plant assets. If the residual value is zero, the carrying value of a fully depreciated asset is zero until the asset is disposed of. If such an asset is discarded, no gain or loss results.

KEY POINT: A fully depreciated asset is kept on the books as long as it is still being used in the business. When a physical count of plant assets is made and reconciled with the general ledger control account and the subsidiary ledger, all assets must be accounted for.

In the illustration, however, the discarded equipment has a carrying value of $1,850 at the time of its disposal. The carrying value is computed from the T accounts above as machinery of $6,500 less accumulated depreciation of $4,650. A loss equal to the carrying value should be recorded when the machine is discarded, as follows:

A = L + OE
+ −
−

Sept. 30	Accumulated Depreciation, Machinery	4,650	
	Loss on Disposal of Machinery	1,850	
	Machinery		6,500
	Discarded machine no longer used in the business		

Gains and losses on disposals of plant assets are classified as other revenues and expenses on the income statement.

STOP AND THINK!
When would the disposal of long-term assets result in no gain or loss?
If cash received for the assets equals their residual value, then no gain or loss occurs. ■

■ PLANT ASSETS SOLD FOR CASH The entry to record a plant asset sold for cash is similar to the one just illustrated, except that the receipt of cash should also be recorded. The following entries show how to record the sale of a machine under three assumptions about the selling price. In the first case, the $1,850 cash received is exactly equal to the $1,850 carrying value of the machine; therefore, no gain or loss occurs.

A = L + OE
+
+
−

Sept. 30	Cash	1,850	
	Accumulated Depreciation, Machinery	4,650	
	Machinery		6,500
	Sale of machine for carrying value; no gain or loss		

In the second case, the $1,000 cash received is less than the carrying value of $1,850, so a loss of $850 is recorded.

A = L + OE
\+ −
\+
−

Sept. 30	Cash	1,000	
	Accumulated Depreciation, Machinery	4,650	
	Loss on Sale of Machinery	850	
	Machinery		6,500
	Sale of machine at less than carrying value; loss of $850 ($1,850 − $1,000) recorded		

KEY POINT: For an asset discarded or sold for cash, the gain (loss) on disposal of the asset equals cash received minus carrying value.

In the third case, the $2,000 cash received exceeds the carrying value of $1,850, so a gain of $150 is recorded.

A = L + OE
\+ +
\+
−

Sept. 30	Cash	2,000	
	Accumulated Depreciation, Machinery	4,650	
	Gain on Sale of Machinery		150
	Machinery		6,500
	Sale of machine at more than the carrying value; gain of $150 ($2,000 − $1,850) recorded		

Exchanges of Plant Assets

Businesses also dispose of plant assets by trading them in on the purchase of other plant assets. Exchanges may involve similar assets, such as an old machine traded in on a newer model, or dissimilar assets, such as a cement mixer traded in on a truck. In either case, the purchase price is reduced by the amount of the trade-in allowance.

Basically, accounting for exchanges of plant assets is similar to accounting for sales of plant assets for cash. If the trade-in allowance received is greater than the carrying value of the asset surrendered, there has been a gain. If the allowance is less, there has been a loss. There are special rules for recognizing these gains and losses, depending on the nature of the assets exchanged:

Exchange	Losses Recognized	Gains Recognized
For financial accounting purposes		
Of dissimilar assets	Yes	Yes
Of similar assets	Yes	No
For income tax purposes		
Of dissimilar assets	Yes	Yes
Of similar assets	No	No

CLARIFICATION NOTE: For assets to be similar, they must be used for similar purposes. A desktop computer, for example, is similar to a laptop computer. Dissimilar assets, such as a truck and a cement mixer, are not used for similar purposes.

PARENTHETICAL NOTE: Recognizing losses but not gains on similar assets follows the convention of conservatism.

KEY POINT: For exchanges of dissimilar assets, the gain or loss on exchange equals the trade-in allowance minus carrying value of the old asset.

For both financial accounting and income tax purposes, both gains and losses are recognized when a company exchanges dissimilar assets. Assets are dissimilar when they perform different functions or do not meet specific monetary and business criteria for being considered similar assets. For financial accounting purposes, most exchanges are considered exchanges of dissimilar assets. In rare cases, when exchanges meet the specific criteria for exchanges of similar assets, the gains are not recognized. In these cases, you could think of the trade-in as an extension of the life and usefulness of the original machine. Instead of recognizing a gain at the time of the exchange, the company records the new machine at the sum of the carrying value of the older machine plus any cash paid.[10]

For income tax purposes, similar assets are defined as those performing the same function. Neither gains nor losses on exchanges of these assets are recognized in computing a company's income tax liability. Thus, in practice, accountants face cases in which both gains and losses are recognized (exchanges of dissimilar assets), cases in which losses are recognized and gains are not (exchanges of similar assets for financial reporting purposes), and cases in which neither gains nor losses are recognized (exchanges of similar assets for income tax purposes). Since all these options are used in practice, they are all illustrated in the following sections.

CLARIFICATION NOTE: There is no relationship between carrying value and trade-in value. Carrying value is original cost minus accumulated depreciation to date, whereas trade-in value is fair market value on the date of the exchange.

LOSS ON THE EXCHANGE RECOGNIZED A loss is recognized for financial accounting purposes on all exchanges in which a material loss occurs. A loss occurs when the trade-in allowance is less than the carrying value of the old asset. To illustrate the recognition of a loss, let us assume that the firm in our earlier example exchanges the machine for a newer, more modern machine on the following terms:

List price of new machine	$12,000
Trade-in allowance for old machine	(1,000)
Cash payment required	$11,000

In this case, the trade-in allowance ($1,000) is less than the carrying value ($1,850) of the old machine. The loss on the exchange is $850 ($1,850 − $1,000). This entry records the transaction under the assumption that the loss is to be recognized:

A = L + OE
+ −
+
−
−

Sept. 30	Machinery (new)	12,000	
	Accumulated Depreciation, Machinery	4,650	
	Loss on Exchange of Machinery	850	
	Machinery (old)		6,500
	Cash		11,000
	Exchange of machines		

KEY POINT: For income tax purposes, gains and losses on the exchange of similar assets are not recognized.

LOSS ON THE EXCHANGE NOT RECOGNIZED In the previous example, in which a loss was recognized, the new asset was recorded at the purchase price of $12,000 and a loss of $850 was recorded. If the transaction involves similar assets and is to be recorded for income tax purposes, the loss should not be recognized. In this case, the cost basis of the new asset will reflect the effect of the unrecorded loss. The cost basis is computed by adding the cash payment to the carrying value of the old asset:

Carrying value of old machine	$ 1,850
Cash paid	11,000
Cost basis of new machine	$12,850

Note that no loss is recognized in the entry to record this transaction:

A = L + OE
+
+
−
−

Sept. 30	Machinery (new)	12,850	
	Accumulated Depreciation, Machinery	4,650	
	Machinery (old)		6,500
	Cash		11,000
	Exchange of machines		

Note that the new machinery is reported at the purchase price of $12,000 plus the unrecognized loss of $850. The nonrecognition of the loss on the exchange is, in effect, a postponement of the loss. Since depreciation of the new machine will be computed based on a cost of $12,850 instead of $12,000, the "unrecognized" loss results in more depreciation each year on the new machine than if the loss had been recognized.

KEY POINT: For exchanges of assets, the cash payment on the exchange equals list price of the new asset minus trade-in allowance of the old asset.

GAIN ON THE EXCHANGE RECOGNIZED Gains on exchanges are recognized for accounting purposes when dissimilar assets are involved. To illustrate the recognition of a gain, we continue with our example, assuming the following terms and assuming the machines being exchanged serve different functions:

List price of new machine	$12,000
Trade-in allowance for old machine	(3,000)
Cash payment required	$ 9,000

Here, the trade-in allowance ($3,000) exceeds the carrying value ($1,850) of the old machine by $1,150. Thus, there is a gain on the exchange, assuming the price of the new machine has not been inflated to allow for an excessive trade-in value. In other words, a gain exists if the trade-in allowance represents the fair market value of the old machine. In that case, the transaction is recorded as follows:

A = L + OE				
+ +	Sept. 30	Machinery (new)	12,000	
+		Accumulated Depreciation, Machinery	4,650	
−		Gain on Exchange of Machinery		1,150
−		Machinery (old)		6,500
		Cash		9,000
		Exchange of machines		

■ **Gain on the Exchange Not Recognized** When similar assets are exchanged, gains are not recognized for either accounting or income tax purposes. The cost basis of the new machine must reflect the effect of the unrecorded gain. This cost basis is computed by adding the cash payment to the carrying value of the old asset:

Carrying value of old machine	$ 1,850
Cash paid	9,000
Cost basis of new machine	$10,850

The entry to record the transaction is as follows:

A = L + OE				
+	Sept. 30	Machinery (new)	10,850	
+		Accumulated Depreciation, Machinery	4,650	
−		Machinery (old)		6,500
−		Cash		9,000
		Exchange of machines		

As with the nonrecognition of losses, the nonrecognition of the gain on an exchange is, in effect, a postponement of the gain. In this illustration, when the new machine is eventually discarded or sold, its cost basis will be $10,850 instead of its original price of $12,000. Since depreciation will be computed on the cost basis of $10,850, the "unrecognized" gain is reflected in lower depreciation each year on the new machine than if the gain had been recognized.

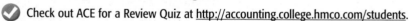

Check out ACE for a Review Quiz at http://accounting.college.hmco.com/students.

Accounting for Natural Resources

LO5 Identify the issues related to accounting for natural resources and compute depletion.

RELATED TEXT ASSIGNMENTS
Q: 19, 20
SE: 9
E: 10
FRA: 5

CLARIFICATION NOTE: Natural resources are not intangible assets. Natural resources are correctly classified as components of property, plant, and equipment.

Natural resources are shown on the balance sheet as long-term assets with such descriptive titles as Timberlands, Oil and Gas Reserves, and Mineral Deposits. The distinguishing characteristic of these assets is that they are converted to inventory by cutting, pumping, mining, or other extraction methods. Natural resources are recorded at acquisition cost, which may include some costs of development. As the resource is extracted and converted to inventory, the asset account must be proportionally reduced. The carrying value of oil reserves on the balance sheet, for example, is reduced by a small amount for each barrel of oil pumped. As a result, the original cost of the oil reserves is gradually reduced, and depletion is recognized in the amount of the decrease.

Depletion

The term *depletion* is used to describe not only the exhaustion of a natural resource but also the proportional allocation of the cost of a natural resource to the units extracted. The costs are allocated in a way that closely resembles the production method used to calculate depreciation. When a natural resource is purchased or developed, there must be an estimate of the total units that will be available, such

ENRICHMENT NOTE: When determining the total units available for depletion, management uses only the total units that are economically feasible to extract. This follows the cost-benefit principle—that is, when the cost of extracting a mineral is greater than the expected profit from the sale of the mineral, the company stops extracting it.

as barrels of oil, tons of coal, or board-feet of lumber. The depletion cost per unit is determined by dividing the cost of the natural resource (less residual value, if any) by the estimated number of units available. The amount of the depletion cost for each accounting period is then computed by multiplying the depletion cost per unit by the number of units extracted and sold. For example, for a mine having an estimated 1,500,000 tons of coal, a cost of $1,800,000, and an estimated residual value of $300,000, the depletion charge per ton of coal is $1:

$$\frac{\$1{,}800{,}000 - \$300{,}000}{1{,}500{,}000 \text{ tons}} = \$1 \text{ per ton}$$

Thus, if 115,000 tons of coal are mined and sold during the first year, the depletion charge for the year is $115,000. This charge is recorded as follows:

A = L + OE
− −

Dec. 31	Depletion Expense, Coal Deposits	115,000	
	Accumulated Depletion, Coal Deposits		115,000
	To record depletion of coal mine: $1 per ton for 115,000 tons mined and sold		

On the balance sheet, data for the mine would be presented as follows:

KEY POINT: The matching rule dictates that the extracted resource be treated as an asset until it is sold. At that point, the asset cost is converted into an expense.

Coal deposits	$1,800,000	
Less accumulated depletion	115,000	$1,685,000

Sometimes a natural resource is not sold in the year it is extracted. It is important to note that it would then be recorded as a depletion *expense* in the year it is *sold*. The part not sold is considered inventory.

Depreciation of Closely Related Plant Assets

PARENTHETICAL NOTE: A company may abandon equipment that is still in good working condition. It may cost the company more to dismantle the equipment and move it to another site than to abandon it.

The extraction of natural resources generally requires special on-site buildings and equipment (e.g., conveyors, drills, and pumps). If the useful life of those assets is longer than the estimated time it will take to deplete the resource, a special problem arises. Because such long-term assets are often abandoned and have no useful purpose once all the resources have been extracted, they should be depreciated on the same basis as the depletion. For example, if machinery with a useful life of ten years is installed on an oil field that is expected to be depleted in eight years, the machinery should be depreciated over the eight-year period, using the production method. That way, each year's depreciation will be proportional to the year's depletion. If one-sixth of the oil field's total reserves is pumped in one year, then the depreciation should be one-sixth of the machinery's cost minus the residual value. If the useful life of a long-term plant asset is less than the expected life of the resource, the shorter life should be used to compute depreciation. In such cases, or when an asset will not be abandoned once all reserves have been depleted, other depreciation methods, such as straight-line or declining-balance, are appropriate.

STOP AND THINK!
When would annual depletion not equal depletion expense?
Annual depletion refers to units extracted, but depletion expense includes only units sold. So annual depletion does not equal depletion expense when units extracted do not equal units sold. ■

Development and Exploration Costs in the Oil and Gas Industry

The costs of exploring and developing oil and gas resources can be accounted for under one of two methods. Under the **successful efforts method**, the cost of successful exploration—for example, producing an oil well—is a cost of the resource. It should be recorded as an asset and depleted over the estimated life of the resource. The cost of an unsuccessful exploration—such as the cost of a dry well—is written off immediately as a loss. Because of these immediate write-offs, successful efforts accounting is considered the more conservative method and is used by most large oil companies. Exploration-minded independent oil companies, on the other hand, argue that the cost of dry wells is part of the overall cost of the systematic development of an oil field and is thus a part of the cost of producing wells. Under this **full-costing method**, all costs, including the cost of dry wells, are recorded as assets and depleted over the estimated life of the producing resources. This method tends to improve a company's earnings performance in its early years. Either method is permitted by the Financial Accounting Standards Board.[11]

Check out ACE for a Review Quiz at http://accounting.college.hmco.com/students.

Accounting for Intangible Assets

LO6 Identify the issues related to accounting for intangible assets, including research and development costs and goodwill.

RELATED TEXT ASSIGNMENTS
Q: 21, 22, 23, 24, 25, 26
SE: 10
E: 11
P: 5
SD: 3, 5, 6
FRA: 2, 3, 5, 6

www.heinz.com

KEY POINT: Generally, intangible assets, including goodwill, are recorded only when purchased. An exception is the cost of internally developed computer software after a working prototype has been developed.

The purchase of an intangible asset is a special kind of capital expenditure. An intangible asset is both long term and nonphysical. Its value comes from the long-term rights or advantages it offers its owner. The most common examples—goodwill, trademarks, brand names, copyrights, patents, licenses or franchises, leaseholds, leasehold improvements, technology, noncompete covenants, and customer lists—are described in Table 1. Some current assets, such as accounts receivable and certain prepaid expenses, also have no physical substance, but they are not classified as intangible assets because they are short term.

Figure 7 shows the percentage of companies that report the various types of intangible assets. For some companies, intangible assets make up a substantial portion of total assets. As noted in the Decision Point at the beginning of the chapter, goodwill, trademarks, and other intangible assets of H. J. Heinz Company amount to almost $3.5 billion, or 35 percent of total assets. How these assets are accounted for will have a substantial effect on Heinz's performance.

Intangible assets are accounted for at acquisition cost—that is, the amount that was paid for them. Some intangible assets, such as goodwill and trademarks, may be acquired at little or no cost. Even though they may have great value and be needed for profitable operations, they should not appear on the balance sheet unless they have been purchased from another party at a price established in the marketplace.

The accounting issues connected with intangible assets, other than goodwill, are the same as those connected with other long-lived assets. The Accounting Principles Board, in its *Opinion No. 17*, lists them as (1) determining an initial carrying amount, (2) accounting for that amount after acquisition under normal business conditions—that is through periodic write-off or amortization—in a manner similar to depreciation, and (3) accounting for that amount if the value declines substantially and permanently.[12] In addition to these three problems, an intangible

Figure 7
Intangible Assets Separately Reported by 600 Large Companies

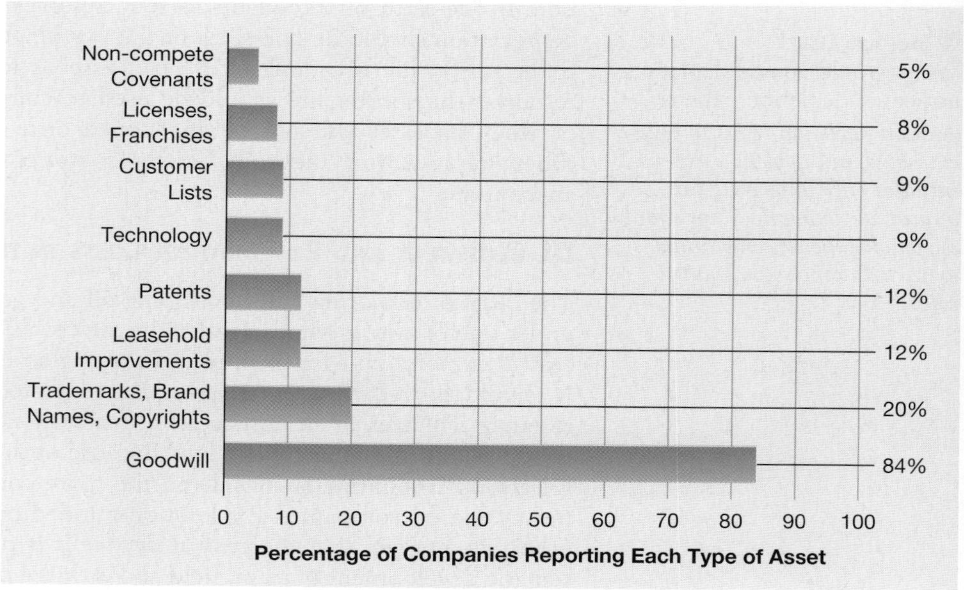

Source: Data from *Accounting Trends and Techniques,* 2002

TABLE 1. Accounting for Intangible Assets

Type	Description	Accounting Treatment
Goodwill	The excess of the amount paid for the purchase of a business over the fair market value of the net assets.	Debit Goodwill for the acquisition cost, and perform impairment review annually.
Trademark, brand name	A registered symbol or name that can be used only by its owner to identify a product or service.	Debit Trademark or Brand Name for the acquisition cost, and amortize it over a reasonable life.
Copyright	An exclusive right granted by the federal government to reproduce and sell literary, musical, and other artistic materials and computer programs for a period of the author's life plus 70 years.	Record at acquisition cost, and amortize over the useful life, which is often much shorter than the legal life. For example, the cost of paperback rights to a popular novel would typically be amortized over a useful life of two to four years.
Patent	An exclusive right granted by the federal government for a period of 20 years to make a particular product or use a specific process. A design may be granted a patent for 14 years.	The cost of successfully defending a patent in a patent infringement suit is added to the acquisition cost of the patent. Amortize over the useful life, which may be less than the legal life.
License, franchise	A right to an exclusive territory or market, or the right to use a formula, technique, process, or design.	Debit License or Franchise for the acquisition cost, and amortize it over a reasonable life.
Leasehold	A right to occupy land or buildings under a long-term rental contract. For example, Company A, which owns the right to use but does not want to use a retail location, sells or subleases to Company B the right to use it for ten years in return for one or more rental payments. Company B has purchased a leasehold.	Debit Leasehold for the amount of the rental payment, and amortize it over the remaining life of the lease. Payments to the lessor during the life of the lease should be debited to Lease Expense.
Leasehold improvements	Improvements to leased property that become the property of the lessor (the owner of the property) at the end of the lease.	Debit Leasehold Improvements for the cost of improvements, and amortize the cost of the improvements over the remaining life of the lease.
Technology	Capitalized costs associated with software developed for sale, lease, or internal use.	Record the amount of capitalizable software production costs, and amortize over the estimated economic life of the product.
Noncompete covenant	A contract limiting the rights of others to compete in a specific industry or line of business for a specified period.	Record at the acquisition cost, and amortize over the contract period.
Customer list	A list of customers or subscribers.	Debit Customer Lists for amount paid, and amortize over the expected life.

Focus on Business Practice

Take a Closer Look at Subscriber Lists!

One of the most valuable intangible assets some companies have is a list of subscribers. For example, the Newark Morning Ledger Co., a newspaper chain, purchased a chain of Michigan newspapers whose list of 460,000 subscribers was valued at $68 million. The U.S. Supreme Court upheld the company's right to amortize the value of the subscriber list because the company showed that the list had a limited useful life. The Internal Revenue Service had argued that the list had an indefinite life and therefore could not provide tax deductions through amortization. This ruling will benefit other types of businesses that purchase everything from bank deposits to pharmacy prescription files.[13]

asset, because it has no physical substance, may sometimes be impossible to identify. For these reasons, its value and its useful life may be quite hard to estimate.

The Accounting Principles Board has decided that a company should record the costs of intangible assets acquired from others as assets. However, the company should record as expenses the costs of developing intangible assets. Also, intangible assets that have a determinable useful life, such as patents, copyrights, and leaseholds, should be written off through periodic amortization over that useful life in much the same way that plant assets are depreciated. Even though some intangible assets, such as brand names and trademarks, have no measurable limit on their lives, they should still be amortized over a reasonable length of time.

CLARIFICATION NOTE: Useful life refers to how long an intangible asset will be contributing income to a firm.

To illustrate these procedures, assume that Soda Bottling Company purchases a patent on a unique bottle cap for $18,000. The entry to record the patent would include $18,000 in the asset account Patents. Note that if Soda Bottling Company had developed the bottle cap internally instead of purchasing it from others, the costs of developing the cap, such as salaries of researchers, supplies used in testing, and costs of equipment, would have been expensed as incurred.

Assume now that Soda's management determines that although the patent for the bottle cap will last for 20 years, the product using the cap will be sold only for the next six years. The entry to record the annual amortization expense would be for $3,000 ($18,000 ÷ 6 years). Note that the Patents account is reduced directly by the amount of the amortization expense. This is in contrast to the treatment of other long-term asset accounts, for which depreciation or depletion is accumulated in separate contra accounts.

If the patent becomes worthless before it is fully amortized, the remaining carrying value is written off as a loss by removing it from the Patents account.

Research and Development Costs

Most successful companies carry out research and development (R&D) activities, often in a separate department. R&D activities include development of new products, testing of existing and proposed products, and pure research. The costs of these activities are substantial for many companies. In a recent year, General Motors spent $6.6 billion on R&D, or about 4 percent of its revenues.[14] R&D costs can be even greater in high-tech fields like pharmaceuticals. For example, Abbott Laboratories recently spent $1.4 billion, or almost 10 percent of revenues, on R&D, and Roche Group spent almost $4 billion, or 14 percent of revenues.[15]

www.gm.com

www.abbott.com

www.roche.com

In the past, some companies recorded as assets R&D costs that could be directly traced to the development of specific patents, formulas, or other rights. Other costs,

Focus on International Business

Lack of Comparability Is a Real Problem!

Worldwide variability in accounting practice causes problems for those who want to compare the financial statements of companies from different countries. For example, the method of accounting for R&D costs differs, depending on the country in which a company files its financial report. In Germany, Mexico, and the United States, a company must expense its R&D costs, whereas in France, Australia, and Japan, a company may expense R&D or capitalize it (record it as an asset) if it meets certain criteria. Companies complying with the European Directives (European laws affecting financial reporting) have a choice of expensing or capitalizing R&D costs, but companies complying with International Accounting Standards (IAS) must expense research costs and capitalize development costs that meet certain conditions.[16]

such as those for testing and pure research, were treated as expenses of the accounting period and deducted from income. Since then, the Financial Accounting Standards Board has stated that all R&D costs should be treated as revenue expenditures and charged to expense in the period in which they are incurred.[17] The board argues that it is too hard to trace specific costs to specific profitable developments. Also, the costs of research and development are continuous and necessary for the success of a business and so should be treated as current expenses. To support this conclusion, the board cites studies showing that 30 to 90 percent of all new products fail and that 75 percent of new-product expenses go to unsuccessful products. Thus, their costs do not represent future benefits.

Computer Software Costs

The costs that companies incur in developing computer software for sale or lease or for their own internal use are considered research and development costs until the product has proved technologically feasible. Thus, costs incurred before that point should be charged to expense when incurred. A product is deemed technologically feasible when a detailed working program has been designed. Once that occurs, all software production costs are recorded as assets, such as Technology, and are amortized over the estimated economic life of the product using the straight-line method. If at any time the company cannot expect to realize from a software product the amount of its unamortized costs on the balance sheet, the asset should be written down to the amount expected to be realized.[18]

Leasehold Improvements

As noted in Table 1, improvements to leased property that become the property of the lessor (the owner of the property) at the end of the lease are called leasehold improvements. Such improvements are common for both small and large businesses. A study of large companies showed that 19 percent list leasehold improvements separately; the percentage is likely to be much higher for small businesses, since they generally operate in leased premises.[19] The improvement costs are amortized over the remaining term of the lease or the useful life of the improvement, whichever is shorter. Leasehold improvements are often classified as tangible assets in the property, plant, and equipment section of the balance sheet but are included in the intangible asset section because the improvements revert to the lessor at the end of the lease and are therefore more of a right than a tangible asset.

Goodwill

Stop and Think!
Why would a company spend millions of dollars on goodwill?
The company must be paying for anticipated superior earnings and believes it will more than recoup the goodwill it purchased. ■

The term *goodwill* means different things to different people. In most cases, the term is taken to mean the good reputation of a company. From an accounting standpoint, goodwill exists when a purchaser pays more for a business than the fair market value of the net assets if purchased individually. Because the purchaser has paid more than the fair market value of the physical assets, there must be intangible assets. If the company being purchased does not have patents, copyrights, trademarks, or other identifiable intangible assets of value, the excess payment is assumed to be for goodwill. Goodwill exists because most businesses are worth more as going concerns than as collections of assets. Goodwill reflects all the factors that allow a company to earn a higher-than-market rate of return on its assets, including customer satisfaction, good management, manufacturing efficiency, the advantages of holding a monopoly, good locations, and good employee relations. The payment above and beyond the fair market value of the tangible assets and other specific intangible assets is properly recorded in the Goodwill account.

The FASB has stated that purchased goodwill is an asset to be reported as a separate line item on the balance sheet and is subject to an annual impairment review. The impairment review requires a company to determine the reporting-unit level

FOCUS ON BUSINESS PRACTICE

Wake up, Goodwill Is Growing!

As Figure 7 shows, 84 percent of 600 large companies separately report goodwill as an asset. Because much of the growth of these companies has come through purchasing other companies, goodwill as a percentage of total assets has also grown. For some, the amount of goodwill is material:[20]

	Goodwill (in billions)	Percentage of Total Assets
General Mills <www.generalmills.com>	$8,473	51.2
Sara Lee Corporation <www.saralee.com>	$3,314	24.1
Tribune Company <www.tribune.com>	$5,419	38.5

on which goodwill is to be tested and the specific methodology to calculate the fair value of the reporting unit. If the fair value of goodwill is less than its carrying value on the balance sheet, then goodwill is considered impaired. Impairment results in reducing goodwill to its fair value and reporting the impairment charge on the income statement. A company can perform the fair value measurement for each reporting unit at any time as long as the measurement date is consistent from year to year.[21]

Goodwill should not be recorded unless it is paid for in connection with the purchase of a whole business. The amount to be recorded as goodwill can be determined by writing the identifiable net assets up to their fair market values at the time of purchase and subtracting the total from the purchase price. For example, assume that the owners of Company A agree to sell the company for $11,400,000. If the net assets (total assets − total liabilities) are fairly valued at $10,000,000, then the amount of the goodwill is $1,400,000 ($11,400,000 − $10,000,000). If the fair market value of the net assets is later determined to be more or less than $10,000,000, an entry is made in the accounting records to adjust the assets to the fair market value. The goodwill would then represent the difference between the adjusted net assets and the purchase price of $11,400,000.

KEY POINT: Goodwill equals purchase price minus adjusted net asset value.

Check out ACE for a Review Quiz at http://accounting.college.hmco.com/students.

SPECIAL PROBLEMS OF DEPRECIATING PLANT ASSETS

SO7 Apply depreciation methods to problems of partial years, revised rates, groups of similar items, special types of capital expenditures, and cost recovery.

RELATED TEXT ASSIGNMENTS
Q: 27, 28, 29, 30, 31, 32
E: 12, 13, 14, 15
P: 3, 8
FRA: 1

The illustrations used so far in this chapter have been simplified to explain the concepts and methods of depreciation. In actual business practice, there is often a need to (1) calculate depreciation for partial years, (2) revise depreciation rates based on new estimates of useful life or residual value, (3) group like items when calculating depreciation, (4) account for special types of capital expenditures, and (5) use the accelerated cost recovery method for tax purposes. The next sections discuss these five cases.

DEPRECIATION FOR PARTIAL YEARS

So far, most illustrations of depreciation methods have assumed that plant assets were purchased at the beginning or end of an accounting period. Usually, however, businesses buy assets when they are needed and sell or discard them when they are no longer useful or needed. The time of year is normally not a factor in the decision. Consequently, it is often necessary to calculate depreciation for partial years.

For example, assume that a piece of equipment is purchased for $3,600 and that it has an estimated useful life of six years and an estimated residual value of $600. Assume also that it is purchased on September 5 and that the yearly accounting period ends on December 31. Depreciation must be recorded for four months, September through December, or four-twelfths of the year. This factor is applied to the calculated depreciation for the entire year. The four months' depreciation under the straight-line method is calculated as follows:

$$\frac{\$3{,}600 - \$600}{6 \text{ years}} \times 4/12 = \$167$$

For the other depreciation methods, most companies compute the first year's depreciation and then multiply by the partial year factor. For example, if the company used the double-declining-balance method on the preceding equipment, the depreciation on the asset would be computed as follows:

$$\$3{,}600 \times 1/3 \times 4/12 = \$400$$

Typically, the depreciation calculation is rounded off to the nearest whole month because a partial month's depreciation is rarely material and the calculation is easier. In this case, depreciation was recorded from the beginning of September even though the purchase was made on September 5.

For all methods, the remainder (eight-twelfths) of the first year's depreciation is recorded in the next annual accounting period together with four-twelfths of the second year's depreciation.

Revision of Depreciation Rates

ENRICHMENT NOTE: A poor estimate can occur when a defective piece of equipment is purchased.

CLARIFICATION NOTE: A change in an accounting estimate is not considered the correction of an error, but rather a revision based on new information.

Because a depreciation rate is based on an estimate of an asset's useful life, the periodic depreciation charge is seldom precise. It is sometimes very inadequate or excessive. This situation may result from an underestimate or overestimate of the asset's useful life or from a wrong estimate of the residual value. What action should be taken when it is found that after several years of use, a piece of equipment will last less time—or longer—than originally thought? Sometimes, it is necessary to revise the estimate of useful life so that the periodic depreciation expense increases or decreases. Then, to reflect the revised situation, the remaining depreciable cost of the asset is spread over the remaining years of useful life.

With this technique, the annual depreciation expense is increased or decreased to reduce the asset's carrying value to its residual value at the end of its remaining useful life. For example, assume that a delivery truck was purchased for $7,000 and has a residual value of $1,000. At the time of the purchase, the truck was expected to last six years, and it was depreciated on the straight-line basis. However, after two years of intensive use, it is determined that the truck will last only two more years, but that its estimated residual value at the end of the two years will still be $1,000. In other words, at the end of the second year, the truck's estimated useful life is reduced from six years to four years. At that time, the asset account and its related accumulated depreciation account would appear as follows:

KEY POINT: Allocate the remaining depreciable cost over the estimated remaining life.

Delivery Truck

Cost	7,000		

Accumulated Depreciation, Delivery Truck

		Depreciation, year 1	1,000
		Depreciation, year 2	1,000

The remaining depreciable cost is computed as follows:

Cost	minus	Depreciation Already Taken	minus	Residual Value
$7,000	−	$2,000	−	$1,000 = $4,000

The new annual periodic depreciation charge is computed by dividing the remaining depreciable cost of $4,000 by the remaining useful life of two years. Therefore, the new periodic depreciation charge is $2,000. The annual adjusting entry for depreciation for the next two years would be as follows:

A = L + OE
−   −

Dec. 31	Depreciation Expense, Delivery Truck	2,000	
	Accumulated Depreciation, Delivery Truck		2,000
	To record depreciation expense for the year		

This method of revising depreciation is used widely in industry. It is also supported by *Opinion No. 9* and *Opinion No. 20* of the Accounting Principles Board of the AICPA.

Group Depreciation

To say that the estimated useful life of an asset, such as a piece of equipment, is six years means that the average piece of equipment of that type is expected to last six years. In reality, some pieces may last only two or three years, and others may last eight or nine years, or longer. For this reason, and for reasons of convenience, large companies group similar items, such as trucks or pieces of office equipment, to calculate depreciation. This method is called **group depreciation**. Group depreciation is widely used in all fields of industry and business. A survey of large businesses indicated that 65 percent used group depreciation for all or part of their plant assets.[22]

Special Types of Capital Expenditures

Companies make capital expenditures not only for plant assets, natural resources, and intangible assets but also for additions and betterments. An **addition** is an enlargement to the physical layout of a plant asset. As an example, if a new wing is added to a building, the benefits from the expenditure will be received over several years, and the amount paid for it should be debited to the asset account. A **betterment** is an improvement that does not add to the physical layout of a plant asset. For example, installing an air-conditioning system is a betterment that will offer benefits over a period of years; thus, its cost should be charged to an asset account.

ENRICHMENT NOTE:
Other examples of betterments include replacing stairs with an escalator in a department store and paving a gravel parking lot.

Revenue expenditures for plant equipment include the repairs necessary to keep an asset in good working condition. Repairs fall into two categories: ordinary repairs and extraordinary repairs. **Ordinary repairs** are necessary to maintain an asset in good operating condition to achieve its originally intended useful life. Trucks must have periodic tune-ups, their tires and batteries must be regularly replaced, and other routine repairs must be made. Offices must be painted regularly, and broken tiles or woodwork must be replaced. Such repairs are a current expense.

ENRICHMENT NOTE:
Putting a new motor in a cement mixer or replacing the roof on a building, thereby extending the useful life of the asset, are other examples of extraordinary repairs.

Extraordinary repairs are repairs of a more significant nature—they affect the estimated residual value or estimated useful life of an asset. For example, a boiler for heating a building may be given a complete overhaul, at a cost of several thousand dollars, that will extend its useful life by five years. Typically, extraordinary repairs are recorded by debiting the Accumulated Depreciation account, under the assumption that some of the depreciation previously recorded has now been eliminated. The effect of this reduction in the Accumulated Depreciation account is to increase the carrying value of the asset by the cost of the extraordinary repair. Consequently, the new carrying value of the asset should be depreciated over the new estimated useful life.

Let us assume that a machine that cost $10,000 has no residual value and an estimated useful life of ten years. After eight years, the accumulated depreciation under the straight-line method is $8,000, and the carrying value is $2,000 ($10,000 − $8,000). At that point, the machine is given a major overhaul costing $1,500. This expenditure extends the machine's useful life three years beyond the original ten years. The entry for the extraordinary repair would be as follows:

A = L + OE				

+
−
	Jan. 4	Accumulated Depreciation, Machinery
		  Cash
		    Extraordinary repair
		    to machinery
			1,500	
				1,500

The annual periodic depreciation for each of the five years remaining in the machine's useful life would be calculated as follows:

Carrying value before extraordinary repairs	$2,000
Extraordinary repairs	1,500
Total	$3,500

$$\text{Annual periodic depreciation} = \frac{\$3,500}{5 \text{ years}} = \$700$$

If the machine remains in use for the five years expected after the major overhaul, the total of the five annual depreciation charges of $700 will exactly equal the new carrying value, including the cost of the extraordinary repair.

COST RECOVERY FOR FEDERAL INCOME TAX PURPOSES

The Tax Reform Act of 1986 is arguably the most sweeping revision of federal tax laws since the original enactment of the Internal Revenue Code in 1913. First, it allows a company to expense the first $17,500 (which increases to $25,000 by tax year 2003) of equipment expenditures rather than recording them as an asset. Second, it allows a new method of writing off expenditures recorded as assets, the **Modified Accelerated Cost Recovery System (MACRS)**. MACRS discards the concepts of estimated useful life and residual value. Instead, it requires that a cost recovery allowance be computed (1) on the unadjusted cost of property being recovered, and (2) over a period of years prescribed by the law for all property of similar types. The accelerated method prescribed under MACRS for most property other than real estate is 200 percent declining balance with a half-year convention (only one half-year's depreciation is allowed in the year of purchase, and one half-year's depreciation is taken in the last year). In addition, the period over which the cost may be recovered is specified. Recovery of the cost of property placed in service after December 31, 1986, is calculated as prescribed in the 1986 law.

Congress hoped that MACRS would encourage businesses to invest in new plant and equipment by allowing them to write off such assets rapidly. MACRS accelerates the write-off of these investments in two ways. First, the prescribed recovery periods are often shorter than the estimated useful lives used for calculating depreciation for the financial statements. Second, the accelerated method allowed under the new law enables businesses to recover most of the cost of their investments early in the depreciation process.

CLARIFICATION NOTE: MACRS depreciation is used for tax purposes only. It cannot be used for financial reporting.

Tax methods of depreciation are not usually acceptable for financial reporting under generally accepted accounting principles because the recovery periods are shorter than the depreciable assets' estimated useful lives.

Chapter Review

REVIEW OF LEARNING OBJECTIVES

LO1 Identify the types of long-term assets and explain the management issues related to accounting for them.

Long-term assets are assets that are used in the operation of a business, are not intended for resale, and have a useful life of more than one year. Long-term assets are either tangible or intangible. In the former category are land, plant assets, and natural resources. In the latter are trademarks, patents, franchises, goodwill, and other rights. The accounting issues associated with long-term assets relate to the decision to acquire the assets, the means of financing the assets, and the methods of accounting for the assets.

LO2 Distinguish between capital and revenue expenditures, and account for the cost of property, plant, and equipment.

It is important to distinguish between capital expenditures, which are recorded as assets, and revenue expenditures, which are recorded as expenses of the current period. The error of classifying one as the other will have an important effect on net income. The acquisition cost of property, plant, and equipment includes all expenditures that are reasonable and necessary to get such an asset in place and ready for use. Among these expenditures are purchase price, installation cost, freight charges, and insurance during transit.

LO3 Define *depreciation* and compute depreciation under the straight-line, production, and declining-balance methods.

Depreciation is the periodic allocation of the cost of a plant asset over its estimated useful life. It is recorded by debiting Depreciation Expense and crediting a related contra-asset account called Accumulated Depreciation. Factors that affect the computation of depreciation are cost, residual value, depreciable cost, and estimated useful life. Depreciation is commonly computed by the straight-line method, the production method, or an accelerated method. The straight-line method is related directly to the passage of time, whereas the production method is related directly to use. An accelerated method, which results in relatively large amounts of depreciation in earlier years and reduced amounts in later years, is based on the assumption that plant assets provide greater economic benefit in their earlier years than in later years. The most common accelerated method is the declining-balance method.

LO4 Account for the disposal of depreciable assets.

Long-term depreciable assets may be disposed of by being discarded, sold, or exchanged. When long-term assets are disposed of, it is necessary to record the depreciation up to the date of disposal and to remove the carrying value from the accounts by removing the cost from the asset account and the depreciation to date from the accumulated depreciation account. If a long-term asset is sold at a price that differs from its carrying value, the gain or loss should be recorded and reported on the income statement. In recording exchanges of similar plant assets, a gain or loss may arise. Losses, but not gains, should be recognized at the time of the exchange. When a gain is not recognized, the new asset is recorded at the carrying value of the old asset plus any cash paid. For income tax purposes, neither gains nor losses are recognized in the exchange of similar assets. When dissimilar assets are exchanged, gains and losses are recognized under both accounting and income tax rules.

LO5 Identify the issues related to accounting for natural resources and compute depletion.

Natural resources are depletable assets that are converted to inventory by cutting, pumping, mining, or other forms of extraction. Natural resources are recorded at cost as long-term assets. They are allocated as expenses through depletion charges as the resources are sold. The depletion charge is based on the ratio of the resource extracted to the total estimated resource. A major issue related to this subject is accounting for oil and gas reserves.

LO6 Identify the issues related to accounting for intangible assets, including research and development costs and goodwill.

The purchase of an intangible asset should be treated as a capital expenditure and recorded at acquisition cost, which in turn should be amortized over the useful life of the asset. The FASB requires that research and development costs be treated as revenue expenditures and charged as expenses in the periods of expenditure. Software costs are treated as research and development costs and expensed until a feasible working program is developed, after which time the costs may be capitalized and amortized over a reasonable estimated life. Goodwill is the excess of the amount paid for the purchase of a business over the fair market value of the net assets and is usually related to the superior earning potential of the business. It should be recorded only if paid for in connection with the purchase of a business, and it should be reviewed annually for possible impairment.

Supplemental Objective

SO7 Apply depreciation methods to problems of partial years, revised rates, groups of similar items, special types of capital expenditures, and cost recovery.

In actual business practice, many factors affect depreciation calculations. It may be necessary to calculate depreciation for partial years because assets are bought and sold throughout the year, or to revise depreciation rates because of changed conditions. Because it is often difficult to estimate the useful life of a single item, and because it is more convenient, many large businesses group similar items for purposes of depreciation. Companies must also consider certain special capital expenditures when calculating depreciation. For example, expenditures for additions and betterments are capital expenditures. Extraordinary repairs, which increase the residual value or extend the life of an asset, are also treated as capital expenditures, but ordinary repairs are revenue expenditures. For income tax purposes, rapid write-offs of depreciable assets are allowed under the Modified Accelerated Cost Recovery System. Such rapid write-offs are not usually acceptable for financial accounting because the shortened recovery periods violate the matching rule.

Review of Concepts and Terminology

The following concepts and terms were introduced in this chapter:

LO3 **Accelerated method:** A method of depreciation that allocates relatively large amounts of the depreciable cost of an asset to earlier years and reduced amounts to later years.

SO7 **Addition:** An enlargement to the physical layout of a plant asset.

LO1 **Amortization:** The periodic allocation of the cost of an intangible asset to the periods it benefits.

LO1 **Asset impairment:** Loss of revenue-generating potential of a long-lived asset before the end of its useful life; the difference between an asset's carrying value and its fair value, as measured by the present value of the expected cash flows.

SO7 **Betterment:** An improvement that does not add to the physical layout of a plant asset.

LO6 **Brand name:** A registered name that can be used only by its owner to identify a product or service.

LO2 **Capital expenditure:** An expenditure for the purchase or expansion of a long-term asset, recorded in an asset account.

LO1 **Carrying value:** The unexpired part of the cost of an asset, not its market value. Also called *book value.*

LO6 **Copyright:** An exclusive right granted by the federal government to reproduce and sell literary, musical, and other artistic materials and computer programs for a period of the author's life plus 70 years.

LO6 **Customer list:** A list of customers or subscribers.

LO3 **Declining-balance method:** An accelerated method of depreciation in which depreciation is computed by applying a fixed rate to the carrying value (the declining balance) of a tangible long-lived asset.

LO1 **Depletion:** The exhaustion of a natural resource through mining, cutting, pumping, or other extraction, and the way in which the cost is allocated.

LO3 **Depreciable cost:** The cost of an asset less its residual value.

LO1 **Depreciation:** The periodic allocation of the cost of a tangible long-lived asset (other than land and natural resources) over its estimated useful life.

LO3 **Double-declining-balance method:** An accelerated method of depreciation in which a fixed rate equal to twice the straight-line percentage is applied to the carrying value (the declining balance) of a tangible long-lived asset.

LO3 **Estimated useful life:** The total number of service units expected from a long-term asset.

LO2 **Expenditure:** A payment or an obligation to make future payment for an asset or a service.

SO7 **Extraordinary repairs:** Repairs that affect the estimated residual value or estimated useful life of an asset thereby increasing its carrying value.

LO6 **Franchise:** The right or license to an exclusive territory or market.

LO5 **Full-costing method:** A method of accounting for the costs of exploring and developing oil and gas resources in which all costs are recorded as assets and depleted over the estimated life of the producing resources.

LO6 **Goodwill:** The excess of the cost of a group of assets (usually a business) over the fair market value of the net assets if purchased individually.

SO7 **Group depreciation:** The grouping of similar items to calculate depreciation.

LO1 **Intangible assets:** Long-term assets with no physical substance whose value is based on rights or advantages accruing to the owner.

LO6 **Leasehold:** A right to occupy land or buildings under a long-term rental contract.

LO6 **Leasehold improvements:** Improvements to leased property that become the property of the lessor at the end of the lease.

LO6 **License:** The right to use a formula, technique, process, or design.

LO1 **Long-term assets:** Assets that have a useful life of more than one year, are acquired for use in the operation of a business, and are not intended for resale. Less commonly called *fixed assets.*

SO7 **Modified Accelerated Cost Recovery System (MACRS):** A mandatory system of depreciation for income tax purposes, enacted by Congress in 1986, that requires a cost recovery allowance to be computed (1) on the unadjusted cost of property being recovered, and (2) over a period of years prescribed by the law for all property of similar types.

LO1 **Natural resources:** Long-term assets purchased for the economic value that can be taken from the land and used up.

LO6 **Noncompete covenant:** A contract limiting the rights of others to compete in a specific industry or line of business for a specified period.

LO3 **Obsolescence:** The process of becoming out of date, which is a factor in the limited useful life of tangible assets.

SO7 **Ordinary repairs:** Repairs necessary to maintain an asset in good operating condition, which are recorded as current period expenses.

LO6 **Patent:** An exclusive right granted by the federal government for a period of 20 years to make a particular product or use a specific process or design.

LO3 **Physical deterioration:** Limitations on the useful life of a depreciable asset resulting from use and from exposure to the elements.

LO3 **Production method:** A method of depreciation that assumes depreciation is solely the result of use and that allocates depreciation based on the units of output or use during each period of an asset's useful life.

LO3 **Residual value:** The estimated net scrap, salvage, or trade-in value of a tangible asset at the estimated date of disposal. Also called *salvage value* or *disposal value.*

LO2 **Revenue expenditure:** An expenditure related to repair, maintenance, and operation of a long-term asset, recorded by a debit to an expense account.

LO3 **Straight-line method:** A method of depreciation that assumes depreciation depends only on the passage of time and that allocates an equal amount of depreciation to each accounting period in an asset's useful life.

LO5 **Successful efforts method:** A method of accounting for the costs of exploring and developing oil and gas resources in which successful exploration is recorded as an asset and depleted over the estimated life of the resource and all unsuccessful efforts are immediately written off as losses.

LO1 **Tangible assets:** Long-term assets that have physical substance.

LO6 **Technology:** Capitalized costs associated with software developed for sale, lease, or internal use and amortized over the estimated economic life of the software.

LO6 **Trademark:** A registered symbol or brand name that can be used only by its owner to identify a product or service.

Review Problem

Comparison of Depreciation Methods

LO3 Norton Construction Company purchased a cement mixer on January 2, 20x4, for \$14,500. The mixer was expected to have a useful life of five years and a residual value of \$1,000. The company engineers estimated that the mixer would have a useful life of 7,500 hours. It was used 1,500 hours in 20x4, 2,625 hours in 20x5, 2,250 hours in 20x6, 750 hours in 20x7, and 375 hours in 20x8. Norton Construction Company's year end is December 31.

REQUIRED ▶

1. Compute the depreciation expense and carrying value for 20x4 to 20x8, using the following methods: (a) straight-line, (b) production, and (c) double-declining-balance.
2. Prepare the adjusting entry to record the depreciation for 20x4 that you calculated in 1(a).

3. Show the balance sheet presentation for the cement mixer after the entry in **2** on December 31, 20x4.
4. What conclusions can you draw from the patterns of yearly depreciation?

Answer to Review Problem

1. Depreciation computed:

Depreciation Method	Year	Computation	Depreciation	Carrying Value
a. Straight-line	20x4	$13,500 × 1/5	$2,700	$11,800
	20x5	13,500 × 1/5	2,700	9,100
	20x6	13,500 × 1/5	2,700	6,400
	20x7	13,500 × 1/5	2,700	3,700
	20x8	13,500 × 1/5	2,700	1,000
b. Production	20x4	$\$13{,}500 \times \frac{1{,}500}{7{,}500}$	$2,700	$11,800
	20x5	$13{,}500 \times \frac{2{,}625}{7{,}500}$	4,725	7,075
	20x6	$13{,}500 \times \frac{2{,}250}{7{,}500}$	4,050	3,025
	20x7	$13{,}500 \times \frac{750}{7{,}500}$	1,350	1,675
	20x8	$13{,}500 \times \frac{375}{7{,}500}$	675	1,000
c. Double-declining-balance	20x4	$14,500 × .4	$5,800	$ 8,700
	20x5	8,700 × .4	3,480	5,220
	20x6	5,220 × .4	2,088	3,132
	20x7	3,132 × .4	1,253*	1,879
	20x8		879*†	1,000

* Rounded.

† Remaining depreciation to reduce carrying value to residual value ($1,879 − $1,000 = $879).

2. Adjusting entry prepared—straight-line method:

20x4			
Dec. 31	Depreciation Expense, Cement Mixer	2,700	
	Accumulated Depreciation, Cement Mixer		2,700
	To record depreciation expense, straight-line method		

3. Balance sheet presentation for 20x4 shown:

Property, plant, and equipment	
Cement mixer	$14,500
Less accumulated depreciation	2,700
	$11,800

4. Conclusions drawn from depreciation patterns: The pattern of depreciation for the straight-line method differs significantly from that for the double-declining-balance method. In the earlier years, the amount of depreciation under the double-declining-balance method is significantly greater than the amount under the straight-line method. In the later years, the opposite is true. The carrying value under the straight-line method is greater than that under the double-declining-balance method at the end of all years except the fifth year. Depreciation under the production method differs from that under the other methods in that it follows no regular pattern. It varies with the amount of use. Consequently, depreciation is greatest in 20x5 and 20x6, which are the years of greatest use. Use declined significantly in the last two years.

Chapter Assignments

Building Your Knowledge Foundation

Questions

1. What are the characteristics of long-term assets?
2. Which of the following items would be classified as plant assets on the balance sheet? (a) A truck held for sale by a truck dealer, (b) an office building that was once the company headquarters but is now to be sold, (c) a typewriter used by a secretary of the company, (d) a machine that is used in manufacturing operations but is now fully depreciated, (e) pollution-control equipment that does not reduce the cost or improve the efficiency of a factory, (f) a parking lot for company employees.
3. Why is land different from other long-term assets?
4. What do accountants mean by the term *depreciation*, and what is its relationship to depletion and amortization?
5. What is asset impairment, and how does it affect the valuation of long-term assets?
6. How do cash flows relate to the decision to acquire a long-term asset, and how does the useful life of an asset relate to the means of financing it?
7. Why is it useful to think of a plant asset as a bundle of services?
8. What is the distinction between revenue expenditures and capital expenditures, why is it important, and what in general is included in the cost of a long-term asset?
9. Which of the following expenditures stemming from the purchase of a computer system would be charged to the asset account? (a) The purchase price of the equipment, (b) interest on the debt incurred to purchase the equipment, (c) freight charges, (d) installation charges, (e) the cost of special communications outlets at the computer site, (f) the cost of repairing a door that was damaged during installation, (g) the cost of adjustments to the system during the first month of operation.
10. Bert's Grocery obtained bids on the construction of a receiving dock at the back of its store. The lowest bid was $22,000. The company decided to build the dock itself, however, and was able to do so for $20,000, which it borrowed. The activity was recorded as a debit to Buildings for $22,000 and credits to Notes Payable for $20,000 and Gain on Construction for $2,000. Do you agree with the entry?
11. A firm buys technical equipment that is expected to last twelve years. Why might the equipment have to be depreciated over a shorter period of time?
12. A company purchased a building five years ago. The market value of the building is now greater than it was when the building was purchased. Explain why the company should continue depreciating the building.
13. Evaluate the following statement: "A parking lot should not be depreciated because adequate repairs will make it last forever."
14. Is the purpose of depreciation to determine the value of equipment? Explain your answer.
15. Contrast the assumption underlying the straight-line depreciation method with the assumption underlying the production depreciation method.
16. What is the principal argument supporting an accelerated depreciation method?
17. If a plant asset is sold during the year, why should depreciation be computed for the partial year prior to the date of the sale?
18. If a plant asset is discarded before the end of its useful life, how is the amount of loss measured?
19. Blackfeet Mining Company computes the depletion rate of ore to be $2 per ton. During 20xx the company mined 400,000 tons of ore and sold 370,000 tons. What is the total depletion expense for the year?
20. Under what circumstances can a mining company depreciate its plant assets over a period of time that is less than their useful lives?

21. Because accounts receivable have no physical substance, can they be classified as intangible assets?
22. Under what circumstances can a company have intangible assets that do not appear on the balance sheet?
23. How does the Financial Accounting Standards Board recommend that research and development costs be treated?
24. After spending three years developing a new software program for designing office buildings, Drew Mason Architects recently completed the detailed working program. How does accounting for the costs of software development differ before and after the completion of a successful working program?
25. How is accounting for software development costs similar to and different from accounting for research and development costs?
26. Under what conditions should goodwill be recorded? Should it remain in the records permanently once it is recorded?
27. What basic procedure should be followed in revising a depreciation rate?
28. On what basis can depreciation be taken on a group of assets rather than on individual items?
29. What will be the effect on future years' income of charging an addition to a building to repair expense?
30. In what ways do an addition, a betterment, and an extraordinary repair differ?
31. How does an extraordinary repair differ from an ordinary repair? What is the accounting treatment for each?
32. What is the difference between depreciation for accounting purposes and the Modified Accelerated Cost Recovery System for income tax purposes?

Short Exercises

LO1 Management Issues

SE 1. Indicate whether each of the following actions is primarily related to (a) acquisition of long-term assets, (b) financing of long-term assets, or (c) choosing methods and estimates related to long-term assets:

1. Deciding between common stock and long-term notes for the raising of funds
2. Relating the acquisition cost of a long-term asset to the cash flows generated by the asset
3. Determining how long an asset will benefit the company
4. Deciding to use cash flows from operations to purchase long-term assets
5. Determining how much an asset will sell for when it is no longer useful to the company

LO2 Determining Cost of Long-Term Assets

SE 2. Standard Auto purchased a neighboring lot for a new building and parking lot. Indicate whether each of the following expenditures is properly charged to (a) Land, (b) Land Improvements, or (c) Buildings.

1. Paving costs
2. Architects' fee for building design
3. Cost of clearing the property
4. Cost of the property
5. Building construction costs
6. Lights around the property
7. Building permit
8. Interest on the construction loan

LO2 Group Purchase

SE 3. Arney Company purchased property with a warehouse and parking lot for $750,000. An appraiser valued the components of the property if purchased separately as follows:

Land	$200,000
Land improvements	100,000
Building	500,000
Total	$800,000

Determine the cost to be assigned to each component.

LO3 Straight-Line Method

SE 4. Waybury Fitness Center purchased a new step machine for $5,500. The apparatus is expected to last four years and have a residual value of $500. What will be the depreciation expense for each year under the straight-line method?

SE 5. **LO3 Production Method**

Assuming that the step machine in **SE 4** has an estimated useful life of 8,000 hours and was used for 2,400 hours in year 1, for 2,000 hours in year 2, for 2,200 hours in year 3, and for 1,400 hours in year 4, how much would depreciation expense be in each year?

SE 6. **LO3 Double-Declining-Balance Method**

Assuming that the step machine in **SE 4** is depreciated using the double-declining-balance method, how much would depreciation expense be in each year?

SE 7. **LO4 Disposal of Plant Assets: No Trade-In**

West Coast Printing had a piece of equipment that cost $8,100 and on which $4,500 of accumulated depreciation had been recorded. The equipment was disposed of on January 4, the first day of business of the current year.

1. Calculate the carrying value of the equipment.
2. Calculate the gain or loss on the disposal under each of the following assumptions:
   a. It was discarded as having no value.
   b. It was sold for $1,500 cash.
   c. It was sold for $4,000 cash.

SE 8. **LO4 Disposal of Plant Assets: Trade-In**

For each of the following assumptions and referring to the equipment mentioned in **SE 7,** compute the gain (loss) on the exchange, the cash payment required, and the amount at which the new equipment would be recorded:

1. The equipment was traded in on dissimilar equipment that had a list price of $12,000. A $3,800 trade-in was allowed, and the balance was paid in cash. Gains and losses are to be recognized.
2. The equipment was traded in on dissimilar equipment that had a list price of $12,000. A $1,750 trade-in was allowed, and the balance was paid in cash. Gains and losses are to be recognized.
3. Same as **2,** except the items are similar and gains and losses are not to be recognized.

SE 9. **LO5 Natural Resources**

Ledgemore Company purchased land containing an estimated 4,000,000 tons of ore for $8,000,000. The land will be worth $1,200,000 without the ore after eight years of active mining. Although the equipment needed for the mining will have a useful life of 20 years, it is not expected to be usable and will have no value after the mining on this site is complete. Compute the depletion charge per ton and the amount of depletion expense for the first year of operation, assuming that 600,000 tons of ore were mined and sold. Also, compute the first-year depreciation on the mining equipment using the production method, assuming a cost of $9,600,000 with no residual value.

SE 10. **LO6 Intangible Assets: Computer Software**

Osaka created a new software application for PCs. Its costs during research and development were $500,000, and its costs after the working program was developed were $350,000. Although its copyright may be amortized over 40 years, management believes that the product will be viable for only five years. How should the costs be accounted for? At what value will the software appear on the balance sheet after one year?

EXERCISES

E 1. **LO1 Management Issues**

Indicate whether each of the following actions is primarily related to (a) acquisition of long-term assets, (b) financing of long-term assets, or (c) choosing methods and estimates related to long-term assets:

1. Deciding to use the production method of depreciation
2. Allocating costs on a group purchase
3. Determining the total units a machine will produce
4. Deciding to borrow funds to purchase equipment
5. Estimating the savings a new machine will yield and comparing the amount to cost
6. Deciding whether to rent or buy a piece of equipment

E 2. **LO1 Purchase Decision—Present Value Analysis**

Management is considering the purchase of a new machine for a cost of $12,000. It is estimated that the machine will generate positive net cash flows of $3,000 per year for five years and will have a disposal price at the end of that time of $1,000. Assuming an interest rate of 9 percent, determine if management should purchase the machine. Use Tables 3 and 4 in the appendix on future value and present value tables to determine the net present value of the new machine.

E 3. **LO2 Determining Cost of Long-Term Assets**

Denver Manufacturing purchased land next to its factory to be used as a parking lot. Expenditures were as follows: purchase price, $150,000; broker's fees, $12,000; title search and other fees, $1,100; demolition of a shack on the property, $4,000; general grading of property, $2,100; paving parking lots, $20,000; lighting for parking lots,

$16,000; and signs for parking lots, $3,200. Determine the amounts that should be debited to the Land account and the Land Improvements account.

LO2 Group Purchase

E 4. Jodie Williams purchased a car wash for $480,000. If purchased separately, the land would have cost $120,000, the building $270,000, and the equipment $210,000. Determine the amount that should be recorded in the new business's records for land, building, and equipment.

LO2 LO3 Cost of Long-Term Asset and Depreciation

E 5. Dewees Brown purchased a used tractor for $35,000. Before the tractor could be used, it required new tires, which cost $2,200, and an overhaul, which cost $2,800. Its first tank of fuel cost $150. The tractor is expected to last six years and have a residual value of $4,000. Determine the cost and depreciable cost of the tractor and calculate the first year's depreciation under the straight-line method.

LO3 Depreciation Methods

E 6. North End Oil Company purchased a drilling truck for $90,000. North End expected the truck to last five years or 200,000 miles, with an estimated residual value of $15,000 at the end of that time. During 20x5, the truck was driven 48,000 miles. North End's year end is December 31. Compute the depreciation for 20x5 under each of the following methods, assuming that the truck was purchased on January 13, 20x4: (1) straight-line, (2) production, and (3) double-declining-balance. Using the amount computed in **3**, prepare the entry in journal form to record depreciation expense for the second year and show how the Drilling Truck account would appear on the 20x5 balance sheet.

LO3 Double-Declining-Balance Method

E 7. Aburri Burglar Alarm Systems Company purchased a word processor for $2,240. It has an estimated useful life of four years and an estimated residual value of $240. Compute the depreciation charge for each of the four years using the double-declining-balance method.

LO4 Disposal of Plant Assets

E 8. A piece of equipment that cost $32,400 and on which $18,000 of accumulated depreciation had been recorded was disposed of on January 2, the first day of business of the current year. For each of the following assumptions, compute the gain (loss) on the disposal or exchange. In addition, for assumptions **4, 5** and **6**, compute the cash payment required and the amount at which the new equipment would be recorded.

1. It was discarded as having no value.
2. It was sold for $6,000 cash.
3. It was sold for $18,000 cash.
4. It was traded in on dissimilar equipment having a list price of $48,000. A $16,200 trade-in was allowed, and the balance was paid in cash. Gains and losses are to be recognized.
5. It was traded in on dissimilar equipment having a list price of $48,000. A $7,500 trade-in was allowed, and the balance was paid in cash. Gains and losses are to be recognized.
6. Same as **5**, except the items are similar and gains and losses are not to be recognized.

LO4 Disposal of Plant Assets

E 9. Sunshire Company purchased a computer on January 2, 20x4, at a cost of $5,000. It is expected to have a useful life of five years and a residual value of $500. Assuming that the computer is disposed of on July 1, 20x7, record the partial year's depreciation for 20x7 using the straight-line method, and record the disposal under each of the following assumptions:

1. The computer is discarded.
2. The computer is sold for $800.
3. The computer is sold for $2,200.
4. The computer is exchanged for a new computer with a list price of $9,000. A $1,200 trade-in is allowed on the cash purchase. The accounting approach to gains and losses is followed.
5. Same as **4**, except a $2,400 trade-in is allowed.
6. Same as **4**, except the income tax approach is followed.
7. Same as **5**, except the income tax approach is followed.
8. Same as **4**, except the computer is exchanged for dissimilar office equipment.
9. Same as **5**, except the computer is exchanged for dissimilar office equipment.

Book value 1,850

LO3 LO5 Natural Resource Depletion and Depreciation of Related Plant Assets

E 10. Seropoulos Mining Company purchased land containing an estimated 10 million tons of ore for a cost of $8,800,000. The land without the ore is estimated to be worth $1,600,000. The company expects that all the usable ore can be mined in 10 years. Buildings costing $1,000,000 with an estimated useful life of 30 years were erected on the site. Equipment costing $960,000 with an estimated useful life of 10 years was installed. Because of the remote location, neither the buildings nor the equipment has an estimated residual value. During its first year of operation, the company mined and sold 800,000 tons of ore.

1. Compute the depletion charge per ton.
2. Compute the depletion expense that Seropoulos Mining should record for the year.
3. Determine the depreciation expense for the year for the buildings, making it proportional to the depletion.
4. Determine the depreciation expense for the year for the equipment under two alternatives: (a) making the expense proportional to the depletion and (b) using the straight-line method.

E 11.
LO6 Amortization of Copyrights and Trademarks

1. Maddox Publishing Company purchased the copyright to a basic computer textbook for $20,000. The usual life of a textbook is about four years. However, the copyright will remain in effect for another 50 years. Calculate the annual amortization of the copyright.
2. Weyland Company purchased a trademark from a well-known supermarket for $160,000. The management of the company argued that because the trademark's value would last forever and might even increase, no amortization should be charged. Calculate the minimum amount of annual amortization that should be charged, according to guidelines of the appropriate Accounting Principles Board opinion.

E 12.
SO7 Depreciation Methods and Partial Years

Using the data given for North End Oil Company in **E 6,** compute the depreciation for calendar year 20x4 under each of the following methods, assuming that the truck was purchased on July 1, 20x4, and was driven 20,000 miles during 20x4: (1) straight-line, (2) production, and (3) double-declining-balance.

E 13.
SO7 Revision of Depreciation Rates

Mt. Sinai Hospital purchased a special x-ray machine. The machine, which cost $311,560, was expected to last ten years, with an estimated residual value of $31,560. After two years of operation (and depreciation charges using the straight-line method), it became evident that the x-ray machine would last a total of only seven years. The estimated residual value, however, would remain the same. Given this information, determine the new depreciation charge for the third year on the basis of the revised estimated useful life.

E 14.
LO2 SO7 Special Types of Capital Expenditures

Tell whether each of the following transactions related to an office building is a revenue expenditure (RE) or a capital expenditure (CE). In addition, indicate whether each transaction is an ordinary repair (OR), an extraordinary repair (ER), an addition (A), a betterment (B), or none of these (N).

1. The hallways and ceilings in the building are repainted at a cost of $8,300.
2. The hallways, which have tile floors, are carpeted at a cost of $28,000.
3. A new wing is added to the building at a cost of $175,000.
4. Furniture is purchased for the entrance to the building at a cost of $16,500.
5. The air-conditioning system is overhauled at a cost of $28,500. The overhaul extends the useful life of the air-conditioning system by ten years.
6. A cleaning firm is paid $200 per week to clean the newly installed carpets.

E 15.
SO7 Extraordinary Repairs

Marino Manufacturing has an incinerator that originally cost $187,200 and now has accumulated depreciation of $132,800. The incinerator has completed its 15th year of service in an estimated useful life of 20 years. At the beginning of the 16th year, the company spent $42,800 repairing and modernizing the incinerator to comply with pollution-control standards. Therefore, the incinerator is now expected to last 10 more years instead of 5. It will not, however, have more capacity than it did in the past or a residual value at the end of its useful life.

1. Prepare the entry in journal form to record the cost of the repair.
2. Compute the carrying value of the incinerator after the entry.
3. Prepare the entry to record straight-line depreciation for the current year.

PROBLEMS

P 1.
LO2 Determining Cost of Assets

Constanza Computers constructed a new training center in 20x4. You have been hired to manage the training center. A review of the accounting records shows the following expenditures debited to an asset account called Training Center:

Attorney's fee, land acquisition	$ 17,450
Cost of land	299,000
Architect's fee, building design	51,000
Building	510,000
Parking lot and sidewalk	67,800
Electrical wiring, building	82,000
Landscaping	27,500
Cost of surveying land	4,600
Training equipment, tables, and chairs	68,200
Installation of training equipment	34,000
Cost of grading the land	7,000
Cost of changes in building to soundproof rooms	29,600
Total account balance	$1,198,150

During the center's construction, an employee of Constanza Computers worked full time overseeing the project. He spent two months on the purchase and preparation of the site, six months on the construction, one month on land improvements, and one month on equipment installation and training room furniture purchase and setup. His salary of $32,000 during this ten-month period was charged to Administrative Expense. The training center was placed in operation on November 1.

REQUIRED Prepare a schedule with the following four column (Account) headings: Land, Land Improvements, Building, and Equipment. Place each of the above expenditures in the appropriate column. Total the columns.

P 2. **LO3 Comparison of Depreciation Methods**

Harrington Manufacturing Company purchased a robot for $720,000 at the beginning of year 1. The robot has an estimated useful life of four years and an estimated residual value of $60,000. The robot, which should last 20,000 hours, was operated 6,000 hours in year 1; 8,000 hours in year 2; 4,000 hours in year 3; and 2,000 hours in year 4.

REQUIRED

1. Compute the annual depreciation and carrying value for the robot for each year assuming the following depreciation methods: (a) straight-line, (b) production, and (c) double-declining-balance.
2. Prepare the adjusting entry in journal form that would be made each year to record the depreciation calculated under the straight-line method.
3. Show the balance sheet presentation for the robot after the adjusting entry in year 2 using the straight-line method.
4. What conclusions can you draw from the patterns of yearly depreciation and carrying value in 1?

P 3. **LO3 SO7 Depreciation Methods and Partial Years**

Ellen Leblanc purchased a laundry company. In addition to the washing machines, Leblanc installed a tanning machine and a refreshment center. Because each type of asset performs a different function, Leblanc has decided to use different depreciation methods. Data on each type of asset are summarized in the table below. The tanning machine was operated for 2,100 hours in 20x5, 3,000 hours in 20x6, and 2,400 hours in 20x7.

Asset	Date Purchased	Cost	Installation Cost	Residual Value	Estimated Life	Depreciation Method
Washing machines	3/5/x5	$15,000	$2,000	$2,600	4 years	Straight-line
Tanning machine	4/1/x5	34,000	3,000	1,000	7,500 hours	Production
Refreshment center	10/1/x5	3,400	600	600	10 years	Double-declining-balance

REQUIRED Assume the fiscal year ends December 31. Compute the depreciation expense for each item and the total depreciation expense for 20x5, 20x6, and 20x7. Round your answers to the nearest dollar and present them in a table with the headings shown below.

			Depreciation		
Asset	Year	Computations	20x5	20x6	20x7

P 4. **LO4 Recording Disposals**

Masterson Construction Company purchased a road grader for $29,000. The machine is expected to have a useful life of five years and a residual value of $2,000.

REQUIRED ▶ Prepare entries in journal form to record the disposal of the road grader at the end of the second year, after the depreciation is recorded, assuming that the straight-line method is used and making the following separate assumptions:

a. The road grader is sold for $20,000 cash.
b. The road grader is sold for $16,000 cash.
c. The road grader is traded in on a dissimilar piece of machinery costing $33,000, a trade-in allowance of $20,000 is given, the balance is paid in cash, and gains or losses are recognized.
d. The road grader is traded in on a dissimilar piece of machinery costing $33,000, a trade-in allowance of $16,000 is given, the balance is paid in cash, and gains or losses are recognized.
e. Same as **c,** except it is traded for a similar road grader and Masterson Construction Company follows accounting rules for the recognition of gains or losses.
f. Same as **d,** except it is traded for a similar road grader and Masterson Construction Company follows accounting rules for the recognition of gains or losses.
g. Same as **c,** except it is traded for a similar road grader and gains or losses are not recognized for income tax purposes.
h. Same as **d,** except it is traded for a similar road grader and gains or losses are not recognized for income tax purposes.

P 5. **LO6 Amortization of License, Leasehold, and Leasehold Improvements**

Part A: On January 2, Baby Doll, Inc., purchased the exclusive license to make dolls based on the characters in a popular new television series called "Sky Pirates." The license cost $2,100,000, and there was no termination date on the rights. Immediately after signing the contract, the company sued a rival firm that claimed it had already received the exclusive license to the series characters. Baby Doll successfully defended its rights at a cost of $360,000.

During the first year and the next, Baby Doll marketed toys based on the series. Because a successful television series lasts about five years, the company felt it could market the toys for three more years. However, before the third year of the series could get under way, a controversy arose between its two stars and its producer. As a result, the stars refused to work the third year, and the show was canceled, rendering the exclusive rights worthless.

REQUIRED ▶ Prepare entries in journal form to record the following: (a) purchase of the exclusive license; (b) successful defense of the license; (c) amortization expense, if any, for the first year; and (d) write-off of the license as worthless.

Part B: Valerie Spare purchased a six-year sublease on a building from the estate of the former tenant. It was a good location for her business, and the annual rent of $3,600, which had been established ten years before, was low. The cost of the sublease was $9,450.

To use the building, Spare had to make certain alterations. She moved some panels at a cost of $1,700 and installed others for $6,100. She also added carpet, lighting fixtures, and a sign at costs of $2,900, $3,100, and $1,200, respectively. All items except the carpet would last for at least twelve years. The expected life of the carpet was six years. None of the improvements would have a residual value.

REQUIRED ▶ Prepare entries in journal form to record the following: (a) the payment for the sublease; (b) the payments for the alterations, panels, carpet, lighting fixtures, and sign; (c) the lease payment for the first year; (d) the amortization expense, if any, associated with the sublease; and (e) the amortization expense, if any, associated with the alterations, panels, carpet, lighting fixtures, and sign.

Alternate Problems

P 6. **LO2 Determining Cost of Assets**

Patroni Company began operation on January 2 of 20x5. At the end of the year, the company's auditor discovered that all expenditures involving long-term assets had been debited to an account called Fixed Assets. An analysis of the Fixed Assets account, which had a year-end balance of $5,289,944, disclosed that it contained the following items:

Cost of land	$ 633,200
Surveying costs	8,200
Transfer of title and other fees required by the county	1,840
Broker's fees for land	42,288
Attorney's fees associated with land acquisition	14,096
Cost of removing timber from land	100,800
Cost of grading land	8,400
Cost of digging building foundation	69,200
Architect's fee for building and land improvements (80 percent building)	129,600
Cost of building construction	1,420,000
Cost of sidewalks	22,800
Cost of parking lots	108,800
Cost of lighting for grounds	160,600
Cost of landscaping	23,600
Cost of machinery	1,978,000
Shipping cost on machinery	110,600
Cost of installing machinery	352,400
Cost of testing machinery	44,200
Cost of changes in building to comply with safety regulations pertaining to machinery	25,080
Cost of repairing building that was damaged in the installation of machinery	17,800
Cost of medical bill for injury received by employee while installing machinery	4,800
Cost of water damage to building during heavy rains prior to opening the plant for operation	13,640
Account balance	$5,289,944

Patroni Company sold the timber it cleared from the land to a firewood dealer for $10,000. This amount was credited to Miscellaneous Income.

During the construction period, two of Patroni's supervisors devoted full time to the construction project. They earn annual salaries of $96,000 and $84,000, respectively. They spent two months on the purchase and preparation of the land, six months on the construction of the building (approximately one-sixth of which was devoted to improvements on the grounds), and one month on machinery installation. The plant began operation on October 1, and the supervisors returned to their regular duties. Their salaries were debited to Factory Salaries Expense.

REQUIRED ▶ Prepare a schedule with the following column headings: Land, Land Improvements, Buildings, Machinery, and Expense. Place each of the above expenditures in the appropriate column. Negative amounts should be shown in parentheses. Total the columns.

P 7. **LO3 Comparison of Depreciation Methods**

Mount Royal Construction Company purchased a new crane for $360,500 at the beginning of year 1. The crane has an estimated residual value of $35,000 and an estimated useful life of six years. The crane is expected to last 10,000 hours. It was used 1,800 hours in year 1; 2,000 in year 2; 2,500 in year 3; 1,500 in year 4; 1,200 in year 5; and 1,000 in year 6.

REQUIRED ▶

1. Compute the annual depreciation and carrying value for the new crane for each of the six years (round to nearest dollar where necessary) under each of the following methods: (a) straight-line, (b) production, and (c) double-declining-balance.
2. Prepare the adjusting entry that would be made each year to record the depreciation calculated under the straight-line method.
3. Show the balance sheet presentation for the crane after the adjusting entry in year 2 using the straight-line method.
4. What conclusions can you draw from the patterns of yearly depreciation and carrying value in 1?

P 8. **LO3 SO7 Depreciation Methods and Partial Years**

Sao Company operates three types of equipment. Because of the equipment's varied functions, company accounting policy requires the application of three different depreciation methods. Data on this equipment are summarized in the table that follows.

Equipment	Date Purchased	Cost	Installation Cost	Estimated Residual Value	Estimated Life	Depreciation Method
1	1/12/x4	$171,000	$ 9,000	$18,000	10 years	Double-declining-balance
2	7/9/x4	191,100	15,900	21,000	10 years	Straight-line
3	10/2/x4	290,700	8,100	33,600	20,000 hours	Production

Equipment 3 was used for 2,000 hours in 20x4; for 4,200 hours in 20x5; and for 3,200 hours in 20x6.

REQUIRED ▶ Assuming that the fiscal year ends December 31, compute the depreciation expense on each type of equipment and the total depreciation expense for 20x4, 20x5, and 20x6 by filling in a table with the headings shown below.

		Depreciation		
Equipment No.	Computations	20x4	20x5	20x6

SKILLS DEVELOPMENT CASES

Conceptual Analysis

SD 1.

LO1 Nature of Depreciation and
LO3 Amortization and Estimated Useful Lives

A change in the estimated useful lives of long-term assets can have a significant effect. For instance, General Motors Corp. <www.gm.com> states,

> . . . the Corporation revised the estimated service lives of its plants and equipment and special tools retroactive to January 1, 1987. These revisions, which were based on 1987 studies of actual useful lives and periods of use, recognized current estimates of service lives of the assets and had the effect of reducing 1987 depreciation and amortization charges by $1,236.6 million or $2.53 per share of $1⅔ par value common stock.[23]

General Motors' income before income taxes for the year was $2,005.4 million. Discuss the purpose of depreciation and amortization. What is estimated service life, and on what basis did General Motors change the estimates of the service lives of plants and equipment and special tools? What was the effect of this change on the corporation's income before income taxes? Is it likely that the company is in better condition economically as a result of the change? Does the company have more cash at the end of the year as a result? (Ignore income tax effects.)

SD 2.

LO3 Change of Depreciation Method

Several years ago, Polaroid Corporation <www.polaroid.com>, a manufacturer of instant cameras and film, changed from an accelerated depreciation method for financial reporting purposes to the straight-line method for newly acquired assets. As noted in its annual report:

> The company changed its method of depreciation for financial reporting for the cost of buildings, machinery, and equipment . . . from a primarily accelerated method to the straight-line method.[24]

What reasons can you give for Polaroid's choosing to switch to a straight-line method of depreciation? Discuss which of the two depreciation methods is more conservative. Polaroid's deteriorating financial position led it to declare bankruptcy in 2001. Could this accounting change have been a signal that the company was in trouble?

SD 3.

LO6 Brands

Hilton Hotels Corporation <www.hilton.com> and Marriott International <www.marriott.com> provide hospitality services. Hilton Hotels' well-known brands include Hilton, Doubletree, Hampton Inn, Embassy Suites, Red Lion Hotels and Inns, and Homewood Suites. Marriott also owns or manages properties with recognizable brand names, such as Marriott Hotels, Resorts and Suites; Ritz-Carlton; Renaissance Hotels; Residence Inn; Courtyard; and Fairfield Inn.

On its balance sheet, Hilton Hotels Corporation includes brands (net of amortization) of $1,048 million, or 11.3 percent of total assets. Marriott International, however, does not list brands among its intangible assets.[25] What principles of accounting for intangibles would cause Hilton to record brands as an asset while Marriott does not? How will these differences in accounting for brands generally affect the net income and return on assets of these two competitors?

Ethical Dilemma

LO2 Ethics and Allocation of Acquisition Costs

SD 4. Signal Company has purchased land and a warehouse for $18,000,000. The warehouse is expected to last 20 years and to have a salvage value equal to 10 percent of its cost. The chief financial officer (CFO) and the controller are discussing the allocation of the purchase price. The CFO believes that the largest amount possible should be assigned to the land because this action will improve reported net income in the future. Depreciation expense will be lower because land is not depreciated. He suggests allocating one-third, or $6,000,000, of the cost to the land. This results in depreciation expense each year of $540,000 [($12,000,000 − $1,200,000) ÷ 20 years]. The controller disagrees, arguing that the smallest amount possible, say one-fifth of the purchase price, should be allocated to the land, thereby saving income taxes, since the depreciation, which is tax deductible, will be greater. Under this plan, annual depreciation would be $648,000 [($14,400,000 − $1,440,000) ÷ 20 years]. The annual tax savings at a 30 percent tax rate is $32,400 [($648,000 − $540,000) × .30]. How will this decision affect the company's cash flows? Ethically, how should the purchase cost be allocated? Who will be affected by the decision?

Group Activity: Divide the class into groups and have each develop the position of the CFO or controller for presentation and debate.

LO2 LO6 Ethics of Aggressive Accounting Policies

SD 5. Is it ethical to choose aggressive accounting practices to advance a company's business? During the 1990s, America Online (AOL) <www.aol.com>, the largest Internet service provider in the United States, was one of the hottest stocks on Wall Street. After its initial stock offering in 1992, its stock price shot up several thousand percent. Accounting is very important to a company like AOL because earnings enable it to sell shares of stock and raise more cash to fund its growth. In its early years, AOL was one of the most aggressive companies in its choice of accounting principles. AOL's strategy called for building the largest customer base in the industry. Consequently, it spent many millions of dollars each year marketing its services to new customers. Such costs are usually recognized as operating expenses in the year in which they are incurred. However, AOL treated these costs as long-term assets, called "deferred subscriber acquisition costs," and expensed them over several years, because it said the average customer was going to stay with the company for three years or more. The company also recorded research and development costs as "product development costs" and amortized them over five years. Both of these practices are justifiable theoretically, but they are not common practice. If the standard, more conservative practice had been followed, the company would have had a net loss in every year it has been in business.[26] This result would have greatly limited AOL's ability to raise money and grow.

Explain in your own words AOL management's rationale for adopting the accounting policies that it did. What could go wrong with such a plan? How would you evaluate the ethics of AOL's actions? Who benefits from the actions? Who is harmed by these actions?

Research Activity

LO1 LO2 LO3 LO6 Individual Field Trip

SD 6. Visit a fast-food restaurant. Make a list of all the intangible and property, plant, and equipment assets you can identify. For each one, identify one management issue that relates to that asset. In addition, give examples of at least one capital expenditure and one revenue expenditure that is applicable to property, plant, and equipment assets. Bring your list to class for discussion.

Decision-Making Practice

SD 7.

LO1 Purchase Decision and Time Value of Money

Morningside Machine Works has obtained a subcontract to manufacture parts for a new military aircraft. The parts are to be delivered over the next five years, and the company will be paid as the parts are delivered.

To make the parts, Morningside Machine Works will have to purchase new equipment. Two types are available. Type A is conventional equipment that can be put into service immediately; Type B requires one year to be put into service but is more efficient than Type A. Type A requires an immediate cash investment of $1,000,000 and will produce enough parts to provide net cash receipts of $340,000 each year for the five years. Type B may be purchased by signing a two-year non-interest-bearing note for $1,346,000. It is projected that Type B will produce net cash receipts of zero in year 1, $500,000 in year 2, $600,000 in year 3, $600,000 in year 4, and $200,000 in year 5. Neither type of equipment can be used on other contracts or will have any useful life remaining at the end of the contract. Morningside currently pays an interest rate of 16 percent to borrow money.

1. What is the present value of the investment required for each type of equipment? (Use Table 3 in the appendix on future value and present value tables.)
2. Compute the net present value of each type of equipment based on your answer in **1** and the present value of the net cash receipts projected to be received. (Use Tables 3 and 4 in the appendix on future value and present value tables.)
3. Write a memorandum to the board of directors that recommends the option that appears to be best for Morningside. Explain your reasoning and include **1** and **2** as attachments.

FINANCIAL REPORTING AND ANALYSIS CASES

Interpreting Financial Reports

FRA 1.

LO3 Effects of Change in
SO7 Accounting Method

Depreciation expense is a significant cost for companies in which plant assets are a high proportion of assets. The amount of depreciation expense in a given year is affected by estimates of useful life and choice of depreciation method. In 2004, Century Steelworks Company, a major integrated steel producer, changed the estimated useful lives for its major production assets. It also changed the method of depreciation for other steelmaking assets from straight-line to the production method.

The company's 2004 annual report states, "A recent study conducted by management shows that actual years-in-service figures for our major production equipment and machinery are, in most cases, higher than the estimated useful lives assigned to these assets. We have recast the depreciable lives of such assets so that equipment previously assigned a useful life of 8 to 26 years now has an extended depreciable life of 10 to 32 years."

The report goes on to explain that the new production method of depreciation "recognizes that depreciation of production equipment and machinery correlates directly to both physical wear and tear and the passage of time. The production method of depreciation, which we have now initiated, more closely allocates the cost of these assets to the periods in which products are manufactured."

The report summarizes the effects of both actions on the year 2004 as shown in the following table:

Incremental Increase in Net Income	In Millions	Per Share
Lengthened lives	$11.0	$ .80
Production method		
Current year	7.3	.53
Prior years	2.8	.20
Total increase	$21.1	$1.53

During 2004, Century Steelworks reported a net loss of $83,156,500 ($6.03 per share). Depreciation expense for 2004 was $87,707,200.

In explaining the changes the company has made, the controller of Century Steelworks was quoted in an article in *Business Journal* as follows: "There is no reason for Century Steelworks to continue to depreciate our assets more conservatively than our competitors do." But the article also quotes an industry analyst who argues that by slowing its method of depreciation, Century Steelworks could be viewed as reporting lower-quality earnings.

1. Explain the accounting treatment when there is a change in the estimated lives of depreciable assets. What circumstances must exist for the production method to produce the effect it did in relation to the straight-line method? What would Century Steelworks' net income or loss have been if the changes had not been made? What might have motivated management to make the changes?
2. What does the controller of Century Steelworks mean when he says that Century had been depreciating "more conservatively than our competitors do"? Why might the changes at Century Steelworks indicate, as the analyst asserts, "lower-quality earnings"? What risks might Century face as a result of its decision to use the production method of depreciation?

International Company

FRA 2.

LO6 **Accounting for Goodwill: U.S. and IAS rules**

For most pharmaceutical companies, intangible assets, such as goodwill, patents, licenses, and trademarks, make up a significant percentage of total assets. For example, for Roche Group <www.roche.com>, intangible assets constitute 22.8 percent of total assets, and for Baxter International <www.baxter.com>, 14.2 percent.[27] For both companies, goodwill represents the largest portion of intangible assets.

Before 2000, Roche Group, a Swiss company, charged any goodwill resulting from acquisitions against equity immediately. However, in 2000, in accordance with a change in International Accounting Standards (IAS), Roche began recording goodwill as an asset and amortizing it over a period of up to 20 years. This IAS change brought U.S. and IAS companies into closer agreement on accounting for goodwill. At that time, companies like Baxter International, which comply with U.S. GAAP, recorded goodwill resulting from acquisitions as an asset and amortized it over periods not to exceed 40 years. However, as of 2002, U.S. companies, while continuing to record purchased goodwill as an asset, were no longer required to amortize any existing or new goodwill. Both IAS and U.S. GAAP require companies to apply the impairment test annually to ensure that goodwill is not overvalued.

What impact did accounting for goodwill under IAS and U.S. GAAP have on cash flows and net income in the year 2002? In your opinion, which accounting treatment for goodwill (U.S. or IAS) is better? State your reasons.

Toys "R" Us Annual Report

FRA 3.

LO1 **Long-Term Assets**
LO2
LO3
LO6

1. Refer to the balance sheets and to the note on property and equipment in the notes to the financial statements in the Toys "R" Us <www.tru.com> annual report to answer the following questions: What percentage of total assets in the most recent year was property and equipment? What is the most significant type of property and equipment? Does Toys "R" Us have a significant investment in land? What other kinds of things are included in the property and equipment category? (Ignore leased property under capital leases for now.)
2. Refer to the summary of significant accounting policies and to the note on property and equipment in the Toys "R" Us annual report. What method of depreciation does Toys "R" Us use? How long does management estimate its buildings to last as compared with furniture and equipment? What does this say about the company's need to remodel its stores?
3. Refer again to the note on property and equipment. What are leasehold improvements? How significant are leasehold improvements, and what are their effects on the earnings of the company?

Comparison Case: Toys "R" Us and Walgreen Co.

FRA 4.
LO1 Long-Term Assets and Cash Flows

Refer to the annual report of Toys "R" Us <www.tru.com> and to the financial statements of Walgreens <www.walgreens.com> in the Supplement to Chapter 6 to answer the following:

1. Prepare a table that shows the net amount each company spent on property and equipment (from the statement of cash flows), the total property and equipment (from the balance sheet), and the percentage of the first figure to the second for each of the past two years. Which company grew its property and equipment at a faster rate?
2. Which other note to the financial statements is helpful in evaluating the cash flows related to property and equipment? (**Hint:** In what way do Toys "R" Us and Walgreens gain use of property and equipment other than by purchase?) How important is this method of obtaining use of assets to these companies? Which company makes greater use of the method?

Fingraph® Financial Analyst™

FRA 5.
LO1 LO3 LO5 LO6 Comparison of Long-Term Assets

Choose any two companies from the list of Fingraph companies on the Needles Accounting Resource Center Web Site at http://accounting.college.hmco.com/students. The industry should be one in which long-term assets are likely to be important, such as the airline, manufacturing, consumer products, consumer food and beverage, or computer industry. Access the Microsoft Excel spreadsheets for the companies you selected. For parts **1**, **3**, and **4**, click on the URL at the top of each company's spreadsheet for a link to the company's web site and annual report.

1. In the annual reports of the companies you have selected, read the long-term asset section of the balance sheet and any reference to long-term assets in the summary of significant accounting policies or notes to the financial statements. What are the most important long-term assets for each company? What depreciation methods do the companies use? Do any long-term assets appear to be characteristic of the industry? What intangible assets do the companies have, and how important are they?
2. Using the Fingraph CD-ROM software, display and print in tabular and graphic form the Balance Sheet Analysis page. Prepare a table that compares the gross and net amounts for property, plant, and equipment.
3. Locate the statements of cash flows in the two companies' annual reports. Prepare another table that compares depreciation (and amortization) expense from the operating activities section with the net purchases of property, plant, and equipment (net capital expenditures) from the investing activities section for two years. Does depreciation (and amortization) expense exceed replacement of long-term assets? Are the companies expanding or reducing their property, plant, and equipment?
4. Find and read references to long-term assets and capital expenditures in management's discussion and analysis in each annual report.
5. Write a one-page executive summary that highlights the most important long-term assets and the accounting policies for long-term assets, and that compares the investing activities of the two companies, including reference to management's assessment. Include the Fingraph page and your tables with your report.

Internet Case

FRA 6.
LO3 LO4 LO6 SEC and Forms 10-K

Public corporations are required not only to communicate with their stockholders by means of an annual report but also to submit an annual report to the Securities and Exchange Commission (SEC). The annual report to the SEC is called a Form 10-K and is a source of the latest information about a company. Through the Needles Accounting Resource Center Web Site at http://accounting.college.hmco.com/students, access the SEC's EDGAR files to locate either H. J. Heinz Company's <www.heinz.com> or Ford Motor Company's <www.ford.com> Form 10-K. Find the financial statements and the notes to the financial statements. Scan through the notes to the financial statements and prepare a list of information related to long-term assets, including intangibles. For instance, what depreciation methods does the company use? What are the useful lives of its property, plant, and equipment? What intangible assets does the company have? Does the company have goodwill? How much does the company spend on research and development? In the statement of cash flows, how much did the company spend on new property, plant, and equipment (capital expenditures)? Summarize your results and be prepared to discuss them as well as your experience in using the SEC's EDGAR database.

Group Activity: Divide students into groups according to the company researched and have each group compile a comprehensive list of information about its company.

12

Chapter 12 presents the management issues associated with current liabilities and payroll accounting.

Current Liabilities

Learning Objectives

LO1 Identify the management issues related to recognition, valuation, classification, and disclosure of current liabilities.

LO2 Identify, compute, and record definitely determinable and estimated current liabilities.

LO3 Distinguish *contingent liabilities* from *commitments.*

Supplemental Objective

SO4 Compute and record the liabilities associated with payroll accounting.

DECISION POINT

A USER'S FOCUS

US Airways, Inc. <www.usairways.com> Liabilities are one of the three major parts of the balance sheet. They are legal obligations for the future payment of assets or the future performance of services that result from past transactions. The current and long-term liabilities of US Airways, Inc., which has total assets of almost $8 billion, are shown in the Financial Highlights.[1] Current maturities of long-term debt; accounts payable; accrued aircraft rent; accrued salaries, wages, and vacation; and other accrued expenses will for the most part require an outlay of cash in the next year. Traffic balances payable will require payments to other airlines, but those may be partially offset by amounts owed by other airlines. Unused tickets are tickets already paid for by passengers and represent services that must be performed. Long-term debt will require cash outlays in future years. Altogether these liabilities represent over 75 percent of total assets. How does the decision of US Airways' management to incur so much debt relate to the goals of the business?

Liabilities are important because they are closely related to the goals of profitability and liquidity. Liabilities are sources of cash for operating and financing activities when they are incurred, but they are also obligations that use cash when they are paid. Achieving the appropriate level of liabilities is critical to business success. A company that has too few liabilities may not be earning up to its potential. A company that has too many liabilities, however, may be incurring excessive risks. In the case of US Airways, the company became vulnerable when there was a down-

What factors other than a downturn in air travel caused US Airways to file for bankruptcy?

turn in air travel as occurred in 2001–2002. Because of problems with liquidity, US Airways had to file for bankruptcy in 2002 in order to continue operating. This chapter focuses on the management and accounting issues involving current liabilities, including payroll liabilities and contingent liabilities.

Financial Highlights
(In millions)

Current Liabilities	**2001**	2000
Current maturities of long-term debt	$ 159	$ 284
Accounts payable	598	506
Traffic balances payable and unused tickets	817	890
Accrued aircraft rent	249	349
Accrued salaries, wages, and vacation	367	319
Other accrued expenses	742	475
Total current liabilities	$2,932	$2,823
Long-term debt, net of current maturities	$3,515	$2,688

MANAGEMENT ISSUES RELATED TO ACCOUNTING FOR CURRENT LIABILITIES

LO1 Identify the management issues related to recognition, valuation, classification, and disclosure of current liabilities.

RELATED TEXT ASSIGNMENTS
Q: 1, 2, 3, 4, 5
SE: 1, 2
E: 1, 2
P: 1
SD: 5
FRA: 1, 3, 4, 5, 6

The primary reason for incurring current liabilities is to meet needs for cash during the operating cycle. The proper identification and management of current liabilities requires an understanding of how these liabilities are recognized, valued, classified, and disclosed.

MANAGING LIQUIDITY AND CASH FLOWS

The operating cycle is the process of converting cash to purchases, to sales, to accounts receivable, and back to cash. Most current liabilities arise in support of this cycle, as when accounts payable arise from purchases of inventory, accrued expenses arise from operating costs, and unearned revenues arise from customers' advance payments. Short-term debt is used to raise cash during periods of inventory buildup or while waiting for collection of receivables. Cash is used to pay current maturities of long-term debt and to pay off liabilities arising from operations.

Failure to manage the cash flows related to current liabilities can have serious consequences for a business. For instance, if suppliers are not paid on time, they may withhold shipments that are vital to a company's operations. Continued failure to pay current liabilities can lead to bankruptcy. To evaluate a company's ability to pay its current liabilities, three measures of liquidity—working capital, the current ratio, and the quick ratio—are often used. Current liabilities are a key component of each of these measures. They typically equal from 25 to 50 percent of total assets.

www.usairways.com

As shown below (in millions of dollars), US Airways' short-term liquidity as measured by working capital was negative in 2000 and 2001:

	Current Assets	−	Current Liabilities	=	Working Capital
2001	$1,793	−	$2,932	=	($1,139)
2000	$2,571	−	$2,823	=	($ 252)

ENRICHMENT NOTE:
Unused tickets are often a significant liability for airlines and other service providers. The receipt of cash is usually incidental to revenue recognition.

This measure highlights the reason why US Airways faced a problem with short-term liquidity. It is common for airlines to have low or negative working capital because unearned ticket revenue is a current liability, but the cash from these ticket sales is quickly consumed in operations. On the assumption that only a small portion of unearned ticket revenues will be repaid to customers, unearned ticket revenue might be excluded from current liabilities for purposes of analysis. The healthiest airlines have positive working capital when unearned ticket revenue is excluded. However, for US Airways, the negative working capital of $1,139 million exceeded the traffic balances and unused tickets of $817 million in 2001.

Another consideration in managing liquidity and cash flows is the amount of time creditors are willing to give a company to pay its accounts payable. Common measures of this time are the **payables turnover** and the **average days' payable**. The payables turnover is the number of times, on average, that accounts payable are paid in an accounting period and shows the relative size of a company's accounts payable. The average days' payable shows how long, on average, a company takes to pay its accounts payables.

www.radioshack.com

For example, RadioShack Corporation, which operates more than 8,000 electronics stores, must carefully plan its purchases and payables. It had accounts payable of $312.6 million in 2002 and $206.7 million in 2001. Its purchases are determined by cost of goods sold adjusted for the change in inventory. An increase in inventory means purchases were more than cost of goods sold; a decrease in inventory means that purchases were less than cost of goods sold. RadioShack's cost of goods sold in 2002 was $2,338.9 million, and its inventory increased by $21.4 million.[2] Its payables turnover is computed as follows:

FIGURE 1
Payables Turnover for Selected Industries

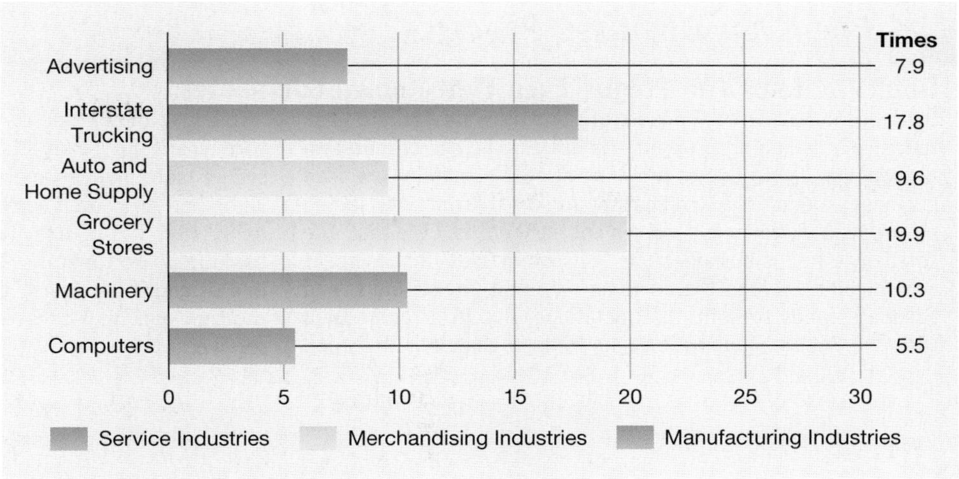

Source: Data from Dun & Bradstreet, *Industry Norms and Key Business Ratios,* 2001–2002.

STOP AND THINK!
Is a decreasing payables turnover good or bad for a company?

Other things being equal, a decreasing payables turnover is good because it means the average days' payable is greater, thus allowing the company more time to pay its bills. The company will not have to borrow as much to finance its operating cycle of inventory turnover and receivables turnover. ■

$$\text{Payables Turnover} = \frac{\text{Cost of Goods Sold} \pm \text{Change in Merchandise Inventory}}{\text{Average Accounts Payable}}$$

$$= \frac{\$2{,}338.9 + \$21.4}{(\$312.6 + \$206.7) \div 2}$$

$$= \frac{\$2{,}360.3}{\$259.7} = 9.1 \text{ times}$$

To find the average days' payable, the number of days in a year is divided by the payables turnover:

$$\text{Average Days' Payable} = \frac{365 \text{ days}}{\text{Payables Turnover}} = \frac{365 \text{ days}}{9.1} = 40.1 \text{ days}$$

The payables turnover of 9.1 times and the resulting average days' payable of 40.1 days are consistent with customary 30-day credit terms.

Figures 1 and 2 show the payables turnover and average days' payable for various industries. To get a full picture of a company's operating cycle and liquidity position, these ratios should be considered in relation to the inventory turnover and the receivables turnover and their related days' ratios.

FIGURE 2
Average Days' Payable for Selected Industries

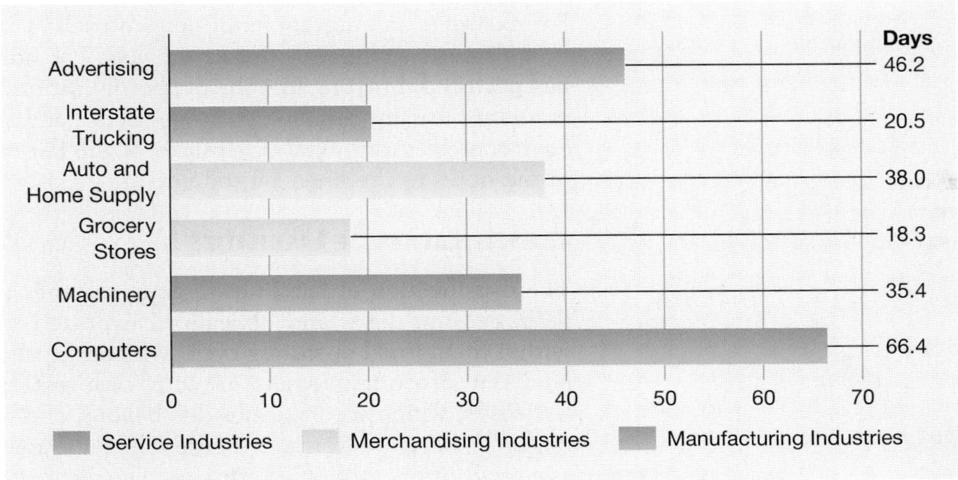

Source: Data from Dun & Bradstreet, *Industry Norms and Key Business Ratios,* 2001–2002.

Focus on Business Practice

Debt Problems Can Plague Even Well-Known Companies.

In a recent Wall Street horror story that illustrates the importance of managing current liabilities, Xerox Corporation <www.xerox.com>, one of the most storied names in American business, found itself combating rumors that it was facing bankruptcy. Following a statement by Xerox's CEO that the company's financial model was "unsustainable," management was forced to defend the company's liquidity by saying it had adequate funds to continue operations. But in a report filed with the SEC, management acknowledged that it had tapped into its $7 billion line of bank credit for more than $3 billion to pay off short-term debt that was coming due. Unable to secure more money from any other source to pay such debts, Xerox had no choice but to turn to the line of credit from its bank. Had it run out, the company might well have gone bankrupt.[3] Fortunately, Xerox was able to restructure its line of credit to stay in business, but it is still in a perilous position and may have to sell itself to another company to survive.

Recognition of Liabilities

Timing is important in the recognition of liabilities. Failure to record a liability in an accounting period very often goes along with failure to record an expense. The two errors lead to an understatement of expense and an overstatement of income.

A liability is recorded when an obligation occurs. This rule is harder to apply than it might appear. When a transaction obligates a company to make future payments, a liability arises and is recognized, as when goods are bought on credit. However, current liabilities often are not represented by direct transactions. One of the key reasons for making adjusting entries at the end of an accounting period is to recognize unrecorded liabilities. Among these accrued liabilities are salaries payable and interest payable. Other liabilities that can only be estimated, such as taxes payable, must also be recognized through adjusting entries.

On the other hand, companies often enter into agreements for future transactions. For instance, a company may agree to pay an executive $150,000 a year for a period of three years, or a public utility may agree to buy an unspecified quantity of coal at a certain price over the next five years. Such contracts, though they are definite commitments, are not considered liabilities because they are for future—not past—transactions. As there is no current obligation, no liability is recognized.

Valuation of Liabilities

On the balance sheet, a liability is generally valued at the amount of money needed to pay the debt or at the fair market value of goods or services to be delivered. For most liabilities, the amount is definitely known, but for some, it must be estimated. For example, an automobile dealer who sells a car with a one-year warranty must provide parts and service during the year. The obligation is definite because the sale has occurred, but the amount of the obligation can only be estimated. Such estimates are usually based on past experience and anticipated changes in the business environment. Additional disclosures of the fair value of liabilities may be required in the notes to the financial statements.

Classification of Liabilities

The classification of liabilities directly matches the classification of assets. **Current liabilities** are debts and obligations expected to be satisfied within one year or within the normal operating cycle, whichever is longer. Such liabilities are normally paid out of current assets or with cash generated from operations. **Long-term liabilities**, which are liabilities due beyond one year or beyond the normal operating cycle, have a different purpose. They are used to finance long-term assets, such as aircraft in the case of US Airways. The distinction between current and long-term liabilities is important because it affects the evaluation of a company's liquidity.

www.usairways.com

DISCLOSURE OF LIABILITIES

To explain some accounts, supplemental disclosure in the notes to the financial statements may be required. For example, if a company has a large amount of notes payable, an explanatory note may disclose the balances, maturities, interest rates, and other features of the debts. Any special credit arrangements, such as issues of commercial paper and lines of credit, should also be disclosed. For example, Goodyear Tire & Rubber Company, which manufactures and sells tires, vehicle components, industrial rubber products, and rubber-related chemicals, disclosed its short-term debt arrangements in the notes to its financial statements, as follows:

www.goodyear.com

ENRICHMENT NOTE: Financial liabilities, such as loans, notes, and other borrowings, are considered financial instruments. The market value of financial instruments is reported in the notes to the financial statements.

> **Short Term Debt and Financing Arrangements**
> At December 31, 2002, Goodyear had short term committed and uncommitted credit arrangements totaling $.97 billion, of which $.68 billion were unused. These arrangements are available to the Company or certain of its international subsidiaries through various domestic and international banks at quoted market interest rates. There are no commitment fees or compensating balances associated with these arrangements. Goodyear had outstanding debt obligations, which by their terms are due within one year, amounting to $653.2 million at December 31, 2002, compared to $364.7 million at December 31, 2001.[4]

This type of disclosure is helpful in assessing whether a company has additional borrowing power, because unused lines of credit allow a company to borrow on short notice, up to the agreed credit limit, with little or no negotiations.

Check out ACE for a Review Quiz at http://accounting.college.hmco.com/students.

COMMON CATEGORIES OF CURRENT LIABILITIES

LO2 Identify, compute, and record definitely determinable and estimated current liabilities.

RELATED TEXT ASSIGNMENTS
Q: 6, 7, 8, 9, 10, 11, 12, 13, 14, 15, 16
SE: 3, 4, 5, 6, 7, 8
E: 3, 4, 5, 6, 7, 8
P: 1, 2, 3, 4, 6, 7, 8
SD: 1, 2, 3, 4, 5
FRA: 3, 6

Current liabilities fall into two major groups: (1) definitely determinable liabilities and (2) estimated liabilities.

DEFINITELY DETERMINABLE LIABILITIES

Current liabilities that are set by contract or by statute and can be measured exactly are called **definitely determinable liabilities**. The related accounting problems are to determine the existence and amount of each such liability and to see that it is recorded properly. Definitely determinable liabilities include accounts payable, bank loans and commercial paper, notes payable, accrued liabilities, dividends payable, sales and excise taxes payable, current portions of long-term debt, payroll liabilities, and unearned revenues.

KEY POINT: On the balance sheet, the order of presentation for current liabilities is not as strict as for current assets. Generally, Accounts Payable or Notes Payable appears first, and the rest follow.

■ **ACCOUNTS PAYABLE** Accounts payable, sometimes called *trade accounts payable,* are short-term obligations to suppliers for goods and services. The amount in the Accounts Payable account is generally supported by an accounts payable subsidiary ledger, which contains an individual account for each person or company to which money is owed.

www.usairways.com

■ **BANK LOANS AND COMMERCIAL PAPER** Management often establishes a **line of credit** with a bank; this arrangement allows the company to borrow funds when they are needed to finance current operations. For example, US Airways states in a note to its financial statements that "the Company has in place a $190 million 364-day secured revolving credit facility and a $250 million three-year secured revolving credit facility to provide liquidity for its operations."[5] Although a promissory note for the full amount of the line of credit is signed when the credit is granted, the company has great flexibility in using the available funds. The company can increase its borrowing up to the limit when it needs cash and reduce the amount borrowed when it generates enough cash of its own. Both the amount borrowed and the interest rate charged by the bank may change daily. The bank may require the company to meet certain financial goals (such as maintaining specific profit margins, current ratios, or debt to equity ratios) to retain the line of credit.

CLARIFICATION NOTE: Only the used portion of the line of credit is recognized as a liability in the financial statements.

Companies with excellent credit ratings may borrow short-term funds by issuing **commercial paper**, unsecured loans that are sold to the public, usually through professionally managed investment firms. The portion of a line of credit currently borrowed and the amount of commercial paper issued are usually combined with notes payable in the current liabilities section of the balance sheet. Details are disclosed in a note to the financial statements.

NOTES PAYABLE Short-term notes payable are obligations represented by promissory notes. These notes may be used to secure bank loans, to pay suppliers for goods and services, and to secure credit from other sources.

The interest may be stated separately on the face of the note (Case 1 in Figure 3), or it may be deducted in advance by discounting it from the face value of the note (Case 2 in Figure 3). The entries to record the note in each case are as follows:

Case 1
A = L + OE
\+ \+

Case 2
A = L + OE
\+ −
    \+

Case 1—Interest Stated Separately

Aug. 31	Cash	5,000	
	Notes Payable		5,000
	Issued 60-day, 12% promissory note with interest stated separately		

Case 2—Interest in Face Amount

Aug. 31	Cash	4,900	
	Discount on Notes Payable	100	
	Notes Payable		5,000
	Issued 60-day promissory note with $100 interest included in face amount		

CLARIFICATION NOTE: The effective interest rate on the loan in Case 2 is 12.24% ($100/$4,900 × 360/60). For ease of computation, 360 days are used to compute interest on notes.

Note that in Case 1 the money received equaled the face value of the note, whereas in Case 2 the money received ($4,900) was less than the face value ($5,000) of the note. The amount of the discount equals the amount of the interest for 60 days. Although the dollar amount of interest on each of these notes is the same, the effective interest rate is slightly higher in Case 2 because the amount

FIGURE 3
Two Promissory Notes: One with Interest Stated Separately; One with Interest in Face Amount

CASE 1: INTEREST STATED SEPARATELY

Chicago, Illinois   August 31, 20xx

Sixty days after date I promise to pay First Federal Bank the sum of $5,000 with interest at the rate of 12% per annum.

Sandra Caron
Caron Corporation

CASE 2: INTEREST IN FACE AMOUNT

Chicago, Illinois   August 31, 20xx

Sixty days after date I promise to pay First Federal Bank the sum of $5,000.

Sandra Caron
Caron Corporation

received is slightly less ($4,900 in Case 2 versus $5,000 in Case 1). Discount on Notes Payable is a contra account to Notes Payable and is deducted from Notes Payable on the balance sheet.

On October 30, when the note is paid, each alternative is recorded as follows:

Case 1
A = L + OE
− − −

Case 2
A = L + OE
− −
A = L + OE
+ −

Case 1—Interest Stated Separately

Oct. 30	Notes Payable	5,000	
	Interest Expense	100	
	Cash		5,100
	Payment of note with interest stated separately		
	$\$5{,}000 \times .12 \times \frac{60}{360} = \$100$		

Case 2—Interest in Face Amount

Oct. 30	Notes Payable	5,000	
	Cash		5,000
	Payment of note with interest included in face amount		
30	Interest Expense	100	
	Discount on Notes Payable		100
	Interest expense on note payable		

■ **ACCRUED LIABILITIES** A key reason for making adjusting entries at the end of an accounting period is to recognize and record any liabilities that are not already in the accounting records. This practice applies to any type of liability. As you will see, accrued liabilities can include estimated liabilities.

Here the focus is on interest payable, a definitely determinable liability. Interest accrues daily on interest-bearing notes. At the end of the accounting period, an adjusting entry should be made in accordance with the matching rule to record the interest obligation up to that point. Let us again use the example of the two notes presented in Figure 3. If we assume that the accounting period ends on September 30, or 30 days after the issuance of the 60-day notes, the adjusting entries for each case would be as follows:

Case 1
A = L + OE
+ −

Case 2
A = L + OE
+ −

Case 1—Interest Stated Separately

Sept. 30	Interest Expense	50	
	Interest Payable		50
	To record interest expense for 30 days on note with interest stated separately		
	$\$5{,}000 \times .12 \times \frac{30}{360} = \$50$		

Case 2—Interest in Face Amount

Sept. 30	Interest Expense	50	
	Discount on Notes Payable		50
	To record interest expense for 30 days on note with interest included in face amount		
	$\$100 \times \frac{30}{60} = \$50$		

KEY POINT: Both of these entries have exactly the same impact on the financial statements.

In Case 2, Discount on Notes Payable will now have a debit balance of $50, which will become interest expense during the next 30 days.

■ **DIVIDENDS PAYABLE** Cash dividends are a distribution of earnings by a corporation. The payment of dividends is solely the decision of the corporation's board of directors. A liability does not exist until the board declares the dividends. There is usually a short time between the date of declaration and the date of payment of dividends. During that short time, the dividends declared are considered current liabilities of the corporation.

■ **SALES AND EXCISE TAXES PAYABLE** Most states and many cities levy a sales tax on retail transactions. There is a federal excise tax on some products, such as automobile tires. A merchant who sells goods subject to these taxes must collect the taxes and forward them periodically to the appropriate government agency. The amount of tax collected represents a current liability until it is remitted to the government. For example, assume that a merchant makes a $100 sale that is subject to a 5 percent sales tax and a 10 percent excise tax. Assuming that the sale takes place on June 1, the entry to record the sale is as follows:

A = L + OE + + + +	June 1	Cash	115	
		Sales		100
		Sales Tax Payable		5
		Excise Tax Payable		10
		Sales of merchandise and collection of sales and excise tax		

The sale is properly recorded at $100, and the taxes collected are recorded as liabilities to be remitted at the proper times to the appropriate government agencies.

CURRENT PORTIONS OF LONG-TERM DEBT If a portion of long-term debt is due within the next year and is to be paid from current assets, then that current portion is properly classified as a current liability. For example, suppose that a $500,000 debt is to be paid in installments of $100,000 per year for the next five years. The $100,000 installment due in the current year should be classified as a current liability. The remaining $400,000 should be classified as a long-term liability. Note that no journal entry is necessary. The total debt of $500,000 is simply reclassified when the financial statements are prepared, as follows:

Current liabilities	
Current portion of long-term debt	$100,000
Long-term liabilities	
Long-term debt	400,000

PAYROLL LIABILITIES For most organizations, the cost of labor and related payroll taxes is a major expense. In some industries, such as banking and airlines, payroll costs represent more than half of all operating costs. Payroll accounting is important because complex laws and significant liabilities are involved. The employer is liable to employees for wages and salaries and to various agencies for amounts withheld from wages and salaries and for related taxes. The term **wages** refers to payment for the services of employees at an hourly rate. The term **salaries** refers to the compensation of employees who are paid at a monthly or yearly rate.

Because payroll accounting applies only to the employees of an organization, it is important to distinguish between employees and independent contractors. Employees are paid a wage or salary by the organization and are under its direct supervision and control. Independent contractors are not employees of the organization, so they are not accounted for under the payroll system. They offer services to the organization for a fee, but they are not under its direct control or supervision. Certified public accountants, advertising agencies, and lawyers, for example, may act as independent contractors.

Figure 4 provides an illustration of payroll liabilities and their relationship to employee earnings and employer taxes and other costs. Two important observations may be made. First, the amount payable to employees is less than the amount of earnings. This occurs because employers are required by law or are requested by employees to withhold certain amounts from wages and send them directly to government agencies or other organizations. Second, the total employer liabilities exceed employee earnings because the employer must pay additional taxes and make other contributions, such as for pensions and medical care, that increase the cost and liabilities. The most common withholdings, taxes, and other payroll costs are described next.

FOCUS ON BUSINESS PRACTICE

Small Businesses Offer Benefits, Too.

A survey of small businesses in the Midwest shows the percentages of respondents that offer the following benefits:[6]

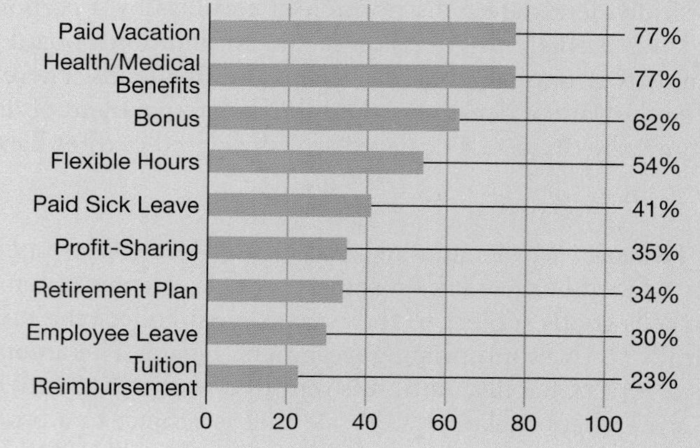

FIGURE 4
Illustration of Payroll Liabilities

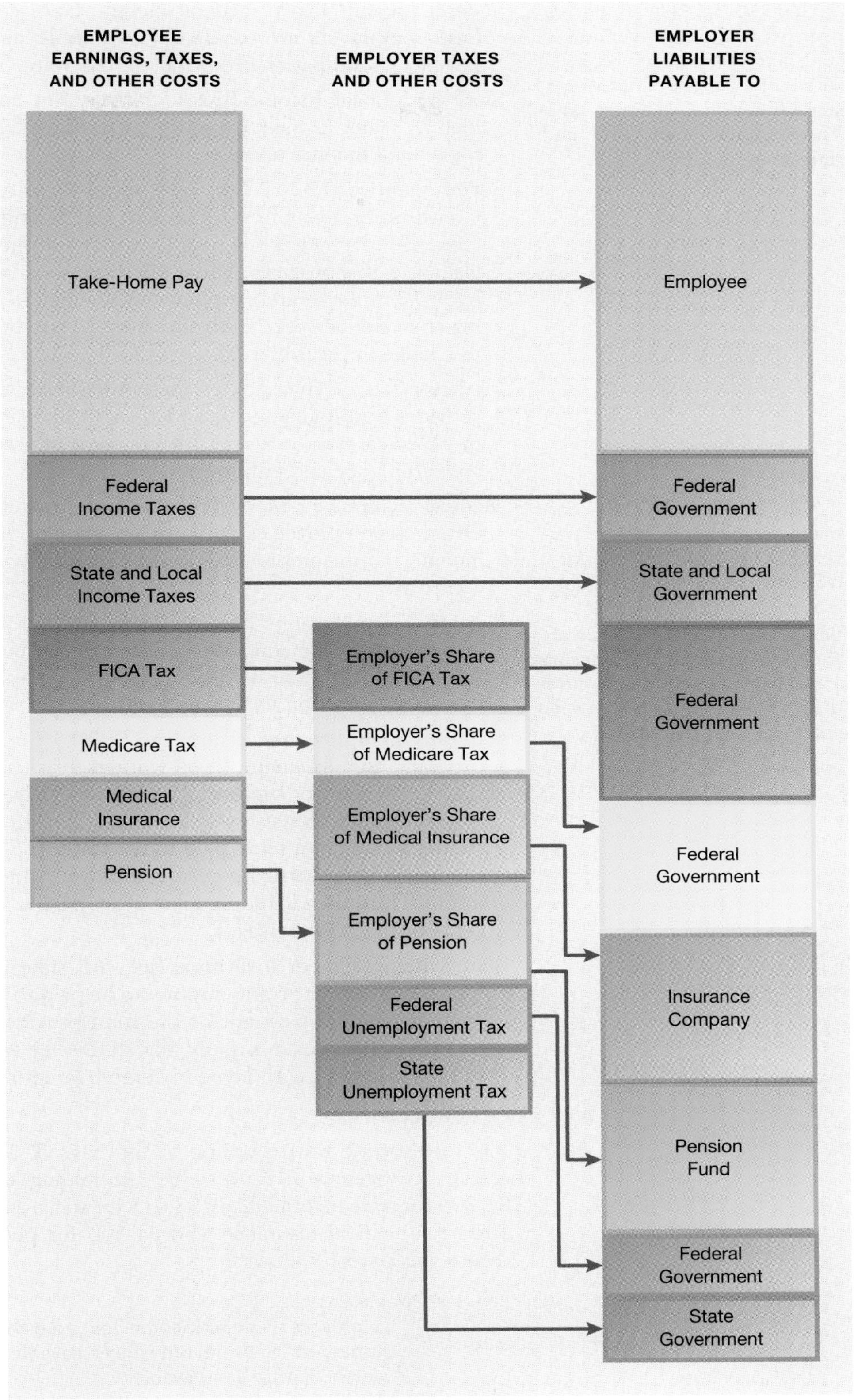

KEY POINT: The employee bears all the tax for federal, state, and local income taxes. The employer and employee share FICA and Medicare taxes. The employer bears FUTA and state unemployment taxes.

Federal Income Taxes Federal income taxes are collected on a "pay as you go" basis. Employers are required to withhold appropriate taxes from employees' paychecks and pay them to the United States Treasury.

State and Local Income Taxes Most states and some local governments have income taxes. In most cases, the procedures for withholding are similar to those for federal income taxes.

Social Security (FICA) Tax The social security program (the Federal Insurance Contribution Act) offers retirement and disability benefits and survivor's benefits. About 90 percent of the people working in the United States fall under the provisions of this program. The 2003 social security tax rate of 6.2 percent was paid by *both* employee and employer on the first $87,000 earned by an employee during the calendar year. Both the rate and the base to which it applies are subject to change in future years.

Medicare Tax A major extension of the social security program is Medicare, which provides hospitalization and medical insurance for persons over age 65. In 2003, the Medicare tax rate was 1.45 percent of gross income, with no limit, paid by *both* employee and employer.

ENRICHMENT NOTE: For many organizations, a large portion of the cost of labor is not reflected in employees' regular paychecks. Vacation pay, sick pay, personal days, health insurance, life insurance, and pensions are some of the additional costs that may be negotiated between employers and employees.

Medical Insurance Many organizations provide medical benefits to employees. Often, the employee contributes a portion of the cost through withholdings from income and the employer pays the rest, usually a greater amount, to the insurance company.

Pension Contributions Many organizations also provide pension benefits to employees. In a manner similar to that for medical insurance, a portion of the pension contribution is withheld from the employee's income and the rest is paid by the organization to the pension fund.

Federal Unemployment Insurance (FUTA) Tax This tax is intended to pay for programs to help unemployed workers. It is paid *only* by employers and recently was 6.2 percent of the first $7,000 earned by each employee (this amount may vary from state to state). Against this federal tax, the employer is allowed a credit for unemployment taxes paid to the state. The maximum credit is 5.4 percent of the first $7,000 earned by each employee. Most states set their rate at this maximum. Thus, the FUTA tax most often paid is .8 percent (6.2 percent − 5.4 percent) of the taxable wages.

State Unemployment Insurance Tax All state unemployment programs provide for unemployment compensation to be paid to eligible unemployed workers. This compensation is paid out of the fund provided by the 5.4 percent of the first $7,000 (or whatever amount the state sets) earned by each employee. In some states, employers with favorable employment records may be entitled to pay less than 5.4 percent.

To illustrate the recording of the payroll, assume that on February 15 total employee wages are $32,500, with withholdings of $5,400 for federal income taxes, $1,200 for state income taxes, $2,015 for social security tax, $471 for Medicare tax, $900 for medical insurance, and $1,300 for pension contributions. The entry to record this payroll follows:

A = L + OE				
+ −	Feb. 15	Wages Expense	32,500	
+		Employees' Federal Income Taxes Payable		5,400
+		Employees' State Income Taxes Payable		1,200
+		Social Security Tax Payable		2,015
+		Medicare Tax Payable		471
+		Medical Insurance Premiums Payable		900
+		Pension Contributions Payable		1,300
		Wages Payable		21,214
		To record payroll		

Note that the employees' take-home pay is $21,214, although $32,500 was earned.

Using the same data, the additional employer taxes and other benefits costs would be recorded as follows, assuming that the payroll taxes correspond to the discussion above and that the employer pays 80 percent of the medical insurance premiums and half of the pension contributions:

A = L + OE				
+ −	Feb. 15	Payroll Taxes and Benefits Expense	9,401	
+		Social Security Tax Payable		2,015
+		Medicare Tax Payable		471
+		Medical Insurance Premiums Payable		3,600
+		Pension Contributions Payable		1,300
+		Federal Unemployment Tax Payable		260
+		State Unemployment Tax Payable		1,755
		To record payroll taxes and other costs		

Note that the payroll taxes and benefits increase the total cost of the payroll to $41,901 ($9,401 + $32,500), which exceeds by almost 29 percent the amount earned by employees. This is a typical situation.

■ **UNEARNED REVENUES** **Unearned revenues** represent obligations for goods or services that the company must provide in a future accounting period in return for an advance payment from a customer. For example, a publisher of a monthly magazine who receives annual subscriptions totaling $240 would make the following entry:

A = L + OE			
+ +	Cash	240	
	Unearned Subscriptions		240
	Receipt of annual subscriptions in advance		

The publisher now has a liability of $240 that will be reduced gradually as monthly issues of the magazine are mailed:

A = L + OE			
− +	Unearned Subscriptions	20	
	Subscription Revenues		20
	Delivery of monthly magazine issues		

Many businesses, such as repair companies, construction companies, and special-order firms, ask for a deposit or advance from a customer before they will begin work. Such advances are also current liabilities until the goods or services are actually delivered.

ESTIMATED LIABILITIES

KEY POINT: Estimated liabilities are recorded and presented on the financial statements in the same way as definitely determinable liabilities. The only difference is that estimated liabilities involve some uncertainty in their computation.

Estimated liabilities are definite debts or obligations whose exact dollar amount cannot be known until a later date. Since there is no doubt about the existence of the legal obligation, the primary accounting problem is to estimate and record the amount of the liability. Examples of estimated liabilities are income taxes, property taxes, product warranties, and vacation pay.

■ **INCOME TAXES** The income of a corporation is taxed by the federal government, most state governments, and some cities and towns. The amount of income taxes liability depends on the results of operations. Often the results are not known until after the end of the year. However, because income taxes are an expense in the year in which income is earned, an adjusting entry is necessary to record the estimated tax liability. The entry is as follows:

A = L + OE				
+ −	Dec. 31	Income Taxes Expense	53,000	
		Estimated Income Taxes Payable		53,000
		To record estimated federal income taxes		

Sole proprietorships and partnerships do *not* pay income taxes. Their owners must report their share of the firm's income on their individual tax returns.

ENRICHMENT NOTE: The process of accruing property tax each month could be applied to income taxes if a company desires monthly financial statements.

■ PROPERTY TAX PAYABLE Property taxes are levied on real property, such as land and buildings, and on personal property, such as inventory and equipment. Property taxes are a main source of revenue for local governments. They are usually assessed annually against the real and personal property involved. Because the fiscal years of local governments and their assessment dates rarely correspond to a company's fiscal year, it is necessary to estimate the amount of property tax that applies to each month of the year.

KEY POINT: Recording product warranty expense in the year of the sale follows the matching rule.

■ PRODUCT WARRANTY LIABILITY When a firm places a warranty on its product (or its service) at the time of sale, a liability exists for the length of the warranty. The cost of the warranty is properly debited to an expense account in the period of sale because it is a feature of the product sold and thus is included in the price the customer pays for the product. On the basis of experience, it should be possible to estimate the amount the warranty will cost in the future. Some products will require little warranty service; others may require much. Thus, there will be an average cost per product.

For example, assume a muffler company guarantees that it will replace free of charge any muffler it sells that fails during the time the buyer owns the car. The company charges a small service fee for replacing the muffler. This warranty is an important selling feature for the firm's mufflers. In the past, 6 percent of the mufflers sold have been returned for replacement under the warranty. The average cost of a muffler is $50. Assume that during July, the company sold 350 mufflers. The accrued liability would be recorded as an adjustment at the end of July as shown below:

A = L + OE
    +   −

July 31	Product Warranty Expense	1,050	
	Estimated Product Warranty Liability		1,050
	To record estimated product warranty expense:		
	Number of units sold	350	
	Rate of replacement under warranty	× .06	
	Estimated units to be replaced	21	
	Estimated cost per unit	× $ 50	
	Estimated liability for product warranty	$1,050	

When a muffler is returned for replacement under the warranty, the cost of the muffler is charged against the Estimated Product Warranty Liability account. For example, assume that on December 5, a customer returns with a defective muffler

FOCUS ON BUSINESS PRACTICE

Those Little Coupons Can Add Up.

Many companies promote their products by issuing coupons that offer "cents off" or other enticements. Since four out of five shoppers use coupons, companies are forced by competition to distribute them. The total value of unredeemed coupons, each of which represents a potential liability for the issuing company, is truly staggering. NCH Promotional Services <www.wattsgroup.com>, a company owned by Dun & Bradstreet, estimates that almost 300 billion coupons are issued annually. Of course, the liability depends on how many of the coupons will actually be redeemed. NCH estimates that number at approximately 6 billion, or about 2 percent. Thus, a big advertiser that puts a cents-off coupon in Sunday papers to reach 60 million people can be faced with liability for 1,200,000 coupons. The total value of coupons redeemed each year is estimated at more than $4 billion.[7]

Focus on Business Practice

Are Frequent-Flier Miles a Liability or a Revenue?

In the early 1980s, American Airlines, Inc. <www.aa.com> developed a frequent-flier program that gives free trips and other awards to customers based on the number of miles they fly on the airline. Since then, many other airlines have instituted similar programs, and it is estimated that 38 million people now participate in them. Today, U.S. airlines have more than 3 trillion "miles" outstanding. Seven to eight percent of all passengers are traveling on free tickets. Estimated liabilities for these tickets have become an important consideration in evaluating an airline's financial position. Complicating the estimate is that almost half the miles have been earned on purchases from hotels, car rental and telephone companies, and Internet service providers like AOL, and through the use of credit cards. In these cases, the companies giving the miles must pay the airlines at the rate of $.02 per mile. Thus, a free ticket obtained with 25,000 miles provides revenue to the airline of $500. In a recent year, airlines took in more than $2 billion from this source.[8]

and pays a $20 service fee to have the muffler replaced. Assume that this particular muffler cost $40. The entry is as follows:

A = L + OE
\+ − +
−

Dec. 5	Cash	20	
	Estimated Product Warranty Liability	40	
	Service Revenue		20
	Merchandise Inventory		40
	Replacement of muffler under warranty		

Stop and Think!
Do adjusting entries involving estimated liabilities and accruals ever affect cash flows?
They never affect cash flows at the time of the entry, but they may require the payment of a liability in the future. ■

■ **Vacation Pay Liability** In most companies, employees accrue paid vacation as they work during the year. For example, an employee may earn two weeks of paid vacation for each 50 weeks of work. Therefore, the person is paid 52 weeks' salary for 50 weeks' work. Theoretically, the cost of the two weeks' vacation should be allocated as an expense over the whole year so that month-to-month costs will not be distorted. The vacation pay represents 4 percent (two weeks' vacation divided by 50 weeks) of a worker's pay. Every week worked earns the employee a small fraction (4 percent) of vacation pay.

Vacation pay liability can represent a substantial amount of money. As noted in this chapter's Decision Point, US Airways reported at its 2001 year end accrued salaries, wages, and vacation liabilities of $367 million.

www.usairways.com

Suppose that a company with a vacation policy of two weeks of paid vacation for each 50 weeks of work has a payroll of $21,000, of which $1,000 was paid to employees on vacation for the week ended April 20. Because of turnover and rules regarding term of employment, it is assumed that only 75 percent of employees will ultimately collect vacation pay. The computation of vacation pay expense based on the payroll of employees not on vacation ($21,000 − $1,000) is as follows: $20,000 × 4 percent × 75 percent = $600. The entry to record vacation pay expense for the week ended April 20 is as follows:

A = L + OE
\+ −

Apr. 20	Vacation Pay Expense	600	
	Estimated Liability for Vacation Pay		600
	Estimated vacation pay expense		

At the time employees receive their vacation pay, an entry is made debiting Estimated Liability for Vacation Pay and crediting Cash or Wages Payable. This entry records the $1,000 paid to employees on vacation during August:

A* = L + OE
− −
*Assumes cash paid.

Aug. 31	Estimated Liability for Vacation Pay	1,000	
	Cash (or Wages Payable)		1,000
	Wages of employees on vacation		

The treatment of vacation pay presented in this example may also be applied to other payroll costs, such as bonus plans and contributions to pension plans.

Check out ACE for a Review Quiz at http://accounting.college.hmco.com/students.

Contingent Liabilities and Commitments

LO3 Distinguish *contingent liabilities* from *commitments.*

RELATED TEXT ASSIGNMENTS
Q: 17, 18
SE: 3
SD: 2, 4
FRA: 2, 3, 5, 6, 7

KEY POINT: Contingencies are recorded when they are probable and can be reasonably estimated.

The FASB requires companies to disclose in a note to their financial statements any contingent liabilities and commitments they may have. A **contingent liability** is not an existing obligation. Rather, it is a potential liability because it depends on a future event arising out of a past transaction. For instance, a construction company that built a bridge may have been sued by the state for using poor materials. The past transaction is the building of the bridge under contract. The future event is the outcome of the lawsuit, which is not yet known.

The FASB has established two conditions for determining when a contingency should be entered in the accounting records: (1) the liability must be probable, and (2) it can be reasonably estimated.[9] Estimated liabilities like the income taxes liability, warranty liability, and vacation pay liability that we described earlier meet those conditions. Therefore, they are accrued in the accounting records.

In a survey of 600 large companies, the most common types of contingencies reported were litigation, which can involve many different issues, and environmental concerns.[10] The notes in an annual report of General Motors Corporation, the world's largest automobile maker, describe contingent liabilities as follows:

www.gm.com

> Litigation is subject to uncertainties and the outcome of individual litigated matters is not predictable with assurance. Various legal actions, governmental investigations, claims, and proceedings are pending against the Corporation, including those arising out of alleged product defects; employment-related matters; governmental regulations relating to safety, emissions, and fuel economy; product warranties; financial services; dealer, supplier, and other contractual relationships and environmental matters. . . . After discussion with counsel, it is the opinion of management that such liability is not expected to have a material adverse effect on the Corporation's consolidated financial condition or results of operations.[11]

STOP AND THINK!
When would a commitment be recognized in the records?
When a transaction has occurred, such as when a purchase agreement is followed up and completed or when a lease payment is made. ■

A **commitment** is a legal obligation that does not meet the technical requirements for recognition as a liability. The most common examples are purchase agreements and leases.[12] For example, in a note to its financial statements, US Airways states: "The Company had 65 A320 aircraft on firm order, 182 aircraft subject to reconfirmation prior to scheduled delivery, and options for 63 additional aircraft." The note goes on to say, "The company leases certain aircraft and ground equipment, in addition to the majority of the ground facilities."[13] It then summarizes the amounts of the lease obligations.

www.usairways.com

Check out ACE for a Review Quiz at http://accounting.college.hmco.com/students.

Payroll Accounting Illustrated

SO4 Compute and record the liabilities associated with payroll accounting.

RELATED TEXT ASSIGNMENTS
Q: 19, 20, 21
SE: 9, 10
E: 9, 10, 11
P: 5
SD: 5

Earlier in this chapter, the liabilities associated with payroll accounting were identified and discussed. This section will focus on the calculations, records, and control requirements of payroll accounting. To demonstrate the concepts, the illustrations are shown in manual format, but, in actual practice, most businesses (including small businesses) use a computer to process payroll.

Computation of an Employee's Take-Home Pay

Besides setting minimum wage levels, the federal Fair Labor Standards Act (also called the Wages and Hours Law) regulates overtime pay. Employers who take part in interstate commerce must pay overtime to employees who work beyond 40 hours a week or more than eight hours a day. This pay must be at least one and one-half times the regular rate. Work on Saturdays, Sundays, or holidays may also call for overtime pay or some sort of premium pay under separate wage agreements. Overtime pay under union or other employment contracts may exceed these minimums.

For example, suppose that the employment contract of Robert Jones calls for a regular wage of $8 an hour, one and one-half times the regular rate for work over eight hours in any weekday, and twice the regular rate for work on Saturdays, Sundays, or holidays. He works the following days and hours during the week of January 18, 20xx:

Day	Total Hours Worked	Regular Time	Overtime
Monday	10	8	2
Tuesday	8	8	0
Wednesday	8	8	0
Thursday	9	8	1
Friday	10	8	2
Saturday	2	0	2
	47	40	7

Jones's wages would be calculated as follows:

Regular time	40 hours × $8	$320
Overtime, weekdays	5 hours × $8 × 1.5	60
Overtime, weekend	2 hours × $8 × 2	32
Total wages		$412

Once Jones's wages are known, his take-home pay can be calculated. Since his total earnings for the week of January 18 are $412.00, his social security tax is 6.2 percent, or $25.54 (he has not earned over $87,000), and his Medicare tax is 1.45 percent, or $5.97. The amount to be withheld for federal income taxes depends in part on Jones's earnings and in part on the number of his exemptions. All employees are required by law to indicate exemptions by filing a Form W-4 (Employee's Withholding Exemption Certificate). Every employee is entitled to one exemption for himself or herself and one for each dependent.

Based on the information in Form W-4, the amount of withholding is determined by referring to a withholding table provided by the Internal Revenue Service. For example, the withholding table in Figure 5 shows that for Jones, a married employee who has a total of four exemptions and is paid weekly, the withholding on total wages of $412 is $31. Actual withholding tables change periodically to reflect changes in tax rates and tax laws. Assume also that Jones's union dues are $2.00, his medical insurance premiums are $7.60, his life insurance premium is $6.00, he places $15.00 per week in savings bonds, and he contributes $1.00 per week to United Charities. Jones's net (take-home) pay can now be computed:

KEY POINT: The expense to the company is the gross earnings, not the net take-home pay.

Total earnings		$412.00
Deductions		
Federal income taxes withheld	$31.00	
Social security tax	25.54	
Medicare tax	5.97	
Union dues	2.00	
Medical insurance	7.60	
Life insurance	6.00	
Savings bonds	15.00	
United Charities contribution	1.00	
Total deductions		94.11
Net (take-home) pay		$317.89

FIGURE 5
Sample Withholding Table

WEEKLY PAYROLL PERIOD—EMPLOYEE MARRIED												
		And the number of withholding allowances claimed is—										
And the wages are—		0	1	2	3	4	5	6	7	8	9	10 or more
At least	*But less than*	The amount of income tax to be withheld will be—										
$300	$310	$37	$31	$26	$20	$14	$ 9	$ 3	$ 0	$ 0	$0	$0
310	320	38	33	27	22	16	10	5	0	0	0	0
320	330	40	34	29	23	17	12	6	1	0	0	0
330	340	41	36	30	25	19	13	8	2	0	0	0
340	350	43	37	32	26	20	15	9	4	0	0	0
350	360	44	39	33	28	22	16	11	5	0	0	0
360	370	46	40	35	29	23	18	12	7	1	0	0
370	380	47	42	36	31	25	19	14	8	2	0	0
380	390	49	43	38	32	26	21	15	10	4	0	0
390	400	50	45	39	34	28	22	17	11	5	0	0
400	410	52	46	41	35	29	24	18	13	7	1	0
410	420	53	48	42	37	31	25	20	14	8	3	0
420	430	55	49	44	38	32	27	21	16	10	4	0

PAYROLL REGISTER

The **payroll register**, which is prepared each pay period, is a detailed listing of the firm's total payroll. A payroll register is presented in Exhibit 1. Note that the name, hours, earnings, deductions, and net pay of each employee are listed. Compare the entry for Robert Jones in the payroll register with the January 18 entry in Robert Jones's employee earnings record, presented in Exhibit 2. Except for the first column, which lists the employee names, and the last two columns, which show

EXHIBIT 1
Payroll Register

Payroll Register — Pay Period: Week ended January 18

		Earnings			Deductions								Payment		Distribution	
Employee	Total Hours	Regular	Overtime	Gross	Federal Income Taxes	Social Security Tax	Medicare Tax	Union Dues	Medical Insurance	Life Insurance	Savings Bonds	Other: A—United Charities	Net Earnings	Check No.	Sales Wages Expense	Office Wages Expense
Linda Duval	40	160.00		160.00	11.00	9.92	2.32		5.80				130.96	923		160.00
John Franks	44	160.00	24.00	184.00	14.00	11.41	2.67	2.00	7.60			A 10.00	136.32	924	184.00	
Samuel Goetz	40	400.00		400.00	53.00	24.80	5.80		10.40	14.00		A 3.00	289.00	925	400.00	
Robert Jones	47	320.00	92.00	412.00	31.00	25.54	5.97	2.00	7.60	6.00	15.00	A 1.00	317.89	926	412.00	
Billie Matthews	40	160.00		160.00	14.00	9.92	2.32		5.80				127.96	927		160.00
Rosaire O'Brien	42	200.00	20.00	220.00	22.00	13.64	3.19	2.00	5.80				173.37	928	220.00	
James Van Dyke	40	200.00		200.00	20.00	12.40	2.90		5.80				158.90	929		200.00
		1,600.00	136.00	1,736.00	165.00	107.63	25.17	6.00	48.80	20.00	15.00	14.00	1,334.40		1,216.00	520.00

EXHIBIT 2
Employee Earnings Record

Employee Earnings Record

Employee's Name Robert Jones	**Social Security Number** 444-66-9999		
Address 777 20th Street	**Sex** Male	**Employee No.**	705
Marshall, Michigan 52603	**Single** ____ **Married** X	**Weekly Pay Rate**	
Date of Birth September 20, 1962	**Exemptions (W-4)** 4	**Hourly Rate**	$8
Position Sales Assistant	**Date of Employment** July 15, 1988	**Date Employment Ended**	

20xx		Earnings			Deductions								Payment		
Period Ended	Total Hours	Regular	Overtime	Gross	Federal Income Taxes	Social Security Tax	Medicare Tax	Union Dues	Medical Insurance	Life Insurance	Savings Bonds	Other: A—United Charities	Net Earnings	Check No.	Cumulative Gross Earnings
Jan 4	40	320.00	0	320.00	17.00	19.84	4.64	2.00	7.60	6.00	15.00	A 1.00	246.92	717	320.00
11	44	320.00	48.00	368.00	23.00	22.82	5.34	2.00	7.60	6.00	15.00	A 1.00	285.24	822	688.00
18	47	320.00	92.00	412.00	31.00	25.54	5.97	2.00	7.60	6.00	15.00	A 1.00	317.89	926	1,100.00

the wage or salary as either sales or office expense, the columns are the same. The columns help employers record the payroll in the accounting records and meet legal reporting requirements. The last two columns in Exhibit 1 are needed to divide the expenses in the accounting records into selling and administrative categories.

RECORDING THE PAYROLL

The journal entry for recording the payroll is based on the column totals from the payroll register. The journal entry to record the January 18 payroll follows. Note that each account debited or credited is a total from the payroll register. If the payroll register is considered a special-purpose journal, the column totals can be posted directly to the ledger accounts, with the correct account numbers shown at the bottom of each column.

ENRICHMENT NOTE: The credits in the January 18 entry would be presented as current liabilities on the financial statements. Because most of them are small, they probably would be aggregated into "Other Payables" or a similar category.

Jan. 18	Sales Wages Expense	1,216.00	
	Office Wages Expense	520.00	
	Employees' Federal Income Taxes Payable		165.00
	Social Security Tax Payable		107.63
	Medicare Tax Payable		25.17
	Union Dues Payable		6.00
	Medical Insurance Premiums Payable		48.80
	Life Insurance Premiums Payable		20.00
	Savings Bonds Payable		15.00
	United Charities Payable		14.00
	Wages Payable		1,334.40
	To record payroll		

A = L + OE: + + + + + + + + + (L); − − (OE)

EMPLOYEE EARNINGS RECORD

KEY POINT: Payroll is one of the easiest elements of a business to computerize.

Each employer must keep a record of earnings and withholdings for each employee. Most companies today use computers to maintain such records, but some small companies may still use manual records. The manual form of **employee earnings**

Focus on Business Ethics

Why Is Payroll Fraud Common?

Payroll fraud is a common form of financial wrongdoing because there are strong motivations for both the employee and the employer to cheat. Some employees want to be paid cash "under the table" to avoid income, social security, and Medicare taxes. Some employers may wish to avoid paying their share of social security and Medicare taxes as well as other payroll taxes and employee benefits. Therefore, the Internal Revenue Service cracks down on cheaters. It investigates, for example, the relationships between restaurants' revenues and the tip income that employees report on their tax returns. Severe penalties, including prison terms, can result from false reporting. Good accounting records and controls over payroll help ensure compliance with the law.

record for Robert Jones is shown in Exhibit 2. This form is designed to help the employer meet legal reporting requirements. Each deduction must be shown to have been paid to the proper agency, and the employee must receive a report of the deductions made each year.

Most of the columns in Exhibit 2 are self-explanatory. Note, however, the column on the far right for cumulative gross earnings (total earnings to date). This record helps the employer comply with the rule of applying social security and unemployment taxes only up to the maximum wage levels. At the end of the year, the employer reports to the employee on Form W-2, the Wage and Tax Statement, the total earnings and tax deductions for the year, which the employee uses to complete his or her individual tax return. The employer sends a copy of the W-2 to the Internal Revenue Service. Thus, the IRS can check whether the employee has reported all income earned from that employer.

Recording Payroll Taxes

According to Exhibit 1, the gross payroll for the week ended January 18 was \$1,736.00. Because it was the first month of the year, all employees had accumulated less than the \$87,000 and \$7,000 maximum taxable salaries. Therefore, the total social security tax was \$107.63 and the total Medicare tax was \$25.17 (equal to the tax on employees), the total FUTA tax was \$13.89 (.008 × \$1,736.00), and the total state unemployment tax was \$93.74 (.054 × \$1,736.00). The entry to record this expense and related liability is as follows:

A = L + OE	Date	Account	Debit	Credit
− (OE)	Jan. 18	Payroll Taxes Expense	240.43	
+ (L)		Social Security Tax Payable		107.63
+ (L)		Medicare Tax Payable		25.17
+ (L)		Federal Unemployment Tax Payable		13.89
+ (L)		State Unemployment Tax Payable		93.74
		To record payroll taxes		

Payment of Payroll and Payroll Taxes

After the weekly payroll is recorded, as illustrated earlier, a liability of \$1,334.40 exists for wages payable. How this liability will be paid depends on the system used by the company. Many companies use a special payroll account against which payroll checks are drawn. Under this system, a check for total net earnings for this payroll (\$1,334.40) must be drawn on the regular checking account and deposited in the special payroll account before the payroll checks are issued to the employees. If a voucher system is combined with a special payroll account, a voucher for the total wages payable is prepared and recorded in the voucher register as a debit to Payroll Bank Account and a credit to Vouchers Payable.

The combined social security and Medicare taxes (both employees' and employer's shares) and the federal income taxes must be paid at least quarterly. More frequent payments are required when the total liability exceeds \$500. The federal unemployment insurance tax is paid yearly if the amount is less than $100. If the liability for the federal unemployment insurance tax exceeds $100 at the end of any quarter, a payment is necessary. Payment dates vary among the states. Other payroll deductions must be paid in accordance with the particular contracts or agreements involved.

Check out ACE for a Review Quiz at http://accounting.college.hmco.com/students.

Chapter Review

Review of Learning Objectives

LO1 Identify the management issues related to recognition, valuation, classification, and disclosure of current liabilities.

Liabilities are legal obligations for future payment of assets or future performance of services. They result from past transactions and should be recognized at the time a transaction obligates a company to make future payments. They are valued at the amount of money necessary to satisfy the obligation or at the fair value of goods or services that must be delivered. Liabilities are classified as current or long term. Supplemental disclosure is required when the nature or details of the obligations would help in understanding the liability. Liabilities are an important consideration in assessing a company's liquidity. Key measures are working capital, payables turnover, and average days' payable.

LO2 Identify, compute, and record definitely determinable and estimated current liabilities.

Two principal categories of current liabilities are definitely determinable liabilities and estimated liabilities. Although definitely determinable liabilities, such as accounts payable, notes payable, accrued liabilities, dividends payable, and the current portion of long-term debt, can be measured exactly, the accountant must still be careful not to overlook existing liabilities in these categories. Estimated liabilities, such as liabilities for income taxes, property taxes, and product warranties, definitely exist, but the amounts must be estimated and recorded properly.

LO3 Distinguish *contingent liabilities* from *commitments.*

A contingent liability is a potential liability that arises from a past transaction and is dependent on a future event. Examples of contingent liabilities are lawsuits, income tax disputes, discounted notes receivable, guarantees of debt, and failure to follow government regulations. A commitment is a legal obligation, such as a purchase agreement, that is not recorded as a liability.

Supplemental Objective

SO4 Compute and record the liabilities associated with payroll accounting.

Computations for payroll liabilities must be made for the compensation to each employee, for withholdings from each employee's total pay, and for the employer's portion of payroll taxes. The salary and deductions for each employee are recorded each pay period in the payroll register. From the payroll register, the details of each employee's earnings are transferred to the employee's earnings record. The column totals of the payroll register are used to prepare an entry that records the payroll and accompanying liabilities. The employer's share of social security and Medicare taxes and the federal and state unemployment taxes as well as any liabilities for other fringe benefits must then be recorded.

Review of Concepts and Terminology

The following concepts and terms were introduced in this chapter:

LO1 **Average days' payable:** How long, on average, a company takes to pay its accounts payable; 365 days divided by payables turnover.

LO2 **Commercial paper:** Unsecured loans sold to the public, usually through professionally managed investment firms, as a means of borrowing short-term funds.

LO3 **Commitment:** A legal obligation that does not meet the technical requirements for recognition as a liability.

LO3 **Contingent liability:** A potential liability that arises from a past transaction and is dependent on a future event.

LO1 **Current liabilities:** Debts and obligations expected to be satisfied within one year or within the normal operating cycle, whichever is longer.

LO2 **Definitely determinable liabilities:** Current liabilities that are set by contract or statute and that can be measured exactly.

SO4 **Employee earnings record:** A record of earnings and withholdings for an individual employee.

LO2 **Estimated liabilities:** Definite debts or obligations whose exact amounts cannot be known until a later date.

LO2 **Line of credit:** An arrangement with a bank that allows a company to borrow funds as needed.

LO1 **Long-term liabilities:** Debts or obligations due beyond one year or beyond the normal operating cycle.

LO1 **Payables turnover:** The number of times, on average, that accounts payable are paid in an accounting period; cost of goods sold plus (or minus) change in merchandise inventory divided by average accounts payable.

SO4 **Payroll register:** A detailed listing of a firm's total payroll that is prepared each pay period.

LO2 **Salaries:** Compensation of employees who are paid at a monthly or yearly rate.

LO2 **Unearned revenues:** Revenues received in advance for goods or services that will not be delivered during the current accounting period.

LO2 **Wages:** Payment for services of employees at an hourly rate.

Review Problem

Notes Payable Transactions and End-of-Period Entries

LO2 McLaughlin, Inc., whose fiscal year ends June 30, 20xx, completed the following transactions involving notes payable:

May 11	Purchased a small crane by issuing a 60-day, 12 percent note for $54,000. The face of the note does not include interest.
16	Obtained a $40,000 bank loan to finance a temporary increase in receivables by signing a 90-day, 10 percent note. The face value includes interest.
June 30	Made the end-of-year adjusting entry to accrue interest expense.
30	Made the end-of-year adjusting entry to recognize interest expired on the note.
30	Made the end-of-year closing entry pertaining to interest expense.
July 10	Paid the note plus interest on the crane purchase.
Aug. 14	Paid off the note to the bank.

REQUIRED ▶ Prepare entries in journal form for the above transactions.

Answer to Review Problem

20xx			
May 11	Equipment	54,000	
	Notes Payable		54,000
	Purchased crane with 60-day, 12% note		

May 16	Cash	39,000	
	Discount on Notes Payable	1,000	
	Notes Payable		40,000
	Obtained loan from bank by signing 90-day, 10% note; discount equals $40,000 × .10 × 90/360 = $1,000		
June 30	Interest Expense	900	
	Interest Payable		900
	Accrued interest expense $54,000 × .12 × 50/360 = $900		
30	Interest Expense	500	
	Discount on Notes Payable		500
	Recognized interest on note $1,000 × 45/90 = $500		
30	Income Summary	1,400	
	Interest Expense		1,400
	Closed interest expense		
July 10	Notes Payable	54,000	
	Interest Payable	900	
	Interest Expense	180	
	Cash		55,080
	Paid note on equipment $54,000 × .12 × 10/360 = $180		
Aug. 14	Notes Payable	40,000	
	Cash		40,000
	Paid bank loan		
14	Interest Expense	500	
	Discount on Notes Payable		500
	Interest expense on matured note $1,000 − $500 = $500		

Chapter Assignments

BUILDING YOUR KNOWLEDGE FOUNDATION

QUESTIONS

1. What are liabilities?
2. Why is the timing of liability recognition important in accounting?
3. At the end of the accounting period, Janson Company had a legal obligation to accept delivery of and pay for a truckload of hospital supplies the following week. Is this legal obligation a liability?
4. Ned Johnson, a star college basketball player, received a contract from the Midwest Blazers to play professional basketball. The contract calls for a salary of $300,000 a year for four years, dependent on his making the team in each of those years. Should this contract be considered a liability and recorded on the books of the basketball team?
5. What is the rule for classifying a liability as current?
6. What are a line of credit and commercial paper? Where do they appear on the balance sheet?
7. A bank is offering Diane Wedge two alternatives for borrowing $2,000. The first alternative is a $2,000, 12 percent, 30-day note. The second alternative is a $2,000, 30-day note discounted at 12 percent. (a) What entries are required by

Diane Wedge to record the two loans? (b) What entries are needed by Wedge to record the payment of the two loans? (c) Which alternative favors Wedge, and why?

8. Where should the Discount on Notes Payable account appear on the balance sheet?
9. When can a portion of long-term debt be classified as a current liability?
10. What are three types of employer-related payroll liabilities?
11. How does an employee differ from an independent contractor?
12. Who pays social security and Medicare taxes?
13. Why are unearned revenues classified as liabilities?
14. What is definite about an estimated liability?
15. Why are income taxes payable considered to be estimated liabilities?
16. When does a company incur a liability for a product warranty?
17. What is a contingent liability, and how does it differ from a commitment?
18. What are some examples of contingent liabilities? For what reason is each a contingent liability?
19. What role does the W-4 form play in determining the withholding for estimated federal income taxes?
20. How can the payroll register be used as a special-purpose journal?
21. Why is an employee earnings record necessary, and how does it relate to the W-2 form?

SHORT EXERCISES

LO1 Issues in Accounting for Liabilities

SE 1. Indicate whether each of the following actions relates to (a) managing liquidity and cash flow, (b) recognition of liabilities, (c) valuation of liabilities, (d) classification of liabilities, or (e) disclosure of liabilities:

1. Determining that a liability will be paid in less than one year
2. Estimating the amount of a liability
3. Providing information about when liabilities are due and their interest rates
4. Determining when a liability arises
5. Assessing working capital and payables turnover

LO1 Measuring Short-Term Liquidity

SE 2. Stratton Company has current assets of $130,000 and current liabilities of $80,000, of which accounts payable are $70,000. Stratton's cost of goods sold is $460,000, its merchandise inventory increased by $20,000, and accounts payable were $50,000 the prior year. Calculate Stratton's working capital, payables turnover, and average days' payable.

LO2 LO3 Types of Liabilities

SE 3. Indicate whether each of the following is (a) a definitely determinable liability, (b) an estimated liability, (c) a commitment, or (d) a contingent liability:

1. Dividends Payable
2. Pending litigation
3. Income Taxes Payable
4. Current portion of long-term debt
5. Vacation Pay Liability
6. Guaranteed loans of another company
7. Purchase agreement

LO2 Interest Expense: Interest Not Included in Face Value of Note

SE 4. On the last day of August, Swift Company borrowed $60,000 on a bank note for 60 days at 10 percent interest. Assume that interest is stated separately. Prepare the following entries in journal form: (1) August 31, recording of note; and (2) October 30, payment of note plus interest.

LO2 Interest Expense: Interest Included in Face Value of Note

SE 5. Assume the same facts as in **SE 4,** except that interest of $1,000 is included in the face amount of the note and the note is discounted at the bank on August 31. Prepare the following entries in journal form: (1) August 31, recording of note; and (2) October 30, payment of note and recording of interest expense.

SE 6. **LO2 Payroll Entries** The following payroll totals for the month of April are from the payroll register of Corelli Corporation: salaries, $223,000.00; federal income taxes withheld, $31,440.00; social security tax withheld, $13,826.00; Medicare tax withheld, $3,233.50; medical insurance deductions, $6,580.00; and salaries subject to unemployment taxes, $156,600.00. Prepare entries in journal form to record (1) the monthly payroll and (2) employer's payroll expense, assuming social security and Medicare taxes equal to the amounts for employees, a federal unemployment insurance tax of .8 percent, a state unemployment tax of 5.4 percent, and medical insurance premiums for which the employer pays 80 percent of the cost.

SE 7. **LO2 Product Warranty Liability** Diamante Corp. manufactures and sells travel clocks. Each clock costs $25 to produce and sells for $50. In addition, each clock carries a warranty that provides for free replacement if it fails during the two years following the sale. In the past, 5 percent of the clocks sold have had to be replaced under the warranty. During October, Diamante sold 52,000 clocks, and 2,800 clocks were replaced under the warranty. Prepare entries in journal form to record the estimated liability for product warranties during the month and the clocks replaced under warranty during the month.

SE 8. **LO2 Vacation Pay Liability** The employees of Larue Services receive two weeks of paid vacation each year. Seventy percent of the employees qualify for vacation. Assuming the September payroll is $150,000, including $12,000 paid to employees on vacation, how much is the vacation pay expense for September? What is the ending balance of the Estimated Liability for Vacation Pay account, assuming a beginning balance of $16,000?

SE 9. **SO4 Payroll Taxes** Karma Company and its employees are subject to a 6.2 percent social security tax on wages up to $87,000 and a 1.45 percent Medicare tax with no limit. The company is subject to a 5.4 percent state unemployment tax and a .8 percent federal unemployment tax up to $7,000 per employee. The company has two employees: A. Ballo, who has cumulative earnings of $88,000 and earned $7,000 in the month of December, and C. Dureo, who has cumulative earnings of $5,000 and earned $1,000 during December. Compute the total payroll taxes for the employees and the employer for December.

SE 10. **SO4 Payroll Earnings, Withholdings, and Taxes** Last week, Manuel Karmelo worked 44 hours. He is paid $10 per hour and receives one and one-half times his regular rate for hours worked over 40. Karmelo has withholdings of $45 for federal income taxes, $10 for state income taxes, $23 for health insurance, 6.2 percent for social security tax, and 1.45 percent for Medicare tax. Compute Karmelo's take-home pay. Also compute the total cost of Karmelo to his employer, assuming that Karmelo's cumulative wages are over the limit for unemployment taxes and that the company makes a health-care contribution of $75.

EXERCISES

E 1. **LO1 Issues in Accounting for Liabilities** Indicate whether each of the following actions relates to (a) managing liquidity and cash flows, (b) recognition of liabilities, (c) valuation of liabilities, (d) classification of liabilities, or (e) disclosure of liabilities:

1. Setting a liability at the fair market value of goods to be delivered
2. Relating the payment date of a liability to the length of the operating cycle
3. Recording a liability in accordance with the matching rule
4. Providing information about financial instruments on the balance sheet
5. Estimating the amount of "cents-off" coupons that will be redeemed
6. Categorizing a liability as long-term debt
7. Measuring working capital
8. Comparing average days' payable with last year

E 2. **LO1 Measuring Short-Term Liquidity** In 20x1, Telos Company had current assets of $310,000 and current liabilities of $200,000, of which accounts payable were $130,000. Cost of goods sold was $850,000, merchandise inventory increased by $40,000, and accounts payable were $110,000 in the prior year. In 20x2, Telos had current assets of $420,000 and current liabilities of $320,000, of which accounts payable were $150,000. Cost of goods sold was $950,000, and merchandise inventory decreased by $30,000. Calculate Telos's working capital, payables turnover, and average days' payable for 20x1 and 20x2. Assess Telos's liquidity and cash flows in relation to the change in payables turnover from 20x1 to 20x2.

E 3. LO2 **Interest Expense: Interest Not Included in Face Value of Note**

On the last day of October, Shealy Company borrows $30,000 on a bank note for 60 days at 12 percent interest. Interest is not included in the face amount. Prepare the following entries in journal form: (1) October 31, recording of note; (2) November 30, accrual of interest expense; and (3) December 30, payment of note plus interest.

E 4. LO2 **Interest Expense: Interest Included in Face Value of Note**

Assume the same facts as in **E 3,** except that interest is included in the face amount of the note and the note is discounted at the bank on October 31. Prepare the following entries in journal form: (1) October 31, recording of note; (2) November 30, recognition of interest accrued on note; and (3) December 30, payment of note and recording of interest expense.

E 5. LO2 **Sales and Excise Taxes**

Web Design Service billed its customers a total of $980,400 for the month of August, including 9 percent federal excise tax and 5 percent sales tax.

1. Determine the proper amount of service revenue to report for the month.
2. Prepare an entry in journal form to record the revenue and related liabilities for the month.

E 6. LO2 **Payroll Entries**

At the end of October, the payroll register for Lakeside Tool and Die Corporation contained the following totals: wages, $185,500; federal income taxes withheld, $47,442; state income taxes withheld, $7,818; social security tax withheld, $11,501; Medicare tax withheld, $2,689.75; medical insurance deductions, $6,435; and wages subject to unemployment taxes, $28,620.

Prepare entries in journal form to record the (1) monthly payroll and (2) employer payroll expenses, assuming social security and Medicare taxes equal to the amount for employees, a federal unemployment insurance tax of .8 percent, a state unemployment tax of 5.4 percent, and medical insurance premiums for which the employer pays 80 percent of the cost.

E 7. LO2 **Product Warranty Liability**

Hoopes Company manufactures and sells electronic games. Each game costs $25 to produce and sells for $45. In addition, each game carries a warranty that provides for free replacement if it fails during the two years following the sale. In the past, 7 percent of the games sold had to be replaced under the warranty. During July, Hoopes sold 26,000 games, and 2,800 games were replaced under the warranty.

1. Prepare an entry in journal form to record the estimated liability for product warranties during the month.
2. Prepare an entry in journal form to record the games replaced under warranty during the month.

E 8. LO2 **Vacation Pay Liability**

Syracuse Corporation gives three weeks' paid vacation to each employee who has worked at the company for one year. Based on studies of employee turnover and previous experience, management estimates that 65 percent of the employees will qualify for vacation pay this year.

1. Assume that Syracuse's July payroll is $600,000, of which $40,000 is paid to employees on vacation. Figure the estimated employee vacation benefit for the month.
2. Prepare an entry in journal form to record the employee benefit for July.
3. Prepare an entry in journal form to record the pay to employees on vacation.

E 9. SO4 **Social Security, Medicare, and Unemployment Taxes**

Munro Company is subject to a 5.4 percent state unemployment insurance tax and a .8 percent federal unemployment insurance tax after credits. Assume both federal and state unemployment taxes apply to the first $7,000 earned by each employee. Social security and Medicare taxes in effect at this time are 6.2 and 1.45 percent, respectively. The social security tax is levied for both employee and employer on the first $87,000 earned by each employee during the year.

During the current year, the cumulative earnings for each employee of the company are as follows:

Employee	Cumulative Earnings	Employee	Cumulative Earnings
Basmani, J.	$28,620	Van Trapp, M.	$16,760
Cohen, A.	5,260	Harwit, P.	6,420
Derbye, G.	32,820	Lemaire, C.	51,650
Carbone, R.	30,130	Papyani, D.	32,100
Sourdiffe, B.	89,000	Menzek, V.	36,645
Conniger, N.	5,120	Woo, S.	5,176

1. Prepare and complete a schedule with the following columns: Employee Name, Cumulative Earnings, Earnings Subject to Social Security Tax, Earnings Subject to Medicare Tax, and Earnings Subject to Unemployment Taxes. Total the columns.
2. Compute the social security and Medicare taxes and the federal and state unemployment taxes for Munro Company for the year.

SO4 Net Pay Calculation and Payroll Entries

E 10. Lynne Featherstone is an employee whose overtime pay is regulated by the Fair Labor Standards Act. Her hourly rate is $8, and during the week ended July 11, she worked 42 hours. She claims two exemptions on her W-4 form. So far this year she has earned $8,650. Each week $12 is deducted from her paycheck for medical insurance.

1. Compute the following items related to the pay for Lynne Featherstone for the week of July 11: (a) total pay, (b) federal income taxes withholding (use Figure 4), (c) social security and Medicare taxes (assume rates of 6.2 percent and 1.45 percent, respectively), and (d) net pay.
2. Prepare an entry in journal form to record the wages expense and related liabilities for Lynne Featherstone for the week ended July 11.

SO4 Payroll Transactions

E 11. Jian-Jin Loo earns a salary of $90,000 per year. Social security and Medicare taxes are, respectively, 6.2 percent on salary up to $87,000 and 1.45 percent on total salary. Federal unemployment insurance taxes are 6.2 percent of the first $7,000; however, a credit is allowed equal to the state unemployment insurance taxes of 5.4 percent on the $7,000. During the year, $15,000 was withheld for federal income taxes, $3,000 for state income taxes, and $1,500 for medical insurance.

1. Prepare an entry in journal form summarizing the payment of $90,000 to Loo during the year.
2. Prepare an entry in journal form summarizing the employer payroll taxes and other costs on Loo's salary for the year. Assume the company pays 80 percent of the total premiums for medical insurance.
3. Determine the total amount paid by Jian-Jin Loo's employer to employ Loo for the year.

PROBLEMS

LO1 LO2 Identification of Current Liabilities

K/R

P 1. Neil Fusco opened a small television repair shop, Fusco Television Repair, on January 2, 20x0. The shop also sells a limited number of television sets. In January 20x1, Fusco realized he had never filed any tax reports for his business and therefore probably owes a considerable amount of taxes. Since he has limited experience in running a business, he has brought you all his business records, including a checkbook, canceled checks, deposit slips, suppliers' invoices, a notice of annual property taxes of $4,620 due to the city, and a promissory note to his father-in-law for $5,000. He wants you to determine what his business owes the government and other parties.

You analyze all his records and determine the following as of December 31, 20x0:

Unpaid invoices for televisions	$ 18,000
Television sales (excluding sales tax)	88,540
Cost of Televisions Sold	62,250
Workers' salaries	20,400
Repair revenues	120,600
Current assets	32,600
Television inventory	23,500

You learn that the company has deducted $952 from the two employees' salaries for federal income taxes owed to the government. The current social security tax is 6.2 percent on maximum earnings of $87,000 for each employee, and the current Medicare tax is 1.45 percent (no maximum earnings). The FUTA tax is 5.4 percent to the state and .8 percent to the federal government on the first $7,000 earned by each employee, and each employee earned more than $7,000. Fusco has not filed a sales tax report to the state (5 percent of sales).

REQUIRED

1. Given these limited facts, determine Fusco Television Repair's current liabilities as of December 31, 20x0.
2. What additional information would you want from Fusco to satisfy yourself that all current liabilities have been identified?

3. Evaluate Fusco's liquidity by calculating working capital, payables turnover, and average days' payable. Comment on the results. (Assume average accounts payable were the same as year-end accounts payable.)

P 2. LO2 Notes Payable Transactions and End-of-Period Entries

Iron's Paper Company, whose fiscal year ends December 31, completed the following transactions involving notes payable:

20x3

Nov. 25 Purchased a new loading cart by issuing a 60-day, 10 percent note for $43,200.

Dec. 16 Borrowed $50,000 from the bank to finance inventory by signing a 90-day note. The face value of the note includes interest of $1,500. Proceeds received were $48,500.

31 Made the end-of-year adjusting entry to accrue interest expense.

31 Made the end-of-year adjusting entry to recognize the discount expired on the note.

20x4

Jan. 24 Paid off the loading cart note.

Mar. 16 Paid off the inventory note to the bank.

REQUIRED ▶

1. Prepare entries in journal form for the notes payable transactions.
2. In the transaction of December 16, would the bank be better off making the loan with the interest stated separately instead of included in the $50,000? Why or why not?

P 3. LO2 Product Warranty Liability

The Galway Company manufactures and sells food processors, which it guarantees for five years. If a processor fails, it is replaced free, but the customer is charged a service fee for handling. In the past, management has found that only 3 percent of the processors sold required replacement under the warranty. The average food processor costs the company $240. At the beginning of September, the account for estimated liability for product warranties had a credit balance of $208,000. During September, 250 processors were returned under the warranty. Service fees of $9,860 were collected for handling. During the month, the company sold 2,800 food processors.

REQUIRED ▶

1. Prepare entries in journal form to record (a) the cost of food processors replaced under warranty and (b) the estimated liability for product warranties for processors sold during the month.
2. Compute the balance of the Estimated Product Warranty Liability account at the end of the month.
3. If the company's product warranty liability is underestimated, what are the effects on current and future years' income?

P 4. LO2 Payroll Entries

At the end of October, the payroll register for Golinski Corporation contained the following totals: sales salaries, $176,220; office salaries, $80,880; administrative salaries, $113,900; federal income taxes withheld, $94,884; state income taxes withheld, $15,636; social security tax withheld, $23,002; Medicare tax withheld, $5,379.50; medical insurance premiums, $12,870; life insurance premiums, $11,712; union dues deductions, $1,368; and salaries subject to unemployment taxes, $57,240. Fifty percent of medical and life insurance premiums are paid by the employer.

REQUIRED ▶ Prepare entries in journal form to record the (1) accrual of the monthly payroll, (2) payment of the net payroll, (3) accrual of employer's payroll taxes and expenses (assuming social security and Medicare taxes equal to the amount for employees, a federal unemployment insurance tax of .8 percent, and a state unemployment tax of 5.4 percent), and (4) payment of all liabilities related to the payroll (assuming that all are paid at the same time).

P 5. SO4 Payroll Register and Related Entries

Hendrik Dairy Company has seven employees. Employees paid hourly receive a set rate for regular hours plus one and one-half times their hourly rate for overtime hours. They are paid every two weeks. The salaried employees are paid monthly on the last biweekly payday of each month. The employees and company are subject to social security tax of 6.2 percent up to a maximum of $87,000 for each employee and to Medicare tax of 1.45 percent. The unemployment insurance tax rates are 5.4 percent for the state and .8 percent for the federal government. The unemployment insurance tax applies to the first $7,000 earned by each employee and is levied only on the employer.

The company maintains a supplemental benefits plan that includes medical insurance, life insurance, and additional retirement funds for employees. Under the plan, each employee contributes 4 percent of her or his gross income as a payroll withholding, and the company matches the amount. Data for the November 30 payroll, the last payday of November, follow.

Employee	Hours Regular	Hours Overtime	Pay Rate	Cumulative Gross Pay Excluding Current Pay Period	Federal Income Taxes to Be Withheld
Eggers, D.	80	5	$ 8.00	$ 4,867.00	$ 71.00
Gosligan, W.	80	4	6.50	3,954.00	76.00
Valmont, P.*	Salary	—	5,000.00	55,000.00	985.00
Norelli, V.	80	—	5.00	8,250.00	32.00
Appia, L.*	Salary	—	2,000.00	20,000.00	294.00
Tou, M.	80	20	10.00	12,000.00	103.00
Voss, B.*	Salary	—	1,500.00	15,000.00	210.00

*Denotes administrative personnel; the rest are sales. P. Valmont's cumulative gross pay includes a $5,000 bonus paid early in the year.

REQUIRED ▶

1. Prepare a payroll register for the pay period ended November 30. The payroll register should have the following columns:

   Employee
   Total Hours
   Earnings
   - Regular
   - Overtime
   - Gross
   - Cumulative

   Deductions
   - Federal Income Taxes
   - Social Security Tax
   - Medicare Tax
   - Supplemental Benefits Plan

   Net Pay
   Distribution
   - Sales Wages Expense
   - Administrative Salaries Expense

2. Prepare an entry in journal form to record the payroll and related liabilities for deductions for the period ended November 30.
3. Prepare entries in journal form to record the employer's payroll taxes and contribution to the supplemental benefits plan.
4. Prepare the November 30 entries (a) to transfer sufficient cash from the company's regular checking account to a special payroll disbursement account and (b) to pay the employees.

ALTERNATE PROBLEMS

LO2 Notes Payable Transactions and End-of-Period Entries

P 6. Aragian Corporation, whose fiscal year ends June 30, completed the following transactions involving notes payable:

20xx

May 11 Signed a 90-day, $132,000 note payable to Eastern Shore Bank for a working capital loan. The face value included interest of $3,960. Proceeds received were $128,040.

21 Obtained a 60-day extension on a $36,000 trade account payable owed to a supplier by signing a 60-day, $36,000 note. Interest is in addition to the face value, at the rate of 14 percent.

June 30 Made the end-of-year adjusting entry to accrue interest expense.

30 Made the end-of-year adjusting entry to recognize discount expired on the note.

July 20 Paid off the note plus interest due the supplier.

Aug. 9 Paid the amount due to the bank on the 90-day note.

REQUIRED ▶

1. Prepare entries in journal form for the notes payable transactions.
2. In the transaction of May 11, would the bank be better off making the loan with the interest stated separately or with it included in the loan amount? Why or why not?

P 7. **LO2 Product Warranty Liability**

Sparkle Bright Company is engaged in the retail sale of washing machines. Each machine has a 24-month warranty on parts. If a repair under warranty is required, a charge for the labor is made. Management has found that 20 percent of the machines sold require some work before the warranty expires. Furthermore, the average cost of replacement parts has been $120 per repair. At the beginning of June, the account for the estimated liability for product warranties had a credit balance of $28,600. During June, 112 machines were returned under the warranty. The cost of the parts used in repairing the machines was $17,530, and $18,884 was collected as service revenue for the labor involved. During the month, Sparkle Bright Company sold 450 new machines.

REQUIRED ▶

1. Prepare entries in journal form to record each of the following: (a) the warranty work completed during the month, including related revenue; (b) the estimated liability for product warranties for machines sold during the month.
2. Compute the balance of the Estimated Product Warranty Liability account at the end of the month.
3. If the company's product warranty liability is overestimated, what are the effects on current and future years' income?

P 8. **LO2 Payroll Entries**

The following payroll amounts for the month of April were taken from the payroll register of Weiskauf Corporation: sales salaries, $116,400; office salaries, $57,000; general salaries, $49,600; social security tax withheld, $13,826; Medicare tax withheld, $3,233.50; income taxes withheld, $31,440; medical insurance premiums, $3,290; life insurance premiums, $1,880; salaries subject to unemployment taxes, $156,600. Fifty percent of medical and life insurance premiums are paid by the employee. The rest are paid by the employer.

REQUIRED ▶ Prepare entries in journal form to record the following: (1) accrual of the monthly payroll, (2) payment of the net payroll, (3) accrual of employer's payroll taxes and expenses (assuming social security and Medicare taxes equal to the amounts for employees, a federal unemployment insurance tax of .8 percent, and a state unemployment tax of 5.4 percent), and (4) payment of all liabilities related to the payroll (assuming that all are paid at the same time).

Skills Development Cases

Conceptual Analysis

SD 1. **LO2 Frequent-Flier Plan**

America South Airways instituted a frequent-flier program under which passengers accumulate points toward a free flight based on the number of miles they fly on the airline. One point was awarded for each mile flown, with a minimum of 750 miles being given for any flight. Because of competition in 2001, the company began a bonus plan under which passengers receive triple the normal mileage points. In the past, about 1.5 percent of passenger miles were flown by passengers who had converted points to free flights. With the triple mileage program, it is expected that a 2.5 percent rate will be more appropriate for future years. During 2001, the company had passenger revenues of $966.3 million and passenger transportation operating expenses of $802.8 million before depreciation and amortization. Operating income was $86.1 million. What is the appropriate rate to use to estimate free miles? What would be the effect of the estimated liability for free travel by frequent fliers on 2001 net income? Describe several ways to estimate the amount of this liability. Be prepared to discuss the arguments for and against recognizing this liability.

SD 2. **LO2 LO3 Nature and Recognition of an Estimated Liability**

The decision to recognize and record a liability is sometimes a matter of judgment. People who use General Motors <www.gm.com> credit cards earn rebates toward the purchase or lease of GM vehicles in relation to the amount of purchases they make with their cards. General Motors chooses to treat these outstanding rebates as a commitment in the notes to its financial statements:

> GM sponsors a credit card program . . . that offers rebates that can be applied primarily against the purchase or lease of GM vehicles. The amount of rebates available to qualified cardholders (net of deferred program income) was $4.0 billion, $3.9 billion, and $3.8 billion at December 31, 2002, 2001, and 2000, respectively.[14]

Using the two criteria established by the FASB for recording a contingency, explain GM's reasoning in treating this liability as a commitment in the notes, where it will likely receive less attention by analysts, rather than including it on the income statement as an expense and on the balance sheet as an estimated liability. Do you agree with this position? (**Hint:** Apply the matching rule.)

Ethical Dilemma

SD 3. **LO2 Known Legal Violations**

Chop Shop Restaurant is a large steak restaurant in the suburbs of Chicago. Joe Murray, an accounting student at a nearby college, recently secured a full-time accounting job at the restaurant. He felt fortunate to have a good job that accommodated his class schedule because the local economy was very bad. After a few weeks on the job, Murray realized that his boss, the owner of the business, was paying the kitchen workers in cash and was not withholding federal and state income taxes or social security and Medicare taxes. Murray understands that federal and state laws require these taxes to be withheld and paid to the appropriate agency in a timely manner. He also realizes that if he raises this issue, he could lose his job. What alternatives are available to Murray? What action would you take if you were in his position? Why did you make this choice?

Group Activity: Use in class groups. Debrief by asking each group for an alternative. Then debate the ethics of each alternative.

Research Activity

SD 4. **LO2 LO3 Basic Research Skills**

Indexes for business periodicals, in which you can look up topics of interest, are available in your school library. Three of the most important of these indexes are the *Business Periodicals Index*, *The Wall Street Journal Index*, and the *Accountants' Index*. Using one or more of these indexes, locate and photocopy two articles related to bank financing, commercial paper, product warranties, airline frequent-flier plans, or contingent liabilities. Keep in mind that you may have to look under related topics to find an article. For example, to find articles about contingent liabilities, you might look under litigation, debt guarantees, or environmental losses. For each of the two articles, write a short summary of the situation and tell how it relates to accounting for the topic as described in the text. Be prepared to discuss your results in class.

Decision-Making Practice

SD 5. **LO1 LO2 SO4 Identification of Current Liabilities**

Sandra Miller opened a bicycle repair shop, Miller Bicycles, in 20x3. She also sold bicycles. The new business was such a success that she hired two assistants on June 1, 20x3. In December, Miller realized that she had failed to file any tax reports for her business since its inception and therefore probably owed a considerable amount of taxes. Since Miller has limited experience in running a business, she has brought all her business records to you and is asking for help. The records include a checkbook, canceled checks, deposit slips, invoices from her suppliers, a notice of annual property taxes of $9,240 due to the city on January 1, 20x4, and a one-year promissory note to the bank for $10,000. She wants you to determine what her business owes the government and other parties. You analyze all her records and determine the following:

Unpaid supplies invoices	$ 6,320
Sales (excluding sales tax)	177,080
Workers' salaries	40,800
Repair revenues	241,200

You learn that the company has deducted $1,904 from the two employees' salaries for federal income taxes owed to the government. The current social security tax is 6.2 percent on maximum earnings of $87,000 for each employee, and the current Medicare tax is 1.45 percent (no maximum earnings). The FUTA tax is 5.4 percent to the state and .8 percent to the federal government on the first $7,000 earned by each employee, and each employee earned more than $7,000. Miller has not filed a sales tax report to the state (5 percent of sales).

1. Given these limited facts, determine Miller Bicycle's current liabilities as of December 31, 20x4.
2. What additional information would you want from Miller to satisfy yourself that all current liabilities have been identified?

Financial Reporting and Analysis Cases

Interpreting Financial Reports

FRA 1. LO1 **Comparison of Two Companies' Ratios with Industry Ratios**

Both Sun Microsystems Inc. <www.sun.com> and Cisco Systems <www.cisco.com> are in the computer industry. These data (in thousands) are for their fiscal year ends:[15]

	Sun	Cisco
Accounts payable	$ 1,050,000	$ 644,000
Cost of goods sold	10,049,000	11,221,000
Increase (decrease) in inventory	492,000	452,000

Compare the payables turnover ratio and average days' payable for both companies. Comment on the results. How are cash flows affected by average days' payable? How do Sun Microsystems' and Cisco Systems' ratios compare with the computer industry ratios shown in Figures 1 and 2 in this chapter? (Use year-end amounts for ratios.)

FRA 2. LO3 **Classic Case: Contingent Liabilities**

In its 1986 annual report, Texaco, Inc. <www.texaco.com>, one of the world's largest oil companies, reported its loss in the biggest damage judgment rendered to that date:

> **Note 17.** Contingent Liabilities
> Pennzoil Litigation
>
> *State Court Action.* On December 10, 1985, the 151st District Court of Harris County, Texas, entered judgment for Pennzoil Company of $7.5 billion actual damages, $3 billion punitive damages, and approximately $600 million prejudgment interest in *Pennzoil Company v. Texaco, Inc.*, an action in which Pennzoil claims that Texaco, Inc., tortiously interfered with Pennzoil's alleged contract to acquire a 3/7ths interest in Getty. Interest began accruing on the judgment at the simple rate of 10% per annum from the date of judgment. Texaco, Inc., believes that there is no legal basis for the judgment, which it believes is contrary to the evidence and applicable law. Texaco, Inc., is pursuing all available remedies to set aside or to reverse the judgment. . . .
>
> The outcome of the appeal on the preliminary injunction and the ultimate outcome of the Pennzoil litigation are not presently determinable, but could have a material adverse effect on the consolidated financial position and the results of the consolidated operations of Texaco, Inc.[16]

At December 31, 1986, Texaco's retained earnings were $12.882 billion, and its cash and marketable securities totaled $3.0 billion. Its net income for 1986 was $.725 billion.

After a series of court reversals and filing for bankruptcy in 1987, Texaco announced in December 1987 an out-of-court settlement with Pennzoil for $3.0 billion. Although less than the original amount, it is still the largest damage payment in history.

1. What two conditions established by the FASB must a contingent liability meet before it is recorded in the accounting records? Does the situation described in "Note 17. Contingent Liabilities" meet those conditions? Explain your answer.
2. Do the events of 1987 change your answer to **1**? Explain your response.
3. How would the settlement have affected Texaco's retained earnings, cash and marketable securities, and net income?

International Company

FRA 3. LO1 LO2 LO3 **Classification and Disclosure of Current Liabilities and Contingent Liabilities**

Man Nutzfahrzeuge Aktiengesellschaft <www.mannutzfahrzeuge.de>, a German firm, is one of the world's largest truck companies. Accounting in Germany differs in some respects from that in the United States. A good example is the placement and classification of liabilities. On the balance sheet, Man places liabilities below a detailed stockholders' equity section. Man does not distinguish between current and long-term liabilities; however, a note to the financial statements does disclose the amount of the liabilities due within one year. Those liabilities are primarily what we call *definitely determinable liabilities,* such as loans, accounts payable, and notes payable. Estimated liabilities do not seem to appear in this category. There is an asset category called *current assets,* similar to that used in the United States. In another note to the financial statements, Man lists what it calls *contingent liabilities,* which have not been recorded and do not appear on the balance sheet. These include liabilities for hire and leasing contracts, guarantees of loans of other companies, and warranties on trucks.[17] What do you think of combining all liabilities, short- and long-term, in a single item on the balance sheet? Should any contingent liabilities be recorded and shown on the balance sheet?

Toys "R" Us Annual Report

FRA 4. LO1 **Short-Term Liabilities and Seasonality**

Refer to the balance sheet and the liquidity and capital resources section of management's discussion in the Toys "R" Us annual report <www.tru.com>. Compute the payables turnover for 2002 for Toys "R" Us. How does it compare with the payables turnover ratios for the industries shown in Figure 1? Toys "R" Us is a seasonal business. Would you expect short-term borrowings and accounts payable to be unusually high or unusually low at the balance sheet date of February 1, 2003? How does management use short-term financing to meet its needs for cash during the year?

Comparison Case: Toys "R" Us and Walgreen Co.

FRA 5. LO1 **Payables Analysis and** LO3 **Commitments and Contingencies**

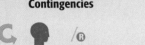

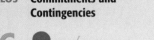

Refer to the financial statements and notes for Toys "R" Us <www.tru.com> and Walgreens <www.walgreens.com> in the Supplement to Chapter 6.

1. Compute the payables turnover and average days' payable for Toys "R" Us and Walgreens for the past two years. Accounts payable in 2000 were $1,152 million for Toys "R" Us and $1,364.0 million for Walgreens. The merchandise inventory for Toys "R" Us in 2000 was $2,307 million, and for Walgreens, $2,830.8 million. Which company makes most use of creditors to finance the operating cycle's needs?
2. Read each company's note on commitments and contingencies. What commitments and contingencies do the companies have in common? For which company does this information seem to be most important? Why is it important to consider this information in connection with payables analysis?

Fingraph® Financial Analyst™

FRA 6. LO1 **Comparison of Current** LO2 **Liabilities and Working** LO3 **Capital**

Choose any two companies from the list of Fingraph companies on the Needles Accounting Resource Center Web Site at http://accounting.college.hmco.com/students. The industry should be one in which current liabilities are likely to be important, such as the airline, manufacturing, consumer products, or computer industry. Access the Microsoft Excel spreadsheets for the companies you selected. Click the URL at the top of each company's spreadsheet to link to the company's web site and annual report.

1. In the annual reports of the companies you have selected, read the current liability section of the balance sheet and any reference to current liabilities in the summary of significant accounting policies or notes to the financial statements. What are the most important current liabilities for each company? Do any current liabilities appear to be characteristic of the industry? Which current liabilities are definitely determinable, and which appear to be accrued liabilities?
2. Using the Fingraph CD-ROM software, display and print in tabular and graphic form the Current Assets and Current Liabilities Analysis page. Prepare a table that compares the current ratio and working capital for both companies for two years.
3. Find and read references to current liabilities in the liquidity analysis section of management's discussion and analysis in each annual report.
4. Write a one-page executive summary that highlights the most important types of current liabilities for this industry and that compares the current ratio and working capital trends of the two companies, including reference to management's assessment. Include the Fingraph page and your table with your report.

Internet Case

FRA 7. LO3 **Investigation of Status of Famous Contingencies**

In addition to the Texaco <www.texaco.com> case in **FRA 2,** other famous contingency liability cases include suits against RJR Nabisco <www.nabisco.com>, Philip Morris <www.philipmorris.com>, and Waste Management, Inc. <www.wm.com>. Investigate the current status of any one of these cases by going to the company's web site and finding its latest annual report. Look in the notes to the financial statements under "Contingencies." Report what you find about the case, including whether it has been settled or is no longer being reported.

13

Chapter 13 discusses the characteristics of the partnership form of business and examines accounting issues relating to formation, division of income, dissolution, and liquidation of partnerships.

Partnerships

Learning Objectives

LO1 Identify the principal characteristics, advantages, and disadvantages of the partnership form of business.

LO2 Record partners' investments of cash and other assets when a partnership is formed.

LO3 Compute and record the income or losses that partners share, based on stated ratios, capital balance ratios, and partners' salaries and interest.

LO4 Record a person's admission to or withdrawal from a partnership.

LO5 Compute the distribution of assets to partners when they liquidate their partnership.

DECISION POINT

A USER'S FOCUS

KPMG LLP <www.kpmg.com> Many people think of partnerships as relatively small business organizations, and usually they are right. However, some partnerships, among them law firms, investment companies, real estate companies, and accounting firms, are very large. An example is KPMG LLP, which is a member firm in KPMG International, a professional services organization with offices in 150 countries. KPMG LLP provides accounting and auditing services, tax services, and management consulting services. With over 1,500 partners and 98,000 employees, it is one of the largest partnerships in the world. In 2002, the firm was growing rapidly, with revenues of over $10 billion, about half of which came from outside the United States. How does a partnership this large organize to accomplish its objectives?[1]

KPMG LLP is organized as a limited liability partnership. In a normal partnership, the personal financial resources of all partners are subject to risk of loss if the partnership suffers a loss it cannot bear. Accounting firms are at risk of suffering large losses as a result of lawsuits from investors who lose money investing in a company audited by the accounting firm. Because KPMG is organized as a limited liability partnership, the partners are liable to the extent of their partnership interest in the firm, but their personal assets are not subject to risk.

Why did KPMG organize itself as a limited liability partnership?

Financial Highlights
(in millions of dollars)

	2002	2001
Annual revenue	$10,720	$10,320

PARTNERSHIP CHARACTERISTICS

LO1 Identify the principal characteristics, advantages, and disadvantages of the partnership form of business.

RELATED TEXT ASSIGNMENTS
Q: 1, 2, 3, 4, 5, 6, 7
SE: 1
SD: 1, 3, 4
FRA: 1, 2, 3

The Uniform Partnership Act, which has been adopted by most states, defines a **partnership** as "an association of two or more persons to carry on as co-owners of a business for profit." Partnerships are treated as separate entities in accounting, but legally there is no economic separation between them and their owners. They differ in many ways from the other forms of business. Here we describe some of their important characteristics.

VOLUNTARY ASSOCIATION

KEY POINT: Partnerships and sole proprietorships are not legal entities; corporations are. All three, however, are considered accounting entities.

A partnership is a voluntary association of individuals rather than a legal entity in itself. Therefore, a partner is responsible under the law for his or her partners' actions within the scope of the business. A partner also has unlimited liability for the debts of the partnership. Because of these potential liabilities, a partner must be allowed to choose the people who join the partnership. A person should select as partners individuals who share his or her business objectives.

PARTNERSHIP AGREEMENT A partnership is easy to form. Two or more competent people simply agree to be partners in a common business purpose. Their agreement is known as a **partnership agreement**. The partnership agreement does not have to be in writing. However, good business practice calls for a written document that clearly states the details of the arrangement, including the name, location, and purpose of the business; the names of the partners and their respective duties; the investments of each partner; the method of distributing income and losses; and the procedures for the admission and withdrawal of partners, the withdrawal of assets allowed each partner, and the liquidation (termination) of the business.

LIMITED LIFE Because a partnership is formed by an agreement between partners, it has a **limited life**. It may be dissolved when a new partner is admitted; a partner withdraws, goes bankrupt, is incapacitated (to the point that he or she cannot perform as obligated), retires, or dies; or the terms of the partnership agreement are met (e.g., when the project for which the partnership was formed is completed). However, if the partners want the partnership to continue legally, the partnership agreement can be written to cover each of these situations. For example, the partnership agreement can state that if a partner dies, the remaining partner or partners must purchase the deceased partner's capital at book value from the heirs.

MUTUAL AGENCY Each partner is an agent of the partnership within the scope of the business. Because of this **mutual agency**, any partner can bind the partnership to a business agreement as long as he or she acts within the scope of the company's normal operations. For example, a partner in a used-car business can bind the partnership through the purchase or sale of used cars. But this partner cannot bind the partnership to a contract to buy men's clothing or any other goods that are not related to the used-car business. Because of mutual agency, it is very important for an individual to choose business partners who have integrity and who share his or her business objectives.

KEY POINT: Unlimited liability means that potential responsibility for debts is not limited by one's investment, as it is in a corporation. Each person is personally liable for all debts of the partnership, including those arising from contingent liabilities such as lawsuits. Liability can be avoided only by filing for personal bankruptcy.

UNLIMITED LIABILITY All partners have **unlimited liability** for their company's debt, which means that each partner is personally liable for all the debts of the partnership. If a partnership cannot pay its debts, creditors must first satisfy their claims from the assets of the business. If these assets are not enough to pay all debts, the creditors can seek payment from the personal assets of each partner. If one partner's personal assets are used up before the debts are paid, the creditors can

Focus on International Business

How Do Partnerships Facilitate International Investment?

American businesses are expanding into emerging markets throughout the world. Many of these markets, such as those of Hungary, Poland, the Czech Republic, India, and China, are in the process of privatizing public entities. This means that operations such as steel mills, cement factories, and utilities that were previously run by the government are being converted into private enterprises. Many countries require that local investors own a substantial proportion of the newly formed businesses. One way of accomplishing this is to form joint ventures, which match a country's need for outside capital and operational know-how with investors' interest in business expansion and profitability. Joint ventures often take the form of partnerships among two or more corporations and other investors. Any income or losses from operations will be divided among the participants according to a predetermined agreement.

Stop and Think!
Why is it important for people to form partnerships with people whom they can trust?
Because of mutual agency, unlimited liability, and co-ownership of property, the risks of being a partner are high. This puts a premium on honesty and trust among the partners. Further, goodwill among partners is important in making decisions and distributing income. ■

claim additional assets from the remaining partners who are able to pay. Each partner, then, can be required by law to pay all the debts of the partnership.

■ **Co-ownership of Partnership Property** When individuals invest property in a partnership, they give up the right to their separate use of the property. The property becomes an asset of the partnership and is owned jointly by the partners.

■ **Participation in Partnership Income** Each partner has the right to share in the company's income and the responsibility to share in its losses. The partnership agreement should state the method of distributing income and losses to each partner. If the agreement describes how income should be shared but does not mention losses, losses are distributed in the same way as income. If the agreement does not describe the method of income and loss distribution, the partners must by law share income and losses equally.

KEY POINT: There is no federal income tax on partnerships. However, an informational return must be filed, and partners are taxed at their personal rates. There may be state or local business taxes assessed on a partnership, however. One example of this is the Michigan Single Business Tax.

■ **Advantages and Disadvantages of Partnerships** Partnerships have both advantages and disadvantages. One advantage is that a partnership is easy to form, change, and dissolve. Also, a partnership facilitates the pooling of capital resources and individual talents; it has no corporate tax burden (because a partnership is not a legal entity for tax purposes, it does not have to pay a federal income tax, as do corporations, but must file an informational return); and it gives the partners a certain amount of freedom and flexibility.

On the other hand, partnerships have the following disadvantages: the life of a partnership is limited; one partner can bind the partnership to a contract (mutual agency); the partners have unlimited personal liability; and it is more difficult for a

Focus on Business Practice

Corporations That Look Like Partnerships

Several types of corporations have been created to mimic the characteristics of partnerships in certain ways. *S corporations* are corporations that U.S. tax laws treat in a manner similar to partnerships. S corporations do not pay income taxes like normal corporations. The income or loss of the S corporation is distributed to the stockholders (which are limited to a small number), who report and pay taxes on the income or loss on their personal tax returns. This avoids the problem of double taxation. *Limited liability corporations* are corporations that professional firms such as accounting and consultancy firms mostly use to limit the liability of the partners, who in this form of business are stockholders. *Special-purpose entities (SPEs)*, which have gained notoriety because of the Enron case, are actually quite common. They are separately distinct from the company that forms them and are used by companies to raise money by selling certain assets such as receivables. By meeting certain conditions, the company that sets them up can legitimately avoid including the debt of the SPEs on its balance sheet. Enron used SPEs extensively and fraudulently to hide debt and other commitments of the company.

Focus on Business Practice

How Do Limited Partnerships Help Finance Big Projects?

Limited partnerships are sometimes used in place of the corporate form to raise funds from the public. Because possible investor losses are normally restricted to the amount of the investment, the limited partnership has some characteristics of the corporate form. Limited partnerships are used to obtain financing for many projects, such as locating and drilling oil and gas wells, manufacturing airplanes, and developing real estate (including shopping centers, office buildings, and apartment complexes). For example, Alliance Capital Management Limited Partnership is one of the largest investment advisors, managing more than $90 billion in assets for corporate and individual investors. The company's partnership units, or shares of ownership, sell on the New York Stock Exchange and can be purchased by the individual investor. In 2003, the units were selling at about $28 each and paid an annual dividend of $2.50 per share.[2]

partnership to raise large amounts of capital and to transfer ownership interests than it is for a corporation.

Other Forms of Association

Two other common forms of association that are a type of partnership or similar to a partnership are limited partnerships and joint ventures.

ENRICHMENT NOTE:
Many types of organizations have been created by law. They include S corporations and limited partnerships. Each provides legal (especially tax) advantages and disadvantages.

Limited Partnerships A **limited partnership** is a special type of partnership that, like corporations, confines the limited partner's potential loss to the amount of his or her investment. Under this type of partnership the unlimited liability disadvantage of a partnership can be overcome. Usually, the limited partnership has a general partner who has unlimited liability but allows other partners to limit their potential loss. The potential loss of all partners in an ordinary partnership is limited only by personal bankruptcy laws.

Joint Ventures In today's global environment, more companies are looking to form alliances similar to partnerships, called *joint ventures*, with other companies rather than to venture out on their own. A **joint venture** is an association of two or more entities for the purpose of achieving a specific goal, such as the manufacture of a product in a new market. Many joint ventures have an agreed-upon limited life. The entities forming joint ventures usually involve companies but can sometimes involve governments, especially in emerging economies. A joint venture brings together the resources, technical skills, political ties, and other assets of each of the parties for a common goal. Profits and losses are shared on an agreed-upon basis.

Focus on Business Technology

Joint Ventures and the Internet

The Internet is fostering the formation of many joint ventures by companies that are normally competitors. Among recent developments of this type are the following:

- Eight metals companies, including Allegheny Technologies Inc. and Alcoa Inc. <www.alcoa.com>, have formed a joint venture to establish online service to provide products to businesses in the metals industries.
- Accor <www.accorhotels.com>, Europe's largest hotel chain; Hilton International <www.hilton.com>; and Forte Hotels <www.forte-hotels.com> have launched an Internet joint venture enabling customers to make online bookings at their hotels. This counters a similar effort involving seven other hotel chains including Marriott <www.marriott.com>, Hyatt <www.hyatt.com>, and Holiday Inn <www.holidayinn.com>.
- General Motors Corporation <www.gm.com> and other companies have formed an Internet joint venture to consolidate and coordinate the purchase of parts and supplies in the manufacture of automobiles.

Check out ACE for a Review Quiz at http://accounting.college.hmco.com/students.

ACCOUNTING FOR PARTNERS' EQUITY

LO2 Record partners' investments of cash and other assets when a partnership is formed.

RELATED TEXT ASSIGNMENTS
Q: 8
SE: 2
E: 1
P: 1, 5
SD: 3

Although accounting for a partnership is very similar to accounting for a sole proprietorship, there are differences. One is that the owner's equity in a partnership is called **partners' equity**. In accounting for partners' equity, it is necessary to maintain separate Capital and Withdrawals accounts for each partner and to divide the income and losses of the company among the partners.

The differences in the Capital accounts of a sole proprietorship and a partnership are as follows:

SOLE PROPRIETORSHIP | PARTNERSHIP

Blake, Capital	
	50,000

Desmond, Capital	
	30,000

Frank, Capital	
	40,000

Blake, Withdrawals	
12,000	

Desmond, Withdrawals	
5,000	

Frank, Withdrawals	
6,000	

In the partners' equity section of the balance sheet, the balance of each partner's Capital account is listed separately:

Liabilities and Partners' Equity

Total liabilities		$28,000
Partners' equity		
Desmond, capital	$25,000	
Frank, capital	34,000	
Total partners' equity		59,000
Total liabilities and partners' equity		$87,000

STOP AND THINK!
When accounts receivable are transferred into a partnership, at what amount should they be recorded?

Accounts receivable should be transferred in at their net realizable value. Thus, the gross amount of accounts receivable should be recorded, and a related contra account Allowance for Uncollected Accounts should also be recorded so that the net amount is the amount that the partnership will realize. ■

Each partner invests cash, other assets, or both in the partnership according to the partnership agreement. Noncash assets should be valued at their fair market value on the date they are transferred to the partnership. The assets invested by a partner are debited to the proper account, and the total amount is credited to the partner's Capital account.

To show how partners' investments are recorded, let's assume that Jerry Adcock and Rose Villa have agreed to combine their capital and equipment in a partnership to operate a jewelry store. According to their partnership agreement, Adcock will invest $28,000 in cash and $37,000 worth of furniture and displays, and Villa will invest $40,000 in cash and $30,000 worth of equipment. Related to the equipment is a note payable for $10,000, which the partnership assumes. The entries to record the partners' initial investments are as follows:

A = L + OE
\+   +
\+

20x3			
July 1	Cash	28,000	
	Furniture and Displays	37,000	
	Jerry Adcock, Capital		65,000
	Initial investment of Jerry Adcock in Adcock and Villa		

A = L + OE
\+ + +
\+

1	Cash	40,000	
	Equipment	30,000	
	Notes Payable		10,000
	Rose Villa, Capital		60,000
	Initial investment of Rose Villa in Adcock and Villa		

KEY POINT: Old book values from previous entities are irrelevant to the new entity.

KEY POINT: Villa's noncash contribution is equal to the fair market value of the equipment less the amount owed on the equipment.

The values assigned to the assets would be included in the partnership agreement. These values can differ from those carried on the partners' personal books. For example, the equipment that Rose Villa contributed had a value of only $22,000 on her books, but its market value had increased considerably after she purchased it. The book value of Villa's equipment is not important. The fair market value of the equipment at the time of transfer *is* important, however, because that value represents the amount of money Villa has invested in the partnership. Later investments are recorded in the same way.

Check out ACE for a Review Quiz at http://accounting.college.hmco.com/students.

DISTRIBUTION OF PARTNERSHIP INCOME AND LOSSES

LO3 Compute and record the income or losses that partners share, based on stated ratios, capital balance ratios, and partners' salaries and interest.

RELATED TEXT ASSIGNMENTS
Q: 9, 10, 11
SE: 3, 4, 5
E: 2, 3, 4
P: 1, 2, 5, 6
SD: 2
FRA: 1

A partnership's income and losses can be distributed according to whatever method the partners specify in the partnership agreement. Income in this form of business normally has three components: return to the partners for the use of their capital (called *interest on partners' capital*), compensation for services the partners have rendered (partners' salaries), and other income for any special contributions individual partners may make to the partnership or risks they may take. The breakdown of total income into its three components helps clarify how much each partner has contributed to the firm.

If all partners contribute equal capital, have similar talents, and spend the same amount of time in the business, then an equal distribution of income and losses would be fair. However, if one partner works full time in the firm and another devotes only a fourth of his or her time, then the distribution of income or losses should reflect the difference. (This concept would apply to any situation in which the partners contribute unequally to the business.)

KEY POINT: The division of income is one area in which a partnership differs from a corporation. In corporations, each common share receives an equal dividend. Partners can use any method they agree on to divide partnership income.

Distributing income and losses among partners can be accomplished by using stated ratios or capital balance ratios or by paying the partners' salaries and interest on their capital and sharing the remaining income according to stated ratios. *Salaries* and *interest* here are not *salaries expense* or *interest expense* in the ordinary sense of the terms. They do not affect the amount of reported net income. Instead, they refer to ways of determining each partner's share of net income or loss on the basis of time spent and money invested in the partnership.

STATED RATIOS

One method of distributing income and losses is to give each partner a stated ratio of the total income or loss. If each partner is making an equal contribution to the firm, each can assume the same share of income and losses. It is important to understand that an equal contribution to the firm does not necessarily mean an equal capital investment in the firm. One partner may be devoting more time and talent to the firm, whereas another may have made a larger capital investment. And if the partners contribute unequally to the firm, unequal stated ratios can be appropriate.

KEY POINT: The computations of each partner's share of net income are relevant to the closing entries in which the Income Summary account is closed to the partners' Capital accounts.

Let's assume that Adcock and Villa had a net income last year of $30,000. Their partnership agreement states that the percentages of income and losses distributed to Jerry Adcock and Rose Villa should be 60 percent and 40 percent, respectively. The computation of each partner's share of the income and the entry to show the distribution are as follows:

Adcock ($30,000 × .60)	$18,000
Villa ($30,000 × .40)	12,000
Net income	$30,000

A = L + OE	20x4			
− + +	June 30	Income Summary	30,000	
		Jerry Adcock, Capital		18,000
		Rose Villa, Capital		12,000
		Distribution of income for the year to the partners' Capital accounts		

Capital Balance Ratios

If invested capital produces the most income for the partnership, then income and losses may be distributed according to capital balances. The ratio used to distribute income and losses here may be based on each partner's capital balance at the beginning of the year or on the average capital balance of each partner during the year. The partnership agreement must describe the method to be used.

Ratios Based on Beginning Capital Balances To show how the first method works, let's look at the beginning capital balances of the partners in Adcock and Villa. At the start of the fiscal year, July 1, 20x3, Jerry Adcock, Capital showed a $65,000 balance and Rose Villa, Capital showed a $60,000 balance. (Actually, these balances reflect the partners' initial investment; the partnership was formed on July 1, 20x3.) The total partners' equity in the firm, then, was $125,000. Each partner's capital balance at the beginning of the year divided by the total partners' equity at the beginning of the year is that partner's beginning capital balance ratio:

	Beginning Capital Balance	Beginning Capital Balance Ratio
Jerry Adcock	$ 65,000	65,000 ÷ 125,000 = .52 = 52%
Rose Villa	60,000	60,000 ÷ 125,000 = .48 = 48%
	$125,000	

The income that each partner should receive when distribution is based on beginning capital balance ratios is determined by multiplying the total income by each partner's capital ratio. If we assume that income for the year was $140,000, Jerry Adcock's share of that income was $72,800, and Rose Villa's share was $67,200.

Jerry Adcock	$140,000 × .52 =	$ 72,800
Rose Villa	140,000 × .48 =	67,200
		$140,000

Ratios Based on Average Capital Balances If Adcock and Villa use beginning capital balance ratios to determine the distribution of income, they do not consider any investments or withdrawals made during the year. But investments and withdrawals usually change the partners' capital ratios. If the partners believe their capital balances will change dramatically during the year, they can choose average capital balance ratios as a fairer means of distributing income and losses.

The following T accounts show the activity over the year in Adcock and Villa's partners' Capital and Withdrawals accounts:

Jerry Adcock, Capital

Debit	Credit
	7/1/x3 65,000

Jerry Adcock, Withdrawals

Debit	Credit
1/1/x4 10,000	

Rose Villa, Capital

Debit	Credit
	7/1/x3 60,000
	2/1/x4 8,000

Rose Villa, Withdrawals

Debit	Credit
11/1/x3 10,000	

Jerry Adcock withdrew $10,000 on January 1, 20x4, and Rose Villa withdrew $10,000 on November 1, 20x3, and invested an additional $8,000 of equipment on February 1, 20x4. Again, the income for the year's operation (July 1, 20x3, to June 30, 20x4) was $140,000. The calculations for the average capital balances and the distribution of income are as follows:

Average Capital Balances

Partner	Date	Capital Balance	×	Months Unchanged	=	Total		Average Capital Balance
Adcock	July–Dec.	$65,000	×	6	=	$390,000		
	Jan.–June	55,000	×	6	=	330,000		
				12		$720,000	÷ 12 =	$ 60,000
Villa	July–Oct.	$60,000	×	4	=	$240,000		
	Nov.–Jan.	50,000	×	3	=	150,000		
	Feb.–June	58,000	×	5	=	290,000		
				12		$680,000	÷ 12 =	56,667
						Total average capital		$116,667

Average Capital Balance Ratios

$$\text{Adcock} = \frac{\text{Adcock's Average Capital Balance}}{\text{Total Average Capital}} = \frac{\$60{,}000}{\$116{,}667} = .514 = 51.4\%$$

$$\text{Villa} = \frac{\text{Villa's Average Capital Balance}}{\text{Total Average Capital}} = \frac{\$56{,}667}{\$116{,}667} = .486 = 48.6\%$$

Distribution of Income

Partner	Income	×	Ratio	=	Share of Income
Adcock	$140,000	×	.514	=	$ 71,960
Villa	140,000	×	.486	=	68,040
				Total income	$140,000

Notice that to determine the distribution of income (or loss), you must determine the average capital balances, the average capital balance ratios, and each partner's share of income or loss. To compute each partner's average capital balance, you must examine the changes that have occured during the year in each partner's capital balance, changes that are the product of further investments and withdrawals. The partner's beginning capital is multiplied by the number of months the balance remains unchanged. After the balance changes, the new balance is multiplied by the number of months it remains unchanged. The process continues until the end of the year. The totals of these computations are added, and then they are divided by 12 to determine the average capital balances. Once the average capital balances are determined, the method of figuring capital balance ratios for sharing income and losses is the same as the method used for beginning capital balances.

Salaries, Interest, and Stated Ratios

KEY POINT: Partnership income or loss cannot be divided solely on the basis of salaries or interest. An additional component, such as stated ratios, is needed.

Partners' contributions to a firm are usually not equal. To make up for the inequality, a partnership agreement can allow for partners' salaries, interest on partners' capital balances, or both in the distribution of income. Again, salaries and interest of this kind are not deducted as expenses before the partnership income is determined. They represent a method of arriving at an equitable distribution of income or loss.

To illustrate an allowance for partners' salaries, we assume that Adcock and Villa agree to annual salaries of $8,000 and $7,000, respectively, and to divide any

STOP AND THINK!
What is a disadvantage of receiving a large salary as part of a partner's distribution of income?

If the partnership is not very profitable, partners with the large salaries will see reductions in their respective capital accounts to the extent that the salary distribution exceeds their distributions for income or loss for the year. ■

remaining income equally between them. Each salary is charged to the appropriate partner's Withdrawals account when paid. Assuming the same $140,000 income for the first year, the calculations for Adcock and Villa are as follows:

	Income of Partner		
	Adcock	**Villa**	**Income Distributed**
Total Income for Distribution			$140,000
Distribution of Salaries			
Adcock	$ 8,000		
Villa		$ 7,000	(15,000)
Remaining Income After Salaries			$125,000
Equal Distribution of Remaining Income			
Adcock ($125,000 × .50)	62,500		
Villa ($125,000 × .50)		62,500	(125,000)
Remaining Income			—
Income of Partners	$70,500	$69,500	$140,000

Salaries allow for differences in the services that partners provide the business. However, they do not take into account differences in invested capital. To allow for capital differences, each partner can receive, in addition to salary, a stated interest on his or her invested capital. Suppose that Jerry Adcock and Rose Villa agree to annual salaries of $8,000 and $7,000, respectively, as well as 10 percent interest on their beginning capital balances, and to share any remaining income equally. The calculations for Adcock and Villa, assuming income of $140,000, are as follows:

	Income of Partner		
	Adcock	**Villa**	**Income Distributed**
Total Income for Distribution			$140,000
Distribution of Salaries			
Adcock	$ 8,000		
Villa		$ 7,000	(15,000)
Remaining Income After Salaries			$125,000
Distribution of Interest			
Adcock ($65,000 × .10)	6,500		
Villa ($60,000 × .10)		6,000	(12,500)
Remaining Income After Salaries and Interest			$112,500
Equal Distribution of Remaining Income			
Adcock ($112,500 × .50)	56,250		
Villa ($112,500 × .50)		56,250	(112,500)
Remaining Income			—
Income of Partners	$70,750	$69,250	$140,000

CLARIFICATION NOTE: If there is a negative balance after salaries or salaries and interest have been distributed, the terms *Remaining Income After Salaries* and *Remaining Income After Salaries and Interest* become *Negative Balance After Salaries* and *Negative Balance After Salaries and Interest*. The computation proceeds in exactly the same way, regardless of whether the balance is positive or negative.

FOCUS ON BUSINESS PRACTICE

What Are the Risks of Being a Partner in an Accounting Firm?

Partners in large accounting firms can make over $250,000 per year, with top partners drawing over $800,000. However, consideration of those incomes should take into account the risks that partners take and the fact that the incomes of partners in small accounting firms are often much lower.

Partners are not compensated in the same way as managers in corporations. Partners' income is not guaranteed, but rather is based on the performance of the partnership. Also, each partner is required to make a substantial investment of capital in the partnership. This capital remains at risk for as long as the partner chooses to stay in the partnership. For instance, in one notable instance, when a large firm was convicted of destroying evidence in the Enron case, the partners lost their total investments as well as their income when their firm was subjected to lawsuits and other losses. The firm was eventually liquidated.

ENRICHMENT NOTE: When negotiating a partnership agreement, be sure to look at (and negotiate) the impact of both profits (net income) and losses.

If the partnership agreement allows for the distribution of salaries or interest or both, the amounts must be allocated to the partners even if profits are not enough to cover the salaries and interest. In fact, even if the company has a loss, these allocations must still be made. The negative balance, or loss, after the allocation of salaries and interest must be distributed according to the stated ratio in the partnership agreement, or equally if the agreement does not mention a ratio.

For example, let's assume that Adcock and Villa agreed to the following conditions, with much higher annual salaries, for the distribution of income and losses:

	Salaries	Interest	Beginning Capital Balance
Adcock	$70,000	10 percent of beginning	$65,000
Villa	60,000	capital balances	60,000

The computations for the distribution of the income and loss, again assuming income of $140,000, are as follows:

KEY POINT: Using salaries and interest to divide income or loss among partners has no effect on the income statement. They are not expenses. Partners' salaries and interest are used only to allow the equitable division of the partnership's net income.

	Income of Partner: Adcock	Income of Partner: Villa	Income Distributed
Total Income for Distribution			$140,000
Distribution of Salaries			
Adcock	$70,000		
Villa		$60,000	(130,000)
Remaining Income After Salaries			$ 10,000
Distribution of Interest			
Adcock ($65,000 × .10)	6,500		
Villa ($60,000 × .10)		6,000	(12,500)
Negative Balance After Salaries and Interest			($ 2,500)
Equal Distribution of Negative Balance*			
Adcock ($2,500 × .50)	(1,250)		
Villa ($2,500 × .50)		(1,250)	2,500
Remaining Income			—
Income of Partners	$75,250	$64,750	$140,000

*Notice that the negative balance is distributed equally because the agreement does not indicate how income and losses should be distributed after salaries and interest are paid.

EXHIBIT 1
Partial Income Statement for Adcock and Villa

Adcock and Villa
Partial Income Statement
For the Year Ended June 30, 20x4

Net income		$140,000
Distribution to the partners		
Adcock		
Salary distribution	$70,000	
Interest on beginning capital balance	6,500	
Total	$76,500	
One-half of remaining negative amount	(1,250)	
Share of net income		$ 75,250
Villa		
Salary distribution	$60,000	
Interest on beginning capital balance	6,000	
Total	$66,000	
One-half of remaining negative amount	(1,250)	
Share of net income		64,750
Net income distributed		$140,000

On the income statement for the partnership, the distribution of income or losses is shown below the net income figure. Exhibit 1 shows how this is done.

Check out ACE for a Review Quiz at http://accounting.college.hmco.com/students.

DISSOLUTION OF A PARTNERSHIP

LO4 Record a person's admission to or withdrawal from a partnership.

RELATED TEXT ASSIGNMENTS
Q: 12, 13
SE: 6, 7, 8, 9
E: 5, 6
P: 3, 5, 7
SD: 3, 5

Dissolution of a partnership occurs whenever there is a change in the original association of partners. When a partnership is dissolved, the partners lose their authority to continue the business as a going concern. The fact that the partners lose this authority does not necessarily mean that the business operation is ended or interrupted. However, it does mean—from a legal and accounting standpoint—that the separate entity ceases to exist. The remaining partners can act for the partnership in finishing the affairs of the business or in forming a new partnership that will be a new accounting entity. The dissolution of a partnership takes place through, among other events, the admission of a new partner, the withdrawal of a partner, or the death of a partner.

ADMISSION OF A NEW PARTNER

BUSINESS-WORLD EXAMPLE: Dissolution of a partnership is a legal issue. Consider Ernst & Young, which admits over one hundred partners each year. The entity continues to operate despite the legal changes it must make.

The admission of a new partner dissolves the old partnership because a new association has been formed. Dissolving the old partnership and creating a new one requires the consent of all the original partners and the ratification of a new partnership agreement. When a new partner is admitted, a new partnership agreement should be in place.

An individual can be admitted to a partnership in one of two ways: by purchasing an interest in the partnership from one or more of the original partners or by investing assets in the partnership.

KEY POINT: Admission of a new partner never has an impact on net income. Regardless of the price a new partner pays, there are never any income statement accounts in the entry to admit a new partner.

PURCHASING AN INTEREST FROM A PARTNER When a person purchases an interest in a partnership from an original partner, the transaction is a personal one between these two people. However, the interest purchased must be transferred from the Capital account of the selling partner to the Capital account of the new partner.

Suppose that Jerry Adcock decides to sell his interest of $70,000 in Adcock and Villa to Richard Davis for $100,000 on August 31, 20x5, and that Rose Villa agrees to the sale. The entry to record the sale on the partnership books looks like this:

A = L + OE	Date	Account	Debit	Credit
	20x5			
	Aug. 31	Jerry Adcock, Capital	70,000	
−		Richard Davis, Capital		70,000
+		Transfer of Jerry Adcock's equity to Richard Davis		

KEY POINT: When a partner sells his or her interest directly to a new partner, the partner, not the partnership, realizes the gain or loss. In this case, Adcock has a gain of $30,000, but the assets, liabilities, and total equity of the partnership do not change.

Notice that the entry records the book value of the equity, not the amount Davis pays. The amount Davis pays is a personal matter between Adcock and him. Because the amount paid does not affect the assets or liabilities of the firm, it is not entered in the records.

Here's another example of a purchase: Assume that Richard Davis purchases half of Jerry Adcock's $70,000 interest in the partnership and half of Rose Villa's interest, assumed to be $80,000, by paying a total of $100,000 to the two partners on August 31, 20x5. The entry to record this transaction on the partnership books would be as follows:

A = L + OE	Date	Account	Debit	Credit
	20x5			
−	Aug. 31	Jerry Adcock, Capital	35,000	
−		Rose Villa, Capital	40,000	
+		Richard Davis, Capital		75,000
		Transfer of half of Jerry Adcock's and Rose Villa's equity to Richard Davis		

CLARIFICATION NOTE: If the account did not reflect the current value of the assets, the asset accounts (and Capital accounts) would need to be adjusted before admitting the new partner.

INVESTING ASSETS IN A PARTNERSHIP When a new partner is admitted through an investment in the partnership, both the assets and the partners' equity in the firm increase. The increase occurs because the assets the new partner invests become partnership assets, and as partnership assets increase, partners' equity increases. For example, assume that Jerry Adcock and Rose Villa have agreed to allow Richard Davis to invest $75,000 in return for a one-third interest in their partnership. The Capital accounts of Jerry Adcock and Rose Villa are $70,000 and $80,000, respectively. Davis's $75,000 investment equals a one-third interest in the firm after the investment is added to the previously existing capital of the partnership:

Jerry Adcock, Capital	$ 70,000
Rose Villa, Capital	80,000
Davis's investment	75,000
Total capital after Davis's investment	$225,000
One-third interest = $225,000 ÷ 3 =	$ 75,000

The entry to record Davis's investment is as follows:

A = L + OE	Date	Account	Debit	Credit
	20x5			
+ +	Aug. 31	Cash	75,000	
		Richard Davis, Capital		75,000
		Admission of Richard Davis for a one-third interest in the company		

BONUS TO THE OLD PARTNERS A partnership is sometimes so profitable or otherwise advantageous that a new investor is willing to pay more than the actual

KEY POINT: The original partners receive a bonus because the entity is worth more as a going concern than the fair market value of the net assets would otherwise indicate. That is, the new partner is paying for unrecorded partnership value.

dollar interest he or she receives in the partnership. For instance, suppose an individual pays $100,000 for an $80,000 interest in a partnership. The $20,000 excess of the payment over the interest purchased is a **bonus** to the original partners. The bonus must be distributed to the original partners according to the partnership agreement. When the agreement does not cover the distribution of bonuses, a bonus should be distributed to the original partners in accordance with the method for distributing income and losses.

Assume that the Adcock and Villa Company has operated for several years and that the partners' capital balances and the stated ratios for distribution of income and loss are as follows:

Partners	Capital Balances	Stated Ratios
Adcock	$160,000	55%
Villa	140,000	45
	$300,000	100%

Richard Davis wants to join the firm. He offers to invest $100,000 on December 1 for a one-fifth interest in the business and income. The original partners agree to the offer. This is the computation of the bonus to the original partners:

Partners' equity in the original partnership		$300,000
Cash investment by Richard Davis		100,000
Partners' equity in the new partnership		$400,000
Partners' equity assigned to Richard Davis ($400,000 × ⅕)		$ 80,000
Bonus to the original partners		
Investment by Richard Davis	$100,000	
Less equity assigned to Richard Davis	80,000	$ 20,000
Distribution of bonus to original partners		
Jerry Adcock ($20,000 × .55)	$ 11,000	
Rose Villa ($20,000 × .45)	9,000	$ 20,000

This is the entry that records Davis's admission to the partnership:

A = L + OE	Date	Account	Debit	Credit
	20x5			
+	Dec. 1	Cash	100,000	
+		Jerry Adcock, Capital		11,000
+		Rose Villa, Capital		9,000
+		Richard Davis, Capital		80,000
		Investment by Richard Davis for a one-fifth interest in the firm, and the bonus distributed to the original partners		

ENRICHMENT NOTE: Human capital plays a large part in the profitability of entities traditionally organized as partnerships (for example, accounting firms, legal firms, and medical practices). When a new partner is admitted, this human capital is recognized in the Capital account of the new partner who receives a bonus.

BONUS TO THE NEW PARTNER There are several reasons that a partnership might want a new partner. A partnership in financial trouble might need additional cash. Or the partners might want to expand the firm's markets and need more capital for this purpose than they themselves can provide. Also, the partners might know a person who would bring a unique talent to the firm. Under these conditions, a new partner may be admitted to the partnership with the understanding that part of the original partners' capital will be transferred (credited) to the new partner's Capital account as a bonus.

For example, suppose that Jerry Adcock and Rose Villa have invited Richard Davis to join the firm. Davis is going to invest $60,000 on December 1 for a one-fourth interest in the company. The stated ratios for distribution of income or loss

STOP AND THINK!
If the value of a partnership is worth far more than the book value of the assets on the balance sheet, would a new partner entering the partnership be more likely to pay a bonus to the old partners or receive a bonus from the old partners?
The new partner would more likely pay a bonus to the old partners because the value of the incoming partner's share of the partnership would be more than the amounts on the balance sheet. The old partners will want compensation for the value of the proportionate share the new partner is getting. ■

for Adcock and Villa are 55 percent and 45 percent, respectively. If Davis is to receive a one-fourth interest in the firm, the interest of the original partners represents a three-fourths interest in the business. The computation of Davis's bonus is as follows:

Total equity in partnership		
Jerry Adcock, Capital		$160,000
Rose Villa, Capital		140,000
Investment by Richard Davis		60,000
Partners' equity in the new partnership		$360,000
Partners' equity assigned to Richard Davis ($360,000 × ¼)		$ 90,000
Bonus to new partner		
Equity assigned to Richard Davis	$90,000	
Less cash investment by Richard Davis	60,000	$ 30,000
Distribution of bonus from original partners		
Jerry Adcock ($30,000 × .55)	$16,500	
Rose Villa ($30,000 × .45)	13,500	$ 30,000

The entry to record the admission of Richard Davis to the partnership is shown below:

A = L + OE				
+ −	20x5 Dec. 1	Cash	60,000	
−		Jerry Adcock, Capital	16,500	
+		Rose Villa, Capital	13,500	
		Richard Davis, Capital		90,000
		To record the investment by Richard Davis of cash and a bonus from Adcock and Villa		

KEY POINT: There is no impact on the income statement of a partnership when a partner withdraws. The only change is on the balance sheet.

WITHDRAWAL OF A PARTNER

Since a partnership is a voluntary association, a partner usually has the right to withdraw at any time. However, to avoid disputes when a partner does decide to withdraw or retire, a partnership agreement should describe the procedures to be followed. The agreement should specify (1) whether an audit will be performed, (2) how the assets will be reappraised, (3) how a bonus will be determined, and (4) by what method the withdrawing partner will be paid.

A partner who wants to withdraw from a partnership can do so in one of several ways. The partner can sell his or her interest to another partner or to an out-

FOCUS ON BUSINESS PRACTICE

Can Withdrawal of Partners Harm a Partnership?

The withdrawal of partners can cause a financial strain on a partnership, as when Goldman, Sachs & Co., the last major Wall Street investment company still organized as a partnership, was scrambling to raise more than $250 million to compensate for the withdrawal of twenty-three partners. The retirements caused a decrease in equity capital of about $400 million, which represented almost 10 percent of the firm's capital. Goldman was looking for private investors to make up for the losses.[3] The majority of Wall Street investment companies, such as Merrill Lynch & Co., Inc., and Salomon Brothers Inc., are organized as corporations. An advantage of this form of organization is that managers who want to leave their jobs can sell their stock to other investors without affecting the firm's capital.

FIGURE 1
Alternative Ways for a Partner to Withdraw

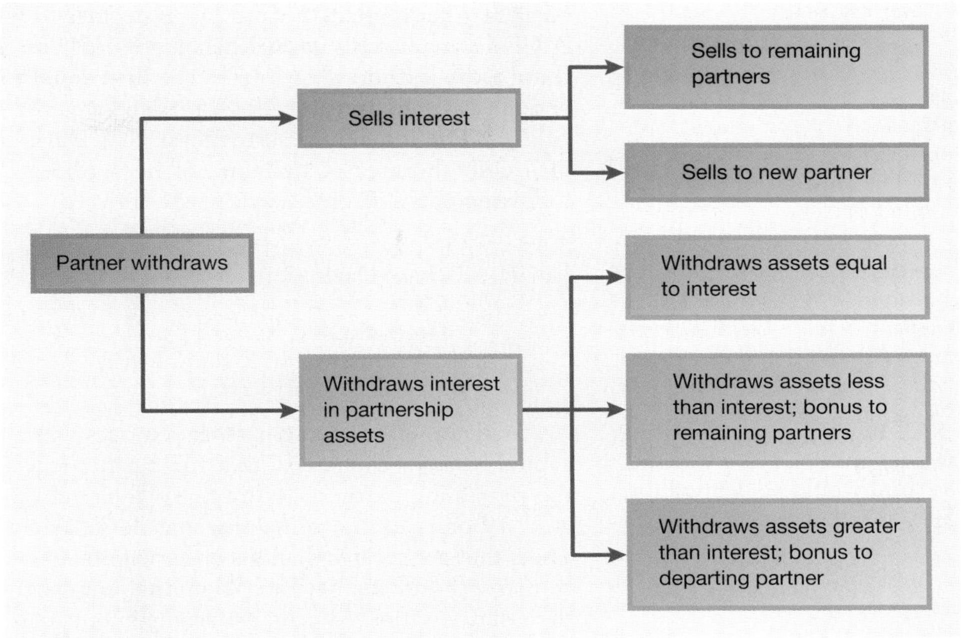

sider with the consent of the remaining partners, or the partner can withdraw assets equal to his or her capital balance, less than his or her capital balance (in this case, the remaining partners receive a bonus), or greater than his or her capital balance (in this case, the withdrawing partner receives a bonus). These alternatives are illustrated in Figure 1.

KEY POINT: Selling a partnership interest does not affect the assets and liabilities of the partnership. Therefore, total equity remains unchanged. The only effect of a partner's selling his or her interest to the existing partners or to a new partner is the change of names in the partners' equity section of the balance sheet.

■ **WITHDRAWAL BY SELLING INTEREST** When a partner sells his or her interest to another partner or to an outsider with the consent of the other partners, the transaction is personal; it does not change the partnership assets or the partners' equity. For example, let's assume that the capital balances of Adcock, Villa, and Davis are $140,000, $100,000, and $60,000, respectively, for a total of $300,000.

Villa wants to withdraw from the partnership and is reviewing two offers for her interest. The offers are (1) to sell her interest to Davis for $110,000 or (2) to sell her interest to Judy Jones for $120,000. The remaining partners have agreed to either potential transaction. Because Davis and Jones would pay for Villa's interest from their personal assets, the partnership accounting records would show only the transfer of Villa's interest to Davis or Jones. The entries to record these possible transfers are as follows:

1. If Villa's interest is purchased by Davis:

A = L + OE			
−	Rose Villa, Capital	100,000	
+	Richard Davis, Capital		100,000
	Sale of Villa's partnership interest to Davis		

2. If Villa's interest is purchased by Jones:

A = L + OE			
−	Rose Villa, Capital	100,000	
+	Judy Jones, Capital		100,000
	Sale of Villa's partnership interest to Jones		

■ **WITHDRAWAL BY REMOVING ASSETS** A partnership agreement can allow a withdrawing partner to remove assets from the firm equal to his or her capital balance. Assume that Richard Davis decides to withdraw from Adcock, Villa, Davis & Company. Davis's capital balance is $60,000. The partnership agreement states that he can withdraw cash from the firm equal to his capital balance. If there is not enough cash, he must accept a promissory note from the new partnership for the balance. The remaining partners ask that Davis take only $50,000 in cash because of a cash shortage at the time of his withdrawal; he agrees to this request. The following entry records Davis's withdrawal:

A = L + OE
− + −

20x5			
Jan. 21	Richard Davis, Capital	60,000	
	Cash		50,000
	Notes Payable, Richard Davis		10,000
	Withdrawal of Richard Davis from the partnership		

KEY POINT: Even if a bonus was involved, Davis's Capital account would be debited for $60,000 to eliminate it.

When a withdrawing partner removes assets that represent less than his or her capital balance, the equity that the partner leaves in the business is divided among the remaining partners according to their stated ratios. This distribution is considered a bonus to the remaining partners. When a withdrawing partner takes out assets that are greater than his or her capital balance, the excess is treated as a bonus to the withdrawing partner. The remaining partners absorb the bonus according to their stated ratios. Alternative arrangements can be spelled out in the partnership agreement.

Death of a Partner

When a partner dies, the partnership is dissolved because the original association has changed. The partnership agreement should state the actions to be taken. Normally, the books are closed, and financial statements are prepared. Those actions are necessary to determine the capital balance of each partner on the date of the death. The agreement may also indicate whether an audit should be conducted, assets appraised, and a bonus recorded, as well as the procedures for settling with the deceased partner's heirs. The remaining partners may purchase the deceased's equity, sell it to outsiders, or deliver specified business assets to the estate. If the firm intends to continue, a new partnership must be formed.

Check out ACE for a Review Quiz at http://accounting.college.hmco.com/students.

Liquidation of a Partnership

LO5 Compute the distribution of assets to partners when they liquidate their partnership.

RELATED TEXT ASSIGNMENTS
Q: 14, 15
SE: 10
E: 7, 8
P: 4, 5, 8

The **liquidation** of a partnership is the process of ending the business, of selling enough assets to pay the partnership's liabilities, and distributing any remaining assets among the partners. Liquidation is a special form of dissolution. When a partnership is liquidated, the business will not continue.

The partnership agreement should indicate the procedures to be followed in the case of liquidation. Usually, the books are adjusted and closed, with the income or loss distributed to the partners. As the assets of the business are sold, any gain or loss should be distributed to the partners according to the stated ratios. As cash becomes available, it must be applied first to outside creditors, then to loans from partners, and finally to the partners' capital balances.

The process of liquidation can have a variety of financial outcomes. We look at two: (1) assets sold for a gain and (2) assets sold for a loss. For both alternatives, we make the assumptions that the books have been closed for Adcock, Villa, Davis & Company and that the following balance sheet exists before liquidation:

STUDY NOTE: Be sure to consider the liquidation procedure step by step. To liquidate a partnership, the partners first must sell the assets and pay the liabilities (or distribute them to the partners). Second, any gains or losses from the sales of assets must be allocated to the partners. Third, when only cash remains, it is paid to the partners. Fourth, when a partner has a negative capital balance, he or she is obligated to pay the deficiency. Otherwise, the remaining partners must absorb the deficiency.

Adcock, Villa, Davis & Company
Balance Sheet
February 2, 20x6

Assets		Liabilities	
Cash	$ 60,000	Accounts payable	$120,000
Accounts receivable	40,000	**Partners' Equity**	
Merchandise inventory	100,000		
Plant assets (net)	200,000	Adcock, Capital	85,000
Total assets	$400,000	Villa, Capital	95,000
		Davis, Capital	100,000
		Total liabilities and partners' equity	$400,000

STOP AND THINK!
When a partnership is dissolved, what is an alternate approach to selling all the assets and distributing the proceeds, and what decisions will have to be made if this approach is taken?

The partners may decide to divide up the assets among themselves. In this case, they will have to decide on the value of the assets and who gets which assets. They will also have to decide how to pay the liabilities. And they will have to settle the capital accounts, just as they would if cash were involved. ■

The stated ratios of Adcock, Villa, and Davis are 3:3:4, or 30, 30, and 40 percent, respectively.

GAIN ON SALE OF ASSETS

Suppose that the following transactions took place in the liquidation of Adcock, Villa, Davis & Company:

1. The accounts receivable were collected for $35,000.
2. The inventory was sold for $110,000.
3. The plant assets were sold for $200,000.
4. The accounts payable of $120,000 were paid.
5. The gain of $5,000 from the realization of the assets was distributed according to the partners' stated ratios.
6. The partners received cash equivalent to the balances of their Capital accounts.

These transactions are summarized in the statement of liquidation in Exhibit 2. The journal entries with their assumed transaction dates are as follows:

TERMINOLOGY NOTE: Notice the proper use of the term *realization* in the February 13 and 14 entries. *Realization* means "conversion into cash."

A = L + OE	Date	Account	Debit	Credit	Explanation on Statement of Liquidation
	20x6				
+ − / −	Feb. 13	Cash	35,000		1
		Gain or Loss from Realization	5,000		
		Accounts Receivable		40,000	
		Collection of accounts receivable			
+ + / −	14	Cash	110,000		2
		Merchandise Inventory		100,000	
		Gain or Loss from Realization		10,000	
		Sale of inventory			

EXHIBIT 2
Statement of Liquidation Showing Gain on Sale of Assets

Adcock, Villa, Davis & Company
Statement of Liquidation
February 2–20, 20x6

Explanation	Cash	Other Assets	Accounts Payable	Adcock, Capital (30%)	Villa, Capital (30%)	Davis, Capital (40%)	Gain (or Loss) from Realization
Balance 2/2/x6	$ 60,000	$340,000	$120,000	$85,000	$95,000	$100,000	
1. Collection of Accounts Receivable	35,000	(40,000)					($ 5,000)
	$ 95,000	$300,000	$120,000	$85,000	$95,000	$100,000	($ 5,000)
2. Sale of Inventory	110,000	(100,000)					10,000
	$205,000	$200,000	$120,000	$85,000	$95,000	$100,000	$ 5,000
3. Sale of Plant Assets	200,000	(200,000)					
	$405,000	—	$120,000	$85,000	$95,000	$100,000	$ 5,000
4. Payment of Liabilities	(120,000)		(120,000)				
	$285,000		—	$85,000	$95,000	$100,000	$ 5,000
5. Distribution of Gain (or Loss) from Realization				1,500	1,500	2,000	(5,000)
	$285,000			$86,500	$96,500	$102,000	—
6. Distribution of Cash to Partners	(285,000)			(86,500)	(96,500)	(102,000)	
	—			—	—	—	

A = L + OE	Feb. 16	Cash	200,000		3
+		Plant Assets		200,000	
−		Sale of plant assets			
A = L + OE	16	Accounts Payable	120,000		4
− −		Cash		120,000	
		Payment of accounts payable			
A = L + OE	20	Gain or Loss from Realization	5,000		5
−		Jerry Adcock, Capital		1,500	
+		Rose Villa, Capital		1,500	
+		Richard Davis, Capital		2,000	
+		Distribution of the gain on assets ($10,000 gain minus $5,000 loss) to the partners			

A = L + OE				
− −	Feb. 20	Jerry Adcock, Capital	86,500		6
−		Rose Villa, Capital	96,500	
−		Richard Davis, Capital	102,000	
		Cash		285,000
		Distribution of cash to the partners		

Notice that the cash distributed to the partners is the balance in their respective Capital accounts. Cash is not distributed according to the partners' stated ratios.

Loss on Sale of Assets

KEY POINT: The case here is almost the same as the previous one because losses are allocated on the same basis as gains. The only difference is that entry 3 in this case (a loss) and entry 5 in the first case (a gain) switch the debits and credits.

We discuss two cases involving losses on the sale of a company's assets. In the first, the losses are small enough to be absorbed by the partners' capital balances. In the second, one partner's share of the losses is too large for his capital balance to absorb.

When a firm's assets are sold at a loss, the partners share the loss on liquidation according to their stated ratios. For example, assume that during the liquidation of Adcock, Villa, Davis & Company, the total cash received from the collection of accounts receivable and the sale of inventory and plant assets was $140,000. The statement of liquidation appears in Exhibit 3.

Exhibit 3
Statement of Liquidation Showing Loss on Sale of Assets

Adcock, Villa, Davis & Company
Statement of Liquidation
February 2–20, 20x6

Explanation	Cash	Other Assets	Accounts Payable	Adcock, Capital (30%)	Villa, Capital (30%)	Davis, Capital (40%)	Gain (or Loss) from Realization
Balance 2/2/x6	$ 60,000	$340,000	$120,000	$85,000	$95,000	$100,000	
1. Collection of Accounts Receivable and Sale of Inventory and Plant Assets	140,000	(340,000)					($200,000)
	$200,000	—	$120,000	$85,000	$95,000	$100,000	($200,000)
2. Payment of Liabilities	(120,000)		(120,000)				
	$ 80,000		—	$85,000	$95,000	$100,000	($200,000)
3. Distribution of Gain (or Loss) from Realization				(60,000)	(60,000)	(80,000)	200,000
	$ 80,000			$25,000	$35,000	$ 20,000	—
4. Distribution of Cash to Partners	(80,000)			(25,000)	(35,000)	(20,000)	
	—			—	—	—	

The journal entries for the transactions summarized in the statement of liquidation in Exhibit 3 are as follows:

A = L + OE	Date	Account	Debit	Credit	Explanation on Statement of Liquidation
	20x6				
+ −	Feb. 15	Cash	140,000		1
−		Gain or Loss from Realization	200,000		
−		Accounts Receivable		40,000	
−		Merchandise Inventory		100,000	
		Plant Assets		200,000	
		Collection of accounts receivable and the sale of inventory and plant assets			
− −	16	Accounts Payable	120,000		2
		Cash		120,000	
		Payment of accounts payable			
−	20	Jerry Adcock, Capital	60,000		3
−		Rose Villa, Capital	60,000		
−		Richard Davis, Capital	80,000		
+		Gain or Loss from Realization		200,000	
		Distribution of the loss on assets to the partners			
− −	20	Jerry Adcock, Capital	25,000		4
−		Rose Villa, Capital	35,000		
−		Richard Davis, Capital	20,000		
		Cash		80,000	
		Distribution of cash to the partners			

KEY POINT: This example (a loss) uses a compound entry for what was included in entries 1, 2, and 3 in the first example (a gain). If you have difficulty with the concept, here is an opportunity to break the entry down into its three component parts.

In some liquidations, a partner's share of the loss is greater than his or her capital balance. In such a situation, because partners are subject to unlimited liability, the partner must make up the deficit in his or her Capital account from personal assets. For example, suppose that after the sale of assets and the payment of liabilities, the remaining assets and partners' equity of Adcock, Villa, Davis & Company look like this:

Assets		
Cash		$ 30,000
Partners' Equity		
Adcock, Capital	$25,000	
Villa, Capital	20,000	
Davis, Capital	(15,000)	$ 30,000

Richard Davis must pay $15,000 into the partnership from personal funds to cover his deficit. If he pays cash to the partnership, the following entry would record the cash contribution:

A = L + OE	Date	Account	Debit	Credit
	20x6			
+	Feb. 20	Cash	15,000	
+		Richard Davis, Capital		15,000
		Additional investment of Richard Davis to cover the negative balance in his Capital account		

After Davis pays $15,000, there is enough cash to pay Adcock and Villa their capital balances and, thus, to complete the liquidation. The transaction is recorded in the following way:

	20x6			
A = L + OE — — —	Feb. 20	Jerry Adcock, Capital	25,000	
		Rose Villa, Capital	20,000	
		Cash		45,000
		Distribution of cash to the partners		

If a partner does not have the cash to cover his or her obligations to the partnership, the remaining partners share the loss according to their established stated ratios. Remember that all partners have unlimited liability. As a result, if Richard Davis cannot pay the $15,000 deficit in his Capital account, Adcock and Villa must share the deficit according to their stated ratios. Each has a 30 percent stated ratio, so each must pay 50 percent of the losses that Davis cannot pay. The new stated ratios are computed as follows:

	Old Ratios	New Ratios	
Adcock	30%	30 ÷ 60 = .50 =	50%
Villa	30	30 ÷ 60 = .50 =	50
	60%		100%

And the entries to record the transactions are as follows:

	20x6			
A = L + OE — — +	Feb. 20	Jerry Adcock, Capital	7,500	
		Rose Villa, Capital	7,500	
		Richard Davis, Capital		15,000
		Transfer of Davis's deficit to Adcock and Villa		
A = L + OE — — —	20	Jerry Adcock, Capital	17,500	
		Rose Villa, Capital	12,500	
		Cash		30,000
		Distribution of cash to the partners		

Davis's inability to meet his obligations at the time of liquidation does not relieve him of his liabilities to Adcock and Villa. If he is able to pay his liabilities at some time in the future, Adcock and Villa can collect the amount of Davis's deficit that they absorbed.

Check out ACE for a Review Quiz at http://accounting.college.hmco.com/students.

Chapter Review

Review of Learning Objectives

LO1 Identify the principal characteristics, advantages, and disadvantages of the partnership form of business.

A partnership has several major characteristics that distinguish it from the other forms of business. It is a voluntary association of two or more people who combine their talents and resources to carry on a business. Their joint effort should be supported by a partnership agreement that spells out the venture's operating procedures. A partnership is dissolved by a partner's admission, withdrawal, or death, and therefore has a limited life. Each partner acts as an agent of the partnership within the scope of normal operations and is personally liable for the partnership's debts. Property invested in the partnership becomes an asset of the partnership, owned jointly by all the partners. And, finally, each partner has the right to share in the company's income and the responsibility to share in its losses.

The advantages of a partnership are the ease of its formation and dissolution, the opportunity to pool several individuals' talents and resources, the lack of corporate tax burden, and the freedom of action each partner enjoys. The disadvantages are the limited life of a partnership, mutual agency, the unlimited personal liability of the partners, and the difficulty of raising large amounts of capital and transferring partners' interest. Two other common forms of association that are a type of partnership or similar to a partnership are limited partnerships and joint ventures.

LO2 Record partners' investments of cash and other assets when a partnership is formed.

A partnership is formed when the partners contribute cash, other assets, or a combination of both to the business. The details are stated in the partnership agreement. Initial investments are recorded with a debit to Cash or another asset account and a credit to the investing partner's Capital account. The recorded amount of the other assets should be their fair market value on the date of transfer to the partnership. In addition, a partnership can assume an investing partner's liabilities. When this occurs, the partner's Capital account is credited with the difference between the assets invested and the liabilities assumed.

LO3 Compute and record the income or losses that partners share, based on stated ratios, capital balance ratios, and partners' salaries and interest.

The partners must share income and losses in accordance with the partnership agreement. If the agreement says nothing about the distribution of income and losses, the partners share them equally. Common methods used for distributing income and losses include stated ratios, capital balance ratios, and salaries and interest on capital investments. Each method tries to measure the individual partner's contribution to the operations of the business.

Stated ratios usually are based on the partners' relative contributions to the partnership. When capital balance ratios are used, income or losses are divided strictly on the basis of each partner's capital balance. The use of salaries and interest on capital investment takes into account both efforts (salary) and capital investment (interest) in dividing income or losses among the partners.

LO4 Record a person's admission to or withdrawal from a partnership.

An individual is admitted to a partnership by purchasing a partner's interest or by contributing additional assets. When an interest is purchased, the withdrawing partner's capital is transferred to the new partner. When the new partner contributes assets to the partnership, it may be necessary to recognize a bonus shared or borne by the original partners or by the new partner.

A person can withdraw from a partnership by selling his or her interest in the business to the remaining partners or a new partner or by withdrawing company assets. When assets are withdrawn, the amount can be equal to, less than, or greater than the partner's capital interest. When assets that have a value less than or greater than the partner's interest are withdrawn, a bonus is recognized and distributed among the remaining partners or to the departing partner.

LO5 Compute the distribution of assets to partners when they liquidate their partnership.

The liquidation of a partnership entails selling the assets necessary to pay the company's liabilities and then distributing any remaining assets to the partners. Any gain or loss on the sale of the assets is shared by the partners according to their stated ratios. When a partner has a deficit balance in a Capital account, that partner must contribute personal assets equal to the deficit. When a partner does not have personal assets to cover a capital deficit, the deficit must be absorbed by the solvent partners according to their stated ratios.

Review of Concepts and Terminology

The following concepts and terms were introduced in this chapter:

LO4 **Bonus:** An amount that accrues to the original partners when a new partner pays more to the partnership than the interest received or that accrues to the new partner when the amount paid to the partnership is less than the interest received.

LO4 **Dissolution:** The loss of authority to continue a partnership as a separate entity due to a change in the original association of partners.

LO1 **Joint venture:** An association of two or more entities for the purpose of achieving a specific goal, such as the manufacture of a product in a new market.

LO1 **Limited life:** A characteristic of a partnership; the fact that any event that breaches the partnership agreement—including the admission, withdrawal, or death of a partner—terminates the partnership.

LO1 **Limited partnership:** A form of partnership in which limited partners' liabilities are limited to their investment.

LO5 **Liquidation:** A special form of dissolution in which a business ends by selling assets, paying liabilities, and distributing any remaining assets to the partners.

LO1 **Mutual agency:** A characteristic of a partnership; the authority of each partner to act as an agent of the partnership within the scope of the business's normal operations.

LO2 **Partners' equity:** The owner's equity in a partnership.

LO1 **Partnership:** An association of two or more people to carry on as co-owners of a business for profit.

LO1 **Partnership agreement:** The contractual relationship between partners that identifies the details of their partnership.

LO1 **Unlimited liability:** A characteristic of a partnership; the fact that each partner has personal liability for all the debts of the partnership.

Review Problem

Distribution of Income and Admission of a Partner

LO3 LO4 Jack Holder and Dan Williams reached an agreement in 20x7 to pool their resources and form a partnership to manufacture and sell university T-shirts. In forming the partnership, Holder and Williams contributed $100,000 and $150,000, respectively. They drafted a partnership agreement stating that Holder was to receive an annual salary of $6,000 and Williams was to receive 3 percent interest annually on his original investment of $150,000 in the business. Income and losses after salary and interest were to be shared by Holder and Williams in a 2:3 ratio.

REQUIRED ▶

1. Compute the income or loss that Holder and Williams share, and prepare the required entries in journal form, assuming the partnership made $27,000 income in 20x7 and suffered a $2,000 loss in 20x8 (before salary and interest).
2. Assume that Jean Ratcliffe offers Holder and Williams $60,000 for a 15 percent interest in the partnership on January 1, 20x9. Holder and Williams agree to Ratcliffe's offer because they need her resources to expand the business. On January 1, 20x9, the balance in Holder's Capital account is $113,600, and the balance in Williams's Capital account is $161,400. Record the admission of Ratcliffe to the partnership, assuming that her investment represents a 15 percent interest in the total partners' capital and that a bonus will be distributed to Holder and Williams in the ratio of 2:3.

ANSWER TO REVIEW PROBLEM

1. Compute the income or loss distribution to the partners.

	Income of Partner		Income
	Holder	Williams	Distributed
20x7			
Total Income for Distribution			$27,000
Distribution of Salary			
Holder	$ 6,000		(6,000)
Remaining Income After Salary			$21,000
Distribution of Interest			
Williams ($150,000 × .03)		$ 4,500	(4,500)
Remaining Income After Salary and Interest			$16,500
Distribution of Remaining Income			
Holder ($16,500 × ⅖)	6,600		
Williams ($16,500 × ⅗)		9,900	(16,500)
Remaining Income			—
Income of Partners	$12,600	$14,400	$27,000
20x8			
Total Loss for Distribution			($ 2,000)
Distribution of Salary			
Holder	$ 6,000		(6,000)
Negative Balance After Salary			($ 8,000)
Distribution of Interest			
Williams ($150,000 × .03)		$ 4,500	(4,500)
Negative Balance After Salary and Interest			($12,500)
Distribution of Negative Balance			
Holder ($12,500 × ⅖)	(5,000)		
Williams ($12,500 × ⅗)		(7,500)	12,500
Remaining Loss			—
Income and Loss of Partners	$ 1,000	($ 3,000)	($ 2,000)

Entry in Journal Form—20x7

Income Summary	27,000	
Jack Holder, Capital		12,600
Dan Williams, Capital		14,400
Distribution of income for the year to the partners' Capital accounts		

Entry in Journal Form—20x8

Dan Williams, Capital	3,000	
Income Summary		2,000
Jack Holder, Capital		1,000
Distribution of the loss for the year to the partners' Capital accounts		

2. Record the admission of a new partner.

Capital Balance and Bonus Computation

Ratcliffe, Capital = (Original Partners' Capital + New Partner's Investment) × 15%
= ($113,600 + $161,400 + $60,000) × .15 = $50,250
Bonus = New Partner's Investment − Ratcliffe, Capital
= $60,000 − $50,250
= $9,750

Distribution of Bonus

Holder	= $9,750 × ⅖ =	$3,900
Williams	= $9,750 × ⅗ =	5,850
	Total bonus	$9,750

Entry in Journal Form

20x9			
Jan. 1	Cash	60,000	
	Jack Holder, Capital		3,900
	Dan Williams, Capital		5,850
	Jean Ratcliffe, Capital		50,250
	Sale of a 15 percent interest in the partnership to Jean Ratcliffe and the bonus paid to the original partners		

Chapter Assignments

Building Your Knowledge Foundation

Questions

1. Briefly define *partnership,* and list several important characteristics of the partnership form of business.
2. Leon and Jon are partners in a drilling operation. Leon purchased a drilling rig to be used in the partnership's operations. Is Leon's purchase binding on Jon even though Jon was not involved in it? Explain your answer.
3. What is the meaning of unlimited liability when applied to a partnership? Describe a form of partnership that limits investors' liability.
4. The partnership agreement for Anne and Jin-Li does not disclose how they will share income and losses. How would the income and losses be shared in this partnership?
5. What are several key advantages of a partnership? What are some disadvantages?
6. How does a limited partnership overcome a key disadvantage of ordinary partnerships?
7. What form of association is becoming more prevalent in conducting global business? Define it.
8. Charles contributes $10,000 in cash and a building with a book value of $40,000 and fair market value of $50,000 to the Charles and Dean partnership. What is the balance of Charles's Capital account in the partnership?
9. Oscar Perez and Leah Torn are forming a partnership. What are some factors they should consider in deciding how income is to be divided?

10. Sue and Ari share income and losses in their partnership in a 3:2 ratio. The firm's net income for the current year is $80,000. How would the distribution of income be recorded in the journal?
11. Kathy and Roger share income in their partnership in a 2:4 ratio. Kathy and Roger receive salaries of $6,000 and $10,000, respectively. How would they share a net income of $22,000 before salaries?
12. Carol purchases Mary's interest in the Mary and Leo partnership for $62,000. Mary has a $57,000 capital interest in the partnership. How would this transaction be recorded in the partnership books?
13. Dan and Augie each own a $50,000 interest in a partnership. They agree to admit Bea as a partner by selling her a one-third interest for $80,000. How large a bonus will be distributed to Dan and Augie?
14. Describe the ways in which the dissolution of a partnership differs from the liquidation of a partnership.
15. In the liquidation of a partnership, José's Capital account showed a $5,000 debit balance after all the creditors had been paid. What obligation does José have to the partnership?

SHORT EXERCISES

SE 1. LO1 **Partnership Characteristics**

Indicate whether each statement below is a reflection of (a) voluntary association, (b) a partnership agreement, (c) limited life, (d) mutual agency, or (e) unlimited liability.

1. A partner may be required to pay the debts of the partnership out of personal assets.
2. A partnership must be dissolved when a partner is admitted, withdraws, retires, or dies.
3. Any partner can bind the partnership to a business agreement.
4. A partner does not have to remain a partner if he or she does not want to.
5. Details of the arrangements among partners are specified in a written contract.

SE 2. LO2 **Partnership Formation**

Bob contributes cash of $12,000, and Kim contributes office equipment that cost $10,000 but is valued at $8,000 to the formation of a new partnership. Prepare the entry in journal form to form the partnership.

SE 3. LO3 **Distribution of Partnership Income**

During the first year, the Bob and Kim partnership (see **SE 2**) earned an income of $5,000. Assume the partners agreed to share income and losses in the ratio of the beginning balances of their capital accounts. How much income should be transferred to each Capital account?

SE 4. LO3 **Distribution of Partnership Income**

During the first year, the Bob and Kim partnership (see **SE 2**) earned an income of $5,000. Assume the partners agreed to share income and losses by figuring interest on the beginning capital balances at 10 percent and dividing the remainder equally. How much income should be transferred to each Capital account?

SE 5. LO3 **Distribution of Partnership Income**

During the first year, the Bob and Kim partnership (see **SE 2**) earned an income of $5,000. Assume the partners agreed to share income and losses by figuring interest on the beginning capital balances at 10 percent, allowing a salary of $6,000 to Bob, and dividing the remainder equally. How much income (or loss) should be transferred to each Capital account?

SE 6. LO4 **Withdrawal of a Partner and Admission of a Partner**

After the partnership has been operating for a year, the Capital accounts of Bob and Kim are $15,000 and $10,000, respectively. Kim withdraws from the partnership by selling her interest in the business to Sonia for $8,000. What will be the Capital account balances of the partners in the new Bob and Sonia partnership? Prepare the journal entry to record the transfer of ownership on the partnership books.

SE 7. LO4 **Admission of a New Partner**

After the partnership has been operating for a year, the Capital accounts of Bob and Kim are $15,000 and $10,000, respectively. Sonia buys a one-sixth interest in the partnership by investing cash of $11,000. What will be the Capital account balances of the partners in the new Bob, Kim, and Sonia partnership, assuming a bonus to the old partners, who share income and losses equally? Prepare the entry in journal form to record the transfer of ownership on the partnership books.

SE 8. **LO4 Admission of a New Partner** After the partnership has been operating for a year, the Capital accounts of Bob and Kim are $15,000 and $10,000, respectively. Sonia buys a one-fourth interest in the partnership by investing cash of $5,000. What will be the Capital account balances of the partners in the new Bob, Kim, and Sonia partnership, assuming that the new partner receives a bonus and that Bob and Kim share income and losses equally? Prepare the entry in journal form to record the transfer of ownership on the partnership books.

SE 9. **LO4 Withdrawal of a Partner** After the partnership has been operating for several years, the Capital accounts of Bob, Kim, and Sonia are $25,000, $16,000, and $9,000, respectively. Sonia decides to leave the partnership and is allowed to withdraw $9,000 in cash. Prepare the entry in journal form to record the withdrawal on the partnership books.

SE 10. **LO5 Liquidation of a Partnership** After the partnership has been operating for a year, the Capital accounts of Bob and Kim are $15,000 and $10,000, respectively. The firm has cash of $12,000 and office equipment of $13,000. The partners decide to liquidate the partnership. The office equipment is sold for only $4,000. Assuming the partners share income and losses in the ratio of one-third to Bob and two-thirds to Kim, how much cash will be distributed to each partner in liquidation?

EXERCISES

E 1. **LO2 Partnership Formation** Henri Mikels and Alex Jamison are watch repairmen who want to form a partnership and open a jewelry store. They have an attorney prepare their partnership agreement, which indicates that assets invested in the partnership will be recorded at their fair market value and that liabilities will be assumed at book value.

The assets contributed by each partner and the liabilities assumed by the partnership are as follows:

Assets	Henri Mikels	Alex Jamison	Total
Cash	$40,000	$30,000	$70,000
Accounts receivable	52,000	20,000	72,000
Allowance for uncollectible accounts	4,000	3,000	7,000
Supplies	1,000	500	1,500
Equipment	20,000	10,000	30,000
Liabilities			
Accounts payable	32,000	9,000	41,000

Prepare the entry in journal form necessary to record the original investments of Mikels and Jamison in the partnership.

E 2. **LO3 Distribution of Income** Elijah Samuels and Tony Winslow agreed to form a partnership. Samuels contributed $200,000 in cash, and Winslow contributed assets with a fair market value of $400,000. The partnership, in its initial year, reported net income of $120,000. Calculate the distribution of the first year's income to the partners under each of the following conditions:

1. Samuels and Winslow failed to include stated ratios in the partnership agreement.
2. Samuels and Winslow agreed to share income and losses in a 3:2 ratio.
3. Samuels and Winslow agreed to share income and losses in the ratio of their original investments.
4. Samuels and Winslow agreed to share income and losses by allowing 10 percent interest on original investments and sharing any remainder equally.

E 3. **LO3 Distribution of Income or Losses: Salary and Interest** Assume that the partnership agreement of Samuels and Winslow in **E 2** states that Samuels and Winslow are to receive salaries of $20,000 and $24,000, respectively; that Samuels is to receive 6 percent interest on his capital balance at the beginning of the year; and that the remainder of income and losses are to be shared equally. Calculate the distribution of the income or losses under the following conditions:

1. Income totaled $120,000 before deductions for salaries and interest.
2. Income totaled $48,000 before deductions for salaries and interest.
3. There was a loss of $2,000.
4. There was a loss of $40,000.

E 4. **LO3 Distribution of Income: Average Capital Balance**

Barbara and Karen operate a furniture rental business. Their capital balances on January 1, 20x7, were $160,000 and $240,000, respectively. Barbara withdrew cash of $32,000 from the business on April 1, 20x7. Karen withdrew $60,000 cash on October 1, 20x7. Barbara and Karen distribute partnership income based on their average capital balances each year. Income for 20x7 was $160,000. Compute the income to be distributed to Barbara and Karen using their average capital balances in 20x7.

E 5. **LO4 Admission of a New Partner: Recording a Bonus**

Ernie, Ron, and Denis have equity in a partnership of $40,000, $40,000, and $60,000, respectively, and they share income and losses in a ratio of 1:1:3. The partners have agreed to admit Henry to the partnership. Prepare entries in journal form to record the admission of Henry to the partnership under the following conditions:

1. Henry invests $60,000 for a 20 percent interest in the partnership, and a bonus is recorded for the original partners.
2. Henry invests $60,000 for a 40 percent interest in the partnership, and a bonus is recorded for Henry.

E 6. **LO4 Withdrawal of a Partner**

Danny, Steve, and Luis are partners. They share income and losses in the ratio of 3:2:1. Luis's Capital account has a $120,000 balance. Danny and Steve have agreed to let Luis take $160,000 of the company's cash when he retires from the business. What entry in journal form must be made on the partnership's books when Luis retires, assuming that a bonus to Luis is recognized and absorbed by the remaining partners?

E 7. **LO5 Partnership Liquidation**

Assume the following assets, liabilities, and partners' equity in the Ming and Demmick partnership on December 31, 20xx:

Assets	=	**Liabilities**	+	**Ming, Capital**	+	**Demmick, Capital**
$160,000	=	$10,000	+	$90,000	+	$60,000

The partnership has no cash. When the partners agree to liquidate the business, the assets are sold for $120,000, and the liabilities are paid. Ming and Demmick share income and losses in a ratio of 3:1.

1. Prepare a statement of liquidation.
2. Prepare entries in journal form for the sale of assets, payment of liabilities, distribution of loss from realization, and final distribution of cash to Ming and Demmick.

E 8. **LO5 Partnership Liquidation**

Ariel, Mandy, and Tisha are partners in a tanning salon. The assets, liabilities, and capital balances as of July 1, 20x7, are as follows:

Assets	$480,000
Liabilities	160,000
Ariel, Capital	140,000
Mandy, Capital	40,000
Tisha, Capital	140,000

Because competition is strong, business is declining, and the partnership has no cash, the partners have decided to sell the business. Ariel, Mandy, and Tisha share income and losses in a ratio of 3:1:1, respectively. The assets were sold for $260,000, and the liabilities were paid. Mandy has no other assets and will not be able to cover any deficits in her Capital account. How will the ending cash balance be distributed to the partners?

PROBLEMS

P 1. **LO2 Partnership Formation**
LO3 and Distribution of Income

In January 20x3, Edie Rivera and Babs Bacon agreed to produce and sell chocolate candies. Rivera contributed $240,000 in cash to the business. Bacon contributed the building and equipment, valued at $220,000 and $140,000, respectively. The partnership had an income of $84,000 during 20x3 but was less successful during 20x4, when income was only $40,000.

REQUIRED ▶

1. Prepare the entry to record the investment of both partners in the partnership.
2. Determine the share of income for each partner in 20x3 and 20x4 under each of the following conditions: (a) The partners agreed to share income equally. (b) The partners failed to agree on an income-sharing arrangement. (c) The partners agreed to share income according to the ratio of their original investments. (d) The partners agreed to share income by allowing interest of 10 percent on their original investments and dividing the remainder equally. (e) The partners agreed to share income by allowing salaries of $40,000 for Rivera and $28,000 for Bacon, and dividing the remainder equally. (f) The partners agreed to share income by paying salaries of

$40,000 to Rivera and $28,000 to Bacon, allowing interest of 9 percent on their original investments, and dividing the remainder equally.
3. What are some of the factors that need to be considered in choosing the plan of partners' income sharing among the options shown in Part 2?

P 2. **LO3 Distribution of Income: Salary and Interest**

Naomi and Petri are partners in a tennis shop. They have agreed that Naomi will operate the store and receive a salary of $104,000 per year. Petri will receive 10 percent interest on his average capital balance during the year of $500,000. The remaining income or losses are to be shared by Naomi and Petri in a 2:3 ratio.

REQUIRED ▶ Determine each partner's share of income and losses under each of the following conditions. In each case, the income or loss is stated before the distribution of salary and interest.

1. Income was $168,000.
2. Income was $88,000.
3. The loss was $25,600.

P 3. **LO4 Admission and Withdrawal of a Partner**

Marnie, Stacie, and Samantha are partners in Woodware Company. Their capital balances as of July 31, 20x4, are as follows:

Marnie, Capital		Stacie, Capital		Samantha, Capital	
	45,000		15,000		30,000

Each partner has agreed to admit Connie to the partnership.

REQUIRED ▶
1. Prepare the journal entries to record Connie's admission to or Marnie's withdrawal from the partnership under each of the following conditions: (a) Connie pays Marnie $12,500 for 20 percent of Marnie's interest in the partnership. (b) Connie invests $20,000 cash in the partnership and receives an interest equal to her investment. (c) Connie invests $30,000 cash in the partnership for a 20 percent interest in the business. A bonus is to be recorded for the original partners on the basis of their capital balances. (d) Connie invests $30,000 cash in the partnership for a 40 percent interest in the business. The original partners give Connie a bonus according to the ratio of their capital balances on July 31, 20x4. (e) Marnie withdraws from the partnership, taking $52,500. The excess of withdrawn assets over Marnie's partnership interest is distributed according to the balances of the Capital accounts. (f) Marnie withdraws by selling her interest directly to Connie for $60,000.
2. When a new partner enters a partnership, why would the new partner pay a bonus to the old partners, or why would the old partners pay a bonus to the new partner?

P 4. **LO5 Partnership Liquidation**

Caruso, Evans, and Weisman are partners in a retail lighting store. They share income and losses in the ratio of 2:2:1, respectively. The partners have agreed to liquidate the partnership. Here is the partnership balance sheet before the liquidation:

Caruso, Evans, and Weisman Partnership
Balance Sheet
August 31, 20x7

Assets		Liabilities	
Cash	$ 280,000	Accounts payable	$ 360,000
Other assets	880,000	**Partners' Equity**	
Total assets	$1,160,000		
		Caruso, Capital	400,000
		Evans, Capital	240,000
		Weisman, Capital	160,000
		Total liabilities and partners' equity	$1,160,000

The other assets were sold on September 1, 20x7, for $720,000. Accounts payable were paid on September 4, 20x7. The remaining cash was distributed to the partners on September 11, 20x7.

REQUIRED ▶

1. Prepare a statement of liquidation.
2. Prepare the following entries in journal form: (a) the sale of the other assets, (b) payment of the accounts payable, (c) the distribution of the loss from realization, and (d) the distribution to the partners of the remaining cash.

P 5. The following events pertain to a partnership formed by Mark Raymond and Stan Bryden to operate a floor-cleaning company:

LO2 LO3 LO4 LO5 Comprehensive Partnership Transactions

20x4

Feb. 14 The partnership was formed. Raymond transferred to the partnership $80,000 cash, land worth $80,000, a building worth $480,000, and a mortgage on the building of $240,000. Bryden transferred to the partnership $40,000 cash and equipment worth $160,000.

Dec. 31 During 20x4, the partnership earned income of just $84,000. The partnership agreement specifies that income and losses are to be divided by paying salaries of $40,000 to Raymond and $60,000 to Bryden, allowing 8 percent interest on beginning capital investments, and dividing any remainder equally.

20x5

Jan. 1 To improve the prospects for the company, the partners decided to take in a new partner, Chuck Menzer, who had experience in the floor-cleaning business. Menzer invested $156,000 for a 25 percent interest in the business. A bonus was transferred in equal amounts from the original partners' Capital accounts to Menzer's Capital account.

Dec. 31 During 20x5, the company earned income of $87,200. The new partnership agreement specified that income and losses would be divided by paying salaries of $60,000 to Bryden and $80,000 to Menzer (no salary to Raymond), allowing 8 percent interest on beginning capital balances after Menzer's admission, and dividing the remainder equally.

20x6

Jan. 1 Because it appeared that the business could not support the three partners, the partners decided to liquidate the partnership. The asset and liability accounts of the partnership were as follows: Cash, $407,200; Accounts Receivable (net), $68,000; Land, $80,000; Building (net), $448,000; Equipment (net), $236,000; Accounts Payable, $88,000; and Mortgage Payable, $224,000. The equipment was sold for $200,000. The accounts payable were paid. The loss was distributed equally to the partners' Capital accounts. A statement of liquidation was prepared, and the remaining assets and liabilities were distributed. Raymond agreed to accept cash plus the land and building at book value and the mortgage payable as payment for his share. Bryden accepted cash and the accounts receivable for his share. Menzer was paid in cash.

REQUIRED ▶ Prepare entries in journal form to record all of the facts above. Support your computations with schedules, and prepare a statement of liquidation in connection with the January 1, 20x6, entries.

Alternate Problems

P 6. Jacob, Deric, and Jason are partners in the South Central Company. The partnership agreement states that Jacob is to receive 8 percent interest on his capital balance at the beginning of the year, Deric is to receive a salary of $100,000 a year, and Jason will be paid interest of 6 percent on his average capital balance during the year. Jacob, Deric, and Jason will share any income or loss after salary and interest in a 5:3:2 ratio. Jacob's capital balance at the beginning of the year was $600,000, and Jason's average capital balance for the year was $720,000.

LO3 Distribution of Income: Salaries and Interest

REQUIRED ▶ Determine each partner's share of income and losses under the following conditions. In each case, the income or loss is stated before the distribution of salary and interest.

1. Income was $545,200.
2. Income was $155,600.
3. The loss was $56,800.

P 7.
LO4 Admission and Withdrawal of a Partner

Peter, Mara, and Vanessa are partners in the Image Gallery. As of November 30, 20xx, the balance in Peter's Capital account was $50,000, the balance in Mara's was $60,000, and the balance in Vanessa's was $90,000. Peter, Mara, and Vanessa share income and losses in a ratio of 2:3:5.

REQUIRED

1. Prepare entries in journal form for each of the following independent conditions: (a) Bob pays Vanessa $100,000 for four-fifths of Vanessa's interest. (b) Bob is to be admitted to the partnership with a one-third interest for a $100,000 cash investment. (c) Bob is to be admitted to the partnership with a one-third interest for a $160,000 cash investment. A bonus, based on the partners' ratio for income and losses, is to be distributed to the original partners when Bob is admitted. (d) Bob is to be admitted to the partnership with a one-third interest for an $82,000 cash investment. A bonus is to be given to Bob on admission. (e) Peter withdraws from the partnership, taking $66,000 in cash. (f) Peter withdraws from the partnership by selling his interest directly to Bob for $70,000.
2. In general, when a new partner enters a partnership, why would the new partner pay a bonus to the old partners, or why would the old partners pay a bonus to the new partner?

P 8.
LO5 Partnership Liquidation

The balance sheet of the Rose Partnership as of July 31, 20xx, follows.

Rose Partnership
Balance Sheet
July 31, 20xx

Assets		Liabilities	
Cash	$ 6,000	Accounts payable	$480,000
Accounts receivable	120,000	**Partners' Equity**	
Inventory	264,000		
Equipment (net)	462,000	Gerri, Capital	72,000
Total assets	$852,000	Susi, Capital	180,000
		Mari, Capital	120,000
		Total liabilities and partners' equity	$852,000

The partners—Gerri, Susi, and Mari—share income and losses in the ratio of 5:3:2. Because of a mutual disagreement, Gerri, Susi, and Mari have decided to liquidate the business.

Assume that Gerri cannot contribute any additional personal assets to the company during liquidation and that the following transactions occurred during liquidation: (a) Accounts receivable were sold for 60 percent of their book value. (b) Inventory was sold for $276,000. (c) Equipment was sold for $300,000. (d) Accounts payable were paid in full. (e) Gain or loss from realization was distributed to the partners' Capital accounts. (f) Gerri's deficit was transferred to the remaining partners in their new income and loss ratio. (g) The remaining cash was distributed to Susi and Mari.

REQUIRED

1. Prepare a statement of liquidation.
2. Prepare entries in journal form to liquidate the partnership and distribute any remaining cash.

SKILLS DEVELOPMENT CASES

Conceptual Analysis

LO1 Partnership Agreement

SD 1. Form a partnership with one or two of your classmates. Assume that the two or three of you are forming a small service business. For example, you might form a company that hires college students to paint houses during the summer or to provide landscaping services.

Working together, draft a partnership agreement for your business. The agreement can be a simple one, with just a sentence or two for each provision. However, it should include the name, location, and purpose of the business; the names of the partners and their respective duties; the investments of each partner; methods for distributing profits and losses; and procedures for dealing with the admission or withdrawal of partners, the withdrawal of assets, the death of a partner, and liquidation of the business. Include a title, date, and signature lines.

Group Activity: Assign groups to prepare partnership agreements.

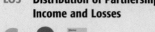

LO3 Distribution of Partnership Income and Losses

SD 2. Landow, Donovan, and Hansa, who are forming a partnership to operate an antiques gallery, are discussing how income and losses should be distributed. Among the facts they are considering are the following:

a. Landow will contribute cash for operations of $100,000, Donovan will contribute a collection of antiques that is valued at $300,000, and Hansa will not contribute any assets.
b. Landow and Hansa will handle day-to-day business operations. Hansa will work full time, and Landow will devote about half-time to the partnership. Donovan will not devote time to day-to-day operations. A full-time clerk in a retail store would make about $20,000 in a year, and a full-time manager would receive about $30,000.
c. The current interest rate on long-term bonds is 8 percent.

Landow, Donovan, and Hansa have just hired you as the partnership's accountant. Write a memorandum describing an equitable plan for distributing income and losses. Outline the reasons why you believe this plan is equitable. According to your plan, which partner will gain the most if the partnership is very profitable, and which will lose the most if the partnership has large losses?

Ethical Dilemma

LO1 Death of a Partner
LO2
LO4

SD 3. South Shore Realty was started 20 years ago when T. S. Tyler, R. C. Strong, and A. J. Hibbert established a partnership to sell real estate near Galveston, Texas. The partnership has been extremely successful. In 20xx, Tyler, the senior partner, who in recent years had not been very active in the partnership, died. Unfortunately, the partnership agreement is vague about how the partnership interest of a partner who dies should be valued. It simply states that "the estate of a deceased partner shall receive compensation for his or her interest in the partnership in a reasonable time after death." The attorney for Tyler's family believes that the estate should receive one-third of the assets of the partnership based on the fair market value of the net assets (total assets less total liabilities). The total assets of the partnership are $10 million in the accounting records, but the assets are worth at least $20 million. Because the firm's total liabilities are $4 million, the attorney is asking for $5.3 million (one-third of $16 million). Strong and Hibbert do not agree, but all parties want to avoid a protracted, expensive lawsuit. They have decided to put the question to an arbitrator, who will make a determination of the settlement.

Here are some other facts that may or may not be relevant. The current balances in the partners' Capital accounts are $1.5 million for Tyler, $2.5 million for Strong, and $2.0 million for Hibbert. Net income in 20xx is to be distributed to the Capital accounts in the ratio of 1:4:3. Before Tyler's semiretirement, the distribution ratio was 3:3:2. Assume you or your group is the arbitrator, and develop what you would consider a fair distribution of assets to Tyler's estate. Defend your solution.

Research Activity

SD 4.
LO1 **Basic Research Skills**

The limited partnership is a form of business that was particularly important to the U.S. economy in the 1980s. To find the latest developments or to study the practical applications of a particular subject, such as limited partnerships, it is helpful to use periodical indexes in the library to find articles relating to that subject. Three periodical indexes relevant to accounting and business are *The Accountant's Index*, the *Business Periodicals Index*, and *The Wall Street Journal Index*. Use one or more of those periodical indexes in your college or university library to find three articles about limited partnerships. Sometimes the articles are not listed under the heading "Limited Partnerships"; instead, they appear under the uses of limited partnerships. Some examples are real estate, investments, research and development, and cattle or livestock. Write a short summary of each article, relating the content of the article to the content of this chapter or explaining why the limited partnership form of business was important in the situation described in the article.

Decision-Making Practice

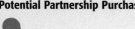

SD 5.
LO4 **Potential Partnership Purchase**

The A-One Fitness Center, owned by Abe Hines and Mario Saconi, has been very successful since its inception five years ago. Hines and Saconi work 10 to 11 hours a day at the business. They have decided to expand by opening up another fitness center in the north part of town. Hines has approached you about becoming a partner in the business. He and Saconi are interested in you because of your experience in operating a small gym. Also, they need additional funds to expand their business. Projected income after the expansion but before partners' salaries for the next five years is as follows:

20x3	20x4	20x5	20x6	20x7
$100,000	$120,000	$130,000	$140,000	$150,000

Currently, Hines and Saconi each draw a $25,000 salary and share remaining profits equally. They are willing to give you an equal share of the business for $142,000. You will receive a $25,000 salary and one-third of the remaining profits. You would work the same hours as Hines and Saconi. Your salary for the next five years where you currently work is expected to be as follows:

20x3	20x4	20x5	20x6	20x7
$34,000	$38,000	$42,000	$45,000	$50,000

Here is financial information for the A-One Fitness Center:

Current Assets	$ 45,000	Long-Term Liabilities	$100,000
Plant and Equipment, net	365,000	Abe Hines, Capital	140,000
Current Liabilities	50,000	Mario Saconi, Capital	120,000

1. Compute your capital balance if you decide to join Hines and Saconi in the fitness center partnership.
2. Analyze your expected income for the next five years.
3. Should you invest in the A-One Fitness Center?
4. Assume that you do not consider Hines and Saconi's offer of partnership to be a good one. Develop a counteroffer that you would be willing to accept (be realistic).

FINANCIAL REPORTING AND ANALYSIS CASES

Interpreting Financial Reports

FRA 1.
LO1 LO3 **Effects of Lawsuit on Partnership**

The Springfield Clinic is owned and operated by ten local doctors as a partnership. Recently, a paralyzed patient sued the clinic for malpractice, for a total of $20 million. The clinic carries malpractice liability insurance in the amount of $10 million. There is no provision for the possible loss from this type of lawsuit in the partnership's financial statements. The condensed balance sheet for 20xx is as follows:

Springfield Clinic
Condensed Balance Sheet
December 31, 20xx

Assets		
Current assets	$246,000	
Property, plant, and equipment (net)	750,000	
Total assets		$996,000
Liabilities and Partners' Equity		
Current liabilities	$180,000	
Long-term debt	675,000	
Total liabilities		$855,000
Partners' equity		141,000
Total liabilities and partners' equity		$996,000

1. How should information about the lawsuit be disclosed in the December 31, 20xx, financial statements of the partnership?
2. Assume that the clinic and its insurance company settle out of court by agreeing to pay a total of $10.1 million, of which $100,000 must be paid by the partnership. What effect will the payment have on the clinic's December 31, 20xx, financial statements? Discuss the effect of the settlement on the Springfield Clinic doctors' personal financial situations.

International Company

FRA 2.
LO1 **International Joint Ventures**

Nokia <www.nokia.com>, the Finnish telecommunications company, has formed an equally owned joint venture with Capital Corporation, a state-owned Chinese company, to develop a center for the manufacture and development of telecommunications equipment in China, the world's fastest-growing market for this kind of equipment. The main aim of the development is to persuade Nokia's suppliers to move close to the company's main plant. The Chinese government looks favorably on companies that involve local suppliers.[4] What advantages does a joint venture have over a single company in entering a new market in another country? What are the potential disadvantages?

Toys "R" Us Annual Report

This activity is not appropriate for this chapter.

Fingraph® Financial Analysis™

This activity is not appropriate for this chapter.

Comparison Case

This activity is not appropriate for this chapter.

Internet Case

LO1 Comparison of Career Opportunities in Partnerships and Corporations

FRA 3. Accounting firms are among the world's largest partnerships and provide a wide range of attractive careers for business and accounting majors. Through the Needles Accounting Resource Center Web Site at http://accounting.college.hmco.com/students, you can explore careers in public accounting by linking to the web site of one of the Big Four accounting firms. The firms are Deloitte & Touche, Ernst & Young, KPMG International, and PricewaterhouseCoopers. Each firm's home page has a career opportunity section. For the firm you choose, compile a list of facts about the firm—size, locations, services, and career opportunities. Do you have the interest and background for a career in public accounting? Why or why not? How do you think working for a large partnership would differ from or be the same as working for a large corporation? Be prepared to discuss your findings in class.

Appendix A

International Accounting

As businesses grow, they naturally look for new sources of supply and new markets in other countries. Today, it is common for businesses to operate in more than one country, and many of these so-called *multinational* or *transnational corporations* operate throughout the world.

The extent of a company's international operations can be found in its annual report in the segment information note to the financial statements. The annual report will also contain a description of the company's international operations.

www.pepsico.com

For example, the Frito Lay segment of PepsiCo, Inc., obtains more than one-third of its $13 billion in revenues from countries outside the United States. PepsiCo's annual report contains the following description of this division's international operations:

> Frito-Lay International manufactures, markets, sells and distributes salty and sweet snacks. Products include Walkers brand snack foods in the United Kingdom, Smith's brand snack foods in Australia, Sabritas brand snack foods and Alegro and Gamesa brand sweet snacks in Mexico. Many of our U.S. brands have been introduced internationally such as Lay's and Ruffles brand potato chips, Doritos and Tostitos brand tortilla chips, Fritos brand corn chips and Cheetos brand cheese-flavored snacks. Principal international snack markets include Mexico, the United Kingdom, Brazil, Spain, the Netherlands, Australia and South Africa.[1]

www.ibm.com
www.nestle.com
www.michelin.com
www.unilever.com
www.sony.com

Table 1 shows the extent of the foreign revenues of five large U.S. corporations. IBM, for example, has operations in 80 countries and receives almost 60 percent of its sales from outside the United States. Other industrial countries, such as Switzerland, France, Germany, Great Britain, the Netherlands, and Japan, have also given rise to numerous worldwide corporations. Nestlé, the large Swiss food company, makes 98 percent of its sales outside Switzerland. Other companies that make more than half their sales outside their home countries include Michelin, the French tire maker; Unilever, the British/Netherlands consumer products company; and Sony, the Japanese electronics company. More than five hundred companies are listed on at least one stock exchange outside their home countries.

Sophisticated investors no longer restrict their investment activities to domestic securities markets. Many Americans invest in foreign securities markets, and

TABLE 1. Extent of Foreign Revenues for Selected U.S. Companies

Company	Foreign Revenues (millions)	Total Revenues (millions)	Foreign Revenues (percentage)
Exxon Mobil <www.exxonmobil.com>	$158,403	$228,439	69.3
IBM <www.ibm.com>	50,377	87,548	57.5
Ford <www.ford.com>	51,691	170,064	30.4
General Motors <www.gm.com>	48,233	184,632	26.1
PepsiCo <www.pepsico.com>	7,259	20,438	35.5

Source: Form 10-K of each company.

FIGURE 1
Value of Securities Traded on the World's Stock Markets

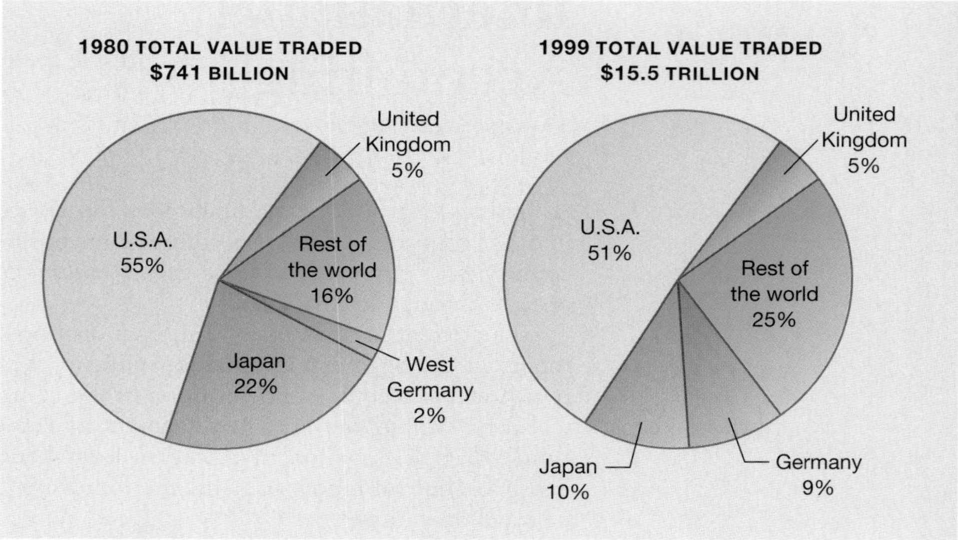

Source: International Finance Corporation, *Emerging Stock Markets Factbook,* © 2000.

non-Americans invest heavily in the stock market in the United States. Figure 1 shows that from 1980 to 1999, the total value of securities traded on the world's stock markets increased over twentyfold, with the U.S. share of the pie declining from 55 to 51 percent.

EFFECTS OF FOREIGN BUSINESS TRANSACTIONS

Foreign business transactions have two major effects on accounting. First, most sales or purchases of goods and services in other countries involve different currencies. Thus, one currency needs to be translated into another, using exchange rates.* An *exchange rate* is the value of one currency stated in terms of another. For example, an English company purchasing goods from a U.S. company and paying in U.S. dollars must exchange British pounds for U.S. dollars before making payment. In effect, currencies are goods that can be bought and sold. Table 2 lists the exchange rates of several currencies in terms of dollars. It shows the exchange rate for the British pound as $1.61. Like the price of any good or service, these prices change daily according to supply and demand. Accounting for these price changes in recording foreign transactions and preparing financial statements for foreign subsidiaries are discussed in the next two sections.

The second major effect of international business on accounting is that financial standards differ from country to country, which makes it difficult to compare companies from different countries. The obstacles to achieving comparability and some of the progress in solving the problem are discussed later in this appendix.

TABLE 2. Partial Listing of Foreign Exchange Rates

Country	Price in $ U.S.	Country	Price in $ U.S.
Britain (pound)	1.61	Hong Kong (dollar)	0.128
Canada (dollar)	0.704	Japan (yen)	0.008
Europe (euro)	1.12	Mexico (peso)	0.10

Source: The Wall Street Journal, May 5, 2003.

*At the time this chapter was written, exchange rates were fluctuating rapidly. The examples, exercises, and probems in this book use exchange rates in the general range for the countries involved.

ACCOUNTING FOR TRANSACTIONS IN FOREIGN CURRENCIES

A U.S. manufacturer may expand by selling its product to foreign customers, or it may lower its product cost by buying a less expensive part from a source in another country. In previous chapters of the text, all purchases and sales were recorded in dollars, and it was assumed that the dollar is a uniform measure in the same way that the inch and the centimeter are. But in the international marketplace, a transaction may take place in Japanese yen, British pounds, or some other currency. The values of these currencies in relation to the dollar rise and fall daily. Thus, if there is a delay between the date of sale or purchase and the date of receipt or payment, the amount of cash involved may differ from that originally agreed upon.

■ **FOREIGN SALES** When a domestic company sells merchandise abroad, it may bill either in its own country's currency or in the foreign currency. If the billing and payment are both in the domestic currency, no accounting problem arises. For example, assume that a U.S. maker of precision tools sells $160,000 worth of its products to a British company and bills the British company in dollars. The entry to record the sale and receipt of payment is familiar:

Date of Sale

A = L + OE + +	Accounts Receivable, British company Sales	160,000	 160,000

Date of Receipt

A = L + OE + −	Cash Accounts Receivable, British company	160,000	 160,000

However, if the U.S. company bills the British company in British pounds and accepts payment in pounds, the U.S. company may incur an *exchange gain or loss*. A gain or loss will occur if the exchange rate between dollars and pounds changes between the date of sale and the date of receipt. Since gains and losses tend to offset one another, a single account is used during the year to accumulate the activity. The net exchange gain or loss is reported on the income statement. For example, assume that the sale of $160,000 above was billed at £100,000, reflecting an exchange rate of 1.60 (that is, $1.60 per pound) on the sale date. Now assume that by the date of receipt, the exchange rate has fallen to 1.50. The entries to record the transactions follow:

Date of Sale

A = L + OE
+   +
	Accounts Receivable, British company
	  Sales
	    £100,000 × $1.60 = $160,000
		160,000	
			160,000

Date of Receipt

A = L + OE
+   −
−
	Cash
	Exchange Gain or Loss
	  Accounts Receivable, British company
	    £100,000 × $1.50 = $150,000
		150,000
		10,000
			
			160,000

The U.S. company has incurred an exchange loss of $10,000 because it agreed ' accept a fixed number of British pounds in payment for its products, and the va' of each pound dropped before the payment was made. Had the value of the po in relation to the dollar increased, the U.S. company would have made an exch gain.

FOREIGN PURCHASES The same logic applies to purchases as to sales, except that the relationship of exchange gains and losses to changes in exchange rates is reversed. For example, assume that the U.S. toolmaker purchases parts from a Japanese supplier for $15,000. If the purchase and payment are made in U.S. dollars, no accounting problem arises.

Date of Purchase

A = L + OE + −	Purchases Accounts Payable, Japanese company	15,000	 15,000

Date of Payment

A = L + OE − −	Accounts Payable, Japanese company Cash	15,000	 15,000

However, the Japanese company may bill the U.S. company in yen and be paid in yen. If so, the U.S. company will incur an exchange gain or loss if the exchange rate changes between the date of purchase and the date of payment. For example, assume that the transaction is for ¥2,500,000 and that the exchange rates on the dates of purchase and payment are $.0090 and $.0085 per yen, respectively. The entries are as follows:

Date of Purchase

A = L + OE + −	Purchases Accounts Payable, Japanese company ¥2,500,000 × $.0090 = $22,500	22,500	 22,500

Date of Payment

A = L + OE − − +	Accounts Payable, Japanese company Exchange Gain or Loss Cash ¥2,500,000 × $.0085 = $21,250	22,500	 1,250 21,250

In this case, the U.S. company received an exchange gain of $1,250 because it agreed to pay a fixed ¥2,500,000, and between the dates of purchase and payment, the exchange value of the yen decreased in relation to the dollar.

REALIZED VERSUS UNREALIZED EXCHANGE GAIN OR LOSS The preceding illustrations dealt with completed transactions (in the sense that payment was made). In each case, the exchange gain or loss was recognized on the date of receipt or payment. If financial statements are prepared between the sale or purchase and the receipt or payment and exchange rates have changed, there will be unrealized gains or losses. The Financial Accounting Standards Board's *Statement No. 52* requires that exchange gains and losses "be included in determining net income for the period in which the exchange rate changes."[2] The requirement includes interim (quarterly) statements and applies whether or not a transaction is complete.

This ruling has caused much debate. Critics charge that it gives too much weight to fleeting changes in exchange rates, causing random changes in earnings that hide long-run trends. Others believe that the use of current exchange rates to value receivables and payables as of the balance sheet date is a major step toward economic reality (current values). To illustrate, we use the preceding case, in which a U.S. company buys parts from a Japanese supplier. We assume that the transaction has not been completed by the balance sheet date, when the exchange rate is $.0080 per yen:

	Date	Exchange Rate ($ per Yen)
Date of purchase	Dec. 1	.0090
Balance sheet date	Dec. 31	.0080
Date of payment	Feb. 1	.0085

The accounting effects of the unrealized gain are as follows:

	Dec. 1	Dec. 31	Feb. 1
Purchase recorded in U.S. dollars (billed as ¥2,500,000)	$22,500	$22,500	$22,500
Dollars to be paid to equal ¥2,500,000 (¥2,500,000 × exchange rate)	22,500	20,000	21,250
Unrealized gain (or loss)	—	$ 2,500	
Realized gain (or loss)			$ 1,250

A = L + OE + −	Dec. 1	Purchases Accounts Payable, Japanese company	22,500	 22,500
A = L + OE − +	Dec. 31	Accounts Payable, Japanese company Exchange Gain or Loss	2,500	 2,500
A = L + OE − − −	Feb. 1	Accounts Payable, Japanese company Exchange Gain or Loss Cash	20,000 1,250	 21,250

In this case, the original sale was billed in yen by the Japanese company. Following the rules of *Statement No. 52,* an exchange gain of $2,500 is recorded on December 31, and an exchange loss of $1,250 is recorded on February 1. Even though these large fluctuations do not affect the net exchange gain of $1,250 for the whole transaction, the effect on each year's income statements may be important.

Restatement of Foreign Subsidiary Financial Statements

Companies often expand by establishing or buying foreign subsidiaries. If a company owns more than 50 percent of a foreign subsidiary and thus exercises control, then the foreign subsidiary should be included in the consolidated financial statements. The reporting of foreign subsidiaries is covered by FASB *Statement No. 52.* The consolidation procedure is the same as the one we described for domestic subsidiaries, except that the statements of the foreign subsidiary must be restated in the reporting currency before consolidation takes place. The *reporting currency* is the currency in which the consolidated financial statements are presented, which for U.S. companies is usually the U.S. dollar. Clearly, it makes no sense to combine the assets of a Mexican subsidiary stated in pesos with the assets of the U.S. parent company stated in dollars. Thus, *restatement* in the currency of the parent company is necessary.

The method of restatement depends on the foreign subsidiary's *functional currency,* which is the currency of the place where the subsidiary carries on most of its business. Generally, it is the currency in which a company earns and spends its cash. The functional currency used depends on the kind of foreign operation in which the subsidiary takes part.

There are two broad types of foreign operation. Type I includes those that ar fairly self-contained and integrated within a certain country or economy. Type includes those that are mainly a direct and integral part or extension of the par company's operations. As a rule, Type I subsidiaries use the currency of the c try in which they are located, and Type II subsidiaries use the currency of the ent company. If the parent is a U.S. company, the functional currency of a subsidiary will be the currency of the country where the subsidiary carries on its business, and the functional currency of a Type II subsidiary will be the U.S. dollar. *Statement No. 52* makes an exception when a Type I subsidiary operates in a country where there is hyperinflation (as a rule of thumb, more than 100 percent cumulative inflation over three years), such as Brazil or Argentina. In such a case, the subsidiary is treated as a Type II subsidiary, with the functional currency being the U.S. dollar. Restatements in these situations do not affect cash flows because they are done simply for the convenience of preparing consolidated statements.

International Accounting Standards

International investors need to compare the financial position and results of operations of companies from different countries. At present, however, few standards of accounting are recognized worldwide.[3] For example, LIFO is the most popular method of valuing inventory in the United States, but it is not acceptable in most European countries. Historical cost is strictly followed in Germany, replacement cost is used by some companies in the Netherlands, and a mixed system, allowing lower of cost or market in some cases, is used in the United States and Britain. Even the formats of financial statements differ from country to country. In Britain and France, for example, the order of the balance sheets is almost the reverse of that in the United States. In those countries, property, plant, and equipment is the first listing in the assets section.

A number of major problems stand in the way of setting international standards. One is that accountants and users of accounting information have not been able to agree on the goals of financial statements. Differences in the way the accounting profession has developed in various countries, in the laws regulating companies, and in governmental and other requirements present other hurdles. Further difficulties are created by differences among countries in the basic economic factors affecting financial reporting, inconsistencies in practices recommended by the accounting profession in different countries, and the influence of tax laws on financial reporting.

Probably the best hopes for finding areas of agreement among different countries are the International Accounting Standards Board (IASB) and the International Federation of Accountants (IFAC).

The role of the IASB is to contribute to the development and adoption of accounting principles that are relevant, balanced, and comparable throughout the world by formulating and publicizing accounting standards and encouraging their observance in the presentation of financial statements.[4] The standards issued by the IASB are generally followed by large multinational companies that are clients of international accounting firms. The IASB has been especially helpful to companies in developing economies that do not have the financial history or resources to develop accounting standards. The IASB is currently engaged in a major project to improve financial reporting worldwide by introducing a set of international accounting standards that will be acceptable to the world's securities regulators, such as the SEC in the United States. If successful, the effort should make it easier for companies to raise equity capital and list their stocks in other countries.

The IFAC, formed in 1977, also includes most of the world's accountancy organizations. It fully supports the work of the IASB and recognizes the IASB as the sole body with responsibility and authority to issue pronouncements on international accounting standards. The IFAC's principal role is to assure quality audits and financial statements prepared in accordance with international accounting standards. It attempts to accomplish this objective by issuing international auditing standards and monitoring the practice of international firms.

The European Community is also attempting to harmonize accounting standards. One of its directives requires certain minimum, uniform reporting and disclosure standards for financial statements. Other directives deal with uniform rules for preparing consolidated financial statements and qualifications of auditors. More importantly, the European Community has agreed to require international accounting standards beginning in 2005 for all companies that seek financing across borders. This is an important step for recognition of international accounting standards and for the goal of a single European market. It will leave the United States as the only major market that does not accept international accounting standards.

The road to international harmony is not easy. However, there is reason for optimism because an increasing number of countries are recognizing the appropriateness of uniform accounting standards in international trade and commerce.

PROBLEMS

P 1. Recording International Transactions: Fluctuating Exchange Rate

Part A: Wooster Corporation purchased a special-purpose machine from Konigsberg Corporation on credit for E 50,000. At the date of purchase, the exchange rate was $.90 per euro. On the date of the payment, which was made in euros, the value of the euro was $.95. Prepare entries in journal form to record the purchase and payment in Wooster Corporation's accounting records.

Part B: U.S. Corporation made a sale on account to U.K. Company on November 15 in the amount of £300,000. Payment was to be made in British pounds on February 15. U.S. Corporation's fiscal year is the same as the calendar year. The British pound was worth $1.70 on November 15, $1.58 on December 31, and $1.78 on February 15. Prepare entries in journal form to record the sale, year-end adjustment, and collection on U.S. Corporation's books.

P 2. International Transactions

Dolfsky Import/Export Company, whose year end is October 31, engaged in the following transactions (exchange rates in parentheses):

Aug.	12	Sold goods to a Mexican firm for $20,000; terms n/30 in U.S. dollars (peso = $.131).
	24	Purchased goods from a Japanese firm for $40,000; terms n/20 in yen (yen = $.0080).
Sept.	2	Sold goods to a British firm for $48,000; terms n/30 in pounds (pound = $1.60).
	11	Received payment in full for August 12 sale (peso = $.128).
	13	Paid for the goods purchased on August 24 (yen = $.0088).
	21	Purchased goods from an Italian firm for $28,000; terms n/10 in U.S. dollars (euro = $.90).
	30	Purchased goods from a Japanese firm for $35,200; terms n/60 in yen (yen = $.0088).
Oct.	2	Paid for the goods purchased on September 21 (euro = $.85).
	3	Received payment in full for the goods sold on September 2 (pound = $1.50).
	8	Sold goods to a French firm for $66,000; terms n/30 in euros (euro = $.88).
	19	Purchased goods from a Mexican firm for $37,000; terms n/30 in U.S. dollars (peso = $.135).
	31	Made year-end adjusting entries for incomplete foreign exchange transactions (euro = $.85; peso = $.130; pound = $1.40; yen = $.0100).
Nov.	9	Received payment for the goods sold on October 8 (euro = $.87).
	18	Paid for the goods purchased on October 19 (peso = $.132).
	28	Paid for the goods purchased on September 30 (yen = $.0090).

REQUIRED ▶ Prepare entries in journal form for these transactions.

Appendix B
Long-Term Investments

www.pepsico.com

Companies make long-term investments for a variety of reasons. For instance, PepsiCo makes investments in operations critical to the distribution of its products, such as its investments in PepsiCo Bottling Company. It also makes investments to expand its markets, as in its purchases of Tropicana, South Beach Beverage, and Quaker Oats. These are stock investments, but a company can also make long-term investments in bonds. Investments in bonds can be a way of ensuring that an affiliate company has sufficient long-term capital, or it can simply be a way of making a relatively secure investment. The following sections discuss the classifications of bonds and stocks and the methods used to account for such investments.

Long-Term Investments in Bonds

Like all investments, investments in bonds are recorded at cost, which, in this case, is the price of the bonds plus the broker's commission. When bonds are purchased between interest payment dates, the purchaser must also pay an amount equal to the interest that has accrued on the bonds since the last interest payment date. Then, on the next interest payment date, the purchaser receives an interest payment for the whole period. The payment for accrued interest should be recorded as a debit to Interest Income, which will be offset by a credit to Interest Income when the semiannual interest is received.

Subsequent accounting for a corporation's long-term bond investments depends on the classification of the bonds. If the company plans at some point to sell the bonds, they are classified as *available-for-sale securities*. If the company plans to hold the bonds until they are paid off on their maturity date, they are considered *held-to-maturity securities.* Except in industries like insurance and banking, it is unusual for companies to buy the bonds of other companies with the express purpose of holding them until they mature, which can be in 10 to 30 years. Thus, most long-term bond investments are available-for-sale securities. Such bonds are accounted for at fair value, much as equity or stock investments are; fair value is usually the market value. When bonds are intended to be held to maturity, they are accounted for not at fair value but at cost, adjusted for the amortization of their discount or premium. The procedure is similar to accounting for long-term bond liabilities, except that separate accounts for discounts and premiums are not used.

KEY POINT: The fair value of bonds is closely related to interest rates. An increase in interest rates lowers the fair value of bonds, and vice versa.

Long-Term Investments in Stocks

All long-term investments in stocks are recorded at cost, in accordance with generally accepted accounting principles. The treatment of the investment in the accounting records after the initial purchase depends on the extent to which the investing company can exercise *significant influence* or *control* over the operating and financial policies of the other company. The Accounting Principles Board (APB) defined these important terms in its *Opinion No. 18*.

NT: Influence and lated specifically gs, not debt

Significant influence is an investing firm's ability to affect the operating and financial policies of the company whose shares it owns, even though it holds 50 percent or less of the voting stock. Indications of significant influence include representation on the board of directors, participation in policymaking, and material

TABLE 1. Accounting Treatments of Long-Term Investments in Stocks

Level of Ownership	Percentage of Ownership	Accounting Treatment
Noninfluential and noncontrolling	Less than 20%	Cost initially; investment adjusted subsequent to purchase for changes in market value
Influential but noncontrolling	Between 20% and 50%	Equity method; investment valued subsequently at cost plus investor's share of income (or minus investor's share of loss) minus dividends received
Controlling	More than 50%	Financial statements consolidated

transactions, exchange of managerial personnel, and technological dependency between the two companies. For the sake of uniformity, the APB decided that without proof to the contrary, ownership of 20 percent or more of the voting stock should be presumed to confer significant influence.* Ownership of less than 20 percent of the voting stock does not confer significant influence.

Control is an investing firm's ability to decide the operating and financial policies of the other company. Control exists when the investor owns more than 50 percent of the voting stock of the company in which it has invested.

Thus, in the absence of information to the contrary, a noninfluential and noncontrolling investment would be less than 20 percent ownership. An influential but noncontrolling investment would be 20 to 50 percent ownership. And a controlling investment would be more than 50 percent ownership. The accounting treatment differs for each kind of investment. Table 1 summarizes these treatments.

■ NONINFLUENTIAL AND NONCONTROLLING INVESTMENT Available-for-sale securities are debt or equity securities that are not classified as trading or held-to-maturity securities. When equity securities are involved, a further criterion is that they be noninfluential and noncontrolling investments of less than 20 percent of the voting stock. The Financial Accounting Standards Board requires a *cost-adjusted-to market method* for accounting for available-for-sale securities. Under this method, available-for-sale securities must be recorded initially at cost and thereafter adjusted periodically through the use of an allowance account to reflect changes in the market value.[1]

Available-for-sale securities are classified as long term if management intends to hold them for more than one year. When accounting for long-term available-for-sale

*The Financial Accounting Standards Board pointed out in its *Interpretation No. 35* (May 1981) that this rule is not a rigid one. All relevant facts and circumstances should be examined to determine whether significant influence exists. The FASB noted five circumstances that may negate significant influence: (1) The company files a lawsuit against the investor or a complaint with a government agency; (2) the investor tries but fails to become a director; (3) the investor agrees not to increase its holdings; (4) the company is operated by a small group that ignores the investor's wishes; (5) the investor tries but fails to obtain company information that is not available to other stockholders.

securities, the unrealized gain or loss resulting from the adjustment is not reported on the income statement. Instead, the gain or loss is reported as a special item in the stockholders' equity section of the balance sheet and in comprehensive income disclosure.

At the end of each accounting period, the total cost and the total market value of these long-term stock investments must be determined. If the total market value is less than the total cost, the difference must be credited to a contra-asset account called Allowance to Adjust Long-Term Investments to Market. Because of the long-term nature of the investment, the debit part of the entry, which represents a decrease in value below cost, is treated as a temporary decrease and does not appear as a loss on the income statement. It is shown in a contra-stockholders' equity account called Unrealized Loss on Long-Term Investments.* Thus, both of these accounts are balance sheet accounts. If the market value exceeds the cost, the allowance account is added to Long-Term Investments, and the unrealized gain appears as an addition to stockholders' equity.

When long-term investments in stock are sold, the difference between the sale price and the cost of the stock is recorded and reported as a realized gain or loss on the income statement. Dividend income from such investments is recorded by a debit to Cash and a credit to Dividend Income. For example, assume the following facts about the long-term stock investments of Coleman Corporation:

June 1, 20x3	Paid cash for the following long-term investments: 10,000 shares of Durbin Corporation common stock (representing 2 percent of outstanding stock) at $25 per share; 5,000 shares of Kotes Corporation common stock (representing 3 percent of outstanding stock) at $15 per share.
Dec. 31, 20x3	Quoted market prices at year end: Durbin common stock, $21; Kotes common stock, $17.
Apr. 1, 20x4	Change in policy required sale of 2,000 shares of Durbin common stock at $23.
July 1, 20x4	Received cash dividend from Kotes equal to $.20 per share.
Dec. 31, 20x4	Quoted market prices at year end: Durbin common stock, $24; Kotes common stock, $13.

KEY POINT: On April 1, 20x4, a *change in policy* requires the sale. This points out that intent is often the only difference between long-term investments and short-term investments.

Entries to record these transactions are as follows:

Investment

A = L + OE
\+
−

20x3			
June 1	Long-Term Investments	325,000	
	Cash		325,000
	Investments in Durbin common stock (10,000 shares × $25 = $250,000) and Kotes common stock (5,000 shares × $15 = $75,000)		

Year-End Adjustment

A = L + OE
− −

20x3			
Dec. 31	Unrealized Loss on Long-Term Investments	30,000	
	Allowance to Adjust Long-Term Investments to Market		30,000
	To record reduction of long-term investment to market		

*If the decrease in market value of the long-term investment is deemed permanent, a different procedure is followed to record the decline. A loss account on the income statement is debited instead of the Unrealized Loss account.

Company	Shares	Market Price	Total Market	Total Cost
Durbin	10,000	$21	$210,000	$250,000
Kotes	5,000	17	85,000	75,000
			$295,000	$325,000

Total Cost − Total Market Value = $325,000 − $295,000 = $30,000

Sale

	Date	Account	Debit	Credit
	20x4			
A = L + OE	Apr. 1	Cash	46,000	
+ −		Loss on Sale of Investments	4,000	
−		Long-Term Investments		50,000
		Sale of 2,000 shares of Durbin common stock		
		2,000 × $23 = $46,000		
		2,000 × $25 = 50,000		
		Loss $ 4,000		

Dividend Received

	Date	Account	Debit	Credit
	20x4			
A = L + OE	July 1	Cash	1,000	
+ +		Dividend Income		1,000
		Receipt of cash dividend from Kotes stock		
		5,000 × $.20 = $1,000		

Year-End Adjustment

	Date	Account	Debit	Credit
	20x4			
A = L + OE	Dec. 31	Allowance to Adjust Long-Term Investments to Market	12,000	
+ +		Unrealized Loss on Long-Term Investments		12,000
		To record the adjustment in long-term investment so it is reported at market		

The adjustment equals the previous balance ($30,000 from the December 31, 20x3, entry) minus the new balance ($18,000), or $12,000. The new balance of $18,000 is the difference at the present time between the total market value and the total cost of all investments. It is figured as follows:

Company	Shares	Market Price	Total Market	Total Cost
Durbin	8,000	$24	$192,000	$200,000
Kotes	5,000	13	65,000	75,000
			$257,000	$275,000

Total Cost − Total Market Value = $275,000 − $257,000 = $18,000

The Allowance to Adjust Long-Term Investments to Market and the Unrealized Loss on Long-Term Investments are reciprocal contra accounts, each with the same dollar balance, as shown by the effects of these transactions on the T accounts:

Contra-Asset Account

Allowance to Adjust Long-Term Investments to Market

20x4	12,000	20x3	30,000
		Bal. 20x4	18,000

Contra-Stockholders' Equity Account

Unrealized Loss on Long-Term Investment

20x3	30,000	20x4	12,000
Bal. 20x4	18,000		

The Allowance account reduces long-term investments by the amount by which the cost of the investments exceeds market; the Unrealized Loss account reduces stockholders' equity by a similar amount. The opposite effects will exist if market value exceeds cost, resulting in an unrealized gain.

INFLUENTIAL BUT NONCONTROLLING INVESTMENT As we have noted, ownership of 20 percent or more of a company's voting stock is considered sufficient to influence the company's operations. When this is the case, the stock investment should be accounted for using the *equity method*. The equity method presumes that an investment of 20 percent or more is not a passive investment and that the investor should therefore share proportionately in the success or failure of the company. The three main features of this method are as follows:

1. The investor records the original purchase of the stock at cost.
2. The investor records its share of the company's periodic net income as an increase in the Investment account, with a corresponding credit to an income account. Similarly, it records its share of a periodic loss as a decrease in the Investment account, with a corresponding debit to a loss account.
3. When the investor receives a cash dividend, the asset account Cash is increased, and the Investment account is decreased.

To illustrate the equity method of accounting, we assume the following facts about an investment by Vassor Corporation: On January 1 of the current year, Vassor acquired 40 percent of the voting common stock of Block Corporation for $180,000. With this share of ownership, Vassor can exert significant influence over Block's operations. During the year, Block reported net income of $80,000 and paid cash dividends of $20,000. Vassor recorded these transactions as follows:

Investment

A = L + OE
+
−
	Investment in Block Corporation
	  Cash
	    Investment in Block Corporation common stock
		180,000	
			180,000

Recognition of Income

A = L + OE
+ +
	Investment in Block Corporation
	  Income, Block Corporation Investment
	    Recognition of 40% of income reported by Block Corporation
	    40% × $80,000 = $32,000
		32,000	
			32,000

Receipt of Cash Dividend

A = L + OE
+
−
	Cash
	  Investment in Block Corporation
	    Cash dividend from Block Corporation
	    40% × $20,000 = $8,000
		8,000	
			8,000

STUDY POINT: Under the equity method, dividends received are credited to the Investment account because the dividends represent a return from or a decrease in the investment in Block Corporation.

The balance of the Investment in Block Corporation account after these transactions is $204,000, as shown here:

Investment in Block Corporation

Investment	180,000	Dividend received	8,000
Share of Income	32,000		
Balance	204,000		

ENRICHMENT NOTE:
Parents and subsidiaries are separate legal entities even though they combine their financial reports at year end.

■ **CONTROLLING INVESTMENT** Some investing firms that own less than 50 percent of the voting stock of a company exercise such powerful influence that for all practical purposes, they control the policies of the other company. Nevertheless, ownership of more than 50 percent of the voting stock is required for accounting recognition of control. When a firm has a controlling interest, a parent-subsidiary relationship is said to exist. The investing company is known as the *parent company;* the other company is a *subsidiary*. Because the two corporations are separate legal entities, each prepares separate financial statements. However, owing to their special relationship, they are viewed for public financial reporting purposes as a single economic entity. For this reason, they must combine their financial statements into a single set of statements called *consolidated financial statements*.

Accounting for consolidated financial statements is complex and is usually the subject of an advanced accounting course. However, most large public corporations have subsidiaries and must prepare consolidated financial statements. It is therefore important to have some understanding of accounting for consolidations.

PROBLEMS

P 1. **Methods of Accounting for Long-Term Investments**

Diversified Corporation has the following long-term investments:

1. 60 percent of the common stock of Down Corporation
2. 13 percent of the common stock of West Lake, Inc.
3. 50 percent of the nonvoting preferred stock of Involе Corporation
4. 100 percent of the common stock of its financing subsidiary, DCF, Inc.
5. 35 percent of the common stock of the French company Maison de Boutaine
6. 70 percent of the common stock of the Canadian company Alberta Mining Company

For each of these investments, tell which of the following methods should be used for external financial reporting, and why.

a. Cost adjusted to market method
b. Equity method
c. Consolidation of parent and subsidiary financial statements

P 2. **Long-Term Investment Transactions**

Red Bud Corporation made the following transactions in its Long-Term Investments account over a two-year period:

20x4
Apr. 1 Purchased with cash 20,000 shares of Season Company stock for $152 per share.
June 1 Purchased with cash 15,000 shares of Abbado Corporation stock for $72 per share.
Sept. 1 Received a $1 per share dividend from Season Company.
Nov. 1 Purchased with cash 25,000 shares of Frankel Corporation stock for $110 per share.
Dec. 31 Market values per share of shares held in the Long-Term Investments account were as follows: Season Company, $140; Abbado Corporation, $32; and Frankel Corporation, $122.

20x5
Feb. 1 Because of unfavorable prospects for Abbado Corporation, Abbado stock was sold for cash at $40 per share.
May 1 Purchased with cash 10,000 shares of Schulian Corporation for $224 per share.
Sept. 1 Received $2 per share dividend from Season Company.
Dec. 31 Market values per share of shares held in the Long-Term Investments account were as follows: Season Company, $160; Frankel Corporation, $140; and Schulian Corporation, $200.

REQUIRED ▶ Prepare entries to record these transactions in the Red Bud Corporation records. Assume that all investments represent less than 20 percent of the voting stock of the company whose stock was acquired.

Long-Term Investments: Equity Method

P 3. The Modi Company owns 40 percent of the voting stock of the Vivanco Company. The Investment account for this company on the Modi Company's balance sheet had a balance of $600,000 on January 1, 20xx. During 20xx, the Vivanco Company reported the following quarterly earnings and dividends paid:

Quarter	Earnings	Dividends Paid
1	$ 80,000	$ 40,000
2	60,000	40,000
3	160,000	40,000
4	(40,000)	40,000
	$260,000	$160,000

The Modi Company exercises a significant influence over the operations of the Vivanco Company and therefore uses the equity method to account for its investment.

REQUIRED ▶

1. Prepare the entries in journal form that the Modi Company must make each quarter in accounting for its investment in the Vivanco Company.
2. Prepare a T account for the investment in common stock of the Vivanco Company. Enter the beginning balance, relevant portions of the entries made in **1**, and the ending balance.

Appendix C

The Time Value of Money

Simple Interest and Compound Interest

Interest is the cost associated with the use of money for a specific period of time. Because interest is a cost associated with time, and "time is money," it is also an important consideration in any business decision. *Simple interest* is the interest cost for one or more periods, under the assumption that the amount on which the interest is computed stays the same from period to period. *Compound interest* is the interest cost for two or more periods, under the assumption that after each period the interest of that period is added to the amount on which interest is computed in future periods. In other words, compound interest is interest earned on a principal sum that is increased at the end of each period by the interest for that period.

■ **Example—Simple Interest** Joe Sanchez accepts an 8 percent, $30,000 note due in ninety days. How much will he receive in total at that time? Remember that the formula for calculating simple interest is as follows:

$$\begin{aligned} \text{Interest} &= \text{Principal} \times \text{Rate} \times \text{Time} \\ &= \$30{,}000 \times 8/100 \times 90/360 \\ &= \$600 \end{aligned}$$

Therefore, the total that Sanchez will receive is calculated as follows:

$$\begin{aligned} \text{Total} &= \text{Principal} + \text{Interest} \\ &= \$30{,}000 + \$600 \\ &= \$30{,}600 \end{aligned}$$

■ **Example—Compound Interest** Ann Clary deposits $5,000 in a savings account that pays 6 percent interest. She expects to leave the principal and accumulated interest in the account for three years. How much will her account total at the end of three years? Assume that the interest is paid at the end of the year and is added to the principal at that time, and that this total in turn earns interest. The amount at the end of three years is computed as follows:

(1) Year	(2) Principal Amount at Beginning of Year	(3) Annual Amount of Interest (Col. 2 × 6%)	(4) Accumulated Amount at End of Year (Col. 2 + Col. 3)
1	$5,000.00	$300.00	$5,300.00
2	5,300.00	318.00	5,618.00
3	5,618.00	337.08	5,955.08

At the end of three years, Clary will have $5,955.08 in her savings account. Note that the annual amount of interest increases each year by the interest rate times the interest of the previous year. For example, between year 1 and year 2, the interest increased by $18 ($318 – $300), which exactly equals 6 percent times $300.

Future Value of a Single Invested Sum at Compound Interest

Another way to ask the question in the example of compound interest above is, What is the future value of a single sum ($5,000) at compound interest (6 percent) for three years? *Future value* is the amount that an investment will be worth at a future date if invested at compound interest. A businessperson often wants to know future value, but the method of computing the future value illustrated above is too time-consuming in practice. Imagine how tedious the calculation would be if the example were ten years instead of three. Fortunately, there are tables that simplify solving problems involving compound interest. Table 1, showing the future value of $1 after a given number of time periods, is an example. It is actually part of a larger table, Table 1 in the appendix on future value and present value tables. Suppose that we want to solve the problem of Clary's savings account above. We simply look down the 6 percent column in Table 1 until we reach the line for three periods and find the factor 1.191. This factor, when multiplied by $1, gives the future value of that $1 at compound interest of 6 percent for three periods (years in this case). Thus, we solve the problem as follows:

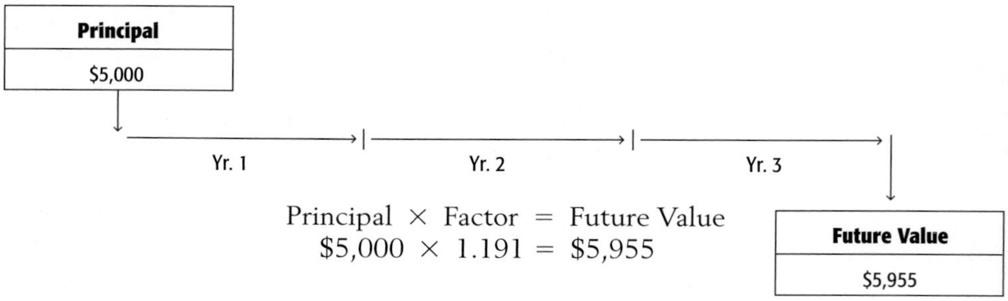

Principal × Factor = Future Value
$5,000 × 1.191 = $5,955

Except for a rounding difference of $.08, the answer is exactly the same as that calculated earlier.

Table 1. Future Value of $1 after a Given Number of Time Periods

Periods	1%	2%	3%	4%	5%	6%	7%	8%	9%	10%	12%	14%	15%
1	1.010	1.020	1.030	1.040	1.050	1.060	1.070	1.080	1.090	1.100	1.120	1.140	1.150
2	1.020	1.040	1.061	1.082	1.103	1.124	1.145	1.166	1.188	1.210	1.254	1.300	1.323
3	1.030	1.061	1.093	1.125	1.158	1.191	1.225	1.260	1.295	1.331	1.405	1.482	1.521
4	1.041	1.082	1.126	1.170	1.216	1.262	1.311	1.360	1.412	1.464	1.574	1.689	1.749
5	1.051	1.104	1.159	1.217	1.276	1.338	1.403	1.469	1.539	1.611	1.762	1.925	2.011
6	1.062	1.126	1.194	1.265	1.340	1.419	1.501	1.587	1.677	1.772	1.974	2.195	2.313
7	1.072	1.149	1.230	1.316	1.407	1.504	1.606	1.714	1.828	1.949	2.211	2.502	2.660
8	1.083	1.172	1.267	1.369	1.477	1.594	1.718	1.851	1.993	2.144	2.476	2.853	3.059
9	1.094	1.195	1.305	1.423	1.551	1.689	1.838	1.999	2.172	2.358	2.773	3.252	3.518
10	1.105	1.219	1.344	1.480	1.629	1.791	1.967	2.159	2.367	2.594	3.106	3.707	4.046

Source: Excerpt from Table 1 in the appendix on future value and present value tables.

FUTURE VALUE OF AN ORDINARY ANNUITY

Another common problem involves an *ordinary annuity,* which is a series of equal payments made at the end of equal intervals of time, with compound interest on these payments.

The following example shows how to find the future value of an ordinary annuity. Assume that Ben Katz makes a \$200 payment at the end of each of the next three years into a savings account that pays 5 percent interest. How much money will he have in his account at the end of the three years? One way of computing the amount is shown in the following table.

(1) Year	(2) Beginning Balance	(3) Interest Earned (5% × Col. 2)	(4) Periodic Payment	(5) Accumulated at End of Period (Col. 2 + Col. 3 + Col. 4)
1	—	—	\$200	\$200.00
2	\$200.00	\$10.00	200	410.00
3	410.00	20.50	200	630.50

Katz would have \$630.50 in his account at the end of three years, consisting of \$600.00 in periodic payments and \$30.50 in interest.

This calculation can also be simplified by using Table 2. We look down the 5 percent column until we reach three periods and find the factor 3.153. This factor, when multiplied by \$1, gives the future value of a series of three \$1 payments at compound interest of 5 percent. Thus, we solve the problem as follows:

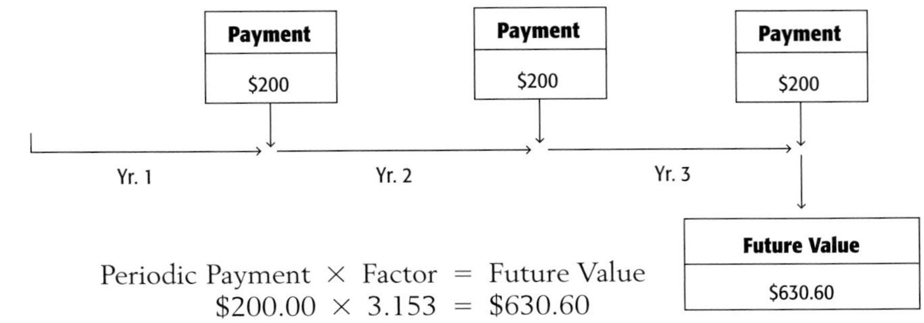

Periodic Payment × Factor = Future Value
\$200.00 × 3.153 = \$630.60

Except for a rounding difference of \$.10, this result is the same as our earlier one.

PRESENT VALUE

Suppose that you had the choice of receiving \$100 today or one year from today. Intuitively, you would choose to receive the \$100 today. Why? You know that if you have the \$100 today, you can put it in a savings account to earn interest, so that you will have more than \$100 a year from today. Therefore, we can say that an amount to be received in the future (future value) is not worth as much today as an amount to be received today (present value) because of the cost associated with the passage of time. In fact, present value and future value are closely related. *Present value* is the amount that must be invested now at a given rate of interest to produce a given future value. For example, assume that Sue Dapper needs $1,000 one year from now. How much should she invest today to achieve that goal if the interest rate is 5 percent? From earlier examples, the following equation may be established.

$$\begin{aligned} \text{Present Value} \times (1.0 + \text{Interest Rate}) &= \text{Future Value} \\ \text{Present Value} \times 1.05 &= \$1{,}000.00 \\ \text{Present Value} &= \$1{,}000.00 \div 1.05 \\ \text{Present Value} &= \$952.38 \end{aligned}$$

Thus, to achieve a future value of $1,000.00, a present value of $952.38 must be invested. Interest of 5 percent on $952.38 for one year equals $47.62, and these two amounts added together equal $1,000.00.

PRESENT VALUE OF A SINGLE SUM DUE IN THE FUTURE When more than one time period is involved, the calculation of present value is more complicated. Consider the following example. Don Riley wants to be sure of having $4,000 at the end of three years. How much must he invest today in a 5 percent savings account to achieve this goal? Adapting the above equation, we compute the present value of $4,000 at compound interest of 5 percent for three years in the future.

Year	Amount at End of Year		Divide by		Present Value at Beginning of Year
3	$4,000.00	÷	1.05	=	$3,809.52
2	3,809.52	÷	1.05	=	3,628.11
1	3,628.11	÷	1.05	=	3,455.34

Riley must invest a present value of $3,455.34 to achieve a future value of $4,000.00 in three years.

This calculation is again made much easier by using the appropriate table. In Table 3, we look down the 5 percent column until we reach three periods and find the factor .864. This factor, when multiplied by $1, gives the present value of $1 to be received three years from now at 5 percent interest. Thus, we solve the problem as shown on the next page.

TABLE 2. Future Value of an Ordinary Annuity of $1 Paid in Each Period for a Given Number of Time Periods

Periods	1%	2%	3%	4%	5%	6%	7%	8%	9%	10%	12%	14%	15%
1	1.000	1.000	1.000	1.000	1.000	1.000	1.000	1.000	1.000	1.000	1.000	1.000	1.000
2	2.010	2.020	2.030	2.040	2.050	2.060	2.070	2.080	2.090	2.100	2.120	2.140	2.150
3	3.030	3.060	3.091	3.122	3.153	3.184	3.215	3.246	3.278	3.310	3.374	3.440	3.473
4	4.060	4.122	4.184	4.246	4.310	4.375	4.440	4.506	4.573	4.641	4.779	4.921	4.993
5	5.101	5.204	5.309	5.416	5.526	5.637	5.751	5.867	5.985	6.105	6.353	6.610	6.742
6	6.152	6.308	6.468	6.633	6.802	6.975	7.153	7.336	7.523	7.716	8.115	8.536	8.754
7	7.214	7.434	7.662	7.898	8.142	8.394	8.654	8.923	9.200	9.487	10.09	10.73	11.07
8	8.286	8.583	8.892	9.214	9.549	9.897	10.26	10.64	11.03	11.44	12.30	13.23	13.73
9	9.369	9.755	10.16	10.58	11.03	11.49	11.98	12.49	13.02	13.58	14.78	16.09	16.79
10	10.46	10.95	11.46	12.01	12.58	13.18	13.82	14.49	15.19	15.94	17.55	19.34	20.30

Source: Excerpt from Table 2 in the appendix on future value and present value tables.

Table 3. Present Value of $1 to Be Received at the End of a Given Number of Time Periods

Periods	1%	2%	3%	4%	5%	6%	7%	8%	9%	10%
1	0.990	0.980	0.971	0.962	0.952	0.943	0.935	0.926	0.917	0.909
2	0.980	0.961	0.943	0.925	0.907	0.890	0.873	0.857	0.842	0.826
3	0.971	0.942	0.915	0.889	0.864	0.840	0.816	0.794	0.772	0.751
4	0.961	0.924	0.888	0.855	0.823	0.792	0.763	0.735	0.708	0.683
5	0.951	0.906	0.863	0.822	0.784	0.747	0.713	0.681	0.650	0.621
6	0.942	0.888	0.837	0.790	0.746	0.705	0.666	0.630	0.596	0.564
7	0.933	0.871	0.813	0.760	0.711	0.665	0.623	0.583	0.547	0.513
8	0.923	0.853	0.789	0.731	0.677	0.627	0.582	0.540	0.502	0.467
9	0.914	0.837	0.766	0.703	0.645	0.592	0.544	0.500	0.460	0.424
10	0.905	0.820	0.744	0.676	0.614	0.558	0.508	0.463	0.422	0.386

Source: Excerpt from Table 3 in the appendix on future value and present value tables.

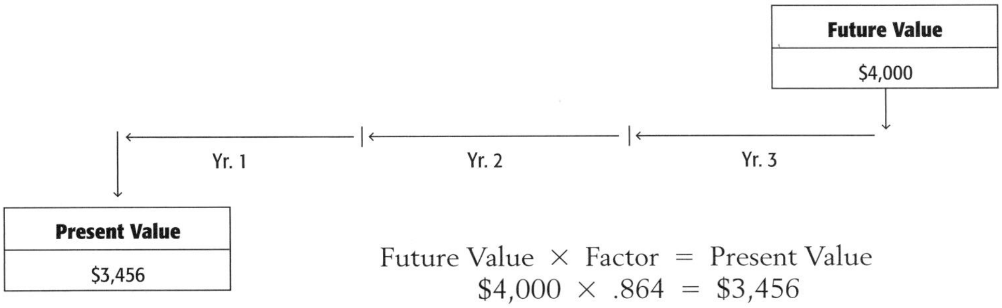

Future Value × Factor = Present Value
$4,000 × .864 = $3,456

Except for a rounding difference of $.66, this result is the same as the one above.

Present Value of an Ordinary Annuity It is often necessary to compute the present value of a series of receipts or payments. When we calculate the present value of equal amounts equally spaced over a period of time, we are computing the present value of an ordinary annuity.

For example, assume that Kathy Foster has sold a piece of property and is to receive $15,000 in three equal annual payments of $5,000, beginning one year from today. What is the present value of this sale, assuming a current interest rate of 5 percent? This present value may be computed by calculating a separate present value for each of the three payments (using Table 3) and summing the results, as shown in the table below.

Future Receipts (Annuity)				Present Value Factor at 5 Percent (from Table 3)		Present Value
Year 1	Year 2	Year 3				
$5,000			×	.952	=	$ 4,760
	$5,000		×	.907	=	4,535
		$5,000	×	.864	=	4,320
Total Present Value						$13,615

The present value of this sale is \$13,615. Thus, there is an implied interest cost (given the 5 percent rate) of \$1,385 associated with the payment plan that allows the purchaser to pay in three installments.

We can make this calculation more easily by using Table 4. We look down the 5 percent column until we reach three periods and find the factor 2.723. This factor, when multiplied by \$1, gives the present value of a series of three \$1 payments (spaced one year apart) at compound interest of 5 percent. Thus, we solve the problem as shown below.

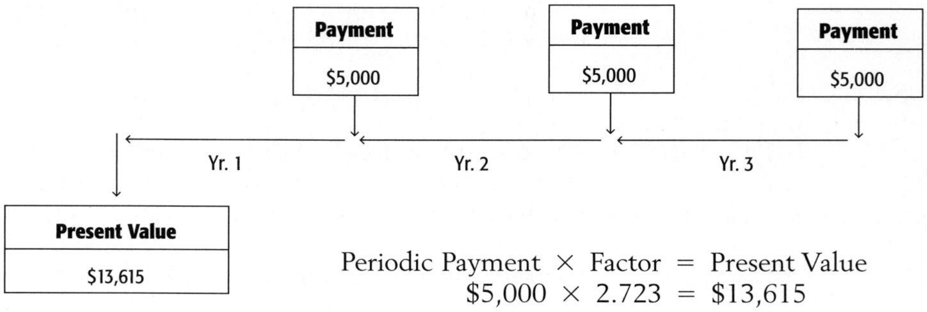

$$\text{Periodic Payment} \times \text{Factor} = \text{Present Value}$$
$$\$5{,}000 \times 2.723 = \$13{,}615$$

This result is the same as the one computed earlier.

Time Periods

In all of the previous examples, and in most other cases, the compounding period is one year, and the interest rate is stated on an annual basis. However, in each of the four tables, the left-hand column refers not to years but to periods. This wording is intended to accommodate compounding periods of less than one year. Savings accounts that record interest quarterly and bonds that pay interest semiannually are cases in which the compounding period is less than one year. To use the tables in such cases, it is necessary to (1) divide the annual interest rate by the number of periods in the year, and (2) multiply the number of periods in one year by the number of years.

For example, assume that a \$6,000 note is to be paid in two years and carries an annual interest rate of 8 percent. Compute the maturity (future) value of the note, assuming that the compounding period is semiannual. Before using the table, it is

Table 4. Present Value of an Ordinary Annuity of \$1 Received Each Period for a Given Number of Time Periods

Periods	1%	2%	3%	4%	5%	6%	7%	8%	9%	10%
1	0.990	0.980	0.971	0.962	0.952	0.943	0.935	0.926	0.917	0.909
2	1.970	1.942	1.913	1.886	1.859	1.833	1.808	1.783	1.759	1.736
3	2.941	2.884	2.829	2.775	2.723	2.673	2.624	2.577	2.531	2.487
4	3.902	3.808	3.717	3.630	3.546	3.465	3.387	3.312	3.240	3.170
5	4.853	4.713	4.580	4.452	4.329	4.212	4.100	3.993	3.890	3.791
6	5.795	5.601	5.417	5.242	5.076	4.917	4.767	4.623	4.486	4.355
7	6.728	6.472	6.230	6.002	5.786	5.582	5.389	5.206	5.033	4.868
8	7.652	7.325	7.020	6.733	6.463	6.210	5.971	5.747	5.535	5.335
9	8.566	8.162	7.786	7.435	7.108	6.802	6.515	6.247	5.995	5.759
10	9.471	8.983	8.530	8.111	7.722	7.360	7.024	6.710	6.418	6.145

Source: **Excerpt from Table 4 in the appendix on future value and present value tables.**

necessary to compute the interest rate that applies to each compounding period and the total number of compounding periods. First, the interest rate to use is 4 percent (8% annual rate ÷ 2 periods per year). Second, the total number of compounding periods is 4 (2 periods per year × 2 years). From Table 1, therefore, the maturity value of the note is computed as follows:

Principal	×	Factor	=	Future Value
$6,000	×	1.170	=	$7,020

The note will be worth $7,020 in two years.

This procedure for determining the interest rate and the number of periods when the compounding period is less than one year may be used with all four tables.

APPLICATIONS OF PRESENT VALUE TO ACCOUNTING

The concept of present value is widely applicable in the discipline of accounting. Here, the purpose is to demonstrate its usefulness in some simple applications. In-depth study of present value is deferred to more advanced courses.

IMPUTING INTEREST ON NON-INTEREST-BEARING NOTES Clearly there is no such thing as an interest-free debt, regardless of whether the interest rate is explicitly stated. The Accounting Principles Board has declared that when a long-term note does not explicitly state an interest rate (or if the interest rate is unreasonably low), a rate based on the normal interest cost of the company in question should be assigned, or imputed.[1]

The following example applies this principle. On January 1, 20x0, Gato purchased merchandise from Haines by issuing an $8,000 non-interest-bearing note due in two years. Gato can borrow money from the bank at 9 percent interest. Gato paid the note in full after two years.

Note that the $8,000 note represents partly a payment for merchandise and partly a payment of interest for two years. In recording the purchase and sale, it is necessary to use Table 3 to determine the present value of the note. The calculation follows.

Future Payment	×	Present Value Factor (9%, 2 years)	=	Present Value
$8,000	×	.842	=	$6,736

The imputed interest cost is $1,264 ($8,000 − $6,736) and is recorded as a discount on notes payable in Gato's records and as a discount on notes receivable in Haines's records.

The entries necessary to record the purchase in the Gato records and the sale in the Haines records are as follows:

Gato Journal

A = L + OE	Account	Debit	Credit
− −	Purchases	6,736	
+	Discount on Notes Payable	1,264	
	Notes Payable		8,000

Haines Journal

Account	Debit	Credit	A = L + OE
Notes Receivable	8,000		+ +
Discount on Notes Receivable		1,264	−
Sales		6,736	

On December 31, 20x0, the adjustments to recognize the interest expense and interest income are as follows:

Gato Journal

A = L + OE	Account	Debit	Credit
+ −	Interest Expense	606.24	
	Discount on Notes Payable		606.24

Haines Journal

Account	Debit	Credit	A = L + OE
Discount on Notes Receivable	606.24		+ +
Interest Income		606.24	

The interest is calculated by multiplying the amount of the original purchase by the interest rate for one year ($6,736.00 × .09 = $606.24). When payment is made on December 31, 20x0, the following entries are made in the respective journals.

Gato Journal

A = L + OE	Account	Debit	Credit
− + −	Interest Expense	657.76	
−	Notes Payable	8,000.00	
	Discount on Notes Payable		657.76
	Cash		8,000.00

Haines Journal

Account	Debit	Credit	A = L + OE
Discount on Notes Receivable	657.76		+ +
Cash	8,000.00		+
Interest Income		657.76	−
Notes Receivable		8,000.00	

The interest entries represent the remaining interest to be expensed or realized ($1,264 − $606.24 = $657.76). This amount approximates (because of rounding differences in the table) the interest for one year on the purchase plus last year's interest [($6,736 + $606.24) × .09 = $660.80].

■ **VALUING AN ASSET** An asset is recorded because it will provide future benefits to the company that owns it. These future benefits are the basis for the definition of an asset. Usually, the purchase price of the asset represents the present value of these future benefits. It is possible to evaluate a proposed purchase price for an asset by comparing that price with the present value of the asset to the company.

For example, Sam Hurst is thinking of buying a new machine that will reduce his annual labor cost by $700 per year. The machine will last eight years. The interest rate that Hurst assumes for making managerial decisions is 10 percent. What is the maximum amount (present value) that Hurst should pay for the machine?

The present value of the machine to Hurst is equal to the present value of an ordinary annuity of $700 per year for eight years at compound interest of 10 percent. Using the factor from Table 4, we compute the value as follows:

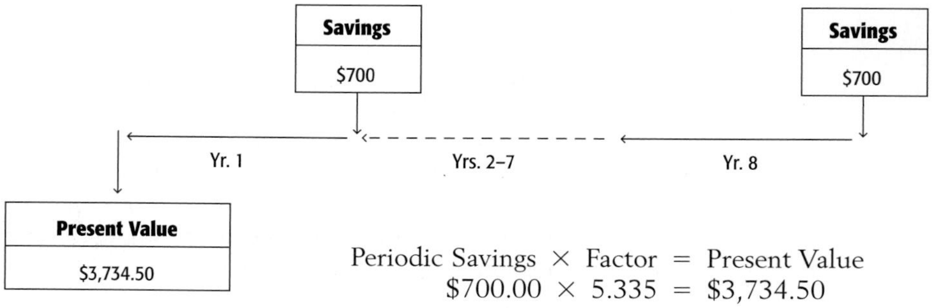

Periodic Savings	×	Factor	=	Present Value
$700.00	×	5.335	=	$3,734.50

Hurst should not pay more than $3,734.50 for the new machine because this amount equals the present value of the benefits that will be received from owning the machine.

■ **DEFERRED PAYMENT** A seller will sometimes agree to defer payment for a sale in order to encourage the buyer to make the purchase. This practice is common, for example, in the farm implement industry, where the farmer needs the equipment in the spring but cannot pay for it until the fall crop is in. Assume that Plains Implement Corporation sells a tractor to Dana Washington for $50,000 on February 1, agreeing to take payment ten months later, on December 1. When this type of agreement is made, the future payment includes not only the sales price of the tractor but also an implied (imputed) interest cost. If the prevailing annual interest rate for such transactions is 12 percent compounded monthly, the actual sale (purchase) price of the tractor would be the present value of the future payment, computed using the factor from Table 3 (10 periods, 1 percent), as follows:

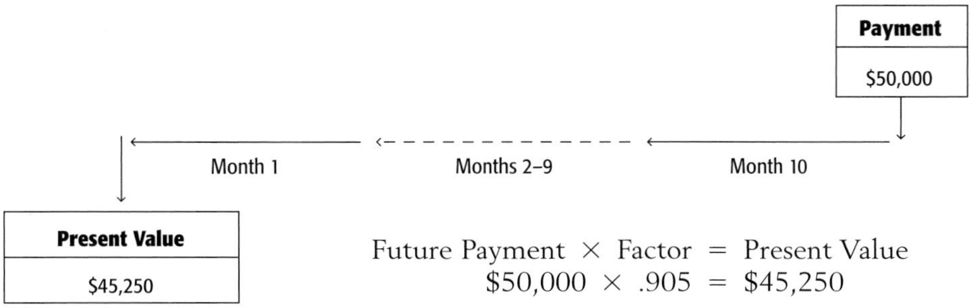

Future Payment	×	Factor	=	Present Value
$50,000	×	.905	=	$45,250

The present value, $45,250, is recorded in Washington's purchase records and in Plains's sale records. The balance consists of interest income. Washington records the purchase and Plains records the sale using the following entries:

A = L + OE	Washington Journal				Plains Journal			A = L + OE
+ +	Feb. 1	Tractor Accounts Payable Purchased tractor	45,250	 45,250	Accounts Receivable Sales Sold tractor	45,250	 45,250	 + +

When Washington pays for the tractor, the entries are as follows:

A = L + OE	Washington Journal				Plains Journal			A = L + OE
− − −	Dec. 1	Accounts Payable Interest Expense Cash Paid on account, including imputed interest expense	45,250 4,750	 50,000	Cash Accounts Receivable Interest Income Received on account from Washington, including imputed interest earned	50,000	 45,250 4,750	 − + +

■ **INVESTMENT OF IDLE CASH** Childware Corporation, a toy manufacturer, has just completed a successful selling season and has $10,000,000 in cash to invest for six months. The company places the cash in a money market account expected to pay 12 percent annual interest. Interest is compounded and credited to the company's account monthly. How much cash will the company have at the end of six months, and what entries will be made to record the investment and the monthly interest? The future value factor from Table 1 is based on six monthly periods of 1 percent (12 percent divided by 12 months), and the future value is computed as follows:

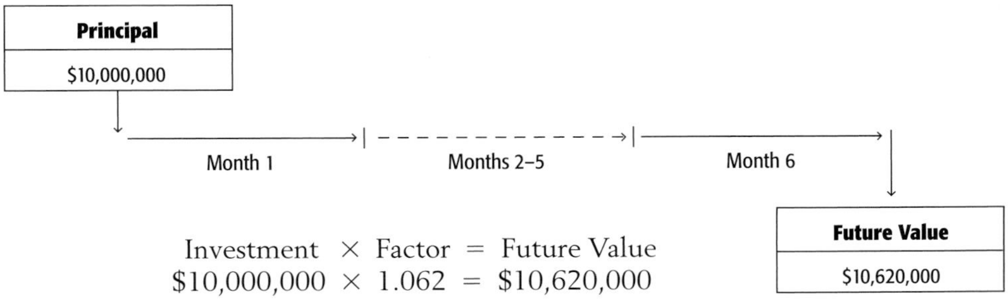

Investment	×	Factor	=	Future Value
$10,000,000	×	1.062	=	$10,620,000

When the investment is made, the following entry is made:

A = L + OE	Short-Term Investments	10,000,000	
+	Cash		10,000,000
−	Made investment of cash		

After the first month, the interest is recorded by increasing the Short-Term Investments account.

A = L + OE	Short-Term Investments	100,000	
+ +	Interest Income		100,000
	Earned one month's interest income		
	$10,000,000 × .01 = $100,000		

After the second month, the interest is earned on the new balance of the Short-Term Investments account.

A = L + OE	Short-Term Investments	101,000	
+ +	Interest Income		101,000
	Earned one month's interest income		
	$10,100,000 × .01 = $101,000		

Entries would continue in a similar manner for four more months, at which time the balance of Short-Term Investments would be about $10,620,000. The actual amount accumulated may vary from this total because the interest rate paid on money market accounts can vary over time as a result of changes in market conditions.

■ ACCUMULATION OF A FUND When a company owes a large fixed amount due in several years, management would be wise to accumulate a fund with which to pay off the debt at maturity. Sometimes creditors, when they agree to provide a loan, require that such a fund be established. In establishing the fund, management must determine how much cash to set aside each period in order to pay the debt. The amount will depend on the estimated rate of interest the investments will earn. Assume that Vason Corporation agrees with a creditor to set aside cash at the end of each year to accumulate enough to pay off a $100,000 note due in five years. Since the first contribution to the fund will be made in one year, five annual contributions will be made by the time the note is due. Assume also that the fund is projected to earn 8 percent, compounded annually. The amount of each annual payment is calculated using Table 2 (5 periods, 8 percent), as follows:

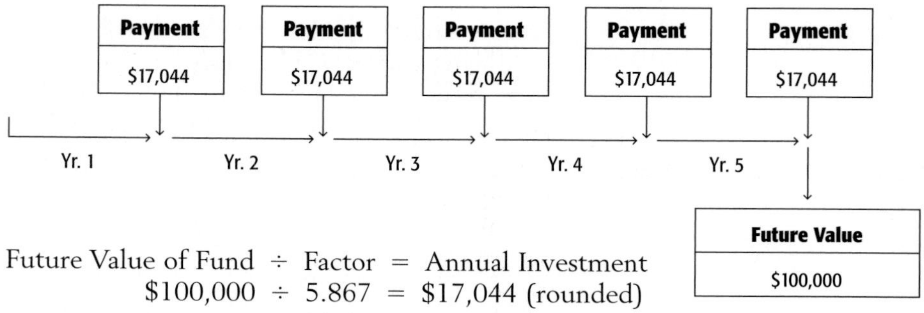

Future Value of Fund ÷ Factor = Annual Investment
$100,000 ÷ 5.867 = $17,044 (rounded)

Each year's contribution to the fund is $17,044, which is recorded as follows:

A = L + OE	Loan Repayment Fund	17,044	
+	Cash		17,044
−	Recorded annual contribution to loan repayment fund		

Other Accounting Applications There are many other applications of present value in accounting, including accounting for installment notes, valuing a bond, and recording lease obligations. Present value is also applied in such areas as pension obligations; premium and discount on debt; depreciation of property, plant, and equipment; capital expenditure decisions; and generally any problem in which time is a factor.

Exercises

Tables 1 to 4 in the appendix on future value and present value tables may be used where appropriate to solve these exercises.

Future Value Calculations

E 1. Wieland receives a one-year note for $3,000 that carries a 12 percent annual interest rate for the sale of a used car.

Compute the maturity value under each of the following assumptions: (1) The interest is simple interest. (2) The interest is compounded semiannually. (3) The interest is compounded quarterly. (4) The interest is compounded monthly.

Future Value Calculations

E 2. Find the future value of (1) a single payment of $20,000 at 7 percent for ten years, (2) ten annual payments of $2,000 at 7 percent, (3) a single payment of $6,000 at 9 percent for seven years, and (4) seven annual payments of $6,000 at 9 percent.

Future Value Calculations

E 3. Assume that $40,000 is invested today. Compute the amount that would accumulate at the end of seven years when the interest rate is (1) 8 percent compounded annually, (2) 8 percent compounded semiannually, and (3) 8 percent compounded quarterly.

Future Value Calculations

E 4. Calculate the accumulation of periodic payments of $1,000 made at the end of each of four years, assuming (1) 10 percent annual interest compounded annually, (2) 10 percent annual interest compounded semiannually, (3) 4 percent annual interest compounded annually, and (4) 16 percent annual interest compounded quarterly.

Future Value Applications

E 5.
a. Two parents have $20,000 to invest for their child's college tuition, which they estimate will cost $40,000 when the child enters college twelve years from now.

   Calculate the approximate rate of annual interest that the investment must earn to reach the $40,000 goal in twelve years. (**Hint:** Make a calculation; then use Table 1 in the appendix on future value and present value tables.)
b. Ted Pruitt is saving to purchase a summer home that will cost about $64,000. He has $40,000 now, on which he can earn 7 percent annual interest.

   Calculate the approximate length of time he will have to wait to purchase the summer home. (**Hint:** Make a calculation; then use Table 1 in the appendix on future value and present value tables.)

Working Backward from a Future Value

E 6. Gloria Faraquez has a debt of $90,000 due in four years. She wants to save enough money to pay it off by making annual deposits in an investment account that earns 8 percent annual interest.

Calculate the amount she must deposit each year to reach her goal. (**Hint:** Use Table 2 in the appendix on future value and present value tables; then make a calculation.)

Determining an Advance Payment

E 7. Ellen Saber is contemplating paying five years' rent in advance. Her annual rent is $9,600.

Calculate the single sum that would have to be paid now for the advance rent, if we assume compound interest of 8 percent.

E 8. Present Value Calculations

Find the present value of (1) a single payment of $24,000 at 6 percent for twelve years, (2) twelve annual payments of $2,000 at 6 percent, (3) a single payment of $5,000 at 9 percent for five years, and (4) five annual payments of $5,000 at 9 percent.

E 9. Present Value of a Lump-Sum Contract

A contract calls for a lump-sum payment of $60,000. Find the present value of the contract, assuming that (1) the payment is due in five years, and the current interest rate is 9 percent; (2) the payment is due in ten years, and the current interest rate is 9 percent; (3) the payment is due in five years, and the current interest rate is 5 percent; and (4) the payment is due in ten years, and the current interest rate is 5 percent.

E 10. Present Value of an Annuity Contract

A contract calls for annual payments of $1,200. Find the present value of the contract, assuming that (1) the number of payments is seven, and the current interest rate is 6 percent; (2) the number of payments is fourteen, and the current interest rate is 6 percent; (3) the number of payments is seven, and the current interest rate is 8 percent; and (4) the number of payments is fourteen, and the current interest rate is 8 percent.

E 11. Non-Interest-Bearing Note

On January 1, 20x0, Pendleton purchased a machine from Leyland by signing a two-year, non-interest-bearing $32,000 note. Pendleton currently pays 12 percent interest to borrow money at the bank.

Prepare entries in Pendleton's and Leyland's journals to (1) record the purchase and the note, (2) adjust the accounts after one year, and (3) record payment of the note after two years (on December 31, 20x2).

E 12. Valuing an Asset for the Purpose of Making a Purchasing Decision

Oscaro owns a service station and has the opportunity to purchase a car wash machine for $30,000. After carefully studying projected costs and revenues, Oscaro estimates that the car wash machine will produce a net cash flow of $5,200 annually and will last for eight years. Oscaro believes that an interest rate of 14 percent is adequate for his business.

Calculate the present value of the machine to Oscaro. Does the purchase appear to be a correct business decision?

E 13. Deferred Payment

Johnson Equipment Corporation sold a precision tool machine with computer controls to Borst Corporation for $800,000 on January 1, agreeing to take payment nine months later, on October 1. Assuming that the prevailing annual interest rate for such a transaction is 16 percent compounded quarterly, what is the actual sale (purchase) price of the machine tool, and what journal entries will be made at the time of the purchase (sale) and at the time of the payment (receipt) on the records of both Borst and Johnson?

E 14. Investment of Idle Cash

Scientific Publishing Company, a publisher of college books, has just completed a successful fall selling season and has $5,000,000 in cash to invest for nine months, beginning on January 1. The company placed the cash in a money market account that is expected to pay 12 percent annual interest compounded monthly. Interest is credited to the company's account each month. How much cash will the company have at the end of nine months, and what entries are made to record the investment and the first two monthly (February 1 and March 1) interest amounts?

E 15. Accumulation of a Fund

Laferia Corporation borrowed $3,000,000 from an insurance company on a five-year note. Management agreed to set aside enough cash at the end of each year to accumulate the amount needed to pay off the note at maturity. Since the first contribution to the fund will be made in one year, four annual contributions are needed. Assuming that the fund will earn 10 percent compounded annually, how much will the annual contribution to the fund be (round to nearest dollar), and what will be the journal entry for the first contribution?

E 16.
Negotiating the Sale of a Business

Horace Raftson is attempting to sell his business to Ernando Ruiz. The company has assets of $900,000, liabilities of $800,000, and owner's equity of $100,000. Both parties agree that the proper rate of return to expect is 12 percent; however, they differ on other assumptions. Raftson believes that the business will generate at least $100,000 per year of cash flows for twenty years. Ruiz thinks that $80,000 in cash flows per year is more reasonable and that only ten years in the future should be considered. Using Table 4 in the appendix on future value and present value tables, determine the range for negotiation by computing the present value of Raftson's offer to sell and of Ruiz's offer to buy.

Appendix D

Future Value and Present Value Tables

Table 1 provides the multipliers necessary to compute the future value of a *single* cash deposit made at the *beginning* of year 1. Three factors must be known before the future value can be computed: (1) the time period in years, (2) the stated annual rate of interest to be earned, and (3) the dollar amount invested or deposited.

■ **EXAMPLE—TABLE 1** Determine the future value of $5,000 deposited now that will earn 9 percent interest compounded annually for five years. From Table 1, the necessary multiplier for five years at 9 percent is 1.539, and the answer is

$$\$5{,}000 \times 1.539 = \$7{,}695$$

TABLE 1. Future Value of $1 After a Given Number of Time Periods

Periods	1%	2%	3%	4%	5%	6%	7%	8%	9%	10%	12%	14%	15%
1	1.010	1.020	1.030	1.040	1.050	1.060	1.070	1.080	1.090	1.100	1.120	1.140	1.150
2	1.020	1.040	1.061	1.082	1.103	1.124	1.145	1.166	1.188	1.210	1.254	1.300	1.323
3	1.030	1.061	1.093	1.125	1.158	1.191	1.225	1.260	1.295	1.331	1.405	1.482	1.521
4	1.041	1.082	1.126	1.170	1.216	1.262	1.311	1.360	1.412	1.464	1.574	1.689	1.749
5	1.051	1.104	1.159	1.217	1.276	1.338	1.403	1.469	1.539	1.611	1.762	1.925	2.011
6	1.062	1.126	1.194	1.265	1.340	1.419	1.501	1.587	1.677	1.772	1.974	2.195	2.313
7	1.072	1.149	1.230	1.316	1.407	1.504	1.606	1.714	1.828	1.949	2.211	2.502	2.660
8	1.083	1.172	1.267	1.369	1.477	1.594	1.718	1.851	1.993	2.144	2.476	2.853	3.059
9	1.094	1.195	1.305	1.423	1.551	1.689	1.838	1.999	2.172	2.358	2.773	3.252	3.518
10	1.105	1.219	1.344	1.480	1.629	1.791	1.967	2.159	2.367	2.594	3.106	3.707	4.046
11	1.116	1.243	1.384	1.539	1.710	1.898	2.105	2.332	2.580	2.853	3.479	4.226	4.652
12	1.127	1.268	1.426	1.601	1.796	2.012	2.252	2.518	2.813	3.138	3.896	4.818	5.350
13	1.138	1.294	1.469	1.665	1.886	2.133	2.410	2.720	3.066	3.452	4.363	5.492	6.153
14	1.149	1.319	1.513	1.732	1.980	2.261	2.579	2.937	3.342	3.798	4.887	6.261	7.076
15	1.161	1.346	1.558	1.801	2.079	2.397	2.759	3.172	3.642	4.177	5.474	7.138	8.137
16	1.173	1.373	1.605	1.873	2.183	2.540	2.952	3.426	3.970	4.595	6.130	8.137	9.358
17	1.184	1.400	1.653	1.948	2.292	2.693	3.159	3.700	4.328	5.054	6.866	9.276	10.760
18	1.196	1.428	1.702	2.026	2.407	2.854	3.380	3.996	4.717	5.560	7.690	10.580	12.380
19	1.208	1.457	1.754	2.107	2.527	3.026	3.617	4.316	5.142	6.116	8.613	12.060	14.230
20	1.220	1.486	1.806	2.191	2.653	3.207	3.870	4.661	5.604	6.728	9.646	13.740	16.370
21	1.232	1.516	1.860	2.279	2.786	3.400	4.141	5.034	6.109	7.400	10.800	15.670	18.820
22	1.245	1.546	1.916	2.370	2.925	3.604	4.430	5.437	6.659	8.140	12.100	17.860	21.640
23	1.257	1.577	1.974	2.465	3.072	3.820	4.741	5.871	7.258	8.954	13.550	20.360	24.890
24	1.270	1.608	2.033	2.563	3.225	4.049	5.072	6.341	7.911	9.850	15.180	23.210	28.630
25	1.282	1.641	2.094	2.666	3.386	4.292	5.427	6.848	8.623	10.830	17.000	26.460	32.920
26	1.295	1.673	2.157	2.772	3.556	4.549	5.807	7.396	9.399	11.920	19.040	30.170	37.860
27	1.308	1.707	2.221	2.883	3.733	4.822	6.214	7.988	10.250	13.110	21.320	34.390	43.540
28	1.321	1.741	2.288	2.999	3.920	5.112	6.649	8.627	11.170	14.420	23.880	39.200	50.070
29	1.335	1.776	2.357	3.119	4.116	5.418	7.114	9.317	12.170	15.860	26.750	44.690	57.580
30	1.348	1.811	2.427	3.243	4.322	5.743	7.612	10.060	13.270	17.450	29.960	50.950	66.210
40	1.489	2.208	3.262	4.801	7.040	10.290	14.970	21.720	31.410	45.260	93.050	188.900	267.900
50	1.645	2.692	4.384	7.107	11.470	18.420	29.460	46.900	74.360	117.400	289.000	700.200	1,084.000

Where r is the interest rate and n is the number of periods, the factor values for Table 1 are

$$\text{FV Factor} = (1 + r)^n$$

Situations requiring the use of Table 2 are similar to those requiring Table 1 except that Table 2 is used to compute the future value of a *series* of *equal* annual deposits at the end of each period.

■ **EXAMPLE—TABLE 2** What will be the future value at the end of 30 years if $1,000 is deposited each year on January 1, beginning in one year, assuming 12 percent interest compounded annually? The required multiplier from Table 2 is 241.3, and the answer is

$$\$1{,}000 \times 241.3 = \$241{,}300$$

The factor values for Table 2 are

$$\text{FVa Factor} = \frac{(1 + r)^n - 1}{r}$$

TABLE 2. Future Value of $1 Paid in Each Period for a Given Number of Time Periods

Periods	1%	2%	3%	4%	5%	6%	7%	8%	9%	10%	12%	14%	15%
1	1.000	1.000	1.000	1.000	1.000	1.000	1.000	1.000	1.000	1.000	1.000	1.000	1.000
2	2.010	2.020	2.030	2.040	2.050	2.060	2.070	2.080	2.090	2.100	2.120	2.140	2.150
3	3.030	3.060	3.091	3.122	3.153	3.184	3.215	3.246	3.278	3.310	3.374	3.440	3.473
4	4.060	4.122	4.184	4.246	4.310	4.375	4.440	4.506	4.573	4.641	4.779	4.921	4.993
5	5.101	5.204	5.309	5.416	5.526	5.637	5.751	5.867	5.985	6.105	6.353	6.610	6.742
6	6.152	6.308	6.468	6.633	6.802	6.975	7.153	7.336	7.523	7.716	8.115	8.536	8.754
7	7.214	7.434	7.662	7.898	8.142	8.394	8.654	8.923	9.200	9.487	10.090	10.730	11.070
8	8.286	8.583	8.892	9.214	9.549	9.897	10.260	10.640	11.030	11.440	12.300	13.230	13.730
9	9.369	9.755	10.160	10.580	11.030	11.490	11.980	12.490	13.020	13.580	14.780	16.090	16.790
10	10.460	10.950	11.460	12.010	12.580	13.180	13.820	14.490	15.190	15.940	17.550	19.340	20.300
11	11.570	12.170	12.810	13.490	14.210	14.970	15.780	16.650	17.560	18.530	20.650	23.040	24.350
12	12.680	13.410	14.190	15.030	15.920	16.870	17.890	18.980	20.140	21.380	24.130	27.270	29.000
13	13.810	14.680	15.620	16.630	17.710	18.880	20.140	21.500	22.950	24.520	28.030	32.090	34.350
14	14.950	15.970	17.090	18.290	19.600	21.020	22.550	24.210	26.020	27.980	32.390	37.580	40.500
15	16.100	17.290	18.600	20.020	21.580	23.280	25.130	27.150	29.360	31.770	37.280	43.840	47.580
16	17.260	18.640	20.160	21.820	23.660	25.670	27.890	30.320	33.000	35.950	42.750	50.980	55.720
17	18.430	20.010	21.760	23.700	25.840	28.210	30.840	33.750	36.970	40.540	48.880	59.120	65.080
18	19.610	21.410	23.410	25.650	28.130	30.910	34.000	37.450	41.300	45.600	55.750	68.390	75.840
19	20.810	22.840	25.120	27.670	30.540	33.760	37.380	41.450	46.020	51.160	63.440	78.970	88.210
20	22.020	24.300	26.870	29.780	33.070	36.790	41.000	45.760	51.160	57.280	72.050	91.020	102.400
21	23.240	25.780	28.680	31.970	35.720	39.990	44.870	50.420	56.760	64.000	81.700	104.800	118.800
22	24.470	27.300	30.540	34.250	38.510	43.390	49.010	55.460	62.870	71.400	92.500	120.400	137.600
23	25.720	28.850	32.450	36.620	41.430	47.000	53.440	60.890	69.530	79.540	104.600	138.300	159.300
24	26.970	30.420	34.430	39.080	44.500	50.820	58.180	66.760	76.790	88.500	118.200	158.700	184.200
25	28.240	32.030	36.460	41.650	47.730	54.860	63.250	73.110	84.700	98.350	133.300	181.900	212.800
26	29.530	33.670	38.550	44.310	51.110	59.160	68.680	79.950	93.320	109.200	150.300	208.300	245.700
27	30.820	35.340	40.710	47.080	54.670	63.710	74.480	87.350	102.700	121.100	169.400	238.500	283.600
28	32.130	37.050	42.930	49.970	58.400	68.530	80.700	95.340	113.000	134.200	190.700	272.900	327.100
29	33.450	38.790	45.220	52.970	62.320	73.640	87.350	104.000	124.100	148.600	214.600	312.100	377.200
30	34.780	40.570	47.580	56.080	66.440	79.060	94.460	113.300	136.300	164.500	241.300	356.800	434.700
40	48.890	60.400	75.400	95.030	120.800	154.800	199.600	259.100	337.900	442.600	767.100	1,342.000	1,779.000
50	64.460	84.580	112.800	152.700	209.300	290.300	406.500	573.800	815.100	1,164.000	2,400.000	4,995.000	7,218.000

TABLE 3. Present Value of $1 to Be Received at the End of a Given Number of Time Periods

Periods	1%	2%	3%	4%	5%	6%	7%	8%	9%	10%	12%
1	0.990	0.980	0.971	0.962	0.952	0.943	0.935	0.926	0.917	0.909	0.893
2	0.980	0.961	0.943	0.925	0.907	0.890	0.873	0.857	0.842	0.826	0.797
3	0.971	0.942	0.915	0.889	0.864	0.840	0.816	0.794	0.772	0.751	0.712
4	0.961	0.924	0.888	0.855	0.823	0.792	0.763	0.735	0.708	0.683	0.636
5	0.951	0.906	0.883	0.822	0.784	0.747	0.713	0.681	0.650	0.621	0.567
6	0.942	0.888	0.837	0.790	0.746	0.705	0.666	0.630	0.596	0.564	0.507
7	0.933	0.871	0.813	0.760	0.711	0.665	0.623	0.583	0.547	0.513	0.452
8	0.923	0.853	0.789	0.731	0.677	0.627	0.582	0.540	0.502	0.467	0.404
9	0.914	0.837	0.766	0.703	0.645	0.592	0.544	0.500	0.460	0.424	0.361
10	0.905	0.820	0.744	0.676	0.614	0.558	0.508	0.463	0.422	0.386	0.322
11	0.896	0.804	0.722	0.650	0.585	0.527	0.475	0.429	0.388	0.350	0.287
12	0.887	0.788	0.701	0.625	0.557	0.497	0.444	0.397	0.356	0.319	0.257
13	0.879	0.773	0.681	0.601	0.530	0.469	0.415	0.368	0.326	0.290	0.229
14	0.870	0.758	0.661	0.577	0.505	0.442	0.388	0.340	0.299	0.263	0.205
15	0.861	0.743	0.642	0.555	0.481	0.417	0.362	0.315	0.275	0.239	0.183
16	0.853	0.728	0.623	0.534	0.458	0.394	0.339	0.292	0.252	0.218	0.163
17	0.844	0.714	0.605	0.513	0.436	0.371	0.317	0.270	0.231	0.198	0.146
18	0.836	0.700	0.587	0.494	0.416	0.350	0.296	0.250	0.212	0.180	0.130
19	0.828	0.686	0.570	0.475	0.396	0.331	0.277	0.232	0.194	0.164	0.116
20	0.820	0.673	0.554	0.456	0.377	0.312	0.258	0.215	0.178	0.149	0.104
21	0.811	0.660	0.538	0.439	0.359	0.294	0.242	0.199	0.164	0.135	0.093
22	0.803	0.647	0.522	0.422	0.342	0.278	0.226	0.184	0.150	0.123	0.083
23	0.795	0.634	0.507	0.406	0.326	0.262	0.211	0.170	0.138	0.112	0.074
24	0.788	0.622	0.492	0.390	0.310	0.247	0.197	0.158	0.126	0.102	0.066
25	0.780	0.610	0.478	0.375	0.295	0.233	0.184	0.146	0.116	0.092	0.059
26	0.772	0.598	0.464	0.361	0.281	0.220	0.172	0.135	0.106	0.084	0.053
27	0.764	0.586	0.450	0.347	0.268	0.207	0.161	0.125	0.098	0.076	0.047
28	0.757	0.574	0.437	0.333	0.255	0.196	0.150	0.116	0.090	0.069	0.042
29	0.749	0.563	0.424	0.321	0.243	0.185	0.141	0.107	0.082	0.063	0.037
30	0.742	0.552	0.412	0.308	0.231	0.174	0.131	0.099	0.075	0.057	0.033
40	0.672	0.453	0.307	0.208	0.142	0.097	0.067	0.046	0.032	0.022	0.011
50	0.608	0.372	0.228	0.141	0.087	0.054	0.034	0.021	0.013	0.009	0.003

Table 3 is used to compute the value today of a single amount of cash to be received sometime in the future. To use Table 3, you must first know: (1) the time period in years until funds will be received, (2) the stated annual rate of interest, and (3) the dollar amount to be received at the end of the time period.

■ **EXAMPLE—TABLE 3** What is the present value of $30,000 to be received 25 years from now, assuming a 14 percent interest rate? From Table 3, the required multiplier is .038, and the answer is

$$\$30{,}000 \times .038 = \$1{,}140$$

14%	15%	16%	18%	20%	25%	30%	35%	40%	45%	50%	Periods
0.877	0.870	0.862	0.847	0.833	0.800	0.769	0.741	0.714	0.690	0.667	1
0.769	0.756	0.743	0.718	0.694	0.640	0.592	0.549	0.510	0.476	0.444	2
0.675	0.658	0.641	0.609	0.579	0.512	0.455	0.406	0.364	0.328	0.296	3
0.592	0.572	0.552	0.516	0.482	0.410	0.350	0.301	0.260	0.226	0.198	4
0.519	0.497	0.476	0.437	0.402	0.328	0.269	0.223	0.186	0.156	0.132	5
0.456	0.432	0.410	0.370	0.335	0.262	0.207	0.165	0.133	0.108	0.088	6
0.400	0.376	0.354	0.314	0.279	0.210	0.159	0.122	0.095	0.074	0.059	7
0.351	0.327	0.305	0.266	0.233	0.168	0.123	0.091	0.068	0.051	0.039	8
0.308	0.284	0.263	0.225	0.194	0.134	0.094	0.067	0.048	0.035	0.026	9
0.270	0.247	0.227	0.191	0.162	0.107	0.073	0.050	0.035	0.024	0.017	10
0.237	0.215	0.195	0.162	0.135	0.086	0.056	0.037	0.025	0.017	0.012	11
0.208	0.187	0.168	0.137	0.112	0.069	0.043	0.027	0.018	0.012	0.008	12
0.182	0.163	0.145	0.116	0.093	0.055	0.033	0.020	0.013	0.008	0.005	13
0.160	0.141	0.125	0.099	0.078	0.044	0.025	0.015	0.009	0.006	0.003	14
0.140	0.123	0.108	0.084	0.065	0.035	0.020	0.011	0.006	0.004	0.002	15
0.123	0.107	0.093	0.071	0.054	0.028	0.015	0.008	0.005	0.003	0.002	16
0.108	0.093	0.080	0.060	0.045	0.023	0.012	0.006	0.003	0.002	0.001	17
0.095	0.081	0.069	0.051	0.038	0.018	0.009	0.005	0.002	0.001	0.001	18
0.083	0.070	0.060	0.043	0.031	0.014	0.007	0.003	0.002	0.001		19
0.073	0.061	0.051	0.037	0.026	0.012	0.005	0.002	0.001	0.001		20
0.064	0.053	0.044	0.031	0.022	0.009	0.004	0.002	0.001			21
0.056	0.046	0.038	0.026	0.018	0.007	0.003	0.001	0.001			22
0.049	0.040	0.033	0.022	0.015	0.006	0.002	0.001				23
0.043	0.035	0.028	0.019	0.013	0.005	0.002	0.001				24
0.038	0.030	0.024	0.016	0.010	0.004	0.001	0.001				25
0.033	0.026	0.021	0.014	0.009	0.003	0.001					26
0.029	0.023	0.018	0.011	0.007	0.002	0.001					27
0.026	0.020	0.016	0.010	0.006	0.002	0.001					28
0.022	0.017	0.014	0.008	0.005	0.002						29
0.020	0.015	0.012	0.007	0.004	0.001						30
0.005	0.004	0.003	0.001	0.001							40
0.001	0.001	0.001									50

The factor values for Table 3 are

$$\text{PV Factor} = (1 + r)^{-n}$$

Table 3 is the reciprocal of Table 1.

TABLE 4. Present Value of $1 Received Each Period for a Given Number of Time Periods

Periods	1%	2%	3%	4%	5%	6%	7%	8%	9%	10%	12%
1	0.990	0.980	0.971	0.962	0.952	0.943	0.935	0.926	0.917	0.909	0.893
2	1.970	1.942	1.913	1.886	1.859	1.833	1.808	1.783	1.759	1.736	1.690
3	2.941	2.884	2.829	2.775	2.723	2.673	2.624	2.577	2.531	2.487	2.402
4	3.902	3.808	3.717	3.630	3.546	3.465	3.387	3.312	3.240	3.170	3.037
5	4.853	4.713	4.580	4.452	4.329	4.212	4.100	3.993	3.890	3.791	3.605
6	5.795	5.601	5.417	5.242	5.076	4.917	4.767	4.623	4.486	4.355	4.111
7	6.728	6.472	6.230	6.002	5.786	5.582	5.389	5.206	5.033	4.868	4.564
8	7.652	7.325	7.020	6.733	6.463	6.210	5.971	5.747	5.535	5.335	4.968
9	8.566	8.162	7.786	7.435	7.108	6.802	6.515	6.247	5.995	5.759	5.328
10	9.471	8.983	8.530	8.111	7.722	7.360	7.024	6.710	6.418	6.145	5.650
11	10.368	9.787	9.253	8.760	8.306	7.887	7.499	7.139	6.805	6.495	5.938
12	11.255	10.575	9.954	9.385	8.863	8.384	7.943	7.536	7.161	6.814	6.194
13	12.134	11.348	10.635	9.986	9.394	8.853	8.358	7.904	7.487	7.103	6.424
14	13.004	12.106	11.296	10.563	9.899	9.295	8.745	8.244	7.786	7.367	6.628
15	13.865	12.849	11.938	11.118	10.380	9.712	9.108	8.559	8.061	7.606	6.811
16	14.718	13.578	12.561	11.652	10.838	10.106	9.447	8.851	8.313	7.824	6.974
17	15.562	14.292	13.166	12.166	11.274	10.477	9.763	9.122	8.544	8.022	7.120
18	16.398	14.992	13.754	12.659	11.690	10.828	10.059	9.372	8.756	8.201	7.250
19	17.226	15.678	14.324	13.134	12.085	11.158	10.336	9.604	8.950	8.365	7.366
20	18.046	16.351	14.878	13.590	12.462	11.470	10.594	9.818	9.129	8.514	7.469
21	18.857	17.011	15.415	14.029	12.821	11.764	10.836	10.017	9.292	8.649	7.562
22	19.660	17.658	15.937	14.451	13.163	12.042	11.061	10.201	9.442	8.772	7.645
23	20.456	18.292	16.444	14.857	13.489	12.303	11.272	10.371	9.580	8.883	7.718
24	21.243	18.914	16.936	15.247	13.799	12.550	11.469	10.529	9.707	8.985	7.784
25	22.023	19.523	17.413	15.622	14.094	12.783	11.654	10.675	9.823	9.077	7.843
26	22.795	20.121	17.877	15.983	14.375	13.003	11.826	10.810	9.929	9.161	7.896
27	23.560	20.707	18.327	16.330	14.643	13.211	11.987	10.935	10.027	9.237	7.943
28	24.316	21.281	18.764	16.663	14.898	13.406	12.137	11.051	10.116	9.307	7.984
29	25.066	21.844	19.189	16.984	15.141	13.591	12.278	11.158	10.198	9.370	8.022
30	25.808	22.396	19.600	17.292	15.373	13.765	12.409	11.258	10.274	9.427	8.055
40	32.835	27.355	23.115	19.793	17.159	15.046	13.332	11.925	10.757	9.779	8.244
50	39.196	31.424	25.730	21.482	18.256	15.762	13.801	12.234	10.962	9.915	8.305

Table 4 is used to compute the present value of a *series* of *equal* annual cash flows.

■ **EXAMPLE—TABLE 4** Arthur Howard won a contest on January 1, 2002, in which the prize was $30,000, the money was payable in 15 annual installments of $2,000 every December 31, beginning in 2002. Assuming a 9 percent interest rate, what is the present value of Mr. Howard's prize on January 1, 2002? From Table 4, the required multiplier is 8.061, and the answer is:

$$\$2{,}000 \times 8.061 = \$16{,}122$$

The factor values for Table 4 are

$$\text{PVa Factor} = \frac{1 - (1 + r)^{-n}}{r}$$

Table 4 is the columnar sum of Table 3. Table 4 applies to *ordinary annuities,* in which the first cash flow occurs one time period beyond the date for which the present value is to be computed.

14%	15%	16%	18%	20%	25%	30%	35%	40%	45%	50%	Periods
0.877	0.870	0.862	0.847	0.833	0.800	0.769	0.741	0.714	0.690	0.667	1
1.647	1.626	1.605	1.566	1.528	1.440	1.361	1.289	1.224	1.165	1.111	2
2.322	2.283	2.246	2.174	2.106	1.952	1.816	1.696	1.589	1.493	1.407	3
2.914	2.855	2.798	2.690	2.589	2.362	2.166	1.997	1.849	1.720	1.605	4
3.433	3.352	3.274	3.127	2.991	2.689	2.436	2.220	2.035	1.876	1.737	5
3.889	3.784	3.685	3.498	3.326	2.951	2.643	2.385	2.168	1.983	1.824	6
4.288	4.160	4.039	3.812	3.605	3.161	2.802	2.508	2.263	2.057	1.883	7
4.639	4.487	4.344	4.078	3.837	3.329	2.925	2.598	2.331	2.109	1.922	8
4.946	4.772	4.607	4.303	4.031	3.463	3.019	2.665	2.379	2.144	1.948	9
5.216	5.019	4.833	4.494	4.192	3.571	3.092	2.715	2.414	2.168	1.965	10
5.453	5.234	5.029	4.656	4.327	3.656	3.147	2.752	2.438	2.185	1.977	11
5.660	5.421	5.197	4.793	4.439	3.725	3.190	2.779	2.456	2.197	1.985	12
5.842	5.583	5.342	4.910	4.533	3.780	3.223	2.799	2.469	2.204	1.990	13
6.002	5.724	5.468	5.008	4.611	3.824	3.249	2.814	2.478	2.210	1.993	14
6.142	5.847	5.575	5.092	4.675	3.859	3.268	2.825	2.484	2.214	1.995	15
6.265	5.954	5.669	5.162	4.730	3.887	3.283	2.834	2.489	2.216	1.997	16
6.373	6.047	5.749	5.222	4.775	3.910	3.295	2.840	2.492	2.218	1.998	17
6.467	6.128	5.818	5.273	4.812	3.928	3.304	2.844	2.494	2.219	1.999	18
6.550	6.198	5.877	5.316	4.844	3.942	3.311	2.848	2.496	2.220	1.999	19
6.623	6.259	5.929	5.353	4.870	3.954	3.316	2.850	2.497	2.221	1.999	20
6.687	6.312	5.973	5.384	4.891	3.963	3.320	2.852	2.498	2.221	2.000	21
6.743	6.359	6.011	5.410	4.909	3.970	3.323	2.853	2.498	2.222	2.000	22
6.792	6.399	6.044	5.432	4.925	3.976	3.325	2.854	2.499	2.222	2.000	23
6.835	6.434	6.073	5.451	4.937	3.981	3.327	2.855	2.499	2.222	2.000	24
6.873	6.464	6.097	5.467	4.948	3.985	3.329	2.856	2.499	2.222	2.000	25
6.906	6.491	6.118	5.480	4.956	3.988	3.330	2.856	2.500	2.222	2.000	26
6.935	6.514	6.136	5.492	4.964	3.990	3.331	2.856	2.500	2.222	2.000	27
6.961	6.534	6.152	5.502	4.970	3.992	3.331	2.857	2.500	2.222	2.000	28
6.983	6.551	6.166	5.510	4.975	3.994	3.332	2.857	2.500	2.222	2.000	29
7.003	6.566	6.177	5.517	4.979	3.995	3.332	2.857	2.500	2.222	2.000	30
7.105	6.642	6.234	5.548	4.997	3.999	3.333	2.857	2.500	2.222	2.000	40
7.133	6.661	6.246	5.554	4.999	4.000	3.333	2.857	2.500	2.222	2.000	50

An *annuity due* is a series of equal cash flows for N time periods, but the first payment occurs immediately. The present value of the first payment equals the face value of the cash flow; Table 4 then is used to measure the present value of $N - 1$ remaining cash flows.

EXAMPLE—TABLE 4 Determine the present value on January 1, 2002, of 20 lease payments; each payment of $10,000 is due on January 1, beginning in 2002. Assume an interest rate of 8 percent.

$$\text{Present Value} = \text{Immediate Payment} + \begin{cases}\text{Present Value of 19 Subsequent} \\ \text{Payments at 8\%}\end{cases}$$

$$= \$10{,}000 + (\$10{,}000 \times 9.604) = \$106{,}040$$

Endnotes

Chapter 1

1. Walgreen Co., *Annual Report*, 2002.
2. *Statement of Financial Accounting Concepts No. 1*, "Objectives of Financial Reporting by Business Enterprises" (Norwalk, Conn.: Financial Accounting Standards Board, 1978), par. 9.
3. Ibid.
4. Christopher D. Ittner, David F. Larcker, and Madhav V. Rajan, "The Choice of Performance Measures in Annual Bonus Contracts," *The Accounting Review*, April 1997.
5. Walgreen Co., *Annual Report*, 2002.
6. Kathy Williams and James Hart, "Microsoft: Tooling the Information Age," *Management Accounting*, May 1996, p. 42.
7. *Statement of the Accounting Principles Board No. 4*, "Basic Concepts and Accounting Principles Underlying Financial Statements of Business Enterprises" (New York: American Institute of Certified Public Accountants, 1970), par. 138.
8. Touche Ross & Co., "Ethics in American Business" (New York: Touche Ross & Co., 1988), p. 7.
9. "Global Ethics Codes Gain Importance as a Tool to Avoid Litigation and Fines," *The Wall Street Journal*, August 19, 1999.
10. *Statement Number IC*, "Standards of Ethical Conduct for Management Accountants" (Montvale, N.J.: Institute of Management Accountants, 1983, revised 1997).
11. J.C. Penney Company, Inc., *Annual Report*, 1995.
12. Nikhil Deogun, "Coca-Cola Reports 27% Drop in Profits Hurt by Weakness in Foreign Markets," *The Wall Street Journal*, January 27, 1999.
13. Southwest Airlines Co., *Annual Report*, 1996.
14. Queen Sook Kim, "Lechters Inc. Files for Chapter 11, Arranges Financing," *The Wall Street Journal*, May 22, 2001.
15. Charles Schwab Corporation, *Annual Report*, 2001.
16. Robert Frank, "Facing a Loss, Lego Narrates a Sad Toy Story," *The Wall Street Journal*, January 22, 1999.

Chapter 2

1. "Boeing Scores a Deal to Sell 15 Planes for Long-Haul Routes," *The Wall Street Journal*, October 5, 2000.
2. The Boeing Co., *Annual Report*, 1994.
3. Craig S. Smith, "China Halts New Purchases of Jets," *The Wall Street Journal*, February 9, 1999.
4. The Boeing Co., *Annual Report*, 2000.
5. Patricia Kranz, "Rubles? Who Needs Rubles?" *BusinessWeek*, April 13, 1998; Andrew Higgins, "Lacking Money to Pay, Russian Firms Survive on Deft Barter System," *The Wall Street Journal*, August 27, 1998.
6. Intel Corp., *Annual Report*, 2002.
7. Shawn Young, "Lucent Revises Its Revenue Downward," *The Wall Street Journal*, December 22, 2000.
8. Nike, Inc., *Annual Report*, 2002.
9. Mellon Bank, *Annual Report*, 2000.
10. Ajinomoto Company, *Annual Report*, 2000.

Chapter 3

1. Kelly Services, *Annual Report*, 2002.
2. *Statement of Financial Accounting Concepts No. 1*, "Objectives of Financial Reporting by Business Enterprises" (Norwalk, Conn.: Financial Accounting Standards Board, 1978), par. 44.
3. Thomas J. Phillips Jr., Michael S. Luehlfing, and Cynthia M. Daily, "The Right Way to Recognize Revenue," *Journal of Accountancy*, June 2001.
4. "Revenue Recognition in Financial Statements," *Staff Accounting Bulletin No. 10* (Securities and Exchange Commission, 1999).
5. Michael Schroeder and Elizabeth MacDonald, "SEC Expects More Big Cases on Accounting," *The Wall Street Journal*, December 24, 1998.
6. PricewaterhouseCoopers presentation, 1999.
7. Lyric Opera of Chicago, *Annual Report*, 2001.
8. The Walt Disney Company, *Annual Report*, 2001.
9. H. J. Heinz Company, *Annual Report*, 2001.
10. Takashimaya Company, Limited, *Annual Report*, 2000.

Chapter 4

1. Dell Compter Corporation, *Annual Report*, 2002.
2. Adapted from H & R Block, Inc., *Annual Report*, 2002.
3. Nestlé S.A., *Annual Report*, 2000.

Chapter 5

1. Target, *Annual Report*, 2002.
2. Ibid.
3. "Shop Online—Pickup at the Store," *BusinessWeek*, June 12, 2000; Nick Wingfield, "As Web Sales Grow Mail-Order Sellers Are Benefiting the Most," *The Wall Street Journal*, May 2, 2001.
4. Joel Millman, "Here's What Happens to Many Lovely Gifts After Santa Rides Off," *The Wall Street Journal*, December 26, 2001.
5. Matthew Rose, "Magazine Revenue at Newsstands Falls in Worst Year Ever," *The Wall Street Journal*, May 15, 2001.
6. Matthew Schifrin, "The Big Squeeze," *Forbes*, March 11, 1996.
7. Wal-Mart Stores, Inc., *Annual Report*, 2000; Kmart Corp., *Annual Report*, 2000.

Chapter 6

1. General Mills, Inc., *Annual Report*, 2001.
2. "Objectives of Financial Reporting by Business Enterprises," *Statement of Financial Accounting Concepts No. 1* (Norwalk, Conn.: Financial Accounting Standards Board, 1978), pars. 32–54.
3. "Qualitative Characteristics of Accounting Information," *Statement of Financial Accounting Concepts No. 1* (Norwalk, Conn.: Financial Accounting Standards Board, 1980), par. 20.
4. Accounting Principles Board, "Accounting Changes," *Opinion No. 20* (New York: American Institute of Certified Public Accountants, 1971), par. 17.
5. Securities and Exchange Commission, *Staff Accounting Bulletin No. 99*, 1999.
6. Reynolds Metals Company, *Annual Report*, 1998.
7. Ray J. Groves, "Here's the Annual Report. Got a Few Hours?" *The Wall Street Journal Europe*, August 26–27, 1994.
8. Roger Lowenstein, "Investors Will Fish for Footnotes in 'Abbreviated' Annual Reports," *The Wall Street Journal*, September 14, 1995.
9. General Mills, *Annual Report*, 2001.
10. Ibid.
11. National Commission on Fraudulent Financial Reporting, *Report of the National Commission on Fraudulent Financial Reporting* (Washington, D.C., 1987), p. 2.
12. Arthur Levitt, "The Numbers Game," NYU Center for Law and Business, September 28, 1998.
13. "Ex-Chairman of Cendant Is Indicted," *The Wall Street Journal*, March 1, 2001; "SEC Sues Former Sunbeam Executive," *Chicago Tribune*, May 16, 2001; "Enron: A Wake-up Call," *The Wall Street*

Journal, December 4, 2001; "SEC List of Accounting-Fraud Probes Grows," *The Wall Street Journal*, July 6, 2001.
14. *Accounting Research and Terminology Bulletin*, final edition (New York: American Institute of Certified Public Accountants, 1961), p. 20.
15. "Debt vs. Equity: Whose Call Counts," *BusinessWeek*, July 19, 1999.
16. Roger Lowenstein, "The '20% Club' No Longer Is Exclusive," *The Wall Street Journal*, May 4, 1995.
17. "SEC Probes Lucent Accounting Practices," *The Wall Street Journal*, February 9, 2001.
18. Albertson's Inc., *Annual Report*, 2001; Great Atlantic & Pacific Tea Company, *Annual Report*, 2001.
19. GlaxoSmithKline PLC, *Annual Report*, 2000.
20. Toys "R" Us, *Annual Report*, 1987.

Chapter 7

1. Lee Copeland, "Donnelley Goes Dutch in Software Conversion," *Chicago Tribune*, June 3, 2002.
2. News item, *Crain's Chicago Business*, October 2001.
3. AICPA Press Release, Jan. 2, 2003
4. News item, *The Wall Street Journal*, July 29, 1999.
5. Michael Totty, "The Next Phase," *The Wall Street Journal*, May 21, 2001.
6. Frank Potter, "Event-to-Knowledge: A New Metric for Finance Department Efficiency," *Strategic Finance*, July 2001.
7. Walgreens, *Annual Report*, 1993.
8. Anthony Bianco, "Virtual Bookstores to Get Real," *BusinessWeek*, October 27,1997.

Chapter 8

1. Ron Winslow and George Anders, "How New Technology Was Oxford's Nemesis," *The Wall Street Journal*, December 11, 1997.
2. Circuit City Stores, *Annual Report*, 2001.
3. *Professional Standards*, vol. 1 (New York: American Institute of Certified Public Accountants, June 1, 1999), Sec. AU 322.07.
4. "1998 Fraud Survey," KPMG Peat Marwick, 1998.
5. *Professional Standards*, vol. 1, Sec. AU 325.16.
6. Lynette Khalfani, "Information-Destruction Finds Lucrative Business in Going to Waste," *The Wall Street Journal*, December 6, 1996.
7. "B-to-B Communities," *Business 2.0*, December 1999.
8. Amy Merrick, "Starbucks Accuses Employee, Husband of Embezzling $3.7 Million from Firm," *The Wall Street Journal*, November 20, 2000.

Chapter 9

1. Pioneer Corporation, *Annual Report*, 2001.
2. "So Much for Detroit's Cash Cushion," *BusinessWeek*, November 5, 2001.
3. Michael Selz, "Big Customers' Late Bills Choke Small Suppliers," *The Wall Street Journal*, June 22, 1994.
4. Pioneer Corporation, *Annual Report*, 2001.
5. Circuit City Stores, Inc., *Annual Report*, 2001.
6. Pioneer Corporation, *Annual Report*, 2001.
7. *Accounting Trends & Techniques* (New York: American Institute of CPAs, 2000), p. 130.
8. *Statement of Financial Accounting Standards No. 115*, "Accounting for Certain Investments in Debt and Equity Securities" (Norwalk, Conn.: Financial Accounting Standards Board, 1993).
9. Pioneer Corporation, *Annual Report*, 2001.
10. "Bad Loans Rattle Telecom Vendors," *BusinessWeek*, February 19, 2001.
11. Craig S. Smith, "Chinese Companies Writing Off Old Debt," *The Wall Street Journal*, December 28, 1995.
12. Information based on promotional brochures of Mitsubishi Electric Corp.
13. Elizabeth McDonald, "Unhatched Chickens," *Forbes*, February 19, 2001.
14. Philips Electronics N.V., *Annual Report*, 2001; Heineken N.V., *Annual Report*, 2001.

Chapter 10

1. J.C. Penney Company, Inc., *Annual Report*, 2002.
2. Illinois Tool Works, Inc., *Annual Report*, 2002.
3. American Institute of Certified Public Accountants, *Accounting Research Bulletin No. 43* (New York: AICPA, 1953), ch. 4.
4. Gary McWilliams, "Whirlwind on the Web," *BusinessWeek*, April 7, 1997.
5. Karen Lundebaard, "Bumpy Ride," *The Wall Street Journal*, May 21, 2001.
6. American Institute of Certified Public Accountants, *Accounting Research Bulletin No. 43* (New York: AICPA, 1953), ch. 4.
7. Micah Frankel and Robert Trezevant, "The Year-End LIFO Inventory Purchasing Decision: An Empirical Test," *The Accounting Review*, April 1994.
8. American Institute of Certified Public Accountants, *Accounting Trends & Techniques* (New York: AICPA, 2002).
9. "As Rite Aid Grew, CEO Seemed Unable to Manage His Empire," *The Wall Street Journal*, October 20, 1999; "RentWay Details Improper Bookkeeping," *The Wall Street Journal*, June 8, 2001.
10. International Paper Company, *Annual Report*, 2001.
11. American Institute of Certified Public Accountants, *Accounting Trends & Techniques* (New York: AICPA, 2002).
12. "Cisco's Numbers Confound Some," *International Herald Tribune*, April 19, 2001; "Kmart Posts $67 Million Loss Due to Markdowns," *The Wall Street Journal*, November 10, 2000.
13. American Institute of Certified Public Accountants, *Accounting Trends & Techniques* (New York: AICPA, 2002).
14. Exxon Mobil, *Annual Report*, 2000.
15. Adapted from Hershey Foods Corp., *Annual Report*, 2000.
16. "SEC Case Judge Rules Crazy Eddie Principals Must Pay $72.7 Million," *The Wall Street Journal*, May 11, 2000.
17. Crane Company, *Annual Report*, 2000.
18. Pioneer Corporation, *Annual Report*, 2001; Yamaha Motor Co., Ltd., *Annual Report*, 2001.

Chapter 11

1. H. J. Heinz Company, *Annual Report*, 2002.
2. *Statement of Financial Accounting Standards No. 144*, "Accounting for the Impairment or Disposal of Long-Lived Assets" (Norwalk, Conn.: Financial Accounting Standards Board, 2001).
3. David Henry, "The Numbers Game," *BusinessWeek*, May 14, 2001.
4. H. J. Heinz Company, *Annual Report*, 2002.
5. Ford Motor Company, *Annual Report*, 2002.
6. *Statement of Position No. 98-1*, "Accounting for the Costs of Computer Software Developed or Planned for Internal Use" (New York: American Institute of Certified Public Accountants, 1996).
7. *Statement of Financial Accounting Standards No. 34*, "Capitalization of Interest Cost" (Norwalk, Conn.: Financial Accounting Standards Board, 1979), par. 9–11.
8. Jared Sandberg, Deborah Solomon, and Rebecca Blumenstein, "Inside WorldCom's Unearthing of a Vast Accounting Scandal," *The Wall Street Journal*, June 27, 2002.
9. *Financial Accounting Standards: Original Pronouncements as of July 1, 1977* (Norwalk, Conn.: Financial Accounting Standards Board, 1977), ARB No. 43, Ch. 9, Sec. C, par. 5.
10. Accounting Principles Board, *Opinion No. 29*, "Accounting for Nonmonetary Transactions" (New York: American Institute of Certified Public Accountants, 1973); Emerging Issues Task Force, *EITF Issue Summary 86-29*, "Nonmonetary Transactions: Magnitude of Boot and the Exceptions to the Use of Fair Value" (Norwalk, Conn.: Financial Accounting Standards Board, 1986).
11. *Statement of Financial Accounting Standards No. 25*, "Suspension of Certain Accounting Requirements for Oil and Gas Producing

Companies" (Norwalk, Conn.: Financial Accounting Standards Board, 1979).

12. Adapted from Accounting Principles Board, *Opinion No. 17*, "Intangible Assets" (New York: American Institute of Certified Public Accountants, 1970), par. 2.
13. "What's in a Name?" *Time*, May 3, 1993.
14. General Motors, *Annual Report*, 2000.
15. Abbott Laboratories, *Annual Report*, 2000; Roche Group, *Annual Report*, 2000.
16. Allan B. Afterman, *International Accounting, Financial Reporting and Analysis* (New York: Warren, Gorham & Lamont, 1995).
17. *Statement of Financial Accounting Standards No. 2*, "Accounting for Research and Development Costs" (Norwalk, Conn.: Financial Accounting Standards Board, 1974), par. 12.
18. *Statement of Financial Accounting Standards No. 86*, "Accounting for the Costs of Computer Software to be Sold, Leased, or Otherwise Marketed" (Norwalk, Conn.: Financial Accounting Standards Board, 1985).
19. *Accounting Trends & Techniques*, 2002.
20. General Mills, *Annual Report*, 2002; Sara Lee Corporation, *Annual Report*, 2002; Tribune Company, *Annual Report*, 2002.
21. *Statement of Financial Accounting Standards No. 144*, "Accounting for the Impairment or Disposal of Long-Lived Assets" (Norwalk, Conn.: Financial Accounting Standards Board, 2001).
22. Edward P. McTague, "Accounting for Trade-Ins of Operational Assets," *National Public Accountant* (January 1986), p. 39.
23. General Motors Corp., *Annual Report*, 1987.
24. Polaroid Corporation, *Annual Report*, 1997.
25. Hilton Hotels Corporation, *Annual Report*, 2000; Marriott International, *Annual Report*, 2000.
26. "Stock Gives Case the Funds He Needs to Buy New Technology," *BusinessWeek*, April 15, 1996.
27. Roche Group, *Annual Report*, 2000; Baxter International, Inc., *Annual Report*, 2000.

Chapter 12

1. US Airways, Inc., *Annual Report*, 2001.
2. RadioShack Corporation, *Annual Report*, 2002.
3. Pamela L. Moore, "How Xerox Ran Short of Black Ink," *BusinessWeek*, October 30, 2000.
4. Goodyear Tire & Rubber Company, *Annual Report*, 2002.
5. US Airways, Inc., *Annual Report*, 2002.
6. Andersen Enterprise Group, cited in *Crain's Chicago Business*, July 5, 1999.
7. Raju Narisetti, "P&G Ad Chief Plots Demise of the Coupon," *The Wall Street Journal*, April 17, 1996; Renae Merle, "Slowdown Is Business Boon for Coupon Seller Valassis," *The Wall Street Journal*, May 1, 2001.
8. Scott McCartney, "Free Airline Miles Become a Potent Tool for Selling Everything," *The Wall Street Journal*, April 16, 1996; "You've Got Miles," *BusinessWeek*, March 6, 2000.
9. *Statement of Financial Accounting Standards No. 5*, "Accounting for Contingencies" (Norwalk, Conn.: Financial Accounting Standards Board, 1975).
10. American Institute of Certified Public Accountants, *Accounting Trends & Techniques*, 2002.
11. General Motors Corp., *Annual Report*, 2000.
12. American Institute of Certified Public Accountants, *Accounting Trends & Techniques*, 2002.
13. US Airways, Inc., *Annual Report*, 2000.
14. General Motors Corp., *Annual Report*, 2002.
15. Sun Micosystems Inc., *Annual Report*, 2001; Cisco Systems, *Annual Report*, 2001.
16. Texaco, Inc., *Annual Report*, 1986.
17. Man Nutzfahrzeuge Aktiengesellschaft, *Annual Report*, 1997.

Chapter 13

1. KPMG International, Internet site www.kpmg.com, February 10, 2002. KPMG has announced plans to separate its consulting practice as a corporation.
2. Information excerpted from the 1990 and 2002 annual reports of Alliance Capital Management Limited Partnership; *The Wall Street Journal*, February 10, 2003.
3. Anita Raghavan, "Goldman Scrambles to Find $250 Million in Equity Capital from Private Investors," *The Wall Street Journal*, September 15, 1994.
4. "Nokia Unveils Plans for Chinese Centre," *Financial Times London*, May 9, 2000.

Chapter 14

1. Cisco Systems, Inc., *Annual Report*, 2002.
2. Copyright © 2000 by Houghton Mifflin Company. Reproduced by permission from *The American Heritage Dictionary of the English Language, Fourth Edition*.
3. *Statement of Position No. 98-5*, "Report on the Costs of Start up Activities" (New York: American Institute of Certified Public Accountants, 1998).
4. Deborah Solomon, "AT&T Slashes Dividends 83%, Cuts Forecasts," *The Wall Street Journal*, December 21, 2002.
5. Abbott Laboratories, *Annual Report*, 2002.
6. Ibid.
7. American Institute of Certified Public Accountants, *Accounting Trends & Techniques* (New York: AICPA, 2001).
8. *Statement of Accounting Standards No. 123*, "Accounting for Stock-Based Compensation" (Norwalk, Conn.: Financial Accounting Standards Board, 1995).
9. Ruth Simon and Ianthe Jeanne Dugan, "Options Overdose," *The Wall Street Journal*, June 4, 2001.
10. Suzanne McGee, "Europe's New Markets for IPOs of Growth Start-Ups Fly High," *The Wall Street Journal*, February 22, 1999.
11. Microsoft Corporation, Inc., *Annual Report*, 1997.
12. G. Christian Hill, "Microsoft Plans Preferred Issue of $750 Million," *The Wall Street Journal*, December 3, 1996.
13. American Institute of Certified Public Accountants, *Accounting Trends & Techniques* (New York: AICPA, 2001).
14. Robert McGough, Suzanne McGee, and Cassell Bryan-Low, "Buyback Binge Now Creates Big Hangover," *The Wall Street Journal*, December 18, 2000.
15. "Avaya Prices Public Offering of Common Stock" and "Avaya Completes Sale of Approximately $200 Million Common Stock," *The Wall Street Journal Online*, March 22, 2002.
16. Tom Herman, "Preferreds' Rich Yields Blind Some Investors to Risks," *The Wall Street Journal*, March 24, 1992.
17. Stanley Ziemba, "USAir Defers Dividends on Preferred Stock," *Chicago Tribune*, September 30, 1994.
18. Susan Carey, "US Airways to Redeem Preferred Owned by Berkshire Hathaway," *The Wall Street Journal*, February 4, 1998.
19. Roche Group, *Annual Report*, 2001.

Chapter 15

1. AMR Corporation, *Annual Report*, 2002.
2. *Statement of Financial Accounting Standards No. 130*, "Reporting Comprehensive Income" (Norwalk, Conn.: Financial Accounting Standards Board, 1997).
3. American Institute of Certified Public Accountants, *Accounting Trends & Techniques* (New York: American Institute of Certified Public Accountants, 2002).
4. Cited in *The Week in Review* (Deloitte Haskins & Sells), February 28, 1985.
5. "Up to the Minute, Down to the Wire," *Twentieth Century Mutual Funds Newsletter*, 1996.

6. American Institute of Certified Public Accountants, *Accounting Trends & Techniques* (New York: American Institute of Certified Public Accountants, 2001).
7. Robert Manor and Melita Marie Garza, "Company's Accounting May Prove Hard to Criminalize," *Chicago Tribune*, January 11, 2002.
8. Sears, Roebuck and Co., *Annual Report*, 1997.
9. *Statement of Financial Accounting Standards No. 109*, "Accounting for Income Taxes" (Norwalk, Conn.: Financial Accounting Standards Board, 1992).
10. American Institute of Certified Public Accountants, *Accounting Trends & Techniques* (New York: American Institute of Certified Public Accountants, 2002).
11. Accounting Principles Board, *Opinion No. 30*, "Reporting the Results of Operations" (New York: American Institute of Certified Public Accountants, 1973), par. 20.
12. Ibid.
13. American Institute of Certified Public Accountants, *Accounting Trends & Techniques* (New York: American Institute of Certified Public Accountants, 2002).
14. Accounting Principles Board, *Opinion No. 20*, "Accounting Changes" (New York: American Institute of Certified Public Accountants, 1971), par. 20.
15. David Cairns International, *IAS Survey Update*, July 2001.
16. American Institute of Certified Public Accountants, *Accounting Trends & Techniques* (New York: American Institute of Certified Public Accountants, 2002).
17. Accounting Principles Board, *Opinion No. 15*, "Earnings per Share" (New York: American Institute of Certified Public Accountants, 1969), par. 12.
18. Minnesota Mining and Manufacturing Company, *Annual Report*, 2000.
19. *Statement of Financial Accounting Standards No. 128*, "Earnings per Share and the Disclosure of Information About Capital Structure" (Norwalk, Conn.: Financial Accounting Standards Board, 1997).
20. Tribune Company, *Annual Report*, 2002.
21. Skandia Group, *Annual Report*, 2000.
22. *Accounting Research Bulletin No. 43* (New York: American Institute of Certified Public Accountants, 1953), chap. 7, sec. B, par. 10.
23. Ibid., par. 13.
24. Robert O'Brien, "Techs' Chill Fails to Stem Stock Splits," *The Wall Street Journal*, June 8, 2000.
25. Rebecca Buckman, "Microsoft Posts Hefty 18% Revenue Rise," *The Wall Street Journal*, January 18, 2002; William M. Bulkeley, "IBM Reports 13% Decline in Net Income," *The Wall Street Journal*, January 18, 2002.
26. "Technology Firms Post Strong Earnings but Stock Prices Decline Sharply," *The Wall Street Journal*, January 21, 1988; Donald R. Seace, "Industrials Plunge 57.2 Points—Technology Stocks' Woes Cited," *The Wall Street Journal*, January 21, 1988.
27. The Washington Post Company, *Annual Report*, 2000.
28. Yamaha Motor Company, Ltd., *Annual Report*, 2001.

Chapter 16

1. AT&T Corporation, *Annual Report*, 2002.
2. "Canadian Airline's Demise Adds to Industry Woes," *The Washington Post*, November 16, 2001; "A Striking End for Air Afrique," British Broadcasting Company, November 26, 2001; "Small Airlines Adapting Quicker," Associated Press, November 22, 2001; "Swiss Air Rescue Hopes Brighten," British Broadcasting Company, November 21, 2001.
3. AT&T Corporation, *Annual Report*, 2002.
4. Ibid.
5. Quentin Hardy, "Japanese Companies Need to Raise Cash, but First a Bond Market Must Be Built," *The Wall Street Journal*, October 20, 1992.
6. Bill Barnhart, "Bond Bellwether," *Chicago Tribune*, December 4, 1996.
7. Accounting Principles Board, *Opinion No. 21*, "Interest on Receivables and Payables" (New York: American Institute of Certified Public Accountants, 1971), par. 15.
8. *Statement of Financial Accounting Standards No. 13*, "Accounting for Leases" (Norwalk, Conn.: Financial Accounting Standards Board, 1976), par. 10.
9. Philip Morris Companies, Inc., *Annual Report*, 2000.
10. *Statement of Financial Accounting Standards No. 87*, "Employers' Accounting for Pensions" (Norwalk, Conn.: Financial Accounting Standards Board, 1985).
11. *Statement of Financial Accounting Standards No. 106*, "Employers' Accounting for Postretirement Benefits Other than Pensions" (Norwalk, Conn.: Financial Accounting Standards Board, 1990).
12. Stanley Ziemba, "TWA, American Revise O'Hare Gate Agreement," *The Wall Street Journal*, May 13, 1992.
13. FedEx Corporation, *Annual Report*, 2001.
14. "More Hotels Won't Be Able to Pay Debt from Operations, Study Says," *The Wall Street Journal*, October 30, 2001.
15. Amazon.com, Press Release, January 28, 1999.
16. NEC Corporation, *Annual Report*, 2001; Sanyo Electric Co., *Annual Report*, 2001.

Chapter 17

1. Marriott International, Inc., *Annual Report*, 2002, adapted.
2. *Statement of Financial Accounting Standards No. 95*, "Statement of Cash Flows" (Norwalk, Conn.: Financial Accounting Standards Board, 1987); *Statement of Financial Accounting Concepts No. 1*, "Objectives of Financial Reporting for Business Enterprises" (Norwalk, Conn.: Financial Accounting Standards Board, 1978), par. 37–39.
3. Marriott International, Inc., *Annual Report*, 2002.
4. Gary Slutsker, "Look at the Birdie and Say: 'Cash Flow,'" *Forbes*, October 25, 1993.
5. Jonathan Clements, "Yacktman Fund Is Bloodied but Unbowed," *The Wall Street Journal*, November 8, 1993.
6. Jeffrey Laderman, "Earnings, Schmearnings—Look at the Cash," *BusinessWeek*, July 24, 1989.
7. "Deadweight on the Markets," *BusinessWeek*, February 19, 2001.
8. Marriott International, Inc., *Annual Report*, 2002.
9. American Institute of Certified Public Accountants, *Accounting Trends & Techniques* (New York: AICPA, 2001).
10. Pallavi Gogoi, "Cash-Rich, So?" *BusinessWeek*, March 19, 2001.
11. "Cash Flow Shortfall in Quarter May Lead to Default on Loan," *The Wall Street Journal*, September 4, 2001.
12. Enron Corporation, *Press Release*, October 16, 2001.
13. Sony Corporation, *Annual Report*, 2000; Canon, Inc., *Annual Report*, 2000.

Chapter 18

1. Sun Microsystems, *Proxy Statement*, 2001.
2. Phyllis Plitch, "Firms Embrace Pro Forma Way on Earnings," *The Wall Street Journal*, January 22, 2002.
3. David Henry, "The Numbers Game," *BusinessWeek*, May 14, 2001.
4. *Statement of Financial Accounting Standards No. 131*, "Segment Disclosures" (Norwalk, Conn.: Financial Accounting Standards Board, 1997).
5. Sun Microsystems, Inc. *Annual Report*, 2001.
6. William H. Beaver, "Alternative Accounting Measures as Indicators of Failure," *Accounting Review*, January 1968; Edward Altman, "Financial Ratios, Discriminant Analysis and the Prediction of Corporate Bankruptcy," *Journal of Finance*, September 1968.
7. Sun Microsystems, Inc., "Management's Discussion and Analysis," *Annual Report*, 2001.
8. Ibid.
9. *Forbes*, November 13, 1978, p. 154.
10. Elizabeth MacDonald, "Firms Say SEC Earnings Scrutiny Goes Too Far," *The Wall Street Journal*, February 1, 1999.
11. H. J. Heinz Company, *Annual Report*, 2001.
12. Pfizer, Inc., *Annual Report*, 2000; Roche Group, *Annual Report*, 2000.

Chapter 19

1. Frederic M. Biddle, "A Little Gas Fuels Hope for a New Type of Electric Car," *The Wall Street Journal*, July 9, 1999.
2. Northiko Shirouzu, "Honda Bucks Industry Wisdom, Aiming to Be Small and Efficient," *The Wall Street Journal*, July 9, 1999.
3. *Statement No. 1A* (New York: Institute of Management Accountants, 1982).
4. Andra Gumbus and Susan D. Johnson, "The Balanced Scorecard at Futura Industries," *Strategic Finance*, July 2003.
5. Presentation by management of Baxter International, October 2001.
6. American Institute of Certified Public Accountants, "The New Finance," www.aicpa.org.
7. Peter Brewer, "Putting Strategy into the Balanced Scorecard," *Strategic Finance*, January 2002.
8. American Institute of Certified Public Accountants, "Summary of Sarbanes-Oxley Act of 2002," www.aicpa.org/info/sarbanes_oxley_summary.htm; Securities and Exchange Commission, "Final Rule: Certification of Disclosure in Companies' Quarterly and Annual Reports," August 28, 2002, www.sec.gov/rules/final/33-8124.htm.
9. Gregory L. White, "GM Appears to Step Back from Proposal," *The Wall Street Journal*, March 30, 1999.

Chapter 20

1. Southwest Airlines, "Fact Sheet," www.southwest.com.
2. Melanie Trottman, "Vaunted Southwest Slips in On-Time Performance," *The Wall Street Journal*, September 25, 2002.
3. Robert Frank and Sarah Ellison, "Meltdown in Chocolatetown," *The Wall Street Journal*, September 19, 2002.
4. United Parcel Service, "About UPS," www.ups.com.
5. Lisa de Moraes, "Conan the Cost: NBC's Thrifty Numbers Game," *The Washington Post*, February 8, 2002.

Chapter 21

1. Robert L. Simison, "Toyota Finds Way to Make Custom Car in 5 Days," *The Wall Street Journal*, August 6, 1999.
2. John M. Parkinson, "Equivalent Units in Process Costing" (paper presented at the meeting of the American Accounting Association, August 2002).
3. Associated Press, "$75 Screws? The Pentagon Pays It," *The Gainesville Sun*, March 19, 1998.
4. William A. Sahlman, "How to Write a Great Business Plan," *Harvard Business Review*, July–August 1997.

Chapter 22

1. Dan Morse, "Tennessee Producer Tries New Tactic in Sofas: Speed," *The Wall Street Journal*, November 19, 2002.
2. Gary Cokins, "Learning to Love ABC," *Journal of Accountancy*, August 1999.
3. Mylene Mangalindan, "Oracle Puts Priority on Customer Service," *The Wall Street Journal*, January 21, 2003.
4. Lance Thompson, "Examining Methods of VBM," *Strategic Finance*, December 2002.
5. Paulette Thomas, "Electronics Firm Ends Practice Just in Time," *The Wall Street Journal*, October 29, 2002.
6. Gina Imperato, "Time for Zero Time," *Net Company*, Fall 1999.
7. Sally Beatty, "Levi's Strive to Keep a Hip Image," *The Wall Street Journal*, January 23, 2003.

Chapter 23

1. Kraft Foods, "Profile," www.kraft.com.
2. Kraft Foods, "Inside Kraft: A Company Overview," http://164.109.16.145/investors/overview.html.

Chapter 24

1. Johnson & Johnson, "Our Company," www.jnj.com.
2. Omar Aguilar, "How Strategic Performance Management Is Helping Companies Create Business Value," *Strategic Finance*, January 2003.
3. Enterprise Rent-a-Car, "Overview," "Facts," "History," www.enterprise.com.
4. Richard Barrett, "From Fast Close to Fast Forward," *Strategic Finance*, January 2003.
5. Jeremy Hope and Robin Fraser, "Who Needs Budgets?" *Harvard Business Review*, February 2003.
6. Ibid.
7. Minnesota Mining and Manufacturing Company, "About 3M," www.3m.com.

Chapter 25

1. Erin White, "How Stogy Turned Stylish," *The Wall Street Journal*, May 3, 2002.
2. Katy McLaughlin, "Factory Tours," *The Wall Street Journal*, October 29, 2002.
3. David E. Keys and Anton Van Der Merwe, "Gaining Effective Organizational Control with RCA," *Strategic Finance*, May 2002.
4. Gabriel Kahn, "Still Going for Gold," *The Wall Street Journal*, January 28, 2003.
5. Curtis C. Verschoor, "Ethical Corporations Are Still More Profitable," *Strategic Finance*, June 2003.

Chapter 26

1. PEAKS Resorts, www.peakscard.com.
2. Rich Teerlink, "Harley's Leadership U-Turn," *Harvard Business Review*, July–August 2000.
3. Marc J. Epstein and Jean-François Manzoni, "The Balanced Scorecard and Tableau de Bord: Translating Strategy into Action," *Management Accounting*, August 1997.
4. Jill Rosenfeld, "Information as if Understanding Mattered," *Fast Company*, March 2000.
5. "Blue Jeans to Help Keep Cars Quiet: Who Thinks This Stuff Up?" *Fast Company*, May 2000.
6. Ans Kolk, "Green Reporting," *Harvard Business Review*, January–February 2000.
7. Russ Banham, "Better Budgets," *Journal of Accountancy*, February 2000.
8. Julia Flynn, "Use of Performance-Based Pay Spreads Across Continental Europe, Survey Says," *The Wall Street Journal*, November 17, 1999.

Chapter 27

1. Stephanie Miles, "What's a Check?" *Wall Street Journal*, October 21, 2002, p. R5.
2. Miles, p. R5.
3. Michael Liedtke, "Keeping the Books," *The Gainesville Sun*, August 22, 2002.
4. Alan Fuhrman, "Your e-Banking Future," *Strategic Finance*, April, 2002.
5. Paulette Thomas, "Case Study: Electronics Firm Ends Practice Just in Time," *The Wall Street Journal*, October 29, 2002.
6. From a speech by Jim Croft, vice president of finance and administration of the Field Museum, Chicago, November 14, 2000.

Appendix A

1. PepsiCo., Inc., *Annual Report*, 2000.
2. *Statement of Financial Accounting Standards No. 52*, "Foreign Currency Translation" (Norwalk, Conn.: Financial Accounting Standards Board, 1981), par. 15.
3. *Financial Reporting: An International Survey* (New York: Price Waterhouse, May 1995).
4. "International Accounting Standards Committee Objectives and Procedures," *Professional Standards* (New York: American Institute of Certified Public Accountants, 1988), vol. B, sec. 9000, par. 24–27.

Appendix B

1. *Statement of Financial Accounting Standards No. 115*, "Accounting for Certain Investments in Debt and Equity Securities" (Norwalk, Conn.: Financial Accounting Standards Board, 1993).

Appendix C

1. Accounting Principles Board, *Opinion No. 21*, "Interest on Receivables and Payables" (New York: American Institute of Certified Public Accountants, 1971), par. 13.

COMPANY NAME INDEX

Abbott Laboratories, 500, 598, 599–600
Accenture, 363, 1123
Accor, 560
Ace Hardware, 11
Air Afrique, 671
Ajinomoto Company, 85–86
Albertson's Inc., 252
Alcoa Inc., 560, 647, 896
Allegheny Technologies Inc., 560
Alliance Capital Management Limited Partnership, 560
Allstate Insurance Co., 997
Amazon.com, 84, 104, 232, 362, 481, 601, 627, 705–706, 756, 1134–1135
American Airlines, Inc., 537, 628–629, 704
American Century Services Corp., 630
American Express, 632
America Online (AOL), 93, 180, 519, 537, 625, 627, 757
Ameritech Corp., 405
AMR Corporation, 628–629, 638
Amtrak, 1009
AOL Time Warner Inc., 93, 180, 519, 537, 625, 627, 757
Apple Computer, Inc., 598, 647, 896, 1097
Association for Investment Management and Research, 630
AT&T Corporation, 598–599, 611, 654, 668–669, 671–672, 674, 675, 804
AutoLiv, Inc., 446
Avaya, Inc., 623
Avon, 788

Babies "R" Us, 257
Bank of America, 409, 632, 1052, 1128–1129, 1130, 1134, 1143
BankOne, 409
Barnes & Noble, 211, 362, 450
Baxter International, 521, 802
Beijing Li-Ning Sports Goods Company, 1068
Bell South, 677
Berkshire Hathaway, 626
Blockbuster Entertainment Corporation, 450, 966
The Boeing Company, 44–45, 46, 222, 488, 892, 1051
Boise Cascade, 896
Borders, 362, 876
BP Corporation, 411–412
Brinker International, Inc., 1098, 1099(table)
Bristol-Myers Squibb, 139, 1108

Caesars World Inc., 91
Canon, Inc., 746, 748
Caterpillar Inc., 139, 896
Century 21, 884
Charles Schwab & Co., Inc., 41–42, 757
Chase Manhattan, 623, 647
ChemLawn, 1084–1085
Chico's, 836
Chili's Grill and Bar, 1098, 1099(table)
Circuit City Stores, Inc., 177, 366, 401, 407–408
Cisco Systems, Inc., 330, 415, 458, 481, 554, 592–593, 597, 599, 601
Citibank, 409, 623, 836–837
Claire's Stores, Inc., 169
Coach, Inc., 1048–1049, 1051
Coca-Cola Company, 23(table), 39, 235, 677, 768, 896, 1104, 1171
Coleman, 209
Columbia HCA Healthcare, 677
CompuCredit, 438
CompuServe, 757
Continental Airlines, Inc., 44–45, 46, 670, 973
Coors, 896
Costco Wholesale Corporation, 176
Crane Company, 476
Crate & Barrel, 401
Crazy Eddie, Inc., 476
Crown Cork & Seal, 896

DaimlerChrysler Corp., 405, 887, 966, 1097, 1098, 1108–1109
Dayton-Hudson Corporation, 1123
Daytons Stores, 1123
Defense Department, U.S., 892
Dell Computer Corporation, 128–129, 132, 164, 224–225, 225(exh.), 226(fig.), 228(exh.), 228–229, 229(fig.), 236(fig.), 237, 253, 255, 444, 473, 808, 881, 926
Deloitte & Touche, 23(table)
Delta Airlines, 488, 973
Department of Defense, 892
Department of Energy, U.S., 481
Dillard Dept. Stores, Inc., 169–170, 406
Disney, 91, 125, 235, 677
DocuShred, Inc., 374
Domino's Pizza, 1085
Dow Chemical Company, 139, 918
Dun & Bradstreet Corp., 536, 754, 757
Du Pont, 23(table)

Eastman Kodak, 805, 896
eBay Inc., 627
Eclipsys, 93
Eddie Bauer Inc., 401
Emerson Electric, 896
Energy, U.S. Department of, 481
Engelhard Corporation, 896
England, Inc., 924–925
Enron Corporation, 25, 219, 220, 374, 559, 634, 746, 747, 753, 799, 812
Enterprise Rent-a-Car, 849, 1005, 1009
Ernst & Young, 23(table), 218
Ethan Allen, Inc., 857
ExxonMobil, 14, 23(table), 410–412, 473, 896, 1173(table)

Federal Express Corporation (FedEx), 704, 805, 967
Fermi National Accelerator Laboratory (Fermilab), 481
Field Museum of Chicago, 1147
Financial Executives Research Foundation, 693
Fleetwood Enterprises, Inc., 91, 743–744
FMCC (Ford Motor Credit Co.), 407
Forbes, 1127
Ford Motor Company, 23(table), 405, 407, 437, 483, 522, 929, 1103, 1173(table)
Ford Motor Credit Co. (FMCC), 407
Forte Hotels, 560
Fruit of the Loom, 209

The Gap, 7
Gateway, Inc., 881

General Electric, 23(table), 805, 1104
General Mills, Inc., 5, 212–213, 219, 502
General Motors Acceptance Corp. (GMAC), 407
General Motors Corporation, 23(table), 405, 407, 500, 518, 538, 552–553, 560, 599, 802, 804, 830, 836, 886, 887, 1104, 1173(table)
Getty Oil, 554
Gillette Company, 139, 647
GlaxoSmithKline PLC, 253–255
GMAC (General Motors Acceptance Corp.), 407
Goldman, Sachs & Co., 570, 598
Goodyear Tire & Rubber Company, 529, 711, 756, 788, 968
Great Atlantic & Pacific Tea Company (A&P), 252

Harley-Davidson, Inc., 804, 884, 1093, 1098
Harrods, 210
Heineken N.V., 438
Helene Curtis Corp., 788
Hershey Foods Corp., 322, 475–476, 849
Hertz, 1098
Hewlett-Packard, 611, 805
Hilton Hotels Corp., 5, 518–519
Hilton International, 560
H.J. Heinz Company, 91, 125–126, 478–479, 498, 789–790
Holiday Inn, 560
The Home Depot, Inc., 404–405, 450
Honda Motor Company, 792–793, 802, 833
H&R Block, Inc., 163, 876, 884, 1043
HSBC Bank USA, 623
Hudsons Stores, 1123
Humana, 836–837
Hyatt, 560

IBM (International Business Machines), 23(table), 437, 623, 662–663, 677, 802, 1173, 1173(table)
Illinois Tool Works, Inc., 442
Indian Motorcycle Corporation, 876
Inspector General, U.S. Office of the, 892
Intel Corporation, 5, 43, 48, 611, 647, 663, 1008–1009, 1097
International Business Machines (IBM), 23(table), 437, 623, 662–663, 677, 802, 1173, 1173(table)
International Paper Co., 457, 1171
Intuit Corporation, 361, 1138

J.C. Penney Company, Inc., 39, 329, 413, 439, 440–441, 442, 443, 444–445, 473
JDS Uniphase, 756
Jiffy Lube, 1098, 1099(table)
John Deere, 836, 1008–1009
John H. Daniel Company, 882–883, 886
Johnson & Johnson, 1002–1003, 1004
J.P. Morgan Investment Management Inc., 41
Juniper Networks, 647

Kellogg Company, 896
Kelly Services, 88–89, 91
Kids "R" Us, 257
Kinko's, 1098, 1099(table)
Kmart, 210, 211, 458
KnowledgeWare, 93
Kodak, 805, 896
Koss Corporation, 940, 1145
KPMG LLP, 23(table), 556–557
Kraft Foods, 964–965, 966, 975, 1051, 1097

Land O'Lakes, 933
Land Rover, 968
Lands' End, 177, 211
La-Z-Boy, Inc., 924
Lechters, Inc., 41
Lego Group, 42
Lehman Brothers Inc., 232
Levi Strauss & Co., 884, 963
Liberty Mutual Insurance Company, 1052
The Limited, 443
L.L. Bean, 177
Lowe's, 1009
Lucent Technologies, Inc., 56, 93, 251, 415, 481
Lyric Opera of Chicago, 124

Macy's, 406, 443
Man Nutzfahrzeuge Aktiengesellschaft, 554–555
Marriott International, Inc., 518–519, 560, 708–710, 714–717, 749
Mars, 849
Marshall Field's, 406, 1123
May SWS Securities, 421
Maytag Corporation, 477
McDonald's, 23(table), 231, 437, 832–833, 978
Mellon Bank, 85
Merck, 1004
Mergent, Inc., 757, 758(exh.), 788
Merrill Lynch Lynch & Co., Inc., 570
Mervyn's, 1123
MGM-UA Communications Co., 91
Michelin, 1173
Microsoft Corporation, 10, 43, 604, 611, 662
Midway Airlines, 670, 671
Minnesota Mining and Manufacturing Company (3M), 640, 896, 1046–1047
Mitsubishi Corp., 436, 1043
Montgomery Ward, 325
Monsanto, 1097, 1123
Moody's Investor Services, Inc., 757, 788, 790–791
Motorola, 415, 805, 836, 850–851

Nabisco, 654, 896
NCH Promotional Services, 536
NEC Corporation, 706
Neiman Marcus, 176
Nestlé S.A., 163, 849, 1173
Netscape Communications Corporation, 625–626
Neuer Markt, 601
Newark Morning Ledger Co., 500
Nike, Inc., 83–84, 229–230, 230(exh.), 802
Nokia, 590
Nordstrom, 406, 1009, 1098
Nortel Networks, 415
Nouveau Marche, 601
Nvidia, 647

Office Depot, 177
Office of the Inspector General, U.S., 892
Official Airline Guide, 834
Oracle Corporation, 86–87, 324, 929
Orkin Exterminating Company, 884
Owens Corning, 896
Oxford Health Plans, Inc., 364–365, 371

Peachtree Software, 361
Pennzoil Company, 554
PeopleSoft, 324, 363, 929
Pep Boys, 836
PepsiCo Bottling Company, 1180
PepsiCo Inc., 757, 758(exh.), 788, 1173, 1173(table), 1180
Pepsi Cola North America, 933
Pfizer, Inc., 790
Philip Morris Companies, Inc., 555, 692, 849
Philips Electronics N.V., 438
Phillips Petroleum, 139
Piedmont Airlines, 488
Pillsbury, 212

Pioneer Corporation, 402–403, 406, 408, 412, 476–477
Pitney Bowes, 931
Polaroid Corporation, 518
PPG Industries, 1167
Preussag, 639
PricewaterhouseCoopers, 23(table), 363
Procter & Gamble, 23(table)

Quaker Oats, 1180
Qualcomm, 415

RadioShack Corporation, 526–527
Rambus Inc., 647
Real Networks Inc., 601
Reebok International Ltd., 5
RentWay, Inc., 456
Revlon, 788
Reynolds Metals Company, 217
Risk Management Association, 757
Rite Aid Corp., 456
RJR Nabisco, 555
Robert Morris Associates, 757
Roche Group, 500, 521, 626, 790
Royal Dutch/Shell, 1108
RR Donnelley, 322–323, 324, 325
Rubbermaid, 209
Russell Stover Candies, 849

Safeway Inc., 329, 704
Salomon Brothers Inc., 570
Sam's Clubs, 176
Sanyo Electric Co., 706
SAP, 324, 929
Sara Lee Corporation, 502
Sears, Roebuck and Co., 401, 407, 413, 439, 443, 634, 836
Sears Roebuck Acceptance Corp. (SRAC), 407
Shanghai Industrial Sewing Machine, 416
Shanghai Steel Tube, 416
Simon & Schuster, 180
Skandia Group, 644
Sony Corporation, 5, 746, 748, 802, 850–851, 975, 1173
South Beach Beverage, 1180
Southwest Airlines Co., 5, 39, 834–835, 838, 839, 849, 973
Sprint Corp., 601, 966
SRAC (Sears Roebuck Acceptance Corp.), 407
Standard & Poor's, 706, 757, 788
Starbucks Corporation, 399
Sunbeam Corporation, 209, 220
Sun Microsystems, Inc., 86–87, 554, 750–751, 759–772, 760–764(exh.), 762–764(fig.), 766(fig.), 767(exh.), 769(exh.), 771(exh.)
Swiss Air, 670, 671

Taco Bell, 857
Takashimaya Company, Ltd., 126
Talbots, 1009
Tandy Corporation, 401
Target, 166–167, 170, 329, 443, 1123
Texaco Inc., 410–412, 554, 555
3M (Minnesota Mining and Manufacturing Company), 640, 896, 1046–1047
Tiffany & Co., 176, 647
Toyota Motor Company, 5–6, 833, 884, 886, 887
Toys "R" Us, 42–43, 86, 91, 126, 163–164, 211, 255, 257–263, 262(fig.), 264, 362, 401, 438–439, 442, 477, 521, 522, 555, 627, 632, 666, 706, 748, 790–791, 849–850, 1043
Trans World Airlines (TWA), 670, 671, 704
Travelocity.com, 104
Tribune Company, 502, 641–642
Tropicana, 1180
Tupperware, 896
TWA (Trans World Airlines), 670, 671, 704
Twentieth Century Mutual Funds, 630

Unilever, 1138, 1173
United Nations, 1004
United Parcel Service (UPS), 444, 849, 857, 967, 1009, 1084–1085, 1104
U.S. Department of Defense, 892
U.S. Department of Energy, 481
U.S. Office of the Inspector General, 892
U.S. Postal Service (USPS), 932, 973
United Way, 1004, 1098
UPS (United Parcel Service), 444, 849, 857, 967, 1009, 1084–1085, 1104
USAA, 805, 836–837, 997
US Airways, Inc., 488, 524–525, 526, 528, 529–530, 537, 538, 626, 671
USPS (U.S. Postal Service), 932, 973

Vail Resorts, 1090–1091, 1092–1095, 1094(fig.), 1095(fig.)
Vanguard Airlines, 488
Verizon, 966
Vicorp Restaurants, 1099

Walgreen Co., 2–3, 7, 42–43, 86, 126, 164, 211, 255, 264, 331, 439, 477, 522, 555, 627, 666, 706, 748, 790–791
Wall Street Journal, 757
Wal-Mart Stores, Inc., 209, 210, 211, 235, 409, 450, 804, 849–850, 963, 968, 1098, 1099(table)
The Walt Disney Company, 91, 125, 235, 677
Washington Post Company, 665–666
Waste Management, Inc., 555
Webvan Group, Inc., 722
Wells Fargo, 623, 968
Wendy's International Inc., 5
Western Airlines, 488
Westinghouse Electric, 933
WorldCom, 219, 220, 487, 753, 799, 1022
W.R. Grace & Co., 788
Wrigley's, 849

Xerox Corporation, 23(table), 528

Yahoo!, 627, 757
Yamaha Motor Company, Ltd., 476–477, 666

SUBJECT INDEX

Note: **Boldface** type indicates key terms.

ABC, *see* Activity-based costing (ABC)
ABM, *see* Activity-based management (ABM)
Abnormal balance, 62
Absorption costing income statement, profit center performance evaluation using, 1101–1103, 1102(exh.)
Accelerated methods, 490, 490–491, 492, 492(fig.)
Account(s), 16
accumulated depreciation, 99(fig.), 99–100
adjusting, 93(exh.), 93–94
balance of, 52
chart of, 48, 49–50(exh.)
clearing, 890
after closing, 136, 137–138(exh.)
contra, 99–100
controlling (control), 332
owner's equity, 50, 51(fig.)
permanent (real), 130
temporary (nominal), 130
titles of, 50–51
uncollectible, *see* Uncollectible accounts
see also specific accounts
Account balance, 52
Accounting, 4
development of, 8
as information system, 4(fig.), 4–8
Accounting cycle, 130
Accounting equation, 14, 14–19
transactions' effects on, 16–19
Accounting information
processing, 7–8
users of, 8(fig.), 8–10
see also Financial statement(s); Report(s); *specific financial statements*
Accounting information systems, 322–348, **324**
computerized accounting systems and, *see* Computerized accounting systems
design principles for, 324–325
Internet and, *see* Internet
special-purpose journals in, *see* Special-purpose journals; *specific journals*
Accounting period issue, 91
Accounting policies, 46
Accounting practices
adoption in emerging economies, 416
changes in, cumulative effect of, 639
operating decisions and, 455
quality of earnings and, 631–633
Accounting Principles Board (APB)
on amortization of bond discount, 680
on depreciation, 503
on earnings per share, 640
on extraordinary items, 638–639
on imputing interest on noninterest-bearing notes, 1193
on influence and control, 1180
on intangible assets, 498, 500
Opinion No. 9 of, 503
Opinion No. 10 of, 1180
Opinion No. 17 of, 498
Opinion No. 20 of, 503
Opinion No. 30 of, 638–639
Accounting rate-of-return method, 1152, 1152–1153
Accounting standards
international accounting and, 1174, 1178–1179
international comparability of, 500
Accounts payable, 15, 529
Accounts Payable account, 18, 19, 385
expense recognition and, 93
under periodic inventory system, 183
Accounts receivable, 15, **413,** 413(fig.), 413–420
collection of, 18
installment, 413
job order costing system and, 891
uncollectible, *see* Uncollectible accounts
Accounts Receivable account, 18, 90
under periodic inventory system, 184
revenue recognition and, 93
in subsidiary ledgers, 332
Accounts receivable aging method, 416, 416–419, 417(exh.), 418(fig.)
Accrual(s), 95
adjusting entries for accrued expenses and, 100–101, 101(fig.)
adjusting entries for accrued revenues and, 103(fig.), 103–104
year-end, of bond interest expense, 686–688
Accrual accounting, 92, 92–95
adjustments and, *see* Adjusting entries; Adjustments
cash flows and, 107
performance measures and, 94–95
recognition of revenues and expenses and, 93
Accrued expenses, 100
adjusting entries for, 100–101, 101(fig.)
Accrued liabilities, 88, 89, 531
Accrued revenues, adjusting entries for, 103(fig.), 103–104
Accumulated depreciation accounts, 99, 99(fig.), 99–100, 724
Activity-based costing (ABC), 805, 856, 856–860, **934,** 934–938
cost hierarchy and bill of activities and, 934–937
reports and, 929
for selling and administrative activities, 937–938, 938(exh.)
Activity-based management (ABM), 805, 928, 928–938
just-in-time operating philosophy compared with, 945–946, 946(table)
in service organizations, 930–931, 931(fig.)
Activity-based systems, 926, 926–927
management cycle and, 927(fig.), 927–928
see also Activity-based management (ABM); Just-in-time (JIT) *entries*
Actual costing, 841, 841–842
Additions, 504
Adjusted trial balance, 104, 104–105, 105(exh.), 106(exh.)
merchandising business and, 185
Adjusting entries, 95, 95(fig.), 95–104
for accrued expenses, 100–101, 101(fig.)

for accrued revenues, 103(fig.), 103–104
for deferred expenses, 96–100
for deferred revenues, 101–102, 102(fig.)
for merchandising business using periodic inventory system, 185
for merchandising business using perpetual inventory system, 187
for promissory notes, 423
on work sheet, 144, 144(exh.)
Adjustments, 93(exh.), 93–104
Aging of accounts receivable, 416
AICPA, *see* American Institute of Certified Public Accountants (AICPA)
Airline industry
bankruptcies in, 671
debt financing in, 670–671
fixed costs in, 839
frequent-flier miles and, 537
pricing in, 973
Allowance for Doubtful Accounts account, 415
Allowance for Uncollectible Accounts account, 414, 414–415, 417, 420
Allowance method, 414, 414–415
Allowance to Adjust Long-Term Investments to Market account, 1182, 1183–1184
American Institute of Certified Public Accountants (AICPA), 24
on consistency, 217
on depreciation, 487
on inventory cost, 446
Amortization, 482(fig.)
of bond discounts, 678–682
of bond premium, 682–685
Annual reports
accounting policies summary in, 46
components of, 257–263
Annual Statement Studies, 757
Annuities, ordinary, 1148–1149, 1189, 1190(table)
Annuities due, 1205
APB, *see* Accounting Principles Board (APB)
Arithmetica, Geometrica, Proportioni et Proportionalita, 8
Articles of incorporation, 594
Asset(s), 15
carrying value of, 1144
cash flows to, 715, 770, 771(exh.)
on classified balance sheet, 220, 222–223
current, 220, 222, 721
depreciation of, *see* Depreciation
intangible, 223, 498, 498(fig.), 499(table), 500–502
investing in partnership, 568
long-term, *see* Long-term assets; Plant assets
net, 15
noncash, issuance of stock for, 608–609
other, 220
plant (fixed; long-lived; operating; tangible), *see* Plant assets
preference as to, 605
purchase by incurring liabilities, 17
purchase with cash, 16
removal from partnership, 571–572
return on, 768, 769(exh.)
short-term, *see* Short-term financial assets
valuing, 1194
Asset impairment, 480
Asset turnover, 232, 768, 769(exh.), **1104**
ATMs (automated teller machines), 409
Audit committees, 594
Audit trail, 380
Authorization, as control activity, 367
Authorized stock, 597
Automated teller machines (ATMs), 409
Available-for-sale securities, 412, 1180, 1181
Average-cost method, 448, 448–449
Average days' inventory on hand, 445, 766, 767(exh.)
Average days' payable, 526, 527, 527(fig.), **766,** 767(exh.)
Average days' sales uncollected, 405, 406, **766,** 767(exh.)
Avoidable costs, 1138

Backflush costing, 942, 942–945, 943(fig.), 944(fig.)
Bad debts, *see* Uncollectible accounts
Bad Debts Expense account, 415
Balance(s), 52
abnormal, 62
compensating, 408
normal, 61
trial, *see* Trial balance
Balanced scorecard, 808, 808–809, 809(fig.), **1092,** 1092–1095
management cycle and, 1092–1095
Balance sheet, 21(exh.), **22**
in annual report, 259
budgeted, 1022, 1024(exh.)
classified, 220, 221(exh.), 222–225
disclosure of bonds on, 674
reading and graphing, 224–225, 225(exh.), 226(fig.)
Balance Sheet column, merchandising business and, 186–187, 188–189
Bank loans, 529–530
Bank reconciliations, 375, 375–378
illustration of, 376–377, 377(exh.)
recording transactions after, 377–378
Bank statement, 373(fig.)
Bar codes, 172
Barron's, 757
Base year, 759
Basic earnings per share, 640, 640–642
Batch-level activities, 934, 934–935
Batch posting, 328
Beginning inventory, 181
Benchmarking, 809–810, **810**
Bennett, Steve, 1138
Betterments, 504
"Big baths," 633
Bill of activities, 935, 936(exh.), 937
Boards of directors, 594
Bond(s), 673, 673–789, 1180
balance sheet disclosure of, 674
callable, 688
convertible, 689
costs of issuing, 677
coupon, 674
interest rates on, 675–676
issued at discount, 676
issued at face value, 674–675
issued at premium, 676–677
100-year, 677
prices of, 675
registered, 673–674
retirement of, 688–689
sale between interest dates, 685–686, 687(fig.)
secured, 673
serial, 673
statement of cash flows and, 725
term, 673
unsecured, 673
year-end accrual of interest expense for, 686–688
zero coupon, 679
Bond certificates, 673
Bond discounts, amortizing, 678–682
Bond indentures, 673
Bonding, 368
Bond issues, 673
Bond premium, amortization of, 682–685

Bonds Payable account, bonds issued at discount and, 676
Bonuses, 569
to new partners, 569–570
to old partners, 568–569
Bookkeeping, 8, 51–54
T account and, 51–52
transaction analysis and processing in, 52–54, 53(fig.)
Book of original entry, *see* Journal *entries*
Book value, 100, 480, **648,** 648–649, 1144
in capital investment analysis, 1144
Book value per share, 648
Brand names, 499(table)
Breakeven analysis, 976–980, 977(fig.)
Breakeven point, 976
contribution margin to determine, 978–979
for multiple products, 979(fig.), 979–980
Budget(s), 1004
capital expenditures, 1019–1020
cash, 1020(table), 1020–1022, 1021–1023(exh.)
cost of goods manufactured, 1018, 1018(exh.)
direct labor, 1014–1015, 1016(exh.)
direct materials purchases, 1014, 1015(exh.)
financial, 1008, 1018–1022
implementation of, 1025
manufacturing overhead, 1015, 1016(exh.), 1017
master, *see* Master budget
operating, 170–171, 171(exh.), 1008, 1011–1018
production, 1012–1013, 1013(exh.)
sales, 1011–1012, 1013(exh.)
selling and administrative expense, 1017, 1017(exh.)
Budget committee, 1025
Budgeted balance sheet, 1022, 1024(exh.)
Budgeted income statement, 1018, 1018–1019, 1019(exh.)
Budgeting, 1002–1027, **1004**
goals and, 1004–1005
management cycle and, 1006–1008, 1007(fig.)
participative, 1006
Buildings
acquisition cost of, 486
see also Plant assets
Business, 4
goals and activities of, 4–6, 6(fig.)
international, *see* International business
performance measures for, 6–7
Business organization forms, 12–14, 13(table)
see also specific forms
Business periodicals
as information source for financial statement analysis, 757
as users of accounting information, 10
Business plans, 797
Business transactions, 11
analysis and processing in bookkeeping, 52–54, 53(fig.)
analysis of, illustration of, 54–61, 602
classification of, 331
document-less, 330
effects on accounting equation, 16–19
in foreign currencies, 1175–1177
see also International accounting
measurement of, *see* Measurement
merchandising, internal control over, 368–375
not recorded in special-purpose journals, 343, 343(exh.)
recording after bank reconciliation, 377–378
recording of, as control activity, 367
Buyers, big, power of, 405

Callable bonds, 688
Callable preferred stock, 606
Call price, 606, **688**
Candy industry, market share in, 849
Capital
contributed (paid-in), 224
cost of, 1106–1107, 1149
legal, 597
working, 230–231
see also Owner's equity
Capital account, 17, 18–19, 19, 50
closing Income Summary account balance to, 135–136, 136(exh.)
dissolution of partnership and, 568
distribution of partnership income/losses and, 563
dividends and, 224
partners' equity and, 561
under periodic inventory system, 191
Capital balance ratios, 563–564
Capital budgeting, 1143–1144
Capital expenditures, 485
Capital expenditures budget, 1019, 1019–1020
Capital investment analysis, 1143, 1143–1144, 1147
Capital investment decisions, 1143, 1143–1153
accounting rate-of-return method for, 1152–1153
capital investment analysis and, 1143–1144
measures used in, 1144–1145
net present value method for, 1149–1151
payback period method for, 1151–1152
time value of money and, 1146–1149
Capital leases, 691
Capital Stock account, 607
Capital structure, 641
Carrying value, 100, 480, 648–649, **1144**
in capital investment analysis, 1144
Cash, 408, 408–409, **711**
"burn rate" for, 722
idle, investment of, 1195–1196
plant assets sold for, 493–494
purchase of assets with, 16
receipts of, control of, 370–371
see also Petty cash *entries*
Cash account, 17, 18–19, 19, 711, 712
bonds issued at discount and, 676
job order costing system and, 891
under periodic inventory system, 184
Cash basis of accounting, 92
Cash budget, 1020, 1020(table), 1020–1022, 1021–1023(exh.)
Cash disbursements, control of, 371–373(fig.), 374–375
Cash disbursements journal, 340, 341(exh.), 342–343
Cash equivalents, 408, 711
Cash flow(s), 22
from accrual-based information, 107
in capital investment analysis, 1144
classification of, 712–714, 713(fig.)
evaluating adequacy of, 770, 771(exh.)
free, 715–717, 770, 771(exh.)
inventory measurement and, 457
liquidity and, 526–527, 527(fig.)
quality of earnings and, 634–635
Cash flow management, 168, 168(fig.), 168–170, 169(fig.)

Cash flows to assets, 715, 770,
771(exh.)
Cash flows to sales, 715, 770,
771(exh.)
Cash flow yield(s), 715, 770,
771(exh.)
Cash gap, 168–170, 169(fig.)
Cash-generating efficiency, 714,
714–715
Cash inflows, net, 1144
Cash payments journal, 340,
341(exh.), 342–343
Cash receipts journal, 338,
339(exh.), 340
Cash reserves, 405
Cash sales receipts, control of,
370–371
Cash Short or Over account, 379
Category killers, 450
Certified public accountants
(CPAs), 23, reports of, 23–24
CFOs (chief financial officers),
functions of, 10
Chart of accounts, 48, 49–50(exh.)
Check(s), 373(fig.), **374,** 374–375
processing time for, 1133
voucher, 381
Check authorization, 373(fig.), **374**
Checkmarks, in general journal, 64
Check registers, 382, 382–383
Chief financial officers (CFOs),
functions of, 10
Classification, 48, 56
Classified financial statements, 220,
230–237
liquidity evaluation using,
230–231
profitability evaluation using,
231–237
Clearing accounts, 890
Closely held corporations, 257
Closing entries, 130, 132(fig.),
132–239
accounts after closing and, 136,
137–138(exh.)
for merchandising business using
periodic inventory system,
190(exh.), 190–191
for merchandising business using
perpetual inventory system,
187, 187(exh.)
required, 132–136, 133(exh.)
on work sheet, 145
CM (contribution margin), 978–979
Codes of professional conduct,
25–26
Collection, of accounts receivable,
18
Commas, in financial reports, 66
Commercial paper, 530
Commitments, 538
Common-size statements, 762,
763(exh.), 763(fig.), 764(exh.),
764(fig.), 765
Common stock, 602
statement of cash flows and, 726
Common Stock account, 607, 608,
646
Common Stock Distributable
account, 646
Comparability, 216
Comparability principle, 325
Compensating balances, 408
Complex capital structure, 641
Compound entries, 63
Compound interest, 1146,
1146–1147, 1187–1188,
1188(table)
Comprehensive income, 630
Computer(s), 8
networking, 326
software costs and, 501
Computerized accounting systems,
325–328
adjustments using, 104
general ledger systems, 326,
327(fig.), 328, 328(fig.)
interest and amortization tables
and, 684
spreadsheet software and,
325–326
trial balance and, 62
value of, 325
Condensed financial statements,
226
Confidentiality, 342
Conglomerate companies, 755–756
Connors, John, 10
Conservatism, 217, 217–218
Consignments, 447
Consistency, 216
Consolidated financial statements,
1185
Consumers, as users of accounting
information, 10
Contingent liabilities, 407, 538
Continuing operations, income
from, 630
Continuity issue, **91,** 91–92
Continuous improvement, 804,
804–807
achieving, 806(fig.), 806–807
activity-based management and,
805
just-in-time operating philosophy
and, 804
theory of constraints and, 806
total quality management and,
805
Contra accounts, 99, 99–100
Allowance to Adjust Long-Term
Investments to Market account,
1182, 1183–1184
Purchases Discounts account, 192
Sales Returns and Allowances
account, 174, 180–181
Unamortized Bond Discount
account, 676
Unrealized Loss on Long-Term
Investments account, 1182,
1183–1184
Contributed capital, 224
Contribution margin (CM), 978,
978–979
Control
internal, *see* Internal control(s)
long-term investment in stock
and, 1180, 1181
Control activities, 366
Control environment, 366
Controllable costs and revenues,
1098
Controlling (control) accounts, 332
Controlling interest, 1181,
1181(table), 1185
Control principle, 324
Conventions, 216
for interpreting accounting
information, 216–219
Conversion costs, 843, 843(fig.),
897, 941
equivalent production for, 898
Conversion Costs account, backflush
costing and, 945
Convertible bonds, 689
Convertible preferred stock, 605,
605–606
Copyrights, 499(table)
Core competencies, 802
Core values, 966
Corporations, 13, 13(table), 13–14,
14(fig.), **594,** 594–614
advantages of, 596
disadvantages of, 596–597
dividends and, *see* Dividend(s)
equity financing and, 597–598
formation of, 594–595, 595(fig.)
limited liability, 559
management of, 594–597,
595(fig.)
owner's equity in, 224
private (closely held), 257
resembling partnerships, 559
S corporations, 559
size of, 13, 14
stockholders' equity and,
601–602, 602(fig.)
stock of, *see* Common stock;
Dividend(s); Preferred stock;
Stock *entries*

stock options and, 600, 601
Cost(s), 47
of acquisition of plant assets, 485–487
assigning in new manufacturing environment, 941–942, 942(table)
avoidable, 1138
behavior of, 839
classification in new manufacturing environment, 941
classifications of, 837–840, 838(fig.)
of computer software, 501
controllable, 1098
controlling using variance analysis, 1056, 1057(fig.), 1058
conversion, 843, 843(fig.), 897, 898, 941
depreciable, 488
development and exploration, in oil and gas industry, 497–498
differential (incremental), 1132
direct, 838
of doing business, *see* Expenses
expired, 91
fixed, 839, 971–972, 972(fig.)
indirect, 838
mixed, 972(fig.), 972–975
net, of purchases, 181
opportunity, 1133–1134
original (historical), 47
overhead, *see* Manufacturing overhead costs
period (noninventoriable), 840
prime, 843, 843(fig.)
product (inventoriable), *see* Product cost(s)
research and development, 500–501
of sales, 174–175
standard, 1050–1051
start-up and organization, 598
sunk, 1132–1133
of television talent, 860
traceability of, 838
value-adding and nonvalue-adding, 839
variable, 968–970, 969(fig.)
Cost allocation, 851, 851–861
ABC approach for, 856–860
estimates and, 854
of manufacturing overhead costs, 852, 853(fig.), 854–860, 855(fig.)
for service organizations, 860–861
traditional approach for, 854–856, 855(fig.), 856
Cost behavior, 964–987, **966**
breakeven analysis and, 976–980, 977(fig.)
cost-volume-profit analysis and, *see* Cost-volume-profit (CVP) analysis
of fixed costs, 971–972, 972(fig.)
management cycle and, 966–967, 967(fig.)
of mixed costs, 972(fig.), 972–975
of variable costs, 968–970, 969(fig.)
Cost-benefit convention, 218, 218–219
Cost-benefit principle, 324
Cost centers, 1097, 1097–1098, 1099(table)
discretionary, 1097–1098, 1099(table)
evaluating performance using flexible budgeting, 1100–1101, 1101(exh.)
Cost drivers, 851
Cost flows, 447
of manufacturing costs, 846(fig.), 846–847
process costing system and, 894–896, 895(fig.)
Cost hierarchy, 934, 934–935, 935(table)
Cost information
management cycle and, 836(fig.), 836–837
organizations and, 837
Costing
activity-based, *see* Activity-based costing (ABC)
backflush, 942–945, 943(fig.), 944(fig.)
job order, *see* Job order costing systems
process, *see* Process costing systems
product, *see* Product costing systems
standard, 1050–1052
see also Variance analysis
variable (full), profit center performance evaluation using, 1101–1103, 1102(exh.)
Cost objects, 851
Cost of capital, 1106, 1106–1107, **1149**
Cost of goods manufactured, 847
Cost of goods manufactured budget, 1018, 1018(exh.)
Cost of goods sold, 174, 174–175, 181
income statement and, 849
Cost of Goods Sold account, 184, 846, 852
backflush costing and, 943, 945
closing, 187, 187(exh.)
job order costing system and, 891
under periodic inventory system, 180–181
under perpetual inventory system, 172, 173, 179, 180, 185
process costing system and, 897
Cost-plus contracts, 892, 892–893
Cost pools, 851
Cost principle, 47
alternatives to, 48
Cost savings, 1144
Costs of quality, 805
Cost-volume-profit (CVP) analysis, 975, 975–976
for manufacturing businesses, 980–984, 983(exh.)
for service businesses, 984–985
Coupon(s), 536
Coupon bonds, 674
Couric, Katie, 860
CPAs (certified public accountants), reports of, 23–24
Credit, 52
Credit analysts, 232
Credit cards, 170, 178, 933–934
Creditors
statement of cash flows and, 712
as users of accounting information, 9–10
as users of financial performance evaluation, 752–753
Credit policies, 405–406, 406(fig.), 407(fig.)
Credit services, as information source for financial statement analysis, 757
Crossfooting, 142, 340
Cumulative effect of accounting changes, 639
Cumulative preferred stock, 604
Current assets, 220, 222
changes in, statement of cash flows and, 721
Current liabilities, 223, 528, 528–545
changes in, statement of cash flows and, 721–722
contingent, 538
definitely determinable, 529–535
estimated, 535–537
payroll accounting and, *see* Payroll accounting
Current manufacturing costs, 847
Current position, assessment of, 753
Current ratio, 231, 231(fig.), **766,** 767(exh.)
Customer lists, 499(table)
Customer numbers, 330

Customer service, technology and, 331
CVP, *see* Cost-volume-profit (CVP) analysis

Dalton, Dick, 892
Dashboard system, 1096
Data processing, 324
electronic, *see* Computerized accounting systems; Technology
manual, 330
Date(s)
for bonds, 420–421, 603
for promissory notes, 420–421
Date of declaration, 603
Date of payment, 603
Date of record, 603
Death, of partner, 572
Debentures, 672
Debit, 52
Debit cards, 170, 409
Debt(s)
bad, *see* Uncollectible accounts
early extinguishment of, 688
long-term, *see* Bond *entries;* Long-term liabilities
Debt to equity ratio, 234, 234–235, 235(fig.), **768,** 769(exh.), 770
Decimal points, in financial reports, 66
Decision makers, 8(fig.), 8–10
Decision making, 1128–1156
capital investment decisions and, *see* Capital investment decisions
incremental analysis for, *see* Incremental analysis
management cycle and, 1130–1132, 1131(fig.)
short-run decision analysis and, 1130–1132, 1131(fig.)
Declining-balance method, 490, 490–491
Deferrals, 95
adjusting entries for deferred expenses and, 96–100
adjusting entries for deferred revenues and, 101–102, 102(fig.)
Deferred Income Taxes account, 636, 636–637
Deferred payment, 1194–1195
Deficit, 642
Defined benefit plans, 692
Defined contribution plans, 692
Definitely determinable liabilities, 529, 529–535
Delivery Expense account, 176
under perpetual inventory system, 180
Depletion, 482(fig.), 496–497
Depreciable cost, 488
Depreciation, 98, 482(fig.), 487–491, 502–505
accumulated, 99(fig.), 99–100
adjusting entries for, 98–100
in capital investment analysis, 1144–1145
of closely related plant assets, 497
comparison of methods for computing, 491, 491(fig.)
cost recovery for income tax purposes and, 505
declining-balance method for computing, 490–491
disposal of depreciable assets and, 492–496
factors affecting computation of, 488–489
group, 504
for partial years, 502–503
production method for computing, 489–490
revision of depreciation rates and, 503
of special types of capital expenditures, 504–505
statement of cash flows and, 720
straight-line method for computing, 489
Development costs, in oil and gas industry, 497–498
Differential analysis, *see* Incremental analysis
Differential costs, 1132
Diluted earnings per share, 641, 641–642
Direct charge-off method, 413–414, **414**
Direct costs, 838
Direct labor budget, 1014, 1014–1015, 1016(exh.)
Direct labor costs, 840
standard costs for, 1052–1053
Direct labor efficiency variance, 1061
Direct labor rate standard, 1053
Direct labor rate variance, 1061
Direct labor time standard, 1053
Direct labor variances, 1060–1062
Direct materials costs, 840
equivalent production for, 897–898
standard costs for, 1052
Direct materials price standard, 1052
Direct materials price variance, 1058, 1058–1059
Direct materials purchases budget, 1014, 1015(exh.)
Direct materials quantity standard, 1052
Direct materials quantity variance, 1059
Direct materials variances, 1058–1060, 1060(fig.)
Direct method, 717
Disclosure
of bonds on balance sheet, 674
of liabilities, 529
Discontinued operations, 638
Discount(s), 675
on bonds, 675–676
sales, 177, 191
trade, 176
Discounting, 408
Discount on Common Stock account, 608
Discretionary cost centers, 1097, 1097–1098, 1099(table)
Dishonored notes, 423
Disposal, of depreciable assets, 492–496
Disposal value, 488
in capital investment analysis, 1145
Dissolution (of partnership), **567,** 567–572
by admission of new partner, 567–570
by death of partner, 572
by withdrawal of partner, 570–572, 571(fig.)
Diversified companies, 755, 755–756
Dividend(s), 224
liquidating, 602
policies for, 598
preference as to, 603–605
stock, 644–647
Dividend income, 412
Dividends in arrears, 604
Dividends payable, 531
Dividends yield, 598, 771(exh.), **772**
Documents, internal control and, 367
Dollar amounts, in financial reports, 66
Dollar signs, in financial statements, 66
Double-declining-balance method, 490
Double-entry bookkeeping, 8, 51–54
T account and, 51–52
transaction analysis and processing in, 52–54, 53(fig.)
Double taxation, 596, 596–597
Drawing account, *see* Withdrawals account

Duality, principle of, 51
Due care, 25
Dun & Bradstreet Corp., 757
Duration of note, 421, 421–422

Early extinguishment of debt, 688
Earned Capital account, 224
Earnings before interest and taxes (EBT), 768
Earnings per share, 640–642
Ebanking, 1139
Ebbers, Bernard, 1022
EBT (earnings before interest and taxes), 768
Ecommerce, *see* Electronic commerce (ecommerce)
Economic planners, as users of accounting information, 10
Economic profit, 768
Economic value added (EVA), 768, **1106,** 1106(exh.), 1106–1107, 1107(fig.)
Economy, value chains and, 929
Edgar, 329
EDI (electronic data interchange), 329
Effective interest method, 680
  for amortization of bond discount, 680–682, 681(table), 682(fig.)
  for amortization of bond premium, 683–684, 684(table), 685(fig.)
Effective interest rate, 675, 679
EFT (electronic funds transfer), 409
E2K (event-to-knowledge) management, 330
Electronic commerce (ecommerce), 104, **329**
  global, 807
  voucher systems and, 380
Electronic data interchange (EDI), 329
Electronic funds transfer (EFT), 409
Electronic work sheets, 146
Emerging economies, accounting practices in, 416
Employee earnings record, 541–542
Employee's Withholding Exemption Certificate, 539
Ending inventory, 181
Engineering method, 973
Enterprise resource planning (ERP) systems, 324
Equipment, acquisition cost of, 486
Equities, 14
Equity
  owner's, 15
  residual, 15, 602
  return on, 235–236, 236(fig.), 599–600, 768, 769(exh.)
  stockholders,' components of, 601–602, 602(fig.)
  trading on, 670
Equity financing, 597–598
Equity method, for accounting for stock investments, 1184
Equivalent production, 897, 897–898, 898(fig.)
  for conversion costs, 898
  for direct materials, 897–898
ERP (enterprise resource planning) systems, 324
Estimated liabilities, 535, 535–637
Estimated useful life, 488, 488–489
Estimation
  inventory valuation by, 459–460
  of overhead rate, 854
  quality of earnings and, 631–633
  of uncollectible accounts expense, 415
Ethics, 25, 25–26
  accounting misstatements and, 220
  budgeting and, 1022
  confidentiality and, 342
  core values and, 966
  deceptive use of accounting principles and, 93
  of decision between long-term assets and expenses, 487
  of electronic funds transfer, 409
  financial reporting and, 219–220
  frauds and, 367
  inventory overstatement and, 456
  management's responsibility for financial statements and, 812
  professional, 25–26
  profits and, 1069
  pro-forma statements and, 756
  recycling and, 1103
  standards of ethical conduct and, 810, 812–813(exh.), 813
  truthfulness of financial statements and, 56
  unit costs and, 892
  whistle-blowing and, 634
European Community, accounting standards and, 1179
EVA (economic value added), 768, 1106(exh.), 1106–1107, 1107(fig.)
Event-to-knowledge (E2K) management, 330
Exchange, of plant assets, 494–496
Exchange gains/losses, 1175
  realized versus unrealized, 1176–1177
Exchange rates, 12, 1174, 1174(table)
Ex-dividend stock, 603
Executing stage of management cycle
  activity-based cost information and, 928
  balanced scorecard and, 1093–1094
  budgeting and, 1007
  cost behavior and, 966
  cost information and, 837
  management accounting and, 798(fig.), 798–799
  product cost information and, 885
  short-run decision analysis and, 1130–1131
  standard costs and, 1050
Expenditure(s), 485
Expenses, 16, 18–19, **90,** 90–91
  accrued, 100–101, 101(fig.)
  deferred, 96–100
  income taxes, 635(table), 635–638
  long-term assets versus, 487
  operating, 176
  other, 226
  prepaid, 96–98, 97(fig.)
  recognition of, 93
Expired costs, 91
Explanatory notes, in annual report, 261
Exploration costs, in oil and gas industry, 497–498
Extensible Business Reporting Language (XBRL), 329
Extraordinary items, 638, 638–639
Extraordinary repairs, 504

Face interest rate, 675
Face value, bonds issued at, 674–675
Facility-level activities, 935
Factor(s), 407
Factoring, 407
Factory burden, 840
Factory overhead, 840
  see also Manufacturing overhead costs
Factory Payroll account, 890
Factory tours, 1050
FASB, *see* Financial Accounting Standards Board (FASB)
Fast-food restaurants, supersizing meals in, 978
Federal Reserve Board, 10
Federal Unemployment Insurance tax, 534
FICA tax, 534
FIFO costing method, 896
  for preparing process cost report, 899, 900(exh.), 901–903
FIFO (first-in, first-out) method, 449

Financial accounting, 7
management accounting compared with, 794, 795(table), 796
Financial Accounting Standards Board (FASB), 24
on available-for-sale securities accounting, 1181
on comprehensive income, 630
on conglomerates, 755–756
on cost-benefit convention, 218–219
on exchange gains and losses, 1176, 1177
on full disclosure, 218
on goodwill, 501–502
on long-term leases, 691
on noncash investing and financing transactions, 713–714
on objectives of financial reporting, 214
on other postretirement benefits, **693**
on pension expense, 693
on qualitative characteristics of accounting information, 215
on reporting of foreign subsidiaries, 1177, 1178
on short-term investments, 409
Statement No. 13 of, 691
Statement No. 52 of, 1176, 1177, 1178
Statement No. 87 of, 693
Statement No. 131 of, 755–756
Financial advisors and analysts, as users of accounting information, 10
Financial budgets, 1008, 1018–1022
Financial highlights, in annual report, 258
Financial information
conventions for interpretation of, 216–219
qualitative characteristics of, 214–216, 215(fig.)
Financial leverage, 670
Financial performance evaluation, 750–774, **752**
external users of, 752–753
horizontal analysis for, 759, 760(exh.), 761(exh.)
information sources for, 756–757
internal users of, 752
ratio analysis for, 765–772
Sarbanes-Oxley Act and, 753
standards for, 754–756
trend analysis for, 760–762, 762(exh.), 762(fig.)
vertical analysis for, 762, 763(exh.), 763(fig.), 764(exh.), 764(fig.), 765
Financial position, 14
Financial press
as information source for financial statement analysis, 757
as user of accounting information, 10
Financial statement(s), 7
adjusted trial balance in preparation of, 104–105, 105(exh.), 106(exh.)
in annual report, 258–260
classified, *see* Classified financial statements
common-size, 762, 763(exh.), 763(fig.), 764(exh.), 764(fig.), 765
condensed, 226
consolidated, 1185
cost classifications for, 839–840, 840(table)
dollar signs in, 66
of foreign subsidiaries, restatement of, 1177–1178
GAAP and, 23
interim, 128, 263, 756
inventory systems and, 454, 454(fig.)
notes to, in annual report, 260–261
preparing using work sheet, 145(exh.), 145–146, 146(exh.)
pro forma, 756, 1008
relationships among, 19, 21(exh.), 22–23
truthfulness of, 56
see also specific statements
Financial statement analysis, *see* Financial performance evaluation
Financial Times, 757
Financing
equity, 597–598
of long-term assets, 483
Financing activities, 6, 712, 712–713
statement of cash flows preparation and, 725–727
Financing period, 168, 168–170, 169(fig.)
Finished Goods Inventory account, 844, 846, 847, 851, 852
backflush costing and, 943, 945
job order costing system and, 890–891
process costing system and, 896–897, 902
First-in, first-out (FIFO) method, 449
Fiscal year, 91
Fixed assets, *see* Long-term assets; Plant assets
Fixed costs, 839, 971, 971–972, 972(fig.)
in airline industry, 839
Fixed overhead budget variance, 1066
Fixed overhead volume variance, 1066, 1066–1068
Flexibility principle, 325
Flexible budget(s), 1055
analyzing manufacturing overhead variances using, 1063(exh.), 1063–1064
cost center performance evaluation using, 1100–1101, 1101(exh.)
in variance analysis, 1054–1056, 1055–1057(exh.)
Flexible budget formula, 1055, 1055–1056
FOB destination, 177
FOB shipping point, 177
Folio column, *see* Post. Ref. column
Footings, 52
Forbes, 757
Form 8-K, 757
Form 10-K, 257, 757
Form 10-Q, 757
Form W-4, 539
Fortune, 757
Franchises, 499(table)
Fraud, 367
payroll, 542
Fraudulent financial reporting, 219, 219–220
Free cash flow, 715–717, **770,** 771(exh.)
Freight In account, under periodic inventory system, 183, 190–191
Freight Out Expense account, 176
under perpetual inventory system, 180
Frequent-flier miles, 537
Full-costing method, 497, 497–498
profit center performance evaluation using, 1101–1103, 1102(exh.)
Full disclosure, 218
Full product cost, 926
Functional currency, 1177
Fund accumulation, 1196
FUTA tax, 534
Future potential, assessment of, 753
Future value, 1147, 1188–1189
of ordinary annuity, 1189, 1190(table)
of single sum at compound interest, 1188, 1188(table)
tables of, 1200, 1200(table)–1201(table)

GAAP, *see* Generally accepted accounting principles (GAAP)

Gains
exchange, 1175, 1176–1177
on exchange of assets, 495–496
from extraordinary items, 639
quality of earnings and, 633
on sale of partnership assets, 573–575, 574(exh.)
statement of cash flows and, 720–721
GASB (Governmental Accounting Standards Board), 24
Gas industry, development and exploration costs in, 497–498
General journal, 63, 63–64
General ledger, 48, 64–66
ledger account form in, 64(exh.), 64–65
posting to, 65(exh.), 65–66
General Ledger Software, 326
General ledger systems, 326, 327(fig.), 328, 328(fig.)
structure of, 326, 328, 328f
Generally accepted accounting principles (GAAP), 23, 23–24
financial statements and, 23–24
independent CPAs' reports and, 23
organizations influencing, 24
Global business, *see* International business
Goals
budgeting and, 1004–1005
coordination of, 1109
linking to objectives and targets, 1108
Goethe, 51
Going concern, 92
Goods available for sale, 181
Goods flow, 447
Good units, 1060
Goodwill, 499(table), 501–502
Governmental Accounting Standards Board (GASB), 24
Governmental organizations, 10
Graphical user interfaces (GUIs), 326
Gross margin, 175, 175–176
Gross margin method, 460, 460(table)
Gross profit, 175–176
Gross profit method, 460, 460(table)
Gross sales, 174
Group depreciation, 504
Group purchases, 487
GUIs (graphical user interfaces), 326

Handbook of Dividend Achievers, 757, 758
Held-to-maturity securities, 410, 1180
High-low method, 974, 974–975
Hill, Eleanor, 892
Historical cost, 47
Horizontal analysis, 759, 760(exh.), 761(exh.)

IASB (International Accounting Standards Board), 1178
Ideal capacity, 968
IFAC (International Federation of Accountants), 1178
IMA, *see* Institute of Management Accountants (IMA)
Impairment reviews, 501–502
Imprest system, 378
In balance, defined, 62
Income, 88–113
comprehensive, 630
dividend, 412
interest, 412
measurement issues and, 91–92
net, *see* Net income
operating, 975
residual, 1104–1105, 1106(exh.)
taxable, 635
Income from continuing operations, 630
Income from operations, 226
Income statement, 21(exh.), **22,** 226–230, 227(exh.)
absorption costing, profit center performance evaluation using, 1101–1103, 1102(exh.)
budgeted, 1018–1019, 1019(exh.)
cost of goods sold and, 849
for merchandising businesses, 173–176, 174(fig.), 175(exh.)
quality of earnings and, 630–631, 631(exh.)
reading and graphing data from, 228(exh.), 228–230, 229(fig.), 230(exh.)
Income statement column, merchandising business and, 186–187, 188–189
Income Summary account, 130
closing process and, 130, 132(fig.), 132–139
under periodic inventory system, 188, 190, 191
Income tax(es), 535–638, 635(table)
in capital investment analysis, 1145
of corporations, 596–597
cost recovery and, 505
deferred, 636–637
inventory systems and, 454–455
net of taxes and, 637–638
payroll accounting and, 534
Income tax allocation, 636
Income taxes payable, 531–532
Incremental analysis, 1132, 1132–1143
irrelevant costs and revenues and, 1132–1133, 1133(exh.)
opportunity costs and, 1133–1134
for outsourcing decisions, 1134–1136, 1135(exh.)
for sales mix decisions, 1140–1141, 1141(exh.)
for segment probability decisions, 1137–1140, 1139(exh.)
for sell or process-further decisions, 1142–1143, 1143(exh.)
for special order decisions, 1136–1137, 1137(exh.)
Incremental costs, 1132
Independence, 25
Independent auditors' report, in annual report, 261–263, 262(fig.)
Independent verification, for internal control, 367–368
Index numbers, 761
Indirect costs, 838
Indirect labor costs, 840
Indirect manufacturing costs, 840
Indirect material costs, 840
Indirect method, 717
for preparing statement of cash flows, 717–718, 717–720, 719f, 720(exh.)
Industry norms, for financial statement analysis, 754–756, 755(exh.)
Industry Norms and Key Business Ratios, 754, 757
Influential but noncontrolling interest, 1180–1181, 1181(table), 1184
Information and communication, 366
Initial public offerings (IPOs), 597, 597–598
Inspection time, 941
Installment accounts receivable, 413
Institute of Management Accountants (IMA), 25
Code of Professional Conduct for Management Accountants of, 25–26, 812–813(exh.)
definition of management accounting, 794
Intangible assets, 223, 498, 498(fig.), 499(table), 500–502
Intangible resources, 482(fig.)
Integrated programs, 326
Integrity, 25
Interest, 422, 1146, 1187–1188
imputing on noninterest-bearing notes, 1193–1194

on partners' capital, 562
on promissory notes, 422
Interest (in company)
controlling, 1181, 1181(table), 1185
influential but noncontrolling, 1180–1181, 1181(table), 1184
noninfluential and noncontrolling, 1180–1181, 1181(table)
Interest (in partnership), 564–567, 567(exh.)
purchase of, 568
sale of, 571
Interest coverage ratio, 671, 769(exh.), 770
Interest expense, for bonds, year-end accrual of, 686–688
Interest income, 412
Interest rates
on bonds, 675–676
on promissory notes, 422
Interim financial statements, 128, **756**
in annual report, 263
Internal control(s), 172, 172–173, 364–389, 366
activities of, 367–368
bank reconciliations for, 375–378
components of, 366–367
limitations of, 368
management goals and, 369
management's responsibility for, 366
over merchandising transactions, 368–375
petty cash procedures for, 378–379
voucher systems for, 380–385
Internal Revenue Service (IRS), 24
International accounting, 1173(table), 1173–1179, 1174(fig.)
accounting standards for, 500, 1174, 1178–1179
exchange rates and, 1174, 1174(table)
foreign purchases and, 1176
foreign sales and, 1175
realized versus unrealized exchange gain or loss and, 1176–1177
restatement of foreign subsidiary financial statements and, 1177–1178
International Accounting Standards (IASs), 500
International Accounting Standards Board (IASB), 1178
International business
accounting changes and, 639
accounting practices in emerging economies and, 416
airline bankruptcies and, 671
budgeting and, 1006
capital investment and, 1145
closing and, 139
comparability of accounting standards and, 500
continuous improvement to address global competition and, *see* Continuous improvement
cost-volume-profit analysis and, 976
dashboard system and, 1096
ebanking and, 1139
ecommerce and, 807
European stock markets and, 601
hybrid costing systems and, 887
just-in-time operating philosophy and, 940
partnerships and, 559
privatization and, 99
reserves and, 644
standard costing and, 1068
statement of cash flows and, 714
valuation of transactions in, 47
International Federation of Accountants (IFAC), 1178
Internet, 328, 328–330
financial reports on, 757
joint ventures and, 560
support of value chain, 802
uses of, 329–330
Internet retailing, 177
Inventoriable costs, *see* Product cost(s)
Inventory
beginning, 181
ending, 181
under just-in-time operating philosophy, 939
in manufacturing businesses, accounts for, 843–847
in merchandising businesses, *see* Merchandise inventory
physical, 172–173
see also Merchandise inventory; *specific inventory accounts*
Inventory cost, 446, 446–447
goods flow versus cost flow and, 447
merchandise in transit and, 446(fig.), 446–447
merchandise on hand not included in inventory and, 447
Inventory systems
financial statements and, 454, 454(fig.)
income taxes and, 454–455
perpetual, 171–172
see also Periodic inventory system; Perpetual inventory system
Inventory turnover, 444, 444–446, 445(fig.), **766,** 767(exh.)
Inventory valuation
by estimation, 459–460
at lower of cost or market, 457–458
under periodic inventory system, 447–450
under perpetual inventory system, 451–453, 453(fig.)
Investing activities, 6, 712
statement of cash flows preparation and, 722–725
Investment(s), 222
capital, *see* Capital investment *entries*
of idle cash, 1195–1196
long-term, 409, 1180–1185
owner's, 15, 16
in partnership, 568
short-term, *see* Short-term investments
statement of cash flows and, 723
Investment advisory services, as information source for financial statement analysis, 757
Investment centers, 1098, 1099(table), 1103–1108
economic value added and, 1106(exh.), 1106–1107, 1107(fig.)
multiple performance measures for, 1108
residual income and, 1104–1105, 1106(exh.)
return on investment and, 1103(exh.), 1103–1104, 1105(fig.)
Investors
statement of cash flows and, 712
as users of accounting information, 9
as users of financial performance evaluation, 752–753
Invoice, 373(fig.), **374**
IPOs (initial public offerings), 597–598
IRS (Internal Revenue Service), 24
Issued stock, 602
Item-by-item method, 458
Item column, in general ledger, 64–65

JIT, *see* Just-in-time (JIT) *entries*
Job order(s), 886
Job order cost cards, 844, **886**
for manufacturing businesses, 892

Job order costing systems, 886, 887–894
job order cost cards and, 892
in manufacturing businesses, 887–891, 888–889(exh.)
in service organizations, 892–894, 893(fig.)
Joint products, 1142
Joint ventures, 560
Journal(s), 63
general, 63–64
special-purpose, *see* Special-purpose journals
Journal entries, 63
adjusting, *see* Adjusting entries
closing, *see* Closing entries
compound, 63
reversing, 140–141
Journal form, 54
Journalizing, 63
Just-in-time (JIT) operating environment, 446
Just-in-time (JIT) operating philosophy, 804, 938, 938–946
activity-based management compared with, 945–946, 946(table)
backflush costing and, 942–945, 943(fig.), 944(fig.)
continuous improvement of work environment and, 941
minimum inventory levels and, 939
multiskilled work force and, 940
preventive maintenance and, 940
product costs in, 941–942
product quality and, 940
pull-through production and, 939
quick setup and flexible work cells and, 939–940

Kaplan, Robert S., 1092
King, Larry, 860

Land, acquisition cost of, 486
Land improvements, acquisition cost of, 486
Last-in, first-out (LIFO) method, 449, 449–450, 450(fig.), 452
LCM (lower-of-cost-or-market) rule, 457–458
Lease(s)
capital, 691
long-term, 690–692, 691(table)
operating, 690
Leasehold(s), 499(table)
Leasehold improvements, 499(table), 501
Ledger(s), 48
subsidiary, 332
Ledger account form, 64, 64(exh.), 64–65
Legal capital, 597
Letterman, David, 860
Letter to stockholders, 257–258
Liabilities, 15, 524–545
accrued, 88, 89, 531
classification of, 528
on classified balance sheet, 223
contingent, 407, 538
current, *see* Current liabilities
disclosure of, 529
estimated, 535–537
long-term, 223, 528
managing liquidity and cash flows and, 526–527, 527(fig.)
payment of, 17
payroll, 532, 533(fig.), 534–535
purchase of assets by incurring, 17
recognition of, 528
valuation of, 528
Liability, unlimited, 558–559
Licenses, 499(table)
Life
limited, 558
useful, estimated, 488–489
LIFO liquidation, 455
LIFO method, *see* Last-in, first-out (LIFO) method
Limited liability corporations, 559
Limited life, 558
Limited partnerships, 560
Linear approximation, 970
Lines of credit, 529, 529–530
Li-Ning, 1068
Liquidating dividends, 602
Liquidation (of partnership), **572,** 572–577
gain on sale of assets and, 573–575, 574(exh.)
loss on sale of assets and, 575(exh.), 575–577
Liquidity, 5, 5–6, **230,** 526–527, 527(fig.), 528
evaluation of, 230–231, 766, 766(fig.), 767(exh.)
Loans, from banks, 529–530
Long-lived assets, *see* Plant assets
Long-term assets, 478–509, **480**
decision to acquire, 481–483
depreciation of, *see* Depreciation
expenses versus, 487
financing, 483
intangible, 498, 498(fig.), 499(table), 500–502
matching rule applied to, 484, 484(fig.)
natural resources, 496–498
see also Plant assets
Long-term debt, current portions of, 532
Long-term investments, 409, 1180–1185
in bonds, 1180
in stocks, 1180–1185, 1181(table)
Long-term leases, 690–692, 691(table)
Long-term liabilities, 223, 528, 668–696
amount of debt to carry and, 671(fig.), 671–672
bonds, *see* Bond *entries*
decision to issue long-term debt and, 670
leases, 690–692, 691(table)
mortgages payable, 690
other postretirement benefits, 693
pensions, 692–693
types of debt and, 672
Losses
exchange, 1175, 1176–1177
on exchange of assets, 495
from extraordinary items, 639
net, 16, 90
quality of earnings and, 633
on sale of partnership assets, 575(exh.), 575–577
statement of cash flows and, 720–721
Lower-of-cost-or-market (LCM) rule, 457, 457–458
LP column, *see* Post. Ref. column

MACRS (modified accelerated cost recovery system), 505
Mail, cash received through, control of, 370
Major category method, 458, 459(table)
Make-or-buy decisions, 1134
Management, 9
basic functions of, 9
goals of, internal control and, 369
responsibility for financial statements, 812
statement of cash flows and, 712
as users of accounting information, 9
as users of financial performance evaluation, 752
Management accounting, 7, 794, 794–800
financial accounting compared with, 794, 795(table), 796
management cycle and, 796(fig.), 796–800
support of value chain analysis, 802–804, 803(exh.)

Management information systems (MISs), 8
Management's discussion and analysis, in annual report, 258
Managers, cost variances for evaluating performance of, 1069, 1070(exh.)
Manual data processing, 330
Manufacturing businesses
 cost reporting and inventory accounting in, 849, 850(fig.), 850–851
 cost-volume-profit analysis for, 980–984, 983(exh.)
 job order costing system for, 887–891, 888–889(exh.)
 tours of, 1050
Manufacturing cost flow, 846, 846(fig.), 846–847
Manufacturing Overhead account, 844, 852
 job order costing system and, 890, 891
 Manufacturing overhead budget, 1015, 1016(exh.), 1017
 Manufacturing overhead costs, 840
 allocating, 852, 853(fig.), 854–860, 855(fig.)
 over- and underapplied, 852
Manufacturing overhead variances, 1062–1069
 analyzing using flexible budgets, 1063(exh.), 1063–1064
Margin(s), 803
 gross, 175–176
 segment, 1138
Margin of safety, 976
Marketable securities, 409
 see also Short-term investments
Market interest rate, 675, 679
Market price, of companies, stock splits and, 647
Market share, in candy industry, 849
Market strength, evaluating, 770, 771(exh.), 772
Market value, 458
Master budget, 1008, 1008–1011, 1009–1011(fig.)
Matching rule, 92
 applying to inventories, 442–443
 long-term assets and, 484, 484(fig.)
Materiality, 217
Materials Inventory account, 843–844, 846, 850–851
 backflush costing and, 942
 job order costing system and, 889–890
Materials request form, 844
Maturity date, 420, 420–421
Maturity value, 422
 of promissory notes, 422
Measurement, 11–12, 44–68
 accounts and, 48, 49–50, 50–51
 clarification issue and, 48
 double-entry system and, 51–54
 of income, *see* Income
 of inventory, *see* Inventory cost; Inventory systems; Inventory valuation
 money measure and, 11–12
 object of, 11
 of profitability, 90–91
 recognition issue and, 46–47
 recording and posting transactions and, 63–66
 separate entity concept and, 12
 transaction analysis illustration and, 54–61, 60(exh.)
 trial balance and, 61(exh.), 61–63, 62(table)
 valuation issue and, 47–48
Medical insurance, payroll accounting and, 534
Medicare tax, 534
Merchandise in transit, cost of, 446(fig.), 446–447
Merchandise inventory, 168, 440–466, **442**
 cost of, *see* Inventory cost
 evaluating level of, 444–446, 445(fig.)
 impact of inventory decisions and, 443, 444(fig.)
 loss of, 458
 matching rule applied to, 442–443
 overstatement of, 456
 valuation of, *see* Inventory valuation
 see also Inventory systems; *specific inventory systems*
Merchandise Inventory account, 850
 under periodic inventory system, 180–181, 182–183, 184, 188
 under perpetual inventory system, 172, 173, 178, 179, 180, 185
Merchandising businesses, 166–195, **168**
 adjusting entries for, 187
 cash flow management and, 168(fig.), 168–170, 169(fig.)
 closing entries for, 187, 187(exh.), 190(exh.), 190–191
 control of, 172–173
 income statement for, 173–176, 174(fig.), 175(exh.)
 inventory systems for, 171–172
  see also Inventory systems; *specific inventory systems*
 profitability management and, 170–171, 171(exh.)
 purchases discounts and, 191–192
 sales discounts and, 191
 terms of sale and, 176–178
 work sheet for, 185–187, 186(exh.), 188–191, 189(exh.)
Merchandising transactions, internal control over, 368–375
Mergent's, 757
MISs (management information systems), 8
Mission, 796, 796–797
Misstatements, inventory measurement and, 455–457
Mixed costs, 972, 972(fig.), 972–975
 engineering method of separating, 973
 high-low method for, 974–975
 scatter diagram method for, 973–974, 974(fig.)
 statistical methods for, 975
Modified accelerated cost recovery system (MACRS), 505
Money, time value of, *see* Time value of money
Money measure, 11, 11–12
Monitoring, 367
Moody's Investors Service, Inc., 757
Mortgages(s), 690
Mouse, 326
Moving time, 941
Multistep form (of income statement), **226,** 226–227, 227(exh.)
Mutual agency, 558

Natural resources, 482(fig.), 496–498
 depletion of, 496–497
 depreciation of closely related plant assets and, 497
 development and exploration costs in oil and gas industry and, 497–498
Net assets, 15
Net cash inflows, 1144
Net cost of purchases, 181
Net income, 16, 90, 176
 in capital investment analysis, 1144
Net losses, 16, 90
Net of taxes, 637, 637–638
Net present value method, 1149, 1149–1151
 advantages of, 1149–1150
 illustration of, 1150–1151
Net purchases, 181
Net sales, 174

Net worth, *see* Owner's equity
Neuer Markt, 601
New manufacturing environment, *see* Just-in-time (JIT) operating philosophy
New York Stock Exchange (NYSE), 7
Nominal accounts, 130
Noncash investing and financing transactions, 713, 713–714
Noncompete covenants, 499(table)
Noncumulative preferred stock, 604
Nonfinancial measures, in service organizations, 810, 811(exh.)
Noninfluential and noncontrolling interest, 1180–1181, 1181(table)
Noninventoriable costs, 840
Nonoperating items, 638–640
  accounting changes, 639–640
  discontinued operations, 638
  extraordinary items, 638–639
  quality of earnings and, 633–634
Nonvalue-adding activities, 805, 932
  process value analysis and, 933–934
  in service organizations, 932
Nonvalue-adding costs, 839
No-par stock, 606, 608
Normal balance, 61
Normal capacity, 968
Normal costing, 842
Norton, David P., 1092
Notes payable, 420, 530(fig.), 530–531
Notes receivable, 420
  see also Promissory notes
Notes Receivable account, 90
Notes to the financial statements, in annual report, 260–261
Not-for-profit organizations, 10
  capital investment analysis for, 1147
Nouveau Marche, 601
NYSE (New York Stock Exchange), 7

Objectives, linking of goals to, 1108
Objectivity, 25
O'Brien, Conan, 860
Obsolescence, 488
Oil industry, development and exploration costs in, 497–498
100-year bonds, 677
Operating activities, 6, 712
  statement of cash flows preparation and, 717–722, 718–720(exh.), 719(fig.)
Operating assets, 222–223
Operating budgets, 170, 170–171, 171(exh.), **1008**
Operating capacity, 968, 968–969
Operating cycle, 168, 168(fig.), **766**
Operating decisions, accounting methods and, 455
Operating expenses, 176
Operating income, 975
Operating leases, 690
Operating objectives, 797
Operations
  discontinued, 638
  income from, 226
Opinion section, of auditors' report, 262(fig.), 262–263
Opportunity costs, 1133, 1133–1134
Ordinary annuities, 1148, 1148–1149
Ordinary repairs, 504
Organization charts, 1098, 1098–1100, 1100(fig.)
Original cost, 47
Other assets, 220
Other postretirement benefits, 693
Other revenues and expenses, 226
Outsourcing, 802, 1134, 1134–1136, 1135(exh.)
Outstanding stock, 602
Overapplied overhead costs, 852
Overhead rates
  applying, 858–860
  estimation of, 854
  planning, 857–858, 858(fig.), 859(table)
  predetermined, 852
Owner's equity, 15
  business form and, 223–224
  on classified balance sheet, 223–224
Owner's investments, 15, 16
Owner's withdrawals, 15, 19

Pacioli, Fra Luca, 8, 51
Paid-in Capital in Excess of Par Value account, 646
Paid-in Capital in Excess of Stated Value account, 607, 608
Paid-in Capital, Retirement of Stock account, 611
Paid-in Capital, Treasury Stock account, 610–611
Parent company, 1185
Participative budgeting, 1006
Partner(s), in accounting firms, risks of being, 566
Partners' equity, 223
Partners' equity, 561, 561–562
Partnership(s), 13, 13(table), 14(fig.), 556–579, **558**
  advantages and disadvantages of, 559
  characteristics of, 558–560
  corporations resembling, 559
  dissolution of, 567–572
  distribution of income and losses of, 562–567
  international investment and, 559
  limited, 560
  liquidation of, 572–577
  owner's equity in, 223
  partners' equity and, 561–562
Partnership agreement, 558
Partnership income/losses
  distribution of, 562–567
  participation in, 559
Par value, 597
Par value stock, 607–608
Past performance
  assessment of, 753
  as standard for financial statement analysis, 754
Patents, 499(table)
Payables turnover, 526, 527, 527(fig.), **766,** 767(exh.)
Payback period method, 1151, 1151–1152
Payment
  deferred, 1194–1195
  of liabilities, 17
  of long-term debt, timing of, 672
  of payroll and payroll taxes, 542–543
Payroll accounting, 538–543
  computation of take-home pay and, 538–539, 540(fig.)
  employee earnings record and, 541–542
  fraud and, 542
  payment of payroll and payroll taxes and, 542–543
  payroll register and, 540(exh.), 540–541, 541(exh.)
  recording payroll and, 541
  recording payroll taxes and, 542
Payroll Bank Account account, 542
Payroll liabilities, 532, 533(fig.), 534–535
Payroll register, 540, 540(exh.), 540–541, 541(exh.)
Payroll taxes
  payment of, 542–543
  recording, 542
Peachtree Complete Accounting, 326, 327(fig.)
Pension(s), 692–693
Pension contributions, payroll accounting and, 534
Pension funds, 692
Pension plans, 692

P/E (price/earnings) ratio, 598, 771(exh.), 772
Percentage of net sales method, 415, 415–416, 418(fig.), 418–419
Performance-based pay, 1108, 1108–1109
Performance evaluation
for managers, cost variances for, 1069, 1070(exh.)
product cost information for, 903
Performance management and evaluation systems, 1096
Performance measure(s), 6, 6–7, **807,** 807–810
balanced scorecard and, 808–809, 809(fig.)
benchmarking and, 809–810
in management cycle, 807–808
Performance measurement, 1090–1112, **1096**
incentives and goals and, 1108–1109
multiple measures for, 1108
object of, 1096
quality of earnings and, 634–635
responsibility accounting for, *see* Investment centers; Responsibility accounting
Period costs, 840
Periodic inventory system, 82(exh.), 181–185, 183(fig.)
pricing inventory under, 447–450
work sheet for merchandising business using, 188–191, 189(exh.)
Periodicity, 91
Permanent accounts, 130
Perpetual inventory system, 171, 171–172, 178–181
merchandise purchase transactions under, 178–179
merchandise sales transactions under, 179–181
pricing inventory under, 451–453, 453(fig.)
work sheet for merchandising business using, 185–187, 186(exh.)
Personal account, *see* Withdrawals account
Personnel procedures, internal control and, 368
Petty Cash account, 379
Petty cash fund, 378, 378–379
establishing, 378
making disbursements from, 378–379
reimbursing, 379
Petty cash vouchers, 378, 378–379, 379(exh.)
Physical controls, 367
Physical deterioration, 488
Physical inventory, 172, 172–173
Planning
activity-based cost information and, 927–928
balanced scorecard and, 1092–1093, 1094(fig.)
budgeting and, 1007
cost behavior and, 966
cost information and, 836–837
management accounting and, 796–798, 797(fig.)
product cost information and, 884
short-run decision analysis and, 1130
standard costs and, 1050
strategic, 1004
Plant assets, 222–223
acquisition cost of, 485–487
closely related to natural resources, depreciation of, 497
depreciation of, *see* Depreciation
discarding, 492–493
exchanges of, 494–496
sale of, 492–494
statement of cash flows and, 724–725
Plant Assets account, 724
Portfolio, 752
Post. Ref. column
in cash payments journal, 342
in cash receipts journal, 338, 340
in general journal, 64
in general ledger, 65, 66
in purchases journal, 337
in sales journal, 334, 335
Post-closing trial balance, 139, 139(exh.)
Posting, 65. 65(exh.), 65–66
batch, 328
real-time, 328
Potentially dilutive securities, 641
Practical capacity, 968
Predetermined overhead rate, 852
Preferred stock, 602, 603–606
callable, 606
convertible, 605–606
cumulative, 604
noncumulative, 604
preference as to assets, 605
preference as to dividends, 603–605
Preferred Stock account, 607
Premiums, 676
on bonds, 676–677
Prepaid expenses, 96
adjusting entries for, 96–98, 97(fig.)
Present value, 1147, 1147–1149, 1189–1192
of ordinary annuity, 1148–1149, 1191–1192, 1192(table)
of single sum due in future, 1147–1148, 1190–1191, 1191(table)
tables of, 1201(table)–1205(table), 1201–1205
valuing bonds using, 677–678
President's Council of Economic Advisers, 10
Preventive maintenance, in just-in-time operating philosophy, 940
Price(s)
of bonds, 675
call (redemption), 606, 688
Price/earnings (P/E) ratio, 598, 771(exh.), **772**
Primary processes, 800
in value chain analysis, 801–802
Prime costs, 843, 843(fig.)
Principle of duality, 51
Private corporations, 257
Process costing systems, 886, 894–897
cost flows through Work in Process Inventory accounts and, 896–897
FIFO costing method for preparing report and, 899, 900(exh.), 901–903
patterns of product flows and cost flows and, 894–896, 895(fig.)
for two or more production departments, 902–903
Process cost report, 896
FIFO costing method for preparing, 899, 900(exh.), 901–903
Processing time, 941
Process value analysis (PVA), 933, 933–934
Procurement cards, 933–934
Product(s)
joint, 1142
quality of, *see* Continuous improvement; Quality
Product cost(s), 839, 839–840, 840(table), 840–843
computation of product unit cost and, 841(table), 841–843
management cycle and, 884(fig.), 884–885
performance evaluation and, 903
prime cost and conversion cost and, 843, 843(fig.)

shifting patterns of, 841
Product costing systems, 882–906, **885,** 885–887
hybrid, 887
job order, *see* Job order costing systems
process, *see* Process costing systems
Product flows, process costing system and, 894–896, 895(fig.)
Production, time required for, 890
Production budget, **1012,** 1012–1013, 1013(exh.)
Production method, 489, 489–490
Product-level activities, 935
Product quality, in just-in-time operating philosophy, 940
Product unit cost, 841, 841(table), 841–843
Product warranty liability, 536–537
Professional ethics, 25, 25–26
Profit, 90, 975
economic, 768
ethics and, 1069
gross, 175–176
see also Cost-volume-profit (CVP) analysis
see also Net income
Profitability, 5, 5–6, **231**
desirable level of, 235
evaluation of, 231–237, 766, 768, 769(exh.)
in fast-food industry, 978
measurement of, 90–91
of segments, incremental analysis for decisions about, 1137–1140, 1139(exh.)
Profitability management, 170, 170–171, 171(exh.)
Profit centers, 1098, 1099(table)
evaluating performance using flexible budgeting, 1101–1103, 1102(exh.)
Profit margin, 232, 768, 769(exh.), **1104**
Pro forma statements, 756, **1008**
Promissory notes, 420
accounting entries for, 422–423
computations for, 420–422
dishonored, 423
Property, plant, and equipment, 222, 222–223
see also Plant assets
Property taxes, 536
Proprietorship, *see* Owner's equity
Public companies, 257
Pull-through production, 939
Purchase(s)
of assets by incurring liabilities, 17
of assets with cash, 16
control of, 371–373(fig.), 374–375
foreign, 1176
group, 487
of interest from partners, 568
of materials, 844
net, 181
net cost of, 181
under perpetual inventory system, 178–179
of treasury stock, 610
Purchase order, 373(fig.), **374,** 844
Purchase request, 844
Purchase requisition, 373(fig.), **374**
Purchases account, 183
under periodic inventory system, 190–191
Purchases discounts, 191, 191–192
Purchases Discounts account, 192
Purchases journal, 335, 335–338, 336(exh.), 337(exh.)
Purchases Returns and Allowances account, 184
under periodic inventory system, 183
Push-through method, 939
PVA (process value analysis), 933–934

Qualitative characteristics, 214–216, **215,** 215(fig.)
Quality
costs of, 805
in just-in-time operating philosophy, 940
see also Continuous improvement
Quality of earnings, 630, 630–635
accounting method and estimate choices and, 631-633
corporate income statement and, 630–631, 631(exh.)
effect on cash flows and performance measures, 634–635
gains and losses and, 633
nonoperating items and, 633–634
reasons to study, 630
write-downs and restructurings and, 633
Queue time, 941
QuickBooks, 326
Quick ratio, 402, 766, 767(exh.)

Ratio analysis, 765, 765–772
of cash flow adequacy, 770, 771(exh.)
of cash-generating efficiency, 714–715
of liquidity, 766, 766f, 767(exh.)
of long-term solvency, 768, 769(exh.), 770
of market strength, 770, 771(exh.), 772
of profitability, 231–237, 766, 768, 769(exh.)
Real accounts, 130
Realizable value, 458
Real-time posting, 328
Receivable turnover, 405, 406, **766,** 767(exh.)
Receiving report, 373(fig.), **374,** 844
Recognition, 46, 46–47, 56
of expenses, 93
of liabilities, 528
of revenues, 93
Recognition point, 46
Records, internal control and, 367
Recourse, factoring and, 407
Redemption price, 606, 688
Registered bonds, 673, 673–674
Regression analysis, 975
Regulatory agencies, as users of accounting information, 10
Relevance, 215
Relevant range, 970
Reliability, 216
Report(s)
activity-based costing, 929
of CPAs, in annual report, 261–263, 262(fig.)
fraudulent, 219–220
of independent CPAs, 23–24
objectives of, 214
presentation of, 66
process cost, FIFO method for preparing, 899, 900(exh.), 901–903
see also Financial statement(s); *specific financial statements*
Reporting currency, 1177
Reporting stage of management cycle
activity-based cost information and, 928
balanced scorecard and, 1095, 1095(fig.)
budgeting and, 1008
cost behavior and, 966–967
cost information and, 837
management accounting and, 799–800, 800(exh.)
product cost information and, 885
short-run decision analysis and, 1132
standard costs and, 1051
Report of management's responsibilities, in annual report, 261
Research and development costs, 500–501
Reserve(s)

cash, 405
international business and, 644
Reserve for Bad Debts account, 415
Residual equity, 15, **602**
Residual income (RI), 1104, 1104–1105, 1106(exh.)
Residual value, 488
in capital investment analysis, 1145
Responsibility accounting, 1097, 1097–1108
responsibility centers and, 1097–1098
see also Cost centers; Investment centers; Profit centers; Revenue centers
Responsibility centers, 1097, 1097–1098
see also Cost centers; Investment centers; Profit centers; Revenue centers
Restatement, of foreign subsidiary financial statements, 1177–1178
Restriction on retained earnings, 644
Restructurings, 633
Retail businesses, cost reporting and inventory accounting in, 849–850, 850(fig.)
Retail method, 459, 459–460, 460(table)
Retained earnings, 642, 644
restrictions on, 644
statement of cash flows and, 726
Retained Earnings account, 224, 611
Retirement
of bonds, 688–689
of treasury stock, 611–612
Return on assets, 232, 232–234, 233(fig.), 234(fig.), **768,** 769(exh.)
Return on equity, 235, 235–236, 236(fig.), **599,** 599–600, **768,** 769(exh.)
Return on investment (ROI), 1103, 1103(exh.), 1103–1104, 1105(fig.)
Revenue(s), 16, 17, **90**
accrued, 103(fig.), 103–104
controllable, 1098
deferred, 101–102, 102(fig.)
other, 226
unearned, 102, 535
Revenue centers, 1098, 1099(table)
Revenue expenditures, 485
Revenue recognition, 93
Reversing entries, 140, 140–141
Reviewing stage of management cycle
activity-based cost information and, 928
balanced scorecard and, 1094–1095
budgeting and, 1008
cost behavior and, 966–967
cost information and, 837
management accounting and, 799
product cost information and, 885
short-run decision analysis and, 1131–1132
standard costs and, 1050–1051
RI (residual income), 1104–1105, 1106(exh.)
Risk assessment, 366, 753
Risk Management Association, 757
Robert Morris Associates, 757
ROI (return on investment), 1103(exh.), 1103–1104, 1105(fig.)
Rolling forecasts, 1008
Rule-of-thumb measures, for financial statement analysis, 754

Salaries, 532
of partners, 564–567, 567(exh.)
Sales, 174
of bonds between interest dates, 685–686, 687(fig.)
cash flows to, 715, 770, 771(exh.)
collecting on, 415
cost of, 174–175
foreign, 1175
gross, 174
of interest in partnership, 571
net, 174
of partnership assets, 573–577, 574(exh.), 575(exh.)
under perpetual inventory system, 179–181
of plant assets, 492–494
terms of, 176–178
of treasury stock, 610–611
Sales account
job order costing system and, 891
under periodic inventory system, 191
Sales budget, 1011, 1011–1012, 1013(exh.)
Sales discounts, 177, 191
Sales Discounts account, 191
Sales forecasts, 1012
Sales invoice, 846
Sales journal, 333, 333–335, 333–335(exh.)
Sales mix, 979, 979(fig.)
Sales mix decisions, 1140
incremental analysis for, 1140–1141, 1141(exh.)
Sales returns, 180
Sales Returns and Allowances account, 174, 180
under periodic inventory system, 180–181, 185, 190–191
Sales taxes payable, 531–532
Salvage value, 488
Sarbanes-Oxley Act, 219–220, **753,** 812
Scatter diagrams, 973, 973–974, 974(fig.)
Scope section, of auditors' report, 262, 262(fig.)
S corporations, 559
Seasonal cycle, managing cash needs during, 404(fig.), 404–405
Secured bonds, 673
Securities and Exchange Commission (SEC), 24
on accrual accounting, 94
on cost-benefit convention, 218–219
deceptive use of accounting principles and, 93
Edgar and, 329
Form 10-K of, 257
on full disclosure, 218
materiality and, 217
reports filed with, 757, 799, 812
stock registration with, 257
as user of accounting information, 10
Securitization, 407, 407–408
Segment(s), 638
decision to drop, 1138
Segment margins, 1138
Segment probability decisions, incremental analysis for, 1137–1140, 1139(exh.)
Seiberling, Frank, 711
Selling and administrative activities, activity-based costing for, 937–938, 938(exh.)
Selling and administrative expense budget, 1017, 1017(exh.)
Sell or process-further decisions, 1142
incremental analysis for, 1142–1143, 1143(exh.)
Separate entity, 12
Separation of duties, 368
Servers, 326
Service businesses, 168
activity-based management in, 930–931, 931(fig.)
cost allocation in, 860–861
cost reporting in, 849, 850(fig.)
cost-volume-profit analysis for, 984–985
job order costing in, 892–894, 893(fig.)

nonfinancial data in, 810, 811(exh.)
value-adding and nonvalue-adding activities in, 932, 933(table)
Share buybacks, 611
Shares of stock, 594
Shipping documents, 846
Shoplifting, 173
Short-run decision(s), incremental analysis for, *see* Incremental analysis
Short-run decision analysis, 1130, 1130–1132, 1131
Short-term financial assets, 402, 402–427
accounts receivable and, *see* Accounts receivable
cash and cash equivalents and, 408–409
credit policies and, 405–406, 406(fig.), 407(fig.)
financing receivables and, 407–408
investments as, 409–412
managing cash needs during seasonal cycles and, 404(fig.), 404–405
notes receivable, *see* Promissory notes
Short-term investments, 409, 409–512
available-for-sale securities, 412
dividend and interest income and, 412
held-to-maturity securities, 410
trading securities, 410–412
Significant influence, 1180–1181
Simple capital structure, 641
Simple interest, 1146, 1187
Single-step form (of income statement), 117(exh.), **227,** 227–228
Social security tax, 534
Software costs, 501
Sole proprietorships, 13, 13(table), 14(fig.), 223
Source documents, 54, 326, 328
Special order decisions, 1136
incremental analysis for, 1136–1137, 1137(exh.)
Special-purpose entities (SPEs), 559
Special-purpose journals, 330, 330–343
cash payments journal, 34(fig.)(exh.), 340, 342–343
cash receipts journal, 338, 339(exh.), 340
flexibility of, 343
purchases journal, 335–338, 336(exh.), 337(exh.)
sales journal, 333–335, 333–335(exh.)
transactions not recorded in, 343, 343(exh.)
Specific identification method, 448
SPEs (special-purpose entities), 559
Split-off point, 1142
Spoilage, 173
Spreadsheets, 325, 325–326
Stakeholders, 1093
Standard cost(s), 1050, 1050–1051
computing, 1052–1054
management cycle and, 1050–1051, 1051(fig.)
total standard unit cost, 1053–1054
Standard costing, 842, 842–843, **1050,** 1050–1052
relevance in today's business environment, 1051–1052
see also Variance analysis
Standard direct labor cost, 1052, 1052–1053
Standard direct materials cost, 1052
Standard fixed overhead rate, 1053
Standard manufacturing overhead cost, 1053
Standard & Poor's, 757
Standard variable overhead rate, 1053
Start-up and organization costs, 598
Stated ratios, 562–563, 564–567, 567(exh.)
Stated value, 607
Statement of cash flows, 21(exh.), **22,** 22–23, 708–729, **711**
in annual report, 259–260
cash-generating efficiency and, 714–715
classification of cash flows and, 712–714, 713(fig.)
financing activities and, 725–727
format of, 714
free cash flow and, 715–717
international use of, 714
investing activities and, 722–725
operating activities and, 717–722, 718–720(exh.), 719(fig.)
purposes of, 712
uses of, 712
Statement of changes in stockholders' equity, *see* Statement of stockholders' equity
Statement of cost of goods manufactured, 847, 847–849, 848(exh.)
Statement of earnings, in annual report, 259
Statement of owner's equity, 21(exh.), **22**
Statement of stockholders' equity, 642, 643(exh.), 644
in annual report, 260
Statements of Financial Accounting Standards, 24
State unemployment insurance tax, 534
Stock
authorized, 597
book value of, 648–649
common, *see* Common stock
earnings per share and, 640–642
ex-dividend, 603
Initial public offerings of, 597–598
issued, 602
long-term investments in, 1180–1185, 1181(table)
outstanding, 602
par value, 597
preferred, *see* Preferred stock
share buybacks and, 611
shares of, 594
treasury, *see* Treasury stock
Stock certificates, 597
Stock dividends, 644, 644–647
Stock Dividends Declared account, 646
Stockholders, 7, 594
Stockholders' equity, components of, 601–602, 602(fig.)
Stock issuance, 606–609
for noncash assets, 608–609
of no-par stock, 608
of par value stock, 607–608
Stock markets, 7
European, 601
Stock option plans, 600, 601
Stock splits, 647, 647–648
Storage time, 941
Straight-line method, 489, 679
for amortization of bond discount, 679–680
for amortization of bond premium, 683
for depreciation, 489
Strategic objectives, 797
Strategic planning, 1004
Subscriber lists, 500
Subsidiaries, 1185
Subsidiary ledgers, 332
Successful efforts method, 497
Summary of Significant Accounting Policies, 46
in annual report, 260
Sunk costs, 1132, 1132–1133
Supplementary information notes, in annual report, 263

Supply chain (network), **798,** 798–799, **929,** 929–930, 930(fig.)
Supply-chain management, 329, 446
Support services, 800
in value chain analysis, 801–802

T accounts, 51–52, **52**
Tangible assets, 482(fig.)
see also Plant assets
Targets, linking of goals to, 1108
Taxable income, 635
Tax authorities, as users of accounting information, 10
Technology, 499(table)
airline industry pricing and, 973
bar codes and, 172
challenges faced by businesses and, 329
check processing and, 1133
computer networks and, 326
credit versus debit cards and, 170
customer numbers and, 330
customer service and, 331
ecommerce and, 104, 329
electronic work sheets and, 146
flexible budget and, 1055
interest and amortization tables and, 684
internal control and, 370
Internet retailing, 177
inventory turnover and, 444
LIFO inventory valuation and, 452
product costs and, 841
rolling forecasts and, 1008
simplicity and, 1098
time savings and, 330
see also Computerized accounting systems; Internet
Telecommunications industry, cash flows in, 716
Television talent, cost of, 860
Temporary accounts, 130
Terms of sale, 176–178
Theft, of inventory, 173
Theoretical capacity, 968
Theory of constraints (TOC), 806
Throughput time, 941
Time
for check processing, 1133
in new manufacturing environment, 941
Time and motion studies, 973
Time cards, 844
Time periods, for compounding interest, 1192–1193
Time value of money, 1146, 1146–1149, 1187–1197
accounting applications of, 1193–1197
future value and, 1188(table), 1188–1189, 1190(table)
interest and, 1146–1147, 1187–1188
present value and, 1147–1149, 1189–1192, 1191(table), 1192(table)
time periods and, 1192–1193
TOC (theory of constraints), 806
Total direct labor cost variance, 1060, 1060–1061, 1062(fig.)
Total direct materials cost variance, 1058
Total fixed overhead variance, 1066
Total manufacturing costs, 847
Total manufacturing overhead variance, 1064
Total quality management (TQM), 805
Total variable overhead variance, 1064, 1064–1065, 1065(fig.)
TQM (total quality management), 805
Trackballs, 326
Trade credit, 413
Trade discounts, 176
Trademarks, 499(table)
Trading on the equity, 670
Trading securities, 410, 410–412
Treasury stock, 600, **609,** 609–612
purchase of, 610
retirement of, 611–612
sale of, 610–611
statement of cash flows and, 726–727, 727(exh.)
Trend analysis, 760, 760–762, 762(exh.), 762(fig.)
Trial balance, 61, 61(exh.), 61–63, 62(table)
adjusted, 104–105, 105(exh.), 106(exh.), 185
post-closing, 139

Unamortized Bond Discount account, 676
Uncollectible accounts, 413, 413–420
allowance method for, 414–415
direct charge-off method for, 413–414
estimating expense of, 415–419
recovery of written off accounts receivable and, 419–420
writing off, 419
Uncollectible Accounts Expense account, 414
Underapplied overhead costs, 852
Understandability, 215
Underwriters, 597
Unearned revenues, 102, 535
Unemployment insurance tax, 534
Uniform Partnership Act, 558
Unit-level activities, 934
Universal product codes (UPCs), 172
Unlimited liability, 558, 558–559
Unrealized Loss on Long-Term Investments account, 1182, 1183–1184
Unsecured bonds, 673
UPCs (universal product codes), 172
Useful life, estimated, 488–489
Usefulness, 215

Vacation pay liability, 537
Valuation, 47, 47–48, 56
of assets, 1194
of bonds, using present value, 677–678
of liabilities, 528
Value, 47
carrying (book), 100, 480, 648–649, 1144
disposal, in capital investment analysis, 1145
face, bonds issued at, 674–675
future, *see* Future value
market, 458
maturity, of promissory notes, 422
par, 597
present, *see* Present value
realizable, 458
residual (disposal; salvage), 488
residual, in capital investment analysis, 1145
stated, 607
time, of money, *see* Time value of money
Value added, economic, 1106(exh.), 1106–1107, 1107(fig.)
Value-adding activities, 805, 932
process value analysis and, 933–934
in service organizations, 932, 933(table)
Value-adding costs, 839
Value-based management (VBM), 933
Value chain, 800
Internet support of, 802
Value chain(s), 929, 929–930
Value chain analysis, 800–804, 801(fig.)
advantages of, 802
management's support of, 802–804, 803(exh.)
primary processes and support services and, 801–802